Photo Credits

Prologue: *Logos courtesy of Certified Accountants' Association of Canada, Chartered Accountants of Canada, and the Society of Management Accountants of Canada;* Chapter 1: *Bernard Mendoza/Tony Stone Images;* Chapter 2: *Sharon Hoogstraten;* Chapter 3: *Courtesy of Imperial Oil;* Chapter 4: *Sharon Hoogstraten;* Chapter 5: *Michael Poselli;* Chapter 6: *Sharon Hoogstraten;* Chapter 7: *Sharon Hoogstraten;* Chapter 8: *Sharon Hoogstraten;* Chapter 9: *George Kavanagh/Tony Stone Images;* Chapter 10: *Sharon Hoogstraten;* Chapter 11: *Chris Speedie/Tony Stone Images;* Chapter 12: *Michael Rosenfeld/Tony Stone Images;* Chapter 13: *Sharon Hoogstraten;* Chapter 14: *Sharon Hoogstraten;* Chapter 15: *Courtesy of Corel Corporation;* Chapter 16: *Sharon Hoogstraten;* Chapter 17: *Sharon Hoogstraten;* Chapter 18: *Sharon Hoogstraten;* Chapter 19: *Stewart Cohen/Tony Stone Images.*

Irwin Book Team

Publisher:	*Roderick T. Banister*
Developmental editor:	*Sabira Hussain*
Marketing manager:	*Murray Moman*
Project editor:	*Waivah Clement*
Production supervisor:	*Bob Lange*
Assistant manager, graphics:	*Charlene R. Perez*
Senior designer:	*Heidi J. Baughman*
Coordinator, Graphic and Desktop Services:	*Keri Johnson*
Photo researcher:	*Randall Nicholas/ Nicholas Communications, Inc.*
Compositor:	*York Graphic Services, Inc.*
Typeface:	*10½ /12½ Times Roman*
Printer:	*Von Hoffmann Press, Inc.*

Times Mirror Higher Education Group

ISBN 0-256-17496-2
Library of Congress Catalog Number 95–80682

Printed in the United States of America
1 2 3 4 5 6 7 8 9 0 VH 3 2 1 0 9 8 7 6

TO THE INSTRUCTOR

We are pleased to present the Eighth Canadian Edition of *FUNDAMENTAL ACCOUNTING PRINCIPLES.* As in previous editions, we have provided complete coverage of financial and managerial accounting at an introductory level. Although many schools use all 27 chapters in the book, we realize that a number of schools do not have the appropriate course time to cover all of the chapters. With this in mind, the Eighth Canadian Edition is available in the following formats to provide you with the flexibility that you need to cover courses of varying lengths:

1. *Fundamental Accounting Principles,* Volume I (Chapters 1–10), ISBN 0-256-17506-3, softcover.
2. *Fundamental Accounting Principles,* Volume I with Working Papers, ISBN 0-256-20964-2, softcover.
3. *Fundamental Accounting Principles,* Volume II (Chapters 11–19), ISBN 0-256-17507-1, softcover.
4. *Fundamental Accounting Principles,* Volume II with Working Papers, ISBN 0-256-20965-0, softcover.
5. *Fundamental Accounting Principles,* Volume III (Managerial, Chapters 20–27), ISBN 0-256-20956-1, softcover.
6. *Fundamental Accounting Principles,* Volume III with Working Papers, ISBN 0-256-20966-9, softcover.
7. *Financial Accounting Principles,* Eighth Canadian Edition (Chapters 1–19), ISBN 0-256-17496-2, hardcover.

Any of the volumes identified above can also be packaged together at a savings to your students. If you are interested in exploring packaging options, please contact your local Times Mirror Professional Publishing Ltd. representative or the College Division at 1-800-268-4178 or 905-470-6739 in the Toronto area.

FINANCIAL ACCOUNTING PRINCIPLES

EIGHTH CANADIAN EDITION

KERMIT D. LARSON
University of Texas—Austin

MORTON NELSON
Wilfrid Laurier University

MICHAEL ZIN
Professor Emeritus
University of Windsor

RAY F. CARROLL
Dalhousie University

Represented in Canada by:

Times Mirror
Professional Publishing Ltd.

IRWIN

Toronto • Chicago • Bogotá • Boston • Buenos Aires
Caracas • London • Madrid • Mexico City • Sydney

Preface

The tradition of *Financial Accounting Principles* includes clear explanations of accounting concepts and practices with closely related assignment material. Recent editions also reflect an educational philosophy we call *action learning*. We are firmly convinced that students learn most effectively when their study activities are designed to emphasize active behaviour. The eighth Canadian edition continues this focus on the effective use of student study time.

By providing a wide variety of action-oriented items in the text and in support of the text, we hope to encourage student involvement within the classroom as well as during study outside of class. Newly developed and thoroughly revised assignment materials provide an extensive basis for varied assignments that stimulate interest, promote a sense of accomplishment, show the real-world relevance of the subject matter, and sharpen the analytical and communications abilities of each student. In addition, the study guide and the computerized tutorial give students a number of action-learning opportunities.

The eighth Canadian edition has changed *Financial Accounting Principles* in many important ways. Extensive input obtained through surveys, focus groups, reviewers, and personal correspondence has driven the revision plan. Instructors confirm several trends that are affecting the world of accounting. The trends most prevalent in accounting education today include the visual orientation of students, the need for flexibility and innovation in the classroom, new pedagogy, and the impact of technology. The many changes that have been integrated throughout this revision are in response to these trends.

Chapter Opening Scenarios

NEW FEATURES

A scenario at the beginning of each chapter raises questions related to the material covered in the chapter. Later in the chapter, one or more references show how the ideas being explained at that point apply to the company described in the chapter opening. Even before students read a chapter, they realize from the opening scenarios that what they will be learning is useful in solving real problems.

Use of Colour

Conscious, deliberate thought and effort have gone into the use of colour to add more interest and appeal to the book. More importantly, colour is used as a code to aid in learning. Blue indicates financial statements and reports that provide accounting information to be used in decision making. The primary documents that accountants generate for themselves as they develop informative statements and reports are green. Finally, documents that serve as sources of the data that go into accounting reports are yellow.

Progress Checks with Answers

A new feature in this edition is a series of Progress Checks integrated in each chapter. These review questions follow the discussion related to a learning objective. The goal is to have students stop momentarily and reflect on whether they should spend more time studying a given section of the text before moving on. Answers to the Progress Check questions are provided at the end of each chapter.

Excerpts and Assignments from Annual Reports

The financial statements of Imperial Oil Limited and other companies are used throughout as a basis for discussing the different aspects of the financial statements. In this way, the relevance of the discussion to actual decision situations is emphasized. Most chapters also contain one or more assignments relating to the annual report of Geac Computer Corporation Limited.

Using the Information

A new section at the end of each financial chapter reinforces real-world business applications. Most of these sections use real-world examples and many of them relate directly to the company vignettes that open the chapters. A few examples of Using the Information topics are

> Debt ratio—Chapter 2
> Business segment information—Chapter 6
> Return on total assets—Chapter 12
> Price-earnings ratio—Chapter 16
> Cash flow analyses—Chapter 18

Enhanced Emphasis on Critical Thinking, Analysis, and Communication Skills

The assignment material in the book has been extensively revised. Many assignments have been reoriented to increase the emphasis on critical thinking and communication skills. For example, the requirements for selected problems in each chapter now include a *preparation component* and a separate *Analysis Component*.

The Analysis Component generally requires students to think about the financial statement consequences of alternative situations. Students learn to consider the consequences of alternatives and the resulting effects on their interpretation of the results. This complements the more usual preparation component of the end-of-chapter assignments.

Quick Study (Five-Minute Exercises)

Instructors indicate an increasing reliance on shorter problem material for use as in-class illustrations and as homework assignments. Undoubtedly the prospect of solving problems in a short time and the rapid feedback of having done so successfully are motivating factors that lead students to extend their study efforts. Accordingly, this edition contains a new category of very short exercises that are identified as Quick Study. At least one exercise is provided for each learning objective.

Additional Problems

In response to requests for more and varied problem material, we have replaced the alternate problems which previously mirrored the main problems with new, different problems. The traditional alternate problems are available in a separate booklet.

Concept Testers

To encourage additional study of important glossary terms, all chapters conclude the assignment material with a *concept tester* in the form of a short crossword puzzle.

Features about which our adopters have expressed enthusiasm have been retained. These include integrated learning objectives, illustrative diagrams, acetate overlays, "As a Matter of Ethics" cases, "As a Matter of Opinion" interviews, the comprehensive accounting cycle illustration, the summary in terms of learning objectives, chapter glossaries, demonstration problems with solutions and the various forms of problem material including Questions, Exercises, Problems, Provocative Problems, Analytical and Review Problems, the Serial Problem and Comprehensive Review Problems (after Chapters 4, 6, 13, and 22 in Volume III).

FEATURES RETAINED

Expanded Prologue

An important change in this edition is an expanded Prologue that describes the accounting function in the context of other organizational functions such as finance, human resources, research and development, production, marketing, and executive management. The Prologue also explains the work accountants do—including their certifications and the fields within which they work—and the pervasive importance of ethics in accounting. As a separate learning unit, the Prologue emphasizes the overall importance of these topics to the understanding of the role accounting plays in providing information to a variety of decision makers.

CONTENT-SPECIFIC CHANGES

Financial Statement Orientation of Chapter 1

As a result of the Prologue revision, Chapter 1 is now a much shorter and more manageable learning unit with a clear focus on financial statements. This includes the information contained in the statements, the basic concepts that guide the development and use of accounting information, and the relationship of the statements to the transactions and events in the life of a business. Appendix A following Chapter 1 now describes the process by which generally accepted accounting principles are established.

Deletions in Chapters 4 and 5

Reviewers and adopters have overwhelmingly encouraged limiting the early examples in the book to proprietorships. As a result, the discussion of partnerships and corporations has been moved from the body of Chapter 4 to Appendix D following Chapter 4. Corporations are considered in the early chapters only as necessary to support student interaction with the financial statements at the back of the book and to recognize the existence of alternative forms of business organization.

Work sheets are now presented as an *optional* step in the accounting cycle. However, we also describe several reasons why an understanding of work sheets is useful. In addition, a more concise discussion of the adjusting entry method of accounting for inventories has reduced the size of the appendix at the end of Chapter 5.

Discounting Notes Receivable

The revision of Chapter 8 recognizes the fact that an increasing number of companies routinely convert their receivables into cash without waiting to receive customer payments. In dealing with this modern business practice, the discussion of discounting notes receivable has been supplemented with a more general examination of the various ways receivables may be converted into cash.

Topics Related to Inventories

The discussion in Chapter 9 of lower of cost or market has been simplified to avoid the details of considering ceiling and floor limits on market value. The treatment of markups and markdowns has been eliminated from the discussion of the retail inventory method. Reviewers agree that all of these topics are better left to intermediate level courses.

Topics Related to Capital Assets

To help students appreciate the differences between financial accounting and tax accounting, we continue to discuss accelerated amortization. However, the discussion has been condensed to exclude the calculations that underlie the apportioning of accelerated amortization between accounting periods. We also eliminated the discussions of capital asset subsidiary records.

Consolidated Financial Statements

Adopters indicate that the consolidated statements chapter in prior editions was the one they most frequently omitted. Nevertheless, long-term investments are an important financial consideration in evaluating many companies. The answer was to eliminate the consolidated statements chapter and to develop a more balanced set of asset chapters. As a result, Chapter 12 completes the asset coverage by discussing natural resources, intangible assets, and long-term investments. The long-term investments portion naturally concludes with a discussion of investments in international operations. The appendix on investments in equity securities from the seventh Canadian edition has been eliminated.

Leases and Accounting for Corporate Income Taxes

In Chapter 13, the discussion of leases has been significantly shortened. Students learn the differences between capital and operating leases without having to journalize the entries related to capital leases. Also, Appendix H, "Accounting for Corporate Income taxes," has been retained.

Streamlined Coverage of Partnerships and Corporations

Reviewers suggested that we compress the coverage of partnerships and corporations and eliminate seldom used procedures and material that is best left for more advanced textbooks. In response, we streamlined discussion of material in these chapters and eliminated coverage of obsolete or nonessential material such as participating preferred, par value shares and the appendix on treasury stock.

Segmental Reporting

The illustration and discussion of segmental reporting have been eliminated from Chapter 19. However, a short section at the close of Chapter 6 recognizes that operating in several business segments complicates the design of the accounting system. Then, the use of business segment information by decision makers is briefly discussed.

To provide instructors flexibility in planning course content, the eighth Canadian edition includes several appendixes. Those that clearly relate to a single chapter are placed at the end of the chapter. Appendixes F, G, H, and I appear at the end of the book.

APPENDIXES AND END-OF-TEXT ITEMS

Comprehensive List of Accounts Used in Exercises and Problems

This list provides students with the large variety of accounts that companies use and that are needed to solve the exercises and problems provided in the text. This list is located at the end of this text.

For the Instructor

SUPPLEMENTS

The support package for *Financial Accounting Principles* includes many items to assist the instructor. They include the following:

- *Solutions Manuals,* Volumes I and II which have more extensive supporting calculations in this edition.
- *Solutions Transparencies,* Volumes I and II which include all exercises, problems, and comprehensive problems. These transparencies are now printed in boldface in a new, exceptionally large typeface so that visibility from a distance is strikingly improved.
- *Teaching Transparencies,* many of which are now in colour.

- *Powerpoint Slides,* developed by Bruce MacLean of Dalhousie University, which are designed to support teaching the course using a computer, data display, and an overhead projector.
- *Video tapes,* available upon adoption, which reinforce important topics and procedures. They may be used in the classroom or media lab.
- *Instructor's Resource Manual,* prepared by Ray Carroll of Dalhousie University, which includes sample course syllabi, suggested homework assignments, a series of lecture outlines, demonstration problems, suggested points for emphasis, and background material for discussing ethics in accounting.
- *Testbank,* which contains a wide variety of test questions, including true-false, multiple-choice, quantitative, matching, and essay questions of varying levels of difficulty.
- *Computest,* a computerized version of the manual testbank for more efficient use, which is available in Macintosh, Windows, or DOS versions. The extensive features of this test-generator program include random question selection based on the user's specification of learning objectives, type of question, and level of difficulty.
- *Teletest.* By calling a toll-free number, users can specify the content of exams and have laser-printed copies of the exams mailed or faxed to them.
- *SPATS (Spreadsheet Applications Template Software),* prepared by Jack Terry and Christopher L. Polselli, C.A., which includes Lotus 1-2-3 (or the equivalent) templates for selected problems and exercises from the text. The templates gradually become more complex, requiring students to build a variety of formulas. What-if questions are added to show the power of spreadsheets and a simple tutorial is included. Instructors may request a free master template for students to use or copy, or students can buy shrinkwrapped versions at a nominal fee. Both DOS and Windows versions are available.
- *Tutorial Software,* prepared by Leland Mansuetti, Keith Weidkamp, and J. Russell Curtis of the British Columbia Institute of Technology. Multiple-choice, true-false, journal entry review and glossary review questions are randomly accessed by students. Explanations of right and wrong answers are provided and scores are tallied. Instructors may request a free master template for students to use or copy, or students can buy shrinkwrapped versions for a nominal fee. Both DOS and Windows versions are available.
- *Solutions Manual to accompany the practice sets* will include detailed solutions to all of the practice sets accompanying the text.

For the Student

In addition to the text, the package of support items for the student includes the following:

- *Working Papers,* Volumes I and II, which include working papers for the exercises, problems, serial problem and comprehensive problems.
- The *Study Guide,* Volumes I and II, which provides a basis for independent study and review and has been expanded to include multiple-choice and true/false questions as well as several additional problems with solutions for each chapter and appendix.

- *Check Figures* for the problems.
- *Barns Bluff Camping Equipment,* by Barrie Yackness of the British Columbia Institute of Technology and Terrie Kroshus. A manual, single proprietorship practice set with business papers that may be assigned after Chapter 7. This practice set is also available in an Alternate Edition prepared by Tilly Jensen of the Northern Alberta Institute of Technology.
- *Student's Name Book Centre,* by Harvey C. Freedman of Humber College of Applied Arts and Technology. A manual, single proprietorship practice set covering a one-month accounting cycle. The set includes business papers and can be assigned after Chapter 7. This practice set is also available in an Alternate Edition.

ACKNOWLEDGMENTS

We are grateful for the encouragement, suggestions, reviews, and counsel provided by students, colleagues, and instructors from across the country. A tremendous amount of useful information was gathered from over 300 responses to an Introductory Accounting Survey organized by the publisher. Although the identities of the respondents were anonymous to the authors, we learned a great deal from you and appreciate the detail you provided.

Many of the improvements in the Eighth Canadian Edition were based on the input from the reviewers of the seventh edition or the manuscript for the eighth edition. We want to thank this important group of people for their contributions to this edition. They include:

Peter McNeil, C.A.
Camosun College

Paul Molgat
Red Deer College

Donna P. Grace
Sheridan College

Tilly Jensen
Northern Alberta Institute of Technology

Terry Fegarty
Seneca College of Applied Arts and Technology

Gregg Tranter
Southern Alberta Institute of Technology

Barrie Yackness
British Columbia Institute of Technology

Sheila Simpson
Humber College of Applied Arts and Technology

We also want to recognize the contribution of Robert Nichols of the British Columbia Institute of Technology who prepared the update of the payroll liabilities chapter and solutions for this edition.

Last but not least, we gratefully acknowledge the contribution from students, faculty members, and secretarial staff at the University of Windsor, Wilfrid Laurier University, and Dalhousie University. Special thanks go to Sharon Roth and Sandra J. Berlasty at the University of Windsor, Allan Russel at Wilfrid Laurier University, and Helen Cruickshanks and Carmen Tam at Dalhousie University.

Kermit D. Larson
Morton Nelson
Michael Zin
Ray Carroll

To the Student

Financial Accounting Principles is designed to get you actively involved in the learning process so you will learn quickly and more thoroughly. The more time you spend expressing what you are learning, the more effectively you will learn. In accounting, you do this primarily by answering questions and solving problems. But this is not the only way to learn. You also can express your ideas by using the book's wide margins for taking notes, summarizing a phrase, or writing down a question that remains unanswered in your mind. Ideas that pop into your head can lead to fruitful exploration. These notes will assist in your later review of the material, and the simple process of writing them will help you learn.

To guide your study, *learning objectives* are listed near the beginning of each chapter. Read these objectives to form some expectations about what you will learn from studying the chapter. Think of them as your goals while you study. Each learning objective is repeated in the margin at the point the chapter begins to provide material related to that objective. You will find each objective repeated at the end of each chapter in the summary. The exercises and problem assignments following each chapter also are coded to these objectives.

As you progress in your study of each chapter, you will periodically encounter Progress Check questions relating to the material you have just studied. Answer the questions and compare your answers with the correct answers at the end of each chapter. If you are not able to answer the questions correctly, review the preceding section of the chapter before going on.

Several features of the text emphasize the real-world usefulness of the material in the book. For example, the *opening paragraphs* of each chapter raise questions about a real business. As you progress through the chapter, keep a sharp eye out for points in the discussion that apply to the scenario in the opening paragraphs. You will find brief inserts entitled *"As a Matter of Opinion"* in which business and community leaders tell how they use accounting in making decisions.

The use of colour in the book has been carefully planned to facilitate your learning. For example, the financial statements and reports that accounting provides as information to be used in decision making are blue. The primary documents that accountants generate for their own use as they develop informative statements and reports are green. Documents that serve as sources of the data that go into an accounting system are yellow.

As you read the text, you will learn many important new terms. These key terms are printed in black boldface the first time they appear, and they are listed again in a *glossary* after each chapter. In addition, you can find these key terms in the index at the end of the book. As a reinforcement to learning, but also as a light break from regular study, all chapters close with a *crossword puzzle* that involves some of the glossary terms.

Computer technology is changing the way businesses operate and will continue to be a driving force in the twenty-first century. To reflect this change and to give you practice with software, some of the assignments in the book are preloaded on a set of computer templates called *SPATS*. These assignments are identified with the following logo:

Ask your instructor or check your school's bookstore for information about other supplemental items that are available to assist your study. The *tutorial software* contains multiple-choice, true/false, journal entry review, and glossary review questions to help you prepare for exams. The *study guide* reviews learning objectives and provides practice problems for each chapter. *Working papers* provide familiarity with the actual framework used in creating accounting information.

Accounting can be an informative, relevant, and engaging field of inquiry. *Financial Accounting Principles* offers many tools to lead you into an understanding of the importance of accounting. Read, discuss, and enjoy! What you learn in this course will be useful in your personal and professional affairs for the rest of your life.

Contents in Brief

Contents

Your Introduction to Business, Accounting, and Ethics

Accountancy is the fastest growing of the professions. These are the accounting bodies that provide education and professional training in Canada.

aren White and Mark Smith are currently undergraduates in a business program. They have been assigned a case in one of their business courses. In the case, Jarrett and Wilson have decided to start a new business which would seek contracts with companies in the Hamilton area to provide a shuttle service for their employees to and from Pearson airport. They began operations under the name of JW Shuttle.

Jarrett and Wilson agreed that since Jarrett had the original idea and had done a substantial amount of the work to get started, Jarrett should receive 75% and Wilson 25% of any income the business earned during its first year of operations.

Karen and Mark understand that the amount of income reported in the first year depends on the methods used to measure the income. More precisely, the total income for the first two years will include $30,000 that will either be recognized in the first year or the second year, depending on the accounting method used. Based on projections through the end of the second year, the following table shows the results of the two alternatives:

	First Year	Second Year	Total
Using Method A:			
Reported income	$40,000	$40,000	$80,000
Allocation to Jarrett and Wilson:			
Jarrett (75% and 50%)	30,000	20,000	50,000
Wilson (25% and 50%)	10,000	20,000	30,000
Using Method B:			
Reported income	$10,000	$70,000	$80,000
Allocation to Jarrett and Wilson:			
Jarrett (75% and 50%)	7,500	35,000	42,500
Wilson (25% and 50%)	2,500	35,000	37,500

LEARNING OBJECTIVES

After studying the Prologue, you should be able to:

1. **Describe the main purpose of accounting and its role in organizations.**
2. **Describe the external role of accounting for organizations.**
3. **List the main fields of accounting and the activities carried on in each field.**
4. **State several reasons for the importance of ethics in accounting.**
5. **Define or explain the words and phrases listed in the prologue glossary.**

What goes on in business and other organizations? How are their activities carried out? Who is responsible for them? And, what part does accounting play? This prologue answers these questions and explains why your study of accounting is important even if you are not planning to be an accountant. You also learn about different kinds of accountants and the work they do. Finally, we consider the great importance of ethics in business and accounting.

ACCOUNTING AND ITS ROLE IN ORGANIZATIONS

LO 1

Describe the main purpose of accounting and its role in organizations.

The main purpose of **accounting** is to provide useful information to people who make rational investment, credit, and similar decisions.[1] Because accountants serve decision makers by providing them with financial information that helps them make better decisions, accounting is often described as a service activity. Decision makers who use accounting information include present and potential investors, lenders, managers, suppliers, and customers.

Accounting provides information about all profit-oriented businesses. Accountants also supply information about nonprofit organizations such as churches, hospitals, museums, schools, and various government agencies. The people who use accounting information about nonprofit organizations include their managers and people who donate to or pay taxes to them, use their services, or otherwise work with them. Whether you are planning to be an accountant, an employee, a manager within an organization, or an external user of the information, your knowledge of accounting will help you achieve more success in your career.

WHAT GOES ON IN ORGANIZATIONS?

Illustration PR–1 shows the major activities of businesses that manufacture and sell products. Businesses such as airlines and express delivery companies that sell services have similar activities. So do governmental and nonprofit organizations. The following paragraphs describe these functions in more detail.

Finance. Every organization needs money to operate and grow. Organizations use money to acquire equipment, buildings, vehicles, and financial holdings. The finance function has the task of planning how to obtain money from sources such as payments from customers, loans from banks, and new investments from owners. Government organizations acquire cash by collecting taxes and fees, while nonprofit organizations acquire most of their cash from contributions by donors. In preparing plans, the finance department identifies and evaluates alternative

---

[1]*CICA Handbook,* "Financial Statement Concepts," par. 1000.12.

Illustration PR-1 Activities within an Organization

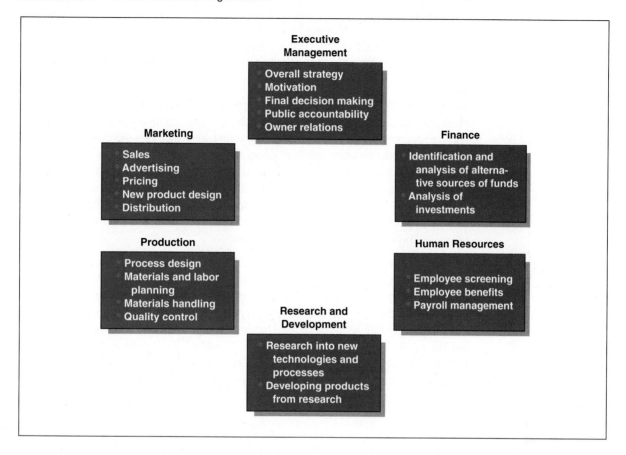

sources of funds. In addition, finance analyzes alternative investment opportunities to identify which to take and which to reject.

Human Resources. All organizations require efforts from people. As a result, employees must be located, screened, hired, trained, compensated, promoted, and counseled. And, they may be released from employment by being retired or laid off. The human resources function is responsible for handling these tasks. In large companies, literally hundreds of employees may be engaged in looking after the other employees.

Research and Development. All organizations need to find new ways to meet the needs of their customers and others. Thus, research into new technologies and products or services is essential. This may be as simple as testing a new recipe for pizza or as complex as creating a more powerful computer. Once research is completed, the development process uses the new knowledge to design or modify specific products or services. If organizations are to survive, this function is essential.

Production. Many companies produce and then sell goods to their customers. Producing these goods requires planning and coordinating many specific activities. These activities include designing the production process, acquiring materials used in production, and selecting the workers' skills to be applied. In addition, materials handling systems must be in place to ensure that raw materials and finished goods are delivered on time. Production management also requires paying a great deal of attention to the quality of the goods. Similar activities in retail and service organizations ensure that quality merchandise and services are delivered to consumers.

Marketing. Companies can sell goods and services only if customers are willing to buy them. Marketing provides customers with information about goods and services and encourages them to make purchases. This includes sales efforts that involve contacting customers directly. Marketing also includes advertising that provides information to large numbers of potential customers. Another activity is to set prices that are low enough to encourage sales and high enough to earn profits. Marketing also involves identifying new products that might meet customers' needs. It includes developing systems that distribute products to customers when and where they need them. These activities are sometimes summed up as the four P's of marketing—product, promotion, price, and place.

Executive Management. All organizations must have leadership, vision, and coordination. Long-term strategies need to be established, and employees must be motivated to do their best. In addition, major decisions have to be made. These tasks are the duty of the company's executive managers, who also represent the company in dealing with the public. In some companies, the owner or owners carry out the executive management functions. In others, key employees take on these responsibilities. They may be called the president, the chief executive officer, or the chair of the board of directors. In nonprofit organizations, the top managers often are called executive directors.

USING ACCOUNTING TO SERVE INTERNAL NEEDS

The internal role of accounting is to serve the organization's various functions by providing information that helps them complete their tasks. By providing this information, accounting helps the organization reach its overall goals. Illustration PR–2 shows some of the information accounting provides within an organization.

The finance function uses information about actual cash flows as a basis for projecting future cash flows and evaluating past decisions. Human resources can carry out its work more effectively if it has information about the company's employees, including payroll costs. Research and development managers need information about the costs they already have incurred so they can decide whether to continue their projects. Marketing managers also use accounting information, especially reports about the company's sales and its marketing costs.

The production division of a company depends heavily on accounting information to determine whether its operating costs are occurring as expected. In carrying out its work, the production department operates within a set of *internal controls* designed by the accounting department. To promote efficiency and prevent unauthorized use of the company's resources, these controls specify procedures that must be followed before certain actions can take place. For example, internal controls may require a manager's approval before any materials are moved to the production line. Internal controls also dictate procedures that are necessary to ensure that accounting reports about production activities are dependable and useful. You will learn more about internal control procedures in Chapter 7.

Illustration PR-2 The Internal Role of Accounting

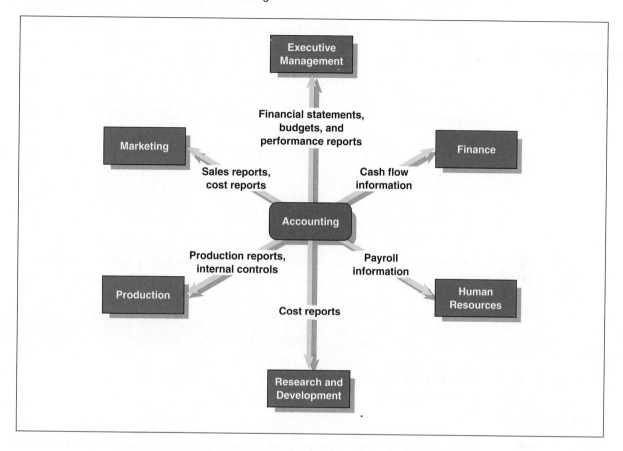

Because executive management has overall responsibility for the organization, it depends heavily on accounting information to understand what is happening. One important set of reports includes the *financial statements*. We explain the contents, usefulness, and limits of these statements throughout this book. (Chapter 1 introduces you to the four primary financial statements.) Executive management also receives and uses budget reports that describe future plans. After events have unfolded, accounting provides performance reports that help the managers to understand what was done well and to identify where improvements might be made.

Perhaps the most important point to learn at this stage is that accounting activities are not important by themselves. They are important only because they provide information that is useful to other parts of the organization.

Progress Check
(Answers to Progress Checks are provided at the end of the Prologue.)

PR-1   The primary function of accounting is to provide financial information: *(a)* To an organization's managers; *(b)* To an organization's creditors; *(c)* That is useful in making rational investment, credit, and similar decisions.

PR-2   Identify six different categories of activities carried on within most organizations.

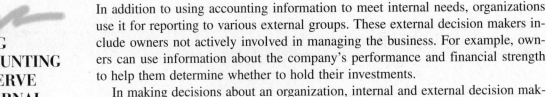

USING ACCOUNTING TO SERVE EXTERNAL NEEDS

LO 2

Describe the external role of accounting for organizations

In addition to using accounting information to meet internal needs, organizations use it for reporting to various external groups. These external decision makers include owners not actively involved in managing the business. For example, owners can use information about the company's performance and financial strength to help them determine whether to hold their investments.

In making decisions about an organization, internal and external decision makers generally begin by asking questions. The answers are often based on accounting information. For example, owners and managers use accounting information to help them answer questions like these:

- What resources does the organization own?
- What debts does it owe?
- How much income is it earning?
- Are the expenses appropriate for the amount of sales?
- Are customers' accounts being collected promptly?

Other decision makers include people who loan money to the organization. These lenders, also called *creditors*, need information to decide whether the company has enough financial strength and profits to pay its debts. For example, they look for answers to questions like these:

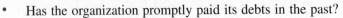

- Has the organization promptly paid its debts in the past?
- Does it have the ability to pay its current debts?
- Does it have good prospects for future earnings?
- Should it be granted additional credit now?

Accounting information is used by voters, legislators, and officials who are concerned about a government agency's receipts and expenditures. Contributors to a nonprofit organization also use accounting information to understand what happens to their donations.

A company's employees have a special interest in knowing whether an organization represents a stable source of employment. They can use accounting information to help them understand their employer's financial health and performance.

Some government agencies are charged with regulating business activities. They often need financial information to carry out that responsibility. Other government agencies are responsible for collecting income taxes. As you know from personal experience, taxpayers use accounting information to determine how much income they have and how much tax they owe.

We explained earlier that executive management is responsible for an organization's relationships with external decision makers. As the diagram on page 5 shows, accounting provides most of the financial information that executive management presents to external decision makers. An objective of this book is to explain the contents and usefulness of the financial statements created for these reporting activities.

Some accounting information is designed to satisfy the needs of a particular external party. For example, information provided to the government for tax calculations may differ significantly from the information in the financial statements. We describe the work of tax accountants later in the Prologue.

Because accounting and bookkeeping both are concerned with financial information and records, some people mistakenly think that they are the same thing. In fact, accounting involves much more than bookkeeping. Although bookkeeping is critical to developing useful accounting information, it is only the clerical part of accounting. That is, **bookkeeping** is the part of accounting that records transactions and other events, either manually or with computers. In contrast, accounting involves analyzing transactions and events, deciding how to report them in financial statements, and interpreting the results. Accounting also involves designing and implementing systems to produce useful reports and to control the operations of an organization. Accounting involves more professional expertise and judgment than bookkeeping because accountants must analyze complex and unusual events.

Whether you want to be an accountant, plan to hold some other position in an organization, or expect to be an investor or creditor, you will benefit by understanding how accounting information is developed. To gain this understanding, initially you will study some basic bookkeeping practices. Later in the book, you will use this knowledge to learn how accountants present financial data in meaningful reports. Eventually, you will be able to use the reports more effectively because you will understand how the information has been processed.

THE DIFFERENCE BETWEEN ACCOUNTING AND BOOKKEEPING

Since computers first became available in the 1950s, they have spread throughout our everyday lives and the business world. Computers are widely used in accounting because they efficiently store, process, and summarize large quantities of financial data. Furthermore, computers perform these functions quickly with limited operator involvement. Thus, computers reduce the time, effort, and cost of processing data while improving clerical accuracy. As a result of these advantages, most accounting systems are now computerized. Even so, manual accounting systems are still used by a surprisingly large number of small businesses.

To prepare, analyze, and use accounting information in today's world, you need to understand the important role computers play in most accounting systems. In essence, computers are tools that help accountants provide useful information for decision makers. The huge growth in the number and power of computers has greatly changed how accountants and other people work. However, computers have not eliminated the need for people to learn about accounting. A strong demand exists for people who can design accounting systems, supervise their operation, analyze complex transactions, and interpret reports. A strong demand also exists for people who can make good decisions because they clearly understand how accounting information relates to business activities. While computers have taken over many routine tasks, they are not substitutes for qualified people with abilities to generate and apply accounting information.

ACCOUNTING AND COMPUTERS

Progress Check

PR-3   Accounting's external function is to provide: *(a)* assurance that management has complied with all laws; *(b)* information to users who are not involved in the organization's daily activities; *(c)* information that managers use to control business operations.

PR-4   What is the relationship between accounting and bookkeeping?

WHY STUDY ACCOUNTING?

Because of the wide range of questions that are answered with accounting information, you will almost certainly use accounting in your future career. (In fact, you probably already use some accounting information as a result of having a credit card or chequing account.) To use accounting effectively, you need to understand the unique accounting words and terms widely used in business.

You should also understand the concepts and procedures that are followed in generating accounting information. One important benefit of this understanding is that it will make you aware of the limitations of accounting information. For example, much of it is based on estimates rather than precise measurements. By understanding how these estimates are made, you will be able to avoid misinterpreting the information.

Another very good reason for studying accounting is to make it the basis for an interesting and rewarding career. The next section of this prologue describes what accountants do.

THE TYPES OF ACCOUNTANTS

LO 3

List the main fields of accounting and the activities carried on in each field.

One way to classify accountants is to identify the kinds of work they perform. In general, accountants work in these three broad fields:

- Financial accounting
- Managerial accounting
- Tax accounting

These fields provide a variety of information to different users. We describe the activities of accountants in these fields later in this prologue.

Another way to classify accountants is to identify the kinds of organizations in which they work. Most accountants are **private accountants.** A private accountant works for a single employer, which is often a business. A large business might employ a hundred or more private accountants, but most companies have fewer.

Many other accountants are **public accountants.** Public accountants provide their services to many different clients. They are called *public accountants* because their services are available to the public. Some public accountants are self-employed. Many others work for public accounting firms that may have thousands of employees or only a few. Canada's leading public accounting firms as of 1995 are:

Firm	Revenue (000's)
KPMG Peat Marwick Thorne	$475,100
Deloitte & Touche	406,000
Ernst & Young	366,000
Coopers & Lybrand	284,927
Arthur Andersen	280,573
Price Waterhouse	240,000
Doane Raymond Grant Thornton	204,400
BDO Dunwoody Ward Mallette	119,103

Source: *The Bottom Line,* April 1995, p. 9.

Government accountants work for local, provincial, and federal government agencies. Some government accountants perform accounting services for their own agencies. Other government accountants are involved with business regulation. Still others investigate violations of laws.

Accounting is a profession like law and medicine because accountants have special abilities and responsibilities. The professional status of an accountant is often indicated by one or more certificates.

Professional Certification

In Canada, there are a number of accounting organizations providing education and professional training. These include the provincial **Institutes of Chartered Accountants,** the **Certified General Accountants' Associations**, and the **Societies of Management Accountants**. Successful completion of the prescribed courses of instruction and practical experience lead to the following designations:

> **Chartered Accountant (CA)**
> **Certified General Accountant (CGA)**
> **Certified Management Accountant (CMA)**

Activities of the three accounting organizations that have shaped accounting thought have been their education and the publication programs. Each has an extensive educational program and has maintained the publication of journals which enjoy wide readership.

In the past decade reliance on postsecondary accounting education has become a significant part of the educational process and complements the extensive correspondence, university distance study, and lecture programs of the **Certified General Accountants' Association of Canada (CGAAC).** The provincial bodies of the **Canadian Institute of Chartered Accountants (CICA)** require a university degree with specified courses. A university degree is required also by some of the provincial bodies of the **Society of Management Accountants of Canada (SMAC).**[2]

Accountancy is the fastest growing of the professions. This growth is in response to the expansion and complexity of the economy, the increasing involvement of the accountant in the process of management decision making, and a growing number of financial reporting activities.

Accountants practice in three fields—financial, managerial, and tax accounting. The actual work done by an accountant depends on both the field and the type (private, public, or government) of accounting in which the person is employed. Illustration PR–3 identifies the specific activities of the three types of accountants within these fields.

THE FIELDS OF ACCOUNTING

Financial Accounting

Financial accounting provides information to decision makers who are not involved in the day-to-day operations of an organization. As we described earlier, these external decision makers include investors, creditors, and others. The information is distributed primarily through general purpose financial statements. Financial

[2] As of January 1995, the provincial Societies of Management Accountants of Ontario and east require a university degree; the four provincial societies in the west do not require university degrees. The Associations of Certified General Accountants do not require university degrees.

Illustration PR-3   Activities of Accountants

Types of Accountants	Fields of Accounting		
	Financial Accounting	**Managerial Accounting**	**Tax Accounting**
Private accountants	Preparing financial statements	General accounting Cost accounting Budgeting Internal auditing	Preparing tax returns Planning
Public accountants	Auditing financial statements	Providing management advisory services	Preparing tax returns Planning
Government accountants	Preparing financial statements Reviewing financial reports Writing regulations Assisting companies Investigating violations	General accounting Cost accounting Budgeting Internal auditing	Reviewing tax returns Assisting taxpayers Writing regulations Investigating violations

statements describe the condition of the organization and the events that happened during the year. Chapter 1 explains the form and contents of financial statements.

The Financial Accounting column of Illustration PR–3 shows that financial statements are prepared by a company's private accountants. However, many companies issue their financial statements only after an **audit.** An audit is an independent review and test of an organization's accounting systems and records; it is performed to add credibility to the financial statements.[3] For example, banks require audits of the financial statements of companies applying for large loans. Also, federal and provincial laws require companies to have audits before their securities (shares and bonds) can be sold to the public. Thereafter, their financial statements must be audited as long as the securities are traded.

To perform an audit, auditors examine the financial statements and the accounting system. Their objective is to decide whether the statements reflect the company's financial position and operating results in agreement with **generally accepted accounting principles (GAAP).** These principles are rules adopted by the accounting profession as guides for measuring and reporting the financial condition and activities of a business. You will learn more about GAAP in Chapter 1 and in many of the following chapters.

When an audit is completed, the auditors prepare a report that expresses their professional opinion about the financial statements. The auditors' report must accompany the statements when they are distributed.

As the first column of Illustration PR–3 shows, some government accountants prepare financial statements. These statements describe the financial status of gov-

---

[3]To achieve this result, audits are performed by independent professionals who are public accountants. Little or no credibility would be added to the statements if they were audited by a company's own employees.

ernment agencies and results of events occurring during the year. The financial statements of governmental bodies are usually audited by the auditor general (federal), provincial auditors, and/or independent accountants.

Other government accountants are involved with regulating financial accounting practices used by businesses. For example, some accountants work for the provincial **Securities Commissions** which regulate securities markets, including the flow of information from companies to the public. Securities Commission accountants review companies' financial reports that are distributed to the public to be sure that the reports comply with the appropriate regulations.

As we mentioned briefly, some government accountants investigate possible violations of laws and regulations. For example, accountants who work for the provincial Securities Commissions (e.g., the Ontario Securities Commission) investigate crimes related to securities. Other accountants investigate financial frauds and white-collar crimes in their capacity as officers of the RCMP and provincial police forces.

Managerial Accounting

The field of managerial accounting involves providing information to an organization's managers. Managerial accounting reports often include much of the same information used in financial accounting. However, managerial accounting reports also include a great deal of information that is not reported outside the company.

Look at the upper and lower sections of the Managerial Accounting column in Illustration PR–3. Notice that private and government accountants have the same four major activities. The middle section of the column shows that public accountants also perform activities related to managerial accounting. These activities are described next.

General Accounting. The task of recording transactions, processing the recorded data, and preparing reports for managers is called **general accounting.** General accounting also includes preparing the financial statements that executive management presents to external users. An organization's own accountants usually design the accounting information system, often with help from public accountants. The general accounting staff is supervised by a chief accounting officer, who is often called the **controller.** (See the organization chart on page 12.) This title stems from the fact that accounting information is used to control the organization's operations.

Cost Accounting. To plan and control operations, managers need information about the nature of costs incurred. **Cost accounting** is a process of accumulating the information managers need about operating costs. It helps managers identify, measure, and control these costs. Cost accounting may involve accounting for the costs of products, services, or specific activities. Cost accounting information is also useful for evaluating each manager's performance. Large companies usually employ many cost accountants because cost accounting information is so important.

Budgeting. Budgeting is the process of developing formal plans for an organization's future activities. A primary goal of budgeting is to give managers from different areas in the organization a clear understanding of how their activities affect the entire organization. After the budget has been put into effect, it provides a basis for evaluating actual performance.

Organization Chart of Controller's Department

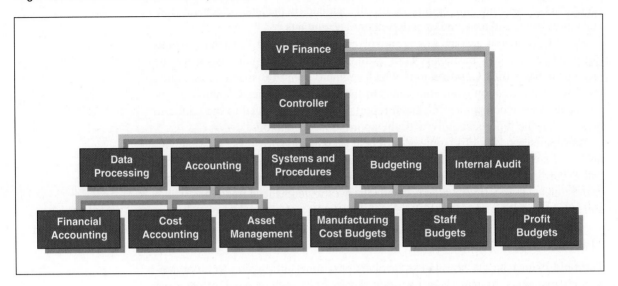

Internal Auditing. Just as independent auditing adds credibility to financial statements, **internal auditing** adds credibility to reports produced and used within an organization. Internal auditors not only examine record-keeping processes but also assess whether managers are following established operating procedures. In addition, internal auditors evaluate the efficiency of operating procedures. Almost all large companies and government agencies employ internal auditors.

Management Advisory Services. Public accountants participate in managerial accounting by providing **management advisory services** to their clients. Independent auditors gain an intimate knowledge of a client's accounting and operating procedures when they conduct their examinations. As a result, auditors are in an excellent position to offer suggestions for improving the company's procedures. Most clients expect these suggestions as a useful by-product of the audit. For example, public accountants often help companies design and install new accounting and internal control systems. This effort includes offering advice on selecting new computer systems. Other advice might relate to budgeting procedures or employee benefit plans.

Tax Accounting

Income taxes raised by federal and provincial governments are based on the income earned by taxpayers. These taxpayers include both individuals and corporate businesses. The amount of taxes is based on what the laws define to be income. Tax accountants help taxpayers comply with these laws by preparing their tax returns. Another **tax accounting** activity involves planning future transactions to minimize the amount of tax to be paid. The Tax Accounting column of Illustration PR–3 identifies the activities of accountants in this field.

Large companies usually have their own private accountants who are responsible for preparing tax returns and doing tax planning. However, large companies may consult with public accountants when they need special tax expertise. Most small companies rely on public accountants for their tax work.

Many accountants are employed on the government side of the tax process. For example, Revenue Canada employs numerous tax accountants. **Revenue Canada** has the duty of collecting federal taxes and otherwise enforcing tax laws. Most Revenue Canada accountants review tax returns filed by taxpayers, while others offer assistance to taxpayers and help write regulations. Still others investigate possible violations of tax laws.

Summary

The preceding discussion shows how important accounting is for most organizations. Regardless of your career goals, you will surely use accounting information and work with accountants. The discussion also shows the variety of opportunities available if you find accounting to be enjoyable and challenging. Next we consider the important role of ethics in business and accounting.

Progress Check

PR-5 The services performed by public accountants generally include: *(a)* income tax services, management advisory services, and independent auditing; *(b)* general accounting, independent auditing, and budgeting; *(c)* government accounting, private accounting, and independent auditing.

PR-6 What are the three broad fields of accounting?

PR-7 What is the purpose of an audit? Describe what public accountants do when they perform an audit.

THE IMPORTANCE OF ETHICS IN ACCOUNTING

LO 4
State several reasons for the importance of ethics in accounting.

As a student, you realize that ethics and ethical behaviour are important features of any society. Disappointing stories in the media often remind us how much ethics affect our society. These stories tell us about attempts to defraud the elderly and other vulnerable people, missed child support payments, harassment, misconduct by public figures, bribery of government officials, and the use of insider information for personal gain in the stock market. Events like these make it difficult for people to trust each other. If trust is lacking, our commercial and personal lives are much more complicated, inefficient, and unpleasant.

In this section of the Prologue, we introduce the meaning of ethics in general and describe how ethics affect business and accounting in particular. Because the purpose of accounting is to provide useful information that can be trusted, it is essential that accountants be ethical. How could the users of accounting information rely on it if they could not trust accountants? The need to avoid this difficult situation has prompted the development of special ethics for accountants.

The Meaning of Ethics

Ethics are the "principles that determine the rightness or wrongness of particular acts or activities." Ethics are also "accepted standards of good behaviour . . . in a profession or trade."[4] Ethics and laws often coincide, with the result that many unethical actions (such as theft and physical violence) are also illegal. Other actions

---

[4]*The New Lexicon Webster's Dictionary of the English Language* (New York: Lexington Publications, 1989), p. 324.

may not be against the law but are generally recognized as unethical. For example, the crime of perjury (not telling the truth) occurs only if the liar has been put under an oath. However, not telling the truth is nearly always unethical.[5] Because of differences between laws and ethics, we cannot count on laws to keep people ethical.

In some cases, a person may face difficulty in deciding whether an action is right or wrong. In these situations, the most ethical choice may be to take a course of action that avoids any doubt about the ethical correctness of the action. For example, financial statement readers would not trust an auditor's report on the statements if the auditor's financial success depended on the success of the reporting company.

Should this prevent an auditor from investing in a client if the investment is only a small part of the auditor's personal wealth? To avoid the question of how much would be too much, ethics rules for auditors simply forbid any direct investment in their clients' securities, regardless of the amount.[6] Also, auditors cannot accept contingent fees that depend on amounts reported in a client's financial statements.[7] These rules are designed to prevent conflicts of interest or even the possibility that the auditor might appear to lack independence.

Many controversial issues that we face in school, the workplace, or elsewhere have ethical implications. These ethical issues are an unavoidable part of life. However, a commitment to being ethical requires us to think carefully before we act to be certain that we are making ethical choices. Our success in making those choices affects how we feel about ourselves and how others feel about us. In fact, our combined individual choices greatly affect the quality of our entire society and the individual experience that each of us enjoys.

Beyond these general ideas, how do ethics relate to business, and more specifically, how do they relate to accounting?

Ethics in Business

We discuss ethics at the beginning of this book because business activity is so central to everyone's life and because useful accounting information is so important for business. Recent history shows that many people have been concerned about what they see as low ethical standards in business. For example, a survey of more than 1,100 executives, deans of business schools, and members of the U.S. Congress showed that 94% of the respondents agreed with the statement that "the business community is troubled by ethical problems."[8] However, we can be encouraged because the survey also showed that the vast majority of the respondents believed high ethical standards are followed by companies that are successful over the long run. This second finding confirms an old saying: "Good ethics is good business." Ethical business practices build trust, which in turn promotes loyalty and productive relationships with customers, suppliers, and employees. As a result, good ethics contribute to a company's reputation and eventually its success.

Because of the important public interest in business ethics, many companies have adopted their own codes of ethics. These codes establish standards for inter-

---

[5]The usual exceptions to this rule involve protecting another person against harm.

[6]Institute of Chartered Accountants of Ontario, *Member's Handbook.*

[7]Ibid.

[8]Touche Ross & Co., *Ethics in American Business* (New York, 1988), pp. 1-2.

As a Matter of Opinion

Mr. Wray received his BA from McMaster University and his LLB from Osgoode Hall Law School. He is a Fellow of the Institute of Chartered Accountants of Ontario and a member of the Ontario Bar. He is the chair of the Interprovincial Committee to Harmonize the Rules of Professional Conduct which govern the ethics of Chartered Accountants across Canada. He has been a partner in Price Waterhouse since 1977, specializing in taxation and forensic accounting.

The accounting profession has earned high regard because of its ethical standards. Our standards require ethical behaviour in our relationships with our clients and our employers. They also require ethical behaviour in our dealings with the public and its interests. And, our standards require us to render high-quality professional services. By adhering to the concepts of objectivity, integrity, and independence, and by continued striving for quality, the profession has won a respected place in the entire business community and among the other professions.

As a student of accounting, be aware of the ethical implications of all that you study. As a member of the accounting profession, or any other profession, practice ethics in all that you do. By doing so, you will bring honour to yourself and your profession.

Donald G. Wray, FCA

nal activities and for relationships with customers, suppliers, regulators, the public, and even competitors. Companies often use their codes as public statements of their commitment to ethical business practices. More importantly, they serve as guides for employees to follow.

Ethics in Accounting

As we mentioned earlier, ethics are important in accounting because accountants are expected to provide useful information for decision makers. These decisions can have a profound effect on many individuals, businesses, and other institutions. As a result, accountants often face ethical issues as they consider what information should be provided to decision makers. Accountants' choices can affect such things as the amount of money a company pays in taxes or distributes to its shareholders. The information can affect the price that a buyer pays for a business or the amount of compensation paid to a company's managers. Internal information can affect judgments about the success of a company's specific products or divisions. If inadequate accounting information would cause a successful division to be closed, its employees, customers, and suppliers would be significantly harmed. Accountants need to consider all these effects in deciding what information will be most useful for these important decisions.

In response to the need for guidance for accountants, ethics codes have been adopted and enforced by professional accounting organizations. These include the provincial Institutes of Chartered Accountants, Associations of Certified General Accountants, and Societies of Management Accountants. To keep their codes up to date, these organizations continually monitor their effectiveness and applicability to new ways of operating. The As a Matter of Opinion box presents the views of Donald G. Wray, FCA, the 1994–95 president of the Public Accountants Council of Ontario, on the importance of ethical behaviour for accountants and others.

As an example of an ethical accounting issue, recall the JW Shuttle business described at the beginning of the Prologue. This case shows how accounting can affect the allocation of wealth between people. Wilson receives $7,500 more and Jarrett receives $7,500 less if Method B is used instead of Method A.

More information is needed in this case to help Jarrett and Wilson decide which method should be used. However, in explaining the appropriate uses of Method A and Method B, the accountant has an ethical responsibility to be fair to both parties. Knowing that Method B is more favourable to Wilson, the accountant must be careful to avoid giving a biased argument in favor of Method B.

Accountants and managers often face situations that are similar to the JW Shuttle case. For example, many companies pay their managers bonuses based on the amount of income reported. Generally, the managers benefit from the use of accounting alternatives that accelerate the reporting of income. However, those alternatives reduce the money available to invest for the benefit of the owners.

Another ethics issue in accounting involves the confidential nature of the information that accountants deal with in their work. For example, auditors have access to salary records and plans for the future. Their clients could be damaged if the auditors released this information to others. To prevent this, auditors' ethics require them to keep information confidential. In addition, internal accountants are not supposed to use confidential information for personal advantage.

These examples show why accountants, their clients, and the public need ethical guidance and commitment. Guidance provides a basis for knowing which actions to take and commitment provides the courage to do what needs to be done. Guidance also tells clients what they can rightfully expect from their accountants and gives the public a basis for having confidence in financial statements. In fact, the performance of the entire economy depends to a considerable extent on having financial information that is trustworthy.

The Ethical Challenge

As you proceed in your study of accounting, you will encounter many other situations in which ethical issues are raised. We encourage you to explore these issues. We also urge you to remember that accounting must be done ethically if it is to be an effective tool in the service of society. Of all the principles of accounting that you learn from this book, the need for ethics is certainly the most fundamental.

In your own approach to life, you are in control of your ethical standards and the ethical decisions that you make. Each of us is individually free to shape our personal morals. To paraphrase former U.S. Supreme Court Chief Justice Earl Warren, it can be said that civilized society "floats on a sea of ethics." It is your choice how you elect to navigate this sea. Do not be misled into thinking that your choice does not matter. Eventually, your choice affects everyone, and that is the ethical challenge each of us faces.

Progress Check

PR-8   All of the provincial accounting bodies have adopted codes of ethics. Is this true or false?

PR-9   Ethical rules prevent auditors from accepting certain kinds of contingent fees. Is this true of false?

LO 1. Describe the main purpose of accounting and its role in organizations. The main purpose of accounting is to provide useful information to people who make rational investment, credit, and similar decisions. These decision makers include present and potential investors, lenders, and other users. The other users include managers of organizations, suppliers who sell to them, and customers who buy from them. Internally, accounting provides information that managers use in the following areas of activity: finance, human resources, research and development, production, marketing, and executive management.

LO 2. Describe the external role of accounting for organizations. In addition to using accounting information to meet internal needs, organizations also report accounting information to various external parties. These external decision makers include people who invest in the organizations and people who loan money to them. Lenders need information to assess whether the company has enough financial strength and profitability to pay its debts.

LO 3. List the main fields of accounting and the activities carried on in each field. Accountants work in private, public, and government accounting. All three have members who work in financial, managerial, and tax accounting. Financial accountants prepare or audit financial statements that are distributed to people who are not involved in day-to-day management. Managerial accountants provide information to people who are involved in day-to-day management. Managerial accounting activities include general accounting, cost accounting, budgeting, internal auditing, and management advisory services. Tax accounting includes preparing tax returns and tax planning.

LO 4. State several reasons for the importance of ethics in accounting. Ethics are principles that determine the rightness or wrongness of particular acts or activities. Ethics are also principles of conduct that govern an individual or a profession. The foundation for trust in business activities is the expectation that people are trustworthy. Ethics are especially important for accounting because users of the information have to trust that it has not been manipulated. Without ethics, accounting information could not be trusted, and economic activity would be much more difficult to accomplish.

SUMMARY OF THE PROLOGUE IN TERMS OF LEARNING OBJECTIVES

GLOSSARY

Accounting a service activity that provides useful information to people who make rational investment, credit, and similar decisions to help them make better decisions. p. 2

Audit a thorough check of an organization's accounting systems and records that adds credibility to financial statements; the specific goal is to determine whether the statements reflect the company's financial position and operating results in agreement with generally accepted accounting principles. p. 10

Bookkeeping the part of accounting that records transactions and other events, either manually or with computers. p. 7

Budgeting the process of developing formal plans for future activities, which then serve as a basis for evaluating actual performance. p. 11

CA Chartered Accountant, p. 9.

CGA Certified General Accountant, p. 9.

CGAAC Certified General Accountants' Association of Canada, the national professional organization of Certified General Accountants, p. 9.

CICA Canadian Institute of Chartered Accountants, the national professional organization of Chartered Accountants, p. 9.

CMA Certified Management accountant, p. 9

Controller   the chief accounting officer of an organization. p. 11

Cost accounting   a managerial accounting activity designed to help managers identify, measure, and control operating costs. p. 11

Ethics   principles that determine the rightness or wrongness of particular acts or activities; also accepted standards of good behavior in a profession or trade. p. 13

GAAP   the abbreviation for *generally accepted accounting principles.* p. 10

General accounting   the task of recording transactions, processing the recorded data, and preparing reports for managers; also includes preparing the financial statements that executive management presents to external users. p. 11

Generally accepted accounting principles (GAAP) rules adopted by the accounting profession as guides for measuring and reporting the financial condition and activities of a business. p. 10

Government accountants   accountants employed by local, provincial, and federal government agencies. p. 8

Internal auditing   an activity that adds credibility to reports produced and used within an organization; internal auditors not only examine record-keeping processes but also assess whether managers are following established operating procedures; internal auditors also evaluate the efficiency of operating procedures. p. 12

Management advisory services   the public accounting activity in which suggestions are offered for improving a company's procedures; the suggestions may concern new accounting and internal control systems, new computer systems, budgeting, and employee benefit plans. p. 12

Private accountants   accountants who work for a single employer, which is often a business. p. 8

Public accountants   accountants who provide their services to many different clients. p. 8

Revenue Canada   the federal agency that has the duty of collecting federal taxes and otherwise enforcing tax laws. p. 12

Securities Commissions   the agencies that regulate securities markets, including the flow of information from companies to the public. p. 11

SMAC   Society of Management Accountants of Canada, the national professional organization of Certified Management Accountants, p. 9.

Tax accounting   the field of accounting that includes preparing tax returns and planning future transactions to minimize the amount of tax; involves private, public, and government accountants. p. 12

QUESTIONS

1. What is the main purpose of accounting?
2. Describe the internal role of accounting for organizations.
3. What are three or four questions that business owners might try to answer by looking to accounting information?
4. Why should people study accounting since computers are used to process accounting data?
5. Why do provinces license public accountants?
6. Identify the three types of services typically offered by public accountants.
7. What title is frequently used for an organization's chief accounting officer? Why?

8. Identify four managerial accounting activities performed by private and government accountants.
9. Identify two management advisory services typically provided by public accountants.
10. Identify several examples of the types of work performed by government accountants.
11. What do tax accountants do in addition to preparing tax returns?
12. Identify the auditing firm that audited the financial statements of Geac Computer Corporation Ltd., in Appendix I at the end of this book.

CONCEPT TESTER

Test your understanding of the concepts introduced in this chapter by completing the following crossword puzzle.

Across Clues

2. Accountants who provide their services to many different clients.
4. The chief accounting officer of an organization.
5. The national accounting body that provides extensive correspondence, distance study and lecture programs.
7. The process of developing formal plans for future activities.

Down Clues

1. Rules adopted as guides for reporting the financial condition and activities of a business.
3. The part of accounting that records transactions and other events.
5. A certification of professional competence in management accounting.
6. The national organization of CAs.

ANSWERS TO PROGRESS CHECKS

PR–1 *c*

PR–2 The activities are finance, human resources, research and development, production, marketing, and executive management.

PR–3 *b*

PR–4 Bookkeeping is the part of accounting that records transactions and other events, either manually or with computers. Accounting activities are concerned with identifying how transactions and events should be described in financial statements. Accounting activities also involve designing and implementing systems that make it possible to produce useful reports and to control the operations of an organization. Accounting involves more professional expertise and judgment than bookkeeping because accountants must analyze complex and unusual events. Also, accountants must be able to interpret and explain the information in the financial reports.

PR–5 *a*

PR–6 The three broad fields of accounting are financial, managerial, and tax accounting.

PR–7 The purpose of an audit is to add credibility to financial statements. When performing an audit, auditors examine financial statements and the accounting records used to prepare them. During the audit, they decide whether the statements reflect the company's financial position and operating results in agreement with generally accepted accounting principles.

PR–8 True

PR–9 True

CHAPTER 1

Financial Statements and Accounting Principles

Many organizations provide accounting information to managers and other decision makers in the form of financial statements. The statements help to describe the organization's financial health and performance using a condensed and highly informative format.

*H*aving solved the Jarrett and Wilson case, Karen White and Mark Smith are ready for their next challenge! One of their assignments is to examine financial statements to determine if an investment in a company would be useful as part of a long-term savings program. One investment possibility that has been suggested to them is Imperial Oil Limited. Karen and Mark know that the company's major businesses include natural resources, petroleum products, and chemicals.

Karen and Mark are trying to understand the financial information contained in Imperial's annual report.

Imperial Oil Limited SELECTED FINANCIAL DATA (in millions)	Year Ended December 31	
	1994	1993
For the year:		
Total revenues	$8,911	$8,795
Net earnings	359	279
At year end:		
Total assets	$11,928	$12,861
Shareholders' equity	5,995	6,566

LEARNING OBJECTIVES

After studying Chapter 1, you should be able to:

1. **Describe the information presented in financial statements, be able to prepare simple financial statements, and analyze a business's performance with the return on equity ratio.**
2. **Explain the accounting principles introduced in the chapter.**
3. **Describe single proprietorships, partnerships, and corporations, including any differences in the owners' responsibilities for the debts of the organizations.**
4. **Analyze business transactions to determine their effects on the accounting equation.**
5. **Define or explain the words and phrases listed in the chapter glossary.**

After studying Appendix A at the end of the chapter, you should be able to:

6. **Describe the process by which generally accepted accounting principles are established.**

In this chapter, you start to learn about the information accountants provide to decision makers in financial statements. Next, you study some general principles that guide accountants in developing these statements. The discussion in Appendix A also describes some of the organizations that regulate and influence financial accounting. To continue your introduction to business, this chapter explains several ways a business can be organized. The chapter also shows you how accountants analyze business transactions to generate useful information. This is important for understanding why financial statements are useful. Finally, the chapter explains the return on equity ratio, which you can use in evaluating a company's operating success during a reporting period.

FINANCIAL STATEMENTS

LO 1

Describe the information presented in financial statements, be able to prepare simple financial statements, and analyze a business's performance with the return on equity ratio.

Accounting exists for the purpose of providing useful information to people who make rational investment, credit, and similar decisions.[1] These decision makers include investors, lenders, managers, suppliers, customers, and other interested people. Be sure to read the As a Matter of Opinion box to learn how one decision maker uses accounting information to help him fulfill his responsibilities as a manager in a regional municipality.

Many organizations provide accounting information to managers and other decision makers in the form of financial statements. The statements are useful because they help to describe the organization's financial health and performance in a condensed and highly informative format. Because they give an overall view of the entire organization, financial statements are a good place to start your study of accounting. We begin by looking at the income statement and the balance sheet.

The Income Statement

Look at the **income statement** in Illustration 1–1 (page 24). The income statement shows whether the business earned a profit (also called *net income.*) A company

---

[1]*CICA Handbook,* "Financial Statement Concepts," par. 1000.12.

As a Matter of Opinion

Mr. Parent received his BBA from Wilfrid Laurier University and his MBA from the University of Toronto. He has been a certified member of the Society of Management Accountants of Ontario since 1991. He is presently the Manager of Financial Services in the Regional Municipality of Waterloo's Finance Department. He works with the Community Health and Social Services Departments with a combined annual operating budget in excess of $170 million.

*I find the practice of accounting in the public sector to be challenging and reward-*ing. Today, all levels of government are being challenged to rethink how services will be provided to the public. My accounting education allows me to examine the intricacies of the many different programs the Municipality offers. This enables me to advise senior management and Council of the financial impacts of proposed initiatives. Often the impact of proposed changes will have differing implications for various stakeholders. Accountants in these situations must take a broad view of the issues when making their recommendations.

Wm. Lee Parent, MBA, CMA

earns a **net income** if its revenues exceed its expenses. A company incurs a **net loss** if its expenses exceed its revenues. In Illustration 1–1, observe that the income statement does not simply report the amount of net income or net loss. Instead, it lists the types and amounts of the revenues and expenses. As another example, **Canadian Pacific Limited** classifies the revenues and expenses on its income statement into the following categories: energy, forest products, real estate and hotels, and telecommunications and manufacturing. This detailed information is more useful for decision making than just a simple net income or loss number.

Revenues are inflows of cash or other assets received in exchange for providing goods or services to customers. Revenues also may occur from decreases in liabilities, for example, providing goods and services for which payment was received in advance.[2] For now, think of assets as economic resources owned by a business and liabilities as the debts owed by a business. Later, we define these terms more completely.

The income statement in Illustration 1–1 shows that the business of Clear Copy earned revenues of $3,900 by providing copy services to customers during the month of December. Examples of revenues for other businesses include sales of products, rent, commissions, and interest.

Expenses are costs incurred by a firm in the process of earning revenue and are measured by the cost of goods and services consumed in the operation of the business.[3] The income statement in Illustration 1–1 shows that Clear Copy used an employee's services. This cost is reported as salaries expense of $700. The business also used services in the form of office space rented to the business by the owner of the building. This cost is reported in Illustration 1–1 as rent expense of $1,000.

Notice that the heading in Illustration 1–1 names the business, states that the report is an income statement, and shows the time period covered by the statement. Information about the time period is important for evaluating the company's

---

[2]*CICA Handbook,* "Financial Statement Concepts," par. 1000.37.

[3]Ibid., par. 1000.38.

Illustration 1–1
Income Statement for
Clear Copy

CLEAR COPY
Income Statement
For Month Ended December 31, 1996

Revenues:
   Copy services revenue $3,900

Operating expenses:
   Rent expense $1,000
   Salaries expense   700

   Total operating expenses   1,700

Net income $2,200

performance. For example, you need to know that Clear Copy earned the $2,200 net income during a one-month period to judge whether that amount is satisfactory.

The Balance Sheet

The purpose of the **balance sheet** is to provide information that helps users understand a company's financial status as of a given date. As a result, the balance sheet often is called the **statement of financial position.** The balance sheet describes financial position by listing the types and dollar amounts of assets, liabilities, and equity of the business. (Equity is the difference between a company's assets and its liabilities.)

Illustration 1–2 presents the balance sheet for Clear Copy as of December 31, 1996. Unlike the income statement that refers to a period of time, the balance sheet describes conditions that exist at a point in time. Thus, the heading shows the specific date on which the assets and liabilities are identified and measured. The amounts in the balance sheet are stated as of the close of business on that date.

The balance sheet in Illustration 1–2 reports that the company owned three different assets at the close of business on December 31, 1996. The assets were cash, store supplies, and copy equipment. The total dollar amount for these assets was $38,000. The balance sheet also shows that there were liabilities of $6,200. Owner's equity was $31,800. This amount is the difference between the assets and the liabilities.

Notice that the total amounts on the two sides of the balance sheet are equal. This equality is why the statement is called a *balance sheet*. The name also reflects the fact that the statement reports the balances of the assets, liabilities, and equity on a given date.

ASSETS, LIABILITIES, AND EQUITY

In general, the **assets** of a business are the items (economic resources) owned by the business and expected to benefit future operations.[4] One familiar asset is cash. Another asset consists of amounts owed to the business by its customers for goods and services sold to them on credit. This asset is called **accounts receivable.** In general, individuals who owe amounts to the business are called its **debtors.** Other

---

[4]Ibid., par. 1000.29.

Illustration 1-2
Balance Sheet for
Clear Copy

CLEAR COPY
Balance Sheet
December 31, 1996

Assets		Liabilities	
Cash	$ 8,400	Accounts payable	$ 6,200
Store supplies	3,600	**Owner's Equity**	
Copy equipment	26,000	Terry Dow, capital	31,800
		Total liabilities and	
Total assets	$38,000	owner's equity	$38,000

assets owned by businesses include merchandise held for sale, supplies, equipment, buildings, and land. Assets also can be intangible rights, such as those granted by a patent or copyright.

The **liabilities** of a business are its debts. These debts normally require future payment in assets or the rendering of services, or both.[5] One common liability consists of amounts owed for goods and services bought on credit. This liability is called **accounts payable.** Other liabilities are salaries and wages owed to employees, taxes payable, notes payable, and interest payable.

A liability represents a claim against a business. In general, those who have the right to receive payments from a company are called its **creditors.** From the creditor's viewpoint, a liability is the right to be paid by a business. (In effect, one company's payable is another company's receivable.) If a business fails to pay its debts, the law gives creditors the right to force the sale of its assets to obtain the money to meet their claims. When the assets are sold under these conditions, the creditors are paid first, up to the full amount of their claims, with the remainder (the residual) going to the owner of the business.

Creditors often use a balance sheet to help them decide whether to loan money to a business. They can use the balance sheet to compare the amounts of existing liabilities and assets. A loan is less risky if the liabilities are small in comparison to the assets. There is less risk because there is a larger cushion if the assets are sold for less than the amounts shown on the balance sheet. On the other hand, a loan is more risky if the liabilities are large compared to the assets. The risk is greater because it is more likely that the assets cannot be sold for enough cash to pay all the debts.

Equity is defined as "the residual interest in the assets of an entity that remains after deducting its liabilities."[6] Equity is also called **net assets.** If a business is organized as a corporation (which we describe later), the owners of the business are called shareholders or stockholders and the equity is called *shareholders' (stockholders') equity.* Because Clear Copy is owned by one person and is not a corporation, the equity section in Illustration 1–2 is simply called *owner's equity.*

Earlier we defined net income as the difference between revenue and expense for a time period. Net income is also the change in owner's equity that occurred during the period as a result of the company's major or central operations. By

---

[5]Ibid., par. 1000.32.

[6]Ibid., par. 1000.35.

describing this change, the income statement links the company's balance sheets as of the beginning and end of the reporting period. The following diagram represents the relationship between these two statements.

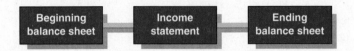

We use this background on the balance sheet and income statement to explain more about financial accounting. The next sections of the chapter describe the principles that guide the practice of financial accounting.

Progress Check
(Answers to Progress Checks are provided at the end of the chapter.)

1-1   Which set of information is reported on an income statement? *(a)* Assets, liabilities, and owner's equity; *(b)* Revenues, expenses, and owner's equity; *(c)* Assets, liabilities, and net income; *(d)* Revenues, expenses, and net income.

1-2   What do accountants mean by the term *expense?*

GENERALLY ACCEPTED ACCOUNTING PRINCIPLES (GAAP)

LO 2

Explain the accounting principles introduced in the chapter.

In the Prologue, we explained that financial accounting practice is governed by a set of rules called *generally accepted accounting principles,* or *GAAP*. To use and interpret financial statements effectively, you need to have a basic understanding of these principles.

A primary purpose of GAAP is to make the information in financial reports relevant, reliable, and comparable. Information that is relevant has the capacity to affect the decisions made by financial statement users. Reliable information is necessary if decision makers are to depend on it. In addition, the information should allow statement users to compare companies. These comparisons are more likely to be useful if all companies use similar practices. GAAP impose limits on the variety of accounting practices that companies can use, thereby making the financial statements more useful.

The Development of GAAP

Prior to the 1930s, GAAP developed through common usage. In effect, a practice was considered suitable if it was acceptable to most accountants. This history is still reflected in the phrase *generally accepted.* However, as the accounting profession grew and the world of business became more complex, many people were not satisfied with the profession's progress in providing useful information.

The desire for improvement caused many accountants, managers, and government regulators to want more uniformity in practice. Thus, in the 1930s, they began to give authority for defining accepted principles to small groups of experienced professional accountants. Since then, a series of committees or boards have had authority to establish GAAP. In general, the authority of these groups has increased over time. We describe the present arrangement for establishing GAAP in Appendix A at the end of this chapter.

Broad and Specific Accounting Principles

GAAP include both broad and specific principles. The broad principles describe the basic assumptions and general guidelines that accountants follow in preparing financial statements. The specific principles provide more detailed rules that accountants follow in reporting the results of various business activities. The broad principles stem from observing long-used accounting practices. In contrast, the specific principles are established more often by the rulings of authoritative bodies.

As a user of financial statements, an understanding of both broad and specific principles will give you insight as to what the information means. It will also help you know what the information does not mean and thereby avoid using it incorrectly. Because the broad principles are especially helpful for learning about accounting, we emphasize them in the early chapters of the book. The broad principles include the following:[7]

	First Introduced	
	Chapter	**Page**
Business entity principle	1	28
Objectivity principle	1	28
Cost principle	1	28
Going-concern principle	1	29
Revenue recognition principle	1	35
Time period principle	3	128
Matching principle	3	130
Conservatism principle	8	410
Materiality principle	8	417
Full-disclosure principle	8	425
Consistency principle	9	456

Specific principles are especially important for understanding individual items in the financial statements. They are described throughout the book as we come to them.

At the beginning of this chapter, we said that the purpose of accounting is to provide useful information to people who make rational investment, credit, and similar decisions. In fact, this description of the purpose of accounting comes from "Financial Statement Concepts," section 1000, in the *CICA Handbook*. This section defines several accounting concepts that should be understood by financial statement users as well as accountants. For example, we relied on these concepts in preceding discussions when we defined revenues, expenses, assets, liabilities, and equity.

Another purpose of the concepts is to describe the characteristics that make accounting information useful for decisions. Earlier, we referred to the section's commonsense ideas that information is useful only if it has both *relevance* and *reliability.*

UNDERSTANDING GENERALLY ACCEPTED ACCOUNTING PRINCIPLES

---

[7]In describing these accounting principles, some writers have used different words to mean the same thing. For example, broad principles also have been called *concepts, theories, assumptions,* and *postulates.* We call them *principles,* but don't be confused if you see them called by other names in other books.

We will begin our discussion of accounting principles by describing some of the broad principles (listed on page 27) that will help you understand financial statements and the procedures used to prepare them.

Business Entity Principle

The **business entity principle** requires every business to be accounted for separately and distinctly from its owner or owners. This principle also requires separate accounting for other entities that might be controlled by the same owners. The reason behind this principle is that separate information for each business is relevant to decisions that the users of the information make.

To illustrate, suppose that the owner of a business wants to see how well it is doing. To be useful, the financial statements for the business should not mix the owner's personal transactions with the business's transactions. For example, the owner's personal expenses should not be subtracted from the company's revenues on its income statement because they do not contribute to the company's success. Thus, the income statement should not report such things as the owner's personal entertainment and transportation expenses. Otherwise, the company's reported net income would be understated and the business would appear less profitable than it really is.

In summary, a company's reports should not include its owner's personal transactions, assets, and liabilities or the transactions, assets, and liabilities of another business. If this principle is not carefully followed, the reported information about the company's financial position and net income is not useful for rational investment and credit decisions.

Objectivity Principle

The **objectivity principle** requires financial statement information to be supported by evidence other than someone's opinion or imagination. Information would not be reliable if it were based only on what the statement preparer thinks might be true. The preparer might be too optimistic or too pessimistic. In the worst case, an unethical preparer might try to mislead financial statement users by deliberately misrepresenting the truth. The objectivity principle is intended to make financial statements useful by ensuring that they present reliable information.

Cost Principle

The **cost principle** requires financial statement information to be based on costs incurred in business transactions. Sales and purchases are examples of **business transactions.** Business transactions are exchanges of economic consideration between two parties. The consideration may include such things as goods, services, money, or rights to collect money. In applying the cost principle, cost is measured on a cash or cash equivalent basis. If cash is given for an asset or service, the cost of the asset or service is measured as the entire amount of cash paid. If something other than cash is exchanged (such as an old vehicle traded in for a new one), cost is measured as the cash equivalent value of what was given up or of the item received, whichever is more clearly evident.[8]

---

[8]*CICA Handbook,* "Non-monetary Transactions," par. 3830.05.

The *cost principle* is accepted because it puts relevant information in the financial statements. Cost is the amount initially sacrificed to purchase an asset or service. Cost also approximates the market value of the asset or service when it was acquired. Information about the amount sacrificed and the initial market value of what was received is generally thought to be relevant to decisions. Complying with the cost principle provides this information.

In addition, the cost principle is consistent with the *objectivity principle.* Most accountants believe that information based on actual costs is more likely to be objective than information based on estimates of values. For example, reporting purchases of assets and services at cost is more objective than reporting the manager's estimate of their value. Thus, financial statements based on costs are believed to be more reliable because the information is more objective.

To illustrate, suppose that a business pays $50,000 for land used in its operations. The cost principle tells us to record the purchase at $50,000. It would make no difference if the buyer thinks that the land is worth at least $60,000. The cost principle requires the purchase to be recorded at the cost of $50,000. However, you learn in later chapters that to provide more useful information, objective estimates of value are sometimes reported instead of costs.

Going-Concern Principle

The **going-concern principle** (also called the **continuing-concern principle**) requires financial statements to reflect the assumption that the business will continue operating instead of being closed or sold. Thus, a company's balance sheet does not report the liquidation values of operating assets that are being held for long-term use. Instead, these assets are reported at amounts based on their cost. Many accountants have argued that the going-concern principle leads to reporting relevant information because many decisions about a business are made with the expectation that it will continue to exist in the future.

As a result of applying the cost and going-concern principles, a company's balance sheet seldom describes what the company is worth. Thus, if a company is to be bought or sold, the buyer and seller are well advised to obtain additional information from other sources such as a professional appraiser.[9]

The going-concern principle must be ignored if the company is expected to fail or be liquidated. In these cases, the going-concern principle and the cost principle do not apply. Instead, estimated market values are relevant and costs are not relevant.

Progress Check

1-3   **Name and describe two qualities of useful information identified by the "Financial Statement Concepts."**

1-4   **Why are the personal activities of a business owner excluded from the financial statements of the owner's business?**

---

[9]GAAP require supplemental disclosures (in the notes to the financial statements) of the current market values of many assets and liabilities.

1-5   **If a company finds a bargain on some equipment worth $40,000 to the company and is able to buy the equipment for $25,000, what amount should be reported for the equipment on the company's balance sheet prepared immediately after the purchase? Which principle governs your answer?**

LEGAL FORMS OF BUSINESS ORGANIZATIONS

LO 3

Describe single proprietorships, partnerships, and corporations, including any differences in the owners' responsibilities for the debts of the organizations.

This section of the chapter describes three legal forms for business organizations. The forms are *single proprietorships, partnerships,* and *corporations.* The particular form chosen for a company creates some differences in its financial statements.

Single Proprietorships and Partnerships

A **single proprietorship** (or **sole proprietorship**) is owned by one person and is not organized under federal or provincial laws as a corporation. Small retail stores and service enterprises are often operated as single proprietorships. No special legal requirements must be met to start this kind of business. As a result, single proprietorships are the most numerous of all types of businesses.

A **partnership** is owned by two or more people, called partners, and is not organized as a corporation. Like a single proprietorship, no special legal requirements must be met in starting a partnership. All that is required is an agreement between the partners to operate a business together. The agreement can be either oral or written. However, a written partnership agreement may help the partners avoid or resolve later disputes.

In a strict legal sense, single proprietorships and partnerships are not separate from their owners. Thus, for example, a court can order an owner to sell personal assets to pay the debts of a proprietorship or partnership. In fact, an owner's personal assets may have to be sold to satisfy *all* the debts of a proprietorship or a partnership, even if this amount exceeds the owner's equity in the company. This unlimited liability feature of proprietorships and partnerships is an important disadvantage.

Despite the lack of separate legal existence from their owners, the *business entity principle* applies to the financial statements of single proprietorships and partnerships. That is, relevant information for ordinary investment and credit decisions is more likely to be reported in the financial statements if each business is treated as being separate from its owner or owners.

Corporations

A **corporation** is a separate legal entity chartered (or *incorporated*) under federal or provincial laws. Unlike proprietorships or partnerships, corporations are legally separate and distinct from their owners.

A corporation's equity is divided into units called **shares** or *stocks* and its owners are called **shareholders** or *stockholders*. For example, **Pier 1 Imports, Inc.,** is a corporation that had issued 37,617,000 shares at the close of its 1994 business year. In other words, Pier 1's equity was divided into 37,617,000 units. A shareholder who owned 376,617 shares would own 1% of the company.

When a corporation issues only one class of shares, it is called **common shares,** *common stock,* or *capital stock.* We discuss other classes of shares in Chapter 15 (Volume II).

A very important characteristic of a corporation is its status as a separate legal entity. This characteristic means that the corporation is responsible for its own acts and its own debts. As a result, the corporation's shareholders are not personally liable for these acts and debts. This limited liability feature is a major advantage of corporations over proprietorships and partnerships.

The separate legal status of a corporation also means that it can enter into its own contracts. For example, a corporation can buy, own, and sell property in its own name. It also can sue and be sued in its own name. In short, the separate legal status enables a corporation to conduct its business affairs with all the rights, duties, and responsibilities of a person. Of course, a corporation lacks a physical body and must act through its managers, who are its legal agents.

In addition, the separate legal status of a corporation means that its life is not limited by its owners' lives or by a need for them to remain owners. Thus, a shareholder can sell or transfer shares to another person without affecting the operations of the corporation.

There are fewer corporations in Canada than proprietorships and partnerships. However, the corporate form of business offers advantages for accumulating and managing capital resources. As a result, corporations control the most economic wealth.

Differences in Financial Statements

Despite the major legal differences among the three forms of businesses, there are only a few differences in their financial statements.

One difference is in the equity section of the balance sheet. A proprietorship's balance sheet lists the capital balance beside the single owner's name. Partnership balance sheets use the same approach, unless there are too many owners for their names to fit in the available space. The names of a corporation's shareholders are not listed in the balance sheet. Instead, the total shareholders' equity is divided into **contributed capital** (also called **paid-in capital**) and **retained earnings.** Contributed capital is created by the shareholders' investments. Retained earnings are created by the corporation's income earning activities.

Another difference exists in the term used to describe payments by a company to its owners. When an owner of a proprietorship or a partnership receives cash from the company, the payments are called **withdrawals.** When owners of a corporation receive cash from the company, the payments are called **dividends.** Withdrawals and dividends are not reported on a company's income statement because they are not expenses incurred to generate revenues but represent reductions in equity.

Another difference involves reporting of payments to a company's managers when the managers are also owners. Because a corporation is a separate legal entity, salaries paid to its managers are reported as expenses on its income statement. In contrast, if the owner of a single proprietorship is also its manager, no salary expense is reported on the income statement for these services. The same is true for a partnership. This different treatment requires special consideration when analyzing the income statement. Our discussion at the end of this chapter describes this analysis in more detail.

To keep things simple while you are beginning to learn accounting, the examples in the first portion of this book are all based on single proprietorships. Chapters 14, 15, and 16 (Volume II) provide additional information about the financial statements of partnerships and corporations.

Progress Check

1-6 A single proprietorship: *(a)* divides its equity into shares; *(b)* is a separate legal entity; *(c)* is owned by one person who is personally responsible for all its debts.

1-7 Why are a proprietor's withdrawals not reported on the company's income statement?

USING THE BALANCE SHEET EQUATION TO PROVIDE USEFUL INFORMATION

LO 4

Analyze business transactions to determine their effects on the accounting equation.

Up to this stage, you have learned that financial statements describe the financial activities of a business. You also know that many of these activities (for example, purchases and sales) involve business transactions. To clearly understand the information in the statements, you need to see how an accounting system captures relevant data from the transactions, classifies and saves it, and then organizes it on the financial statements. We begin to explain this in the next section of the chapter. Our explanation continues through Chapter 4. We start with a simple example.

The beginning point for accounting systems is the definition of *owner's equity* as the difference between an organization's assets and liabilities. This definition can be stated as the following equation for a single proprietorship:

$$\text{Assets} - \text{Liabilities} = \text{Owner's Equity}$$

Creditors and owners provide the resources for acquiring the assets. Like any equation, this one can be modified by rearranging the terms. The following modified form of the equation is called the **balance sheet equation:**

$$\text{Assets} = \text{Liabilities} + \text{Owner's Equity}$$

Because it serves as the basis for financial accounting information, the balance sheet equation also is called the **accounting equation.** The next section shows you how to use this equation to keep track of changes in a company's assets, liabilities, and owner's equity in a way that provides useful information.

THE EFFECTS OF TRANSACTIONS ON THE ACCOUNTING EQUATION

A transaction is an exchange between two parties of such things as goods, services, money, or rights to collect money. Because the two parties exchange assets and liabilities, transactions affect the components of the accounting equation. Importantly, each and every transaction always leaves the equation in balance. That is, the total assets always equal the sum of the liabilities and the equity regardless of what happens in a transaction. We show how this equality is preserved by looking at the transactions of a new small business called Clear Copy.

Transaction 1. On December 1, 1996, Terry Dow formed a new photocopying store that was organized as a single proprietorship. Dow planned to be the manager of the store as well as its owner. The marketing plan for the store is to focus primarily on serving business customers who place relatively large orders. Dow

	Assets				Owner's Equity	
	Cash	+	Store Supplies	+	Copy Equipment	=	Terry Dow, Capital	Explanation of Change

	Cash		Store Supplies		Copy Equipment		Terry Dow, Capital	Explanation of Change
(1)	$30,000						$30,000	Investment
(2)	– 2,500		+$2,500					
Bal.	$27,500		$2,500				$30,000	
(3)	–20,000				+$20,000			
Bal.	$ 7,500 +		$2,500	+	$20,000	=	$30,000	

Illustration 1–3
Changes in the
Balance
Sheet Equation
Caused
by Asset Purchases for
Cash

invested $30,000 cash in the new company and deposited it in a bank account opened under the name of Clear Copy. After this event, the cash (an asset) and the owner's equity each equal $30,000; as you can see, the accounting equation is in balance:

$$\text{Assets} \quad = \quad \text{Owner's Equity}$$

$$\underline{\text{Cash, } \$30,000} \qquad \underline{\text{Terry Dow, Capital, } \$30,000}$$

The equation shows that the business has one asset, cash, equal to $30,000. It has no liabilities, and the owner's equity is $30,000.

Transactions 2 and 3. In its second business transaction, Clear Copy used $2,500 of its cash to purchase store supplies. In a third transaction, Clear Copy spent $20,000 to buy photocopying equipment. These events, which we call transactions 2 and 3, were both exchanges of cash for other assets. Neither transaction produced an expense because no value was lost to the company. The purchases merely changed the form of the assets from cash to supplies and equipment.

The effects of these transactions are shown in colour in the equations in Illustration 1–3. Observe that the decreases in cash are exactly equal to the increases in the store supplies and the copy equipment. As a result, the equation remains in balance after each transaction.

Transaction 4. Next, Dow decided that the business needed more store supplies and additional copy equipment. The items to be purchased would have a total cost of $7,100. However, as shown on the last line of the first column in Illustration 1–3, the business had only $7,500 in cash after transaction 3. Because these purchases would use almost all of Clear Copy's cash, Dow arranged to purchase them on credit from Handy Supply Company. That is, Clear Copy took delivery of the items in exchange for a promise to pay for them later. The supplies cost $1,100, the copy equipment cost $6,000, and the total liability to Handy Supply is $7,100.

The effects of this purchase are shown in Illustration 1–4 as transaction 4. Notice that the purchase increased total assets by $7,100 while the company's liabilities (called *accounts payable*) increased by the same amount. The transaction did not create an expense, so the amount of equity remained unchanged from the original $30,000 balance.

Illustration 1–4   Changes in the Balance Sheet Equation Caused by Asset Purchases on Credit, Revenues Received in Cash, and Expenses Paid in Cash

	Cash	+	Store Supplies	+	Copy Equipment	=	Accounts Payable	+	Terry Dow, Capital	Explanation of Change
			Assets				Liabilities		Owner's Equity	
Bal.	$7,500		$2,500		$20,000				$30,000	
(4)			+1,100		+ 6,000		+$7,100			
Bal.	$7,500		$3,600		$26,000		$7,100		$30,000	
(5)	+2,200								+ 2,200	Revenue
Bal.	$9,700		$3,600		$26,000		$7,100		$32,200	
(6)	−1,000								− 1,000	Expense
Bal.	$8,700		$3,600		$26,000		$7,100		$31,200	
(7)	− 700								−700	Expense
Bal.	$8,000	+	$3,600	+	$26,000	=	$7,100	+	$30,500	

Transaction 5. A primary objective of a business is to increase its owner's wealth. This goal is met when the business produces a profit (also called *net income*). A net income is reflected in the accounting equation as a net increase in owner's equity. Clear Copy's method of generating revenues is to sell photocopying services to its customers. The business produces a net income only if its revenues are greater than the expenses incurred in earning them. As you should expect, the process of earning copy services revenues and incurring expenses creates changes in the accounting equation.

We can see how the accounting equation is affected by earning revenues in transaction 5. In this transaction, Clear Copy provided copying services to a customer on December 10 and immediately collected $2,200 cash. Illustration 1–4 shows that this event increased cash by $2,200 and increased owner's equity by $2,200. This increase in equity is identified in the last column as a revenue because it was earned by providing services. This information can be used later to prepare the income statement.

Transactions 6 and 7. Also on December 10, Clear Copy paid $1,000 rent to the owner of the building in which its store is located. Paying this amount allowed Clear Copy to occupy the space for the entire month of December. The effects of this event are shown in Illustration 1–4 as transaction 6. On December 12, Clear Copy paid the $700 salary of the company's only employee. This event is reflected in Illustration 1–4 as transaction 7.

Both transactions 6 and 7 produced expenses for the business. That is, they used up cash for the purpose of providing services to customers. Unlike the asset purchases in transactions 2 and 3, the cash payments in transactions 6 and 7 acquired services. The benefits of these services do not last beyond the end of the month. The equations in Illustration 1–4 show that both transactions reduced cash and Terry Dow's equity. Thus, the accounting equation remains in balance after each event. The last column in Illustration 1–4 shows that these decreases were expenses. This information is useful when the income statement is prepared.

Summary. We said before that a business produces a net income when its revenues exceed its expenses. Net income increases owner's equity. If the expenses exceed the revenues, a net loss occurs and equity is decreased. Remember that the amount of net income or loss is not affected by transactions completed between a business and its owner. Thus, Terry Dow's initial investment of $30,000 is not income to the business, even though it increased the equity.

To keep things simple and to emphasize the fact that revenues and expenses produce changes in equity, the illustrations in this first chapter add the revenues directly to owner's equity and subtract the expenses directly from owner's equity. In actual practice, however, information about the revenues and expenses is accumulated separately and the amounts are added to or subtracted from owner's equity. We describe more details about this process in Chapters 2, 3, and 4.

Because of the importance of earning revenues for a company's success, we briefly interrupt the description of Clear Copy's transactions to describe the *revenue recognition principle*. This principle guides us in knowing when to record a company's revenue so that it can be usefully reported in the income statement.

Managers need guidance in deciding when to recognize revenue. (*Recognize* means to record an event for the purpose of reporting its effects in the financial statements.) For example, if revenue is recognized too early, the income statement reports net income sooner than it should and the business looks more profitable than it really is. On the other hand, if the revenue is not recognized on time, the income statement shows lower amounts of revenue and net income than it should and the business looks less profitable than it really is. In either case, the income statement does not provide decision makers with useful information about the company's success.

The question of when revenue should be recognized on the income statement is addressed by the **revenue recognition principle** (also called the **realization principle**). This principle includes three important guidelines:

1. *Revenue should be recognized at the time it is earned.* The whole process of getting ready to provide services, finding customers, convincing them to buy, and providing a service contributes to the earning of revenue. However, the amount of revenue earned at any point in the process usually cannot be determined reliably until the entire process is complete. This does not occur until the business acquires the right to collect the selling price. Therefore, in most cases, revenue should not be recognized on the income statement until the earnings process is essentially complete. For most businesses, the earnings process is completed only when services are rendered or when the seller transfers ownership of goods sold to the buyer. For example, suppose that a customer pays in advance of taking delivery of a good or service. Because the earnings process is not completed, the seller should not recognize any revenue. Instead, the seller must actually complete the earnings process before recognizing the revenue.[10] This practice is known as the *sales basis of* revenue recognition.

REVENUE RECOGNITION PRINCIPLE

LO 2

Explain the accounting principles introduced in the chapter.

---

[10]*CICA Handbook,* "Revenue," par. 3400.06–.09.

Illustration 1-5   Changes in the Balance Sheet Equation Caused by Noncash Revenues, the Later Receipt of Cash, the Payment of Payables, and Withdrawals by the Owner

	Cash	+	Accounts Receivable	+	Store Supplies	+	Copy Equipment	=	Accounts Payable	+	Terry Dow, Capital	Explanation of Change
					Assets				**Liabilities**		**Owner's Equity**	
Bal.	$8,000				$3,600		$26,000		$7,100		$30,500	
(8)			+$1,700								+ 1,700	Revenue
Bal.	$8,000		$1,700		$3,600		$26,000		$7,100		$32,200	
(9)	+1,700		−1,700									
Bal.	$9,700		$ 0		$3,600		$26,000		$7,100		$32,200	
(10)	− 900								− 900			
Bal.	$8,800		$ 0		$3,600		$26,000		$6,200		$32,200	
(11)	− 400										− 400	Withdrawal
Bal.	$8,400	+	$ 0	+	$3,600	+	$26,000	=	$6,200	+	$31,800	

2. *The inflow of assets associated with revenue does not have to be in the form of cash.* The most common noncash asset acquired by the seller in a revenue transaction is an account receivable from a customer. These transactions, called *credit sales,* occur because it is convenient for the customer to get the goods or services now and pay for them later. (Remember that Clear Copy took advantage of this convenience in transaction 4 when it bought supplies and equipment on credit.) If objective evidence shows that the seller has the right to collect the account receivable, the seller should recognize the revenue. When the cash is collected later, no additional revenue is recognized. Instead, collecting the cash simply changes the form of the asset from a receivable to cash.

3. *The amount of recognized revenue should be measured as the cash received plus the cash equivalent value (fair market value) of any other asset or assets received.* For example, if the transaction creates an account receivable, the seller should recognize revenue equal to the value of the receivable, which is usually equivalent to the amount of cash to be collected.

The notes to a company's financial statements should include an explanation of the specific approach to revenue recognition used by the company. For example, **Magna International, Inc.** states in its 1994 annual report that "Revenue from sales of manufactured products is recognized upon shipment to customers."

THE EFFECTS OF ADDITIONAL TRANSACTIONS ON THE ACCOUNTING EQUATION

To show how the revenue recognition principle works, we return to the example of Clear Copy.

Transactions 8 and 9. Assume that Clear Copy provided copy services for a customer and billed that customer $1,700. This event is identified as transaction 8 in Illustration 1–5. Ten days later, the customer paid Clear Copy the full $1,700, shown in transaction 9.

Illustration 1–5 shows that transaction 8 created a new asset, the account receivable from the customer. The $1,700 increase in assets produces an equal increase in owner's equity. Notice that this increase in equity is identified as a revenue in the last column of Illustration 1–5.

Transaction 9 occurred when the customer in transaction 8 paid the account receivable. This event merely converted the receivable to cash. Because transaction 9 did not increase total assets and did not affect liabilities, equity did not change. Thus, this transaction did not create any new revenue. The revenue was generated when Clear Copy rendered the services, not when the cash was collected. This emphasis on the earning process instead of cash flows reflects the goal of providing useful information in the income statement by applying the *revenue recognition principle.*

Transaction 10. In transaction 10, Clear Copy paid $900 to Handy Supply Company on December 24. The $900 payment relates to the earlier purchase of equipment from Handy. (The amount due Handy for the supplies purchase remains unpaid.) Illustration 1–6 shows that this transaction decreased Clear Copy's cash by $900 and decreased its liability to Handy Supply by the same amount. As a result, there was no reduction in owner's equity. This event did not create an expense, even though cash flowed out of the company.

Transaction 11. Another type of event, the payment of cash to the company's owner, is identified in Illustration 1–5 as transaction 11. In this case, Clear Copy paid $400 to Terry Dow to use for personal living expenses. Traditionally, a company's payments of cash (or other assets) to its owner are called *withdrawals.* Notice that this decrease in owner's equity is not called an expense in Illustration 1–5. Withdrawals are not expenses because they do not create revenues for the company. And because withdrawals are not expenses, they are not used to calculate net income.

Summary. Illustration 1–6 presents the effects of the entire series of 11 transactions for Clear Copy. Take time now to see that the equation remains in balance after each transaction. This is because the effects of each transaction are always in balance. In transactions 1, 5, and 8, total assets and equity increased by equal amounts. In transactions 2, 3, and 9, one asset increased while another decreased by an equal amount. Transaction 4 increased total assets and a liability by equal amounts. In transactions 6, 7, and 11, assets and equity decreased by equal amounts. Finally, transaction 10 decreased an asset and a liability by the same amount. The equality of these effects is central to the working of double entry accounting. You learn more about double entry accounting in the next chapter.

Progress Check

1-8   **A new business has the following transactions: (1) the owner invested $3,600 cash; (2) supplies were purchased for $2,600 cash; (3) services were provided to a customer for $2,300 cash; (4) a salary of $1,000 was paid to an employee; and (5) $3,000 cash was borrowed from the bank. After these transactions, total assets, total liabilities, and total owner's equity are:** (a) **$7,900, $5,300, $2,600;** (b) **$7,900, $3,000, $4,900;** (c) **$7,900, $3,000, $3,600.**

1-9   **Is it possible for a transaction to increase a liability without affecting any other asset, liability, or owner's equity? Explain.**

Illustration 1-6 Changes in the Balance Sheet Equation Caused by Noncash Revenues, the Later Receipt of Cash, the Payment of Payables, and Withdrawals by the Owner

	Cash	+ Accounts Receivable	+ Store Supplies	+ Copy Equipment	= Accounts Payable	+ Terry Dow, Capital	Explanation of Change
(1)	$30,000					$30,000	Investment
(2)	− 2,500		+$2,500				
Bal.	$27,500		$2,500			$30,000	
(3)	−20,000			+$20,000			
Bal.	$ 7,500		$2,500	$20,000		$30,000	
(4)			+1,100	+ 6,000	+$7,100		
Bal.	$7,500		$3,600	$26,000	$7,100	$30,000	
(5)	+2,200					+2,200	Revenue
Bal.	$9,700		$3,600	$26,000	$7,100	$32,200	
(6)	−1,000					−1,000	Expense
Bal.	$8,700		$3,600	$26,000	$7,100	$31,200	
(7)	− 700					− 700	Expense
Bal.	$8,000		$3,600	$26,000	$7,100	$30,500	
(8)		+$1,700				+1,700	Revenue
Bal.	$8,000	$1,700	$3,600	$26,000	$7,100	$32,200	
(9)	+1,700	−1,700					
Bal.	$9,700	$ 0	$3,600	$26,000	$7,100	$32,200	
(10)	− 900				− 900		
Bal.	$8,800	$ 0	$3,600	$26,000	$6,200	$32,200	
(11)	− 400					− 400	Withdrawal
Bal.	$8,400 +	$ 0 +	$3,600 +	$26,000 =	$6,200 +	$31,800	

Above the columns: **Assets** (Cash + Accounts Receivable + Store Supplies + Copy Equipment), **Liabilities** (Accounts Payable), **Owner's Equity** (Terry Dow, Capital; Explanation of Change)

UNDERSTANDING MORE ABOUT THE FINANCIAL STATEMENTS

Up to this point, you have learned about only two financial statements: the income statement and the balance sheet. GAAP also require companies to include two other statements in their reports. They are the statement of changes in owner's equity and the statement of changes in financial position.

The following diagram shows how all four financial statements are linked:

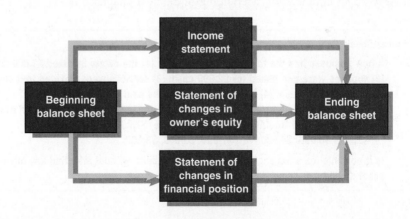

The income statement describes how owner's equity changed during the period through the company's income earning activities. The statement of changes in owner's equity describes all changes in equity, including net income, new investments by the owner, and withdrawals by the owner. The statement of changes in financial position describes how the amount of cash changed between the beginning and ending balance sheets. The statement of changes in financial position also describes many of the changes in the company's other assets and liabilities. Thus, most of the company's activities are described by the three statements in the middle, while the balance sheets describe the company's financial position before and after those activities occurred.

The Income Statement

The top section of Illustration 1–7 shows Clear Copy's income statement as it appeared in Illustration 1–1. Now you can see that it is based on the information about revenues and expenses recorded in the owner's equity column in Illustration 1–6.

In the income statement, the copy services revenue of $3,900 resulted from transactions 5 and 8. If the business had earned other kinds of revenues, they would have been listed separately to help users understand more about the company's activities. The income statement then lists the rent and salaries expenses incurred in transactions 6 and 7. The types of expenses are identified to help users form a more complete picture of the events of the time period. Finally, the income statement presents the amount of net income earned during the month.

The Statement of Changes in Owner's Equity

The **statement of changes in owner's equity** presents information about everything that happened to equity during the reporting period. The statement shows the beginning equity, the events that increased it (new investments by the owner and net income), and the events that decreased it (withdrawals and a net loss instead of net income).

The middle section of Illustration 1–7 shows the statement of changes in owner's equity for Clear Copy. The heading refers to December 1996 because the statement describes events that happened during that month. The beginning balance of equity is stated as of the beginning of business on December 1. It is zero because the business did not exist before then. An existing business would report the balance as of the end of the prior reporting period. The Clear Copy statement shows that $30,000 of equity was created by Dow's initial investment. It also shows the $2,200 net income earned during the month. This item links the income statement to the statement of changes in owner's equity. The statement also reports Dow's $400 withdrawal and the $31,800 equity balance at the end of the month.

The Balance Sheet

The lower section of Illustration 1–7 presents Clear Copy's balance sheet (the same statement appeared in Illustration 1–2). The heading shows that the statement describes the company's financial condition at the close of business on December 31, 1996.

The left side of the balance sheet lists the company's assets: cash, store supplies, and copy equipment. The right side of the balance sheet shows that the

Illustration 1–7   Financial Statements for Clear Copy

CLEAR COPY
Income Statement
For Month Ended December 31, 1996

Revenues:		
Copy services revenue		$3,900
Operating expenses:		
Rent expense	$1,000	
Salaries expense	700	
Total operating expenses		1,700
Net income		$2,200

CLEAR COPY
Statement of Changes in Owner's Equity
For Month Ended December 31, 1996

Terry Dow, capital, December 1, 1996		$ –0–
Plus: Investments by owner	$30,000	
Net income	2,200	32,200
Total		$32,200
Less withdrawals by owner		400
Terry Dow, capital, December 31, 1996		$31,800

CLEAR COPY
Balance Sheet
December 31, 1996

Assets		Liabilities	
Cash	$ 8,400	Accounts payable . . .	$ 6,200
Store supplies	3,600	**Owner's Equity**	
Copy equipment . .	26,000	Terry Dow, capital . . .	31,800
		Total liabilities and	
Total assets	$38,000	owner's equity	$38,000

company owes $6,200 on accounts payable. If any other liabilities had existed (such as bank loans), they would have been listed in this section. The equity section shows an ending balance of $31,800. Note the link between the statement of changes in owner's equity and the balance sheet.

The Statement of Changes in Financial Position

The fourth financial statement is the **statement of changes in financial position,** which describes where cash came from and where it went during the period. The statement also shows how much cash was on hand at the beginning of the period and how much was left at the end. This information is important because good cash management is essential if a business is to prosper or even survive.

The statement of changes in financial position, covered in Chapter 18, has complexities that you do not have the background to grasp at this stage of your course. You should, however, be able to prepare a schedule of cash changes during the pe-

CLEAR COPY
Schedule of Cash Changes
For Month Ended December 31, 1996

Cash inflows:		
Investment by owner	$30,000	
Receipts from customers	3,900	
Total cash inflows		$33,900
Cash outflows:		
Payment to employee	$ 700	
Payment of rent	1,000	
Payment for store supplies	2,500	
Payment for copy equipment	20,000	
Payment on account payable	900	
Withdrawal by owner	400	
Total cash outflows		25,500
Increase in cash		$ 8,400
Cash balance, December 1, 1996		–0–
Cash balance, December 31, 1996		$ 8,400

Illustration 1–8
A Schedule of Cash Changes for Clear Copy

riod. Illustration 1–8 shows the schedule of cash changes for Terry Dow's business. The information reported in the schedule was taken from the first column (labeled Cash) of Illustration 1–6. The heading identifies December as the time period covered by the statement.

An important reason for recording and reporting information about a company's assets, liabilities, equity, and net income is to help the owner judge the business venture's relative success compared to other activities or investments. One way to describe this success is to calculate the **return on equity ratio,** which equals the amount of income achieved in a period divided by the amount of owner's equity. The formula for this ratio is as follows:

$$\text{Return on equity} = \frac{\text{Net income}}{\text{Beginning owner's equity}}$$

Recall from the beginning of this chapter the story of Karen White and Mark Smith, who are considering the investment in **Imperial Oil.** In starting to analyze that company, they could use the financial information presented on page 21 to calculate Imperial Oil's 1994 return on equity, as follows:

$$\frac{\text{Net earnings}}{\text{Beginning shareholders' equity}} = \frac{\$359}{\$6,566} = 5.5\%$$

Interpreting the rate of return achieved by a company requires an understanding of several factors. For example, the rate should be compared with the rates that could be earned on other kinds of investments.

In the example of Clear Copy, the financial statements show that Terry Dow earned a return on equity at the rate of 7.3% for the month of December. To find this rate, we divide $2,200 of net income by the $30,000 beginning balance of owner's equity.

USING THE INFORMATION— RETURN ON EQUITY

LO 1
Describe the information presented in financial statements, be able to prepare simple financial statements, and analyze a company's performance with the return on equity ratio.

Dow's rate for December is high compared to most investments and may appear very appealing. Recall, however, that the income reported for a single proprietorship does not reflect any expense for the effort exerted by the owner in managing its operations.

Dow should compare this rate with other investment alternatives to determine whether Clear Copy is producing an adequate return on equity. Because 7.3% for the month appears very high it is likely that Dow will be encouraged to stay in the business. However, we have not completely measured the income for the month. Chapters 2 and 3 introduce additional revenues and expenses, the net effect of which will be to reduce the net income amount shown here.

Progress Check

1-10 What financial statement item appears on both the income statement and the statement of changes in owner's equity?

1-11 What financial statement item appears on both the statement of changes in owner's equity and the balance sheet?

1-12 Why might a business owner calculate the return on equity ratio?

SUMMARY OF THE CHAPTER IN TERMS OF LEARNING OBJECTIVES

LO 1. Describe the information presented in financial statements, be able to prepare simple financial statements, and analyze a company's performance with the return on equity ratio. The income statement shows a company's revenues, expenses, and net income or loss. The balance sheet lists a company's assets, liabilities, and owner's equity. The statement of changes in owner's equity shows the effects on owner's equity from investments by the owner, withdrawals, and net income or net loss. The statement of changes in financial position shows the changes in cash that resulted from operating, investing, and financing activities. The financial statements are prepared with information about the effects of each transaction on the accounting equation. The company's performance can be analyzed by comparing the company's return on equity with rates on other investments available to the owner.

LO 2. Explain the accounting principles introduced in the chapter. Accounting principles help accountants produce relevant and reliable information. Among others, broad accounting principles include the business entity principle, the objectivity principle, the cost principle, the going-concern principle, and the revenue recognition principle.

LO 3. Describe single proprietorships, partnerships, and corporations, including any differences in the owners' responsibilities for the debts of the organizations. A single (or sole) proprietorship is an unincorporated business owned by one individual. A partnership differs from a single proprietorship in that it has more than one owner. Proprietors and partners are personally responsible for the debts of their businesses. A corporation is a separate legal entity. As such, its owners are not personally responsible for its debts.

LO 4. Analyze business transactions to determine their effects on the accounting equation. The accounting equation states that Assets = Liabilities +

Owner's Equity. Business transactions always have at least two effects on the elements in the accounting equation. The equation is always in balance when business transactions are properly recorded.

After several months of planning, Barbara Schmidt started a haircutting business called The Cutlery. The following events occurred during its first month:

a. On August 1, Schmidt put $3,000 cash into a chequing account in the name of The Cutlery. She also invested $15,000 of equipment that she already owned.

b. On August 2, $600 cash was paid for furniture for the shop.

c. On August 3, $500 cash was paid to rent space in a strip mall for August.

d. On August 4, the shop was furnished by installing the old equipment and some new equipment that was bought on credit for $1,200. This amount is to be repaid in three equal payments at the end of August, September, and October.

e. On August 5, The Cutlery opened for business. Receipts from cash sales in the first week and a half of business (ended August 15) were $825.

f. On August 17, $125 was paid to an assistant for working during the grand opening.

g. Cash receipts from sales during the second half of August were $930.

h. On August 31, an installment was paid on the account payable.

i. On August 31, Schmidt withdrew $900 cash for her personal use.

Required

1. Arrange the following asset, liability, and owner's equity titles in a table similar to the one in Illustration 1–6: Cash, Furniture, Store Equipment, Accounts Payable, and Barbara Schmidt, Capital. Show the effects of each transaction on the equation. Explain each of the changes in owner's equity.

2. Prepare an income statement for August.

3. Prepare a statement of changes in owner's equity for August.

4. Prepare a balance sheet as of August 31.

5. Prepare a schedule of cash changes for the month of August.

6. Determine the return on equity ratio for August.

Planning the Solution

- Set up a table with the appropriate columns, including a final column for describing the events that affect owner's equity.

- Analyze each transaction and show its effects as increases or decreases in the appropriate columns. Be sure that the accounting equation remains in balance after each event.

- To prepare the income statement, find the revenues and expenses in the last column. List those items on the statement, calculate the difference, and label the result as *net income* or *net loss*.

- Use the information in the Explanation of Change column to prepare the statement of changes in owner's equity.

- Use the information on the last row of the table to prepare the balance sheet.

- To prepare the schedule of cash changes follow the example in Illustration 1–8.

- Calculate the return on equity by dividing net income by the beginning equity.

Solution to Demonstration Problem

1.

	Assets			= Liabilities +	Owner's Equity	
	Cash +	Furniture +	Store Equipment	= Accounts Payable	+ Barbara Schmidt, Capital	Explanation of Change
a.	$3,000			$15,000	$18,000	Investment
b.	− 600	$600				
Bal.	$2,400	$600	$15,000		$18,000	
c.	− 500				− 500	Expense
Bal.	$1,900	$600	$15,000		$17,500	
d.			+1,200	+$1,200		
Bal.	$1,900	$600	$16,200	$1,200	$17,500	
e.	+ 825				+ 825	Revenue
Bal.	$2,725	$600	$16,200	$1,200	$18,325	
f.	− 125				− 125	Expense
Bal.	$2,600	$600	$16,200	$1,200	$18,200	
g.	+ 930				+ 930	Revenue
Bal.	$3,530	$600	$16,200	$1,200	$19,130	
h.	− 400			− 400		
Bal.	$3,130	$600	$16,200	$ 800	$19,130	
i.	− 900				− 900	Withdrawal
Bal.	$2,230 +	$600 +	$16,200 =	$ 800 +	$18,230	

2.

THE CUTLERY
Income Statement
For Month Ended August 31

Revenues:		
Sales		$1,755
Operating expenses:		
Rent expense	$500	
Salaries expense	125	
Total operating expenses		625
Net income		$1,130

3.

THE CUTLERY
Statement of Changes in Owner's Equity
For Month Ended August 31

Barbara Schmidt, capital, August 1		$ 0
Plus: Investments by owner	$18,000	
Net income	1,130	19,130
Total		$19,130
Less withdrawals by owner		(900)
Barbara Schmidt, capital, August 31		$18,230

4.
THE CUTLERY
Balance Sheet
August 31

Assets		Liabilities	
Cash.	$ 2,230	Accounts payable	$ 800
Furniture.	600	**Owner's Equity**	
Store equipment	16,200	Barbara Schmidt, capital . . .	18,230
		Total liabilities and	
Total assets	$19,030	owner's equity	$19,030

5.
THE CUTLERY
Schedule of Cash Changes
For Month Ended August 31

Cash inflows:
Investment by owner $3,000
Receipts from customers   1,755
Total cash inflows $4,755
Cash outflows:
Payment to employee . . . . $ 125
Payment of rent   500
Payment for furniture   600
Payment on account payable   400
Withdrawal by owner   900
Total cash outflows   2,525
Increase in cash $2,230
Cash balance, August 1, 1996   0
Cash balance, August 31, 1996 . . . . $2,230

6.   Return on equity $= \dfrac{\text{Net income}}{\text{Beginning owner's equity}} = \dfrac{\$1,130}{\$18,000} = 6.3\%$

Developing Accounting Standards

ACCOUNTING PRINCIPLES, AUDITING STANDARDS, AND FINANCIAL ACCOUNTING

LO 6
Describe the process by which generally accepted accounting principles are established.

Generally accepted accounting principles are not natural laws like the laws of physics or other sciences. Instead, GAAP are identified in response to the needs of users and others affected by accounting. Thus, GAAP are subject to change as needs change.

Three groups of people are most directly affected by financial reporting: preparers, auditors, and users. The following diagram shows the relationship between the financial statements and these groups.

Private accountants prepare the financial statements. To give users more confidence in the statements, independent auditors usually examine the financial statements and develop an audit report. The statements and the audit report are then distributed to the users.

Illustration A–1 expands this diagram to show how accounting principles and auditing standards relate to the financial reporting process. First, in Illustration A–1, we show that GAAP are applied in preparing the financial statements. Preparers use GAAP to decide what procedures to follow as they account for business transactions and put the statements together.

Second, in Illustration A–1, we show that audits are performed in accordance with **generally accepted auditing standards (GAAS)** which are developed by the CICA's **Auditing Standards Board (ASB).** GAAS are the rules adopted by the accounting profession as guides for conducting audits of financial statements. GAAS tell auditors what they must do in their audits to determine whether the financial statements comply with GAAP.

Applying both GAAP and GAAS assures users that financial statements include relevant, reliable, and comparable information. The audit does not, however, ensure that they can safely invest in or loan to the company. The audit does not reduce the risk that the company's products and services will not be successfully marketed or that other factors, such as the loss of a key executive, could cause it to fail.

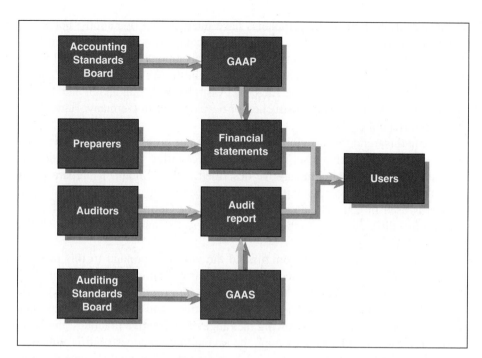

Illustration A-1
Generally Accepted
Accounting Principles
(GAAP), Generally
Accepted Auditing
Standards (GAAS),
and the Groups that
Participate in Financial
Accounting

In Illustration A–1, we also identify the two organizations that are the primary authoritative sources of GAAP and GAAS. The primary authoritative source of GAAP is the **Accounting Standards Board (AcSB).** The board members, supported by a research staff, use their collective knowledge to identify problems in financial accounting and to find ways to solve them. The board also seeks advice from groups and individuals affected by GAAP. The advice comes via comments on the board's "exposure drafts" on specific issues. The finalized recommendations are published as part of the *CICA Handbook.*

The Accounting Standards Board gains its authority from both law and the members of the Canadian Institute of Chartered Accountants. Under the regulations of the Canada Business Corporations Act, the accounting standards for external reporting set out in the *CICA Handbook* have the force of law. Also, in 1969 the CICA adopted paragraph 1500.06, which states:

> Where the accounting treatment or statement presentation does not follow the
> recommendations of this *Handbook,* the practice used should be explained
> in notes to the financial statements with an indication of the reason why the
> recommendation concerned was not followed.

A number of other professional organizations support the Accounting Standards Board's process by providing input. In summary, the Accounting Standards Board's job is to improve financial reporting while balancing the interests of the affected groups.

In today's world, people in different countries engage in business with each other more easily than in the past. A company in Canada might sell its products all over the world. Another company in Singapore might raise cash by selling shares to Canadian and Japanese investors. At the same time, it might borrow from creditors in Saudi Arabia and Germany.

**HOW
ACCOUNTING
PRINCIPLES
ARE
ESTABLISHED**

**INTERNATIONAL
ACCOUNTING
STANDARDS**

An increasing number of companies have international operations. For example, **Four Seasons Hotels, Inc.,** is a Canadian company with operations in lodging and contract services. Most of the company's operations are in the United States. However, the company also managed properties in the West Indies, New Zealand, Thailand, Hong Kong, Malaysia, England, Australia, Fiji, Singapore, and Taiwan. It also has properties under construction or development in Germany, Hawaii, and the Czech Republic.

Despite this trend toward global business, a major problem exists because each country has its own unique set of acceptable accounting practices. Consider, for example, the Singapore company we described earlier. Should it prepare financial statements that comply with Singapore accounting standards, or with the standards used in Canada, Japan, Saudi Arabia, or Germany? Should it have to prepare five different sets of reports to gain access to financial markets in all five countries?

Accounting organizations from around the world responded to this problem by creating the International Accounting Standards Committee **(IASC)** in 1973. With headquarters in London, the IASC issues *International Accounting Standards* that identify preferred accounting practices and then encourages their worldwide acceptance. By narrowing the range of alternative practices, the IASC hopes to create more harmony among the accounting practices of different countries. If standards could be harmonized, a single set of financial statements could be used by one company in all financial markets.

In many countries, the bodies that set accounting standards have encouraged the IASC to reduce the differences. The CICA's Accounting Standards Committee has provided this encouragement and technical assistance. However, the IASC does not have the authority to impose its standards on companies. Although progress has been slow, interest is growing in moving Canadian GAAP toward the IASC's preferred practices.

Progress Check

A-1   Which body currently establishes generally accepted accounting principles in Canada? *(a)* The Ontario Securities Commission; *(b)* Parliament; *(c)* The AcSB; *(d)* The IASC.

A-2   What is the difference between GAAP and GAAS?

A-3   Is it true that Canadian companies with operations in foreign countries are required to prepare their financial statements according to the rules established by the IASC?

SUMMARY OF APPENDIX A IN TERMS OF LEARNING OBJECTIVES

LO 6. Describe the process by which generally accepted accounting principles are established. Specific accounting principles for financial accounting are established in Canada by the Accounting Standards Board (AcSB), with input from various interested parties. Auditing standards are established by the Auditing Standards Board (ASB), another committee of the Canadian Institute of Chartered Accountants (CICA). The International Accounting Standards Committee (IASC) identifies preferred practices and encourages their adoption throughout the world.

GLOSSARY

Accounting equation a description of the relationship between a company's assets, liabilities, and equity; expressed as Assets = Liabilities + Owner's Equity; also called the *balance sheet equation*. p. 32

Accounts payable liabilities created by buying goods and services on credit. p. 25

Accounts receivable assets created by selling goods and services on credit. p. 24

AcSB the Accounting Standards Board; the authoritative committee of the CICA that identifies generally accepted accounting principles. p. 47

ASB the Auditing Standards Board; the authoritative committee of the CICA that identifies generally accepted auditing standards. p. 46

Assets items (economic resources) owned by the business and expected to benefit future operations. p. 24

Balance sheet a financial statement providing information that helps users understand a company's financial status; lists the types and dollar amounts of assets, liabilities, and equity as of a specific date; also called the *statement of financial position*. p. 24

Balance sheet equation another name for the *accounting equation*. p. 32

Business entity principle the principle that requires every business to be accounted for separately and distinctly from its owner or owners; based on the goal of providing relevant information about the business. p. 28

Business transaction an exchange between two parties of economic consideration, such as goods, services, money, or rights to collect money. p. 28

CICA Handbook the publication of the CICA that establishes generally accepted accounting principles in Canada p. 47

Common shares the name given to a corporation's shares when it issues only one kind or class of shares, also known as *common stock*. p. 31

Continuing-concern principle another name for the *going-concern principle*. p. 29

Contributed capital the category of shareholders' equity created by the shareholders' investments, also called *paid-in capital*. p. 31

Corporation a business chartered, or incorporated, as a separate legal entity under federal or provincial laws. p. 30

Cost principle the accounting principle that requires financial statement information to be based on costs in-curred in business transactions; it requires assets and services to be recorded initially at the cash or cash-equivalent amount given in exchange. p. 28

Creditors individuals or organizations entitled to receive payments from a company. p. 25

Debtors individuals or organizations that owe amounts to a business. p. 24

Dividends payments of cash by a corporation to its shareholders. p. 31

Equity the difference between a company's assets and its liabilities; more precisely, the residual interest in the assets of an entity that remains after deducting its liabilities; also called *net assets*. p. 25

Expenses costs incurred by a firm in the process of earning revenue; measured by the cost of goods and services consumed in the operation of the business. p. 23

GAAS the abbreviation for *generally accepted auditing standards*. p. 46

Generally accepted auditing standards rules adopted by the accounting profession as guides for conducting audits of financial statements. p. 46

Going-concern principle the rule that requires financial statements to reflect the assumption that the business will continue operating instead of being closed or sold, unless evidence shows that it will not continue; also called *continuing-concern* principle: p. 29

IASC International Accounting Standards Committee; a committee that attempts to create more harmony among the accounting practices of different countries by identifying preferred practices and encouraging their worldwide acceptance. p. 48

Income statement the financial statement that shows whether the business earned a profit or suffered a loss; it lists the types and amounts of the revenues and expenses. p. 22

Liabilities debts owed by a business or organization; normally require future payments in assets or the rendering of services, or both p. 25

Net assets assets minus liabilities; another name for *equity*. p. 25

Net income the excess of revenues over expenses for a period. p. 23

Net loss the excess of expenses over revenues for a period. p. 23`

Objectivity principle the accounting guideline that requires financial statement information to be supported by evidence other than someone's opinion or imagination;

objectivity adds to the reliability and usefulness of accounting information. p. 28

Paid-in capital   another name for *contributed capital.*
p. 31

Partnership   a business that is owned by two or more
people and that is not organized as a corporation. p. 30

Realization principle   another name for the *revenue
recognition principle.* p. 35

Retained earnings   the category of shareholders' equity
created by a corporation's profitable activities. p. 31

Return on equity ratio   the ratio of net income to beginning owner's equity; used to judge a business's success compared to other activities or investments; may be
modified for proprietorships or partnerships by subtracting the value of the owner's efforts in managing the
business from the reported income. p. 41

Revenue recognition principle   the rule that (1) requires revenue to be recognized at the time it is earned,
(2) allows the inflow of assets associated with revenue to
be in a form other than cash, and (3) measures the
amount of revenue as the cash plus the cash equivalent
value of any noncash assets received from customers in
exchange for goods or services. p. 35

Revenues   inflows of cash or other assets received in
exchange for providing goods or services to customers;
may also occur as decreases in liabilities. p. 23

Shareholders   the owners of a corporation; also called
stockholders. p. 30

Shares   units of ownership in a corporation; also called
stock. p. 30

Single proprietorship   a business owned by one individual that is not organized as a corporation. p. 30

Sole proprietorship   another name for a *single proprietorship.* p. 30

Statement of changes in financial position   a financial
statement that describes where a company's cash came
from and where it went during the period. p. 40

Statement of changes in owner's equity   a financial
statement that shows the beginning balance of owner's equity, the changes in equity that resulted from new investments by the owner, net income (or net loss), and withdrawals, and the ending balance. p. 39

Statement of financial position   another name for the
balance sheet. p. 24

Withdrawal   a payment from a proprietorship or partnership to its owner or owners. p. 31

SYNONYMOUS TERMS

Accounting equation   balance sheet equation.
Balance sheet   statement of financial position; position
statement.
Economic resources   assets.
Equity   net assets; owner's equity.

Going-concern principle   continuing-concern principle.
Revenue recognition principle   realization principle.
Shareholders   stockholders.
Single proprietorship   sole proprietorship.

QUESTIONS

1. What information is presented in an income statement?
2. What do accountants mean by the term *revenue?*
3. Why does the user of an income statement need to know the time period that it covers?
4. What information is presented in a balance sheet?
5. Define (a) assets, (b) liabilities, (c) equity, and (d) net assets.
6. Identify two categories of generally accepted ac-counting principles.
7. What AcSB recommendations identify generally ac-cepted accounting principles?
8. What does the objectivity principle require for in-formation presented in financial statements? Why?
9. A business shows office stationery on the balance sheet at its $430 cost, although it cannot be sold for more than $10 as scrap paper. Which accounting principles require this treatment?
10. Why is the revenue recognition principle needed? What does it require?
11. What events or activities change owner's equity?
12. Identify four financial statements that a business presents to its owners and other users.

13. What should a company's return on equity ratio be compared with to determine whether the owner has made a good investment?

14. Find the financial statements of Geac Computer Corporation Limited in Appendix I. To what level of significance are the dollar amounts rounded? What time period does the income statement cover?

Geac

15. Review the financial statements of Geac Computer Corporation Limited in Appendix I. What is the amount of total assets reported at April 30, 1994? How much net cash was provided by operating activities during the 1994 year?

Geac

QUICK STUDY (Five-Minute Exercises)

Name the financial statement on which each of the following items appears:

a. Rent expense.	e. Service fees earned.
b. Store equipment.	f. Accounts payable.
c. Cash received from customers.	g. Repayment of bank loan.
d. Owner, withdrawals.	h. Supplies.

QS 1–1
(LO 1)

Identify which broad accounting principle describes most directly each of the following practices:

QS 1–2
(LO 2)

a. If $15,000 cash is paid to buy land, the land should be reported on the purchaser's balance sheet at $15,000.

b. Jan Jacobson owns Freeland Bakery and also owns Westside Supplies, both of which are sole proprietorships. In having financial statements prepared for the bakery, Jacobson should be sure that the expense transactions of Westside Supplies are excluded from the statements.

c. In December, 1995, Bartel Great Outdoors received a customer's order to provide two experienced guides for a June 1996 fishing trip in the Yukon. Bartel should record the revenue for the service in June 1996, not in December 1995.

For each of the following situations, determine whether the business is a sole proprietorship, partnership, or corporation.

QS 1–3
(LO 3)

a. The equity of Foster Company is divided into 10,000 common shares.

b. Metal Roofing Company is owned by Chris Fisher, who is personally liable for the debts of the business.

c. Jerry Forrentes and Susan Montgomery own Money Services, a company that cashes payroll cheques for individuals and provides a variety of personal services. Neither Forrentes nor Montgomery has personal responsibility for the debts of Money Services.

d. Nancy Kerr and Frank Maples own Downtown Runners, a courier service. Both Kerr and Maples are personally liable for any debts of the business.

QS 1–4
(LO 4)

Determine the missing amount for each of the following equations:

	Assets	=	Liabilities	+	Owner's Equity
a.	$ 25,000		$13,500		?
b.	$100,000		?		$28,500
c.	?		$62,500		$31,800

QS 1–5
(LO 4)

Use the accounting equation to determine:

a. The owner's equity in a business that has $249,800 of assets and $168,300 of liabilities.

b. The liabilities of a business having $100,600 of assets and $84,000 of owner's equity.

c. The assets of a business having $25,100 of liabilities and $75,000 of owner's equity.

QS 1–6
(LO 1)

In its 1993 financial statements, the Boeing Company, which is the largest aerospace company in North America, reported the following:

Sales and other operating revenues	$25,438 million
Net earnings (net income)	1,244 million
Total assets	20,450 million
Total beginning-of-year shareholders' equity	8,056 million
Total end-of-year shareholders' equity	8,983 million

Calculate the return on beginning equity.

EXERCISES

Exercise 1–1
Effects of transactions on the accounting equation
(LO 4)

The following equation shows the effects of five transactions on the assets, liabilities, and owner's equity of Dr. Kirby's dental practice. Write short descriptions of the probable nature of each transaction.

	Cash	+	Accounts Receivable	+	Office Supplies	+	Land	=	Accounts Payable	+	M. Kirby, Capital
	$15,000				$5,000		$29,000				$49,000
a.	− 6,000						+ 6,000				
	$ 9,000				$5,000		$35,000				$49,000
b.					+ 800				$ 800		
	$ 9,000				$5,800		$35,000		$ 800		$49,000
c.			$2,100								+ 2,100
	$ 9,000		$2,100		$5,800		$35,000		$ 800		$51,100
d.	− 800								− 800		
	$ 8,200		$2,100		$5,800		$35,000		$ 0		$51,100
e.	+ 2,100		−2,100								
	$10,300	+	$ 0	+	$5,800	+	$35,000	=	$ 0	+	$51,100

Exercise 1–2
Analyzing the accounting equation
(LO 4)

Chris Bevit began operating a new consulting firm on January 15. The accounting equation showed the following balances after each of the company's first five transactions. Analyze the equations and describe each of the five transactions with their amounts.

After Transaction	Cash	+ Accounts Receivable	+ Office Supplies	+ Office Furniture	= Accounts Payable	+ C. Bevit, Capital
a.	$60,000	$ 0	$ 0	$ 0	$ 0	$60,000
b.	58,000	0	3,500	0	1,500	60,000
c.	42,000	0	3,500	16,000	1,500	60,000
d.	42,000	4,000	3,500	16,000	1,500	64,000
e.	35,000	4,000	3,500	16,000	1,500	57,000

A business had the following amounts of assets and liabilities at the beginning and end of a recent year:

Exercise 1–3
Determining net income
(LO 1, 4)

	Assets	Liabilities
Beginning of the year	$150,000	$60,000
End of the year	240,000	92,000

Determine the net income earned or net loss incurred by the business during the year under each of the following unrelated assumptions:

a.   The owner made no additional investments in the business and withdrew no assets during the year.

b.   The owner made no additional investments in the business during the year but withdrew $3,500 per month to pay personal living expenses.

c.   The owner withdrew no assets during the year but invested an additional $65,000 cash in the business.

d.   The owner withdrew $4,500 per month to pay personal living expenses and invested an additional $20,000 cash in the business at the end of the year.

Cathy Egan began a professional practice on July 1 and plans to prepare financial statements at the end of each month. During July, Egan completed these transactions:

Exercise 1–4
The effects of
transactions on the
accounting equation
(LO 1, 4)

a.   Invested $25,000 cash and equipment that had a $5,000 fair market (cash equivalent) value.

b.   Paid $800 rent for office space for the month.

c.   Purchased $6,000 of additional equipment on credit.

d.   Completed work for a client and immediately collected $1,000 cash.

e.   Completed work for a client and sent a bill for $3,500 to be paid within 30 days.

f.   Purchased $4,000 of additional equipment for cash.

g.   Paid an assistant $1,200 as wages for the month.

h.   Collected $2,500 of the amount owed by the client described in transaction e.

i.   Paid for the equipment purchased in transaction c.

Required

Create a table like the one in Illustration 1–6, using the following headings for the columns: Cash; Accounts Receivable; Equipment; Accounts Payable; and Cathy Egan, Capital. Then, use additions and subtractions to show the effects of the transactions on the elements of the equation. Show new totals after each transaction. Once you have completed the table, determine Egan's income for July. Determine the return on Egan's initial investment for the month of July.

Exercise 1–5
The effects of
transactions on the
accounting equation
(LO 4)

Following are seven pairs of changes in elements of the accounting equation. Provide an example of a transaction that creates the described effects:

a.   Decreases an asset and decreases equity.

b.   Decreases an asset and decreases a liability.

c.   Decreases a liability and increases a liability.

d.   Increases an asset and decreases an asset.

e.   Increases an asset and increases a liability.

f.   Increases an asset and increases equity.

g.   Increases a liability and decreases equity.

Exercise 1–6
Income statement
(LO 1)

On July 1, Maia Mears began the practice of tax accounting under the name of Maia Mears, Accountant. On July 31, the company's records showed the following items. Use this information to prepare a July income statement for the business.

Cash	$ 4,000	Owner's withdrawals	$1,500
Accounts receivable	5,000	Tax fees earned	5,000
Office supplies	750	Miscellaneous expenses	180
Tax library	12,000	Rent expense	850
Office equipment	9,000	Salaries expense	2,000
Accounts payable	2,500	Telephone expense	220
Owner's investments	28,000		

Exercise 1–7
Statement of changes in
owner's equity
(LO 1)

Use the facts in Exercise 1–6 to prepare a July statement of changes in owner's equity for the business of Maia Mears, Accountant.

Exercise 1–8
Balance sheet
(LO 1)

Use the facts in Exercise 1–6 to prepare a July 31 balance sheet for the business of Maia Mears, Accountant.

Exercise 1–9
Information in financial
statements
(LO 1)

Match each of these numbered items with the financial statement or statements on which it should be presented. Indicate your answer by writing the letter or letters for the correct statement in the blank space next to each item.

A. Income statement   C. Balance sheet
B. Statement of changes   D. Statement of changes in financial position
   in owner's equity

___ 1. Cash received from customers.   ___ 5. Accounts payable.

___ 2. Office supplies.   ___ 6. Investments of cash by owner.

___ 3. Rent expense paid in cash.   ___ 7. Accounts receivable.

___ 4. Consulting fees earned and received as cash. ___ 8. Cash withdrawals by owner.

Exercise 1–10
Missing information
(LO 4)

Calculate the amount of the missing item in each of the following independent cases:

	a	b	c	d
Owner's equity, January 1	$ 0	$ 0	$ 0	$ 0
Owner's investments during the year	80,000	?	42,000	50,000
Owner's withdrawals during the year	?	(36,000)	(20,000)	(21,000)
Net income (loss) for the year	21,000	54,000	(6,000)	?
Owner's equity, December 31	68,000	66,000	?	57,000

Match each of these numbered descriptions with the term it best describes. Indicate your answer by writing the letter for the correct principle in the blank space next to each description.

Exercise 1–11
Accounting principles
(LO 2)

A. Broad principle
B. Cost principle
C. Business entity principle
D. Revenue recognition principle

E. Specific principle
F. Objectivity principle
G. Going-concern principle

___1. Requires every business to be accounted for separately from its owner or owners.

___2. Requires financial statement information to be supported by evidence other than someone's opinion or imagination.

___3. Usually created by a pronouncement from an authoritative body.

___4. Requires financial statement information to be based on costs incurred in transactions.

___5. Derived from long-used accounting practices.

___6. Requires financial statements to reflect the assumption that the business will continue operating instead of being closed or sold.

___7. Requires revenue to be recorded only when the earnings process is complete.

Use the information for each of the following independent cases to calculate the company's return on equity:

Exercise 1–12
Return on equity
(LO 1)

	a	b	c	d
Beginning equity	$25,000	$400,000	$150,000	$286,400
Net income	5,400	108,000	45,750	88,965

PROBLEMS

Ranca Carr secured her license and opened an architect's office. During its first year, the following transactions affected Carr's business:

Problem 1–1
Analyzing the effects of transactions on the accounting equation
(LO 4)

a. Carr sold a personal investment in Royal Bank for $44,000, and deposited $30,000 of the proceeds in a bank account opened in the name of the business.

b. Carr invested $15,000 of her own personal office equipment in the business.

c. The business paid $150,000 for a small building to be used as an office. It paid $25,000 in cash and signed a note payable promising to pay the balance over several years.

d. Purchased $2,000 of office supplies for cash.

e. Purchased $18,000 of office equipment on credit.

f. Completed a project design on credit and billed the client $2,000 for the work.

g. Paid a local newspaper $500 for an announcement that the office had opened.

h. Designed a house for a client and collected a $9,000 cash commission on completion of the construction.

i. Made a $1,000 payment on the equipment purchased in transaction e.

j. Received $1,500 from the client described in transaction f.

k. Paid $1,250 cash for the office secretary's wages.

l. Carr withdrew $4,000 from the company bank account to pay personal living expenses.

Required

Preparation component:

1. Create a table like the one in Illustration 1–6, using the following headings for the columns: Cash; Accounts Receivable; Office Supplies; Office Equipment; Building; Accounts Payable; Notes Payable; and Ranca Carr, Capital. Leave space for an Explanation column to the right of the Capital column.

2. Use additions and subtractions to show the transactions' effects on the elements of the equation. Show new totals after each transaction. Also, indicate next to each change in the owner's equity whether it was caused by an investment, a revenue, an expense, or a withdrawal.

3. Once you have completed the table, determine the company's net income.

4. Determine the return on the beginning-of-period equity, which consisted of the two amounts invested by Carr in transactions *a* and *b*.

Analysis component:

5. State whether you think the practice is a good use of Carr's money, if an investment in low-risk bonds would have returned 6% for the same period.

Problem 1–2
Balance sheet and income statement
(LO 1, 3)

Benny Gates graduated from college in May with a degree in photographic arts. On June 1, Gates invested $30,000 in a new business under the name Benny Gates, Photographer. Gates plans on preparing financial statements for the business at the end of each month. The following transactions occurred during the first month:

June 1 Rented the furnished office and darkroom equipment of a photographer who was retiring. Gates paid $1,600 cash for the rent.

2 Purchased photography supplies for $840 cash.

4 Paid $400 cash for the month's cleaning services.

7 Completed work for a client and immediately collected $300 cash.

13 Completed work for Carl Simone on credit, $1,500.

15 Paid $425 cash for an assistant's salary for the first half of the month.

20 Received payment in full for the work completed for Carl Simone on June 13.

20 Completed work for Wendy Nation on credit, $1,400

21 Purchased additional photography supplies on credit, $500.

25 Completed work for Billie Carr on credit, $950.

26 Picked up brochures to be used right away to advertise the studio. Gates purchased them from a printer at a cost of $180, which he is to pay within 30 days.

28 Received full payment from Wendy Nation for the work completed on June 20.

June	29	Paid for the photography supplies purchased on June 21.
	30	Paid $100 cash for the month's telephone bill.
	30	Paid $240 cash for the month's utilities.
	30	Paid $425 cash for an assistant's salary for the second half of the month.
	30	Purchased insurance protection for the next 12 months (beginning July 1) by paying a $1,500 premium. Because none of this insurance protection had been used up, it was considered to be an asset called Prepaid Insurance.
	30	Gates withdrew $560 from the business for personal use.

Required

1. Arrange the following asset, liability, and owner's equity titles in an equation like Illustration 1–6: Cash; Accounts Receivable; Prepaid Insurance; Photography Supplies; Accounts Payable; and Benny Gates, Capital. Include an Explanation column for changes in owner's equity.

2. Show the effects of the transactions on the elements of the equation by recording increases and decreases in the appropriate columns. Indicate an increase with a + and a decrease with a − before the amount. Do not determine new totals for the items of the equation after each transaction. Next to each change in Benny Gates, Capital, state whether it was caused by an investment, a revenue, an expense, or a withdrawal. Determine the final total for each item and verify that the equation is in balance.

3. Prepare an income statement for June, a statement of changes in owner's equity for June, and a June 30 balance sheet.

The accounting records of Carmen King's dental practice show the following assets and liabilities as of the end of 1996 and 1997:

Problem 1–3
Calculating and interpreting net income and preparing a balance sheet
(LO 1, 3)

	December 31	
	1996	**1997**
Cash	$35,000	$ 12,500
Accounts receivable	19,000	14,900
Dental supplies	3,000	2,200
Dental equipment	92,000	98,000
Office equipment	36,000	36,000
Land		30,000
Building		120,000
Accounts payable	5,000	25,000
Note payable		70,000

Late in December 1997 (just before the amounts in the second column were calculated), King purchased a small office building in the name of the practice, Carmen King, D.D.S., and moved the practice from rented quarters to the new building. The building and the land it occupies cost $150,000. The practice paid $80,000 in cash and a note payable was signed for the balance. King had to invest an additional $35,000 cash in the practice to enable it to pay the $80,000. The practice earned a satisfactory net income during 1997, which enabled King to withdraw $3,000 per month from the practice for personal living expenses.

Required

Preparation component:

1. Prepare balance sheets for the business as of the end of 1996 and the end of 1997. (Remember that owner's equity equals the difference between the assets and the liabilities.)

2. By comparing the owner's equity amounts from the balance sheets and using the additional information presented in the problem, prepare a calculation to show how much net income was earned by the business during 1997.

3. Calculate the return on equity for the dental practice, using the beginning balance of owner's equity for the year.

Analysis component:

4. Consider the possibility that King might have organized the business as a corporation which would have paid King a salary of $25,000. Would organizing the business as a corporation instead of as a proprietorship affect your evaluation of return on equity? Explain why.

Problem 1–4
Analyzing transactions and preparing financial statements
(LO 1, 3)

Thom Stone began a new financial planning practice and completed these transactions during April:

April 1 Transferred $28,000 from a personal savings account to a checking account opened in the name of the business, Thom Stone, C.F.P.

1 Rented the furnished office of a planner who was retiring, and paid cash for the month's rent of $400.

2 Purchased the retiring person's professional library for $7,000 by paying $1,600 in cash and agreeing to pay the balance in six months.

4 Purchased office supplies by paying $450 cash.

6 Completed planning work for Karl Hubbell and immediately collected $500 for doing the work.

9 Purchased $1,900 of office equipment on credit.

15 Completed planning work for Carol Banks on credit in the amount of $2,000.

19 Purchased $250 of office supplies on credit.

21 Paid for the office equipment purchased on April 9.

25 Billed Sy Young $300 for planning work; the balance is due in 30 days.

29 Received $2,000 from Carol Banks for the work completed on April 15.

30 Paid the office assistant's salary of $1,600.

30 Paid the monthly utility bills of $220.

30 Withdrew $500 from the business for personal living expenses.

Required

Preparation component:

1. Arrange the following asset, liability, and owner's equity titles in an equation like Illustration 1–6: Cash; Accounts Receivable; Office Supplies; Professional Library; Office Equipment; Accounts Payable; and Thom Stone, Capital. Leave space for an Explanation column to the right of Thom Stone, Capital.

2. Use additions and subtractions to show the effects of each transaction on the items in the equation. Show new totals after each transaction. Next to each change in owner's equity, state whether the change was caused by an investment, a revenue, an expense, or a withdrawal.

3. Use the increases and decreases in the last column of the equation to prepare an income statement and a statement of changes in owner's equity for the month. Also prepare a balance sheet as of the end of the month.

4. Calculate the return on equity for the month, using the initial investment as the beginning balance of equity.

Analysis component:

5. Assume that the investment transaction on April 1 had been for $20,000 instead of $28,000 and the $8,000 difference had been borrowed from a bank. Explain the effect of this change on total assets, total liabilities, owner's equity, and return on equity.

The following financial statement information is known about five unrelated companies:

Problem 1–5
Missing information
(LO 1)

	Company A	Company B	Company C	Company D	Company E
December 31, 1996:					
Assets	$90,000	$70,000	$58,000	$40,000	$82,000
Liabilities	47,000	45,000	28,000	19,000	?
December 31, 1997:					
Assets	96,000	82,000	?	62,500	75,000
Liabilities	?	55,000	38,000	32,000	50,000
During 1997:					
Owner investments ..	10,000	3,000	15,500	?	3,000
Net income	15,000	?	9,000	6,000	12,000
Owner withdrawals ..	5,000	7,000	6,500	0	6,000

Required

1. Answer the following questions about Company A:
   a. What was the owner's equity on December 31, 1996?
   b. What was the owner's equity on December 31, 1997?
   c. What was the amount of liabilities owed on December 31, 1997?
2. Answer the following questions about Company B:
   a. What was the owner's equity on December 31, 1996?
   b. What was the owner's equity on December 31, 1997?
   c. What was the net income for 1997?
3. Calculate the amount of assets owned by Company C on December 31, 1997.
4. Calculate the amount of owner investments in Company D made during 1997.
5. Calculate the amount of liabilities owed by Company E on December 31, 1996.

Identify how each of the following transactions affects the company's financial statements. For the balance sheet, identify how each transaction affects total assets, total liabilities, and owner's equity. For the income statement, identify how each transaction affects Net Income. For the statement of changes in financial position, identify how each transaction affects cash flows from operating activities, cash flows from financing activities, and cash flows from investing activities. If there is an increase, place a + in the column or columns. If

Problem 1–6
Identifying the effects of transactions on the financial statements
(LO 1, 3)

there is a decrease, place a − in the column or columns. If there is both an increase and a decrease, place + / − in the column or columns. The line for the first transaction is completed as an example.

Transaction	Balance Sheet			Income Statement	Statement of Changes in Financial Position		
	Total Assets	Total Liabilities	Equity	Net Income	Operating	Financing	Investing
1 Owner invests cash	+		+			+	
2 Sell services for cash							
3 Acquire services on credit							
4 Pay wages with cash							
5 Owner withdraws cash							
6 Borrow cash with note payable							
7 Sell services on credit							
8 Buy office equipment for cash							
9 Collect receivable from (7)							
10 Buy asset with note payable							

Problem 1–7
Analytical essay
(LO 4)

Review the facts presented in Problem 1–2. Now assume that all of the company's revenue transactions generated cash (that is, none had been made on credit). Also assume that all of the expense and purchase transactions used cash and none were on credit. Describe the differences, if any, these alternate assumptions would create for the income statement, the statement of changes in owner's equity, and the balance sheet. Construct your answer in general terms without stating the actual dollar amounts of each difference. Be certain to explain why each statement would or would not be affected by the changes in the assumptions.

Review the facts presented in Problem 1–1 for transactions *f* and *j*. Identify the transaction that creates a revenue and explain your answer. Then explain why the other transaction did not create a revenue. Next, review the facts for transactions *d* and *k*. Identify the transaction that creates an expense for the current reporting period and explain your answer. Finally, explain why the other transaction did not create an expense.

Problem 1–8
Analytical essay
(LO 2, 4)

Carol Olds secured her broker's license and opened a real estate office. During a short period, she completed these transactions:

Problem 1–9
Effects of transactions on the accounting equation
(LO 4)

a. Sold for $62,500 a personal investment in General Electric shares, which she had inherited, and deposited $60,000 of the proceeds in a bank account opened in the name of the business, Carol Olds, Realtor.

b. Purchased for $150,000 a small building to be used as an office. She paid $45,000 in cash and signed a note payable promising to pay the balance over a period of years.

c. Purchased office equipment for cash, $11,600.

d. Took from home for use in the business office equipment having a $700 fair value.

e. Purchased on credit office supplies, $100, and office equipment, $5,000.

f. Paid the local paper $165 for advertising.

g. Completed a real estate appraisal for a client on credit and billed the client $250 for the work done.

h. Sold a house and collected a $10,000 cash commission on completion of the sale.

i. Carol Olds withdrew $2,000 from the business to pay personal expenses.

j. The client paid for the appraisal of transaction *g*.

k. Made a $2,500 installment payment on the amount owed from transaction *e*.

l. Paid the office secretary's wages, $950.

Required

1. Arrange the following asset, liability, and owner's equity titles in an equation like Illustration 1–6: Cash; Accounts Receivable; Office Supplies; Office Equipment; Building; Accounts Payable; Notes Payable; and Carol Olds, Capital. Leave space for an Explanation column to the right of Carol Olds, Capital.

2. Show by additions and subtractions the effects of each transaction on the elements of the equation. Show new totals after each transaction. Next to each change in Carol Olds, Capital, state whether the change was caused by an investment, a revenue, an expense, or a withdrawal.

Gary Meyer graduated from law school in May 1996, and on June 1 began a law practice by investing $5,000 in cash in the practice. He also transferred to the business office equipment having a cash value of $8,500. Then, he completed these additional transactions during June:

Problem 1–10
Analyzing transactions and preparing financial statements
(LO 1, 3)

June   1   Rented the office of a lawyer who was retiring and paid the rent for June, $800.

        1   Moved from home to the law office law books acquired at university. (In other words, invested the books in the practice.) The books had a $600 fair value.

June	2	Purchased office supplies for cash, $120.
	4	Purchased additional law books costing $1,500. Paid $500 in cash and promised to pay the balance within 90 days.
	5	Completed legal work for a client and immediately collected $500 for the work done.
	10	Completed legal work for Village Bank on credit, $1,500.
	15	Purchased additional office supplies on credit, $50.
	20	Received $1,500 from Village Bank for the work completed on June 10.
	25	Completed legal work for Astor Realty on credit, $1,300.
	30	Made a $300 installment payment on the law books purchased on June 4.
	30	Paid the June telephone bill, $70.
	30	Paid the office secretary's wages, $1,200.
	30	Gary Meyer took $1,400 out of the business for his personal use.

Required

1. Arrange the following asset, liability, and owner's equity titles in an equation like Illustration 1–6: Cash; Accounts Receivable; Office Supplies; Law Library; Office Equipment; Accounts Payable; and Gary Meyer, Capital. Leave space for an Explanation column to the right of Gary Meyer, Capital.
2. Show by additions and subtractions the effects of each transaction on the elements of the equation. Show new totals after each transaction. Next to each change in Gary Meyer, Capital, state whether the change was caused by an investment, a revenue, an expense, or a withdrawal.
3. Analyze the items in the last column of the equation and prepare a June income statement for the practice.
4. Prepare a June statement of changes in owner's equity.
5. Prepare a June 30 balance sheet.

Problem 1–11
Preparation of balance sheet; calculation of net income
(LO 1, 3)

The accounting records of Viola Nunez's medical practice show the following assets and liabilities as of the end of 1995 and 1996:

	December 31	
	1995	**1996**
Cash	$ 9,600	$ 1,600
Accounts receivable	5,700	7,000
Office supplies	1,000	800
Automobile	4,800	4,800
Office equipment	18,500	23,200
Land		70,000
Building		125,000
Accounts payable	1,400	1,600
Notes payable		145,000

During the last week of December 1996 (just before the amounts above were calculated), Dr. Nunez purchased a small office building in the name of the medical practice, Viola Nunez, M.D., and moved her practice from rented quarters to the new building. The building and the land it occupies cost $195,000; the practice paid $50,000 in cash and signed a note payable for the balance. Dr. Nunez had to invest an additional $40,000 in the practice to enable it to pay the $50,000. The practice earned a satisfactory net income during 1995, which enabled Dr. Nunez to withdraw $3,200 per month from the practice to pay her personal living expenses.

Required

1. Prepare two balance sheets for the business, as of the end of 1995 and the end of 1996. (Remember that the owner's equity equals assets less liabilities.)
2. Using the information presented above and by comparing the owner's equity in the balance sheets, prepare a calculation to show the net income earned by the business during 1996.

An analysis of cash and accounts receivable transactions of Townsend Office Services for the month of October 1996 indicates the following:

Problem 1–12
Analyzing transactions and preparing financial statements
(LO 1, 4)

Cash account:
Beginning balance	$ 900
Sandy Townsend, additional investment	9,000
Collection of accounts receivable	4,500
Payment of office rent for 3 months (Oct.–Dec.)	1,800
Rental payment for office equipment (for October)	450
Payment of wages including Townsend of $2,250	5,250
Payment of utilities, telephone, and advertising	900
Partial payment for office supplies (cost $1,500)	750

Accounts receivable:
Beginning balance	1,800
Billings during the month	6,750
Collection of accounts receivable	4,500

Additional information

$1,400 of office supplies were on hand on October 31.

Required

1. Prepare the October income statement.
2. Prepare the October 31 balance sheet.
3. Determine the October 1, 1996, balance in Sandra Townsend's capital account.

Megan Brinks ran out of money at the end of the first semester of her sophomore year in college. She had to go to work, but she could not find a satisfactory job. However, since she had an automobile, she decided to go into business for herself. Consequently, she began Megan's Delivery Service with no assets other than the automobile, which had a fair market value of $8,400. She kept no accounting records; and now, at the year-end, she has engaged you to determine the net income earned by the service during its first year. You find that the service has a $700 year-end bank balance plus $50 of undeposited cash. Local stores owe the service $125 for delivering packages during the past month. In the last week of the year, Megan sold the automobile for $7,500, and used the cash proceeds to help buy a new delivery truck that cost $16,800. The service still owes a finance company $7,000 as a result of the truck's purchase. Also, when the truck was purchased, Megan borrowed $1,500 from her father to help make the down payment. The loan was made to the delivery service, was interest free, and has not been repaid. Finally, since the service has been profitable from the beginning, Megan has withdrawn $300 of its earnings each week for the 52 weeks of its existence to pay personal living expenses.

Problem 1–13
Analytical essay
(LO 4)

Determine and present a calculation to prove the net income earned by the business during the first year of its operations.

Problem 1–14
Identifying the effects of transactions on the financial statements
(LO 1, 3)

Identify how each of the following transactions affects the company's financial statements. For the balance sheet, identify how each transaction affects total assets, total liabilities, and owner's equity. For the income statement, identify how each transaction affects Net Income. For the statement of changes in financial position, identify how each transaction affects cash flows from operating activities, cash flows from financing activities, and cash flows from investing activities. If there is an increase, place a "+" in the column or columns. If there is a decrease, place "−" in the column or columns. If there is both an increase and a decrease, place "+/−" in the column or columns. The line for the first transaction is completed as an example.

	Balance Sheet			Income Statement	Statement of Changes in Financial Position		
Transaction	**Total Assets**	**Total Liabilities**	**Equity**	**Net Income**	**Operating**	**Financing**	**Investing**
1 Owner invests cash	+		+			+	
2 Buy store equipment for cash							
3 Buy asset with note payable							
4 Sell services for cash							
5 Acquire services on account							
6 Sell services on credit							
7 Borrow cash from bank							
8 Collect receivable from (6)							
9 Owner withdraws cash							
10 Pay wages with cash							

Problem 1–15
Analytical essay
(LO 4)

Review the facts presented in Problem 1–10. Now assume that all of the company's revenue transactions generated cash (that is, none had been made on credit). Also assume that all of the expense and purchase transactions used cash and none were on credit. Describe the differences, if any, these alternate assumptions would create for the income statement, the statement of changes in owner's equity, and the balance sheet. Construct your answer in general terms without stating the actual dollar amounts of each difference. Be certain to explain why each statement would or would not be affected by the changes in the assumptions.

Review the facts presented in Problem 1–9 for transactions *g* and *j*. Identify the transactions that creates a revenue and explain your answer. Then explain why the other transaction did not create a revenue. Next, review the facts for transactions *e* and *l*. Identify the transaction that creates an expense for the current reporting period and explain your answer. Finally, explain why the other transaction did not create an expense.

Problem 1–16
Analytical essay
(LO 2, 4)

PROVOCATIVE PROBLEMS

On Friday, September 3, Ann Walker invested $1,000 cash in a small enterprise to participate in a local flea market set up in her neighbourhood for the Labour Day weekend. In the name of her business, Ann's Bangles and Baubles, she paid $250 rent for space in the market to sell various kinds of costume jewellery. She also paid $50 cash for plastic jewellery boxes and paid her teenage children $130 to build a booth just for the market. Because she didn't plan to do this again until the next year, she planned to abandon the booth after the market closed. Walker purchased her jewellery from a local wholesaler at a total cost of $900 but because she had only $570 in cash, could not pay the full price in cash. However, the wholesaler knew that Walker's credit was good and agreed to accept $500 in cash and the promise that she would pay the $400 balance the day after the market closed. Over the weekend, she sold most of the jewellery for $2,000 cash and paid an assistant $90 cash for helping her. When the market closed, Walker estimated that her unsold goods could be returned to the wholesaler for their original cost of $60. Because of the large number of sales, none of the jewellery boxes was left.

Walker cannot decide whether this venture might be a good thing to repeat in the future. She needs to know whether she earned a satisfactory profit for the time and money that she put into it. Use the methods described in the chapter to develop the information. Prepare an income statement and a statement of changes in owner's equity for the four-day period ending on Monday, September 6. Also prepare a balance sheet as of the close of business on September 6. Then, evaluate whether you think her effort was suitably rewarded by the results, assuming that she could have earned $540 in wages on another job.

**Provocative Problem
1–1**
Weekend market
(LO 1, 3)

Geac Computer Corporation Limited, is in the business of manufacturing and marketing computer systems as well as software and other related products and services. The financial statements and other information from Geac's 1994 annual report are included in Appendix I at the end of the book. Use information from that report to answer the following questions:

**Provocative Problem
1–2**
Financial statement
analysis case
(LO 1)

1. Examine Geac's consolidated balance sheet. To what level of significance are the dollar amounts rounded?
2. What is the closing date of Geac's most recent annual reporting period?
3. What amount of net income did Geac have during the 1994 year?
4. How much cash (and cash equivalents) did the company hold at the end of the 1994 reporting period?
5. What was the net amount of cash provided by the company's operating activities during the 1994 year?
6. Did the company's investing activities for 1993 create a net cash inflow or outflow? What was the amount of the net flow?
7. Compare 1994's results to 1993's results to determine whether the company's total revenues increased or decreased. If so, what was the amount of the increase or decrease?

8. What was the change in the company's net income between 1994 and 1993?

9. What amount was reported as total assets at the end of the 1994 reporting period?

10. Calculate the return on beginning shareholders' equity that Geac achieved in 1994.

Provocative Problem 1–3
Dofasco Inc.
(LO 3)

Dofasco Inc. is one of Canada's leading steel producers. In a recent annual report, the notes to the financial statements included the following comments:

14. RELATED PARTY TRANSACTIONS

Mr J.D. Leitch, a director and chairman of the Corporation [Dofasco], is a director of Upper Lakes Group Inc., which controls ULS Corporation. During 1993, the Corporation was required by contract to offer ULS Corporation its entire requirements for water transport of the Corporation's bulk raw materials to Hamilton, and ULS Corporation was required to provide such transport. Freight rates are negotiated annually. Shipping charges totalled $28.5 million in 1993 (1992–$34.6 million).

The Corporation purchases iron ore pellets under contract from the Quebec Cartier Mining Company at market prices and on normal trade terms. [Authors' note: Dofasco owns 50% of QCM.] Total pellet purchases from QCM amounted to $96.1 million in 1993 (1992–$90.9 million). At December 31, 1993 the Corporation owed QCM $10.1 million (1992–$7.3 million).

Required

Explain why Dofasco might have included these comments in its report. What accounting principle might be compromised by related-party transactions like the ones described?

ANALYTICAL AND REVIEW PROBLEMS

A & R Problem 1–1

Allan Russell began his Auto Repair Shop the first part of this month. The balance sheet, prepared by an inexperienced part-time bookkeeper is shown below:

RUSSELL AUTO REPAIR SHOP
Balance Sheet
November 30, 1996

Assets		Liabilities and Owner's Equity	
Cash	$ 4,500	Parts and supplies	$ 7,875
Accounts payable	24,750	Accounts receivable	33,750
Equipment	15,750	Prepaid rent	2,250
Allan Russell, capital	19,125	Mortgage payable	20,250
Total assets	$64,125	Total equities	$64,125

Required

1. Prepare a correct balance sheet.
2. Explain why the incorrect balance sheet can be in balance.

A & R Problem 1–2

Gitanjli Datt began the practice of law the first day of October with an initial investment of $7,500 in cash. After completing the first month of practice, the financial statements were being prepared by Jim Graham, the secretary/bookkeeper Ms. Datt had hired. The statements were completed, and Ms. Datt almost burst out laughing when she saw them. She had completed a course in legal accounting in law school and knew the statements prepared by Mr. Graham left much to be desired. Consequently, she asks you to revise the statements. The Graham version is presented below:

GITANJLI DATT, LAWYER
Balance Sheet
October 31, 1996

Assets		Owner's Equity	
Cash	$2,700	G. Datt, capital . . .	$5,250
Prepaid rent	1,500		
Supplies expense	300		
Accounts payable	750		$5,250
	$5,250		

GITANJLI DATT, LAWYER
Income Statement
For the Month Ended October 31, 1996

Revenues:		
Legal fees	$8,250	
Accounts receivable	1,500	$ 9,750
Expenses:		
Salaries expense	$2,100	
Telephone expense	150	
Rent expense	1,500	
Supplies	750	
Law library	6,000	10,500
Loss		$ 750

Required

Prepare the corrected financial statements for Gitanjli Datt.

CONCEPT TESTER

Test your understanding of the concepts introduced in this chapter by completing the following crossword puzzle.

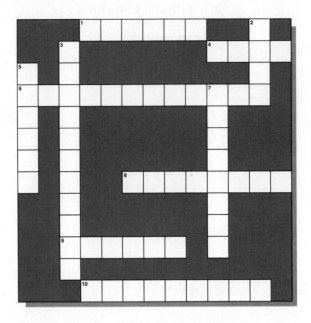

Across Clues

1. Equity of a corporation divided into units.
4. Generally accepted accounting principles.
6. The owners of a corporation.
8. Inflows of assets received in exchange for goods and services provided to customers.
9. The difference between a company's assets and liabilities.
10. Payments of cash by a corporation to its shareholders.

Down Clues

2. Generally accepted auditing standards.
3. Debts owed by a business organization.
5. Property or economic resources owned by a business.
7. Outflows or the using up of assets as a result of the major operations of a business.

ANSWERS TO PROGRESS CHECKS

1–1 *d*

1–2 An expense is a cost incurred by a firm in the process of earning revenue.

1–3 "Financial Statement Concepts" identifies relevance and reliability as two qualities of useful information.

1–4 A company's financial statements present its activities separately from its owner's activities because separate information is necessary for evaluating the company.

1–5 The equipment should be reported at its $25,000 cost, according to the cost principle.

1–6 *c*

1–7 A proprietor's withdrawals are not reported on the company's income statement because they are not expenses incurred to generate revenues.

1–8 *b*

1–9 No. If a liability increases, one or more of three other things must happen: an asset increases, or equity decreases, or another liability decreases.

1–10 Net income appears on both the income statement and the statement of changes in owner's equity.

1–11 The owner's capital account balance at the end of the period appears on both the statement of changes in owner's equity and the balance sheet.

1–12 Owners use the return on equity ratio to describe the success of the business in a way that can be compared to other investment opportunities.

A–1 *c*

A–2 GAAP are the principles that govern the reporting of information in the financial statements. GAAS, on the other hand, are the standards that guide auditors in performing an audit.

A–3 No. The IASC does not have the authority to impose standards. The Canadian company must comply with the GAAP established by the CICA's AcSB.

CHAPTER 2

Recording Transactions

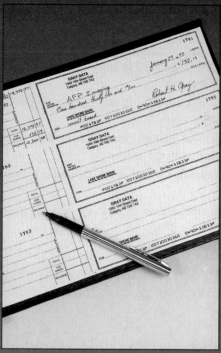

Whether an organization is small or large, an important key to gathering useful information is a system that records the effects of transactions as soon as they occur. Double-entry accounting serves this purpose very well.

n their continuing examination of Imperial's 1994 financial statements, Karen White and Mark Smith decided to read the narrative part of the report. As is true for most companies, Imperial includes a letter from the executive officers in their annual report. Karen and Mark found this "Letter to Shareholders from the Chairman and President" interesting and informative. They were particularly interested in the statement: "First, there is our financial position, one of the strongest in the industry. This gives us flexibility and allows us to manage through periods of uncertainty and volatility, such as we have recently experienced in crude-oil pricing." As Karen and Mark only started their first course in accounting, they wondered how "strength of financial position" is measured.

IMPERIAL OIL LIMITED
Selected financial data
(in millions)

December 31	Total Assets	Total Liabilities*	Total Shareholders' Equity
1994	$11,928	$5,933	$5,995
1993	12,861	6,295	6,566
1992	13,135	6,499	6,636
1991	13,491	6,701	6,790
1990	14,458	7,593	6,865

*Including deferred income taxes.

LEARNING OBJECTIVES

After studying Chapter 2, you should be able to:

1. **Describe the events recorded in accounting systems and the importance of source documents and business papers in those systems.**
2. **Describe how accounts are used to record information about the effects of transactions, how code numbers are used to identify each account, and the meaning of the words *debit* and *credit*.**
3. **Describe how debits and credits are used to analyze transactions and record their effects in the accounts.**
4. **Record transactions in a General Journal, describe balance column accounts, and post entries from the journal to the ledger.**
5. **Prepare a trial balance and explain its usefulness. Calculate a company's debt ratio.**
6. **Define or explain the words and phrases listed in the chapter glossary.**

In Chapter 1, you learned how the accounting equation (Assets = Liabilities + Owner's Equity) is affected by business transactions. In this chapter, you learn how the effects of transactions are recorded in accounts. All accounting systems, small or large, manual or computerized, use procedures similar to those described in this chapter. No matter how unusual or complicated a business may be, these procedures are the first steps in a process that leads to financial statements.

We begin by describing how source documents provide useful information about transactions. Then, we describe accounts and explain how they are used. Next, we explain debits and credits and use them to show how transactions affect the accounts. With this background in place, we describe the process of recording events in the journal and ledger. The chapter concludes by describing how to use a company's debt ratio to assess risk.

THE ACCOUNTING PROCESS

LO 1

Describe the events recorded in accounting systems and the importance of source documents and business papers in those systems.

Chapter 1 explains that accounting provides useful financial information to decision makers. To generate this information, a company uses an accounting process that analyzes economic events, records the results, and classifies and summarizes the information in reports and financial statements. These reports and statements are provided to individuals who find the information to be useful for making investment, credit, and other decisions about the entity. You can see the overall steps in this process in the flowchart in Illustration 2–1.

Business Transactions and Other Events

Notice that the economic events in Illustration 2–1 consist of business transactions and other events. Recall from Chapter 1 that business transactions are exchanges of economic consideration between two parties. Also, remember that a company's accounting equation is affected by transactions. The accounting process begins by analyzing transactions to determine how they affect the equation. Then, those effects are recorded in accounting records, informally referred to as *the books*. Additional processing steps summarize and classify the effects of all transactions. The process is not complete until it provides useful information to decision makers in financial statements or other reports.

Illustration 2-1   The Accounting Process

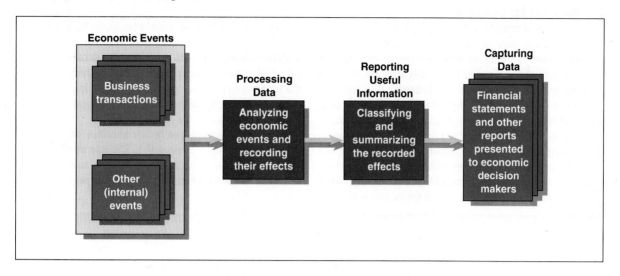

Because business transactions are exchanges between the entity and some other person or organization, they are sometimes called **external transactions.** Other economic events, called **internal transactions,** can affect the accounting equation. These events are not transactions with outside parties. For example, suppose that a company uses a machine in its operations. As the machine is used, its total remaining usefulness decreases. This using up of the machine's economic benefit is an economic event that decreases assets and decreases owner's equity.

Other events that can affect a company's accounting equation include natural events such as floods that destroy assets and create losses. In a few circumstances, changes in the market values of certain assets are also recorded. Economic events like these are not transactions between the company and other parties. We explain the analysis and recording of these economic events in Chapter 3.

Companies use various documents and other papers when they conduct business. These **business papers** include sales tickets, cheques, purchase orders, bills to customers, bills from suppliers, employee earnings records, and bank statements. Business papers are also called **source documents** because they are the source of the information recorded with accounting entries. Source documents may be printed on paper or they may exist only in computer records.

SOURCE DOCUMENTS AND BUSINESS PAPERS

For example, when you buy a pocket calculator on credit, the store prepares at least two copies of a sales ticket. One copy is given to you. Another is sent to the store's accounting department and triggers an entry in the system to record the sale. (In many systems, this copy is sent electronically without a physical document.) Or, if you pay cash for the calculator, the sale is rung up on a cash register that records and stores the amount of each sale.

Some cash registers print the amount of each sale on a paper tape locked inside the register. Most newer registers store the data electronically. In either case, the proper keyboard commands at the end of the day cause the cash register to determine the total cash sales for that day. This total is then used to record the day's sales in the accounting records. These systems are designed to ensure that the

As a Matter of Ethics

While taking classes toward her business degree, Kim Li accepted a part-time job at a busy fast food restaurant in a large downtown mall. As a new employee, she received training from the restaurant's assistant manager, including instructions on operating the cash register. The assistant manager explained that the formal policy is to ring up each sale when an order is placed and the cash is received.

The assistant manager also told Li that the pressure of the noon-hour rush makes it easier to just accept the customers' cash and make change without ringing up the sales. The assistant manager explained that the formal policy is ignored because it is more important to serve the customers promptly to keep them from going to any of the other restaurants in the mall. Then, after two o'clock, the assistant manager adds up the cash in the drawer and rings up sufficient sales to equal the collected amount. This way, the record in the register always comes out right and there are no problems to explain when the manager arrives at four o'clock to handle the dinner traffic.

Li sees the advantages in this shortcut but wonders whether something is wrong with it. She also wonders what will happen if the manager comes in early some day and finds out that she isn't following the formal policy.

accounting records include all transactions. They also help prevent mistakes and theft. The As a Matter of Ethics case above describes a challenge created by an instruction to overlook these accounting procedures. Read the case and think about what you would do if you were Kim Li.

Both buyers and sellers use sales tickets (also called *invoices*) as source documents. For example, if the new calculator is going to be used in your business, your copy of the invoice is a source document. It provides information to record the purchase in accounting records for your business.

To summarize, business papers are the starting point in the accounting process. These source documents, especially if they are created outside the business, provide objective evidence about transactions and the amounts to be recorded for them. As you learned in Chapter 1, this type of evidence is important because it makes the reported information more reliable and useful.

Years ago, most accounting systems required pen and ink to manually record and process data about transactions. Today, only very small companies use manual systems. Now, large and small companies use computers to record and process the data. However, you will find it easier to understand the steps in the accounting process by learning to prepare accounting data manually. Despite the differences, the general concepts you learn by studying manual methods apply equally well to computerized accounting systems. More importantly, these concepts help you use financial statements because you understand the source of their information.

Progress Check
(Answers to Progress Checks are provided at the end of the chapter.)

2-1   Which of the following are examples of accounting source documents? *(a)* Journals and ledgers; *(b)* Income statements and balance sheets; *(c)* External transactions and internal transactions; *(d)* Bank statements and sales tickets; *(e)* All of the above.

2-2   What kinds of economic events affect a company's accounting equation?

2-3   Why are business papers called source documents?

---

different kinds of revenues and expenses. Examples of possible revenue accounts are *Sales, Commissions Earned, Professional Fees Earned, Rent Earned,* and *Interest Earned.* Examples of expense accounts are *Advertising Expense, Store Supplies Expense, Office Salaries Expense, Office Supplies Expense, Rent Expense, Utilities Expense,* and *Insurance Expense.*

You can get an idea of the variety of accounts that a company might use by looking at the list of accounts at the end of this text. It lists the accounts you need to solve the exercises and problems in this book.[1]

THE LEDGER AND THE CHART OF ACCOUNTS

Accounts may have different physical forms, depending on the system. In computerized systems, accounts are stored in files on floppy or hard disks. In manual systems, each account may be a separate page in a loose-leaf book or a separate card in a tray of cards. Regardless of their physical form, the collection of all accounts is called the **ledger.** If the accounts are in files on a hard disk, those files are the ledger. If the accounts are pages in a book or cards in a file, the book or file is the ledger. In other words, a ledger is simply a group of accounts.

A company's size affects the number of accounts needed in its accounting system. A small company may get by with as few as 20 or 30 accounts, while a large company may use several thousand. The **chart of accounts** is a list of all accounts used by a company. The chart also includes an identification number assigned to each account. To be efficient, companies assign their account identification numbers in a systematic manner. For example, a small business might use this numbering system for its accounts:

101–199   Asset accounts
201–299   Liability accounts
301–399   Owner's equity accounts
401–499   Revenue accounts
501–699   Operating expense accounts

Although this system provides for 99 asset accounts, a company may not use all of them. The numbers create a three-digit code that conveys information to the company's accountants and bookkeepers. For example, the first digit of the code numbers assigned to the asset accounts is a 1, while the first digit assigned to the liability accounts is a 2, and so on. In each case, the first digit of an account's number reveals whether the account appears on the balance sheet or the income statement. The second and third digits may also relate to the accounts' categories. We describe account numbering systems more completely in the next chapter.

In its simplest form, an account looks like the letter T:

USING T-ACCOUNTS

(Name)	
(Left side)	(Right side)

---

[1]Remember that different companies may use account titles that are different from the titles in the list. For example, a company might use Interest Revenue instead of Interest Earned or Rental Expense instead of Rent Expense. All that is required is that an account title describe the item it represents.

Because of its shape, this simple form is called a **T-account.** Notice that the T format gives the account a left side, a right side, and a convenient place for its name.

The shape of a T-account provides one side for recording increases in the item and the other side for recording decreases. For example, the following T-account represents Clear Copy's cash account after the transactions in Chapter 1:

		Cash		
Investment by owner	30,000	Purchase of store supplies	2,500
Copy services revenue earned	2,200	Purchase of copy equipment	20,000
Collection of account receivable	1,700	Payment of rent	1,000
		Payment of salary	700
		Payment of account payable	900
		Withdrawal by owner	400

Calculating the Balance of an Account

An **account balance** is simply the difference between the increases and decreases recorded in the account. Thus, for example, the balance of an asset account is the amount of that asset on the date the balance is calculated. The balance of a liability account is the amount owed on the date of the balance. Putting the increases on one side of the account and the decreases on the other makes it easy to find an account's balance. To determine the balance, simply find the total increases shown on one side (including the beginning balance), find the total decreases shown on the other side, and then subtract the sum of the decreases from the sum of the increases.

For example, the total increases in Clear Copy's Cash account were $33,900, the total decreases were $25,500, and the account balance is $8,400. This T-account shows how to calculate the $8,400 balance:

		Cash		
Investment by owner	30,000	Purchase of store supplies	2,500
Copy services revenue earned	2,200	Purchase of copy equipment	20,000
Collection of account receivable	1,700	Payment of rent	1,000
		Payment of salary	700
		Payment of account payable	900
		Withdrawal by owner	400
Total increases	**33,900**	Total decreases	**25,500**
Less decreases	**−25,500**		
Balance	**8,400**		

Debits and Credits

In accounting terms, the left side of a T-account is called the **debit** side, often abbreviated Dr. The right side is called the **credit** side, abbreviated Cr.[2] To enter

---

[2]These abbreviations are remnants of 18th-century English bookkeeping practices that used the terms *Debitor* and *Creditor* instead of *debit* and *credit*. These abbreviations use the first and last letters from the words, just as we still do for *Saint* (St.) and *Doctor* (Dr.).

amounts on the left side of an account is to *debit* the account. To enter amounts on the right side is to *credit* the account. The difference between the total debits and the total credits in an account is the account balance. When the sum of the debits exceeds the sum of the credits, the account has a debit balance. It has a credit balance when the sum of the credits exceeds the sum of the debits.

From looking at the Cash account, you might think that the terms *debit* and *credit* mean *increase* and *decrease.* That is not correct. Whether a debit is an increase or decrease depends on the type of account. Similarly, whether a credit increases or decreases an account depends on the type of account. In any account, however, a debit and a credit have opposite effects. That is, in an account where a debit is an increase, a credit is a decrease. And, if a debit is a decrease in a particular account, a credit is an increase.

When we work with T-accounts, a debit simply means an entry on the left side and a credit simply means an entry on the right side. For example, notice how Terry Dow's initial investment in Clear Copy is recorded in the Cash and capital accounts:

Cash		Terry Dow, Capital	
Investment 30,000			Investment 30,000

Notice that the cash increase is recorded on the left side of the Cash account with a $30,000 debit entry; the corresponding increase in owner's equity is recorded on the right side of the capital account with a $30,000 credit entry. This method of recording the transaction is an essential feature of *double-entry accounting,* which we explain in the next section.

Debits and credits are neither favourable nor unfavourable. The actual effect depends on what is debited and credited. For example, a debit to an asset might be considered favourable, while a debit to an expense might be considered unfavourable. On the other hand, a credit to a liability might be considered unfavourable while a credit to a revenue would be favourable. These practices will become more clear after studying the transactions later in this chapter.

Progress Check

2-4 **Which of the following answers properly classifies these commonly used accounts? (1) Prepaid Rent, (2) Unearned Fees, (3) Buildings, (4) Owner's Capital, (5) Wages Payable, (6) Office Supplies.**

	Assets	Liabilities	Owner's Equity
a.	1,6	2,5	3,4
b.	1,3,6	2,5	4
c.	1,3,6	5	2,4

2-5 **What are accounts? What is a ledger?**

2-6 **What determines the quantity and types of accounts used by a company?**

2-7 **Does debit always mean increase and credit always mean decrease?**

USING DEBITS
AND CREDITS
IN DOUBLE-
ENTRY
ACCOUNTING

LO 3

Describe how debits and
credits are used to ana-
lyze transactions and
record their effects in the
accounts.

In **double-entry accounting,** every transaction affects and is recorded in at least two accounts. When recording each transaction, *the total amount debited must equal the total amount credited.* Because each transaction is recorded with total debits equal to total credits, the sum of the debits for all entries must equal the sum of the credits for all entries. Furthermore, the sum of the debit account balances in the ledger must equal the sum of the credit account balances. The only reason the sum of the debit balances would not equal the sum of the credit balances would be that an error has occurred. Thus, an important result of double-entry accounting is that many errors are avoided by being sure that the debits and credits for each transaction are equal.

According to traditional double-entry accounting, increases in assets are recorded on the debit side of asset accounts.[3] Why are asset accounts given debit balances? There is no specific reason. The choice is simply a convention that makes it easier for accountants by having all accounting systems work the same way. Then, because asset accounts have debit balances, increases in those balances are recorded with debits and decreases are recorded with credits.

Because asset accounts have debit balances and because debits must equal credits, liability accounts and owner's equity accounts must have credit balances. This follows from the logic of the accounting equation (Assets = Liabilities + Owner's Equity). Therefore, increases in liability and owner's equity accounts are recorded with credit entries. In other words, if asset increases are recorded with debit entries, equal debits and credits for a transaction are possible only if increases in liabilities and owner's equity are recorded as credits. To summarize, double-entry accounting systems record increases and decreases in balance sheet accounts as follows:

Assets		=	Liabilities		+	Owner's Equity	
Debit for increases	Credit for decreases		Debit for decreases	Credit for increases		Debit for decreases	Credit for increases

The practices shown in these T-accounts can be expressed as the following rules for recording transactions in a double-entry accounting system:

1. Increases in assets are debited to asset accounts; therefore, decreases in assets are recorded with credit entries to asset accounts.

2. Increases in liabilities are credited to liability accounts; therefore, decreases in liabilities are recorded with debit entries to liability accounts.

3. Increases in owner's equity are credited to owner's equity accounts; therefore, decreases in owner's equity are recorded with debit entries to owner's equity accounts.

Debits and credits may be confusing because of previous exposure to the terms. When you make a deposit to your chequing account, the bank credits your account's balance. To understand this practice, decide whether your chequing account is an asset or a liability to the bank. How does your deposit affect the bank's assets and liabilities?

---

[3]These double-entry practices originated in 15th-century Italy and have stood the test of more than 500 years of change and progress in business.

Chapter 1 taught you that owner's equity is increased by owner's investments and by revenues. You also learned that owner's equity is decreased by expenses and by withdrawals. Therefore, the following rules also apply:

4. The owner's investments are credited to the owner's capital account because they increase equity.
5. The owner's withdrawals of assets are debited to the owner's withdrawals account because they decrease equity.
6. Revenues are credited to revenue accounts because they increase equity. The system should include a separate account for each type of revenue.
7. Expenses are debited to expense accounts because they decrease equity. The system should include a separate account for each type of expense.

At this stage, you may find it helpful to memorize these rules. You will use them over and over in the course of your study. Before long, the rules will become second nature to you.

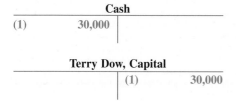

EXAMPLES OF DEBITS AND CREDITS

The following transactions for Clear Copy will help you learn how to apply these debit and credit rules. Study each transaction carefully to be sure that you understand it before you go on to the next one.

Each transaction is numbered so you can identify the transaction's effects on the accounts. You should recognize the first 11 transactions because they were used in Chapter 1 to show how transactions affect the accounting equation. In this chapter, we add five more transactions (numbers 12 through 16) to illustrate different kinds of events.

Before recording a transaction, the bookkeeper first analyzes it to determine what was increased or decreased. Then, the debit and credit rules are applied to decide how to record the increases or decreases. The bookkeeper's analysis for each of the example transactions appears next to the T-accounts. Study each analysis carefully to be sure that you understand the process.

1. On December 1, Terry Dow invested $30,000 in Clear Copy.

Cash		
(1)	30,000	

Terry Dow, Capital		
	(1)	30,000

Analysis of the transaction: The transaction increased the company's cash. At the same time, it increased Dow's equity. Increases in assets are debited and increases in owner's equity are credited. Therefore, record the transaction with a debit to Cash and a credit to Terry Dow, Capital, for $30,000.

2. Purchased store supplies by paying $2,500 cash.

Store Supplies		
(2)	2,500	

Cash			
(1)	30,000	(2)	2,500

Analysis of the transaction: The cost of the store supplies is increased by the purchase and cash is decreased. Increases in assets are debited and decreases are credited. Therefore, record the transaction with a debit to Store Supplies and a credit to Cash for $2,500.

3. Purchased copying equipment by paying $20,000 cash.

Copy Equipment	
(3) 20,000	

Cash	
(1) 30,000	(2) 2,500
	(3) 20,000

Analysis of the transaction: The cost of the copying equipment is increased and cash is decreased. Increases in assets are debited and decreases are credited. Debit Copy Equipment and credit Cash for $20,000.

4. Purchased $1,100 of store supplies and $6,000 of copying equipment on credit from Handy Supply Company.

Store Supplies	
(2) 2,500	
(4) 1,100	

Copy Equipment	
(3) 20,000	
(4) 6,000	

Accounts Payable	
	(4) 7,100

Analysis of the transaction: This transaction increased two assets, store supplies and copy equipment. It also created a new liability. Increases in assets are debits and increases in liabilities are credits. Therefore, debit Store Supplies for $1,100, debit Copy Equipment for $6,000, and credit Accounts Payable for $7,100.

5. Provided copying services to a customer and immediately collected $2,200 cash.

Cash	
(1) 30,000	(2) 2,500
(5) 2,200	(3) 20,000

Copy Services Revenue	
	(5) 2,200

Analysis of the transaction: This revenue transaction increased both assets and owner's equity. Increases in assets are debits and increases in owner's equity are credits. Revenue accounts are increased with credits because revenues increase owner's equity. Therefore, debit Cash $2,200 to record the increase in assets. Credit Copy Services Revenue $2,200 to increase owner's equity and to accumulate information for the income statement.

6. Paid $1,000 cash for rent for December.

Rent Expense	
(6) 1,000	

Cash	
(1) 30,000	(2) 2,500
(5) 2,200	(3) 20,000
	(6) 1,000

Analysis of the transaction: The cost of renting the store during December is an expense, which decreases owner's equity. Because decreases in owner's equity are debits, expenses are recorded as debits. Therefore, debit Rent Expense $1,000 to decrease owner's equity and to accumulate information for the income statement. Also, credit Cash $1,000 to record the decrease in assets.

7. Paid $700 cash for the employee's salary for the pay period ended on December 12.

Salaries Expense	
(7)	700

Cash			
(1)	30,000	(2)	2,500
(5)	2,200	(3)	20,000
		(6)	1,000
		(7)	700

Analysis of the transaction: The employee's salary is an expense that decreased owner's equity. Debit Salaries Expense $700 to decrease owner's equity and to accumulate information for the income statement. Also, credit Cash $700 to record the decrease in assets.

8. Completed copying work on credit and billed the customer $1,700 for the services.

Accounts Receivable	
(8)	1,700

Copy Services Revenue			
		(5)	2,200
		(8)	1,700

Analysis of the transaction: This revenue transaction gave Clear Copy the right to collect $1,700 from the customer. Thus, it increased both assets and owner's equity. Therefore, debit Accounts Receivable $1,700 for the increase in assets and credit Copy Services Revenue $1,700 to increase owner's equity and to accumulate information for the income statement.

9. The customer paid the $1,700 account receivable created in transaction 8.

Cash			
(1)	30,000	(2)	2,500
(5)	2,200	(3)	20,000
(9)	1,700	(6)	1,000
		(7)	700

Accounts Receivable			
(8)	1,700	(9)	1,700

Analysis of the transaction: One asset was increased and another decreased. Debit Cash $1,700 to record the increase in cash, and credit Accounts Receivable $1,700 to record the decrease in the account receivable.

10. Paid Handy Supply Company $900 cash on the $7,100 owed for the supplies and equipment purchased on credit in transaction 4.

Accounts Payable			
(10)	900	(4)	7,100

Cash			
(1)	30,000	(2)	2,500
(5)	2,200	(3)	20,000
(9)	1,700	(6)	1,000
		(7)	700
		(10)	900

Analysis of the transaction: A payment to a creditor decreases an asset and a liability by the same amount. Decreases in liabilities are debited, and decreases in assets are credited. Debit Accounts Payable $900 and credit Cash $900.

11. Terry Dow withdrew $400 from Clear Copy for personal living expenses.

Terry Dow, Withdrawals

(11)	400	

Cash

(1)	30,000	(2)	2,500
(5)	2,200	(3)	20,000
(9)	1,700	(6)	1,000
		(7)	700
		(10)	900
		(11)	400

Analysis of the transaction: This event reduced owner's equity and assets by the same amount. The Terry Dow, Withdrawals account is debited $400 to decrease owner's equity and to accumulate information for the statement of changes in owner's equity. Cash is credited $400 to record the asset reduction.

12. Signed a contract with a customer and accepted $3,000 cash in advance of providing any services.

Cash

(1)	30,000	(2)	2,500
(5)	2,200	(3)	20,000
(9)	1,700	(6)	1,000
(12)	3,000	(7)	700
		(10)	900
		(11)	400

Unearned Copy Services Revenue

		(12)	3,000

Analysis of the transaction: The $3,000 inflow of cash increased assets but a revenue was not earned. Instead, the transaction creates a liability that will be satisfied by doing the client's copying work in the future. Record the asset increase by debiting Cash for $3,000 and record the liability increase by crediting Unearned Copy Services Revenue for $3,000.

13. Paid $2,400 cash for the premium on a two-year insurance policy.

Prepaid Insurance

(13)	2,400	

Cash

(1)	30,000	(2)	2,500
(5)	2,200	(3)	20,000
(9)	1,700	(6)	1,000
(12)	3,000	(7)	700
		(10)	900
		(11)	400
		(13)	2,400

Analysis of the transaction: The advance payment of the insurance premium creates an asset (a prepaid expense) by decreasing another asset. The new asset is recorded with a $2,400 debit to Prepaid Insurance and the payment is recorded with a $2,400 credit to Cash.

14. Paid $120 cash for additional store supplies.

15. Paid $230 cash for the December utilities bill.

16. Paid $700 cash for the employee's salary for two weeks ended December 26.

Store Supplies

(2)	2,500	
(4)	1,100	
(14)	120	

Analysis of the transactions: These transactions are similar because each of them decreased cash. They are different from each other because the store supplies are assets while the utilities and employee's salary are expenses. The $120 cost of the supplies should be debited to the Store Supplies asset account, while the $230 for utilities and the $700 salary should be debited to separate expense accounts. Each transaction requires its own credit to Cash.

	Utilities Expense		
(15)	230		

	Salaries Expense		
(7)	700		
(16)	700		

	Cash		
(1)	30,000	(2)	2,500
(5)	2,200	(3)	20,000
(9)	1,700	(6)	1,000
(12)	3,000	(7)	700
		(10)	900
		(11)	400
		(13)	2,400
		(14)	120
		(15)	230
		(16)	700

ACCOUNTS AND THE ACCOUNTING EQUATION

Illustration 2–3 shows the accounts of Clear Copy after the 16 transactions have been recorded and the balances computed. The three columns in the illustration relate the accounts to the assets, liabilities, and owner's equity elements of the accounting equation. When we take the totals of the balance in each of the three columns, we find that total assets are $40,070 ($7,950 + $0 + $2,400 + $3,720 + $26,000). The total liabilities are $9,200 ($6,200 + $3,000), and the total of the equity accounts is $30,870 ($30,000 − $400 + $3,900 − $1,000 − $1,400 − $230). Thus, the total assets of $40,070 equals the $40,070 sum of the liabilities and the owner's equity ($9,200 + $30,870). The withdrawals, revenue, and expense accounts in the box record the events that change equity; their balances are reported as events on the income statement and statement of changes in owner's equity. Their balances are eventually combined with the balance of the capital account to produce the amount of equity reported on the balance sheet. Chapter 4 describes the bookkeeping (closing) process for combining these balances.

Progress Check

2-8 Double-entry accounting requires that:
 a. All transactions that create debits to asset accounts must create credits to liability or owner's equity accounts.
 b. A transaction that requires a debit to a liability account must require a credit to an asset account.
 c. Every transaction must be recorded with total debits equal to total credits.

2-9 What kinds of transactions increase owner's equity? What kinds decrease owner's equity?

2-10 Why are most accounting systems called double-entry?

Illustration 2-3 The Ledger for Clear Copy

	Assets			=		Liabilities		+		Owner's Equity	

Assets = **Liabilities** + **Owner's Equity**

Cash

(1)	30,000	(2)	2,500
(5)	2,200	(3)	20,000
(9)	1,700	(6)	1,000
(12)	3,000	(7)	700
		(10)	900
		(11)	400
		(13)	2,400
		(14)	120
		(15)	230
		(16)	700
Total	36,900	Total	28,950
	−28,950		
Balance	7,950		

Accounts Receivable

(8)	1,700	(9)	1,700

Prepaid Insurance

(13)	2,400	

Store Supplies

(2)	2,500	
(4)	1,100	
(14)	120	
Balance	3,720	

Copy Equipment

(3)	20,000	
(4)	6,000	
Balance	26,000	

Accounts Payable

(10)	900	(4)	7,100
Total	900	Total	7,100
			−900
		Balance	6,200

Unearned Copy Services Revenue

		(12)	3,000

Terry Dow, Capital

		(1)	30,000

Terry Dow, Withdrawals

(11)	1,500	

Copy Services Revenue

		(5)	2,200
		(8)	1,700
		Balance	3,900

Rent Expense

(6)	1,000	

Salaries Expense

(7)	700	
(16)	700	
Balance	1,400	

Utilities Expense

(15)	230	

The accounts in this box record increases and decreases in owner's equity. Their balances are reported on the income statement or the statement of changes in owner's equity.

$40,070	=	**$9,200**	+	**$30,870**

TRANSACTIONS ARE FIRST RECORDED IN THE JOURNAL

In the preceding pages, we used debits and credits to show how transactions affect accounts. This process of analyzing transactions and recording their effects directly in the accounts is helpful as a learning exercise. However, real accounting systems do not record transactions directly in the accounts. If the bookkeeper recorded the effects directly in the accounts, errors would be easily made and difficult to track down and correct.

To help avoid errors, accounting systems record transactions in a **journal** before recording them in the accounts. This practice provides a complete record of each transaction in one place and links the debits and credits for each transaction. After the debits and credits for each transaction are entered in the journal, they are transferred to the ledger accounts. This two-step process produces useful records for the auditor about a company's transactions. At the same time, the process helps the bookkeeper avoid errors. And, if errors are made, the process makes it easier to find and correct them.

The process of recording transactions in a journal is called *journalizing.* The process of transferring journal entry information to the ledger is called **posting.** This sequence of steps is represented in Illustration 2–4. Various source documents provide the evidence that transactions have occurred. Next, these transactions are recorded in the journal. Finally, the journal entries are posted to the ledger. This sequence causes the journal to be called the **book of original entry** while the ledger is sometimes called the **book of final entry.**

LO 4

Record transactions in a General Journal, describe balance column accounts, and post entries from the journal to the ledger.

The General Journal

The most flexible type of journal is the **General Journal.** The General Journal can be used to record any kind of transaction. A journal entry records this information about each transaction:

1. The transaction's date.
2. The names of the affected accounts.
3. The amount of each debit and credit.
4. An explanation of the transaction.
5. The identifying numbers of the accounts.

Illustration 2–5 shows how the first four transactions for Clear Copy would be recorded in a typical General Journal in a manual system. The General Journals used in computerized systems may look like the manual journal page, or they may differ. Regardless of their form or appearance, journals serve the same purpose in every system.

Notice that the fourth entry in Illustration 2–5 uses three accounts to record the credit purchase of store supplies and additional copying equipment. A transaction that affects at least three accounts is recorded in the General Journal with a **compound journal entry.**

Recording Transactions in a General Journal

A bookkeeper follows routine procedures when recording entries in the General Journal. The following steps were used to record the entries in Illustration 2–5. As you read these steps, compare them to the illustration to see how they produced the journal entries:

1. Enter the year at the top of the first column of the first line on the page.
2. Enter the month on the first line of the journal entry in the first column. (Successive entries in the same month on the same page of the journal would not show the month again.)
3. Enter the day's date for the transaction in the second column on the first line of each entry.

Illustration 2-4   The Sequence of Steps in Recording Transactions

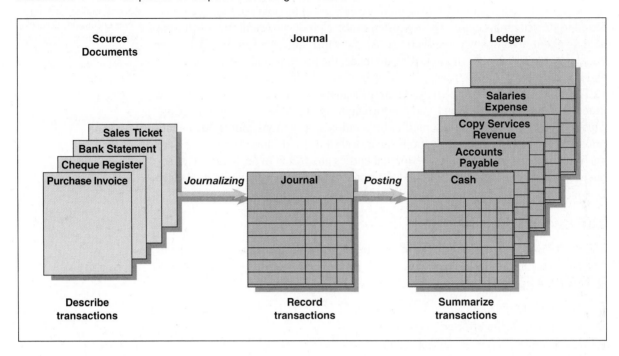

4. Enter the names of the accounts to be debited. The account titles are taken from the chart of accounts and are aligned with the left margin of the Account Titles and Explanation column.

5. Enter the amount debited to each account in the Debit column of the journal on the same line as the account title.

6. Enter the names of the accounts to be credited. The account titles are taken from the chart of accounts and are indented far enough from the left margin of the column to distinguish them from the debited accounts (perhaps as much as an inch).

7. Enter the amount credited to each account in the Credit column of the journal on the same line as the account title.

8. Provide a brief explanation of the transaction to help an auditor or other person understand what happened. The explanation is indented about half as far as the credited account titles to avoid confusing the explanation with either a debit or credit entry. (For clarity, this book italicizes the explanations.)

9. Skip a single line between each journal entry to keep them separate.

Once the journalizing process is completed, the journal entry provides a complete and useful description of the event's effects on the organization.

In a manual system, nothing is entered in the **Posting Reference (PR) column** when a transaction is initially recorded in the journal. As a control over the

Illustration 2-5   A General Journal Showing Transactions for Clear Copy

GENERAL JOURNAL							Page 1	
Date		Account Titles and Explanation	PR	Debit			Credit	
1996 Dec.	1	Cash		30,000	00			
		Terry Dow, Capital					30,000	00
		Investment by owner.						
	2	Store Supplies		2,500	00			
		Cash					2,500	00
		Purchased supplies for cash.						
	3	Copy Equipment		20,000	00			
		Cash					20,000	00
		Purchased copy equipment for cash.						
	6	Store Supplies		1,100	00			
		Copy Equipment		6,000	00			
		Accounts Payable					7,100	00
		Purchased supplies and equipment on credit.						

posting process, the account numbers are not entered until the entries are posted to the ledger. (Because the old word for page was *folio,* and because each account used to be a separate page in a book, the Posting Reference column in the journal is occasionally called the *folio column.*)

Computerized Journals.   Journals in computerized accounting systems serve the same purpose of providing a complete record of each transaction. In some systems, they even look like the manual journal page in Illustration 2–5. In addition, they may include error-checking routines that ensure the debits in the entry equal the credits. They often provide shortcuts that allow the computer operator to enter account numbers instead of names, or to enter the account names and numbers with pull-down menus or other easy-to-use techniques.

T-accounts are used in textbooks and accounting classes to show how accounts work. T-accounts are helpful because they allow you to disregard some details and concentrate on the main ideas. Actual accounting systems, however, use **balance column accounts** like the one in Illustration 2–6.

BALANCE COLUMN ACCOUNTS

The balance column account format is similar to a T-account because it has columns for entering each debit and credit. It is different because it provides space for the entry's date and any explanation that might be needed. It also has a third column for showing the balance of the account after each entry is posted. As a result, the amount on the last line in this column is the account's current balance. For example, Clear Copy's Cash account in Illustration 2–6 was debited on December 1 for the $30,000 investment by Terry Dow. As a result, the account had a $30,000 debit balance. The account was then credited on December 2 for $2,500, and its new $27,500 balance was entered in the third column. On December 3, it was credited again, this time for $20,000, and its balance was reduced to $7,500. Finally, the Cash account was debited for $2,200 on December 10, and its balance was increased to $9,700.

When the balance column format is used, the heading of the Balance column does not indicate whether the account has a debit or credit balance. However, this omission should not create any problems because every account has a *normal balance*. The normal balance of each type of account (asset, liability, owner's equity, revenue, or expense) is the same as the debit or credit entry used to record an increase in the account. The table below shows the normal balances for accounts.

Type of Account	Increases Are Recorded as	Normal Balance
Asset	Debits	Debit
Liability	Credits	Credit
Owner's equity:		
Capital	Credits	Credit
Withdrawals	Debits	Debit
Revenue	Credits	Credit
Expense	Debits	Debit

Abnormal Balances. Some unusual events may cause an account to have an abnormal balance. For example, a credit customer might accidentally pay its balance twice, which would give the account receivable a credit balance instead of a zero balance. If an abnormal balance is created, the bookkeeper can identify it by circling the amount or by entering the balance in red or some other nonstandard colour. Many computerized systems automatically provide a code beside the balance, such as *dr* or *cr* to identify the kind of balance.

Zero Balances. If an account has a zero balance, it is customary to indicate that fact by writing zeros or a dash in the Balance column. This practice avoids confusion between a zero balance and an accidentally omitted balance.

POSTING JOURNAL ENTRIES

Illustration 2–4 on page 90 shows that journal entries are posted to the accounts in the ledger. To ensure that the ledger is up to date, journal entries are posted as promptly as possible, which may be daily, weekly, or as time permits. All entries need to be posted before the end of the reporting period to provide the accounts with updated balances when the financial statements are prepared.

Illustration 2-6   The Cash Account for Clear Copy in the Balance Column Format

Cash							Account No. 101	
Date		Explanation	PR	Debit		Credit		Balance
1996 Dec.	1		G1	30,000	00			30,000	00
	2		G1			2,500	00	27,500	00
	3		G1			20,000	00	7,500	00
	10		G1	2,200	00			9,700	00

When posting the entries to the ledger, the bookkeeper copies the debits in the journal entries into the accounts as debits, and copies the journal entries' credits into the accounts as credits. The diagram in Illustration 2–7 identifies the six steps used in a manual system to post each debit and credit from the journal entry. Use the diagram to see how these six steps are completed:

For the debit:

1. Find the account that was debited in the journal entry.
2. Enter the date of the journal entry in the account on the next available line for the debit.
3. Write the amount debited in the journal entry in the debit column of the account.
4. To show where the debit came from, enter the letter *G* and the journal page number in the Posting Reference (PR) column for the account. (The letter *G* shows that the posted entry came from the General Journal. Other journals are identified by their own letters. We discuss other journals in Chapter 6.
5. Calculate and enter the account's new balance in the third column.
6. To show that the posting process is complete, enter the account number in the Posting Reference column on the entry's line in the journal. (If posting is interrupted, the bookkeeper can use the journal's Posting Reference column to take up the process where it was stopped.)

For the credit:

Repeat the six steps. However, the credit amount is entered in the Credit column and has a credit effect on the account balance.

Notice that step 6 in the posting procedure for either the debit or the credit of an entry inserts the account number in the journal's Posting Reference column. This creates a link between the ledger and the journal entry. This link provides a cross-reference that helps the bookkeeper and the auditor trace an amount from one record to the other.

Illustration 2-7   Six Steps for Posting a General Journal Entry to the Ledger

(1) Find the account	(3) Post the entered amount	(5) Enter the account balance
(2) Enter the date	(4) Enter the journal page	(6) Enter the account number

GENERAL JOURNAL   Page 1

Date	Account Titles and Explanation	PR	Debit	Credit
1996 Dec. 1	Cash	101	30,000 00	
	Terry Dow, Capital	301		30,000 00
	Investment by owner.			

LEDGER

Cash   Account No. 101

Date	Explanation	PR	Debit	Credit	Balance
1996 Dec. 1		G1	30,000 00		30,000 00

Terry Dow, Capital   Account No. 301

Date	Explanation	PR	Debit	Credit	Balance
1996 Dec. 1		G1		30,000 00	30,000 00

Posting in Computerized Systems. Computerized accounting systems do not require any additional effort by the operator to post the journal entries to the ledger. The programs in the systems are designed to automatically transfer the debit and credit entries from the journal into the database. In effect, the journal entries are posted directly into the accounts in the ledger without any additional steps.

Many systems include error-detection routines that test the reasonableness of the journal entry and the account balance when the new entry is recorded. Computerized data processing is discussed in Chapter 6.

Progress Check

2-11   The owner of Davis Company invested $15,000 cash and land with a fair market value of $23,000 in the business. The company also assumed responsibility for an $18,000 note payable originally issued to finance the purchase of the land. The journal entry to record this investment consists of: *(a)* One debit and one credit; *(b)* Two debits and one credit; *(c)* Two debits and two credits; or *(d)* Debits that total $38,000 and credits that total $33,000.

2-12   What is a compound journal entry?

2-13   Why are posting reference numbers entered in the journal when entries are posted to the accounts?

PREPARING AND USING THE TRIAL BALANCE

LO 5

Prepare a trial balance, explain its usefulness, and calculate a company's debt ratio.

Recall that a double-entry accounting system records every transaction with equal debits and credits. As a result, the bookkeeper can tell that an error has occurred if the sum of the debit entries in the ledger does not equal the sum of the credit entries. The bookkeeper also knows that an error has occurred if the sum of the debit account balances does not equal the sum of the credit balances.

One purpose for preparing a **trial balance** is to find out if the debit and credit account balances are equal. A trial balance is a summary of the ledger that is a list of the accounts and their balances. The account balances are placed in either the debit or credit column of the trial balance. Illustration 2–8 presents the trial balance for Clear Copy after the 16 entries described earlier in the chapter have been posted to the ledger (shown in Illustration 2–3).

The trial balance also serves as a helpful internal document for preparing the financial statements. The task of preparing the statements is simplified if the accountant can take the account balances from the trial balance instead of looking them up in the ledger. (Chapter 3 describes the statement preparation process in more detail.)

The bookkeeper uses these five steps to prepare a trial balance:

1. Find the balance of each account in the ledger.
2. List each account and place its balance beside it. Debit balances are entered in the Debit column and credit balances are entered in the Credit column. (If an account has a zero balance, it may be included in the trial balance with a zero in the column for its normal balance.)
3. Compute the total of the debit balances.
4. Compute the total of the credit balances.
5. Verify that the sum of the debit balances equals the sum of the credit balances.

The trial balance for Clear Copy in Illustration 2–8 is presented in a typical format. Notice that the total of the debit balances equals the total of the credit balances. If

Illustration 2-8 Trial Balance Drawn from the Ledger of Clear Copy

CLEAR COPY
Trial Balance
December 31, 1996

	Debit	Credit
Cash	$ 7,950	
Accounts receivable	0	
Prepaid insurance	2,400	
Store supplies	3,720	
Copy equipment	26,000	
Accounts payable		$ 6,200
Unearned copy services revenue		3,000
Terry Dow, capital		30,000
Terry Dow, withdrawals	400	
Copy services revenue		3,900
Rent expense	1,000	
Salaries expense	1,400	
Utilities expense	230	
Total	$43,100	$43,100

the two totals were not equal, we would know that at least one error had occurred. However, the fact that the two totals are equal does not prove that all errors were avoided.

The Information Provided by a Trial Balance

When a trial balance does not balance (that is, the columns are not equal), we know that at least one error has occurred. The error (or errors) may have occurred during these steps in the accounting process: (1) preparing journal entries, (2) posting journal entries to the ledger, (3) calculating account balances, (4) copying account balances to the trial balance, or (5) totaling the trial balance columns.

If the trial balance does balance, the accounts are likely to be free from errors that create unequal debits and credits. However, bookkeeping accuracy is not assured if the column totals are equal because some errors do not create unequal debits and credits. For example, the bookkeeper may debit a correct amount to the wrong account in preparing the journal entry or in posting a journal entry to the ledger. This error would cause two accounts to have incorrect balances but the trial balance would not be out of balance. Another error would be to record an equal debit and credit of an incorrect amount. This error would give the two accounts incorrect balances but would not create unequal debits and credits. As a result, the fact that the trial balance column totals are equal does not prove that all journal entries have been recorded and posted correctly. However, equal totals do suggest that several types of errors probably have not occurred.

Searching for and Correcting Errors

If the trial balance does not balance, at least one error has occurred. The error (or errors) needs to be found and corrected before going on to prepare the financial statements. The search for the error is more efficient if the bookkeeper checks the journalizing, posting, and trial balance preparation steps in reverse order.

First, the bookkeeper should verify that the trial balance columns were correctly added. Second, if that step does not find the error, the bookkeeper should verify that account balances were accurately copied from the ledger. Third, the book-keeper should check to see if a debit or credit balance was mistakenly listed in the trial balance as a credit or debit. (A clue to this kind of error would be that the difference between the total debits and total credits in the trial balance would equal twice the amount of the incorrectly listed account balance.)

If the error remains undiscovered, the bookkeeper's fourth step is to recalculate each account balance. Then, if the error is not found, it is necessary to verify that each journal entry was properly posted to the accounts. Finally, the only remaining (and least likely) source of the error would be an original journal entry that did not have equal debits and credits.

One frequent error is called a *transposition*. This error occurs when two digits are switched or transposed within a number. For example, a $691 debit in a journal entry may be posted to the ledger as $619. If this happens and it is the only error, the difference between the two trial balance columns is evenly divisible by nine. For example, suppose that a posting error places a $619 debit in an account instead of the journal's correct amount of $691. As a result, the total credits in the trial balance would be larger than the total debits by $72 ($691 − $619). This number is evenly divisible by 9 ($72/9 = 8). Furthermore, the quotient (8) equals the difference between the two transposed numbers. The number of digits in the quotient also signals the location of the transposition. In this example, the fact that the quotient (8) has only one digit tells us that the transposition occurred in the first digit of the transposed numbers, starting from the right.[4]

Correcting Errors

If errors are discovered in either the journal or the ledger, they need to be corrected to ensure that the financial statements provide useful information. The approach to correcting the records depends on the nature of the errors and when they are discovered.

If an error in a journal entry is discovered before the error is posted, it can be corrected in a manual system by drawing a line through the incorrect information. Then, the correct information can be written above it to create a record of the change for the auditor. (Most computerized systems allow the operator to simply replace the incorrect information.) If a correct amount in the journal was posted incorrectly in the ledger, the bookkeeper can correct it the same way.

If an error in a journal entry is not discovered before it is posted, the correction may have to be done differently. For example, suppose that a journal entry incorrectly debited (or credited) the wrong account. If the journal entry has already been posted to that incorrect account, the bookkeeper generally does not strike through both erroneous entries in the journal and ledger. Instead, the usual practice is to correct the error in the original journal entry by creating another journal entry. This *correcting entry* removes the amount from the wrong account and moves it to the

---

[4] If the transposition error had posted $961 instead of the correct $691, the difference would have been $270, and the quotient would have been $30 ($270/9). The fact that the quotient has two digits tells us to carefully examine the second digits from the right for a transposition of two numbers with a difference of 3.

right account. For example, suppose that the bookkeeper recorded a purchase of office supplies with this incorrect debit in the journal entry to the Office Equipment account and then posted it to the accounts in the ledger:

Oct.	14	Office Equipment	1,600.00	
		Cash		1,600.00
		To record the purchase of office supplies.		

As a result of posting this incorrect entry, the Office Supplies account balance is too small (understated) by $1,600 and the Office Equipment account balance is too large (overstated) by the same amount. Three days later, the error is discovered and the following entry is made to correct both account balances:

Oct.	17	Office Supplies	1,600.00	
		Office Equipment		1,600.00
		To correct the entry of October 14 that incorrectly debited Office Equipment instead of Office Supplies.		

The credit in the correcting entry cancels the error from the first entry, and the debit correctly records the supplies. The explanation in the correcting entry allows the auditor to know exactly what happened. There are no specific guidelines for writing journal entry explanations. As mentioned earlier in the chapter, the explanation should be short but provide enough information to describe why the entry was made.

Similar correcting entries may be needed in computerized accounting systems. The exact procedure depends on the particular program being used.

OTHER FORMATTING CONVENTIONS

When amounts are entered manually on ruled accounting paper in a journal, ledger, or trial balance, commas are not needed to indicate thousands and decimal points are not needed to separate dollars and cents. However, commas and decimal points are used in financial statements and other reports.

As a matter of convenience, dollar signs are not used in journals and ledgers. However, they do appear in financial statements and other reports, including trial balances. This book follows the practice of putting a dollar sign beside the first amount in each column of numbers and the first amount appearing after a ruled line indicating that an addition or subtraction has been performed. The financial statements in Illustrations 1–7 and 1–8 on pages 40 and 41 demonstrate how dollar signs are used in this book. Different companies use various conventions for dollar signs. For example, some companies use dollar signs beside only the first and last numbers in the columns in the financial statements.

If an amount entered manually in a ledger or a journal consists of even dollars without cents, a convenient shortcut uses a dash in the cents column instead of two zeros. To simplify the illustrations, this book usually shows exact dollar amounts.

Even small companies seldom show decimal points or cents in their financial statements. Normally, the amounts are rounded, perhaps to the nearest dollar but often to a higher level. **Imperial Oil Limited** is typical of many very large companies in that it rounds its financial statement amounts to the nearest million dollars.

With so much emphasis in this chapter on bookkeeping activities, it might be easy to temporarily overlook the fact that accounting records are created for the purpose of providing useful information in financial statements. This chapter closes by describing a ratio that users apply to assess a company's risk of inability to pay its debts as they become due.

USING THE INFORMATION– THE DEBT RATIO

Almost all companies finance some portion of their assets with liabilities and the remaining portion with owner's equity. A company that finances a relatively large portion of its assets with liabilities is said to have a high degree of financial leverage.

You learn more about financial leverage in later chapters. However, you should understand that financial leverage involves risk. Because liabilities must be repaid and also require a company to pay interest, the risk of liabilities is that the company may not be able to make the required payments. In general, the risk is higher if a company is highly leveraged.

One way to evaluate the risk associated with a company's use of liabilities to finance its assets is to calculate and evaluate the **debt ratio.** This ratio describes the relationship between the amounts of the company's liabilities and assets, as follows:

$$\text{Debt ratio} = \frac{\text{Total liabilities}}{\text{Total assets}}$$

To see how the debt ratio is applied, consider the example of **Imperial Oil Limited** discussed at the beginning of the chapter. Using the data that was presented on page 71, the company's debt ratios at the end of each year from 1990 through 1994 are as follows:

		1994	1993	1992	1991	1990
a.	Total liabilities*	$ 5,933	$ 6,295	$ 6,499	$ 6,701	$ 7,593
b.	Total assets*	11,928	12,861	13,135	13,491	14,458
c.	Debt ratio (a ÷ b)	.497	.489	.495	.497	.525

Evaluating a company's debt ratio depends on several factors such as the nature of its operations, its ability to generate cash flows, the economic conditions at the time, and the industry in which it operates. Thus, it is not possible to say that a specific debt ratio is good for all companies. However, notice that Imperial's debt ratio was rather constant (range of .489 to .525) over the five-year period. Recall that according to the company's management, Imperial's financial position is one of the strongest in the industry and gives it the flexibility to manage through periods of uncertainty.

Progress Check

2-14   **Which of the following terms describes a list of all of a company's accounts and their identifying numbers?** *(a)* **A journal;** *(b)* **A ledger;** *(c)* **A trial balance;** *(d)* **A source document; or** *(e)* **A chart of accounts.**

2-15   **When are dollar signs used in accounting reports?**

2-16   **A $4,000 debit to Store Equipment in a journal entry was incorrectly posted to the ledger as a $4,000 credit, and the account had a resulting debit balance of $20,000. What is the effect of the error on the trial balance column totals?**

2-17   **Which debt ratio implies more risk, ignoring other factors?** *(a)* **6.6;** *(b)* **5.0.**

SUMMARY OF THE CHAPTER IN TERMS OF LEARNING OBJECTIVES

LO 1. Describe the events recorded in accounting systems and the importance of source documents and business papers in those systems. Accounting systems record transactions and other events that affect a company's assets, liabilities, and equity. The other events include internal transactions that use up assets or external events that cause the company's assets or liabilities to change. Source documents describe information that is recorded with accounting entries.

LO 2. Describe how accounts are used to record information about the effects of transactions, how code numbers are used to identify each account, and the meaning of the words *debit* and *credit*. Accounts are the basic building blocks of accounting systems. In one sense, accounts are symbols of the company's assets, liabilities, owner's equity, revenues, and expenses. In another sense, accounts are special records used to store information about transactions. The ledger is the collection of accounts used by an organization. Each account is assigned an identification number based on a code that indicates what kind of account it is. Debits record increases in assets, withdrawals, and expenses. Credits record decreases in these same accounts. Credits also record increases in liabilities, the owner's capital account, and revenues, while debits record decreases in these accounts.

LO 3. Describe how debits and credits are used to analyze transactions and record their effects in the accounts. To understand how a transaction affects a business, determine what accounts were increased or decreased. Every transaction affects at least two accounts, and the sum of the debits for each transaction equals the sum of the credits. As a result, the effects of business transactions never create an imbalance in the accounting equation (Assets = Liabilities + Owner's Equity).

LO 4. Record transactions in a General Journal, describe balance column accounts, and post entries from the journal to the ledger. Transactions are first recorded in a journal that provides a record of all their effects in one location. Second, each entry in the journal is posted to the accounts in the ledger. This process places information in the accounts that is used to produce the company's financial statements. Balance column accounts are widely used in accounting systems. These accounts include columns for debit entries, credit entries, and the balance after each entry.

LO 5. Prepare a trial balance, explain its usefulness, and calculate a company's debt ratio. A trial balance is a list of the accounts in the ledger that shows their debit and credit balances in separate columns. The trial balance is a convenient summary of the ledger's contents. It also reveals the existence of some kinds of errors if the sum of the debit account balances does not equal the sum of the credit account balances. A company's debt ratio is the ratio between its total liabilities and total assets. It provides information about the risk a company faces by using liabilities to finance its assets.

This demonstration problem is based on the same facts as the demonstration problem at the end of Chapter 1. The following events occurred during the first month of Barbara Schmidt's new haircutting business called The Cutlery:

a. On August 1, Schmidt put $3,000 cash into a chequing account in the name of The Cutlery. She also invested $15,000 of equipment that she already owned.

b. On August 2, she paid $600 cash for furniture for the shop.

c. On August 3, she paid $500 cash to rent space in a strip mall for August.

d. On August 4, she furnished the shop by installing the old equipment and some new equipment that she bought on credit for $1,200. This amount is to be repaid in three equal payments at the end of August, September, and October.

e. On August 5, The Cutlery opened for business. Receipts from cash sales in the first week and a half of business (ended August 15) were $825.

f. On August 17, Schmidt paid $125 to an assistant for working during the grand opening.

g. Cash receipts from sales during the second half of August were $930.

h. On August 31, Schmidt paid an installment on the accounts payable.

i. On August 31, she withdrew $900 cash for her personal use.

Required

1. Prepare general journal entries for the preceding transactions.
2. Open the following accounts: Cash, 101; Furniture, 161; Store Equipment, 165; Accounts Payable, 201; Barbara Schmidt, Capital, 301; Barbara Schmidt, Withdrawals, 302; Haircutting Services Revenue, 403; Wages Expense, 623; and Rent Expense, 640.
3. Post the journal entries to the ledger accounts.
4. Prepare a trial balance as of August 31.

*   Analyze each transaction to identify the accounts affected by the transaction and the amount of each effect.

*   Use the debit and credit rules to prepare a journal entry for each transaction.

*   Post each debit and each credit in the journal entries to the appropriate ledger accounts and cross-reference each amount in the Posting Reference columns in the journal and account.

*   Calculate each account balance and list the accounts with their balances on a trial balance.

*   Verify that the total debits in the trial balance equal total credits.

*Planning the
Solution*

Solution to
Demonstration
Problem

1.   General journal entries:

Date		Account Titles and Explanations	PR	Debit	Credit
Aug.	1	Cash	101	3,000.00	
		Store Equipment	165	15,000.00	
		Barbara Schmidt, Capital	301		18,000.00
		Owner's initial investment.			
	2	Furniture	161	600.00	
		Cash	101		600.00
		Purchased furniture for cash.			
	3	Rent Expense	640	500.00	
		Cash	101		500.00
		Paid rent for August.			
	4	Store Equipment	165	1,200.00	
		Accounts Payable	201		1,200.00
		Purchased additional equipment on credit.			
	15	Cash	101	825.00	
		Haircutting Services Revenue	403		825.00
		Cash receipts from ten days of operations.			
	17	Wages Expense	623	125.00	
		Cash	101		125.00
		Paid wages to assistant.			
	31	Cash	101	930.00	
		Haircutting Services Revenue	403		930.00
		Cash receipts from second half of August.			
	31	Accounts Payable	201	400.00	
		Cash	101		400.00
		Paid an installment on accounts payable.			
	31	Barbara Schmidt, Withdrawals	302	900.00	
		Cash	101		900.00
		Owner withdrew cash from the business.			

2. 3.   Accounts in the ledger:

	Cash					Account No. 101
Date		Explanation	PR	Debit	Credit	Balance
Aug.	1		G1	3,000.00		3,000.00
	2		G1		600.00	2,400.00
	3		G1		500.00	1,900.00
	15		G1	825.00		2,725.00
	17		G1		125.00	2,600.00
	31		G1	930.00		3,530.00
	31		G1		400.00	3,130.00
	31		G1		900.00	2,230.00

Furniture   Account No. 161

Date		Explanation	PR	Debit	Credit	Balance
Aug.	2		G1	600.00		600.00

Store Equipment   Account No. 165

Date		Explanation	PR	Debit	Credit	Balance
Aug.	1		G1	15,000.00		15,000.00
	4		G1	1,200.00		16,200.00

Accounts Payable   Account No. 201

Date		Explanation	PR	Debit	Credit	Balance
Aug.	4		G1		1,200.00	1,200.00
	31		G1	400.00		800.00

Barbara Schmidt, Capital   Account No. 301

Date		Explanation	PR	Debit	Credit	Balance
Aug.	1		G1		18,000.00	18,000.00

Barbara Schmidt, Withdrawals   Account No. 302

Date		Explanation	PR	Debit	Credit	Balance
Aug.	31		G1	900.00		900.00

Haircutting Services Revenue   Account No. 403

Date		Explanation	PR	Debit	Credit	Balance
Aug.	15		G1		825.00	825.00
	31		G1		930.00	1,755.00

Wages Expense   Account No. 623

Date		Explanation	PR	Debit	Credit	Balance
Aug.	17		G1	125.00		125.00

Rent Expense   Account No. 640

Date		Explanation	PR	Debit	Credit	Balance
Aug.	3		G1	500.00		500.00

4.

THE CUTLERY
Trial Balance
August 31, 1996

	Debit	Credit
Cash	$ 2,230	
Furniture	600	
Store equipment	16,200	
Accounts payable		$ 800
Barbara Schmidt, capital		18,000
Barbara Schmidt, withdrawals	900	
Haircutting services revenue		1,755
Wages expense	125	
Rent expense	500	
Totals	$20,555	$20,555

GLOSSARY

Account a place or location within an accounting system in which the increases and decreases in a specific asset, liability, owner's equity, revenue, or expense are recorded and stored. p. 75

Account balance the difference between the increases (including the beginning balance) and decreases recorded in an account. p. 80

Balance column account an account with debit and credit columns for recording entries and a third column for showing the balance of the account after each entry is posted. p. 91

Book of final entry another name for a ledger. p. 89

Book of original entry another name for a journal. p. 89

Business papers various kinds of documents and other papers that companies use when they conduct their business; sometimes called *source documents*. p. 73

Capital account an account used to record the owner's investments in the business plus any more or less permanent changes in the owner's equity. p. 78

Chart of accounts a list of all accounts used by a company; includes the identification number assigned to each account. p. 79

Compound journal entry a journal entry that affects at least three accounts. p. 89

Credit an entry that decreases asset and expense accounts, or increases liability, owner's equity, and revenue accounts; recorded on the right side of a T-account. p. 80

Debit an entry that increases asset and expense accounts, or decreases liability, owner's equity, and revenue accounts; recorded on the left side of a T-account. p. 80

Debt ratio the ratio between a company's liabilities and assets; used to describe the risk associated with the company's debts. p. 99

Double-entry accounting an accounting system that records the effects of transactions and other events in at least two accounts with equal debits and credits. p. 82

External transactions exchanges between the entity and some other person or organization. p. 73

General Journal the most flexible type of journal; can be used to record any kind of transaction. p. 89

Internal transactions a term occasionally used to describe economic events that affect an entity's accounting equation but that are not transactions between two parties. p. 73

Journal a record in which the effects of transactions are first recorded; amounts are posted from the journal to the ledger; also called the *book of original entry*. p. 88

Ledger the collection of all accounts used by a business. p. 79

Posting the process of copying journal entry information to the ledger. p. 89

Posting Reference (PR) column a column in journals and accounts used to cross-reference journal and ledger entries. p. 90

Prepaid expenses assets created by payments for economic benefits that are not used until later; as the benefits are used up, the cost of the assets becomes an expense. p. 76

Promissory note an unconditional written promise to pay a definite sum of money on demand or on a defined future date (or dates). p. 75

Source documents another name for *business papers*; these documents are the source of information recorded with accounting entries. p. 73

T-account a simple account form widely used in accounting education to illustrate how debits and credits work. p. 80

Trial balance a summary of the ledger that lists the accounts and their balances; the total debit balances should equal the total credit balances. p. 95

Unearned revenues liabilities created by advance cash payments from customers for products or services; satisfied by delivering the products or services in the future. p. 77

Withdrawals account the account used to record the transfers of assets from a business to its owner; also known as *personal account* or *drawing account*. p. 78

SYNONYMOUS TERMS

Business papers source documents.
Journal book of original entry.
Ledger book of final entry.

Posting Reference column folio column.
Withdrawals account drawing account; personal account.

QUESTIONS

1. What are the three fundamental steps in the accounting process?

2. What is the difference between a note receivable and an account receivable?

3. If assets are valuable resources and asset accounts have debit balances, why do expense accounts have debit balances?

4. Why does the bookkeeper prepare a trial balance?

5. Should a transaction be recorded first in a journal or the ledger? Why?

6. Are debits or credits listed first in general journal entries? Are the debits or the credits indented?

7. What kinds of transactions can be recorded in a General Journal?

8. If a wrong amount was journalized and posted to the accounts, how should the error be corrected?

9. Why is the evidence provided by business papers important to accounting?

10. If a transaction has the effect of decreasing an asset, is the decrease recorded as a debit or as a credit? If the transaction has the effect of decreasing a liability, is the decrease recorded as a debit or as a credit?

11. Why are some accounting systems called *double-entry* accounting systems?

12. What entry (debit or credit) would you make to (*a*) increase a revenue, (*b*) decrease an expense, (*c*) record an owner's withdrawals, and (*d*) record an owner's investment?

13. Why are the rules of debit and credit the same for both liability and owner's equity accounts?

14. What kinds of errors would cause the column totals of a trial balance to be unequal? What are some examples of errors that would not be revealed by a trial balance?

15. What is the purpose of posting reference numbers that are entered in the journal at the time entries are posted to the accounts?

QUICK STUDY (Five-Minute Exercises)

QS 2–1
(LO 1)

Select the items from the following list that are likely to serve as source documents:

a.	Sales ticket.	*e.*	Invoice from supplier.
b.	Trial balance.	*f.*	Balance sheet.
c.	Bank statement.	*g.*	Utility bill.
d.	Income statement.	*h.*	Owner's withdrawals account.

QS 2–2
(LO 2)

Indicate the financial statement on which each of the following accounts appears, using IS for income statement, SCOE for the statement of changes in owner's equity, and BS for balance sheet:

a.	Accounts Receivable.	*f.*	Salaries Expense.
b.	Consulting Services Revenue.	*g.*	Owner, Capital.
c.	Owner, Withdrawals.	*h.*	Interest Payable.
d.	Land.	*i.*	Office Supplies.
e.	Unearned Rent.	*j.*	Interest Earned.

QS 2–3
(LO 3)

Indicate whether a debit or credit is necessary to decrease the normal balance of each of the following accounts:

a.	Accounts Receivable.	*f.*	Salaries Expense.
b.	Consulting Services Revenue.	*g.*	Owner, Capital.
c.	Owner, Withdrawals.	*h.*	Interest Payable.
d.	Land.	*i.*	Office Supplies.
e.	Unearned Rent.	*j.*	Interest Earned.

QS 2–4
(LO 2, 3)

Identify whether a debit or credit entry would be made to record the indicated change in each of the following accounts:

a.	To increase Rent Earned.	*f.*	To decrease Unearned Fees.
b.	To increase Owner, Withdrawals.	*g.*	To increase Rent Expense.
c.	To decrease Owner, Capital.	*h.*	To increase Accounts Payable.
d.	To decrease Cash.	*i.*	To increase Office Equipment.
e.	To decrease Prepaid Insurance.	*j.*	To decrease Accounts Receivable.

QS 2–5
(LO 4)

Prepare journal entries for the following transactions:

a. On January 3, Jan Davis opened a new consulting business by investing $5,000 cash.
b. On January 5, Davis purchased office supplies on credit for $250.
c. On January 14, Davis received $1,600 in return for providing consulting services to a customer.

QS 2-6
(LO 5)

A trial balance has total debits of $14,000 and total credits of $17,000. Which one of the following errors would create this imbalance? Explain.

a. A $1,500 debit to Wages Expense in a journal entry was incorrectly posted to the ledger as a $1,500 credit, leaving the Wages Expense account with a $2,000 debit balance.

b. A $3,000 debit to Wages Expense in a journal entry was incorrectly posted to the ledger as a $3,000 credit, leaving the Wages Expense account with a $500 debit balance.

c. A $1,500 credit to Fees Earned in a journal entry was incorrectly posted to the ledger as a $1,500 debit, leaving the Fees Earned account with a $4,200 credit balance.

EXERCISES

Complete the following table by (1) identifying the type of account listed on each line, (2) entering debit or credit in the blank spaces to identify the kind of entry that would increase or decrease the account balance, and (3) identifying the normal balance of the account.

Exercise 2–1
Increases, decreases, and normal balances of accounts
(LO 2, 3)

	Account	Type of Account	Increase	Decrease	Normal Balance
a.	Accounts payable				
b.	Accounts receivable				
c.	B. Baxter, capital				
d.	B. Baxter, withdrawals				
e.	Cash				
f.	Equipment				
g.	Fees earned				
h.	Land				
i.	Postage expense				
j.	Prepaid insurance				
k.	Rent expense				
l.	Unearned revenue				

Franklin Consulting Company recently notified a client that it would have to pay a $32,000 fee for consulting services. Unfortunately, the client did not have enough cash to pay the entire bill. Fran Franklin, the owner of the company, agreed to accept the following items in full payment: $5,000 cash and computer equipment worth $50,000. Franklin also had to assume responsibility for a $23,000 note payable related to the equipment. Which of the following effects would be recorded by Franklin for this transaction? (Your answer may include more than one of the listed effects. Some of the effects of the transaction may not be listed.)

Exercise 2–2
Analyzing the effects of a transaction on the accounts
(LO 3)

a. $23,000 increase in a liability account.
b. $5,000 increase in the cash account.
c. $5,000 increase in a revenue account.
d. $32,000 increase in the F. Franklin, Capital account.
e. $32,000 increase in a revenue account.

Open the following T-accounts: Cash; Accounts Receivable; Office Supplies; Office Equipment; Accounts Payable; R. J. Wainwright, Capital; Services Revenue; and Utilities Expense. Next, record these transactions of the Wainwright Company by recording the debit and credit entries directly in the T-accounts. Use the letters beside each transaction to identify the entries. Finally, determine the balance of each account.

Exercise 2–3
Recording the effects of transactions directly in T-accounts
(LO 3)

a. R. J. Wainwright invested $8,500 cash in the business.
b. Purchased $250 of office supplies for cash.
c. Purchased $4,700 of office equipment on credit.
d. Received $1,000 cash as fees for services provided to a customer.
e. Paid for the office equipment purchased in transaction c.
f. Billed a customer $1,800 as fees for services.
g. Paid the monthly utility bills with $350 cash.
h. Collected $750 of the account receivable created in transaction f.

Exercise 2–4
Preparing a trial balance
(LO 5)

After recording the transactions of Exercise 2–3 in T-accounts and calculating the balance of each account, prepare the trial balance for the ledger. Use November 30, 1996, as the date.

Exercise 2–5
Effects of posting errors on the trial balance
(LO 5)

Complete the following table by filling in the blanks. For each of the listed posting errors, enter in column (1) the amount of the difference that the error would create between the two trial balance columns (show a zero if the columns would balance). If there would be a difference between the two columns, identify in column (2) the trial balance column that would be larger. The answer for the first error is provided as an example.

	Description	(1) Difference between Debit and Credit Columns	(2) Column with the Larger Total
a.	A $1,600 debit to Utilities Expense was posted as a $1,060 debit.	$540	credit
b.	A $28,000 debit to Automobiles was posted as a debit to Accounts Payable.		
c.	A $3,300 credit to Fees Earned was posted as a $330 credit.		
d.	A $960 debit to Office Supplies was not posted at all.		
e.	A $1,500 debit to Prepaid Rent was posted as a debit to Rent Expense.		
f.	A $2,700 credit to Cash was posted twice as two credits to the Cash account.		
g.	A $6,600 debit to the owner's withdrawals account was debited to the owner's capital account.		

Exercise 2–6
Analyzing a trial balance error
(LO 5)

As the bookkeeper for a company, you are disappointed to learn that the column totals in your new trial balance are not equal. After going through a careful analysis, you have discovered only one error. Specifically, the balance of the Office Equipment account has a debit balance of $15,600 on the trial balance. However, you have figured out that a correctly recorded credit purchase of a computer for $3,500 was posted from the journal to the ledger with a $3,500 debit to Office Equipment and another $3,500 debit to Accounts Payable. Answer each of the following questions and present the dollar amount of any misstatement.

a.   Is the balance of the Office Equipment account overstated, understated, or correctly stated in the trial balance?

b.   Is the balance of the Accounts Payable account overstated, understated, or correctly stated in the trial balance?

c.   Is the debit column total of the trial balance overstated, understated, or correctly stated?

d.   Is the credit column total of the trial balance overstated, understated, or correctly stated?

e. If the debit column total of the trial balance is $240,000 before correcting the error, what is the total of the credit column?

On January 1, Rob Gregory created a new business called RG Public Relations Consulting. Near the end of the year, he hired a new bookkeeper without making a careful reference check. As a result, a number of mistakes have been made in preparing the following trial balance:

Exercise 2–7
Preparing a corrected trial balance
(LO 5)

RG PUBLIC RELATIONS CONSULTING
Trial Balance
December 31

	Debit	Credit
Cash	$ 11,000	
Accounts receivable		$ 15,800
Office supplies	5,300	
Office equipment	41,000	
Accounts payable		18,930
R. Gregory, capital	51,490	
R. Gregory, withdrawals	18,000	
Services revenue		45,600
Wages expense		12,000
Rent expense		9,600
Advertising expense		2,500
Totals	$126,790	$104,680

Gregory's analysis of the situation has uncovered these errors:

a. The sum of the debits in the Cash account is $74,350 and the sum of the credits is $61,080.

b. A $550 payment from a credit customer was posted to Cash but was not posted to Accounts Receivable.

c. A credit purchase of office supplies for $800 was completely unrecorded.

d. A transposition error occurred in copying the balance of the Services Revenue account to the trial balance. The correct amount was $46,500.

Other errors were made in placing account balances in the trial balance columns and in taking the totals of the columns. Use all this information to prepare a correct trial balance.

Use the information in each of the following situations to calculate the unknown amount:

Exercise 2–8
Analyzing account entries and balances
(LO 2, 3)

1. During June, Sunnyside Company had $65,000 of cash receipts and $67,500 of cash disbursements. The June 30 Cash balance was $11,200. Determine how much cash the company had on hand at the close of business on May 31.

2. On May 31, Sunnyside Company had a $65,000 balance in Accounts Receivable. During June, the company collected $59,300 from its credit customers. The June 30 balance in Accounts Receivable was $67,000. Determine the amount of sales on account that occurred in June.

3. Sunnyside Company had $98,000 of accounts payable on May 31 and $91,000 on June 30. Total purchases on account during June were $180,000. Determine how much cash was paid on accounts payable during June.

Seven transactions were posted to these T-accounts. Provide a short description of each transaction. Include the amounts in your descriptions.

Exercise 2–9
Analyzing transactions from T-accounts
(LO 2, 3)

Cash				Truck	
(a)	3,500	(b)	1,800	(a)	5,500
(e)	1,250	(c)	300		
		(f)	1,200	**Accounts Payable**	
		(g)	350	(f)	1,200	(d)	4,800

Plumbing Supplies			Accounts Payable	

Plumbing Supplies			**Vinnie Doran, Capital**	
(c)	300			(a)	11,800
(d)	100				

Prepaid Insurance			**Plumbing Fees Earned**	
(b)	1,800			(e)	1,250

Plumbing Equipment			**Gas and Oil Expense**	
(a)	2,800		(g)	350	
(d)	4,700				

Exercise 2–10
General journal entries
(LO 4)

Use the information in the T-accounts in Exercise 2–9 to prepare general journal entries for the seven transactions. (Omit the account numbers.)

Exercise 2–11
General journal entries
(LO 4)

Prepare general journal entries to record the following transactions of Wayne's Water-Taxi Service.

May 1   Wayne Oldham invested $15,000 cash and a boat with a $65,000 fair value in a new company that will operate a water-taxi service in the harbour.

1   Rented space in a marina by paying $6,000 for the next three months in advance.

2   Purchased a two-way radio for the boat for $2,800 cash.

15   Collected $5,300 in fares over the preceding two weeks.

31   Paid $1,750 cash for gas and oil used by the boat during May.

Exercise 2–12
T-accounts and the trial balance
(LO 3, 5)

Use the information provided in Exercise 2–11 to prepare a May 31 trial balance for Wayne's Water-Taxi Service. First, open these T-accounts: Cash; Prepaid Rent; Boat; Equipment; Wayne Oldham, Capital; Fares Earned; and Gas and Oil Expense. Then post the general journal entries to the T-accounts. Finally, prepare the trial balance.

Exercise 2–13
Analyzing and journalizing revenue transactions
(LO 4)

Examine the following transactions and identify those that created revenues for the business. Prepare general journal entries to record those transactions and explain why the other transactions did not create revenues.

a.   Received $25,500 cash from Dr. J. Runner, the owner of the medical practice.

b.   Provided $900 of medical services to a patient on credit.

c.   Received $1,050 cash for medical services provided to patient.

d.   Received $6,100 from a patient in payment for medical services to be provided next year.

e.   Received $3,000 from a patient in partial payment of an account receivable.

f.   Borrowed $100,000 from the bank by signing a promissory note.

Examine the following transactions and identify those that created expenses for the business. Prepare general journal entries to record those transactions and explain why the other transactions did not create expenses.

a. Paid $9,400 cash for medical supplies purchased 30 days previously.

b. Paid the $750 salary of the doctor's assistant.

c. Paid $30,000 cash for medical equipment.

d. Paid utility bill with $620 cash.

e. Paid $700 to the owner of the medical practice as a withdrawal.

Exercise 2–14
Analyzing and journalizing expense transactions
(LO 4)

Calculate the debt ratio for each of the following cases:

Exercise 2–15
Calculating the debt ratio
(LO 5)

Case	Assets	Liabilities	Owner's Equity
1	$290,000	$110,000	$180,000
2	61,000	51,000	10,000
3	205,000	101,000	104,000
4	177,000	22,000	155,000
5	124,000	92,000	32,000
6	180,000	60,000	120,000

PROBLEMS

Bobbie Benson opened a consulting firm and completed these transactions during June.

a. Invested $40,000 cash and office equipment with a $15,000 fair value in a business called Benson Consulting.

b. Purchased land and a small office building. The land was worth $15,000, and the building was worth $85,000. The purchase price was paid with $20,000 cash and a long-term note payable for $80,000.

c. Purchased $1,200 of office supplies on credit.

d. Bobbie Benson transferred title of an automobile to the business. The car was worth $9,000.

e. Purchased $3,000 of additional office equipment on credit.

f. Paid $750 salary to an assistant.

g. Provided services to a client and collected $3,000 cash.

h. Paid $400 for the month's utilities.

i. Paid account payable created in transaction c.

j. Purchased $10,000 of new office equipment by paying $9,300 cash and trading in old equipment with a recorded cost of $700.

k. Completed $2,600 of services for a client. This amount is to be paid within 30 days.

l. Paid $750 salary to an assistant.

m. Received $1,900 payment on the receivable created in transaction k.

n. The owner withdrew $2,000 cash from the business.

Problem 2–1
Recording transactions in T-accounts; preparing a trial balance
(LO 2, 3, 5)

Required

1. Open the following T-accounts: Cash; Accounts Receivable; Office Supplies; Automobiles; Office Equipment; Building; Land; Accounts Payable; Long-Term Notes Payable; Bobbie Benson, Capital; Bobbie Benson, Withdrawals; Fees Earned; Salaries Expense; and Utilities Expense.

2. Record the effects of the listed transactions by entering debits and credits directly in the T-accounts. Use the transaction letters to identify each debit and credit entry.

3. Determine the balance of each account and prepare a trial balance as of June 30.

Problem 2–2
Recording transactions in T-accounts; preparing a trial balance
(LO 2, 3, 5)

At the beginning of March, Avery Wilson created a custom computer programming company called Softouch. The following transactions occurred during the month:

a. Created the business by investing $35,000 cash, office equipment with a value of $2,000, and $15,000 of computer equipment.

b. Purchased land for an office. The land was worth $18,000, which was paid with $1,800 cash and a long-term note payable for $16,200.

c. Purchased a portable building with $25,000 cash and moved it onto the land.

d. Paid $2,000 cash for the premiums on two one-year insurance policies.

e. Provided services to a client and collected $1,900 cash.

f. Purchased additional computer equipment for $7,500. Paid $3,500 cash and signed a long-term note payable for the $4,000 balance.

g. Completed $4,000 of services for a client. This amount is to be paid within 30 days.

h. Purchased $750 of additional office equipment on credit.

i. Completed another software job for $6,000 on credit.

j. Received a bill for rent on a computer that was used on the completed job. The $400 rent must be paid within 30 days.

k. Collected $2,400 from the client described in transaction g.

l. Paid $500 wages to an assistant.

m. Paid the account payable created in transaction h.

n. Paid $225 cash for some repairs to an item of computer equipment.

o. The owner wrote a $3,200 cheque on the company's bank account to pay some personal expenses.

p. Paid $500 wages to an assistant.

q. Paid $1,000 cash to advertise in the local newspaper.

Required

1. Open the following T-accounts: Cash; Accounts Receivable; Prepaid Insurance; Office Equipment; Computer Equipment; Building; Land; Accounts Payable; Long-Term Notes Payable; Avery Wilson, Capital; Avery Wilson, Withdrawals; Fees Earned; Wages Expense; Computer Rental Expense; Advertising Expense; and Repairs Expense.

2. Record the transactions by entering debits and credits directly in the accounts. Use the transaction letters to identify each debit and credit. Prepare a trial balance as of March 31.

3. Calculate the company's debt ratio. Use $78,675 as the ending total assets.

Problem 2–3
Recording transactions in T-accounts; preparing a trial balance
(LO 4, 5)

Wayne Seale completed these transactions during a short period:

a. Began business as an excavating contractor by investing cash. $37,500; office equipment, $2,200; and excavating machinery, $67,500.

b. Purchased for $37,500 land to be used as an office site and for parking equipment. Paid $15,000 in cash and signed a promissory note payable for the balance.

c.   Purchased additional excavating machinery costing $32,650. Paid $10,150 in cash and signed a promissory note payable for the balance.

d.   Paid $6,700 cash for a used prefabricated building and moved it on the land for use as an office.

e.   Completed an excavating job and immediately collected $1,275 in cash for the work.

f.   Prepaid the premium on an insurance policy giving one year's protection, $960.

g.   Completed an $1,875 excavating job for City-Wide Contractors on credit.

h.   Paid the wages of the equipment operator, $1,200.

i.   Paid $250 cash for repairs to excavating machinery.

j.   Received $1,875 from City-Wide Contractors for the work of transaction (g).

k.   Completed a $1,200 excavating job for SMK Contractors on credit.

l.   Received and recorded as an account payable a $165 bill for the rent of a special machine used on the SMK Contractors job.

m.   Purchased additional office equipment on credit, $790.

n.   Wayne Seale withdrew $750 from the business for personal use.

o.   Paid the wages of the equipment operator, $1,350.

p.   Paid the $165 account payable resulting from renting the machine of transaction (l).

q.   Paid for gas and oil consumed by the excavating machinery, $335.

Required

1.   Open the following T-accounts; Cash; Accounts Receivable; Prepaid Insurance; Office Equipment; Machinery; Building; Land; Accounts Payable; Notes Payable; Wayne Seale, Capital; Wayne Seale, Withdrawals; Excavating Revenue; Machinery Repairs Expense; Wages Expense; Machinery Rentals Expense; and Gas and Oil Expense.

2.   Record the transactions by entering debits and credits directly in the accounts. Use the transaction letters to identify each debit and credit.

3.   Prepare a trial balance using the current date and headed Wayne Seale, Contractor.

Carrie Ford opened a new accounting practice called Carrie Ford, Public Accountant, and completed these transactions during March:

Problem 2–4
Preparing and posting general journal entries; preparing a trial balance
(LO 4, 5)

Mar. 1   Invested $25,000 in cash and office equipment that had a fair value of $6,000.

     1   Prepaid $1,800 cash for three months' rent for an office.

     3   Made credit purchases of office equipment for $3,000 and office supplies for $600.

     5   Completed work for a client and immediately received $500 cash.

     9   Completed a $2,000 project for a client, who will pay within 30 days.

   11   Paid the account payable created on March 3.

   15   Paid $1,500 cash as the annual premium on an insurance policy.

   20   Received $1,600 as partial payment for the work completed on March 9.

   23   Completed work for another client for $660 on credit.

   27   Carrie Ford withdrew $1,800 cash from the business to pay some personal expenses.

Mar. 30   Purchased $200 of additional office supplies on credit.

      31   Paid $175 for the month's utility bill.

Required

1. Prepare general journal entries to record the transactions.

2. Open the following accounts (use the balance column format): Cash (101); Accounts Receivable (106); Office Supplies (124); Prepaid Insurance (128); Prepaid Rent (131); Office Equipment (163); Accounts Payable (201); Carrie Ford, Capital (301); Carrie Ford, Withdrawals (302); Accounting Fees Earned (401); and Utilities Expense (690).

3. Post the entries to the accounts and enter the balance after each posting.

4. Prepare a trial balance as of the end of the month.

Problem 2–5
Interpreting journals,
posting, and analyzing
trial balance errors
(LO 4, 5)

Ada Evans started a business called The Pine Bough on August 1 and completed several transactions during the month. Her accounting and bookkeeping skills are not well-polished, and she needs some help gathering information at the end of the month. She recorded the following journal entries during the month:

Aug.	1	Cash	15,000.00	
		Automobiles	11,000.00	
		Ada Evans, Capital		26,000.00
	3	Store Supplies	323.00	
		Cash		323.00
	7	Cash	500.00	
		Accounts Receivable	2,500.00	
		Fees Earned		3,000.00
	8	Store Equipment	3,200.00	
		Accounts Payable		3,200.00
	15	Cash	400.00	
		Fees Earned		400.00
	17	Prepaid Insurance	625.00	
		Cash		625.00
	23	Cash	2,500.00	
		Accounts Receivable		2,500.00
	25	Accounts Payable	3,200.00	
		Cash		3,200.00
	27	Office Equipment	4,700.00	
		Ada Evans, Capital		4,700.00
	28	Ada Evans, Withdrawals	1,230.00	
		Cash		1,230.00
	29	Store Supplies	727.00	
		Accounts Payable		727.00
	31	Salaries Expense	1,570.00	
		Cash		1,570.00

Based on these entries, Evans prepared the following trial balance:

THE PINE BOUGH
Trial Balance
August 31

Cash	$11,452	
Accounts receivable	0	
Store supplies	1,500	
Prepaid insurance	625	
Automobiles	11,000	
Office equipment	7,400	
Store equipment		$ 3,200
Accounts payable		7,270
Ada Evans, capital		30,700
Ada Evans, withdrawals	123	
Fees earned		3,400
Salaries expense	1,750	
Totals	$33,850	$44,570

Required

Preparation component:

Evans remembers something about trial balances and realizes that the preceding one has at least one error. To help her find the mistakes, set up the following balance column accounts and post the entries to them: Cash (101); Accounts Receivable (106); Store Supplies (125); Prepaid Insurance (128); Automobiles (151); Office Equipment (163); Store Equipment (165); Accounts Payable (201); Ada Evans, Capital (301); Ada Evans, Withdrawals (302); Fees Earned (401); and Salaries Expense (622).

Analysis component:

Although Evans's journal entries are correct, she forgot to provide explanations of the events. Analyze each entry and present a reasonable explanation of what happened. Then, prepare a correct trial balance and describe the errors that Evans made.

Jan Dell started a new business, Dimple Dell Day Care, and completed these transactions during October of the current year:

Problem 2–6
Journalizing, posting, and preparing financial statements
(LO 4, 5)

Oct. 1 Invested $35,000 in cash, $2,500 in teaching supplies, and school equipment worth $9,000.

2 Paid $750 cash for one month's rent for suitable space in a shopping centre.

3 Paid a liability insurance policy premium of $1,400 for the first month.

4 Purchased a van for picking up the kids by paying $14,000 cash.

10 Purchased $800 of additional teaching supplies on credit.

21 Paid $4,000 cash for helpers' salaries.

23 Paid one-half of the account payable created on October 10.

28 Collected $9,000 cash from customers.

29 Paid $1,150 for the month's utility bills.

31 Withdrew $1,200 cash from the business to pay some personal expenses.

Required

1. Open the following accounts: Cash (101); Teaching Supplies (126); Automobiles (151); School Equipment (167); Accounts Payable (201); Jan Dell, Capital (301); Jan Dell, Withdrawals (302); Day Care Fees Earned (401); Salaries Expense (622); Insurance Expense (637); Rent Expense (640); and Utilities Expense (690).

2. Prepare general journal entries to record the transactions, post them to the accounts, and prepare a trial balance as of October 31.

3. Prepare an income statement for the month ended October 31.

4. Prepare a statement of changes in owner's equity for the month ended October 31.

5. Prepare a balance sheet dated October 31.

Problem 2–7
Journalizing, posting, and preparing financial statements
(LO 4, 5)

Amy Tuck graduated from law school with a law degree in June of the current year, and during July she completed these transactions:

July 1 Began the practice of law by investing $3,000 in cash and law books acquired in school and having a $1,200 fair value.

1 Rented the furnished office of a lawyer who was retiring and paid the rent (expense) for July, $725.

2 Purchased law books costing $1,125 under an agreement calling for a $150 down payment and the balance in monthly installments. Paid the down payment and recorded the remaining $975 as an account payable.

5 Purchased office supplies on credit, $70.

6 Took out a liability insurance policy giving one year's protection and paid the premium (expense) for the month of July, $50.

8 Completed legal work for a client and immediately collected $450 for the work done.

12 Paid for the office supplies purchased on credit on July 5.

16 Completed legal work for York Bank on credit, $1,275.

22 Amy Tuck wrote a $30 cheque on the bank account of the legal practice to pay her home telephone bill.

24 Received $1,275 from York Bank for the work completed July 16.

26 Completed legal work for Royal Realty on credit, $900.

30 Paid the telephone bill of the legal practice, $40.

31 Paid the salary of the office secretary, $1,350.

31 Prepaid the rent on the office for August and September, $1,450.

31 Prepaid the liability insurance premium for the next 11 months, $550.

Required

1. Open the following accounts: Cash; Accounts Receivable; Prepaid Rent; Prepaid Insurance; Office Supplies; Law Library; Accounts Payable; Amy Tuck, Capital; Amy Tuck, Withdrawals; Legal Fees Earned; Rent Expense; Salaries Expense; Telephone Expense; and Insurance Expense.

2. Prepare general journal entries to record the transactions, post to the accounts, and prepare a trial balance titled Amy Tuck, Lawyer.

3. Prepare an income statement for the month ended July 31.

4. Prepare a statement of changes in owner's equity for the month ended July 31.
5. Prepare a balance sheet dated July 31.

Joan Conrod opened a real estate business and during a short period as an agent completed these business transactions:

a. Invested $42,000 in cash and office equipment with a $6,000 fair value in a real estate agency she called Conrod Realty.
b. Purchased land valued at $30,000 cash and a small office building valued at $105,000, paying $35,000 cash and signing a note payable to pay the balance over a period of years.
c. Purchased office supplies on credit, $60.
d. Joan Conrod contributed her personal automobile, which had a $7,200 fair value, for exclusive use in the business.
e. Purchased additional office equipment on credit, $720.
f. Paid the office secretary's salary, $600.
g. Sold a house and collected an $8,500 cash commission on the sale.
h. Paid $150 for newspaper advertising that had appeared.
i. Paid for the supplies purchased on credit in transaction (c).
j. Purchased a new typewriter for the business, paying $840 cash plus an old typewriter carried in the accounting records at $140.
k. Completed a real estate appraisal on credit and billed the client $210 for the appraisal.
l. Paid the secretary's salary, $600.
m. Received payment in full for the appraisal of transaction (k).
n. Joan Conrod withdrew $1,500 from the business to pay personal expenses.

Required

1. Open the following T-accounts: Cash; Accounts Receivable; Office Supplies; Office Equipment; Automobile; Land; Building; Accounts Payable; Notes Payable; Joan Conrod, Capital; Joan Conrod, Withdrawals; Commissions Earned; Appraisal Fees Earned; Office Salaries Expense; and Advertising Expense.
2. Record the transactions by entering debits and credits directly in the accounts. Use the transaction letters to identify each debit and credit amount.
3. Determine the balance of each account in the ledger and prepare a trial balance using the current date and the title Conrod Realty.

Adam Uppe, Public Accountant, completed these transactions during September of the current year:

Sept. 1 Began a public accounting practice by investing $4,200 in cash and office equipment having a $4,800 fair value.
1 Prepaid two months' rent in advance on suitable office space, $1,800.
2 Purchased on credit office equipment, $420, and office supplies, $75.
4 Completed accounting work for a client and immediately received payment of $180 cash.
8 Completed accounting work on credit for Frontier Bank, $700.

Problem 2–8
Recording transactions in T-accounts; preparing a trial balance
(LO 3, 4, 5)

Problem 2–9
Posting from general journal entries; preparing a trial balance
(LO 3, 4, 5)

Sept. 10   Paid for the items purchased on credit on September 2.

14   Paid the annual $750 premium on an insurance policy.

18   Received payment in full from Frontier Bank for the work completed on September 8.

24   Completed accounting work on credit for Travis Realty, $500.

28   Adam Uppe withdrew $300 cash from the practice to pay personal expenses.

29   Purchased additional office supplies on credit, $45.

30   Paid the September utility bills, $165.

Required

1.   Open the following accounts: Cash; Accounts Receivable; Office Supplies; Prepaid Insurance; Prepaid Rent; Office Equipment; Accounts Payable; Adam Uppe, Capital; Adam Uppe, Withdrawals; Accounting Fees Earned; and Utilities Expense.

2.   Prepare general journal entries to record the transactions.

3.   Post to the accounts.

4.   Prepare a trial balance. Title the trial balance Adam Uppe, Public Accountant.

Problem 2–10
Analytical essay
(LO 3)

Consider the facts in Problem 2–2 and focus on transactions *h* and *o*. Explain how transaction *h* affects the balance sheet, income statement, and statement of changes in owner's equity differently from transaction *o*. Describe how the effects of transaction *o* would differ if the company's owner had written the cheque to pay the company's property taxes instead of the described purpose.

Problem 2–11
Analytical essay
(LO 3, 5)

Consider the facts in Problem 2–4 and assume that the following mistakes were made in journalizing and posting the transactions. Explain how each mistake would affect the account balances and the column totals in the trial balance.

a.   The March 1 investment by Ford was recorded correctly in the journal but the debit to Cash was incorrectly posted to the Cash account as $52,000.

b.   The March 5 transaction was incorrectly recorded in the journal as a collection of an account receivable.

c.   In recording the March 15 transaction in the journal, the account that should have been debited was credited and the account that should have been credited was debited.

d.   The March 30 transaction was recorded correctly in the journal, and the debit was correctly posted, but the credit was not posted at all.

e.   The $175 payment on March 31 was recorded incorrectly in both accounts in the journal as a $715 payment.

Problem 2–12
Analytical essay
(LO 3, 5)

A trial balance may be in balance, yet there may be errors in specific accounts. Explain how the following may occur as a result of errors:

a.   Understated liability and understated asset.

b.   Overstated asset and overstated owner's equity.

c.   Understated asset and understated owner's equity.

d.   One asset understated and another asset overstated.

e.   One liability understated and another liability overstated.

SERIAL PROBLEM

This comprehensive problem starts in this chapter and continues in Chapters 3, 4, and 5. Because of its length, this problem is most easily solved if you use the Working Papers that accompany this text.)

Emerald Computer Services

On October 1, 1996, Tracy Green created a single proprietorship called Emerald Computer Services. Emerald will provide consulting services, including computer system installations and custom program development. Green has adopted the calendar year for reporting and expects to prepare the company's first set of financial statements as of December 31, 1996. The initial chart of accounts for the accounting system includes these items:

Account	No.	Account	No.
Cash	101	Tracy Green, Capital	301
Accounts Receivable	106	Tracy Green, Withdrawals	302
Computer Supplies	126	Computer Services Revenue	403
Prepaid Insurance	128	Wages Expense	623
Prepaid Rent	131	Advertising Expense	655
Office Equipment	163	Mileage Expense	676
Computer Equipment	167	Miscellaneous Expenses	677
Accounts Payable	201	Repairs Expense, Computer	684

Required

1. Prepare journal entries to record each of the following transactions for Emerald Computer Services.

2. Open balance column accounts for the company and post the journal entries to them.

Transactions:

Oct. 1   Tracy Green invested $30,000 cash in the business, along with a $12,000 computer system and $6,000 of office equipment.

2   Rented office space for $750 per month and paid the first four months' rent in advance.

3   Purchased computer supplies on credit for $880 from AAA Supply Co.

4   Paid $1,440 cash for one year's premium on a property and liability insurance policy.

5   Billed Bravo Productions $2,200 for installing a new computer.

7   Paid for the computer supplies purchased from AAA Supply Co.

9   Hired Fran Sims as a part-time assistant for $125 per day, as needed. These wages will be paid once each month.

11   Billed Bravo Productions another $800 for services.

14   Received $2,200 from Bravo Productions on their account.

16   Paid $470 to repair computer equipment damaged when moving into the new office.

18   Paid $1,240 for an advertisement in the local newspaper.

21   Received $800 from Bravo Productions on their account.

24   Paid Fran Sims for seven days' work.

27   Billed Charles Company $2,150 for services.

31   Paid $2,000 to Tracy Green for personal use.

Nov.   1   Reimbursed Tracy Green for business usage of her automobile, 700 kilometres at $0.25 per km.

     4   Received $3,100 cash from Delta Fixtures, Inc., for computer services.

     6   Purchased $640 of computer supplies from AAA Supply Co.

     7   Billed Fox Run Estates $2,900 for services.

    10   Notified by Alpha Printing Co. that Emerald's bid of $2,500 for an upcoming project was accepted.

    17   Paid $150 for Tracy Green's home utilities bill.

    19   Received $1,250 from Charles Company against the bill dated October 27.

    21   Donated $500 to the United Way in the company's name.

    24   Completed work for Alpha Printing Co. and sent them a bill for $2,500.

    26   Sent another bill to Charles Company for the past due amount of $900.

    27   Paid $2,000 to Tracy Green as a withdrawal.

    28   Reimbursed Tracy Green for business usage of her automobile, 800 kilometres at $0.25 per km.

    30   Paid Fran Sims for 14 days' work.

PROVOCATIVE PROBLEMS

Provocative Problem 2–1

Ella Fant, interior decorator

(LO 2)

Ella Fant operates an interior decorating business. For the first few months of the company's life (through May), the accounting records were maintained by an outside bookkeeping service. According to those records, Fant's capital balance was $10,000 as of May 31. To save on expenses, Fant decided to keep the records herself. She managed to record June's transactions properly, but was a bit rusty when the time came to prepare the financial statements. Her first versions of the balance sheet and income statement follow; Fant is bothered that the company operated at a loss during the month, even though she had been very busy. Use the account balances included in the original financial statements to prepare revised statements (except for the capital account), including a statement of changes in owner's equity for the month.

ELLA FANT INTERIORS
Income Statement
June 30

Revenue:		
Investments by owner		$ 725
Unearned professional fees		10,575
Total		$11,300
Operating expenses:		
Prepaid insurance	$ 750	
Rent expense	450	
Telephone expense	300	
Professional library	8,000	
Travel and entertainment expense	3,100	
Utilities expense	400	
Withdrawals by owner	325	
Total operating expenses		13,325
Net income (loss)		$(2,025)

ELLA FANT INTERIORS
Balance Sheet
For Month Ended June 30

Assets		Liabilities	
Cash	$13,000	Accounts payable	$ 2,725
Accounts receivable	2,900	Professional fees earned	8,400
Insurance expense	250	Total liabilities	$11,125
Prepaid rent	900		
Office supplies	250	**Owner's Equity**	
Land	12,000	Ella Fant, capital	34,975
Salaries expense	3,300		
Short-term notes payable	13,500	Total liabilities and	
Total assets	$46,100	owner's equity	$46,100

At the end of the summer, Pat Hand closed down a small business that operated in Paradise Park. The business rented out two-passenger bicycles and sold shirts, sunglasses, and hats. Hand started the summer with $9,000 in cash and an agreement to rent a small building in the park for up to five years. The $2,400 annual rent must be paid every year, even though the business is open from only June 1 through August 31. At the beginning of the summer, Hand paid cash for the first year's rent and nine bicycles at the price of $250 each.

Over the summer, Hand also purchased shirts, sunglasses, and hats on credit for the total cost of $6,000. By August 31, all but $125 of the payables were paid. Over the summer, cash had been paid for $650 of utility bills and $3,000 of wages to several part-time workers. The owner had also withdrawn $250 cash from the business each week for 13 weeks.

The summer's revenues included $7,500 in bicycle rentals and $13,500 for shirts, sunglasses, and hats. All revenue was collected in cash, except for $80 owed by a local day care centre for some shirts.

Upon closing on August 31, Hand returned the unsold inventory of sunglasses to the distributor for a full cash refund of their $50 original cost. The owner took home the unsold inventory of shirts and hats as gifts for friends and family. Their original cost was $135. Finally, each of the nine used bicycles was sold for $110 cash.

Use the information to prepare an income statement describing the summer's business activities for the three months ended August 31. Also prepare a statement of changes in owner's equity for the same three months and a balance sheet as of August 31. The company's name is Paradise Pedals. As a first step in gathering the data, develop a list of brief explanations of the transactions. Next, post the amounts directly to T-accounts without using a general journal. Then use the T-account balances to prepare the statements. (Record the shirts, hats, and sunglasses in an account called Cost of Goods Sold and then reduce the balance for the unsold merchandise. Also record the difference between the original cost and the selling price of the bicycles in an account called Amortization Expense.)

Refer to the financial statements and related information for Geac Computer, Corporation Limited in Appendix I. Find the answers to the following questions by analyzing the information in the report:

1. What four broad categories of expenses are reported on Geac's income statement (Consolidated Statements of Operations)?

2. What five current assets are reported on Geac's balance sheet?

Provocative Problem 2–2
Pat Hand, seasonal business operator
(LO 4, 5)

Provocative Problem 2–3
Financial statement analysis case
(LO 2)

3. What three current liabilities are reported on Geac's balance sheet?

4. What dollar amounts of provisions for income taxes are reported by Geac on its income statements for the annual reporting periods ending in 1994 and 1993?

5. Using the sum of the company's total liabilities, what is Geac's debt ratio at the end of the 1994 year? How does this compare to the ratio at the end of the 1993 year?

Provocative Problem 2–4
Ethical issues essay

Review the As a Matter of Ethics case on page 74. Discuss the nature of the dilemma faced by Kim Li and evaluate the alternative courses of action that she should consider.

ANALYTICAL AND REVIEW PROBLEMS

A & R Problem 2–1

Lester Fenwick started a real estate agency and completed seven transactions, including Fenwick's initial investment of $8,500 cash. After these transactions, the ledger included the following accounts with their normal balances:

Cash	$11,300
Office supplies	330
Prepaid insurance	1,600
Office equipment	8,250
Accounts payable	8,250
Lester Fenwick, capital	8,500
Lester Fenwick, withdrawals	3,900
Commissions earned	12,000
Advertising expense	3,370

Required

Preparation component:

Prepare a trial balance for the business.

Analysis component:

Analyze the accounts and balances and prepare a list that describes each of the seven transactions and its amount. Also, present a schedule that shows how the transactions resulted in the $11,300 Cash balance.

A & R Problem 2–2

Sabira Hussain began a computer consulting business called Aribas Computer Services. She invested $25,000 and her automobile which had a market value of $18,000. The business was an instant success; however, she could not say the same about her bookkeeper who prepared the following trial balance:

ARIBAS COMPUTER SERVICES
Trial Balance
September 30, 1996

Cash	$26,200	
Accounts receivable	4,000	
Supplies	4,800	
Automobile	21,000	
Accounts payable		$ 0
Sabira Hussain, Capital		56,000
Total	$56,000	$56,000

Upon seeing the trial balance, Hussain dismissed the bookkeeper and asked you to help her until she found a replacement. With Hussain's help you were able to determine the following:

a. Consulting fees earned and billed during September amounted to $16,000 of which $9,000 was collected.

b. Office equipment purchased but not as yet paid for, $3,000.

c. Supplies purchased for cash, $1,800.

d. Paid $1,800 for two months' office rent.

e. Wages paid for September, $2,200.

f. Hussain withdrew $3,000 for living expenses.

Required

1. List the errors the bookkeeper made.

2. Prepare a corrected trial balance.

3. Explain why the original trial balance balanced.

CONCEPT TESTER

Test your understanding of the concepts introduced in this chapter by completing the following crossword puzzle.

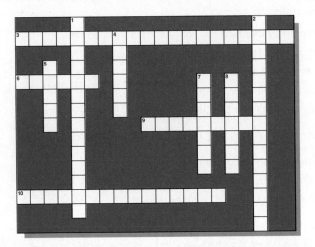

Across Clues

3. Exchanges between the entity and some other person or organization (2 words).

6. An entry that decreases assets and expenses but increases other financial statement items.

9. Total liabilities divided by total assets (2 words).

10. A list of the accounts used by a company, with identifying numbers (3 words).

Down Clues

1. An unconditional written promise to pay a definite sum on demand or a given future date (2 words).

2. Documents that are the source of information recorded with accounting entries (2 words).

4. The collection of all accounts used by a business.

5. An entry that increases assets and expenses or decreases other financial statement items.

7. A record in which the effects of transactions are first recorded.

8. The process of copying journal entry information to the ledger.

ANSWERS TO PROGRESS CHECKS

2–1 *d*

2–2 External and internal transactions.

2–3 Business papers are called source documents because they provide information about an entity's transactions that is used as a basis for recording the transactions in the accounting records.

2–4 *b*

2–5 Business papers are important because of the objectivity principle, which requires that accounting be based on verifiable evidence whenever possible.

2–6 A company's size affects the number of accounts it uses.

2–7 No. For example, a debit increases an expense account and decreases a revenue account.

2–8 *c*

2–9 Owner's equity is increased by revenues and by owner's investments in the business. Owner's equity is decreased by expenses and owner's withdrawals.

2–10 The name *double-entry* is used because all transactions are recorded in at least two accounts, a debit in one account and a credit in another.

2–11 *c*

2–12 A journal entry with more than one debit or credit items.

2–13 To indicate that the item has been posted to the account in the ledger.

2–14 *e*

2–15 The use of the dollar sign may vary from company to company. However, most use dollar signs beside only the first and last numbers in the columns in the financial statements.

2–16 The debit column is understated by $4,000 and the credit column is overstated by $4,000, a difference of $8,000.

2–17 *a*

CHAPTER 3

Although most economic events that affect an organization occur as external transactions, other kinds of events also change its assets, liabilities, and net income. The adjusting process records these events so that the financial statements present more useful information.

Adjusting the Accounts and Preparing the Statements

ince their first encounter in the school library with Imperial Oil Limited, Karen White and Mark Smith have continued to study the company's 1994 Annual Report. Although their familiarity with financial statements is very limited, they did note just how large a company Imperial is. Its assets approached $13 billion and annual sales $9 billion in 1994.

Examining the balance sheet, Karen and Mark observed that a variety of assets were identified as "current assets." Likewise, several liabilities were identified as "current liabilities." White and Smith wondered why these items were segregated from the other items on the statement and described as current. Perhaps they are related to each other in some important way.

IMPERIAL OIL LIMITED
(in millions)

| | Year Ended December 31 | |
	1994	1993
Total current assets	$2,797	$2,899
Total current liabilities	1,581	1,593

LEARNING OBJECTIVES

After studying Chapter 3, you should be able to:

1. **Explain why financial statements are prepared at the end of regular accounting periods, why the accounts must be adjusted at the end of each period, and why the accrual basis of accounting produces more useful income statements and balance sheets than the cash basis.**

2. **Prepare adjusting entries for prepaid expenses, amortization, unearned revenues, accrued expenses, and accrued revenues.**

3. **Prepare a schedule that includes the unadjusted trial balance, the adjustments, and the adjusted trial balance; use the adjusted trial balance to prepare financial statements; and prepare entries to record cash receipts and cash disbursements related to accrued assets and liabilities.**

4. **Define each asset and liability category for the balance sheet, prepare a classified balance sheet, and calculate the current ratio.**

5. **Define or explain the words and phrases listed in the chapter glossary.**

After studying Appendix B at the end of Chapter 3, you should be able to:

6. **Explain why some companies record prepaid and unearned items in income statement accounts and prepare adjusting entries when this procedure is used.**

In business for a century, Imperial Oil Limited, realizes the importance of communicating its position through its annual reports. For example, the company used its 1993 annual report to point out that it was selling less productive assets and changing its sales mix to emphasize more profitable products. In 1994 the company pointed out the resulting success. To accurately present this financial picture, a company must have an effective accounting system in place.

You learned in Chapter 2 that companies use accounting systems to collect information about transactions and other economic events. That chapter showed you how journals and ledgers are used to capture information about external transactions. This chapter explains how the accounting system gathers information about economic events that are not transactions with outside parties. The process involves adjusting the account balances at the end of the reporting period to reflect the economic events that are sometimes called internal transactions. As a result, the adjusted accounts contain the amounts to be reported on the financial statements according to generally accepted accounting principles. The chapter ends with a description of the current ratio, which is used by decision makers to assess the company's ability to pay its liabilities in the near future.

ACCOUNTING PERIODS AND FISCAL YEARS

To be useful, information must reach decision makers frequently and promptly. To provide this timely information, accounting systems are designed to produce periodic reports at regular intervals. As a result, the accounting process is based on the **time period principle.** According to this principle, an organization's activities are identified with specific time periods, such as a month, a three-month quarter, or a year. Then, financial statements are prepared for each reporting period. The time periods covered by the reports are called **accounting periods.** Most organizations use one year as their primary accounting period. As a result, they prepare annual financial statements. However, nearly all organizations also prepare **interim financial reports** that cover one or three months of activity.

LO 1
Explain why financial statements are prepared at the end of regular accounting periods, why the accounts must be adjusted at the end of each period, and why the accrual basis of accounting produces more useful income statements and balance sheets than the cash basis.

The annual reporting period is not always the same as the calendar year ending December 31. In fact, an organization can adopt a **fiscal year** consisting of any 12 consecutive months. For example, most banks use October 31 as the end of the fiscal period. An acceptable variation of this is to adopt an annual reporting period of 52 weeks.[1]

Companies that do not experience much seasonal variation in sales volume within the year often choose the calendar year as their fiscal year. On the other hand, companies that experience major seasonal variations in sales often choose a fiscal year that corresponds to their **natural business year.** The natural business year ends when sales activities are at their lowest point during the year. For example, the natural business year for retail stores ends around January 31, after the Christmas and January selling seasons. As a result, they often start their annual accounting periods on February 1.

WHY ARE THE ACCOUNTS ADJUSTED AT THE END OF AN ACCOUNTING PERIOD?

During an accounting period, the normal process is to record the economic events that occur in the form of external transactions (with outside parties). After all external transactions are recorded, several accounts in the ledger need to be updated before their balances appear in the financial statements. This need arises from the fact that some economic events remain unrecorded because they did not occur as external transactions.

For example, the costs of some assets expire as time passes. Notice that the third item in the trial balance of Clear Copy in Illustration 3–1 is Prepaid insurance and that it has a balance of $2,400. This amount is the original cost of the premium for two years of insurance protection beginning on December 1, 1996. By December 31, 1996, one month's coverage has been used up, and $2,400 is no longer the cost of the remaining prepaid insurance. Because the coverage costs an average of $100 per month ($2,400/24 months), the Prepaid Insurance account balance should be reduced by that amount. In addition, the income statement should report $100 as insurance expense.

Similarly, the $3,720 balance in the Store Supplies account includes the cost of some supplies that were consumed during December. The cost of these supplies should be reported as an expense of the month. Because of these unrecorded events, the balances of the Prepaid Insurance and Store Supplies accounts should be *adjusted* before they are presented on the December 31 balance sheet.

Another adjustment is necessary because one month of the copy equipment's useful life has expired. In addition, the balances of the Unearned Copy Services Revenue, Copy Services Revenue, and Salaries Expense accounts should be adjusted before they appear on the December income statement.

The next section of the chapter explains how the adjusting process is accomplished. As you study the material, remember that our goal is to provide useful information in the financial statements.

---

[1] Some companies actually choose a 52-week fiscal year, with the result that their annual reports end on a different date each year. The Oshawa Group uses a 52- or 53-week fiscal period with the end of the fiscal year falling on the last day of the last full week in January.

Illustration 3–1

CLEAR COPY
Trial Balance
December 31, 1996

	Debit	Credit
Cash	$ 7,950	
Accounts receivable	0	
Prepaid insurance	2,400	
Store supplies	3,720	
Copy equipment	26,000	
Accounts payable		$ 6,200
Unearned copy services revenue		3,000
Terry Dow, capital		30,000
Terry Dow, withdrawals	400	
Copy services revenue		3,900
Rent expense	1,000	
Salaries expense	1,400	
Utilities expense	230	
Total	$43,100	$43,100

THE ADJUSTING PROCESS

The adjusting process is consistent with two accounting principles, the *revenue recognition principle* and the *matching principle.* Chapter 1 explained that the *revenue recognition principle* requires revenue to be reported on the income statement only when it is earned, not before and not after. For most firms, revenue is earned when a service or a product is delivered to the customer. For example, if Clear Copy provides copy services to a customer during December, the revenue is earned during December. As a result, it should be reported on the December income statement, even if the customer paid for the services in November or will pay for them in January. One major goal for the adjusting process is to ensure that revenue is reported, or recognized, in the time period when it is earned.

The goal of the **matching principle** is to report expenses on the income statement in the same accounting period as the revenues that were earned as a result of the expenses. For example, assume that a business earns revenues during December while it operates out of rented store space. According to the *revenue recognition principle,* the business should report its revenues on the December income statement. In earning those revenues, the business incurs rent expense. The *matching principle* tells us that the rent should be reported on the income statement for December, even if the rent was paid in November or will be paid in January. As a result, the rent expense for December is matched with December's revenues. This matching of expenses with revenues is a major goal of the adjusting process.

Matching expenses with revenues often requires a company to predict future events. To use financial statements wisely, you need to understand that they are based on predictions and therefore include measurements that are not precise. For example, **The Walt Disney Company's** 1993 annual report explains that the company allocates film production costs among years based on a ratio of actual revenues to date from the film divided by its predicted total gross revenues.

When the adjusting process assigns revenues to the periods in which they are earned and matches expenses with the revenues, the company is using **accrual basis accounting.** The objective of the accrual basis is to report the economic effects of revenues and expenses when they are earned or incurred, not when cash is received or paid.

The alternative to accrual accounting is **cash basis accounting.** Under the cash basis, revenues are recognized when cash is received and expenses are reported when cash is paid. For example, if revenue is earned in December but cash is not received from the customer until January, the cash basis reports the revenue in January. Because revenues are reported when cash is received and expenses are deducted when cash is paid, cash basis net income for a period is the difference between revenues received in cash (called *receipts*) and expenses paid with cash (called *expenditures* or *disbursements*).

The conclusion of "Financial Statement Concepts" is: "Items recognized in financial statements are accounted for in accordance with the accrual basis of accounting. The accrual basis of accounting recognizes the effect of transactions and events in the period in which the transactions and events occur, regardless of whether there has been a receipt or payment of cash or its equivalent."[2] Some concerns use a cash basis, but it is acceptable only if the amount of prepaid, unearned, and accrued items is unimportant. One important benefit of accrual accounting is that it makes the information on accounting statements comparable from period to period.

For example, Clear Copy paid $2,400 for two years of insurance coverage beginning on December 1. Under accrual accounting, $100 of insurance expense is reported on the December 1996 income statement. During 1997, $1,200 of expense will be reported (the average monthly cost is $100). During 1998, $1,100 expense will be reported for the first 11 months of the year. This allocation of the insurance cost among the three fiscal years is represented graphically in Illustration 3–2.

In contrast, a cash basis income statement for December 1996 would report insurance expense of $2,400. The income statements for 1997 and 1998 would not report any insurance expense from this policy. To provide useful information about the company's activities and assets, the accrual basis shows that each of the 24 months had $100 of insurance expense. The balance sheet also reports the remaining unexpired premium as the cost of the prepaid insurance asset. However, the cash basis would never report an asset. In summary, the cash basis information would be less useful for decisions because the reported income for 1996, 1997, and 1998 would not reflect comparable measures of the cost of having insurance in those years.

The accrual basis is generally accepted for external reporting because it produces more useful information. The cash basis is not acceptable for a balance sheet or income statement because it provides incomplete information about assets, liabilities, revenues, and expenses.

ACCRUAL BASIS COMPARED WITH CASH BASIS ACCOUNTING

---

[2] *CICA Handbook,* par. 1000.41.

Illustration 3–2 Allocating the $2,400 Cost of Insurance Protection for 24 Months Beginning December 1, 1996

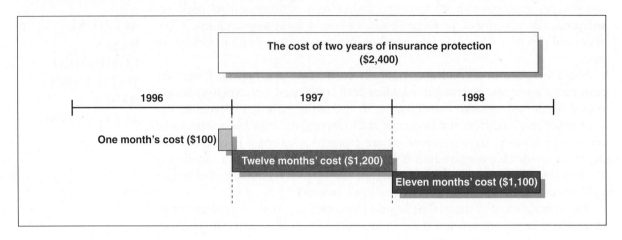

Progress Check

(Answers to Progress Checks are provided at the end of the chapter.)

3–1   **A company's annual reporting period:** *(a)* **Is called the fiscal year;** *(b)* **Always ends at the close of the natural business year;** *(c)* **Always ends at the close of the calendar business year;** *(d)* **Cannot be divided into shorter interim periods.**

3–2   **Why do companies prepare interim financial statements?**

3–3   **Which accounting principles lead most directly to the adjustment process?**

3–4   **Is the cash basis of accounting consistent with the matching principle?**

3–5   **On April 1, 1996, Collins Company paid a $4,800 premium for two years of insurance coverage. Under the cash basis, how much insurance expense will be reported in 1997?**

ADJUSTING SPECIFIC ACCOUNTS

LO 2

Prepare adjusting entries for prepaid expenses, depreciation, unearned revenues, accrued expenses, and accrued revenues.

The process of adjusting the accounts is similar to the process used to analyze and record transactions. Each account balance and the economic events that affect it are analyzed to determine whether an adjustment is needed. If an adjustment is needed, an **adjusting entry** is recorded to bring the asset or liability account balance up to date. The adjustment also updates the related expense or revenue account. Like other journal entries, adjusting entries are posted to the accounts. The following paragraphs explain why adjusting entries are needed to provide useful information.

Adjusting entries for prepaid expenses, amortization, and unearned revenues involve previously recorded assets and liabilities. These entries are made to record the effects of economic events (including the passing of time) that have changed these assets and liabilities. On the other hand, adjusting entries for accrued expenses and accrued revenues involve liabilities and assets that have not yet been recorded. Adjusting entries record the effects of economic events that created these liabilities and assets as well as the related expenses and revenues.

Prepaid Expenses

A prepaid expense is an economic benefit paid for in advance of its use. When it is paid for, the company acquires an asset that will expire or be used up. As the asset is used, its cost becomes an expense.

Prepaid Insurance. For example, recall that Clear Copy paid $2,400 for two years of insurance protection that went into effect on December 1, 1996. (The allocation of this cost to 1996, 1997, and 1998 is described in Illustration 3–2.) As each day of December went by, some of the benefit of the insurance protection expired, and a portion of the asset's cost became an expense. By December 31, one month's insurance coverage had expired. This expense is measured as $100, which is 1/24 of $2,400. The following adjusting entry records the expense with a debit, and reduces the cost of the asset with a credit to the asset account:

		Adjustment a		
Dec.	31	Insurance Expense	100.00	
		Prepaid Insurance		100.00
		To record the expense created by expired insurance.		

Posting the adjusting entry has the following effect on the accounts:

Prepaid Insurance				**Insurance Expense**		
Dec. 26	2,400	Dec. 31	100	Dec. 31	100	
	− 100					
Balance	2,300					

After the entry is posted, the $100 balance in Insurance Expense and the $2,300 balance in Prepaid Insurance are ready to be presented on the financial statements.

The allocation process in Illustration 3–2 shows that another adjusting entry in 1997 transfers $1,200 from Prepaid Insurance to Insurance Expense. A third adjusting entry in 1998 transfers the remaining $1,100 to the expense account.

Store Supplies. Store supplies are another prepaid expense that is adjusted. For example, Clear Copy purchased $3,720 of store supplies in December and used some of them up during the month. Consuming these supplies created an expense equal to their cost. However, the daily consumption of the supplies was not recorded in the accounts because the information was not needed. Due to the fact that the account balances are not presented in financial statements until the end of the month, bookkeeping effort can be reduced by making only one adjusting entry to record the total cost of all supplies consumed in the month.

Because an income statement is to be prepared for December, the cost of the store supplies used during the month needs to be recognized as an expense. To learn the amount used, Terry Dow counts (or, takes an inventory of) the remaining unused supplies. Then, the cost of the remaining supplies is deducted from the cost of the purchased supplies. For example, suppose that Dow finds that $2,670 of supplies remain out of the $3,720 purchased in December. The $1,050 difference between these two amounts is the cost of the consumed supplies. This amount is the month's store supplies expense. This adjusting entry records the expense with a debit and reduces the asset account balance with an equal credit:

		Adjustment b		
Dec.	31	Store Supplies Expense	1,050.00	
		Store Supplies		1,050.00
		To record the expense created by using store supplies.		

Posting the adjusting entry has the following effect on the accounts:

Store Supplies				Store Supplies Expense	
Dec. 2	2,500	Dec. 31	1,050	Dec. 31	1,050
6	1,100				
26	120				
Total	3,720	Total	1,050		
	− 1,050				
Balance	2,670				

As a result, the balance of the store supplies account now equals the $2,670 cost revealed by the manager's inventory.

Other Prepaid Expenses. Unlike the two previous examples, some prepaid expenses are both acquired and fully used up within a single accounting period. For example, a company usually pays monthly rent on the first day of each month. Every month, the payment creates a prepaid expense that fully expires by the end of the month. In these cases, the bookkeeper can ignore the fact that the payment creates an asset and record the payment with a debit to the expense account instead of the asset account. (These practices are described more completely in Appendix B at the end of this chapter.)

Amortization[3]

In accounting, the term **capital assets** describes tangible long-lived assets that are used to produce or sell goods and services. Examples of capital assets are land, buildings, machines, vehicles, and professional libraries. Except for land, capital assets eventually wear out or otherwise lose their usefulness and value. Therefore, income statements should report the cost of using these assets as expenses during their useful lives. The expense created by allocating the original cost of assets is called **amortization.** Amortization expense is recorded with an adjusting entry similar to the entries to record the using up of prepaid expenses. However, the entry is slightly more complicated because a special account is used to record the reduced asset balance.

---

[3]In 1990, the revised *CICA Handbook*, section 3060, recommended use of the term *amortization* instead of *depreciation,* but the use of *depreciation* was not ruled out. Also, *fixed assets* was replaced by *capital assets.* It may take several years for the new terminology to be widely implemented by companies; thus, *depreciation* and *depletion* may continue in use for some time.

For example, Clear Copy uses copy equipment to earn revenue. This equipment's cost should be amortized to provide a complete income statement. Early in December, Clear Copy made two purchases of equipment for $20,000 and $6,000. Using information received from the manufacturer and other sources, Terry Dow predicts that the equipment will have a four-year useful life. Dow also predicts that the company will be able to sell the equipment for $8,000 at the end of the four years. Therefore, the net cost expected to expire over the useful life is $18,000 ($26,000 − $8,000). When this net cost is divided by the 48 months in the asset's predicted life, the result is an average monthly cost of $375 ($18,000/48). This average cost is recorded as amortization expense for each month with this adjusting entry:

		Adjustment c		
Dec.	31	Amortization Expense	375.00	
		Accumulated Amortization, Copy Equipment		375.00
		To record the expense created by using the copying equipment.		

Posting the adjusting entry has the following effect on the accounts:

Copy Equipment			**Amortization Expense, Copy Equipment**	
Dec. 3	20,000		Dec. 31	375
6	6,000			
Total	26,000			

Accumulated Amortization, Copy Equipment		
	Dec. 31	375

After the entry is posted, the Copy Equipment account and its related Accumulated Amortization, Copy Equipment account together show the December 31 balance sheet amounts for this asset. The Amortization Expense, Copy Equipment account shows the amount of expense that will appear on the December income statement.

In most cases, a decrease in an asset account is recorded by entering a credit directly in the account. However, note in the illustrated accounts that this procedure is not followed in recording amortization. Instead, amortization is recorded in a **contra account.** A contra account's balance is subtracted from a related account's balance to provide more information than simply the net amount. In this example, the contra account is Accumulated Amortization, Copy Equipment.

Why are contra accounts used to record amortization? Contra accounts allow balance sheet readers to observe both the original cost of the assets and the estimated amount of amortization that has been charged to expense in the past. By knowing both the original cost and the accumulated amortization, decision makers can more completely assess the company's productive capacity and the potential need to replace the assets. For example, Clear Copy's balance sheet shows both the $26,000 original cost of the equipment and the $375 balance in the accumulated amortization contra account. This information lets statement users see that the equipment is almost new. In contrast, if Clear Copy simply reported the net remaining cost of $25,625, the users would not know whether the equipment is new or so old that it needs immediate replacement.

Note the words **accumulated amortization** in the title of the contra account. This reflects the fact that this account reports the total amount of amortization expense recognized in all prior periods since the assets were put into service. For example, the Copy Equipment and the Accumulated Amortization accounts would look like this on February 28, 1997, after three monthly adjusting entries:

Copy Equipment			Accumulated Amortization, Copy Equipment		
Dec. 3	20,000			Dec. 31	375
6	6,000			Jan. 31	375
				Feb. 28	375
Total	26,000			Total	1,125

These account balances would be presented on the February 28 balance sheet as follows:

Copy equipment	$26,000
Less accumulated amortization	1,125
Net	$24,875

Later chapters describe how other contra accounts are used in other situations.

Unearned Revenues

An unearned revenue is a liability created when a customer's payment is received in advance of delivering the goods or services. For example, Clear Copy has unearned revenue. On December 26, Terry Dow agreed to provide copying services for a customer for the fixed fee of $1,500 per month. On that day, the customer paid the first two months' fees in advance to cover the period from December 27 to February 26. This entry records the cash receipt:

Dec.	26	Cash	3,000.00	
		Unearned Copy Services Revenue		3,000.00
		Received advanced payment for copying services to		
		be provided over two months.		

This advance payment increased cash and created an obligation to do copying work over the next two months. By December 31, the business provided five days' service and earned one-sixth of the $1,500 revenue for the first month. This amount is $250 ($1,500/6). The company also discharged one-twelfth of the total $3,000 liability because five days is one-twelfth of two months. According to the *revenue recognition principle,* the $250 of revenue should appear on the December income statement. Notice that the event that caused the earning of revenue was simply the passage of time. There was no external transaction. The following adjusting entry updates the accounts by reducing the liability and recognizing the earned revenue:

		Adjustment d		
Dec.	31	Unearned Copy Services Revenue	250.00	
		Copy Services Revenue ($1,500/6)		250.00
		Earned revenue that was received in advance.		

The accounts look like this after the entry is posted:

Unearned Copy Services Revenue		Copy Services Revenue	
Dec. 31 250	Dec. 26 3,000		Dec. 10 2,200
			12 1,700
			31 250

In effect, the adjusting entry transfers $250 of earned revenue from the liability account to the revenue account.

Accrued Expenses

Most expenses are recorded when they are paid with cash. In making the journal entry to record the transaction, the credit to the Cash account is accompanied by a debit to the expense account. However, because some expenses incurred during the period have not been paid for, they may remain unrecorded at the end of an accounting period. These incurred but unpaid expenses are called **accrued expenses.** One typical example of an accrued expense is the unpaid wages earned by employees for work they have already completed.

Accrued Salaries. For example, Clear Copy's only employee earns $70 per day or $350 for a five-day workweek that begins on Monday and ends on Friday. The employee's salary is paid every two weeks on Friday. On the 12th and the 26th of December, these wages were paid, recorded in the journal, and posted to the ledger. The Salaries Expense and Cash accounts show these entries:

December 1997						
S	M	T	W	T	F	S
	1	2	3	4	5	6
7	8	9	10	11	12	13
14	15	16	17	18	19	20
21	22	23	24	25	26	27
28	29	30	31			

Cash		Salaries Expense	
Dec. 12 700		Dec. 12 700	
26 700		26 700	

The calendar for December 1997 in the margin shows us that three working days (December 29, 30, and 31) come after the December 26 payday. Thus, the employee earned three days' salary at the close of business on Wednesday, December 31. Because this salary had not been paid, the expense was not recorded. But, the financial statements would be incomplete if they failed to report this additional expense and the liability to the employee for the unpaid salary. Therefore, this adjusting entry should be recorded on December 31 to produce a complete record of the company's expenses and liabilities:

		Adjustment e		
Dec.	31	Salaries Expense	210.00	
		Salaries Payable		210.00
		To record three days' accrued salary.		

After this entry is posted, the Salaries Expense and liability accounts appear as follows:

Salaries Expense			Salaries Payable	
Dec. 12	700		Dec. 31	210
26	700			
31	210			
Total	1,610			

As a result of this entry, $1,610 of salaries expense is reported on the income statement. In addition, the balance sheet reports a $210 liability to the employee.

Accrued Interest Expense. Another typical accrued expense is interest incurred on accounts and notes payable. Interest expense is incurred simply with the passage of time. Therefore, unless interest is paid on the last day of the accounting period, some additional amount will have accrued since the previous payment. A company's financial statements will be incomplete unless this expense and additional liability are recorded. The adjusting entry for interest is similar to the one used to accrue the unpaid salary.

Accrued Revenues

Many revenues are recorded when cash is received from the customer. Other revenues are recorded when goods and services are sold on credit. However, some earned revenues may remain unrecorded at the end of the accounting period. Although these **accrued revenues** are earned, they are unrecorded because the customer has not yet paid for them or the seller has not yet billed the customer. For example, suppose that Clear Copy agreed to provide copying services for a bank at a fixed fee of $2,700 per month. The terms of the agreement call for Clear Copy to provide services from the 12th of December, 1996, through the 11th of the following month. The bank will pay $2,700 cash to Clear Copy on January 11, 1997, when the service period is over.

As of December 31, 1996, 20 days of services have been provided to the bank. However, because Clear Copy has not yet been paid, it has not recorded the earning of the revenue. Because 20 days equal two-thirds of a month, Clear Copy has earned two-thirds of one month's fee, or $1,800 ($2,700 × 2/3). According to the *revenue recognition principle,* this revenue should be reported on the December income statement because it was earned in that month. In addition, the balance sheet should report that the bank owes the company $1,800. Clear Copy makes this adjusting entry to record the effects of the agreement:

Dec.	31	Adjustment f Accounts Receivable	1,800.00	
		Copy Services Revenue		1,800.00
		To record 20 days' accrued revenue.		

The debit to the receivable reflects the fact that the bank owes Clear Copy for the provided services. After this entry is posted, the affected accounts look like this:

Accounts Receivable						**Copy Services Revenue**		
Dec. 12	1,700	Dec. 22	1,700			Dec. 10	2,200	
31	1,800					12	1,700	
						31	250	
						31	1,800	
						Balance	5,950	

Accounts receivable are reported on the balance sheet at $1,800, and $5,950 of revenues are reported on the income statement.

Accrued Interest Income. We mentioned earlier that interest is an accrued expense recorded with an adjusting entry. Interest is also an accrued revenue when a company is entitled to receive it from a debtor. If a company has notes or accounts receivable that produce interest income, the bookkeeper records an adjusting entry to recognize any accrued but uncollected interest revenue. The entry also records the interest receivable from the debtor as an asset.

Take time to read the As a Matter of Ethics case on page 139. It tells about pressure being applied to an accountant to omit some adjusting entries that are needed to present complete financial statements. Consider the situation and determine what you would do if you were in this accountant's place.

Progress Check

3-6 At the end of its 1996 fiscal year, Corona Company omitted an adjustment to record $200 of accrued service revenues. The effect of the error is to: *(a)* Overstate 1996 net income by $200; *(b)* Overstate 1996 revenues by $200; *(c)* Understate total assets by $200; *(d)* Overstate total assets by $200.

3-7 What is a contra account?

3-8 What is an accrued expense? Give an example.

3-9 How does an unearned revenue arise? Give an example of an unearned revenue.

THE ADJUSTED TRIAL BALANCE

LO 3

Prepare a schedule that includes the unadjusted trial balance, the adjustments, and the adjusted trial balance; use the adjusted trial balance to prepare financial statements; and prepare entries to record cash receipts and cash disbursements related to accrued assets and liabilities.

An **unadjusted trial balance** is prepared before adjustments have been recorded. As you might expect, an **adjusted trial balance** uses the account balances after the adjusting entries have been posted to the ledger. In Illustration 3–3, parallel columns show the unadjusted trial balance, the adjustments, and the adjusted trial balance for Clear Copy as of December 31, 1996. Notice that several new accounts have been added because of the adjusting entries. (The order of the accounts also has been changed to match the order of the account numbers listed inside the book's front and back covers.) Also notice that the letters in the adjustments columns identify the debits and credits that were recorded with adjusting entries presented earlier in the chapter.

PREPARING FINANCIAL STATEMENTS FROM THE ADJUSTED TRIAL BALANCE

Chapter 2 explained that the trial balance summarizes the information in the ledger by showing the account balances. This summary is easier to work with than the entire ledger when preparing financial statements. The accountant uses the adjusted trial balance for this purpose because it includes the balances that should appear in the statements.

Illustrations 3–4 and 3–5 show how the account balances are transferred from the adjusted trial balance to the statements. For completeness, the trial balance includes the identification numbers for the accounts.

Because the amount of net income is used on the statement of changes in owner's equity, the first phase of the preparation process produces the company's income statement. The arrows in the lower section of Illustration 3–4 show how the balances of the revenue and expense accounts are transferred into the income statement. The revenue is listed on the statement first, and then the expenses. The total expenses are subtracted from the revenues to find the net income of $1,585.

Illustration 3–3 The Unadjusted Trial Balance, Adjustments, and Adjusted Trial Balance for Clear Copy as of December 31, 1996

	Unadjusted Trial Balance		Adjustments		Adjusted Trial Balance	
Cash	7,950				7,950	
Accounts receivable			(f) 1,800		1,800	
Store supplies	3,720			(b)1,050	2,670	
Prepaid insurance	2,400			(a) 100	2,300	
Copy equipment	26,000				26,000	
Accumulated amortization, copy equipment				(c) 375		375
Accounts payable		6,200				6,200
Salaries payable				(e) 210		210
Unearned copy services revenue		3,000	(d) 250			2,750
Terry Dow, capital		30,000				30,000
Terry Dow, withdrawals	400				400	
Copy services revenue		3,900		(d) 250 (f) 1,800		5,950
Amortization expense, copy equipment			(c) 375		375	
Salaries expense	1,400		(e) 210		1,610	
Insurance expense			(a) 100		100	
Rent expense	1,000				1,000	
Store supplies expense			(b)1,050		1,050	
Utilities expense	230				230	
Totals	43,100	43,100	3,785	3,785	45,485	45,485

The second phase prepares the statement of changes in owner's equity. In developing this statement, the accountant combines the net income from the income statement with the balances of Terry Dow's capital and withdrawals accounts. The $30,000 capital account balance came from the initial investment in December. (In other situations, the accountant would have to analyze the capital account to identify the beginning balance and any new investments made during the period.) The bottom line of the statement shows the owner's equity on December 31.

The third phase of the preparation process is represented in Illustration 3–5. In this phase, the balances of the asset and liability accounts are transferred to the asset and liability sections of the balance sheet. Notice how the balance of the accumulated amortization account is shown as a deduction from the cost of the copy equipment. Also, notice that the December 31 balance of Terry Dow's capital is taken from the statement of changes in owner's equity. The $30,000 balance of the capital account cannot be used on the balance sheet because it does not include the changes in equity created by the month's revenues, expenses, and withdrawals. (The next chapter explains how the capital account is updated through the closing process.) The completed balance sheet shows the total cost of the company's assets, its total liabilities, and the owner's equity.

Illustration 3–4 Preparing the Income Statement and the Statement of Changes in Owner's Equity from the Adjusted Trial Balance

PHASE TWO: Prepare the statement of changes in owner's equity

CLEAR COPY
Adjusted Trial Balance
December 31, 1996

Acct. No.	Title	Debit	Credit
101	Cash	$ 7,950	
106	Accounts receivable	1,800	
125	Store supplies	2,670	
128	Prepaid insurance	2,300	
167	Copy equipment	26,000	
168	Accumulated amortization, copy equipment		$ 375
201	Accounts payable		6,200
209	Salaries payable		210
236	Unearned copy services revenue		2,750
301	Terry Dow, capital		30,000
302	Terry Dow, withdrawals	400	
403	Copy services revenue		5,950
614	Amortization expense, copy equipment	375	
622	Salaries expense	1,610	
637	Insurance expense	100	
641	Rent expense	1,000	
651	Store supplies expense	1,050	
690	Utilities expense	230	
	Totals	$45,485	$45,485

CLEAR COPY
Statement of Changes in Owner's Equity for
Month Ended December 31, 1996

Terry Dow, capital, November 30, 1996		$ –0–
Plus:		
Investments by owner	$30,000	
Net Income	1,585	
Total additions		31,585
Total		$31,585
Less withdrawals by owner		400
Terry Dow, capital, December 31, 1996		$31,185

CLEAR COPY
Income Statement
December 31, 1996

Revenues:		
Copy services revenues		$ 5,950
Operating Expenses:		
Amortization expense, copy equipment	$ 375	
Salaries expense	1,610	
Insurance expense	100	
Rent expense	1,000	
Store supplies expense	1,050	
Utilities expense	230	
Total operating expenses		4,365
Net income		$1,585

PHASE ONE: Prepare the income statement

Illustration 3-5 Preparing the Balance Sheet from the Adjusted Trial Balance and the Statement of Changes in Owner's Equity

CLEAR COPY
Adjusted Trial Balance
December 31, 1996

Acct. No.	Title	Debit	Credit
101	Cash	$ 7,950	
106	Accounts receivable	1,800	
125	Store supplies	2,670	
128	Prepaid insurance	2,300	
167	Copy equipment	26,000	
168	Accumulated amortization, copy equipment		$ 375
201	Accounts payable		6,200
209	Salaries payable		210
236	Unearned copy services revenue		2,750
301	Terry Dow, capital		30,000
302	Terry Dow, withdrawals	400	
403	Copy services revenue		5,950
614	Amortization expense, copy equipment	375	
622	Salaries expense	1,610	
637	Insurance expense	100	
641	Rent expense	1,000	
651	Store supplies expense	1,050	
690	Utilities expense	230	
	Totals	$45,485	$45,485

PHASE THREE: Prepare the balance sheet

CLEAR COPY
Balance Sheet
December 31, 1996

Assets

Cash		$ 7,950
Accounts receivable		1,800
Store supplies		2,670
Prepaid insurance		2,300
Copy equipment	$26,000	
Less accumulated amortization	(375)	25,625
Total assets		$40,345

Liabilities

Accounts payable	$ 6,200	
Salaries payable	210	
Unearned copy services revenue	2,750	
Total liabilities		$ 9,160

Owner's Equity

Terry Dow, capital, December 31, 1996		31,185
Total liabilities and owner's equity		$40,345

Statement of Changes in Owner's Equity (from Illustration 3–4)

REMOVING
ACCRUED
ASSETS AND
LIABILITIES
FROM THE
ACCOUNTS

Revenues that are accrued at the end of an accounting period result in cash receipts from customers during the next period. In addition, expenses that were accrued at the end of an accounting period result in cash payments during the next period to settle the unpaid liabilities. This section explains how the accrued assets and accrued liabilities are removed from the accounts.

Accrued Expenses

Earlier, Clear Copy recorded three days of accrued wages for its employee with this adjusting entry:

Dec.	31	Salaries Expense	210.00	
		Salaries Payable		210.00
		To record three days' accrued salary.		

When the next payday comes on Friday, January 9, the following entry removes the accrued liability and records additional salaries expense for January:

Jan.	9	Salaries Payable (3 days at $70)	210.00	
		Salaries Expense (7 days at $70)	490.00	
		Cash		700.00
		Paid two weeks' salary, including three days accrued in December		

The first debit in the January 9 entry records the payment of the liability for the three days' salary accrued on December 31. The second debit records the salary for January's first seven working days (including the New Year's Day holiday) as an expense of the new accounting period. The credit records the total amount of cash paid to the employee.

Accrued Revenue

On December 31, the following adjusting entry was made to record 20 days' accrued revenue earned under Clear Copy's contract with the bank:

Dec.	31	Accounts Receivable	1,800.00	
		Copy Services Revenue		1,800.00
		To record 20 days' accrued revenue.		

When the first month's fee is received on January 11, the company makes the following entry to eliminate the receivable and recognize the revenue earned in January:

Jan.	11	Cash	2,700.00	
		Accounts Receivable		1,800.00
		Copy Services Revenue		900.00
		Received cash for accrued and earned copy services revenue.		

The first credit in the entry records the collection of the receivable. The second credit records the earned revenue.

Progress Check

3–10 The following information has been taken from Jones Company's unadjusted and adjusted trial balances:

| | Unadjusted | | Adjusted | |
	Debit	Credit	Debit	Credit
Prepaid insurance	$6,200		$5,900	
Salaries payable				$1,400

The adjusting entries must have included these items:
a. A $300 debit to Prepaid Insurance and a $1,400 credit to Salaries Payable.
b. A $300 credit to Prepaid Insurance and a $1,400 debit to Salaries Payable.
c. A $300 credit to Insurance Expense and a $1,400 debit to Salaries Expense.

3–11 What types of accounts are taken from the adjusted trial balance to prepare an income statement?

3–12 In preparing financial statements from an adjusted trial balance, which statement is prepared second?

3–13 On December 31, 1996, Hall Company recorded $1,600 of accrued salaries. On January 5 (the next payday), salaries of $8,000 were paid. From this you know that: (a) The company uses cash basis accounting; (b) The January 5 entry includes a $6,400 credit to Cash; (c) The salaries expense assigned to 1997 is $6,400.

Up to this point, we have presented only **unclassified balance sheets.** (For example, see Illustration 3–5.) However, the information on a balance sheet is more useful if assets and liabilities are classified into relevant groups. Readers of these **classified balance sheets** have more information to use in making their decisions. For example, they can use the data to assess the likelihood that funds will be available to meet the liabilities when they become due.

Businesses do not all use the same system of classifying assets and liabilities on their balance sheets. However, most businesses classify them as shown in Illustration 3–6. Assets are classified as (1) current assets, (2) investments, (3) capital assets, and (4) intangible assets. Liabilities are either (1) current liabilities or (2) long-term liabilities. We explain the nature of these classes next.

CLASSIFYING BALANCE SHEET ITEMS

LO 4

Define each asset and liability category for the balance sheet, prepare a classified balance sheet, and calculate the current ratio.

Illustration 3-6   A Classified Balance Sheet

NATIONAL ELECTRICAL SUPPLY CO.
Balance Sheet
December 31, 1996

Assets

Current assets:

Cash	$ 6,500	
Temporary investments	2,100	
Accounts receivable	4,400	
Notes receivable	1,500	
Merchandise inventory	27,500	
Prepaid expenses	2,400	
Total current assets		$ 44,400

Investments:

Chrysler Corporation common shares	$ 18,000	
Land held for future expansion	48,000	
Total investments		66,000

Capital assets:

Plant and equipment:

Store equipment	$ 33,200		
Less accumulated amortization	8,000	$ 25,200	
Buildings	$170,000		
Less accumulated amortization	45,000	125,000	
Land		73,200	
Total plant and equipment			223,400

Intangible asset:

Trademark		10,000
Total assets		$343,800

Liabilities

Current liabilities:

Accounts payable	$ 15,300	
Wages payable	3,200	
Notes payable	3,000	
Current portion of long-term liabilities	7,500	
Total current liabilities		$ 29,000

Long-term liabilities:

Notes payable (net of current portion)	150,000	
Total liabilities		$179,000

Owner's Equity

B. Brown, capital		164,800
Total liabilities and owner's equity		$343,800

Current Assets

Current assets are cash and other assets that are reasonably expected to be sold, collected, or consumed within one year or within the normal **operating cycle of the business,** whichever is longer. In addition to cash, current assets typically include temporary investments in marketable securities, accounts receivable, notes receivable, goods expected to be sold to customers (called *merchandise* or *inventory*), and prepaid expenses.

The Operating Cycle. The length of a company's operating cycle depends on its activities. The diagrams in Illustration 3–7 represent the phases of operating cycles for service and merchandising companies. For a company that sells services, the operating cycle is the average time between paying the employees who perform the services and receiving the cash from customers. For a company that sells goods, the operating cycle is the average time between paying for the merchandise and receiving cash from customers.

Most operating cycles are shorter than one year. As a result, most companies use a one-year period in deciding which assets are current. However, a few companies have an operating cycle longer than one year. For example, a company may routinely allow customers to take several years to pay for their purchases. Some producers of beverages and other products allow their products to age for several years. In both cases, these companies use the longer operating cycle in deciding which assets are current.[4]

Other Details. The balance sheet in Illustration 3–6 lists current assets first. This practice gives a prominent position to assets that are most easily converted into cash. Items within the current asset category are traditionally listed in the order of how quickly they will be converted to cash. Prepaid expenses are usually listed last because they will not be converted to cash.

A company's individual prepaid expenses are usually small compared to other assets on the balance sheet. As a result, they are often combined and shown as a single item. Thus, it is likely that the Prepaid expenses item in Illustration 3–6 includes such things as prepaid insurance, prepaid rent, office supplies, and store supplies.

Investments

The second balance sheet classification is long-term investments. In many cases, notes receivable and investments in shares and bonds are not current assets because they will be held for more than one year (or one operating cycle). Investments also include land that is not being used in operations because it is held for future expansion. Notice that the temporary investments on the second line in Illustration 3–6 are current assets and are not presented in the Investments section. We explain the differences between temporary and long-term investments in a later chapter.

Capital Assets

Earlier, we described capital assets as tangible long-lived assets that are used to produce or sell goods and services. Examples include equipment, vehicles, buildings, and land. Two key phrases in the definition are *long-lived* and *used to produce or sell goods and services*. Although it is tangible and has a long life, land held for future expansion is not a capital asset because it is not used to produce or sell goods and services.

The term *capital assets* is often used as a balance sheet caption. Other widely used titles for the same category are *Property, plant, and equipment*, or *Land, buildings, and equipment*. The order of the listing of the types of capital assets within the category varies among organizations.

---

[4]In these unusual situations, the companies provide supplemental information about their current assets and liabilities to allow users to compare them with other companies.

Illustration 3-7   The Phases of Operating Cycles for Companies that Sell Services and Merchandise

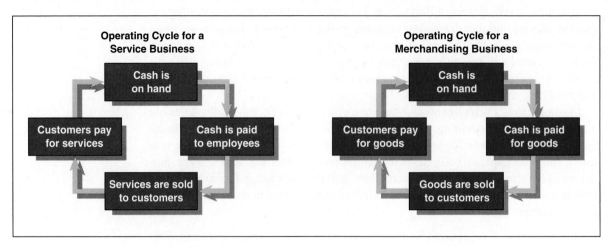

Intangible Assets

Some assets that are used to produce or sell goods and services do not have a physical form. These assets are called **intangible assets.** Examples of intangible assets are goodwill, patents, trademarks, copyrights, and franchises. Their value comes from the privileges or rights granted to or held by the owner.

Current Liabilities

Obligations due to be paid or liquidated within one year (or the operating cycle) are classified as **current liabilities.** Current liabilities are usually satisfied by paying out current assets. Typical current liabilities are accounts payable, notes payable, wages payable, taxes payable, interest payable, and unearned revenues. Also, any portion of a long-term liability due to be paid within one year (or a longer operating cycle) is a current liability. Illustration 3–6 shows how the current portion of long-term liabilities is usually described on a balance sheet. Unearned revenues are classified as current liabilities because they will be settled by delivering goods or services within the year (or the operating cycle). Different companies present current liabilities in different orders. Generally, the first position goes to the liabilities that will be paid first.

Long-Term Liabilities

The second liability classification consists of **long-term liabilities.** These liabilities are not due to be paid within one year, or the operating cycle. Notes payable and bonds payable are usually long-term liabilities. If a company has both short- and long-term notes payable, it probably uses separate accounts for them in its ledger.

EQUITY ON THE BALANCE SHEET

The format of the balance sheet's equity section depends on whether the company is a single proprietorship, a partnership, or a corporation.

Single Proprietorships and Partnerships

If a business is a single proprietorship, the equity section consists of a single line showing the owner's equity as of the balance sheet date. For example, the balance sheet in Illustration 3–5 shows "Terry Dow, capital, December 31, 1996" and the amount of $31,185. When total liabilities exceed total assets, the negative equity amount (often called a *deficit*) is subtracted from total liabilities.

If a business is organized as a partnership, separate equity accounts are used for each partner. Changes in each partner's equity are reported in a statement of changes in partners' equity that is similar to the statement of changes in owner's equity. The balance sheet shows the equity of each partner in a format like this:

Partners' Equity	
Shirley Tucker, capital	$17,300
Mark Jackson, capital	24,800
Total partners' equity	$42,100

Corporations

Corporations are established under provincial or federal laws. These laws may require the company's financial statements to distinguish between the equity created by investments from shareholders and the equity created by the corporation's net incomes less any reductions for **dividends.** A dividend is a distribution, generally a cash payment, made by a corporation to its shareholders. A cash dividend reduces the assets and the equity of a corporation in the same way that a withdrawal reduces the assets and equity of a proprietorship.

As described in Chapter 1, a corporation's total shareholders' equity is divided into **contributed capital** (also called *paid-in capital*) and **retained earnings.** Contributed capital is created by the shareholders' investments, and retained earnings are created by the corporation's profitable activities (cumulative net income less net losses and dividends). The components of shareholders' equity are usually shown on a corporate balance sheet like this:

Shareholders' Equity	
Contributed capital: Common shares . . .	$400,000
Retained earnings	124,400
Total shareholders' equity	$524,400

If a corporation issues only one kind of shares, they are called **common shares** or *share capital-common*. (Other types of classes or shares are described in Chapter 15.) The $400,000 amount assigned to common share capital in the example is the amount invested in the corporation by its original shareholders when they bought the shares from the corporation. The retained earnings of $124,400 represents the shareholders' equity arising from prior years' net incomes in excess of any net losses and dividends paid to the shareholders.

ALTERNATIVE BALANCE SHEET FORMATS

Different companies choose different formats for their balance sheets. For example, the balance sheet in Illustration 1–7 (on p. 40) places the liabilities and shareholder's equity to the right of the assets. This format creates an **account form balance sheet.** If the items are arranged vertically, as shown in Illustration 3–6, the format creates a **report form balance sheet.** Both forms are widely used, and neither is considered more useful than the other.

USING CODE NUMBERS FOR ACCOUNTS

We described a possible three-digit account numbering system in Chapter 2. In these systems, the code number assigned to an account not only identifies the account but also provides information about the account's financial statement category.

In the following simple system, the first digit in an account's number identifies its primary balance sheet or income statement category. For example, account numbers beginning with a 1 are assigned to asset accounts and account numbers beginning with a 2 are assigned to liability accounts. Under this system, the following numbers could be assigned to the accounts of a company that buys and sells merchandise:

101–199	**Assets**
201–299	**Liabilities**
301–399	**Owner's Equity** (including withdrawals)
401–499	**Revenues**
501–599	**Cost of Goods Sold** (these accounts are described in Chapter 5)
601–699	**Operating Expenses**
701–799	**Gains**
801–899	**Losses**

In this system, the second digit of each account number identifies its subclassification within the primary category, as follows:

101–199	**Assets**
101–139	Current assets (second digit is 0, 1, 2, or 3)
141–149	Long-term investments (second digit is 4)
151–179	Capital assets (second digit is 5, 6, or 7)
181–189	Natural resources (second digit is 8)
191–199	Intangible assets (second digit is 9)
201–299	**Liabilities**
201–249	Current liabilities (second digit is 0, 1, 2, 3, or 4)
251–299	Long-term liabilities (second digit is 5, 6, 7, 8, or 9)

Finally, the third digit completes the unique code for each account. For example, specific current asset accounts might be assigned the following numbers:

101–199	**Assets**
101–139	Current assets
101	Cash
106	Accounts Receivable

110	Rent Receivable
128	Prepaid Insurance

This code is used for the accounts listed inside the front and back covers of the book.

A three-digit account numbering system may be adequate for many smaller businesses. However, a numbering system for a more complex business might use four, five, or even more digits.

Most financial statement users find it helpful to evaluate a company's ability to pay its debts in the near future. This ability affects decisions by suppliers about allowing the company to buy on credit. It affects decisions by banks about lending money to the company and the terms of the loan, including the interest rate, due date, and any assets to be pledged as security against the loan. The ability to pay debts also affects a business owner's decisions about obtaining cash to pay existing debts when they come due.

The **current ratio** is widely used to describe the company's ability to pay its short-term obligations. It is calculated by dividing the current assets by the current liabilities:

$$\text{Current ratio} = \frac{\text{Current assets}}{\text{Current liabilities}}$$

Using the data for **Imperial Oil Limited,** presented at the beginning of the chapter, the current ratios at the end of 1994 and 1993 are calculated as follows:

$$\text{Current ratio} = \frac{\$2,899}{\$1,593} = 1.82$$

Note that the ratio decreased slightly from the end of 1993 to the end of 1994. Both values suggest that the company's short-term obligations could be satisfied with the short-term resources on hand. If the ratio were to be closer to one, the company might expect to face more difficulty in paying the liabilities. If the ratio were less than one, the company would be more likely to have difficulty because its current liabilities would be greater than its current assets.

USING THE INFORMATION— THE CURRENT RATIO

Progress Check

3-14 Which of the following assets should be classified as current assets? Which should be classified as capital assets? *(a)* Land used in operating the business; *(b)* Office supplies; *(c)* Receivables from customers due in 10 months; *(d)* Insurance protection for the next nine months; *(e)* Trucks used to provide services to customers; *(f)* Trademarks used in advertising the company's services.

3-15 Identify two examples of assets classified as investments on the balance sheet.

3-16 Which category of liabilities is used in the calculation of the current ratio?

3-17 On the balance sheet of a corporation, the shareholders' equity is divided into two categories. What are they?

LO 1. Explain why financial statements are prepared at the end of regular accounting periods, why the accounts must be adjusted at the end of each period, and why the accrual basis of accounting produces more useful income statements and balance sheets than the cash basis. Companies prepare reports once each year. They also prepare interim financial statements because decision makers need information frequently and promptly. Adjusting entries are needed to capture information about unrecorded events that are not external transactions. The revenue recognition principle requires adjustments to ensure that revenue is reported when it is earned. The matching principle requires adjustments to ensure that expenses are reported in the same period as the revenue that was earned as a result of the expenses.

Accrual accounting is preferred to cash basis accounting because accrual accounting reports the economic effects of events when they occur, not when the cash flows happen. In addition to accrual basis financial statements, however, GAAP requires companies to report a statement of changes in financial position (SCFP) on a cash or cash equivalent basis. You will learn the preparation of the SCFP in Chapter 18.

LO 2. Prepare adjusting entries for prepaid expenses, amortization, unearned revenues, accrued expenses, and accrued revenues. Adjusting entries are used *(a)* to record expenses when prepaid expenses expire, *(b)* to record amortization expense as the cost of using plant and equipment assets, *(c)* to record revenues when the company converts unearned revenues to earned revenues, *(d)* to accrue expenses and related liabilities, and *(e)* to accrue revenues and related assets.

LO 3. Prepare a schedule that includes the unadjusted trial balance, the adjustments, and the adjusted trial balance; use the adjusted trial balance to prepare financial statements; and prepare entries to record cash receipts and cash disbursements related to accrued assets and liabilities. The effects of adjustments can be shown in a six-column schedule that presents the unadjusted trial balance in the first two columns, the adjusting entries in the next two columns, and the adjusted trial balance in the final two columns. The adjusted trial balance shows all ledger accounts, including assets, liabilities, revenues, expenses, and owner's equity. As a result, it can be used to prepare the income statement, the statement of changes in owner's equity, and the balance sheet.

Payments of accrued expenses in the next accounting period are recorded with a debit to the accrued liability and may include another debit for any additional expense incurred since the beginning of the new period. When accrued revenues are collected, the entry credits the previously recorded asset (a receivable) and may include another credit for any additional revenue earned during the new period.

LO 4. Define each asset and liability category for the balance sheet, prepare a classified balance sheet, and calculate the current ratio. Classified balance sheets usually report three categories of assets: current assets, investments, capital assets—tangible and intangible. The two categories of liabilities are current and long-term. Owner's equity for proprietorships and partners' equity for partnerships are reported by putting the capital account balances on the balance sheet. A corporation reports shareholders' equity as contributed capital and retained earnings. A company's current ratio describes its ability to pay its current liabilities out of its current assets. The value of the ratio equals the amount of the current assets divided by the current liabilities.

The following information relates to Best Plumbing Company on December 31, 1997. The company uses the calendar year as its annual reporting period.

DEMONSTRATION PROBLEM

a. The company's weekly payroll is $2,800, paid every Friday for a five-day work-week. December 31, 1997, falls on a Wednesday, but the employees will not be paid until Friday, January 2, 1998.

b. Eighteen months earlier, on July 1, 1996, the company purchased equipment that cost $10,000 and had no salvage value. Its useful life is predicted to be five years.

c. On October 1, 1997, the company agreed to work on a new housing project. For installing plumbing in 24 new homes, the company was paid $144,000 in advance. When the $144,000 cash was received on October 1, 1997, that amount was credited to the Unearned Plumbing Revenue account. Between October 1 and December 31, 1997, work on 18 homes was completed.

d. On September 1, 1997, the company purchased a one-year insurance policy for $1,200. The transaction was recorded with a $1,200 debit to Prepaid Insurance.

Required

1. Prepare the adjusting entries needed on December 31, 1997, to record the previously unrecorded effects of the events.

2. Complete the following table describing your adjusting entries. Your answer should indicate the amount entered in the listed accounts by each entry; the amount of the asset or liability that will appear on the December 31, 1997, balance sheet; and whether the item on the balance sheet will be a current asset, an item related to plant and equipment, a current liability, or a long-term liability:

Entry	Account	Amount in the Entry	Amount on the Balance Sheet	Balance Sheet Category
a	Wages Payable			
b	Accumulated Amortization, Equipment			
c	Unearned Plumbing Revenue			
d	Prepaid Insurance			

3. Complete the following table describing your adjusting entries. Your answer should indicate how much the entry changed (if at all) the company's reported income, its reported total assets, and its reported total liabilities. If the change is a decrease, enter the amount in parentheses:

Entry	Reported Net Income	Reported Total Assets	Reported Total Liabilities
a			
b			
c			
d			

Planning the Solution

- Analyze the information for each situation to determine which accounts need to be updated with an adjustment.
- Calculate the size of each adjustment and prepare the necessary journal entries.
- Show the amount entered by each adjustment in the designated accounts, determine the adjusted balance, and then determine the balance sheet classification that the account falls within.
- Determine each entry's effect on reported net income, reported total assets, and reported total liabilities.

Solution to Demonstration Problem

Adjusting journal entries.

a.	Dec.	31	Wages Expense	1,680.00	
			Wages Payable		1,680.00
			To accrue wages for the last three days of the year ($2,800 × 3/5).		
b.	Dec.	31	Amortization Expense, Equipment	2,000.00	
			Accumulated Amortization, ... Equipment		2,000.00
			To record amortization expense for the full year ($10,000/5 = $2,000).		
c.	Dec.	31	Unearned Plumbing Revenue	108,000.00	
			Plumbing Services Revenue		108,000.00
			To recognize plumbing revenues earned ($144,000 × 18/24).		
d.	Dec.	31	Insurance Expense	400.00	
			Prepaid Insurance		400.00
			To adjust for the expired portion of insurance ($1,200 × 4/12).		

Entry	Account	Amount in the Entry	Amount on the Balance Sheet	Balance Sheet Category
a	Wages Payable	$1,680 cr	$1,680	Current liability
b	Accumulated Amortization, Equipment	$2,000 cr	$3,000	Plant and equipment
c	Unearned Plumbing Revenue	$108,000 dr	$36,000	Current liability
d	Prepaid Insurance	$400 cr	$800	Current asset

Entry	Reported Net Income	Reported Total Assets	Reported Total Liabilities
a	$(1,680)	no effect	$1,680
b	$(2,000)	$(2,000)	no effect
c	$108,000	no effect	$(108,000)
d	$(400)	$(400)	no effect

Recording Prepaid and Unearned Items in Income Statement Accounts

The discussion in Chapter 3 emphasized the fact that prepaid expenses are assets at the time they are purchased. Therefore, at the time of purchase, we recorded prepaid expenses with debits to asset accounts. Then, at the end of the accounting period, adjusting entries transferred the cost that had expired to expense accounts. We also recognized that some prepaid expenses are purchased and will fully expire before the end of the accounting period. In these cases, you can avoid having to make adjusting entries if you charge the prepaid items to expense accounts at the time of purchase.

Some companies follow a practice of recording all prepaid expenses with debits to expense accounts. Then, at the end of the accounting period, if any amounts remain unused or unexpired, adjusting entries are made to transfer the cost of the unused portions from the expense accounts to prepaid expense (asset) accounts. This practice is perfectly acceptable. The reported financial statements are exactly the same under either procedure.

To illustrate the differences between the two procedures, recall that on December 26, Clear Copy paid for 24 months of insurance coverage that began on December 1. We recorded that payment with a debit to an asset account but could have recorded a debit to an expense account. The alternatives are as follows:

PREPAID EXPENSES

LO 6

Explain why some companies record prepaid and unearned items in income statement accounts and prepare adjusting entries when this procedure is used.

			Payment Recorded as Asset		Payment Recorded as Expense	
Dec.	26	Prepaid Insurance	2,400.00			
		Cash		2,400.00		
	26	Insurance Expense			2,400.00	
		Cash				2,400.00

At the end of the accounting period (December 31), insurance protection for one month has expired. That means $2,400/24 = \$100$ of the asset expired and became an expense of December. The required adjusting entry depends on how the original payment was recorded. The alternative adjusting entries are:

	Payment Recorded as Asset	Payment Recorded as Expense
Adjusting entries:		
Dec. 31 Insurance Expense	100.00	
Prepaid Insurance	100.00	
31 Prepaid Insurance		2,300.00
Insurance Expense		2,300.00

When these entries are posted to the accounts, you can see that the two alternative procedures give the same results. Regardless of which procedure is followed, the December 31 adjusted account balances show prepaid insurance of $2,300 and insurance expense of $100.

Payment Recorded as Asset Prepaid Insurance			Payment Recorded as Expense Prepaid Insurance	
Dec. 26	2,400	Dec. 31 100	Dec. 31 2,300	
	−100			
Bal.	2,300			

Insurance Expense		Insurance Expense		
Dec. 31 100		Dec. 26	2,400	Dec. 31 2,300
			−2,300	
		Bal.	100	

To continue the example for another month, assume that on January 1, Clear Copy paid $750 to purchase a second insurance policy. This policy provides protection for three months beginning January 1. Therefore, the total cost of unexpired insurance on January 1 was $2,300 + $750 = $3,050. On January 31, $250 of the second policy's cost (one month's worth) had expired. Since $100 of the first insurance policy and $250 of the second insurance policy expired during January, the adjusting entry on January 31 must be designed to report an insurance expense of $350 and a prepaid insurance asset of $3,050 − $350 = $2,700. Depending on how the original payments were recorded, the alternative adjusting entries are:

	Payment Recorded as Asset	Payment Recorded as Expense
Adjusting entries:		
Jan. 31 Insurance Expense	350.00	
Prepaid Insurance	350.00	
31 Prepaid Insurance		400.00
Insurance Expense		400.00

Note that if the insurance payments are debited to an expense account, the required adjusting entry increases the Prepaid Insurance account balance $400, from $2,300 to $2,700. The credit in the entry reduces the Insurance Expense account debit balance from $750 to $350.

The procedures for recording unearned revenues are similar to those used to record prepaid expenses. Receipts of unearned revenues may be recorded with credits to liability accounts (as described in Chapter 3) or they may be recorded with credits to revenue accounts. The adjusting entries at the end of the period are different, depending on which procedure is followed. Nevertheless, either procedure is acceptable. The amounts reported in the financial statements are exactly the same, regardless of which procedure is used.

UNEARNED REVENUES

To illustrate the alternative procedures of recording unearned revenues, recall that on December 26, Clear Copy received $3,000 in payment for copying services to be provided over the two-month period beginning December 15. In Chapter 3, that receipt was recorded with a credit to a liability account. The alternative would be to record it with a credit to a revenue account. Both alternatives follow:

			Receipt Recorded as a Liability		Receipt Recorded as a Revenue	
Dec.	26	Cash	3,000.00			
		Unearned Copy Services Revenue		3,000.00		
	26	Cash			3,000.00	
		Copy Services Revenue				3,000.00

By the end of the accounting period (December 31), Clear Copy had earned $750 of this revenue. That means $750 of the liability had been satisfied. Depending on how the original receipt was recorded, the required adjusting entry is as follows:

			Receipt Recorded as Liability		Receipt Recorded as Revenue	
Adjusting entries:						
Dec.	31	Unearned Copy Services Revenue . .	750.00			
		Copy Services Revenue		750.00		
	31	Copy Services Revenue			2,250.00	
		Unearned Copy Services Revenue				2,250.00

After these entries are posted, you can see that the two alternative procedures give the same results. Regardless of which procedure is followed, the December 31 adjusted account balances show unearned copy services revenue of $2,250 and copy services revenue of $750.

Receipt Recorded as a Liability				Receipt Recorded as a Revenue	
Unearned Copy Services Revenue				**Unearned Copy Services Revenue**	
Dec. 31	750	Dec. 26	3,000	Dec. 31	2,250
			−750		
		Bal.	2,250		

Copy Services Revenue			Copy Services Revenue			
	Dec. 31	750	Dec. 31	2,250	Dec. 26	3,000
						−2,250
					Bal.	750

SUMMARY OF APPENDIX B IN TERMS OF LEARNING OBJECTIVES

LO 6. Explain why some companies record prepaid and unearned items in income statement accounts and prepare adjusting entries when this procedure is used. Because many prepaid expenses expire during the same period they are purchased, some companies choose to charge all prepaid expenses to expense accounts at the time they are purchased. When this is done, end-of-period adjusting entries are required to transfer any unexpired amounts from the expense accounts to appropriate asset accounts. Also, unearned revenues may be credited to revenue accounts at the time cash is received. If so, end-of-period adjusting entries are required to transfer any unearned amounts from the revenue accounts to appropriate unearned revenue accounts.

GLOSSARY

Account form balance sheet a balance sheet that is arranged so that the assets are listed on the left and the liability and owner's equity items are listed on the right. p. 150

Accounting period the length of time into which the life of a business is divided for the purpose of preparing periodic financial statements. p. 128

Accrual basis of accounting a system of accounting in which the adjustment process is used to assign revenues to the periods in which they are earned and to match expenses with revenues. p. 131

Accrued expenses expenses incurred during an accounting period but that prior to end-of-period adjustments, remain unrecorded because payment is not due. p. 137

Accrued revenues revenues earned during an accounting period but that, prior to end-of-period adjustments, remain unrecorded because payment has not been received. p. 138

Accumulated amortization the total amount of amortization recorded against an asset or group of assets during the entire time the asset or assets have been owned. p. 136

Adjusted trial balance a trial balance that shows the account balances after they have been revised to reflect the effects of end-of-period adjustments. p. 140

Adjusting entry a journal entry made at the end of an accounting period for the purpose of assigning revenues to the period in which they are earned, assigning ex-

penses to the period in which the expiration of benefit is incurred, and to update related liability and asset accounts. p. 132

Amortization the expiration of the usefulness of capital assets (plant, equipment, and intangibles), and the related process of allocating the cost of such assets to expense of the periods during which the assets are used. p. 134

Capital assets tangible, long-lived assets held for use in the production or sale of other assets of services. p. 134

Cash basis of accounting an accounting system in which revenues are reported in the income statement when cash is received and expenses are reported when cash is paid. p. 131

Classified balance sheet a balance sheet that shows assets and liabilities grouped in meaningful subclasses. p. 145

Common shares the name given to a corporation's shares when it issues only one kind or class of shares. p. 149

Contra account an account the balance of which is subtracted from the balance of an associated account to show a more proper amount for the item recorded in the associated account. p. 135

Contributed capital the portion of a corporation's equity that represents investments in the corporation by its shareholders. p. 149

Current assets cash or other assets that are reasonably expected to be realized in cash or to be sold or consumed within one year or one operating cycle of the business, whichever is longer. p. 146

Current liabilities obligations due to be paid or liqui-dated within one year or one operating cycle of the busi-ness, whichever is longer. p. 148

Dividends a distribution, generally of assets, made by a corporation to its shareholders. p. 149

Fiscal year any 12 consecutive months used by a busi-ness as its annual accounting period. p. 129

Intangible assets economic benefits or resources with-out physical substance, the value of which stems from the privileges or rights that accrue to their owner. p. 148

Interim financial reports financial reports of a busi-ness that are based on one-month or three-month ac-counting periods. p. 129

Long-term liabilities obligations not due to be paid within one year or the current operating cycle of the business. p. 148

Matching principle accounting requirements that ex-penses be reported in the same accounting period as the revenues that were earned as a result of the expenses. p. 130

Natural business year the 12-month period that ends when the activities of a business are at their lowest point. p. 129

Operating cycle of a business the average time a busi-ness takes to pay cash for salaries of employees or to pay for merchandise and then to receive cash from cus-tomers in exchange for the sale of the services or mer-chandise. pp. 146

Plant and equipment same as capital assets. p. 147

Report form balance sheet a balance sheet with a ver-tical format that shows the assets above the liabilities and the liabilities above the owner's equity. p. 150

Retained earnings the portion of a corporation's equity that represents its cumulative net income less net losses and dividends. p.149

Time period principle identifying the activities of a business as occurring during specific time periods such as months, or three-month periods, or years so that peri-odic financial reports of the business can be prepared. p. 128

Unadjusted trial balance trial balance before adjust-ments have been recorded. p. 140

Unclassified balance sheet a balance sheet that pre-sents a single list of assets and a single list of liabilities with no attempt to divide them into classes. p. 145

SYNONYMOUS TERMS

Accumulated amortization allowance for amortization.
Amortization depreciation.
Capital assets property, plant, and equipment; land, buildings, and equipment; plant assets; fixed assets

Common shares capital stock

The letter[B] *identifies the questions, quick studies, exercises, and problems that are based on Appendix B at the end of the chapter.*

QUESTIONS

1. What type of business is most likely to select a fis-cal year that corresponds to the natural business year instead of the calendar year?

2. What kind of assets require adjusting entries to record amortization?

3. What contra account is used when recording and reporting the effects of amortization? Why is it used?

4. How is an unearned revenue classified on the bal-ance sheet?

5. What is an accrued revenue? Give an example.

6. What is the difference between the cash and ac-crual bases of accounting?

7. What classes of assets and liabilities are shown on a typical classified balance sheet?

8. What is a company's operating cycle?

9. What are the characteristics of capital assets?

10. When financial statements are prepared from an adjusted trial balance, why should the income statement be prepared first? What statement is prepared next?

11. Which accounting principles provide the basis for the adjustment process?

[B]12. Bee Company records revenues received in advance with credits to liability accounts, while Cee Company records revenues received in advance with credits to revenue accounts. Will these companies have differences in their financial statements because of this difference in their procedures? Why or why not?

QUICK STUDY (Five-Minute Exercises)

QS 3–1
(LO 1)

In its first year of operations, Blaine Company earned $26,000 in revenues and received $22,000 cash from customers. The company incurred expenses of $15,000 but had not paid for $1,500 of them at year-end. In addition, Blaine prepaid $2,500 for expenses that would be incurred the next year. Calculate the first year's net income under a cash basis and calculate the first year's net income under an accrual basis.

QS 3–2
(LO 2)

In recording its transactions during the year, Founder Company records prepayments of expenses in asset accounts and receipts of unearned revenues in liability accounts. At the end of its annual accounting period, the company must make three adjusting entries. They are *(a)* to accrue salaries expense, *(b)* to adjust the Unearned Services Revenue account to recognize earned revenue, and *(c)* to record the earning of services revenue for which cash will be received the following period. For each of these adjusting entries, use the numbers assigned to the following accounts to indicate the correct account to be debited and the correct account to be credited.

1. Prepaid Salaries Expense
2. Cash
3. Salaries Payable
4. Accounts Receivable

5. Salaries Expense
6. Services Revenue Earned
7. Unearned Services Revenue

QS 3–3
(LO 2)

In making adjusting entries at the end of its accounting period, Fulmer Company failed to record $700 of insurance premiums that had expired. This cost had been initially debited to the Prepaid Insurance account. The company also failed to record accrued salaries payable of $400. As a result of these oversights, the financial statements for the reporting period will *(a)* understate net income by $400, *(b)* understate assets by $700, *(c)* overstate liabilities by $400, *(d)* understate expenses by $1,100.

QS 3–4
(LO 3)

The following information has been taken from Jones Company's unadjusted and adjusted trial balances:

	Unadjusted		Adjusted	
	Debit	Credit	Debit	Credit
Prepaid insurance	$6,200		$5,900	
Salaries payable				$1,400

The adjusting entries must have included these items:

a.   A $300 credit to Prepaid Insurance and a $1,400 debit to Salaries Payable.

b.   A $300 debit to Insurance Expense and a $1,400 debit to Salaries Payable.

c.   A $300 debit to Insurance Expense and a $1,400 debit to Salaries Expense.

Calculate Nickel Company's current ratio given the following information about its assets and liabilities:

QS 3–5
(LO 4)

Accounts receivable	$17,000
Accounts payable	11,000
Buildings	35,000
Cash	4,000
Long-term notes payable	20,000
Office supplies	800
Prepaid insurance	3,500
Unearned services revenue	3,000

Blalock Company initially records prepaid and unearned items in income statement accounts. In preparing adjusting entries at the end of the company's first accounting period:

ᴮQS 3–6
(LO 6)

a.   Unpaid salaries will be recorded with a debit to Prepaid Salaries and a credit to Salaries Expense.

b.   The cost of unused office supplies will be recorded with a debit to Supplies Expense and a credit to Office Supplies.

c.   Unearned fees will be recorded with a debit to Consulting Fees Earned and a credit to Unearned Consulting Fees.

d.   Earned but unbilled consulting fees will be recorded with a debit to Unearned Consulting Fees and a credit to Consulting Fees Earned.

e.   None of the above is correct.

EXERCISES

Prepare adjusting journal entries for the financial statements for the year ended December 31, 1996, for each of these independent situations:

Exercise 3–1
Adjusting entries for expenses
(LO 2)

a.   The Supplies account had a $150 debit balance on January 1, 1996; $1,340 of supplies were purchased during the year; and the December 31, 1996, count showed that $177 of supplies are on hand.

b.   The Prepaid Insurance account had a $2,800 debit balance at December 31, 1996, before adjusting for the costs of any expired coverage. An analysis of the company's insurance policies showed that $2,300 of coverage had expired.

c.   The Prepaid Insurance account had a $3,500 debit balance at December 31, 1996, before adjusting for the costs of any expired coverage. An analysis of the company's insurance policies showed that $520 of unexpired insurance remained in effect.

d.   Amortization on the company's equipment for 1996 was estimated to be $8,000.

e.   Six months' property taxes are estimated to be $5,400. They have accrued since June 30, 1996, but are unrecorded and unpaid at December 31, 1996.

Exercise 3–2
Adjusting entries for
accrued expenses
(LO 2, 3)

The Haywood Company has five part-time employees, and each earns $120 per day. They are normally paid on Fridays for work completed on Monday through Friday of the same week. They were all paid in full on Friday, December 28, 1996. The next week, all five of the employees worked only four days because New Year's Day was an unpaid holiday. Show the adjusting entry that would be recorded on Monday, December 31, 1996, and the journal entry that would be made to record paying the employees' wages on Friday, January 4, 1997.

Exercise 3–3
Identifying adjusting
entries
(LO 2)

For each of these adjusting entries, enter the letter of the explanation that most closely describes the transaction in the blank space beside the entry:

a. To record the year's consumption of a prepaid expense.

b. To record accrued interest expense.

c. To record accrued income.

d. To record the year's amortization expense.

e. To record the earning of previously unearned income.

f. To record accrued salaries expense.

```
___ 1. Amortization Expense ........................   99,000.00
          Accumulated Amortization ..................              99,000.00
___ 2. Insurance Expense ............................    6,000.00
          Prepaid Insurance ..........................               6,000.00
___ 3. Interest Receivable ..........................   22,000.00
          Interest Earned ............................              22,000.00
___ 4. Salaries Expense .............................   37,500.00
          Salaries Payable ...........................              37,500.00
___ 5. Interest Expense .............................   63,000.00
          Interest Payable ...........................              63,000.00
___ 6. Unearned Professional Fees ...................   86,000.00
          Professional Fees Earned ..................              86,000.00
```

Exercise 3–4
Missing data in supplies
expense calculations
(LO 2)

Determine the missing amounts in each of these four independent situations:

	a.	b.	c.	d.
Supplies on hand—January 1	$100	$ 800	$ 680	?
Supplies purchased during the year	700	2,700	?	$12,000
Supplies on hand—December 31	250	?	920	1,600
Supplies expense for the year	?	650	4,800	13,150

Exercise 3–5
Adjustments and
payments of accrued
items
(LO 2, 3)

The following three situations require adjusting journal entries to prepare financial statements as of June 30. For each situation, present the adjusting entry and the entry that would be made to record the payment of the accrued liability during July.

a. The total weekly salaries expense for all employees is $6,000. This amount is paid at the end of the day on Friday of each week with five working days. June 30 falls on Tuesday of this year, which means that the employees had worked two days since the last payday. The next payday is July 3.

b. The company has a $390,000 note payable that requires 0.8% interest to be paid each month on the 20th of the month. The interest was last paid on June 20 and the next payment is due on July 20.

c. On June 1, the company retained a lawyer at a flat monthly fee of $1,000. This amount is payable on the 12th of the following month

On March 1, 1996, a company paid a $32,400 premium on a three-year insurance policy for protection beginning on that date. Fill in the blanks in the following table:

Exercise 3–6
Amounts of cash and accrual basis expenses
(LO 1, 2)

Balance Sheet Asset under the:			Insurance Expense under the:		
	Accrual Basis	Cash Basis		Accrual Basis	Cash Basis
31/12/96	$_____	$_____	1996	$_____	$_____
31/12/97	_____	_____	1997	_____	_____
31/12/98	_____	_____	1998	_____	_____
31/12/99	_____	_____	1999	_____	_____
			Total	$_____	$_____

The owner of a duplex apartment building prepares annual financial statements based on a March 31 fiscal year.

Exercise 3–7
Unearned and accrued revenues
(LO 2, 3)

a. The tenants of one of the apartments paid five months' rent in advance on November 1, 1996. The monthly rental is $1,000 per month. Because more than one month's rent was paid in advance, the journal entry credited the Unearned Rent account when the payment was received. No other entry had been recorded prior to March 31, 1997. Give the adjusting journal entry that should be recorded on March 31, 1997.

b. On January 1, 1997, the tenants of the other apartment moved in and paid the first month's rent. The $900 payment was recorded with a credit to the Rent Earned account. However, the tenants have not paid the rent for February or March. They have agreed to pay it as soon as possible. Give the adjusting journal entry that should be recorded on March 31, 1997.

c. On April 3, 1997, the tenants described in part b paid $2,700 rent for February, March, and April. Give the journal entry to record the cash collection.

Use the following adjusted trial balance of the Hamburg Trucking Company to prepare (a) an income statement for the year ended December 31, 1996; (b) a statement of changes in owner's equity for the year ended December 31, 1996; and (c) an unclassified balance sheet as of December 31, 1996. The owner did not make any new investments during 1996.

Exercise 3–8
Preparing financial statements
(LO 3)

	Debit	Credit
Cash	$ 5,500	
Accounts receivable	18,000	
Office supplies	2,000	
Trucks	180,000	
Accumulated amortization, trucks		$ 45,000
Land	75,000	
Accounts payable		11,000
Interest payable		3,000
Long-term notes payable		52,000
B. Hamburg, capital		161,000
B. Hamburg, withdrawals	19,000	
Trucking fees earned		128,000
Amortization expense, trucks	22,500	
Salaries expense	60,000	
Office supplies expense	7,000	
Repairs expense, trucks	11,000	
Total	$400,000	$400,000

Exercise 3–9
Preparing a classified
balance sheet and
calculating the current
ratio
(LO 4)

Use the information provided in Exercise 3–8 to prepare a classified balance sheet for the Hamburg Trucking Company as of December 31, 1996. Determine the value of the current ratio as of the balance sheet date.

Exercise 3–10
Identifying the effects of
adjusting entries
(LO 2, 3)

Following are two income statements for the Carlton Financial Consulting Co. for the year ended December 31. The left column was prepared before any adjusting entries were recorded and the right column includes the effects of adjusting entries. Analyze the statements and prepare the adjusting entries that must have been recorded. Thirty percent of the additional consulting fees were earned but not billed and the other 70% were earned by performing services that the customers had paid for in advance.

CARLTON FINANCIAL CONSULTING CO.
Income Statements
For Year Ended December 31

	Before Adjustments	After Adjustments
Revenues:		
Consulting fees earned	$ 48,000	$ 60,000
Commissions earned	85,000	85,000
Total revenues	$133,000	$145,000
Operating expenses:		
Amortization expense, computers		$ 3,000
Amortization expense, office furniture		3,500
Salaries expense	$ 25,000	29,900
Insurance expense		2,600
Rent expense	9,000	9,000
Office supplies expense		960
Advertising expense	6,000	6,000
Utilities expense	2,500	2,640
Total operating expenses	$ 42,500	$ 57,600
Net income	$ 90,500	$ 87,400

Exercise 3–11
Calculating the current
ratio
(LO 4)

Calculate the current ratio in each of the following cases:

	Current Assets	Current Liabilities
Case 1	$84,000	$31,000
Case 2	96,000	75,000
Case 3	45,000	48,000
Case 4	84,500	82,600
Case 5	65,000	97,000

BExercise 3–12
Adjustments for prepaid
items recorded in expense
and revenue accounts
(LO 6)

The Elder Painting Co. was organized on December 1 by Terry Elder. In setting up the bookkeeping procedures, Elder decided to debit expense accounts when the company prepays its expenses and to credit revenue accounts when customers pay for services in advance. Prepare journal entries for items *a* through *d* and adjusting entries as of December 31 for items *e* through *g:*

a. Shop supplies were purchased on December 1 for $1,000.

b. The company prepaid insurance premiums of $480 on December 2.

c. On December 15, the company received an advance payment of $4,000 from one customer for two painting projects.

d. On December 28, the company received $1,200 from a second customer for painting services to be performed in January.

e. By counting them on December 31, Elder determined that $640 of shop supplies were on hand.

f. An analysis of the insurance policies in effect on December 31 showed that $80 of insurance coverage had expired.

g. As of December 31, only one project had been completed. The fee for this particular project was $2,100.

The Falcon Company experienced the following events and transactions during March:

Mar. 1 Received $1,000 in advance of performing work for T. Carson.

5 Received $4,200 in advance of performing work for B. Gamble.

10 Completed the job for T. Carson.

16 Received $3,750 in advance of performing work for S. Curtin.

25 Completed the job for B. Gamble.

31 The job for S. Curtin is still unfinished.

a. Give journal entries (including any adjusting entry as of the end of the month) to record these events using the procedure of initially crediting the Unearned Fees account when a payment is received from a customer in advance of performing services.

b. Give journal entries (including any adjusting entry as of the end of the month) to record these events using the procedure of initially crediting the Fees Earned account when a payment is received from a customer in advance of performing services.

c. Under each method, determine the amount of earned fees that should be reported on the income statement for March and the amount of unearned fees that should appear on the balance sheet as of March 31.

Exercise 3–13
Alternative procedures for revenues received in advance
(LO 6)

PROBLEMS

The Montgomery Company's annual accounting period ends on December 31, 1997. The following information concerns the adjusting entries to be recorded as of that date:

Problem 3–1
Adjusting journal entries
(LO 2, 3)

a. The Office Supplies account started the year with a $1,000 balance. During 1997, the company purchased supplies at a cost of $4,200, which was added to the Office Supplies account. The inventory of supplies on hand at December 31 had a cost of $880.

b. An analysis of the company's insurance policies provided these facts:

Policy	Date of Purchase	Years of Coverage	Total Cost
1	April 1, 1996	2	$5,280
2	April 1, 1997	3	4,356
3	August 1, 1997	1	900

The total premium for each policy was paid in full at the purchase date, and the Prepaid Insurance account was debited for the full cost.

c. The company has five employees who earn a total of $700 in salaries for every working day. They are paid each Monday for their work in the five-day workweek ending on the preceding Friday. December 31, 1996, falls on Tuesday, and all five employees worked the first two days of the week. Because New Year's Day is a paid holiday, they will be paid salaries for five full days on Monday, January 6, 1997.

d. The company purchased a building on August 1, 1996. The building cost $570,000 and is expected to have a $30,000 salvage value at the end of its predicted 30-year life.

e. Because the company is not large enough to occupy the entire building, it arranged to rent some space to a tenant at $800 per month, starting on November 1, 1996. The rent was paid on time on November 1, and the amount received was credited to the Rent Earned account. However, the tenant has not paid the December rent. The company has worked out an agreement with the tenant, who has promised to pay both December's and January's rent in full on January 15. The tenant has agreed not to fall behind again.

f. On November 1, the company also rented space to another tenant for $725 per month. The tenant paid five months' rent in advance on that date. The payment was recorded with a credit to the Unearned Rent account.

Required

1. Use the information to prepare adjusting entries as of December 31, 1996.

2. Prepare journal entries to record the subsequent cash transactions described in parts c and e.

Problem 3–2
Adjusting entries and the adjusted trial balance
(LO 3, 4)

Miller Realty's unadjusted trial balance on December 31, 1996, the end of its annual accounting period, is as follows:

MILLER REALTY
Trial Balance
December 31, 1996

Cash	$ 2,910	
Prepaid insurance	1,375	
Office supplies	435	
Office equipment	9,375	
Accumulated amortization, office equipment		$ 2,880
Automobile	19,150	
Accumulated amortization, automobile		3,225
Accounts payable		335
Unearned management fees		675
Don Miller, capital		16,700
Don Miller, withdrawals	27,900	
Sales commissions earned		61,920
Office salaries expense	15,450	
Advertising expense	1,245	
Rent expense	7,200	
Telephone expense	695	
Totals	$85,735	$85,735

Required

1. Set up accounts for the items in the trial balance plus these additional accounts: Accounts Receivable; Office Salaries Payable; Management Fees Earned; Insurance Expense; Office Supplies Expense; Amortization Expense, Office Equipment; and Amortization Expense, Automobile. Enter the trial balance amounts in the accounts.

2. Use the information that follows to prepare and post adjusting entries:
   a. An examination of insurance policies shows $1,085 of expired insurance.

   b. An inventory shows $120 of unused office supplies on hand.

   c. Estimated annual amortization on the office equipment is $1,225.

   d. Estimated annual amortization on the automobile is $2,665.

   e. The December telephone bill arrived after the trial balance was prepared, and its $60 amount was not included in the trial balance amounts. Also, a $165 bill for newspaper advertising that had appeared in December was not included in the trial balance amounts.

   f. A client who was taking a tour around the world signed a contract with Miller Realty for the management of his apartment building. The contract calls for a $225 monthly fee, and management began on December 1. The client paid three months' fees in advance, and the amount paid was credited to the Unearned Management Fees account.

   g. Miller Realty agreed to manage the small office building of a second client for $250 per month payable at the end of each three months. The contract was signed on November 15, and one and one-half months' fees have accrued.

   h. The one office employee is paid weekly; and on December 31, two days' wages at $120 per day have accrued.

3. After posting the adjusting entries, prepare an adjusted trial balance, an income statement, a statement of changes in owner's equity, and a classified balance sheet. Miller's capital account balance of $16,700 consists of a $6,700 balance on December 31, 1995, plus a $10,000 investment during 1996.

Carl Carter owns and operates Carter Carpentry School. The school provides training to individuals who pay tuition directly to the business, and also offers extension training to groups in off-site locations. The school's unadjusted trial balance as of December 31, 1996, follows. Facts that require eight adjusting entries on December 31, 1996, are presented after the table:

Problem 3–3
Adjusting entries and financial statements
(LO 3, 4)

CARTER CARPENTRY SCHOOL
Unadjusted Trial Balance

Cash	$ 13,000	
Accounts receivable		
Teaching supplies	5,000	
Prepaid insurance	7,500	
Prepaid rent	1,000	
Professional library	15,000	
Accumulated amortization, professional library		$ 4,500
Equipment	35,000	
Accumulated amortization, equipment		8,000
Accounts payable		18,000
Salaries payable		
Unearned extension fees		5,500
Carl Carter, capital		31,800
Carl Carter, withdrawals	20,000	
Tuition fees earned		51,000
Extension fees earned		19,000
Amortization expense, equipment		
Amortization expense, professional library		
Salaries expense	24,000	
Insurance expense		
Rent expense	11,000	
Teaching supplies expense		
Advertising expense	3,500	
Utilities expense	2,800	
Totals	$137,800	$137,800

Additional facts:

a. An analysis of the company's policies shows that $1,500 of insurance coverage has expired.

b. An inventory shows that teaching supplies costing $1,300 are on hand at the end of the year.

c. The estimated annual amortization on the equipment is $6,000.

d. The estimated annual amortization on the professional library is $3,000.

e. The school offers off-campus services for specific employers. On November 1, the company agreed to do a special six-month course for a client. The contract calls for a monthly fee of $1,100, and the client paid the first five months' fees in advance. When the cash was received, the Unearned Extension Fees account was credited.

f. On October 15, the school agreed to teach a four-month class for an individual for $1,500 tuition per month payable at the end of the class. The services have been provided as agreed, and no payment has been received.

g. The school's only employee is paid weekly. As of the end of the year, two days' wages have accrued at the rate of $100 per day.

h. The balance in the Prepaid Rent account represents the rent for December.

Required

1. Enter the unadjusted trial balance in the first two columns of a six-column table like the one shown in Illustration 3–3.

2. Enter the adjusting entries in the Adjustments columns of the table. Identify the debits and credits of each entry with the letters in the list of additional facts. Complete the adjusted trial balance.

3. Prepare the company's income statement and statement of changes in owner's equity for 1996, and prepare the classified balance sheet as of December 31, 1996. The owner did not make additional investments in the business during the year.

In the following six-column table for the Decker Company, the first two columns contain the unadjusted trial balance for the company as of March 31, 1996. The last two columns contain the adjusted trial balance as of the same date.

Problem 3–4
Comparing the unadjusted and adjusted trial balances and preparing financial statements
(LO 3, 4)

	Unadjusted Trial Balance		Adjustments		Adjusted Trial Balance	
Cash	$ 13,500				$ 13,500	
Accounts receivable	6,000				11,230	
Office supplies	9,000				1,500	
Prepaid insurance	3,660				2,440	
Office equipment	36,000				36,000	
Accumulated amortization, office equipment		$ 6,000				$ 9,000
Accounts payable		4,650				5,100
Interest payable						400
Salaries payable						3,300
Unearned consulting fees .		8,000				7,150
Long-term notes payable .		22,000				22,000
Webster Decker, capital ..		14,210				14,210
Webster Decker, withdrawals	15,000				15,000	
Consulting fees earned ..		78,000				84,080
Amortization expense, office equipment					3,000	
Salaries expense	35,500				38,800	
Interest expense	700				1,100	
Insurance expense					1,220	
Rent expense	6,600				6,600	
Office supplies expense ..					7,500	
Advertising expense	6,900				7,350	
Totals	$132,860	$132,860			$145,240	$145,240

Required

Preparation component:

1. Prepare the company's income statement and the statement of changes in owner's equity for the year ended March 31, 1996. The owner did not make any new investments during the year.

2. Prepare the company's classified balance sheet as of March 31, 1996.

3. Calculate the company's current ratio and debt ratio as of March 31, 1996.

Analysis component:

4. Analyze the differences between the unadjusted and adjusted trial balances to determine the adjustments that must have been made. Show the results of your analysis by inserting the adjusting journal entries that must have been recorded by the company in the two middle columns. Label each entry with a letter, and provide a short description of the purpose for recording it. (Use the Working Papers that accompany the text or recreate the table.)

Problem 3–5
Adjusting entries and the adjusted trial balance
(LO 3, 4)

The unadjusted trial balance of United Moving and Storage follows:

UNITED MOVING AND STORAGE
Trial Balance
December 31, 1996

Cash	$ 3,360	
Accounts receivable	815	
Prepaid insurance	5,370	
Office supplies	480	
Investment in Trail, Inc., common shares	25,000	
Office equipment	5,475	
Accumulated amortization, office equipment		$ 2,520
Trucks	66,300	
Accumulated amortization, trucks		17,300
Building	207,000	
Accumulated amortization, building		42,900
Land	26,250	
Franchise	20,000	
Unearned storage fees		2,595
Long-term notes payable		180,000
Dennis Mead, capital		81,170
Dennis Mead, withdrawals	36,000	
Revenue from moving services		135,170
Storage fees earned		11,660
Office salaries expense	17,100	
Drivers' and helpers' wages expense	39,945	
Gas, oil, and repairs expense	4,020	
Interest expense	16,200	
Totals	$473,315	$473,315

Required

1. Set up accounts for the items in the trial balance plus these additional accounts: Salaries and Wages Payable; Insurance Expense; Office Supplies Expense; Amortization Expense, Office Equipment; Amortization Expense, Trucks; and Amortization Expense, Building. Enter the trial balance amounts in the accounts.

2. Use the information that follows to prepare and post adjusting entries:
   a. Insurance premiums of $4,225 expired during the year.

   b. An inventory shows $165 of unused office supplies on hand.

   c. Estimated amortization on the office equipment, $775; (*d*) on the trucks, $8,000; and (*e*) on the building, $9,300.

f.   Of the $2,595 balance in the Unearned Storage Fees account, $1,985 was earned by the year-end.

g.   Accrued storage fees earned but unrecorded at year-end totaled $515.

h.   There were $200 of earned but unrecorded office salaries and $1,135 of earned but unrecorded drivers' and helpers' wages at the year-end.

3. Prepare an adjusted trial balance, an income statement for the year, a statement of changes in owner's equity, and a classified year-end balance sheet. Mead's $81,170 capital balance reflects the December 31, 1995, balance plus a January 15, 1996, investment of $30,000. A $9,000 installment on the long-term note payable is due within one year.

James Piper, a lawyer, has always kept his records on a cash basis; at the end of 1996, he prepared the following cash basis income statement:

Problem 3–6
Accrual basis income statement
(LO 3)

JAMES PIPER, LAWYER
Income Statement
For Year Ended December 31, 1996

Revenues	$95,500
Expenses	40,450
Net income	$ 55,050

In preparing the statement, the following amounts of prepaid, unearned, and accrued items were ignored at the end of 1995 and 1996:

	End of 1995	1996
Prepaid expenses	$ 2,310	1,800
Accrued expenses	2,595	3,270
Unearned revenues	3,300	5,430
Accrued revenues	4,550	3,660

Required

Under the assumptions that the 1995 prepaid expenses were consumed or expired in 1996, the 1995 unearned revenues were earned in 1996, and the 1995 accrued items were either paid or received in cash in 1996, prepare a 1996 accrual basis income statement for James Piper's law practice. Attach to your statement calculations showing how you arrived at each 1996 income statement amount.

Problem 3–7
Preparing financial
statements from the
adjusted trial balance and
computing ratios
(LO 3, 4)

This adjusted trial balance is for the Krumbell Wrecking Co. as of December 31, 1996:

	Debit	Credit
Cash	$ 11,000	
Accounts receivable	22,000	
Interest receivable	5,000	
Notes receivable (due in 90 days)	80,000	
Office supplies	4,000	
Trucks	90,000	
Accumulated amortization, trucks		$ 36,000
Equipment	70,000	
Accumulated amortization, equipment ...		5,000
Land	35,000	
Accounts payable		44,000
Interest payable		6,000
Salaries payable		5,500
Unearned wrecking fees		11,000
Long-term notes payable		65,000
W. Krumbell, capital		123,900
W. Krumbell, withdrawals	19,000	
Wrecking fees earned		210,000
Interest earned		8,000
Amortization expense, trucks	9,000	
Amortization expense, equipment	5,000	
Salaries expense	90,000	
Wages expense	16,000	
Interest expense	12,000	
Office supplies expense	13,000	
Advertising expense	25,000	
Repairs expense, trucks	8,400	
Total	$514,400	$514,400

Required

1. Use the information in the trial balance to prepare (*a*) the income statement for the year ended December 31, 1996 (under the assumption that the owner made no new investments during the year); (*b*) the statement of changes in owner's equity for the year ended December 31, 1996; and (*c*) the classified balance sheet as of December 31, 1996.

2. Calculate the following ratios for the company:
   a. Current ratio as of December 31, 1996.
   b. Debt ratio as of December 31, 1996.

ᴮ**Problem 3–8**
Recording prepaid
expenses and unearned
revenues
(LO 2, 6)

The following events occurred for a company during the last two months of its fiscal year ended December 31:

Nov. 1 Paid $1,000 for future newspaper advertising.

    1 Paid $1,440 for insurance through October 31 of the following year.

   30 Received $2,200 for future services to be provided to a customer.

Dec. 1 Paid $1,800 for the services of a consultant, to be received over the next three months.

   15 Received $5,100 for future services to be provided to a customer.

Dec. 31 Of the advertising paid for on November 1, $600 worth had not yet been published by the newspaper.

31 Part of the insurance paid for on November 1 had expired.

31 Services worth $800 had not yet been provided to the customer who paid on November 30.

31 One-third of the consulting services paid for on December 1 had been received.

31 The company had performed $2,000 of the services that the customer had paid for on December 15.

Required

Preparation component:

1. Prepare entries for the above events under the approach that records prepaid expenses as assets and records unearned revenues as liabilities. Also, prepare adjusting entries at the end of the year.

2. Prepare journal entries under the approach that records prepaid expenses as expenses and records unearned revenues as revenues. Also, prepare adjusting entries at the end of the year.

Analysis component:

3. Explain why the alternative sets of entries in requirements 1 and 2 do not result in different financial statement amounts.

Carmen Tam purchased Pecan Grove, a mobile home park, last September 1, and she has operated it four months without keeping formal accounting records. However, she has deposited all receipts in the bank and has kept an accurate chequebook record of payments. An analysis of the cash receipts and payments follows:

Problem 3–9
Accrual basis income statement
(LO 3, 5)

	Receipts	Payments
Investment	$52,000	
Purchased Pecan Grove:		
Office equipment	$ 1,500	
Buildings and improvements	90,000	
Land	105,000	
Total	$196,500	
Less long-term note payable signed ..	145,000	
Cash paid		$51,500
Insurance premium paid		1,140
Office supplies purchased		144
Wages paid		4,000
Utilities paid		450
Property taxes paid		1,500
Owner's withdrawals of cash		4,800
Mobile home space rentals collected	19,380	
Totals	$71,380	$63,534
Cash balance, December 31		7,846
Totals	$71,380	$71,380

Ms. Tam wants you to prepare an accrual basis income statement for the village for the four-month period she has operated the business, a statement of changes in owner's equity, and a December 31 balance sheet. You ascertain the following (T-accounts may be helpful in organizing the data):

The buildings and improvements were estimated to have a 25-year remaining life when purchased and at the end of that time will be wrecked. It is estimated that the sale of salvaged materials will just pay the wrecking costs and the cost of clearing the site. The office equipment is in good condition. At the time of purchase, Ms. Tam estimated she would use the equipment for three years and would then trade it in on new equipment of like kind. She thought $150 a fair estimate of what she would receive for the old equipment when she traded it in at the end of three years.

The $1,140 payment for insurance was for a policy taken out on September 1. The policy's protection was for one year beginning on that date. Ms. Tam estimates that one-third of the office supplies purchased have been used. She also says that the one employee of the park earns $50 per day for a five-day week that ends on Friday. The employee was paid last week but has worked four days, December 28 through 31, for which he has not been paid.

Included in the $19,380 of mobile home rentals collected is $360 received from a tenant for three months' rent beginning on December 1. Also, a tenant has not paid his $120 rent for the month of December.

The long-term note payable requires an annual payment of 12% interest on the beginning principal balance plus a $6,000 annual payment on the principal. The first payment is due next September 1. The property tax payment was for one year's taxes that were paid on October 1 for the tax year beginning on September 1, the day Ms. Tam purchased the business

BProblem 3–10
Recording prepayments and unearned items in income statement accounts
(LO 2, 6)

Waivah Company debits expense accounts when recording prepaid expenses; it credits revenue accounts when recording unearned receipts. The following information was available on December 31, 1996, the end of the company's annual accounting period.

a. The Store Supplies account had a $340 debit balance at the beginning of the year, $1,250 of supplies were purchased during the year, and an inventory of unused supplies at the year-end totaled $620.

b. An examination of insurance policies showed two policies, as follows:

Policy	Date of Purchase	Life of Policy	Cost
1 ...	May 1, 1994	3 years	$2,340
2 ...	October 1, 1996	2 years	2,280

Insurance Expense was debited for the cost of each policy at the time of its purchase. However, the correct amount of Prepaid Insurance was recorded during the adjustment processes at the end of 1994 and 1995.

c. On October 15, 1996, Waivah Company agreed to provide consulting services to a client and received advance payment of $8,500. At year-end, the client agreed that three-fourths of the services had been provided.

d. The company occupies most of the space in its building but it also rents space to one tenant. The tenant agreed on November 1 to rent a small amount of space at $750 per month, and on that date paid three months' rent in advance.

e. The Office Supplies account had a $550 debit balance at the beginning of the year and $750 of supplies were purchased during the year. A year-end inventory of office supplies indicated that supplies amounting to $990 had been used during the year.

Required

Prepare adjusting journal entries dated December 31, 1996, prior to the preparation of annual financial statements. For item (b), prepare a separate adjusting entry for each insurance policy.

Review the information presented in paragraphs c, d, and e of Problem 3–1. Describe how each of the following errors from 1997 would affect the company's income statements for 1997 and 1998 and its balance sheets as of December 31, 1997, and 1998 (treat each case as independent from the others). None of the errors were repeated in 1998, but they remained undiscovered until well into 1999.

Problem 3–11
Analytical essay
(LO 1, 2)

1. The company mistakenly recorded the $1,400 of accrued salary expense described in part c as if the amount was only $1,000. However, the employees were paid the correct amount of $1,400 on January 6, 1998. At that time, the Salaries Payable account was debited for $1,000 and the remainder of the $3,500 payment to the employees was debited to the Salaries Expense account for 1998.

2. The company failed to record the $7,500 amortization expense on the building described in part d.

3. The company failed to record the $800 of accrued rent income described in part e. Instead, the revenue was recorded on January 15 as income earned in 1998.

On November 1, 1996, Carson Company and Winslow Company each paid $6,000 for six months' rent on their offices. Carson recorded its payment with a debit to the Prepaid Rent account. On the other hand, Winslow debited the Rent Expense account for $6,000. Both companies use calendar years as their accounting periods. Describe the differences between the adjusting entries the two companies should make on December 31, 1996. Be sure to explain how the two companies' different bookkeeping procedures affect the financial statements.

ᴮProblem 3–12
Analytical essay
(LO 1, 2, 6)

SERIAL PROBLEM

(This comprehensive problem was introduced in Chapter 2 and continues in Chapters 4 and 5. If the Chapter 2 segment has not been completed, the assignment can begin at this point. However, you will need to use the facts presented on pages 119-20 in Chapter 2. Because of its length, this problem is most easily solved if you use the Working Papers that accompany this text.)

Emerald Computer Services

After the success of its first two months, Tracy Green has decided to continue operating Emerald Computer Services. (The transactions that occurred in these months are described in Chapter 2.) Before proceeding into December, Green adds these new accounts to the chart of accounts for the ledger:

Account	No.
Accumulated Amortization, Office Equipment	164
Accumulated Amortization, Computer Equipment ...	168
Wages Payable	210
Unearned Computer Fees	233
Amortization Expense, Office Equipment	612
Amortization Expense, Computer Equipment	613
Insurance Expense	637
Rent Expense	640
Computer Supplies Expense	652

Required

1. Prepare journal entries to record each of the following transactions for Emerald Computer Services. Post the entries to the accounts in the ledger.

2. Prepare adjusting entries to record the events described on December 31. Post the entries to the accounts in the ledger.

3. Prepare an adjusted trial balance as of December 31, 1996.

4. Prepare an income statement for the three months ended December 31, 1996.

5. Prepare a statement of changes in owner's equity for the three months ended December 31, 1996.

6. Prepare a balance sheet as of December 31, 1996.

Transactions and other data:

Dec. 3 Paid $700 to the Town Centre Mall for the company's share of mall advertising costs.

4 Paid $400 to repair the company's computer.

6 Received $2,500 from Alpha Printing Co. for the receivable from the prior month.

10 Paid Fran Sims for six days' work at the rate of $125 per day.

12 Notified by Alpha Printing Co. that Emerald's bid of $4,000 on a proposed project was accepted. The company paid an advance of $1,000.

13 Purchased $770 of computer supplies on credit from AAA Supply Co.

15 Sent a reminder to Fox Run Estates to pay the fee for services originally recorded on November 7.

19 Completed project for Delta Fixtures, Inc., and received $3,750 cash.

21 Paid $2,000 to Tracy Green as a cash withdrawal.

22–26 Took the week off for the holidays.

28 Received $1,900 from Fox Run Estates on their receivable.

29 Reimbursed Tracy Green for business usage of her automobile, 400 kilometres at $0.25 per km.

31 The following information was collected to be used in adjusting entries prior to preparing financial statements for the company's first three months:

a. The December 31 inventory of computer supplies was $480.

b. Three months have passed since the annual insurance premium was paid.

c. As of the end of the year, Fran Sims has not been paid for four days of work at the rate of $125 per day.

d. The computer is expected to have a four-year life with no salvage value.

e. The office equipment is expected to have a three-year life with no salvage value.

f. Prepaid rent for three of the four months has expired.

PROVOCATIVE PROBLEMS

The 1996 and 1997 balance sheets for Phillips Law Practice reported the following assets and liabilities:

Provocative Problem
3–1
Phillips Law Practice
(LO 1, 2)

	1996	1997
Accounts receivable ...	$45,000	$62,000
Prepaid insurance	4,800	3,600
Interest payable	5,750	9,250
Unearned legal fees	17,000	25,000

The company's records show that the following amounts of cash were spent and received during 1997:

Cash spent to pay insurance premiums ..	$ 12,500
Cash spent to pay interest	14,000
Cash received on accounts receivable ...	120,000
Cash received in advance for legal fees ..	108,000

Calculate the amounts to be reported on Phillips Law Practice's 1997 income statement for (*a*) insurance expense, (*b*) interest expense, and (*c*) total legal fees earned.

Early in January, Chris Williams created a new business called We-Fix-Anything. Unfortunately, Williams has not maintained any double-entry accounting records, although all cash receipts and disbursements have been carefully recorded. In addition, all unpaid invoices for the company's expenses and purchases are kept in a file until they are paid. The cash records have been summarized in this schedule:

Provocative Problem
3–2
We-Fix-Anything
(LO 2, 3, 4, 6)

Cash received:		
Investment by owner	$43,000	
Customer repairs	66,000	
Total		$109,000
Cash paid:		
Shop equipment	$21,200	
Repair supplies	25,000	
Rent	8,400	
Insurance premiums	900	
Newspaper advertising	2,000	
Utility bills	1,600	
Employee's wages	8,000	
Chris Williams	20,000	
Total cash payments		87,100
Cash balance as of December 31 ..		$ 21,900

Williams wants to know the net income for the first year and the company's financial position at the end of the year. Provide this information by preparing an accrual basis income statement, a statement of changes in owner's equity, and a classified balance sheet. Also compute the current ratio and the debt ratio.

The following information will help you: The shop equipment was bought in January and is predicted to have a useful life of 10 years, with a $1,200 salvage value. There is a $4,000 unpaid invoice in the file; it is for supplies that have been purchased and received. An inventory shows that $8,200 of supplies are on hand at the end of the year. The shop space is rented for $600 per month under a five-year lease. The lease contract required Williams to pay the first and the final two months' rents in advance. The insurance premiums acquired two policies on January 2. The first is a one-year policy that cost $500, and the second is a two-year policy that cost $400. There are $190 of earned but unpaid wages and customers owe the shop $3,750 for services they have received.

Provocative Problem 3–3
Financial statement analysis case
(LO 4)

Geac

Refer to the financial statements and related information for Geac Computer Corporation Limited in Appendix I. Find the answers to the following questions by analyzing the information in the report.

1. Does the company present a classified balance sheet? What title is given to the financial statement?

2. Identify the classifications of assets presented on the balance sheet.

3. What is the total amount of accumulated depreciation and amortization as of April 30, 1994?

4. What is the company's current ratio at the end of its 1993 and 1992 fiscal years?

Provocative Problem 3–4
Ethical issues essay
(LO 2, 3, 4, 6)

Review the As a Matter of Ethics case on page 139. Describe the ethical dilemma faced by Bill Palmer and describe the alternative courses of action that he might take. Explain how your answer would differ given the following assumptions: *(a)* Palmer knows that the company's financial statements are not going to be audited; *(b)* Palmer knows that the president's bonus depends on the amount of income reported in the first year; and *(c)* Palmer's job depends on complying with the president's wishes.

ANALYTICAL AND REVIEW PROBLEMS

A & R Problem 3–1

The Salaries Payable account of James Bay Company Limited appears below:

Salaries Payable			
Entries during 1996	155,648	Bal. Jan. 1, 1996	9,008
		Entries during 1996	155,360

The company records the salary expense and related liability at the end of each week and pays the employees on the last Friday of the month.

Required

Calculate:

1. Salary expense for 1996.

2. How much was paid to employees in 1996 for work done in 1995?

3. How much was paid to employees in 1996 for work done in 1996?

4. How much will be paid to employees in 1997 for work done in 1996?

The records for Jan Kauffman's home nursing business were kept on the cash basis instead of the accrual basis. However, the company is now applying for a loan and the bank wants to know what its net income for 1997 was under generally accepted accounting principles. Here is the income statement for 1997 under the cash basis:

A & R Problem 3–2

KAUFFMAN'S HOME NURSING
Income Statement (Cash Basis)
For Year Ended December 31, 1997

Revenues	$175,000
Expenses	110,000
Net income	$ 65,000

This additional information was gathered to help the accountant convert the income statement to the accrual basis:

	As of 31/12/96	As of 31/12/97
Accrued revenues	$ 4,000	$5,500
Unearned revenues	22,000	7,000
Accrued expenses	4,900	3,000
Prepaid expenses	9,000	6,900

All prepaid expenses from the beginning of the year were consumed or expired, all unearned revenues from the beginning of the year were earned, and all accrued expenses and revenues from the beginning of the year were paid or collected.

Required

Prepare an accrual basis income statement for this business for 1997. Provide schedules that explain how you converted from cash revenues and expenses to accrual revenues and expenses.

CONCEPT TESTER

Test your understanding of the concepts introduced in this chapter by completing the following crossword puzzle.

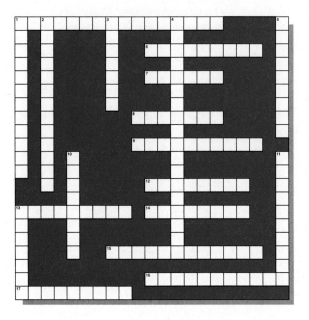

Across Clues

1. Time period covered by financial reports (2 words).

6. Distribution to shareholders.

7. An account, the balance of which is subtracted from the balance of the associated account.

8. Expenses incurred but unpaid.

9. Time period of twelve consecutive months (2 words).

12. Classification of liabilities to be paid beyond a year (2 words).

13. End of period entry to recognize revenue earned but unrecorded.

14. Principle that requires reporting of expenses in the same accounting period as resulting revenues.

15. Indicator of ability to pay short-term obligations (2 words).

16. Total of amortization recorded since acquisition of a capital asset.

17. Definition of unearned revenue.

Down Clues

1. Term recommended by AcSB instead of depreciation.

2. Long-term assets used by businesses (2 words).

3. Financial reports for one or three months.

4. Principle that requires reporting of revenues when earned (2 words).

5. Recognition of revenue when cash is received (2 words).

10. Trial balance that shows account balances after they have been revised by end-of-period procedure.

11. Balance sheet with meaningful groupings.

13. Basis of accounting for external financial statements.

ANSWERS TO PROGRESS CHECKS

3–1 *a*

3–2 Interim financial statements are prepared to provide decision makers information frequently and promptly.

3–3 The revenue recognition principle and the matching principle.

3–4 No, the cash basis is not consistent with the matching principle because it does not always report expenses in the same period as the revenues that were earned as a result of the expenses.

3–5 No expense is reported in 1997. Under the cash basis, the entire $4,800 is reported as expense in 1996 when the premium was paid.

3–6 *c*

3–7 The balance of a contra account is subtracted from the balance of a related account so that more complete information than simply the net amount is provided.

3–8 An accrued expense is an incurred expense that is not recorded prior to adjusting entries because it has not been paid. An example is unpaid salaries earned by employees prior to the year-end.

3–9 An unearned revenue arises when cash is received from a customer before the service is provided to the customer. Magazine subscription receipts are an example.

3–10 *c*

3–11 Revenue accounts and expense accounts.

3–12 The statement of changes in owner's equity is prepared second.

3–13 *c*

3–14 Current assets: *b, c, d.*
Capital assets: *a, e.*

3–15 Share investments that will be held longer than one year or the current operating cycle. Land held for plant expansion.

3–16 Current liabilities.

3–17 Contributed capital and retained earnings.

A systematic approach is essential for efficient and accurate processing of large amounts of information. Whether work sheets are on paper or computerized, they help provide this structure. Proprietorships, partnerships, and corporations all use similar work sheets.

The Work Sheet and the Closing Process

aralleling Karen White and Mark Smith's progress in the study of accounting was their continued interest in the examination of the annual report of Imperial Oil Limited. They reread the "Letter to Shareholders." On this reading they were particularly interested in the statement: "First, we intend to improve the sales mix by emphasizing more profitable products."

White and Smith have now completed the study of Chapter 3. They intend to use their newfound knowledge to test whether Imperial is indeed improving its profitability.

IMPERIAL OIL LIMITED
Selected financial data
(in millions)

	1994	1993	1992	1991	1990
Net earnings (income) ..	$ 359	$ 279	$ 195	$ 162	$ 256
Revenue	9,011	8,903	9,147	9,502	11,303

LEARNING OBJECTIVES

After studying Chapter 4, you should be able to:

1. **Explain why work sheets are useful, prepare a work sheet for a service business, and prepare financial statements from the information in a work sheet.**

2. **Explain why the temporary accounts are closed at the end of each accounting period and prepare closing entries and a post-closing trial balance for a service business.**

3. **Describe each step in the accounting cycle.**

4. **Calculate the profit margin ratio and describe what it reveals about a company's performance.**

5. **Define or explain the words and phrases listed in the chapter glossary.**

After studying Appendix C at the end of Chapter 4, you should be able to:

6. **Explain when and why reversing entries are used and prepare reversing entries.**

After studying Appendix D at the end of Chapter 4, you should be able to:

7. **Explain the nature of a corporation's retained earnings and their relationship to the declaration of dividends.**

8. **Prepare entries to record the declaration and payment of a dividend and to close the temporary accounts of a corporation.**

This chapter continues your study of the accounting process by describing procedures that the accountant performs at the end of each reporting period. You learn about an optional work sheet that accountants use to draft adjusting entries and the financial statements. Studying the work sheet allows you to get an overall perspective on the steps in the accounting cycle. The chapter also describes the closing process that prepares the revenue, expense, and withdrawals accounts for the next reporting period and updates the owner's capital account. In addition, the chapter describes the profit margin ratio that decision makers use to assess a company's performance.

USING WORK SHEETS AT THE END OF ACCOUNTING PERIODS

LO 1

Explain why work sheets are useful, prepare a work sheet for a service business, and prepare financial statements from the information in a work sheet.

When organizing the information presented in formal reports to internal and external decision makers, accountants prepare numerous analyses and informal documents. These informal documents are important tools for accountants. Traditionally, they are called **working papers.** One widely used working paper is the **work sheet.** Normally, the work sheet is not distributed to decision makers. It is prepared and used by accountants.

Why Study the Work Sheet?

As we stated previously, preparing a work sheet is an optional procedure. When a business has only a few accounts and adjustments, preparing a work sheet is not necessary. Also, computerized accounting systems provide financial statements without first generating a work sheet. Nevertheless, there are several reasons why an understanding of work sheets is helpful:

1. In a manual accounting system involving many accounts and adjustments, the work sheet helps the accountant avoid errors.

2. Studying the work sheet is an effective way for you to see the entire accounting process from beginning to end. In a sense, it gives a bird's-eye view of the process between the occurrence of economic events and the presentation of their effects in financial statements. This knowledge helps managers and other decision makers understand the information in the statements.

3. After a company has tentatively prepared its financial statements, the auditors of the statements often use a work sheet as a basis for planning and organizing the audit. Also, they may use a work sheet to reflect any additional adjustments that appear necessary as a result of the audit.

4. Accountants often use work sheets to prepare interim (monthly or quarterly) financial statements.

5. A modified form of the work sheet is sometimes used to show the effects of proposed transactions.

Where Does the Work Sheet Fit into the Accounting Process?

In practice, the work sheet is an optional step in the accounting process that can simplify the accountant's efforts in preparing financial statements. When a work sheet is used, it is prepared before making the adjusting entries at the end of the reporting period. The work sheet gathers information about the accounts, the needed adjustments, and the financial statements. When it is finished, the work sheet contains information that is recorded in the journal and then presented in the statements.

Illustration 4–1 shows a blank work sheet. Notice that it has five sets of double columns for the

PREPARING THE WORK SHEET

1. Unadjusted trial balance.
2. Adjustments.
3. Adjusted trial balance.
4. Income statement.
5. Statement of changes in owner's equity and the balance sheet.

Note that a separate set of double columns is not provided for the statement of changes in owner's equity. Because that statement includes only a few items, they are simply listed with the balance sheet items. A work sheet can be completed manually or with a computer. In fact, the format is well-suited for using a spreadsheet program.

Step 1—Enter the Unadjusted Trial Balance

Turn the first transparency over to create Illustration 4–2. This illustration shows how the accountant starts preparing the work sheet by listing the number and title of every account expected to appear on the company's financial statements. Then, the unadjusted debit or credit balances of the accounts are found in the ledger and recorded in the first two columns. Because these columns serve as the unadjusted trial balance, the totals of the columns should be equal.

Illustration 4–2 uses the information for Clear Copy from Chapter 2 to show step 1. The account balances include the effects of December's external transactions. They do not reflect any of the adjustments described in Chapter 3.

In some cases, the accountant determines later that additional accounts need to be inserted on the work sheet. If the work sheet is completed manually, the additional accounts are inserted below the initial list. If a computer spreadsheet program is used, the new lines are easily inserted between existing lines.

Because a later phase in the example requires two lines for the Copy Services Revenue account, Illustration 4–2 includes an extra blank line below that account. If this need is not anticipated when the work sheet is being prepared manually, the accountant can squeeze two entries on one line.

Step 2—Enter the Adjustments and Prepare the Adjusted Trial Balance

Turn the next overlay page to create Illustration 4–3. The work sheet now appears as it would after step 2 is completed. Step 2 begins by entering adjustments for economic events that were not external transactions. These include adjustments for prepaid expenses, amortization, unearned revenues, accrued expenses, and accrued revenues. The illustration shows the six adjustments for Clear Copy that were explained in Chapter 3:

a. Expiration of $100 of prepaid insurance.

b. Consumption of $1,050 of store supplies.

c. Amortization of copy equipment by $375.

d. Earning of $250 of previously unearned revenue.

e. Accrual of $210 of salaries owed to the employee.

f. Accrual of $1,800 of revenue owed by a customer.

To be sure that equal debits and credits are entered, the components of each adjustment are identified on the work sheet with a letter. Some accountants explain the adjustments with a list at the bottom of the work sheet or on a separate page.[1] To test for accuracy, they add the totals of the two columns to confirm that they are equal.

After the adjustments are entered on the work sheet, the adjusted trial balance is prepared by combining the adjustments with the unadjusted balances. Debits and credits are combined just as they would be in determining an account's balance. For example, the Prepaid Insurance account in Illustration 4–3 has a $2,400 debit balance in the unadjusted trial balance. This is combined with the $100 credit entry (a) in the Adjustments columns to give the account a $2,300 debit balance in the adjusted trial balance. Salaries Expense has a $1,400 balance in the unadjusted trial balance and is combined with the $210 debit entry (e) in the Adjustments columns. When the debit balance is combined with the debit from the adjustment, the account

---

[1]Auditors' work sheets cross-reference each adjustment to a detailed analysis and other supporting evidence.

USE THE FOLLOWING OVERLAYS (ILLUSTRATIONS 4-1 THROUGH 4-6) IN THE DISCUSSION OF WORKSHEETS.

Illustration 4–1 Preparing the Work Sheet at the End of the Accounting Period

CLEAR COPY CO.
Work Sheet
For Month Ended December 31, 19X1

The heading should identify the entity, the document, and the time period.

No.	Title	Unadjusted Trial Balance		Adjustments		Adjusted Trial Balance		Income Statement		Statement of Changes in Owner's Equity and Balance Sheet	
	Account	Dr.	Cr.	Dr.	Cr.	Dr.	Cr.	Dr.	Cr.	Dr.	Cr.

The work sheet can be prepared manually or with a computer spreadsheet program.

The worksheet collects and summarizes the information used to prepare financial statements, adjusting entries, and closing entries.

Illustration 4-6 Step Five: Prepare the Financial Statements from the Work Sheet Information

CLEAR COPY CO.
Income Statement
For Month Ended December 31, 19X1

Revenues:		
Copy services revenue		$5,950
Operating expenses:		
Depreciation expense, copy equipment	$ 375	
Salaries expense	1,610	
Insurance expense	100	
Rent expense	1,000	
Store supplies expense	1,050	
Utilities expense	230	
Total operating expenses		4,365
Net income		$1,585

CLEAR COPY CO.
Statement of Changes in Owner's Equity
For Month Ended December 31, 19X1

Terry Dow, Capital, November 30, 19X1		$ 0
Plus:		
Investments by owner	$30,000	
Net income	1,585	31,585
Total		$31,585
Less withdrawals by owner		400
Terry Dow, capital, December 31, 19X1		$31,185

CLEAR COPY CO.
Balance Sheet
December 31, 19X1

Assets

Cash		$ 7,950
Accounts receivable		1,800
Store supplies		2,670
Prepaid insurance		2,300
Copy equipment	$26,000	
Accumulated depreciation, copy equipment	(375)	25,625
Total assets		$40,345

Liabilities

Accounts payable		$ 6,200
Salaries payable		210
Unearned copy services revenue		2,750
Total liabilities		$ 9,160

Owner's Equity

Terry Dow, capital		31,185
Total liabilities and owner's equity		$40,345

has a $1,610 debit balance in the adjusted trial balance. The totals of the Adjusted Trial Balance columns should confirm that debits equal credits.

Step 3—Extend the Adjusted Trial Balance Amounts to the Financial Statement Columns

Turn the third transparency over to create Illustration 4–4 and to see the effects of step 3. In this step, the accountant assigns each adjusted account balance to its financial statement. This is done by extending each amount to the appropriate column across the page. The revenue and expense balances are extended to the Income Statement columns. The asset, liability, and owner's capital and withdrawals account balances are extended to the Statement of Changes in Owner's Equity and Balance Sheet columns. Accounts with debit balances in the adjusted trial balance are extended to the Debit columns and accounts with credit balances are extended to the Credit columns.

Next, the columns are totaled. Notice that the paired column totals are not equal. This occurs because the sum of the expenses debit balances does not equal the sum of the revenue credit balances. This also creates an equal and opposite imbalance in the Statement of Changes in Owner's Equity and Balance Sheet columns. Step 4 deals with this imbalance.

Step 4—Enter the Net Income (or Loss) and Balance the Financial Statement Columns

To see the completed work sheet, turn the final transparent overlay to create Illustration 4–5. Step 4 begins by entering Net income and Totals on the next two lines in the account title column. Next, the accountant computes the net income by finding the excess of the Income Statement Credit column total over the Debit column total. This amount is inserted on the net income line in the Debit column, and a new total is computed for each column. (If the initial total of the debits is greater than the initial total credits, the expenses exceed the revenues and the company has incurred a net loss. If so, the difference is entered in the Credit column instead of the Debit column.) The total debits and total credits in the Income Statement columns are now equal.

The accountant next enters the net income in the last Credit column of the work sheet. (If there is a net loss, it is entered in the last Debit column.) Notice that this entry causes the total debits in the last two columns to equal the total credits.

Even if all five pairs of columns balance, the work sheet may not be free of errors. For example, if the accountant incorrectly extends an asset account's balance to the Income Statement Debit column, the columns balance but net income is understated. Or, if an expense is extended to the Statement of Changes in Owner's Equity and Balance Sheet Debit column, the columns balance but the net income is overstated. Although these errors may not be immediately obvious, they are discovered when the accountant begins to actually prepare the financial statements. For example, it would be apparent that an asset does not belong on the income statement or that an expense does not belong on the balance sheet.

At this point, the work sheet is complete. If the accountant discovers new information or an error, the change can easily be included in the work sheet, especially if it is being prepared with a computer spreadsheet.

PREPARING ADJUSTING ENTRIES FROM THE WORK SHEET

Entering the adjustments in the Adjustments columns of a work sheet does not get these adjustments into the ledger accounts. Therefore, after completing the work sheet, adjusting entries like the ones described in Chapter 3 must be entered in the General Journal and posted to the accounts in the ledger. The work sheet makes this easy because its Adjustments columns provide the information for these entries. If adjusting entries are prepared from the information in Illustration 4–3, you will see that they are the same adjusting entries we discussed in the last chapter.

PREPARING FINANCIAL STATEMENTS FROM THE WORK SHEET

A work sheet is not a substitute for the financial statements. The work sheet is nothing more than a supporting tool that the accountant uses at the end of an accounting period to help organize the data. However, as soon as it is completed, the accountant uses the work sheet to prepare the financial statements.

The sequence is the same as we have seen before. The income statement is completed first. The net income is then combined with the owner's investments, withdrawals, and beginning capital balance on the statement of changes in owner's equity. In doing this, the accountant analyzes the owner's capital account to separate the beginning balance from any new investments made during the reporting period. Finally, the balance sheet is completed by using the ending balance of owner's equity from the statement of changes in owner's equity.

WHY USE A WORK SHEET?

At this point, it should be clear that we ended up with exactly the same financial statements and adjusting entries that we developed in Chapter 3 without using a work sheet. So, why prepare a work sheet?

First, the example in this chapter is greatly simplified. Real companies have many more adjusting entries and accounts than Clear Copy. A work sheet makes it easier to organize all the additional information. As we mentioned earlier in the chapter, auditors often use work sheets to plan and organize their work. In fact, they may request that a company provide a work sheet showing the adjustments made prior to the audit.

Second, the work sheet can be used to prepare *interim* financial statements without recording the adjusting entries in the journal and ledger. Thus, a company can prepare statements each month or quarter and avoid taking the time to formally journalize and post the adjustments except once at the end of each year. All large companies with publicly traded ownership prepare interim financial reports, usually on a quarterly basis. Some of them also include summaries of the past year's quarterly data in their annual reports.

Also, companies may use a work sheet format to show the effects of proposed transactions. In doing this, they enter their adjusted financial statements amounts in the first two columns, arranging them to appear in the form of financial statements. Then, the proposed transactions are inserted in the second two columns. The extended amounts in the last columns show the effects of the proposed transactions on the financial statements. These final columns are called **pro forma statements,** because they show the statements as if the proposed transactions had already occurred.

Because the work sheet is an informal working paper, its format is not dictated by generally accepted accounting principles. For example, some accountants omit the Adjusted Trial Balance columns. Others use different work sheet columns to draft the *closing entries* described later in the chapter. Some work sheets have separate columns for the statement of changes in owner's equity and the balance sheet. The decision about which format is preferred rests with the accountant who creates the work sheet.

ALTERNATE FORMATS OF THE WORK SHEET

Progress Check
(Answers to Progress Checks are provided at the end of the chapter.)

4–1   On a work sheet, the $99,400 salaries expense balance was incorrectly extended from the Adjusted Trial Balance column to the Statement of Changes in Owner's Equity and Balance Sheet Debit column. As a result of this error, *(a)* the Adjusted Trial Balance columns will not balance; *(b)* revenues on the work sheet will be understated; *(c)* net income on the work sheet will be overstated.

4–2   Where does the accountant obtain the amounts entered in the Unadjusted Trial Balance columns of the work sheet?

4–3   What is the advantage of using a work sheet to prepare adjusting entries?

4–4   From a 10-column work sheet, the accountant prepares the financial statements in what order?

After the financial statements are completed and the adjusting entries are recorded, the next step in the accounting cycle is to journalize and post **closing entries.** Closing entries are designed to transfer the end-of-period balances in the revenue, expense, and withdrawals accounts to the owner's capital account. These entries are necessary because:

CLOSING ENTRIES

LO 2
Explain why the temporary accounts are closed at the end of each accounting period and prepare closing entries and a post-closing trial balance for a service business.

1. Revenues increase owner's equity, while expenses and withdrawals decrease owner's equity.

2. During an accounting period, these increases and decreases are temporarily accumulated in the revenue, expense, and withdrawals accounts rather than in the owner's capital account.

3. By transferring the effects of revenues, expenses, and withdrawals from the revenue, expense, and withdrawals accounts to the owner's capital account, closing entries install the correct end-of-period balance in the owner's capital account.

4. Closing entries also cause the revenue, expense, and withdrawals accounts to begin each new accounting period with zero balances.

Remember that an income statement reports the revenues earned and expenses incurred during one accounting period and is prepared from information recorded in the revenue and expense accounts. Also, the statement of changes in owner's equity reports the changes in the owner's capital account during one period and uses the information accumulated in the withdrawals account. Because the revenue, expense, and withdrawals accounts accumulate information for only one period and then must be ready to do the same thing the next period, they must start each period with zero balances.

To close the revenue and expense accounts, the accountant transfers their balances first to a summary account called **Income Summary.** Then, the Income Summary balance, which is the net income or loss, is transferred to the owner's capital account. Finally, the accountant transfers the owner's withdrawals account balance to the owner's capital account. After the closing entries are posted, the revenue, expense, Income Summary, and withdrawals accounts have zero balances. Thus, these accounts are said to be closed or cleared.

Illustration 4–7 diagrams the four entries that close the revenue, expense, Income Summary, and withdrawals accounts of Clear Copy on December 31, 1996. The preclosing balances of the accounts in the illustration are taken from the adjusted trial balance in Illustration 4–5.

Entry 1. The first closing entry transfers the credit balances in the revenue accounts to the Income Summary account. In general journal form, the entry is:

Dec.	31	Copy Services Revenue	5,950.00	
		Income Summary		5,950.00
		To close the revenue account and create the Income Summary account.		

Note that this entry closes the revenue account by giving it a zero balance. If the company had several different revenue accounts, this entry would be a compound entry that included a debit to each of them. This clearing of the accounts allows them to be used to record new revenues in the upcoming year.

The Income Summary account is created especially for the closing process and is used only during that process. The $5,950 credit balance in Income Summary equals the total revenues for the year.

Entry 2. The second closing entry transfers the debit balances in the expense accounts to the Income Summary account. This step concentrates all the expense account debit balances in the Income Summary account. It also closes each expense account by giving it a zero balance. That allows it to be used to record new expenses in the upcoming year. The second closing entry for Clear Copy is:

Dec.	31	Income Summary	4,365.00	
		Amortization Expense, Copy Equipment		375.00
		Salaries Expense		1,610.00
		Insurance Expense		100.00
		Rent Expense		1,000.00
		Store Supplies Expense		1,050.00
		Utilities Expense		230.00
		To close the expense accounts.		

Illustration 4–7 shows that posting this entry gives each expense account a zero balance and prepares it to accept entries for expenses in 1997. The entry also makes the balance of the Income Summary account equal to December's net income of

Illustration 4–7 Closing Entries for Clear Copy

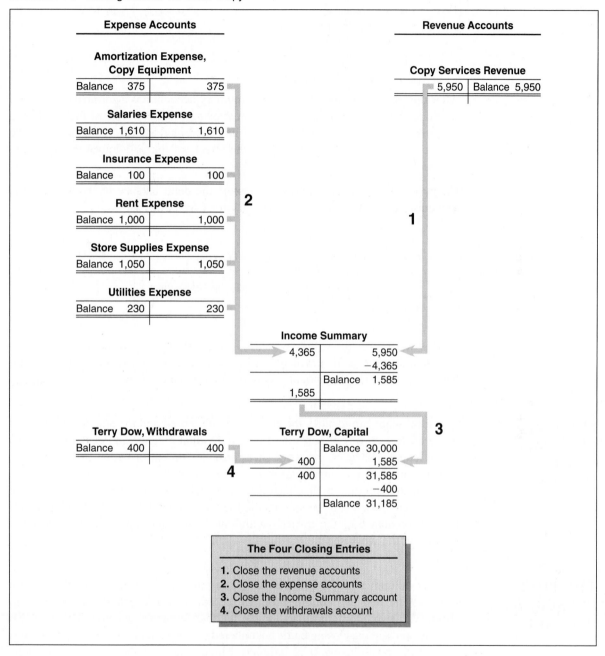

$1,585. In effect, all the debit and credit balances of the expense and revenue accounts have now been concentrated in the Income Summary account.

Entry 3. The third closing entry transfers the balance of the Income Summary account to the owner's capital account. This entry closes the Income Summary account and adds the company's net income to the owner's capital account:

Dec.	31	Income Summary	1,585.00	
		Terry Dow, Capital		1,585.00
		To close the Income Summary account and add the net income to the capital account.		

After this entry is posted, the Income Summary account has a zero balance. It will continue to have a zero balance until the closing process occurs at the end of the next year. The owner's capital account has been increased by the amount of the net income, but still does not include the effects of the withdrawal that occurred in December.

Entry 4. The final closing entry transfers the debit balance of the withdrawals account to the capital account. This entry for Clear Copy is:

Dec.	31	Terry Dow, Capital	400.00	
		Terry Dow, Withdrawals		400.00
		To close the withdrawals account and reduce the balance of the capital account.		

This entry gives the withdrawals account a zero balance, which allows it to accumulate the next year's payments to the owner. It also reduces the capital account balance to the $31,185 amount reported on the balance sheet.

SOURCES OF CLOSING ENTRY INFORMATION

The accountant can identify the accounts to be closed and the amounts to be used in the closing entries by referring to the individual revenue and expense accounts in the ledger. However, the work sheet provides this information in a more convenient format. To locate the information on the work sheet, look again at the income statement columns in Illustration 4–5. All accounts with balances in these columns are closed and the amounts in the work sheet are used in the closing entries. The balance of the owner's withdrawals account appears in the last debit column in the work sheet.

THE POST-CLOSING TRIAL BALANCE

The six-column table in Illustration 4–8 summarizes the effects of the closing process. The first two columns contain the adjusted trial balance from the work sheet, with two additional lines for the Income Summary account. The next two columns present the closing entries, numbered (1) through (4). The last two columns contain the **post-closing trial balance,** which lists the balances of the accounts that were not closed.[2] These accounts represent the company's assets, liabilities, and owner's equity as of the end of 1996. These items and amounts are the same as those presented in the balance sheet in Illustration 4–6.

---

[2] Some accountants use work sheets that include these four columns instead of the financial statement columns. The financial statements are not changed by choosing one or the other.

Illustration 4–8 The Adjusted Trial Balance, Closing Entries, and Post-Closing Trial Balance for Clear Copy

	Adjusted Trial Balance		Closing Entries		Post-Closing Trial Balance	
Cash	7,950				7,950	
Accounts receivable	1,800				1,800	
Store supplies	2,670				2,670	
Prepaid insurance	2,300				2,300	
Copy equipment	26,000				26,000	
Accumulated amortization,						
copy equipment		375				375
Accounts payable		6,200				6,200
Salaries payable		210				210
Unearned copy services revenue		2,750				2,750
Terry Dow, capital		30,000	(4) 400	(3) 1,585		31,185
Terry Dow, withdrawals	400			(4) 400		
Copy services revenue		5,950	(1) 5,950			
Amortization expense,						
copy equipment	375			(2) 375		
Salaries expense	1,610			(2) 1,610		
Insurance expense	100			(2) 100		
Rent expense	1,000			(2) 1,000		
Store supplies expense	1,050			(2) 1,050		
Utilities expense	230			(2) 230		
Income summary			(2) 4,365	(1) 5,950		
			(3) 1,585			
Totals	45,485	45,485	12,300	12,300	40,720	40,720

Instead of preparing the six-column table in Illustration 4–8, the post-closing trial balance is often prepared as a separate two-column table, as in Illustration 4–9. Regardless of the format, the post-closing trial balance is the last step in the annual accounting process.

Permanent (Real) Accounts and Temporary (Nominal) Accounts

Asset, liability, and owner's capital accounts are not closed as long as the company continues to own the assets, owe the liabilities, and have owner's equity. Because these accounts are not closed, they are called **permanent accounts** or **real accounts.** These accounts are permanent because they describe real conditions that are perceived to exist.

In contrast, the terms **temporary accounts** and **nominal accounts** describe the revenue, expense, Income Summary, and withdrawals accounts. These terms are used because the accounts are opened at the beginning of the year, used to record events, and then closed at the end of the year. These accounts are temporary because they describe nominal events or changes that have occurred rather than real conditions that continue to exist.

Illustration 4-9
Separate Post-Closing
Trial Balance for Clear
Copy

The Post Closing Trial Balance		
Cash	$ 7,950	
Accounts receivable	1,800	
Store supplies	2,670	
Prepaid insurance	2,300	
Copy equipment	26,000	
Accumulated amortization, copy equipment .		$ 375
Accounts payable		6,200
Salaries payable		210
Unearned copy services revenue		2,750
Terry Dow, capital		31,185
Totals	$40,720	$40,720

THE LEDGER FOR CLEAR COPY

To complete the Clear Copy example, look at Illustration 4–10, the company's entire ledger as of December 31, 1996. Review the accounts and observe that the temporary accounts (the withdrawals account and all accounts with numbers greater than 400) have been closed.

CLOSING ENTRIES FOR CORPORATIONS

Up to this point, our examples of closing entries have related to the activities and accounts of single proprietorships. However, closing entries for corporations are very similar. The first two closing entries are exactly the same. In other words, a corporation's revenue and expense accounts are closed to the Income Summary account. The last two entries are different.

Recall from Chapter 3 that a corporation's balance sheet presents the shareholders' equity as contributed capital and retained earnings. As a result, the third closing entry for a corporation closes the Income Summary account to the Retained Earnings account. For example, **Petro-Canada** reported a net income of $162 million in 1993, which means that was the credit balance in the Income Summary account after the revenue and expense accounts were closed. The company's third closing entry would have updated the Retained Earnings account as follows:

Dec.	31	Income Summary	162,000,000.00	
		Retained Earnings		162,000,000.00
		To close the Income Summary account and update Retained Earnings.		

The fourth closing entry is also different because corporations use a Dividends Declared account instead of a withdrawals account. The accounting practices for dividends paid to shareholders are described in Appendix D and in Chapter 16. Coverage of corporations, at this point, is limited to closing entries. For a more complete coverage of partnership and corporation accounting refer to Appendix D at the end of this chapter and Chapters 14, 15 and 16.

Illustration 4–10 The Ledger for Clear Copy as of December 31, 1996 (after adjustments and closing entries have been posted)

Asset Accounts:

	Cash			Acct. No. 101	
Date		Expl.	Debit	Credit	Balance
1996					
Dec.	1		30,000		30,000
	2			2,500	27,500
	3			20,000	7,500
	10		2,200		9,700
	12			1,000	8,700
	12			700	8,000
	22		1,700		9,700
	24			900	8,800
	24			400	8,400
	26		3,000		11,400
	26			2,400	9,000
	26			120	8,880
	26			230	8,650
	26			700	7,950

	Store Supplies			Acct. No. 125	
Date		Expl.	Debit	Credit	Balance
1996					
Dec.	2		2,500		2,500
	6		1,100		3,600
	26		120		3,720
	31			1,050	2,670

	Prepaid Insurance			Acct. No. 128	
Date		Expl.	Debit	Credit	Balance
1996					
Dec.	26		2,400		2,400
	31			100	2,300

	Copy Equipment			Acct. No. 167	
Date		Expl.	Debit	Credit	Balance
1996					
Dec.	3		20,000		20,000
	6		6,000		26,000

	Accounts Receivable			Acct. No. 106	
Date		Expl.	Debit	Credit	Balance
1996					
Dec.	12		1,700		1,700
	22			1,700	0
	31		1,800		1,800

	Accumulated Amortization, Copy Equipment			Acct. No. 168	
Date		Expl.	Debit	Credit	Balance
1996					
Dec.	31			375	375

Liability and Equity Accounts:

	Accounts Payable			Acct. No. 201	
Date		Expl.	Debit	Credit	Balance
1996					
Dec.	6			7,100	7,100
	24		900		6,200

	Unearned Copy Services Revenue			Acct. No. 236	
Date		Expl.	Debit	Credit	Balance
1996					
Dec.	26			3,000	3,000
	31		250		2,750

	Salaries Payable			Acct. No. 209	
Date		Expl.	Debit	Credit	Balance
1996					
Dec.	31			210	210

Illustration 4–10 *(concluded)*

<table>
<tr><td colspan="6" align="center">Terry Dow, Capital   Acct. No. 301</td></tr>
<tr><td colspan="2">Date</td><td>Expl.</td><td>Debit</td><td>Credit</td><td>Balance</td></tr>
<tr><td>1996</td><td></td><td></td><td></td><td></td><td></td></tr>
<tr><td>Dec.</td><td>1</td><td></td><td></td><td>30,000</td><td>30,000</td></tr>
<tr><td></td><td>31</td><td></td><td></td><td>1,585</td><td>31,585</td></tr>
<tr><td></td><td>31</td><td></td><td>400</td><td></td><td>31,185</td></tr>
</table>

<table>
<tr><td colspan="6" align="center">Terry Dow,
Withdrawals   Acct. No. 302</td></tr>
<tr><td colspan="2">Date</td><td>Expl.</td><td>Debit</td><td>Credit</td><td>Balance</td></tr>
<tr><td>1996</td><td></td><td></td><td></td><td></td><td></td></tr>
<tr><td>Dec.</td><td>24</td><td></td><td>400</td><td></td><td>400</td></tr>
<tr><td></td><td>31</td><td></td><td></td><td>400</td><td>0</td></tr>
</table>

Revenue and Expense Accounts (including Income Summary):

<table>
<tr><td colspan="6" align="center">Copy Services Revenue   Acct. No. 403</td></tr>
<tr><td colspan="2">Date</td><td>Expl.</td><td>Debit</td><td>Credit</td><td>Balance</td></tr>
<tr><td>1996</td><td></td><td></td><td></td><td></td><td></td></tr>
<tr><td>Dec.</td><td>10</td><td></td><td></td><td>2,200</td><td>2,200</td></tr>
<tr><td></td><td>12</td><td></td><td></td><td>1,700</td><td>3,900</td></tr>
<tr><td></td><td>31</td><td></td><td></td><td>250</td><td>4,150</td></tr>
<tr><td></td><td>31</td><td></td><td></td><td>1,800</td><td>5,950</td></tr>
<tr><td></td><td>31</td><td></td><td>5,950</td><td></td><td>0</td></tr>
</table>

<table>
<tr><td colspan="6" align="center">Amortization Expense,
Copy Equipment   Acct. No. 614</td></tr>
<tr><td colspan="2">Date</td><td>Expl.</td><td>Debit</td><td>Credit</td><td>Balance</td></tr>
<tr><td>1996</td><td></td><td></td><td></td><td></td><td></td></tr>
<tr><td>Dec.</td><td>31</td><td></td><td>375</td><td></td><td>375</td></tr>
<tr><td></td><td>31</td><td></td><td></td><td>375</td><td>0</td></tr>
</table>

<table>
<tr><td colspan="6" align="center">Salaries Expense   Acct. No. 622</td></tr>
<tr><td colspan="2">Date</td><td>Expl.</td><td>Debit</td><td>Credit</td><td>Balance</td></tr>
<tr><td>1996</td><td></td><td></td><td></td><td></td><td></td></tr>
<tr><td>Dec.</td><td>12</td><td></td><td>700</td><td></td><td>700</td></tr>
<tr><td></td><td>26</td><td></td><td>700</td><td></td><td>1,400</td></tr>
<tr><td></td><td>31</td><td></td><td>210</td><td></td><td>1,610</td></tr>
<tr><td></td><td>31</td><td></td><td></td><td>1,610</td><td>0</td></tr>
</table>

<table>
<tr><td colspan="6" align="center">Insurance Expense   Acct. No. 637</td></tr>
<tr><td colspan="2">Date</td><td>Expl.</td><td>Debit</td><td>Credit</td><td>Balance</td></tr>
<tr><td>1996</td><td></td><td></td><td></td><td></td><td></td></tr>
<tr><td>Dec.</td><td>31</td><td></td><td>100</td><td></td><td>100</td></tr>
<tr><td></td><td>31</td><td></td><td></td><td>100</td><td>0</td></tr>
</table>

<table>
<tr><td colspan="6" align="center">Rent Expense   Acct. No. 641</td></tr>
<tr><td colspan="2">Date</td><td>Expl.</td><td>Debit</td><td>Credit</td><td>Balance</td></tr>
<tr><td>1996</td><td></td><td></td><td></td><td></td><td></td></tr>
<tr><td>Dec.</td><td>12</td><td></td><td>1,000</td><td></td><td>1,000</td></tr>
<tr><td></td><td>31</td><td></td><td></td><td>1,000</td><td>0</td></tr>
</table>

<table>
<tr><td colspan="6" align="center">Store Supplies Expense   Acct. No. 651</td></tr>
<tr><td colspan="2">Date</td><td>Expl.</td><td>Debit</td><td>Credit</td><td>Balance</td></tr>
<tr><td>1996</td><td></td><td></td><td></td><td></td><td></td></tr>
<tr><td>Dec.</td><td>31</td><td></td><td>1,050</td><td></td><td>1,050</td></tr>
<tr><td></td><td>31</td><td></td><td></td><td>1,050</td><td>0</td></tr>
</table>

<table>
<tr><td colspan="6" align="center">Utilities Expense   Acct. No. 690</td></tr>
<tr><td colspan="2">Date</td><td>Expl.</td><td>Debit</td><td>Credit</td><td>Balance</td></tr>
<tr><td>1996</td><td></td><td></td><td></td><td></td><td></td></tr>
<tr><td>Dec.</td><td>26</td><td></td><td>230</td><td></td><td>230</td></tr>
<tr><td></td><td>31</td><td></td><td></td><td>230</td><td>0</td></tr>
</table>

<table>
<tr><td colspan="6" align="center">Income Summary   Acct. No. 901</td></tr>
<tr><td colspan="2">Date</td><td>Expl.</td><td>Debit</td><td>Credit</td><td>Balance</td></tr>
<tr><td>1996</td><td></td><td></td><td></td><td></td><td></td></tr>
<tr><td>Dec.</td><td>31</td><td></td><td></td><td>5,950</td><td>5,950</td></tr>
<tr><td></td><td>31</td><td></td><td>4,365</td><td></td><td>1,585</td></tr>
<tr><td></td><td>31</td><td></td><td>1,585</td><td></td><td>0</td></tr>
</table>

Progress Check

4-5   When closing entries are prepared:
      a. The accounts for expenses, revenues, and the owner's withdrawals are closed to the Income Summary account.
      b. The final balance of the Income Summary account equals net income or net loss for the period.
      c. All temporary accounts have zero balances when the process is completed.

4-6   Why are revenue and expense accounts called temporary? Are there any other temporary accounts?

4-7   What accounts are listed on the post-closing trial balance?

4-8   What account is used by a corporation to close the Income Summary account?

Chapters 2, 3, and 4 have described the accounting procedures that are completed during each reporting period. They begin with recording external transactions in the journal and end with preparing the post-closing trial balance. Because these steps are repeated each period, they are often called the **accounting cycle.** A flow

A REVIEW OF THE ACCOUNTING CYCLE

LO 3
Describe each step in the accounting cycle.

Step	Description
1. **Journalizing**	Analyzing transactions and recording debits and credits in a journal.
2. **Posting**	Copying the debits and credits from the journal entries to the accounts in the ledger.
3. **Preparing an unadjusted trial balance**	Summarizing the ledger accounts and partially testing clerical accuracy. (If a work sheet is used, this is done on the work sheet.)
4. **Completing the work sheet (optional)**	Identifying the effects of adjustments on the financial statements before entering them in the ledger and posting them to the accounts; also drafting the adjusted trial balance, extending the adjusted amounts to the appropriate financial statement columns, and determining the size of the net income or net loss.
5. **Adjusting the accounts**	Identifying necessary adjustments to bring the account balances up to date; journalizing and posting entries to record the adjustments in the accounts. (If the work sheet is prepared, the information in the adjustments columns is used for the entries.)
6. **Preparing the financial statements**	Using the information on the adjusted trial balance (or the work sheet) to prepare an income statement, a statement of changes in owner's equity, a balance sheet, and a statement of changes in financial position. (Techniques for preparing the changes in financial position statement are described in Chapter 18.)
7. **Closing the temporary accounts**	Preparing journal entries to close the revenue, expense, and withdrawals accounts and to update the owner's capital (or retained earnings) account. These entries are posted to the ledger.
8. **Preparing a post-closing trial balance**	Testing the clerical accuracy of the adjusting and closing procedures.

Illustration 4–11   The Accounting Cycle

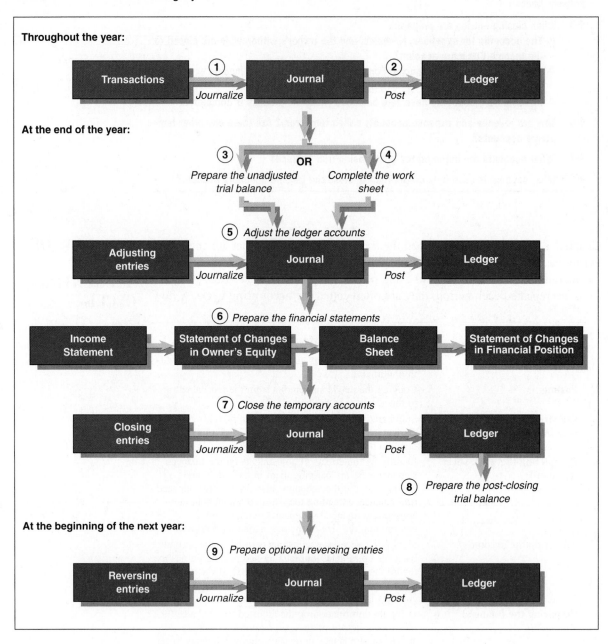

chart in Illustration 4–11 shows the steps in order. Steps 1 and 2 take place every day as the company engages in business transactions. The other steps are completed at the end of the accounting period. Review this illustration and the list of the steps to be sure that you understand how each one helps accountants provide useful information in the financial statements.

Illustration 4–11 also identifies an optional ninth step of making reversing entries at the beginning of the following period. These entries are described in Appendix C, which begins on page 204.

A Practical Point

Normally, accountants are not able to make all of the adjusting and closing entries on the last day of the fiscal year. Information about the economic events that require adjustments often is not available until after several days or even a few weeks. As a result, the adjusting and closing entries are recorded later but dated as of the last day of the year. This means the financial statements reflect what is known on the date that they are prepared instead of what was known on the financial statement date.

For example, a company might receive a utility bill on January 14 for costs incurred from December 1 through December 31. Upon receiving the bill, the company's accountant records the expense and the payable as of December 31. The income statement for December reflects the full expense and the December 31 balance sheet includes the payable, even though the exact amounts were not actually known on December 31.

Progress Check

4-9   The steps in the accounting cycle _(a)_ are concluded by preparing a post-closing trial balance; _(b)_ are concluded by preparing a balance sheet; or _(c)_ begin with preparing the unadjusted trial balance.

4-10   At what point in the accounting cycle is the work sheet prepared?

By now, it should be clear that accountants go to great lengths to ensure that a company's financial statements reflect up-to-date information about its assets, liabilities, revenues, and expenses. A primary goal of this effort is to provide information that helps internal and external decision makers evaluate the results achieved in the reporting period. This includes evaluating management's success in generating profits. The information may suggest ways to achieve better results and also helps users predict future results.

In using accounting information to evaluate the results of operations, one widely used ratio relates the company's net income to its sales. The ratio is called the **profit margin** or the **return on sales,** and is calculated with this formula:

$$\text{Profit margin} = \frac{\text{Net income}}{\text{Revenues}}$$

In effect, this ratio measures the average portion of each dollar of revenue that ends up as profit.

Recall from the beginning of the chapter that Karen White and Mark Smith desired to test whether Imperial Oil Limited was improving its profitability. The company's profit margins during several years were:

USING THE INFORMATION— THE PROFIT MARGIN

LO 4

Calculate the profit margin ratio and describe what it reveals about a company's performance.

(in millions)

	1994	1993	1992	1991	1990
Net revenue (income)	$ 359	$ 279	$ 195	$ 162	$ 256
Revenue	9,011	8,903	9,147	9,502	11,303
Profit margin	4.0%	3.1%	2.1%	1.7%	2.3%

Note the positive trend in Imperial's profit margin in the last three years. However, this may be less favourable because the company's sales volume decreased 20% during the same period. Consequently, one may conclude that although the trend in Imperial's profit margin is favourable, you cannot conclude that the absolute values are good without further investigation, such as comparisons with other companies in the same industry.

Progress Check

4-11   **The profit margin is the ratio between a company's net income and total** *(a)* **expenses;** *(b)* **assets;** *(c)* **liabilities; or** *(d)* **revenues.**

4-12   **If a company had a profit margin of 22.5% and net income of $1,012,500, what was the total amount of its revenues for the reporting period?**

SUMMARY OF THE CHAPTER IN TERMS OF LEARNING OBJECTIVES

LO 1. Explain why work sheets are useful, prepare a work sheet for a service business, and prepare financial statements from the information in a work sheet. Accountants often use work sheets at the end of an accounting period in the process of preparing adjusting entries, the adjusted trial balance, and the financial statements. The work sheet is only a tool for accountants and is not distributed to investors or creditors. The work sheet described in this chapter has five pairs of columns for the unadjusted trial balance, the adjustments, the adjusted trial balance, the income statement, and the statement of changes in owner's equity and the balance sheet. Other formats are used in practice.

The income statement is prepared from the Income Statement columns of the work sheet by taking the revenues from the Credit column and the expenses from the Debit column. The net income is the difference between the debits and credits. The statement of changes in owner's equity combines the preclosing balance of the capital account (including the beginning balance plus any new investments), the net income from the Income Statement columns, and the owner's withdrawals. The balance sheet combines all assets, contra assets, and liabilities from the last two columns of the work sheet with the ending balance of owner's equity presented in the statement of changes in owner's equity.

LO 2. Explain why the temporary accounts are closed at the end of each accounting period and prepare closing entries and a post-closing trial balance for a service business. The temporary accounts are closed at the end of each accounting period for two reasons. First, this process updates the owner's equity account to include the effects of all economic events recorded for the year. Second, it prepares the revenue, expense, and withdrawals accounts for the next reporting period by giving them zero balances. The revenue and expense account balances are initially transferred to the Income Summary account, which is then closed to the owner's capital account. Finally, the withdrawals account is closed to the capital account.

LO 3. Describe each step in the accounting cycle. The accounting cycle consists of eight steps: (1) journalizing external transactions and (2) posting the entries during the year, and at the end of the year: (3) preparing either an unadjusted trial balance or (4) a work sheet, (5) preparing and posting adjusting entries, (6) preparing the financial statements, (7) preparing and posting closing entries, and (8) preparing the post-closing trial balance.

LO 4. Calculate the profit margin ratio and describe what it reveals about a company's performance. The profit margin ratio describes a company's income earning activities by showing the period's net income as a percentage of total revenue. It is found by dividing the reporting period's net income by the revenue for the same period. The ratio can be usefully interpreted only in light of additional facts about the company and its industry.

This six-column table shows the December 31, 1996, adjusted trial balance of Westside Appliance Repair Company:

DEMONSTRATION PROBLEM

	Adjusted Trial Balance		Closing Entries		Post-Closing Trial Balance	
Cash	83,300					
Notes receivable	60,000					
Prepaid insurance	19,000					
Prepaid rent	5,000					
Equipment	165,000					
Accumulated amortization, equipment ..		52,000				
Accounts payable		37,000				
Long-term notes payable		58,000				
B. Westside, capital		173,500				
B. Westside, withdrawals	25,000					
Repair services revenue		294,000				
Interest earned		6,500				
Amortization expense, equipment	26,000					
Wages expense	179,000					
Rent expense	47,000					
Insurance expense	7,000					
Interest expense	4,700					
Income summary						
Totals	621,000	621,000				

The beginning balance of the capital account was $140,500, and the owner invested $33,000 cash in the company on June 15, 1996.

Required

1. Prepare closing entries for Westside Appliance Repair Co.
2. Complete the six-column schedule.
3. Post the closing entries to this capital account:

B. Westside, Capital   **Account No.** 301

Date	Explanation	Debit	Credit	Balance
1996				
Jan. 1	Beginning balance			140,500.00
June 15	New investment		33,000.00	173,500.00

• Prepare entries to close the revenue accounts to Income Summary, to close the expense accounts to Income Summary, to close Income Summary to the capital account, and to close the withdrawals account to the capital account.

Planning the Solution

- Enter the four closing entries in the second pair of columns in the six-column schedule, and then extend the balances of the asset and liability accounts to the third pair of columns.

- Enter the post-closing balance of the capital account in the last column. Examine the totals of the columns to verify that they are equal.

- Post the third and fourth closing entries to the capital account.

Solution to Demonstration Problem

1.

Dec.	31	Repair Services Revenue	294,000.00	
		Interest Earned	6,500.00	
		Income Summary		300,500.00
		To close the revenue accounts and create the Income Summary account.		
	31	Income Summary	263,700.00	
		Amortization Expense, Equipment		26,000.00
		Wages Expense		179,000.00
		Rent Expense		47,000.00
		Insurance Expense		7,000.00
		Interest Expense		4,700.00
		To close the expense accounts.		
	31	Income Summary	36,800.00	
		B. Westside, Capital		36,800.00
		To close the Income Summary account and add the net income to the capital account.		
	31	B. Westside, Capital	25,000.00	
		B. Westside, Withdrawals		25,000.00
		To close the withdrawals account and reduce the balance of the capital account.		

2.

	Adjusted Trial Balance		Closing Entries		Post-Closing Trial Balance	
Cash	83,300				83,300	
Notes receivable	60,000				60,000	
Prepaid insurance	19,000				19,000	
Prepaid rent	5,000				5,000	
Equipment	165,000				165,000	
Accumulated amortization, equipment ..		52,000				52,000
Accounts payable		37,000				37,000
Long-term notes payable		58,000				58,000
B. Westside, capital		173,500	(4) 25,000	(3) 36,800		185,300
B. Westside, withdrawals	25,000			(4) 25,000		
Repair services revenue		294,000	(1) 294,000			
Interest earned		6,500	(1) 6,500			
Amortization expense, equipment	26,000			(2) 26,000		
Wages expense	179,000			(2) 179,000		
Rent expense	47,000			(2) 47,000		
Insurance expense	7,000			(2) 7,000		
Interest expense	4,700			(2) 4,700		
Income summary			(2) 263,700	(1) 300,500		
....		(3) 36,800				
Totals	621,000	621,000	626,000	626,000	332,300	332,300

3.

B. Westside, Capital   Account No. 301

Date		Explanation	Debit	Credit	Balance
1996					
Jan.	1	Beginning balance			140,500.00
June	15	New investment		33,000.00	173,500.00
Dec.	31	Net income		36,800.00	210,300.00
	31	Withdrawals	25,000.00		185,300.00

Reversing Entries

LO 6

Explain when and why reversing entries are used and prepare reversing entries.

Reversing entries are optional entries that relate to accrued assets and liabilities created by adjusting entries at the end of a reporting period. Reversing entries are used for the practical purpose of simplifying a company's bookkeeping process.

Illustration C–1 shows how reversing entries work. The top of the diagram shows the adjusting entry that Clear Copy recorded on December 31, 1996, for the employee's earned but unpaid salary. The entry recorded three days' salary to increase December's total salary expense to $1,610. The entry also recognized a liability of $210. The expense is reported on December's income statement and the expense account is closed. As a result, the ledger on January 1, 1997, reflects a $210 liability and a zero balance in the Salaries Expense account. At this point, the choice is made between using or not using reversing entries.

BOOKKEEPING WITHOUT REVERSING ENTRIES

The path down the left side of Illustration C–1 was described in Chapter 3. When the next payday occurs on January 9, the bookkeeper records the payment with a compound entry that debits both the expense and liability accounts. Posting the entry creates a $490 balance in the expense account and reduces the liability account balance to zero because the debt has been settled.

The disadvantage of this approach is the complex entry on January 9. Paying the accrued liability causes the entry to differ from the routine entries made on all other paydays. To construct the proper entry on January 9, the bookkeeper must be informed of the effect of the adjusting entry. Reversing entries overcome this disadvantage.

BOOKKEEPING WITH REVERSING ENTRIES

The right side of Illustration C–1 shows how a reversing entry on January 1 overcomes the disadvantage of the complex January 9 entry. The reversing entry is the exact opposite of the adjusting entry recorded on December 31. In other words, the Salaries Payable liability is debited for $210, with the result that the account has a zero balance after the entry is posted. Technically, the Salaries Payable account now understates the liability, but no problem exists because financial statements will not be prepared before the liability is settled on January 9.

The credit to the Salaries Expense account is unusual because it gives the account an *abnormal credit balance.* This account's balance is also temporary and does not cause a problem because financial statements will not be prepared before January 9.

As a result of the reversing entry, the January 9 entry to record the payment is simple. Notice that it debits the Salaries Expense account for the full $700 paid. This entry is the same as all other entries made to record 10 days' salary for the employee.

Look next at the accounts on the lower right side of Illustration C–1. After the payment entry is posted, the Salaries Expense account has the $490 balance that

Illustration C–1 Reversing Entries for Accrued Expenses

Accrue salaries expense on December 31, 1996

Salaries Expense ———————— 210
   Salaries Payable ——————— 210

Salaries Expense

Date	Expl.	Debit	Credit	Balance
1996				
Dec. 12	(7)	700		700
26	(16)	700		1,400
31	(e)	210		1,610

Salaries Payable

Date	Expl.	Debit	Credit	Balance
1996				
Dec. 31	(e)		210	210

No reversing entry recorded on January 1, 1997

NO ENTRY

Salaries Expense

Date	Expl.	Debit	Credit	Balance
1997				

Salaries Payable

Date	Expl.	Debit	Credit	Balance
1996				
Dec. 31	(e)		210	210
1997				

Reversing entry recorded on January 1, 1997

Salaries Payable ———————— 210
   Salaries Expense ———————— 210

Salaries Expense

Date	Expl.	Debit	Credit	Balance
1997				
Jan. 1			210	(210)

Salaries Payable

Date	Expl.	Debit	Credit	Balance
1996				
Dec. 31	(e)		210	210
1997		210		0
Jan. 1				

Pay the accrued and current salaries on January 9, the first payday in 1997

Salaries Expense ———————— 490
Salaries Payable ———————— 210
   Cash ————————— 700

Salaries Expense

Date	Expl.	Debit	Credit	Balance
1997				
Jan. 9		490		490

Salaries Payable

Date	Expl.	Debit	Credit	Balance
1996				
Dec. 31	(e)		210	210
1997				0
Jan. 9		210		

Salaries Expense ———————— 700
   Cash ————————— 700

Salaries Expense

Date	Expl.	Debit	Credit	Balance
1997				
Jan. 1		700	210	(210)
Jan. 9				490

Salaries Payable

Date	Expl.	Debit	Credit	Balance
1996				
Dec. 31	(e)		210	210
1997				0
Jan. 1		210		

Under both approaches, the expense and liability accounts have the same balances after the subsequent payment on January 9:

Salaries Expense——————— $ 490
Salaries Payable ——————— $ 0

it should have to reflect seven days' salary of $70 per day. The zero balance in the Salaries Payable account is now correct. Then, the lower section of the illustration shows that the expense and liability accounts have exactly the same balances whether reversing occurs or not.

As a general rule, adjusting entries that create new asset or new liability accounts are the best candidates for reversing.

SUMMARY OF APPENDIX C IN TERMS OF LEARNING OBJECTIVES

LO 6. **Explain when and why reversing entries are used and prepare reversing entries.** Optional reversing entries can be applied to accrued assets and liabilities, including accrued interest earned, accrued interest expense, accrued taxes, and accrued salaries or wages. The goal of reversing entries is to simplify subsequent journal entries. The financial statements are not affected by the choice. Reversing entries are used simply as a matter of convenience in bookkeeping.

Accounting for Partnerships and Corporations

In the early chapters we use the "Proprietorship Approach," that is, the accounting model is based on a single proprietor. Accounting for partnerships and corporations is discussed in detail in Chapters 14, 15, and 16. Appendix D to this chapter facilitates those individuals who desire to introduce accounting for partnerships and corporations at this stage.

Accounting for a partnership is like accounting for a single proprietorship except for transactions that directly affect the partners' capital and withdrawals accounts. These transactions require a capital account and a withdrawals account for each partner. To close the Income Summary account, make a compound entry that allocates to each partner his or her share of the net income or loss such as the following:

Dec.	31	Income Summary	7,000.00	
		Julie Ehlers, Capital		3,000.00
		Megan Brinkoeter, Capital		4,000.00
		To close the Income Summary account.		

CORPORATE ACCOUNTING

LO 7
Explain the nature of a corporation's retained earnings and their relationship to the declaration of dividends.

Accounting for a corporation also differs from that of a single proprietorship for transactions that affect the equity accounts of the corporation. The accounts of a corporation are designed to distinguish between equity resulting from amounts invested in the corporation by its shareholders and equity resulting from earnings. This distinction is important because a corporation generally cannot pay a legal dividend unless it has shareholders' equity resulting from earnings. In making the distinction, two kinds of shareholders' equity accounts are kept: (1) *contributed capital accounts* and (2) *retained earnings accounts.* Amounts invested in a corporation (contributed) by its shareholders are shown in contributed capital accounts such as the Common Share account. Shareholders' equity resulting from earnings is shown in a retained earnings account.

To demonstrate corporate accounting, assume that five persons secured a certificate of incorporation for a new corporation. Each invested $10,000 in the corporation by buying 1,000 of its common shares. The corporation's entry to record their investments is

Jan.	5	Cash	50,000.00	
		Common Shares		50,000.00
		Issued 5,000 common shares for cash.		

If during its first year the corporation earned $20,000, the entry to close its Income Summary account is

Dec.	31	Income Summary	20,000.00	
		Retained Earnings		20,000.00
		To close the Income Summary account.		

If these are the only entries that affected the Common Shares and Retained Earnings accounts during the first year, the corporation's year-end balance sheet will show the shareholders' equity as follows:

Shareholders' Equity

Share capital–common: 5,000 shares outstanding ..	$50,000	
Retained earnings	20,000	
Total shareholders' equity		$70,000

Because a corporation is a separate legal entity, the names of its shareholders usually are of little interest to a balance sheet reader and are not shown in the equity section. However, in this case, the section does show that the net asset or equity of the corporation is $70,000. Of this amount, $50,000 resulted from the issuance of shares to the shareholders and $20,000 was the result of net income that has not been paid out as dividends.

Perhaps the concept of retained earnings would be clearer if the balance sheet item were labeled "Shareholders' equity resulting from earnings." However, the retained earnings caption is commonly used; it does not represent a specific amount of cash or any other asset. These are shown in the asset section of the balance sheet. Retained earnings represent the shareholders' equity resulting from earnings.

LO 8

Prepare entries to record the declaration and payment of a dividend and to close the temporary accounts of a corporation.

To continue, assume that on January 10 of the corporation's second year, its board of directors met and by vote declared a $1 per share dividend payable on February 1 to the January 25 **shareholders of record** (shareholders according to the corporation's records). The entry to record the declaration of the dividend is as follows:

Jan.	10	Cash Dividends Declared	5,000.00	
		Common Dividend Payable		5,000.00
		Declared a $1 per share dividend.		

The **Cash Dividends Declared**[1] account is a temporary account that serves the same function for a corporation as does a withdrawals account for a proprietorship. At the end of each period, the Cash Dividends Declared account is closed to Retained Earnings. The entry to record the payment of the dividend is as follows:

Feb.	01	Common Dividend Payable	5,000.00	
		Cash		5,000.00
		Paid the dividend declared on January 10.		

Note from the two entries that the dividend declaration reduces shareholders' equity and increases liabilities, while the payment of the dividend reduces the corporation's assets and liabilities. The net result is to reduce assets and shareholders' equity just as a withdrawal of cash by the owner of a single proprietorship reduces assets and the owner's equity.

A cash dividend is normally paid by mailing cheques to the shareholders. Also, in this case, three dates are normally involved in a dividend declaration and payment. They are (1) the **date of declaration**, (2) the **date of record**, and (3) the **date of payment**. On the date of declaration, the dividend becomes a liability of the corporation. However, if some shareholders sell their shares to new investors in time for the new shareholders to be listed in the corporation's records on the date of record, the new shareholders will receive the dividend on the date of payment. Otherwise, the dividend will be paid to the old shareholders.

A dividend must be formally voted by a corporation's board of directors. Also, courts have generally held that the board is the final judge of when a dividend should be paid. Therefore, shareholders have no right to a dividend until it is declared. However, as soon as a cash dividend is declared, it becomes a liability of the corporation, normally a current liability, and must be paid. Furthermore, shareholders have the right to sue and force payment of a cash dividend once it is declared.

If during its second year (1996) the corporation suffered a $7,000 net loss, the entries to close its Income Summary and Dividends Declared accounts are:

1996 Dec.	31	Retained Earnings	7,000.00	
		Income Summary		7,000.00
		To close the Income Summary account.		
	31	Retained Earnings	5,000.00	
		Cash Dividends Declared		5,000.00
		To close the Cash Dividends Declared account.		

Now assume that during 1997, the corporation paid no dividends but suffered a net loss of $14,000. The entry to close the Income Summary account at the end of 1997 is

---

[1] Some corporations prefer to debit retained earnings directly at the time of dividend declaration. The Cash Dividend Declared account is used to illustrate the parallelism in accounting for withdrawals in proprietorships and partnerships and dividends in corporate accounting.

1997					
Dec.	31	Retained Earnings		14,000.00	
		Income Summary			14,000.00
		To close the Income Summary account.			

Posting these entries has the following effects on the Retained Earnings account:

	Retained Earnings				Acct. No. 318	
Date		**Explanation**	**PR**	**Debit**	**Credit**	**Balance**
1995						
Dec.	31	Net income	G4		20,000.00	20,000.00
1996						
Dec.	31	Net loss	G5	7,000.00		13,000.00
	31	Cash dividends declared	G7	5,000.00		8,000.00
1997						
Dec.	31	Net loss	G9	14,000.00		6,000.00 Dr.

Due to the dividend and the net losses, the Retained Earnings account has a $6,000 debit balance. A debit balance in a Retained Earnings account indicates a negative amount of retained earnings. A corporation with a negative amount of retained earnings is said to have a **deficit**. A deficit may be shown on a corporation's balance sheet as follows:

Shareholders' Equity	
Share capital–common: 5,000 shares outstanding ..	$50,000
Deduct retained earnings deficit	(6,000)
Total shareholders' equity	$44,000

In most jurisdictions, a corporation with a deficit is not allowed to pay a cash dividend. This legal requirement is intended to protect the creditors of the corporation. Because a corporation is a separate legal entity, it is responsible for its own debts. However, the corporation's shareholders normally are not responsible for the corporation's debts. Therefore, if a corporation's creditors are to be paid, they must be paid from the corporation's assets. By making dividends illegal when there is a deficit, a corporation in financial difficulty is prevented from paying its assets in dividends and leaving nothing for payment of its creditors. (You will learn more about partnerships and corporations in Chapters 14, 15, and 16.)

SUMMARY OF APPENDIX D IN TERMS OF LEARNING OBJECTIVES

LO 7. Explain the nature of a corporation's retained earnings and their relationship to the declaration of dividends. Retained earnings is the total amount of net incomes a corporation has earned since it was organized, less the total of losses and the total of dividends declared.

LO 8. Prepare entries to record the declaration and payment of a dividend and to close the temporary accounts of a corporation. Dividend declarations are recorded with a debit to a temporary account called Dividends Declared and a credit to a liability account. Payment in cash is recorded like any other liability.

GLOSSARY

Accounting cycle eight recurring steps performed each accounting period, starting with recording transactions in the journal and continuing through the post-closing trial balance. p. 197

Cash Dividends Declared a temporary account that serves the same function for a corporation as does a withdrawals account for a proprietorship and that is closed to Retained Earnings at the end of each accounting period. p. 209

Closing entries journal entries recorded at the end of each accounting period to prepare the revenue, expense, and withdrawals accounts for the upcoming year and update the owner's capital account for the events of the year just finished. p. 189

Date of declaration the date on which a dividend is declared by vote of a corporation's board of directors. p. 209

Date of payment the date on which a dividend liability of a corporation is satisfied by mailing cheques to the shareholders. p. 209

Date of record the date on which the shareholders who are listed in a corporation's records are determined to be those who will receive a dividend. p. 209

Deficit a negative amount (debit balance) of retained earnings. p. 210

Income Summary the special account used only in the closing process to temporarily hold the amounts of revenues and expenses before the net difference is added to (or subtracted from) the owner's capital account or the Retained Earnings account for a corporation. p. 190

Nominal accounts another name for *temporary accounts*. p. 193

Permanent accounts accounts that are used to describe assets, liabilities, and owner's equity; they are not closed as long as the company continues to own the assets, owe the liabilities, or have owner's equity; the balances of these accounts appear on the balance sheet. p. 193

Post-closing trial balance a trial balance prepared after the closing entries have been posted; the final step in the accounting cycle. p. 192

Profit margin the ratio of a company's net income to its revenues; measures the average proportion of each dollar of revenue that ends up as profit. p. 199

Pro forma statements statements that show the effects of the proposed transactions as if the transactions had already occurred. p. 188

Real accounts another name for *permanent accounts*. p. 193

Return on sales another name for *profit margin*. p. 199

Reversing entries optional entries recorded at the beginning of a new year that prepare the accounts for simplified journal entries subsequent to accrual adjusting entries. p. 204

Shareholders of record the shareholders of a corporation as reflected in the records of the corporation. p. 208

Temporary accounts accounts that are used to describe revenues, expenses, and owner's withdrawals; they are closed at the end of the reporting period. p. 193

Work sheet a 10-column spreadsheet used to draft a company's unadjusted trial balance, adjusting entries, adjusted trial balance, and financial statements; an optional step in the accounting process. p. 184

Working papers analyses and other informal reports prepared by accountants when organizing the useful information presented in formal reports to internal and external decision makers. p. 184

SYNONYMOUS TERMS

Permanent accounts real accounts; balance sheet accounts

Temporary accounts nominal accounts

The letters C and D identify the questions, quick studies, exercises, and problems based on Appendixes C and D at the end of the chapter.

QUESTIONS

1. What tasks are performed with the work sheet?
2. Why are the debit and credit entries in the Adjustments columns of the work sheet identified with letters?

3. What internal document is produced by combining the amounts in the Unadjusted Trial Balance columns with the amounts in the Adjustments columns of the work sheet?

4. What two purposes are accomplished by recording closing entries?

5. What are the four closing entries?

6. What accounts are affected by closing entries? What accounts are not affected?

7. Describe the similarities and differences between adjusting and closing entries.

8. What is the purpose of the Income Summary account?

9. Explain whether an error has occurred if a post-closing trial balance includes an Amortization Expense, Building account.

C10. How are the financial statements of a company affected by the accountant's choice to use or not use reversing entries?

C11. How do reversing entries simplify a company's bookkeeping efforts?

C12. If a company accrued unpaid salaries expense of $500 at the end of a fiscal year, what reversing entry could be made? When would it be made?

QUICK STUDY (Five-Minute Exercises)

QS 4–1
(LO 1)

In preparing a work sheet, indicate the financial statement debit column to which a normal balance of each of the following accounts should be extended. Use IS for the Income Statement Debit column and BS for the Statement of Changes in Owner's Equity or Balance Sheet Debit column.

1. Accounts receivable
2. Owner, withdrawals
3. Prepaid insurance
4. Insurance expense
5. Equipment
6. Amortization expense, equipment

QS 4–2
(LO 1)

The following information is from the work sheet for Pursley Company as of December 31, 1996. Using this information, determine the amount that should be reported for A. Pursley, capital on the December 31, 1996, balance sheet.

	Income Statement		Statement of Changes in Owner's Equity and Balance Sheet	
	Dr.	Cr.	Dr.	Cr.
A. Pursley, capital				50,000
A. Pursley, withdrawals			32,000	
Totals	125,000	184,000		

QS 4–3
(LO 2)

Using the information presented in QS 4–2, prepare the entries to close the Income Summary and the withdrawals accounts.

QS 4–4
(LO 3)

List the following steps of the accounting cycle in the proper order:

a. Preparing the post-closing trial balance.
b. Journalizing and posting adjusting entries.
c. Preparing the unadjusted trial balance.
d. Journalizing and posting closing entries.
e. Journalizing transactions.
f. Posting the transaction entries.
g. Preparing the financial statements.
h. Completing the work sheet.

Gruene Corporation had net income of $75,850 and revenue of $410,000 for the year ended December 31, 1996. Calculate Gruene's profit margin.

QS 4–5
(LO 4)

On December 31, 1996, Ace Management Co. prepared an adjusting entry for $9,800 of earned but unrecorded rent revenue. On January 20, 1997, Ace received rent payments in the amount of $15,500. Assuming Ace uses reversing entries, prepare the 1997 entries pertaining to the rent transactions.

^CQS 4–6
(LO 6)

EXERCISES

These accounts are from the Adjusted Trial Balance columns in a company's 10-column work sheet. In the blank space beside each account, write the letter of the appropriate financial statement column to which a normal account balance should be extended.

A. Debit column for the income statement

B. Credit column for the income statement

C. Debit column for the statement of changes in owner's equity and balance sheet

D. Credit column for the statement of changes in owner's equity and balance sheet

Exercise 4–1
Extending adjusted
account balances on a
work sheet
(LO 1)

___ 1. R. Jefferson, Withdrawals

___ 2. Interest Earned

___ 3. Accumulated Amortization, Machinery

___ 4. Service Fees Revenue

___ 5. Accounts Receivable

___ 6. Rent Expense

___ 7. Amortization Expense, Machinery

___ 8. Accounts Payable

___ 9. Cash

___ 10. Office Supplies

___ 11. R. Jefferson, Capital

___ 12. Wages Payable

___ 13. Machinery

___ 14. Insurance Expense

___ 15. Interest Expense

___ 16. Interest Receivable

Use the following information from the Adjustments columns of a 10-column work sheet to prepare adjusting journal entries:

Exercise 4–2
Preparing adjusting
entries from work sheet
information
(LO 1)

No.	Title	Adjustments Debit	Adjustments Credit
109	Interest receivable	(d) 380	
124	Office supplies		(b) 1,350
128	Prepaid insurance		(a) 1,000
164	Accumulated amortization, office equipment ..		(c) 3,500
209	Salaries payable		(e) 660
409	Interest earned		(d) 380
612	Amortization expense, office equipment	(c) 3,500	
620	Office salaries expense	(e) 660	
636	Insurance expense, office equipment	(a) 432	
637	Insurance expense, store equipment	(a) 568	
650	Office supplies expense	(b) 1,350	
	Totals	6,890	6,890

The following unadjusted trial balance contains the accounts and balances of the Fine Painting Co. as of December 31, 1996, the end of its fiscal year:

Exercise 4–3
Preparing a work sheet
(LO 1)

No.	Title	Debit	Credit
101	Cash	$18,000	
126	Supplies	12,000	
128	Prepaid insurance	2,000	
167	Equipment	23,000	
168	Accumulated amortization, equipment .		$ 6,500
209	Salaries payable		
301	B. Fine, capital		31,900
302	B. Fine, withdrawals	6,000	
404	Services revenue		36,000
612	Amortization expense, equipment		
622	Salaries expense	11,000	
637	Insurance expense		
640	Rent expense	2,400	
652	Supplies expense		
	Totals	$74,400	$74,400

Required

Use the following information about the company's adjustments to complete a 10-column work sheet for the company:

a.   The cost of expired insurance coverage was $300.

b.   The cost of unused supplies on hand at the end of the year was $1,600.

c.   Amortization of the equipment for the year was $3,250.

d.   Earned but unpaid salaries at the end of the year were $250.

Exercise 4–4
Adjusting and closing entries
(LO 2)

Use the information in Exercise 4–3 to prepare adjusting and closing journal entries for Fine Painting Co. (It is helpful but not mandatory to solve Exercise 4–3 first.)

Exercise 4–5
Completing the income statement columns and preparing closing entries
(LO 1, 2)

These partially completed Income Statement columns from a 10-column work sheet are for the Winston Sail'em Boat Rental Company. Use the information to determine the amount that should be entered on the Net income line of the work sheet. In addition, draft closing entries for the company. The owner's name is C. Winston, and the preclosing balance of the withdrawals account is $18,000.

	Debit	Credit
Rent earned		99,000
Salaries expense	35,300	
Insurance expense	4,400	
Dock rental expense	12,000	
Boat supplies expense	6,220	
Amortization expense, boats	21,500	
Totals		
Net income		
Totals		

Exercise 4–6
Extending accounts in the work sheet
(LO 1)

The Adjusted Trial Balance columns of a 10-column work sheet for the Plummer Plumbing Co. follow. Complete the work sheet by extending the account balances into the appropriate financial statement columns and by entering the amount of net income for the reporting period.

No.	Title	Adjusted Trial Balance	
101	Cash	$ 8,200	
106	Accounts receivable	24,000	
153	Trucks	41,000	
154	Accumulated amortization, trucks		$ 16,500
193	Franchise	30,000	
201	Accounts payable		14,000
209	Salaries payable		3,200
233	Unearned fees		2,600
301	F. Plummer, capital		64,500
302	F. Plummer, withdrawals	14,400	
401	Plumbing fees earned		79,000
611	Amortization expense, trucks	11,000	
622	Salaries expense	31,500	
640	Rent expense	12,000	
677	Miscellaneous expenses	7,700	
	Totals	$179,800	$179,800
	Net income		
	Totals		

The adjusted trial balance for Plummer Plumbing Co. follows. Prepare a table with two columns under each of the following headings: Adjusted Trial Balance, Closing Entries, and Post-Closing Trial Balance. Complete the table by providing four closing entries and the post-closing trial balance.

Exercise 4–7
Preparing closing entries and the post-closing trial balance
(LO 2)

No.	Title	Adjusted Trial Balance	
101	Cash	$ 8,200	
106	Accounts receivable	24,000	
153	Trucks	41,000	
154	Accumulated amortization, trucks		$ 16,500
193	Franchise	30,000	
201	Accounts payable		14,000
209	Salaries payable		3,200
233	Unearned fees		2,600
301	F. Plummer, capital		64,500
302	F. Plummer, withdrawals	14,400	
401	Plumbing fees earned		79,000
611	Amortization expense, trucks	11,000	
622	Salaries expense	31,500	
640	Rent expense	12,000	
677	Miscellaneous expenses	7,700	
901	Income summary		
	Totals	$179,800	$179,800

The following balances of the retained earnings and temporary accounts are for High Ridge, Inc., from its adjusted trial balance:

Exercise 4–8
Closing entries for a corporation
(LO 2)

	Debit	Credit
Retained earnings		$43,200
Services revenue		62,000
Interest earned		5,800
Salaries expense	$23,500	
Insurance expense	4,050	
Rental expense	6,400	
Supplies expense	3,100	
Amortization expense, trucks	10,600	

Required

a. Prepare the closing entries for this corporation.

b. Determine the amount of retained earnings to be reported on the company's balance sheet.

Exercise 4–9
Preparing and posting
closing entries
(LO 2, 3)

Open the following T-accounts with the provided balances. Prepare closing journal entries and post them to the accounts.

B. Holley, Capital			Rent Expense		
	Dec. 31	44,000	Dec. 31	9,600	

B. Holley, Withdrawals			Salaries Expense		
Dec. 31	21,000		Dec. 31	24,000	

Income Summary			Insurance Expense		
			Dec. 31	3,500	

Services Revenue			Amortization Expense		
	Dec. 31	77,000	Dec. 31	15,000	

Exercise 4–10
Calculating the profit
margin
(LO 4)

Use the following information to calculate the profit margin for each case:

	Net Income	Revenue
a.	$ 1,745	$ 10,540
b.	48,372	131,651
c.	55,102	84,262
d.	27,513	450,266
e.	39,632	144,638

CExercise 4–11
Reversing entries
(LO 6)

The following information was used to prepare adjusting entries for the Maritime Company as of August 31, the end of the company's fiscal year:

a. The company has earned $3,000 of unrecorded service fees.

b. The expired portion of prepaid insurance is $2,400.

c. The earned portion of the Unearned Fees account balance is $1,700.

d. Amortization expense for the office equipment is $3,300.

e. Employees have earned but have not been paid salaries of $2,250.

Required

Prepare the reversing entries that would simplify the bookkeeping effort for recording subsequent events related to these adjustments.

CExercise 4–12
Reversing entries
(LO 6)

The following two conditions existed for Lomax Company on September 30, 1996, the end of its fiscal year:

a. Lomax rents a building from its owner for $2,400 per month. By a prearrangement, the company delayed paying September's rent until October 5. On this date, the company paid the rent for both September and October.

b. Lomax rents space in a building it owns to a tenant for $655 per month. By pre-arrangement, the tenant delayed paying the September rent until October 8. On this date, the tenant paid the rent for both September and October.

Required

1. Prepare the adjusting entries that Lomax should record for these situations as of September 30.

2. Assuming that Lomax does not use reversing entries, prepare journal entries to record Lomax's payment of rent on October 5 and the collection of rent on October 8 from Lomax's tenant.

3. Assuming that Lomax does use reversing entries, prepare those entries and the journal entries to record Lomax's payment of rent on October 5 and the collection of rent on October 8 from Lomax's tenant.

A corporation debited Cash Dividends Declared for $50,000 during the year ended December 31. The items that follow appeared in the Income Statement columns of the work sheet prepared at year-end. Prepare closing journal entries for the corporation.

ᴰExercise 4–13
Closing entries for a corporation
(LO 8)

	Income Statement	
	Debit	**Credit**
Services revenue		285,700
Office salaries expense	187,000	
Rent expense	18,000	
Insurance expense	4,400	
Office supplies expense	400	
Amortization expense, office equipment ..	5,100	
	214,900	285,700
Net income	70,800	
	285,700	285,700

1. On a sheet of notepaper, open the following T-accounts: Cash, Accounts Receivable, Equipment, Notes Payable, Common Dividend Payable, Common Shares, Retained Earnings, Income Summary, Cash Dividends Declared, Services Revenue, and Operating Expenses.

ᴰExercise 4–14
Recording corporate transactions in T-accounts
(LO 8)

2. Record directly in the T-accounts these transactions of a new corporation:

a. Issued common shares for $150,000 cash.

b. Purchased equipment for $146,500 cash.

c. Sold and delivered $30,000 of services on credit.

d. Collected $27,000 of accounts receivable.

e. Paid $18,000 of operating expenses.

f. Declared cash dividends of $7,500.

g. Paid the dividends declared in (f).

h. Purchased $12,000 of additional equipment, giving $5,000 in cash and a $7,000 promissory note.

i. Closed the revenue accounts, (j) the expense accounts, (k) Income Summary, and (l) Cash Dividends Declared.

3. Answer these questions:

   a. Does the corporation have retained earnings?

   b. Does it have any cash?

   c. If the corporation has retained earnings, why does it not also have cash?

   d. Can the corporation legally declare additional cash dividends?

   e. Can it pay additional cash dividends?

   f. What does the balance of the Notes Payable account tell the financial statement reader about the makeup of the corporation's assets?

   g. Explain what the balance of the Common Shares account represents.

   h. Explain what the balance of the Retained Earnings account represents.

PROBLEMS

Problem 4–1
The work sheet, adjusting and closing entries, financial statements, and profit margin
(LO 1, 2, 4)

Dunagin's Repairs opened for business on January 1, 1996. By the end of the year, the company's unadjusted trial balance appeared as follows:

DUNAGIN'S REPAIRS
Unadjusted Trial Balance
December 31, 1996

No.	Title	Debit	Credit
101	Cash	$ 3,000	
124	Office supplies	3,800	
128	Prepaid insurance	2,650	
167	Equipment	48,000	
168	Accumulated amortization, equipment		
201	Accounts payable		$ 12,000
210	Wages payable		
301	R. Dunagin, capital		30,000
302	R. Dunagin, withdrawals	15,000	
401	Repair fees earned		77,750
612	Amortization expense, equipment		
623	Wages expense	36,000	
637	Insurance expense		
640	Rent expense	9,600	
650	Office supplies expense		
690	Utilities expense	1,700	
	Totals	$119,750	$119,750

Required

Preparation component:

1. Enter the unadjusted trial balance on a 10-column work sheet and complete the work sheet using this information:

   a. An inventory of the office supplies at the end of the year showed that $700 of supplies were on hand.

   b. The cost of expired insurance coverage was $660.

   c. The year's amortization on the equipment was $4,000.

   d. The earned but unpaid wages at the end of the year were $500.

2. Present the adjusting entries and closing entries as they would appear in the journal.

3. Use the information in the work sheet to prepare an income statement, a statement of changes in owner's equity, and a classified balance sheet.

4. Determine the company's profit margin.

Analysis component:

5. Assume that the facts presented in requirement 1 differ as follows:

    a. None of the $2,650 prepaid insurance had expired.

    b. There were no earned but unpaid wages at the end of the year.

    Describe the changes in the financial statements that would result from these assumptions.

This unadjusted trial balance is for Blue Max Construction as of the end of its fiscal year. The beginning balance of the owner's capital account was $12,660 and the owner invested another $15,000 cash in the company during the year.

Problem 4–2
Work sheet, journal entries, financial statements, and profit margin
(LO 1, 2, 4)

BLUE MAX CONSTRUCTION
Unadjusted Trial Balance
September 30, 1997

No.	Title	Debit	Credit
101	Cash	$ 18,000	
126	Supplies	9,400	
128	Prepaid insurance	6,200	
167	Equipment	81,000	
168	Accumulated amortization, equipment ..		$ 20,250
201	Accounts payable		4,800
203	Interest payable		
208	Rent payable		
210	Wages payable		
213	Estimated business taxes payable		
251	Long-term notes payable		25,000
301	T. Morrison, capital		27,660
302	T. Morrison, withdrawals	36,000	
401	Construction fees earned		140,000
612	Amortization expense, equipment		
623	Wages expense	41,000	
633	Interest expense	1,500	
637	Insurance expense		
640	Rent expense	13,200	
652	Supplies expense		
683	Business taxes expense	5,000	
684	Repairs expense	2,510	
690	Utilities expense	3,900	
	Totals	$217,710	$217,710

Required

1. Prepare a 10-column work sheet for 1997, starting with the unadjusted trial balance and including these additional facts:

    a. The inventory of supplies at the end of the year had a cost of $2,500.

    b. The cost of expired insurance for the year is $4,000.

    c. Annual amortization on the equipment is $9,000.

d. The September utilities expense was not included in the trial balance because the bill arrived after it was prepared. Its $400 amount needs to be recorded.

e. The company's employees have earned $1,500 of accrued wages.

f. The lease for the office requires the company to pay total rent for the year equal to 10% of the company's annual revenues. The rent is paid to the building owner with monthly payments of $1,100. If the annual rent exceeds the total monthly payments, the company must pay the excess before October 31. If the total is less than the amount previously paid, the building owner will refund the difference by October 31.

g. Additional business taxes of $800 have been assessed on the company but have not been paid or recorded in the accounts.

h. The long-term note payable bears interest at 1% per month, which the company is required to pay by the 10th of the following month. The balance of the Interest Expense account equals the amount paid during the year. The interest for September has not yet been paid or recorded. In addition, the company is required to make a $5,000 payment on the note on November 30, 1997.

2. Use the work sheet to prepare the adjusting and closing entries.

3. Prepare an income statement, a statement of changes in owner's equity, and a classified balance sheet. Calculate the company's profit margin for the year.

4. Analyze the following independent errors and describe how each would affect the 10-column work sheet. Explain whether the error is likely to be discovered in completing the work sheet and, if not, the effect of the error on the financial statements.

a. The adjustment for supplies consumption credited Supplies for $2,500 and debited the same amount to Supplies Expense.

b. When completing the adjusted trial balance in the work sheet, the $18,000 cash balance was incorrectly entered in the Credit column.

Problem 4–3
End-of-period accounting procedures
(LO 1, 2, 3)

The unadjusted trial balance of Doc's Delivery Service is as follows:

DOC'S DELIVERY SERVICE
Unadjusted Trial Balance
December 31, 1996

Cash	$ 785	
Accounts receivable	1,000	
Prepaid insurance	3,415	
Office supplies	365	
Prepaid rent	375	
Office equipment	3,690	
Accumulated amortization, office equipment		$ 855
Delivery equipment	22,185	
Accumulated amortization, delivery equipment		4,725
Accounts payable		1,335
Unearned delivery service revenue		825
Mark Welby, capital		34,355
Mark Welby, withdrawals	18,000	
Delivery service revenue		62,325
Rent expense	3,750	
Telephone expense	515	
Office salaries expense	15,090	
Delivery wages expense	30,480	
Gas, oil, and repairs expense	4,770	
Totals	$104,420	$104,420

Required

1. Enter the unadjusted trial balance on a work sheet form and complete the work sheet using the information that follows:

    a. Expired insurance on the office equipment, $165, and on the delivery equipment, $2,665.

    b. An inventory showed $180 of unused office supplies on hand.

    c. Estimated amortization on the office equipment, $435, and (d) on the delivery equipment, $3,495.

    e. In December 1995, the company had prepaid the January 1996 rent for garage and office space occupied by the delivery service. This amount appears as the balance of the Prepaid Rent account. Rents for February through November were paid each month and debited to the Rent Expense account. As of December 31, 1996, the December rent had not been paid.

    f. The delivery service has contracts with three stores for the delivery of packages on a fixed-fee basis. Two of the stores made advance payments on their contracts, and the amounts paid were credited to the Unearned Delivery Service Revenue account. An examination of the contracts shows that $480 of the $825 paid was earned by the end of the accounting period. The third store's contract provides for a $380 monthly fee to be paid at the end of each month's service. One-half of a month's revenue has accrued on this contract but it is unrecorded.

    g. A $125 bill for repairs to a delivery truck during December arrived in the mail after the trial balance was prepared. The bill is unpaid and unrecorded.

    h. Office salaries, $60, and delivery wages, $145, have accrued but are unpaid and unrecorded.

2. Prepare an income statement, a statement of changes in owner's equity, and a classified balance sheet.

3. Journalize adjusting and closing entries.

4. Post the adjusting and closing entries to the accounts and prepare a post-closing trial balance. (If the working papers are not being used, omit this requirement.)

Your examination of the books of Dr. Milton Vacon, a local general practitioner, revealed that his nurse/secretary followed the cash basis of accounting in all matters with the exception of equipment. The equipment, which cost $42,000 at the time Dr. Vacon started practice (January 2, 1995), was set up as an asset and to date has not been amortized. The equipment had an estimated useful life of 10 years at which time it could be sold for an estimated $2,000. Upon further examination you were able to identify the relevant data as follows:

Problem 4–4
Financial statement preparation
(LO 1)

	1995	1996	1997
Reported income	$91,000	$96,000	$89,000
Supplies on hand at year-end	500	300	1,200
Wages not paid at year-end	1,600	1,800	1,500
Billings to the Provincial Hospital Insurance during December for which a cheque has not been received	10,000	8,000	12,000
Miscellaneous expenses owing at year-end	1,300	1,700	1,200
Cash on hand and in bank at year-end	6,000	5,000	8,000

Required

1. Compute the correct net income for each year using the accrual basis of accounting (show all supporting calculations).

2. Prepare the December 31, 1997, balance sheet. (Assume there were no other asset or liability accounts than the ones given above).

Problem 4–5
All steps in the accounting cycle (covers two accounting cycles)
(LO 1, 2, 3)

Tami Martin opened a real estate office she called Martin Realty. During May she completed these transactions:

May 3   Invested in the real estate agency $3,000 in cash and an automobile having a $15,000 fair value.

3   Rented furnished office space and paid one month's rent, $750.

4   Purchased office supplies for cash, $225.

8   Paid the premium on a one-year insurance policy, $1,080.

14   Paid the salary of the office secretary for two weeks, $600.

16   Sold a house and collected an $8,010 commission.

28   Paid the salary of the office secretary for two weeks, $600.

31   Paid the May telephone bill, $75.

31   Paid for gas and oil used in the agency car during May, $90.

Required Work for May

1. Open these accounts: Cash; Prepaid Insurance; Office Supplies; Automobile; Accumulated Depreciation, Automobile; Salaries Payable; Tami Martin, Capital; Tami Martin, Withdrawals; Income Summary; Commissions Earned; Rent Expense; Salaries Expense; Gas, Oil, and Repairs Expense; Telephone Expense; Insurance Expense; Office Supplies Expense; and Amortization Expense, Automobile.

2. Prepare and post journal entries to record the transactions.

3. Prepare an unadjusted trial balance on a work sheet form and complete the work sheet using the following information:

    a. Two-thirds of a month's insurance has expired.

    b. An inventory shows $185 of unused office supplies remaining.

    c. Estimated amortization on the automobile, $250.

    d. Earned but unpaid salary of the office secretary, $60.

4. Prepare an income statement and a statement of changes in owner's equity for May, and prepare a May 31 classified balance sheet.

5. Journalize and post adjusting and closing entries.

6. Prepare a post-closing trial balance.

During June, Tami Martin completed these transactions:

June 1   Paid the June rent on the office space, $750.

4   Purchased additional office supplies for cash, $45.

11   Paid the salary of the office secretary for two weeks, $600.

15   Tami Martin withdrew $3,000 cash from the business for personal use.

18   Sold a building lot and collected a $2,200 commission.

25   Paid the salary of the office secretary for two weeks, $600.

30   Paid for gas and oil used in the agency car during June, $80.

30   Paid the June telephone bill, $65.

Required Work for June

1. Prepare and post journal entries to record the transactions.

2. Prepare an unadjusted trial balance on a work sheet form and complete the work sheet using the following information:

   a. One month's insurance has expired.

   b. An office supplies inventory shows $185 of unused supplies.

   c. Estimated amortization on the automobile, $250.

   d. Earned but unpaid secretary's salary, $180.

3. Prepare an income statement and a statement of changes in owner's equity for June and prepare a June 30 classified balance sheet.

4. Journalize and post adjusting and closing entries.

5. Prepare a post-closing trial balance.

On June 1, Jo Farr created a new travel agency called International Tours. These events occurred during the company's first month:

<table>
<tr><td>June 1</td><td>Farr created the new company by investing $20,000 cash and computer equipment worth $30,000.</td></tr>
<tr><td>2</td><td>The company rented furnished office space by paying $1,600 rent for the first month.</td></tr>
<tr><td>3</td><td>The company purchased $1,200 of office supplies for cash.</td></tr>
<tr><td>10</td><td>The company paid $3,600 for the premium on a one-year insurance policy.</td></tr>
<tr><td>14</td><td>The owner's assistant was paid $800 for two weeks' salary.</td></tr>
<tr><td>24</td><td>The company collected $6,800 of commissions from airlines on tickets obtained for customers.</td></tr>
<tr><td>28</td><td>The assistant was paid another $800 for two weeks' salary.</td></tr>
<tr><td>29</td><td>The company paid the month's $750 telephone bill.</td></tr>
<tr><td>30</td><td>The company paid $350 cash to repair the company's computer.</td></tr>
<tr><td>30</td><td>The owner withdrew $1,425 cash from the business.</td></tr>
</table>

Problem 4–6
Performing the steps in the accounting cycle
(LO 1, 2, 3)

The company's chart of accounts included these accounts:

101	Cash	405	Commissions Earned
106	Accounts Receivable	612	Amortization Expense, Computer
124	Office Supplies		Equipment
128	Prepaid Insurance	622	Salaries Expense
167	Computer Equipment	637	Insurance Expense
168	Accumulated Amortization,	640	Rent Expense
	Computer Equipment	650	Office Supplies Expense
209	Salaries Payable	684	Repairs Expense
301	J. Farr, Capital	688	Telephone Expense
302	J. Farr, Withdrawals	901	Income Summary

Required

1. Use the balance-column format to create each of the listed accounts.

2. Prepare journal entries to record the transactions for June and post them to the accounts.

3. Prepare a 10-column work sheet that starts with the unadjusted trial balance as of June 30. Use the following information to draft the adjustments for the month:

   a. Two-thirds of one month's insurance coverage was consumed.

   b. There were $800 of office supplies on hand at the end of the month.

    c.   Amortization on the computer equipment was estimated to be $825.

    d.   The assistant had earned $160 of unpaid and unrecorded salary.

    e.   The company had earned $1,750 of commissions that had not yet been billed.

     Complete the remaining columns of the worksheet.

4.   Prepare journal entries to record the adjustments drafted on the work sheet and post them to the accounts.

5.   Prepare an income statement, a statement of changes in owner's equity, and a balance sheet.

6.   Prepare journal entries to close the temporary accounts and post them to the accounts.

7.   Prepare a separate post-closing trial balance.

Problem 4–7
Financial reporting
problem
(LO 1)

The following balance sheet was prepared at the end of the company's fiscal year:

TENDER TUNES
Balance Sheet
December 31, 1996

Assets

Current assets:

Cash		$ 6,500
Prepaid insurance		600
Total current assets		8,600
Capital assets:		
Automobiles	$42,000	
Accumulated amortization, automobiles	(17,000)	$25,000
Office equipment	$40,000	
Accumulated amortization, office equipment	(13,500)	26,500
Total capital assets		51,500
Total assets		$60,100

Liabilities

Current liabilities:	
Accounts payable	$ 4,200
Interest payable	400
Salaries payable	1,100
Unearned fees	1,800
Total current liabilities	$ 7,500
Noncurrent liabilities:	
Long-term notes payable	40,000
Total liabilities	$47,500

Owner's Equity

Charlie Griffin, capital	12,600
Total liabilities and owner's equity	$60,100

The company's accountant also prepared and posted the following adjusting and closing entries:

Dec.	31	Insurance Expense	800.00	
		Prepaid Insurance		800.00
		To record consumed insurance coverage.		

31	Office Supplies Expense	4,100.00	
	Office Supplies		4,100.00
	To record consumed office supplies.		

31	Amortization Expense, Automobiles	8,500.00	
	Accumulated Amortization,		
	Automobiles		8,500.00
	To record amortization on automobiles.		

31	Amortization Expense, Office Equipment	3,500.00	
	Accumulated Amortization,		
	Office Equipment		3,500.00
	To record amortization on equipment.		

31	Unearned Fees	730.00	
	Fees Earned		730.00
	To record earning of fees paid in advance.		

31	Salaries Expense	1,100.00	
	Salaries Payable		1,100.00
	To record accrued salaries.		

31	Interest Expense	400.00	
	Interest Payable		400.00
	To record accrued interest expense.		

31	Fees Earned	61,000.00	
	Income Summary		61,000.00
	To close the revenue account and open the		
	Income Summary account.		

31	Income Summary	45,960.00	
	Amortization Expense, Automobiles		8,500.00
	Amortization Expense, Office Equipment		3,500.00
	Salaries Expense		15,000.00
	Interest Expense		3,200.00
	Insurance Expense		800.00
	Rent Expense		7,200.00
	Office Supplies Expense		4,100.00
	Gas, Oil, and Repairs Expense		2,350.00
	Telephone Expense		1,310.00
	To close the expense accounts.		

31	Income Summary	15,040.00	
	Charlie Griffin, Capital		15,040.00
	To close Income Summary.		

31	Charlie Griffin, Capital	16,000.00	
	Charlie Griffin, Withdrawals		16,000.00
	To close withdrawals account.		

Use the information in the balance sheet and the journal entries to complete a 10-column work sheet. (The five steps should be completed in reverse order.)

^C**Problem 4–8**
Adjusting, reversing, and
subsequent entries
(LO 6)

The unadjusted trial balance for Milton's Pool Parlor as of December 31, 1996, follows:

MILTON'S POOL PARLOR
December 31, 1996

	Unadjusted Trial Balance	
Cash	$ 11,000	
Accounts receivable		
Supplies	4,500	
Equipment	150,000	
Accumulated amortization, equipment		$ 15,000
Interest payable		
Salaries payable		
Unearned membership fees		24,000
Notes payable		50,000
U. Milton, capital		58,250
U. Milton, withdrawals	30,000	
Membership fees earned		90,000
Amortization expense, equipment		
Salaries expense	38,000	
Interest expense	3,750	
Supplies expense		
Totals	$237,250	$237,250

Required

1. Prepare a six-column table with two columns under each of the following headings: Unadjusted Trial Balance, Adjustments, and Adjusted Trial Balance. Complete the table by entering adjustments that reflect the following information:

   a. As of December 31, employees have earned $800 of unpaid and unrecorded wages. The next payday is January 4, and the total wages to be paid will be $1,200.

   b. The cost of supplies on hand at December 31 is $1,800.

   c. The note payable requires an interest payment to be made every three months. The amount of unrecorded accrued interest at December 31 is $1,250, and the next payment is due on January 15. This payment will be $1,500.

   d. An analysis of the unearned membership fees shows that $16,000 remains unearned at December 31.

   e. In addition to the membership fees included in the revenue account balance, the company has earned another $12,000 in fees that will be collected on January 21. The company is also expected to collect $7,000 on the same day for new fees earned during January.

   f. Amortization expense for the year is $15,000.

2. Prepare journal entries for the adjustments drafted in the six-column table.

3. Prepare journal entries to reverse the effects of the adjusting entries that involve accruals.

4. Prepare journal entries to record the cash payments and collections that are described for January.

Leeward Service Company's unadjusted trial balance on December 31, 1996, the end of its annual accounting period, is as follows:

^CProblem 4–9
Adjusting, closing, and reversing entries
(LO 2, 6)

LEEWARD SERVICE COMPANY
Unadjusted Trial Balance
December 31, 1996

Cash	$ 73,725	
Notes receivable	37,500	
Office supplies	4,200	
Land	45,000	
Unearned service fees		$ 18,000
Notes payable		90,000
J. Boat, capital		37,500
J. Boat, withdrawals	60,000	
Service fees earned		267,000
Interest earned		2,550
Rent earned		12,375
Salaries expense	193,500	
Insurance expense	4,950	
Interest expense	8,550	
Totals	$427,425	$427,425

Information necessary to prepare adjusting entries is as follows:

a. Employees, who are paid $7,500 every two weeks, have earned $5,250 since the last payment. The next payment of $7,500 will be on January 4.

b. Leeward rents office space to a tenant who has paid only $450 of the $1,125 rent for December. On January 12, the tenant will pay the remainder along with the rent for January.

c. An inventory of office supplies discloses $675 of unused supplies.

d. Premiums for insurance against injuries to employees are paid monthly. The $450 premium for December will be paid January 12.

e. Leeward owes $90,000 on a note payable that requires quarterly payments of accrued interest. The quarterly payments of $2,700 each are made on the 15th of January, April, July, and October.

f. An analysis of Leeward's service contracts with customers shows that $6,300 of the amount customers have prepaid remains unearned.

g. Leeward has a $37,500 note receivable on which interest of $175 has accrued. On January 22, the note and the total accrued interest of $575 will be repaid to Leeward.

h. Leeward has earned but unrecorded revenue for $8,250 for services provided to a customer who will pay for the work on January 24. At that time, the customer will also pay $3,100 for services Leeward will perform in early January.

Required

1. Prepare adjusting journal entries.
2. Prepare closing journal entries.
3. Prepare reversing entries.
4. Prepare journal entries to record the January 1997 cash receipts and cash payments identified in the above information.

On December 31, 1996, the Castle Rock Company recorded a $10,000 liability to its employees for wages earned in 1996 that will be paid on January 5, the first pay day in 1997. In addition, they will receive another $5,000 for wages earned in 1997. The accountant did

^CProblem 4–10
Analytical Essay
(LO 6)

not prepare a reversing entry as of January 1, 1997, but did not inform the bookkeeper about the liability accrued for the wages. As a result, the bookkeeper recorded a $15,000 debit to Wages Expense on January 5, and a $15,000 credit to Cash.

Describe the effects of this error on the financial statements for 1996. Describe any erroneous account balances that will exist during 1997. Suggest a reasonable point in time at which the error would be discovered.

Problem 4–11
Analytical Essay
(LO 6)

On December 31, 1996, the Big Rock Company recorded a $15,000 liability to its employees for wages earned in 1996 that will be paid on January 5, the first pay day in 1997. In addition, they will receive another $7,500 for wages earned in 1997. The accountant did not prepare a reversing entry as of January 1, 1997, but did not inform the bookkeeper about the liability accrued for the wages. As a result, the bookkeeper recorded a $22,500 debit to Wages Expense on January 5, and a $22,500 credit to Cash.

Also in 1996, two-thirds of work was completed on a contract the total value of which was $30,000. On completion of the contract in 1997, the bookkeeper recorded $30,000 debit to cash and a $30,000 credit to contract revenue. No account was taken in 1996 of the work on the contract.

Describe the effects of these errors on the financial statements for 1996. Describe any erroneous account balances that will exist during 1997. Suggest a reasonable point in time at which the errors would be discovered.

ᴰProblem 4–12
Closing entries for
partnerships and
corporations
(LO 8)

Carol Boyce, Sarah Reed, and John Hudson started a business on January 7, 1995, and each invested $75,000 in the business. During 1995, the business lost $30,240, and during 1996, it earned $83,550. On January 5, 1997, the three owners agreed to pay out to themselves $36,000 of the accumulated earnings of the business. On January 9, 1997, the $36,000 was paid out.

Required

1. Assume that the business is a partnership and the partners share net incomes and net losses equally. Give the entries to record the investments and to close the Income Summary account at the end of 1995 and again at the end of 1996. Also assume that the partners shared equally in the $36,000 of earnings paid out. Give the entry to record the withdrawals.

2. Assume that the business is organized as a corporation and that each owner invested $75,000 in it by buying 7,500 of its common shares. Give the entry to record the investments. Also, give the entries to close the Income Summary account at the end of 1995 and again at the end of 1996 and to record the declaration and payment of the $1.60 per share dividend. (Ignore corporate income taxes and assume that the three owners are the corporation's board of directors.)

ᴰProblem 4–13
Closing entries for
partnerships and
corporations
(LO 8)

On January 7, 1995, John Aspen, Sarah Khan, and Paul Glen started a business in which John Aspen invested $10,000. Sarah Khan invested $20,000, and Paul Glen invested $40,000. During 1995, the business lost $70,000; and during 1996, it earned $24,500. On January 5, 1997, the three business owners agreed to pay out to themselves $14,000 of the accumulated earnings of the business, and on January 10, the $14,000 was paid out.

Required

1. Assume that the business is a partnership and that the partners share net incomes and net losses in proportion to their investments. Give the entries to record the

investments and to close the Income Summary account at the end of 1995 and again at the end of 1996. Also assume that the partners paid out the accumulated earnings in proportion to their investments. Give the entry to record the withdrawals.

2. Assume that the business is organized as a corporation and that the owners invested in the corporation by buying its common shares at $5 per share, with John Aspen buying 2,000 shares, Sarah Khan buying 4,000 shares, and Paul Glen buying 8,000 shares. Give the entry to record the investments. Also, give the entries to close the Income Summary account at the end of 1995 and again at the end of 1996. Then give the entries to record the declaration and payment of the $1 per share dividend. (Ignore corporation income taxes and assume the investors are the corporation's board of directors.)

SERIAL PROBLEM

(The first two segments of this comprehensive problem were in Chapters 2 and 3, and the final segment is presented in Chapter 5. If the Chapter 2 and 3 segments have not been completed, the assignment can begin at this point. However, you should use the facts on pages 119–120 in Chapter 2 and pages 175–176 in Chapter 3. Because of its length, this problem is most easily solved if you use the Working Papers that accompany this text.)

Emerald Computer Services

The transactions of Emerald Computer Services for October through December 1996 have been recorded in the problem segments in Chapters 2 and 3, as well as the year-end adjusting entries. Prior to closing the revenue and expense accounts for 1996, the accounting system is modified to include the Income Summary account, which is given the number 901.

Required

1. Record and post the appropriate closing entries.
2. Prepare a post-closing trial balance.

PROVOCATIVE PROBLEMS

During his second year in college, Wesley Smith inherited Strongarm Moving Service when his father died. He immediately dropped out of school and took over management of the business. At the time he took over, Wesley recognized he knew little about accounting. However, he reasoned that since the business performed its services strictly for cash, if the cash of the business increased, the business was doing OK. Therefore, he was pleased as he watched the cash balance grow from $2,100 when he took over to $25,715 at year-end. Furthermore, since he had withdrawn $30,000 from the business to buy a new car and to pay personal expenses, he reasoned that the business must have earned $48,850 during the year. He arrived at $48,850 by adding the $23,615 increase in cash to the $30,000 he had withdrawn from the business. Wesley was shocked when he received the income statement that follows and learned that the business had earned less than the amounts withdrawn.

Provocative Problem 4–1
Strongarm Moving Service
(Review problem)

STRONGARM MOVING SERVICE
Income Statement
For Year Ended December 31, 1996

Revenue from moving services		$120,565
Operating expenses:		
Salaries and wages expense	$54,825	
Gas, oil, and repairs expense	4,835	
Telephone expense	525	
Taxes expense	3,710	
Insurance expense	3,485	
Office supplies expense	375	
Amortization expense, office equipment . .	600	
Amortization expense, trucks	9,375	
Amortization expense, building	7,500	
Total operating expenses		85,230
Net income		$ 35,335

After thinking about the statement for several days, Wesley asked you to explain how, in a year in which the cash increased $18,850 and he withdrew $30,000, the business earned only $35,335. In examining the accounts of the business, you note that accrued salaries and wages payable at the beginning of the year were $185 but increased to $575 at year's end. Also, the accrued taxes payable were $675 at the beginning of the year but had increased to $715 at year-end. Also, the balance of the Prepaid Insurance account was $300 less and the balance of the Office Supplies account was $75 less at the end of the year than at the beginning. However, except for the changes in these accounts, the change in cash, and the changes in the balances of the accumulated amortization accounts, there were no other changes in the balances of the concern's asset and liability accounts between the beginning of the year and the end. Back your explanation with a calculation that accounts for the increase in the business's cash.

Provocative Problem
4–2
Red River Car Wash
(LO 1, 2, 3)

Use the following information to complete a 10-column work sheet for Red River Car Wash. Instead of the usual column headings, use the following headings on the work sheet:

Unadjusted Trial Balance: Debit and Credit

Adjustments: Debit and Credit

Adjusted Trial Balance: Debit and Credit

Closing Entries: Debit and Credit

Post-Closing Trial Balance: Debit and Credit

Unadjusted Trial Balance

No.	Title	Debit	Credit
101	Cash	$ 3,200	
106	Accounts receivable	500	
126	Soap supplies	6,000	
128	Prepaid insurance	2,100	
167	Equipment	15,000	
168	Accumulated amortization, equipment . .		$ 4,000
201	Accounts payable		1,350
210	Salaries payable		
301	K. McGowan, capital		25,900
302	K. McGowan, withdrawals	13,500	
401	Fees earned		44,450
612	Amortization expense, equipment		
623	Wages expense	18,000	
637	Insurance expense		
640	Rent expense	6,000	
652	Soap supplies expense		
690	Utilities expense	11,400	
901	Income summary		
	Totals	$75,700	$75,700

Use this information for the adjustments:

a. Three customers owe the company $550 for services provided but not billed.

b. A count of the supplies shows that $3,700 has been consumed.

c. The insurance coverage expired at the rate of $35 per month for 12 months.

d. The annual amortization expense for the equipment is $2,000.

e. December's utility costs of $135 were not included in the unadjusted trial balance.

f. The employees had earned $623 of accrued wages as of December 31.

As the end of the calendar year is approaching, Controller Jerry James is getting the Woodward Company's accounting department ready to prepare the annual financial statements. One concern is the expense of the services provided by an external consultant under a three-month contract that runs from November 30, 1996, through February 28, 1997. The total fee for the contract is based on the hours of the consultant's time, with the result that the total fee is not known.

The controller is concerned that the company's financial statements could not be prepared until March because the amount of consulting expense will not be known until then. To avoid this problem, the controller has asked you to prepare a letter to Pat Patterson, the consultant, that would ask for a progress report by the end of the first week of January. This report would specifically identify the hours and charges that will be billed for the consultant's time in December.

Draft the letter that will be sent to Patterson requesting this information. It will be signed by the controller on December 15, 1996.

Provocative Problem 4–3
Woodward Company
(LO 3)

Review the consolidated balance sheet and the consolidated statement of operations of Geac Computer Corporation Limited in Appendix I at the end of this book. Assume that a ledger account exists for each item in these statements. Prepare the closing entries and a post-closing trial balance for the company as of April 30, 1994. (Note: Check "Notes to Consolidated Financial Statements" for contra account balances.)

Provocative Problem 4–4
Financial statement analysis case
(LO 4)

Geac

ANALYTICAL AND REVIEW PROBLEMS

A & R Problem 4–1   The owner of Dynamo Stores has come to you for assistance because his bookkeeper has just moved to another city. The following is the only information his bookkeeper left him.

(1)   Balance sheets as of December 31, 1996 and 1997.

	1996	1997
Assets	$150,000	$120,000
Liabilities	$ 45,000	$ 30,000
Capital	105,000	90,000
	$150,000	$120,000

(2)   The owner withdrew $75,000 in 1997 for his personal use.

(3)   The business incurred total expenses of $120,000 for 1997, of which $90,000 was for wages and $30,000 for advertising.

Required

1.   Compute the total revenue and net income for 1997.

2.   Prepare closing or clearing entries for 1997 (omit narratives).

A & R Problem 4–2   The partially completed work sheet for the current fiscal year of Sandy's Delivery Service appears below:

Required

1.   Complete the work sheet.

2.   Journalize the adjusting and closing entries (omit narratives).

SANDY'S DELIVERY SERVICE
Work Sheet
For the Year Ended December 31, 1996

Account Titles	Trial Balance		Adjustments		Adjusted Trial Balance		Income Statement		Balance Sheet	
	Dr.	Cr	Dr.	Cr.	Dr.	Cr.	Dr.	Cr.	Dr.	Cr.
Cash	10,650									
Accounts receivable	5,000				6,000					
Supplies on hand	2,400								600	
Prepaid insurance	2,400									
Prepaid rent	1,800									
Delivery trucks					40,000					
Accounts payable		3,130				3,130				
Unearned delivery fees		3,500								2,000
Sandra Berlasty, capital, Dec. 31, 1996		50,000								
Sandra Berlasty, drawing	3,000									
Delivery service revenue		15,700								
Advertising expense	600									
Gas and oil expense	680									
Salaries expense	5,600									
Utilities expense	200									
	72,330	72,330								
Insurance expense							800			
Rent expense					900					
Supplies expense										
Amortization expense—delivery trucks										
Accumulated amortization—delivery trucks										2,000
Accrued salaries payable										400
Net income										

CONCEPT TESTER

Test your understanding of the concepts introduced in this chapter by completing the following crossword puzzle.

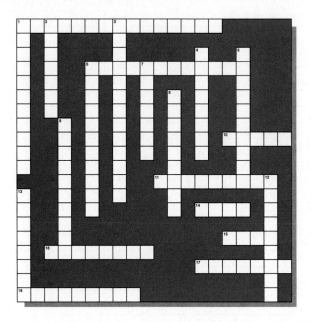

Across Clues

1. Recurring steps performed each accounting period (2 words).

6. Ratio of net income to revenue (2 words).

10. Number of recurring steps performed each accounting period.

11. Term used to describe asset, liability and owner equity accounts.

14. Another name for permanent accounts.

15. Balance in nominal accounts after posting closing entries.

16. Trial balance that shows account balances revised by end-of-period procedure.

17. Another name for temporary accounts.

18. Distribution to shareholders.

Down Clues

1. Total amount of amortization recorded against an asset.

2. End-of-period entries to render zero balances in nominal accounts.

3. Special account used only in the closing process (2 words).

4. Financial statements that show the ef/

5. Assets with no physical form.

6. Trial balance that tests the accuracy of adjusting and closing procedure (2 words).

7. Financial statements prepared at intervals during a fiscal period.

8. A 10-column spreadsheet (2 words).

9. Balance sheet with meaningful groupings of assets and liabilities.

12. Term used to describe revenue, expense, and other withdrawal accounts.

13. Trial balance that shows account balances revised by end-of-period procedure.

COMPREHENSIVE PROBLEM

Following is the unadjusted trial balance of Piper's Plumbing and Heating as of November 30, 1996. The account balances include the effects of transactions during the first 11 months of the year.

Piper's Plumbing and Heating
(Review of Chapters 1–4)

PIPER'S PLUMBING AND HEATING
Unadjusted Trial Balance
November 30, 1996

No.	Title	Debit	Credit
101	Cash	$ 17,000	
124	Office supplies	9,400	
126	Repair supplies	86,500	
128	Prepaid insurance	2,400	
153	Trucks	82,000	
154	Accumulated amortization, trucks ...		$ 40,000
173	Building	185,000	
174	Accumulated amortization, building ..		32,000
201	Accounts payable		13,500
210	Wages payable		
233	Unearned heating fees		3,700
301	Bill Piper, capital		174,600
302	Bill Piper, withdrawals	30,000	
401	Plumbing fees earned		180,000
402	Heating fees earned		95,000
606	Amortization expense, building		
611	Amortization expense, trucks		
623	Wages expense	65,000	
637	Insurance expense		
650	Office supplies expense		
652	Repair supplies expense		
669	Gas, oil, and repairs expense	13,500	
672	General and administrative expenses ..	48,000	
	Totals	$538,800	$538,800

The following transactions occurred during December 1996:

Dec. 2 Received $1,000 for completed heating work.

5 Paid $11,325 on accounts payable.

6 Paid $4,100 insurance premium in advance.

7 Received $3,300 cash for plumbing work completed.

10 Purchased $1,500 of repair supplies on credit.

14 Paid $3,000 for wages earned December 1 to 14.

17 Purchased $325 of office supplies on credit.

21 Received $2,200 cash for plumbing work completed and $14,000 cash for heating work.

24 Paid $1,430 for truck repairs related to an accident.

28 Paid $3,300 for wages earned December 15 to 28.

30 Received $600 cash for plumbing work completed and $4,500 cash for heating work.

Required

1. Use the balance column format to create the accounts listed in the November 30 trial balance. Enter the unadjusted November 30 balances in the accounts.

2. Prepare and post journal entries to record the transactions for December; omit entering the account numbers in the posting reference column.

3. Prepare a 10-column work sheet as of December 31. Start by entering the unadjusted balances from the accounts as of that date. Continue by entering adjustments for the following items, and then complete the rest of the work sheet.

    a. At the end of the year, the office supplies inventory was $730.

    b. At the end of the year, the repair supplies inventory was $7,600.

    c. At the end of the year, the unexpired portion of the prepaid insurance was $3,800.

    d. Annual amortization on the trucks was $20,000.

    e. Annual amortization on the building was $5,000.

    f. At the end of the year, the employees had earned $990 in accrued wages.

    g. At the end of the year, the balance of unearned heating fees was $600.

4. Prepare adjusting journal entries and post them to the accounts.

5. Prepare an income statement and a statement of changes in owner's equity for 1996 and a balance sheet as of December 31, 1996. The owner did not make any new investments during the year.

6. Prepare closing journal entries and post them to the accounts.

7. Prepare a post-closing trial balance.

ANSWERS TO PROGRESS CHECKS

4–1 c

4–2 The amounts in the Unadjusted Trial Balance columns are taken from the account balances in the ledger.

4–3 The work sheet offers the advantage of providing an overview of the information in the accounts and helps accountants organize the data.

4–4 Income statement, statement of changes in owner's equity, balance sheet.

4–5 c

4–6 Revenue and expense accounts are called temporary because they are opened and closed every reporting period. The Income Summary and owner's withdrawals accounts are also temporary accounts.

4–7 Permanent accounts are listed on the post-closing trial balance. These accounts include the asset, liability, and owner's capital accounts.

4–8 A corporation closes the Income Summary account to the Retained Earnings account.

4–9 a

4–10 A work sheet is prepared at the end of the reporting period after all transactions have been journalized and posted, but before adjustments have been recorded.

4–11 d

4–12 Profit margin = Net income/Total revenue. Therefore, Total revenue = Net income/Profit margin. Total revenue = $1,012,500/22.5% = $4,500,000.

Accounting for Merchandising Activities

[M]any companies earn profits by buying merchandise and selling it to [cu]stomers. Accounting helps managers to determine the amount of [in]come earned by these companies and the cost of the inventory they [ha]ve on hand.

*K*aren White and Mark Smith's continued interest in Imperial Oil Limited brought them back to both the company's financial statements and the section in Chapter 3 discussing the current ratio. They focused on the part that stated: "The current ratio is widely used to describe the company's ability to pay its short-term obligations." White and Smith then examined the composition of Imperial's current assets and the level of current liabilities, presented in the table below:

White and Smith left the school library wondering how items such as "Inventories of crude oil and products" and "materials, supplies and prepaid expenses" could be used to pay the current liabilities. They intended to raise this issue in their next accounting class.

IMPERIAL OIL LIMITED
(in millions)

December 31	1994	1993
Current assets:		
Cash	$ 409	$ 605
Marketable securities at cost	859	874
Accounts receivable	1,045	889
Inventories of crude oil and products	384	402
Materials, supplies and prepaid expenses	100	129
Total current assets	$2,797	$2,899
Total current liabilities	$1,581	$1,593

LEARNING OBJECTIVES

After studying Chapter 5, you should be able to:

1. **Describe merchandising activities, analyze their effects on financial statements, and record sales of merchandise.**
2. **Describe how the ending inventory and the cost of goods sold are determined with perpetual and periodic inventory accounting systems.**
3. **Describe various formats for income statements and prepare closing entries for a merchandising business.**
4. **Complete a work sheet that includes the inventory-related accounts.**
5. **Calculate the acid-test ratio and describe what it reveals about a company's liquidity.**
6. **Define or explain the words and phrases in the chapter glossary.**

After studying Appendix E at the end of Chapter 5, you should be able to:

7. **Explain an adjusting entry approach to recording the change in the Merchandise Inventory account.**

The first four chapters in this book used only service companies as examples of businesses that prepare financial statements. This chapter introduces some of the business and accounting practices used by companies that engage in merchandising activities. These companies buy goods and then resell them to customers. This chapter shows how the financial statements describe the special transactions and assets related to these activities. In particular, you will learn about the additional financial statement elements created by merchandising activities. To help you understand where the information comes from, we describe how accountants close the accounts of merchandising companies and design income statements.

THE NATURE OF MERCHANDISING ACTIVITIES

LO 1

Describe merchandising activities, analyze their effects on financial statements, and record sales of merchandise.

The first four chapters have described the financial statements and accounting records of Clear Copy. Because it provides services to its customers, Clear Copy is a service company. Other examples of service companies include **Greyhound Lines Inc.; Air Canada; Price Waterhouse;** and **Richardson Greenshields of Canada Limited.** In return for services provided to its customers, a service company receives commissions, fares, or fees as revenue. Its net income for a reporting period is the difference between its revenues and the operating expenses incurred in providing the services.

In contrast, a merchandising company earns net income by buying and selling **merchandise,** which consists of goods that the company acquires for the purpose of reselling them to customers.[1] To achieve a net income, the revenue from selling the merchandise needs to exceed not only the cost of the merchandise sold to customers but also the company's other operating expenses for the reporting period.

---

[1] A merchandising company can be either a wholesaler or a retailer. Wholesalers buy goods from manufacturers and sell them to retailers or other wholesalers. Retailers buy goods from wholesalers and sell them to individual customers.

The accounting term for the revenues from selling merchandise is *sales* and the term used to describe the expense of buying and preparing the merchandise is *cost of goods sold*.[2] The company's other expenses are often called *operating expenses.* This condensed income statement for Meg's Mart shows you how these three elements of net income are related to each other:

MEG'S MART
Condensed Income Statement
For Year Ended December 31, 1997

Net sales	$314,700
Cost of goods sold	(230,400)
Gross profit from sales	$ 84,300
Total operating expenses	(62,800)
Net income	$ 21,500

This income statement tells us that Meg's Mart sold goods to its customers for $314,700. The company acquired those goods at a total cost of $230,400. As a result, it earned $84,300 of **gross profit,** which is the difference between the net sales and the cost of goods sold. In addition, the company incurred $62,800 of operating expenses and achieved $21,500 of net income for the year.

A merchandising company's balance sheet includes an additional element that is not on the balance sheet of a service company. In Illustration 5–1, we present the classified balance sheet for Meg's Mart. Notice that the current asset section includes an item called **merchandise inventory.** Even though they also have inventories of supplies, most companies simply refer to merchandise on hand as *inventory.* This asset consists of goods the company owns on the balance sheet date and holds for the purpose of selling to its customers. The $21,000 amount listed for the inventory is the costs incurred to buy the goods, ship them to the store, and otherwise make them ready for sale.

The next sections of the chapter provide more information about these unique elements of the financial statements for merchandising companies.

This schedule shows how Meg's Mart calculates its *net sales* for 1997:

**TOTAL
REVENUE
FROM SALES**

MEG'S MART
Calculation of Net Sales
For Year Ended December 31, 1997

Sales		$321,000
Less: Sales returns and allowances	$2,000	
Sales discounts	4,300	6,300
Net sales		$314,700

---

[2]Many service companies also use the word *sales* to describe their revenues.

Illustration 5-1
Classified Balance
Sheet for a
Merchandising
Company

MEG'S MART
Balance Sheet
December 31, 1997

Assets

Current assets:
Cash	$ 8,200	
Accounts receivable	11,200	
Merchandise inventory	21,000	
Prepaid expenses	1,100	
Total current assets		$41,500

Capital assets:
Office equipment	$ 4,200		
Less accumulated amortization	1,400	$ 2,800	
Store equipment	$30,000		
Less accumulated amortization	6,000	24,000	
Total capital assets			26,800
Total assets			$68,300

Liabilities

Current liabilities:
Accounts payable	$16,000	
Salaries payable	800	
Total liabilities		$16,800

Owner's Equity

Meg Harlowe, capital	51,500
Total liabilities and owner's equity	$68,300

The components of this calculation are described in the following paragraphs.

Sales

The sales item in this calculation is the total cash and credit sales made by the company during the year. Each cash sale was rung up on one of the company's cash registers. At the end of each day, the total cash sales for the day were recorded with a journal entry like this one for November 3:

Nov.	3	Cash	1,205.00	
		Sales		1,205.00
		Sold merchandise for cash.		

This entry records the fact that the cash received from customers represents sales revenue earned by the company.

In addition, a journal entry would be prepared each day to record the credit sales made on that day. For example, this entry records $450 of credit sales on November 3:

Nov.	3	Accounts Receivable	450.00	
		Sales		450.00
		Sold merchandise on credit.		

This entry records the increase in the company's assets in the form of the accounts receivable and records the revenue from the credit sales.[3]

Sales Returns and Allowances

To meet their customers' needs, most companies allow customers to return any unsuitable merchandise for a full refund. If a customer keeps the unsatisfactory goods and is given a partial refund of the selling price, the company is said to have provided a sales *allowance.* Either way, returns and allowances involve dissatisfied customers and the possibility of lost future sales. To monitor the extent of these problems, managers need information about actual returns and allowances. Thus, many accounting systems record returns and allowances in a separate *contra-revenue* account like the one used in this entry to record a $200 cash refund:

Nov.	3	Sales Returns and Allowances	200.00	
		Cash		200.00
		Customer returned defective merchandise.		

The company could record the refund with a debit to the Sales account. Although this would provide the same measure of net sales, it would not provide information that the manager can use to monitor the refunds and allowances. By using the Sales Returns and Allowances contra account, the information is readily available. To simplify the reports provided to external decision makers, published income statements usually omit this detail and present only the amount of net sales.

Sales Discounts

When goods are sold on credit, the expected amounts and dates of future payments need to be clearly stated to avoid misunderstandings. The **credit terms** for a sale describe the amounts and timing of payments that the buyer agrees to make in the future. The specific terms usually reflect the ordinary practices of most companies in the industry. For example, companies in one industry might expect to be paid 10 days after the end of the month in which a sale occurred. These credit terms would be stated on sales invoices or tickets as "n/10 EOM," with the abbreviation **EOM** standing for "end of the month." In another industry, invoices may normally be due and payable 30 calendar days after the invoice date. These terms are abbreviated as "n/30," and the 30-day period is called the **credit period.**

When the credit period is long, the seller often grants a **cash discount** if the customer pays promptly. These early payments are desirable because the seller re-

[3]Chapter 8 describes how stores account for sales to customers who use third-party credit cards, such as those issued by banks.

ceives the cash more quickly and can use it to carry on its activities. In addition, prompt payments reduce future efforts and costs of billing customers. These advantages are usually worth the cost of offering the discounts.

If cash discounts for early payment are granted, they are described in the credit terms on the invoice. For example, the terms of 2/10, n/60 mean that a 60-day credit period passes before full payment is due. However, to encourage early payment, the seller allows the buyer to deduct 2% of the invoice amount from the payment if it is made within 10 days of the invoice date. The **discount period** is the period in which the reduced payment can be made.

At the time of a credit sale, the seller does not know that the customer will pay within the discount period and take advantage of a cash discount. As a result, the discount is usually not recorded until the customer pays within the discount period. For example, suppose that Meg's Mart completed a credit sale on November 12 at a gross selling price of $100, subject to terms of 2/10, n/60. This entry records the sale:

Nov.	12	Accounts Receivable	100.00	
		Sales		100.00
		Sold merchandise under terms of 2/10,		
		n/60.		

Even though the customer may pay less than the gross price, the entry records the receivable and the revenue as if the full amount will be collected.

In fact, the customer has two alternatives. One option is to wait 60 days until January 11 and pay the full $100. If this is done, Meg's Mart records the collection as follows:

Jan.	11	Cash	100.00	
		Accounts Receivable		100.00
		Collected account receivable.		

The customer's other option is to pay $98 within a 10-day period that runs through November 22. If the customer pays on November 22, Meg's Mart records the collection with this entry:

Nov.	22	Cash	98.00	
		Sales Discounts	2.00	
		Accounts Receivable		100.00
		Received payment for the November 12		
		sale less the discount.		

Cash discounts granted to customers are called **sales discounts.** Because management needs to monitor the amount of cash discounts to assess their effectiveness and their cost, they are recorded in a contra-revenue account called Sales Discounts.

The balance of this account is deducted from the balance of the Sales account when calculating the company's net sales. Although information about the amount of discounts is useful internally, it is seldom reported on income statements distributed to external decision makers.

Progress Check

(Answers to Progress Checks are provided at the end of the chapter.)

5–1   Which of the following items is not unique to the financial statements of merchandising companies? *(a)* Cost of goods sold; *(b)* Accounts receivable; *(c)* Merchandise inventory.

5–2   What is a merchandising company's gross profit?

5–3   Why are sales returns and allowances and sales discounts recorded in contra-revenue accounts instead of in the Sales account? Is this information likely to be reported outside the company?

5–4   How long are the credit and discount periods under credit terms of 2/10, n/60?

A merchandising company's balance sheet includes a current asset called *inventory* and its income statement includes the item called *cost of goods sold*. Both of these items are affected by the company's merchandise transactions. The amount of the asset on the balance sheet equals the cost of the inventory on hand at the end of the fiscal year. The amount of the cost of goods sold is the cost of the merchandise that was sold to customers during the year.

Two different inventory accounting systems may be used to collect information about the cost of the inventory on hand and the cost of goods sold. They are described in the following paragraphs.

Periodic and Perpetual Inventory Systems

The two basic types of inventory accounting systems are called *perpetual* and *periodic*. As suggested by their name, **perpetual inventory systems** maintain a continuous record of the amount of inventory on hand. This perpetual record is maintained by adding the cost of each newly purchased item to the inventory account and subtracting the cost of each sold item from the account. When an item is sold, its cost is recorded in the Cost of Goods Sold account. Whenever posting is up to date during the period, users of perpetual systems can determine the cost of merchandise on hand by looking at the balance of the inventory account. They can also determine the cost of goods sold thus far during the period by referring to the Cost of Goods Sold account.

Before computers were used widely, perpetual systems were generally applied only by businesses that made a limited number of sales each day, such as automobile dealers or major appliance stores. Because there were relatively few transactions, the perpetual accounting system could be operated efficiently. However, the availability of improved technology has greatly increased the number of companies that use perpetual systems.

Under **periodic inventory systems,** a company does not continuously update its records of the quantity and cost of goods that are on hand or sold. Instead, the company simply records the cost of new merchandise in a temporary *Purchases*

MEASURING INVENTORY AND COST OF GOODS SOLD

LO 2

Describe how the ending inventory and the cost of goods sold are determined with perpetual and periodic inventory accounting systems.

account. When merchandise is sold, only the revenue is recorded. Then, when financial statements are prepared, the company takes a *physical inventory* by counting the quantities of merchandise on hand. The total cost is determined by relating the quantities to records that show each item's original cost. This total cost is then used to determine the cost of goods sold.

Traditionally, periodic systems were used by companies such as drug and department stores that sold large quantities of low-valued items. Without computers and scanners, it was not feasible for accounting systems to track such small items as toothpaste, pain killers, clothing, and housewares through the inventory and into the customers' hands.

Although perpetual systems are now more affordable, they are still not used by all merchandising companies. As a result, it will be helpful for you to understand how periodic systems work. In addition, studying periodic systems will help you visualize the flow of goods through inventory without having to learn the more complicated sequence of journal entries used in perpetual systems. (More information on perpetual systems is provided in Chapter 9. However, at this stage you may wish to consider journal-entry comparison of the two systems: comparison is provided in the footnote at the bottom of this page.[4])

CALCULATING THE COST OF GOODS SOLD WITH A PERIODIC INVENTORY SYSTEM

As mentioned earlier, a store that uses a periodic inventory system does not record the cost of merchandise items when they are sold. Rather, the accountant waits until the end of the reporting period and determines the cost of all the goods sold during the period. To make this calculation, the accountant must have information about:

1. The cost of merchandise on hand at the beginning of the period.
2. The cost of merchandise purchased during the period.
3. The cost of unsold goods on hand at the end of the period.

Look at Illustration 5–2 to see how this information can be used to measure the cost of goods sold for Meg's Mart.

In Illustration 5–2, note that Meg's Mart had $251,400 of goods available for sale during the period. They were available because the company had $19,000 of goods on hand when the period started and purchased an additional $232,400 of goods during the year.

The available goods either were sold during the period or on hand at the end of the period. Because the count showed that $21,000 were on hand at the end of the year, we can conclude that $230,400 must have been sold. This schedule presents the calculation:

---

[4]Periodic

Purchase of goods:

Purchases xxx
    Accounts payable xxx

Sales of goods:

Accounts receivable   xxx
    Sales xxx

No entry; the impact of the cost of the goods is via an end-of-period update of inventory and the closing of purchases and related accounts.

Perpetual

Inventory xxx
    Accounts payable xxx
Accounts receivable xxx
    Sales xxx
Cost of goods sold xxx
    Inventory xxx

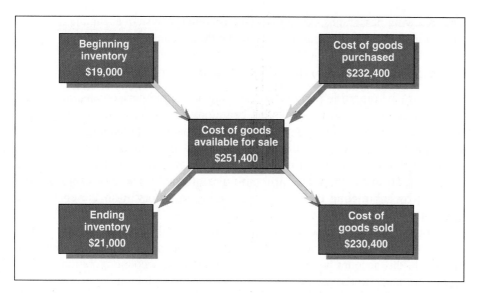

Illustration 5-2
The Flow of Goods
and Costs through
Inventory

MEG'S MART
Calculation of Cost of Goods Sold
For Year Ended December 31, 1997

Beginning inventory	$ 19,000
Cost of goods purchased	232,400
Cost of goods available for sale	$251,400
Less ending inventory	(21,000)
Cost of goods sold	$230,400

Note that if any three of the items in this calculation are known, they can be used to calculate the fourth. For example, **Example** Corporation's 1996 annual report disclosed the following information:

Beginning merchandise inventories	$2,269 million
Ending merchandise inventories	1,579 million
Cost of sales	$6,717 million

The cost of Example's purchases during 1996 can be calculated as follows:

Ending merchandise inventories	$1,579 million
Cost of sales	6,717 million
Cost of goods that must have been available for sale	$8,296 million
Less beginning merchandise inventories	2,269 million
Cost of goods purchased	$6,027 million

---

The following paragraphs explain how the accounting system accumulates the information that the accountant needs to make these calculations.

Measuring and Recording Merchandise Inventory

Because a new reporting period starts as soon as the old period ends, the ending inventory of one period is always the beginning inventory of the next. When a periodic inventory system is used, the dollar amount of the ending inventory is determined by (1) counting the unsold items in the store and the stockroom, (2) multiplying the counted quantity of each type of good by its cost, and (3) adding all the costs of the different types of goods. The cost of goods sold is found by subtracting the cost of the ending inventory from the cost of the goods available for sale.

Through the closing process described later in the chapter, the periodic system records the cost of the ending inventory in the *Merchandise Inventory* account. The balance in this account is not changed during the next accounting period. In fact, entries are made to the Merchandise Inventory account only at the end of the period. Thus, neither the purchases of new merchandise nor the cost of goods sold is entered in the Merchandise Inventory account. As a result, as soon as any goods are purchased or sold in the current period, the account no longer shows the cost of the merchandise on hand. Because the account's balance describes the beginning inventory of the period, it cannot be used on a new balance sheet without being updated by the closing entries described later in this chapter.

Recording the Cost of Purchased Merchandise

To determine the cost of purchased merchandise, the gross purchase price must be adjusted for the effects of (1) any cash discounts provided by the suppliers, (2) any returns and allowances for unsatisfactory items received from the suppliers, and (3) any freight costs paid by the buyer to get the goods into the buyer's inventory. For example, the cost of the goods purchased by Meg's Mart for 1997 is calculated as follows:

MEG'S MART
Calculation of Cost of Goods Purchased
For Year Ended December 31, 1997

Purchases		$235,800
Less: Purchases returns and allowances	$1,500	
Purchases discounts	4,200	5,700
Net purchases		$230,100
Add transportation-in		2,300
Cost of goods purchased		$232,400

The following paragraphs explain how these amounts are accumulated in the accounts.

The Purchases Account. Under a periodic inventory system, the cost of merchandise bought for resale is debited to a temporary account called *Purchases*. For example, Meg's Mart records a $1,200 credit purchase of merchandise on November 2 with this entry:

Nov.	2	Purchases	1,200.00	
		Accounts Payable		1,200.00
		Purchased merchandise on credit, invoice		
		dated November 2, terms 2/10, n/30.		

The Purchases account accumulates the cost of all merchandise bought during a period. The account is a holding place for information used at the end of the period to calculate the cost of goods sold.

Trade Discounts. When a manufacturer or wholesaler prepares a catalogue of the items it offers for sale, each item is given a **list price,** which is also called a *catalogue price*. The list price generally is not the intended selling price of the item. Instead, the intended selling price equals the list price reduced by a given percentage called a **trade discount.**

The amount of the trade discount usually depends on whether the buyer is a wholesaler, a retailer, or the final consumer. For example, a wholesaler that buys large quantities is granted a larger discount than a retailer that buys smaller quantities. Regardless of its amount, a trade discount is a reduction in a list price that is applied to determine the actual sales price of the goods to a customer.

Trade discounts are commonly used by manufacturers and wholesalers to change selling prices without republishing their catalogues. When the seller wants to change the selling prices, it can notify its customers merely by sending them a new set of trade discounts to apply to the catalogue prices.

Because list prices are not intended to reflect the negotiated sales value of the merchandise, neither the buyer nor the seller enters the list prices and the trade discounts in their accounts. Instead, they record the actual sales price (the list price less the trade discount). For example, if a manufacturer deducts a 40% trade discount on an item listed in its catalogue at $2,000, the selling price is $1,200, which is [$2,000 − (40% × $2,000)]. The seller records the credit sale as follows:

Nov.	2	Accounts Receivable	1,200.00	
		Sales		1,200.00
		Sold merchandise on credit.		

The buyer also records the purchase at $1,200. For example, see the previous entry to record the purchase by Meg's Mart.

Purchases Discounts. When stores buy merchandise on credit, they may be offered cash discounts for paying within the discount period. The buyer refers to these cash discounts as **purchases discounts.** When the buyer pays within the discount period, the accounting system records a credit to a contra-purchases account called *Purchases Discounts*. The following entry uses this account to record the payment for the merchandise purchased on November 2:

As a Matter of Ethics

Renee Fleck was recently hired by Mid-Mart, a medium-size retailing company that purchases most of its merchandise on credit. She overlapped on the new job for several days with the outgoing employee in her position, Martin Hull, so that he could help her learn the ropes.

One of Fleck's responsibilities is to see that the payables are paid promptly to maintain the company's credit standing with its suppliers and to take advantage of all cash discounts. Hull told Fleck that the current system has accomplished both goals easily and has also made another contribution to the company's profits. He explained that the computer system has been programmed to prepare cheques for amounts net of the cash discounts. Even though the cheques are dated as of the last day of the discount period, they are not mailed until five days later. Because the accounts are always paid, the company has had virtually no trouble with its suppliers. "It's simple," Hull explained to Fleck. "We get the free use of the cash for an extra five days, and who's going to complain? Even when somebody does, we just blame the computer system and the people in the mail room."

A few days later, Hull had departed and Fleck assumed her new duties. The first invoice that she examined had a 10-day discount period on a $10,000 purchase. The transaction occurred on April 9 subject to terms of 2/10, n/30. Fleck had to decide whether she should mail the $9,800 cheque on April 19 or wait until the 24th.

Nov.	12	Accounts Payable	1,200.00	
		Purchases Discounts (2% × $1,200)		24.00
		Cash		1,176.00
		Paid for the purchase of November 2 less the discount.		

By recording the amount of discounts taken in a separate contra account, the accountant can help managers keep track of the company's performance in taking advantage of discounts. For example, if all purchases are made on credit and all suppliers offer a 2% discount, the balance of the Purchases Discounts contra account should equal 2% of the balance of the Purchases account. If the accountant did not use the contra account, the $24 credit entry would be recorded as a reduction of the Purchases account balance. As a result, it would be more difficult to determine whether discounts were taken.

The accountant uses the balance of the Purchases Discounts account to compute the net cost of the purchases for the period. However, published financial statements usually do not include this calculation because it is useful only for managers.

A Cash Management Technique. To ensure that discounts are not missed, most companies set up a system to pay all invoices within the discount period. Furthermore, careful cash management ensures that no invoice is paid until the last day of the discount period. A helpful technique for reaching both of these goals is to file each invoice in such a way that it automatically comes up for payment on the last day of its discount period. For example, a simple manual system uses 31 folders, one for each day in the month. After an invoice is recorded in the journal, it is placed in the file folder for the last day of its discount period. Thus, if the last day of an invoice's discount period is November 12, it is filed in folder number 12. Then, the invoice and any other invoices in the same folder are removed and paid on November 12. Computerized systems can accomplish the same result by using a code that identifies the last date in the discount period. When that date is reached, the computer automatically provides a reminder that the account should be paid. Another way a company can gain more control over purchase discounts is by using the *net method of recording purchases*. This method is discussed in Chapter 7.

Read the As a Matter of Ethics case and consider what you would do if you were faced with the situation it describes.

Purchases Returns and Allowances. Sometimes, merchandise received from a supplier is not acceptable and must be returned. In other cases, the purchaser may keep imperfect but marketable merchandise because the supplier grants an allowance, which is a reduction in the purchase price.

Even though the seller does not charge the buyer for the returned goods or gives an allowance for imperfect goods, the buyer incurs costs in receiving, inspecting, identifying, and possibly returning defective merchandise. The occurrence of these costs can be signaled to the manager by recording the cost of the returned merchandise or the seller's allowance in a separate contra-purchases account called *Purchases Returns and Allowances*. For example, this journal entry is recorded on November 14 when Meg's Mart returns defective merchandise for a $265 refund of the original purchase price:

Nov.	14	Accounts Payable	265.00	
		Purchases Returns and Allowances		265.00
		Returned defective merchandise.		

As we described for Purchases Discounts, the accountant uses the balance of the Purchases Returns and Allowances account to compute the net cost of goods purchased during the period. However, published financial statements generally do not include this detailed information.

Discounts and Returned Merchandise. If part of a shipment of goods is returned within the discount period, the buyer can take the discount only on the remaining balance of the invoice. For example, suppose that Meg's Mart is offered a 2% cash discount on $5,000 of merchandise. Two days later, the company returns $800 of the goods before the invoice is paid. When the liability is paid within the discount period, Meg's Mart can take the 2% discount only on the $4,200 balance. Thus, the discount is $84 (2% × $4,200) and the cash payment must be $4,116 ($4,200 − $84).

Transportation Costs. Depending on the terms negotiated with its suppliers, a company may be responsible for paying the shipping costs for transporting the acquired goods to its own place of business. Because these costs are necessary to make the goods ready for sale, the cost principle requires them to be added to the cost of the purchased goods.

The freight charges could be recorded with a debit to the Purchases account. However, more complete information about these costs is provided to management if they are debited to a special supplemental account called *Transportation-In*. The accountant adds this account's balance to the net purchase price of the acquired goods to find the total cost of goods purchased. (See the schedule on page 246.)

The use of this account is demonstrated by the following entry, which records a $75 freight charge for incoming merchandise:

Nov.	24	Transportation-In	75.00	
		Cash		75.00
		Paid freight charges on purchased merchandise.		

Because detailed information about freight charges is relevant only for managers, it is seldom found in external financial statements.

Freight paid to bring purchased goods into the inventory is accounted for separately from freight paid on goods sent to customers. The shipping cost of incoming goods is included in the cost of goods sold, while the shipping cost for outgoing goods is a selling expense.

Identifying Ownership Responsibilities and Risks. When a merchandise transaction is planned, the buyer and seller need to establish which party will be responsible for paying any freight costs and which will bear the risk of loss during transit.

The basic issue to be negotiated is the point at which ownership is transferred from the buyer to the seller. The place of the transfer is called the **FOB** point, which is the abbreviation for the phrase, *free on board*. The meaning of different FOB points is explained by the diagram in Illustration 5–3.

Under an *FOB shipping point* agreement (also called *FOB factory*), the buyer accepts ownership at the seller's place of business. As a result, the buyer is responsible for paying the shipping costs and bears the risk of damage or loss while the goods are in shipment. In addition, the goods are part of the buyer's inventory while they are in transit because the buyer already owns them.

Alternatively, an *FOB destination* agreement causes ownership of the goods to pass at the buyer's place of business. If so, the seller is responsible for paying the shipping charges and bears the risk of damage or loss in transit. Furthermore, the seller should not record the sales revenue until the goods arrive at the destination because the transaction is not complete before that point in time.

Compaq Computer Corporation originally shipped all of its products under FOB factory agreements. However, customers' shipping companies proved to be undependable in picking up shipments at scheduled times and caused backups at the plant, missed deliveries, and disappointed end users. The company changed its agreements to FOB destination and cleared up these problems.

Debit and Credit Memoranda

Buyers and sellers often find they need to adjust the amount that is owed between them. For example, purchased merchandise may not meet specifications, unordered goods may be received, different quantities may be received than were ordered and billed, and billing errors may occur.

Illustration 5–3 Identifying Ownership Responsibilities and Risks

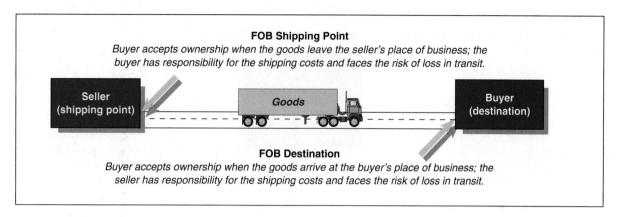

In some cases, the original balance can be adjusted by the buyer without a negotiation. For example, a seller may make an error on an invoice. If the buying company discovers the error, it can make its own adjustment and notify the seller by sending a **debit memorandum** or a **credit memorandum.** A debit memorandum is a business document that informs the recipient that the sender has *debited* the account receivable or payable. It provides the notification with words like these: "We debit your account," followed by the amount and an explanation. On the other hand, a credit memorandum informs the recipient that the sender has credited the receivable or payable. See Illustration 5–4 for two situations that involve these documents.

The debit memorandum in Illustration 5–4 is based on a case in which a buyer initially records an invoice as an account payable and later discovers an error by the seller that overstated the total bill by $100. The buyer corrects the balance of its liability and formally notifies the seller of the mistake with a debit memorandum reading: "We have debited your account for $100 because of an error." Additional information is provided about the invoice, its date, and the nature of the error. The buyer sends a *debit* memorandum because the correction debits the account payable to reduce its balance. The buyer's debit to the payable is offset by a credit to the Purchases account.

When the seller receives its copy of the debit memorandum, it records a *credit* to the buyer's account receivable to reduce its balance. An equal debit is recorded in the Sales account. Neither company uses a contra account because the adjustment was created by an error.

In other situations, an adjustment can be made only after negotiations between the buyer and the seller. For example, suppose that a buyer claims that some merchandise does not meet specifications. The amount of the allowance to be given by the seller can be determined only after discussion. Assume that a buyer accepts delivery of merchandise and records the transaction with a $750 debit to the Purchases account and an equal credit to Accounts Payable. Later, the buyer discovers that some of the merchandise is flawed. After a phone call, the seller agrees to grant a $250 allowance against the original purchase price.

The seller records the allowance with a debit to the Sales Returns and Allowances contra account and a credit to Accounts Receivable. Then, the seller formally

Illustration 5–4   The Use of Debit and Credit Memoranda

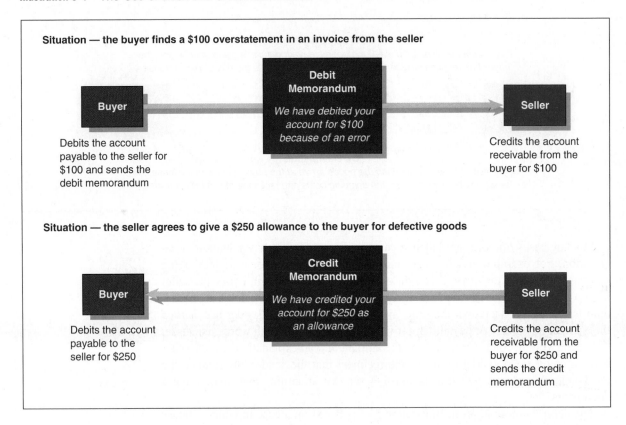

Situation — the buyer finds a $100 overstatement in an invoice from the seller

Buyer

Debits the account payable to the seller for $100 and sends the debit memorandum

Debit Memorandum

We have debited your account for $100 because of an error

Seller

Credits the account receivable from the buyer for $100

Situation — the seller agrees to give a $250 allowance to the buyer for defective goods

Buyer

Debits the account payable to the seller for $250

Credit Memorandum

We have credited your account for $250 as an allowance

Seller

Credits the account receivable from the buyer for $250 and sends the credit memorandum

notifies the buyer of the allowance with a credit memorandum. A *credit* memorandum is used because the adjustment credited the receivable to reduce its balance. When the buyer receives the credit memorandum, it debits Accounts Payable and credits Purchases Returns and Allowances.

Inventory Shrinkage

Merchandising companies lose merchandise in a variety of ways, including shoplifting and deterioration while an item is on the shelf or in the warehouse. These losses are called **shrinkage.**

Even though perpetual inventory systems track all goods as they move into and out of the company, they are not able to directly measure shrinkage. However, these systems allow the accountant to calculate shrinkage by comparing a physical count with recorded quantities.

Because periodic inventory systems do not identify quantities on hand, they cannot provide direct measures of shrinkage. In fact, all that they can determine is the cost of the goods on hand and the goods that passed out of the inventory. The amount that passed out includes the cost of goods sold, stolen, or destroyed. For example, suppose that shoplifters took merchandise that cost $500. Because the goods were not on hand for a physical count, the ending inventory's cost is $500 smaller than it would have been. As a result, the $500 is included in the cost of the goods sold.

Chapter 9 describes perpetual systems and how they provide more complete information about shrinkage. Chapter 9 also describes how an accountant can estimate shrinkage when a periodic system is used.

Progress Check

5–5 Which of the following items is subtracted from the list price of merchandise to determine the actual sales price? *(a)* Freight-in; *(b)* Trade discount; *(c)* Purchases discount; *(d)* Purchases return and/or allowance.

5–6 How is the cost of goods sold determined with a periodic inventory accounting system?

5–7 What is the meaning of the abbreviation *FOB*? What is the meaning of the term *FOB destination?*

Generally accepted accounting principles do not require companies to use exactly the same financial statement formats. In fact, practice shows that many different formats are used. This section of the chapter describes several possible formats that Meg's Mart could use for its income statement.

In Illustration 5–5, we present a **classified income statement** that would probably be distributed only to the company's managers because of the details that it includes. The sales and cost of goods sold sections are the same as the calculations presented earlier in the chapter. The difference between the net sales and cost of goods sold is the gross profit for the year.

Also notice that the operating expenses section classifies the expenses into two categories. **Selling expenses** include the expenses of promoting sales through displaying and advertising the merchandise, making sales, and delivering goods to customers. **General and administrative expenses** support the overall operations of a business and include the expenses of activities such as accounting, human resource management, and financial management.

Some expenses may be divided between categories because they contribute to both activities. For example, Illustration 5–5 reflects the fact that Meg's Mart divided the total rent expense of $9,000 for its store building between the two categories. Ninety percent ($8,100) was selling expense and the remaining 10% ($900) was general and administrative expense.[5] The cost allocation should reflect an economic relationship between the prorated amounts and the activities. For example, the allocation in this case could be based on relative rental values.

In Illustration 5–6, we use the **multiple-step income statement** format that is sometimes used in external reports. The only difference between this format and the one in Illustration 5–5 is that it leaves out the detailed calculations of net sales and cost of goods sold. The format is called multiple-step because it shows several intermediate totals between sales and net income.

In contrast, we present a **single-step income statement** for Meg's Mart in Illustration 5–7. This simpler format includes cost of goods sold as an operating

ALTERNATIVE INCOME STATEMENT FORMATS

LO 3
Describe various formats for income statements and prepare closing entries for a merchandising business.

---

[5]These expenses can be recorded in a single account or in two separate accounts. If they are recorded in one account, the accountant allocates its balance between the two expenses when preparing the statements.

Illustration 5–5   Classified Income Statement for Internal Use

MEG'S MART
Income Statement
For Year Ended December 31, 1997

Sales			$321,000
Less: Sales returns and allowances		$2,000	
Sales discounts		4,300	6,300
Net sales			$314,700
Cost of goods sold:			
Merchandise inventory, December 31, 1996		$19,000	
Purchases	$235,800		
Less: Purchases returns and allowances	$1,500		
Purchases discounts	4,200	5,700	
Net purchases		$230,100	
Add transportation-in		2,300	
Cost of goods purchased		232,400	
Goods available for sale		$251,400	
Merchandise inventory, December 31, 1997		21,000	
Cost of goods sold			230,400
Gross profit from sales			$ 84,300
Operating expenses:			
Selling expenses:			
Amortization expense, store equipment	$ 3,000		
Sales salaries expense	18,500		
Rent expense, selling space	8,100		
Store supplies expense	1,200		
Advertising expense	2,700		
Total selling expenses		$33,500	
General and administrative expenses:			
Amortization expense, office equipment	$ 700		
Office salaries expense	25,300		
Insurance expense	600		
Rent expense, office space	900		
Office supplies expense	1,800		
Total general and administrative expenses		29,300	
Total operating expenses			62,800
Net income			$ 21,500

expense and presents only one intermediate total for total operating expenses. Many companies use this format in their published financial statements.

In practice, many companies use formats that combine some of the features of both the single- and multiple-step statements. As long as the income statement elements are presented logically, management can choose the format that it wants to use.[6]

---

[6]Later chapters describe other possible elements, such as extraordinary gains and losses, that must be presented in specified locations on the income statement.

Illustration 5-6
Multiple-Step Income
Statement

MEG'S MART
Income Statement
For Year Ended December 31, 1997

Net sales		$314,700
Cost of goods sold		230,400
Gross profit from sales		$ 84,300
Operating expenses:		
Selling expenses:		
Amortization expense, store equipment ...	$ 3,000	
Sales salaries expense	18,500	
Rent expense, selling space	8,100	
Store supplies expense	1,200	
Advertising expense	2,700	
Total selling expenses		$33,500
General and administrative expenses:		
Amortization expense, office equipment ..	$ 700	
Office salaries expense	25,300	
Insurance expense	600	
Rent expense, office space	900	
Office supplies expense	1,800	
Total general and administrative expenses .		29,300
Total operating expenses		62,800
Net income		$ 21,500

Illustration 5-7
Single-Step Income
Statement

MEG'S MART
Income Statement
For Year Ended December 31, 1997

Net sales		$314,700
Cost of goods sold	$230,400	
Selling expenses	33,500	
General and administrative expenses	29,300	
Total operating expenses		293,200
Net income		$ 21,500

To help you understand how information flows through the accounting system into the financial statements, we now discuss the process for closing the temporary accounts of merchandising companies. The process is demonstrated with data from the adjusted trial balance for Meg's Mart in Illustration 5–8. In addition, the accountant knows from a physical count that the cost of the ending inventory is $21,000.

The trial balance includes these unique accounts for merchandising activities: Merchandise Inventory, Sales, Sales Returns and Allowances, Sales Discounts, Purchases, Purchases Returns and Allowances, Purchases Discounts, and Transportation-In. Their presence in the ledger causes the four closing entries to be slightly different from the ones described in Chapter 4.

CLOSING ENTRIES FOR MERCHANDISING COMPANIES

Illustration 5–8
Adjusted Trial Balance

MEG'S MART
Adjusted Trial Balance
December 31, 1997

Cash	$ 8,200	
Accounts receivable	11,200	
Merchandise inventory	19,000	
Office supplies	550	
Store supplies	250	
Prepaid insurance	300	
Office equipment	4,200	
Accumulated amortization, office equipment		$ 1,400
Store equipment	30,000	
Accumulated amortization, store equipment		6,000
Accounts payable		16,000
Salaries payable		800
Meg Harlowe, capital		34,000
Meg Harlowe, withdrawals	4,000	
Sales		321,000
Sales returns and allowances	2,000	
Sales discounts	4,300	
Purchases	235,800	
Purchases returns and allowances		1,500
Purchases discounts		4,200
Transportation-in	2,300	
Amortization expense, store equipment	3,000	
Amortization expense, office equipment	700	
Office salaries expense	25,300	
Sales salaries expense	18,500	
Insurance expense	600	
Rent expense, office space	900	
Rent expense, selling space	8,100	
Office supplies expense	1,800	
Store supplies expense	1,200	
Advertising expense	2,700	
Totals	$384,900	$384,900

Entry 1—Record the Ending Inventory and Close the Temporary Accounts that Have Credit Balances

The first entry adds the $21,000 cost of the ending inventory to the balance of the Merchandise Inventory account. It also closes the temporary accounts that have credit balances, including the Sales account and the two contra-purchases accounts. The first closing entry for Meg's Mart is:

Dec.	31	Merchandise Inventory	21,000.00	
		Sales	321,000.00	
		Purchases Returns and Allowances	1,500.00	
		Purchases Discounts	4,200.00	
		Income Summary		347,700.00
		To close temporary accounts with credit balances and record the ending inventory.		

Posting this entry gives zero balances to the three temporary accounts that had credit balances in the adjusted trial balance. It also momentarily increases the balance of the Merchandise Inventory account to $40,000. However, the next entry reduces the balance of this account.

Entry 2—Remove the Beginning Inventory and Close the Temporary Accounts that Have Debit Balances

The second entry subtracts the cost of the beginning inventory from the Merchandise Inventory account. It also closes the temporary accounts that have debit balances, including the expense accounts, the two contra-sales accounts, the Purchases account, and the Transportation-In account. The second closing entry for Meg's Mart is:

Dec.	31	Income Summary	326,200.00	
		Merchandise Inventory		19,000.00
		Sales Returns and Allowances		2,000.00
		Sales Discounts		4,300.00
		Purchases		235,800.00
		Transportation-In		2,300.00
		Amortization Expense, Store Equipment		3,000.00
		Amortization Expense, Office Equipment		700.00
		Office Salaries Expense		25,300.00
		Sales Salaries Expense		18,500.00
		Insurance Expense		600.00
		Rent Expense, Office Space		900.00
		Rent Expense, Selling Space		8,100.00
		Office Supplies Expense		1,800.00
		Store Supplies Expense		1,200.00
		Advertising Expense		2,700.00
		To close temporary accounts with debit balances and to remove the beginning inventory balance.		

Posting this entry reduces the balance of the Merchandise Inventory account to $21,000, which is the amount determined by the physical count on December 31, 1997. It also gives zero balances to the 14 temporary accounts that had debit balances.

After posting the first two closing entries, the Merchandise Inventory account appears as follows:

Merchandise Inventory   **Acct. No.** 119

Date		Explanation	Debit	Credit	Balance
1996					
Dec.	31	Ending balance for 1996			19,000.00
1997					
Dec.	31	First closing entry	21,000.00		40,000.00
	31	Second closing entry		19,000.00	21,000.00

As mentioned earlier in the chapter, the $21,000 balance will remain unchanged throughout 1998 until the accounts are closed at the end of that year.

Entry 3—Close the Income Summary Account to the Owner's Capital Account

The third closing entry for a merchandising company is the same as the third closing entry for a service company. It closes the Income Summary account and updates the balance of the owner's capital account. The third closing entry for Meg's Mart is:

Dec.	31	Income Summary	21,500.00	
		Meg Harlowe, Capital		21,500.00
		To close the Income Summary account.		

The $21,500 amount in the entry is the net income reported on the income statement.

Entry 4—Close the Owner's Withdrawals Account to the Owner's Capital Account

The fourth closing entry for a merchandising company is the same as the fourth closing entry for a service company. It closes the owner's withdrawals account and reduces the balance of the owner's capital account to the amount shown on the balance sheet. The fourth closing entry for Meg's Mart is:

Dec.	31	Meg Harlowe, Capital	4,000.00	
		Meg Harlowe, Withdrawals		4,000.00
		To close the withdrawals account.		

When this entry is posted, all the temporary accounts are cleared and ready to record events in 1998. In addition, the owner's capital account has been fully updated to reflect the events of 1997.

Progress Check

5–8   Which of the following accounts is not unique to a merchandising company? *(a)* Merchandise Inventory; *(b)* Purchases Returns and Allowances; *(c)* Advertising Expense; *(d)* Transportation-In; *(e)* Purchases.

5–9   Which income statement format shows the detailed calculations of net sales and cost of goods sold? Which format does not present any intermediate totals (other than total expenses)?

5–10 Which of the four closing entries includes a credit to Merchandise Inventory?

Illustration 5–9 presents a version of the work sheet that the accountant for Meg's Mart could prepare in the process of developing its 1997 financial statements. It differs in two ways from the 10-column work sheet described in Chapter 4.

The first difference is the deletion of the adjusted trial balance columns. Many accountants delete these columns simply to reduce the size of the work sheet. This has nothing to do with the fact that Meg's Mart is a retail business. The omission of the columns causes the accountant to first compute the adjusted balances and then extend them directly into the financial statement columns.

The second difference appears on the line for the Merchandise Inventory account. The unadjusted trial balance includes the beginning inventory balance of $19,000. This amount is extended into the Debit column for the income statement. Then, the ending balance is entered in the Credit column for the income statement and the Debit column for the balance sheet. This step allows the cost of goods sold to be included in net income while the correct ending balance is included for the balance sheet.

The adjustments in the work sheet reflect the following economic events:

(a) Expiration of $600 of prepaid insurance.
(b) Consumption of $1,200 of store supplies.
(c) Consumption of $1,800 of office supplies.
(d) Amortization of the store equipment for $3,000.
(e) Amortization of the office equipment for $700.
(f) Accrual of $300 of unpaid office salaries and $500 of unpaid store salaries.

Once the adjusted amounts are extended into the financial statement columns, the accountant uses the information to develop the company's financial statements.

A WORK SHEET FOR A MERCHANDISING COMPANY

LO 4

Complete a work sheet for a merchandising company and explain the difference between the closing entry and adjusting entry approaches to updating the Merchandise Inventory account.

You have learned in this chapter that a company's current assets may include a merchandise inventory. Thus, you can understand that a major part of a company's current assets may not be available immediately for paying its existing liabilities. The inventory must be sold and the resulting accounts receivable must be collected before cash is available. As a result, the current ratio (which we described in Chapter 3) may not be an adequate indicator of a company's ability to pay its current liabilities.

Another measure that financial statement users often use to evaluate a company's ability to settle its current debts with its existing assets is the **acid-test ratio.** The acid-test ratio is similar to the current ratio, but differs because it excludes the less liquid current assets. The acid-test ratio is calculated just like the current ratio except that its numerator omits inventory and prepaid expenses. The remaining current assets (cash, temporary investments, and receivables) are called the company's *quick assets*. The formula for the ratio is

$$\text{Acid-test ratio} = \frac{\text{Quick assets}}{\text{Current liabilities}}$$

Recall the discussion of **Imperial Oil Limited** at the beginning of the chapter. The acid-test ratios for Imperial Oil are computed as follows:

USING THE INFORMATION— THE ACID-TEST RATIO

LO 5

Calculate the acid-test ratio and describe what it reveals about a company's liquidity.

Illustration 5–9   Work Sheet for Meg's Mart for the Year Ended December 31, 1997

No.	Account	Unadjusted Trial Balance Dr.	Cr.	Adjustments Dr.	Cr.	Income Statement Dr.	Cr.	Statement of Changes in Owner's Equity and Balance Sheet Dr.	Cr.
101	Cash	8,200						8,200	
106	Accounts receivable	11,200						11,200	
119	**Merchandise inventory**	**19,000**				19,000	21,000	21,000	
124	Office supplies	2,350			(c) 1,800			550	
125	Store supplies	1,450			(b) 1,200			250	
128	Prepaid insurance	900			(a) 600			300	
163	Office equipment	4,200						4,200	
164	Accum. amort., office equipment		700		(e) 700				1,400
165	Store equipment	30,000						30,000	
166	Accum. amort., store equipment		3,000		(d) 3,000				6,000
201	Accounts payable		16,000						16,000
209	Salaries payable				(f) 800				800
301	Meg Harlowe, capital		34,000						34,000
302	Meg Harlowe, withdrawals	4,000						4,000	
413	Sales		321,000				321,000		
414	Sales returns and allowances	2,000				2,000			
415	Sales discounts	4,300				4,300			
505	Purchases	235,800				235,800			
506	Purchases returns and allowances		1,500				1,500		
507	Purchases discounts		4,200				4,200		
508	Transportation-in	2,300				2,300			
612	Amort. expense, store equipment			(d) 3,000		3,000			
613	Amort. expense, office equipment			(e) 700		700			
620	Office salaries expense	25,000		(f) 300		25,300			
621	Sales salaries expense	18,000		(f) 500		18,500			
637	Insurance expense			(a) 600		600			
641	Rent expense, office space	900				900			
642	Rent expense, selling space	8,100				8,100			
650	Office supplies expense			(c) 1,800		1,800			
651	Store supplies expense			(b) 1,200		1,200			
655	Advertising expense	2,700				2,700			
	Totals	380,400	380,400	8,100	8,100	326,200	347,700	79,700	58,200
	Net income					21,500			21,500
	Totals					347,700	347,700	79,700	79,700

		End of Year	
	Acid-Test Ratios	1994	1993
	($409 + $859 + $1,045)/$1,581	1.5	
	($605 + $874 + $899)/$1,593		1.5

In contrast, the current ratios (current assets/current liabilities) for Imperial Oil have these values:

	End of Year	
Current Ratios	1994	1993
$2,797/$1,581	1.8	
$2,899/$1,593		1.8

A traditional rule of thumb is that an acid-test ratio value of at least 1.0 suggests the company is not likely to face a liquidity crisis in the near future. However, a value less than 1.0 may not be threatening if the company can generate enough cash from sales or the accounts payable are not due until later in the year. On the other hand, a value more than 1.0 may hide a liquidity crisis if the payables are due at once but the receivables will not be collected until late in the year. These possibilities reinforce the point that a single ratio is seldom enough to indicate strength or weakness. However, it can identify areas that the analyst should look into more deeply.

Progress Check

5-11 **Which assets are defined as quick assets for the purpose of calculating the acid-test ratio?** *(a)* **Cash, temporary investments, and prepaid expenses;** *(b)* **Merchandise inventory and prepaid expenses;** *(c)* **Merchandise inventory and temporary investments;** *(d)* **Cash, temporary investments, and receivables.**

5-12 **Which ratio is a more strict test of a company's ability to meet its obligations in the very near future, the acid-test ratio or the current ratio?**

SUMMARY OF THE CHAPTER IN TERMS OF LEARNING OBJECTIVES

LO 1. Describe merchandising activities, analyze their effects on financial statements, and record sales of merchandise. Merchandising companies purchase and sell products. Their financial statements include the cost of the merchandise inventory in the current assets on the balance sheet and sales and cost of goods sold on the income statement. The difference between sales and cost of goods sold is called gross profit.

The seller of merchandise records the sale at the list price less any trade discount. Any returns or allowances are recorded in a contra account to provide information to the manager. When cash discounts from the sales price are offered and the customers pay within the discount period, the seller records the discounts in a contra-sales account.

LO 2. Describe how the ending inventory and the cost of goods sold are determined with perpetual and periodic inventory accounting systems. A perpetual inventory system continuously tracks the cost of goods on hand and the cost of goods sold. A periodic system merely accumulates the cost of goods purchased during the year and does not provide continuous information about the cost of the inventory or the sold goods. At year-end, the cost of the inventory is determined and used to calculate the cost of goods sold. The cost of goods available for sale equals the beginning inventory plus the cost of goods purchased. The cost of goods sold equals the cost of goods available for sale minus the cost of the ending inventory. The cost of goods purchased is affected by purchases discounts, purchases returns and allowances, and transportation-in. These amounts are recorded in contra and supplemental accounts to provide information to management. The contra and supplemental accounts are seldom reported in external statements.

LO 3. Describe various formats for income statements and prepare closing entries for a merchandising business. Companies have flexibility in choosing formats for their income statements. Internal statements show more details, including the calculations of net sales and the cost of goods sold. Classified income statements describe expenses incurred in different activities. Multiple-step statements include several intermediate totals and single-step statements do not.

In the closing entry approach, the Merchandise Inventory account is updated in the process of making closing entries. The ending inventory amount is added to the account as part of the entry that closes the income statement accounts with credit balances. The beginning inventory amount is removed from the account as part of the entry that closes the income statement accounts with debit balances.

LO 4. Complete a work sheet that includes the inventory-related accounts. The work sheet for a merchandising company uses special entries to update the inventory. The beginning inventory balance is extended into the Income Statement Debit column and the cost of the ending inventory is entered in the Income Statement Credit column and Balance Sheet Debit column. Many accountants omit the adjusted trial balance columns to reduce the size of the work sheet.

LO 5. Calculate the acid-test ratio and describe what it reveals about a company's liquidity. The acid-test ratio is used to assess a company's ability to pay its current liabilities with its existing quick assets (cash, temporary investments, and receivables). The costs of the merchandise inventory and prepaid expenses are not included in the numerator. A ratio value equal to or greater than one is usually considered to be adequate.

DEMONSTRATION PROBLEM

Use the following adjusted trial balance and additional information to complete the requirements:

YE OLDE JUNQUE AND STUFF
Adjusted Trial Balance
December 31, 1997

Cash	$ 19,000	
Merchandise inventory	52,000	
Store supplies	1,000	
Equipment	40,000	
Accumulated amortization, equipment		$ 16,500
Accounts payable		8,000
Salaries payable		1,000
Ann Teak, capital		69,000
Ann Teak, withdrawals	8,000	
Sales		320,000
Sales discounts	20,000	
Purchases	147,000	
Purchases discounts		12,000
Transportation-in	11,000	
Amortization expense	5,500	
Salaries expense	60,000	
Insurance expense	12,000	
Rent expense	24,000	
Store supplies expense	6,000	
Advertising expense	21,000	
Totals	$426,500	$426,500

A physical count shows that the cost of the year's ending inventory is $50,000.

Required

1. Prepare schedules that calculate the company's net sales and cost of goods sold for the year.
2. Present a single-step income statement for 1997.
3. Prepare closing entries.

Planning the Solution

- The calculation of net sales deducts discounts from sales. The calculation of cost of goods sold adds the cost of goods purchased for the year to the beginning inventory and then subtracts the cost of the ending inventory.

- To prepare the single-step income statement, find the net sales and then list the operating expenses. Use the cost of goods sold number calculated in the first requirement.

- The first closing entry debits the inventory account for the cost of the ending inventory and debits all temporary accounts with credit balances. The second closing entry credits the inventory account with the cost of the beginning inventory and credits all temporary accounts with debit balances. The third entry closes the Income Summary account to the owner's capital account, and the fourth closing entry closes the owner's withdrawals account to the owner's capital account.

Solution to Demonstration Problem

1.

Sales		$320,000
Less sales discounts		(20,000)
Net sales		$300,000
Beginning inventory		$ 52,000
Purchases	$147,000	
Less purchases discounts	(12,000)	
Plus transportation-in	11,000	
Cost of goods purchased		146,000
Cost of goods available for sale		$198,000
Less ending inventory		(50,000)
Cost of goods sold		$148,000

2.

YE OLDE JUNQUE AND STUFF
Income Statement
For Year Ended December 31, 1997

Net sales.		$300,000
Operating expenses:		
Cost of goods sold.	$148,000	
Amortization expense.	5,500	
Salaries expense	60,000	
Insurance expense	12,000	
Rent expense	24,000	
Store supplies expense	6,000	
Advertising expense.	21,000	
Total expenses.		276,500
Net income.		$ 23,500

3.

Dec.	31	Merchandise Inventory	50,000.00	
		Sales	320,000.00	
		Purchases Discounts	12,000.00	
		Income Summary		382,000.00
		To close temporary accounts with credit balances and record the ending inventory.		
Dec.	31	Income Summary	358,500.00	
		Merchandise Inventory		52,000.00
		Sales Discounts		20,000.00
		Purchases		147,000.00
		Transportation-In		11,000.00
		Amortization Expense		5,500.00
		Salaries Expense		60,000.00
		Insurance Expense		12,000.00
		Rent Expense		24,000.00
		Store Supplies Expense		6,000.00
		Advertising Expense		21,000.00
		To close temporary accounts with debit balances and to remove the beginning inventory balance.		
Dec.	31	Income Summary	23,500.00	
		Ann Teak, Capital		23,500.00
		To close the Income Summary account.		
Dec.	31	Ann Teak, Capital	8,000.00	
		Ann Teak, Withdrawals		8,000.00
		To close the withdrawals account.		

The Adjusting Entry Approach to Recording the Change in the Merchandise Inventory Account

In the previous sections, the change in the Merchandise Inventory account was recorded in the process of making closing entries. This closing entry approach is widely used in practice. However, it is not the only bookkeeping method that can be applied at the end of the year. Another approach is to record the change in the Merchandise Inventory account with adjusting entries. When this approach is followed, the first two closing entries do not include changes in the Merchandise Inventory account. This adjusting entry approach is preferred by some accountants. It is also used by many computerized accounting systems that do not allow the Merchandise Inventory account (a permanent account) to be changed in the closing process.

LO 7

Explain an adjusting entry approach to recording the change in the Merchandise Inventory account.

The Adjusting Entries

Under the adjusting entry approach, Meg's Mart removes the beginning balance from the Merchandise Inventory account by recording this adjusting entry at the end of 1997:

Dec.	31	Income Summary	19,000.00	
		Merchandise Inventory		19,000.00
		To remove the beginning balance from the Merchandise Inventory account.		

The second adjusting entry produces the correct ending balance in the Merchandise Inventory account:

Dec.	31	Merchandise Inventory	21,000.00	
		Income Summary		21,000.00
		To insert the correct ending balance into the Merchandise Inventory account.		

After this entry is posted, the Merchandise Inventory account has a $21,000 debit balance. In addition, the Income Summary account has a $2,000 credit balance.

The Closing Entries

If the two adjusting entries for inventory are used, the closing entries differ only by not including the Merchandise Inventory account. Thus, Meg's Mart records the following two closing entries for 1997 under the adjusting entry approach:

Dec.	31	Sales	321,000.00	
		Purchases Returns and Allowances	1,500.00	
		Purchases Discounts	4,200.00	
		Income Summary		326,700.00
		To close temporary accounts with credit balances.		

Dec.	31	Income Summary	307,200.00	
		Sales Returns and Allowances		2,000.00
		Sales Discounts		4,300.00
		Purchases		235,800.00
		Transportation-In		2,300.00
		Amortization Expense, Store Equipment		3,000.00
		Amortization Expense, Office Equipment		700.00
		Office Salaries Expense		25,300.00
		Sales Salaries Expense		18,500.00
		Insurance Expense		600.00
		Rent Expense, Office Space		900.00
		Rent Expense, Selling Space		8,100.00
		Office Supplies Expense		1,800.00
		Store Supplies Expense		1,200.00
		Advertising Expense		2,700.00
		To close temporary accounts with debit balances.		

The third and fourth entries are the same as before, although now the amount debited to the Income Summary account is based on four previous entries instead of two:

Dec.	31	Income Summary	21,500.00	
		Meg Harlowe, Capital		21,500.00
		To close the Income Summary account.		
Dec.	31	Meg Harlowe, Capital	4,000.00	
		Meg Harlowe, Withdrawals		4,000.00
		To close the withdrawals account.		

The Adjusting Entry Approach and the Work Sheet. If the accountant uses the adjusting entry approach to update the inventory account, the two adjustments are included in the adjustments columns in the work sheet, and a line for the Income Summary account is inserted at the bottom of the work sheet.

Progress Check

5-13 In which of the following columns is the ending inventory entered on the work sheet when the closing entry approach is used to record the change in inventory? *(a)* Unadjusted Trial Balance Debit Column; *(b)* Adjustments Debit column; *(c)* Income Statement Debit column; *(d)* Income Statement Credit column; *(e)* Balance Sheet Credit column.

5-14 Will the reported amounts of ending inventory and net income differ if the adjusting entry approach to recording the change in inventory is used instead of the closing entry approach?

LO 7. Explain an adjusting entry approach to recording the change in the Merchandise Inventory account. The adjusting entry approach to recording the ending inventory in the accounts uses two adjusting entries that remove the beginning cost from and add the ending cost to the Merchandise Inventory account. This approach is often used in computer systems.

SUMMARY OF APPENDIX E IN TERMS OF LEARNING OBJECTIVE

GLOSSARY

Acid-test ratio a ratio used to assess the company's ability to settle its current debts with its existing assets; it is the ratio between a company's quick assets (cash, temporary investments, and receivables) and its current liabilities. p. 259

Cash discount a reduction in a debt that is granted by a seller to a purchaser in exchange for the purchaser's making payment within a specified period of time called the discount period. p. 241

Classified income statement an income statement format that classifies items in significant groups and shows detailed calculations of sales and cost of goods sold. p. 253

Credit memorandum a notification that the sender has entered a credit in the recipient's account maintained by the sender. p. 251

Credit period the time period that can pass before a customer's payment is due. p. 241

Credit terms the description of the amounts and timing of payments that a buyer agrees to make in the future. p. 241

Debit memorandum a notification that the sender has entered a debit in the recipient's account maintained by the sender. p. 251

Discount period the time period in which a cash discount is available. p. 242

EOM the abbreviation for *end-of-month*; used to describe credit terms for some transactions. p. 241

FOB the abbreviation for *free on board;* the designated point at which ownership of goods passes to the buyer; FOB shipping point (or factory) means that the buyer pays the shipping costs and FOB destination means that the seller pays the shipping costs. p. 250

General and administrative expenses expenses that support the overall operations of a business and include the expenses of such activities as providing accounting services, human resource management, and financial management. p. 253

Gross profit the difference between net sales and the cost of goods sold. p. 239

List price the nominal price of an item before any trade discount is deducted. p. 247

Merchandise goods acquired for the purpose of reselling them to customers. p. 238

Merchandise inventory goods a company owns on any given date and holds for the purpose of selling them to its customers. p. 239

Multiple-step income statement an income statement format that shows several intermediate totals between sales and net income. p. 253

Periodic inventory system a method of accounting that records the cost of inventory purchased but does not track the quantity on hand or sold to customers; the records are updated periodically to reflect the results of physical counts of the items on hand. p. 243

Perpetual inventory system a method of accounting that maintains continuous records of the amount of inventory on hand and sold. p. 243

Purchases discount a cash discount taken against an amount owed to a supplier of goods. p. 247

Sales discount a cash discount taken by customers against an amount owed to the seller. p. 242

Selling expenses the expenses of promoting sales by displaying and advertising the merchandise, making sales, and delivering goods to customers. p. 253

Shrinkage inventory losses that occur as a result of shoplifting or deterioration. p. 252

Single-step income statement an income statement format that does not present intermediate totals other than total expenses. p. 253

Trade discount a reduction below a list or catalogue price that is negotiated in setting the selling price of goods. p. 247

SYNONYMOUS TERMS

Actual sales price invoice price
FOB factory FOB shipping point
Gross profit gross margin

List price catalogue price
Merchandise goods

The letter E identifies the questions, quick studies, exercises, and problems based on Appendix E at the end of the chapter.

QUESTIONS

1. What item on the balance sheet is unique to merchandising companies? What items on the income statement are unique to merchandising companies?

2. Explain how a business can earn a gross profit on its sales and still have a net loss.

3. Why would a company offer a cash discount?

4. What is the difference between a sales discount and a purchases discount?

5. In counting the ending inventory, an employee omitted the contents of one shelf that contained merchandise with a cost of $2,300. How would this omission affect the company's balance sheet and income statement?

6. Distinguish between cash discounts and trade discounts. Is the amount of a trade discount on purchased merchandise recorded in the Purchases Discounts account?

7. Why would a company's manager be concerned about the quantity of its purchases returns if its suppliers allow unlimited returns?

8. What do the sender and the recipient of a debit memorandum record in their accounts?

9. What is the difference between single-step and multiple-step income statement formats?

10. Does the beginning or ending inventory appear on the unadjusted trial balance of a company that uses a periodic inventory system?

11. How and when is cost of goods sold determined in a store that uses a periodic inventory system?

12. When is the cost of goods sold recorded when a company uses a perpetual inventory system?

13. Why should the manager of a business be interested in the amount of its sales returns and allowances?

14. Since sales returns and allowances are subtracted from sales on the income statement, why not save the effort of this subtraction by debiting all such returns and allowances directly to the Sales account?

QUICK STUDY (Five-Minute Exercises)

Calculate net sales and gross profit in each of the following situations:

QS 5–1
(LO 1)

	a	b	c	d
Sales	$125,000	$505,000	$33,700	$256,700
Sales discounts	3,200	13,500	300	4,000
Sales returns and allowances	19,000	3,000	6,000	600
Cost of goods sold	67,600	352,700	22,300	123,900

A company purchased merchandise that cost $165,000 during the year that just ended. Determine the company's cost of goods sold in each of the following four situations:

QS 5–2
(LO 2)

a. There were no beginning or ending inventories.

b. There was a beginning inventory of $35,000 and no ending inventory.

c. There was a $30,000 beginning inventory and a $42,000 ending inventory.

d. There was no beginning inventory but there was a $21,000 ending inventory.

Given the following accounts with normal year-end balances, prepare the entry to close the income statement accounts that have debit balances (entry 2):

QS 5–3
(LO 3)

Merchandise inventory	$ 34,800
Jan Dean, capital	115,300
Jan Dean, withdrawals	4,000
Sales	157,200
Sales returns and allowances	3,500
Sales discounts	1,700
Purchases	102,000
Purchases returns and allowances	8,100
Purchases discounts	2,000
Transportation-in	5,400
Amortization expense	7,300
Salaries expense	29,500
Miscellaneous expenses	1,900

Refer to the information in QS 5–3. Prepare the entry to close the income statement accounts that have debit balances (entry 2) assuming the business uses the adjusting entry approach to record the change in merchandise inventory.

^EQS 5–4
(LO 4)

Use the following information to calculate the acid-test ratio:

QS 5–5
(LO 5)

Cash	$1,000
Accounts receivable	2,500
Inventory	6,000
Prepaid expenses	500
Accounts payable	3,750
Other current liabilities	1,250

EXERCISES

Exercise 5–1
Merchandising terms
(LO 1, 2)

Insert the letter for each term in the blank space beside the definition that it most closely matches:

A. Cash discount	E. FOB shipping point	H. Purchases discount
B. Credit period	F. Gross profit	I. Sales discount
C. Discount period	G. Inventory	J. Trade discount
D. FOB destination		

____ 1. An agreement that ownership of goods is transferred at the buyer's place of business.

____ 2. The time period in which a cash discount is available

____ 3. The difference between net sales and the cost of goods sold.

____ 4. A reduction in a receivable or payable that is granted if it is paid within the discount period.

____ 5. A cash discount taken against an amount owed to a supplier of goods.

____ 6. An agreement that ownership of goods is transferred at the seller's place of business.

____ 7. A reduction below a list or catalogue price that is negotiated in setting the selling price of goods.

____ 8. A cash discount taken by customers against an amount owed to the seller.

____ 9. The time period that can pass before a customer's payment is due.

____ 10. The goods that a company owns and expects to sell to its customers.

Exercise 5–2
Calculating cost of goods sold
(LO 2)

Determine each of the missing numbers in the following situations:

	a	b	c
Purchases	$45,000	$80,000	$61,000
Purchases discounts	2,000	?	1,300
Purchases returns and allowances	1,500	3,000	2,200
Transportation-in	?	7,000	8,000
Beginning inventory	3,500	?	18,000
Cost of goods purchased	44,700	79,000	?
Ending inventory	2,200	15,000	?
Cost of goods sold	?	83,200	68,260

Exercise 5–3
Recording journal entries for merchandise transactions
(LO 2)

Prepare journal entries to record the following transactions for a retail store:

March 2   Purchased merchandise from Alfa Company under the following terms: $1,800 invoice price, 2/15, n/60, FOB factory.

       3   Paid $125 for shipping charges on the purchase of March 2.

       4   Returned to Alfa Company unacceptable merchandise that had an invoice price of $300.

     17   Sent a cheque to Alfa Company for the March 2 purchase, net of the discount and the returned merchandise.

March 18 Purchased merchandise from Bravo Company under the following terms: $2,500 invoice price, 2/10, n/30, FOB destination.

21 After brief negotiations, received a credit memorandum from Bravo Company granting a $700 allowance on the purchase of March 18.

28 Sent a cheque to Bravo Company paying for the March 18 purchase, net of the discount and the allowance.

On May 12, Wilcox Company accepted delivery of $20,000 of merchandise and received an invoice dated May 11, with terms of 3/10, n/30, FOB Garner Company's factory. When the goods were delivered, Wilcox Company paid $185 to Express Shipping Service for the delivery charges on the merchandise. The next day, Wilcox Company returned $800 of defective goods to the seller, which received them one day later. On May 21, Wilcox Company mailed a cheque to Garner Company for the amount owed on that date. It was received the following day.

Exercise 5–4
Analyzing and recording merchandise transactions and returns
(LO 1, 2)

Required

a. Present the journal entries that Wilcox Company should record for these transactions.

b. Present the journal entries that Garner Company should record for these transactions.

Sandra's Store purchased merchandise from a manufacturer with an invoice price of $11,000 and credit terms of 3/10, n/60, and paid within the discount period.

Exercise 5–5
Analyzing and recording merchandise transactions and discounts
(LO 1, 2)

Required

a. Prepare the journal entries that the purchaser should record for the purchase and payment.

b. Prepare the journal entries that the seller should record for the sale and collection.

c. Assume that the buyer borrowed enough cash to pay the balance on the last day of the discount period at an annual interest rate of 8% and paid it back on the last day of the credit period. Calculate how much the buyer saved by following this strategy. (Use a 365-day year.)

The following information appeared in a company's income statement:

Exercise 5–6
Calculating expenses and cost of goods sold
(LO 1, 2)

Sales	$300,000
Sales returns	15,000
Sales discounts	4,500
Beginning inventory	25,000
Purchases	180,000
Purchases returns and allowances	6,000
Purchases discounts	3,600
Transportation-in	11,000
Gross profit from sales	105,000
Net income	55,000

Required

Calculate the *(a)* total operating expenses, *(b)* cost of goods sold, and *(c)* ending inventory.

Exercise 5–7
Calculating expenses
and income
(LO 1, 2)

Fill in the blanks in the following income statements. Identify any losses by putting the amount in parentheses.

	a	b	c	d	e
Sales	$40,000	$85,000	$24,000	$?	$59,000
Cost of goods sold:					
Beginning inventory	$ 4,000	$ 6,200	$ 5,000	$ 3,500	$ 6,400
Purchases	24,000	?	?	16,000	14,000
Ending inventory	?	(5,400)	(6,000)	(3,300)	?
Cost of goods sold	$22,700	$31,800	$?	$?	$14,000
Gross profit	$?	$?	$ 2,500	$22,800	$?
Expenses	6,000	21,300	8,100	1,300	15,000
Net income (loss)	$?	$31,900	$ (5,600)	$21,500	$?

Exercise 5–8
Multiple-step income
statement and other
calculations
(LO 3)

The following accounts and balances are taken from the year-end adjusted trial balance of the Vintage Shop, a single proprietorship. Use the information in these columns to complete the requirements.

	Debit	Credit
Merchandise inventory	$ 28,000	
Sales		$425,000
Sales returns and allowances	16,500	
Sales discounts	4,000	
Purchases	240,000	
Purchases returns and allowances		18,000
Purchases discounts		2,000
Transportation-in	6,000	
Selling expenses	35,000	
General and administrative expenses ..	95,000	

The count of the ending inventory shows that its cost is $37,000.

Required

a.   Calculate the company's net sales for the year.

b.   Calculate the company's cost of goods purchased for the year.

c.   Calculate the company's cost of goods sold for the year.

d.   Prepare a multiple-step income statement for the year that lists net sales, cost of goods sold, gross profit, the operating expenses, and net income.

Exercise 5–9
Classified income
statement
(LO 3)

Use the information provided in Exercise 5–8 to prepare a classified income statement that shows the calculations of net sales and cost of goods sold.

Exercise 5–10
Closing entries
(LO 3)

The Vintage Shop described in Exercise 5–8 is owned and operated by Otto Vintage. The ending balance of Vintage's withdrawals account is $25,000. Prepare four closing entries for this company. Post the entries to a balance column account for Merchandise Inventory that includes the beginning balance.

The Vintage Shop described in Exercise 5–8 is owned and operated by Otto Vintage. The ending balance of Vintage's withdrawals account is $25,000. Assume that the company uses the adjusting entry approach to update its inventory account. Prepare adjusting and closing journal entries for this company, and post them to a balance column account for Merchandise Inventory that includes the beginning balance.

ᴱExercise 5–11
Adjusting entry
approach
(LO 7)

The following closing entries for Fox Fixtures Co. were made on March 31, the end of its annual accounting period:

Exercise 5–12
Preparing reports from
closing entries
(LO 3)

1.

Merchandise Inventory	11,000.00	
Sales	445,000.00	
Purchases Returns and Allowances	22,000.00	
Purchases Discounts	11,400.00	
Income Summary		489,400.00

To close temporary accounts with credit balances and record the ending inventory.

2.

Income Summary	453,300.00	
Merchandise Inventory		15,000.00
Sales Returns and Allowances		25,000.00
Sales Discounts		16,000.00
Purchases		286,000.00
Transportation-In		8,800.00
Selling Expenses		69,000.00
General and Administrative Expenses		33,500.00

To close temporary accounts with debit balances and to remove the beginning inventory balance.

Required

Use the information in the closing entries to prepare:

a. A calculation of net sales.

b. A calculation of cost of goods purchased.

c. A calculation of cost of goods sold.

d. A multiple-step income statement for the year that lists net sales, cost of goods sold, gross profit, the operating expenses, and net income.

The following unadjusted trial balance was taken from the ledger of Johnson's Newsstand at the end of its fiscal year. (To reduce your effort, the account balances are relatively small.)

Exercise 5–13
Preparing a work sheet
for a merchandising
proprietorship
(LO 4)

JOHNSON'S NEWSSTAND
Unadjusted Trial Balance
December 31

No.	Title	Debit	Credit
101	Cash	$ 3,700	
106	Accounts receivable	1,800	
119	Merchandise inventory	1,200	
125	Store supplies	600	
201	Accounts payable		$ 140
209	Salaries payable		
301	Tod Johnson, capital		5,785
302	Tod Johnson, withdrawals	375	
413	Sales		6,000
414	Sales returns and allowances	145	
505	Purchases	3,200	
506	Purchases discounts		125
507	Transportation-in	80	
622	Salaries expense	700	
640	Rent expense	250	
651	Store supplies expense		
	Totals	$12,050	$12,050

Required

Use the preceding information and the following additional facts to complete an eight-column work sheet for the company (do not include columns for the adjusted trial balance).

a.   The ending inventory of store supplies was $450.

b.   Accrued salaries at the end of the year were $60.

c.   The ending merchandise inventory was $1,360.

Exercise 5–14
Acid-test ratio
(LO 5)

Calculate the current and acid-test ratios in each of the following cases:

	Case X	Case Y	Case Z
Cash	$ 800	$ 910	$1,100
Temporary investments			500
Receivables		990	800
Inventory	2,000	1,000	4,000
Prepaid expenses	1,200	600	900
Total current assets	$4,000	$3,500	$7,300
Current liabilities	$2,200	$1,100	$3,650

PROBLEMS

Problem 5–1
Journal entries for
merchandising activities
(LO 1, 2)

Prepare general journal entries to record the following transactions of the Belton Company and determine the cost of goods purchased and net sales for the month. (Use a separate account for each receivable and payable; for example, record the purchase on July 1 in Accounts Payable—Jones Co.)

July 1   Purchased merchandise from the Jones Company for $3,000 under credit terms of 1/15, n/30, FOB factory.

July 2   Sold merchandise to Terra Co. for $800 under credit terms of 2/10, n/60, FOB shipping point.

3   Paid $100 for freight charges on the purchase of July 1.

8   Sold $1,600 of merchandise for cash.

9   Purchased merchandise from the Keene Co. for $2,300 under credit terms of 2/15, n/30, FOB destination.

12   Received a $200 credit memorandum acknowledging the return of merchandise purchased on July 9.

13   Received the balance due from the Terra Co. for the credit sale dated July 2, net of the discount.

16   Paid the balance due to the Jones Company within the discount period.

19   Sold merchandise to Urban Co. for $1,250 under credit terms of 2/10, n/60, FOB shipping point.

21   Issued a $150 credit memorandum to Urban Co. for an allowance on goods sold on July 19.

22   Received a debit memorandum from Urban Co. for an error that overstated the total invoice by $50.

24   Paid the Keene Co. the balance due after deducting the discount.

30   Received the balance due from the Urban Co. for the credit sale dated July 19, net of the discount.

31   Sold merchandise to Terra Co. for $5,000 under credit terms of 2/10, n/60, FOB shipping point.

Prepare general journal entries to record the following transactions of Schafer Merchandising:

Problem 5–2
Journal entries for merchandising transactions
(LO 1, 2)

Oct. 1   Purchased merchandise on credit, terms 2/10, n/30, $7,200.

2   Sold merchandise for cash, $750.

7   Purchased merchandise on credit, terms 2/10, n/30, $5,250, FOB the seller's factory.

7   Paid $225 cash for freight charges on the merchandise shipment of the previous transaction.

8   Purchased delivery equipment on credit, $12,000.

12   Sold merchandise on credit, terms 2/15, 1/30, n/60, $3,000.

13   Received a $750 credit memorandum for merchandise purchased on October 7 and returned for credit.

13   Purchases office supplies on credit, $240, n/30.

15   Sold merchandise on credit, terms 2/10, 1/30, n/60, $2,100.

15   Paid for the merchandise purchased on October 7, less the return and the discount.

16   Received a credit memorandum for unsatisfactory office supplies purchased on October 13 and returned, $60.

19   Issued a $210 credit memorandum to the customer who purchased merchandise on October 15 and returned a portion for credit.

25   Received payment for the merchandise sold on October 15, less the return and applicable discount.

27   The customer of October 12 paid for the purchase of that date, less the applicable discount.

31   Paid for the merchandise purchased on October 1.

Problem 5–3
Income statements and
closing entries
(LO 1, 2, 3)

On December 31, 1996, the end of Seaside Sales' annual accounting period, the financial statement columns of its work sheet appeared as follows:

	Income Statement		Balance Sheet	
	Debit	**Credit**	**Debit**	**Credit**
Merchandise inventory	69,330	66,545	66,545	
Other assets			487,785	
Debra Kelso, capital				200,000
Liabilities				312,370
Debra Kelso, withdrawals			50,000	
Sales		963,720		
Sales returns and allowances	5,715			
Sales discounts	14,580			
Purchases	651,735			
Purchases returns and allowances		2,730		
Purchases discounts		8,970		
Transportation-in	9,205			
Sales salaries expense	80,080			
Rent expense, selling space	33,000			
Store supplies expense	1,620			
Amortization expense, store equipment ...	8,910			
Office salaries expense	65,945			
Rent expense, office space	3,000			
Office supplies expense	735			
Insurance expense	3,390			
Amortization expense, office equipment ..	2,760			
	950,005	1,041,965	604,330	512,370
Net income	91,960			91,960
	1,041,965	1,041,965	604,330	604,330

Required

1. Prepare a 1996 classified, multiple-step income statement for Seaside, showing in detail the expenses and the items that make up cost of goods sold.

2. Prepare compound closing entries for Seaside.

3. Open a Merchandise Inventory account and enter a December 31, 1995, balance of $69,330. Then post those portions of the closing entries that affect the account.

4. Prepare a single-step income statement. Condense each revenue and expense category into a single item.

The December 31, 1996, year-end, unadjusted trial balance of the ledger of Eastman Store, a single proprietorship business, is as follows:

Problem 5–4
Proprietorship work sheet, income statement, and closing entries
(LO 2, 3, 4)

EASTMAN STORE
Unadjusted Trial Balance
December 31, 1996

Cash	$ 7,305	
Merchandise inventory	47,000	
Store supplies	1,715	
Office supplies	645	
Prepair insurance	3,840	
Store equipment	57,735	
Accumulated amortization, store equipment		$ 9,575
Office equipment	14,130	
Accumulated amortization, office equipment		3,670
Accounts payable		4,680
Bob Eastman, capital		93,585
Bob Eastman, withdrawals	31,500	
Sales		478,850
Sales returns and allowances	3,185	
Sales discounts	5,190	
Purchases	331,315	
Purchases returns and allowances		1,845
Purchases discounts		4,725
Transportation-in	2,810	
Sales salaries expense	34,710	
Rent expense, selling space	24,000	
Advertising expense	1,220	
Store supplies expense	–0–	
Amortization expense, store equipment	–0–	
Office salaries expense	27,630	
Rent expense, office space	3,000	
Office supplies expense	–0–	
Insurance expense	–0–	
Amortization expense, office equipment	–0–	
Totals	$596,930	$596,930

Required

1. Copy the unadjusted trial balance on a work sheet form and complete the work sheet using the following information:
   a. Store supplies inventory, $385.
   b. Office supplies inventory, $180.
   c. Expired insurance, $2,765.
   d. Amortization on the store equipment, $5,865.
   e. Amortization on the office equipment, $1,755.
   f. Ending merchandise inventory, $48,980.
2. Journalize closing entries for the store.
3. Open a balance column Merchandise Inventory account and enter a December 31, 1995, balance of $47,000. Then post those portions of the closing entries that affect the account.

The following amounts appeared on the Gershwin Company's adjusted trial balance as of October 31, the end of its fiscal year:

Problem 5–5
Income statement calculations and formats
(LO 1, 2, 3)

	Debit	Credit
Merchandise inventory	$ 25,000	
Other assets	140,000	
Liabilities		$ 37,000
G. Gershwin, capital		117,650
G. Gershwin, withdrawals	17,000	
Sales		210,000
Sales returns and allowances	15,000	
Sales discounts	2,250	
Purchases	90,000	
Purchases returns and allowances		4,300
Purchases discounts		1,800
Transportation-in	3,100	
Sales salaries expense	28,000	
Rent expense, selling space	10,000	
Store supplies expense	3,000	
Advertising expense	18,000	
Office salaries expense	16,000	
Rent expense, office space	2,500	
Office supplies expense	900	
Totals	$370,750	$370,750

A physical count shows that the cost of the ending inventory is $27,000.

Required

1. Calculate the company's net sales for the year.

2. Calculate the company's cost of goods purchased for the year.

3. Calculate the company's cost of goods sold for the year.

4. Present a multiple-step income statement that lists the company's net sales, cost of goods sold, and gross profit, as well as the components and amounts of selling expenses and general and administrative expenses.

5. Present a condensed single-step income statement that lists these expenses: cost of goods sold, selling expenses, and general and administrative expenses.

Problem 5–6
Closing entries and interpreting information about discounts and returns
(LO 1, 3)

Use the data for the Gershwin Company in Problem 5–5 to meet the following requirements:

Required

Preparation component:

1. Prepare closing entries for the company as of October 31.

Analysis component:

2. All of the company's purchases were made on credit and the suppliers uniformly offer a 3% discount. Does it appear that the company's cash management system is accomplishing the goal of taking all available discounts?

3. In prior years, the company has experienced a 4% return rate on its sales, which means that approximately 4% of its gross sales were for items that were eventually returned outright or that caused the company to grant allowances to customers. How does this year's record compare to prior years' results?

Refer to the Gershwin Company data in Problem 5-5 and notice that the adjusted trial balance reflects the closing entry approach to account for merchandise inventory. Now assume that the company has decided to switch to the adjusting entry approach.

Required

Preparation component:

1. Prepare adjusting entries to update the Merchandise Inventory account at October 31 and then prepare closing entries for the company as of October 31.

Analysis component:

2. All of the company's purchases were made on credit and the suppliers uniformly offer a 2.1% discount. Does it appear that the company's cash management system is accomplishing the goal of taking all available discounts?

3. In prior years, the company has experienced a 9% return rate on its sales, which means that approximately 9% of its gross sales were for items that were eventually returned outright or that caused the company to grant allowances to customers. How does this year's record compare to prior years' results?

The following unadjusted trial balance was prepared at the end of the fiscal year for Ruth's Place:

EProblem 5-7
Adjusting entries, closing entries, and interpreting information about discounts and returns
(LO 1, 3, 4)

Problem 5-8
Work sheet, income statements, and acid-test ratio
(LO 3, 4, 5)

RUTH'S PLACE
Unadjusted Trial Balance
December 31

101	Cash	$ 4,000	
119	Merchandise inventory	9,900	
125	Store supplies	5,000	
128	Prepaid insurance	2,000	
165	Store equipment	45,000	
166	Accumulated amortization, store equipment		$ 6,000
201	Accounts payable		8,000
301	Ruth Helm, capital		35,200
302	Ruth Helm, withdrawals	3,500	
413	Sales		90,000
415	Sales discounts	1,000	
505	Purchases	38,000	
506	Purchases returns and allowances		800
508	Transportation-in	1,800	
612	Amortization expense, store equipment		
622	Salaries expense	16,000	
637	Insurance expense		
640	Rent expense	5,000	
651	Store supplies expense		
655	Advertising expense	8,800	
	Totals	$140,000	$140,000

Required

1. Use the unadjusted trial balance and the following information to prepare an eight-column work sheet for the company:

   a. The ending inventory of store supplies is $650.

   b. Expired insurance for the year is $1,200.

c. Amortization expense for the year is $9,000.

d. The ending merchandise inventory is $11,500.

2. Prepare a detailed multiple-step income statement that would be used by the store's owner.

3. Prepare a single-step income statement that would be provided to decision makers outside the company.

4. Compute the company's current and acid-test ratios as of December 31.

Problem 5–9
Proprietorship work sheet, financial statements, and closing entries
(LO 1, 2, 4)

The unadjusted trial balance of Classic Threads on December 31, 1996, the end of the annual accounting period, is as follows:

CLASSIC THREADS
Unadjusted Trial Balance
December 31, 1996

Cash	$ 10,275	
Accounts receivable	22,665	
Merchandise inventory	51,845	
Store supplies	2,415	
Office supplies	775	
Prepaid insurance	3,255	
Store equipment	61,980	
Accumulated amortization, store equipment		$ 10,830
Office equipment	12,510	
Accumulated amortization, office equipment		2,825
Accounts payable		8,310
Salaries payable		–0–
Sally Fowler, capital		106,015
Sally Fowler, withdrawals	15,000	
Sales		562,140
Sales returns and allowances	5,070	
Purchases	385,085	
Purchases returns and allowances		1,820
Purchases discounts		4,710
Transportation-in	5,125	
Sales salaries expense	43,220	
Rent expense, selling space	20,250	
Store supplies expense	–0–	
Amortization expense, store equipment	–0–	
Office salaries expense	48,330	
Rent expense, office space	8,850	
Office supplies expense	–0–	
Insurance expense	–0–	
Amortization expense, office equipment	–0–	
Totals	$696,650	$696,650

Required

1. Copy the unadjusted trial balance on a work sheet form and complete the work sheet using the information that follows:

    a. Ending store supplies inventory, $445.

    b. Ending office supplies inventory, $225.

    c. Expired insurance, $2,805.

    d. Amortization on the store equipment, $5,415.

    e. Amortization on the office equipment, $1,485.

f. Accrued sales salaries payable, $445; and accrued office salaries payable, $210.

g. Ending merchandise inventory, $54,365.

2. Prepare a multiple-step income statement showing in detail the expenses and the items that make up cost of goods sold.

3. Prepare a statement of changes in owner's equity. On December 31, 1995, the Sally Fowler, Capital account had a balance of $36,015. Early in 1996, Ms. Fowler invested an additional $70,000 in the business.

4. Prepare a year-end classified balance sheet with the prepaid expenses combined.

5. Prepare adjusting and closing entries.

Briefly explain why a company's manager would want the accounting system to record a customer's return of unsatisfactory goods in the Sales Returns and Allowances account instead of the Sales account. In addition, explain whether the information would be useful for external decision makers.

Problem 5–10
Analytical Essay
(LO 1)

A retail company's accountant recently compiled the cost of the ending merchandise inventory to use in preparing the financial statements. In developing the measure, the accountant did not know that $10,000 of incoming goods had been shipped by a supplier on December 31 under an FOB factory agreement. These goods had been recorded as a purchase, but they were not included in the physical count because they were not on hand. Explain how this overlooked fact would affect the company's financial statements and these ratios: debt ratio, current ratio, profit margin, and acid-test ratio.

Problem 5–11
Analytical Essay
(LO 2)

SERIAL PROBLEM

(The first three segments of this comprehensive problem were presented in Chapters 2, 3, and 4. If those segments have not been completed, the assignment can begin at this point. However, the student will need to use the facts presented on pages 119–20 in Chapter 2, pages 175–76 in Chapter 3, and page 229 in Chapter 4. Because of its length, this problem is most easily solved if students use the Working Papers that accompany this text.)

Emerald Computer Services

Earlier segments of this problem have described how Tracy Green created Emerald Computer Services on October 1, 1996. The company has been successful, and its list of customers has started to grow. To accommodate the growth, the accounting system is ready to be modified to set up separate accounts for each customer. The following list of customers includes the account number used for each account and any balance as of the end of 1996. Green decided to add a fourth digit with a decimal point to the 106 account number that had been used for the single Accounts Receivable account. This modification allows the existing chart of accounts to continue being used. The list also shows the balances that two customers owed as of December 31, 1996:

Account	No.	Dec. 31 Balance
Alpha Printing Co.	106.1	
Bravo Productions	106.2	
Charles Company	106.3	$ 900
Delta Fixtures, Inc.	106.4	
Echo Canyon Ranch	106.5	
Fox Run Estates	106.6	$1,000
Golf Course Designs, Inc.	106.7	
Hotel Pollo del Mar	106.8	
Indiana Manuf. Co.	106.9	

In response to frequent requests from customers, Green has decided to begin selling computer software. The company will extend credit terms of 1/10, n/30 to customers who purchase merchandise. No cash discount will be available on consulting fees. The following additional accounts were added to the General Ledger to allow the system to account for the company's new merchandising activities:

Account	No.
Merchandise Inventory	119
Sales	413
Sales Returns and Allowances	414
Sales Discounts	415
Purchases	505
Purchases Returns and Allowances	506
Purchases Discounts	507
Transportation-In	508

Because the accounting system does not use reversing entries, all revenue and expense accounts have zero balances as of January 1, 1997.

Required

1. Prepare journal entries to record each of the following transactions for Emerald Computer Services.
2. Post the journal entries to the accounts in the company's General Ledger. (Use asset, liability, and capital accounts that start with the balance as of December 31, 1996.)
3. Prepare a six-column table similar to Illustration 3–3 that presents the unadjusted trial balance, the March 31 adjustments, and the adjusted trial balance.

    Do not prepare closing entries and do not journalize the adjusting entries or post them to the ledger.
4. Prepare an interim income statement for the three months ended March 31, 1997. Use a detailed multiple-step format that shows calculations of net sales, total revenues, cost of goods sold, total expenses, and net income.
5. Prepare an interim statement of changes in owner's equity for the three months ended March 31, 1997.
6. Prepare an interim balance sheet as of March 31, 1997.

Transactions:

Jan. 4   Paid Fran Sims for five days, including one day in addition to the four unpaid days from the prior year.

6   Tracy Green invested an additional $12,000 cash in the business.

7   Purchased $2,800 of merchandise from SoftHead Co. on terms of 1/10, n/30, FOB shipping point.

8   Received $1,000 from Fox Run Estates as final payment on its account.

10   Completed 5-day project for Alpha Printing Co. and billed them $3,000, which is the total price of $4,000 less the advance payment of $1,000.

13   Sold merchandise with a retail value of $2,100 to Delta Fixtures, Inc., with terms of 1/10, n/30, FOB shipping point.

14   Paid $350 for freight charges on the merchandise purchased on January 7.

16   Received $1,500 cash from Golf Course Designs, Inc., for computer services.

17   Paid SoftHead Co. for the purchase on January 7, net of the discount.

Jan. 21 Delta Fixtures, Inc., returned $200 of defective merchandise from its purchase on January 13.

22 Received the balance due from Delta Fixtures, Inc., net of the discount and the credit for the returned merchandise.

23 Returned defective merchandise to SoftHead Co. and accepted credit against future purchases. Its cost, net of the discount, was $198.

26 Sold $2,900 of merchandise on credit to Hotel Pollo del Mar.

28 Purchased $4,000 of merchandise from SoftHead Co. on terms of 1/10, n/30, FOB destination.

29 Received a $198 credit memo from SoftHead Co. concerning the merchandise returned on January 23.

31 Paid Fran Sims for 10 days' work.

Feb. 1 Paid $2,250 to the Town Hall Mall for another three months' rent.

3 Paid SoftHead Co. for the balance due, net of the cash discount, less the $198 amount in the credit memo.

4 Paid $400 to the local newspaper for advertising.

11 Received the balance due from Alpha Printing Co. for fees billed on January 10.

16 Paid $2,000 to Tracy Green as a withdrawal.

23 Sold $1,600 of merchandise on credit to Golf Course Designs, Inc.

26 Paid Fran Sims for 8 days' work.

27 Reimbursed Tracy Green's business automobile usage for 600 km. at $0.25 per kilometre.

Mar. 8 Purchased $1,200 of computer supplies from AAA Supply Co. on credit.

9 Received the balance due from Golf Course Designs, Inc., for merchandise sold on February 23.

15 Repaired the company's computer at the cost of $430.

16 Received $2,130 cash from Indiana Manuf. Co. for computing services.

19 Paid the full amount due to AAA Supply Co. including amounts created on December 13 and March 8.

24 Billed Bravo Productions for $2,950 of computing services.

25 Sold $900 of merchandise on credit to Echo Canyon Ranch.

30 Sold $1,110 of merchandise on credit to Charles Company.

31 Reimbursed Tracy Green's business automobile usage for 400 km. at $0.25 per kilometre.

Information for the March 31 adjustments and financial statements:

a. The March 31 inventory of computing supplies is $670.

b. Three more months have passed since the company purchased the annual insurance policy at the cost of $1,440.

c. Fran Sims has not been paid for 7 days of work.

d. Three months have passed since any prepaid rent cost has been transferred to expense.

e. Amortization on the computer for January through March is $750.

f. Amortization on the office equipment for January through March is $500.

g. The March 31 inventory of merchandise is $2,182.

PROVOCATIVE PROBLEMS

**Provocative Problem
5–1**

Financial Reporting
Problem

(LO 1, 2, 3)

Wanda Wonder, the owner of the WonderFull Store, has operated the company for several years but has never used an accrual accounting system. To have more useful information, Wonder has engaged you to help prepare an income statement for 1997. Based on data that you have gathered from the cash-basis accounting system and other documents, you have been able to prepare the following balance sheets as of the beginning and end of 1997:

	December 31	
	1996	**1997**
Cash	$ 5,400	$ 42,250
Accounts receivable	18,500	22,600
Merchandise inventory	39,700	34,000
Equipment (net of amortization) ...	87,000	56,000
Total assets	$150,600	$154,850
Accounts payable	$ 28,300	$ 36,250
Wages payable	2,200	1,700
Wanda Wonder, capital	120,100	116,900
Total liabilities and owner's equity ..	$150,600	$154,850

The store's cash records also provided the following facts for 1997:

Amount collected on accounts receivable ..	$339,900
Payments for:	
Accounts payable	198,050
Employees' wages	52,000
All other operating expenses	29,000
Withdrawals by the owner	24,000

You have determined that all merchandise purchases and sales were made on credit, and that no equipment was either purchased or sold during the year.

Use the preceding information to calculate the amounts of the company's sales, cost of goods purchased, cost of goods sold, amortization expense, and wages expense for 1997. Then, prepare a multiple-step income statement that shows the company's gross profit.

**Provocative Problem
5–2**

Nan's Nursery

(LO 1, 2, 3)

Nan Hall and Mike Linden were partners in a nursery. They disagreed, closed the business, and ended their partnership. In settlement for her partnership interest, Nan Hall received an inventory of trees, plants, and garden supplies having a $22,500 cost. Since there was nothing practical she could do with the inventory except open a new nursery, she did so by investing the inventory and $18,000 in cash. She used $15,000 of the cash to buy equipment, and she opened for business on May 1. During the succeeding eight months, she paid out $63,750 to creditors for additional trees, plants, and garden supplies and $21,000 in operating expenses. She also withdrew $15,000 for personal expenses, and at the year-end, she prepared the balance sheet that follows:

NAN'S NURSERY
Balance Sheet
December 31, 1996

Cash		$ 8,550	Accounts payable (all for	
Merchandise inventory . . .		26,650	merchandise)	$ 3,300
Equipment	$ 15,000		Nan Hall, capital	45,700
Less amortization	1,200	13,800	Total liabilities and	
Total assets		$49,000	owner's equity	$49,000

Based on the information given, prepare calculations to determine the net income earned by the business, the cost of goods sold, and the amount of its sales. Then prepare an income statement showing the result of the nursery's operations during its first eight months.

Phil Potter worked in the National Bank for 20 years, until his aunt died, leaving him a sizable estate. After sitting around long enough to get bored and see his bank balance dwindle, Phil decided to open a retail paint store. When he started the business on July 1, 1996, Valley Hills had no such store, and it appeared to Phil that the business would succeed.

On July 1, Phil deposited $53,500 in a bank account under the name Phil's Paints. He then paid $12,000 cash for store equipment, which he expected to last 10 years before it became valueless. He also bought merchandise for $37,500 cash, and paid $3,600 in advance for six months' rent.

Phil estimated that most paint stores marked their goods for sale at prices averaging 35% above cost. In other words, an item that cost $10.00 was marked for sale at $13.50. But to entice customers, he decided to mark his merchandise for sale at 30% above cost. Since his overhead would be low, he thought this would still leave a new income equal to 10% of sales.

On December 31, 1996, six months after opening his store, Phil has come to you for advice. He thinks business has been good. However, he doesn't quite understand why his cash balance has fallen to $1,200.

In talking with Phil and examining his records, you determine that the inventory was replaced three times during the six months, each time at a cost of $37,500. All merchandise suppliers have been paid except for $10,850, which is not yet due. A full stock of merchandise (cost of $37,500) is on hand and customers owe Phil $29,100. In addition to the rend paid in advance, Phil paid $14,700 for other expenses.

Prepare an income statement for the business covering the six-month period ended December 31, a statement of changes in owner's equity, a December 31, 1996, balance sheet, and a statement that explains the $1,200 cash balance by showing the cash receipts and cash disbursements during the six months ended December 31.

Provocative Problem 5–3
Phil's Paints
(LO 1, 3)

Use the financial statements for Geac Computer Corporation Limited in Appendix I at the end of the book to find the answers to these questions:

a. Although Geac manufactures most of the goods that it sells, assume that the amounts reported for inventories and cost of sales* were all purchased ready for resale and then calculate the total cost of goods purchased during the fiscal year ended April 30, 1994.

b. Calculate the current and acid-test ratios as of the end of the 1994 and 1993 fiscal years. Comment on what you find.

*Use "costs, excluding amounts shown below" as cost of sales.

Provocative Problem 5–4
Financial statement analysis case
(LO 1, 5)

Geac

Describe the problem faced by Renee Fleck in the As a Matter of Ethics case on page 248 and evaluate her alternative courses of action.

Provocative Problem 5–5
Ethical issue essay

ANALYTICAL AND REVIEW PROBLEMS

A & R Problem 5–1   The partially completed work sheet of Incomplete Data Company appears below:

INCOMPLETE DATA COMPANY
Work Sheet for the Year Ended December 31, 1996

Account Titles	Trial Balance		Adjustments		Income Statement		Balance Sheet	
	Debit	Credit	Debit	Credit	Debit	Credit	Debit	Credit
Cash	34,780							
Accounts receivable							4,600	
Merchandise inventory					31,400	26,400		
Prepaid fire insurance	720						480	
Prepaid rent	4,800							
Office equipment							12,000	
Accum. amort.—office equipment		4,500						
Accounts payable		8,000						
Clay Camp, capital		22,000						
Clay Camp, drawing							20,000	
Sales		300,000						
Sales returns and allowances					1,000			
Purchases	199,200							
Purchases returns and allowances						1,400		
Advertising expense	1,000							
Supplies expense	1,800							
Salaries expense	23,200							
Utilities expense	1,400							
Fire insurance expense								
Rent expense					2,400			
Amort. expense—office equipment					1,500			
Salaries payable								660

Required

1.   Complete the work sheet for the year ended December 31, 1996.

The following are the selected data for the Allen Sales Company for the year 1997.　　**A & R Problem 5–2**

1　Selected closing entries:

Income Summary	273,000	
Purchases Returns and Allowances	2,500	
Purchases		180,000
Freight-In		4,000
Purchase Discounts Lost		200
Sales Salaries Expense		40,000
Advertising Expense		10,000
Rent Expense, Office Space		8,000
Delivery Expense		4,800
Office Salaries Expense		26,000
Amortization, Office Equipment		2,000
Miscellaneous Expense		500
To close expense and other nominal accounts		
G. Allen, Capital	28,000	
G. Allen, Withdrawals		28,000
To close the withdrawals account.		

2.　G. Allen follows the practice of withdrawing half of the annual net income from the business.

3.　There were no sales returns and allowances for the year. However, sales discounts amounted to $2,000.

4.　Inventories:

December 31, 1996—$25,000

December 31, 1997—$20,000

Required

1. Compute the amount of net income for 1997.
2. Compute the amount of sales for 1997.
3. Prepare a classified income statement for 1997.

CONCEPT TESTER

Test your understanding of the concepts introduced in this chapter by completing the following crossword puzzle.

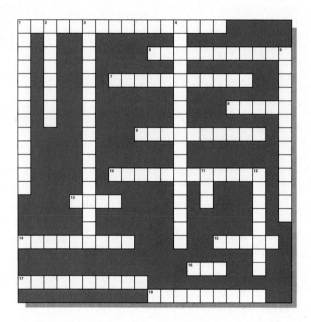

Across Clues

1. Freight charges on goods purchased (2 words).
5. Amounts and timing of payments agreed to by buyers (2 words).
7. Goods bought and sold to others.
8. Term for revenues from selling of merchandise.
9. Income statement format (2 words).
10. Income statement format that discloses gross profit (2 words).
13. Expense of buying and preparing goods sold (abbreviation).
14. Inventory method that recognizes COGS at time of sale.
15. Synonymous term for merchandise.
16. Legal arrangement for identifying location at which title to goods is transferred (abbreviation).
17. Balance sheet that identifies current assets, capital assets, etc.
18. Collection of goods waiting to be sold to customers.

Down Clues

1. Reduction from catalogue price (2 words).
2. Ratio of quick assets to current liabilities (2 words).
3. Cash discount taken against amount owed to supplier (2 words).
4. Total of selling and general administration expenses (2 words).
6. Cash discount taken by customers (2 words).
11. Credit terms (abbreviation).
12. Inventory method which fails to identify amount of shrinkage.

ANSWERS TO PROGRESS CHECKS

5–1 *b*

5–2 Gross profit is the difference between net sales and cost of goods sold.

5–3 Keeping sales returns and allowances and sales discounts separate from sales makes useful information readily available to managers for internal monitoring and decision making. This information is not likely to be reported outside the company because it would not be useful for external decision makers.

5–4 Under credit terms of 2/10, n/60, the credit period is 60 days and the discount period is 10 days.

5–5 *b*

5–6 With a periodic inventory system, the cost of goods sold is determined at the end of an accounting period by adding the cost of goods purchased to the beginning inventory and subtracting the ending inventory.

5–7 FOB means free on board. The term *FOB destination* means that the seller does not transfer ownership of the goods to the buyer until they arrive at the buyer's place of business. Thus, the seller is responsible for paying the shipping charges and bears the risk of damage during shipment.

5–8 *c*

5–9 The classified income statement; the single-step income statement.

5–10 The second closing entry, which closes the income statement accounts with debit balances, includes a credit to Merchandise Inventory to remove the beginning inventory amount.

5–11 *d*

5–12 The acid-test ratio.

5–13 *d*

5–14 Both approaches will report the same ending inventory and net income.

CHAPTER 6

Accounting Systems

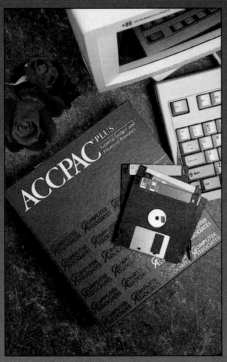

As businesses grow, the number of transactions becomes very large. To handle this load, companies use special accounting methods and records. Today, most companies use the powerful capabilities of computers to achieve accurate and fast information processing.

*K*aren White's friends operated O'Natural, a small business that sells nutritional supplements. During 1995, sales revenue amounted to $37,600. Upon learning that Karen was studying accounting, they invited her to examine their record-keeping system. Upon examination of the accounting records, Karen was amazed at how closely the rather simple system followed what she had learned in the first five chapters of her textbook. She found a single sales and purchases account and a number of asset, liability, and owner's equity accounts.

That evening Karen shared her experience with Mark Smith and the two wondered how complex a system a company such as Imperial Oil Limited needs, with sales over $9 billion and the level of detail the financial statements provide, especially in the notes to the statements. They wondered how this information can be captured by Imperial's accounting system and whether management decisions for a small business might be better served by a more complex accounting system.

Imperial Oil Limited—1994
(amounts in millions)

Total revenues:	
Natural resources	$ 854
Petroleum products	7,313
Chemicals	759
Corporate and other	85
Total revenues	$ 9,011

LEARNING OBJECTIVES

After studying Chapter 6, you should be able to:

1. **Describe the five basic components of an accounting system.**
2. **Describe the types of computers used in large and small accounting systems, the role of software in those systems, and the different approaches to inputting and processing data, including the use of networking.**
3. **Explain special journals and controlling accounts, use them to record transactions, and explain how to test the posting of entries to the Accounts Receivable and Accounts Payable subsidiary ledgers.**
4. **Explain the use of special and general journals in accounting for sales and goods and services taxes and sales returns and allowances, and explain how sales invoices can serve as a Sales Journal.**
5. **Explain the nature and use of business segment information.**
6. **Define or explain the words and phrases listed in the chapter glossary.**

Even in a small business such as O'Natural, a large amount of information must be processed through the accounting system. Thus, the accounting system should be designed to process the information efficiently. As you study this chapter, you will learn some general concepts to follow in designing an efficient accounting system. The chapter begins by explaining the basic components of an accounting system, whether it is a manual or computer-based system. After considering some of the special characteristics of computer-based systems, the chapter then explains some of the labour-saving procedures employed in manual systems. These include efficient ways of processing routine transactions such as credit sales, cash receipts, credit purchases, and cash disbursements.

THE COMPONENTS OF AN ACCOUNTING SYSTEM

LO 1

Describe the five basic components of an accounting system.

Accounting systems consist of people, forms, procedures, and equipment. These systems must be designed to capture data about the transactions of the entity and to generate from that data a variety of financial, managerial, and tax accounting reports. Because all accounting systems must accomplish these same broad objectives, both manual and computerized accounting systems include the same basic components. However, computer-based systems provide more accuracy, speed, efficiency, and convenience.

The five common components of manual and computerized accounting systems are:

* Source documents.
* Input devices.
* Data processor.
* Data storage.
* Output devices.

Illustration 6–1 shows the relationships between these five components.

Illustration 6-1 The Components of an accounting System

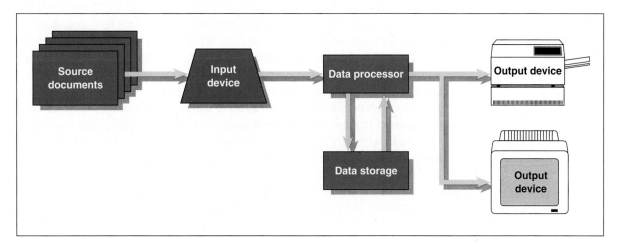

Source Documents

Chapter 2 described some of the business papers that companies use in the process of completing transactions. These business papers are called *source documents* because they provide a basis for making accounting entries. In other words, they provide the data that are entered in and processed by the accounting system. You are no doubt familiar with some kinds of source documents such as bank statements and cheques received from other parties. Other examples of source documents include invoices from suppliers, billings to customers, and employee earnings records.

In manual accounting systems, source documents consist of paper documents. Paper documents are also very important for computerized systems, but some source documents take other forms. For example, some companies send invoices directly from their own computers to their customers' computers. The source documents in this case are computer files.

Accurate source documents are important for the proper functioning of an accounting system. If the information going into the system is faulty and incomplete, the information coming out of the system will also be faulty and incomplete. (In computer jargon, the results of defective input are described as garbage in, garbage out.)

Input Devices

The second component of an accounting system is one or more **input devices.** As shown in Illustration 6–1, an input device transfers the information from source documents to the data processing component of the accounting system. In a computer-based system, this often involves converting the data on the source documents from a written form into electronic signals. In addition to transferring data from source documents to the data processor, input devices are used to tell the data processing component how to process the data.

In prior chapters, you used an input device when you solved exercises and problems by recording the effects of transactions with journal entries. If you recorded transactions using the *SPATS* supplement that accompanies this text, you used the keyboard of a computer as the input device. When you recorded transactions using pencil and paper, you were using these items as the input device for a manual accounting system.

The most common input device for a computer-based accounting system is a keyboard. System operators use keyboards to transfer data from the source documents into the computer. Another input device is a *bar code reader* like those used in grocery and other retail stores. With a bar code reader, the clerk merely moves purchased items over the reader, which picks up their code numbers and sends the data to the computer. Other input devices include *scanners* that read words and numbers directly from source documents.

In both manual and computer systems, companies promote clerical accuracy by using routine procedures to input data. Also, controls should be in place to ensure that only authorized individuals can input data to the accounting system. Such controls help protect the integrity of the system and also allow incorrect input to be traced back to its source.

Data Processor

The third component of an accounting system is the **data processor** which interprets, manipulates, and summarizes recorded information so it can be used in analyses and reports. In manual systems, the primary data processor is the accountant's brain. However, the manual processing of data is not entirely a mental process. That is, the accountant uses the journal, the ledger, the working papers, and such procedures as posting to convert the journal entry data into more useful information. Of course, few if any accounting systems are completely manual. For example, calculators are essential equipment for manual systems.

As a result of technical developments over the last two decades, many manual accounting systems have been replaced by computer-based systems. The data processor in a computer-based system includes both *hardware* and *software.* Hardware is the machinery that performs the steps called for by the software. The software consists of computer programs that specify the operations to be performed on the data. Software actually controls the whole system, including input, file management, processing, and output.

Data Storage

Data storage is an essential component of both manual and computer-based systems. As data is inputted and processed, it must be saved so it can be used as output or processed further. This stockpile of data (a database) should be readily accessible so periodic financial reports can be compiled quickly. In addition, data storage should support the preparation of special purpose reports that managers may request. The accounting database also serves as the primary source of information auditors use when they audit the financial statements. Companies also maintain files of source documents for use by auditors and to clear up errors or disputes.

In manual systems, data storage consists of files of paper documents. However, with a computer-based system, most of the data is stored on floppy diskettes, hard disks, or magnetic tapes. As a result of recent improvements, these devices can store very large amounts of data. For example, floppy diskettes can hold up to two megabytes of information (one megabyte is roughly equivalent to 500 double-spaced typed pages). Small digital-audio-tape (DAT) cassettes can hold hundreds of megabytes of information. Some hard disks can hold thousands of megabytes (1,000 megabytes is a gigabyte). Because of the recent improvements in data storage, accounting systems now can store much more detailed and extensive databases than was possible in the past. As a result, managers have much more information available to help them plan and control business activities.

In a computer-based system, data storage can be on-line (usually on a hard disk), which means that the data can be accessed whenever it is needed by the software. In contrast, when data is stored off-line, the data cannot be accessed until the computer operator inserts a disk or a magnetic tape into a drive.

Generally, we do not use the concepts of on-line and off-line storage in reference to manual accounting systems. However, one might argue that in a manual system, only the data stored in the accountant's brain is on-line; everything else is off-line.

Output Devices

The fifth component of an accounting system is the **output devices.** These allow information to be taken out of the system and placed in the hands of its users. Examples of output include bills to customers, cheques payable to suppliers and employees, financial statements, and a variety of other internal reports.

For computer-based systems, the most common output devices are video screens and printers. Other output devices include telephones or direct phone line connections to the computer systems of suppliers or customers. When requests for output are entered, the data processor searches the database for the needed data, organizes it in the form of a report, and sends the information to an output device.

Depending on the output device, the information may be displayed on a screen, printed on paper, or expressed as a voice over the telephone. For example, a bank customer may call to find out the balance in his or her chequing account. If a touch-tone telephone serves as an input/output device, a recording may ask the customer to enter appropriate identifying information including the number of the account. With this input, the computer searches the database for the information and sends it back over the telephone. If the telephone is not used as an input/output device, the bank employee who answers the phone inputs the information request using a keyboard. The employee then reads the output on a video screen and relays it over the phone to the customer.

Another kind of output involves paying employees without writing paycheques. Instead, the company's computer system may send the payroll data directly to the computer system of the company's bank. Thus, the output of the company's system is an electronic fund transfer (EFT) from the company's bank account to the employees' bank accounts. The output device in this instance is the connection or interface between the computer systems of the company and the bank. Large companies are increasingly using EFTs. In other situations, the company's computer outputs the payroll data on a magnetic tape or disk. The tape or disk is then used by the bank to transfer the funds to the employees' bank accounts.

In addition to the preceding forms of output, many situations require printed output that computer systems produce on laser, impact, or ink-jet printers.

For companies using manual accounting systems, the production of output involves physically searching the records to find the needed data and then organizing it in a written report.

Progress Check
(Answers to Progress Checks are provided at the end of the chapter.)

6–1   Which one of the following components of an accounting system is not likely to include paper documents? *(a)* Source documents; *(b)* Data processor; *(c)* Data storage; *(d)* Output devices.

6–2   What does the data processor component of an accounting system accomplish?

6–3   What uses are made of the data that are stockpiled in the data storage component of an accounting system?

SMALL AND LARGE COMPUTER-BASED SYSTEMS

LO 2

Describe the types of computers used in large and small accounting systems, the role of software in those systems, and the different approaches to inputting and processing data, including the use of networking.

The world has seen radical changes in the use of computers since the first Apple computer was sold in 1980. Many of you are already proficient users of personal computers (PCs) such as those produced by **International Business Machines Corporation (IBM)** or by **Apple Computer, Inc.** These computers (often called *microcomputers*) are physically small, easy to operate, and increasingly inexpensive.

Although the use of microcomputers in business has greatly expanded in recent years, many companies also use larger computers called *mainframes*. These machines are able to process huge quantities of accounting data quickly. In addition, they help businesses perform other important tasks such as analyzing the results of market research, compiling shareholder information, and doing engineering design work for products and production lines. These computers include the AS series of machines produced by IBM and the VAX family manufactured by **Digital Equipment Corporation (DEC).**

CUSTOM-DESIGNED AND OFF-THE-SHELF PROGRAMS

Regardless of its size and speed, every computer does nothing more than execute instructions that are organized as programs. A program consists of a series of very specific instructions for obtaining data from input or storage, processing it, returning it to storage for later use, and sending it to an output device to produce a report.

Illustration 6–2 presents a flowchart of the steps that a computer program might use to process a stack of customer orders for merchandise. When this program is executed in a normal situation, the system creates a shipping order that identifies the products to be sent to customers. If a shipment causes the quantity on hand to fall below the minimum level, the system generates a purchase order to be approved by a manager. If the quantity on hand is less than the customer ordered, the system produces a partial shipping order as well as a report to the customer that the remainder is on back order. Then, if replacements have not been ordered already, the system produces a purchase order. If no units of the desired product are on hand, the system notifies the customer of the back order and issues a purchase

Illustration 6–2   Flowchart for an Order-Processing Program

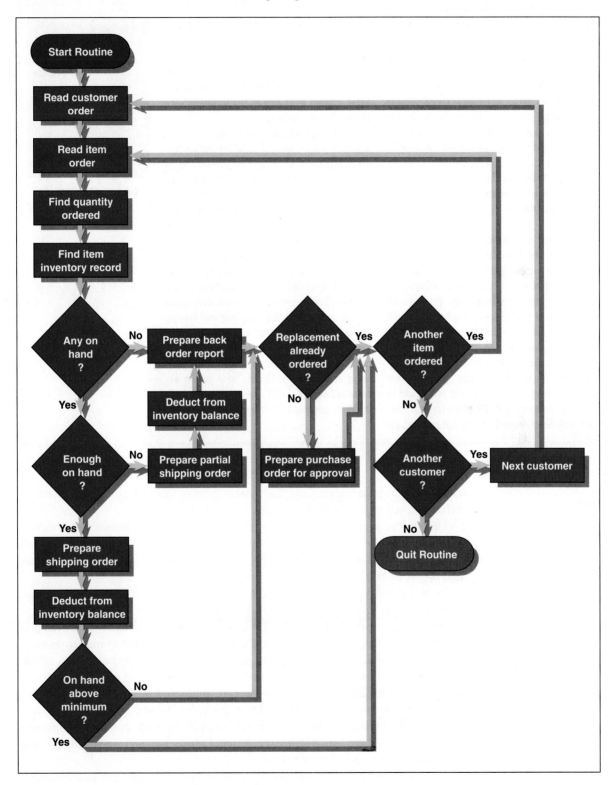

As a Matter of Opinion

Mrs. King graduated from Wilfrid Laurier University with her Honours Bachelor of Business Administration degree in 1986. She received her Chartered Accountant designation in 1987. She currently works in Toronto for the public accounting firm, Arthur Andersen in their Enterprise Group which provides audit, tax and consulting services to family-owned and mid-sized organizations. She has also worked in private industry as a controller for a computer software company. She is the Treasurer of the Toronto Venture Group and a member of the Institute of Chartered Accountants of Ontario.

The advent of microcomputers, local area networks and user friendly software have made it a virtual necessity for companies, regardless of size, to use computer systems in their accounting functions. This has allowed small businesses to eliminate much of the mechanical drudgery in their financial recordkeeping and allowed them to create their financial records much more quickly. But accounting software can be deceptively simple. Many programs do not have built in internal controls to ensure that transactions are captured properly or do not provide au-

dit trails to allow users to track their transactions readily. Accounting programs must also be set up properly at the outset or the financial data that is created may be meaningless. All of these factors can lead to disaster if there is no one in the business with accounting expertise.

Even sophisticated computer systems cannot replace sound accounting knowledge. Many transactions require judgements to be made that can only be made by humans with a clear understanding of the transaction. Similarly, humans trained in accounting and analysis can detect input errors that the computer would rarely, if ever, identify.

Today's accountant must have skills in both areas; computer applications and accounting knowledge. It is important to understand how computer systems work in order to use them effectively without having to pay costly computer consultants every time there is a problem. However, one must never assume that the computer does everything correctly and that is why strong accounting skills are still a necessity in today's complex business environment.

Lorrie L. King, BBA, CA

order, unless one already exists. The system follows this process for each item ordered by each customer until the stack of orders is exhausted.

Despite the apparent complexity of the instructions in Illustration 6–2, this routine is actually incomplete. For example, it does not update the accounting records for sales and accounts receivable, nor does it deal with cash and trade discounts that might be offered to customers.

In the early days of computer systems, each program had to be custom designed using a programming language such as COBOL or FORTRAN. Since then, programmers have developed more flexible and easier-to-use languages. However, programming is a skill that only a limited number of people need to master. Instead, the expanded used of microcomputers has resulted in an increasing variety of off-the-shelf programs that are ready to be used.

Some off-the-shelf programs are general, multipurpose applications that accomplish a variety of different tasks. These programs include familiar word processor programs (such as Microsoft Word® and WordPerfect®), spreadsheet programs (such as Quattro®Pro, Microsoft Excel®, and Lotus® 1-2-3®), and database management programs (such as dBase®).

Other off-the-shelf programs are designed to meet very specific needs of users. These programs include a large number of accounting programs such as AccPac

---

As a Matter of Ethics

A public accountant has a client whose business has grown significantly over the last couple of years and has reached the point where its accounting system has become inadequate for handling both the volume of transactions and management's needs for financial information. The client asks the public accountant which software system would work best for the company.

The public accountant has been offered a 10% com-

mission by a software company for each purchase of its system by one of the public accountant's clients. The price of one of these systems falls within the range specified by the client. Do you think that the public accountant's evaluation of the alternative systems could be affected by this commission arrangement? Should it be? Should the public accountant feel compelled to tell the client about the commission arrangement before making a recommendation?

---

for Windows®, CA Simply Accounting®, AccPac 2000, DacEasy® Accounting, Peachtree® Complete Accounting, and Great Plains® Accounting Series. Off-the-shelf programs are designed to be so user-friendly they guide users through the input steps and then ask which reports are desired.

Many of the off-the-shelf accounting programs save time and minimize errors because they operate as *integrated* systems. In an integrated system, actions taken in one part of the system also produce results in related parts.

For example, when a credit sale is recorded in an integrated system, several parts of the system are updated with one or two simple commands. First, the system stores transaction data (as in a journal) so that you can review the entire entry at a later time. Second, it updates the Cash and Accounts Receivable accounts. Third, it updates a detailed record of the amount owed by the customer. Fourth, it might update a detailed record of the products held for sale to show the number of units sold and the number that remain on hand.

Computers and integrated software programs have dramatically reduced the bookkeeping tasks in accounting. However, do not think that computers have eliminated the need for accountants. Nor should you conclude that success in business no longer requires a knowledge of accounting. The need for accountants and accounting knowledge is created by the need for information, not by the need for pencil and paper. Accountants continue to be in demand because their expertise is necessary to determine what information ought to be produced and what data should be used to produce it. Accountants are also needed to analyze and explain the output. Furthermore, writing new, improved programs requires a knowledge of accounting.

In short, the value of accounting knowledge does not disappear just because mechanical steps are done with a computer. You still need to understand the effects of events on the company and how they are reflected in financial statements and management reports.

BATCH AND ON-LINE SYSTEMS

Accounting systems also differ in how the input is entered and processed. With **batch processing,** the source documents are accumulated for a period of time and then processed all at the same time, such as once a day, week, or month. By comparison, with **on-line processing,** data are entered and processed as soon as source documents are available. As a result, the database is immediately updated.

The disadvantage of batch processing is that the database is not kept up to date during the times that source documents are being accumulated. In many situations, however, companies use batch processing because the database requires only periodic updating. For example, records used in sending bills to customers may require updating only once each month.

On-line processing has the advantage of keeping the database always up to date. However, it is more expensive because the software is more complicated and because it usually requires a much larger investment in hardware. On-line processing applications include airline reservations, credit card records, and rapid response mail-order processing.

COMPUTER NETWORKS

In many circumstances, firms create advantages by linking or networking computers with each other. **Computer networks** allow different users to share access to the same data and the same programs. A relatively small computer network is called a *local area network (LAN)*. This type of network links the machines within an office by special *hard-wired* hookups. For example, many universities have networks in their computer labs. Larger computer networks that are spread over long distances communicate over telephone lines by using *modems*.

In some cases, the need for information requires very large networks. Examples include the system used by **Federal Express Corporation** for tracking its packages and billing its customers and the system used by **The Bay** for monitoring inventory levels in each of its stores. These networks involve many computers (desktops and mainframes) and satellite communications to gather information and to provide ready access to the database from all locations.

We now turn to a discussion of some of the labour-saving procedures used to process transactions in manual systems. However, remember that accounting systems have similar purposes whether they are computer-based or manual in operation. Thus, your understanding of computer-based systems will be improved when you understand manual procedures.

Progress Check

6-4   In a computer-based accounting system:
  a. The accounting software is more efficient if it operates as an integrated system.
  b. The need for accountants is nearly eliminated.
  c. Data about transactions must be entered with on-line processing.
  d. The accountant must have the ability to program the computer.

6-5   What advantages do computer systems offer over manual systems?

6-6   Which of the following allows different computer users to access the same data and programs?   (a) On-line processing;   (b) Electronic Fund Transfers;   (c) Bar code readers;   (d) Local area networks.

SPECIAL JOURNALS

The General Journal is a flexible journal in which you can record any transaction. However, each debit and credit entered in a General Journal must be individually posted. As a result, a firm that uses a General Journal to record all the transactions of its business requires much time and labour to post the individual debits and credits.

One way to reduce the writing and the posting labour is to divide the transactions of a business into groups of similar transactions and to provide a separate **special journal** for recording the transactions in each group. For example, most of the transactions of a merchandising business fall into four groups: sales on credit, purchases on credit, cash receipts, and cash disbursements. When a special journal is provided for each group, the journals are:

LO 3

Explain special journals and controlling accounts, use them to record transactions, and explain how to test the posting of entries to the Accounts Receivable and Accounts Payable subsidiary ledgers.

1. A Sales Journal for recording credit sales.
2. A Purchases Journal for recording credit purchases.
3. A Cash Receipts Journal for recording cash receipts.
4. A Cash Disbursements Journal for recording cash payments.
5. A General Journal for the miscellaneous transactions not recorded in the special journals and also for adjusting, closing, and correcting entries.

The following illustrations show how special journals save time in journalizing and posting transactions. They do this by providing special columns for accumulating the debits and credits of similar transactions. These journals allow you to post the amounts entered in the special columns as column totals rather than as individual amounts. For example, you can save posting labour if you record credit sales for a month in a Sales Journal like the one at the top of Illustration 6–3. As the illustration shows, you do not post the credit sales to the general ledger accounts until the end of the month. Then, you calculate the total sales for the month and post the total as one debit to Accounts Receivable and as one credit to Sales. Only seven sales are recorded in the illustrated journal. However, if you assume the 7 sales represent 700 sales, you can better appreciate the posting labour saved by making only one debit to Accounts Receivable and one credit to Sales.

The special journal in Illustration 6–3 is also called a **columnar journal** because it has columns for recording the date, the customer's name, the invoice number, and the amount of each credit sale. Only credit sales are recorded in it, and they are recorded daily with the information about each sale placed on a separate line. Normally, the information is taken from a copy of the sales ticket or invoice prepared at the time of the sale. However, before discussing the journal further, you need to understand the role played by subsidiary ledgers.

KEEPING A SEPARATE ACCOUNT FOR EACH CREDIT CUSTOMER

In previous chapters, when we recorded credit sales, we debited a single account called Accounts Receivable. However, when a business has more than one credit customer, the accounts must show how much each customer has purchased, how much each customer has paid, and how much remains to be collected from each customer. To provide this information, businesses with credit customers must maintain a separate Account Receivable for each customer.

One possible way of keeping a separate account for each customer would be to keep all of these accounts in the same ledger that contains the financial statement accounts. However, this usually is not done. Instead, the ledger that contains the financial statement accounts, now called the **General Ledger,** continues to hold a single Accounts Receivable account. Then, a supplementary record is established in which a separate account is maintained for each customer. This supplementary record is called the **Accounts Receivable Ledger.** This subsidiary ledger may exist on tape or disk storage in a computerized system. In a manual system, the Accounts Receivable Ledger may take the form of a book or tray that contains the customer accounts. In either case, the customer accounts in the subsidiary ledger are kept separate from the Accounts Receivable account in the General Ledger.

Understand that when debits (or credits) to Accounts Receivable are posted twice (once to Accounts Receivable and once to the customer's account), this does not

Illustration 6–3   Posting from the Sales Journal

Sales Journal				Page 3
Date	**Account Debited**	**Invoice Number**	**PR**	**Amount**
Feb. 2	James Henry	307	√	450.00
7	Albert Smith	308	√	500.00
13	Sam Moore	309	√	350.00
15	Paul Roth	310	√	200.00
22	James Henry	311	√	225.00
25	Frank Booth	312	√	175.00
28	Albert Smith	313	√	250.00
28	Total—Accounts Receivable, Dr.; Sales, Cr.			2,150.00
				(106/413)

Individual amounts are posted daily to the sub-sidiary ledger.

Total is posted at the end of the month to the general ledger accounts.

Accounts Receivable Ledger

Frank Booth

Date	PR	Debit	Credit	Balance
Feb. 25	S3	175.00		175.00

James Henry

Date	PR	Debit	Credit	Balance
Feb. 2	S3	450.00		450.00
22	S3	225.00		675.00

Sam Moore

Date	PR	Debit	Credit	Balance
Feb. 13	S3	350.00		350.00

Paul Roth

Date	PR	Debit	Credit	Balance
Feb. 15	S3	200.00		200.00

Albert Smith

Date	PR	Debit	Credit	Balance
Feb. 7	S3	500.00		500.00
28	S3	250.00		750.00

General Ledger

Accounts Receivable   No. 106

Date	PR	Debit	Credit	Balance
Feb. 28	S3	2,150.00		2,150.00

Sales   No. 413

Date	PR	Debit	Credit	Balance
Feb. 28	S3		2,150.00	2,150.00

Note that the customer accounts are in a subsidiary ledger and the financial statement accounts are in the **General Ledger.**
Explanation columns are omitted from the accounts due to a lack of space.

Illustration 6-4 The Accounts Receivable Controlling Account and Subsidiary Ledger

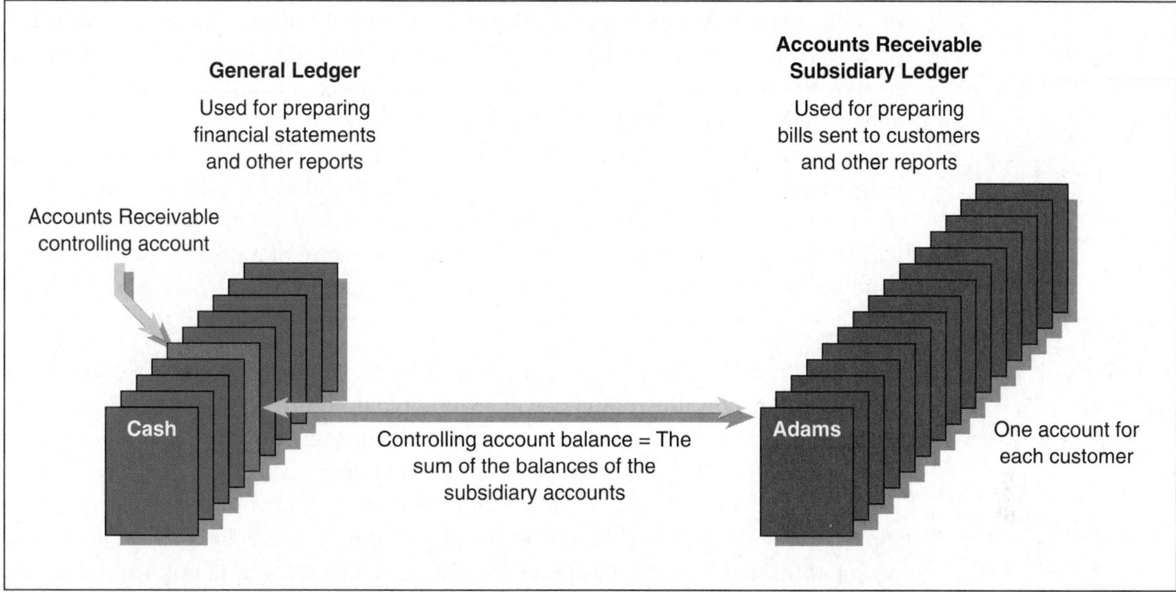

violate the requirement that debits equal credits. The equality of debits and credits is maintained in the General Ledger. The Accounts Receivable Ledger is simply a supplementary record that provides detailed information concerning each customer.

Illustration 6–4 shows the relationship between the Accounts Receivable controlling account and the accounts in the subsidiary ledger. Note that after all items are posted, the balance in the Accounts Receivable account should equal the sum of the balances in the customers' accounts. As a result, the Accounts Receivable account controls the Accounts Receivable Ledger and is called a **controlling account.** Since the Accounts Receivable Ledger is a supplementary record controlled by an account in the General Ledger, it is called a **subsidiary ledger.** After posting is completed, if the Accounts Receivable balance does not equal the sum of the customer account balances, you know an error has been made.

The Accounts Receivable account and the Accounts Receivable Ledger are not the only examples of controlling accounts and subsidiary ledgers. Most companies buy on credit from several suppliers. As a result, a company must keep a separate account for each creditor. To accomplish this, the firm maintains an Accounts Payable controlling account in the General Ledger and a separate account for each creditor in a subsidiary **Accounts Payable Ledger.** The controlling account, subsidiary ledger, and columnar journal techniques demonstrated thus far with accounts receivable also apply to the creditor accounts. The only difference is that a Purchases Journal and a Cash Disbursements Journal are used to record most of the transactions that affect these accounts. You will learn about these journals later in the chapter.

Another situation in which a subsidiary ledger often is used involves equipment. For example, a company with many items of office equipment might keep only one Office Equipment account in its General Ledger. This account would control a subsidiary ledger in which each item of equipment is recorded in a separate account.

MAINTAINING A SEPARATE RECORD FOR EACH ACCOUNT PAYABLE

Recall from the beginning of the chapter the detailed sales information **Imperial Oil** presented in its 1994 annual report. The presentation included the revenue of each major business segment. However, Imperial Oil's accounting system undoubtedly keeps far more detailed sales records than reflected in the annual report. In fact, the company sells thousands of different products and no doubt is able to analyze the sales performance of each one of them.

To some extent, this kind of detail is captured by having many different general ledger sales accounts. However, it also may be captured by using supplementary records that function like subsidiary ledgers. In fact, the concept of a subsidiary ledger may be applied in many different ways to ensure that the accounting system captures sufficient details to support possible analyses managers may want to make.

POSTING THE SALES JOURNAL

When customer accounts are maintained in a subsidiary ledger, a Sales Journal is posted as shown in Illustration 6–3. The individual sales recorded in the Sales Journal are posted each day to the proper customer accounts in the Accounts Receivable Ledger. These daily postings keep the customer accounts up-to-date. This is important in granting credit because the person responsible for granting credit should know the amount the credit-seeking customer currently owes. The source of this information is the customer's account; if the account is not up-to-date, an incorrect decision may be made.

Note the check marks in the Sales Journal's Posting Reference column. They indicate that the sales recorded in the journal were individually posted to the customer accounts in the Accounts Receivable Ledger. Check marks rather than account numbers are used because customer accounts may not be numbered. When the accounts are not numbered, they are arranged alphabetically in the Accounts Receivable Ledger so they can be located easily.

In addition to the daily postings to customer accounts, the Sales Journal's Amount column is totaled at the end of the month. Then, the total is debited to Accounts Receivable and credited to Sales. The credit records the month's revenue from charge sales. The debit records the resulting increase in accounts receivable.

IDENTIFYING POSTED AMOUNTS

When posting several journals to ledger accounts, you should indicate in the Posting Reference column before each posted amount the journal and the page number of the journal from which the amount was posted. Indicate the journal by using its initial. Thus, items posted from the Cash Disbursements Journal carry the initial *D* before their journal page numbers in the Posting Reference columns. Likewise, items from the Cash Receipts Journal carry the letter *R*. Those from the Sales Journal carry the initial *S*. Items from the Purchases Journal carry the initial *P*, and from the General Journal, the letter *G*.

Progress Check

6-7   When special journals are used:
   a. A General Journal is not used.
   b. All cash payments by cheque are recorded in the Cash Disbursements Journal.
   c. All purchase transactions are recorded in the Purchases Journal.
   d. All sales transactions are recorded in the Sales Journal.

6-8   Why does a columnar journal save posting labour?

6-9   **How can debits and credits remain equal when credit sales to customers are posted twice (once to Accounts Receivable and once to the customer's account)?**

6-10   **How can you identify the journal from which a particular amount in a ledger account was posted?**

A Cash Receipts Journal that is designed to save labour through posting column totals must be a multicolumn journal. A multicolumn journal is necessary because different accounts are credited when cash is received from different sources. For example, the cash receipts of a store normally fall into three groups: (1) cash from credit customers in payment of their accounts, (2) cash from cash sales, and (3) cash from other sources. Note in Illustration 6–5 that a special column is provided for the credits that result when cash is received from each of these sources.

Cash from Credit Customers

When a Cash Receipts Journal similar to Illustration 6–5 is used to record cash received in payment of a customer's account, the customer's name is entered in the journal's Account Credited column. The amount credited to the customer's account is entered in the Accounts Receivable Credit column, and the debits to Sales Discounts and Cash are entered in the journal's last two columns.

Look at the Accounts Receivable Credit column. First, observe that this column contains only credits to customer accounts. Second, the individual credits are posted daily to the customer accounts in the subsidiary Accounts Receivable Ledger. Third, the column total is posted at the end of the month as a credit to the Accounts Receivable controlling account. This is the normal recording and posting procedure when using special journals and controlling accounts with subsidiary ledgers. Transactions are normally entered in a special journal column. Then, the individual amounts are posted to the subsidiary ledger accounts and the column totals are posted to the general ledger accounts.

Cash Sales

After cash sales are entered on one or more cash registers and totaled at the end of each day, the daily total is recorded with a debit to Cash and a credit to Sales. When using a Cash Receipts Journal like Illustration 6–5, the debits to Cash are entered in the Cash Debit column, and the credits in a special column headed Sales Credit. By using a separate Sales Credit column, the bookkeeper can post the total cash sales for a month as a single amount, the column total. (Although cash sales are normally journalized daily based on the cash register reading, cash sales are journalized only once each week in Illustration 6–5 to shorten the illustration.)

At the time they record daily cash sales in the Cash Receipts Journal, some bookkeepers, as in Illustration 6–5, place a check mark in the Posting Reference (PR) column to indicate that no amount is individually posted from that line of the journal. Other bookkeepers use a double check ($\sqrt{\sqrt{}}$) to distinguish amounts that are not posted to customer accounts from amounts that are posted.

Miscellaneous Receipts of Cash

Most cash receipts are from collections of accounts receivable and from cash sales. However, other sources of cash include borrowing money from a bank or selling

---

CASH RECEIPTS JOURNAL

LO 3

Explain special journals and controlling accounts, use them to record transactions, and explain how to test the posting of entries to the Accounts Receivable and Accounts Payable subsidiary ledgers.

Illustration 6–5 Posting from the Cash Receipts Journal

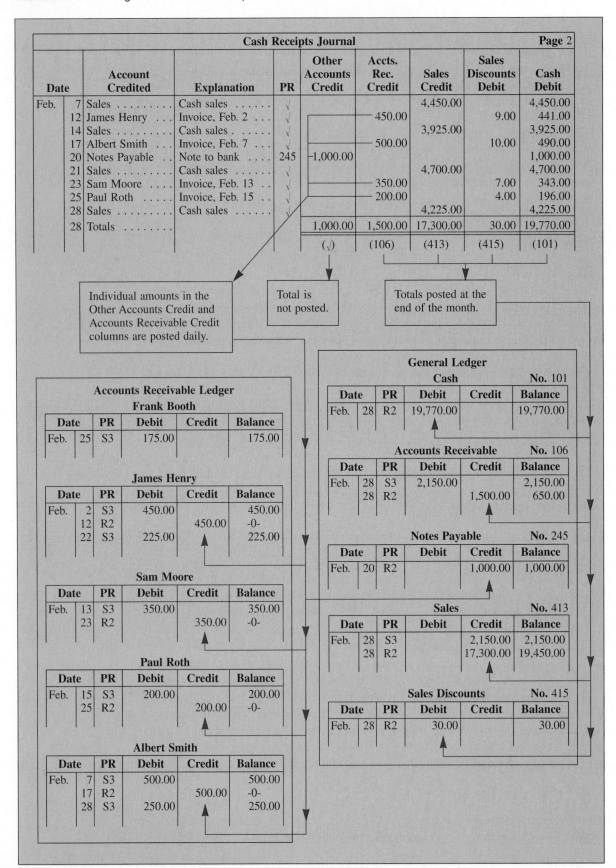

unneeded assets. The Other Accounts Credit column is for receipts that do not occur often enough to warrant a separate column. In most companies, the items entered in this column are few and are posted to a variety of general ledger accounts. As a result, postings are less apt to be omitted if these items are posted daily.

The Cash Receipts Journal's Posting Reference column is used only for daily postings from the Other Accounts and Accounts Receivable columns. The account numbers in the Posting Reference column indicate items that were posted to general ledger accounts. The check marks indicate either that an item (like a day's cash sales) was not posted or that an item was posted to the subsidiary Accounts Receivable Ledger.

Month-End Postings

At the end of the month, the amounts in the Accounts Receivable, Sales, Sales Discounts, and Cash columns of the Cash Receipts Journal are posted as column totals. However, the transactions recorded in any journal must result in equal debits and credits to general ledger accounts. Therefore, to be sure that the total debits and credits in a columnar journal are equal, the bookkeeper must *crossfoot* the column totals before posting them. To *foot* a column of numbers is to add it. To crossfoot, add the debit column totals and add the credit column totals; then compare the two sums for equality. For Illustration 6–5, the column totals appear as follows:

Debit Columns		**Credit Columns**	
Sales discounts debit	$ 30	Other accounts credit	$ 1,000
Cash debit	19,770	Accounts receivable credit	1,500
		Sales credit	17,300
Total	$19,800	Total	$19,800

After crossfooting the journal to confirm that debits equal credits, the bookkeeper posts the totals of the last four columns as indicated in each column heading. Because the individual items in the Other Accounts column are posted daily, the column total is not posted. Note in Illustration 6–5 the check mark below the Other Accounts column. The check mark indicates that the column total was not posted. The account numbers of the accounts to which the remaining column totals were posted are in parentheses below each column.

Posting items daily from the Other Accounts column with a delayed posting of the offsetting items in the Cash column (total) causes the General Ledger to be out of balance during the month. However, this does not matter because posting the Cash column total causes the offsetting amounts to reach the General Ledger before the trial balance is prepared.

POSTING RULE

Now that we have explained the procedures for posting from two different journals to a subsidiary ledger and its controlling account, the rule that governs all such postings should be clear. The rule for posting to a subsidiary ledger and its controlling account is: *The controlling account must be debited periodically for an amount or amounts equal to the sum of the debits that have already been posted to the subsidiary ledger, and it must be credited periodically for an amount or amounts equal to the sum of the credits that have already been posted to the subsidiary ledger.*

PURCHASES JOURNAL

A Purchases Journal with one money column can be used to record purchases of merchandise on credit. However, a Purchases Journal usually is more useful if it is a multicolumn journal in which all credit purchases on account are recorded. Such a journal may have columns similar to those in Illustration 6–6. In the illustrated journal, the invoice date and terms together indicate the date on which payment for each purchase is due. The Accounts Payable Credit column is used to record the amounts credited to each creditor's account. These amounts are posted daily to the individual creditor accounts in a subsidiary Accounts Payable Ledger.

In Illustration 6–6, note that each line of the Account column shows the subsidiary ledger account that should be posted for the amount in the Accounts Payable Credit column. The Account column also shows the general ledger account to be debited when a purchase involves an amount recorded in the Other Accounts Debit column.

In this illustration, note the separate column provided for purchases of office supplies on credit. A separate column such as this is useful whenever several transactions involve debits to a particular account. The Other Accounts Debit column in Illustration 6–6 allows the Purchases Journal to be used for all purchase transactions involving credits to Accounts Payable. The individual amounts in the Other Accounts Debit column typically are posted daily to the indicated general ledger accounts.

At the end of the month, all of the column totals except the Other Accounts Debit column are posted to the appropriate general ledger accounts. After this is done, the balance in the Accounts Payable controlling account should equal the sum of the account balances in the subsidiary Accounts Payable Ledger.

THE CASH DISBURSEMENTS JOURNAL OR CHEQUE REGISTER

The Cash Disbursements Journal, like the Cash Receipts Journal, has columns so that you can post repetitive debits and credits in column totals. The repetitive cash payments involve debits to the Accounts Payable controlling account and credits to both Purchases Discounts and Cash. Most companies usually purchase merchandise on credit. Therefore, a Purchases column is not needed. Instead, the occasional cash purchase is recorded as shown on line 2 of Illustration 6–7.

Observe that the illustrated journal has a column headed Cheque Number (Ch. No.). To gain control over cash disbursements, all payments except for very small amounts should be made by cheque.[1] The cheques should be prenumbered by the printer and should be entered in the journal in numerical order with each cheque's number in the column headed Ch. No. This makes it possible to scan the numbers in the column for omitted cheques. When a Cash Disbursements Journal has a column for cheque numbers, it is often called a **Cheque Register.**

The individual amounts in the Other Accounts Debit column of a Cash Disbursements Journal are normally posted to the appropriate general ledger accounts on a daily basis. The individual amounts in the Accounts Payable Debit column are also posted daily to the named creditors' accounts in the subsidiary Accounts Payable Ledger. At the end of the month, the bookkeeper crossfoots the column totals and posts the Accounts Payable Debit column total to the Accounts Payable

---

[1]In Chapter 7, we discuss a system that is used to control small payments made with currency and coins.

Illustration 6–6   Posting from the Purchases Journal

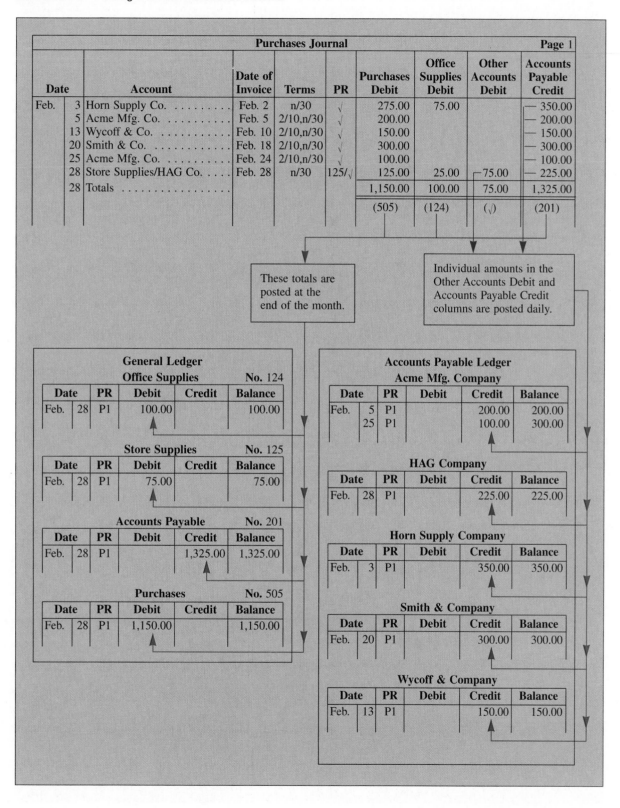

Illustration 6–7 Posting from the Cash Disbursements Journal

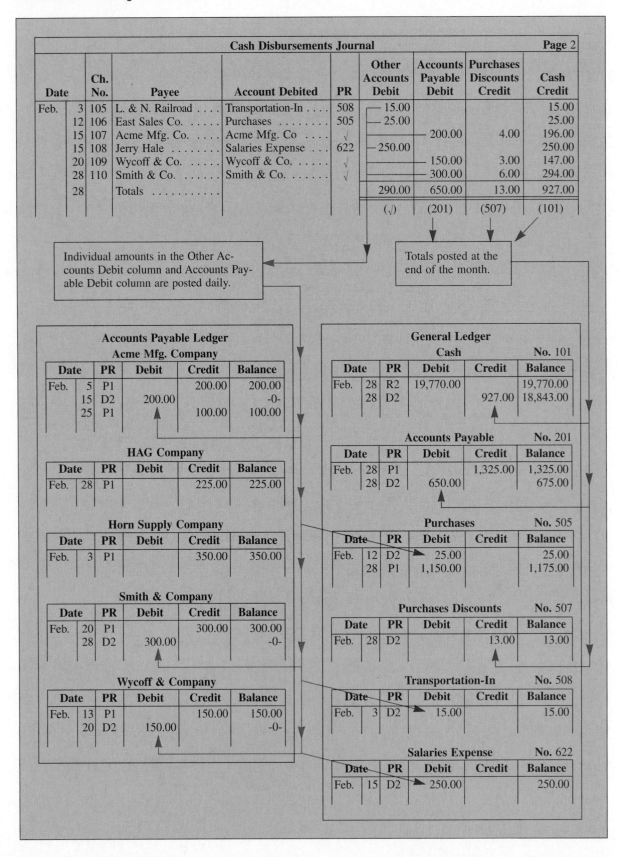

Cash Disbursements Journal						Page 2			
Date	Ch. No.	Payee	Account Debited	PR	Other Accounts Debit	Accounts Payable Debit	Purchases Discounts Credit	Cash Credit
Feb. 3	105	L. & N. Railroad	Transportation-In	508	15.00			15.00
12	106	East Sales Co.	Purchases	505	25.00			25.00
15	107	Acme Mfg. Co.	Acme Mfg. Co	√		200.00	4.00	196.00
15	108	Jerry Hale	Salaries Expense ...	622	250.00			250.00
20	109	Wycoff & Co.	Wycoff & Co.	√		150.00	3.00	147.00
28	110	Smith & Co.	Smith & Co.	√		300.00	6.00	294.00
28		Totals			290.00	650.00	13.00	927.00
					(√)	(201)	(507)	(101)

Individual amounts in the Other Accounts Debit column and Accounts Payable Debit column are posted daily.

Totals posted at the end of the month.

Accounts Payable Ledger

Acme Mfg. Company

Date	PR	Debit	Credit	Balance
Feb. 5	P1		200.00	200.00
15	D2	200.00		-0-
25	P1		100.00	100.00

HAG Company

Date	PR	Debit	Credit	Balance
Feb. 28	P1		225.00	225.00

Horn Supply Company

Date	PR	Debit	Credit	Balance
Feb. 3	P1		350.00	350.00

Smith & Company

Date	PR	Debit	Credit	Balance
Feb. 20	P1		300.00	300.00
28	D2	300.00		-0-

Wycoff & Company

Date	PR	Debit	Credit	Balance
Feb. 13	P1		150.00	150.00
20	D2	150.00		-0-

General Ledger

Cash — No. 101

Date	PR	Debit	Credit	Balance
Feb. 28	R2	19,770.00		19,770.00
28	D2		927.00	18,843.00

Accounts Payable — No. 201

Date	PR	Debit	Credit	Balance
Feb. 28	P1		1,325.00	1,325.00
28	D2	650.00		675.00

Purchases — No. 505

Date	PR	Debit	Credit	Balance
Feb. 12	D2	25.00		25.00
28	P1	1,150.00		1,175.00

Purchases Discounts — No. 507

Date	PR	Debit	Credit	Balance
Feb. 28	D2		13.00	13.00

Transportation-In — No. 508

Date	PR	Debit	Credit	Balance
Feb. 3	D2	15.00		15.00

Salaries Expense — No. 622

Date	PR	Debit	Credit	Balance
Feb. 15	D2	250.00		250.00

controlling account. Then, the Purchases Discounts Credit column total is posted to the Purchases Discounts account and the Cash Credit column total is posted to the Cash account. The Other Accounts column total is not posted.

Periodically, after all posting is completed, the account balances in the General Ledger and the subsidiary ledgers should be tested for accuracy. To do this, the bookkeeper first prepares a trial balance of the General Ledger to confirm that debits equal credits. If the trial balance balances, the accounts in the General Ledger, including the controlling accounts, are assumed to be correct. Second, the subsidiary ledgers are tested by preparing schedules of accounts receivable and accounts payable.

A **schedule of accounts payable** is prepared by listing the accounts in the Accounts Payable Ledger with their balances and calculating the sum of the balances. If the total is equal to the balance of the Accounts Payable controlling account, the accounts in the Accounts Payable Ledger are presumably correct. Illustration 6–8 shows a schedule of accounts payable drawn from the Accounts Payable Ledger of Illustration 6–7.

A **schedule of accounts receivable** is prepared in the same way as a schedule of accounts payable. Also, if its total equals the balance of the Accounts Receivable controlling account, you can assume the accounts in the Accounts Receivable Ledger are correct.

Illustration 6–9 provides a schematic look at the flow of accounting information from the source documents through to the general ledger and trial balance. This flow of information is essentially the same whether a manual or computerized accounting system is being used. The advantage of a computerized system is in its accuracy since the posting of the amounts to the accounts, the accumulation of balances, and the production of the financial statements are done automatically by the program. This assumes, of course, that the initial identification of the accounts and the entering of the amounts are done accurately. A solid knowledge of accounting is still necessary whether a manual or computerized system is being used.

Progress Check

6–11   When special journals and controlling accounts with subsidiary ledgers are used, which of the following is not true?

a. Transactions are first entered in the appropriate special journal.

b. All column totals, except Other Accounts, are posted to the general ledger accounts at month-end.

c. Individual transactions in the Other Accounts columns are posted to the appropriate general ledger accounts at month-end.

6–12   What is the rule for posting to a subsidiary ledger and its controlling account?

6–13   To test the accuracy of amounts posted to Accounts Receivable and Accounts Payable controlling accounts and their subsidiary ledgers:

a. Prepare a trial balance of the General Ledger accounts.

b. Foot and crossfoot the column totals in the journals.

c. Prepare schedules of accounts receivable and accounts payable.

d. Both *a* and *c.*

Illustration 6-8
Schedule of
Accounts Payable,
December 31

Acme Mfg. Company	$100
HAG Company	225
Horn Supply Company	350
Total accounts payable	$675

SALES AND GOODS AND SERVICES TAXES

LO 4
Explain how sales and goods and services taxes are recorded in special journals, how sales invoices can serve as a Sales Journal, and how sales returns and allowances are recorded.

Provincial Sales Tax

All provinces except Alberta require retailers to collect a provincial sales tax (**PST**) from their customers and to periodically remit this tax to the appropriate provincial authority. When special journals are used, a column is provided for PST in the Sales Journal and the Cash Receipts Journal. A record of PST is obtained by recording in the PST column the appropriate amount of PST on cash sales (Cash Receipts Journal) and sales on account (Sales Journal). It should be noted that not all sales are subject to PST.

Goods and Services Tax

The goods and services tax (**GST**) is a 7% tax on almost all goods and services provided in Canada. It is a federal tax on the consumer. However, unlike the PST, businesses pay GST up front but generally receive a full credit or refund for all GST paid. Ultimately, only the final consumer bears the burden of this tax. This is because businesses collect GST on sales, but since they receive full credit for GST paid on their purchases, they only remit the difference to the appropriate federal authority. To illustrate the collection and payment of GST consider the following example.

LM Company assembles riding mowers. It pays $200 for materials which are subject to GST of $14. LM pays the $14 to its suppliers who remit the $14 to Revenue Canada. LM now has a $14 GST credit, that is, prepaid GST.

LM sells the mower to KD Company, a dealer, for $500 and collects $35 in GST. LM remits the $35, minus the $14 input credit, that is, the GST paid to its suppliers. KD now has a $35 GST credit, that is, prepaid GST.

KD sells the mower to CC, the consumer, for $800 and collects $56 in GST. KD remits the $56, minus the $35 GST credit to Revenue Canada.

To summarize:

	GST Paid	GST Collected	GST Remitted
Materials supplier		$14	$14
LM Company	$14	35	21
KD Company	35	56	21
CC (the consumer)	56		$56

The total GST remitted is $56, the same amount that CC, the consumer, paid. The supplier, and LM and KD companies act as collection agents, collecting the tax along each stage of the process.

Illustration 6-9 Flow of Accounting Information

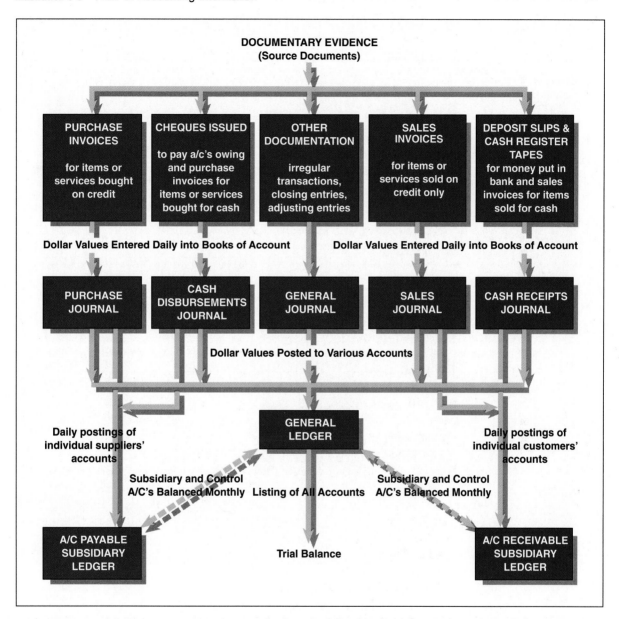

To facilitate the recording of GST, special GST (credit) columns must be provided not only in the Sales Journal and the Cash Receipts Journal, as in the case of PST, but also GST (debit) columns in the Purchases Journal and Cash Disbursements Journal. To illustrate, assume that Berlasty Company uses specialized journals shown in Illustration 6–10. The following transactions were completed and recorded during December:

Dec. 1   Purchases on account, $1,000 from Jason Supply, terms n/30.
　　3   Paid transportation on the Dec. 1 purchase, $30.

Illustration 6-10 Special Journals with PST and GST Columns as Applicable

Purchases Journal

Date	Account Credited	Terms	PR	Accounts Payable Credit	Purchases Debit	Office Supplies Debit	GST Payable Debit
Dec. 1	Jason Supply	n/30		1,070.00	1,000.00		70.00
							70.00
							(225)

Cash Disbursements Journal

Date	Ch. No.	Account Debited	PR	Other Accounts Debit	GST Payable Debit	Accts. Payable Debit	Purch. Disc. Credit	Cash Credit
Dec. 3	256	Transportation-in		30.00	2.10			32.10
9	257	Purchases		500.00	35.00			535.00
28	258	Accts. Pay/Jason Supply				1,070.00		1,070.00
				530.00	37.10	1,070.00		1,637.10
					(225)			

Sales Journal

Date	Account Debited	Invoice No.	PR	Acct. Rec. Debit	PST Payable Credit	GST Payable Credit	Sales Credit
Dec. 30	S. Burns	2734		2,260.00	120.00	140.00	2,000.00
					(224)	(225)	

Cash Receipts Journal

Date	Account Credited	Explanation	PR	Other Accounts Credit	Accts. Rec. Credit	PST Payable Credit	GST Payable Credit	Sales Credit	Cash Debit
Dec. 15						96.00	84.00	1,200.00	1,380.00
						(224)	(225)		

Dec. 9 Purchases for cash, $500.

1 Cash sale, $1,200 (subject to PST and GST).

28 Paid for the Dec. 1 purchase.

30 Sales to S. Burns on account, $2,000 ($1,500 subject to PST and $2,000 subject to GST).

After the posting is completed, as described earlier in the chapter, the PST and GST T-accounts would appear as follows:

PST (224)			GST (225)			
	SJ	120.00	PJ	70.00	SJ	140.00
	CRJ	96.00	CDJ	37.10	CRS	84.00
Balance		216.00	Balance			116.90

On December 31, PST payable amounts to $216 and GST payable amounts to $116.90. The computation of GST is not uniform throughout the country. In some of the provinces, the computation is as illustrated above, that is, PST and GST are computed as a percentage of the selling price. In other provinces, PST is initially computed as a percentage of the selling price and GST is computed as a percentage of the total of the selling price plus the PST. It should also be noted that while GST is a 7% federal tax, thus uniform in each of the provinces, PST is a provincial tax and differs in percentage from province to province. The preceding discussion is based on Ontario's PST of 8%.

In Illustration 6–10, one account was used to record GST on purchases and on sales. Some accountants prefer to record GST on purchases in a Prepaid GST account and GST on sales in a GST Payable account. Thus, if two accounts are used in Illustration 6–10, the GST Payable Debit column in the Purchases Journal and the Cash Disbursements Journal would be changed to Prepaid GST. The Sales Journal and the Cash Receipts Journal would remain as illustrated. The use of one or two accounts to account for GST is a matter of preference; the final result is the same.

Remittance of GST

The GST is administered by Revenue Canada Customs and Excise. Remittance is accompanied by a Goods and Services Tax Return shown in Illustration 6–11.

Frequency of filing returns is dependent on the size of the business. Large businesses (annual sales in excess of $6 million) are required to file GST returns monthly. Medium size businesses (annual sales of $500,000 to $6 million) are required to file quarterly. Small businesses (annual sales up to $500,000) have the option of filing annually but paying quarterly installments. GST for a period must be remitted to Revenue Canada by the end of the month following the month (quarter) collected.

To save labour, some retailers avoid using Sales Journals for credit sales. Instead, they post each sales invoice total directly to the customer's account in the subsidiary Accounts Receivable Ledger. Then, they place copies of the invoices in numerical order in a binder. At the end of the month, they total all the invoices of that month and make a general journal entry to debit Accounts Receivable and credit Sales for the total. In effect, the bound invoice copies act as a Sales Journal. Such a procedure is known as direct posting of sales invoices.

SALES INVOICES AS A SALES JOURNAL

A business that has only a few sales returns may record them in a General Journal with an entry like the following:

SALES RETURNS

Oct.	17	Sales Returns and Allowances	414	17.50	
		Accounts Receivable—George Ball	106/$\sqrt{}$		17.50
		Customer returned merchandise.			

The debit of the entry is posted to the Sales Returns and Allowances account. The credit is posted to both the Accounts Receivable controlling account and to

Illustration 6-11   Goods and Services Tax Return

Revenue Canada
Customs and Excise

Revenu Canada
Douanes et Accise

PROTECTED WHEN COMPLETED
PROTÉGÉ UNE FOIS REMPLI

GOODS AND SERVICES TAX RETURN (Non-personalized)
DÉCLARATION DE LA TAXE SUR LES PRODUITS ET SERVICES (non personnalisée)
Prescribed by the Minister of National Revenue under subsection 238(4) of the Excise Tax Act / Prescrit par le ministre du Revenu national en vertu du paragraphe 238(4) de la Loi sur la taxe d'accise

This return is for use by a GST registrant, or by a person who is required to remit tax where a personalized return is not available for the reporting period.
Cette formule doit être utilisée par les inscrits ou par toute personne tenue de verser la taxe lorsqu'une déclaration personnalisée n'est pas disponible pour la période de déclaration.

- To complete this form, please refer to the Instructions on the back.
Pour remplir cette formule, voir les renseignements au verso de la déclaration.

GST Account Number / Numéro de compte TPS: A 1 2 3 4 9 7 3 4

Reporting Period / Période de déclaration
From/du Y-A 9 5 M 1 0 D-J 0 1   To/au Y-A 9 5 M 1 2 D-J 3 1

Due Date / Date d'échéance
Y-A 9 6 M 0 1 D-J 3 1

Name of Individual or Entity / Raison sociale ou nom
BERLASTY COMPANY

Trading Name if Different from Above / Nom commercial s'il diffère de la raison sociale ou du nom

Mailing Address (No., Street and Apt. Number) / Adresse postale (n°, rue, app.)
125 SUNSET AVENUE

City / Ville
WINDSOR

Province
ONTARIO

Postal Code / Code postal
N9B 3P4

Name of the person we may contact concerning your return / Nom de la personne avec qui nous pouvons communiquer concernant votre déclaration
SANDRA BERLASTY

Telephone No. / N° de téléphone
(519) 253-4232

Personal information provided on this form is protected under the provisions of the Privacy Act and is maintained in Personal Information Bank RCC/P-PU-065.

Les renseignements personnels fournis dans cette formule sont protégés en vertu de la Loi sur la protection des renseignements personnels et sont conservés dans le Répertoire des renseignements personnels RND/P-PU-065.

SECTION TWO - TAX CALCULATIONS
PARTIE DEUX - CALCULS DE LA TAXE

GST Collectible / TPS percevable	103	2 2 4 0 0
GST Adjustments / Redressements de la TPS	104	Ø
Input Tax Credit (ITC) / Crédit de taxe sur les intrants (CTI)	106	– 1 0 7 1 0
ITC Adjustments / Redressements du CTI	107	Ø

SECTION ONE - PERIOD SUMMARY
PARTIE UN - SOMMAIRE DE LA PÉRIODE

Total Taxable Supplies (sales and other revenue) / Total des fournitures taxables (ventes et autres recettes)	101	3 2 0 0 0 0
Total Purchases / Total des achats	102	1 5 3 0 0 0
Paid by instalments / Payée par acomptes provisionnels	110	Ø
Rebates / Remboursements	111	Ø

Add Lines 103 and 104 / Additionnez les montants des lignes 103 et 104 — 105

Total GST and Adjustments for Period / Total de la TPS et des redressements pour cette période: 2 2 4 0 0

Add Lines 106 and 107 / Additionnez les montants des lignes 106 et 107 — 108

Total ITCs and Adjustments / Total du CTI et des redressements: – 1 0 7 1 0

Subtract Line 108 from Line 105 (indicate if negative amount) / Soustrayez le montant de la ligne 108 de celui de la ligne 105 (indiquez s'il s'agit d'un montant négatif) — 109

NET TAX - TAXE NETTE: 1 1 6 9 0

Add Lines 110 and 111 / Additionnez les montants des lignes 110 et 111 — 112

Total Other Credits - Total des autres crédits

Subtract Line 112 from Line 109 (indicate if negative amount) / Soustrayez le montant de la ligne 112 de celui de la ligne 109 (indiquez s'il s'agit d'un montant négatif) — 113

BALANCE - SOLDE: 1 1 6 9 0

OR / OU

Refund Claimed / Remboursement demandé — 114

Payment Enclosed / Paiement inclus — 115: 1 1 6 9 0

If the balance is negative claim a refund, otherwise remit the amount owing. A balance of less than $1.00 will neither be charged nor refunded. All registrants must file a return regardless of the balance. Do not staple or paper clip.

Si le montant du solde est négatif, demandez un remboursement. S'il est positif, vous devez remettre le montant inscrit. Les soldes inférieurs à 1,00 $ ne sont ni exigés ni remboursés. Tous les inscrits doivent produire une déclaration, peu importe le montant du solde. N'utilisez ni agrafes ni trombones.

I hereby certify that the information given in this return and in any documents attached is true, correct and complete in every respect and that I am authorized to sign on behalf of the registrant.

J'atteste que les renseignements fournis dans cette déclaration et dans tout document qui y serait joint sont vrais, exacts et complets sous tous les rapports et que je suis autorisée à signer au nom de l'inscrit.

▶ IT IS A SERIOUS OFFENCE TO MAKE A FALSE RETURN.
LA PRODUCTION D'UNE DÉCLARATION FAUSSE EST UNE INFRACTION GRAVE.

Name / Nom: Sandra Berlasty
Authorized Signature / Signature autorisée: Sandra Berlasty

Title / Titre: Treasurer
Date: January 31, 1996

GST 62 (90/11)

PART 1: DETACH AND FORWARD TO PROCESSING CENTRE
PARTIE 1: DÉTACHEZ ET FAITES PARVENIR AU CENTRE DE TRAITEMENT DES DONNÉES

---

the customer's account. Note the account number and the check mark, 106/√, in the PR column on the credit line. This indicates that both the Accounts Receivable controlling account in the General Ledger and the George Ball account in the Accounts Receivable Ledger were credited for $17.50. Both were credited because the balance of the controlling account in the General Ledger will not equal the sum of the customer account balances in the subsidiary ledger unless both are credited.

Illustration 6–12

		Sales Returns and Allowances Journal				
Date		Account Credited	Explanation	Credit Memo No.	PR	Amount
Oct.	7	Robert Moore	Defective merchandise	203	√	10.00
	14	James Warren	Defective merchandise	204	√	12.00
	18	T. M. Jones	Not ordered	205	√	6.00
	23	Sam Smith	Defective merchandise	206	√	18.00
	31	Sales Returns and Allowances, Dr.; Accts. Receivable, Cr.				46.00
						(414/106)

A company with a large number of sales returns can save posting labour by recording them in a special Sales Returns and Allowances Journal similar to Illustration 6–12. Note that this is in keeping with the idea that a company can design and use a special journal for any group of similar transactions if there are enough transactions to warrant the journal. When using a Sales Returns and Allowances Journal to record returns, the amounts in the journal are posted daily to the customers' accounts. Then, at the end of the month, the journal total is posted as a debit to Sales Returns and Allowances and as a credit to Accounts Receivable.

GENERAL JOURNAL ENTRIES

When special journals are used, a General Journal is always necessary for adjusting, closing, and correcting entries and for a few transactions that cannot be recorded in the special journals. Some of these transactions are purchases returns, purchases of plant assets financed by notes payable, and if a Sales Returns and Allowances Journal is not provided, sales returns.

Progress Check

6-14   If sales taxes must be recorded and special journals are used: *(a)* The sales taxes must be recorded in the General Journal. *(b)* A separate column for sales taxes should be included in the Cash Receipts Journal and the Sales Journal. *(c)* A special Sales Taxes Journal should be used.

6-15   What is direct posting of sales invoices?

6-16   If a company uses special journals for sales, purchases, cash receipts, and cash disbursements, why does it need a General Journal?

USING THE INFORMATION— BUSINESS SEGMENTS

The accounting system a company uses is more complicated when a company is large and operates in more than one line of business. When information is provided about each **business segment** of the company, outside users of the financial statements can gain a better understanding of the overall business. A business segment is a portion of the company that can be separately identified by the products or services that it provides or a geographic market that it serves.

LO 5
Explain the nature and use of business segment information.

Companies that have securities traded in public markets must publish segment information if they have material operations in more than one industry.[2] The required information for each segment includes:

1. Revenues or net sales.
2. Operating profits.
3. Capital expenditures.
4. Depreciation and amortization expense.
5. Identifiable assets.

In addition, they may be required to report (1) a geographical distribution of sales and (2) sales to each major customer that accounts for 10% or more of total sales.

Look again at the net sales information for **Imperial Oil** presented on page 291. This is a typical example of business segment information. Note that the company identified three primary segments: natural resources, petroleum products, and chemicals. In addition, the company reported its geographic distribution of sales.

The usefulness of segment information comes from the fact that different industries and geographical areas often face different levels of risk, profitability, and opportunities for growth. The information helps financial statement readers gain insight about the performance of the segments and the dependence of the entire company on the profits derived from each of the segments.

Progress Check

6-17   The requirements for segment information include presenting each segment's:
(a) Revenues; (b) Operating expenses; (c) Income taxes; (d) Capital expenditures; (e) Both a and d.

SUMMARY OF THE CHAPTER IN TERMS OF LEARNING OBJECTIVES

LO 1. Describe the five basic components of an accounting system. The components of accounting systems include source documents, input devices, the data processor, data storage, and output devices. Both manual and computerized systems must have all five components.

LO 2. Describe the types of computers used in large and small accounting systems, the role of software in those systems, and the different approaches to inputting and processing data, including the use of networking. Depending on the complexity of a company's accounting system, the computers used may be large mainframe computers or smaller microcomputers. If a mainframe computer is used, the software that provides the computer instructions is likely to be custom made for the company. However, an increasing variety of off-the-shelf programs are available, especially for microcomputers. There are many different ways to set up computer systems, including batch and on-line processing, and computer networks.

LO 3. Explain special journals and controlling accounts, use them to record transactions, and explain how to test the posting of entries to the Accounts Receivable and Accounts Payable subsidiary ledgers. Columnar journals are designed so that repetitive debits or credits are entered in separate columns. A typical set of special journals includes a Sales Journal, a Purchases Journal, a Cash

---

[2]*CICA Handbook*, section 1700, "Segmented Information" paragraph .33.

Receipts Journal, and a Cash Disbursements Journal (or Cheque Register). Any transactions that cannot be entered in the special journals are entered in the General Journal.

When many accounts of the same type are required, such as an account receivable for each credit customer, they usually are kept in a separate subsidiary ledger. Then, a single controlling account is maintained in the General Ledger. After all transactions are posted to the accounts in the subsidiary ledger and to the controlling account, the controlling account balance should equal the sum of the account balances in the subsidiary ledger.

LO 4. Explain the use of special and general journals in accounting for sales taxes and sales returns and allowances, and explain how sales invoices can serve as a Sales Journal. To record PST and GST, the Sales Journal and the Cash Receipts Journal should include separate PST and GST Payable columns. When sales invoices substitute for a Sales Journal, the customer accounts in the Accounts Receivable Ledger are posted directly from the sales invoices. Copies of the invoices for each month are then bound and totaled as a basis for recording the sales in the General Ledger. Sales returns and allowances may be recorded in the General Journal, or a special journal for sales returns and allowances may be used. GST paid by the firm is recorded in the Purchases Journal.

LO 5. Explain the nature and use of business segment information. Public companies with material operations in more than one industry must provide separate information for each segment. The information includes revenues, operating profits, capital expenditures, amortization, and identifiable assets. It also includes a geographical distribution of sales and sales to major customers.

GLOSSARY

Accounting system the people, forms, procedures, and equipment that are used to capture data about the transactions of an entity and to generate from that data a variety of financial, managerial, and tax accounting reports. p. 292

Accounts Payable Ledger a subsidiary ledger that contains a separate account for each party that grants credit on account to the entity. p. 303

Accounts Receivable Ledger a subsidiary ledger that contains an account for each credit customer. p. 301

Batch processing an approach to inputting data that accumulates source documents for a period such as a day, week, or month and inputs all of them at the same time. p. 299

Business segment a portion of a company that can be separately identified by the products or services that it provides or a geographic market that it serves. p. 317

Cheque Register a book of original entry for recording cash payments by cheque. p. 308

Columnar journal a book of original entry having columns, each of which is designated as the place for

entering specific data about each transaction of a group of similar transactions. p. 301

Computer network a system in which computers are linked with each other so that different users on different computers can share access to the same data and the same programs. p. 299

Controlling account a general ledger account the balance of which (after posting) equals the sum of the balances of the accounts in a related subsidiary ledger. p. 303

Data processor the component of an accounting system that interprets, manipulates, and summarizes the recorded information so that it can be used in analyses and reports. p. 294

Data storage the component of an accounting system that keeps the inputted data in a readily accessible manner so that financial reports can be drawn from it efficiently. p. 294

General Ledger the ledger that contains the financial statement accounts of a business. p. 301

GST (Goods and Services Tax)   a federal tax on the consumer on almost all goods and services. p. 312

Input device   a means of transferring information from source documents to the data processing component of an accounting system. p. 293

On-line processing   an approach to inputting data whereby the data on each source document is inputted as soon as the document is available. p. 299

Output devices   the means by which information is taken out of the accounting system and made available for use. p. 295

PST (Provincial Sales Tax)   a tax collected by retailers on customer purchases. p. 312

Schedule of accounts payable   a list of the balances of all the accounts in the Accounts Payable Ledger that is summed to show the total amount of accounts payable outstanding. p. 311

Schedule of accounts receivable   a list of the balances of all the accounts in the Accounts Receivable Ledger that is summed to show the total amount of accounts receivable outstanding. p. 311

Special journal   a book of original entry that is designed and used for recording only a specified type of transaction. p. 300

Subsidiary ledger   a group of accounts that show the details underlying the balance of a controlling account in the General Ledger. p. 303

QUESTIONS

1. What are the five basic components of an accounting system?

2. What are source documents? Give some examples.

3. What is the purpose of an input device? Give some examples of input devices for computer systems.

4. What is the difference between data that is stored off-line and data that is stored on-line?

5. What purpose is served by the output devices of an accounting system?

6. What is the difference between batch and on-line processing?

7. When special journals are used, separate special journals normally are used to record each of four different types of transactions. What are these four types of transactions?

8. Why should sales to and receipts of cash from credit customers be recorded and posted daily?

9. Both credits to customer accounts and credits to miscellaneous accounts are individually posted from a Cash Receipts Journal similar to the one in Illustration 6–5. Why not put both kinds of credits in the same column and thus save journal space?

10. What procedures allow copies of a company's sales invoices to be used as a Sales Journal?

11. When a general journal entry is used to record a returned credit sale, the credit of the entry must be posted twice. Does this cause the trial balance to be out of balance? Why or why not?

12. Look in Appendix I at Geac Computer's financial statements. What amount of operating income in 1994 came from operations in Europe? What geographic area generated the largest operating income?

QUICK STUDY (Five-Minute Exercises)

Identify the role in an accounting system played by each of the lettered items by assigning a number from the list on the left:

1. Source documents
2. Input devices
3. Data processor
4. Data storage
5. Output devices

_____ *a.* Bar code reader
_____ *b.* Filing cabinet
_____ *c.* Bank statement
_____ *d.* Calculator
_____ *e.* Computer keyboard
_____ *f.* Floppy diskette
_____ *g.* Computer monitor
_____ *h.* Invoice from a supplier
_____ *i.* Computer hardware and software
_____ *j.* Computer printer

Fill in the blanks:

a. Personal computers, often called _____, are physically small, easy to operate, and increasingly inexpensive.

b. Off-the-shelf programs designed so that actions taken in one part of the system also produce results in related parts are known as _____ systems.

c. With _____ processing, source documents are accumulated for a period of time and then processed all at the same time, such as once a day, week, or month.

d. A computer _____ allows different computer users to share access to the same data and programs.

Sampson Iron Works uses a Sales Journal, a Purchases Journal, a Cash Receipts Journal, a Cash Disbursements Journal, and a General Journal. Sampson recently completed the following transactions. List the transaction letters and next to each letter give the name of the journal in which the transaction should be recorded.

a. Paid a creditor.
b. Sold merchandise for cash.
c. Purchased merchandise on credit.
d. Sold merchandise on credit.
e. Borrowed money from the bank.
f. Purchased shop supplies on credit.
g. Paid an employee's salary.

The Nostalgic Book Shop uses a Sales Journal, a Purchases Journal, a Cash Receipts Journal, a Cash Disbursements Journal, and a General Journal. The following transactions occurred during the month of November. Journalize the November transactions that should be recorded in the General Journal.

Nov. 2   Purchased merchandise on credit for $1,900 from the Randolph Co., terms 2/10, n/30.

Nov. 12   The owner, I. M. Nowalski, contributed an automobile worth $13,500 to the business.

16   Sold merchandise on credit to W. Ryder for $1,100, terms n/30.

19   W. Ryder returned $90 of merchandise originally purchased on November 16.

28   Returned $170 of defective merchandise to the Randolph Co. from the November 2 purchase.

QS 6–5
(LO 5)

A company with publicly traded securities operates in more than one industry. Which of the following items of information about each business segment must the company report?

a.	Revenues	*e.*	Capital expenditures
b.	Net sales	*f.*	Amortization and depreciation
c.	Operating profits	*g.*	Cash flows
d.	Operating expenses	*h.*	Identifiable assets

EXERCISES

Exercise 6–1
The Sales Journal
(LO 3)

Fletcher's Frozen Foods uses a Sales Journal, a Purchases Journal, a Cash Receipts Journal, a Cash Disbursements Journal, and a General Journal. The following transactions occurred during the month of February:

Feb. 2   Sold merchandise to M. Stohl for $356 cash, Invoice No. 5703.

5   Purchased merchandise on credit from Campbell Company, $2,035.

7   Sold merchandise to E. Jason for $950, terms 2/10, n/30, Invoice No. 5704.

8   Borrowed $5,000 by giving a note to the bank.

12   Sold merchandise to L. Patrick for $223, terms n/30, Invoice No. 5705.

16   Received $931 from E. Jason to pay for the purchase of February 7.

19   Sold used store equipment to Green Acres for $500.

25   Sold merchandise to P. Sumo for $428, terms n/30, Invoice No. 5706.

Required

On a sheet of notebook paper, draw a Sales Journal like the one that appears in Illustration 6–3. Journalize the February transactions that should be recorded in the Sales Journal.

Exercise 6–2
The Cash Receipts Journal
(LO 3)

Landmark Map Company uses a Sales Journal, a Purchases Journal, a Cash Receipts Journal, a Cash Disbursements Journal, and a General Journal. The following transactions occurred during the month of September:

Sept. 3   Purchased merchandise on credit for $2,900 from Pace Supply Co.

7   Sold merchandise on credit to N. Jamal for $800, subject to a $16 sales discount if paid by the end of the month.

9   Borrowed $1,750 by giving a note to the bank.

13   Received a capital contribution of $3,500 from R. Galindo, the owner of the company.

18   Sold merchandise to T. Byrd for $199 cash.

22   Paid Pace Supply $2,900 for the merchandise purchased on September 3.

Sept.27 Received $784 from N. Jamal in payment of the September 7 purchase.

30 Paid salaries of $1,500.

Required

On a sheet of notebook paper, draw a multicolumn Cash Receipts Journal like the one that appears in Illustration 6–5. Journalize the September transactions that should be recorded in the Cash Receipts Journal.

Gem Industries uses a Sales Journal, a Purchases Journal, a Cash Receipts Journal, a Cash Disbursements Journal, and a General Journal. The following transactions occurred during the month of July:

Exercise 6–3
The Purchases Journal
(LO 3)

July 1 Purchased merchandise on credit for $7,190 from Angel, Inc., terms n/30.

8 Sold merchandise on credit to H. Baruk for $1,300, subject to a $26 sales discount if paid by the end of the month.

10 J. Powers, the owner of the business, contributed $2,500 cash to the business.

14 Purchased store supplies from Steck & Vaughn on credit for $145, terms n/30.

17 Purchased office supplies on credit from King Mart for $310, terms n/30.

24 Sold merchandise to V. Valdi for $467 cash.

28 Purchased store supplies from Hadlock's for $79 cash.

29 Paid Angel, Inc., $7,190 for the merchandise purchased on July 1.

Required

On a sheet of notebook paper, draw a multicolumn Purchases Journal like the one that appears in Illustration 6–6. Journalize the July transactions that should be recorded in the Purchases Journal.

Neon Art Supply uses a Sales Journal, a Purchases Journal, a Cash Receipts Journal, a Cash Disbursements Journal, and a General Journal. The following transactions occurred during the month of March:

Exercise 6–4
The Cash Disbursements Journal
(LO 3)

Mar. 3 Purchased merchandise for $1,850 on credit from Paige, Inc., terms 2/10, n/30.

9 Issued Cheque No. 210 to Mott & Son to buy store supplies for $369.

12 Sold merchandise on credit to C. Klempt for $625, terms n/30.

17 Issued Cheque No. 211 for $1,000 to repay a note payable to City Bank.

20 Purchased merchandise for $4,700 on credit from LeBeck's, terms 2/10, n/30.

29 Issued Cheque No. 212 to LeBeck's to pay the amount due for the purchase of March 20, less the discount.

31 Paid salary of $1,500 to B. Eldon by issuing Cheque No. 213.

31 Issued Cheque No. 214 to Paige, Inc., to pay the amount due for the purchase of March 3.

Required

On a sheet of notebook paper, draw a multicolumn Cash Disbursements Journal like the one that appears in Illustration 6–7. Journalize the March transactions that should be recorded in the Cash Disbursements Journal.

Exercise 6–5
Special journal
transactions
(LO 3)

Simonetti Pharmacy uses the following journals: Sales Journal, Purchases Journal, Cash Receipts Journal, Cash Disbursements Journal, and General Journal. On June 5, Simonetti purchased merchandise priced at $15,000, subject to credit terms of 2/10, n/30. On June 14, the pharmacy paid the net amount due. However, in journalizing the payment, the bookkeeper debited Accounts Payable for $15,000 and failed to record the cash discount. Cash was credited for the actual amount paid. In what journals would the June 5 and the June 14 transactions have been recorded? What procedure is likely to discover the error in journalizing the June 14 transaction?

Exercise 6–6
Posting to subsidiary
ledger accounts
(LO 3)

At the end of May, the Sales Journal of Cowtown Leather Goods appeared as follows:

Sales Journal

Date		Account Debited	Invoice Number	PR	Amount
May	6	Bud Smith	190		1,780.00
	10	Don Holly	191		2,040.00
	17	Sandy Ford	192		960.00
	25	Don Holly	193		335.00
	31	Total			5,115.00

Cowtown also had recorded the return of merchandise with the following entry:

May	20	Sales Returns and Allowances	165.00	
		Accounts Receivable—Sandy Ford		165.00
		Customer returned merchandise.		

Required

1. On a sheet of notebook paper, open a subsidiary Accounts Receivable Ledger that has a T-account for each customer listed in the Sales Journal. Post to the customer accounts the entries in the Sales Journal and any portion of the general journal entry that affects a customer's account.

2. Open a General Ledger that has T-accounts for Accounts Receivable, Sales, and Sales Returns and Allowances. Post the Sales Journal and any portion of the general journal entry that affects these accounts.

3. Prepare a list or schedule of the accounts in the subsidiary Accounts Receivable Ledger and add their balances to show that the total equals the balance in the Accounts Receivable controlling account.

Exercise 6–7
Accounts Receivable
Ledger
(LO 3, 4)

Skillern Company posts its sales invoices directly and then binds the invoices to make them into a Sales Journal. Sales are subject to a 10% Provincial Sales Tax and the 7% Goods and Services Tax. Skillern had the following sales during January:

Jan.	2	Jay Newton	$ 3,600
	8	Adrian Carr	6,100
	10	Kathy Olivas	13,400
	14	Lisa Mack	20,500
	20	Kathy Olivas	11,200
	29	Jay Newton	7,300
		Total	$62,100

Required

1. On a sheet of notebook paper, open a subsidiary Accounts Receivable Ledger having a T-account for each customer. Post the invoices to the subsidiary ledger.

2. Give the general journal entry to record the end-of-month total of the Sales Journal.

3. Open an Accounts Receivable controlling account and a Sales account and post the general journal entry.

4. Prepare a list or schedule of the accounts in the subsidiary Accounts Receivable Ledger and add their balances to show that the total equals the balance in the Accounts Receivable controlling account.

Following are the condensed journals of Tip-Top Trophy Shop. The journal column headings are incomplete in that they do not indicate whether the columns are debit or credit columns.

Exercise 6–8
Posting from special journals and subsidiary ledgers to T-accounts
(LO 3)

<table>
<tr><th colspan="2">Sales Journal</th></tr>
<tr><th>Account</th><th>Amount</th></tr>
<tr><td>Jack Heinz ....</td><td>2,700</td></tr>
<tr><td>Trudy Stone ....</td><td>7,400</td></tr>
<tr><td>Wayne Day ....</td><td>3,000</td></tr>
<tr><td>Total ....</td><td>13,100</td></tr>
</table>

<table>
<tr><th colspan="2">Purchases Journal</th></tr>
<tr><th>Account</th><th>Amount</th></tr>
<tr><td>Frasier Corp. ....</td><td>3,400</td></tr>
<tr><td>Sultan, Inc. ....</td><td>6,500</td></tr>
<tr><td>McGraw Company ....</td><td>1,700</td></tr>
<tr><td>Total ....</td><td>11,600</td></tr>
</table>

General Journal

...	..	Sales Returns and Allowances	400.00	
..	..	Accounts Receivable—Jack Heinz		400.00
...	..	Accounts Payable—Frasier Corp.	850.00	
..	..	Purchases Returns and Allowances		850.00

Cash Receipts Journal

Account	Other Accounts	Accounts Receivable	Sales	Sales Discounts	Cash
Jack Heinz		2,300		46	2,254
Sales			1,950		1,950
Notes Payable	3,500				3,500
Sales			525		525
Trudy Stone		7,400		148	7,252
Store Equipment	200				200
Totals	3,700	9,700	2,475	194	15,681

Cash Disbursements Journal

Account	Other Accounts	Accounts Payable	Purchases Discounts	Cash
Prepaid Insurance	960			960
Sultan, Inc.		6,500	195	6,305
Frasier Corp.		2,550	51	2,499
Store Equipment	1,570			1,570
Totals	2,530	9,050	246	11,334

Required

1. Prepare T-accounts on notebook paper for the following general ledger and subsidiary ledger accounts. Separate the accounts of each ledger group as follows:

General Ledger Accounts	Accounts Receivable Ledger Accounts
Cash	Wayne Day
Accounts Receivable	Jack Heinz
Prepaid Insurance	Trudy Stone
Store Equipment	
Accounts Payable	
Notes Payable	
Sales	**Accounts Payable Ledger Accounts**
Sales Returns and Allowances	Frasier Corp.
Sales Discounts	McGraw Company
Purchases	Sultan, Inc.
Purchases Returns and Allowances	
Purchases Discounts	

2. Without referring to any of the illustrations in the chapter that show complete column headings for the journals, post the journals to the proper T-accounts.

Exercise 6–9
Errors related to the Purchases Journal
(LO 3, 4)

A company that records credit purchases in a Purchases Journal and records purchases returns in its General Journal made the following errors. List each error by letter, and opposite each letter tell when the error should be discovered:

a. Made an addition error in determining the balance of a creditor's account.

b. Made an addition error in totaling the Office Supplies column of the Purchases Journal.

c. Posted a purchases return to the Accounts Payable account and to the creditor's account but did not post to the Purchases Returns and Allowances account.

d. Posted a purchases return to the Purchases Returns and Allowances account and to the Accounts Payable account but did not post to the creditor's account.

e. Correctly recorded a $4,000 purchase in the Purchases Journal but posted it to the creditor's account as a $400 purchase.

PROBLEMS

Problem 6–1
Special journals, subsidiary ledgers, schedule of accounts receivable
(LO 3)

Niagara Company completed these transactions during April of the current year:

Apr. 2 Purchased merchandise on credit from Flott Company, invoice dated April 2, terms 2/10, n/60, $13,300.

3 Sold merchandise on credit to Linda Hobart, Invoice No. 760, $2,000. (The terms of all credit sales are 2/10, n/30.)

3 Purchased office supplies on credit from Whitewater Inc., $1,380. Invoice dated April 2, terms n/10 EOM.

4 Issued Cheque No. 587 to *Northern Times* for advertising expense, $815.

5 Sold merchandise on credit to Paul Abrams, Invoice No. 761, $6,000.

6 Received an $85 credit memorandum from Whitewater Inc. for office supplies received on April 3 and returned for credit.

9 Purchased store equipment on credit from Cooper's Supply, invoice dated April 9, terms n/10 EOM, $11,125.

Apr. 11   Sold merchandise on credit to Kelly Schaefer, Invoice No. 762, $9,500.

   12   Issued Cheque No. 588 to Flott Company in payment of its April 2 invoice, less the discount.

   13   Received payment from Linda Hobart for the April 3 sale, less the discount.

   13   Sold merchandise on credit to Linda Hobart, Invoice No. 763, $4,100.

   14   Received payment from Paul Abrams for the April 5 sale, less the discount.

   16   Issued Cheque No. 589, payable to Payroll, in payment of the sales salaries for the first half of the month, $9,750. Cashed the cheque and paid the employees.

   16   Cash sales for the first half of the month were $50,840. (Cash sales are usually recorded daily from the cash register readings. However, they are recorded only twice in this problem to reduce the repetitive transactions.)

   17   Purchased merchandise on credit from Sprague Company, invoice dated April 16, terms 2/10, n/30, $12,750.

   18   Borrowed $40,000 from First Provincial Bank by giving a long-term note payable.

   20   Received payment from Kelly Schaefer for the April 11 sale, less the discount.

   20   Purchased store supplies on credit from Cooper's Supply, invoice dated April 19, terms n/10 EOM, $730.

   23   Received a $400 credit memorandum from Sprague Company for defective merchandise received on April 17 and returned.

   23   Received payment from Linda Hobart for the April 13 sale, less the discount.

   25   Purchased merchandise on credit from Flott Company, invoice dated April 24, terms 2/10, n/60, $10,375.

   26   Issued Cheque No. 590 to Sprague Company in payment of its April 16 invoice, less the return and the discount.

   27   Sold merchandise on credit to Paul Abrams, Invoice No. 764, $3,070.

   27   Sold merchandise on credit to Kelly Schaefer, Invoice No. 765, $5,700.

   30   Issued Cheque No. 591, payable to Payroll, in payment of the sales salaries for the last half of the month, $9,750.

   30   Cash sales for the last half of the month were $70,975.

Required

Preparation component:

1.   Open the following general ledger accounts: Cash, Accounts Receivable, Long-Term Notes Payable, Sales, and Sales Discounts. Also open subsidiary accounts receivable ledger accounts for Paul Abrams, Linda Hobart, and Kelly Schaefer.

2.   Prepare a Sales Journal and a Cash Receipts Journal like the ones illustrated in this chapter.

3.   Review the transactions of Niagara Company and enter those transactions that should be journalized in the Sales Journal and those that should be journalized in the Cash Receipts Journal. Ignore any transactions that should be journalized in a Purchases Journal, a Cash Disbursements Journal, or a General Journal.

4.   Post the items that should be posted as individual amounts from the journals. (Normally, such items are posted daily; but since they are few in number in this problem you are asked to post them only once.)

5.   Foot and crossfoot the journals and make the month-end postings.

6.   Prepare a trial balance of the General Ledger and test the accuracy of the subsidiary ledger by preparing a schedule of accounts receivable.

Analysis component:

7.   Assume that the sum of the account balances on the schedule of accounts receivable does not equal the balance of the controlling account in the General Ledger. Describe the steps you would go through to discover the error(s).

Problem 6–2
Special journals, subsidiary ledgers, schedule of accounts payable
(LO 3, 4)

On March 31, Niagara Company had a cash balance of $167,000 and a Long-Term Notes Payable balance of $167,000. The April transactions of Niagara Company included those listed in Problem 6–1.

Required

1.   Open the following general ledger accounts: Cash, Office Supplies, Store Supplies, Store Equipment, Accounts Payable, Long-Term Notes Payable, Purchases, Purchases Returns and Allowances, Purchases Discounts, Sales Salaries Expense, and Advertising Expense. Enter the March 31 balances of Cash and Long-Term Notes Payable ($167,000 each).

2.   Open subsidiary accounts payable ledger accounts for Cooper's Supply, Flott Company, Sprague Company, and Whitewater Inc.

3.   Prepare a General Journal and a Cash Disbursements Journal like the ones illustrated in this chapter. Prepare a Purchases Journal with a debit column for purchases, a debit column for other accounts, and a credit column for accounts payable.

4.   Review the April transactions of Niagara Company and enter those transactions that should be journalized in the General Journal, the Purchases Journal, or the Cash Disbursements Journal. Ignore any transactions that should be journalized in a Sales Journal or Cash Receipts Journal.

5.   Post the items that should be posted as individual amounts from the journals. (Normally, such items are posted daily; but since they are few in number in this problem you are asked to post them only once.)

6.   Foot and crossfoot the journals and make the month-end postings.

7.   Prepare a trial balance and a schedule of accounts payable.

Problem 6–3
Special journals, subsidiary ledgers, trial balance
(LO 3, 4)

(If the Working Papers that accompany this text are not being used, omit this problem.)

It is December 16 and you have just taken over the accounting work of Outdoor Outfitters, whose annual accounting periods end each December 31. The company's previous accountant journalized its transactions through December 15 and posted all items that required posting as individual amounts, as an examination of the journals and ledgers in the Working Papers will show.

The company completed these transactions beginning on December 16:

Dec. 16   Sold merchandise on credit to Ambrose Fielder, Invoice No. 916, $7,700. (Terms of all credit sales are 2/10, n/30.)

17   Received a $1,040 credit memorandum from Weathers Company for merchandise received on December 15 and returned for credit.

17   Purchased office supplies on credit from Gray Supply Company, $615. Invoice dated December 16, terms n/10 EOM.

Dec. 18 Received a $40 credit memorandum from Gray Supply Company for office supplies received on December 17 and returned for credit.

20 Issued a credit memorandum to Amy Oakley for defective merchandise sold on December 15 and returned for credit, $500.

21 Purchased store equipment on credit from Gray Supply Company, invoice dated December 21, terms n/10 EOM, $6,700.

22 Received payment from Ambrose Fielder for the December 12 sale less the discount.

23 Issued Cheque No. 623 to Sunshine Company in payment of its December 15 invoice less the discount.

24 Sold merchandise on credit to Wilson Wilde, Invoice No. 917, $1,200.

24 Issued Cheque No. 624 to Weathers Company in payment of its December 15 invoice less the return and the discount.

25 Received payment from Amy Oakley for the December 15 sale less the return and the discount.

26 Received merchandise and an invoice dated December 25, terms 2/10, n/60, from Sunshine Company, $8,100.

29 Sold a neighboring merchant five boxes of file folders (office supplies) for cash at cost, $50.

30 Marlin Levy, the owner of Outdoor Outfitters, used Cheque No. 625 to withdraw $2,500 cash from the business for personal use.

31 Issued Cheque No. 626 to Jamie Forster, the company's only sales employee, in payment of her salary for the last half of December, $1,620.

31 Issued Cheque No. 627 to Countywide Electric Company in payment of the December electric bill, $510.

31 Cash sales for the last half of the month were $29,600. (Cash sales are usually recorded daily but are recorded only twice in this problem to reduce the repetitive transactions.)

Required

1. Record the transactions in the journals provided.

2. Post to the customer and creditor accounts and also post any amounts that should be posted as individual amounts to the general ledger accounts. (Normally, these amounts are posted daily, but they are posted only once by you in this problem because they are few in number.)

3. Foot and crossfoot the journals and make the month-end postings.

4. Prepare a December 31 trial balance and test the accuracy of the subsidiary ledgers by preparing schedules of accounts receivable and payable.

The Flutie Company completed these transactions during March of the current year:

Mar. 2 Sold merchandise on credit to Leroy Hazzard, Invoice No. 854, $15,800. (Terms of all credit sales are 2/10, n/30.)

3 Purchased office supplies on credit from Arnot Company, $1,120. Invoice dated March 3, terms n/10 EOM.

3 Sold merchandise on credit to Sam Segura, Invoice No. 855, $9,200.

Problem 6–4
Special journals, subsidiary ledgers, trial balance
(LO 3)

Mar. 5   Received merchandise and an invoice dated March 3, terms 2/10, n/30, from Defore Industries, $42,600.

6   Borrowed $36,000 by giving Commerce Bank a long-term promissory note payable.

9   Purchased office equipment on credit from Jett Supply, invoice dated March 9, terms n/10 EOM, $20,850.

10   Sold merchandise on credit to Marjorie Cobb, Invoice No. 856, $4,600.

12   Received payment from Leroy Hazzard for the March 2 sale less the discount.

13   Sent Defore Industries Cheque No. 416 in payment of its March 3 invoice less the discount.

13   Received payment from Sam Segura for the March 3 sale less the discount.

14   Received merchandise and an invoice dated March 13, terms 2/10, n/30, from the Welch Company, $31,625.

15   Issued Cheque No. 417, payable to Payroll, in payment of sales salaries for the first half of the month, $15,900. Cashed the cheque and paid the employees.

15   Cash sales for the first half of the month were $134,680. (Normally, cash sales are recorded daily; however, they are recorded only twice in this problem to reduce the repetitive entries.)

15   *Post to the customer and creditor accounts and also post any amounts that should be posted as individual amounts to the general ledger accounts. (Normally, such items are posted daily; but you are asked to post them on only two occasions in this problem because they are few in number.)*

16   Purchased store supplies on credit from Arnot Company, $1,670. Invoice dated March 16, terms n/10 EOM.

17   Received a credit memorandum from the Welch Company for unsatisfactory merchandise received on March 14 and returned for credit, $2,425.

19   Received a credit memorandum from Jett Supply for office equipment received on March 9 and returned for credit, $630.

20   Received payment from Marjorie Cobb for the sale of March 10 less the discount.

23   Issued Cheque No. 418 to the Welch Company in payment of its invoice of March 13 less the return and the discount.

27   Sold merchandise on credit to Marjorie Cobb, Invoice No. 857, $13,910.

28   Sold merchandise on credit to Sam Segura, Invoice No. 858, $5,315.

31   Issued Cheque No. 419, payable to Payroll, in payment of sales salaries for the last half of the month, $15,900. Cashed the cheque and paid the employees.

31   Cash sales for the last half of the month were $144,590.

31   *Post to the customer and creditor accounts and post any amounts that should be posted as individual amounts to the general ledger accounts.*

31   *Foot and crossfoot the journals and make the month-end postings.*

Required

1.   Open the following general ledger accounts: Cash, Accounts Receivable, Office Supplies, Store Supplies, Office Equipment, Accounts Payable, Long-Term Notes Payable, Sales, Sales Discounts, Purchases, Purchases Returns and Allowances, Purchases Discounts, and Sales Salaries Expense.

2. Open the following accounts receivable ledger accounts: Marjorie Cobb, Leroy Hazzard, and Sam Segura.

3. Open the following accounts payable ledger accounts: Arnot Company, Defore Industries, Jett Supply, and the Welch Company.

4. Enter the transactions in a Sales Journal, a Purchases Journal, a Cash Receipts Journal, a Cash Disbursements Journal, and a General Journal similar to the ones illustrated in this chapter. Post when instructed to do so.

5. Prepare a trial balance and test the accuracy of the subsidiary ledgers by preparing schedules of accounts receivable and payable.

Small Company uses a Cash Disbursements Journal similar to the one shown in Illustration 6–7. In the process of crossfooting the journal at the end of the current month, the company's bookkeeper found that the sum of the debits did not equal the sum of the credits. Describe the procedures you would follow to discover the reason why the journal does not crossfoot correctly.

Problem 6–5
Analytical essay
(LO 3)

Lorber's is a merchandising company that uses the special journals described in this chapter. At the end of the accounting period, the bookkeeper for the company prepared a trial balance and a schedule of accounts receivable. The trial balance is in balance but the sum of the account balances on the schedule of accounts receivable does not equal the balance in the controlling account. Describe the procedures you would follow to discover the reason for the imbalance between the controlling account and the total shown on the schedule of accounts receivable.

Problem 6–6
Analytical essay
(LO 2)

Youngstown Company completed these transactions during May of the current year:

May 1 Issued Cheque No. 101 to *The Weekly Journal* for advertising expense, $1,080.

2 Purchased merchandise on credit from Barclay Company, invoice dated May 1, terms 2/10, n/60, $6,500.

4 Sold merchandise on credit to Mark Loftis, Invoice No. 203, $6,500. (The terms of all credit sales are 2/10, n/60.)

4 Purchased on credit from Nixen Company merchandise, $7,050; and store supplies, $750. Invoice dated May 4, terms n/10 EOM.

5 Sold merchandise on credit to Helen Stone, Invoice No. 204, $12,300.

6 Received a $525 credit memorandum from Nixen Company for unsatisfactory merchandise received on May 4 and returned for credit.

8 Purchased store equipment on credit from Rexor Company, invoice dated May 8, terms n/10 EOM, $17,400.

10 Issued Cheque No. 102 to Barclay Company in payment of its May 1 invoice, less the discount.

12 Sold merchandise on credit to Regina Niser, Invoice No. 205, $4,650.

14 Received payment from Mark Loftis for the May 4 sale, less the discount.

15 Issued Cheque No. 103, payable to Payroll, in payment of the sales salaries for the first half of the month, $4,875. Cashed the cheque and paid the employees.

15 Sold merchandise on credit to Mark Loftis, Invoice No. 206, $7,350.

15 Cash sales for the first half of the month, $14,835. (Cash sales are usually recorded daily from the cash register readings. However, they are recorded only twice in this problem to reduce the repetitive transactions.)

Problem 6–7
Special journals and subsidiary ledgers
(LO 3)

May 15   Received payment from Helen Stone for the May 5 sale, less the discount.

16   Purchased merchandise on credit from Long Company, invoice dated May 16, terms 2/10, n/60, $8,250.

18   Borrowed $15,000 from Pioneer Trust Bank by giving a note payable.

22   Received payment from Regina Niser for the May 12 sale, less the discount.

23   Received a $300 credit memorandum from Long Company for defective merchandise received on May 16 and returned.

24   Purchased on credit from Rexor Company merchandise, $4,410; and store supplies, $540. Invoice dated May 23, terms n/10 EOM.

25   Received payment from Mark Loftis for the May 15 sale, less the discount.

26   Purchased merchandise on credit from Barclay Company, invoice dated May 25, terms 2/10, n/60, $3,900.

26   Issued Cheque No. 104 to Long Company in payment of its May 16 invoice, less the return and the discount.

27   Sold merchandise on credit to Helen Stone, Invoice No. 207, $5,085.

29   Sold merchandise on credit to Regina Niser, Invoice No. 208, $3,495.

31   Issued Cheque No. 105, payable to Payroll, in payment of the sales salaries for the last half of the month, $4,875.

31   Cash sales for the last half of the month were $20,820.

Required

1.   Open the following general ledger accounts: Cash, Accounts Receivable, Notes Payable, Sales, and Sales Discounts. Also open subsidiary accounts receivable ledger accounts for Mark Loftis, Regina Niser, and Helen Stone.

2.   Prepare a Sales Journal and a Cash Receipts Journal like the ones illustrated in this chapter.

3.   Review the transactions of Youngstown Company and enter those transactions that should be journalized in the Sales Journal and those that should be journalized in the Cash Receipts Journal. Ignore any transactions that should be posted in a Purchases Journal, a Cash Disbursements Journal, or a General Journal.

4.   Post the items that should be posted as individual amounts from the journals. (Normally, such items are posted daily; but since they are few in number, in this problem you are asked to post them only once.)

5.   Foot and crossfoot the journals and make the month-end postings.

6.   Prepare a trial balance of the General Ledger and test the accuracy of the subsidiary ledger by preparing a schedule of accounts receivable.

Problem 6–8
Special journals,
subsidiary ledgers,
schedule of
accounts payable
(LO 3, 4)

On April 30, Youngstown Company had a cash balance of $30,000 and a Notes Payable balance of $30,000. The May transactions of Youngstown Company included those listed in Problem 6–7.

Required

1.   Open the following general ledger accounts: Cash, Store Supplies, Office Supplies, Store Equipment, Notes Payable, Accounts Payable, Purchases, Purchases Returns and Allowances, Purchases Discounts, Sales Salaries Expense, and Advertising Expense. Enter the April 30 balances of Cash and Notes Payable ($30,000 each).

2. Open subsidiary accounts payable ledger accounts for Barclay Company, Long Company, Nixen Company, and Rexor Company.

3. Prepare a General Journal, a Purchases Journal, and a Cash Disbursements Journal like the ones illustrated in this chapter.

4. Review the May transactions of Youngstown Company and enter those transactions that should be journalized in the General Journal, the Purchases Journal, or the Cash Disbursements Journal. Ignore any transactions that should be posted in a Sales Journal or Cash Receipts Journal.

5. Post the items that should be posted as individual amounts from the journals. (Normally, such items are posted daily; but since they are few in number, in this problem you are asked to post them only once.)

6. Foot and crossfoot the journals and make the month-end postings.

7. Prepare a trial balance and a schedule of accounts payable.

(If the working papers that accompany this text are not being used, omit this problem.)
It is January 19, and you have just taken over the accounting work of Crowe Company, a concern operating with annual accounting periods that end each January 31. The company's previous accountant journalized its transactions through January 18 and posted all items that required posting as individual amounts, as an examination of the journals and ledgers in the booklet of working papers will show.
The company completed these transactions beginning on January 19:

Problem 6–9
Special journals,
subsidiary ledgers,
and a trial balance
(LO 3)

Jan. 19 Sold merchandise on credit to Brenda Simms, Invoice No. 741, $8,300. (Terms of all credit sales are 2/10, n/60.)

20 Received a $685 credit memorandum from Younger Company for merchandise received on January 17 and returned for credit.

20 Purchased on credit from Reed Suppliers merchandise, $7,350; store supplies, $1,080; and office supplies, $745. Invoice dated January 19, terms n/10 EOM.

22 Issued a credit memorandum to Sam Trent for defective merchandise sold on January 18 and returned for credit, $445.

23 Received a $270 credit memorandum from Reed Suppliers for office supplies received on January 20 and returned for credit.

23 Purchased store equipment on credit from Reed Suppliers, invoice dated January 22, terms n/10 EOM, $9,925.

24 Sold merchandise on credit to Frank Urich, Invoice No. 742, $11,135.

25 Issued Cheque No. 450 to Younger Company in payment of its January 15 invoice less the return and the discount.

25 Received payment from Brenda Simms for the January 15 sale less the discount.

26 Issued Cheque No. 451 to Vax Company in payment of its January 16 invoice less a 2% discount.

28 Received merchandise and an invoice dated January 28, terms 2/10, n/60, from Vax Company, $12,750.

28 Received payment from Sam Trent for the January 18 sale less the return and the discount.

30 Sold a neighbouring merchant a carton of computer ribbons (store supplies) for cash at cost, $405.

Jan. 31   Issued Cheque No. 452 to Valley Power Company in payment of the January hydro bill, $2,495.

31   Issued Cheque No. 453 to Max Davis, the company's only sales employee, in payment of her salary for the last half of January, $1,440.

31   Cash sales for the last half of the month, $54,510. (Cash sales are usually recorded daily but are recorded only twice in this problem in order to reduce the repetitive transactions.)

31   Susan Linder, the owner of Crowe Company, used Cheque No. 454 to withdraw $7,500 cash from the business for personal use.

Required

1.   Record the transactions in the journals provided.

2.   Post to the customer and creditor accounts and also post any amounts that should be posted as individual amounts to the general ledger accounts. (Normally, these amounts are posted daily, but they are posted only once by you in this problem because they are few in number.)

3.   Foot and crossfoot the journals and make the month-end postings.

4.   Prepare a January 31 trial balance and test the accuracy of the subsidiary ledgers by preparing schedules of accounts receivable and payable.

Problem 6–10
Special journals, preparing and proving the trial balance
(LO 3)

Jarrett Company completed these transactions during October of the current year: Sales are subject to a 10% PST and the 7% GST.

Oct. 2   Borrowed $36,000 by giving Regional Bank a promissory note payable.

3   Received merchandise and an invoice dated October 1, terms 2/10, n/60, from Bradley Company, $12,600.

4   Purchased on credit from Abell Company merchandise, $10,950; store supplies, $450; and office supplies, $225. Invoice dated October 3, terms n/10 EOM.

5   Sold merchandise on credit to Omar Hanes, Invoice No. 520, $9,300. (Terms of all credit sales are 2/10, n/60.)

6   Purchased office equipment on credit from Telecore Company, invoice dated October 5, terms n/10 EOM, $14,550.

9   Sold merchandise on credit to Leigh Rogers, Invoice No. 521, $8,850.

10   Sent Bradley Company Cheque No. 312 in payment of its October 1 invoice less the discount.

11   Received merchandise and an invoice dated October 10, terms 2/10, n/60, from Thomas Company, $12,900.

15   Received payment from Omar Hanes for the October 5 sale less the discount.

15   Issued Cheque No. 313, payable to Payroll, in payment of sales salaries for the first half of the month, $7,200. Cashed the cheque and paid the employees.

15   Cash sales for the first half of the month, $44,700. (Normally, cash sales are recorded daily; however, they are recorded only twice in this problem to reduce the number of repetitive entries.)

15   *Post to the customer and creditor accounts and also post any amounts that should be posted as individual amounts to the general ledger accounts. (Normally, such items are posted daily; but you are asked to post them on only two occasions in this problem because they are few in number.)*

Oct. 16 Sold merchandise on credit to Carl Chase, Invoice No. 522, $10,850.

18 Purchased on credit from Abell Company merchandise, $5,475; store supplies, $525; and office supplies, $420. Invoice dated October 17, terms n/10 EOM.

19 Received payment from Leigh Rogers for the October 9 sale less the discount.

20 Received a credit memorandum from Thomas Company for unsatisfactory merchandise received on October 10 and returned for credit, $1,200.

20 Issued Cheque No. 314 to Thomas Company in payment of its invoice of October 10 less the return and the discount.

23 Sold merchandise on credit to Carl Chase, Invoice No. 523, $7,050.

26 Received payment from Carl Chase for the sale of October 16 less the discount.

27 Received a credit memorandum from Telecore Company for office equipment received on December 6 and returned for credit, $750.

28 Sold merchandise on credit to Leigh Rogers, Invoice No. 524. $6,150.

31 Issued Cheque No. 315, payable to Payroll, in payment of sales salaries for the last half of the month, $7,200. Cashed the cheque and paid the employees.

31 Cash sales for the last half of the month, $50,550.

31 *Post to the customer and creditor accounts and post any amounts that should be posted as individual amounts to general ledger accounts.*

31 Foot and crossfoot the journals and make the month-end postings.

Required

1. Open the following general ledger accounts: Cash, Accounts Receivable, Store Supplies, Office Supplies, Office Equipment, Notes Payable, Accounts Payable, Sales, Sales Discounts, Purchases, Purchases Returns and Allowances, Purchases Discounts, and Sales Salaries Expense.

2. Open the following accounts receivable ledger accounts: Carl Chase, Omar Hanes, Leigh Rogers.

3. Open the following accounts payable ledger accounts: Abell Company, Bradley Company, Telecore Company, and Thomas Company.

4. Enter the transactions in a Sales Journal, a Purchases Journal, a Cash Receipts Journal, a Cash Disbursements Journal, and a General Journal similar to the ones illustrated in this chapter. Post when instructed to do so.

5. Prepare a trial balance and test the accuracy of the subsidiary ledgers by preparing schedules of accounts receivable and payable.

Short Company uses a Cash Receipts Journal similar to the one shown in Illustration 6–5. In the process of crossfooting the journal at the end of the current month, the company's bookkeeper found that the sum of the debits did not equal the sum of the credits. Describe the procedures you would follow in an effort to discover the reason why the journal does not crossfoot correctly.

Problem 6–11
Analytical essay
(LO 3)

Ferber's is a merchandising company that uses the special journals described in this chapter. At the end of the accounting period, the bookkeeper for the company prepared a trial balance and a schedule of accounts payable. The trial balance is in balance but the sum of the account balances on the schedule of accounts payable does not equal the balance in the controlling account. Describe the procedures you would follow to discover the reason for the imbalance between the controlling account and the total shown on the schedule of accounts payable.

Problem 6–12
Analytical essay
(LO 2)

PROVOCATIVE PROBLEM

Provocative Problem 6–1
Ethical issues essay

Review the As a Matter of Ethics case presented on page 299. Discuss the problem faced by the public accountant and the factors the public accountant should consider in deciding on a course of action.

ANALYTICAL AND REVIEW PROBLEM

A & R Problem 6–1

The following problem is designed to test your ability in the use of special journals and subsidiary ledgers. The special journals of James Bay Department Store are reproduced below, followed by a number of representative transactions that occurred during the period. The money columns in the journals are numbered to minimize clerical work in recording each transaction.

Accounts Receivable Debit	Sales Credit							PST Credit	GST Credit
	Men's Clothing	Women's Clothing	Appliances	Furniture	Bargain Basement	Other Departments			
1	2	3	4	5	6	7		8	9

Cash Debit	Sales Discounts Debit	Sales Credit						Accounts Receivable Credit	Other Accounts Credit	PST Credit	GST Credit
		Men's Clothing	Women's Clothing	Appliances	Furniture	Bargain Basement	Other Departments				
10	11	12	13	14	15	16	17	18	19	20	21

Purchases Debit						Prepaid GST Debit	Accounts Payable Credit
Men's Clothing	Women's Clothing	Appliances	Furniture	Bargain Basement	Other Departments		
22	23	24	25	26	27	28	29

Accounts Payable Debit	Supplies Expense Debit	Other Accounts Debit	Prepaid GST Debit	Cash Credit
30	31	32	33	34

Debit	Credit
35	36

Transactions (*Note:* All sales are subject to a provincial sales tax (PST) of 8% and the federal goods and services tax (GST) of 7%.)

	Debit	Credit

a. Borrowed $37,500 from Great Northern Bank on note payable.

b. Sale on account $450 to J.C. Snead—Men's Clothing.

c. Sale for cash of baked goods—$15.

d. Purchases of $11,250 on account of goods—Bargain Basement from Lonbec Co.

e. Purchases of $12,300 on account of Appliances from Canlec Inc.

f. Sale on account $2,100 of Furniture to Gates Brown.

g. Sale for cash $1,500 less 5% discount—Appliances.

h. Collection of account receivable from Cec Oak, $900.

i. Payment of account payable to J.T. Inglis, $6,300.

j. J.C. Snead returned for credit a shirt that had a flaw—$60.

Required

1. Identify each of the journals.
2. Journalize by indicating the column number in the spaces provided after each transaction. For example: Purchase for cash of supplies (immediately expensed).

Debit	Credit
31, 33	34

3. Indicate how the data in the special journals are posted to various accounts by filling in the spaces provided with the following posting possibilities.
   a. Posted as a *debit* to some General Ledger account.
   b. Posted as a *debit* to some subsidiary ledger account.
   c. Posted as a *credit* to some General Ledger account.
   d. Posted as a *credit* to some subsidiary ledger account.
   e. Not posted.

Note: The numbers in parentheses are the identification numbers for the money columns of the special journals. For example: (31) money column.

	Posted as
(00) Total of column (34) Example	e
a. Total of column 1.	
b. Detail items of column 3.	
c. Detail items of column 8.	
d. Total of column 9.	
e. Detail items of column 17.	
f. Total of column 20.	
g. Total of column 26.	
h. Detail items of column 27.	
i. Detail items of column 32.	
j. Detail items of column 1.	
k. Total of column 19.	
l. Detail items of column 18.	
m. Total of column 29.	
n. Total of column 5.	
o. Detail items of column 10.	
p. Detail items of column 21.	

COMPREHENSIVE PROBLEM

Regis Company
(LO 3, 4)

(If the Working Papers that accompany this text are not available, omit this comprehensive problem.)

Assume it is Monday, August 1, the first business day of the month, and you have just been hired as the accountant for Regis Company, which operates with monthly accounting periods. All of the company's accounting work has been completed through the end of July and its ledgers show July 31 balances. During your first month on the job, you record the following transactions:

Aug. 1 Issued Cheque No. 1236 to Republic Management Co. in payment of the August rent, $2,650. (Use two lines to record the transaction. Charge 80% of the rent to Rent Expense, Selling Space and the balance to Rent Expense, Office Space.)

2 Sold merchandise on credit to L&M Company, Invoice No. 5725, $4,300. (The terms of all credit sales are 2/10, n/30.)

2 Issued a $125 credit memorandum to Prime, Inc., for defective merchandise sold on July 28 and returned for credit. The total selling price (gross) was $3,375.

3 Received a $570 credit memorandum from Signature Products for merchandise received on July 29 and returned for credit.

4 Purchased on credit from Discount Supplies: merchandise, $26,480; store supplies, $410; and office supplies, $59. Invoice dated August 4, terms n/10 EOM.

5 Received payment from Prime, Inc., for the remaining balance from the sale of July 28 less the August 2 return and the discount.

8 Issued Cheque No. 1237 to Signature Products to pay for the $5,070 of merchandise received on July 29 less the August 3 return and a 2% discount.

9 Sold store supplies to the merchant next door at cost for cash, $250.

10 Purchased office equipment on credit from Discount Supplies, invoice dated August 10, terms n/10 EOM, $2,910.

11 Received payment from L&M Company for the August 2 sale less the discount.

11 Received merchandise and an invoice dated August 10, terms 2/10, n/30, from Mayfair Corp., $6,300.

12 Received a $610 credit memorandum from Discount Supplies for defective office equipment received on August 10 and returned for credit.

15 Issued Cheque No. 1238, payable to Payroll, in payment of sales salaries, $3,800, and office salaries, $2,250. Cashed the cheque and paid the employees.

15 Cash sales for the first half of the month, $42,300. (Such sales are normally recorded daily. They are recorded only twice in this problem to reduce the repetitive entries.)

15 *Post to the customer and creditor accounts. Also, post individual items that are not included in column totals at the end of the month to the general ledger accounts. (Such items are normally posted daily, but you are asked to post them only twice each month because they are few in number.)*

Aug. 16   Sold merchandise on credit to L&M Company, Invoice No. 5726, $2,850.

17   Received merchandise and an invoice dated August 14, terms 2/10, n/60, from Tranh Industries, $9,750.

19   Issued Cheque No. 1239 to Mayfair Corp. in payment of its August 10 invoice less the discount.

22   Sold merchandise on credit to Anchor Services, Invoice No. 5727, $4,900.

23   Issued Cheque No. 1240 to Tranh Industries in payment of its August 14 invoice less the discount.

24   Purchased on credit from Discount Supplies: merchandise, $5,800; store supplies, $450; and office supplies, $200. Invoice dated August 24, terms n/10 EOM.

25   Received merchandise and an invoice dated August 23, terms 2/10, n/30, from Signature Products, $2,200.

26   Sold merchandise on credit to Franzetti Corp., Invoice No. 5728, $10,150.

26   Issued Cheque No. 1241 to HP&L in payment of the July electric bill, $918.

29   The owner of Regis Company, Walt Regis, used Cheque No. 1242 to withdraw $5,000 from the business for personal use.

30   Received payment from Anchor Services for the August 22 sale less the discount.

30   Issued Cheque No. 1243, payable to Payroll, in payment of sales salaries, $3,800, and office salaries, $2,250. Cashed the cheque and paid the employees.

31   Cash sales for the last half of the month were $47,180.

31   *Post to the customer and creditor accounts. Also, post individual items that are not included in column totals at the end of the month to the general ledger accounts.*

31   Foot and crossfoot the journals and make the month-end postings.

Required

1.   Enter the transactions in the appropriate journals and post when instructed to do so.

2.   Prepare a trial balance in the Trial Balance columns of the provided work sheet form and complete the work sheet using the following information:

   a.   Expired insurance, $395.

   b.   Ending store supplies inventory, $1,880.

   c.   Ending office supplies inventory, $360.

   d.   Estimated amortization of store equipment, $405.

   e.   Estimated amortization of office equipment, $235.

   f.   Ending merchandise inventory, $126,000.

3.   Prepare a multiple-step classified August income statement, an August statement of changes in owner's equity, and an August 31 classified balance sheet.

4.   Prepare and post adjusting and closing entries.

5.   Prepare a post-closing trial balance. Also prepare a list of the Accounts Receivable Ledger accounts and a list of the Accounts Payable Ledger accounts. Total the balances of each to confirm that the totals equal the balances in the controlling accounts.

CONCEPT TESTER (LO 5)

Test your understanding of the concepts introduced in this chapter by completing the following crossword puzzle.

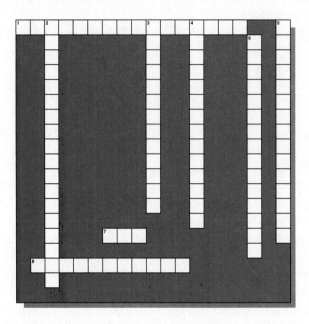

Across Clues

1. The means by which data is captured and reports are generated (2 words).

7. A federal tax on the consumer.

8. Means of transferring information from source documents to an accounting system (2 words).

Down Clues

2. The portion of the general ledger that represents the sum of the balances in the subsidiary ledger (2 words).

3. The book that contains the financial statement accounts (2 words).

4. A book of original entry designed for recording specified transactions (2 words).

5. Accumulating source data for a period of time and inputting them at the same time (2 words).

6. The portion of a company that can be separately identified (2 words).

ANSWERS TO PROGRESS CHECKS

6–1   *b*

6–2   The data processor component interprets, manipulates, and summarizes the recorded information so that it can be used in analyses and reports.

6–3   The data that is saved in data storage is used to prepare periodic financial reports, to prepare special-purpose reports for managers, and to provide a source of information for independent auditors.

6–4   *a*

6–5   Compared to manual systems, computer systems offer more accuracy, speed, efficiency, and convenience.

6–6   *d*

6–7   *b*

6–8   Columnar journals allow you to accumulate repetitive debits and credits and post them as column totals rather than as individual amounts.

6–9   The equality of debits and credits is still maintained within the General Ledger. The subsidiary ledger containing the customer's individual account is used only for supplementary information.

6–10   The initial and page number of the journal from which the amount was posted is entered in the

Posting Reference column of the ledger account next to the amount.

6–11   *c*

6–12   The controlling account must be debited periodically for an amount or amounts equal to the sum of the debits to the subsidiary ledger, and it must be credited periodically for an amount or amounts equal to the sum of the credits to the subsidiary ledger.

6–13   *d*

6–14   *b*

6–15   This refers to the procedure of using copies of sales invoices as a Sales Journal. Each invoice total is posted directly to the customer's account, and all the invoices are totaled at month-end for posting to the General Ledger accounts.

6–16   The General Journal would still be needed for adjusting, closing, and correcting entries, and for miscellaneous transactions such as sales returns, purchases returns, and plant asset purchases.

6–17   *e*

Accounting for Cash and the Principles of Internal Control

Because almost all business activities involve cash, it must be carefully controlled. Internal control systems are designed to make accounting information dependable and to help companies avoid misplacing or misusing their assets.

t the outset of the lecture on Chapter 7, Karen White and Mark Smith's instructor took time to review the fundamental, or basic, accounting system as covered in the first six chapters and to preview some of the interesting topics that will be coming up. She challenged the students to review financial reports of different companies to reinforce their "book learning" and promised to bring to their attention selections she found on topics such as fraud, internal control, temporary investments, inventory pricing, accounting for capital assets and liabilities, and so on.

Her first handout discussed the rise worldwide of white-collar crimes, which cause substantial financial loss and even bankruptcy in some cases. The "Insurance Bureau of Canada estimates that its industry loses about $1 billion annually and the banking industry probably suffers similar losses" due to fraud.[1] In a case involving a $60,000 embezzlement from a church, an analysis of the facts attributed the fraud to the governing board's lack of basic accounting knowledge. In another case, a salesperson with access to the assets and to shipping, receiving, and invoicing documents defrauded the company of $3 million. Other news reports indicate that a wide range of business entities—medical offices, travel agencies, retail operations, utility companies, major unions—are victims of substantial embezzlement. In addition, accounting literature indicates that small businesses and not-for-profit organizations often have weak internal control structures that leave them vulnerable to embezzlement.

---

[1]Gordon Arnault, "Corporate Fraud Is a Growth Industry," *Globe and Mail,* January 17, 1995, p. B28.

LEARNING OBJECTIVES

1. Explain the concept of liquidity and the difference between cash and cash equivalents.

2. Explain why internal control procedures are needed in a large organization and state the broad principles of internal control.

3. Describe internal control procedures used to protect cash received from cash sales, cash received through the mail, and cash disbursements.

4. Explain the operation of a petty cash fund and be able to prepare journal entries to record petty cash fund transactions.

5. Explain why the bank balance and the book balance of cash should be reconciled and be able to prepare a reconciliation.

6. Explain how recording invoices at net amounts helps gain control over cash discounts taken, and calculate days' sales uncollected.

7. Define or explain the words and phrases listed in the chapter glossary.

Cash is an asset that every business owns and uses. Most organizations own at least some assets known as cash equivalents, which are very similar to cash. In studying this chapter, you will learn the general principles of internal control and the specific principles that guide businesses in managing and accounting for cash. It is management's responsibility to set up the policies and procedures to ensure the safeguarding of business assets, including cash. In order to do so, management and employees of organizations should understand and be able to apply basic principles of internal control. If these internal control principles had been followed by the victims described on the previous page, many of the entities might have been saved from financial loss.

The chapter shows you how to establish and use a petty cash fund and how to reconcile a chequing account. Also, you will learn a method of accounting for purchases that helps management determine whether cash discounts on purchases are being lost and, if so, how much has been lost.

CASH, CASH EQUIVALENTS, AND THE CONCEPT OF LIQUIDITY

LO 1

Explain the concept of liquidity and the difference between cash and cash equivalents.

In previous chapters, you learned that a company can own many different kinds of assets such as accounts receivable, merchandise inventory, equipment, buildings, and land. These assets all have value, but most of them are not easily used as a means of payment when buying other assets, acquiring services, or paying off liabilities. Usually, cash must be used as the method of payment. Another way to state this is to say that cash is more *liquid* than these other assets.

In more general terms, the **liquidity** of an asset refers to how easily the asset can be converted into other types of assets or be used to buy services or satisfy obligations. All assets can be evaluated in terms of their relative liquidity. Assets such as cash are said to be **liquid assets** because they can be converted easily into other types of assets or used to buy services or pay liabilities.

As you know, a company needs more than valuable assets to stay in business. That is, the company must own some liquid assets so that bills are paid on time and purchases can be made for cash when necessary.

For financial accounting, the asset *cash* includes not only currency and coins but also amounts on deposit in bank accounts, including chequing accounts (sometimes called demand deposits) and some savings accounts (also called time deposits). In addition, cash includes items that are acceptable for deposit in those accounts, especially customers' cheques made payable to the company.

To increase their return, many companies invest their idle cash balances in assets called **cash equivalents**. These assets are short-term, or temporary, investments that are highly liquid, that is, readily convertible into cash and relatively insensitive to interest and market rate fluctuations. Examples of cash equivalents include short-term investments in treasury bills, commercial paper (short-term corporate notes payable), and money market funds.

Because cash equivalents are so similar to cash, most companies combine them with cash as a single item on the balance sheet. For example, **Canadian Pacific Limited's** balance sheet on December 31, 1993, reported the following:

Cash and temporary investments . . . . $1,667.7 (million)

Canadian Pacific Limited has classified its temporary investments as a cash equivalent.

As you would expect, cash is an important asset for every business. Because cash is so important, companies need to be careful about keeping track of it. They also need to carefully control access to cash by employees and others who might want to take it for their own use. A good accounting system supports both goals. It can keep track of how much cash is on hand, and it helps control who has access to the cash. Because of the special importance of cash, this chapter describes the practices companies follow to account for and protect cash.

The importance of accounting for cash and cash equivalents is highlighted by the fact that a complete set of financial statements includes a statement of changes in financial position, or statement of cash flows. That statement identifies the types of activities that caused changes in cash and cash equivalents. You learn more about that statement in Chapter 18.

Progress Check
(Answers to Progress Checks are provided at the end of the chapter.)

7-1   Why does a company need to own liquid assets?

7-2   Why does a company own cash equivalent assets in addition to cash?

7-3   Which of the following assets should be classified as a cash equivalent? *(a)* Land purchased as an investment; *(b)* Accounts receivable; *(c)* Common shares purchased as a long-term investment; *(d)* A 90-day Treasury bill issued by the Canadian government.

INTERNAL CONTROL

LO 2

Explain why internal control procedures are needed in a large organization and state the broad principles of internal control.

In a small business, the manager often controls the entire operation through personal supervision and direct participation in all its activities. For example, he or she commonly buys all the assets and services used in the business. The manager also hires and supervises all employees, negotiates all contracts, and signs all cheques. As a result, the manager knows from personal contact and observation whether the business actually received the assets and services for which the cheques were written. However, as a business grows, it becomes increasingly difficult to maintain this close personal contact. At some point, the manager must delegate responsibilities and rely on formal procedures rather than personal contact in controlling the operations of the business.

The procedures a company uses to control its operations make up its **internal control system.** A properly designed internal control system encourages adherence to prescribed managerial policies. In doing so, it promotes efficient operations and protects the assets from waste, fraud, and theft. The system also helps ensure that accurate and reliable accounting data are produced.

Specific internal control procedures vary from company to company and depend on such factors as the nature of the business and its size. However, the same broad principles of internal control apply to all companies. These broad principles are:

1. Clearly establish responsibilities.
2. Maintain adequate records.
3. Insure assets and bond employees.
4. Separate record-keeping and custody over assets.
5. Divide responsibility for related transactions.
6. Use mechanical devices whenever feasible.
7. Perform regular and independent reviews.

We discuss these seven principles in the following paragraphs. Throughout, we describe how various internal control procedures prevent fraud and theft. Remember, however, that these procedures are needed to ensure that the accounting records are complete and accurate.

Clearly Establish Responsibilities

To have good internal control, responsibility for each task must be clearly established and assigned to one person. When responsibility is not clearly spelled out, it is difficult to determine who is at fault when something goes wrong. For example, if two sales clerks share access to the same cash register and there is a shortage, it may not be possible to tell which clerk is at fault. Neither can prove that he or she did not cause the shortage. To prevent this problem, one clerk should be given responsibility for making all change. Alternately, the business can use a register with separate cash drawers for each operator.

Maintain Adequate Records

A good record-keeping system helps protect assets and ensures that employees follow prescribed procedures. Reliable records are also a source of information that management uses to monitor the operations of the business. For example, if detailed records of manufacturing equipment and tools are maintained, items are unlikely to be lost or otherwise disappear without any discrepancy being noticed. As another example, expenses and other expenditures are less likely to be debited to the wrong accounts if a comprehensive chart of accounts is established and followed carefully. If the chart is not in place or is not used correctly, management may never discover that some expenses are excessive.

Numerous preprinted forms and internal business papers should be designed and properly used to maintain good internal control. For example, if sales slips are properly designed, sales personnel can record the needed information efficiently without errors or delays to customers. And, if all sales slips are prenumbered and controlled, each salesperson can be held responsible for the sales slips issued to him or her. As a result, a salesperson is not able to pocket cash by making a sale and destroying the sales slip. Computerized point-of-sale systems can achieve the same control results.

Insure Assets and Bond Key Employees

Assets should be covered by adequate casualty insurance, and employees who handle cash and negotiable assets should be bonded. An employee is said to be *bonded* when the company purchases an insurance policy, or a bond, against losses from theft by that employee. Bonding clearly reduces the loss suffered by a theft. It also tends to discourage theft because bonded employees know that an impersonal bonding company must be dealt with when a theft is discovered.

Separate Record-Keeping and Custody over Assets

A fundamental principle of internal control is that the person who has access to or is otherwise responsible for an asset should not maintain the accounting record for that asset. When this principle is followed, the custodian of an asset, knowing that a record of the asset is being kept by another person, is not as likely to misplace, steal, or waste the asset. And, the record-keeper, who does not have access to the asset, has no reason to falsify the record. As a result, two people would have to agree to commit a fraud (called *collusion*) if the asset were stolen and the theft concealed in the records. Because collusion is necessary, the fraud is less likely to happen.

Divide Responsibility for Related Transactions

Responsibility for a transaction or a series of related transactions should be divided between individuals or departments so that the work of one acts as a check on the other. However, this principle does not call for duplication of work. Each employee or department should perform an unduplicated portion.

For example, responsibility for placing orders, receiving the merchandise, and paying the vendors should not be given to one individual or department. Doing so creates a situation in which mistakes and perhaps fraud are more likely to occur. Having a different person check incoming goods for quality and quantity may encourage more care and attention to detail than having it done by the person who placed the order. And designating a third person to approve the payment of the invoice offers additional protection against error and fraud. Finally, giving a fourth person the authority to actually write cheques adds another measure of protection.

Use Mechanical Devices Whenever Feasible

Cash registers, cheque protectors, time clocks, and mechanical counters are examples of control devices that should be used whenever feasible. A cash register with a locked-in tape makes a record of each cash sale. A cheque protector perforates the amount of a cheque into its face, and makes it difficult to change the amount. A time clock registers the exact time an employee arrives on the job and the exact time the employee departs. Using mechanical change and currency counters is faster and more accurate than counting by hand and reduces the possibility of loss.

Perform Regular and Independent Reviews

Even a well-designed internal control system has a tendency to deteriorate as time passes. Changes in personnel and computer equipment present opportunities for shortcuts and other omissions. The stress of time pressures tends to bring about the same results. Thus, regular reviews of internal control systems are needed to be sure that the standard procedures are being followed. Where possible, these reviews should be performed by internal auditors who are not directly involved in operations. From their independent perspective, internal auditors can evaluate the overall efficiency of operations as well as the effectiveness of the internal control system.

Many companies also have audits by independent auditors who are public accountants. After testing the company's financial records, the public accountants give an opinion as to whether the company's financial statements are presented fairly in accordance with generally accepted accounting principles. However, before public accountants decide on how much testing they must do, they evaluate the effectiveness of the internal control system. When making their evaluation, they can find areas for improvement and offer suggestions.

COMPUTERS AND INTERNAL CONTROL

The broad principles of internal control should be followed for both manual and computerized accounting systems. However, computers have several important effects on internal control. Perhaps the most obvious is that computers provide rapid access to large quantities of information. As a result, management's ability to monitor and control business operations can be greatly improved.

Computers Reduce Processing Errors

Computers reduce the number of errors in processing information. Once the data are entered correctly, the possibility of mechanical and mathematical errors is largely eliminated. On the other hand, data entry errors may occur because the process of entering data may be more complex in a computerized system. Also, the lack of human involvement in later processing may cause data entry errors to go undiscovered.

Computers Allow More Extensive Testing of Records

The regular review and audit of computerized records can include more extensive testing because information can be accessed so rapidly. To reduce costs when manual methods are used, managers may select only small samples of data to test. But, when computers are used, large samples or even complete data files can be reviewed and analyzed.

Computerized Systems May Limit Hard Evidence of Processing Steps

Because many data processing steps are performed by the computer, fewer items of documentary evidence may be available for review. However, computer systems can create additional evidence by recording more information, such as who made entries and even when they were made. And, the computer can be programmed to require the use of passwords before making entries so that access to the system is limited. Therefore, internal control may depend more on reviews of the design and operation of the computerized processing system and less on reviews of the documents left behind by the system.

Separation of Duties Must Be Maintained

Because computerized systems are so efficient, companies often need fewer employees. This savings carries the risk that the separation of critical responsibilities may not be maintained. In addition, companies that use computers need employees with special skills to program and operate them. The duties of such employees must be controlled to minimize undetected errors and the risk of fraud. For example, better control is maintained if the person who designs and programs the system does not serve as the operator. Also, control over programs and files related to cash receipts and disbursements should be separated. To prevent fraud, cheque-writing activities should not be controlled by the computer operator. However, achieving a suitable separation of duties can be especially difficult in small companies that have only a few employees.

Recall from the first page of the chapter the case in which $3 million was embezzled. The salesperson in that case had access to both the assets and the documents. Similar access to both the cash and the records may result in cash being embezzled.

Progress Check

7-4 **The broad principles of internal control require that:**
   a. **Responsibility for a series of related transactions (such as placing orders for, receiving, and paying for merchandise) should be given to one person so that responsibility is clearly assigned.**
   b. **Responsibility for specific tasks should be shared by more than one employee so that one serves as a check on the other.**
   c. **Employees who handle cash and negotiable assets should be bonded.**

7-5 **What are some of the effects of computers on internal control?**

INTERNAL CONTROL FOR CASH

Now that we have covered the principles of good internal control in general, it is helpful to see how they are applied to cash, the most liquid of all assets. A good system of internal control for cash should provide adequate procedures for protecting both cash receipts and cash disbursements. In the procedures, three basic guidelines should always be observed:

LO 3

Describe internal control procedures used to protect cash received from cash sales, cash received through the mail, and cash disbursements.

1. Duties should be separated so that people responsible for actually handling cash are not responsible for keeping the cash records.
2. All cash receipts should be deposited in the bank, intact, each day.
3. All cash payments should be made by cheque.

The reason for the first principle is that a division of duties helps avoid errors. It also requires two or more people to collude if cash is to be embezzled (stolen) and the theft concealed in the accounting records. One reason for the second guideline is that the daily deposit of all receipts produces a timely independent test of the accuracy of the count of the cash received and the deposit. It also helps prevent loss or theft and keeps an employee from personally using the money for a few days before depositing it.

Finally, if all payments are made by cheque, the bank records provide an independent description of cash disbursements. This arrangement also tends to prevent thefts of cash. (One exception to this principle allows small disbursements of currency and coins to be made from a petty cash fund. Petty cash funds are discussed later in this chapter.) Note especially that the daily intact depositing of receipts and making disbursements by cheque allows you to use the bank records as a separate and external record of essentially all cash transactions. Later in the chapter, you learn how to use bank records to confirm the accuracy of your own records.

The exact procedures used to achieve control over cash vary from company to company. They depend on such factors as company size, number of employees, the volume of cash transactions, and the sources of cash. Therefore, the procedures described in the following paragraphs illustrate many but not all situations.

Cash from Cash Sales

Cash sales should be recorded on a cash register at the time of each sale. To help ensure that correct amounts are entered, each register should be placed so that customers can read the amounts displayed. Also, clerks should be required to ring up each sale before wrapping the merchandise and should give the customer a receipt. Finally, each cash register should be designed to provide a permanent, locked-in record of each transaction. In some systems, the register is directly connected to a computer. The computer is programmed to accept cash register transactions and enter them in the accounting records. In other cases, the register simply prints a record of each transaction on a paper tape locked inside the register.

We stated earlier that custody over cash should be separated from record-keeping for cash. For cash sales, this separation begins with the cash register. The salesclerk who has access to the cash in the register should not have access to its locked-in record. At the end of each day, the salesclerk should count the cash in the register, record the result, and turn over the cash and this record of the count to an employee in the cashier's office. The employee in the cashier's office, like the salesclerk, has access to the cash and should not have access to the computerized accounting records (or the register tape). A third employee, preferably from the accounting department, examines the computerized record of register transactions (or the register tape) and compares its total with the cash receipts reported by the cashier's office. The computer record (or register tape) becomes the basis for the journal entry to record cash sales. Note that the accounting department employee has access to the records for cash but does not have access to the actual cash. The salesclerk and the employee from the cashier's office have access to the cash but not to the accounting records. Thus, their accuracy is automatically checked, and none of them can make a mistake or divert any cash without the difference being revealed.

Cash Received through the Mail

Control of cash that comes in through the mail begins with the person who opens the mail. Preferably, two people should be present when the mail is opened. One should make a list (in triplicate) of the money received. The list should record each sender's name, the amount, and the purpose for which the money was sent. One copy is sent to the cashier with the money. A second copy goes to the accounting department. A third copy is kept by the clerk who opened the mail. The cashier deposits the money in the bank, and the bookkeeper records the amounts received in the accounting records. Then, when the bank balance is reconciled by a fourth person (this process is discussed later in the chapter), errors or fraud by the clerk, the cashier, or the bookkeeper are detected. They will be detected because the bank's record of the amount of cash deposited and the records of three people must agree. Note how this arrangement makes errors and fraud nearly impossible, unless the employees enter into collusion. If the clerk does not report all receipts accurately, the customers will question their account balances. If the cashier does not deposit all receipts intact, the bank balance does not agree with the bookkeeper's cash balance. The bookkeeper and the fourth person who reconciles the bank balance do not have access to cash and, therefore, have no opportunity to divert any to themselves. Thus, undetected errors and fraud are made highly unlikely.

Cash Disbursements

The previous discussions clearly show the importance of gaining control over cash from sales and cash received through the mail. Most large embezzlements, however, are actually accomplished through payments of fictitious invoices. Therefore, controlling cash disbursements is perhaps even more critical than controlling cash receipts.

As described earlier, the key to controlling cash disbursements is to require all expenditures to be made by cheque, except very small payments from petty cash. And, if authority to sign cheques is assigned to some person other than the business owner, that person should not have access to the accounting records. This separation of duties helps prevent an employee from concealing fraudulent disbursements in the accounting records.

In a small business, the manager usually signs cheques and normally knows from personal contact that the items being paid for were actually received. However, this arrangement is impossible in a larger business. Instead, internal control procedures must be substituted for personal contact. The procedures are designed to assure the cheque signer that the obligations to be paid were properly incurred and should be paid. Often these controls are achieved through a voucher system.

Illustration 7-1   The Accumulation of Documents in the Voucher

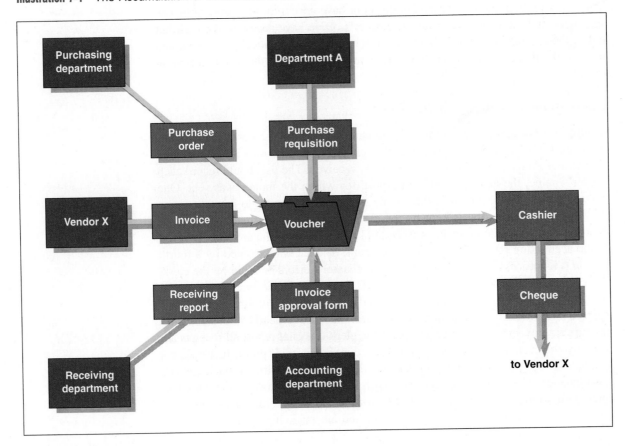

THE VOUCHER SYSTEM AND CONTROL

A **voucher system** is a set of procedures designed to control the incurrence of obligations and disbursements of cash. This kind of system:

1. Establishes procedures for incurring obligations that result in cash disbursements, such as permitting only authorized individuals to make purchase commitments.
2. Provides established procedures for verifying, approving, and recording these obligations.
3. Permits cheques to be issued only in payment of properly verified, approved, and recorded obligations.
4. Requires that every obligation be recorded at the time it is incurred and that every purchase be treated as an independent transaction, complete in itself.

A good voucher system produces these results for every transaction, even if several purchases are made from the same company during a month or other billing period.

When a voucher system is used, control over cash disbursements begins as soon as the company incurs an obligation that will result in cash being paid out. A key factor in making the system work is that only specified departments and individuals are authorized to incur such obligations. Managers should also limit the kind of obligations that each department or individual can incur. For example, in a large retail store, only a specially created purchasing department should be authorized to incur obligations through merchandise purchases. In addition, the procedures for purchasing, receiving, and paying for merchandise should be divided among several departments. These departments include the one that originally requested the purchase, the purchasing department, the receiving department, and the accounting department. To coordinate and control the responsibilities of these departments, several different business papers are used. Illustration 7–1 shows how these papers are accumulated in a **voucher.** A voucher is an internal business paper that is used to accumulate other papers and information needed to control the disbursement of cash and to ensure that the transaction is properly recorded. The following explanation of each paper going into the voucher will show you how companies use this system to gain control over cash disbursements for merchandise purchases.

Purchase Requisition

In a large retail store, department managers generally are not allowed to place orders directly with suppliers. If each manager could deal directly with suppliers, the amount of merchandise purchased and the resulting liabilities would not be well controlled. Therefore, to gain control over purchases and the resulting liabilities, department managers usually are required to place all orders through the purchasing department. When merchandise is needed, the department managers inform the purchasing department of their needs by preparing and signing a **purchase requisition** shown in Illustration 7–2. On the requisition, the manager lists the merchandise needed by the department and requests that it be purchased. Two copies of the purchase requisition are sent to the Purchasing Department. The manager of the requisitioning department (identified in Illustration 7–1 as Department A) keeps a third copy as a backup. The purchasing department sends one copy to the accounting department. When it is received, the accounting department creates a new voucher.

Purchase Order

A **purchase order** is a business paper used by the purchasing department to place an order with the seller, or **vendor,** which usually is a manufacturer or wholesaler. The purchase order such as the one shown in Illustration 7–3 authorizes the vendor to ship the ordered merchandise at the stated price and terms.

When a purchase requisition is received by the purchasing department, it prepares at least four copies of a purchase order. The copies are distributed as follows:

> **Copy 1** is sent to the vendor as a request to purchase and as authority to ship the merchandise.

Illustration 7-2   Purchase Requisition

SUGGESTED SUPPLIER & ADDRESS	**PURCHASE REQUISITION** **Albert Distributing Company** **NOTE:** (1) REQUISITIONER TO COMPLETE ALL UNSHADED AREAS. (2) SUBMIT ALL QUOTATIONS WITH REQUISITION.

ORDERED FROM	REQUISITIONED BY:	EXT.
	DELIVER TO:	EXT.
	DEPARTMENT:	
	BLDG/RM	

DATE REQUISITIONED D M Y	DATE REQUIRED D M Y	SHIP VIA	F.O.B.	RC	TERMS 2%-10 N-30

FOR FEDERAL AND PROVINCIAL
TAX PURPOSES PLEASE GIVE A
BRIEF OUTLINE OF THE
                    END USE ▶

ITEM	QUANTITY	REF. NO.	DESCRIPTION	DUTY	ANNEX CODE	G.S.T.	PROV. TAX	UNIT PRICE	AMOUNT

IF THIS EQUIPMENT REQUIRES INSTALLATION OR SERVICE CONNECTION (e.g. PLUMBING, ELECTRICAL) PLEASE INDICATE   ☐ YES   ☐ NO

AMOUNT	
G.S.T.	
P.S.T.	
TOTAL	

A EXEMPT	B INCL IF APP.	C NOT APP.	D TAXABLE	E EXEMPT	F ZERO RATED	G INCLUDED	H APP. P.S.T. INCL	I LIC	J NOT APP.	K EXEMPT RESEARCH	L EXEMPT PROD.	M PLUS
DUTY			GOODS & SERVICES TAX				PROVINCIAL SALES TAX					

ACCOUNT NUMBER	COMMITTED AMOUNT	
		AUTHORIZED SIGNATURE
		PURCHASE ORDER NUMBER:

Illustration 7-3   Purchase Order

Albert Distributing Company
365 Albert Street
Waterloo, Ontario N2L 3C5
(519) 884-8457

PURCHASE ORDER

No.   335

THIS NUMBER MUST APPEAR ON ALL
CORRESPONDENCE, INVOICES,
SHIPPING PAPERS AND PACKAGES.

(519) 884-8457

SEND INVOICE ONLY TO:

365 Albert Street, Waterloo, Ont. N2L 3C5

VENDOR _____   SHIP TO _____

DATE	DATE TO BE SHIPPED	SHIP VIA	C.O.D. TERMS	FREIGHT TERMS	ADV. ALLOWANCE	SPECIAL ALLOWANCE

ORDERED	PRODUCT NO.	DESCRIPTION	COST EACH	

PURCHASE CONDITIONS

1. Supplier will be responsible for extra freight cost on partial shipment; unless prior permission is obtained.
2. Please acknowledge this order.
3. Please notify us immediately if you are unable to complete order by date specified.

4. All items must be individually packed.
5. **Our purchase order no. must appear on all invoice packages & correspondence.**

IF NOT SHIPPED BY_____ , CANCEL ORDER.   _____
PURCHASING AGENT

VENDOR COPY

Copy 2, with a copy of the purchase requisition attached, is sent to the accounting department, where it is used in approving the payment of the invoice for the purchase; this copy is shown in Illustration 7–1.

Copy 3 is sent to the department originally issuing the requisition to inform its manager that the action has been taken.

Copy 4 is retained on file by the purchasing department.

Invoice

An **invoice** such as the one in Illustration 7–4 is an itemized statement of goods prepared by the vendor that lists the customer's name, the items sold, the sales prices, and the terms of sale. In effect, the invoice is the bill sent to the buyer by the seller. (From the vendor's point of view, it is a *sales invoice*.) The vendor sends the invoice to the buyer or **vendee,** who treats it as a *purchase invoice*. On receiving a purchase order, the vendor ships the ordered merchandise to the buyer and mails a copy of the invoice that covers the shipment. The goods are delivered to the buyer's receiving department and the invoice is sent directly to the buyer's accounting department, where it is placed in the voucher. Illustration 7–1 also presents this document flow.

Receiving Report

Most large companies maintain a special department that receives all merchandise or other purchased assets. When each shipment arrives, this receiving department counts the goods and checks them for damage and agreement with the purchase order. Then, it prepares four or more copies of a **receiving report.** An example of a receiving report is shown in Illustration 7–5. This report is a form used within the business to notify the appropriate persons that ordered goods were received and to describe the quantities and condition of the goods. As shown in Illustration 7–1, one copy is sent to the accounting department and placed in the voucher. Copies are also sent to the original requisitioning department and the purchasing department to notify them that the goods have arrived. The receiving department retains a copy in its files.

Invoice Approval Form

After the receiving report arrives, the accounting department should have copies of these papers on file in the voucher:

1. The *purchase requisition* listing the items to be ordered.
2. The *purchase order* listing the merchandise that was actually ordered.
3. The *invoice* showing the quantity, description, price, and total cost of the goods shipped by the seller.
4. The *receiving report* listing the quantity and condition of the items actually received by the buyer.

With the information on these papers, the accounting department is in a position to make an entry recording the purchase and to approve its eventual payment before the end of the discount period. In approving the invoice for payment, the accounting department checks and compares the information on all the papers. To facilitate the checking procedure and to ensure that no step is omitted, the department commonly uses an **invoice approval form.** (See Illustration 7–6.) This form is a document on which the accounting department notes that it has performed each step in the process of checking an invoice and approving it for recording and payment. An invoice approval form may be a separate business paper that is filed in

Illustration 7–4   Sales Invoice

SALE INVOICE

Albert Distributing Company
365 Albert Street
Waterloo, Ontario N2L 3C5
(519) 884-8457

INVOICE NO. 730

S
O   FIRM NAME _____   Invoice Date _____
L
D   ATTENTION OF _____   Prepared By _____
T
O   ADDRESS _____   Credit Terms _____

    CITY _____ PROVINCE _____ POSTAL CODE

                        Customer Purchase Order   Shipment Date _____

                        Number _____   Shipped Via _____

BO   BO = Back order — will be shipped shortly.   Date _____   Bill of Lading No. _____
DO   DO = Being shipped direct from factory.
NO   NO = Not available — item no longer stocked. Signed By_____
SO   SO = Similar item substituted.

QUANTITY ORDERED	PRODUCT NUMBER	DESCRIPTION	QUANTITY SHIPPED	UNIT PRICE	EXTENSION

TOTAL SALE	
GST	
PST	
TOTAL	
CUSTOMER ACCT. NO.	
INVOICE VERIFIED BY	

IMPORTANT: **ALL RETURNS MUST BE MADE WITHIN 10 DAYS AND ACCOMPANIED BY AN INVOICE COPY AND PACKED IN THE ORIGINAL CARTON.**

CUSTOMER

Illustration 7-5   Receiving Report

RECEIVING REPORT

Albert Distributing Company
365 Albert Street
Waterloo, Ontario N2L 3C5
(519) 884-8457

NO. **73**

DATE	19	PURCHASE ORDER NO. OR RETURN REQUEST NO.
RECEIVED FROM		PREPAID
ADDRESS		COLLECT
FREIGHT CARRIER	FREIGHT BILL NO.	

	QUANTITY	ITEM NO.	DESCRIPTION
1.			
2.			
3.			
4.			
5.			
6.			
7.			
8.			
9.			
10.			
11.			
12.			

REMARKS: CONDITIONS, ETC.

RECEIVED BY	DELIVERED TO

**BE SURE TO
MAKE THIS RECORD
ACCURATE AND COMPLETE**

	By	Date
Purchase order number	____	____
Requisition check	____	____
Purchase order check	____	____
Receiving report check	____	____
Invoice check:		
Price approval	____	____
Calculations	____	____
Terms	____	____
Approved for payment	____	____

Illustration 7-6

An Invoice Approval Form

the voucher or it may be preprinted on the voucher. It also may be stamped on the invoice. For clarity, the flowchart in Illustration 7–1 shows the form as a separate document.

As each step in the checking procedure is finished, the clerk initials the invoice approval form and records the current date. Initials in each space on the form indicate that the following administrative actions have been taken:

1. **Requisition check** . . . . The items on the invoice were actually requisitioned, as shown on the copy of the purchase requisition.

2. **Purchase order check** . . . . The items on the invoice were actually ordered, as shown on the copy of the purchase order.

3. **Receiving report check** . . . The items on the invoice were actually received, as shown on the copy of the receiving report.

4. **Invoice check:**

   Price approval . . . . The invoice prices are stated as agreed with the vendor.

   Calculations . . . . The invoice has no mathematical errors.

   Terms . . . . The terms are stated as agreed with the vendor.

The Voucher

After an invoice is checked and approved, the voucher is complete. At this point, the voucher is a record that summarizes the transaction. The voucher shows that the transaction has been certified as correct and authorizes its recording as an obligation of the buyer. The voucher also contains approval for paying the obligation on the appropriate date. Of course, the actual physical form used for vouchers varies substantially from company to company. In general, they are designed so that the invoice and other documents from which they are prepared are placed inside the voucher, which is often a folder. The information printed on the inside of a typical voucher is shown in Illustration 7–7, and the information on the outside is shown in Illustration 7–8.

The preparation of a voucher requires a clerk to enter the specified information in the proper blanks. The information is taken from the invoice and all the supporting documents filed inside the voucher. Once the steps are completed, the voucher is sent to the appropriate authorized individual, who completes one final

Illustration 7-7
Inside of a Voucher

VALLEY SUPPLY COMPANY   Voucher No. _93–767_
Vancouver, B.C.

Date _____ _Oct. 1, 1996_
Pay to _____ _A. B. Seay Wholesale Company_
City _____ _New Westminster_   Province _____ _British Columbia_

For the following: (attach all invoices and supporting papers)

Date of Invoice	Terms	Invoice Number and Other Details	Amount
Sept. 30, 1996	2/10, n/60	Invoice No. C-11756 Less discount Net amount payable	800.00 16.00 784.00

Payment approved

_____ _N. O. Neal_
Auditor

Illustration 7-8
Outside of a Voucher

Voucher No. _93–767_

ACCOUNTING DISTRIBUTION

Account Debited	Amount
Purchases	800.00
Transportation-In	
Store Supplies	
Office Supplies	
Sales Salaries	
Other	
Total Vouch. Pay. Cr.	800.00

Due date _____ _October 10, 1996_

Pay to _A. B. Seay Wholesale Company_
City _New Westminster_
Province _British Columbia_

Summary of charges:
Total charges _____ _800.00_
Discount _____ _16.00_
Net payment _____ _784.00_

Record of payment:
Paid _____
Cheque No. _____

review of the information, approves the accounts and amounts to be debited (called the *accounting distribution*), and approves the voucher for recording.

After a voucher is approved and recorded, it is filed until its due date, when it is sent to the cashier's office for payment. Here, the person responsible for issuing cheques relies on the approved voucher and its signed supporting documents as proof that the obligation was properly incurred and should be paid. As described earlier, the purchase requisition and purchase order attached to the voucher confirm that the purchase was authorized. The receiving report shows that the items were received, and the invoice approval form verifies that the invoice was checked for errors. As a result, there is little chance for error. There is even less chance for fraud without collusion, unless all the documents and signatures are forged.

Under a voucher system, obligations should be approved for payment and recorded as liabilities as soon as possible after they are incurred. As shown in the example, this practice should be followed for all purchases. It also should be followed for all expenses. For example, when a company receives a monthly telephone bill, the charges (especially long-distance calls) should be examined for accuracy. A voucher should be prepared, and the telephone bill should be filed inside the voucher. The voucher then is recorded with a journal entry. If the amount is due at once, a cheque should be issued. Otherwise, the voucher should be filed for payment on the due date.

The requirement that vouchers be prepared for expenses as they are incurred helps ensure that every expense payment is approved only when adequate information is available. However, invoices or bills for such things as equipment repairs are sometimes not received until weeks after the work is done. If no records of the repairs exist, it may be difficult to determine whether the invoice or bill correctly states the amount owed. Also, if no records exist, it may be possible for a dishonest employee to arrange with an outsider for more than one payment of an obligation, or for payment of excessive amounts, or for payment for goods and services not received. A properly functioning voucher system helps prevent all of these undesirable results. A voucher system may also be computerized. However, similar controls must be instituted to ensure that orders and payments are properly authorized. The major difference is that the records would be computer-generated instead of being manually created.

THE VOUCHER SYSTEM AND EXPENSES

Progress Check

7-6 Regarding internal control procedures for cash receipts:
   a. All cash disbursements, other than from petty cash, should be made by cheque.
   b. An accounting employee should count the cash received from sales and promptly deposit the receipts.
   c. Mail containing cash receipts should be opened by an accounting employee who is responsible for recording and depositing the receipts.

7-7 Do all companies need a voucher system? At what approximate point in a company's growth would you recommend installing a voucher system?

A basic principle for controlling cash disbursements requires that all disbursements be made by cheque. However, an exception to this rule is made for *petty cash disbursements.* Every business must make many small payments for items such as postage, express charges, repairs, and small items of supplies. If firms made such payments by cheque, they would end up writing many cheques for small amounts. This arrangement would be both time consuming and expensive. Therefore, to avoid writing cheques for small amounts, a business should establish a petty cash fund and use the money in this fund to make payments like those listed earlier.

Establishing a petty cash fund requires estimating the total amount of small payments likely to be made during a short period, such as a month. Then, a cheque is drawn by the company cashier's office for an amount slightly in excess of this estimate. This cheque is recorded with a debit to the Petty Cash account (an asset) and a credit to Cash. The cheque is cashed, and the currency is turned over to a

THE PETTY CASH FUND

LO 4

Explain the operation of a petty cash fund and be able to prepare journal entries to record petty cash fund transactions.

member of the office staff designated as the *petty cashier.* This person is responsible for the safekeeping of the cash, for making payments from this fund, and for keeping accurate records.

The petty cashier should keep the petty cash in a locked box in a safe place. As each disbursement is made, the person receiving payment signs a *petty cash receipt* (see Illustration 7–9). The receipt is then placed in the petty cashbox with the remaining money. Under this system, the sum of all the receipts plus the remaining cash should always equal the amount of the fund. For example, a $100 petty cash fund could have *(a)* $100 in cash, *(b)* $80 in cash and $20 in receipts, or *(c)* $10 in cash and $90 in receipts. Notice that each disbursement reduces the cash and increases the sum of the receipts in the petty cashbox. When the cash is nearly gone, the fund should be reimbursed. This provides internal control over the petty cash fund since only one person is responsible for each petty cash fund, and the total of the cash and receipts must equal the amount of the fund.

To reimburse the fund, the petty cashier presents the receipts to the company cashier. The company cashier stamps all receipts *paid* so that they cannot be reused, retains them, and gives the petty cashier a cheque for their sum. When this cheque is cashed and the proceeds returned to the cashbox, the money in the box is restored to its original amount, and the fund is ready to begin a new cycle of operations.

At the time a cheque is written to reimburse the petty cash fund, the petty cashier should sort the paid receipts according to the type of expense or other accounts to be debited in recording payments from the fund. Each group is then totaled, and the totals are used in making the entry to record the reimbursement.

ILLUSTRATION OF A PETTY CASH FUND

To avoid writing numerous cheques for small amounts, a company established a petty cash fund on November 1, designating one of its office clerks, Carl Burns, as petty cashier. A $75 cheque was drawn, cashed, and the proceeds turned over to Burns. The following entry recorded the cheque:

Nov.	1	Petty Cash	75.00	
		Cash		75.00
		Established a petty cash fund.		

Notice that this entry transfers $75 from the regular Cash account to the Petty Cash account. After the petty cash fund is established, the Petty Cash account is not debited or credited again unless the size of the total fund is changed. For example, the fund should be increased if it is being exhausted and reimbursed too frequently. Another entry like the preceding one would be made to record an increase in the size of the fund. That is, there would be a debit to Petty Cash and credit to Cash for the amount of the increase. If the fund is too large, some of the money in the fund should be redeposited in the chequing account. Such a reduction in the fund is recorded with a debit to Cash and a credit to Petty Cash.

Illustration 7-9
A Petty Cash Receipt

```
┌─────────────────────────────────────────────────────────────┐
│                                                               │
│  No _____- 1 -_____                              $   $10.00   │
│                                                               │
│                  RECEIVED OF PETTY CASH                       │
│                                                               │
│                            Date___Nov. 2___  19_96_           │
│                                                               │
│  For _Washing windows_____        │
│                                                               │
│       _____        │
│                                                               │
│  Charge to_____Miscellaneous expenses_____        │
│                                                               │
│       _____        │
│                                                               │
│  Approved by                    Received by                   │
│  CaB                            Bob Jone                      │
│                                                               │
│  TOPS-Form 3008                                               │
│                                                               │
└─────────────────────────────────────────────────────────────┘
```

During November, Carl Burns, the petty cashier, made several payments from the petty cash fund. Each time, he asked the person who received payment to sign a receipt. On November 27, after making a $26.50 payment for repairs to an office computer, Burns noticed that only $3.70 cash remained in the fund. Therefore, he summarized and totaled the petty cash receipts as shown in Illustration 7–10. Then, he gave the summary and the petty cash receipts to the company cashier in exchange for a $71.30 cheque to reimburse the fund. Burns cashed the cheque, put the $71.30 proceeds in the petty cashbox, and was ready to make additional payments from the fund. The reimbursing cheque is recorded with the following journal entry:

Nov.	27	Miscellaneous Expenses	46.50	
		Transportation-In	15.05	
		Delivery Expense	5.00	
		Office Supplies	4.75	
		Cash		71.30
		Reimbursed petty cash.		

Information for this entry came from the petty cashier's summary of payments. Note that the debits in the entry record the petty cash payments. Even if the petty cash fund is not low on funds at the end of an accounting period, it may be reimbursed at that time to record the expenses in the proper period. Otherwise, the financial statements show an overstated petty cash asset and understated expenses or assets that were paid for out of petty cash. (Of course, the amounts involved are seldom if ever significant to users of the financial statements.)

Illustration 7-10
Summary of Petty
Cash Payments

Miscellaneous expenses:		
Nov. 2, washing windows	$10.00	
Nov. 17, washing windows	10.00	
Nov. 27, computer repairs	26.50	$46.50
Transportation-in:		
Nov. 5, delivery of merchandise purchased . . .	$ 6.75	
Nov. 20, delivery of merchandise purchased . .	8.30	15.05
Delivery expense:		
Nov. 18, customer's package delivered		5.00
Office supplies:		
Nov. 15, purchased office supplies		4.75
Total		$71.30

CASH OVER AND SHORT

Sometimes, a petty cashier fails to get a receipt for a payment. Then, when the fund is reimbursed, he or she may forget the purpose of the expenditure. This mistake causes the fund to be short. If, for whatever reason, the petty cash fund is short at reimbursement time, the shortage is recorded as an expense in the reimbursing entry with a debit to the **Cash Over and Short account.** This account is an income statement account that records the income effects of cash overages and cash shortages arising from omitted petty cash receipts and from errors in making change.

Errors in making change are discovered when there are differences between the cash in a cash register and the record of the amount of cash sales. Even though a cashier is careful, some customers may be given too much or too little change. As a result, at the end of a day, the actual cash from a cash register may not equal the cash sales rung up. For example, assume that a cash register shows cash sales of $550 but the actual count of cash in the register is $555. The entry to record the cash sales and the overage would be:

Nov.	23	Cash	555.00	
		Cash Over and Short		5.00
		Sales		550.00
		Day's cash sales and overage.		

On the other hand, if there were a shortage of cash in the register on the next day, the entry to record cash sales and the shortage would look like the following:

Nov.	24	Cash	621.00	
		Cash Over and Short	4.00	
		Sales		625.00
		Day's cash sales and shortage.		

As a Matter of Ethics

Nancy Tucker is an internal auditor for a large corporation and is in the process of making surprise counts of three $200 petty cash funds in various offices in the headquarters building. She arrived at the office of one of the fund custodians shortly before lunch while he was on the telephone. Tucker explained the purpose of her visit, and the custodian asked politely that she come back after lunch so that he could finish the business he was conducting by long distance. She agreed and returned around 1:30. The custodian opened the petty cash box and showed her nine new $20 bills with consecutive serial numbers plus receipts that totaled $20. Would you suggest that the auditor take any further action or comment on these events in her report to management?

Because customers are more likely to dispute being shortchanged, the Cash Over and Short account usually has a debit balance by the end of the accounting period. Because it is a debit, this balance represents an expense. This expense may be shown on the income statement as a separate item in the general and administrative expense section. Or, because the amount is usually small, you can combine it with other small expenses and report them as a single item called *miscellaneous expenses*. If Cash Over and Short has a credit balance at the end of the period, it usually is included as part of *miscellaneous revenues* on the income statement.

Progress Check

7-8   Why are some cash payments made from a petty cash fund?

7-9   Why should a petty cash fund be reimbursed at the end of an accounting period?

7-10   What are two results of reimbursing the petty cash fund?

At least once every month, banks send depositors bank statements that show the activity in their accounts during the month. Different banks use a variety of formats for their bank statements. However, all of them include the following items of information in one place or another:

1.   The balance of the depositor's account at the beginning of the month.
2.   Deposits and any other amounts added to the account during the month.
3.   Cheques and any other amounts deducted from the account during the month.
4.   The account balance at the end of the month.

Of course, all this information is presented as it appears in the bank's records. Examine Illustration 7–11, an example of a typical bank statement, to find the four items just listed.

Enclosed with the monthly statement are the depositor's **canceled cheques** and any debit or credit memoranda that have affected the account. Canceled cheques are cheques that the bank has paid and deducted from the customer's account during the month. Additional deductions that may appear on the bank statement for an individual include withdrawals through automatic teller machines (ATM withdrawals) and periodic payments arranged in advance by the depositor.[2] Other de-

RECONCILING THE BANK BALANCE

LO 5

Explain why the bank balance and the book balance of cash should be reconciled and be able to prepare a reconciliation.

---

[2]Because of the need to make all disbursements by cheque, most business chequing accounts do not allow ATM withdrawals.

Illustration 7-11 A Typical Bank Statement

LONDON BANK LB

VALLEY COMPANY
39 MAPLE STREET
LONDON, ONTARIO
K2M 4K6

LONDON BANK
NOV 30
DAILY
INTEREST
ACCOUNT

BRANCH
LONDON MAIN

ACCOUNT NUMBER
007-500865

BALANCE FORWARD
7,502.02

DATE	SYMBOL	WITHDRAWALS	DEPOSITS	BALANCE
OCT 31	756	1,102.31		6,399.71
OCT 31	757	179.00		6,220.71
NOV 02	NBD		20,000.00	26,220.71
NOV 02	755	835.17		25,385.54
NOV 03	PL	250.00		25,135.54
NOV 04	759	1,116.00		24,019.54
NOV 08	749	32.00		23,987.54
NOV 08	747	4,212.00		19,775.54
NOV 09	751	50.00		19,725.54
NOV 10	762	1,906.81		17,818.73
NOV 14	PL	250.00		17,568.73
NOV 14	764	940.43		16,628.30
NOV 14	750	113.78		16,514.52
NOV 15	CM		2,075.05	18,589.57
NOV 15	770	10,000.00		8,589.57
NOV 15	763	267.29		8,322.28
NOV 15	767	86.46		8,235.82
NOV 17	766	125.00		8,110.82
NOV 17	769	164.00		7,946.82
NOV 21	765	89.78		7,857.04
NOV 23	771	150.00		7,707.04
NOV 24	768	178.29		7,528.75
NOV 30	INT		78.89	7,607.64
NOV 30	S/C	1.00		7,606.64

EXPLANATION OF SYMBOLS

Each transaction is identified by one of the following symbols.
Talk to your branch staff if you have any questions.

AID Investment Certificate Interest	INT Interest	OBC Other Bank Service Charge
CHQ Cheque	JCW Johnny Cash Withdrawal	PAY Payroll Deposit
CM Miscellaneous Credit	MCM Merchant MasterCard Credit	PL Loan Payment
COR Correction	MDM Merchant MasterCard Debit	PWR Powerline Payment
CSB Canada Savings Bond Transaction	MTC MasterTeller Service Charge	RTD Returned Item
DEP Deposit	MTG Mortgage Payment	SC Service Charge
DM Miscellaneous Debit	MTW MasterTeller Withdrawal	SDB Safe Deposit Box Payment
ECM Electronic Funds Credit	NBD No Book Deposit	WD Withdrawal
EDM Electronic Funds Debit	NBW No Book Withdrawal	
ICW Interac Withdrawal	NRT Non Resident Tax	

ductions from the depositor's account may include service charges and fees assessed by the bank, customers' cheques deposited that prove to be uncollectible, and corrections of previous errors. Except for the service charges, the bank notifies the depositor of the deduction in each case with a debit memorandum at the time that the bank reduces the balance. For completeness, a copy of each debit memorandum is usually sent with the monthly statement.[3]

In addition to deposits made by the depositor, the bank may add amounts to the depositor's account. Examples of additions would be amounts the bank has collected on behalf of the depositor and corrections of previous errors. Credit memoranda notify the depositor of all additions when they are first recorded. For completeness, a copy of each credit memorandum may be sent with the monthly statement.

Another item commonly added to the bank balance on the statement is interest earned by the depositor. Some chequing accounts pay the depositor interest based on the average cash balance maintained in the account. The bank calculates the amount of interest earned and credits it to the depositor's account each month. In Illustration 7–11, note that the bank credited $78.89 of interest to the account of Valley Company. (The methods used to calculate interest are discussed in the next chapter.)

When the business deposits all receipts intact and when all payments (other than petty cash payments) are drawn from the chequing account, the bank statement is a device for proving the accuracy of the depositor's cash records. The test of the accuracy begins by preparing a **bank reconciliation;** this analysis explains the difference between the balance of a chequing account in the depositor's records and the balance on the bank statement and is a critical element of internal control for cash.

Need for Reconciling the Bank Balance

For virtually all chequing accounts, the balance on the bank statement does not agree with the balance in the depositor's accounting records. Therefore, to prove the accuracy of both the depositor's records and those of the bank, you must *reconcile* the two balances. In other words, you must explain or account for the differences between them.

Numerous factors cause the bank statement balance to differ from the depositor's book balance. Some are:

1. **Outstanding cheques.** These cheques were written (or drawn) by the depositor, deducted on the depositor's records, and sent to the payees. However, they did not reach the bank for payment and deduction before the statement date.

2. **Unrecorded deposits.** Companies often make deposits at the end of each business day, after the bank is closed. These deposits made in the bank's night depository are not recorded by the bank until the next business day. Therefore, a deposit placed in the night depository on the last day of the month cannot appear on the bank statement for that month. In addition, deposits mailed to the bank toward the end of the month may be in transit and unrecorded when the statement is prepared.

---

[3]A depositor's account is a liability on the bank's records. Thus, a deposit increases the account balance, and the bank records it with a *credit* to the account. Debit memos from the bank produce *credits* on the depositor's books, and credit memos lead to *debits*.

3. **Charges for uncollectible items and for service.** Occasionally, a company deposits a customer's cheque that bounces, or turns out to be uncollectible. Usually, the balance in the customer's account is not large enough to cover the cheque. In these cases, the cheque is called a nonsufficient funds (NSF) cheque. In other situations, the customer's account has been closed. In processing deposited cheques, the bank credits the depositor's account for the full amount. Later, when the bank learns that the cheque is uncollectible, it debits (reduces) the depositor's account for the amount of the cheque. Also, the bank may charge the depositor a fee for processing the uncollectible cheque. At the same time, the bank notifies the depositor of each deduction by mailing a debit memorandum. Although each deduction should be recorded by the depositor on the day the debit memorandum is received, sometimes an entry is not made until the bank reconciliation is prepared.

   Other charges to a depositor's account that a bank might report on the bank statement include the printing of new cheques. Also, the bank may assess a monthly service charge for maintaining the account. Notification of these charges is *not* provided until the statement is mailed.

4. **Credits for collections and for interest.** Banks sometimes act as collection agents for their depositors by collecting promissory notes and other items. When the bank collects an item, it deducts a fee and adds the net proceeds to the depositor's account. At the same time, it sends a credit memorandum to notify the depositor of the transaction. As soon as the memorandum is received, it should be recorded by the depositor. However, these items may remain unrecorded until the time of the bank reconciliation.

   Many bank accounts earn interest on the average cash balance in the account during the month. If an account earns interest, the bank statement includes a credit for the amount earned during the past month. Notification of earned interest is provided only by the bank statement.

5. **Errors.** Regardless of care and systems of internal control for automatic error detection, both banks and depositors make errors. Errors by the bank may not be discovered until the depositor completes the bank reconciliation. Also, the depositor's errors often are not discovered until the balance is reconciled.

Steps in Reconciling the Bank Balance

To obtain the benefits of separated duties, an employee who does not handle cash receipts, process cheques, or maintain cash records should prepare the bank reconciliation. In preparing to reconcile the balance, this employee must gather information from the bank statement and from other sources in the records. The person who performs the reconciliation must do the following:

- Compare the deposits listed on the bank statement with the deposits shown in the accounting records. Identify any discrepancies and determine which is correct. Make a list of any errors or unrecorded deposits.

- Examine all other credits on the bank statement and determine whether each was recorded in the books. These items include collections by the bank, correction of previous bank statement errors, and interest earned by the depositor. List any unrecorded items.

- Compare the canceled cheques listed on the bank statement with the actual cheques returned with the statement. For each cheque, make sure that the correct amount was deducted by the bank and that the returned cheque was properly charged to the company's account. List any discrepancies or errors.

- Compare the canceled cheques listed on the bank statement with the cheques recorded in the books. (To make this process easier, the bank statement normally lists canceled cheques in numerical order.) Prepare a list of any outstanding cheques.

  Although an individual may occasionally write a cheque and fail to record it in the books, companies with reasonable internal controls rarely if ever write a cheque without recording it. Nevertheless, prepare a list of any canceled cheques unrecorded in the books.

- Determine whether any outstanding cheques listed on the previous month's bank reconciliation are not included in the canceled cheques listed on the bank statement. Prepare a list of any of these cheques that remain outstanding at the end of the current month. Send this list to the cashier's office for follow-up with the payees to see if the cheques were actually received.

- Examine all other debits to the account shown on the bank statement and determine whether each was recorded in the books. These include bank charges for newly printed cheques, NSF cheques, and monthly service charges. List those not yet recorded.

When this information has been gathered, the employee can complete the reconciliation like the one in Illustration 7–12 by using these steps:

1. Start with the bank balance of the cash account.
2. Identify and list any unrecorded deposits and any bank errors that understated the bank balance. Add them to the bank balance.
3. Identify and list any outstanding cheques and any bank errors that overstated the bank balance. Subtract them from the bank balance.
4. Compute the adjusted balance. This amount is also called the correct or reconciled balance.
5. Start with the book balance of the cash account.
6. Identify and list any unrecorded credit memoranda from the bank (perhaps for the proceeds of a collected note), interest earned, and any errors that understated the balance. Add them to the book balance.
7. Identify and list any unrecorded debit memoranda from the bank (perhaps for a NSF cheque from a customer), service charges, and any errors that overstated the book balance. Subtract them from the book balance.
8. Compute the reconciled balance. This is also the correct balance.
9. Verify that the two adjusted balances from steps 4 and 8 are equal. If so, they are reconciled. If not, check for mathematical accuracy and for any missing data.

When the reconciliation is complete, the employee should send a copy to the accounting department so that any needed journal entries can be recorded. For

Illustration 7-12
A Typical Bank
Reconciliation

MOUNTAIN COMPANY
Bank Reconciliation
October 31, 1996

①Bank statement balance	$2,050.00	⑤Book balance		$1,404.58
②Add:		⑥Add:		
Deposit of October 31 ...	145.00	Proceeds of note less		
		collection fee	$ 485.00	
		Interest earned	8.42	
		Total	$ 493.42	
Total	$2,195.00	Total		$1,898.00
③Deduct:		⑦Deduct:		
Outstanding checks:		NSF check plus service		
No. 124	$ 150.00	charge	$ 30.00	
No. 126	200.00	Check printing charge	23.00	
Total	$ 350.00	Total	$ 53.00	
④Reconciled balance	$1,845.00	⑧Reconciled balance		$1,845.00

⑨The two balances both equal $1,845.00

example, entries are needed to record any unrecorded debit and credit memoranda and any of the company's mistakes. Another copy should go to the cashier's office, especially if the bank has made an error that needs to be corrected.

ILLUSTRATION OF A BANK RECONCILIATION

We can illustrate a bank reconciliation by preparing one for Mountain Company as of October 31. In preparing to reconcile the bank account, the Mountain Company employee gathered the following facts:

- The bank balance shown on the bank statement was $2,050.

- The cash balance according to the accounting records was $1,404.58.

- A $145 deposit was placed in the bank's night depository on October 31 and was unrecorded by the bank when the bank statement was mailed.

- Enclosed with the bank statement was a copy of a credit memorandum showing that the bank had collected a note receivable for the company on October 23. The note's proceeds of $500 (less a $15 collection fee) were credited to the company's account. This credit memorandum had not been recorded by the company.

- The bank statement also showed a credit of $8.42 for interest earned on the average cash balance in the account. Because there had been no prior notification of this item, it had not been recorded on the company's books.

- A comparison of canceled cheques with the company's books showed that two cheques were outstanding—No. 124 for $150 and No. 126 for $200.

- Other debits on the bank statement that had not been previously recorded on the books included (a) a $23 charge for cheques printed by the bank; and (b) an NSF (nonsufficient funds) cheque for $20 plus the related processing fee of $10. The NSF cheque had been received from a customer, Frank Green, on October 16 and had been included in that day's deposit.

Illustration 7–12 shows the bank reconciliation that reflects these items. The numbers in the circles beside the various parts of the reconciliation correspond to the numbers of the steps listed earlier.

Preparing a bank reconciliation helps locate any errors made by either the bank or the depositor. It also identifies unrecorded items that should be recorded on the company's books. For example, in Mountain Company's reconciliation, the adjusted balance of $1,845.00 is the correct balance as of October 31, 1996. However, at that date, Mountain Company's accounting records show a $1,404.58 balance. Therefore, journal entries must be made to increase the book balance to the correct balance. This process requires four entries. The first is:

Nov.	2	Cash	485.00	
		Collection Expense	15.00	
		Notes Receivable		500.00
		To record the collection fee and proceeds of a note *collected by the bank.*		

This entry records the net proceeds of Mountain Company's note receivable that had been collected by the bank, the expense of having the bank perform that service, and the reduction in the Notes Receivable account.

The second entry records the interest credited to Mountain Company's account by the bank:

Nov.	2	Cash	8.42	
		Interest Earned		8.42
		To record interest earned on the average cash balance *maintained in the chequing account.*		

Interest earned is a revenue, and the entry recognizes both the revenue and the related increase in Cash.

The third entry records the NSF cheque that was returned as uncollectible. The $20 cheque was received from Green in payment of his account and deposited. The bank charged $10 for handling the NSF cheque and deducted $30 from Mountain Company's account. Therefore, the company must reverse the entry made when the cheque was received and also record the $10 processing fee:

Nov.	2	Accounts Receivable—Frank Green	30.00	
		Cash		30.00
		To charge Frank Green's account for his NSF cheque *and for the bank's fee.*		

This entry reflects the fact that Mountain Company followed customary business practice and added the NSF $10 fee to Green's account. Thus, it will try to collect the entire $30 from Green.

The fourth entry debits Miscellaneous Expenses for the cheque printing charge. The entry is:

Nov.	2	Miscellaneous Expenses	23.00	
		Cash		23.00
		Cheque printing charge.		

After these entries are recorded, the balance of cash is increased to the correct amount of $1,845.00 ($1,404.58 + $485.00 + $8.42 − $30.00 − $23.00)

Progress Check

7-11   What is a bank statement?

7-12   What is the meaning of the phrase *to reconcile a bank balance*?

7-13   Why should you reconcile the bank statement balance of cash and the depositor's book balance of cash?

7-14   List items that commonly affect the bank side of a reconciliation and indicate if the items are added or subtracted.

7-15   List items that commonly affect the book side of a reconciliation and indicate if the items are added or subtracted.

OTHER INTERNAL CONTROL PROCEDURES

LO 6

Explain how recording invoices at net amounts helps gain control over cash discounts taken, and calculate days' sales uncollected.

Internal control principles apply to every phase of a company's operations including merchandise purchases, sales, cash receipts, cash disbursements, and owning and operating plant assets. Many of these procedures are discussed in later chapters. At this point, we consider a way that a company can gain more control over *purchases discounts*.

Recall that entries such as the following have recorded the receipt and payment of an invoice for a purchase of merchandise:

Oct.	2	Purchases	1,000.00	
		Accounts Payable		1,000.00
		Purchased merchandise, terms 2/10, n/60.		
	12	Accounts Payable	1,000.00	
		Purchases Discounts		20.00
		Cash		980.00
		Paid the invoice of October 2.		

These entries reflect the **gross method of recording purchases.** That is, the invoice was recorded at its gross amount of $1,000 before considering the cash discount. Many companies record invoices in this way. However, the **net method of recording purchases** records invoices at their *net* amounts (after cash discounts). This method is widely thought to provide more useful information to management.

To illustrate the net method, assume that a company purchases merchandise with a $1,000 invoice price, and terms of 2/10, n/60. On receiving the goods, the purchasing company deducted the offered $20 discount from the gross amount and recorded the purchase at the $980 net amount:

Oct.	2	Purchases	980.00	
		Accounts Payable		980.00
		Purchased merchandise on credit.		

If the invoice for this purchase is paid within the discount period, the entry to record the payment debits Accounts Payable and credits Cash for $980. However, if payment is not made within the discount period and the discount is *lost,* an entry such as the following must be made either before or when the invoice is paid:

Dec.	1	Discounts Lost	20.00	
		Accounts Payable		20.00
		To record the discount lost.		

A cheque for the full $1,000 invoice amount is then written, recorded, and mailed to the creditor.[4]

Advantage of the Net Method

When invoices are recorded at *gross* amounts, the amount of discounts taken is deducted from the balance of the Purchases account on the income statement to arrive at the cost of merchandise purchased. However, the amount of any lost discounts does not appear in any account or on the income statement. Therefore, lost discounts may not come to the attention of management.

On the other hand, when purchases are recorded at *net* amounts, the amount of discounts taken does not appear on the income statement. Instead, an expense for **discounts lost** is brought to management's attention through its appearance on the income statement as an operating expense.

Recording invoices at their net amounts supplies management with useful information about the amount of discounts missed through oversight, carelessness, or some other reason. Thus, this practice gives management better control over the people responsible for paying bills on time so that cash discounts can be taken. When the accounts record the fact that discounts are missed, someone has to explain why. As a result, it is likely that fewer discounts are lost through carelessness.

---

[4]Alternatively, the lost discount can be recorded with the late payment in a single entry.

USING THE INFORMATION— DAYS' SALES UNCOLLECTED

Many companies attract customers by selling to them on credit. As a result, cash flows from customers are postponed until the accounts receivable are collected. To evaluate the liquidity of a company's assets, investors want to know how quickly the company converts its accounts receivable into cash. One way financial statement users evaluate the liquidity of the receivables is to look at the **days' sales uncollected.** This is calculated by taking the ratio between the present balance of receivables and the credit sales over the preceding year, and then multiplying by the number of days in the year. Since the amount of credit sales usually is not reported, net sales is typically used in the calculation. Thus, the formula for the calculation is:

$$\text{Days' sales uncollected} = \frac{\text{Accounts receivable}}{\text{Net sales}} \times 365$$

For example, assume Meg's Mart had accounts receivable of $11,200 at the end of 1996 and net sales of $314,700 for the year. By dividing $11,200 by $314,700, we find that the receivables balance represents 3.56% of the year's sales. Because there are 365 days in a year, the $11,200 balance is 3.56% of 365 days of sales, or 13 days of sales.

The number of days' sales uncollected is used as an estimate of how much time is likely to pass before cash receipts from credit sales equal the amount of the existing accounts receivable. In evaluating this number, financial statement users should compare it to days' sales uncollected calculations for other companies in the same industry. In addition, they may make comparisons between the current and prior periods. To illustrate such a comparison, selected data from the 1993 annual reports of two toy manufacturing companies are used to compute days' sales uncollected:

(*in thousands*)	**TYCO**		**MATTEL**	
Accounts Receivable	$219,036		$580,313	
Net Sales	$730,179	× 365	$2,704,448	× 365
Days' Sales Uncollected	110 days		78 days	

If **TYCO Toys, Inc.**'s management made the preceding comparison, the resulting figures might motivate them to investigate how this compares to last year and how they could improve this ratio. Continuation of a financially sound business requires continuous monitoring of the liquidity of the firm's assets.

Progress Check

7-16   When invoices are recorded at net amounts:
    a. The amount of purchases discounts taken is not recorded in a separate account.
    b. Purchases discounts taken are recorded in a Purchases Discounts account.
    c. The cash expenditures for purchases will always be less than if the invoices are recorded at gross amounts.

7-17   Why is the days' sales uncollected calculation usually based on net sales instead of credit sales?

LO 1. Explain the concept of liquidity and the difference between cash and cash equivalents. The liquidity of an asset refers to how easily the asset can be converted into other types of assets or used to buy services or satisfy obligations. Cash is the most liquid asset. To increase their return, companies may invest their idle cash balances in cash equivalents. These investments are readily convertible to a known amount of cash with market values that are relatively insensitive to interest rate changes. In evaluating the liquidity of a company, financial statement users may calculate days' sales uncollected.

LO 2. Explain why internal control procedures are needed in a large organization and state the broad principles of internal control. Internal control systems are designed to encourage adherence to prescribed managerial policies. In doing so, they promote efficient operations and protect assets against theft or misuse. They also help ensure that accurate and reliable accounting data are produced. Principles of good internal control include establishing clear responsibilities, maintaining adequate records, insuring assets and bonding employees, separating record-keeping and custody of assets, dividing responsibilities for related transactions, using mechanical devices whenever feasible, and performing regular independent reviews of internal control practices.

LO 3. Describe internal control procedures used to protect cash received from cash sales, cash received through the mail, and cash disbursements. To maintain control over cash, custody must be separated from record-keeping for cash. All cash receipts should be deposited intact in the bank on a daily basis, and all payments (except for minor petty cash payments) should be made by cheque. A voucher system helps maintain control over cash disbursements by ensuring that payments are made only after full documentation and approval.

LO 4. Explain the operation of a petty cash fund and be able to prepare journal entries to record petty cash fund transactions. The petty cashier, who should be a responsible employee, makes small payments from the petty cash fund and obtains signed receipts for the payments. The Petty Cash account is debited when the fund is established or increased in size. Petty cash disbursements are recorded with a credit to cash whenever the fund is replenished.

LO 5. Explain why the bank balance and the book balance of cash should be reconciled and be able to prepare a reconciliation. A bank reconciliation is produced to prove the accuracy of the depositor's and the bank's records. In completing the reconciliation, the bank statement balance is adjusted for such items as outstanding cheques and unrecorded deposits made on or before the bank statement date but not reflected on the statement. The depositor's cash account balance is adjusted to the correct balance. The difference arises from such items as service charges, collections the bank has made for the depositor, and interest earned on the average chequing account balance.

LO 6. Explain how recording invoices at net amounts helps gain control over cash discounts taken, and calculate days' sales uncollected. When the net method of recording invoices is used, missed cash discounts are reported as an expense in the income statement. In contrast, when the gross method is used, discounts taken are reported as reductions in the cost of the purchased goods. Therefore, the net method directs management's attention to instances where the company failed to take advantage of discounts.

SUMMARY OF THE CHAPTER IN TERMS OF LEARNING OBJECTIVES

Reconciliation of Phillip Company's bank account as of May 31:

Bank statement balance	$2,304.75		Book balance	$2,268.32
Add:				
Deposit of May 30.	245.62			
Total	2,550.37			
Deduct:			Deduct:	
Outstanding cheques:			NSF cheque plus service charge . .	56.75
No. 376.	185.30		Bank service charges	18.65
No. 382.	172.15			
Total	357.45		Total	75.40
Reconciled balance	$2,192.92		Reconciled balance	$2,192.92

Summary of Phillip Company's bank statement for the month of June:

Date	Symbol	Withdrawl	Deposit	Balance
May 31	Balance forward			2,304.75
June 2	NBD		245.62	2,550.37
June 3	376	185.30		2,365.08
June 5	383	250.00		2,115.07
June 10	NBD		385.70	2,500.77
June 12	384	48.90		2,451.87
June 14	385	152.30		2,299.57
June 18	387	113.78		2,185.79
June 20	NBD		462.95	2,648.74
June 22	389	238.95		2,409.79
June 25	386	138.40		2,271.39
June 26	382	172.15		2,099.24
June 29	391	74.20		2,025.04
June 30	SC	15.70		2,009.34

Summary of June Cheque Register:

Date	No.	Amount
June		
2	383	$ 250.00
5	384	48.90
6	385	152.30
8	386	138.40
10	387	113.78
12	388	186.30
15	389	238.95
16	390	146.40
20	391	74.20
26	392	106.70
29	393	164.80
Total		$1,620.73

Summary of June Cash Receipts:

Date	Amount
June	
9	$ 385.70
18	462.95
29	220.85
Total	$1,069.50

Book cash balance, June 30:

Book balance, May 31	$2,192.92
Add receipts	1,069.50
Total	3,262.42
Deduct cheques	1,620.73
Book balance, June 30	$1,641.69

Required

Prepare a bank reconciliation and any necessary journal entries for Phillip Company for the
month of June.

- Examine the previous month's bank reconciliation for any items that should be carried over to the current month.
- Compare the deposits in the accounting records with the deposits in the bank statement.
- Examine any other credits in the bank statement.
- Compare the canceled cheques in the bank statement with the cheques recorded in the books.
- Examine any other debits in the bank statement.
- Calculate and compare the reconciled bank balance and the reconciled book balance.

Planning the Solution

Reconciliation of Phillip Company's bank account as of June 30:

Solution to Demonstration Problem

Bank statement balance	$2,009.34	Book balance		$1,641.69
Add:				
Deposit of June 29	220.85			
Total	2,230.19			
Deduct:		Deduct:		
Outstanding cheques:		Bank service charge	15.70	
No. 388	186.30			
No. 390	146.40			
No. 392	106.70			
No. 393	164.80			
Total	604.20			
Reconciled balance	$1,625.99	Reconciled balance		$1,625.99

Journal entry:

June	30	Miscellaneous expense	15.70	
		Cash		15.70
		Bank charges.		

GLOSSARY

Bank reconciliation an analysis that explains the difference between the balance of a chequing account shown in the depositor's records and the balance shown on the bank statement. p. 367

Canceled cheques cheques that the bank has paid and deducted from the customer's account during the month. p. 365

Cash equivalents temporary liquid investments that can be easily and quickly converted to cash. p. 345

Cash Over and Short account an income statement account used to record cash overages and cash shortages arising from omitted petty cash receipts and from errors in making change. p. 364

Days' sales uncollected the number of days of average credit sales volume accumulated in the accounts receivable balance, calculated as the product of 374 times the ratio of the accounts receivable balance divided by credit (or net) sales. p. 374

Discounts lost an expense resulting from failing to take advantage of cash discounts on purchases. p. 373

Gross method of recording purchases a method of recording purchases at the full invoice price without deducting any cash discounts. p. 372

Internal control system procedures adopted by a business to encourage adherence to prescribed managerial policies; in doing so, the system also promotes operational efficiencies and protects the business assets from waste, fraud, and theft, and helps ensure that accurate and reliable accounting data are produced. p. 346

Invoice an itemized statement prepared by the vendor that lists the customer's name, the items sold, the sales prices, and the terms of sale. p. 356

Invoice approval form a document on which the accounting department notes that it has performed each step in the process of checking an invoice and approving it for recording and payment. p. 356

Liquid asset an asset, such as cash, that is easily converted into other types of assets or used to buy services or pay liabilities. p. 344

Liquidity a characteristic of an asset that refers to how easily the asset can be converted into another type of asset or used to buy services or satisfy obligations. p. 344

Net method of recording purchases a method of recording purchases at the full invoice price less any cash discounts. p. 373

Outstanding cheques cheques that were written (or drawn) by the depositor, deducted on the depositor's records, and sent to the payees; however, they had not reached the bank for payment and deduction before the statement date. p. 367

Purchase order a business paper used by the purchasing department to place an order with the vendor; authorizes the vendor to ship the ordered merchandise at the stated price and terms. p. 353

Purchase requisition a business paper used to request that the Purchasing Department buy the needed merchandise or other items. p. 352

Receiving report a form used within the business to notify the appropriate persons that ordered goods were received and to describe the quantities and condition of the goods. p. 356

Vendee the buyer or purchaser of goods or services. p. 356

Vendor the seller of goods or services, usually a manufacturer or wholesaler. p. 353

Voucher an internal business paper used to accumulate other papers and information needed to control the disbursement of cash and to ensure that the transaction is properly recorded. p. 352

Voucher system a set of procedures designed to control the incurrence of obligations and disbursements of cash. p. 352

SYNONYMOUS TERMS

Chequing account demand deposit.
Invoice bill.
Purchase order P.O.
Savings account time deposit.

Unrecorded deposits deposits in transit.
Vendee buyer.
Vendor seller.
Write a cheque draw a cheque.

QUESTIONS

1. Which of the following assets is most liquid? Which is least liquid? Merchandise inventory, building, accounts receivable, cash.

2. List the seven broad principles of internal control.

3. Why should the person who keeps the record of an asset not be the person responsible for custody of the asset?

4. Internal control procedures are important in every business, but at what stage in the development of a business do they become critical?

5. Why should responsibility for a sequence of related transactions be divided among different departments or individuals?

6. Why should all receipts be deposited intact on the day of receipt?

7. When merchandise is purchased for a large store, why are department managers not permitted to deal directly with suppliers?

8. When a disbursing officer issues a cheque for a large business, he or she usually cannot know from personal contact that the assets, goods, or services being paid for were received by the business or that the purchase was properly authorized. However, if the company has an internal control system, the officer can depend on it. Exactly which documents does the officer depend on to tell that the purchase

was authorized and that the goods were actually received?

9. Why are some cash payments made from a petty cash fund?

10. What is a petty cash receipt? Who signs a petty cash receipt?

11. Why should you reconcile the bank statement balance of cash and the depositor's book balance of cash?

12. Geac Computer Corporation Limited's consolidated statement of changes in financial position (see Appendix I) describes the changes in cash that occurred during the year ended April 30, 1994. What amount was provided (or used) by investing activities and what amount was provided (or used) by financing activities?

QUICK STUDY (Five-Minute Exercises)

What is the difference between the terms *liquidity* and *cash equivalent?*

**QS 7–1
(LO 1)**

a. What is the main objective of internal control and how is it accomplished?

b. Why should record-keeping for assets be separated from custody over the assets?

**QS 7–2
(LO 2)**

In a good system of internal control for cash that provides adequate procedures for protecting both cash receipts and cash disbursements, three basic guidelines should always be observed. What are these guidelines?

**QS 7–3
(LO 3)**

a. The Petty Cash Fund of the No-Fear Ski Club was established at $50. At the end of the month, the fund contained $4.35 and had the following receipts: film rental $12.50, refreshments for meetings $20.15 (both expenditures to be classified as Entertainment Expenses), postage $4.00, and printing $9.00. Prepare the journal entries to record *(a)* the establishment of the fund; *(b)* the reimbursement at the end of the month.

b. Explain when the Petty Cash account would be credited in a journal entry.

**QS 7–4
(LO 4)**

a. Identify whether each of the following items affects the bank or book side of the reconciliation and indicate if the amount represents an addition or a subtraction.

(1) Bank service charges.

(2) Outstanding cheques.

(3) Debit memos.

(4) Unrecorded deposits.

(5) Interest on average monthly balance.

(6) NSF cheques.

(7) Credit memos.

b. Which of the previous items require a journal entry?

**QS 7–5
(LO 5)**

Which accounting method uses a Discounts Lost account and what is the advantage of this method?

**QS 7–6
(LO 6)**

Refer to Geac Computer financial statements in Appendix I. What was the difference in the number of days' sales collected in 1994 and 1993? According to this ratio analysis, is Geac's collection of receivables improving? Explain your answer.

**QS 7–7
(LO 6)**

Geac

EXERCISES

Exercise 7–1
Analyzing internal
control
(LO 2)

Seinfeld Company is a young business that has grown rapidly. The company's bookkeeper, who was hired two years ago, left town suddenly after the company's manager discovered that a great deal of money had disappeared over the past 18 months. An audit disclosed that the bookkeeper had written and signed several cheques made payable to the bookkeeper's sister, and then recorded the cheques as salaries expense. The sister, who cashed the cheques but had never worked for the company, left town with the bookkeeper. As a result, the company incurred an uninsured loss of $123,000.

Evaluate Seinfeld Company's internal control system and indicate which principles of internal control appear to have been ignored in this situation.

Exercise 7–2
Recommending internal
control procedures
(LO 2, 3)

What internal control procedures would you recommend in each of the following situations?

a.   An antique store has one employee who is given cash and sent to garage sales each weekend. The employee pays cash for merchandise to be resold at the antique store.

b.   Fun in the Sun has one employee who sells sun visors and beach chairs at the beach. Each day, the employee is given enough visors and chairs to last through the day and enough cash to make change. The money is kept in a box at the stand.

Exercise 7–3
Internal control over cash
receipts
(LO 2, 3)

Some of Carver Company's cash receipts from customers are sent to the company in the mail. Carver's bookkeeper opens the letters and deposits the cash received each day. What internal control problem is inherent in this arrangement? What changes would you recommend?

Exercise 7–4
Petty cash fund
(LO 4)

A company established a $400 petty cash fund on March 1. One week later, on March 8, the fund contained $74.50 in cash and receipts for these expenditures: postage, $73.00; transportation-in, $38.00; miscellaneous expenses, $122.00; and store supplies, $92.50.

Prepare the journal entries to (a) establish the fund and (b) reimburse it on March 8. (c) Now assume that the fund was not only reimbursed on March 8 but also increased to $600 because it was exhausted so quickly. Give the entry to reimburse the fund and increase it to $600.

Exercise 7–5
Petty cash fund
(LO 4)

A company established a $300 petty cash fund on May 9. On May 31, the fund had $123.20 in cash and receipts for these expenditures: transportation-in, $24.20; miscellaneous expenses, $66.10; and store supplies, $84.90. The petty cashier could not account for the $1.60 shortage in the fund. Prepare (a) the May 9 entry to establish the fund and (b) the May 31 entry to reimburse the fund and reduce it to $225.

Exercise 7–6
Bank reconciliation
(LO 5)

Cisco Company deposits all receipts intact on the day received and makes all payments by cheque. On April 30, 1996, after all posting was completed, its Cash account showed a $9,540 debit balance. However, Cisco's April 30 bank statement showed only $7,881 on deposit in the bank on that day. Prepare a bank reconciliation for Cisco, using the following information:

a.   Outstanding cheques, $1,440.

b.   Included with the April canceled cheques returned by the bank was a $15 debit memorandum for bank services.

c. Cheque No. 658, returned with the canceled cheques, was correctly drawn for $327 in payment of the utility bill and was paid by the bank on April 22. However, it had been recorded with a debit to Utilities Expense and a credit to Cash as though it were for $372.

d. The April 30 cash receipts, $3,129, were placed in the bank's night depository after banking hours on that date and were unrecorded by the bank at the time the April bank statement was prepared.

Give the journal entries that Cisco Company should make as a result of having prepared the bank reconciliation in the previous exercise.

Exercise 7–7
Adjusting entries resulting from bank reconciliation
(LO 5)

Complete the following bank reconciliation by filling in the missing amounts:

Exercise 7–8
Completion of bank reconciliation
(LO 5)

SAZAR COMPANY
Bank Reconciliation
September 30, 1996

Bank statement balance	$19,260	Book balance of cash	$?
Add:		Add:	
Deposit of September 30	$ 8,575	Collection of note	$15,000
Bank error	?	Interest earned	450
Total	$?	Total	$?
Total	$27,915	Total	$23,640
Deduct:		Deduct:	
Outstanding cheques	?	NSF cheque	$ 550
		Recording error	?
		Service charge	20
		Total	$?
Reconciled balance	$23,010	Reconciled balance	$?

Tiny's Toys had the following transactions during the month of September. Prepare entries to record the transactions assuming Tiny's Toys records invoices *(a)* at gross amounts and *(b)* at net amounts.

Exercise 7–9
Recording invoices at gross or net amounts
(LO 6)

Sept. 3 Received merchandise purchased at a $3,150 invoice price, invoice dated August 31, terms 2/10, n/30.

8 Received a $650 credit memorandum (invoice price) for merchandise received on September 3 and returned for credit.

15 Received merchandise purchased at a $7,000 invoice price, invoice dated September 13, terms 2/10, n/30.

22 Paid for the merchandise received on September 15, less the discount.

29 Paid for the merchandise received on September 3. Payment was delayed because the invoice was mistakenly filed for payment today. This error caused the discount to be lost. The filing error occurred after the credit memorandum received on September 8 was attached to the invoice dated August 31.

Exercise 7–10
Liquidity of accounts
receivable
(LO 6)

Electric Services Company reported net sales for 1995 and 1996 of $345,000 and $520,000. The end-of-year balances of accounts receivable were December 31, 1995, $30,000; and December 31, 1996, $76,000. Calculate the days' sales uncollected at the end of each year and describe any changes in the apparent liquidity of the company's receivables.

PROBLEMS

Problem 7–1
Establishing, reimbursing,
and increasing petty cash
fund
(LO 4)

Serrapede's Trading Company completed the following petty cash transactions during July of the current year:

July   1   Drew a $250 cheque, cashed it, and gave the proceeds and the petty cashbox to Tom Albertson, the petty cashier.

3   Purchased stationery, $37.00.

11   Paid $12.50 postage to express mail a contract to a customer.

14   Paid $11.25 COD charges on merchandise purchased for resale.

17   Paid $29.00 for stamps.

19   Purchased paper for the copy machine, $16.25.

22   Reimbursed Sarah Oliver, the manager of the business, $24.00 for business car usage.

24   Paid $37.50 COD charges on merchandise purchased for resale.

26   Paid City Delivery $12.00 to deliver merchandise sold to a customer.

31   Albertson sorted the petty cash receipts by accounts affected and exchanged them for a cheque to reimburse the fund for expenditures. However, there was only $65.35 in cash in the fund, and he could not account for the shortage. In addition, the size of the petty cash fund was increased to $300.

Required

Preparation component:

1.   Prepare a journal entry to record establishing the petty cash fund.

2.   Prepare a summary of petty cash payments that has these categories: Office supplies, Postage expense, Transportation-in, Auto expense, and Delivery expense. Sort the payments into the appropriate categories and total the expenses in each category.

3.   Prepare the journal entry to record the reimbursement and the increase of the fund.

Analysis component:

4.   Assume that the July 31 transaction reimbursed but did not increase the size of the fund. Also assume that when the payments from petty cash were recorded, the company's bookkeeper made an entry in the following general form:

July	31	xxxxxxxxxxxx (Expense)	xxx	
		xxxxxxxxxxxx (Expense)	xxx	
		xxxxxxxxxxxx (Asset)	xxx	
		Petty Cash		xxx

Explain why this entry is not correct. Also explain the effects of the error on the General Ledger and on the balance sheet.

The Thayer Company has only a General Journal in its accounting system and uses it to record all transactions. However, the company recently set up a petty cash fund to facilitate payments of small items. The following petty cash transactions were noted by the petty cashier as occurring during October (the last month of the company's fiscal year):

Problem 7–2
Petty cash fund; reimbursement and analysis of errors
(LO 4)

Oct. 2 Received a company cheque for $275 to establish the petty cash fund.

16 Received a company cheque to replenish the fund for the following expenditures made since October 2 and to increase the fund to $375.

   a. Payment of $63.50 to *Travis Times* for an advertisement in the newspaper.

   b. Purchased postage stamps for $58.

   c. Purchased office supplies for $70.75.

   d. Payment of $75 for janitorial service.

   e. Discovered that $12.35 remained in the petty cashbox.

31 The petty cashier noted that $182.20 remained in the fund. Having decided that the October 16 increase in the fund was too large, received a company cheque to replenish the fund for the following expenditures made since October 16 but causing the fund to be reduced to $325.

   f. Reimbursement to office manager for business travel, $36.

   g. Purchased office supplies for $57.80.

   h. Paid $52 to Austin Trucking Co. to deliver merchandise sold to a customer.

   i. Payment of $47 COD delivery charges on merchandise purchased for resale.

Required

1. Prepare journal entries to record the establishment of the fund on October 2 and its replenishments on October 16 and on October 31.

2. Explain how the company's financial statements would be affected if the petty cash fund is not replenished and no entry is made on October 31. (Hint: The amount of office supplies that appears on a balance sheet is determined by a physical count of the supplies on hand.)

The following information was available to reconcile Kramer Company's book cash balance with its bank statement balance as of March 31, 1996:

Problem 7–3
Preparation of bank reconciliation and recording adjustments
(LO 5)

a. The March 31 cash balance according to the accounting records was $24,789, and the bank statement balance for that date was $34,686.

b. Cheque No. 573 for $834 and Cheque No. 582 for $300, both written and entered in the accounting records in March, were not among the canceled cheques returned. Two cheques, No. 531 for $1,761 and No. 542 for $285, were outstanding on February 28 when the bank and book statement balances were last reconciled. Cheque No. 531 was returned with the March canceled cheques but Cheque No. 542 was not.

c. When the March cheques were compared with entries in the accounting records, it was found that Cheque No. 567 had been correctly drawn for $1,925 to pay for office supplies but was erroneously entered in the accounting records as though it were drawn for $1,952.

d. Two debit memoranda were included with the returned cheques and were unrecorded at the time of the reconciliation. One of the debit memoranda was for $570 and dealt with an NSF cheque for $555 that had been received from a customer, Barbara White, in payment of her account. It also assessed a $15 fee for processing. The second debit memorandum covered cheque printing and was for $67. These transactions were not recorded by Kramer before receiving the statement.

e. A credit memorandum indicated that the bank had collected a $15,000 note receivable for the company, deducted a $15 collection fee, and credited the balance to the company's account. This transaction was not recorded by Kramer before receiving the statement.

f. The March 31 cash receipts, $5,897, had been placed in the bank's night depository after banking hours on that date and did not appear on the bank statement.

Required

Preparation component:

1. Prepare a bank reconciliation for the company as of March 31.

2. Prepare the general journal entries necessary to bring the company's book balance of cash into conformity with the reconciled balance.

Analysis component:

3. Explain the nature of the messages conveyed by a bank to one of its depositors when the bank sends a debit memo and a credit memo to the depositor.

Problem 7–4
Preparation of bank reconciliation
(LO 5)

Milton Vacon, the controller of the Dartmouth Corporation provided the following information.

Reconciliation of Dartmouth Corporation's bank account as of May 31:

Bank statement balance		$12,304.75	Book balance		$12,568.32
Add:					
Deposit of Apr. 30	2,245.62				
Total		14,550.37			
Deduct:			Deduct:		
Outstanding cheques:			NSF cheque plus service charge		356.75
No. 876	1,185.30		Bank service charges		18.65
No. 882	1,172.15				
Total		$ 2,357.45	Total		375.40
Reconciled balance		$12,192.92	Reconciled balance		$12,192.92

Summary of Dartmouth Corporation's bank statement for the month of June:

Date	Symbol	Withdrawl	Deposit	Balance
May 31	Balance forward			12,304.75
June 2	NBD		2,245.62	14,550.37
June 3	876	1,185.30		13,365.07
June 5	883	2,250.00		11,115.07
June 10	NBD		2,385.70	13,500.77
June 12	884	848.90		12,651.87
June 14	885	1,152.30		11,499.57
June 18	887	1,113.78		10.385.79
June 20	NBD		2,462.95	12,848.74
June 22	889	1,238.95		11,609.79
June 25	886	1,138.40		10,471.39
June 26	882	1,172.15		9,299.24
June 29	891	874.20		8,425.04
June 30	SC	45.70		8,379.34

Summary of June Cheque Register:

Date June	No.	Amount
2	883	$ 2,250.00
5	884	848.90
6	885	1,152.30
8	886	1,138.40
10	887	2,113.78
12	888	1,186.30
15	889	1,238.95
16	890	1,146.40
20	891	974.20
26	892	1,106.70
29	893	1,164.80
Total		$14,320.73

Summary of June Cash Receipts:

Date June	Amount
9	$ 2,385.70
18	2,462.95
29	2,220.85
Total	$ 7,069.50

Book cash balance, June 30:

Book balance, May 31	$12,192.92
Add receipts	7,069.50
Total	19,262.42
Deduct cheques	14,320.73
Book balance, June 30	$ 4,941.69

Required

Prepare a bank reconciliation for Dartmouth Corporation for the month of June.

Mountainview Co. reconciled its bank and book statement balances of cash on October 31 and showed two cheques outstanding at that time, No. 1388 for $1,597 and No. 1393 for $745. The following information was available for the November 30, 1996, reconciliation:

From the November 30 bank statement:

Balance of previous statement on October 31, 1996	27,418.00
5 Deposits and other credits totaling	17,176.00
9 Cheques and other debits totaling	16,342.00
Current balance as of November 30, 1996	28,252.00

Problem 7–5
Preparation of bank reconciliation and recording adjustments
(LO 5)

Chequing Account Transactions

Date	Amount	Transaction Description
Nov. 5	1,698.00 +	Deposit
12	3,426.00 +	Deposit
17	905.00 −	NSF cheque
21	6,297.00 +	Deposit
25	3,618.00 +	Deposit
30	17.00 +	Interest
30	2,120.00 +	Credit memorandum

Date	Cheque No.	Amount	Date	Cheque No.	Amount
Nov. 3	1388	1,597.00	Nov. 22	1404	3,185.00
7	1401*	4,363.00	20	1405	1,442.00
4	1402	1,126.00	28	1407*	329.00
22	1403	614.00	29	1409*	2,781.00

*Indicates a skip in cheque sequence

From Mountainview Co.'s accounting records:

Cash   **Account No. 101**

Date		Explanation	PR	Debit	Credit	Balance
Oct.	31	Balance				25,076.00
Nov.	30	Total receipts	R12	17,474.00		42,550.00
	30	Total disbursements	D23		15,537.00	27,013.00

Cash Receipts Deposited

Date		Cash Debit
Nov.	5	1,698.00
	12	3,426.00
	21	6,297.00
	25	3,618.00
	30	2,435.00
		17,474.00

Cash Disbursements

Cheque No.		Cash Credit
1401		4,363.00
1402		1,126.00
1403		614.00
1404		3,135.00
1405		1,442.00
1406		1,322.00
1407		329.00
1408		425.00
1409		2,781.00
		15,537.00

Cheque No. 1404 was correctly drawn for $3,185 to pay for computer equipment; however, the bookkeeper misread the amount and entered it in the accounting records with a debit to Computer Equipment and a credit to Cash as though it were for $3,135.

The NSF cheque was originally received from a customer, Jerry Skyles, in payment of his account. Its return was not recorded when the bank first notified the company. The credit memorandum resulted from the collection of a $2,150 note for Mountainview by the bank. The bank had deducted a $30 collection fee. The collection has not been recorded.

Required

1. Prepare a November 30 bank reconciliation for the company.

2. Prepare the general journal entries needed to adjust the book balance of cash to the reconciled balance.

The July 31, 1996, credit balance in the Sales account of Cardina Company showed it had sold merchandise for $147,000 during the month. The concern began July with a $280,700 merchandise inventory and ended the month with a $237,000 inventory. It had incurred $34,300 of operating expenses during the month, and it had also recorded the following transactions:

2   Received merchandise purchased at a $6,300 invoice price, invoice dated June 27, terms 2/10, n/30.

5   Received a $1,300 credit memorandum (invoice price) for merchandise received on July 2 and returned for credit.

10 Received merchandise purchased at a $14,000 invoice price, invoice dated July 8, terms 2/10, n/30.

14 Received merchandise purchased at a $7,800 invoice price, invoice dated July 12, terms 2/10, n/30.

17 Paid for the merchandise received on July 10, less the discount.

21 Paid for the merchandise received on July 14, less the discount.

27 Paid for the merchandise received on July 2. Payment was delayed because the invoice was mistakenly filed for payment today. This error caused the discount to be lost. The filing error occurred after the credit memorandum received on July 5 was attached to the invoice dated June 27.

Required

1. Assume that Cardina Company records invoices at gross amounts.
    a. Prepare General Journal entries to record the transactions.
    b. Prepare a July income statement.
2. Assume that Cardina Company records invoices at net amounts.
    a. Prepare General Journal entries to record the transactions.
    b. Prepare a July income statement.

In Problem 7–1, several of the transactions involved payments of cash from a petty cash fund. Nevertheless, the entry to record these payments does not include a credit to Petty Cash. Explain why this is true. Under what circumstances would the entry to record payments from the petty cash fund include a credit to Petty Cash?

The bank statement in Problem 7–5 discloses three places where the canceled cheques returned with the bank statement are not numbered sequentially. In other words, some of the prenumbered cheques in the sequence are missing. There are several possible situations that would explain why the canceled cheques returned with a bank statement might not be numbered sequentially. Describe three situations, each of which is a possible explanation of why the canceled cheques returned with a bank statement are not numbered sequentially.

A concern completed the following petty cash transactions during October of the current year:

Oct. 2 Drew a $125 cheque, cashed it, and turned the proceeds and the petty cashbox over to Norm Bowers, an office clerk who was to act as petty cashier.

5 Paid $9.15 parcel post charges on merchandise sold to a customer and delivered by mail.

8 Purchased office supplies with petty cash, $14.50.

9 Paid $28.35 from petty cash for repairs to an office copier.

Oct. 12 Paid $10 COD delivery charges on merchandise purchased for resale.

15 Paid Mercury Delivery Service $11.25 to deliver merchandise sold to a customer.

21 Gave Dennis Moore, the owner of the business, $20 from petty cash for personal use.

23 Paid $12.55 COD delivery charges on merchandise purchased for resale.

27 Dennis Moore, owner of the business, signed a petty cash receipt and took $12 from petty cash for lunch money.

30 Norm Bowers exchanged his paid petty cash receipts for a cheque reimbursing the fund for expenditures and a shortage of cash in the fund that he could not account for. He reported a cash balance of $2.20 in the fund.

Required

1. Prepare a general journal entry to record the cheque establishing the petty cash fund.

2. Prepare a summary of petty cash payments that has these categories: Office supplies, Transportation-in, Delivery expense, Withdrawals, and Miscellaneous expenses. Sort the payments into the appropriate categories, total the expenses in each category, and prepare the general journal entry to reimburse the fund.

Problem 7–10
Establishing,
reimbursing,
and increasing
petty cash fund
(LO 4)

A business completed these petty cash transactions:

May 4 Drew a $75 cheque to establish a petty cash fund, cashed it, and turned the proceeds and the petty cashbox over to Gayle Bates, an office worker who was appointed petty cashier.

6 Paid $12.55 parcel post charges on merchandise sold to a customer and delivered by mail.

8 Paid $14 to have the office windows washed.

11 Purchased office supplies with petty cash, $25.25.

12 Susan Dixon, owner of the business, signed a petty cash receipt and took $8 from petty cash for coffee money.

14 Paid $13.20 COD delivery charges on merchandise purchased for resale.

15 Gayle Bates noted that only $2 remained in the petty cashbox. Thus, she sorted the petty cash receipts in terms of the accounts affected and exchanged the receipts for a cheque to reimburse the fund. However, since the fund had been exhausted so quickly, the cheque was made sufficiently large to increase the size of the fund to $150.

18 Paid $35 from petty cash for minor repairs to an office machine.

20 Paid $12.75 COD delivery charges on merchandise purchased for resale.

22 Paid A. M. Delivery Service $15.20 to deliver merchandise sold to a customer.

26 Purchased office supplies with petty cash, $18.

27 Susan Dixon, owner of the business, signed a petty cash receipt and took $15 from petty cash for lunch money.

June 1 Paid $16.50 COD delivery charges on merchandise purchased for resale.

5 Purchased paper clips and pencils with petty cash, $10.80.

10 Paid $18.75 COD delivery charges on merchandise purchased for resale.

12 Gayle Bates sorted the petty cash receipts and exchanged them for a cheque to replenish the fund for expenditures and, since there was only $1.50 in cash in the fund, for the unexplained shortage.

Required

1. Prepare a general journal entry to record the cheque establishing the petty cash fund.

2. Prepare a summary of petty cash payments prior to May 15 that has these categories: Delivery expense, Office supplies, Miscellaneous expenses, Withdrawals, and Transportation-in. Sort the payments into the appropriate categories and total each category. Prepare a similar summary of petty cash payments after May 15.

3. Prepare entries to reimburse the fund and increase its size on May 15 and to reimburse the fund on June 12.

The accounting system used by the Franklin Company requires that all entries be journalized in a General Journal. To facilitate payments of small items, Franklin Company recently established a petty cash fund. The following transactions involving the petty cash fund occurred during August (the last month of the company's fiscal year):

Problem 7–11
Petty cash fund;
reimbursement and
analysis of errors
(LO 4)

Aug. 3 A company cheque for $200 was drawn and made payable to the petty cashier to establish the petty cash fund.

    14 A company cheque was drawn to replenish the fund for the following expenditures made since August 1 and to increase the fund to $300:

      a. Purchased postage stamps for $44.

      b. Payment of $42.30 to Meeks Trucking for delivery of merchandise to customers.

      c. Gave Beth Rogers, owner of the business, $50 for personal use.

      d. Paid $60.50 to Appliance Company for repairs of office equipment.

      e. Discovered that only $1.20 remained in the petty cashbox.

    31 The petty cashier noted that $2.60 remained in the fund. Having decided that the August 14 increase in the fund was not large enough, a company cheque was drawn to replenish the fund for the following expenditures made since August 14 and to increase it to $350:

      a. Payment of $97.25 for office supplies to support the company's computer.

      b. Payment of $52.15 for items classified as miscellaneous general expense.

      c. Payment of $63 for janitorial service.

      d. Payment of $85 to Southern Advertising Company for a space advertisement in a weekly newsletter.

Required

1. Prepare general journal entries to record the establishment of the fund on August 3 and its replenishments on August 14 and on August 31.

2. If Franklin Company had failed to replenish the petty cash fund on August 31, what would have been the effect on net income for the fiscal year ended August 31 and on total assets on August 31? Explain your answer. (Hint: The amount of Office Supplies to appear on a balance sheet is determined by a physical count of the supplies on hand.)

The following information was available to reconcile Golf Company's book balance of cash with its bank statement balance as of February 28:

Problem 7–12
Preparation of bank
reconciliation and
recording adjustments
(LO 5)

a. After all posting was completed on February 28, the company's Cash account had a $7,180 debit balance, but its bank statement showed a $9,415 balance.

b.   Cheques No. 217 for $353 and No. 222 for $709 were outstanding on the January 31 bank reconciliation. Cheque No. 222 was returned with the February canceled cheques, but Cheque No. 217 was not.

c.   In comparing the canceled cheques returned with the bank statement with the entries in the accounting records, it was found that Cheque No. 297 for the purchase of office equipment was correctly drawn for $724 but was entered in the accounting records as though it were for $742. It was also found that Cheque No. 331 for $482 and Cheque No. 333 for $240, both drawn in February, were not among the canceled cheques returned with the statement.

d.   A credit memorandum enclosed with the bank statement indicated that the bank had collected a $3,600 noninterest-bearing note for the concern, deducted a $24 collection fee, and had credited the remainder to the concern's account.

e.   A debit memorandum for $464 listed a $452 NSF cheque plus a $12 NSF charge. The cheque had been received from a customer, Jan Bellors, and was among the canceled cheques returned.

f.   Also among the canceled cheques was an $18 debit memorandum for bank services. None of the memoranda had been recorded.

g.   The February 28 cash receipts, $1,952, were placed in the bank's night depository after banking hours on that date, and their amount did not appear on the bank statement.

Required

1. Prepare a bank reconciliation for the company.
2. Prepare entries in general journal form to bring the company's book balance of cash into conformity with the reconciled balance.

Problem 7–13
Preparation of bank reconciliation
(LO 5)

Cindy Estelle, the controller of the Burnaby Corporation provided the following information.

Reconciliation of Burnaby Corporation's bank account as of October 31:

Bank statement balance	$ 9,843.80	Book balance	$10,054.69
Add:			
Deposit of Oct. 30	1,796.50		
Total	11,640.30		
Deduct:		Deduct:	
Outstanding cheques:		NSF cheque plus service	
No. 537	948.24	charge	285.40
No. 542	937.72	Bank service charges	14.95
Total	$ 1,885.96	Total	300.35
Reconciled balance	$ 9,754.34	Reconciled balance	$ 9,754.34

Summary of Burnaby Corporation's bank statement for the month of November:

Date	Symbol	Withdrawl	Deposit	Balance
Oct 31	Balance forward			9,843.80
Nov 2	NBD		1,796.50	11,640.30
Nov 3	536	948.24		10,692.06
Nov 5	543	1,800.00		8,892.06
Nov 10	NBD		1,908.56	10,800.62
Nov 12	544	679.12		10,121.50
Nov 14	545	921.84		9,199.66
Nov 18	547	891.02		8,308.64
Nov 20	NBD		1,970.36	10,279.00
Nov 22	549	991.16		9,287.84
Nov 25	546	910.72		8,377.12
Nov 26	542	937.72		7,439.40
Nov 29	551	699.36		6,740.04
Nov 30	SC	36.50		6,703.54

Summary of June Cheque Register:

Date	No.	Amount
Nov		
2	543	$ 1,800.00
5	544	679.12
6	545	921.84
8	546	910.72
10	547	891.02
12	548	949.04
15	549	991.16
16	550	917.12
20	551	699.36
26	552	885.36
29	553	931.84
Total		$10,576.58

Summary of June Cash Receipts:

Date	Amount
Nov	
9	$ 1,908.56
18	1,970.36
29	1,776.58
Total	5,655.50

Book cash balance, June 30:

Book balance, May 31	$ 9,754.34
Add receipts	5,655.50
Total	15,409.84
Deduct cheques	10,576.58
Book balance, June 30	$ 4,833.26

Required

Prepare a bank reconciliation for Burnaby Corporation for the month of November.

PROVOCATIVE PROBLEMS

The Commerce Company has enjoyed rapid growth since it was created several years ago. Last year, for example, its sales exceeded $4 million. However, its purchasing procedures have not kept pace with its growth. A plant supervisor or department head who needs raw materials, plant assets, or supplies telephones a request to the purchasing department manager. The purchasing department manager then prepares a purchase order in duplicate, sends one copy to the company selling the goods, and keeps the other copy in the files. When the seller's invoice is received, it is sent directly to the purchasing department. When the goods

Provocative Problem 7–1
Analytical Essay
(LO 2, 3)

arrive, receiving department personnel count and inspect the items and prepare only one copy of a receiving report, which is then sent to the purchasing department. The purchasing department manager attaches the receiving report and the file copy of the purchase order to the invoice. If all is in order, the invoice is stamped *approved for payment* and signed by the purchasing department manager. The invoice and its supporting documents then are sent to the accounting department to be recorded and filed until due. On its due date, the invoice and its supporting documents are sent to the office of the company treasurer, and a cheque is prepared and mailed. The number of the cheque is entered on the invoice and the invoice is sent to the accounting department for an entry to record its payment.

Do the procedures of Commerce make it fairly easy for someone in the company to initiate the payment of fictitious invoices by the company? If so, who is most likely to commit the fraud and what would that person have to do to receive payment of a fictitious invoice? What changes should be made in the company's purchasing procedures, and why should each change be made?

Provocative Problem 7–2
Business communications case
(LO 5)

On March 26, Summerfield Office Supply received Miles Brokaw's cheque number 629, dated March 24, in the amount of $1,420. The cheque was to pay for merchandise Brokaw had purchased on February 25. The merchandise was shipped from Summerfield's office at 1715 Westgate Boulevard, Toronto, Ontario M5H 1A2 to Brokaw's home at 823 Congress, Mississauga, Ontario L5H 1K4. On March 27, Summerfield's cashier deposited the cheque in the company's bank account. The bank returned the cheque to Summerfield with the March 31 bank statement. Also included was a debit memorandum indicating that Brokaw's cheque was returned for nonsufficient funds and the bank was charging Summerfield a $25 NSF processing fee. Immediately after reconciling the bank statement on April 2, Marla Decker, Summerfield's accountant, asks you to write a letter for her signature using the company's letterhead stationery. Your letter to Brokaw should explain the amount owed and request prompt payment.

Provocative Problem 7–3
Financial statement analysis case
(LO 1, 6)

For this problem, turn to the financial statements of Geac Computer Corporation Limited, in Appendix I. Use the information presented in the financial statements to answer these questions:

1. For both 1994 and 1993, determine the total amount of cash and short-term investments that Geac held at the end of the year. Determine the percentage that this amount represents of total current assets, total current liabilities, total shareholders' equity, and total assets.

2. For 1994, use the information in the statement of changes in financial position to determine the percentage change between the beginning of the year and end of the year holding of cash and cash equivalents.

3. What was the number of days' sales uncollected at the end of the 1994 fiscal year and at the end of the 1993 fiscal year?

Provocative Problem 7–4
Ethical issue essay

Review the As a Matter of Ethics case on page 365. Discuss the nature of the problem faced by Nancy Tucker and evaluate the alternative courses of action she should consider.

ANALYTICAL AND REVIEW PROBLEMS

The bank statement for October arrived in Friday's mail. You were especially anxious to receive the statement as one of your assignments was to prepare a bank reconciliation for the Saturday meeting. You got around to preparing the reconciliation rather late in the afternoon and found all the necessary data with the exception of the bank balance. The bottom portion of the bank statement was smudged, and several figures, including the balance, were obliterated. A telephone call to the bank was answered by a recording with the information that the bank was closed until 10 A.M. Monday. Since the reconcilation had to be prepared, you decided to plug in the bank balance.

A & R Problem 7–1

In preparation, you assembled the necessary material as follows:

a. Cash balance per books was $6,800.

b. From the canceled cheques returned by the bank you determined that six cheques remained outstanding. The total of these cheques was $2,700.

c. In checking the canceled cheques you noted that Cheque No. 274 was properly made for $418 but was recorded in the cash disbursement journal as $481. The cheque was in payment of an account.

d. Included with the bank statement were two memoranda; the credit memorandum was for collection of a note for $1,200 and $90 of interest thereon and the debit memorandum was for $12 of bank charges.

e. While you were sorting the canceled cheques, one of the cheques caught your attention. You were astounded by the similarity of name with that of your company and the similarity of the cheques. The cheque was for $620 and was obviously in error charged to your company's account.

f. From the deposit book you determined that a $2,500 deposit was made after hours on October 31.

Required

1. Prepare a bank reconciliation statement as of October 31 (plug in the indicated bank balance).

2. Prepare the necessary journal entries.

A & R Problem 7–2   Your assistant prepared the following bank reconciliation statement. Obviously the statement is unacceptable and the task of preparing a proper reconciliation falls upon you.

BRANDON COMPANY
Bank Reconciliation
May 31, 1996

Balance per books May 31		$ 8,000
Add:		
Note collected	$1,000	
Interest on note	110	
Deposit in transit	2,455	3,565
		11,565
Deduct:		
Bank charges	10	
NSF cheque	400	
Outstanding cheques	1,800	
Error in Cheque No. 78 issued for $872 and recorded		
in the books as $827	45	2,255
Indicated bank balance		9,310
Balance per bank statement		8,000
Discrepancy		$ 1,310

Required

1.   Prepare a proper bank reconciliation showing the true cash balance.

2.   Prepare the necessary journal entries.

A & R Problem 7–3   Wanda White acquired a sports equipment distribution business with a staff of six salespersons and two clerks. Because of the trust that Wanda had in her employees—after all, they were all her friends and just like members of the family—she believed that an honour system in regard to the operation of the petty cash fund was adequate. Consequently, Wanda placed $300 in a coffee jar, which, for convenience, was kept in a cupboard in the common room. All employees had access to the petty cash fund and withdrew amounts as required. No vouchers were required for withdrawals. As required, additional funds were placed in the coffee jar and the amount of the replenishment was charged to "miscellaneous selling expense."

Required

1.   From the internal control point of view, discuss the weaknesses of the petty cash fund operation and suggest steps necessary for improvement.

2.   Does the petty cash fund operation as described above violate any of the generally accepted accounting principles? If yes, which and how is the principle(s) violated?

CONCEPT TESTER

Test your understanding of the concepts introduced in this chapter by completing the following crossword puzzle.

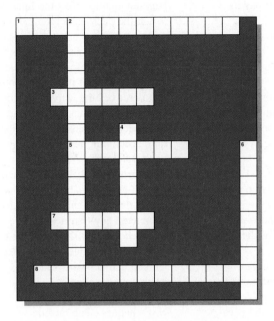

Across Clues

1. A business paper that tells a vendor to ship ordered merchandise at the stated terms (2 words).
3. The seller of goods or services.
5. A statement showing the items sold, price, and terms given by a vendor to a customer.
7. The buyer or purchaser of goods or services.
8. An expense resulting from failing to take a cash discount on purchases (2 words).

Down Clues

2. Investments convertible to a known amount of cash, without undue risk (2 words).
4. Business paper used to accumulate information needed to control disbursements of cash.
6. Asset characteristic; refers to how quickly the asset can be used to pay for other assets.

ANSWERS TO PROGRESS CHECKS

7–1 A company needs to own liquid assets to be able to acquire other assets, buy services, and pay its obligations.

7–2 A company owns cash equivalents because they earn more income than cash does.

7–3 *d*

7–4 *c*

7–5 Computers reduce processing errors, allow more extensive testing of records, tend to limit the amount of hard evidence of processing steps that is available, and highlight the importance of maintaining a separation of duties.

7–6 *a*

7–7 Not necessarily. A voucher system should be used when the manager can no longer control the purchasing procedures through personal supervision and direct participation in the activities of the business.

7–8 If all cash payments were made by cheque, numerous cheques for small amounts would be written. Because this practice would be expensive and often would take too long, a petty cash fund is established to avoid writing cheques for small amounts.

7–9 If the petty cash fund is not reimbursed at the end of an accounting period, the transactions for which petty cash expenditures were made are unrecorded in the accounts and the asset petty cash is overstated. However, these amounts are seldom large enough to affect the financial statements.

7–10 When the petty cash fund is reimbursed, the petty cash transactions are recorded in the accounts. The reimbursement also allows the fund to continue being used for its intended purpose.

7–11 A bank statement is a report prepared by the bank that describes the activity in a depositor's account.

7–12 To reconcile a bank balance means to explain the difference between the cash balance in the depositor's accounting records and the balance on the bank statement.

7–13 The purpose of the bank reconciliation is to determine if any errors have been made by the bank or by the depositor and to determine if the bank has completed any transactions affecting the depositor's account that the depositor has not recorded.

7–14 Outstanding cheques—subtracted
Unrecorded deposits—added

7–15 Bank services charges—subtracted
Debit memos—subtracted
NSF cheques—subtracted
Interest earned—added
Credit memos—added

7–16 *a*

7–17 The calculation is based on net sales because the amount of credit sales normally is not known by statement readers.

Companies rarely operate in today's economy without extending credit to customers. By being careful in granting credit, a business can increase sales without incurring high costs. Accounting information helps managers assess the risk and the success of their credit decisions.

Temporary Investments and Receivables

Karen White and Mark Smith have been asked to look at Imperial Oil Limited's (Esso) financial statements and, in particular, their amounts of temporary investments and receivables. Information from the company's balance sheet follows:

IMPERIAL OIL LIMITED
(in millions)
December 31, 1994

	Current Assets	
Marketable securities at cost		$ 859
Accounts Receivable		1,045
Total Current Assets		$2,797

Esso's marketable securities and accounts receivable represent 68% of the firm's total current assets. Sound financial management of these assets is vital to ensure future liquidity and growth potential. Accounting for these highly liquid assets provides important information to help managers assess the risk and success of their decisions regarding these assets. Economic conditions causing many businesses and consumers to take longer to pay their bills and an increasing amount of defaults due to bankruptcies have made receivables management a top priority today.

LEARNING OBJECTIVES

After studying Chapter 8, you should be able to:

1. **Prepare journal entries to account for temporary investments and explain how lower of cost or market is reported on such investments.**
2. **Prepare entries to account for credit card and debit card sales.**
3. **Prepare entries to account for transactions with credit customers, including accounting for bad debts under the allowance method and the direct write-off method.**
4. **Calculate the interest on promissory notes and prepare entries to record the receipt of promissory notes and their payment or dishonour.**
5. **Explain how receivables can be converted into cash before they are due and calculate accounts receivable turnover.**
6. **Define or explain the words and phrases listed in the chapter glossary.**

The focus of the prior chapter was on accounting for cash, the most liquid of all assets. This chapter continues the discussion of liquid assets by focusing on temporary, or short-term, investments, accounts receivable, and short-term notes receivable. You will learn about current business trends relating to receivables and about accounting regulations for temporary investments. You will then be better able to understand and use the financial statement information related to these current assets.

Because companies use cash to acquire assets and to pay expenses and obligations, good managers plan to maintain a cash balance large enough to meet expected payments plus some surplus for unexpected needs. Also, idle cash balances may exist during some months of each year because of seasonal fluctuations in sales volume. Rather than leave these idle cash balances in chequing accounts that pay little or no interest, most companies invest them in securities that earn higher returns.

TEMPORARY INVESTMENTS

LO 1

Prepare journal entries to account for temporary investments and explain how lower of cost or market is reported on such investments.

Recall from Chapter 7 that cash equivalents are investments that can be easily converted into a known amount of cash; generally, they mature within a relatively short time period. Some investments of idle cash balances do not meet the criteria of cash equivalents but, nevertheless, are classified as current assets. Although these **temporary investments,** or **short-term investments,** do not qualify as cash equivalents, they serve a similar purpose. Like cash equivalents, temporary investments can be converted into cash easily and are an available source of cash to satisfy the needs of current operations. Management usually expects to convert them into cash within one year or the current operating cycle of the business, whichever is longer.[1]

Temporary investments may be made in the form of government or corporate debt obligations (called *debt securities*) or in the form of shares (called *equity securities*). Some investments in debt securities mature within one year or the current operating cycle of the business and will be held until they mature. Other securities that do not mature in the short term can be classified as current assets only if they

---

[1]*CICA Handbook,* section 1510, "Current Assets and Current Liabilities," par. .01.

are marketable. In other words, the reporting company must be able to sell them without excessive delays.

In the notes to their financial statements, companies usually give their definition of cash equivalents and short-term investments. **Corel Corporation,** for example, includes this note:

> Short-term investments are stated at the lower of cost or market. Short-term investments of $52,114,000 and $68,629,000 at November 30, 1992 and 1993, respectively, included with cash consisted principally of government securities, commercial paper, bankers' acceptances, letter loan agreements, term deposit certificates and bearer deposit notes. The carrying amount approximates fair value because of the short maturity of those instruments.

When temporary investments are purchased, you should record them at cost. For example, assume that on January 10 Alpha Company purchased Ford Motor Company's short-term notes payable for $40,000. Alpha's entry to record the transaction is:

Jan.	10	Temporary Investments	40,000.00	
		Cash		40,000.00
		Bought $40,000 of Ford Motor Company notes due		
		May 10.		

Assume that these notes mature on May 10 and that the cash proceeds are $40,000 plus $1,200 interest. When the receipt is recorded, this entry credits the interest to a revenue account:

May	10	Cash	41,200.00	
		Temporary Investments		40,000.00
		Interest Earned		1,200.00
		Received cash proceeds from matured notes.		

To determine the cost of an investment, you must include any commissions paid. For example, assume that on June 2, 1996, Bailey Company purchased 1,000 shares of Northern Telecom common stock as a temporary investment. The purchase price was 30⅛ ($30.125 per share) plus a $625 broker's commission. The entry to record the transaction is:[2]

June	2	Temporary Investments	30,750.00	
		Cash		30,750.00
		Bought 1,000 shares of Nortel stock at 30⅛ plus $625		
		broker's commission.		

---

[2]Share prices are quoted on stock exchanges on the basis of dollars and ⅛ dollars per share. For example, a stock quoted at 23⅛ sold for $23.125 per share and one quoted at 36½ sold for $36.50 per share.

Notice that the commission is not recorded in a separate account.

When cash dividends are received on shares held as an investment, they are credited to a revenue account, as follows:

Dec.	12	Cash	1,000.00	
		Dividends Earned		1,000.00
		Received dividend of $1 per share on 1,000 shares of Nortel stock.		

When a company sells a temporary investment, it records the difference between its cost and the cash proceeds from the sale as a gain or loss. For example, assume that on December 20, 1996, Bailey Company sells 500 shares of Nortel for 28¼ per share less a $120 commission. Bailey receives cash proceeds from the sale of $14,005, or [(500 × $28.25) − $120]. Bailey's cost of the sold shares is $15,375, or one half of the $30,750 original cost of the 1,000 shares. The following entry records the sale:

Dec.	20	Cash	14,005.00	
		Loss on Sale of Temporary Investments	1,370.00	
		Temporary Investments		15,375.00
		Sold 500 Nortel shares at 28¼ less $120 broker's commission.		

Reporting Temporary Investments in the Financial Statements

Temporary investments in marketable securities should be reported on the balance sheet at the **lower of cost or market (LCM)**. To calculate the lower of cost or market, the *total* cost of all marketable securities held as temporary investments (called the *portfolio*) is compared with the *total* market value of the portfolio. Comparison on an item-by-item basis is normally not done.

For example, assume that Bailey Company did not have any temporary investments prior to its purchase of the Nortel shares on June 2, 1996. Later during 1996, Bailey Company purchased two other temporary investments in marketable securities. On December 31, 1996, the lower of cost or market is determined by comparing the total cost and total market value of the entire portfolio, as follows:

Temporary Investments	Cost	Market	LCM
Alcan Aluminium common shares	$42,600	$43,500	
Imperial Oil common shares	30,500	28,200	
Northern Telecom common shares	15,375	14,500	
Total	$88,475	$86,200	$86,200

The difference between the $88,475 cost and the $86,200 market value amounts to a $2,275 loss of market value.

Since all of the temporary investments were purchased during 1996, this $2,275 market value decline occurred entirely during 1996. The following adjusting entry on December 31, 1996, records the loss:

1996					
Dec.	31	Loss on Market Decline of Temporary Investments ...	2,275.00		
		Allowance to Reduce Temporary Investments			
		to Market.			2,275.00
		To record the decline in value of the investments			
		below their original cost.			

The Loss on Market Decline of Temporary Investments account is closed to Income Summary and is reported on the income statement. The Allowance to Reduce Temporary Investments to Market account is a contra asset account. Its balance is subtracted from the total cost of the temporary investments so that on the balance sheet they are reported at the lower of cost or market. For example, the Bailey Company would report its temporary investments as follows:

Current assets:
   Cash and cash equivalents .... $xx,xxx
   Temporary investments, at lower of
      cost or market (cost is $88,475)   86,200

In this example, notice that the $2,275 loss recorded during 1996 is equal to the December 31, 1996, balance in the allowance account. This occurs because we have assumed that no investments were owned prior to 1996. Therefore, the allowance account had a zero balance on December 31, 1995.

If an additional loss occurs in a future year, the allowance account balance after recording that loss probably will not equal the amount of that loss. To see why this is true, assume that on December 31, 1997, the total cost of Bailey Company's temporary investments portfolio is $108,475 and the total market value is $104,700 (assume additions to the investment portfolio during 1997). In other words, market value is $3,775 less than cost. Because the allowance account already has a credit balance of $2,275 as a result of the adjusting entry made on December 31, 1996, the adjusting entry to record the 1997 loss is:

1997					
Dec.	31	Loss on Market Decline of Temporary Investments ...	1,500.00		
		Allowance to Reduce Temporary Investments			
		to Market.			1,500.00
		To record the market decline during 1997.			

Thus, the loss recorded in 1997 is $1,500 and the December 31, 1997, balance in the allowance account is $3,775.

Because temporary investments in marketable equity securities must be reported at the *lower* of cost or market, market value increases above cost are not recorded as gains until the investments are sold. However, if a portfolio of temporary investments has been written down to a market value below cost, later increases in market value up to the original cost are reported on the income statement.[3]

For example, assume that on December 31, 1998, the market value of Bailey Company's temporary investments is $500 less than cost. Since the allowance account had a credit balance of $3,775 at the end of 1997, the December 31, 1998, adjusting entry is:

1998					
Dec.	31	Allowance to Reduce Temporary Investments to Market . .		3,275.00	
		Recovery of Market Value Decline, Temporary			
		Investments			3,275.00
		To adjust the allowance account from $3,775 to $500.			

Notice that the only entries that change the allowance (contra asset) account balance are the end-of-period adjusting entries. The entries to record purchases and sales of investments during a period do not affect the allowance account.

If cost and market are about the same, a company can just report the investments at cost. For example, the 1994 balance sheet for Moore Corporation Limited shows this information:

Current assets:
  Short-term securities, at cost which
    approximates market value $246,481,000

Some people criticize the lower of cost or market method because it is a departure from the *cost principle.* In recent years, however, an increasing number of people have criticized LCM because it does not record all changes in value, including increases above the original cost. In fact, the CICA's Accounting Standards Board is developing a new Handbook section for financial instruments which recommends that temporary investments be reported at market value, whether higher or lower than cost. However, it is not expected that the Canadian standards will change before 1997. Until then we will continue to use LCM.

Progress Check

(Answers to Progress Checks are provided at the end of the chapter.)

8-1   How are temporary investments reported on the balance sheet—at cost or market values?

---

[3]Canadian GAAP is unclear about reversing previous losses when the allowance method is used. General practice appears to accept these recoveries on the basis that they reverse previous increases to the allowance account. Generally, if the direct method is used, any recoveries would not be included.

8-2   Normally, how often would an adjusting entry to record LCM be entered?

8-3   What happens when a previously written-down portfolio increases?

In addition to cash, cash equivalents, and temporary investments, the liquid assets of a business include receivables that result from credit sales to customers. In the following sections, we discuss the procedures to account for sales when customers use credit cards issued by banks or credit card companies. Then, we focus on accounting for credit sales when a business grants credit directly to its customers. This situation requires the company (1) to maintain a separate account receivable for each customer and (2) to account for bad debts that result from credit sales. In addition, we discuss how to account for notes receivable, many of which arise from extending credit to customers.

CREDIT SALES AND RECEIVABLES

Many customers use credit cards such as Visa, MasterCard, or American Express to charge purchases from various businesses. Other retail businesses such as **Eaton's** or **The Bay** issue their own in-house charge cards. This practice gives the customers the ability to make purchases without carrying cash or writing cheques. It also allows them to defer their payments to the credit card company. Further, once credit is established with the credit card company, the customer does not have to open an account with each store. Finally, customers who use credit cards can make single monthly payments instead of several to different creditors.

Another method of paying for purchases is through the use of a **debit card**. A debit card, such as Interac, is similar to a credit card but the customer enters an authorization code at the point of sale and the amount of the purchase is electronically transferred by the bank from the customer's bank account to the merchant's bank account. Accounting for these transactions is similar to the accounting for credit card sales which is illustrated below.

There are good reasons why businesses allow customers to use credit cards instead of maintaining their own accounts receivable. First, the business does not have to evaluate the credit standing of each customer or make decisions about who should get credit and how much. Second, the business avoids the risk of extending credit to customers who cannot or do not pay. Instead, this risk is faced by the credit card company. Third, the business typically receives cash from the credit card company sooner than it would if it granted credit directly to its customers. Fourth, a variety of credit options for customers offers a potential increase in sales volume.

In dealing with some credit cards, usually those issued by banks such as Visa or MasterCard, the business deposits a copy of each credit card sales receipt in its bank account just like it deposits a customer's cheque. Thus, the business receives a credit to its chequing account without delay. Other credit cards, such as American Express, require the business to send a copy of each receipt to the credit card company. Until payment is received, the business has an account receivable from the credit card company. In return for the services provided by the credit card company, a business pays a fee ranging from 2% to 5% of credit card sales. This charge is deducted from the credit to the chequing account or the cash payment to the business.

CREDIT CARD SALES

LO 2
Prepare entries to account for credit card sales.

The procedures used in accounting for credit card sales depend on whether cash is received immediately on deposit or is delayed until paid by the credit card company. If cash is received immediately, as would be the case for a debit card payment, the entry to record $100 of credit or debit card sales with a 4% fee is:

Jan.	25	Cash	96.00	
		Credit Card Expense	4.00	
		Sales		100.00
		To record credit/debit card sales less a 4% credit card expense.		

If the business must send the receipts to the credit card company and wait for payment, this entry on the date of the sales records them:

Jan.	25	Accounts Receivable, Credit Card Company	100.00	
		Sales		100.00
		To record credit card sales.		

When cash is received from the credit card company, the entry to record the receipt and the deduction of the fee is:

Feb.	10	Cash	96.00	
		Credit Card Expense	4.00	
		Accounts Receivable—Credit Card Co		100.00
		To record cash receipt less 4% credit card expense.		

In the last two entries, notice that the credit card expense was not recorded until cash was received from the credit card company. This practice is merely a matter of convenience. By following this procedure, the business avoids having to calculate and record the credit card expense each time sales are recorded. Instead, the expense related to many sales can be calculated once and recorded when cash is received. However, the *matching principle* requires reporting credit card expense in the same period as the sale. Therefore, if the sale and the cash receipt occur in different periods, you must accrue and report the credit card expense in the period of the sale by using an adjusting entry at the end of the year. For example, this year-end adjustment accrues $24 of credit card expense on a $600 receivable that the Credit Card Company has not yet paid.

Dec.	31	Credit Card Expense	24.00	
		Accounts Receivable—Credit Card Company		24.00
		To accrue credit card expense that is unrecorded at the end of the year.		

Then, the following entry records the cash collection in January:

Jan.	5	Cash	576.00	
		Accounts Receivable—Credit Card Company		576.00
		To record collection of the amount due from Credit Card Company.		

Some firms report credit card expense in the income statement as a type of discount that is deducted from sales to get net sales. Other companies classify it as a selling expense or even as an administrative expense. Arguments can be made for all three alternatives but there is little practical difference in the result.

Progress Check

8-4 **In recording credit card sales, when do you debit Accounts Receivable and when do you debit Cash?**

8-5 **When are credit card expenses recorded in situations where sales receipts must be accumulated before they can be sent to the credit card company? When are these expenses incurred?**

8-6 **If payment for a credit card sale has not been received by the end of the accounting period, how do you account for the credit card expense associated with that sale?**

In previous chapters, we recorded credit sales by debiting a single Accounts Receivable account. However, a business with more than one credit customer must design its accounting system to show how much each customer has purchased, how much each customer has paid, and how much remains to be collected from each customer. This information provides the basis for sending bills to the customers. To have this information on hand, businesses that extend credit directly to their customers must maintain a separate account receivable for each of them.

One possible way of keeping a separate account for each customer would be to include all of these accounts in the same ledger that contains the financial statement accounts. However, this approach usually is not used because there are too many customers. Recall from Chapter 6 that the **General Ledger,** which is the ledger that contains the financial statement accounts, has only a single Accounts Receivable account. A supplementary record is established in which a separate account is maintained for each customer. This supplementary record is the **Accounts Receivable Ledger.**

Illustration 8–1 shows the relationship between the Accounts Receivable account in the General Ledger and the individual customer accounts in the Accounts Receivable Ledger. In Part A of Illustration 8–1, notice that the $3,000 sum of the two balances in the Accounts Receivable Ledger is equal to the balance of the Accounts Receivable account in the General Ledger as of February 1. To maintain this relationship, each time that credit sales are posted with a debit to the Accounts Receivable account in the General Ledger, they are also posted with debits to the appropriate

MAINTAINING A SEPARATE ACCOUNT FOR EACH CREDIT CUSTOMER

LO 3
Prepare entries to account for transactions with credit customers, including accounting for bad debts under the allowance method and the direct write-off method.

Illustration 8-1   The Accounts Receivable Account and the Accounts Receivable Ledger

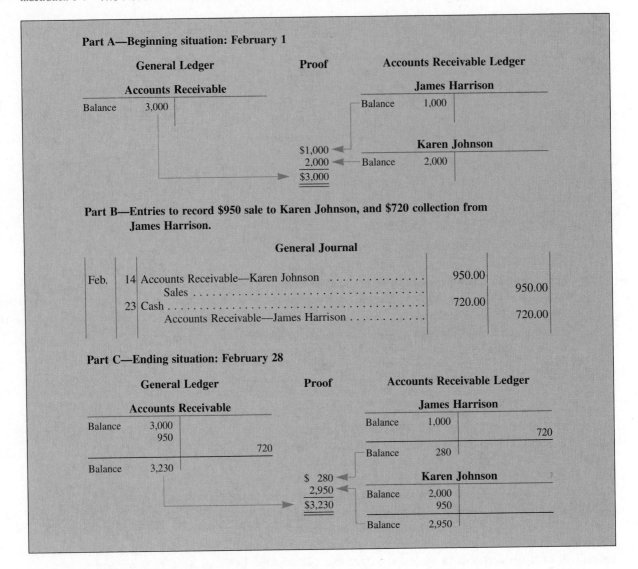

customer accounts in the Accounts Receivable Ledger. Also, cash receipts from credit customers must be posted with credits to both the Accounts Receivable account in the General Ledger and to the appropriate customer accounts.

Part B shows the general journal entry to record a credit sale on February 14 to customer Karen Johnson. It also shows the entry to record the collection of $720 from James Harrison.

Part C presents the General Ledger account and the Accounts Receivable Ledger as of February 28. Notice how the General Ledger account shows the effects of the sales and the collection, and that it has a $3,230 balance. The same events are reflected in the accounts for the two customers: Harrison now has a balance of only $280, and Johnson owes $2,950. The $3,230 sum of their accounts equals the debit balance of the General Ledger account.

Note that posting debits or credits to Accounts Receivable twice does not violate the requirement that debits equal credits. The equality of debits and credits is maintained *in the General Ledger*. The Accounts Receivable Ledger is simply a supplementary record that provides detailed information concerning each customer.

Because the balance in the Accounts Receivable account is always equal to the sum of the balances in the customers' accounts, the Accounts Receivable account is said to control the Accounts Receivable Ledger and is an example of a **controlling account.** And, the Accounts Receivable Ledger is an example of a supplementary record that is controlled by an account in the General Ledger; this kind of supplementary record is called a **subsidiary ledger.**

The Accounts Receivable account and the Accounts Receivable Ledger are not the only examples of controlling accounts and subsidiary ledgers. Most companies buy on credit from several suppliers and must use a controlling account and subsidiary ledger for accounts payable. Another example might be an Office Equipment account that would control a subsidiary ledger in which the cost of each item of equipment is recorded in a separate account.

BAD DEBTS

When a company grants credit to its customers, there usually are a few who do not pay what they promised. The accounts of such customers are called **bad debts.** These bad debt amounts that cannot be collected are an expense of selling on credit.

You might ask why merchants sell on credit if it is likely that some of the accounts prove to be uncollectible. The answer is that they believe granting credit will increase revenues and profits. They are willing to incur bad debt losses if the net effect is to increase sales and profits. Therefore, bad debt losses are an expense of selling on credit that is incurred to increase sales.

The reporting of bad debts expense on the income statement is governed by the *matching principle*. This principle requires that the expenses from bad debts be reported in the same accounting period as the revenues they helped produce.

MATCHING BAD DEBT EXPENSES WITH SALES

Managers realize that some portion of credit sales result in bad debts. However, the fact that a specific credit sale will not be collected does not become apparent until later. If a customer fails to pay within the credit period, most businesses send out several repeat billings and make other efforts to collect. Usually, they do not accept the fact that the customer is not going to pay until every reasonable means of collection has been exhausted. In many cases, this point may not be reached until one or more accounting periods after the period in which the sale was made. Thus, matching this expense with the revenue it produced requires the company to estimate its unknown amount at the end of the year. The **allowance method of accounting for bad debts** accomplishes this matching of bad debts expense with revenues.

ALLOWANCE METHOD OF ACCOUNTING FOR BAD DEBTS

At the end of each accounting period, the allowance method of accounting for bad debts requires estimating the total bad debts expected to result from the period's sales. An allowance is then provided for the loss. This method has two advantages: (1) the expense is charged to the period in which the revenue is recognized; and (2) the accounts receivable are reported on the balance sheet at the estimated amount of cash to be collected.

Recording the Estimated Bad Debts Expense

Under the allowance method of accounting for bad debts, you calculate the estimated bad debts expense at the end of each accounting period. Then, you record it with an adjusting entry. For example, assume that Fritz Company had credit sales of $300,000 during the first year of its operations. At the end of the year, $20,000 remains uncollected. Based on the experience of similar businesses, Fritz Company estimates that $1,500 of accounts receivable will be uncollectible. This estimated expense is recorded with the following adjusting entry:

Dec.	31	Bad Debts Expense	1,500.00	
		Allowance for Doubtful Accounts		1,500.00
		To record the estimated bad debts.		

The debit in this entry causes the expense to appear on the income statement of the year in which the sales were made. As a result, the estimated $1,500 expense of selling on credit is matched with the $300,000 of revenue it helped produce.

Note that the credit of the entry is to a contra account called **Allowance for Doubtful Accounts.** A contra account must be used because at the time of the adjusting entry, you do not know which customers will not pay. Therefore, because specific bad accounts are not identifiable at the time of the adjusting entry, they cannot be removed from the subsidiary Accounts Receivable Ledger. Because the customer accounts are left in the subsidiary ledger, the controlling account for Accounts Receivable cannot be reduced. Instead, the Allowance for Doubtful Accounts account *must* be credited.

Bad Debts in the Accounts and in the Financial Statements

The process of evaluating customers and approving them for credit usually is not assigned to the selling department of a business. Otherwise, given the primary objective of increasing sales, the selling department might not use good judgment in approving customers for credit. Because the sales department is not responsible for granting credit, it should not be held responsible for bad debts expense. Therefore, bad debts expense often appears on the income statement as an administrative expense rather than a selling expense.

Recall from the previous example that Fritz Company has $20,000 of outstanding accounts receivable at the end of its first year of operations. Thus, after the bad debts adjusting entry is posted, the company's Accounts Receivable and Allowance for Doubtful Accounts accounts show these balances:

Accounts Receivable		Allowance for Doubtful Accounts	
Dec. 31 20,000			Dec. 31 1,500

The Allowance for Doubtful Accounts credit balance of $1,500 has the effect of reducing accounts receivable (net of the allowance) to their estimated **realizable**

value. The term *realizable value* means the expected proceeds from converting the assets into cash. Although $20,000 is legally owed to Fritz Company by all of its customers, only $18,500 is likely to be realized in cash collections from customers.

When the balance sheet is prepared, the allowance for doubtful accounts is subtracted from the accounts receivable to show the amount expected to be realized from the accounts. For example, this information could be reported as follows:

Current assets:		
Cash and cash equivalents		$11,300
Temporary investments, at lower of cost or		
market (cost is $16,200)		14,500
Accounts receivable	$20,000	
Less allowance for doubtful accounts	(1,500)	18,500
Merchandise inventory		52,700
Prepaid expenses		1,100
Total current assets		$98,100

In this example, compare the presentations of temporary investments and accounts receivable, and note that contra accounts are subtracted in both cases. Even though the contra account to the Temporary Investments account is not shown on the statement, you can easily determine that its balance is $1,700 by comparing the $16,200 cost with the $14,500 net amount. Sometimes, the contra account to Accounts Receivable is presented in a similar fashion, as follows:

Accounts receivable (net of $1,500 estimated	
uncollectible accounts)	$18,500

Writing Off a Bad Debt

When specific accounts are identified as uncollectible, they are written off against the Allowance for Doubtful Accounts. For example, after spending a year trying to collect from Jack Vale, the Fritz Company finally decided that his $100 account was uncollectible and made the following entry to write it off:

Jan.	23	Allowance for Doubtful Accounts	100.00	
		Accounts Receivable—Jack Vale		100.00
		To write off an uncollectible account.		

Posting the credit of the entry to the Accounts Receivable account removes the amount of the bad debt from the controlling account. Posting it to the Jack Vale account removes the amount of the bad debt from the subsidiary ledger. By removing it from the subsidiary ledger, Fritz Company avoids the cost of sending additional bills to Vale. After the entry is posted, the general ledger accounts appear as follows:

Accounts Receivable			Allowance for Doubtful Accounts		
Dec. 31	20,000			Dec. 31	1,500
		Jan. 23	100	Jan. 23	100

Notice two aspects of the entry and the accounts. First, although bad debts are an expense of selling on credit, the allowance account is debited in the write-off. The expense account is not debited. The expense account is not debited because the estimated expense was previously recorded at the end of the period in which the sale occurred. At that time, the expense was estimated and recorded with an adjusting entry.

Second, although the write-off removed the amount of the account receivable from the ledgers, it did not affect the estimated realizable value of Fritz Company's net accounts receivable, as the following tabulation shows:

	Before	After
Accounts receivable	$20,000	$19,900
Less allowance for doubtful accounts	1,500	1,400
Estimated realizable accounts receivable	$18,500	$18,500

Thus, neither total assets nor net income are affected by the decision to write off a specific account. However, both total assets and net income are affected by the recognition of the year's bad debts expense in the adjusting entry. Again, a primary purpose of writing off a specific account is to avoid the cost of additional collection efforts. Also, the *conservatism principle* would indicate that the accounts receivable should only include those amounts that are reasonably expected to be collected.

Bad Debt Recoveries

When a customer fails to pay and the account is written off, his or her credit standing is jeopardized. Therefore, the customer may choose to voluntarily pay all or part of the amount owed after the account is written off as uncollectible. This payment helps restore the credit standing. Thus, when this event happens, it should be recorded in the customer's subsidiary account where the information will be retained for use in future credit evaluations.

When a company collects an account that was previously written off, it makes two journal entries. The first reverses the original write-off and reinstates the customer's account. The second entry records the collection of the reinstated account. For example, assume that on August 15 Jack Vale pays in full the account that Fritz Company had previously written off. The entries to record the bad debt recovery are:

Aug.	15	Accounts Receivable—Jack Vale	100.00	
		Allowance for Doubtful Accounts		100.00
		To reinstate the account of Jack Vale written off on		
		January 23.		
	15	Cash	100.00	
		Accounts Receivable—Jack Vale		100.00
		Received full payment of account.		

In this case, Jack Vale paid the entire amount previously written off. In other situations, the customer may pay only a portion of the amount owed. The question then arises of whether the entire balance of the account should be returned to accounts receivable or just the amount paid. The answer is a matter of judgment. If you believe the customer will later pay in full, the entire amount owed should be returned. However, only the amount paid should be returned if you believe that no more will be collected.

Progress Check

8-7   In meeting the requirements of the matching principle, why must bad debts expenses be estimated?

8-8   What term describes the balance sheet valuation of accounts receivable less the allowance for doubtful accounts?

8-9   Why is estimated bad debts expense credited to a contra account rather than to the Accounts Receivable controlling account?

ESTIMATING THE AMOUNT OF BAD DEBTS EXPENSE

As you already learned, the allowance method of accounting for bad debts requires an adjusting entry at the end of each accounting period to record management's estimate of the bad debts expense for the period. That entry takes the following form:

Dec.	31	Bad Debts Expense	????	
		Allowance for Doubtful Accounts		????
		To record the estimated bad debts.		

How does a business determine the amount to record in this entry? There are two alternative approaches. One focuses on the income statement relationship between bad debts expense and sales. The other focuses on the balance sheet relationship between accounts receivable and allowance for doubtful accounts. Both alternatives require a careful analysis of past experience.

Estimating Bad Debts by Focusing on the Income Statement

The income statement approach to estimating bad debts is based on the idea that some particular percentage of a company's credit sales for the period will become uncollectible.[4] Hence, in the income statement, the amount of bad debts expense should equal that amount.

For example, suppose that Baker Company had credit sales of $400,000 in 1996. Based on past experience and the experience of similar companies, Baker Company estimates that 0.6% of credit sales will be uncollectible. Using this prediction, Baker Company can expect $2,400 of bad debts expense to result from the year's sales ($400,000 × 0.006 = $2,400). The adjusting entry to record this estimated expense is:

Dec.	31	Bad Debts Expense	2,400.00	
		Allowance for Doubtful Accounts		2,400.00
		To record the estimated bad debts.		

This entry does not mean the December 31, 1996, balance in Allowance for Doubtful Accounts will be $2,400. A $2,400 balance would occur only if the account had a zero balance immediately prior to posting the adjusting entry. For several reasons, however, the unadjusted balance of Allowance for Doubtful Accounts is not likely to be zero.

First, unless Baker Company began business during the current year, the Allowance for Doubtful Accounts would have had a credit balance at the beginning of the year. The beginning-of-year credit balance would have resulted from entries made in past years to record estimated bad debts expense and to write off uncollectible accounts. The cumulative effect of these entries would show up as a credit balance at the beginning of the current year.

Second, because bad debts expense must be estimated each year, the total amount of expense recorded in past years is not likely to equal the amounts that were written off as uncollectible. Although annual expense estimates are based on past experience, some residual difference between recorded expenses and amounts written off should be expected to show up in the unadjusted Allowance for Doubtful Accounts balance.

Third, some of the amounts written off as uncollectible during the current year probably relate to credit sales made during the current year. These debits affect the unadjusted Allowance for Doubtful Accounts balance. In fact, they may cause the account to have a debit balance prior to posting the adjusting entry for bad debts expense.

For these reasons, you should not expect the Allowance for Doubtful Accounts to have an unadjusted balance of zero at the end of the year. As we stated earlier, this means that the adjusted balance reported on the balance sheet normally does not equal the amount of expense reported on the income statement.

Remember that expressing bad debts expense as a percentage of sales is an estimate based on past experience. As new experience is gained over time, the percentage used may appear to have been too large or too small. When this happens, a different rate should be used in future periods.

---

[4]Note that the factor to be considered is *credit* sales. Naturally, cash sales do not produce bad debts, and they generally should not be used in the calculation. However, if cash sales are relatively small compared to credit sales, there is no practical difference in the result.

Estimating Bad Debts by Focusing on the Balance Sheet

The balance sheet approach to estimating bad debts is based on the idea that some portion of the end-of-period accounts receivable balance will not be collected. From this point of view, the goal of the bad debts adjusting entry is to make the Allowance for Doubtful Accounts balance equal to the portion of outstanding accounts receivable estimated to be uncollectible. To obtain this required balance in the Allowance for Doubtful Accounts account, simply compare its balance before the adjustment with the required balance. The difference between the two is debited to Bad Debts Expense and credited to Allowance for Doubtful Accounts. Estimating the required balance of the Allowance account can be done in two ways: (1) by using the simplified approach and (2) by aging the accounts receivable.

The Simplified Balance Sheet Approach. Using the simplified balance sheet approach, a company estimates that a certain percentage of its outstanding receivables will prove to be uncollectible. This estimated percentage is based on past experience and the experience of similar companies. It also may be affected by current conditions such as recent prosperity or economic difficulties faced by the firm's customers. Then, the total dollar amount of all outstanding receivables is multiplied by the estimated percentage to determine the estimated dollar amount of uncollectible accounts. This amount must appear in the balance sheet as the balance of the Allowance for Doubtful Accounts. To put this balance in the account, you must prepare an adjusting entry that debits Bad Debts Expense and credits Allowance for Doubtful Accounts. The amount of the adjustment is the amount necessary to provide the required balance in Allowance for Doubtful Accounts.

For example, assume that Baker Company (of the previous illustration) has $50,000 of outstanding accounts receivable on December 31, 1996. Past experience suggests that 5% of the outstanding receivables are uncollectible. Thus, after the adjusting entry is posted, the Allowance for Doubtful Accounts should have a $2,500 credit balance (5% of $50,000). Assume that before the adjustment the account appears as follows:

Allowance for Doubtful Accounts

		Dec. 31, 1995, balance 2,000
Feb. 6	800	
July 10	600	
Nov. 20	400	
		Unadjusted balance 200

The $2,000 beginning balance appeared on the December 31, 1995, balance sheet. During 1996, accounts of specific customers were written off on February 6, July 10, and November 20. As a result, the account has a $200 credit balance prior to the December 31, 1996, adjustment. The adjusting entry to give the Allowance the required $2,500 balance is:

Dec.	31	Bad Debts Expense	2,300.00	
		Allowance for Doubtful Accounts		2,300.00
		To record the estimated bad debts.		

After this entry is posted, the Allowance has a $2,500 credit balance, as shown here:

Allowance for Doubtful Accounts

		Dec. 31, 1995, balance	2,000
Feb. 6	800		
July 10	600		
Nov. 20	400		
		Unadjusted balance	200
		Dec. 31	2,300
		Dec. 31, 1996, balance	2,500

Aging Accounts Receivable. Both the income statement approach and the simplified balance sheet approach use knowledge gained from past experience to estimate the amount of bad debts expense. Another balance sheet approach produces a more refined estimate based on past experience and on information about current conditions.

This method involves **aging of accounts receivable.** Under this method, each account receivable is examined in the process of estimating the amount that is uncollectible. Specifically, the receivables are classified by how long they have been outstanding. Then, estimates of uncollectible amounts are made under the assumption that the longer an amount is outstanding, the more likely it will be uncollectible.

To age the accounts receivable outstanding at the end of the period, you must examine each account and classify the outstanding amounts by how much time has passed since they were created. The selection of the classes to be used depends on the judgment of each company's management. However, the classes are often based on 30-day (or one month) periods. After the outstanding amounts have been classified (or aged), past experience is used to estimate a percentage of each class that will become uncollectible. These percentages are applied to the amounts in the classes to determine the required balance of the Allowance for Doubtful Accounts. The calculation is completed by setting up a schedule like the one in Illustration 8–2 for Baker Company.

In Illustration 8–2, notice that each customer's account is listed with its total balance. Then, each balance is allocated to five categories based on the age of the unpaid charges that make up the balance. (In computerized systems, this allocation is done automatically.) When all accounts have been aged, the amounts in each category are totaled and multiplied by the estimated percentage of uncollectible accounts for each category. The reasonableness of the percentages used must be reviewed regularly and frequently reflect reactions to the state of the economy.

For example, in Illustration 8–2, Baker Company is owed $3,500 that is 31 to 60 days past due. Baker's management estimates that 10% of the amounts in this age category will not be collected. Thus, the dollar amount of uncollectible accounts in this category is $350 ($3,500 × 10%). The total in the first column tells us that the adjusted balance in Baker Company's Allowance for Doubtful Accounts should be $2,290 ($740 + $325 + $350 + $475 + $400). Because the Allowance has an unadjusted credit balance of $200, the aging of accounts receivable approach requires the following change in its balance:

Illustration 8-2   Estimating Bad Debts by Aging the Accounts

BAKER COMPANY
Schedule of Accounts Receivable by Age
December 31, 1996

Customer's Name	Total	Not Due	1 to 30 Days Past Due	31 to 60 Days Past Due	61 to 90 Days Past Due	Over 90 Days Past Due
Charles Abbot	$ 450.00	$ 450.00				
Frank Allen	710.00			$ 710.00		
George Arden	500.00	300.00	$ 200.00			
Paul Baum	740.00				$ 100.00	$ 640.00
ZZ Services	1,000.00	810.00	190.00			
Totals	$49,900.00	$37,000.00	$6,500.00	$3,500.00	$1,900.00	$1,000.00
Rate		× 2%	× 5%	× 10%	× 25%	× 40%
Estimated uncollectible amounts . . .	$ 2,290.00	$ 740.00	$ 325.00	$ 350.00	$ 475.00	$ 400.00

```
Unadjusted balance   . . . .   $  200 credit
Required balance  . . . . . .    2,290 credit
Required adjustment . . . .   $2,090 credit
```

As a result, Baker should record the following adjusting entry:

Dec.	31	Bad Debts Expense	2,090.00	
		Allowance for Doubtful Accounts		2,090.00
		To record the estimated bad debts.		

For instructional purposes, suppose that Baker's Allowance had an unadjusted *debit* balance of $500. In this case, the calculation of the adjustment amount and the entry would be:

```
Unadjusted balance   . . . .   $  500 debit
Required balance  . . . . . .    2,290 credit
Required adjustment . . . .   $2,790 credit
```

Dec.	31	Bad Debts Expense	2,790.00	
		Allowance for Doubtful Accounts		2,790.00
		To record the estimated bad debts.		

Recall from page 411 that when the income statement approach was used, Baker's bad debts expense for 1996 was estimated to be $2,400. When the simplified balance sheet approach was used (see page 413), the estimate was $2,300. And when aging of accounts receivable was used the first time, the estimate was $2,090. Do not be surprised that the amounts are different; after all, each approach is only an estimate of what will prove to be true. However, the aging of accounts receivable is based on a more detailed examination of specific outstanding accounts and is usually the most reliable.[5]

DIRECT WRITE-OFF METHOD OF ACCOUNTING FOR BAD DEBTS

The allowance method of accounting for bad debts satisfies the requirements of the *matching principle*. Therefore, it is the method that should be used in most cases. However, another method may be suitable under certain limited circumstances. Under this **direct write-off method of accounting for bad debts,** no attempt is made to estimate uncollectible accounts or bad debts expense at the end of each period. In fact, no adjusting entry is made. Instead, bad debts expense is recorded when specific accounts are written off as uncollectible. For example, note the following entry to write off a $52 uncollectible account:

Nov.	23	Bad Debts Expense	52.00	
		Accounts Receivable—Dale Hall		52.00
		To write off the uncollectible account under the direct write-off method.		

The debit of the entry charges the uncollectible amount directly to the current year's Bad Debts Expense account. The credit removes the balance of the account from the subsidiary ledger and from the controlling account.

If an account previously written off directly to Bad Debts Expense is later collected in full, the following entries record the recovery:

Mar.	11	Accounts Receivable—Dale Hall	52.00	
		Bad Debts Expense		52.00
		To reinstate the account of Dale Hall previously written off.		
	11	Cash	52.00	
		Accounts Receivable—Dale Hall		52.00
		In full payment of account.		

Sometimes an amount previously written off directly to Bad Debts Expense is recovered in the year following the write-off. If there is no balance in the Bad Debts Expense account from previous write-offs and no other write-offs are expected, the

---

[5]In many cases, the aging analysis is supplemented with information about specific customers that allows management to decide whether those accounts should be classified as uncollectible. This information often is supplied by the sales and credit department managers.

credit portion of the entry recording the recovery can be made to a Bad Debt Recoveries revenue account.

The direct write-off method usually mismatches revenues and expenses. The mismatch occurs because bad debts expense is not recorded until an account becomes uncollectible, which often does not occur during the same period as the credit sale. Despite this weakness, the direct write-off method may be used when a company's bad debts expenses are very small in relation to other financial statement items such as total sales and net income. In such cases, the direct write-off method is justified by the *materiality principle,* which we explain next.

THE MATERIALITY PRINCIPLE

The basic idea of the **materiality principle** is that the requirements of accounting principles may be ignored if the effect on the financial statements is unimportant to their users. In other words, failure to follow the requirements of an accounting principle is acceptable when the failure does not produce an error or misstatement large enough to influence a financial statement reader's judgment of a given situation.

INSTALLMENT ACCOUNTS AND NOTES RECEIVABLE

Many companies allow their credit customers to make periodic payments over several months. When this is done, the selling company's assets may be in the form of **installment accounts receivable** or notes receivable. As is true for other accounts receivable, the evidence behind installment accounts receivable includes sales slips or invoices that describe the sales transactions. A note receivable, on the other hand, is a written document that promises payment and is signed by the customer. In either case, when payments are made over several months or if the credit period is long, the customer is usually charged interest. Although the credit period of installment accounts and notes receivable may be more than one year, they should be classified as current assets if the company regularly offers customers such terms.

Generally, creditors prefer notes receivable over accounts receivable when the credit period is long and the receivable relates to a single sale for a fairly large amount. Notes also can replace accounts receivable when customers ask for additional time to pay their past-due accounts. In these situations, creditors prefer notes to accounts receivable for legal reasons. If a lawsuit is needed to collect from a customer, a note represents a clear written acknowledgment by the debtor of the debt, its amount, and its terms. Banks and finance companies often use installment accounts, notes receivable, or similar instruments in dealings with their customers.

Progress Check

D & C Boutiques International estimated that, based on an aging of accounts receivable, $6,142 would be uncollectible. The year-end December 31, 1995 balance of the allowance account is a credit of $440.

8-10   **Prepare the year-end adjusting entry.**

8-11   **Using the following information, prepare the appropriate journal entries:**
On January 10, 1996, the $300 account of customer Felix Arthur was determined uncollectible. On April 12, 1996, Felix Arthur paid the account that was determined uncollectible on January 10, 1996.

Illustration 8–3
A Promissory Note

| $1,000.00 | Winnipeg, Manitoba | March 9, 1996 |

Thirty days ___ after date ___ _I, Hugo Brown_ ___ promise to pay to

the order of ___ _Frank Tomlinson_ ___

One thousand and no / 100 - dollars

for value received with interest at ___ _12%_ ___

payable at ___ _National Bank of Winnipeg, Manitoba_ ___

Hugo Brown

PROMISSORY NOTES

LO 4

Calculate the interest on promissory notes and prepare entries to record the receipt of promissory notes and their payment or dishonour.

A **promissory note** is an unconditional written promise to pay a definite sum of money on demand or at a fixed or determinable future date. In the promissory note shown in Illustration 8–3, Hugo Brown promises to pay Frank Tomlinson or to his order (that is, according to Tomlinson's instructions) a definite sum of money ($1,000), called the **principal of the note** at a fixed future date (April 8, 1996). As the one who signed the note and promised to pay it at maturity, Hugo Brown is the **maker of the note.** As the person to whom the note is payable, Frank Tomlinson is the **payee of the note.** To Hugo Brown, the illustrated note is a liability called a _note payable._ To Frank Tomlinson, the same note is an asset called a _note receivable._

The Hugo Brown note bears **interest** at 12%. Interest is the charge assessed for the use of money. To a borrower, interest is an expense. To a lender, it is a revenue. The rate of interest that a note bears is stated on the note.

Calculating Interest

Unless otherwise stated, the rate of interest on a note is the rate charged for the use of the principal for one year. The formula for calculating interest is:

$$\begin{array}{ccccccc} \text{Principal} & & \text{Annual} & & \text{Time of the} & & \\ \text{of the} & \times & \text{rate of} & \times & \text{note expressed} & = & \text{Interest} \\ \text{note} & & \text{interest} & & \text{in years} & & \end{array}$$

For example, interest on a $1,000, 12%, six-month note is calculated as:

$$\$1,000 \times 12\% \times \frac{6}{12} = \$60$$

The **maturity date of a note** is the day on which the note (principal and interest) must be repaid. Many notes mature in less than a full year, and the period covered by them often is expressed in days. When the time of a note is expressed in days, the maturity date is the specified number of days after the note's date. As a simple example, a one-day note dated June 15 matures and is due on June 16. Also, a 90-day note dated July 10 matures on October 8. This October 8 due date is calculated as follows:

Number of days in July	31
Minus the date of the note	10
Gives the number of days the note runs in July	21
Add the number of days in August	31
Add the number of days in September	30
Total through September 30	82
Days in October needed to equal the 90-day time of the note, also the maturity date of the note (October 8)	8
Total time the note runs in days	90

In other situations, the period of a note is expressed in months. In these cases, the note matures and is payable in the month of its maturity on the same day of the month as its original date. For example, a three-month note dated July 10 is payable on October 10.

The amount of interest for a 90-day note with interest at 12% is calculated as follows:[6]

$$\text{Interest} = \text{Principal} \times \text{Rate} \times \frac{\text{Exact days}}{365}$$

or

$$\text{Interest} = \$1{,}000 \times 12\% \times \frac{90}{365} = \$29.59$$

Recording the Receipt of a Note

To simplify record-keeping, notes receivable are usually recorded in a single Notes Receivable account. Only one account is needed because the individual original notes are on hand. Therefore, the maker, rate of interest, due date, and other information may be learned by examining each note.[7]

When a company receives a note at the time of a sale, an entry such as this one is recorded:

Dec.	5	Notes Receivable	650.00	
		Sales		650.00
		Sold merchandise, terms six-month, 9% note.		

A business also may accept a note from an overdue customer as a way of granting a time extension on the past-due account receivable. When this happens, the business may collect part of the past-due balance in cash. This partial payment

---

[6]Specific types of note may legally allow for three days of grace. For example, a 90-day note becomes due and payable on the 93rd day, and interest is calculated for 93 days. Because it is common practice that notes are due and payable on a specified date, illustrations are based on the time period specified on the face of the note. Unless otherwise instructed, you are to solve problems using the specific number of days and a 365-day year.

[7]If the company holds a large number of notes, it may be more efficient to set up a controlling account and a subsidiary ledger.

forces a concession from the customer, reduces the customer's debt (and the seller's risk), and produces a note for a smaller amount. For example, Symplex Company agrees to accept $232 in cash and a $600, 60-day, 15% note from Joseph Cook to settle his $832 past-due account. Symplex makes the following entry to record the receipt of the cash and note:

Oct.	5	Cash	232.00	
		Notes Receivable	600.00	
		Accounts Receivable—Joseph Cook		832.00
		Received cash and a note in settlement of an account.		

When Cook pays the note on the due date, Symplex records the receipt as follows:

Dec.	4	Cash	614.79	
		Notes Receivable		600.00
		Interest Earned		14.79
		Collected the Joseph Cook note including interest of		
		$600 × 15% × 60/365.		

Dishonoured Notes Receivable

Sometimes, the maker of a note is not able to pay the note at maturity. When a note's maker is unable or refuses to pay at maturity, the note is said to be dishonoured. This act of **dishonouring a note** does not relieve the maker of the obligation to pay. Furthermore, the payee should use every legitimate means to collect. However, collection may require lengthy legal proceedings.

The usual practice is to have the balance of the Notes Receivable account show only the amount of notes that have not matured. Therefore, when a note is dishonoured, you should remove the amount of the note from the Notes Receivable account and charge it back to an account receivable from its maker. To illustrate, Symplex Company holds an $800, 12%, 60-day note of George Hart. At maturity, Hart dishonours the note. To remove the dishonoured note from the Notes Receivable account, the company makes the following entry:

Oct.	14	Accounts Receivable—George Hart	815.78	
		Interest Earned		15.78
		Notes Receivable		800.00
		To charge the account of George Hart for his		
		dishonoured note including interest of		
		$800 × 12% × 60/365.		

Charging a dishonoured note back to the account of its maker serves two purposes. First, it removes the amount of the note from the Notes Receivable account, leaving in the account only notes that have not matured. It also records the dishonoured note in the maker's account. The second purpose is important. If the maker of the dishonoured note again applies for credit in the future, his or her account will show all past dealings, including the dishonoured note. Restoring the account also reminds the business to continue collection efforts.

Note that Hart owes both the principal and the interest. Therefore, the entry records the full amount owed in Hart's account and credits the interest to Interest Earned. This procedure assures that the interest will be included in future efforts to collect from Hart.

End-of-Period Adjustments

When notes receivable are outstanding at the end of an accounting period, the accrued interest should be calculated and recorded. This procedure recognizes the interest revenue when it is earned and recognizes the additional asset owned by the note's holder. For example, on December 16, Perry Company accepted a $3,000, 60-day, 12% note from a customer in granting an extension on a past-due account. When the company's accounting period ends on December 31, $14.79 of interest will have accrued on this note ($3,000 $\times$ 12% $\times$ 15/365). The following adjusting entry records this revenue:

Dec.	31	Interest Receivable	14.79	
		Interest Earned		14.79
		To record accrued interest.		

The adjusting entry causes the interest earned to appear on the income statement of the period in which it was earned. It also causes the interest receivable to appear on the balance sheet as a current asset.

Collecting Interest Previously Accrued

When the note is collected, Perry Company's entry to record the cash receipt is:

Feb.	14	Cash	3,059.18	
		Interest Earned		44.39
		Interest Receivable		14.79
		Notes Receivable		3,000.00
		Received payment of a note and its interest.		

Observe that the entry's credit to Interest Receivable records collection of the interest accrued at the end of the previous period. Only the $44.39 of interest earned between January 1 and February 14 is recorded as revenue.

In calculating interest in the foregoing examples, the "exact," or proper, method was used. For classroom purposes, however, instructors may prefer to use a less accurate simplified method of interest calculation in order to focus on comprehension rather than on lengthy procedural calculation. To simplify interest calculations, the following assumptions are made:

ALTERNATIVE METHOD OF INTEREST CALCULATION

1. Treat a year as having 360 days divided into 12 months of 30 days each.
2. Use the exact days of the note; that is, do not give consideration to the days of grace.

Thus, interest on a 90-day, 12%, $1,500 note is calculated as:

$$\$1{,}500 \times \frac{12}{100} \times \frac{90}{360} = \$45$$

To facilitate the use of the alternative method of interest calculation, certain exercises and problems may be designated for use of this method.

Progress Check

8–12 **White Corporation purchased $7,000 of merchandise from Stamford Company on December 16, 1995. Stamford accepted White's $7,000, 90-day, 12% note as payment. Assuming Stamford's annual accounting period ends on December 31 and it does not make reversing entries, prepare entries for Stamford Company on December 16, 1995, and December 31, 1995.**

8–13 **Based on the facts in 8–12, prepare the March 16, 1996, entry assuming White dishonours the note.**

CONVERTING RECEIVABLES INTO CASH BEFORE THEY ARE DUE

LO 5

Explain how receivables can be converted into cash before they are due and calculate accounts receivable turnover.

Many companies grant credit to customers and then hold the receivables until they are paid by the customers. However, some companies convert receivables into cash without waiting until they are due. This is done either by selling the receivables or by using them as security for a loan. In certain industries such as textiles and furniture, this has been a common practice for years. More recently, the practice has spread to other industries, in particular the apparel industry. More small businesses are using sale of receivables as a source of cash, especially those selling to other businesses and government agencies that often delay payment.

Selling Accounts Receivable

A business may sell its accounts receivable to a finance company or bank. The buyer, which is called a *factor,* charges the seller a *factoring fee* and then collects the receivables as they come due. By incurring the factoring fee cost, the seller receives the cash earlier and passes the risk of bad debts to the factor. The seller also avoids the cost of billing and accounting for the receivables.

For example, assume that a business sells $20,000 of its accounts receivable and is charged a 2% factoring fee. The seller records the sale with the following entry:

Aug.	15	Cash	19,600.00	
		Factoring Fee Expense	400.00	
		Accounts Receivable		20,000.00
		Sold accounts receivable for cash, less a 2% factoring fee.		

Factoring has become big business today with 90% of the factoring industry's business coming from textile and apparel businesses.

Pledging Accounts Receivable as Security for a Loan

When a business borrows money and pledges its accounts receivable as security for the loan, the business records the loan with an entry such as the following:

Aug.	20	Cash	35,000.00	
		Notes Payable		35,000.00
		Borrowed money on a note secured by the pledge of		
		accounts receivable.		

Under the pledging arrangement, the risk of bad debts is not transferred to the lender. The borrower retains ownership of the receivables. However, if the borrower defaults on the loan, the creditor has the right to be paid from the cash receipts as the accounts receivable are collected.

Because pledged receivables are committed as security for a loan from a particular creditor, the borrower's financial statements should disclose the fact that accounts receivable have been pledged. For example, the following note to the financial statements provides the necessary information: "Accounts receivable in the amount of $40,000 are pledged as security for a $35,000 note payable to Western National Bank."

Discounting Notes Receivable

Notes receivable also can be converted into cash before they mature, usually by discounting the notes receivable at a bank. This discounting might be done for a number of reasons; perhaps the most common is to allow the holder to avoid having to borrow money by signing its own note. When a note receivable is discounted, the owner endorses and delivers the note to the bank in exchange for cash. The bank holds the note to maturity and then collects its maturity value from the original maker.

To illustrate, assume that on May 28, Symplex Company received a $1,200, 60-day, 12% note dated May 27 from John Owen. It held the note until June 2 and then discounted it at the bank at 14%. Since the maturity date of this note is July 26, the bank must wait 54 days after discounting the note to collect from Owen. These 54 days are called the **discount period,** which is the number of days between the date on which a note is discounted at the bank and its maturity date. The discount period is calculated for this note as follows:

Original period of the note in days		60
Less time held by Symplex Company:		
Number of days in May	31	
Less the date of the note.	27	
Days held in May	4	
Days held in June	2	
Total days held by Symplex		6
Discount period in days		54

At the end of the discount period, the bank expects to collect the maturity value of this note from Owen. The **maturity value of a note** is its principal plus any interest due on its maturity date. The maturity value of the Owen note is

Principal of the note	$1,200.00
Interest on $1,200 for 60 days at 12%	23.67
Maturity value	$1,223.67

In calculating the interest or discount to be charged, banks traditionally base their discount on the maturity value of the note. In this case, we assume the bank has a 14% **discount rate,** which is the rate of interest it charges for lending money by discounting a note. Therefore, in discounting this note, the bank deducts 54 days' interest at 14% from the note's maturity value and gives Symplex Company the remainder. The amount of interest deducted in advance is called the **bank discount,** and the remainder is called the **proceeds of the discounted note.** The bank discount and the proceeds are calculated as follows:

Maturity value of the note	$1,223.67
Less discount on $1,223.67 for 54 days at 14%	25.35*
Proceeds	$1,198.32

*$1,223.67 \times .14 \times (^{54}\!/_{365}) = 25.35

In this case, the proceeds, $1,198.32, are $1.68 less than the $1,200 principal amount of the note. Therefore, Symplex makes this entry to record the discount transaction:

June	2	Cash	1,198.32	
		Interest Expense	1.68	
		Notes Receivable		1,200.00
		Discounted the John Owen note for 54 days at 14%.		

In this entry, note that the $23.67 of interest Symplex would have earned by holding the note to maturity is offset against the $25.35 discount charged by the bank. The $1.68 difference is debited to Interest Expense.

   In the situation just described, the principal of the discounted note exceeded the proceeds. However, in other cases, the proceeds can exceed the principal. When this happens, the difference is credited to Interest Earned. For example, suppose that instead of discounting the John Owen note on June 2, Symplex discounted it on June 26 at 14%. Therefore, the discount period is 30 days, the discount is $14.08, and the proceeds of the note are $1,209.59, calculated as follows:

Maturity value of the note				$1,223.67
Less discount on $1,223.67 for 30 days at 14%				14.08*
Proceeds				$1,209.59

*$1,223.67 × .14 × ($\frac{30}{365}$) = $14.08

Because the proceeds exceed the principal, the transaction is recorded as follows:

June	26	Cash	1,209.59	
		Interest Earned		9.59
		Notes Receivable		1,200.00
		Discounted the John Owen note for 30 days at 14%.		

Notes receivable may be discounted with recourse or without recourse. If a note is discounted with recourse and the original maker of the note fails to pay the bank when the note matures, the original payee of the note must pay. Thus, a company that discounts a note with recourse has a contingent liability until the bank is paid. A **contingent liability** is an obligation to make a future payment if, and only if, an uncertain future event actually occurs. The company should disclose the contingent liability in its financial statements with a note such as: "The company is contingently liable for a $50,000 note receivable discounted with recourse." When a note is discounted *without recourse,* the bank assumes the risk of a bad debt loss and the original payee does not have a contingent liability.

The disclosure of contingent liabilities in the notes is consistent with the **full-disclosure principle.** This principle requires financial statements (including the notes) to present all relevant information about the operations and financial position of the entity. A company should report any facts important enough to affect a statement reader's evaluation of the company's operations, financial position, or cash flows. This principle does not require companies to report excessive detail. It simply means that significant information should not be withheld and that enough information should be provided to make the reports understandable. Examples of items that are reported to satisfy the full-disclosure principle include the following:

FULL-DISCLOSURE PRINCIPLE

Contingent Liabilities. In addition to discounted notes, a company should disclose any items for which the company is contingently liable. Examples are possible additional tax assessments, debts of other parties that the company has guaranteed, and unresolved lawsuits against the company. Information about these facts helps users predict events that might affect the company.

Long-Term Commitments under Contracts. A company should disclose that it has signed a long-term lease requiring material annual payments, even though the obligation does not appear in the accounts. Also, a company should reveal that it has pledged certain of its assets as security for loans. These facts show statement readers that the company has restricted its flexibility. For example, the **Onex Corporation** reported the following in its December 31, 1994 Annual Report:

15. COMMITMENTS AND CONTINGENCIES

a) The estimated total cost to complete approved capital projects of the operating companies at December 31, 1994 is approximately $23,500,000.

b) Outstanding letters of credit of the operating companies amount to $83,300,000 at December 31, 1994. The letters of credit form part of the operating bank credit lines of the companies. Floating-charge debentures on the companies' assets and a pledge of assets form part of the security for these bank credit lines.

Accounting Methods Used. When more than one accounting method can be applied, a company must describe the one it uses, especially when the choice can materially affect reported net income.[8] For example, a company must describe the methods it uses to account for inventory and amortization. (These methods are explained in future chapters.) This information helps users understand how the company determines its net income.

USING THE INFORMATION— ACCOUNTS RECEIVABLE TURNOVER

In Chapter 7, you learned how to calculate *days' sales uncollected,* which provides information about the short-term liquidity of a company. In evaluating short-term liquidity, you also may want to calculate **accounts receivable turnover.** The formula for this ratio is:

$$\text{Accounts receivable turnover} = \frac{\text{Net sales}}{\text{Average accounts receivable}}$$

Recall that days' sales uncollected relates to the accounts receivable balance at the end of the year. In contrast, notice that the denominator in the turnover formula is the average accounts receivable balance during the year. The average is often calculated as:

$$\frac{(\text{The beginning balance} + \text{The ending balance})}{2}$$

This method of estimating the average balance provides a useful result if the seasonal changes in the accounts receivable balances during the year are not too large.

Accounts receivable turnover indicates how often the company converted its average accounts receivable balance into cash during the year. Thus, a turnover of 12 suggests that the average accounts receivable balance was converted into cash 12 times during the year.

Accounts receivable turnover also provides useful information for evaluating how efficient management has been in granting credit to produce revenues. A ratio that is high in comparison with competing companies suggests that management should consider using more liberal credit terms to increase sales. A low ratio suggests that management should consider less liberal credit terms and more aggressive collection efforts to avoid an excessive investment in accounts receivable. The following data was extracted from 1994 annual reports of two companies to illustrate the calculations and comparisons:

---

[8]*CICA Handbook,* section 1505, "Disclosure of Accounting Policies," par. .09.

Anchor Lamina Inc. (In thousands)

$$\text{Accounts receivable turnover} = \frac{\$74,693}{(\$11,446 + \$14,471)/2} = 5.76 \text{ times}$$

Magna International Inc. (In millions)

$$\text{Accounts receivable turnover} = \frac{\$3,568.5}{(\$314.6 + \$536.5)/2} = 8.39 \text{ times}$$

Progress Check

8-14 A garment manufacturer is short of cash but has substantial accounts receivable. What alternatives are available for gaining cash from the accounts receivable prior to receiving payments from the credit customers? Show the entry that would be made for each alternative.

8-15 What does a low accounts receivable turnover ratio indicate? Should a low turnover ratio cause concern? Why or why not?

SUMMARY OF THE CHAPTER IN TERMS OF LEARNING OBJECTIVES

LO 1. Prepare journal entries to account for temporary investments and explain how lower of cost or market is reported on such investments. Temporary investments are recorded at cost; dividends and interest on the investments are recorded in appropriate income statement accounts. On the balance sheet, temporary investments are reported at lower of cost or market. Write-downs to market are credited to a contra account, the Allowance to Reduce Temporary Investments to Market, and the loss is reported in the income statement.

LO 2. Prepare entries to account for credit card or debit card sales. When credit card or debit card receipts are deposited in a bank account, the credit card expense is recorded at the time of the deposit. When credit card receipts must be submitted to the credit card company for payment, Accounts Receivable is debited for the sales amount. Then, credit card expense is recorded when cash is received from the credit card company. However, any unrecorded credit card expense should be accrued at the end of each accounting period.

LO 3. Prepare entries to account for transactions with credit customers, including accounting for bad debts under the allowance method and the direct write-off method. Under the allowance method, bad debts expense is recorded with an adjustment at the end of each accounting period that debits the expense and credits the Allowance for Doubtful Accounts. The amount of the adjustment is determined by focusing on either (*a*) the income statement relationship between bad debts expense and credit sales or (*b*) the balance sheet relationship between accounts receivable and the Allowance for Doubtful Accounts. The latter approach may involve using a simple percentage relationship or aging the accounts. Uncollectible accounts are written off with a debit to the Allowance for Doubtful Accounts. The direct write-off method charges Bad Debts Expense when accounts are written off as uncollectible. This method is suitable only when the amount of bad debts expense is immaterial.

LO 4. Calculate the interest on promissory notes and prepare entries to record the receipt of promissory notes and their payment or dishonour. Interest rates are typically stated in annual terms. When a note's time to maturity is more or less than one year, the amount of interest on the note must be determined by expressing the time as a fraction of one year and multiplying the note's principal by that fraction and the annual interest rate. Dishonoured notes are credited to Notes Receivable and debited to Accounts Receivable and to the account of the maker.

LO 5. Explain how receivables can be converted into cash before they are due and calculate accounts receivable turnover. To obtain cash from receivables before they are due, a company may sell accounts receivable to a factor, who charges a factoring fee. Also, a company may borrow money by signing a note payable that is secured by pledging the accounts receivable. Notes receivable may be discounted at a bank, with or without recourse. The full-disclosure principle requires companies to disclose the amount of accounts receivable that have been pledged and the contingent liability for notes discounted with recourse.

DEMONSTRATION PROBLEM

Garden Company had the following transactions during 1996:

May	8	Purchased 300 common shares of Canadian Pacific as a temporary investment. The cost of $40 per share plus $975 in broker's commissions was paid in cash.
July	14	Wrote off a $750 account receivable arising from a sale several months ago. (Garden Company uses the allowance method.)
Aug.	15	Accepted a $2,000 down payment and a $10,000 note receivable from a customer in exchange for an inventory item that normally sells for $12,000. The note was dated August 15, bears 12% interest, and matures in six months.
Sept.	2	Sold 100 shares of Canadian Pacific at $47 per share, and continued to hold the other 200 shares. The broker's commission on the sale was $225.
Sept.	15	Received $9,850 in return for discounting without recourse the $10,000 note (dated August 15) at the local bank.
Dec.	2	Purchased 400 common shares of Magna International for $60 per share plus $1,600 in commissions. The shares are to be held as a temporary investment.

Required

1. Prepare journal entries to record these transactions on the books of Garden Company.

2. Prepare adjusting journal entries as of December 31, 1996, for the following items (assume 1996 is the first year of operations):

   a. The market prices of the securities held by Garden Company are $48 per share for the Canadian Pacific shares, and $55 per share for the Magna International shares.

   b. Bad debts expense is estimated by an aging of accounts receivable. The unadjusted balance of the Allowance for Doubtful Accounts account is a $1,000 debit, while the required balance is estimated to be a $20,400 credit.

- Examine each item to determine which accounts are affected, and produce the needed journal entries.

- With respect to the year-end adjustments, adjust temporary investments to LCM and record the bad debts expense.

Planning the Solution

1.

Solution to Demonstration Problem

May	8	Temporary Investments	12,975.00	
		Cash		12,975.00
		Purchased 300 shares of Canadian Pacific. Cost is (300 × $40) + $975.		
July	14	Allowance for Doubtful Accounts	750.00	
		Accounts Receivable		750.00
		Wrote off an uncollectible account.		
Aug.	15	Cash	2,000.00	
		Notes Receivable	10,000.00	
		Sales		12,000.00
		Sold merchandise to customer for $2,000 cash and $10,000 note receivable.		
Sept.	2	Cash	4,475.00	
		Gain on Sale of Investment		150.00
		Temporary Investments		4,325.00
		Sold 100 shares of Canadian Pacific for $47 per share less a $225 commission. The original cost is $12,975 × 100/300.		
	15	Cash	9,850.00	
		Interest Expense	150.00	
		Notes Receivable		10,000.00
		Discounted note receivable dated August 15.		

Principal	$10,000
Interest earned ($10,000 × 12% × $\frac{1}{12}$)	100
	$10,100
Proceeds (given)	9,850
Discounting fee	$ 250

Note: Months are used in the calculation because the time period of the note was expressed in months.

Dec.	2	Temporary Investments	25,600.00	
		Cash		25,600.00
		Purchased 400 shares of Magna International for *$60 per share plus $1,600 in commissions.*		
	31	Loss on Temporary Investments	2,650.00	
		Allowance to Reduce Temporary Investments to Market		2,650.00
		To reflect market values of temporary investments.		

Temporary Investments	Shares	Cost per Share	Total Cost	Market Value per Share	Total Market Value	Difference
Canadian Pacific	200	$43.25	$ 8,650	$48.00	$ 9,600	
Magna International . .	400	64.00	25,600	55.00	22,000	
Total			$34,250		$31,600	$2,650

	31	Bad Debts Expense	21,400.00	
		Allowance for Doubtful Accounts		21,400.00
		To adjust the allowance account from $1,000 debit *balance to $20,400 credit balance.*		

GLOSSARY

Accounts Receivable Ledger a supplementary record (also called a subsidiary ledger) having an account for each customer. p. 405

Accounts receivable turnover a measure of how long it takes a company to collect its accounts, calculated by dividing credit sales (or net sales) by the average accounts receivable balance. p. 426

Aging of accounts receivable a process of classifying accounts receivable by how long they have been outstanding for the purpose of estimating the amount of uncollectible accounts. p. 414

Allowance for Doubtful Accounts a contra asset account with a balance equal to the estimated amount of accounts receivable that will be uncollectible. p. 408

Allowance method of accounting for bad debts an accounting procedure that (1) estimates and reports bad debt expense from credit sales during the period of the sales, and (2) reports accounts receivable at the amount of cash proceeds that is expected from their collection (their estimated realizable value). p. 407

Bad debts accounts receivable from customers that are not collected; the amount is an expense of selling on credit. p. 407

Bank discount the amount of interest deducted in advance by the bank when discounting a note. p. 424

Contingent liability an obligation to make a future payment if, and only if, an uncertain future event actually occurs. p. 425

Controlling account a general ledger account with a balance that is always equal to the sum of the balances in a related subsidiary ledger. p. 407

Debit card card issued by a bank or similar financial institution to allow consumers to pay for purchases by a bank transfer authorized at point of sale. p. 403

Direct write-off method of accounting for bad debts a method that makes no attempt to estimate uncollectible accounts or bad debts expense at the end of each period; instead, when an account is found to be uncollectible, it is written off directly to Bad Debts Expense; this method is generally considered to be inferior to the allowance method. p. 416

Discount period the number of days between the day on which a note is discounted at the bank and its maturity date. p. 423

Discount rate the rate of interest a bank charges for lending money by discounting a note. p. 424

Dishonouring a note failure by a promissory note's maker to pay the amount due at maturity. p. 420

Full-disclosure principle the accounting principle that requires financial statements (including the footnotes) to contain all relevant information about the operations and financial position of the entity; it also requires that the information be presented in an understandable manner. p. 425

General Ledger the ledger that contains all the financial statement accounts of an organization. p. 405

Installment accounts receivable accounts receivable that allow the customer to make periodic payments over several months and that typically earn interest for the seller. p. 417

Interest the charge assessed for the use of money. p. 418

Lower of cost or market (LCM) the required method of reporting temporary investments at the lower of the total cost of the securities (called the *portfolio*) or their total market value at the balance sheet date. p. 400

Maker of a note one who signs a note and promises to pay it at maturity. p. 418

Materiality principle the idea that the requirements of an accounting principle may be ignored if the effect on the financial statements is unimportant to their users. p. 417

Maturity date of a note the date on which a note and any interest are due and payable. p. 418

Maturity value of a note its principal plus any interest due on its maturity date. p. 424

Payee of a note the one to whom a promissory note is made payable. p. 418

Principal of a note the amount that the signer of a promissory note agrees to pay back when it matures, not including the interest. p. 418

Proceeds of the discounted note the maturity value of a discounted note minus the interest deducted in advance by the bank. p. 424

Promissory note an unconditional written promise to pay a definite sum of money on demand or at a fixed or determinable future date. p. 418

Realizable value the expected proceeds from converting assets into cash. p. 408

Short-term investments another name for *temporary investments*. p. 398

Subsidiary ledger a collection of accounts (other than general ledger accounts) that contains the details underlying the balance of a controlling account in the General Ledger. p. 407

Temporary investments investments that can be converted into cash quickly (but less quickly than cash equivalents), and that management intends to sell as a source of cash to satisfy the needs of current operations; temporary investments include such things as government or corporate debt obligations and marketable equity securities. p. 398

SYNONYMOUS TERMS

Allowance for doubtful accounts allowance for bad debts.

Common shares common stock

Credit sales charge sales.

Debt obligations debt securities.

Equity investment share or stock investment.

Maker of a note borrower.

Payee of a note lender.

Preferred shares preferred stock.

Shareholders' equity stockholders' equity.

Stocks equity securities.

Temporary investments short-term investments.

QUESTIONS

1. Under what conditions should investments be classified as current assets?

2. If a temporary investment in securities cost $6,780 and was sold for $7,500, how should the difference between the two amounts be recorded?

3. On a balance sheet, what valuation must be reported for temporary investments in securities?

4. If a company purchases temporary investments in securities for the first time, and their fair (market) values fall below cost, what account is credited for the amount of the unrealized loss?

5. If temporary investments that have been written down increase in value, how is the increase in value accounted for?

6. How do businesses benefit from allowing their customers to use credit cards?

7. Explain why writing off a bad debt against the allowance account does not reduce the estimated realizable value of a company's accounts receivable.

8. Why does the Bad Debts Expense account usually not have the same adjusted balance as the Allowance for Doubtful Accounts?

9. Why does the direct write-off method of accounting for bad debts commonly fail to match revenues and expenses?

10. What is the essence of the accounting principle of materiality?

11. Why might a business prefer a note receivable to an account receivable?

12. Review the consolidated balance sheets of Geac Computer Corporation presented in Appendix I. Assuming the company records all of its receivables in one controlling account, what was the balance of that account on April 30, 1994?

QUICK STUDY (Five-Minute Exercises)

QS 8–1
(LO 1)

On January 20, Smythe and O'Shea Co. made a temporary investment in 100 common shares of Computer Links. The purchase price was $62^1/_5$ and the broker's fee was $200. March 20, they received $2 per share in dividends. Prepare the January 20 and March 20 journal entries.

QS 8–2
(LO 1)

During this year, Balzarini Associates acquired temporary investments securities at a cost of $46,000. At December 31 year-end, these securities had a market (fair) value of $44,000.

   a. Prepare the necessary year-end adjustment.

   b. Explain how each account used in requirement *a* would affect or be reported in the financial statements.

QS 8–3
(LO 2)

Journalize the following transactions:

   a. Sold $2,000 in merchandise on Visa credit cards. The sales receipts were deposited in our business account. Visa charges us a 5% fee.

   b. Sold $5,000 on miscellaneous credit cards. Cash will be received within two weeks and a 4% fee will be charged.

QS 8–4
(LO 3)

Arnold Equipment Co. uses the allowance method to account for uncollectibles. On March 1, they wrote off a $4,000 account of a customer, Trukin Co. On May 1, they received a $1,000 payment from Trukin Co.

   a. Make the appropriate entry or entries for March 1.

   b. Make the appropriate entry or entries for May 1.

QS 8–5
(LO 3)

The year-end trial balance of Harpson Co. shows Accounts Receivable of $164,000, Allowance for Doubtful Accounts of $200 (credit), Sales of $600,000. Uncollectibles are estimated to be 1.5% of outstanding Accounts Receivable.

   a. Prepare the December 31 year-end adjustment.

   b. What amount would have been used in the year-end adjustment if the allowance account had a year-end debit balance of $100?

   c. Assume the same facts as presented above except Harpson Co. estimated uncollectibles as 1% of sales. What amount would be used in the adjustment?

On May 2, 1996, Building Corp. received a $9,000, 90-day, 12% note from a customer Sean Conrad as payment on account. Prepare the May 2 and maturity date entries assuming the note is honoured by Conrad.

QS 8–6
(LO 4)

The December 31 trial balance shows a $5,000 balance in Notes Receivable. This balance is from one note dated December 1, with a period of 120 days and 9% interest. Prepare the December 31 and maturity date entries assuming the note is honoured.

QS 8–7
(LO 4)

The following facts were extracted from Orion Corp's comparative balance sheets:

QS 8–8
(LO 5)

	1996	1995
Accounts receivable	$ 514,000	$ 426,000
Sales (net)	1,600,000	1,200,000

Compute the Accounts Receivable turnover for 1996.

EXERCISES

Prepare general journal entries to record the following transactions involving Best Plumbing's temporary investments, all of which occurred during 1996.

Exercise 8–1
Transactions involving
temporary investments
(LO 1)

a. On April 15, paid $90,000 to purchase $90,000 of Westside Company's short-term (60-day) notes payable, which are dated April 15, and pay interest at an 8% rate.

b. On May 10, bought 600 shares of Algoma Steel common shares at 10 1/2 plus a $126 brokerage fee.

c. On June 15, received a cheque from Westside Company in payment of the principal and 60 days' interest on the notes purchased in transaction a.

d. On June 25, paid $75,000 to purchase Stockard Corporation's 7% notes payable, $75,000 principal value, due June 25, 1996.

e. On August 16, received a $1.25 per share cash dividend on the Algoma Steel common shares purchased in transaction b.

f. On September 3, sold 300 shares of Algoma Steel common shares for $15 per share, less a $90 brokerage fee.

g. On December 26, received a cheque from Stockard Corporation for six months' interest on the notes purchased in transaction d.

On December 31, 1996, Compustat Company held the following temporary investments in securities:

Exercise 8–2
Recording LCM of
temporary investments
(LO 1)

	Cost	Market Value
Anchor Lamina Inc. common shares	$37,200	$41,100
Dofasco Inc. common shares	50,400	48,500
Northern Telecom Ltd. common shares . . .	69,600	63,900
Union Gas Ltd. common shares	85,500	84,100

Compustat had no temporary investments prior to 1996. Prepare the December 31 adjusting entry to record the change in market value of the investments.

Exercise 8–3
Adjusting the temporary
investment account to
reflect changes in
market value
(LO 1)

Rexlon Company's annual accounting period ends on December 31. The cost and market value of the company's temporary investments in marketable securities were as follows:

	Total Cost	Total Market Value
Temporary investments:		
On December 31, 1995	$56,250	$52,500
On December 31, 1996	63,750	68,125

Prepare the December 31, 1996, adjusting entry to update the market values of the temporary investments.

Exercise 8–4
Credit card transactions
(LO 2)

Nickels Company allows customers to use two credit cards in charging purchases. With the Dominion Bank card, Nickels receives an immediate credit on depositing sales receipts in its chequing account. Dominion Bank assesses a 3% service charge for credit card sales. The second credit card that Nickels accepts is Canacard. Nickels sends their accumulated receipts to Canacard on a weekly basis and is paid by Canacard approximately 15 days later. Canacard charges 2.5% of sales for using its card. Prepare entries in journal form to record the following credit card transactions of Nickels Company:

May 4 Sold merchandise for $2,500, accepting the customers' Dominion Bank cards. At the end of the day, the Dominion Bank card receipts were deposited in the company's account at the bank.

5 Sold merchandise for $550, accepting the customer's Canacard.

12 Mailed $9,520 of credit card receipts to Canacard, requesting payment.

28 Received Canacard's cheque for the May 12 billing, less the normal service charge.

Exercise 8–5
Subsidiary ledger
accounts
(LO 3)

Littlefield Corporation recorded the following transactions during April 1996:

Apr.	2	Accounts Receivable—Barbara Fowler	2,500.00	
		Sales		2,500.00
	10	Accounts Receivable—Robert Guerrero	260.00	
		Sales		260.00
	18	Accounts Receivable—Chris Layton	1,800.00	
		Sales		1,800.00
	23	Sales Returns and Allowances	562.00	
		Accounts Receivable—Chris Layton		562.00
	30	Accounts Receivable—Barbara Fowler	1,125.00	
		Sales		1,125.00

Required

1. Open a General Ledger having T-accounts for Accounts Receivable, Sales, and Sales Returns and Allowances. Also, open a subsidiary Accounts Receivable Ledger having a T-account for each customer. Post the preceding entries to the general ledger accounts and the customer accounts.

2. List the balances of the accounts in the subsidiary ledger, total the balances, and compare the total with the balance of the Accounts Receivable controlling account.

On December 31, at the end of its annual accounting period, a company estimated its bad debts as one-fourth of 1% of its $1,240,000 of credit sales made during the year, and made an addition to its Allowance for Doubtful Accounts equal to that amount. On the following February 3, management decided the $1,390 account of Colin Smith was uncollectible and wrote it off as a bad debt. Two months later, on April 2, Smith unexpectedly paid the amount previously written off. Give the journal entries required to record these events.

Exercise 8–6
Allowance for doubtful accounts
(LO 3)

At the end of each year, a company uses the simplified balance sheet approach to estimate bad debts. On December 31, 1996, it has outstanding accounts receivable of $176,600 and estimates that 3.5% will be uncollectible. (*a*) Give the entry to record bad debts expense for 1996 under the assumption that the Allowance for Doubtful Accounts had a $1,470 credit balance before the adjustment. (*b*) Give the entry under the assumption that the Allowance for Doubtful Accounts has a $1,235 debit balance before the adjustment.

Exercise 8–7
Bad debts expense
(LO 3)

Prepare journal entries to record these transactions:

Exercise 8–8
Dishonour of a note
(LO 4)

Aug. 12 Accepted a $4,500, three-month, 10% note dated today from Clive Nelson in granting a time extension on his past-due account.

Nov. 12 Nelson dishonoured his note when presented for payment.

Dec. 31 After exhausting all legal means of collecting, wrote off the account of Nelson against the Allowance for Doubtful Accounts.

On March 31, Jester Company had accounts receivable in the amount of $82,500. Prepare journal entries to record the following transactions for April. Also, prepare any notes to the April 30 financial statements that should be reported as a result of these transactions.

Exercise 8–9
Selling and pledging accounts receivable
(LO 5)

Apr. 5 Sold merchandise to customers on credit, $23,600.

8 Sold $6,800 of accounts receivable to Union Bank. Union Bank charges a 1.5% fee.

17 Received payments from customers, $5,200.

24 Borrowed $15,000 from Union Bank, pledging $22,000 of accounts receivable as security for the loan.

The following information is from the financial statements of Fine Furniture Company:

Exercise 8–10
Accounts receivable turnover
(LO 5)

	1996	1995	1994
Net sales	$1,080,000	$860,000	$750,000
Accounts receivable (December 31)	81,900	80,100	76,800

Calculate Fine Furniture's accounts receivable turnover for 1995 and 1996. Compare the two results and give a possible explanation for any significant change.

PROBLEMS

Ridgeway Company had no temporary investments on December 31, 1995, but had the following transactions involving temporary investments during 1996:

Problem 8–1
Accounting for temporary investments
(LO 1)

Jan. 15 Paid $250,000 to buy six-month, Treasury bills, $250,000 principal amount, 6%, dated January 15.

Feb. 7 Purchased 3,000 Royal Bank common shares at $59^{1}/_{2}$ plus a $3,570 brokerage fee.

Feb. 19   Purchased 1,200 Imperial Oil common shares at $62\frac{1}{4}$ plus a $1,494 broker-age fee.

Mar.   1   Paid $50,000 for Treasury notes, $50,000 principal amount, 9%, dated March 1, 1996, due March 1, 1997.

      26   Purchased 2,000 Abitibi Price common shares at $43\frac{3}{8}$ plus a $1,250 broker-age fee.

June   1   Received a $1.60 per share cash dividend on the Royal Bank common shares.

      17   Sold 1,200 Royal Bank common shares at 76 less a $912 brokerage fee.

July 17   Received a cheque for the principal and accrued interest on the Treasury bills that matured on July 15.

Aug.   5   Received a $3.10 per share cash dividend on the Imperial Oil common shares.

Sept. 1   Received a cheque for six months' interest on the Treasury notes purchased on March 1.

       1   Received a $1.75 per share cash dividend on the remaining Royal Bank common shares owned.

Nov.   5   Received a $2.95 per share cash dividend on the Imperial Oil common shares.

On December 31, 1996, the market prices of the equity securities held by Ridgeway Company were Royal Bank, $61\frac{7}{8}$; Imperial Oil, $50\frac{5}{8}$; and Abitibi Price, $33\frac{1}{2}$.

Required

1. Prepare General Journal entries to record the preceding transactions.
2. Prepare a schedule to calculate the lower of cost or market of Ridgeway's temporary investments in marketable equity securities.
3. Prepare adjusting entries, if necessary, to record accrued interest on Ridgeway Company's investments in debt obligations and to reduce the marketable equity securities to the lower of cost or market.

Problem 8–2
Credit sales and credit cards sales
(LO 2)

Werner Company allows a few customers to make purchases on credit. Other customers may use either of two credit cards. The First Bank deducts a 2% service charge for sales on its credit card but immediately credits the chequing account of its commercial customers when credit card receipts are deposited. Werner deposits the First Bank credit card receipts at the close of each business day.

When customers use the National Credit card, Werner Company accumulates the receipts for several days and then submits them to the National Credit Company for payment. National deducts a 3% service charge and usually pays within one week of being billed.

Werner Company completed the following transactions:

Aug.   2   Sold merchandise on credit to L. L. Terry for $985. (Terms of all credit sales are 2/15, n/60; all sales are recorded at the gross price.)

       3   Sold merchandise for $3,980 to customers who used their First Bank credit cards. Sold merchandise for $4,300 to customers who used their National Credit cards.

       5   Sold merchandise for $2,460 to customers who used their National Credit cards.

       7   Wrote off the account of R. Brown against Allowance for Doubtful Accounts. The $278 balance in Brown's account stemmed from a credit sale in December of last year.

Aug. 8   The National Credit card receipts accumulated since August 3 were submitted
           to the credit card company for payment.

      17   Received L. L. Terry's cheque paying for the purchase of August 2.

      19   Received the amount due from National Credit Company.

Required

Prepare General Journal entries to record the preceding transactions and events.

On December 31, 1996, Hallmart Company's records showed the following results for the
year:

Problem 8–3
Estimating bad debts
expense
(LO 3)

Cash sales	$ 601,250
Credit sales	1,178,000

In addition, the unadjusted trial balance included the following items:

Accounts receivable	$356,700 debit
Allowance for doubtful accounts	5,250 debit

Required

1. Prepare the adjusting entry needed on the books of Hallmart to recognize bad debts
    under each of the following independent assumptions:

    a.   Bad debts are estimated to be 1% of total sales.

    b.   Bad debts are estimated to be 2% of credit sales.

    c.   An analysis suggests that 5% of outstanding accounts receivable on December
           31, 1996, will become uncollectible.

2. Show how Accounts Receivable and the Allowance for Doubtful Accounts would
    appear on the December 31, 1996, balance sheet given the facts in requirement 1*(b)*.

3. Show how Accounts Receivable and the Allowance for Doubtful Accounts would
    appear on the December 31, 1996, balance sheet given the facts in requirement 1*(c)*.

Artex Company had credit sales of $1.3 million in 1996. On December 31, 1996, the com-
pany's Allowance for Doubtful Accounts had a credit balance of $6,700. The accountant
for Artex has prepared a schedule of the December 31, 1996, accounts receivable by age,
and on the basis of past experience has estimated the percentage of the receivables in each
age category that will become uncollectible. This information is summarized as follows:

Problem 8–4
Aging accounts
receivable
(LO 3)

December 31, 1996 Accounts Receivable	Age of Accounts Receivable	Expected Percentage Uncollectible
$365,000	Not due (under 30 days)	1.00%
177,000	1 to 30 days past due	2.50
38,000	31 to 60 days past due	7.75
20,000	61 to 90 days past due	45.00
6,000	over 90 days past due	70.00

Required

Preparation component:

1. Calculate the amount that should appear in the December 31, 1996, balance sheet as
    the Allowance for Doubtful Accounts.

2. Prepare the journal entry to record bad debts expense for 1996.

Analysis component:

3.   On June 30, 1997, Artex concluded that a customer's $1,875 receivable (created in 1996) was uncollectible and that the account should be written off. What effect will this action have on Artex's 1997 net income? Explain your answer.

Problem 8–5
Recording accounts receivable transactions and bad debt adjustments
(LO 3)

Gilcrest Company began operations on January 1, 1996. During the next two years, the company completed a number of transactions involving credit sales, accounts receivable collections, and bad debts. These transactions are summarized as follows:

1996

a.   Sold merchandise on credit for $817,500, terms n/30.

b.   Wrote off uncollectible accounts receivable in the amount of $12,500.

c.   Received cash of $476,500 in payment of outstanding accounts receivable.

d.   In adjusting the accounts on December 31, concluded that 1.5% of the outstanding accounts receivable would become uncollectible.

1997

e.   Sold merchandise on credit for $1,017,000, terms n/30.

f.   Wrote off uncollectible accounts receivable in the amount of $19,200.

g.   Received cash of $788,500 in payment of outstanding accounts receivable.

h.   In adjusting the accounts on December 31, concluded that 1.5% of the outstanding accounts receivable would become uncollectible.

Required

Prepare journal entries to record the 1996 and 1997 summarized transactions of Gilcrest and the adjusting entries to record bad debts expense at the end of each year.

Problem 8–6
Journalizing notes receivable and bad debt transactions
(LO 4)

Prepare General Journal entries to record these transactions and events experienced by Ethyl Company:

Jan.   8   Accepted a $4,250, 60-day, 10% note dated this day in granting a time extension on the past-due account of Pat Wilkins.

Mar.   9   Pat Wilkins paid the maturity value of his $4,250 note.

       11   Accepted a $4,950, 60-day, 11% note dated this day in granting a time extension on the past-due account of Paula Mathers.

May   10   Paula Mathers dishonoured her note when presented for payment.

       17   Accepted a $3,000, 90-day, 13% note dated May 15 in granting a time extension on the past-due account of Elmer Mayes.

       25   Discounted the Elmer Mayes note at the bank at 15%.

Aug. 16   Because the company had not received a notice protesting the Elmer Mayes note, assumed that it had been paid.

       17   Accepted a $2,250, 60-day, 11% note dated August 15 in granting a time extension on the past-due account of Steve Rollins.

Sept. 8   Discounted the Steve Rollins note at the bank at 13%.

Oct. 15   Received notice protesting the Steve Rollins note. Paid the bank the maturity value of the note plus a $30 protest fee.

       16   Received a $6,150, 60-day, 12% note dated this day from Martha Watson in granting a time extension on her past-due account.

Nov. 15   Discounted the Martha Watson note at the bank at 15%.

Dec. 16   Received notice protesting the Martha Watson note. Paid the bank the maturity value of the note plus a $30 protest fee.

27   Received payment from Martha Watson of the maturity value of her dishonoured note, the protest fee, and interest on both for 12 days beyond maturity at 12%.

31   Wrote off the accounts of Paula Mathers and Steve Rollins against Allowance for Doubtful Accounts.

Prepare General Journal entries to record the following transactions of Waterloo Company:

1996

Dec. 11   Accepted a $7,500, 90-day, 12% note dated this day in granting Fred Calhoun a time extension on his past-due account.

31   Made an adjusting entry to record the accrued interest on the Fred Calhoun note.

31   Closed the Interest Earned account.

1997

Jan. 10   Discounted the Fred Calhoun note at the bank at 14%.

Mar. 10   Received notice protesting the Fred Calhoun note. Paid the bank the maturity value of the note plus a $30 protest fee.

Mar. 5   Accepted a $2,250, 11%, 60-day note dated this day in granting a time extension on the past-due account of Donna Reed.

29   Discounted the Donna Reed note at the bank at 15%.

May 7   Because no notice protesting the Donna Reed note had been received, assumed that it had been paid.

June 9   Accepted a $3,375, 60-day, 10% note dated this day in granting a time extension on the past-due account of Jack Miller.

Aug. 8   Received payment of the maturity value of the Jack Miller note.

11   Accepted a $4,000, 60-day, 10% note dated this day in granting Roger Addison a time extension on his past-due account.

31   Discounted the Roger Addison note at the bank at 13%.

Oct. 12   Received notice protesting the Roger Addison note. Paid the bank the maturity value of the note plus a $30 protest fee.

Nov. 19   Received payment from Roger Addison of the maturity value of his dishonoured note, the protest fee, and interest on both for 40 days beyond maturity at 10%.

Dec. 23   Wrote off the Fred Calhoun account against Allowance for Doubtful Accounts.

Problem 8–7
Analysis and journalizing of notes receivable transactions
(LO 5)

The Doreen Granger Company had some surplus cash balances on hand and projected that excess cash would continue to be available over the next few years. Following is a series of events and other facts relevant to the temporary investment activity of the company:

1996

May 8   Purchased 1,000 shares of BCE at $40.40 plus $1,515 commission.

July 14   Purchased 2,000 shares of Dupont A at $32.40 plus $2,430 commission.

Sept. 29   Purchased 3,000 shares of Molson A at $19.20 plus $2,160 commission.

Dec. 31   These per share market values were known for the shares in the portfolio: BCE, $50.00; Dupont A, $29.00; Molson A, $14.40.

Problem 8–8
Entries and LCM application for temporary investments
(LO 1)

1997

Feb.   4   Sold 2,000 shares of Dupont A at $20.20 less $1,515 commission.

July   12   Sold 3,000 shares of Molson A, at $17.20 less $1,935 commission.

Aug. 17   Purchased 4,000 shares of Oshawa A at $13.60 plus $2,040 commission.

Dec. 15   Purchased 2,400 shares of Imperial Oil at $40.60 plus $3,654 commission.

       31   These per share market values were known for the shares in the portfolio: BCE, $60.60; Oshawa A, $8.20; Imperial Oil, $34.80.

1998

Jan.   2   Purchased 4,000 shares of Petro Canada at $7.20 plus $1,080 commission.

Feb.   2   Sold 4,000 shares of Oshawa A at $19.80 less $2,970 commission.

May   18   Sold 1,000 shares of BCE at $72.40 less $2,715 commission.

Nov. 28   Purchased 1,000 shares of The Bay at $25.60 plus $960 commission.

       30   Sold 2,400 shares of Imperial Oil at $30.40 less $2,736 commission.

Dec. 31   These per share market values were known for the shares in the portfolio: Petro Canada, $11.40; The Bay, $18.00.

Required

1. Prepare journal entries to record the events and any year-end adjustments needed to record the application of the lower of cost or market method of accounting for temporary investments.

2. Prepare a schedule that shows how the temporary investment portfolio would be described on the balance sheet at the end of each of the three years.

3. Prepare a schedule that shows the components of income (gains and losses, including LCM effects) from these investment activities, and their total effect, for each of the three years. Ignore dividends.

Problem 8–9
Analytical essay
(LO 1)

Cloron Company did not own any temporary investments prior to 1996. After purchasing some temporary investments in 1996, the company's accountant made the following December 31, 1996, adjusting entry:

Dec.	31	Loss on Market Decline of Temporary Investments	2,750.00	
		Allowance to Reduce Temporary Investments		
		to Market		2,750.00
		To adjust temporary investments portfolio		
		to the LCM amount.		

When Cloron's accountant reviewed the year-end adjustments with an office manager of the company, the accountant commented that the previous adjustment might have been different if the company had owned temporary investments on December 31, 1995. The office manager thought the accountant must be confused. The manager said that the December 31, 1996, adjustment was supposed to record a gain that occurred during 1996, and therefore should not be affected by any events that occurred during 1995.

Required

Explain why the accountant's comment is correct.

Review the facts about Hallmart Company in Problem 8–3.

Problem 8–10
Analytical essay
(LO 3)

Required

1. Recall that Allowance for Doubtful Accounts is a contra asset account. Nevertheless, Hallmart's unadjusted trial balance shows that this account has a $5,250 debit balance. Explain how this contra asset account could have a debit balance.
2. In Problem 8–3, requirement 1(c) indicates that 5% of the outstanding accounts receivable ($356,700 × 5% = $17,835) will become uncollectible. Given this conclusion, explain why the adjusting entry should not include a $17,835 credit to Accounts Receivable.

Griffen Company had no temporary investments on December 31, 1996, but had the following transactions involving temporary investments during 1997:

Problem 8–11
Accounting for temporary investments
(LO 1)

Jan. 9   Paid $60,000 to buy six-month Certificate of Deposit, $60,000 principal amount, 8%, dated January 9.

Feb. 2   Purchased 800 shares of Inco common shares at 35½ plus a $400 brokerage fee.

     15   Purchased 600 shares of Seagram common shares at 64¼ plus a $300 brokerage fee.

Mar. 2   Paid $45,000 for Canada Savings Bonds, $45,000 principal amount, 9%, dated March 2, 1997, due March 2, 2001.

     16   Purchased 1,200 shares of Nynex common shares at 55⅛ plus a $975 brokerage fee.

June 2   Received a $0.45 per share cash dividend on the Inco common shares.

     16   Sold 600 shares of Inco common shares at 37 less a $300 brokerage fee.

July 11   Received a cheque for the principal and accrued interest on the Certificate of Deposit that matured on July 9.

Aug. 13   Received a $0.55 per share cash dividend on the Seagram common shares.

Sept. 2   Received a cheque for six months' interest on the Canada Savings Bonds purchased on March 2.

      2   Received a $0.45 per share cash dividend on the remaining Inco common shares owned by Griffen Company.

Nov. 13   Received a $0.55 per share cash dividend on the Seagram common shares.

On December 31, 1997, the market prices of the equity securities held by Griffen Company were: Inco, 38½; Seagram, 63; and Nynex, 47⅞.

Required

1. Prepare general journal entries to record the above transactions.
2. Prepare a schedule to calculate the lower of cost or market of Griffen's temporary investments in marketable equity securities.
3. Prepare adjusting entries, if necessary, to record accrued interest on Griffen Company's investments in debt obligations and to reduce the marketable equity securities to the lower of cost or market.

Problem 8–12
Credit sales and credit
card sales
(LO 2, 3)

Chilton Company allows a few customers to make sales on credit. Other customers may use either of two credit cards. The Canadex Bank makes a 3% service charge for sales on its credit card but immediately credits the chequing account of its commercial customers when credit card receipts are deposited. Chilton deposits the Canadex Bank credit card receipts at the close of each business day.

When customers use the Western Credit Card, Chilton Company accumulates the receipts for two or three days and then submits them to the Western Credit Company for payment. Western makes a 4% service charge and usually pays within one week of being billed.

Chilton Company completed the following transactions:

Apr. 4   Sold merchandise on credit to Joe Blake for $1,750. (Terms of all credit sales are 2/15, n/60.)

5   Sold merchandise for $3,250 to customers who used their Canadex Bank credit cards. Sold merchandise for $3,600 to customers who used their Western credit cards.

6   Sold merchandise for $2,400 to customers who used their Western credit cards.

8   Wrote off the account of T. Kurth against Allowance for Doubtful Accounts. The $500 balance in Kurth's account stemmed from a credit sale in August of last year.

9   The Western credit card receipts accumulated since April 4 were submitted to the credit card company for payment.

19   Received Joe Blake's cheque paying for the purchase of April 4.

20   Received the amount due from Western Credit Company.

Required

Prepare general journal entries to record the above transactions.

Problem 8–13
Estimating bad debts
expense
(LO 3)

On December 31, 1996, Defore Corporation's unadjusted trial balance included the following items:

	Debit	Credit
Cash sales		$360,000
Credit sales		585,000
Accounts receivable	$210,000	
Allowance for doubtful accounts		200

Required

1. Prepare the adjusting entry on the books of Defore Corporation to estimate bad debts under each of the following independent assumptions:
   a.   Bad debts are estimated to be 2% of total sales.
   b.   Bad debts are estimated to be 3.5% of credit sales.
   c.   An analysis suggests that 7.5% of outstanding accounts receivable on December 31, 1996, will become uncollectible.
2. Show how Accounts Receivable and Allowance for Doubtful Accounts would appear on the December 3, 1996, balance sheet given the facts in 1. *b* above.
3. Show how Accounts Receivable and Allowance for Doubtful Accounts would appear on the December 31, 1996, balance sheet given the facts in 1. *c* above.

Software Corporation had credit sales of $6.5 million in 1996. On December 31, 1996, the company's Allowance for Doubtful Accounts had a debit balance of $7,400. The accountant for Software Corporation has prepared a schedule of the December 31, 1996, accounts receivable by age, and on the basis of past experience has estimated the percentage of the receivables in each age category that will become uncollectible. This information is summarized as follows:

Problem 8–14
Aging accounts receivable
(LO 3)

December 31, 1996, Accounts Receivable	Age of Accounts Receivable	Uncollectible Percent Expected
$600,000	Not due (under 30 days)	2
300,000	1 to 30 days past due	3
70,000	31 to 60 days past due	15
40,000	61 to 90 days past due	40
32,000	over 90 days past due	80

Required

1. Calculate the amount that should appear in the December 31, 1996, balance sheet as allowance for doubtful accounts.

2. Prepare the general journal entry to record bad debts expense for 1996.

3. On May 21, 1997, Software Corporation concluded that customer's $9,600 accounts receivable was uncollectible and that the account should be written off. What effect will this action have on Software Corporation's 1997 net income? Explain your answer.

After beginning operations on January 1, 1995, Johanson Company completed a number of transactions during 1995 and 1996 that involved credit sales, accounts receivable collections, and bad debts. These transactions are summarized as follows:

Problem 8–15
Recording accounts receivable transactions and bad debt adjustments
(LO 3)

1995

a. Sold merchandise on credit for $157,800, terms n/30.

b. Received cash of $128,900 in payment of outstanding accounts receivable.

c. Wrote off uncollectible accounts receivable in the amount of $300.

d. In adjusting the accounts on December 31, concluded that 1.5% of the outstanding accounts receivable would become uncollectible.

1996

a. Sold merchandise on credit for $198,800, terms n/30.

b. Received cash of $165,300 in payment of outstanding accounts receivable.

c. Wrote off uncollectible accounts receivable in the amount of $700.

d. In adjusting the accounts on December 31, concluded that 1.5% of the outstanding accounts receivable would become uncollectible.

Required

Prepare general journal entries to record the 1995 and 1996 summarized transactions of Johanson Company and the adjusting entries to record bad debts expense at the end of each year.

Prepare entries in general journal form to record these transactions by Wheat Company:

Problem 8–16
Journalizing notes receivable and bad debts transactions
(LO 3, 4, 5)

Jan. 10 Accepted a $3,000, 60-day, 12% note dated this day in granting a time extension on the past-due account of David Huerta.

Mar. 14 David Huerta dishonoured his note when presented for payment.

Mar. 19   Accepted a $2,100, 90-day, 10% note dated this day in granting a time extension on the past-due account of Rose Jones.

    28   Discounted the Rose Jones note at the bank at 16%.

June 20   Since notice protesting the Rose Jones note had not been received, assumed the note had been paid.

    27   Accepted $700 in cash and a $1,300, 60-day, 12% note dated this day in granting a time extension on the past-due account of Jake Thomas.

July 24   Discounted the Jake Thomas note at the bank at 14%.

Aug. 29   Received notice protesting the Jake Thomas note. Paid the bank the maturity value of the note plus a $20 protest fee.

Sept. 4   Accepted a $1,500, 60-day, 11% note dated this day in granting a time extension on the past-due account of Ginnie Bauer.

Oct. 13   Discounted the Ginnie Bauer note at the bank at 14%.

Nov. 6   Received notice protesting the Ginnie Bauer note. Paid the bank the maturity value of the note plus a $20 protest fee.

Dec. 6   Received payment from Ginnie Bauer of the maturity value of her dishonoured note, the protest fee, and interest at 11% on both for 30 days beyond maturity.

    28   Decided the accounts of David Huerta and Jake Thomas were uncollectible and write them off against Allowance for Doubtful Accounts.

PROVOCATIVE PROBLEMS

Provocative Problem 8–1
Business communications case
(LO 3)

As the accountant for JWest Company, you recently attended a sales managers' meeting devoted to a discussion of the company's credit policies. At the meeting, you reported that bad debts expense for the past year was estimated to be $35,000 and accounts receivable at the end of the year amounted to $645,000 less a $21,000 allowance for doubtful accounts. Chris Albertson, one of the sales managers, expressed confusion over the fact that bad debts expense and the allowance for doubtful accounts were different amounts. To save time at the meeting, you agreed to discuss the matter with Albertson after the meeting.

Because the meeting lasted longer than expected, Albertson had to leave early to catch a plane back to his sales district. As a result, you need to write a memorandum to him explaining why a difference in bad debts expense and the allowance for doubtful accounts is not unusual. (Assume that the company estimates bad debts expense to be 2% of sales.)

Provocative Problem 8–2
Financial reporting problem
(LO 3)

Builders Depot has been in business for six years and has used the direct write-off method of accounting for bad debts. The following information is available from the accounting records for the first five years:

	1995	1994	1993	1992	1991
Sales	$2,243,000	$1,170,000	$2,600,000	$3,400,000	$950,000
Net income	336,200	175,000	390,200	509,500	142,200
Bad debts written off during year	13,940	18,410	47,960	11,720	2,100
Bad debts by year of sale*	21,300	11,990	29,790	32,910	10,640

*Results from classifying bad debt losses so that the losses appear in the same years as the sales that produced them. For example, the $21,300 for 1995 includes $12,500 of bad debts that became uncollectible during 1996.

You are the manager of Builders Depot and want to change the method of accounting for bad debts from the direct write-off method to the allowance method. Kelly Skyles, the president of the company, feels this is not necessary. Prepare a five-year schedule for Skyles showing:

a. Net income if bad debts expense is defined to be bad debts by year of sale.

b. The dollar amount of difference between net income using the direct write-off method and the answer to requirement *a*.

c. The answer to requirement *b* as a percentage of the answer to requirement *a*.

d. Bad debts by year of sale as a percentage of sales.

e. Bad debts written off during the year as a percentage of sales.

Use the schedule to support your argument for using the allowance method to account for bad debts.

Refer to the financial statements and related disclosures from Geac Computer Corporation Ltd.'s 1994 annual report in Appendix I. Based on your examination of this information, answer the following:

Provocative Problem 8–3
Financial statement analysis case
(LO 1, 5)

Geac

1. Geac's most liquid assets include cash and short-term investments, and accounts receivable. What total amount of those assets did Geac have on April 30, 1994?

2. Express Geac's total liquid assets as of April 30, 1994, (as previously defined) as a percentage of current liabilities. Do the same for 1993. Comment on Geac's ability to satisfy current liabilities at the end of fiscal year 1994, as compared to the end of fiscal year 1993.

3. Calculate Geac's accounts receivable turnover for 1994.

ANALYTICAL AND REVIEW PROBLEMS

Shortcash Company required a loan of $15,000 and was offered two alternatives by the Security Bank. The alternatives are:

A & R Problem 8–1*

a. Shortcash would give the bank a one-year $15,000 note payable, dated November 1, 1996, with interest at 9%.

b. Shortcash would give the bank a one-year $16,350 noninterest-bearing note payable dated November 1, 1996. The bank would precalculate and deduct $1,350 of interest from the face amount of the note.

Required

1. Prepare all the necessary entries (including repayment on October 31, 1997) with regard to alternative *a*. Assume that Shortcash Company's fiscal year ends December 31.

2. Repeat the journal entries for alternative *b*.

—————
*Interest to be calculated on a monthly basis.

A & R Problem 8–2   The Tor-Mont Company has been in business three years and has applied for a significant bank loan. Prior to considering the applications, the bank asks you to conduct an audit for the last three years. Concerning accounts receivable, you find that the company has been charging off receivables as they finally proved uncollectible and treating them as expenses at the time of write-off.

Your investigation indicates that receivable losses have approximated (and can be expected to approximate) 2% of net sales. Until this first audit, the company's sales and direct receivable write-off experience was:

		Accounts Written Off In		
Year of Sales	Amount of Sales	1993	1994	1995
1993	$450,000	$1,500	$6,000	$1,800
1994	600,000	—	3,000	7,200
1995	750,000	—	—	4,500

Required

1. Indicate the amount by which net income was understated or overstated each year because the company used the direct write-off method rather than the generally acceptable allowance method.

2. Prepare all the entries for each of the three years that would have been made if Tor-Mont had used the allowance method from the start of the business.

3. Which of the entries in (2) are year-end adjusting entries?

CONCEPT TESTER

Test your understanding of the concepts introduced in this chapter by completing the following crossword puzzle.

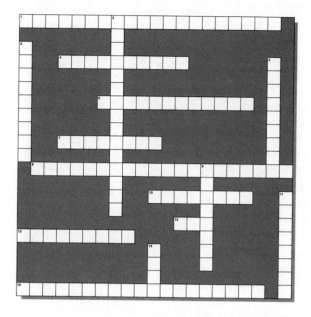

Across Clues

1. Securities which management intends to convert to cash in the near future (2 words).

4. The requirement that information be presented in an understandable manner (2nd of 3 words; also see 14 down, 13 across).

6. The point at which notes are due (2 words).

7. Amounts that are not collected (2 words).

8. The idea that some things may be ignored if they will not affect the decisions of those using financial statements (2 words).

10. A contra asset that estimates uncollectible amounts (3rd of 4 words; also see 3 down, 12 across, 11 down).

12. A contra asset that estimates uncollectible amounts (2nd of 4 words; also see 3 down, 10 across, 11 down).

13. The requirement that information be presented in an understandable manner (3rd of 3 words; also see 14 down, 4 across).

15. An obligation that is dependent upon the occurrence of a future event (2 words).

Down Clues

2. The expected proceeds from converting assets to cash (2 words).

3. A contra asset that estimates uncollectible amounts (1st of 4 words; also see 12 across, 10 across, 11 down).

5. The portion of a note which does not include interest.

9. The charge for the use of money.

11. A contra asset that estimates uncollectible amounts (4th of 4 words; also see 3 down, 12 across, 10 across).

14. The requirement that information be presented in an understandable manner (1st of 3 words; also see 4 across, 13 across).

ANSWERS TO PROGRESS CHECKS

8–1 Temporary investments are reported at lower of cost or market; thus, they may be reported at either cost or market.

8–2 Normally once a period, at the balance sheet date.

8–3 The increase can be reversed and a recovery (gain) is recognized up to the original cost of the investments.

8–4 If cash is received as soon as copies of credit card sales receipts are deposited in the bank, the business debits Cash at the time of the sale. If the business does not receive payment until after it submits the receipts to the credit card company, it debits Accounts Receivable at the time of the sale.

8–5 The credit card expenses are recorded when the cash is received from the credit card company; however, they are incurred at the time of the related sales.

8–6 An adjusting entry must be made to satisfy the matching principle. The credit card expense must be reported in the same period as the sale.

8–7 Bad debts expense must be matched with the sales that gave rise to the accounts receivable. This requires that companies estimate bad debts before they learn which accounts are uncollectible.

8–8 Realizable value.

8–9 The estimated amount of bad debts expense cannot be credited to the Accounts Receivable account because the specific customer accounts that will prove uncollectible cannot be identified and removed from the subsidiary Accounts Receivable Ledger. If the controlling account were credited directly, its balance would not equal the sum of the subsidiary account balances.

8–10
1995
Dec. 31 Bad Debts Expense   5,702
            Allow. for
               Doubtful Acc.   5,702

8–11
1996
Jan. 10 Allowance for
             Doubtful Accounts   300
             Acc. Rec.—
               Felix Arthur   300

Apr. 12 Acc. Rec.—
             Felix Arthur   300
             Allow. for
             Doubtful Acc.   300

    12 Cash   300
             Acc. Rec.—
               Felix Arthur   300

8–12
1995
Dec. 16 Notes Receivable   7,000
             Sales   7,000

Dec. 31 Interest Receivable   35
             Interest Earned   35
             $7,000 \times 12\% \times 15/365$

8–13
1996
Mar. 16 Acc. Rec.—
             White Corp.   7,140
             Interest Earned   105
             Interest Rec.   35
             Notes Rec.   7,000

8–14 Alternatives are (1) selling their accounts receivable to a factor, and (2) pledging the accounts receivable as security for a loan. The entries to record these transactions would take the following form:
(1) Cash
        Factoring Fee Expense
            Accounts Receivable
(2) Cash
            Notes Payable

8–15 A low turnover ratio indicates that the company takes longer to convert its accounts receivables to cash. This should cause concern if the turnover ratio is much lower than the average in the industry.

CHAPTER 9

Inventories and Cost of Goods Sold

Merchandising companies buy and sell large quantities and varieties of goods. These activities lead to complex accounting problems in measuring profits. Companies use several different methods to develop information about their inventories and cost of goods sold.

Karen White and Mark Smith know that there are different accounting policies that can be chosen. Their instructor indicated that the choice of one acceptable accounting approach over another can have a dramatic impact on net income. To illustrate, Moore Corporation Limited, a Canadian company that is the world's largest designer and manufacturer of business forms and related products, systems, and services, provided the following information about inventories in its 1994 annual report.

Notes to Consolidated Financial Statements

1. Summary of accounting policies (in part)

Inventories:

Inventories of raw materials and work in process are valued at the lower of cost and replacement cost and inventories of finished goods at the lower of cost and net realizable value. The cost of the principal raw material inventories and the raw material content of finished goods inventories in the United States is determined on the last-in, first-out basis. The cost of all other inventories is determined on the first-in, first-out basis.

2. Inventories (in thousands)	1994	1993
Raw materials	$ 74,161	$ 77,141
Work in process	27,280	26,321
Finished goods	131,883	141,827
Other	11,178	10,058
	$244,502	$255,347

The excess of the current cost over the last-in, first-out cost of those inventories determined on the latter basis is approximately $40,700,000 at December 31, 1994 (1993–$43,370,000).

If Moore Corporation used the current cost for its US inventories instead of the last-in, first-out basis, its 1994 net income would be increased by $40.7 million. The reason for using the last-in, first-out, method is to reduce the income tax liability for its US operations. Revenue Canada will not allow the use of the last-in, first-out method for Canadian operations.

LEARNING
OBJECTIVES

After studying Chapter 9, you should be able to:

1. **Describe *(a)* how the matching principle relates to accounting for merchandise, *(b)* the types of items that should be included in merchandise inventory, and *(c)* the elements that make up the cost of merchandise.**

2. **Calculate the cost of an inventory based on *(a)* specific invoice prices, *(b)* weighted-average cost, *(c)* FIFO, and *(d)* LIFO, and explain the financial statement effects of choosing one method over the others.**

3. **Explain the effect of an inventory error on the income statements of the current and succeeding years.**

4. **Describe perpetual inventory systems and prepare entries to record merchandise transactions and maintain subsidiary inventory records under a perpetual inventory system.**

5. **Calculate the lower-of-cost-or-market amount of an inventory.**

6. **Use the retail method and the gross profit method to estimate an inventory and calculate merchandise turnover and days' stock on hand.**

7. **Define or explain the words and phrases listed in the chapter glossary.**

The operations of merchandising businesses involve the purchase and resale of tangible goods. In Chapter 5, when we first introduced the topic of accounting for merchandisers, we left several important matters for later consideration. In this chapter, we return to the topic and examine the methods businesses use at the end of each period to assign dollar amounts to merchandise inventory and to cost of goods sold. The principles and procedures that we explain in this chapter are used in department stores, grocery stores, automobile dealerships, and any other businesses that purchase goods for resale. Since these procedures affect the reported amounts of income, assets, and equity, understanding the fundamental concepts of inventory accounting will enhance your ability to use and interpret financial statements.

The assets that a business buys and holds for resale are called *merchandise inventory*. As a rule, the items held as merchandise inventory are sold within one year or one operating cycle. Therefore, merchandise inventory is a current asset, usually the largest current asset on the balance sheet of a merchandiser.

MATCHING MERCHANDISE COSTS WITH REVENUES

Accounting for inventories affects both the balance sheet and the income statement. However, "the method for determining cost should be one that results in the fairest matching of costs against revenues regardless of whether or not the method corresponds to the [order in which the goods leave the firm]."[1] The matching process is already a familiar topic. For inventories, it consists of deciding how much of the cost of the goods that were available for sale during a period should be deducted from the period's revenue and how much should be carried forward as inventory to be matched against a future period's revenue.

---

[1] *CICA Handbook,* section 3030, "Inventories," par. .09.

In a periodic inventory system, when the cost of goods available for sale is allocated between cost of goods sold and ending inventory, the key problem is assigning a cost to the ending inventory. Remember, however, that by assigning a cost to the ending inventory, you are also determining cost of goods sold. This is true because the ending inventory is subtracted from the cost of goods available for sale to determine cost of goods sold.

The following schedule illustrates this relationship:

> Cost of goods sold:
>
>   Beginning inventory
>   + Purchases
>   = Cost of goods available for sale
>   − Ending inventory
>   = Cost of goods sold

LO 1

Describe *(a)* how the matching principle relates to accounting for merchandise; *(b)* the types of items that should be included in merchandise inventory; and *(c)* the elements that make up the cost of merchandise.

ITEMS TO INCLUDE IN MERCHANDISE INVENTORY

The merchandise inventory of a business includes all goods owned by the business and held for sale, regardless of where the goods may be located at the time inventory is counted. In applying this rule, most items present no problem. All that is required is to see that all items are counted, that nothing is omitted, and that nothing is counted more than once. However, goods in transit, goods sold but not delivered, goods on consignment, and obsolete and damaged goods require special attention.

Should merchandise be included in the inventory of a business if the goods are in transit from a supplier to a business on the date the business takes an inventory? The answer to this question depends on whether the rights and risks of ownership have passed from the supplier to the purchaser. If ownership has passed to the purchaser, they should be included in the purchaser's inventory. If the buyer is responsible for paying the freight charges, ownership usually passes as soon as the goods are loaded on the means of transportation. (As mentioned in Chapter 5, the terms would be FOB the seller's factory or warehouse.) On the other hand, if the seller is to pay the freight charges, ownership passes when the goods arrive at their destination (FOB destination).

Goods on consignment are goods shipped by their owner (known as the **consignor**) to another person or firm (called the **consignee**) who is to sell the goods for the owner. Consigned goods belong to the consignor and should appear on the consignor's inventory. For example, a company pays sports celebrities such as Silken Laumann, Wayne Gretzky and Roberto Alomar to sign memorabilia. The autographed baseballs, jerseys, photos, and so on, are then offered to the shopping networks on consignment as well as sold through catalogs and dealers.

Damaged goods and deteriorated or obsolete goods should not be counted in the inventory if they are not salable. If such goods can be sold at a reduced price, they should be included in the inventory at a conservative estimate of their **net realizable value** (sales price less the cost of making the sale). Thus, the accounting period in which the goods deteriorated, were damaged, or became obsolete suffers the resultant loss.

ELEMENTS OF MERCHANDISE COST

As applied to merchandise, cost means the sum of the expenditures and charges directly or indirectly incurred in bringing an article to its existing condition and location.[2] Therefore, the cost of an inventory item includes the invoice price, less any discount, plus any additional or incidental costs necessary to put the item into place and condition for sale. The additional costs may include import duties, transportation-in, storage, insurance, and any other related costs such as those incurred during an aging process (for example, the aging of wine).

All of these costs should be included in the cost of merchandise. When calculating the cost of a merchandise inventory, however, some concerns do not include the incidental costs of acquiring merchandise. They price the inventory on the basis of invoice prices only. As a result, the incidental costs are allocated to cost of goods sold during the period in which they are incurred.

In theory, a share of each incidental cost should be assigned to every unit purchased. This causes a portion of each to be carried forward in the inventory to be matched against the revenue of the period in which the inventory is sold. However, the effort of computing costs on such a precise basis may outweigh the benefit from the extra accuracy. Therefore, many businesses take advantage of the *materiality principle* and charge such costs to cost of goods sold.

TAKING AN ENDING INVENTORY

As you learned in Chapter 5, when a *periodic inventory system* is used, the dollar amount of the ending inventory is determined as follows: count the units of each product on hand, multiply the count for each product by its cost per unit, and add the costs for all products. In making the count, items are less likely to be counted twice or omitted from the count if you use prenumbered **inventory tickets** like the one in Illustration 9–1.

Before beginning the inventory count, a sufficient number of the tickets, at least one for each product on hand, is issued to the employees who make the count. Next, the employees count the quantity of each product. From the count and the price tag attached to the merchandise, the required inventory tickets are filled in and attached to the counted items. By the time the count is completed, inventory tickets should have been attached to all counted items. After checking for uncounted items, the employees remove the tickets and send them to the accounting department. To ensure that no ticket is lost or left attached to merchandise, the accounting department verifies that all the prenumbered tickets issued have been returned.

In the accounting department, the unit and cost data on the tickets are aggregated by multiplying the number of units of each product by its unit cost. This gives the dollar amount of each product in the inventory and the total for all the products is the dollar total of the inventory.

The use of computers has made physical stocktaking somewhat easier by having the computer do the extensions and additions. Scanners can facilitate the transfer of the data into the computer. However, it is still necessary to perform a check on the print-outs to ensure that the data is complete and that there are no errors.

---

[2] Ibid., par. 3030.02.

Illustration 9–1   Inventory Tickets Used to Tag Inventory Items as They Are Counted

INVENTORY TICKET NO. _786_	Quantity counted _____
Item _____	Sales price $ _____
Counted by _____	Cost price $ _____
Checked by _____	Purchase date _____

A common error is one where prices are entered incorrectly so that an item which costs, for example, $50 per hundred, is priced as $50 per unit. This error can significantly overvalue the inventory.

Progress Check
(Answers to Progress Checks are provided at the end of the chapter.)

9–1   Which accounting principle most directly governs the allocation of cost of goods available for sale between the ending inventory and cost of goods sold?

9–2   If Campbell sells goods to Thompson, FOB Campbell's factory, and the goods are still in transit from Campbell to Thompson, which company should include the goods in its inventory?

9–3   Kramer Gallery purchased an original painting for $11,400. Additional costs incurred in obtaining and offering the artwork for sale included $130 for transportation-in, $150 for import duties, $100 for insurance during shipment, $180 for advertising costs, $400 for framing, and $800 for sales salaries. In calculating the cost of inventory, what total cost should be assigned to the painting? *(a)* $11,400; *(b)* $11,530; *(c)* $11,780; *(d)* $12,180.

ASSIGNING COSTS TO INVENTORY ITEMS

LO 2

Calculate the cost of an inventory based on *(a)* specific invoice prices, *(b)* weighted-average cost, *(c)* FIFO, and *(d)* LIFO, and explain the financial statement effects of choosing one method over the others.

One of the major issues in accounting for merchandise involves determining the unit cost amounts that will be assigned to items in the inventory. When all units are purchased at the same unit cost, this process is easy. However, when identical items are purchased at different costs, a problem arises as to which costs apply to the ending inventory and which apply to the goods sold. There are four commonly used methods of assigning costs to goods in the ending inventory and to goods sold. They are (1) specific invoice prices; (2) weighted-average cost; (3) first-in, first-out; and (4) last-in, first-out. All four methods are generally accepted.

To illustrate the four methods under the periodic inventory system, assume that a company has 12 units of Product X on hand at the end of its annual accounting period. Also, assume that the inventory at the beginning of the year and the purchases during the year were as follows:

Jan.	1	Beginning inventory	10 units @ $100 =	$1,000
Mar.	13	Purchased	15 units @ $108 =	1,620
Aug.	17	Purchased	20 units @ $120 =	2,400
Nov.	10	Purchased	10 units @ $125 =	1,250
Total			55 units	$6,270

Specific Invoice Prices

When each item in an inventory can be clearly related to a specific purchase and its invoice, **specific invoice inventory pricing** may be used to assign costs. For example, assume that 6 of the 12 unsold units of Product X were from the November purchase and 6 were from the August purchase. With this information, specific invoice prices can be used to assign costs to the ending inventory and to goods sold as follows:

Total cost of 55 units available for sale		$6,270
Less ending inventory priced by means of specific invoices:		
6 units from the November purchase at $125 each	$750	
6 units from the August purchase at $120 each	720	
Ending inventory (12 units)		1,470
Cost of goods sold		$4,800

Weighted Average

When using **weighted-average inventory pricing,** multiply the per unit costs of the beginning inventory and of each purchase by the number of units in the beginning inventory and each purchase. Then, divide the total of these amounts by the total number of units available for sale to find the weighted-average cost per unit as follows:

```
10 units @ $100 = $1,000
15 units @ $108 =  1,620
20 units @ $120 =  2,400
10 units @ $125 =  1,250
55                 $6,270
$6,270/55 = $114 weighted-average cost per unit
```

After determining the weighted-average cost per unit, use this average to assign costs to the inventory and to the units sold as follows:

Total cost of 55 units available for sale	$6,270
Ending inventory priced on a weighted average cost basis: 12 units at $114 each	1,368
Cost of goods sold	$4,902

First-In, First-Out

First-in, first-out inventory pricing (FIFO) assumes the items in the beginning inventory are sold first. Additional sales are assumed to come in the order in which they were purchased. Thus, the costs of the last items received are assigned to the ending inventory, and the remaining costs are assigned to goods sold. For example, when first-in, first-out is used, the costs of Product X are assigned to the inventory and goods sold as follows:

Total cost of 55 units available for sale		$6,270
Less ending inventory priced on a basis of FIFO:		
10 units from the November purchase at $125 each . .	$1,250	
2 units from the August purchase at $120 each	240	
Ending inventory (12 units)		1,490
Cost of goods sold		$4,780

Understand that FIFO is acceptable whether or not the physical flow of goods actually follows a first-in, first-out pattern. The physical flow of products depends on the nature of the product and the way the products are stored. If a product is perishable (for example, fresh tomatoes), the business attempts to sell them in a first-in, first-out pattern. Other products, for example, bolts or screws kept in a large bin, may tend to be sold on a last-in, first-out basis. In either case, the FIFO method of allocating cost may be used.

Last-In, First-Out

Under the **last-in, first-out inventory pricing (LIFO)** method, the costs of the last goods received are charged to cost of goods sold and matched with revenue from sales. Again, this method is acceptable even though the physical flow of goods may not be on a last-in, first-out basis.

One argument for the use of LIFO is based on the fact that a going concern must replace the inventory items it sells. When goods are sold, replacements are purchased. Thus, a sale causes the replacement of goods. From this point of view, a correct matching of costs with revenues would be to match replacement costs with the sales that made replacements necessary. Although the costs of the most recent purchases are not quite the same as replacement costs, they usually are close approximations of replacement costs. Because LIFO assigns the most recent purchase costs to the income statement, LIFO (compared to FIFO or weighted average) comes closest to matching replacement costs with revenues.

Under LIFO, costs are assigned to the 12 remaining units of Product X and to the goods sold as follows:

Total cost of 55 units available for sale		$6,270
Less ending inventory priced on a basis of LIFO:		
10 units in the beginning inventory at $100 each . .	$1,000	
2 units from the March purchase at $108 each . . .	216	
Ending inventory (12 units)		1,216
Cost of goods sold		$5,054

Notice that when LIFO is used to match costs and revenues, the ending inventory cost is the cost of the oldest 12 units.

Comparison of Methods

In a stable market where prices remain unchanged, the choice of an inventory pricing method is not important. When prices are unchanged over a period of time, all methods give the same cost figures. However, in a changing market where prices are rising or falling, each method may give a different result. These differences are shown in Illustration 9–2, where we assume that Product X sales were $6,000 and operating expenses were $500.

In Illustration 9–2, note the differences that resulted from the choice of an inventory pricing method. Because purchase prices were rising throughout the period, FIFO resulted in the lowest cost of goods sold, the highest gross profit, and the highest net income. On the other hand, LIFO resulted in the highest cost of goods sold, the lowest gross profit, and the lowest net income. As you would expect, the results of using the weighted-average method fall between FIFO and LIFO. The results of using specific invoice prices depend entirely on which units were actually sold.

Each of the four pricing methods is generally accepted, and arguments can be made for using each. In one sense, one might argue that specific invoice prices exactly match costs and revenues. It is clearly the most appropriate method when each unit of product has unique features that affect the cost of that particular unit. However, this method may not be practical except for relatively high-priced items when just a few units are kept in stock and sold. Weighted-average costs tend to smooth out price fluctuations. FIFO provides an inventory valuation on the balance sheet that most closely approximates current replacement cost. LIFO causes the last costs incurred to be assigned to cost of goods sold. Therefore, it results in a better matching of current costs with revenues on the income statement.

Because the choice of an inventory pricing method often has material effects on the financial statements, the choice of a method should be disclosed in the notes to the statements. This information is important to an understanding of the statements and is required by the *full-disclosure principle*.[3]

The Consistency Principle

Because the choice of an inventory pricing method can have a material effect on the financial statements, some companies might be inclined to make a new choice each year. Their objective would be to select whichever method would result in the most favourable financial statements. If this were allowed, however, readers of financial statements would find it extremely difficult to compare the company's financial statements from one year to the next. If income increased, the reader would have difficulty deciding whether the increase resulted from more successful operations or from the change in the accounting method. The **consistency principle** is used to avoid this problem.

---

[3]Ibid., par. 3030.10

	Specific Invoice Prices	Weighted Average	FIFO	LIFO
Sales	$6,000	$6,000	$6,000	$6,000
Cost of goods sold:				
Merchandise inventory, January 1	$1,000	$1,000	$1,000	$1,000
Purchases	5,270	5,270	5,270	5,270
Cost of goods available for sale	$6,270	$6,270	$6,270	$6,270
Merchandise inventory, December 31	1,470	1,368	1,490	1,216
Cost of goods sold	$4,800	$4,902	$4,780	$5,054
Gross profit	$1,200	$1,098	$1,220	$ 946
Operating expenses	500	500	500	500
Income before taxes	$ 700	$ 598	$ 720	$ 446

Illustration 9–2
The Income Statement Effects of Alternative Inventory Pricing Methods

The *consistency principle* requires that a company use the same accounting methods period after period, so that the financial statements of succeeding periods will be comparable.[4] The *consistency principle* is not limited just to inventory pricing methods. Whenever a company must choose between alternative accounting methods, consistency requires that the company continue to use the selected method period after period. As a result, a reader of a company's financial statements may assume that in keeping its records and in preparing its statements, the company used the same procedures employed in previous years. Only on the basis of this assumption can meaningful comparisons be made of the data in a company's statements year after year.

The consistency principle does not require a company to use one inventory valuation method exclusively, however; it can use different methods to value different categories of inventory. For example, **Texaco, Inc.,** includes the following note in its financial statements:

Virtually all inventories of crude oil, petroleum products, and petrochemicals are stated at cost, determined on the last-in, first-out (LIFO) method. Other merchandise inventories are stated at cost, determined on the first-in, first-out (FIFO) method. Inventories are valued at the lower of cost or market. Materials and supplies are stated at average cost.

In achieving comparability, the *consistency principle* does not mean that a company can never change from one accounting method to another. Rather, if a company justifies a different acceptable method or procedure as an improvement in financial reporting, a change may be made. However, when such a change is made, the *full-disclosure principle* requires that the nature of the change, justification for the change, and the effect of the change on net income be disclosed in the notes to the statements.[5]

----

[4]Ibid., par. 1000.23.
[5]Ibid., par. 1506.16.

Progress Check

9–4   A company with the following beginning inventory and purchases ended the period with 30 units on hand:

	Units	Unit Cost
Beginning Inventory	100	$10
Purchases #1	40	12
Purchases #2	20	14

Using the data above, match the following:

					Choices
Ending inventory using	(1)	FIFO	_____	(a)	$ 330
	(2)	LIFO	_____	(b)	$ 400
	(3)	Weighted average	_____	(c)	$ 300
Cost of goods sold using	(1)	FIFO	_____	(a)	$1430
	(2)	LIFO	_____	(b)	$1360
	(3)	Weighted average	_____	(c)	$1460

9–5   In a period of rising prices, which method (LIFO or FIFO) reports the higher net income?

9–6   In a period of rising prices, what effect will LIFO as compared to FIFO have on the balance sheet?

INVENTORY ERRORS— PERIODIC SYSTEM

LO 3

Explain the effect of an inventory error on the income statements of the current and succeeding years.

Companies that use the *periodic inventory system* must be especially careful in taking the end-of-period inventory. If an error is made, it will cause misstatements in cost of goods sold, gross profit, net income, current assets, and owner's equity. Also, the ending inventory of one period is the beginning inventory of the next. Therefore, the error will carry forward and cause misstatements in the succeeding period's cost of goods sold, gross profit, and net income. Furthermore, since the amount involved in an inventory often is large, the misstatements can materially reduce the usefulness of the financial statements.

To illustrate the effects of an inventory error, assume that in each of the years 1994, 1995, and 1996, a company had $100,000 in sales. If the company maintained a $20,000 inventory throughout the period and made $60,000 in purchases in each of the years, its cost of goods sold each year was $60,000 and its annual gross profit was $40,000. However, assume the company incorrectly calculated its December 31, 1994, inventory at $16,000 rather than $20,000. Note the effects of the error in Illustration 9–3.

Observe in Illustration 9–3 that the $4,000 understatement of the December 31, 1994, inventory caused a $4,000 overstatement in 1994 cost of goods sold and a $4,000 understatement in gross profit and net income. Also, because the ending inventory of 1994 became the beginning inventory of 1995, the error caused an understatement in the 1995 cost of goods sold and a $4,000 overstatement in gross profit and net income. However, by 1996 the error had no effect.

In Illustration 9–3, the December 31, 1994, inventory is understated. Had it been overstated, it would have caused opposite results—the 1994 net income would have been overstated and the 1995 income understated.

Illustration 9-3 Effects of Inventory Errors—Periodic Inventory System

	1994		1995		1996	
Sales		$100,000		$100,000		$100,000
Cost of goods sold:						
Beginning inventory	$20,000		$16,000*		$20,000	
Purchases	60,000		60,000		60,000	
Goods for sale	$80,000		$76,000		$80,000	
Ending inventory	16,000*		20,000		20,000	
Cost of goods sold		64,000		56,000		60,000
Gross profit		$ 36,000		$ 44,000		$ 40,000

*Should have been $20,000.

Because inventory errors correct themselves by causing offsetting errors in the next period, you might be inclined to think that they are not serious. Do not make this mistake. Management, creditors, and owners base many important decisions on fluctuations in reported net income. Therefore, inventory errors must be avoided.

Progress Check

9-7 **Falk Company maintains its inventory records on a periodic basis. In making the physical count of inventory at 1996 year-end, an error was made that overstated the 1996 ending inventory by $10,000. Will this error cause cost of goods sold to be over- or understated in 1996? In 1997? By how much?**

The previous discussion of inventories focused on the periodic inventory system. Under the periodic system, the Merchandise Inventory account is updated only once each accounting period, at the end of the period. Then, the Merchandise Inventory account reflects the current balance of inventory only until the first purchase or sale in the following period. Thereafter, the Merchandise Inventory account no longer reflects the current balance.

By contrast, a *perpetual inventory system* updates the Merchandise Inventory account after each purchase and after each sale. As long as all entries have been posted, the account shows the current amount of inventory on hand. The system takes its name from the fact that the Merchandise Inventory account is perpetually up to date. When a perpetual system is used, management is able to monitor the inventory on hand on a regular basis. This aids in planning future purchases.

Before the widespread use of computers in accounting, only companies that sold a limited number of products of relatively high value used perpetual inventory systems. The cost and effort of maintaining perpetual inventory records were simply too great for other types of companies. However, since computers have made the record-keeping chore much easier, an increasing number of firms are switching from periodic to perpetual systems.

PERPETUAL INVENTORY SYSTEMS

LO 4

Describe perpetual inventory systems and prepare entries to record merchandise transactions and maintain subsidiary inventory records under a perpetual inventory system.

COMPARING JOURNAL ENTRIES UNDER PERIODIC AND PERPETUAL INVENTORY SYSTEMS

By using parallel columns in Illustration 9–4, we show the typical journal entries made under periodic and perpetual inventory systems. Observe the entries for the purchase of transaction 1. The perpetual system does not use a Purchases account. Instead, the cost of the items purchased is debited directly to Merchandise Inventory. Also, in transaction 2, the perpetual system credits the cost of purchase returns directly to the Merchandise Inventory account instead of using a Purchases Returns and Allowances account.

Transaction 3 involves the sale of merchandise. Note that the perpetual system requires two entries to record the sale, one to record the revenue and another to record cost of goods sold. Thus, the perpetual system uses a Cost of Goods Sold account. In the periodic system the elements of cost of goods sold are not transferred to such an account. Instead, they are transferred to Income Summary in the process of recording the closing entries.

The closing entries under the two systems are shown as item 4 in Illustration 9–4. Under the periodic system, all of the cost elements related to inventories are transferred to Income Summary. By comparison, under the perpetual system, those cost elements were already recorded in a Cost of Goods Sold account. Thus, the closing entries simply transfer the balance in the Cost of Goods Sold account to Income Summary. Of course, Sales must be closed under both inventory systems. In Illustration 9–4, both inventory systems result in the same amounts of sales, cost of goods sold, and end-of-period merchandise inventory.

SUBSIDIARY INVENTORY RECORDS— PERPETUAL SYSTEM

When a company sells more than one product and uses the perpetual inventory system, the Merchandise Inventory account serves as a controlling account to a subsidiary Merchandise Inventory Ledger. This ledger contains a separate record for each product in stock. This ledger may be computerized or kept on a manual basis. In either case, the record for each product shows the number of units and cost of each purchase, the number of units and cost of each sale, and the resulting balance of product on hand.

Illustration 9–5 shows an example of a subsidiary merchandise inventory record. This particular record is for Product Z, which is stored in Bin 8 of the stockroom. In this case, the record also shows the company's policy of maintaining no more than 25 or no less than 5 units of Product Z on hand.

In Illustration 9–5, note that the beginning inventory consisted of 10 units that cost $10 each. The first transaction occurred on January 5 and was a sale of five units at $17 per unit. Next, 20 units were purchased on January 8 at a cost of $10.50 per unit. Then, three units were sold on January 10 for $17 per unit. The entries to record the January 10 sale are:

Jan.	10	Cash (or Accounts Receivable)	51.00	
		Sales		51.00
		$3 \times \$17.00 = \$51$		
	10	Cost of Goods Sold	30.00	
		Merchandise Inventory		30.00
		$3 \times \$10.00 = \$30$		

In the second entry, notice that the cost per unit assigned to these three units was $10. This indicates that a first-in, first-out basis is being assumed for this product. In

Illustration 9–4 A Comparison of Entries under Periodic and Perpetual Inventory Systems

X Company purchases merchandise for $15 per unit and sells it for $25. The company begins the current period with five units of product on hand, which cost a total of $75.

Periodic			Perpetual		

1. *Purchased on credit 10 units of merchandise for $15 per unit:*

Purchases	150		Merchandise Inventory	150	
Accounts Payable		150	Accounts Payable		150

2. *Returned 3 units of merchandise originally purchased in (1):*

Accounts Payable	45		Accounts Payable	45	
Purchases Returns and Allowances		45	Merchandise Inventory		45

3. *Sold eight units for $200 cash:*

Cash	200		Cash	200	
Sales		200	Sales		200
			Cost of Goods Sold	120	
			Merchandise Inventory		120

4. *Closing entries:*

Merchandise Inventory (Ending)	60		Income Summary	120	
Sales	200		Cost of Goods Sold		120
Purchases Returns and Allowances	45				
Income Summary		305	Sales	200	
			Income Summary		200
Income Summary	225				
Merchandise Inventory (Beginning)		75			
Purchases		150			

	Units	Cost
Beginning inventory	5	$ 75
Purchases	10	150
Purchases returns	(3)	(45)
Goods available	12	$180
Goods sold	(8)	(120)
Ending inventory	4	$ 60

Merchandise Inventory

Transaction No.	Dr.	Cr.	Bal.
Opening Balance			75
1.	150		225
2.		45	180
3.		120	60

addition to FIFO, perpetual inventory systems can be designed to accommodate an average cost flow assumption. Perpetual inventory systems rarely use LIFO in the subsidiary records. If a company wants its financial statements to reflect LIFO, special adjustments are made at the end of each accounting period to convert the balances from FIFO or weighted average to LIFO. The details of using weighted average and LIFO with perpetual systems are explained in a more advanced accounting course.

Illustration 9-5 A Subsidiary Inventory Record Using FIFO

Item	Product Z				Location in stock room	Bin 8			
Maximum	25				Minimum	5			

Date	Received			Sold			Balance		
	Units	Cost	Total	Units	Cost	Total	Units	Cost	Balance
Jan. 1							10	10.00	100.00
Jan. 5				5	10.00	50.00	5	10.00	50.00
Jan. 8	20	10.50	210.00				5	10.00	
							20	10.50	260.00
Jan.10				3	10.00	30.00	2	10.00	
							20	10.50	230.00

All companies should take a physical inventory at least annually, even if a perpetual inventory system is used. By taking a physical inventory, management confirms the accuracy of the perpetual inventory records. When the physical inventory shows that the perpetual records are incorrect, a special adjusting entry should be prepared to update the accounts.

Before the widespread use of computers, many companies avoided the use of a perpetual inventory system in favour of the periodic system. Computers greatly facilitate the record keeping required in a perpetual system. The use of point-of-sale scanners and other systems in grocery and department stores allows management to track the inventory from the receiving dock, to the warehouse, to the store shelf, to the customer. This technology allows better purchase planning and better service to the consumer. In addition, since inventories can be controlled, the amount of inventory and the carrying costs can be reduced.

Progress Check

9-8 What account is used in a perpetual inventory system but not in a periodic system?

9-9 In a perpetual inventory system, which of the following statements are true?
   a. The Merchandise Inventory account balance shows the amount of merchandise on hand.
   b. Subsidiary inventory records are maintained for each type of product.
   c. A sale of merchandise requires two entries, one to record the revenue and one to record the cost of goods sold.
   d. A separate Cost of Goods Sold account is used.
   e. All of the above are correct.

As we have discussed, the cost of the ending inventory is determined by using one of the four pricing methods (FIFO, LIFO, weighted average, or specific invoice prices). However, the cost of the inventory is not necessarily the amount reported on the balance sheet. Generally accepted accounting principles require that the inventory be reported at market value whenever market is lower than cost. Thus, merchandise inventory is shown on the balance sheet at the **lower of cost or market (LCM).**

Determination of Market

In applying lower of cost or market to merchandise inventories, what do accountants mean by the term *market*? For the purpose of assigning a value to merchandise inventory, market can be either *net realizable value* or *replacement cost*. Replacement cost means the price a company would pay if it bought new items to replace those in its inventory. When the cost to replace merchandise drops below original cost, the sales price of the merchandise is also likely to fall. Therefore, the merchandise is worth less to the company and should be written down to replacement cost (or market). Net realizable value means the amount the company expects to receive when it sells the merchandise less any costs of preparing the merchandise for sale, such as repairs, or selling costs, such as commissions. If the net realizable value (NRV) is less than original cost, then the merchandise should be written down to NRV (or market).

The choice of either NRV or replacement cost as the market value depends on which amount is more reliable. Most Canadian companies tend to use NRV as their definition of market value.[6]

LOWER OF COST OR MARKET

LO 5
Calculate the lower-of-cost-or-market amount of an inventory.

Product	Units on Hand	Per Unit Cost	Per Unit Replacement Cost	Total Cost	Total Market	Lower of Cost or Market (by product)
X	20	$8	$7	$160	$140	$140
Y	10	5	6	50	60	50
Z	5	9	7	45	35	35
Total cost originally incurred				$255		
LCM (applied to whole inventory)					$235	
LCM (applied to each product)						$225

Note that when LCM is applied to the whole inventory, the total is $235, which is $20 lower than the $255 cost. And when the method is applied separately to each product, the sum is only $225. In general, a company may apply LCM three different ways:

1. LCM may be applied separately to each product.
2. LCM may be applied to major categories of products.

---

[6]CICA, *Financial Reporting in Canada 1993,* (Toronto: 1993), p. 92.

3. If the products are not too different, LCM may be applied to the inventory as a whole.

THE CONSERVATISM PRINCIPLE

Generally accepted accounting principles require writing inventory down to market when market is less than cost. On the other hand, inventory generally cannot be written up to market when market exceeds cost. If writing inventory down to market is justified, why not also write inventory up to market? What is the reason for this apparent inconsistency?

The reason is that the gain from a market value increase is not realized until a sales transaction provides verifiable evidence of the amount of the gain. But why, then, are inventories written down when market is below cost?

Accountants often justify the lower-of-cost-or-market rule by citing the **conservatism principle.** This principle attempts to guide the accountant in uncertain situations where amounts must be estimated. In general terms, it implies that when "uncertainty exists estimates [should] ensure that assets, revenues and gains are not overstated and conversely, that liabilities, expenses and losses are not understated."[7] Because the value of inventory is uncertain, writing the inventory down when its market value falls is clearly the less optimistic estimate of the inventory's value to the company.

Progress Check

9-10   A company's ending inventory includes the following items:

Product	Units on Hand	Unit Cost	Market Value per Unit
A	20	$ 6	$ 5
B	40	9	8
C	10	12	15

The inventory's lower of cost or market, applied separately to each product, is:
(a) $520; (b) $540; (c) $570; (d) $600.

METHODS OF ESTIMATING INVENTORY VALUE

LO 6

Use the retail method and the gross profit method to estimate an inventory and calculate merchandise turnover and days' stock on hand.

Most companies prepare financial statements on a quarterly or monthly basis. These monthly or quarterly statements are called **interim statements,** because they are prepared between the regular year-end statements. The cost of goods sold information that is necessary to prepare interim statements is readily available if a perpetual inventory system is used. However, a periodic system requires a physical inventory to determine cost of goods sold. To avoid the time-consuming and expensive process of taking a physical inventory each month or quarter, some companies use the **retail inventory method** to estimate cost of goods sold and ending inventory. Then, they take a physical inventory at the end of each year. Other companies also use the retail inventory method to prepare the year-end statements. Another method used to estimate inventories is the gross profit method. However, all companies should take a physical inventory at least once each year to correct any errors or shortages.

---

[7]*CICA Handbook,* section 1000, "Financial Statement Concepts," par. .21(d).

The Retail Method of Estimating Inventories

When the retail method is used to estimate an inventory, the company's records must show the amount of inventory it had at the beginning of the period both at *cost* and at *retail*. You already understand the cost of an inventory. The retail amount of an inventory simply means the dollar amount of the inventory at the marked selling prices of the inventory items.

In addition to the beginning inventory, the accounting records must show the net amount of goods purchased during the period both at cost and at retail. This is the balance of the Purchases account less returns and discounts. Also, the records must show the amount of net sales at retail. With this information, you estimate the ending inventory as follows:

Step 1: Compute the amount of goods available for sale during the period both at cost and at retail.

Step 2: Divide the goods available at cost by the goods available at retail to obtain a **retail method cost ratio.**

Step 3: Deduct net sales (at retail) from goods available for sale (at retail) to determine the ending inventory at retail.

Step 4: Multiply the ending inventory at retail by the cost ratio to reduce the inventory to a cost basis.

Look at Illustration 9–6 to see these calculations.

This is the essence of Illustration 9–6: (1) The company had $100,000 of goods (at marked selling prices) for sale during the period. (2) The cost of these goods was 60% of their $100,000 marked retail sales value. (3) The company's records (its Sales account) showed that $70,000 of these goods were sold, leaving $30,000 (retail value) of unsold merchandise in the ending inventory. (4) Since cost in this store is 60% of retail, the estimated cost of this ending inventory is $18,000.

An ending inventory calculated as in Illustration 9–6 is an estimate arrived at by deducting sales (goods sold) from goods available for sale. As we said before, this method may be used for interim statements or even for year-end statements. Nevertheless, a store must take a physical count of the inventory at least once each year to correct any errors or shortages.

Using the Retail Method to Reduce a Physical Inventory to Cost

In retail stores, items for sale normally have price tags attached that show selling prices. So, when a store takes a physical inventory, it commonly takes the inventory at the marked selling prices of the items on hand. It then reduces the dollar total of this inventory to a cost basis by applying its cost ratio. It does this because the selling prices are readily available and the application of the cost ratio eliminates the need to look up the invoice price of each item on hand.

For example, assume that the company in Illustration 9–6 estimates its inventory by the retail method and takes a physical inventory at the marked selling prices of the goods. Also assume that the total retail amount of this physical inventory is $29,600. The company can calculate the cost for this inventory simply by applying its cost ratio to the inventory total as follows:

$$\$29,600 \times 60\% = \$17,760$$

Illustration 9-6
Calculating the Ending
Inventory Cost by the
Retail Method

			At Cost	At Retail
(Step 1)	Goods available for sale:			
	Beginning inventory		$20,500	$ 34,500
	Net purchases		39,500	65,500
	Goods available for sale		$60,000	$100,000
(Step 2)	Cost ratio: ($60,000/$100,000) × 100 = 60%			
(Step 3)	Deduct net sales at retail			70,000
	Ending inventory at retail			$ 30,000
(Step 4)	Ending inventory at cost ($30,000 × 60%)		$18,000	

The $17,760 cost figure for this company's ending physical inventory is a satisfactory figure for year-end statement purposes. It is also acceptable for income tax purposes.

Inventory Shortage

An inventory determined as in Illustration 9–6 is an estimate of the amount of goods on hand. Since it is determined by deducting sales from goods for sale, it does not reveal any shortages due to breakage, loss, or theft. However, you can estimate the amount of such shortages by comparing the inventory as calculated in Illustration 9–6 with the amount that results from taking a physical inventory.

For example, in Illustration 9–6, we estimated that the ending inventory at retail was $30,000. Then, we assumed that this same company took a physical inventory and counted only $29,600 of merchandise on hand (at retail). Therefore, the company must have had an inventory shortage at retail of $30,000 − $29,600 = $400. Stated in terms of cost, the shortage is $400 × 60% = $240.

Gross Profit Method of Estimating Inventories

Sometimes, a business that does not use a perpetual inventory system or the retail method may need to estimate the cost of its inventory. For example, if the inventory is destroyed by fire or is stolen, the business must estimate the inventory so that it can file a claim with its insurance company. In cases such as this, the cost of the inventory can be estimated by the **gross profit method.** With this method, the historical relationship between cost of goods sold and sales is applied to sales of the current period as a way of estimating cost of goods sold during the current period. Then, cost of goods sold is subtracted from the cost of goods available for sale to get the estimated cost of the ending inventory.

To use the gross profit method, several items of accounting information must be available. This includes information about the normal gross profit margin or rate, the cost of the beginning inventory, the cost of net purchases, transportation-in, and the amount of sales and sales returns.

For example, assume that the inventory of a company was totally destroyed by a fire on March 27, 1996. The company's average gross profit rate during the past five years has been 30% of net sales. On the date of the fire, the company's accounts showed the following balances:

Illustration 9–7
The Gross Profit
Method of Estimating
Inventory

Goods available for sale:		
Inventory, January 1, 1996		$12,000
Net purchases	$20,000	
Add transportation-in	500	20,500
Goods available for sale		$32,500
Less estimated cost of goods sold:		
Sales	$31,500	
Less sales returns	(1,500)	
Net sales	$30,000	
Estimated cost of goods sold (70% × $30,000)		(21,000)
Estimated March 27 inventory and inventory loss		$11,500

Sales	$31,500
Sales returns	1,500
Inventory, January 1, 1996	12,000
Net purchases	20,000
Transportation-in	500

With this information, the gross profit method may be used to estimate the company's inventory loss. To apply the gross profit method, the first step is to recognize that whatever portion of each dollar of net sales was gross profit, the remaining portion was cost of goods sold. Thus, if the company's gross profit rate averages 30%, then 30% of each net sales dollar was gross profit, and 70% was cost of goods sold. In Illustration 9–7, we show how the 70% is used to estimate the inventory that was lost.

To understand Illustration 9–7, recall that an ending inventory is normally subtracted from goods available for sale to determine the cost of goods sold. Then, observe in Illustration 9–7 that the opposite subtraction is made. Estimated cost of goods sold is subtracted from goods available for sale to determine the estimated ending inventory.

As we mentioned, the gross profit method is often used to estimate the amount of an insurance claim. Accountants also use this method to see if an inventory amount determined by management's physical count of the items on hand is reasonable.

USING THE INFORMATION—MERCHANDISE TURNOVER AND DAYS' STOCK ON HAND

In prior chapters, we explained some ratios that you can use to evaluate a company's short-term liquidity. These ratios include the current ratio, the acid-test ratio, days' sales uncollected, and accounts receivable turnover. A company's ability to pay its short-term obligations also depends on how rapidly it sells its merchandise inventory. To evaluate this, you may calculate **merchandise turnover.** The formula for this ratio is:

$$\text{Merchandise turnover} = \frac{\text{Cost of goods sold}}{\text{Average merchandise inventory}}$$

In this ratio, the average merchandise inventory is usually calculated by adding the beginning and ending inventory amounts and dividing the total by two. However, if the company's sales vary by season of the year, you may want to take an average of the inventory amounts at the end of each quarter.

Analysts use merchandise turnover in evaluating short-term liquidity. In addition, they may use it to assess whether management is doing a good job of controlling the amount of inventory kept on hand. A ratio that is high compared to the ratios of competing companies may indicate that the amount of merchandise held in inventory is too low. As a result, sales may be lost because customers are unable to find what they want. A ratio that is low compared to other companies may indicate an inefficient use of assets. In other words, the company may be holding more merchandise than is needed to support its sales volume.

Earlier in this chapter, we explained how the choice of an inventory costing method (such as FIFO, weighted average, or LIFO) affects the reported amounts of inventory and cost of goods sold. The choice of an inventory costing method also affects the calculated amount of merchandise turnover. Therefore, comparing the merchandise turnover ratios of different companies may be misleading unless they use the same costing method.

Another inventory statistic used to evaluate the liquidity of the merchandise inventory is **days' stock on hand.** This is similar to the days' sales uncollected measure described in Chapter 7. The formula for days' stock on hand is:

$$\text{Days' stock on hand} = \frac{\text{Ending inventory}}{\text{Cost of goods sold}} \times 365$$

Notice the difference in the focus of merchandise turnover and days' stock on hand. Merchandise turnover is an average that occurred during an accounting period. By comparison, the focus of days' stock on hand is on the end-of-period inventory. Days' stock on hand is an estimate of how many days it will take to convert the inventory on hand at the end of the period into accounts receivable or cash.

In **The GAP, Inc.'s** 1993 annual report, management reported that they had initiated an aggressive new strategy of selling a more creative mix of merchandise and improving inventory management. This enabled The GAP to realize a 22.6% increase in net earnings for 1993 based on sales that only increased by 11.3%. The following data from The GAP's financial statements show that GAP's days' stock on hand decreased from 68.2 days in 1992 to 56.9 days in 1993 and inventory turnover increased from 5.8 to 6.1 times.

	1993	1992	1991
Cost of goods sold and occupancy expenses ..	$2,121,789	$1,955,553	
Ending merchandise inventory	331,155	365,692	$313,899

Days' stock on hand:

$$1993: \frac{\$331,155}{\$2,121,789} \times 365 = 56.9 \text{ days}$$

$$1992: \frac{\$365,692}{\$1,955,553} \times 365 = 68.2 \text{ days}$$

Progress Check

9-11   The following data relates to Taylor Company's inventory during the year:

	Cost	Retail
Beginning inventory	$324,000	$530,000
Purchases	204,000	348,000
Purchases returns	9,000	13,000
Sales		320,000

Using the retail method, the estimated cost of the ending inventory is:
(a) $545,000;   *(b)* $324,200;   *(c)* $333,200;   *(d)* $314,000;   *(e)* $327,000.

9-12   Describe the method for determining the merchandise turnover figure.

LO 1. Describe *(a)* how the matching principle relates to accounting for merchandise, *(b)* the types of items that should be included in merchandise inventory, and *(c)* the elements that make up the cost of merchandise. The allocation of the cost of goods available for sale between cost of goods sold and ending inventory is an accounting application of the *matching principle*. Merchandise inventory should include all goods that are owned by the business and held for resale. This includes items the business has placed on consignment with other parties but excludes items that the business has taken on consignment from other parties. The cost of merchandise includes not only the invoice price less any discounts but also any additional or incidental costs incurred to put the merchandise into place and condition for sale.

LO 2. Calculate the cost of an inventory based on *(a)* specific invoice prices, *(b)* weighted-average cost, *(c)* FIFO, and *(d)* LIFO, and explain the financial statement effects of choosing one method over the others. When specific invoice prices are used to price an inventory, each item in the inventory is identified and the cost of the item is determined by referring to the item's purchase invoice. With weighted-average cost, the total cost of the beginning inventory and of purchases is divided by the total number of units available to determine the weighted-average cost per unit. Multiplying this cost by the number of units in the ending inventory yields the cost of the inventory. FIFO prices the ending inventory based on the assumption that the first units purchased are the first units sold. LIFO is based on the assumption that the last units purchased are the first units sold. All of these methods are acceptable.

LO 3. Explain the effect of an inventory error on the income statements of the current and succeeding years. When the periodic inventory system is used, an error in counting the ending inventory affects assets (inventory), net income (cost of goods sold), and owner's equity. Since the ending inventory is the beginning inventory of the next period, an error at the end of one period affects the cost of goods sold and the net income of the next period. These next period effects offset the financial statement effects in the previous period.

LO 4. Describe perpetual inventory systems and prepare entries to record merchandise transactions and maintain subsidiary inventory records under a perpetual inventory system. Under a perpetual inventory system, purchases and

SUMMARY OF THE CHAPTER IN TERMS OF LEARNING OBJECTIVES

purchases returns are recorded in the Merchandise Inventory account. At the time sales are recorded, the cost of goods sold is credited to Merchandise Inventory. As a result, the Merchandise Inventory is kept up to date throughout the accounting period.

LO 5. Calculate the lower-of-cost-or-market amount of an inventory. When lower of cost or market is applied to merchandise inventory, market can mean net realizable value or replacement cost. Lower of cost or market may be applied separately to each product, to major categories of products, or to the merchandise inventory as a whole.

LO 6. Use the retail method and the gross profit method to estimate an inventory and calculate merchandise turnover and days' stock on hand. When the retail method is used, sales are subtracted from the retail amount of goods available for sale to determine the ending inventory at retail. This is multiplied by the cost ratio to reduce the inventory amount to cost. To calculate the cost ratio, divide the cost of goods available by the retail value of goods available (including markups but excluding markdowns).

With the gross profit method, multiply sales by $(1 - \text{the gross profit rate})$ to estimate cost of goods sold. Then, subtract the answer from the cost of goods available for sale to estimate the cost of the ending inventory.

Analysts use merchandise turnover and days' stock on hand in evaluating a company's short-term liquidity. They also use merchandise turnover to evaluate whether the amount of merchandise kept in inventory is too high or too low.

DEMONSTRATION PROBLEM

Tale Company uses a periodic inventory system and had the following beginning inventory and purchases during 1996:

		Item X	
Date		Units	Unit Cost
Jan. 1	Inventory	400	$14
Mar. 10	Purchase	200	15
May 9	Purchase	300	16
Sept. 22	Purchase	250	20
Nov. 28	Purchase	100	21

At December 31, 1996, there were 550 units of X on hand.

Required

1. Using the preceding information, apply FIFO inventory pricing and calculate the cost of goods available for sale in 1996, the ending inventory, and the cost of goods sold.

2. In preparing the financial statements for 1996, the bookkeeper was instructed to use FIFO but failed to do so and computed the cost of goods sold according to LIFO. Determine the size of the misstatement of 1996's income from this error. Also determine the effect of the error on the 1997 income. Assume no income taxes.

- Multiply the units of each purchase and the beginning inventory by the appropriate unit costs to determine the total costs. Then, calculate the cost of goods available for sale.
- For FIFO, calculate the ending inventory by multiplying the units on hand by the unit costs of the latest purchases. Then, subtract the ending inventory from the cost of goods available for sale.
- For LIFO, calculate the ending inventory by multiplying the units on hand by the unit costs of the beginning inventory and the earliest purchases. Then, subtract the total ending inventory from the cost of goods available for sale.
- Compare the ending 1996 inventory amounts under FIFO and LIFO to determine the misstatement of 1996 income that resulted from using LIFO. The 1997 and 1996 errors are equal in amount but have opposite effects.

Planning the Solution

1. FIFO basis:

Solution to Demonstration Problem

Jan. 1 inventory (400 @ $14)		$ 5,600
Purchases:		
Mar. 10 purchase (200 @ $15) . . .	$3,000	
May 9 purchase (300 @ $16)	4,800	
Sept. 22 purchase (250 @ $20) . . .	5,000	
Nov. 28 purchase (100 @ $21) . . .	2,100	14,900
Cost of goods available for sale		$20,500
Ending inventory at FIFO cost:		
Nov. 28 purchase (100 @ $21) . . .	$2,100	
Sept. 22 purchase (250 @ $20) . . .	5,000	
May 9 purchase (200 @ $16)	3,200	
FIFO cost of ending inventory . . .		10,300
Cost of goods sold		$10,200

2. LIFO basis:

Cost of goods available for sale		$20,500
Ending inventory at LIFO cost:		
Jan. 1 inventory (400 @ $14)	$5,600	
Mar. 10 purchase (150 @ $15) . . .	2,250	
LIFO cost of ending inventory . . .		7,850
Cost of goods sold		$12,650

If LIFO is mistakenly used when FIFO should have been used, cost of goods sold in 1996 would be overstated by $2,450, which is the difference between the FIFO and LIFO amounts of ending inventory. Income would be understated in 1996 by $2,450. In 1997, income would be overstated by $2,450 because of the understatement of the beginning inventory.

GLOSSARY

Conservatism principle the accounting principle that guides accountants to select the less optimistic estimate when two estimates of amounts to be received or paid are about equally likely. p. 464

Consignee one who receives and holds goods owned by another party for the purpose of selling the goods for the owner. p. 451

Consignor an owner of goods who ships them to another party who will then sell the goods for the owner. p. 451

Consistency principle the accounting requirement that a company use the same accounting methods period after period so that the financial statements of succeeding periods will be comparable. p. 456

Days' stock on hand an estimate of how many days it will take to convert the inventory on hand at the end of the period into accounts receivable or cash; calculated by dividing the ending inventory by cost of goods sold and multiplying the result by 365. p. 468

First-in, first-out (FIFO) inventory pricing the pricing of an inventory under the assumption that the first items received were the first items sold. p. 455

Gross profit inventory method a procedure for estimating an ending inventory in which the past gross profit rate is used to estimate cost of goods sold, which is then subtracted from the cost of goods available for sale to determine the estimated ending inventory. p. 466

Interim statements monthly or quarterly financial statements prepared in between the regular year-end statements. p. 464

Inventory ticket a form attached to the counted items in the process of taking a physical inventory. p. 452

Last-in, first-out (LIFO) inventory pricing the pricing of an inventory under the assumption that the last items received were the first items sold. p. 455

Lower of cost or market (LCM) the required method of reporting merchandise inventory in the balance sheet, in which market may be defined as net realizable value or replacement cost on the date of the balance sheet. p. 463

Merchandise turnover the number of times a company's average inventory was sold during an accounting period, calculated by dividing cost of goods sold by the average merchandise inventory balance. p. 467

Net realizable value the expected sales price of an item less any additional costs to sell. p. 451

Retail inventory method a method for estimating an ending inventory based on the ratio of the amount of goods for sale at cost to the amount of goods for sale at marked selling prices. p. 464

Retail method cost ratio the ratio of goods available for sale at cost to goods available for sale at retail prices. p. 465

Specific invoice inventory pricing the pricing of an inventory where the purchase invoice of each item in the ending inventory is identified and used to determine the cost assigned to the inventory. p. 454

Weighted-average inventory pricing an inventory pricing system in which the unit prices of the beginning inventory and of each purchase are weighted by the number of units in the beginning inventory and each purchase. The total of these amounts is then divided by the total number of units available for sale to find the unit cost of the ending inventory and of the units that were sold. p. 454

SYNONYMOUS TERM

Specific invoice inventory pricing specific identification method.

QUESTIONS

1. Where is merchandise inventory disclosed in the financial statements?

2. Why are incidental costs often ignored in pricing an inventory? Under what accounting principle is this permitted?

3. Give the meanings of the following when applied to inventory: *(a)* FIFO; *(b)* LIFO; *(c)* cost; and *(d)* perpetual inventory.

4. If prices are falling, will the LIFO or the FIFO method of inventory valuation result in the lower cost of goods sold?

5. May a company change its inventory pricing method each accounting period?

6. Does the accounting principle of consistency preclude any changes from one accounting method to another?

7. What effect does the full-disclosure principle have if a company changes from one acceptable accounting method to another?

8. What is meant when it is said that under a periodic inventory system, inventory errors correct themselves?

9. If inventory errors under a periodic inventory system correct themselves, why be concerned when such errors are made?

10. What guidance for accountants is provided by the principle of conservatism?

11. What accounts are used in a periodic inventory system but not in a perpetual inventory system?

12. What is the usual meaning of the word *market* as it is used in determining the lower of cost or market for merchandise inventory?

13. In deciding whether to reduce an item of merchandise to the lower of cost or market, what is the importance of the item's net realizable value?

14. Refer to Geac Computer Corporation's financial statements in Appendix I. On April 30, 1994, what percentage of Geac's current assets was represented by inventory?

QUICK STUDY (Five Minute Exercises)

a. Explain how the matching principle applies to the accounting for inventory.

b. Fun Stuff Inc., a distributor of novelty items, operates out of owner Margaret Falcaro's home. At the end of the accounting period, Falcaro tells us she has 2,000 units of product in her basement, 50 of which were damaged by water leaks and cannot be sold. She also has another 400 units in her van ready to deliver to fill a customer order, terms FOB destination, and has another 100 units out on consignment to a friend who owns a stationery store. How many units should be included in the end-of-the-period inventory?

QS 9–1
(LO 1)

The Victorian Attic, an antique dealer, purchased the contents of an estate for a bulk bid price of $45,000. The terms of the purchase were FOB shipping point and the cost of trans-

QS 9–2
(LO 1)

porting the goods to Victorian Attic was $2,000. Victorian Attic insured the shipment at the cost of $200. Prior to placing the goods in the store, they cleaned and refurbished some merchandise at a cost of $600 for labour and parts. Determine the cost of the inventory acquired in the purchase of the estate contents.

**QS 9–3
(LO 2)**

A company had the following beginning inventory and purchases during a period. What is the cost of the 110 units that remain in the ending inventory, assuming (a) FIFO, (b) LIFO, and (c) weighted average?

	Units	Unit Cost
Beginning inventory on January 1	200	$6.00
Purchase on March 20	50	$6.50
Purchase on July 2	80	$7.00

**QS 9–4
(LO 2)**

Identify the inventory costing method most closely related to each of the following statements assuming a period of rising costs:

a.   Results in a balance sheet inventory closest to replacement costs.

b.   Matches recent costs against revenue.

c.   Provides a tax advantage.

d.   Is best because each unit of product has unique features that affect cost.

e.   Understates current value of inventory on a balance sheet.

**QS 9–5
(LO 3)**

Gardner Company maintains its inventory records on a periodic basis. In taking a physical inventory at the end of 1995, certain units were counted twice. Explain how this error affects the following: (a) cost of goods sold, (b) gross profit, (c) 1995 net income, (d) 1996 net income, (e) the combined two-year income, (f) income in years after 1996.

**QS 9–6
(LO 4)**

a.   Journalize the following transactions under the periodic inventory system and under the perpetual inventory system:

Nov. 2   Purchased and received 100 cases of soda at a cost of $11 per case, FOB destination.

  5   Sold 20 cases of soda on account for $15 per case.

 17   Returned 30 cases of soda to supplier.

b.   Under which of the two alternative inventory systems would the inventory account have a November 17 balance that represented the cost of the 50 cases of soda that remain on hand?

**QS 9–7
(LO 5)**

Media-Tec has the following products in its ending inventory:

Product	Quantity	Cost	Market
A	4	$300	$240
B	15	400	420
C	8	200	180

Calculate lower of cost or market (a) for the inventory as a whole, and (b) applied separately to each product.

**QS 9–8
(LO 6)**

The inventory of Abba Cadabba was destroyed by a fire on April 15. The following data were found in the accounting records:

Jan. 1 inventory	$20,000
Jan. 1–Apr. 15 purchases (net)	38,000
Sales	86,000
Estimated gross profit rate	54%

Determine the cost of the inventory destroyed in the fire.

EXERCISES

Serges Company began a year and purchased merchandise as follows:

Jan.	1	Beginning inventory	80 units @ $60.00 =	$ 4,800
Feb.	16	Purchased	400 units @ $56.00 =	22,400
Sept.	2	Purchased	160 units @ $50.00 =	8,000
Nov.	26	Purchased	320 units @ $46.00 =	14,720
Dec.	4	Purchased	240 units @ $40.00 =	9,600
		Total	1,200 units	$59,520

Exercise 9–1
Alternative cost flow assumptions, periodic inventory system
(LO 2)

Required

The company uses a periodic inventory system, and the ending inventory consists of 300 units, 100 from each of the last three purchases. Determine the share of the $59,520 cost of the units for sale that should be assigned to the ending inventory and to goods sold under each of the following: *(a)* costs are assigned on the basis of specific invoice prices, *(b)* costs are assigned on a weighted-average cost basis, *(c)* costs are assigned on the basis of FIFO, and *(d)* costs are assigned on the basis of LIFO. Which method provides the highest and lowest net income?

Finest Company began a year and purchased merchandise as follows:

Jan.	1	Beginning inventory	80 units @ $40.00 =	$ 3,200
Feb.	16	Purchased	400 units @ $46.00 =	18,400
Sept.	2	Purchased	160 units @ $50.00 =	8,000
Nov.	26	Purchased	320 units @ $56.00 =	17,920
Dec.	4	Purchased	240 units @ $60.00 =	14,400
		Total	1,200 units	$61,920

Exercise 9–2
Alternative cost flow assumptions, periodic inventory system
(LO 2)

Required

The company uses a periodic inventory system, and the ending inventory consists of 300 units, 100 from each of the last three purchases. Determine the share of the $61,920 cost of the units for sale that should be assigned to the ending inventory and to goods sold under each of the following: *(a)* costs are assigned on the basis of specific invoice prices, *(b)* costs are assigned on a weighted-average cost basis, *(c)* costs are assigned on the basis of FIFO, and *(d)* costs are assigned on the basis of LIFO. Which method provides the highest and lowest net income?

Coe Company had $435,000 of sales during each of three consecutive years, and it purchased merchandise costing $300,000 during each of the years. It also maintained a $105,000 inventory from the beginning to the end of the three-year period. However, in accounting under a periodic inventory system, it made an error at the end of 1995 that caused its ending 1995 inventory to appear on its statements at $90,000 rather than the correct $105,000.

Exercise 9–3
Analysis of inventory errors
(LO 3)

Required

1. State the actual amount of the company's gross profit in each of the years.

2. Prepare a comparative income statement like Illustration 9–3 to show the effect of this error on the company's cost of goods sold and gross profit in 1995, 1996, and 1997.

Exercise 9–4
Perpetual inventory
system—FIFO cost flow
(LO 4)

In its beginning inventory on January 1, 1996, Stable Company had 120 units of merchandise that cost $8 per unit. Prepare general journal entries for Stable to record the following transactions during 1996, assuming a perpetual inventory system and a first-in, first-out cost flow.

Apr. 3 Purchased on credit 300 units of merchandise at $10.00 per unit.

       9 Returned 60 defective units from the April 3 purchase to the supplier.

July 16 Purchased for cash 180 units of merchandise at $8.50 per unit.

Aug. 5 Sold 200 units of merchandise for cash at a price of $12.50 per unit.

Dec. 31 Prepare entries to close the revenue and expense accounts to the Income Summary.

Exercise 9–5
Lower of cost or market
(LO 5)

Crystal Corporation's ending inventory includes the following items:

Product	Units on Hand	Unit Cost	NRV per Unit
W	40	$30	$34
X	50	48	40
Y	60	26	24
Z	44	20	20

Net realizable value is determined to be the best measure of market. Calculate lower of cost or market for the inventory (a) as a whole, and (b) applied separately to each product.

Exercise 9–6
Estimating ending
inventory—retail
method
(LO 6)

During an accounting period, Felder Company sold $220,000 of merchandise at marked retail prices. At the period end, the following information was available from its records:

	At Cost	At Retail
Beginning inventory	$ 62,180	$102,000
Net purchases	115,820	176,125

Use the retail method to estimate Felder's ending inventory at cost.

Exercise 9–7
Reducing physical
inventory to cost—
retail method
(LO 6)

Assume that in addition to estimating its ending inventory by the retail method, Felder Company of Exercise 9–6 also took a physical inventory at the marked selling prices of the inventory items. Assume further that the total of this physical inventory at marked selling prices was $50,500. Then, (a) determine the amount of this inventory at cost and (b) determine the store's inventory shrinkage from breakage, theft, or other causes at retail and at cost.

Exercise 9–8
Estimating ending
inventory—gross
profit method
(LO 6)

On January 1, a store had a $216,000 inventory at cost. During the first quarter of the year, it purchased $735,000 of merchandise, returned $10,500, and paid freight charges on purchased merchandise totaling $22,300. During the past several years, the store's gross profit on sales has averaged 25%. Under the assumption the company had $890,000 of sales during the first quarter of the year, use the gross profit method to estimate its inventory at the end of the first quarter.

From the following information for Jester Company, calculate merchandise turnover for 1996 and 1995 and days' stock on hand at December 31, 1996, and 1995.

Exercise 9–9
Merchandise turnover
and days' stock on hand
(LO 6)

	1996	1995	1994
Cost of goods sold	$367,900	$243,800	$223,600
Inventory (December 31)	77,120	69,400	73,200

Comment on Jester's efficiency in using its assets to support increasing sales from 1995 to 1996.

PROBLEMS

Hart Company began a year with 3,000 units of Product A in its inventory that cost $25 each, and it made successive purchases of the product as follows:

Problem 9–1
Alternative cost flows—
periodic system
(LO 2)

Jan. 29	4,500 units @ $30 each
Apr. 4	5,000 units @ $35 each
Sept. 8	4,800 units @ $40 each
Dec. 9	4,500 units @ $45 each

The company uses a periodic inventory system. On December 31, a physical count disclosed that 6,000 units of Product A remained in inventory.

Required

1. Prepare a calculation showing the number and total cost of the units available for sale during the year.

2. Prepare calculations showing the amounts that should be assigned to the ending inventory and to cost of goods sold assuming *(a)* a FIFO basis, *(b)* a LIFO basis, and *(c)* a weighted-average cost basis. Round your calculation of the weighted-average cost per unit to three decimal places.

MDI Company sold 7,800 units of its product at $55 per unit during 1996. Incurring operating expenses of $8 per unit in selling the units, it began the year and made successive purchases of the product as follows:

Problem 9–2
Income statement
comparisons and cost
flow assumptions
(LO 2)

January 1 beginning inventory	800 units costing $30.00 per unit
Purchases:	
March 3	1,000 units costing $31.00 per unit
June 9	2,000 units costing $32.00 per unit
October 17	4,500 units costing $33.00 per unit
December 6	600 units costing $34.00 per unit

Required

Preparation component:

1. Prepare a comparative income statement for the company, showing in adjacent columns the net incomes earned from the sale of the product assuming the company uses a periodic inventory system and prices its ending inventory on the basis of: *(a)* FIFO, *(b)* LIFO, and *(c)* weighted-average cost. Round your calculation of the weighted-average cost per unit to three decimal places.

Analysis component:

2. In comparing the results of the three alternatives, how would they change if MDI had been experiencing declining prices in the aquisition of additional inventory?

Problem 9–3
Analysis of inventory errors
(LO 3)

Ying Company keeps its inventory records on a periodic basis. The following amounts were reported in the company's financial statements:

	Financial Statements for Year Ended December 31		
	1994	**1995**	**1996**
(a) Cost of goods sold	$130,000	$154,000	$140,000
(b) Net income	40,000	50,000	42,000
(c) Total current assets	210,000	230,000	200,000
(d) Owner's equity	234,000	260,000	224,000

In making the physical counts of inventory, the following errors were made:

Inventory on December 31, 1994	Understated	$12,000
Inventory on December 31, 1995	Overstated	6,000

Required

Preparation component:

1. For each of the preceding financial statement items—*(a), (b), (c),* and *(d)*—prepare a schedule similar to the following and show the adjustments that would have been necessary to correct the reported amounts.

	1994	**1995**	**1996**
Cost of goods sold:			
Reported	_____	_____	_____
Adjustments: Dec. 31/94 error . . .	_____	_____	_____
Dec. 31/95 error . . .	_____	_____	_____
Corrected	======	======	======

Analysis component:

2. What is the error in the aggregate net income for the three-year period that resulted from the inventory errors? Explain why this result occurs. Also explain why the understatement of inventory by $12,000 in 1994 resulted in an understatement of equity by the same figure that year.

Problem 9–4
Lower of cost or market
(LO 5)

The following information pertains to the physical inventory of Home Appliance Centre taken at December 31:

	Units on Hand	**Per Unit**	
Product		**Cost**	**NRV**
Kitchen:			
Refrigerators	165	$380	$405
Stoves	120	203	181
Dishwashers	158	140	165
Microwaves	200	50	40
Entertainment:			
Stereos	140	250	312
Televisions	360	304	320

Cleaning/Maintenance:			
Washers	245	190	146
Dryers	280	188	162
Vacuum Cleaners	104	67	79

Required

In each of these independent cases, calculate the lower of cost or market *(a)* for the inventory as a whole, *(b)* for the inventory by major category, and *(c)* for the inventory, applied separately to each product.

The records of The Unlimited provided the following information for the year ended December 31:

Problem 9–5
Retail inventory method
(LO 6)

	At Cost	At Retail
January 1 beginning inventory	$ 160,450	$ 264,900
Purchases	1,113,140	1,828,200
Purchases returns	17,600	34,100
Sales		1,570,200
Sales returns		15,600

Required

1. Prepare an estimate of the company's year-end inventory by the retail method.
2. Under the assumption the company took a year-end physical inventory at marked selling prices that totaled $478,800, prepare a schedule showing the store's loss from theft or other cause at cost and at retail.

Cafferty Company wants to prepare interim financial statements for the first quarter of 1996. The company uses a periodic inventory system but would like to avoid making a physical count of inventory. During the last five years, the company's gross profit rate has averaged 35%. The following information for the year's first quarter is available from its records:

Problem 9–6
Gross profit method
(LO 6)

January 1 beginning inventory	$ 600,520
Purchases	1,890,400
Purchases returns	26,100
Transportation-in	13,800
Sales	2,382,300
Sales returns	18,900

Required

Use the gross profit method to prepare an estimate of the company's March 31 inventory.

Part 1. Draton Company's inventory includes a product that cost $9 per unit. Replacement cost is $8, expected sales price is $12, and additional costs to sell are $2. Explain the reason why the inventory should or should not be written down.

Problem 9–7
Analytical essay
(LO 3)

Part 2. Flavour Company's inventory includes a damaged product that cost $16 per unit. Replacement cost is $15, expected sales price is $17, additional costs that must be incurred to sell the product are $3. Explain the reason why the inventory should not be reported on the balance sheet at $16. At what value should it be reported? Why?

Review the facts about Hart Company presented in Problem 9–1 and notice that Hart uses a periodic inventory system. The facts of Problem 9–1 indicate that Hart Company had 21,800 units of product available for sale, had 6,000 units on hand at the end of the period,

Problem 9–8
Analytical essay
(LO 2, 5)

and, therefore, had sales of 15,800 units during the period. Now assume that the sale occurred as follows:

March 1	4,000 units
June 1	5,000 units
November 1	5,300 units
December 20	1,500 units

Required

1. Explain what effect, if any, these additional facts would have on the solution to requirement 2a and 2b of Problem 9–1.

2. Given the preceding information about the timing of sales, explain whether the Problem 9–1 solution to requirement 2a and 2b would provide the same answers under a perpetual inventory system as it does under a periodic inventory system.

Problem 9–9
Lower of cost or market
(LO 2)

Case 1: In this case, an evaluation of the expected selling price and normal profit margin for each product shows that replacement cost is the best measure of market. The inventory includes:

Product	Units on Hand	Cost	Replacement Cost
A	800	$20	$23
B	900	32	29
C	400	22	21

Case 2: In this case, the inventories of Products D and E have been damaged. If $15 additional cost per unit is paid to repackage the Product D units, they can be sold for $50 per unit. The Product E units can be sold for $70 per unit after paying additional cleaning costs of $18 per unit. The inventory includes:

Product	Units on Hand	Cost	Replacement Cost
D	330	$44	$46
E	500	60	55

Required

In each of the above independent cases, calculate the lower of cost or market (a) for the inventory as a whole and (b) for the inventory, applied separately to each product.

Problem 9–10
Analysis of inventory
errors
(LO 3)

Milicia Company keeps its inventory records on a periodic basis. The following amounts were reported in the company's financial statements:

		Financial Statements for Year Ended December 31		
		1996	**1997**	**1998**
(a)	Cost of goods sold	$ 67,000	$ 75,000	$ 65,000
(b)	Net income	24,000	39,000	21,000
(c)	Total current assets	108,000	115,000	100,000
(d)	Owners' equity	144,000	157,000	162,000

In making the physical counts of inventory, the following errors were made:

Inventory on December 31, 1996	Understated	$9,000
Inventory on December 31, 1997	Overstated	14,000

Required

1. For each of the financial statement items listed above as *(a)*, *(b)*, *(c)*, and *(d)*, prepare a schedule similar to the following and show the adjustments that would have been necessary to correct the reported amounts.

	1996	**1997**	**1998**
Cost of goods sold:			
Reported			
Adjustments: Dec. 31, 1996 error ...			
Dec. 31, 1997 error ...			
Corrected			

2. What is the error in the aggregate net income for the three-year period that resulted from the inventory errors?

The Turner Company sells a product called TurnUp and uses a perpetual inventory system to account for its merchandise. The beginning balance of TurnUps and transactions during January of this year were as follows:

Problem 9–11
Inventory records under FIFO and weighted average—perpetual system
(LO 4)

Jan. 1 Balance: 25 units costing $8 each.
  3 Purchased 50 units costing $9 each.
  7 Sold 20 units.
  19 Sold 15 units.
  21 Purchased 30 units costing $11 each.
  24 Sold 15 units.
  29 Sold 32 units.

Required

1. Under the assumption the concern keeps its records on a FIFO basis, enter the beginning balance and the transactions on a subsidiary inventory record like the one illustrated in this chapter.
2. Under the assumption the concern keeps its inventory records on a weighted average basis, enter the beginning inventory and the transactions on a second subsidiary inventory record.
3. Assume the 32 units sold on January 29 were sold on credit to Sally Rugby at $25 each and prepare general journal entries to record the sale on a FIFO basis.

Calico Stores takes a year-end physical inventory at marked selling prices and uses the retail method to reduce the inventory total to a cost basis for statement purposes. It also uses the retail method to estimate the amount of inventory it should have at the end of a year and by comparison determines any inventory shortage due to shoplifting or other cause. At the end of last year, its physical inventory at marked selling prices totaled $138,200, and the following information was available from its records:

Problem 9–12
Retail inventory method
(LO 5)

	At Cost	**At Retail**
Beginning inventory	$ 52,930	$ 80,200
Purchases	267,840	405,000
Purchases returns	5,520	8,400
Sales		340,000
Sales returns		4,400

Required

1. Use the retail method to estimate the store's year-end inventory at cost.
2. Use the retail method to reduce the company's year-end physical inventory to a cost basis.
3. Prepare a schedule showing the inventory shortage at cost and at retail.

Problem 9–13
Gross profit method
(LO 5)

When the Accessory Store was opened for business on the morning of March 10, it was discovered that thieves had broken in and stolen the store's entire inventory. The following information for the period January 1 through March 10 was available to establish the amount of loss:

January 1 merchandise inventory at cost	$125,100
Purchases	370,000
Purchases returns	3,225
Transportation-in	15,750
Sales	720,400
Sales returns	13,200

Required

Under the assumption the store had earned an average 38% gross profit on sales during the past five years, prepare a statement showing the estimated loss.

Problem 9–14
Gross profit method
(LO 5)

Herbert Florists wants to prepare interim financial statements for the first quarter of 1996. The company uses a periodic inventory system but would like to avoid making a physical count of inventory. During the last five years, the company's gross profit rate has averaged 30%, and the following information for the year's first quarter is available from its records:

January 1 beginning inventory	$ 70,560
Purchases	115,240
Purchases returns	3,900
Transportation-in	9,420
Sales	227,000
Sales returns	5,040

Required

Use the gross profit method to prepare an estimate of the company's March 31 inventory.

PROVOCATIVE PROBLEMS

Provocative Problem 9–1
Sampson's Sporting Goods
(LO 6)

The retail outlet of Samson's Sporting Goods suffered extensive smoke and water damage and a small amount of fire damage on October 5. The company carried adequate insurance, and the insurance company's claims adjuster appeared the same day to inspect the damage. After completing his survey, the adjuster agreed with Sam Corbin, the store's owner, that the inventory could be sold to a company specializing in fire sales for about one-third of its cost. The adjuster offered Corbin $235,400 in full settlement for the damage to the inventory. He suggested that the offer be accepted and said he had authority to deliver at once a cheque for that amount. He also pointed out that a prompt settlement would provide funds to replace the inventory in time for the store to participate in the Christmas shopping season.

Corbin felt the loss might exceed $235,400, but he recognized that a time-consuming count and inspection of each item in the inventory would be required to establish the loss more precisely. He was anxious to get back into business before the Christmas rush, the season making the largest contribution to annual net income, and was reluctant to take the time for the inventory count. Yet, he was also unwilling to take a substantial loss on the insurance settlement.

Corbin asked for and received one day in which to consider the insurance company's offer and immediately went to his records for the following information:

		At Cost	At Retail
a.	January 1 inventory	$ 387,700	$ 640,315
	Purchases, Jan. 1 through Oct. 5	1,347,200	2,250,450
	Net sales, Jan. 1 through Oct. 5		2,261,400

b. On March 1, the remaining inventory of winter sportswear and equipment was marked down from $110,400 to $87,000 and placed on sale in the annual end-of-the-winter-season sale. Two-thirds of the merchandise was sold. The markdown on the remainder was canceled, thereby returning the prices to regular retail amounts. (A markdown cancellation is subtracted from a markdown, and a markup cancellation is subtracted from a markup.)

c. In May, a special line of swimwear proved popular, and 110 suits were marked up from their normal $42.00 retail price to $52.50 per suit. Seventy suits were sold at the higher price; and on August 5, the markup on the remaining 40 suits was canceled and they were returned to their regular $42.00 price.

d. Between January 1 and October 5, markdowns totaling $11,300 were taken on several odd lots of sportswear. Recommend whether or not you think Corbin should accept the insurance company's offer. Back your recommendations with figures.

Provocative Problem 9–2
Modern Furniture Store **(LO 5)**

Modern Furniture Store has been in operation for six years, during which it has earned a 32% average gross profit on sales. However, the night before last, June 2, it suffered a disastrous fire that destroyed its entire inventory, and Marie Lauzon, the store's owner, has filed a $119,040 inventory loss claim with the insurance company. When asked on what she based her claim, she replied that during the day before the fire, she had marked every item in the store down 20% in preparation for the annual summer clearance sale, and during the marking-down process, she had taken an inventory of the merchandise in the store. "Furthermore," she said, "it's a big loss, but every cloud has a silver lining, because I am giving you fellows [the insurance company] the benefit of the 20% markdown in filing this claim."

When it was explained to Madame Lauzon that she had to back her loss claim with more than her word as to the amount of the loss, she produced the following information from her presale inventory and accounting records, which fortunately were in a fireproof vault and were not destroyed in the fire.

1. The store's accounts were closed on Dec. 31 of last year.
2. After posting was completed, the accounts showed the following June 2 balances:

Merchandise inventory, Jan 1 balance	$103,800
Purchases	279,400
Purchases returns	2,950
Freight-in	7,050
Sales	448,100
Sales returns	10,100

3. Madame Lauzon's prefire inventory totaled $148,800 at premarkdown prices.

From the information given, present figures to show the amount of loss suffered by Madame Lauzon. Also, show how she arrived at the amount of her loss claim. Can her presale inventory figure be used to substantiate the actual amount of her loss? If so, use the presale inventory figure to substantiate the actual loss.

Provocative Problem 9–3

Financial statement analysis case

(LO 1, 2)

Geac

Refer to the financial statements and related disclosures from Geac Computer Corporation Limited's 1994 annual report in Appendix I. Based on your examination of this information, answer the following:

1. What was the total amount of inventories held as current assets by Geac at April 30, 1994? At April 30, 1993?
2. Inventories represented what percentage of total assets at April 30, 1994? At April 30, 1993?
3. Comment on the relative size of inventories Geac holds compared to other types of assets.
4. What method did Geac use to determine the inventory amounts reported on its balance sheet?
5. Calculate merchandise turnover for fiscal year 1994 and days' stock on hand at April 30, 1994, and April 30, 1993. (Use "costs, excluding amounts shown below," for cost of goods sold.)

ANALYTICAL AND REVIEW PROBLEMS

A & R Problem 9–1

The following information is taken from the records of Bradford Company for four consecutive operating periods:

	Periods			
	1	2	3	4
Beginning inventory	$29,000	$41,000	$31,000	$37,000
Ending inventory	41,000	31,000	37,000	19,000
Net income	25,000	29,000	33,000	41,000

Assume that the company made the errors below:

Period	Error in Ending Inventory	
1	Overstated	$9,000
2	Understated	7,000
3	Overstated	8,000

Required

1. Compute the revised net income for each of the four periods.
2. Assuming that the company's ending inventory for period 4 is correct, how would these errors affect the total net income for the four periods combined? Explain.

The records of Walker Company as of December 31, 1996, show the following: **A & R Problem 9–2**

	Net Purchases	Net Income	Accounts Payable	Inventory
Balance per company's books	$20,500	$235,000	$22,100	$29,200
(a)				
(b)				
(c)				
(d)				
(e)				
Correct balances				

The accountant of Walker Company discovers in the first week of January 1997 that the following errors were made by his staff.

a. Goods costing $4,500 were in transit (FOB shipping point) and were not included in the ending inventory. The invoice had been received and the purchase recorded.

b. Damaged goods (cost $3,900) that were being held for return to the supplier were included in inventory. The goods had been recorded as a purchase and the entry for the return of these goods had also been made.

c. Inventory items costing $2,600 were incorrectly excluded from the final inventory. These goods had not been recorded as a purchase and had not been paid for by the company.

d. Goods that were shipped FOB destination had not yet arrived and were not included in inventory. However, the invoice had arrived on December 30, 1996, and the purchase for $2,100 was recorded.

e. Goods that cost $2,700 were segregated and not included in inventory because a customer expressed an intention to buy the goods. The sale of the goods for $4,200 had been recorded in December 1996.

Required

Using the format provided above, show the correct amount for net purchases, net income, accounts payable, and inventory for Walker Company as at December 31, 1996.

CONCEPT TESTER

Test your understanding of the concepts introduced in this chapter by completing the following crossword puzzle.

Across Clues

1. One who holds goods for sale that are owned by another party.
2. Principle that calls for less optimistic estimate when two estimates are equally likely.
5. Inventory pricing method that assumes units sold first come from units purchased first.
6. Inventory estimation method based on ratio of cost of goods available to selling price (2 words).
7. Financial statements prepared on a monthly or quarterly basis (2 words).

Down Clues

1. Owner of goods who transfers them to another party who will attempt to sell them for the owner.
2. Principle that calls for using the same accounting methods period after period.
3. Inventory pricing method that assumes units sold come from latest purchases.
4. Required method of reporting inventory at replacement cost when that is less than cost.

ANSWERS TO PROGRESS CHECKS

9–1 The matching principle.

9–2 Thompson.

9–3 *d*

9–4 Ending inventory   (1) *b*
                          (2) *c*
                          (3) *a*
    Cost of goods sold   (1) *b*
                          (2) *c*
                          (3) *a*

9–5 FIFO. LIFO results in a higher cost of goods sold and therefore a lower gross profit, which carries through to a lower net income.

9–6 LIFO will result in a smaller inventory figure on the balance sheet, as compared to FIFO which will result in an inventory figure that is close to current replacement costs.

9–7 The cost of goods sold will be understated by $10,000 in 1996 and overstated by $10,000 in 1997.

9–8 An account used only in a perpetual inventory system is Cost of Goods Sold.

9–9 *e*

9–10 *b*

9–11 *e*

9–12 Merchandise turnover =

$$\frac{\text{Cost of goods sold}}{(\text{Opening inventory} + \text{Closing inventory})/2}$$

Payroll Liabilities

Accounting for employees' wages and salaries is one task that is shared by almost every business entity. Payroll acccounting provides the means to comply with governmental regulations and provides valuable information regarding labour costs.

Karen White and Mark Smith's instructor stressed that wages, salaries and benefits form an important part of the expenses of every business. However, some businesses are more labour intensive than others. The following table compares the proportion of total expenses represented by labour costs for selected Canadian industries.

Wages, Salaries and Benefits as Percent of Total Expenses[1]

Industry	Percent
Insurance and real estate agencies	58.2
Primary steel industries	21.6
Motor vehicle industry	16.7
Department stores	14.2
Television, radio, and stereo stores	14.2
Supermarkets	9.3

[1]Source: CICA, "The Canadian Small Business Financial Performance Survey," 1994 Edition (Toronto: 1994).

LEARNING OBJECTIVES

After studying Chapter 10, you should be able to:

1. **List the taxes and other items frequently withheld from employees' wages.**

2. **Make the calculations necessary to prepare a Payroll Register and prepare the entry to record payroll liabilities.**

3. **Prepare journal entries to record the payments to employees and explain the operation of a payroll bank account.**

4. **Calculate the payroll costs levied on employers and prepare the entries to record the accrual and payment of these amounts.**

5. **Calculate and record employee fringe benefit costs and show the effect of these items on the total cost of employing labour.**

6. **Define or explain the words and phrases listed in the chapter glossary.**

Wages or salaries generally amount to one of the largest expenses incurred by a business. Accounting for employees' wages and salaries is one task that is shared by almost all business entities.

Payroll accounting:

- records cash payments to employees
- provides valuable information regarding labour costs
- accounts for amounts withheld from employees' pay
- accounts for employee (fringe) benefits and payroll costs paid by the employer
- provides the means to comply with governmental regulations on employee compensation

As you study this chapter, you will learn the general processes all businesses follow to account for these items.

ITEMS WITHHELD FROM EMPLOYEES' WAGES

LO 1

List the taxes and other items frequently withheld from employees' wages.

An understanding of payroll accounting and the design and use of payroll records requires some knowledge of the laws and programs that affect payrolls. Many of these require **payroll deductions,** amounts withheld from the wages of employees. Consequently, the more pertinent of these are discussed in the first portion of this chapter before the subject of payroll records is introduced.

Withholding Employees' Income Tax

With few exceptions, employers are required to calculate, collect, and remit to the Receiver General of Canada the income taxes of their employees. Historically, when the first federal income tax law became effective in 1917, it applied to only a few individuals having high earnings. It was not until World War II that income taxes were levied on substantially all wage earners. At that time Parliament recognized that many individual wage earners could not be expected to save sufficient money with which to pay their income taxes once each year. Consequently, Parliament instituted a system of pay-as-you-go withholding of taxes at their source each payday. This pay-as-you-go withholding of employee income taxes requires an employer to act as a tax collecting agent of the federal government.

The amount of income taxes to be withheld from an employee's wages is determined by his or her wages and the amount of **personal tax credits.** Each individual is entitled, in 1995, to some or all of the following annual amounts which are subject to tax credits (as applicable):

1.	Basic personal amount	$6,456
2.	Married or equivalent	5,380
	(with maximum earnings stipulated)	

The total of each taxpayer's personal tax credits is deducted from income to determine the level of income tax deductions from the individual's gross pay. For example, an individual with a gross weekly salary of $500 and personal tax credits of $6,456 (1995 net claim code 1 on the TD1 form) would have $92.55 of income taxes withheld. Another individual with the same gross salary but with personal tax credits of $11,783 (claim code 5) would have $64.40 withheld.

Employers are responsible for determining the amount of income tax owed by each employee every payday and withholding it from his or her pay for that period. However, to do this an employer must know the credits claimed by each employee. Consequently, every employee is required to file with the employer an employee's Personal Tax Credit Return, Form TD1, on which he or she claims the applicable credit. The taxpayer must file a revised Form TD1 each time the exemptions change during a year. The TD1 form is shown in Illustration 10–1.

In determining the amounts of income taxes to be withheld from the wages of employees, employers normally use tax withholding tables provided by Revenue Canada, Taxation. The tables indicate the tax to be withheld from any amount of wages and with any number of credits. The to-be-withheld amounts include both federal and provincial income taxes except for the province of Quebec. The province of Quebec levies and collects its own income tax and its own pension plan contributions. Employers in that province remit separately, to the respective authority, federal and provincial tax deductions. In addition to determining and withholding income taxes from each employee's wages every payday, employers are required to remit the withheld taxes to the Receiver General of Canada each month.

Canada Pension Plan (CPP)

The **Canada Pension Plan** applies, with few exceptions, to everyone who is working. Every employee and self-employed person between the ages of 18 and 70 must make contributions in required amounts to the Canada Pension Plan (CPP). Self-employed individuals are required to periodically remit appropriate amounts to the Receiver General of Canada. Employee contributions are deducted by the employer from salary, wages, or other remuneration paid to the employee. Furthermore, each employer is required to contribute an amount equal to that deducted from the employees' earnings.

Contributions are based on earnings, with the first $3,400 of each employee's annual income being exempt. On earnings above that amount and up to the 1995 ceiling of $34,900 a year, the employee contributes at a rate of 2.7%. The total contribution from both employee and employer is 5.4% on the $31,500 of annual earnings between $3,400 and $34,900. Thus, the maximum contribution to the

Illustration 10-1 TDI Form

Revenue Revenu
Canada Canada

PERSONAL TAX CREDITS RETURN

TD1(E)
Rev. 95

Instructions

You have to complete this return if you have a new employer or payer, and you received one or more of the following types of income:

- salary, wages, commissions, pensions, or any other remuneration; or
- Unemployment Insurance benefits, including training allowances.

Complete a new return no later than seven days after your marital or parental status changes or when you expect a change in your personal credits for the year. It is an offence to file a false return.

If you receive non-employment income, such as a pension or Old Age Security, and you want to have extra tax deducted at source, you can complete Form TD3, *Request for Income Tax Deduction on non-employment income.*

If you have deductions such as registered retirement savings plan contributions, alimony payments, or child care expenses, the amount of tax to be withheld from your income can be reduced. You have to send a written application to your district income tax office. A tax office letter of authority is not needed when a court order states that alimony or maintenance payments have to be deducted at source from an employee's salary.

If you need help, ask your employer or payer, or call the Employer Services Division of your income tax office. The number for this office is listed in the government pages of your telephone book under Revenue Canada.

Confidential calculation on back - Employee's copy

Employer's or payer's copy

Revenue Revenu
Canada Canada

PERSONAL TAX CREDITS RETURN

TD1(E)
Rev. 95

After you complete this return, give it to your employer or payer.

Last name (capital letters)	Usual first name and initials	Employee number

Address	For non-residents only - country of permanent residence	Social insurance number

	Postal code	Date of birth
		Year　Month　Day

1. Basic personal amount

Everyone can claim **$6,456** as the basic personal amount.
- If you choose to claim this amount, enter $6,456.
- If you choose not to claim this amount (e.g., when you have more than one employer or payer and you have already claimed the basic personal amount), **enter 0 in box A** on the other side of this return and do not complete sections 2 to 8. You may with to complete sections 9 to 11.
- If you are a non-resident, and you will be including most of your annual world income (90% or more) when determining your taxable income in Canada, you can claim certain personal amounts. If you are not sure about your non-resident status, or need more information, call the Client Assistance Division of your income tax office   **Credit claimed** $ _____

2. Spousal amount or equivalent-to-spouse amount.

You can claim an amount for supporting your spouse if you are **married or have a common-law spouse**. A common-law spouse is a person of the opposite sex with whom you live in a common-law relationship for any continuous period of at least 12 months, including any period of separation (due to a breakdown in the relationship) of less than 90 days, or with whom you live in a common-law relationship and who is the natural or adoptive parent of your child.

You can claim an equivalent-to-spouse amount if you are **single, divorced, separated, or widowed**, and you support a relative who is:
- residing in Canada (if the relative is your child, the child does not have to reside in Canada);
- living with you in a home you maintain;
- related to you by blood, marriage, or adoption; and
- under 18 years old, except for a relative who has a mental or physical infirmity.

Calculating the amount
If you marry during the year, your spouse's net income includes the income earned before and during the marriage.
If the net income of your spouse or relative for the year will be:
- over $5,918, **enter 0**
- $538 or less, **enter $5,380**; or
- more than $538, complete calculation no. 2 on the back of this return and enter the result as credit claimed.

Any person you claim here cannot be claimed again in section 3.   **Credit claimed** $ _____

3. Amount for disabled dependent relatives

With the introduction of the child tax benefit, there is no amount for dependent children who are under the age of 18 at the end of the year. However, you can claim an amount for each disabled dependant who is:
- your or your spouse's child or grandchild, 18 years old or older, and who has a physical or mental infirmity; or
- your or your spouse's parent, grandparent, brother, sister, aunt, uncle, niece, or nephew, who is 18 years old or older, and who has a physical or mental infirmity and is resident in Canada.

Calculating the amount for a disabled dependent relative:
If your dependant's net income for the year will be:
- $2,690 or less, **enter $1,583** in section 3 of this return; or
- more than $2,690, complete calculation no. 3 on the back of this return and enter the result as credit claimed.
You can claim an amount for each disabled dependent relative you have.   **Credit claimed** $ _____

4. Amount for eligible pension

An eligible pension income includes pension payments received from a pension plan or fund as a life annuity, and foreign pension payments. It does not include payments form the Canada or Quebec Pension Plan, Old Age Security, guaranteed supplements, or lump-sum withdrawals from a pension fund.
If you receive an eligible pension income, you can claim your eligible pension income or $1,000, whichever amount is less.   **Credit claimed** $ _____

5. Age amount

If your estimated net income from all sources for the year will be:
- $25,921 or less, **enter $3,482**;
- over $25,921, but not over $49,134.33, complete calculation no. 5 on the back of this return and **enter** the result as credit claimed; or
- over $49,134.33, **enter $0**.   **Credit claimed** $ _____

Ce formulaire existe aussi en français.

Illustration 10-1 *(concluded)*

Calculation no. 2 • more than $538, calculate:	$ 5,918
Minus: net income of spouse or relative	
Total calculated:	
Report total in section 2 as credit claimed	

Calculation no. 3 • more than $2,690, calculate:	$ 4,273
Minus: dependant's net income	
Total calculated:	
Report total in section 3 as credit claimed	

Calculation no. 5:
• over $25,921, but not over $49,134.33, calculate:

Basic age amount: . . . . $ 3,482 A.

Reduced by:
1. Annual estimated net income. $ _____
2. Less base amount . . . . –$ 25,921
3. Line 1 minus line 2 . . . . = $ _____

4. Line 3 by 15% . . . . –_____ B.

Subtract A from B. If negative, **enter 0** $ =_____

Report total in section 5 as credit claimed

Claim Codes	
Total claim amount	**Claim codes**
No claim amount	0
Minimum $ 6,456	1
$ 6,456.01 - 8,037	2
8,037.01 - 9,619	3
9,619.01 - 11,202	4
11,202.01 - 12,783	5
12,783.01 - 14,364	6
14,364.01 - 15,946	7
15,946.01 - 17,527	8
17,527.01 - 19,109	9
19,109.01 - 20,693	10
$ 20,693.01 - and over Manual calculation required by employer	X
No tax withholding required	E

6. Tuition fees and education amount

Enter your tuition fees, for courses you will take in the year, to attend a university, college, or an institution that the Minister of Human Resources Development has certified . . . . _____

Add $80 for each month in the year that you will be enrolled full-time in a qualifying educational program at a university, college, or a school offering job retraining courses or correspondence courses, as indicated on Form T2202 or T2202A . . . . _____

Subtract any scholarships, fellowships, or bursaries you will receive in the year (do not report the first $500) . . . . _____

Enter the total amount claimed. If you arrive at a negative amount, **enter 0** . . . .   **Credit claimed** $ _____

7. Disability amount

You can claim $4,233 for a person who is severely impaired, mentally or physically, and for whom you will claim the disability amount by using Form T2201, *Disability Tax Credit Certificate*.

Such an impairment has to markedly restrict the person in his or her daily living activities. The impairment has to last, or be expected to last, for a continuous period of at least 12 months.

Enter the total amount claimed: . . . .   **Credit claimed** $ _____

8. Amounts transferred from your spouse, relatives, or dependants

You can transfer any of the following amounts that your spouse, relative, or dependants do not need to reduce their federal income tax to zero.

Age amount - If, this year, your spouse will be 65 or older, you can claim any unused balance of the age amount to a maximum of $3,482 . . . . _____

Pension income amount - If your spouse receives eligible pension income, you can claim any unused balance of the eligible pension amount to a maximum of $1,000 . . . . _____

Disability amount - If your spouse, relatives, or dependants are disabled, you can claim their unused balance of the disability amount to a maximum of $4,233 for each person . . . . _____

Tuition fees and education amount - If you are supporting a spouse, relative, or dependants who are attending a university, college, or a certified educational institution, you can claim their unused balance of tuition fees and education amount to a maximum of $4,000 for each person . . . . _____

Enter the total amount calculated . . . .   **Credit claimed** $ _____

Total all your personal tax credit amounts from sections 1 to 8 . . . . $ _____

Total of credits

At the top of this form, see the claim codes to determine the claim code that applies to you, and enter this code in box **A** . If the total of your tax credits is greater than your employment income for the year, your claim code is "E."

[_____] **A**

Additional information

9. Additional tax to be deducted

If you receive additional income you may find it convenient to have additional tax deducted from each payment. This will help you avoid having to pay tax when you file your income tax return. If so, state the amount of additional tax you want to have deducted from each payment. If you want to change this extra deduction later, you have to complete a new TD1 return. $ _____

10. Deduction for living in a designated area (e.g., Yukon Territory, or Northwest Territories)

If you live in the Yukon Territory, Northwest Territories, or another designated area for more than six months in a row, beginning or ending this year, you can claim:

• $7.50 for each day that you live in the designated area; or
• $15 for each day that you live in the designated area, if during that time you live in a dwelling that you maintain, and you are the only person living in that dwelling who is claiming this deduction.
   For more information, including a list and categories of designated areas, see the income tax guide called *Northern Residents Deduction,* available at any income tax office. $ _____

11. If you reside in **Ontario, Manitoba, Saskatchewan** or **British Columbia**, enter the number of your dependants under 18 years old at the end of the year.

For **Ontario, Manitoba** and **Saskatchewan** residents, only the spouse with the higher net income can indicate an amount.
If you reside in **Ontario, Manitoba** or **British Columbia**, the number of children indicated should not include a child claimed for purposes of the equivalent-to-spouse amount   [_____]

I certify that, to the Best of my knowledge, the information given on this form is correct and complete.

Signature _____   Date _____

Canada Pension Plan is $850.50 each from the employee and the employer. The $3,400 exemption is adjusted for weekly or monthly pay periods by dividing by the appropriate number; that is, 52, 12, and so on.

Employers are responsible for making the proper deductions from their employees' earnings. They remit these deductions each month, together with their own contributions, to the Receiver General of Canada.

Self-employed individuals pay the combined rate for employees and employers, or 5.4% on annual earnings between $3,400 and the exempt ceiling of $34,900.

Unemployment Insurance (UI)

To alleviate hardships caused by interruptions in earnings through unemployment, the federal government, with the concurrence of all provincial governments, implemented an employee/employer-financed unemployment insurance plan. Under the Unemployment Insurance Act, 1971, compulsory **unemployment insurance** coverage was extended to all Canadian workers who are not self-employed. As of January 1, 1995, over 12 million employees, including teachers, hospital workers, and top-level executives, were covered by the insurance plan.

The purpose of an unemployment insurance program is usually twofold:

1. To pay unemployment compensation for limited periods to unemployed individuals eligible for benefits.
2. To establish and operate employment facilities that assist unemployed individuals in finding suitable employment and assist employers in finding employees.

The unemployment insurance fund from which benefits are paid is jointly financed by employees and their employers. Under the current act, in 1995 employers are required to deduct from their employees' wages 3% of insured earnings, to add a contribution of 1.4 times the amount deducted from employees' wages, and to remit both amounts to the Receiver General of Canada. Insured earnings refer to average weekly gross pay in the range of $163 to $815. Employees paid in whole or in part on a time-worked or fixed-salary basis must be employed at least 15 hours in a weekly pay period or earn 20% of the maximum weekly insurable earnings ($815 in 1995) in order to be insurable. The maximum amount deductible per year is $1,271.40 (in 1995). This amount is adjusted for weekly or monthly pay periods by dividing by the appropriate number; that is, 52, 12, and so on.

The Unemployment Insurance Act, in addition to setting rates, requires that an employer

1. Withhold from the wages of each employee each payday an amount of unemployment insurance tax calculated at the current rate.
2. Pay an unemployment insurance tax equal to 1.4 times the amount withheld from the wages of all employees.
3. Periodically remit both the amounts withheld from employees' wages and the employer's tax to the Receiver General of Canada. (Remittance is discussed later in this chapter.)
4. Complete a "Record of Employment" form for employees who experience an "interruption of earnings" because of termination of employment, illness, injury, or pregnancy.

5. Keep a record for each employee that shows among other things wages subject to unemployment insurance and taxes withheld. (The law does not specify the exact form of the record, but most employers keep individual employees earnings records similar to the one shown later in this chapter.)

Weekly Unemployment Benefits

The amount of weekly benefits received by an unemployed individual who qualifies is based on his or her average insurable weekly earnings. The federal government has varied the benefit period from region to region on the basis of percentage and duration of unemployment in the region.

Use of Withholding Tables

Most employers use **wage bracket withholding tables** similar to the one for 1995 shown in Illustration 10–2 in determining Canada Pension Plan and unemployment insurance to be withheld from employees' gross earnings. The illustrated table is for a weekly pay period; different tables are provided for different pay periods. Somewhat similar tables are available for determining income tax withholdings. These tables are also available on computer discs from Revenue Canada for computer applications.

Determining the amount of withholdings from an employee's gross wages is quite easy when withholding tables are used. First, the employee's wage bracket is located in the first two columns. Then the amounts to be withheld for Canada Pension Plan and unemployment insurance are found on the line of the wage bracket in the appropriate columns.

The T-4 Form

Employers are required to report wages and deductions both to each employee and to the local office of Revenue Canada. On or before the last day of February, the employer must give each employee a T-4 summary, a statement that tells the employee

a. Total wages for the preceding year.
b. Taxable benefits received from the employer.
c. Income taxes withheld.
d. Deductions for registered pension plan.
e. Canada Pension Plan contributions.
f. Unemployment insurance deductions.

On or before the last day of February, the employer must forward to the district taxation office copies of the employee's T-4 statements plus a T-4 that summarizes the information contained on the employee's T-4 statements. The T-4 form is shown in Illustration 10–3.

Wages, Hours, and Union Contracts

All provinces have laws establishing maximum hours of work and minimum pay rates. And while the details vary with each province, generally employers are required to pay an employee for hours worked in excess of 40 in any one week at the employee's regular pay rate plus an overtime premium of at least one-half of

Illustration 10-2 1995 Wage Bracket Withholding Tables—UIC and CPP

UNEMPLOYMENT INSURANCE PREMIUMS / COTISATIONS À L'ASSURANCE-CHÔMAGE

For minimum and maximum insurable earnings amounts for various pay periods see Schedule II. For the maximum premium deduction for various pay periods see bottom of this page.

Les montants minimum et maximum des gains assurables pour diverses périodes de paie figurent en annexe II. La déduction maximale de primes pour diverses périodes de paie figure au bas de la présente page.

Remuneration / Rémunération		U.I. Premium Cotisation d'a.-c.	Remuneration / Rémunération		U.I. Premium Cotisation d'a.-c.	Remuneration / Rémunération		U.I. Premium Cotisation d'a.-c.	Remuneration / Rémunération		U.I. Premium Cotisation d'a.-c.
From-de	To-à		From-de	To-à		From-de	To-à		From-de	To-à	
192.17	192.49	5.77	216.17	216.49	6.49	240.17	240.49	7.21	264.17	264.49	7.93
192.50	192.83	5.78	216.50	216.83	6.50	240.50	240.83	7.22	264.50	264.83	7.94
192.84	193.16	5.79	216.84	217.16	6.51	240.84	241.16	7.23	264.84	265.16	7.95
193.17	193.49	5.80	217.17	217.49	6.52	241.17	241.49	7.24	265.17	265.49	7.96
193.50	193.83	5.81	217.50	217.83	6.53	241.50	241.83	7.25	265.50	265.83	
193.84	194.16	5.82	217.84	218.16	6.54	241.84	242.16	7.26	265.84	266.1	
194.17	194.49	5.83	218.17	218.49	6.55	242.17	242.49	7.27	266.17		
194.50	194.83	5.84	218.50	218.83	6.56	242.50	242.83	7.28			
194.84	195.16	5.85	218.84	219.16	6.57	242.84	243.16	7.28			
195.17	195.49	5.86	219.17	219.49	6.58	243.17	243				
195.50	195.83	5.87	219.50	219.83	6.59	243.5					
195.84	196.16	5.88	219.84	220.16	6.60						
196.17	196.49	5.89	220.17	220.49							
196.50	196.83	5.90	220.50	220.							
196.84	197.16	5.91	220.84								
197.17	197.49	5.92									
197.50	197.83	5.93									
197.34	198.16										
198.17	198.49										
198.50	198.83										
198.84	199.16										
199.17	199.49										
199.50	199.83										
199.84	200.16										

CANADA PENSION PLAN CONTRIBUTIONS / COTISATIONS AU RÉGIME DE PENSIONS DU CANADA

WEEKLY PAY PERIOD — PÉRIODE HEBDOMADAIRE DE PAIE 181.33—301.32

Remuneration / Rémunération		C.P.P. R.P.C.	Remuneration / Rémunération		C.P.P. R.P.C.	Remuneration / Rémunération		C.P.P. R.P.C.	Remuneration / Rémunération		C.P.P. R.P.C.
From-de	To-à		From-de	To-à		From-de	To-à		From-de	To-à	
181.33	181.73	2.88	211.33	211.73	3.60	241.33	241.73	4.32	271.33	271.73	5.04
181.74	182.57	2.89	211.74	212.15	3.61	241.74	242.15	4.33	271.74	272.15	5.05
182.16	182.98	2.90	212.16	212.57	3.62	242.16	242.57	4.34	272.16	272.57	5.06
182.58	183.40	2.91	212.58	212.99	3.63	242.58	242.98	4.35	272.58	272.98	5.07
182.99	183.82	2.92	212.99	213.40	3.64	242.99	243.40	4.36	272.99	273.40	5.08
183.83	184.23	2.93	213.41	213.82	3.65	243.41	243.82	4.37	273.41	273.82	5.09
183.41	184.65	2.94	213.83	214.23	3.66	243.83	244.23	4.38	273.83	274.23	5.11
184.24	185.07	2.95	214.24	214.65	3.67	244.24	244.65	4.39	274.24	274.65	5.12
184.66		2.96	214.66	215.07	3.68	244.66	245.07	4.40	274.66	275.07	5.13
185.08	185.48	2.97	215.08	215.48	3.69	245.08	245.48	4.41	275.08	275.48	5.14
185.49	185.90	2.99	215.49	215.90	3.70	245.49	245.90	4.42	275.49	275.90	5.15
185.91	186.73	3.00	215.91	216.32	3.71	245.91	246.32	4.43	275.91	276.31	5.16
186.33	187.15	3.01	216.33	216.73	3.72	246.33	246.73	4.45	276.33	276.73	5.17
186.74	187.57	3.02	216.74	217.15	3.73	246.74	247.15	4.46	276.74	277.15	5.18
187.16	187.98	3.04	217.16	217.57	3.74	247.16	247.57	4.47	277.16	277.57	5.19
187.58	188.40	3.05	217.58	217.98	3.75	247.58	247.99	4.48	277.58	277.98	5.20
187.99	188.82		217.99	218.40	3.76	247.99	248.40	4.49	277.99	278.40	5.21
188.41			218.41	218.82	3.77	248.41	248.82		278.41	278.82	
188.83	189.23	3.06	218.83	219.23	3.78	248.83	249.23	4.50	278.83	279.23	5.22
189.24	189.65	3.07	219.24	219.65	3.79	249.24	249.65	4.51	279.24	279.65	5.23
189.66	190.07	3.08	219.66	220.07	3.80	249.66	250.07	4.52	279.65	280.07	5.25
190.08	190.48	3.09	220.08	220.43	3.81	250.03	250.90	4.53	280.08	280.48	5.26
190.49	190.90	3.10	220.49	221.32	3.82	250.91	251.32	4.54	280.49	280.90	5.27
190.91	191.32	3.11	220.91	221.73	3.83	251.32	251.73	4.55	280.91	281.73	5.28
191.33	191.73	3.12	221.33	222.15	3.85	251.74	252.15	4.57	281.33	282.57	5.29
191.74	192.15	3.14	221.74	222.57	3.86	252.16	252.57	4.58	281.74	282.57	5.30
192.16	192.57		222.10						282.16		
192.58	192.98	3.15	222.58	222.98	3.87	252.58	252.98	4.59	282.58	282.98	5.31
192.99	193.40	3.16	222.99	223.40	3.88	252.99	253.40	4.60	282.99	283.40	5.32
193.41	193.82	3.17	223.41	223.82	3.90	253.41	253.83	4.61	283.41	283.82	5.
193.33	194.2	3.19	223.83		3.93	253.83		4.62	283.83		
						254.24			284.24		

his or her regular rate. This gives an employee an overtime rate of at least 1½ times his or her regular hourly rate for hours in excess of 40 in any one week. In addition, employers commonly operate under contracts with their employees' union that provide even better terms. For example, union contracts often provide for time-and-a-half for work on Saturdays, and double time for Sundays and holidays. When an employer is under a union contract in which the terms are better than those provided for by law, the contract terms take precedence over the law.

In addition to specifying working hours and wage rates, union contracts often provide for the collection of employees' union dues by the employer. Such a requirement commonly provides that the employer shall deduct dues from the wages of each employee and remit the amounts deducted to the union. The employer is usually required to remit once each month reporting each employee's name and the amount deducted from his or her pay.

Illustration 10-3   T-4 Form

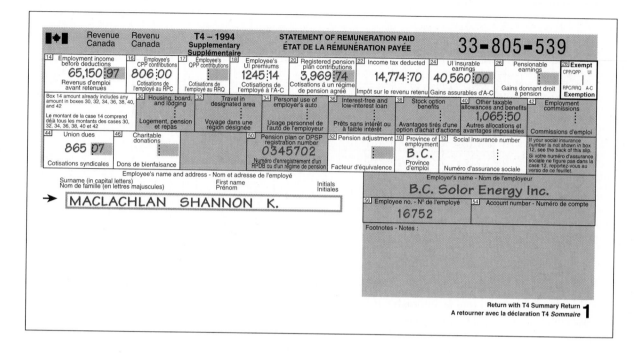

Other Payroll Deductions

In addition to the payroll deductions discussed thus far, employees may individually authorize additional deductions. Some examples of these might be

1. Deductions to accumulate funds for the purchase of Canada Savings Bonds.
2. Deductions to pay health, accident, hospital, or life insurance premiums.
3. Deductions to repay loans from the employer or the employees' credit union.
4. Deductions to pay for merchandise purchased from the company.
5. Deductions for donations to charitable organizations such as the United Way.

Timekeeping

Compiling a record of the time worked by each employee is called **timekeeping.** The method used to compile such a record depends on the nature of the company's business and the number of its employees. In a very small business, timekeeping may consist of no more than notations of each employee's working time made in a memorandum book by the manager or owner. In many companies, however, time clocks are used to record on clock cards each employee's time of arrival and departure. The time clocks are usually placed near entrances to the office, store, or factory. At the beginning of each payroll period, a **clock card** for each employee (see Illustration 10–4) is placed in a rack for use by the employee. Upon arriving at work, each employee takes his or her card from the rack and places it in a slot in the time clock. This actuates the clock to stamp the date and arrival time on the card. The employee then returns the card to the rack. Upon leaving the plant, store, or office for lunch or at the end of the day, the procedure is repeated. The em-

Illustration 10-4   An Employee's Clock Card

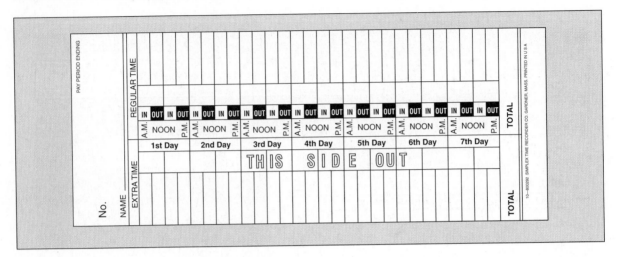

ployee takes the card from the rack, places it in the clock, and the time of departure is automatically stamped. At a result, at the end of each period, the card shows the hours the employee was at work.

Progress Check

10-1   What is the purpose of the federal Unemployment Insurance scheme?

10-2   When must T-4 statements be given to employees?

10-3   What are other typical nonmandatory payroll deductions?

THE PAYROLL REGISTER

LO 2

Make the calculations necessary to prepare a Payroll Register and prepare the entry to record payroll liabilities.

Each pay period the total hours worked as compiled on clock cards or by other means is summarized in a Payroll Register, an example of which is shown in Illustration 10–5. The illustrated register is for a weekly pay period and shows the payroll data for each employee on a separate line.

In Illustration 10–5, the columns under the heading Daily Time show the hours worked each day by each employee. The total of each employee's hours is entered in the column headed Total Hours. If hours worked include overtime hours, these are entered in the column headed O.T. Hours.

The Regular Pay Rate column shows the hourly pay rate of each employee. Total hours worked multiplied by the regular pay rate equals regular pay. Overtime hours multiplied by the overtime premium rate (50% in this case) equals overtime premium pay. And regular pay plus overtime premium pay is the **employee's gross pay.**

The amounts withheld from each employee's gross pay are recorded in the Deductions columns of the payroll register. For example, you determine the income tax deductions by matching the gross pay of each employee to the tax deduction tables and then enter the results in the tax deduction column. Income tax deductions are based on the gross pay less the amounts deducted for unemployment insurance and Canada Pension Plan. The tax tables allow for these adjustments and separate books are available for each province. However, for simplicity, assume that income tax deductions are 20% of the employee's gross pay.

Illustration 10-5 Payroll Register

Employees	Clock Card No.	Daily Time							Total Hours	O.T. Hours	Reg. Pay Rate	Regular Pay	O.T. Premium Pay	Gross Pay	
		M	T	W	T	F	S	S							
Auer, John	118	8	8	8	8	8			40		10.00	400.00		400.00	1
Cheung, Joan	109	0	8	8	8	8	8		40		12.00	480.00		480.00	2
Daljit, Moe	121	8	8	8	8	8	8	4	52	12	15.00	780.00	90.00	870.00	3
Lee, Shannon	104	8	8		8	8	8	4	44	4	14.00	616.00	28.00	644.00	4
Prasad, Sunil	108		8	8	8	8	4	8	44	4	15.00	660.00	30.00	690.00	5
Rupert, Allan	105	8	8	8	8	8			40		12.00	480.00		480.00	6
Totals												3,416.00	148.00	3,564.00	

Payroll Week Ended
Earnings

Register June 11, 1995

	Deductions					Payment		Distribution	
	U.I. Premium	Income Taxes	Hosp. Ins.	C.P.P.	Total Deductions	Net Pay	Cheque No.	Sales Salaries	Office Salaries
1	12.00	80.00	18.00	9.03	119.03	280.97	754	400.00	
2	14.40	96.00	18.00	11.19	139.59	340.41	755	480.00	
3	26.10	174.00	24.00	21.63	245.73	624.27	756		870.00
4	19.32	128.80	18.00	15.62	181.74	462.26	757		644.00
5	20.71	138.00	24.00	16.77	199.48	490.52	758	690.00	
6	14.40	96.00	18.00	11.19	139.59	340.41	759	480.00	
	106.93	712.80	120.00	85.43	1,025.16	2,538.84		2,050.00	1,514.00

As previously stated, the income tax withheld depends on each employee's gross pay and personal tax credits. You can determine these amounts by first referring to the personal tax credits and then to the appropriate wage bracket withholding tables. You then enter them in the column headed Income Taxes.

The column headed Hosp. Ins. shows the amounts withheld to pay for hospital insurance for the employees and their families. The total withheld from all employees is a current liability of the employer until paid to the insurance company. Likewise, the total withheld for employees' union dues is a current liability until paid to the union.

Additional columns may be added to the Payroll register for any other deductions that occur sufficiently often to warrant special columns. For example, a company that regularly deducts amounts from its employees' pay for Canada Savings bonds may add a special column for this deduction.

An employee's gross pay less total deductions is the **employee's net pay** and is entered in the Net Pay column. The total of this column is the amount the employees are to be paid. The numbers of the cheques used to pay the employees are entered in the column headed Cheque No.

The Distribution columns are used to classify the various salaries in terms of different kinds of expense. Here you enter each employee's gross salary in the proper column according to the type of work performed. The column totals then indicate the amounts to be debited to the salary expense accounts.

Recording the Payroll

Generally, a Payroll Register such as the one shown is a supplementary memorandum record. As such, you do not post its information directly to the accounts. Instead, you must first record the payroll with a General Journal entry, which is then posted to the accounts. The entry to record the payroll shown in Illustration 10–5 is:

June	11	Sales Salaries Expense	2,050.00	
		Office Salaries Expense	1,514.00	
		Unemployment Insurance Payable		106.93
		Employees' Income Taxes Payable		712.80
		Employees' Hospital Insurance Payable		120.00
		Canada Pension Plan Payable		85.43
		Payroll Payable		2,538.84
		To record the June 11 payroll.		

The debits of the entry were taken from the Payroll Register's distribution column totals. They charge the employees' gross earnings to the proper salary expense accounts. The credits to UI Payable, Employees' Income Taxes Payable, Employees' Hospital Insurance Payable, and CPP Payable record these amounts as current liabilities. The credit to Payroll Payable (also called Salaries Payable, Wages Payable, or Accrued Salaries Payable, etc.) records as a liability the net amount to be paid to the employees.

Progress Check

10-4   **What constitutes the employee's gross pay?**

10-5   **What is the employee's net pay?**

PAYING THE EMPLOYEES

LO 3

Prepare journal entries to record the payments to employees and explain the operation of a payroll bank account.

Almost every business pays its employees by cheques. In a company that has few employees, these cheques often are drawn on the regular bank account and entered in a Cash Disbursements Journal (or Cheque Register) like the one described in Chapter 6. Since each cheque is debited to the Payroll Payable account, posting labour can be saved by adding a Salaries Payable column in the journal. If such a column is added, entries to pay the employees shown in the Illustration 10–5 payroll will appear as in Illustration 10–6.

Most employers furnish each employee an earnings statement each payday. The statement gives the employee a record of hours worked, gross pay, deductions, and net pay. The statement often takes the form of a detachable paycheque portion that is removed before the cheque is cashed. A paycheque with a detachable earnings statement is reproduced in Illustration 10–7.

Payroll Bank Account

A business with many employees will often use a special **payroll bank account** to pay its employees. When such an account is used, one cheque for the total payroll is drawn on the regular bank account and deposited in the special payroll bank

Illustration 10-6 Cash Disbursements Journal

			Cash Disbursements Journal						
Date	Cheque No.	Payee	Account Debited	PR	Other Accts. Debit	Accts. Pay. Debit	Payroll Pay. Debit	Pur. Dis. Credit	Cash Credit
June 11	754	John Auer	Payroll Pay.				280.97		280.97
June 11	755	Joan Cheung	"				340.41		340.41
June 11	756	Moe Daljit	"				624.27		624.27
June 11	757	Shannon Lee	"				462.26		462.26
June 11	758	Sunil Prasad	"				490.52		490.52
June 11	759	Allan Rupert	"				340.41		340.41

Illustration 10-7 A Payroll Cheque

Employee	Total Hours	O.T. Hours	Reg. Pay Rate	Regular Pay	O.T. Prem. Pay	Gross Pay	U.I. Premium	Income Taxes	C.P. Plan	Hosp. Ins.	Total Deductions	Net Pay
John Auer	40		10.00	400.00		400.00	12.00	80.00	9.03	18.00	119.03	280.97

STATEMENT OF EARNINGS AND DEDUCTIONS FOR EMPLOYEE'S RECORDS—DETACH BEFORE CASHING CHEQUE

VALLEY SALES COMPANY
2590 Dixon Road • Cambridge, Ontario

No. 893

PAY TO THE ORDER OF __John Auer__ Date __June 11, 1995__ $ __280.97__

__Two hundred eighty dollars and ninety-seven cents__ -

Merchants National Bank
Cambridge, Ontario

VALLEY SALES COMPANY

Jane R. Morris

account. Then individual payroll cheques are drawn on this special account. Because only one cheque for the payroll total is drawn on the regular bank account each payday, use of a special payroll bank account simplifies internal control, especially the reconciliation of the regular bank account. It may be reconciled without considering the payroll cheques outstanding, and there may be many of these. Many financial institutions offer a payroll service whereby the employees' net pay is transferred electronically into their accounts. The employer simply transfers the net amount of the payroll to the institution along with the employees' names and the accounts to be credited.

When a company uses a special payroll bank account, it must complete the following steps to pay the employees:

1. Record the information shown on the Payroll Register in the usual manner with a General Journal entry similar to the one previously illustrated. This entry causes the sum of the employees' net pay to be credited to the liability account (Salaries Payable).

2. Have a single cheque written that is payable to Payroll Bank account for the total amount of the payroll and enter the payment in the Cheque Register. This requires a debit to Salaries Payable and a credit to Cash.

3. Have the cheque deposited in the payroll bank account. This transfers an amount of money equal to the payroll total from the regular bank account to the special payroll bank account.

4. Have individual payroll cheques drawn on the special payroll bank account and delivered to the employees. As soon as all employees cash their cheques, the funds in the special account will be exhausted. Typically, companies will arrange for the bank to charge all service costs to the regular bank account.

A special Payroll Cheque Register may be used in connection with a payroll bank account. However, most companies do not use such a register. Instead, the payroll cheque numbers are entered in the Payroll Register so that it serves as a Cheque Register.

Employee's Individual Earnings Record

An **Employee's Individual Earnings Record,** as shown in Illustration 10–8, provides for each employee in one record a full year's summary of the employee's working time, gross earnings, deductions, and net pay. In addition, it accumulates information that

1. Serves as a basis for the employer's payroll tax returns.
2. Indicates when an employee's earnings have reached the maximum amounts for CPP and UI deductions.
3. Supplies data for the T4 slip, which must be given to the employee at the end of the year.

The payroll information on an Employee's Individual Earnings Record is taken from the Payroll Register. The information as to earnings, deductions, and net pay is first recorded on a single line in the Payroll Register. Then, each pay period, the information is posted from the Payroll Register to the earnings record. Note the last column of the record. It shows an employee's cumulative earnings and is used to determine when the earnings reach the maximum amounts taxed and are no longer subject to the various payroll taxes.

Progress Check

10-6   Why would a company use a special payroll bank account?

10-7   What is the purpose of the employee's earnings record?

Illustration 10-8 Employee's Individual Earnings Record

Employee's Name _____John Auer_____ SIN. No. _____123-456-789_____ Employee No. _____114_____

Home
Address _____111 South Greenwood_____ Notify in Case
of Emergency _____Margaret Auer_____ Phone
No. _____964-9834_____

Employed _____May 15, 1993_____ Date of
Termination _____ Reason _____

Date of
Birth _____June 6, 1972_____ Date
Becomes 65 _____June 6, 2037_____ Male (X) Married ( ) Number of
Female ( ) Single (X) Exemptions _0_ Pay
Rate _$10.00_

Occupation _____Clerk_____ Place _____Warehouse_____

Date		Time Lost		Time Worked												
Per. Ends	Paid	Hrs.	Rea-son	Total	O.T. Hours	Reg. Pay	O.T. Prem. Pay	Gross Pay	U.I. Prem.	Income Taxes	Hosp. Ins.	CPP	Total Deduc-tions	Net Pay	Cheque No.	Cumu-lative Pay
Ja 6	Ja 6			40		400.00		400.00	12.00	80.00	18.00	9.03	119.03	280.97	673	280.97
Ja 13	Ja 13			40		400.00		400.00	12.00	80.00	18.00	9.03	119.03	280.97	701	561.94
Ja 20	Ja 20			40		400.00		400.00	12.00	80.00	18.00	9.03	119.03	280.97	743	842.91
Ja 27	Ja 27	4	Sick	36		360.00		360.00	10.80	72.00	18.00	7.95	108.75	251.25	795	1,094.16
Fe 3	Fe 3			40		400.00		400.00	12.00	80.00	18.00	9.03	119.03	280.97	839	1,375.13
Fe 10	Fe 10			40		400.00		400.00	12.00	80.00	18.00	9.03	119.03	280.97	854	1,656.10
Fe 17	Fe 17			40		400.00		400.00	12.00	80.00	18.00	9.03	119.03	280.97	893	1,937.07
Fe 24	Fe 24			40		400.00		400.00	12.00	80.00	18.00	9.03	119.03	280.97	932	2,218.04
Ju 11	Ju 11			40		400.00		400.00	12.00	80.00	18.00	9.03	119.03	280.97	1517	6,432.59

PAYROLL DEDUCTIONS REQUIRED OF THE EMPLOYER

LO 4

Calculate the payroll costs levied on employers and prepare the entries to record the accrual and payment of these amounts.

Under the previous discussion of the Canada Pension Plan, it was pointed out that pension deductions are required in like amounts on both employed workers and their employers. A covered employer is required by law to deduct from the employees' pay the amounts of their Canada Pension Plan, but in addition, the employer must pay an amount equal to the sum of the employees' Canada pension. Commonly, the amount deducted by the employer is recorded at the same time the payroll to which it relates is recorded. Also, since both the employees' and employer's shares are reported on the same form and are paid in one amount, the liability for both is normally recorded in the same liability account, the Canada Pension Plan Payable account.

In addition to the Canada Pension Plan, an employer is required to pay unemployment insurance that is 1.4 times the sum of the employees' unemployment insurance deductions. Most employers record both of these payroll deductions with a General Journal entry that is made at the time the payroll to which they relate is recorded. For example, the entry to record the employer's amounts on the payroll of Illustration 10–5 is:

June	11	Benefits Expense	235.13	
		Unemployment Insurance Payable		149.70
		Canada Pension Plan Payable		85.43
		To record the employer's payroll taxes.		

The debit of the entry records as an expense the payroll taxes levied on the employer, and the credits record the liabilities for the taxes. The $149.70 credit to Unemployment Insurance Payable is 1.4 times the sum of the amounts deducted from the pay of the employees whose wages are recorded in the Payroll Register of Illustration 10–5, and the credit to Canada Pension Plan Payable is equal to the total of the employees' pension plan deductions.

PAYING THE PAYROLL DEDUCTIONS

Income tax, Unemployment Insurance, and Canada Pension Plan amounts withheld each payday from the employees' pay plus the employer's portion of unemployment insurance and Canada Pension Plan are current liabilities until paid to the Receiver General of Canada. The normal method of payment is to pay the amounts due at any chartered bank or remit directly to the Receiver General of Canada. Payment of these amounts is usually required to be made before the 15th of the month following the month that deductions were made from the earnings of the employees. Large employers are required to remit on the 10th and 25th of each month. Payment of these liabilities is recorded in the same manner as payment of any other liabilities.

ACCRUING PAYROLL DEDUCTIONS ON WAGES

Mandatory payroll deductions are levied on wages actually paid. In other words, accrued wages are not subject to payroll deductions until they are paid. Nevertheless, if the requirements of the matching principle are to be met, both accrued wages and the accrued deductions on the wages should be recorded at the end of an accounting period. However, since the amounts of such deductions vary little from one accounting period to the next and often are small in amount, many employers apply the materiality principle and do not accrue payroll deductions.

Progress Check

10-8 **If Marita Company deducted $1,750 for Unemployment Insurance and $1,275 for CPP from its employees in April, what would the benefits expense be for the month?**

10-9 **When are the payments for employee deductions due to the Receiver General?**

EMPLOYEE (FRINGE) BENEFIT COSTS

In addition to the wages earned by employees and the related payroll amounts paid by the employer, many companies provide their employees a variety of benefits. Since the costs of these benefits are paid by the employer and the benefits are in addition to the amount of wages earned, they are often called **employee fringe benefits.** For example, an employer may pay for part (or all) of the employees' medical insurance, life insurance, and disability insurance. Another typical employee benefit involves employer contributions to a retirement income plan. Workers' compensation is required to be paid by employers according to the legislation in each province. Perhaps the most typical employee benefit is vacation pay.

Workers' Compensation

Legislation is in effect in all provinces for payments to employees for an injury or disability arising out of or in the course of their employment. Under the provincial workers' compensation acts, employers are, in effect, required to insure their employees against injury or disability that may arise as a result of employment. Premiums are normally based on (1) accident experience of the industrial classification to which each business is assigned and (2) the total payroll.

Procedures for payment are as follows:

1. At the beginning of each year, every covered employer is required to submit to the Workers' Compensation Board an estimate of his or her expected payroll for the ensuing year.
2. Provisional premiums are then established by the board by relating estimated requirements for disability payments to estimated payroll. Provisional premium notices are then sent to all employers.
3. Provisional premiums are normally payable in from three to six installments during the year.
4. At the end of each year, actual payrolls are submitted to the board, and final assessments are made based on actual payrolls and actual payments. Premiums are normally between 1% and 3% of gross payroll and are borne by the employer.

Employer Contributions to Employee Insurance and Retirement Plans

The entries to record employee benefit costs depend on the nature of the benefit. Some employee retirement plans are quite complicated and involve accounting procedures that are too complex for discussion in this introductory course. In other cases, however, the employer simply makes periodic cash contributions to a retirement fund for each employee and records the amounts contributed as expense. Other employee benefits that require periodic cash payments by the employer include employer payments of insurance premiums for employees.

In the case of employee benefits that simply require the employer to make periodic cash payments, the entries to record the employer's obligations are similar to those used for payroll deductions.[1] For example, assume an employer with five employees has agreed to pay medical insurance premiums of $40 per month for each employee. The employer also will contribute 10% of each employee's salary to a retirement program. If each employee earns $2,500 per month, the entry to record these employee benefits for the month of March is

---

[1]Some payments of employee benefits must be added to the gross salary of the employee for the purpose of calculating income tax, CPP, and UI payroll deductions. However, in this chapter and in the problems at the end of the chapter, the possible effect of employee benefit costs on payroll taxes is ignored to avoid undue complexity in the introductory course.

Mar.	31	Benefits Expense	1,450.00	
		Employees' Medical Insurance Payable		200.00
		Employees' Retirement Program Payable		
		[($2,500 × 5) × 10%]		1,250.00

Vacation Pay

Employers are required to allow their employees paid vacation time (at a minimum rate of 4% of gross earnings) as a benefit of employment. For example, many employees receive 2 weeks' vacation in return for working 50 weeks each year. The effect of a 2-week vacation is to increase the employer's payroll expenses by 4% (2/50 = .04). After five years of service most employees are entitled to a 3-week vacation (i.e., 6%). However, new employees often do not begin to accrue vacation time until after they've worked for a period of time, perhaps as much as a year. The employment contract may say that no vacation is granted until the employee works one year, but if the first year is completed, the employee receives the full 2 weeks. Contracts between the employer and employees may allow for vacation pay in excess of the 4% minimum.

To account for vacation pay, an employer should estimate and record the additional expense during the weeks the employees are working and earning the vacation time. For example, assume that a company with a weekly payroll of $20,000 grants two weeks' vacation after one year's employment. The entry to record the estimated vacation pay is

Date		Benefits Expense	800.00	
		Estimated Vacation Pay Liability		
		($20,000 × .04)		800.00

As employees take their vacations and receive their vacation pay, the entries to record the vacation payroll take the following general form:

Date		Estimated Vacation Pay Liability	xxx	
		Employees' UI and CPP Payable		xxx
		Employees' Income Taxes Payable		xxx
		Other withholding liability accounts such		
		as Employees' Hospital Insurance Payable		xxx
		Payroll Payable		xxx

Mandatory payroll deductions and employee benefits costs are often a major category of expense incurred by a company. They may amount to well over 25% of the salaries earned by employees.

Progress Check

10-10   How is the cost of Workers' Compensation determined?

10-11   Assume a company with an annual payroll of $160,000 grants three weeks' vacation to its employees. Record the estimated vacation pay for the year.

Manually prepared records like the ones described in this chapter are used in many small companies. However, an increasing number of companies use computers to process their payroll. The computer programs are designed to take advantage of the fact that the same calculations are performed each pay period. Also, much of the same information must be entered for each employee in the Payroll Register, on the employee's earnings record, and on the employee's paycheque. The computers simultaneously store or print the information in all three places.

COMPUTERIZED PAYROLL SYSTEMS

LO 1. **List the taxes and other items frequently withheld from employees' wages.** Amounts withheld from employees' wages include federal income taxes, unemployment insurance, and Canada Pension Plan. Payroll costs levied on employers include unemployment insurance, Canada Pension, and workers' compensation.

An employee's gross pay may be the employee's specified wage rate multiplied by the total hours worked plus an overtime premium rate multiplied by the number of overtime hours worked. Alternatively, it may be the given periodic salary of the employee. Taxes withheld and other deductions for items such as union dues, insurance premiums, and charitable contributions are subtracted from gross pay to determine the net pay.

SUMMARY OF THE CHAPTER IN TERMS OF LEARNING OBJECTIVES

LO 2. **Make the calculations necessary to prepare a Payroll Register and prepare the entry to record payroll liabilities.** A Payroll Register is used to summarize all employees' hours worked, regular and overtime pay, payroll deductions, net pay, and distribution of gross pay to expense accounts during each pay period. It provides the necessary information for journal entries to record the accrued payroll and to pay the employees.

LO 3. **Prepare journal entries to record the payments to employees and explain the operation of a payroll bank account.** A payroll bank account is a separate account that is used solely for the purpose of paying employees. Each pay period, an amount equal to the total net pay of all employees is transferred from the regular bank account to the payroll bank account. Then cheques are drawn against the payroll bank account for the net pay of the employees.

LO 4. **Calculate the payroll costs levied on employers and prepare the entries to record the accrual and payment of these amounts.** When a payroll is accrued at the end of each pay period, payroll deductions and levies also should be accrued with a debit to Benefits Expense and credits to appropriate liability accounts.

LO 5. Calculate and record employee fringe benefit costs and show the effect of these items on the total cost of employing labour. Fringe benefit costs that involve simple cash payments by the employee should be accrued with an entry similar to the one used to accrue payroll levies. To account for the expense associated with vacation pay, you should estimate the expense and allocate the estimated amount to the pay periods during the year. These allocations are recorded with a debit to Employees' Benefits Expense and a credit to Estimated Vacation Pay Liability. Then payments to employees on vacation are charged to the estimated liability.

DEMONSTRATION PROBLEM

Presented below are various items of information about three employees of the Deluth Company for the week ending November 25, 1995.

	Billings	Dephir	Singe
Wage rate (per hour)	$ 15	$ 30	$ 18
Overtime premium	50%	50%	50%
Annual vacation	2 weeks	4 weeks	3 weeks
Cumulative wages as of November 18, 1995	$28,500	$52,600	$14,800
For the week (pay period) ended November 25, 1995:			
Hours worked	40	44	48
Medical insurance:			
Deluth's contribution	$ 25	$ 25	$ 25
Withheld from employee	18	18	18
Union dues withheld	50	70	50
Income tax withheld	120	276	187
Unemployment insurance withheld	18	24	24
Canada Pension withheld	16	—	25

Payroll deduction rates:
Income taxes   assume 20% of gross wages
Unemployment insurance   3.0% to a maximum of $24 per week
Canada Pension Plan   2.7% less annual exemption of $3,400; maximum per year is $850.50

Required

In solving the following requirements, round all amounts to the nearest whole dollar. Prepare schedules that determine, for each employee and for all employees combined, the following information:

1. Wages earned for the regular 40-hour week, total overtime pay, and gross wages.
2. Vacation pay accrued for the week.
3. Deductions withheld from the employees' wages.
4. Costs imposed on the employer.
5. Employees' net pay for the week.
6. Employer's total payroll-related cost (wages, mandatory deductions, and fringe benefits).

Present journal entries to record the following:

7. Payroll expense.
8. Payroll deductions and employees' benefits expense.

- Calculate the gross pay for each employee.
- Compute the amounts deducted for each employee and their net pay.
- Compute the employer's share of payroll deductions.
- Prepare the necessary journal entries.

1. The gross wages (including overtime) for the week:

	Billings	**Dephir**	**Singe**	**Total**
Regular wage rate	$ 15	$ 30	$ 18	
Regular hours	× 40	× 44	× 48	
Regular pay	$600	$1,320	$864	$2,784
Overtime premium	$ 7.5	$ 15	$ 9	
Overtime hours	0	× 4	× 8	
Total overtime pay	$ 0	$ 60	$ 72	$ 132
Gross wages	$600	$1,380	$936	$2,916

2. The vacation pay accrued for the week:

	Billings	**Dephir**	**Singe**	**Total**
Annual vacation	2 weeks	4 weeks	3 weeks	
Weeks worked in year	50 weeks	48 weeks	49 weeks	
Vacation pay as a percentage of regular pay	4.00%	8.33%	6.12%	
Regular pay this week	× $600	× $1,320	× $864	
Vacation pay this week	$24	$110	$53	$187

The information in the following table is needed for parts 3 and 4:

			Earnings Subject to	
Employees	**Earnings through November 25**	**Earnings This Week**	**CPP**	**Unemployment Ins.**
Billings	$28,500	$ 600	$ 535	$ 600
Dephir	52,600	1,380	—	815
Singe	14,800	936	871	815
Totals		$2,916	$1,406	$2,230

3. Amounts withheld from the employees:

	Billings	**Dephir**	**Singe**	**Total**
Income tax withheld	$120	$276	$187	$583
CPP withheld	14	—	24	38
UI withheld	18	24	24	66
Totals	$152	$300	$235	$687

4. The costs imposed on the employer:

	Billings	**Dephir**	**Singe**	**Total**
CPP (1.0)	$14	—	$24	$ 38
Unemployment Insurance (1.4)	25	$34	34	93
Totals	$39	$34	$58	$131

5.   The net amount paid to the employees:

	Billings	Dephir	Singe	Total
Regular pay	$600	$1,320	$864	$2,784
Overtime pay	0	60	72	132
Gross pay	$600	$1,380	$936	$2,916
Withholdings:				
Income tax withholding	$120	$ 276	$187	$ 583
CPP withholding	14	—	24	38
UI withholding	18	24	24	66
Medical insurance	18	18	18	54
Union dues	50	70	50	170
Total withholdings	$220	$ 388	$303	$ 911
Net pay to employees	$380	$ 992	$633	$2,005

6.   The total payroll-related cost to the employer:

	Billings	Dephir	Singe	Total
Regular pay	$600	$1,320	$ 864	$2,784
Overtime pay	0	60	72	132
Gross pay	$600	$1,380	$ 936	$2,916
Deductions and fringe benefits:				
CPP	$ 14	$ —	$ 24	$ 38
UI	25	34	34	93
Vacation Pay	24	110	53	187
Medical insurance	25	25	25	75
Total deductions and fringe benefits	$ 88	$ 169	$ 136	$ 393
Total payroll-related cost	$688	$1,549	$1,072	$3,309

7.   Journal entry for salary expense:

1995			
Nov. 25	Salary Expense	2,916.00	
	Employees' Income Taxes Payable		583.00
	Employees' CPP Payable		38.00
	Employees' UI Payable		66.00
	Employees' Medical Insurance Payable		54.00
	Employees' Union Dues Payable		170.00
	Payroll Payable		2,005.00
	To record payroll expense.		

GLOSSARY

Canada Pension Plan   a national contributory retirement pension scheme. p. 491

Clock card   a card issued to each employee that the employee inserts in a time clock to record the time of arrival and departure to and from work. p. 497

Employee fringe benefits   payments by an employer, in addition to wages and salaries, that are made to acquire employee benefits such as insurance coverage and retirement income. p. 504

Employee's gross pay   the amount an employee earns before any deductions for taxes or other items such as union dues or insurance premiums. p. 498

Employee's Individual Earnings Record   a record of an employee's hours worked, gross pay, deductions, net pay, and certain personal information about the employee. p. 502

Employee's net pay the amount an employee is paid, determined by subtracting from gross pay all deductions for taxes and other items that are withheld from the employee's earnings. p. 499

Payroll bank account a special bank account a company uses solely for the purpose of paying employees by depositing in the account each pay period an amount equal to the total employees' net pay and drawing the employees' payroll cheques on that account. p. 500

Payroll deduction an amount deducted from an employee's pay, usually based on the amount of an employee's gross pay. p. 490

Personal tax credits amounts that may be deducted from an individual's income taxes and that determine the amount of income taxes to be withheld. p. 491

Timekeeping the process of recording the time worked by each employee. p. 497

Unemployment insurance an employee/employer-financed unemployment insurance plan. p. 494

Wage bracket withholding table a table showing the amounts to be withheld from employees' wages at various levels of earnings. p. 495

QUESTIONS

1. Who pays the contributions to the Canada Pension Plan?

2. Who pays premiums under the workers' compensation laws?

3. What benefits are paid to unemployed workers for funds raised by the Federal Unemployment Insurance Act?

4. Who pays federal unemployment insurance? What is the rate?

5. What are the objectives of unemployment insurance laws?

6. To whom and when are payroll deductions remitted?

7. What determines the amount that must be deducted from an employee's wages for income taxes?

8. What is a tax withholding table?

9. What is the Canada Pension Plan deduction rate for self-employed individuals?

10. How is a clock card used in recording the time an employee is on the job?

11. How is a special payroll bank account used in paying the wages of employees?

12. At the end of an accounting period a firm's special payroll bank account has a $562.35 balance because the payroll cheques of two employees have not cleared the bank. Should this $562.35 appear on the firm's balance sheet? If so, where?

13. What information is accumulated on an employee's individual earnings record? Why must this information be accumulated? For what purposes is the information used?

14. What payroll charges are levied on the employer? What amounts are deducted from the wages of an employee?

15. What are employee fringe benefits? Name some examples.

QUICK STUDY (Five-Minute Exercises)

A company deducts $260 in unemployment insurance and $205 in Canada pension from the weekly payroll of its employees. How much is the company's expense for these items for the week?

QS 10–1
(LO 1)

Tracon Co. has six employees, each of whom earns $3,000 per month. Income taxes are 20% of gross pay and the company deducts UI and CPP. Prepare the March 31 journal entry to record the payroll for the month.

QS 10–2
(LO 2)

QS 10–3
(LO 3)
Use the information in QS 10–2 to record the payment of the wages to the employees for March assuming that Tracon uses a payroll bank account.

QS 10–4
(LO 3)
Racon Co. has eight employees, each of whom earns $3,500 per month. Income taxes are 20% of gross pay and the company deducts UI and CPP. Prepare the April 30 journal entry to record Racon's payroll expenses for the month.

QS 10–5
(LO 3)
Racon Co. (see QS 10–4) contributes 8% of an employee's salary to a retirement program, medical insurance premiums of $60 per employee, and vacation allowance equivalent to 5% of the employee's salary. Prepare a journal entry to record the fringe benefit costs for April.

EXERCISES

Exercise 10–1
Calculating gross and net pay
(LO 1)
Julie Leung, an employee of the Import Company Limited, worked 48 hours during the week ended January 5. Her pay rate is $20 per hour, and her wages are subject to no deductions other than income taxes, unemployment insurance, and Canada Pension Plan. The overtime premium is 50% and is applicable to any time greater than 40 hours per week. Calculate her regular pay, overtime premium pay, gross pay, UI, CPP, income tax deductions (assume a tax deduction rate of 20%), total deductions, and net pay.

Exercise 10–2
Journalizing payroll information
(LO 3)
On January 5, at the end of its first weekly pay period in the year, Nasah Company's payroll record showed that its sales employees had earned $3,720 and its office employees had earned $2,300. The employees were to have $210 of UI and $150 of CPP withheld plus $1,030 of income taxes, $180 of union dues, and $570 of hospital insurance premiums. Give the General Journal entry to record the payroll.

Exercise 10–3
Calculating payroll deductions and recording the payroll
(LO 1)

The following information as to earnings and deductions for the pay period ended May 17 was taken from a company's payroll records:

Employees' Names	Weekly Gross Pay	Earnings to End of Previous Week	Income Taxes	Health Insurance Deductions
Hellena Chea	$ 720	$12,510	$144.00	$ 24.00
Joseph Lim	610	10,320	91.00	24.00
Dino Patelli	830	15,500	142.00	36.00
Shari Quinata	1,700	29,500	395.00	24.00
	$3,860		$772.00	$108.00

Calculate the employees' UI and CPP withholdings, the amounts paid to each employee, and prepare a General Journal entry to record the payroll. Assume all employees work in the office.

Exercise 10–4
Calculating and recording payroll deductions
(LO 4)

Use the information provided in Exercise 10–3 to complete the following requirements:

1. Prepare a General Journal entry to record the employer's payroll costs resulting from the payroll.
2. Prepare a General Journal entry to record the following employee benefits incurred by the company: (a) health insurance costs equal to the amounts contributed by each employee and (b) contributions equal to 10% of gross pay for each employee's retirement income program.

Manchuran Company's employees earn a gross pay of $20 per hour and work 40 hours each week. Manchuran Company contributes 8% of gross pay to a retirement program for employees and pays medical insurance premiums of $50 per week per employee. What is Manchuran Company's total cost of employing a person for one hour? (Assume that individual wages are less than the $34,900 Canada Pension Plan limit.)

Exercise 10–5
Analyzing total labour costs
(LO 5)

Bellward Corporation grants vacation time of two weeks to those employees who have worked for the company one complete year. After 10 years of service, employees receive four weeks of vacation. The monthly payroll for January totals $320,000 of which 70% is payable to employees with 10 or more years of service. On January 31, record the January expense arising from the vacation policy of the company.

Exercise 10–6
Calculating fringe benefit costs
(LO 5)

O'Riley Company's payroll costs and fringe benefit expenses include the normal CPP and UI contributions, retirement fund contributions of 10% of total earnings, and health insurance premiums of $120 per employee per month. Given the following list of employee annual salaries, payroll costs and fringe benefits constitute what percentage of salaries?

Exercise 10–7
Analyzing the cost of payroll deductions and fringe benefits
(LO 4, 5)

Doherty	$36,000
Fane	61,000
Kahan	59,000
Martin	37,000
Poon	48,000

Sharon Von Hatton is single and earns a weekly salary of $940. In response to a citywide effort to obtain charitable contributions to the local United Way programs, Von Hatton has requested that her employer withhold 2% of her salary (net of CPP, UI, and income taxes—assume a tax deduction rate of 20%). Under this program, what will be Von Hatton's annual contribution to the United Way?

Exercise 10–8
Other payroll deductions
(LO 1)

PROBLEMS

On January 6, at the end of the first weekly pay period of the year, a company's Payroll Register showed that its employees had earned $19,570 of sales salaries and $6,230 of office salaries. Withholdings from the employees' salaries were to include $740 of UI, $660 of CPP, $5,310 of income taxes, $930 of hospital insurance, and $420 of union dues.

Problem 10–1
The Payroll Register and the payroll bank account
(LO 1, 3)

Required

1. Prepare the General Journal entry to record the January 6 payroll.
2. Prepare a General Journal entry to record the employer's payroll expenses resulting from the January 6 payroll.
3. Under the assumption the company uses a payroll bank account and special payroll cheques in paying its employees, give the Cheque Register entry (Cheque No. 542) to transfer funds equal to the payroll from the regular bank account to the payroll bank account.
4. Answer this question: After the Cheque Register entry is made and posted, are additional debit and credit entries required to record the payroll cheques and pay the employees?

Problem 10–2
The Payroll Register, the payroll bank account, and payroll deductions
(LO 1, 3, 4)

The payroll records of Brownlee Corporation provided the following information for the weekly pay period ended December 21:

Employees	Clock Card No.	Daily Time							Pay Rate	Hospital Insurance	Union Dues	Earnings to End of Previous Week
		M	T	W	T	F	S	S				
Ray Loran	11	8	8	8	8	8	4	0	20.00	40.00	16.00	42,000
Kathy Sousa	12	7	8	6	7	8	4	0	18.00	40.00	15.00	46,000
Gary Smith	13	8	8	0	8	8	4	4	16.00	40.00	14.00	21,000
Nicole Parton	14	8	8	8	8	8	0	0	20.00	40.00	16.00	32,000
Diana Wood	15	0	6	6	6	6	8	8	18.00	40.00	15.00	36,000
										200.00	76.00	

Required

1. Enter the relevant information in the proper columns of a Payroll Register and complete the register for CPP and UI deductions. Charge the wages of Kathy Sousa to Office Salaries Expense and the wages of the remaining employees to Service Wages Expense. Calculate income tax deductions at 20% of gross pay.

2. Prepare a General Journal entry to record the Payroll Register information.

3. Make the Cheque Register entry (Cheque No. 399) to transfer funds equal to the payroll from the regular bank account to the payroll bank account under the assumption the company uses special payroll cheques and a payroll bank account in paying its employees. Assume the first payroll cheque is numbered 530 and enter the payroll cheque numbers in the Payroll Register.

4. Prepare a General Journal entry to record the employer's payroll costs resulting from the payroll.

Problem 10–3
The Payroll Register, payroll taxes, and employee fringe benefits
(LO 1, 4, 5)

A company accumulated the following information for the weekly pay period ended December 22:

Employees	Clock Card No.	Daily Time							Pay Rate	Medical Insurance	Union Dues	Earnings to End of Previous Week
		M	T	W	T	F	S	S				
Shannon Fong	21	8	8	8	8	8	4	0	18.00	30.00	20.00	41,000
Karen Horta	22	7	8	6	7	8	4	0	16.00	28.00	18.00	44,000
Garth Koran	23	8	8	0	8	8	4	4	14.00	25.00	16.00	19,000
Nicha Daljit	24	8	8	8	8	8	0	0	18.00	30.00	20.00	34,000
										113.00	74.00	

Required

1. Enter the relevant information in the proper columns of a Payroll Register and complete the register for CPP and UI deductions. Assume the first employee is a salesperson, the second two work in the shop, and the last one works in the office. Calculate income tax deductions at 20% of gross pay.

2. Prepare a General Journal entry to record the Payroll Register information.

3. Make the Cheque Register entry to transfer funds equal to the payroll from the regular bank account to the payroll bank account (Cheque No. 522) under the assumption the company uses special payroll cheques and a payroll bank account in paying its employees. Assume the first payroll cheque is numbered 230 and enter the payroll cheque numbers in the Payroll Register.

4. Prepare a General Journal entry to record the employer's payroll deductions resulting from the payroll.

5. Prepare General Journal entries to accrue employee fringe benefit costs for the week. Assume the company matches the employees' payments for medical insurance and contributes an amount equal to 8% of each employees' gross pay to a retirement program. Also, each employee accrues vacation pay at the rate of 6% of the wages and salaries earned. The company estimates that all employees eventually will be paid their vacation pay.

A company has three employees, each of whom has been employed since January 1, earns $2,600 per month, and is paid on the last day of each month. On March 1, the following accounts and balances appeared in its ledger:

Problem 10–4
General Journal entries for payroll transactions **(LO 3)**

a. Employees Income Taxes Payable, $1,480 (liability for February only).

b. Unemployment Insurance Payable, $475 (liability for February).

c. Canada Pension Plan Payable, $390 (liability for February).

d. Employees' Medical Insurance Payable, $980 (liability for January and February).

During March and April, the company completed the following transactions related to payroll:

Mar. 11 Issued Cheque No. 320 payable to Receiver General of Canada. The cheque was in payment of the February employee income taxes, UI, and CPP amounts due.

31 Prepared a General Journal entry to record the March Payroll Record which had the following column totals:

Income Taxes	UI	CPP	Medical Insur- ance	Total Deduc- tions	Net Pay	Office Salaries	Shop Wages
$1,460	$230	$190	$260	$2,280	$5,660	$2,600	$5,200

31 Recorded the employer's $260 liability for its 50% contribution to the medical insurance plan of employees and 4% vacation pay accrued to the employees.

31 Issued Cheque No. 351 payable to Payroll Bank Account in payment of the March payroll. Endorsed the cheque, deposited it in the payroll bank account, and issued payroll cheques to the employees.

31 Prepared a General Journal entry to record the employer's payroll costs resulting from the March payroll.

Apr. 15 Issued Cheque No. 375 payable to the Receiver General in payment of the March mandatory deductions.

15 Issued Cheque No. 376 payable to All Canadian Insurance Company in payment of the employee medical insurance premiums for the first quarter.

Required

Prepare the necessary Cheque Register and General Journal entries to record the transactions.

Problem 10–5

The Payroll Register and the payroll bank account

(LO 1, 3)

Chechoff Company's first weekly pay period of the year ended on January 8. On that date the column totals of the company's Payroll Register indicated its sales employees had earned $32,500, its office employees had earned $12,800, and its delivery employees had earned $4,800. Withholdings from the employees' salaries included $1,200 of UI, $960 of CPP, $9,700 federal income taxes, $1,620 medical insurance deductions, and $540 of union dues.

Required

1. Prepare the General Journal entry to record the January 8 payroll.
2. Prepare a General Journal entry to record the employer's payroll deductions resulting from the January 8 payroll.
3. Under the assumption the company uses special payroll cheques and a payroll bank account in paying its employees, give the Cheque Register entry (Cheque No. 378) to transfer funds equal to the payroll from the regular bank account to the payroll bank account.
4. Answer this question: After the Cheque Register entry is made and posted, are additional debit and credit entries required to record the payroll cheques and pay the employees?

Problem 10–6

The Payroll Register, the payroll bank account, and payroll deductions

(LO 1, 3, 4)

The following information was taken from the payroll records of Radical Software Company for the weekly pay period ending December 20:

Employees	Clock Card No.	Daily Time							Pay Rate	Hospital Insurance	Union Dues	Earnings to End of Previous Week
		M	T	W	T	F	S	S				
Pam Loella	41	0	8	8	8	8	4	4	18.00	40.00	20.00	40,000
Martan Mann	42	6	7	8	7	8	4	0	16.00	30.00	18.00	31,000
George Singe	43	8	4	0	8	8	4	4	18.00	40.00	20.00	26,000
Nathan Tang	44	8	8	8	8	8	0	4	16.00	30.00	18.00	35,000
Terry Vaughan	45	0	6	6	6	0	0	4	14.00	20.00	10.00	18,000
										160.00	86.00	

Required

1. Enter the relevant information in the proper columns of a Payroll Register and complete the register for CPP and UI deductions. The company pays time-and-a-half for hours in excess of 40 each week. Also, work on Saturdays is paid at time-and-a-half whether the total for the week is over 40 or not. Charge the wages of George Singe to Office Salaries Expense and the wages of the remaining employees to Plant Salaries Expense. Calculate income tax deductions at 20% of gross pay.
2. Prepare a General Journal entry to record the Payroll Register information.
3. Assume the company uses special payroll cheques drawn on a payroll bank account in paying its employees and make the Cheque Register entry (Cheque No. 484) to transfer funds equal to the payroll from the regular bank account to the payroll bank account. Also, assume the first payroll cheque is No. 632 and enter the payroll cheque numbers in the Payroll Register.
4. Prepare a General Journal entry to record the employer's payroll deductions resulting from the payroll.

The following information for the weekly pay period ended December 10 was taken from the records of a company:

Problem 10–7
The Payroll Register, payroll taxes, and employee fringe benefits (LO 1, 3, 5)

Employees	Clock Card No.	Daily Time							Pay Rate	Medical Insurance	Union Dues	Earnings to End of Previous Week
		M	T	W	T	F	S	S				
Ralph Abdoul	61	8	8	8	8	8	4	0	25.00	60.00	22.00	52,000
Ali Johnston	62	7	8	6	7	8	4	0	20.00	60.00	20.00	56,000
Sarah Bigalow	63	8	8	0	8	8	4	4	18.00	60.00	18.00	23,000
Leslie Worbetts	64	8	8	8	8	8	0	0	25.00	60.00	22.00	35,000
Ainsley Vangough	65	0	6	6	6	6	8	8	20.00	60.00	20.00	41,000
										300.00	102.00	

Required

1. Enter the relevant information in the proper columns of a Payroll Register and complete the register for CPP and UI deductions. Assume that the first employee works in the office, the second is a salesperson, and the last two work in the shop. Calculate tax deductions at 20% of gross pay.

2. Prepare a General Journal entry to record the Payroll Register information.

3. Make the Cheque Register entry (Cheque No. 389) to transfer funds equal to the payroll from the regular bank account to the payroll bank account. Assume the first payroll cheque is numbered 632 and enter the payroll cheque numbers in the Payroll Register.

4. Prepare a General Journal entry to record the employer's payroll deductions resulting from the payroll.

5. Prepare a General Journal entry to accrue employee fringe benefit costs for the week. Assume the company matches the employees' payments for medical insurance and contributes an amount equal to 8% of each employees' gross pay to a retirement program. Also, each employee accrues vacation pay at the rate of 6% of the wages and salaries earned. The company estimates that all employees eventually will be paid their vacation pay.

A company has five employees, each of whom has been employed since January 1, earns $1,900 per month, and is paid on the last day of each month. On June 1 the following accounts and balances appeared on its ledger:

Problem 10–8
General Journal entries for payroll transactions (LO 3)

a. Employees' Income Taxes Payable, $1,670. (The balance of this account represents the liability for the May 31 payroll only.)

b. Unemployment Insurance Payable, $820 (liability for May only).

c. Canada Pension Payable, $575 (liability for May).

d. Employees' Medical Insurance Payable, $1,420 (liability for April and May).

During June and July, the company completed the following payroll-related transactions:

June 10   Issued Cheque No. 726 payable to the Receiver General for Canada. The cheque was in payment of the May employee income taxes, CPP, and UI amounts due.

30   Prepared a General Journal entry to record the June Payroll Record which had the following column totals:

Income Taxes	UI	CPP	Medical Insur- ance	Total Deduc- tions	Net Pay	Office Salaries	Shop Wages
$1,960	$285	$240	$620	$3,105	$6,395	$5,700	$3,800

30   Recorded the employer's $620 liability for its 50% contribution to the medical insurance plan of employees and 4% vacation pay accrued to the employees.

30   Issued Cheque No. 766 payable to Payroll Bank Account in payment of the June payroll. Endorsed the check, deposited it in the payroll bank account, and issued payroll cheques to the employees.

30   Prepared a General Journal entry to record the employer's payroll costs resulting from the June payroll.

July 15   Issued Cheque No. 790 payable to Receiver General in payment of the June mandatory deductions.

15   Issued Cheque No. 791 payable to Blacke Insurance Company. The cheque was in payment of the April, May, and June employee health insurance premiums.

Required

Prepare the necessary Cheque Register and General Journal entries to record the transactions.

PROVOCATIVE PROBLEMS

Provocative Problem 10–1
Sharpe Limited
(LO 1, 4)

Sharpe Limited, which has 90 regular employees, has recently received an order for a line of archery equipment from a chain of department stores. The order should be very profitable and will probably be repeated each year. In filling the order, Sharpe can manufacture the various bows and other supplies with present machines and employees. However, it will have to add 30 persons to its work force for 40 hours per week for 20 weeks to finish the crossbows and pack them for shipment.

The company can hire these workers and add them to its own payroll, or it can secure the services of 30 people through Personnel, Inc. Sharpe will pay Personnel, Inc., $15.00 per hour for each hour worked by each person supplied. The people will be employees of Personnel, Inc., and it will pay their wages and all taxes on the wages. On the other hand, if Sharpe Limited employs the workers and places them on its payroll, it will pay them $12 per hour and will also pay the following payroll costs on their wages: Canada Pension Plan and unemployment insurance. The company will also have to pay medical insurance costs of $15 per employee per week.

Should Sharpe Limited place the temporary help on its own payroll, or should it secure their services through Personnel, Inc.? Justify your answer.

VideoConference Company employs a systems specialist at an annual salary of $75,000. The company pays the usual portion of mandatory unemployment insurance and Canada Pension. VideoConference also pays $120 per month for the employee's medical insurance. Effective June 1, the company agreed to contribute 10% of the specialist's gross pay to a retirement program.

What was the total monthly cost of employing the specialist in January, March, July, and December? Assuming the employee works 200 hours each month, what is the cost per hour in January? If the annual gross salary is increased by $5,000, what will be the increase in the total annual costs of employing the specialist?

Provocative Problem 10–2
VideoConference Company
(LO 4, 5)

ANALYTICAL AND REVIEW PROBLEMS

Using current year's withholding tables for Canada Pension Plan, unemployment insurance, and income tax, update the Payroll Register of Illustration 10–5. In computing income tax withholdings, state your assumption as to each employee's personal deductions. Assume that hospital insurance deductions continue at the same amounts as in Illustration 10–5.

A & R Problem 10–1

The following data were taken from the Payroll Register of Eastcoastal Company:

A & R Problem 10–2

```
Gross salary ................... xxx
Employees' income tax deductions .... xxx
UI deductions ................. xxx
CPP deductions ................ xxx
Hospital insurance deductions ........ xxx
Union dues deductions ........... xxx
```

Eastcoastal contributes an equal amount to the hospital insurance plan, in addition to the statutory payroll taxes, and 6% of the gross salaries to a pension program.

Required

Record in General Journal form the payroll, payment of the employees, and remittance to the appropriate authority amounts owing in connection with the payroll. (Note: All amounts are to be indicated as xxx.)

CONCEPT TESTER

Test your understanding of the concepts introduced in this chapter by completing the following crossword puzzle.

Across Clues

1. An item used by employees to record arrival and departure times (2 words).
5. A national retirement scheme (3rd of 3 words; also see 1 down, 5 down).
6. Special bank account used for paying employees (2nd of 3 words; also see 10 across, 2 down).
9. Payment by employers to enhance the employees' wages (2nd of 3 words).
10. Special bank account used for paying employees (1st of 3 words; see also 6 across, 2 down).
11. The amount an employee earns before any deductions (2 words).
12. Payments by employers to enhance the employees' wages (1st of 3 words; also see 9 across, 7 down).
13. A government program to assist those who are out of work (1st of 2 words; also see 8 down).

Down Clues

1. A national retirement scheme (1st of 3 words; also see 5 down, 5 across).
2. Special bank account used for paying employees (3rd of 3 words; also see 10 across, 6 across).
3. An amount subtracted from the employee's pay (2 words).
4. Process of recording when an employee is on the job.
5. A national retirement scheme (2nd of 3 words; also see 1 down, 5 across).
7. Payments by employers to enhance the employees' wages (3rd of 3 words; also see 12 across, 9 across).
8. A government program to assist those who are out of work (2nd of 2 words; also see 13 across).

ANSWERS TO PROGRESS CHECKS

10–1 Unemployment insurance is designed to alleviate hardships caused by interruptions in earnings through unemployment.

10–2 On or before the last day in February.

10–3 Deductions for Canada Savings Bonds, health or life insurance premiums, loan repayments, and donations to charitable organizations.

10–4 Regular pay plus overtime pay.

10–5 Gross pay less all the deductions.

10–6 A payroll bank account simplifies the payments to the employees and the internal control.

10–7 An employee's earnings record serves as a basis for the employer's tax returns, indicates when the maximum CPP and UI deductions have been reached and supplies the data for the employees' T-4 slips.

10–8 $3,725 = ($1,750 \times 1.4) + $1,275$

10–9 Normally by the 15th of the following month; large employers must remit on the 10th and 25th of each month.

10–10 Premiums are based on the accident experience in the specific industry and on the size of the employer's payroll.

10–11 $9,600 = ($160,000 \times .06)$

Capital Assets: Plant and Equipment

...mpanies invest large amounts in plant assets, such as trucks and ...ipment, that are used to produce and distribute goods and provide ...vices to customers. Accounting provides information about the ...ts of obtaining, maintaining, and using these assets.

...s part of their continued study of balance sheet items, Karen White and Mark Smith were given sections of Weston's financial statements. In its December 31, 1994, annual report, George Weston Limited indicated that "Fixed asset investment of $552 million represents another record level and strong commitment to the business. Capital expenditures increased because more opportunities meeting the Company's minimum return levels were identified." George Weston Limited is a broadly based Canadian company founded in 1882 that conducts operations in food processing, food distribution, and resource operations in North America. These diverse businesses operate through Weston Foods, a bakery, dairy, and confectionery food processor; Loblaw Companies, the largest food distributor in Canada; and Weston Resources, a forest products and fish processing company.

GEORGE WESTON LIMITED
NOTES TO CONSOLIDATED FINANCIAL STATEMENTS
(in millions)

	Dec. 31, 1994	Dec. 31, 1993
Fixed Assets	$4,712	$4,327
Less Accumulated Depreciation	2,008	1,865
Net Book Value	$2,704	$2,462

George Weston Limited
Consolidated Cash Flow Statement

Investment:		
Purchase of fixed assets	$ 552	$ 418

LEARNING OBJECTIVES

After studying Chapter 11, you should be able to:

1. **Describe the differences between capital (plant) assets and other kinds of assets, and calculate the cost and record the purchase of plant assets.**

2. **Explain amortization accounting (including the reasons for amortization), calculate amortization by the straight-line and units-of-production methods, and calculate amortization after revising the estimated useful life of an asset.**

3. **Describe the use of accelerated amortization for financial accounting purposes and calculate accelerated amortization under the declining-balance method.**

4. **Describe the difference between revenue and capital expenditures and account properly for costs such as repairs and betterments incurred after the original purchase of capital assets.**

5. **Prepare entries to account for the disposal or exchange of capital assets and explain the use of total asset turnover in evaluating a company's efficiency in using its assets.**

6. **Define or explain the words and phrases listed in the chapter glossary.**

The focus of this chapter is long-term, tangible assets used in the operation of a business. These capital assets represent a major category of investment by businesses. Recent financial press predictions call for an approximate 8% increase in spending related to capital assets. For example, in the **Consumers Packaging Inc.** annual report for the year ended December 31, 1994, management made the following statement: "After spending an average of only $20 million per year on capital expenditures in the years 1991 to 1993, the Company spent $44 million in 1994 and plans to spend $48 million in 1995. In the two years to the end of 1995, the Company will have rebuilt 4 of its 13 furnaces, which normally have a life of 8 to 10 years, and replaced almost half of its glass-forming machines with more modern and productive machines."

Learning fundamental concepts of accounting for plant and equipment will enable you to recognize the direct financial statement impact of business activities like those described above. In studying this chapter, you will learn what distinguishes plant and equipment from other types of assets, how to determine their cost, and how companies allocate their costs to the periods that benefit from their use.

CAPITAL (PLANT) ASSETS COMPARED TO OTHER TYPES OF ASSETS

LO 1

Describe the differences between capital (plant) assets and other kinds of assets, and calculate the cost and record the purchase of plant assets.

Tangible assets that are used in the production or sale of other assets or services and that have a useful life longer than one accounting period are called *capital assets*. In the past, such assets were often described as *plant assets* or *fixed assets*. However, more descriptive terms such as *plant and equipment* or perhaps *property, plant, and equipment* are now used.

The main difference between capital assets and merchandise is that capital assets are held for use while merchandise is held for sale. For example, a business that buys a computer for the purpose of reselling it should report the computer on the balance sheet as merchandise inventory. If the same retailer owns another computer that is used to account for business operations and to prepare reports, it is classified as plant and equipment.

The characteristic that distinguishes capital assets from current assets is the length of their useful lives. For example, supplies are usually consumed within a short time after they are placed in use. Thus, their cost is assigned to the single period in which they are used. By comparison, capital assets have longer useful lives that extend over more than one accounting period. As the usefulness of capital assets expires over these periods, their cost must be allocated among them. This allocation should be accomplished in a rational and systematic manner.[1]

Capital assets are also different than the items that are reported on the balance sheet as long-term investments. Although both are held for more than one accounting period, long-term investments are not used in the primary operations of the business. For example, land that is held for future expansion is classified as a long-term investment. On the other hand, land on which the company's factory is located is a capital asset. In addition, standby equipment held for use in case of a breakdown or during peak periods of production is a capital asset. However, equipment that is removed from service and held for sale is no longer considered a capital asset.

When a capital asset is purchased, it should be recorded at cost. This cost includes all normal and reasonable expenditures necessary to get the asset in place and ready to use. For example, the cost of a factory machine includes its invoice price, less any cash discount for early payment, plus freight, unpacking, and assembling costs. The cost of an asset also includes the costs of installing a machine before placing it in service. Examples are the costs to build a concrete base or foundation for a machine, to provide electrical connections, and to adjust the machine before using it in operations.

An expenditure cannot be charged to and reported as part of the cost of a capital asset unless the expenditure is reasonable and necessary. For example, if a machine is damaged by being dropped during unpacking, the repairs should not be added to its cost. Instead, they should be charged to an expense account. Also, a fine paid for moving a heavy machine on city streets without proper permits is not part of the cost of the machine. However, if proper permits are obtained, their cost is included in the cost of the asset. Sometimes, costs in addition to the purchase price are incurred to modify or customize a new capital asset. These items should be charged to the asset's cost.

When a capital asset is constructed by a business for its own use, cost includes material and labour costs plus a reasonable amount of indirect overhead costs such as the costs of heat, light, power, and amortization on the machinery used to construct the asset. Cost also includes design fees, building permits, and insurance during construction. However, insurance costs for coverage after the asset has been placed in service are an operating expense.

When land is purchased for a building site, its cost includes the total amount paid for the land, including any real estate commissions. Its cost also includes fees for insuring the title, legal fees, and any accrued property taxes paid by the purchaser. In addition, payments for surveying, clearing, grading, draining, and landscaping are included in the cost of land. Other costs of land include assessments

COST OF A CAPITAL ASSET

---

[1] *CICA Handbook,* section 3060, "Capital Assets," par. 31.

by the local government, whether incurred at the time of purchase or later, for such things as installing streets, sewers, and sidewalks. These assessments are included because they add a more or less permanent value to the land.

Land purchased as a building site may have an old building that must be removed. In such cases, the total purchase price should be charged to the Land account. Also, the cost of removing the old building, less any amounts recovered through the sale of salvaged materials, should be charged to the Land account.

Because land has an unlimited life and is not consumed when it is used, it is not subject to amortization. However, **land improvements,** such as parking lot surfaces, fences, and lighting systems, have limited useful lives. Although these costs increase the usefulness of the land, they must be charged to separate Land Improvement accounts so that they can be amortized. Of course, a separate Building account must be charged for the costs of purchasing or constructing a building that will be used as a plant asset.

Land, land improvements, and buildings often are purchased in a single transaction for a lump-sum price. When this occurs, you must allocate the cost of the purchase among the different types of assets, based on their relative market values. These market values may be estimated by appraisal or by using the tax-assessed valuations of the assets.

For example, assume that a company pays $90,000 cash to acquire land appraised at $30,000, land improvements appraised at $10,000, and a building appraised at $60,000. The $90,000 cost is allocated on the basis of appraised values as follows:

	Appraised Value	Percentage of Total	Apportioned Cost
Land	$ 30,000	30%	$27,000
Land improvements	10,000	10	9,000
Building	60,000	60	54,000
Totals	$100,000	100%	$90,000

Progress Check

(Answers to Progress Checks are provided at the end of the chapter.)

11-1   Identify the asset classification for: *(a)* office supplies; *(b)* office equipment; *(c)* merchandise; *(d)* land held for future expansion; *(e)* trucks used in operations.

11-2   Identify the account charged for each of the following expenditures: *(a)* the purchase price of a vacant lot; *(b)* the cost of paving that vacant lot.

11-3   What amount should be recorded as the cost of a new production machine, given the following items related to the machine: gross purchase price, $700,000; duty, $49,000; purchase discount taken, $21,000; freight to move machine to plant, $3,500; assembly costs, $3,000; cost of foundation for machine, $2,500; cost of spare parts to be used in maintaining the machine, $4,200?

Because capital assets are purchased for use, you can think of a capital asset as a quantity of usefulness that contributes to the operations of the business throughout the service life of the asset. And, because the life of any capital asset (other than land) is limited, this quantity of usefulness expires as the asset is used. This expiration of a capital asset's quantity of usefulness is generally described as *amortization*. In accounting, this term describes the process of allocating and charging the cost of the usefulness to the accounting periods that benefit from the asset's use.

The term *amortization* is the general term used for many situations where amounts are allocated to different accounts over varying lengths of time. When the Accounting Standards Board revised and reissued the standard on capital assets (Section 3060), they said that the cost of capital assets should be amortized over their useful lives in a rational and systematic manner. In practice, the term *depreciation* still tends to be used for plant assets such as machinery and buildings, and the term *depletion* still tends to be used for natural resources. Amortization continues to be used for intangible assets and other items such as premium or discount on long-term debt. We will continue to use the terms depreciation and depletion from time to time. Remember that they are terms that are specialized names for amortization.

For example, when a company buys an automobile for use as a plant asset, it acquires a quantity of usefulness in the sense that it obtains a quantity of transportation. The total cost of the transportation is the cost of the car less the expected proceeds to be received when the car is sold or traded in at the end of its service life. This net cost must be allocated to the accounting periods that benefit from the car's use. In other words, the asset's cost must be amortized. Note that the amortization process does not measure the decline in the car's market value each period. Nor does it measure the physical deterioration of the car each period. Under generally accepted accounting principles, amortization is a process of allocating a capital asset's cost to income statements of the years in which it is used.

Because amortization represents the cost of using a capital asset, you should not begin recording amortization charges until the asset is actually put to use providing services or producing products.

The **service life** of a capital asset is the length of time it will be used in the operations of the business. This service life (or useful life) may not be as long as the asset's potential life. For example, although computers have a potential life of six to eight years, a company may plan to trade in its old computers for new ones every three years. In this case, the computers have a three-year service life. Therefore, this company should charge the cost of the computers (less their expected trade-in value) to amortization expense over this three-year period.

Several factors often make the service life of a plant asset hard to predict. Wear and tear from use determine the service life of many assets. However, two additional factors, **inadequacy** and **obsolescence,** often need to be considered.

When a business grows more rapidly than anticipated, the capacity of the assets may become too small for the productive demands of the business. As this happens, the assets become inadequate. Obsolescence, like inadequacy, is hard to anticipate

NATURE OF AMORTIZATION

LO 2

Explain amortization accounting (including the reasons for amortization), calculate amortization by the straight-line and units-of-production methods, and calculate amortization after revising the estimated useful life of an asset.

SERVICE (USEFUL) LIFE OF A CAPITAL ASSET

because the timing of new inventions and improvements normally cannot be predicted. Yet, new inventions and improvements may cause a company to discard an obsolete asset long before it wears out.

Many times, a company is able to predict the service life of a new asset based on the company's past experience with similar assets. In other cases, when it has no experience with a particular type of asset, a company must depend on the experience of others or on engineering studies and judgment.

In its 1994 annual report, **Corel Corporation** disclosed the following information regarding its amortization procedures:

(e) Capital Assets

Capital assets are recorded at cost. Amortization of licenses commences with the market release of each new software product and versions. Depreciation and amortization are calculated using the following rates and bases:

Furniture and equipment	20–33% declining balance
Computer equipment and software	33.3% straight-line
Research and development equipment	20% declining balance
Software licenses and purchased software, clipart libraries and Photo CD libraries	Shorter of the life of the license or 20.0–33.3% straight-line
Leasehold improvements	Straight-line over the term of the lease

SALVAGE VALUE

The total amount of amortization that should be taken over an asset's service life is the asset's cost minus its estimated **salvage value.** The salvage value of a plant asset is the amount that you expect to receive from selling the asset at the end of its life. If you expect an asset to be traded in on a new asset, the salvage value is the estimated trade-in value.

Sometimes, a company must incur additional costs to dispose of plant assets. For example, a company may plan to clean and paint an old machine before offering it for sale. In this case, the estimated salvage value is the expected proceeds from the sale of the asset less the cleaning and painting costs.

ALLOCATING AMORTIZATION

Many amortization methods for allocating a capital asset's total cost among the several accounting periods in its service life have been suggested and used in the past. However, at present, most companies use the *straight-line method* of amortization in their financial accounting records for presentation in their financial statements. Some types of assets are amortized according to the *units-of-production method.* We explain these two methods next and then consider some *accelerated amortization* methods.

Straight-Line Method

Straight-line amortization (or **depreciation**) charges each year in the asset's life with the same amount of expense. To determine the annual expense, the total cost to be amortized over the asset's life is calculated by first subtracting the asset's estimated salvage value from its cost. This total amount to be amortized is then divided by the estimated number of accounting periods in the asset's service life.

Illustration 11-1   The Financial Statement of Straight-Line Amortization.

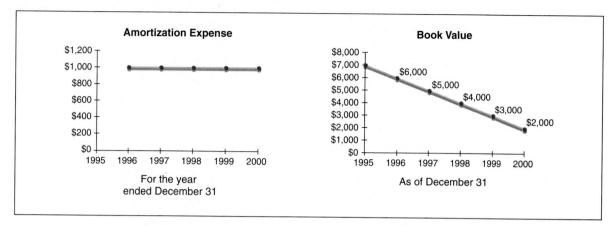

For example, if an asset costs $7,000, has an estimated service life of five years, and has an estimated $2,000 salvage value, its amortization per year by the straight-line method is $1,000. This amount is calculated as follows:

$$\frac{\text{Cost} - \text{Salvage}}{\text{Service life in years}} = \frac{\$7,000 - \$2,000}{5 \text{ years}} = \$1,000 \text{ per year}$$

If this asset is purchased on December 31, 1995, and used throughout its predicted service life of five years, the straight-line method will allocate an equal amount of amortization to each of those years (1996 through 2000). The left graph in Illustration 11–1 shows that this $1,000 per year amount will be reported each year as an expense. The right graph shows the amount that will be reported on each of the six balance sheets that will be produced while the company actually owns the asset. This **book value** of the asset is its original cost less accumulated amortization. The book value goes down by $1,000 each year. Both graphs show why this method is called *straight-line*.

Although most companies use straight-line amortization, other methods are common in certain industries. For example, **Canadian Pacific Limited** uses the units-of-production method in its facilities that produce crude oil and natural gas.

Units-of-Production Method

The purpose of recording amortization, or depreciation, is to provide relevant information about the cost of consuming an asset's usefulness. In general, this means that each accounting period an asset is used should be charged with a fair share of its cost. The straight-line method charges an equal share to each period. If plant assets are used about the same amount in each accounting period, this method produces a reasonable result. However, the use of some plant assets varies greatly from one accounting period to another. For example, a contractor may use a particular piece of construction equipment for a month and then not use it again for a few months.

Because the use of such equipment varies from period to period, **units-of-production amortization** may provide a better matching of expenses with revenues than straight-line amortization. Under the units-of-production method, the cost of an asset minus its estimated salvage value is divided by the total number cost of an asset minus its estimated salvage value is divided by the total number of units that management predicts it will produce during its service life. Units of production may be expressed as units of product or in any other unit of measure such as hours of use or distances driven. In effect, this method computes the amount of amortization per unit of service provided by the asset. Then, the amount of amortization taken in an accounting period is determined by multiplying the units produced in that period by the amortization per unit.

For example, a truck that cost $24,000 has a predicted salvage value of $4,000 and an estimated service life of 200,000 kilometres. The amortization per kilometre, or the amortization per unit of service, is $0.10, which is calculated as follows:

$$\text{Amortization per unit of production} = \frac{\text{Cost} - \text{Salvage value}}{\text{Predicted units of production}}$$

$$= \frac{\$24,000 - \$4,000}{200,000 \text{ kms.}}$$

$$= \$0.10 \text{ per km.}$$

If the truck is driven 32,000 kilometres during its first year, amortization for the first year is $3,200 (32,000 kms. at $.10 per km.). If the truck is driven 24,000 kilometres in the second year, amortization for the second year is 24,000 kilometres times $0.10 per km., or $2,400.

AMORTIZATION FOR PARTIAL YEARS

Of course, capital assets may be purchased or disposed of at any time during the year. When an asset is purchased (or disposed of) at some time other than the beginning or end of an accounting period, amortization must be recorded for part of a year. Otherwise, the year of purchase or the year of disposal is not charged with its share of the asset's amortization.

For example, assume that a machine was purchased and placed in service on October 8, 1996, and that the annual accounting period ends on December 31. The machine cost $4,600; it has an estimated service life of five years and an estimated salvage value of $600. Because the machine was purchased and used nearly three months during 1996, the annual income statement should reflect amortization expense on the machine for that part of the year. The amount of amortization to be reported is often based on the assumption that the machine was purchased on the first of the month nearest the actual date of purchase. Therefore, since the purchase occurred on October 8, three months' amortization is recorded on December 31. If the purchase had been on October 16 or later during October, amortization would be calculated as if the purchase had been on November 1. Using straight-line amortization, the three months' amortization of $200 is calculated as follows:

$$\frac{\$4,600 - \$600}{5} \times \frac{3}{12} = \$200$$

A similar calculation is necessary when the disposal of an asset occurs during a year. For example, suppose that the preceding asset is sold on June 24, 2000. On the date of the disposal, amortization should be recognized. The partial year's amortization, calculated to the nearest whole month, is:

$$\frac{\$4,600 - \$600}{5} \times \frac{6}{12} = \$400$$

In presenting information about the capital assets of a business, both the cost and accumulated amortization of capital assets should be reported. For example, **CGC, Inc.'s** balance sheet at the close of its 1994 fiscal year included the following:

Property, Plant and Equipment

Property, plant and equipment consists of the following:

(in thousands of dollars)	Cost	Accumulated Depletion, Depreciation & Amortization	1994 Net	1993 Net
Land, land improvements and mineral deposits	$ 2,721	$ 511	$ 2,210	$ 2,223
Buildings	19,431	9,034	10,397	10,857
Furniture, fixtures and equipment	89,288	63,769	25,519	27,596
Vehicles	2,682	2,341	341	394
Leasehold improvements	2,341	1,098	1,243	1,318
Construction in progress	5,720	—	5,720	2,824
Total	$122,183	$76,753	$45,430	$45,212

Notice that CGC reported only the amount of accumulated depletion, depreciation, and amortization for all property, plant, and equipment. This is not necessarily the usual practice in published financial statements. In fact, many companies show property, plant, and equipment on one line with the net amount of cost less accumulated amortization. When this is done, however, the amount of accumulated amortization is disclosed in a note. To satisfy the *full-disclosure principle,* companies also describe the amortization method or methods used.[2] Usually, they do this in a note.

Reporting both the cost and the accumulated amortization of capital assets may help balance sheet readers compare the status of different companies. For example, a company that holds assets having an original cost of $50,000 and accumulated amortization of $40,000 may be in quite a different situation than another company with new assets that cost $10,000. Although the net unamortized cost is the same in both cases, the first company may have more productive capacity available but probably is facing the need to replace its older assets. These differences are not conveyed if the balance sheets report only the $10,000 book values.

From the discussion so far, you should recognize that amortization is a process of cost allocation rather than valuation. Capital assets are reported on balance sheets at their remaining unamortized costs (book value), not at market values.

Some people argue that financial statements should report the market value of plant assets. However, this practice has not gained general acceptance. Instead, most accountants believe that financial statements should be based on the *going-concern principle* described in Chapter 1. This principle states that, unless there is adequate evidence to the contrary, the accountant should assume the company will

[2]Ibid., par. 3060.58.

continue in business. This leads to a related assumption that capital assets will be held and used long enough to recover their original cost through the sale of products and services. Therefore, since the capital assets will not be sold, their market values are not reported in the financial statements. Instead, the assets are carried on the balance sheet at cost less accumulated amortization. This is the remaining portion of the original cost that is expected to be recovered in future periods.

Inexperienced financial statement readers may make the mistake of thinking that the accumulated amortization shown on a balance sheet represents funds accumulated to buy new assets when the presently owned assets must be replaced. However, you know that accumulated amortization is a contra account with a credit balance that cannot be used to buy anything. If a business has funds available to buy assets, the funds are shown on the balance sheet as liquid assets such as *Cash,* not as accumulated amortization.

REVISING AMORTIZATION RATES

Because the calculation of amortization or depreciation must be based on an asset's *predicted* useful life, amortization expense is an estimate. Therefore, during the life of an asset, new information may indicate that the original prediction of useful life was inaccurate. If your estimate of an asset's useful life changes, what should be done? The answer is to use the new estimate of the remaining useful life to calculate amortization in the future. In other words, revise the estimate of annual amortization expense in the future by spreading the remaining cost to be amortized over the revised remaining useful life. This approach should be followed whether the amortization method is straight-line, units-of-production, or some other method.

For example, assume that a machine was purchased seven years ago at a cost of $10,500. At that time, the machine was predicted to have a 10-year life with a $500 salvage value. Therefore, it was amortized by the straight-line method at the rate of $1,000 per year [($10,500 − $500)/10 = $1,000]. At the beginning of the asset's eighth year, its book value is $3,500, calculated as follows:

Cost	$10,500
Less seven years' accumulated amortization . . .	7,000
Book value	$ 3,500

At the beginning of its eighth year, the predicted number of years remaining in the useful life is changed from three to five years. The estimated salvage value is also changed to $300. Amortization for each of the machine's five remaining years should be calculated as follows:

$$\frac{\text{Book value} - \text{Revised salvage value}}{\text{Revised remaining useful life}} = \frac{\$3,500 - \$300}{5 \text{ years}} = \$640 \text{ per year}$$

Thus, $640 of amortization should be recorded for the machine at the end of the eighth and each remaining year in its useful life.

Because this asset was amortized at the rate of $1,000 per year for the first seven years, you might contend that amortization expense was overstated during the first seven years. While that view may have merit, accountants have concluded that past years' financial statements generally should not be restated to reflect facts that were not known when the statements were originally prepared.

A revision of the predicted useful life of a plant asset is an example of a **change in an accounting estimate.** Such changes result "from new information or subsequent developments and accordingly from better insight or improved judgment." Generally accepted accounting principles require that changes in accounting estimates, such as a change in estimated useful life or salvage value, be reflected only in future financial statements, not by modifying past statements.[3]

Progress Check

11-4   **For accounting purposes, what is the meaning of the term *amortization*?**

11-5   **Clandestine Gift Shop purchased a new machine for $96,000 on January 1, 1996. Its predicted useful life is five years or 100,000 units of product, and salvage value is $8,000. During 1996, 10,000 units of product were produced. Find the book value of the machine on December 31, 1996, assuming *(a)* straight-line amortization and *(b)* units-of-production amortization.**

11-6   **In early January of 1996, Betty's Brownies acquired mixing equipment at a cost of $3,800. The company estimated that this equipment would be used for three years and then have a salvage of $200. Early in 1998, they changed the estimate to a four-year life with no residual value. Assuming straight-line amortization, how much will be reported as amortization on this equipment for the year ended 1998?**

An annual survey of 300 Canadian companies indicates that straight-line is the most widely used method of amortization. However, note in the following table that **accelerated amortization** methods were used 20% of the time in 1992:

	Amortization Methods Used	
	1992	1991
Straight-line	62%	61%
An accelerated method	20	21
Units-of-production	16	16
Other	2	2
Total	100%	100%

Source: *Financial Reporting in Canada 1993,* Canadian Institute of Chartered Accountants (Toronto: 1993), p. 154.

ACCELERATED AMORTIZATION

LO 3
Describe the use of accelerated amortization for financial accounting purposes and calculate accelerated amortization under the declining-balance method.

Accelerated amortization methods produce larger amortization charges during the early years of an asset's life and smaller charges in the later years. Although more

---

[3]Ibid., par. 1506.25.

As a Matter of Ethics

Fascar Company has struggled financially for more than two years. The economic situation surrounding the company has been depressed and there are no signs of improvement for at least two more years. As a result, net income has been almost zero, and the future seems bleak.

The operations of Fascar require major investments in equipment. As a result, amortization is a large factor in the calculation of income. Because competition in Fascar's industry normally has required frequent replacements of equipment, the equipment has been amortized over only three years. However, Fascar's president has recently instructed Sue Ann Meyer, the

company's accountant, to revise the estimated useful lives of existing equipment to six years and to use a six-year life on new equipment.

Meyer suspects that the president's instruction is motivated by a desire to improve the reported income of the company. In trying to determine whether to follow the president's instructions, Meyer is torn between her loyalty to her employer and her responsibility to the public, the shareholders, and others who use the company's financial statements. She also wonders what the independent accountant who audits the financial statements will think about the change.

than one accelerated method is used in financial reporting, the most commonly used is the declining-balance method.

Declining-Balance Method

Under **declining-balance amortization,** an amortization rate of up to twice the straight-line rate is applied each year to the book value of the asset at the beginning of the year. Because the book value *declines* each year, the amount of amortization gets smaller each year.

The **Income Tax Act** requires that companies use a declining-balance method for calculating the maximum capital cost allowance (amortization or depreciation for tax purposes) that may be claimed in any period. The Act specifies the rates for various classes of assets. For example, a rate of 20% would be used for general machinery and equipment, and a rate of 4% for most buildings. Further discussion of the details of tax accounting for capital assets is deferred to a more advanced course.

When the amortization rate used is twice the straight-line rate, the method is called the *double-declining-balance method.* To use the double-declining-balance method: (1) calculate the straight-line amortization rate for the asset; (2) double it; and (3) calculate amortization expense for the year by applying this rate to the asset's book value at the beginning of that year. Note that the salvage value is not used in the calculation.

For example, assume that the double-declining-balance method is used to calculate amortization on a new $10,000 asset; it has an estimated life of five years and an estimated salvage value of $1,000. The steps to follow are:

1. Divide 100% by five years to determine the straight-line annual amortization rate of 20% per year.
2. Double this 20% rate to get a declining-balance rate of 40% per year.
3. Calculate the annual amortization charges as shown in the following table:

Year	Beginning Book Value	Annual Amortization (40% of Book Value)	Accumulated Amortization at Year-End	Ending Book Value ($10,000 Cost Less Accumulated Amortization)
First	$10,000	$4,000	$4,000	$6,000
Second	6,000	2,400	6,400	3,600
Third	3,600	1,440	7,840	2,160
Fourth	2,160	864	8,704	1,296
Fifth	1,296	296*	9,000	1,000
Total		$9,000		

*Fifth year amortization is $1,296 − $1,000 = $296.

In the table, notice that the annual amortization of $296 for the fifth year does not equal 40% × $1,296, or $518.40. Instead, the $296 was calculated by subtracting the $1,000 salvage value from the $1,296 book value at the beginning of the fifth year. This was done because, according to generally accepted accounting principles, an asset should not be amortized below its salvage value. If the declining-balance procedure had been applied in the fifth year, the $518.40 of annual amortization would have reduced the ending book value to $777.60, which is less than the $1,000 estimated salvage value.

Earlier in the chapter we discussed the calculation of a partial year's amortization when the straight-line method is used. Recall that when an asset is purchased (or disposed of) at some time other than the end of an accounting period, amortization must be recorded for part of a year. Declining-balance amortization does not complicate this calculation. For example, if amortization must be calculated for three months, the annual amount of amortization is simply multiplied by $3/12$. So, if an asset that cost $10,000 is purchased three months before the end of the year and the annual declining-balance amortization rate is 20%, amortization for the last three months is $10,000 \times 20\% \times 3/12 = \$500$.

The following year's amortization would be based on the unamortized balance of $9,500 ($10,000 − $500). Thus, the amortization for the next full year would be $1,900 ($9,500 × .2). Another, somewhat more complex calculation may be used to verify the amortization of $1,900, as follows:

Year 1 $10,000 × 20% × ¾₁₂	$ 500
Year 2 ($10,000 × 20% × ⁹/₁₂) + ($8,000 × 20% × ³/₁₂)	1,900

REVENUE AND CAPITAL EXPENDITURES

By this time, you have learned that some expenditures are recorded as expenses right away while others are recorded as assets with expenses coming later. After a plant asset is acquired and put into service, additional expenditures may be incurred to operate, maintain, repair, and improve it. In recording these additional expenditures, the accountant must decide whether they should be debited to expense accounts or asset accounts. The issue is whether more useful information is provided by reporting these expenditures as current expenses or by adding them to the plant asset's cost and amortizing them over its remaining useful life.

Expenditures that are recorded as expenses and deducted from revenues on the current period's income statement are called **revenue expenditures.** They are reported on the income statement because they do not provide material benefits in future periods. Examples of revenue expenditures that relate to plant assets are supplies, fuel, lubricants, and electrical power.

In contrast to revenue expenditures, **capital expenditures** produce economic benefits that do not fully expire before the end of the current period. Because they are debited to asset accounts and reported on the balance sheet, they are also called **balance sheet expenditures.** Capital expenditures increase or improve the kind or amount of service that an asset provides.

Because the information in the financial statements is affected for several years by the choice you make in recording costs as revenue or capital expenditures, managers must be careful in deciding how to classify them. In making these decisions, it is helpful to identify the costs as repairs, betterments, or purchases of assets with low costs.

Repairs

Repairs are made to keep an asset in normal, good operating condition. These expenditures are necessary if an asset is to provide its expected level of service over its estimated useful life. However, repairs do not extend the useful life beyond the original estimate and do not increase the productivity of the asset beyond the levels originally estimated. For example, machines must be cleaned, lubricated, and adjusted, and small parts must be replaced when they wear out. These repairs typically are made every year, and accountants treat them as *revenue expenditures.* Thus, their costs should be reported on the current income statement as expenses.

Consistent with the guidelines given here, Air Canada expenses routine maintenance and repairs as incurred. However, the cost of scheduled airframe and engine overhauls is capitalized as a betterment because such expenditures are expected to benefit future periods.

Betterments

A **betterment** (or an improvement) occurs when a plant asset is modified to improve service potential. A betterment might increase the physical output or service capacity, lower operating costs, extend the useful life or improve output quality. A betterment often involves adding a component to an asset or replacing one of its old components with an improved or superior component. While a betterment might make an asset more productive, it may not necessarily increase the asset's useful life. For example, replacing the manual controls on a machine with automatic controls reduces future labour costs. But, the machine still wears out just as fast as it would have with the manual controls.

A betterment benefits future periods and should be debited to the asset account as a capital expenditure. Then, the new book value (less salvage) should be amortized over the remaining service life of the asset. For example, suppose that a company paid $80,000 for a machine with an eight-year service life and no salvage value. On January 2, after three years and $30,000 of amortization, it adds an automatic control system to the machine at a cost of $18,000. As a result, the company's labour cost to operate the machine in future periods will be reduced. The cost of the betterment is added to the Machinery account with this entry:

Jan.	2	Machinery	18,000.00	
		Cash		18,000.00
		To record the installation of the automatic control system.		

At this point, the remaining cost to be amortized is $80,000 + $18,000 − $30,000 = $68,000. Because five years remain in the useful life, the annual amortization expense hereafter will be $13,600 per year ($68,000/5 years).

Capital Assets with Low Costs

Even with the help of computers, keeping individual plant asset records can be expensive. Therefore, many companies do not keep detailed records for assets that cost less than some minimum amount such as $50 or $100. Instead, they treat the acquisition as a revenue expenditure and charge the cost directly to an expense account at the time of purchase. As long as the amounts are small, this practice is acceptable under the *materiality principle*. That is, treating these capital expenditures as revenue expenditures is unlikely to mislead a user of the financial statements.

Progress Check

11-7 **At the beginning of the fifth year of a machine's estimated six-year useful life, the machine was completely overhauled and its estimated useful life was extended to nine years in total. The machine originally cost $108,000, and the overhaul cost was $12,000. Prepare the journal entry to record the cost of the overhaul.**

11-8 **What is the difference between revenue expenditures and capital expenditures and how should they be recorded?**

11-9 **What is a betterment? How should a betterment to a machine be recorded?**

A variety of events might lead to the disposal of capital assets. Some assets wear out or become obsolete. Other assets may be sold because of changing business plans. Sometimes, an asset is discarded or sold because it is damaged by a fire or other accident. Regardless of what leads to a disposal, the journal entry or entries related to the disposal should:

CAPITAL ASSET DISPOSALS

1. Record amortization expense up to the date of the disposal and bring the accumulated amortization account up to date.

LO 5

Prepare entries to account for the disposal or exchange of plant assets and explain the use of total asset turnover in evaluating a company's efficiency in using its assets.

2.   Remove the asset and accumulated amortization account balances that relate to the disposal.

3.   Record any cash received or paid as a result of the disposal.

4.   Record any gain or loss that results from comparing the book value of the asset with the cash received or paid as a result of the disposal.

For example, assume a machine that cost $9,000 was totally destroyed in a fire on June 25. Accumulated amortization at the end of the previous year was $3,000 and unrecorded amortization for the first six months of the current year is $500. The following entry brings the accumulated amortization account up to date:

June	25	Amortization Expense	500.00	
		Accumulated Amortization, Machinery		500.00
		To record amortization up to the date of the fire.		

Assume the owner of the machine carried insurance against fire losses and received a $4,400 cash settlement for the loss. The following entry records the loss of the machine and the cash settlement:

June	25	Cash	4,400.00	
		Loss on Fire[4]	1,100.00	
		Accumulated Amortization, Machinery	3,500.00	
		Machinery		9,000.00
		To record the destruction of machinery, the receipt of		
		insurance settlement, and the net loss resulting from		
		the fire.		

Notice that the two entries accomplish all four of the necessary changes that occurred as a result of the asset disposal. Of course, an asset disposal might involve a gain instead of a loss. Also, a disposal might involve a cash payment instead of a receipt. Regardless of the specific facts, entries similar to these must be made so the income statement shows any gain or loss resulting from the disposal and the balance sheet reflects the necessary changes in the asset and accumulated amortization accounts.

EXCHANGING CAPITAL ASSETS

Many capital assets are sold for cash when they are retired from use. Others, such as machinery, automobiles, and office equipment, are commonly exchanged for new assets. In a typical exchange of assets, a trade-in allowance is received on the old asset, and any balance is paid in cash.

Accounting for the exchange of nonmonetary assets depends on whether the old and the new assets are similar in the functions they perform. For example, trading

---

[4]Note that the recorded loss of $1,100 probably does not equal the economic loss from the fire. The economic loss depends on the difference between the cost of replacing the asset and any insurance settlement. A difference between this economic loss and the reported loss arises from the fact that the accounting records do not attempt to reflect the replacement value of plant assets.

an old truck for a new truck is an exchange of similar assets. An example of exchanging dissimilar assets would be trading a parcel of land for a truck.

Exchanges of Dissimilar Assets

If a company exchanges a plant asset for another asset that is *dissimilar* in use or purpose, any gain or loss on the exchange must be recorded. The gain or loss can be determined by comparing the book value of the assets given up with the fair market value of the assets received. For example, assume that a company exchanges an old machine plus $16,500 cash for some merchandise inventory. The old machine originally cost $18,000 and had accumulated amortization of $15,000 at the time of the exchange. Also assume that the fair market value of the merchandise received in the exchange was $21,000. This entry would record the exchange:

Jan.	5	Merchandise Inventory (or Purchases)	21,000.00	
		Accumulated Amortization, Machinery	15,000.00	
		Machinery		18,000.00
		Cash		16,500.00
		Gain on Exchange of Machinery		1,500.00
		Exchanged old machine and cash for merchandise inventory.		

Note that the book value of the assets given up totaled $19,500, which included $16,500 cash plus $3,000 ($18,000 − $15,000) for the machine. Because the merchandise had a fair market value of $21,000, the entry recorded a gain of $1,500 ($21,000 − $19,500).

Another way to calculate the gain or loss is to compare the machine's book value with the trade-in allowance granted for the machine. Since the fair market value of the merchandise was $21,000 and the cash paid was $16,500, the trade-in allowance granted for the machine was $4,500. The difference between the machine's $3,000 book value and the $4,500 trade-in allowance equals the $1,500 gain on the exchange.

Exchanges of Similar Assets

In general, accounting for exchanges of similar assets depends on whether the amount of cash involved is more or less than 10% of the total consideration given up or received. If the amount of cash is more than 10%, the transaction is a monetary transaction and a gain or loss on the exchange is recorded in the same manner as for exchanges of dissimilar assets.

Nonmonetary Exchanges. Accountants have determined that when an exchange of similar assets occurs and the cash involved is less than 10% of the total consideration, an earnings process has not been completed. The usual rule then is that no gain or loss should be recorded on the exchange. Therefore, the cost of the asset received is recorded as the book value of the asset delivered plus any cash paid or minus any cash received.

To illustrate, assume we decide to trade trucks with another company because they are in more convenient locations. Our truck has an original cost of $90,000 and accumulated amortization of $25,000. We have determined that the market value of the truck we are to receive is approximately $65,000, the book value of the truck we are giving up.

The entry to record the exchange when no cash is involved is

Jan.	5	Automotive equipment (new truck)	65,000	
		Accumulated amortization	25,000	
		Automotive equipment (old truck)		90,000

If we assume that we receive $1,000 as part of the exchange, the entry is

Jan.	5	Cash	1,000	
		Automotive equipment (new truck)	64,000	
		Accumulated amortization	25,000	
		Automotive equipment (old truck)		90,000

Notice that no gain is recorded. Instead the truck's cost is recorded as $64,000. This is still a nonmonetary transaction because the cash involved is less than 10% of the total consideration (10% of $65,000 = $6,500) and similar assets are being exchanged.

Now assume that we pay $3,000 as part of the exchange. The entry to record the transaction is

Jan.	5	Automotive equipment (new truck)	65,000	
		Accumulated amortization	25,000	
		Loss on exchange of trucks	3,000	
		Cash		3,000
		Automotive equipment (old truck)		90,000

Although the general rule is that no gains or losses should be recorded on nonmonetary exchanges of similar assets, the maximum amount at which we may record the new asset is its market value. In this example the value of the assets delivered is $68,000 ($3,000 cash plus a truck with a $65,000 book value). However, the market value of the truck received is $65,000. The cost of the truck received must not be recorded at more than $65,000. Therefore, we must record a $3,000 loss.

In nonmonetary exchanges of similar assets, the cost of the asset received is recorded at the book value of the asset given up, minus any cash received or plus any cash paid, as long as this amount is no greater than the market value of the asset being received.[5] A loss might need to be recorded but it is unlikely that a gain would arise.

[5]*CICA Handbook,* section 3830, "Non-Monetary Transactions," par. .10.

We have not yet discussed all of the different assets a business might own. Nevertheless, you can see from this and previous chapters that a company's assets are usually very important factors in determining the company's ability to earn profits. Managers spend a great deal of time and energy deciding which assets a company should acquire, how much should be acquired, and how the assets can be used most efficiently. Outside investors and other financial statement readers are also interested in evaluating whether a company uses its assets efficiently.

One way to describe the efficiency of a company's use of its assets is to calculate **total asset turnover.** The formula for this calculation is

$$\text{Total asset turnover} = \frac{\text{Net sales}}{\text{Average total assets}}$$

In this calculation, average total assets is often approximated by averaging the total assets at the beginning of the year with total assets at the end of the year.

For example, suppose that a company with total assets of $9,650,000 at the beginning of the year and $10,850,000 at the end of the year generated sales of $44,000,000 during the year. The company's total asset turnover for the year is calculated as follows:

$$\text{Total asset turnover} = \frac{\$44,000,000}{(\$9,650,000 + \$10,850,000)/2} = 4.3$$

Thus, in describing the efficiency of the company in using its assets to generate sales, we can say that it turned its assets over 4.3 times during the year. Or, we might say that each $1.00 of assets produced $4.30 of sales during the year.

As is true for other financial ratios, a company's total asset turnover is meaningful only when compared to the results in other years and of similar companies. Interpreting the total asset turnover also requires that users understand the company's operations. Some operations are capital intensive, meaning that a relatively large amount must be invested in assets to generate sales. This suggests a relatively low total asset turnover. On the other hand, if operations are labour intensive, sales are generated more by the efforts of people than the use of assets. Thus, we would expect a higher total asset turnover.

Imperial Oil Limited's asset turnover ratio for 1994 is ($ millions):

$$\frac{\$9,011}{(\$11,928 + \$12,861) \div 2} = 0.73$$

Canadian Tire Corporation Limited's asset turnover ratio for 1994 is ($ thousands):

$$\frac{\$3,599,231}{(\$2,668,863 + \$2,400,279) \div 2} = 1.42$$

Progress Check

11-10 **Melanie Co. acquired equipment on January 10, 1996, at a cost of $42,000. The estimated useful life of equipment was five years with an estimated salvage value of $7,000. On June 27, 1997, the company decided to change their manufacturing methods and sold this equipment for $32,000. Prepare the appropriate entry or entries for June 27, 1997.**

11-11   Standard Company traded an old truck for a new one. The original cost of the old truck was $30,000, and its accumulated amortization at the time of the trade was $23,400. The new truck had a cash price of $45,000. Prepare entries to record the trade assuming Standard received a $3,000 trade-in allowance.

11-12   Using the annual report for Geac Computer Corporation in Appendix I, calculate the total asset turnover for the year ended April 30, 1994.

SUMMARY OF THE CHAPTER IN TERMS OF LEARNING OBJECTIVES

LO 1.   Describe the differences between capital assets and other kinds of assets, and calculate the cost and record the purchase of capital assets. Capital assets are tangible items that have a useful life longer than one accounting period. Capital assets are not held for sale but are used in the production or sale of other assets or services. The cost of capital assets includes all normal and reasonable expenditures necessary to get the assets in place and ready to use. The cost of a lump-sum purchase should be allocated among the individual assets based on their relative market values.

LO 2.   Explain amortization accounting (including the reasons for amortization), calculate amortization by the straight-line and units-of-production methods, and calculate amortization after revising the estimated useful life of an asset. The cost of capital assets that have limited service lives must be allocated to the accounting periods that benefit from their use. The straight-line method of amortization divides the cost minus salvage value by the number of periods in the service life of the asset to determine the amortization expense of each period. The units-of-production method divides the cost minus salvage value by the estimated number of units the asset will produce to determine the amortization per unit. If the estimated useful life of a capital asset is changed, the remaining cost to be amortized is spread over the remaining (revised) useful life of the asset.

LO 3.   Describe the use of accelerated amortization for financial accounting purposes and calculate accelerated amortization under the declining-balance method. Accelerated amortization methods such as the declining-balance method are acceptable for financial accounting purposes if they are based on realistic estimates of useful life.

LO 4.   Describe the difference between revenue and capital expenditures and account properly for costs such as repairs and betterments incurred after the original purchase of capital assets. The benefit of revenue expenditures expires during the current period. Thus, revenue expenditures are debited to expense accounts and matched with current revenues. Capital expenditures are debited to asset accounts because they benefit future periods. Repairs are revenue expenditures. Capital expenditures include betterments. Amounts paid for assets with low costs are technically capital expenditures but can be treated as revenue expenditures if they are not material.

LO 5.   Prepare entries to account for the disposal or exchange of plant assets and explain the use of total asset turnover in evaluating a company's efficiency in using its assets. When a plant asset is discarded or sold, the cost and accumulated amortization are removed from the accounts. Any cash proceeds are recorded and compared to the asset's book value to determine gain or loss. When nonmonetary assets are exchanged and they are dissimilar, either a gain or a loss on disposal is recognized. When similar assets are exchanged in a nonmonetary transaction, gains and losses are seldom recognized. Instead, the new asset account is debited for the book value of the old asset plus any cash paid or minus any cash received. Total asset turnover measures the efficiency of a company's use of its assets to generate sales.

DEMONSTRATION PROBLEM

On July 14, 1996, Truro Company paid $600,000 to acquire a fully equipped factory. The purchase included the following:

Asset	Appraised Value	Estimated Salvage Value	Estimated Service Life	Amortization Method
Land	$160,000			Not amortized
Land improvements . .	80,000	$ −0−	10 years	Straight line
Building	320,000	100,000	10 years	Double declining balance
Machinery	240,000	20,000	10,000 units	Units of production*
Total	$800,000			

*The machinery was used to produce 700 units in 1996 and 1,800 units in 1997.

Required

1. Allocate the total $600,000 cost among the separate assets.
2. Calculate the 1996 (six months) and 1997 amortization expense for each type of asset and calculate the total each year for all assets.

Planning the Solution

• Complete a three-column worksheet showing these amounts for each asset: appraised value, percent of total value, and allocated cost.
• Using the allocated costs, compute the amount of amortization for 1996 (only one-half year) and 1997 for each asset. Then, summarize those calculations in a table showing the total amortization for each year.

Solution to Demonstration Problem

1. Allocation of total cost among the assets:

Asset	Appraised Value	Percent of Total Value	Allocated Cost
Land	$160,000	20%	$120,000
Land improvements	80,000	10	60,000
Building	320,000	40	240,000
Machinery	240,000	30	180,000
Total	$800,000	100%	$600,000

2. Amortization for each asset:

Land Improvements:

Cost	$60,000
Salvage value	−0−
Net cost	$60,000
Service life	10 years
Annual expense ($60,000/10)	$6,000
1996 amortization ($6,000 × 6/12)	$3,000
1997 amortization	$6,000

Building:
  Straight-line rate = 100%/10 = 10%
  Double-declining-balance rate = 10% × 2 = 20%

1996 amortization ($240,000 × 20% × 6/12)	$24,000
1997 amortization [($240,000 − $24,000) × 20%] . .	$43,200

Machinery:

Cost	$180,000
Salvage value	20,000
Net cost	$160,000
Total expected units	10,000
Expected cost per unit ($160,000/10,000)	$ 16

Year	Units × Unit Cost	Amortization
1996	700 × $16	$11,200
1997	1,800 × $16	28,800

Total amortization expense:

	1997	1996
Land improvements	$ 6,000	$ 3,000
Building	43,200	24,000
Machinery	28,800	11,200
Total	$78,000	$38,200

GLOSSARY

Accelerated amortization amortization methods that produce larger amortization charges during the early years of an asset's life and smaller charges in the later years. p. 533

Balance sheet expenditure another name for *capital expenditure.* p. 536

Betterment a modification to an asset to increase its service potential or physical output or to lower its operating costs, extend its useful life, or improve the quality of its output. p. 536

Book value the amount assigned to an item in the accounting records and in the financial statements; for a plant asset, book value is its original cost less accumulated amortization. p. 529

Capital expenditure an expenditure that produces economic benefits that do not fully expire before the end of the current period; because it creates or adds to existing assets, it should appear on the balance sheet as the cost of an asset. Also called a *balance sheet expenditure.* p. 536

Change in an accounting estimate a change in a calculated amount used in the financial statements that results from new information or subsequent developments and from better insight or improved judgment. p. 533

Declining-balance amortization an amortization method in which a plant asset's amortization charge for the period is determined by applying a constant amortization rate each year to the asset's beginning book value. p. 534

Inadequacy a condition in which the capacity of plant assets becomes too small for the productive demands of the business. p. 527

Income Tax Act the codification of the Canadian federal tax laws. p. 534

Land improvements assets that increase the usefulness of land but that have a limited useful life and are subject to amortization. p. 526

Obsolescence a condition in which, because of new inventions and improvements, a capital asset can no longer be used to produce goods or services with a competitive advantage. p. 527

Repairs expenditures made to keep a plant asset in normal, good operating condition; treated as a revenue expenditure. p. 536

Revenue expenditure an expenditure that should appear on the current income statement as an expense and be deducted from the period's revenues because it does not provide a material benefit in future periods. p. 536

Salvage value the amount that management predicts will be recovered at the end of a plant asset's service life through a sale or as a trade-in allowance on the purchase of a new asset. p. 528

Service life the length of time in which a plant asset will be used in the operations of the business. p. 527

Straight-line amortization a method that allocates an equal portion of the total amortization for a plant asset

(cost minus salvage) to each accounting period in its service life. p. 528

Total asset turnover a measure of how efficiently a company uses its assets to generate sales; calculated by dividing net sales by average total assets. p. 541

Units-of-production amortization a method that allocates an equal portion of the total amortization for a plant asset (cost minus salvage) to each unit of product or service that it produces, or on a similar basis, such as hours of use or kilometres driven. p. 529

SYNONYMOUS TERMS

Amortizable cost depreciable cost.

Capital assets plant assets; property, plant, and equipment; fixed assets.

Depletion amortization.

Depreciation amortization.

Service life useful life.

QUESTIONS

1. What characteristics of a capital asset make it different from other assets?

2. What is the balance sheet classification of land held for future expansion? Why is the land not classified as a plant asset?

3. In general, what is included in the cost of a plant asset?

4. What is the difference between land and land improvements?

5. Does the balance of the account, Accumulated Amortization, Machinery, represent funds accumulated to replace the machinery when it wears out? What does the balance of Accumulated Amortization represent?

6. What is the difference between repairs and betterments and how should they be recorded?

7. What accounting principle justifies charging the $75 cost of a plant asset immediately to an expense account?

8. What are some of the events that might lead to the disposal of a plant asset?

9. Should a gain on an exchange of plant assets be recorded?

10. How is total asset turnover calculated? Why would a financial statement user be interested in calculating total asset turnover?

11. Refer to the consolidated balance sheets for Geac Computer Corporation Limited in Appendix I. What phrase does Geac use to describe its capital assets? What is the book value of capital assets as of December 31, 1994, and December 31, 1993?

QUICK STUDY (Five-Minute Exercises)

Explain the difference between *(a)* capital assets and long-term investments; *(b)* capital assets and inventory; and *(c)* capital assets and current assets.

QS 11–1
(LO 1)

Mattituck Lanes installed automatic scorekeeping equipment. The electrical work required to prepare for the installation was $12,000. The invoice price of the equipment was $120,000. Additional costs were $2,000 for delivery and $8,400, sales tax. During the installation, a

QS 11–2
(LO 1)

component of the equipment was damaged because it was carelessly left on a lane and hit by the automatic lane cleaning machine during a daily maintenance run. The cost of repairing the component was $1,500. What is the cost of the automatic scorekeeping equipment?

QS 11–3
(LO 2)

January 5, 1996, Blind Man's Sun acquired sound equipment for concert performances at a cost of $111,800. The rock band estimated that they would use this equipment for four years, during which time they anticipated performing about 12 concerts. They estimated at that point they could sell the equipment for $3,800. During 1996, the band performed four concerts. Calculate the 1996 amortization using (a) straight-line method and (b) the units-of-production method.

QS 11–4
(LO 2)

Refer to the facts in QS 11–3. Assume that Blind Man's Sun chose straight-line amortization but recognized during the second year that due to concert bookings beyond expectations, this equipment would only last a total of three years. The salvage value would remain unchanged. Calculate the revised amortization for the second year and the third year.

QS 11–5
(LO 3)

A fleet of refrigerated delivery trucks acquired on January 4, 1996, at a cost of $620,000 had an estimated useful life of eight years and an estimated salvage value of $100,000. Calculate the 1996 amortization under the double-declining-balance method for financial accounting purposes.

QS 11–6
(LO 4)

a. Classify the following expenditures as revenue or capital expenditures:

    (1) Monthly replacement cost of filters on an air conditioning system, $120.

    (2) Cost of replacing a compressor for a meatpacking firm's refrigeration system that extends the estimated life of the system four years, $40,000.

    (3) The cost of $175,000 for an addition of a new wing on an office building.

    (4) The cost of annual tune-ups for delivery trucks.

b. Prepare the journal entry to record (2) and (3).

QS 11–7
(LO 5)

Dean's Carpet Stores owned an automobile with a $20,000 cost and $18,000 accumulated amortization. In a transaction with a neighbouring computer retailer, Dean exchanged this auto for a computer with a fair market value of $6,000. Dean was required to pay an additional $5,000 cash. Prepare the entry to record this transaction for Dean.

QS 11–8
(LO 5)

Frolic, Inc., owns an industrial machine that cost $19,200 and has been amortized $10,200. Frolic exchanged the machine for a newer model that has a fair value of $24,000. Record the exchange assuming a trade-in allowance of (a) $8,000 and (b) $12,000.

QS 11–9
(LO 5)

Goodyear Tire & Rubber Company reported the following facts in its 1993 annual report: net sales of $11,643.4 million for 1993 and $11,784.9 million for 1992; total end-of-year assets of $8,436.1 million for 1993 and $8,563.7 million for 1992. Calculate the total asset turnover for 1993.

EXERCISES

Exercise 11–1
Cost of a capital asset
(LO 1)

Hot Sox purchased a machine for $23,000, terms 2/10, n/60, FOB shipping point. The seller prepaid the freight charges, $520, adding the amount to the invoice and bringing its total to $23,520. The machine required a special steel mounting and power connections costing

$1,590, and another $750 was paid to assemble the machine and get it into operation. In moving the machine onto its steel mounting, it was dropped and damaged. The repairs cost $380. Later, $60 of raw materials were consumed in adjusting the machine so that it would produce a satisfactory product. The adjustments were normal for this type of machine and were not the result of the damage. However, the items produced while the adjustments were being made were not sellable. Prepare a calculation to show the cost of this machine for accounting purposes. (Assume Hot Sox pays for the purchase within the discount period.)

Piper Plumbing Company paid $184,125 for real estate plus $9,800 in closing costs. The real estate included land appraised at $83,160; land improvements appraised at $27,720; and a building appraised at $87,120. Prepare a calculation showing the allocation of the total cost among the three purchased assets and present the journal entry to record the purchase.

Exercise 11–2
Lump-sum purchase of capital assets
(LO 1)

After planning to build a new manufacturing plant, Jammers Casual Wear purchased a large lot on which a small building was located. The negotiated purchase price for this real estate was $150,000 for the lot plus $80,000 for the building. The company paid $23,000 to have the old building torn down and $34,000 for landscaping the lot. Finally, it paid $960,000 in construction costs, which included the cost of a new building plus $57,000 for lighting and paving a parking lot next to the building. Present a single journal entry to record the costs incurred by Jammers, all of which were paid in cash.

Exercise 11–3
Recording costs of real estate
(LO 1)

Moon Paper Company installed a computerized machine in its factory at a cost of $84,600. The machine's useful life was estimated at 10 years, or 363,000 units of product, with a $12,000 trade-in value. During its second year, the machine produced 35,000 units of product. Determine the machine's second-year amortization under the *(a)* straight-line, *(b)* units-of-production, and *(c)* double-declining-balance methods.

Exercise 11–4
Alternative amortization methods
(LO 2, 3)

On April 1, 1996, Lake Excavating Services purchased a trencher for $500,000. The machine was expected to last five years and have a salvage value of $50,000. Calculate amortization expense for 1997, using *(a)* the straight-line method and *(b)* the double-declining-balance method.

Exercise 11–5
Alternative amortization methods; partial year's amortization
(LO 2, 3)

Gemini Fitness Club used straight-line amortization for a machine that cost $43,500, under the assumption it would have a four-year life and a $4,500 trade-in value. After two years, Gemini determined that the machine still had three more years of remaining useful life, after which it would have an estimated $3,600 trade-in value. *(a)* Calculate the machine's book value at the end of its second year. *(b)* Calculate the amount of amortization to be charged during each of the remaining years in the machine's revised useful life.

Exercise 11–6
Revising amortization rates
(LO 2)

Starnes Enterprises recently paid $156,800 for equipment that will last five years and have a salvage value of $35,000. By using the machine in its operations for five years, the company expects to earn $57,000 annually, after deducting all expenses except amortization. Present a schedule showing income before amortization, amortization expense, and net income for each year and the total amounts for the five-year period, assuming *(a)* straight-line amortization and *(b)* double-declining-balance amortization.

Exercise 11–7
Income statement effects of alternative amortization methods
(LO 2, 3)

In January 1996, Labenski Labs purchased computer equipment for $98,000. The equipment will be used in research and development activities for four years and then sold at an estimated salvage value of $20,000. Prepare schedules showing the amortization assuming *(a)* straight-line amortization and *(b)* double-declining-balance amortization.

Exercise 11–8
Alternative amortization methods
(LO 2, 3)

Exercise 11–9
Repairs and betterments
(LO 4)

Eden Extract Company paid $175,000 for equipment that was expected to last four years and have a salvage value of $20,000. Prepare journal entries to record the following costs related to the equipment:

a. During the second year of the equipment's life, $14,000 cash was paid for a new component that was expected to increase the equipment's productivity by 10% each year.

b. During the third year, $3,500 cash was paid for repairs necessary to keep the equipment in good working order.

c. During the fourth year, $9,300 was paid for repairs that were expected to increase the service life of the equipment from four to six years.

Exercise 11–10
Betterments
(LO 4)

Hot Dog Heaven owns a building that appeared on its balance sheet at the end of last year at its original $374,000 cost less $280,500 accumulated amortization. The building has been amortized on a straight-line basis under the assumption that it would have a 20-year life and no salvage value. During the first week in January of the current year, major structural repairs were completed on the building at a cost of $44,800. The repairs did not increase the building's capacity, but they did extend its expected life for 7 years beyond the 20 years originally estimated.

a. Determine the building's age as of the end of last year.

b. Give the entry to record the repairs, which were paid with cash.

c. Determine the book value of the building after the repairs were recorded.

d. Give the entry to record the current year's amortization.

Exercise 11–11
Partial year's
amortization; disposal
of capital asset
(LO 2, 5)

Plum Hill Industries purchased and installed a machine on January 1, 1996, at a total cost of $185,500. Straight-line amortization was taken each year for four years, based on the assumption of a seven-year life and no salvage value. The machine was disposed of on July 1, 2000, during its fifth year of service. Present the entries to record the partial year's amortization on July 1, 2000, and to record the disposal under each of the following unrelated assumptions: *(a)* The machine was sold for $70,000 cash; and *(b)* Plum Hill received an insurance settlement of $60,000 resulting from the total destruction of the machine in a fire.

Exercise 11–12
Exchanging capital assets
(LO 5)

The Rourke Group traded in an old tractor for a new tractor, receiving a $56,000 trade-in allowance and paying the remaining $164,000 in cash. The old tractor cost $190,000, and straight-line amortization of $105,000 had been recorded under the assumption that it would last eight years and have a $22,000 salvage value. Answer the following questions:

a. What was the book value of the old tractor?

b. What is the loss on the exchange?

c. What amount should be debited to the new Tractor account?

Exercise 11–13
Recording capital asset
disposal or exchange
(LO 5)

On January 2, 1996, Kelly Camera Shop disposed of a machine that cost $84,000 and had been amortized $45,250. Present the journal entries to record the disposal under each of the following unrelated assumptions:

a. The machine was sold for $32,500 cash.

b. The machine was traded in on a new machine of like purpose having a $117,000 cash price. A $40,000 trade-in allowance was received, and the balance was paid in cash.

c. The machine was traded for another machine of like purpose, and Kelly paid $3,000 as part of the exchange. The market value of the machine received is approximately $45,000.

d. The machine was traded for vacant land adjacent to the shop to be used as a parking lot. The land had a fair value of $75,000, and Kelly paid $25,000 cash in addition to giving the seller the machine.

Lamb's Antiques reported net sales of $2,431,000 for 1995 and $3,771,000 for 1996. End of year balances for total assets were: 1994, $793,000; 1995, $850,000; and 1996, $941,000. Calculate Lamb's total asset turnover for 1995 and 1996, and comment on the store's efficiency in the use of its assets.

Exercise 11–14
Evaluating efficient use of assets
(LO 5)

PROBLEMS

In 1996, ProSports paid $1,400,000 for a tract of land and two buildings on it. The plan was to demolish Building One and build a new store in its place. Building Two was to be used as a company office and was appraised at a value of $291,500, with a useful life of 20 years and an $80,000 salvage value. A lighted parking lot near Building One had improvements (Land Improvements One) valued at $185,500 that were expected to last another 14 years and have no salvage value. Without considering the buildings or improvements, the tract of land was estimated to have a value of $848,000. ProSports incurred the following additional costs:

Problem 11–1
Real estate costs; partial year's amortization
(LO 1, 2)

Cost to demolish Building One	$ 211,300
Cost of additional landscaping	83,600
Cost to construct new building (Building Three), having a useful life of 25 years and a $195,050 salvage value ..	1,009,500
Cost of new land improvements near Building Two (Land Improvements Two) which have a 20-year useful life and no salvage value	79,000

Required

1. Prepare a schedule having the following column headings: Land, Building Two, Building Three, Land Improvements One, and Land Improvements Two. Allocate the costs incurred by ProSports to the appropriate columns and total each column.

2. Prepare a single journal entry dated March 31 to record all the incurred costs, assuming they were paid in cash on that date.

3. Using the straight-line method, prepare December 31 adjusting entries to record amortization for the nine months of 1996 during which the assets were in use.

Valley Wide Industries recently negotiated a lump-sum purchase of several assets from a vending machine service company that was going out of business. The purchase was completed on March 1, 1996, at a total cash price of $1,575,000, and included a building, land, certain land improvements, and 12 vehicles. The estimated market value of each asset was: building, $816,000; land, $578,000; land improvements, $85,000; and vehicles, $221,000.

Problem 11–2
Plant asset costs; partial year's amortization; alternative methods
(LO 1, 2, 3)

Required

Preparation component:

1. Prepare a schedule to allocate the lump-sum purchase price to the separate assets that were purchased. Also present the journal entry to record the purchase.

2. Calculate the 1996 amortization expense on the building using the straight-line method, assuming a 15-year life and a $51,300 salvage value.

3. Calculate the 1996 amortization expense on the land improvements assuming an eight-year life and double-declining-balance amortization.

Analysis component:

4. Defend or refute this statement: Accelerated amortization results in lower income over the life of the asset.

Problem 11–3

Alternative amortization methods; partial year's amortization; disposal of plant asset

(LO 2, 3, 5)

Part 1. A machine that cost $105,000, with a four-year life and an estimated $10,000 salvage value, was installed in Patterson Company's factory on January 1. The factory manager estimated that the machine would produce 237,500 units of product during its life. It actually produced the following units: year 1, 60,700; year 2, 61,200; year 3, 59,800; and year 4, 59,100. Note the total number of units produced by the end of year 4 exceeded the original estimate. Nevertheless, the machine should not be amortized below the estimated salvage value.

Required

1. Prepare a calculation showing the amount that should be charged to amortization over the machine's four-year life.

2. Prepare a form with the following column headings:

Year	Straight Line	Units of Production	Double-Declining Balance

Then show the amortization for each year and the total amortization for the machine under each amortization method.

Part 2. Patterson purchased a used machine for $83,500 on January 2. It was repaired the next day at a cost of $1,710 and installed on a new platform that cost $540. The company predicted that the machine would be used for six years and would then have a $7,300 salvage value. Amortization was to be charged on a straight-line basis. A full year's amortization was charged on December 31, the end of the first year of the machine's use. On September 30 of its sixth year in service, it was retired.

Required

1. Prepare journal entries to record the purchase of the machine, the cost of repairing it, and the installation. Assume that cash was paid.

2. Prepare entries to record amortization on the machine on December 31 of its first year and on September 30 in the year of its disposal.

3. Prepare entries to record the retirement of the machine under each of the following unrelated assumptions: (*a*) it was sold for $6,750; (*b*) it was sold for $18,000; and (*c*) it was destroyed in a fire and the insurance company paid $12,000 in full settlement of the loss claim.

Finlay General Contractors completed these transactions involving the purchase and operation of heavy equipment:

1995

June 30   Paid $127,720 cash for a new front-end loader, plus $7,600 in state sales tax and $1,250 for transportation charges. The loader was estimated to have a four-year life and a $17,370 salvage value.

Oct.   4   Paid $1,830 to enclose the cab and install air conditioning in the loader. This increased the estimated salvage value of the loader by $555.

Dec. 31   Recorded straight-line amortization on the loader.

1996

Feb. 16   Paid $460 to repair the loader after the operator backed it into a tree.

July   1   Paid $2,250 to overhaul the loader's engine. As a result, the estimated useful life of the loader was increased by two years.

Dec. 31   Recorded straight-line amortization on the loader.

Required

Prepare journal entries to record the transactions.

Cyber Systems completed the following transactions involving delivery trucks:

1996

Mar. 29   Paid cash for a new delivery truck, $38,830 plus $2,330 sales tax. The truck was estimated to have a five-year life and a $6,000 trade-in value.

Dec. 31   Recorded straight-line amortization on the truck.

1997

Dec. 31   Recorded straight-line amortization on the truck. However, due to new information obtained earlier in the year, the original estimated service life of the truck was changed from five years to four years, and the original estimated trade-in value was increased to $7,000.

1998

July   5   Traded in the old truck and paid $27,130 in cash for a new truck. The new truck was estimated to have a six-year life and a $6,250 trade-in value. The invoice for the exchange showed these items:

Price of the new truck	$45,100
Trade-in allowance granted on the old truck . .	(19,500)
Balance of purchase price	$25,600
Sales tax	1,530
Total paid in cash	$27,130

Dec. 31   Recorded straight-line amortization on the new truck.

Required

Prepare journal entries to record the transactions.

Problem 11–6
Partial year's
amortization; alternative
methods; disposal of
capital assets
(LO 2, 3, 5)

Menck Interiors completed the following transactions involving machinery:

Machine No. 15-50 was purchased for cash on May 1, 1996, at an installed cost of $52,900. Its useful life was estimated to be six years with a $4,300 trade-in value. Straight-line amortization was recorded for the machine at the end of 1996, 1997, and 1998; on April 29, 1999, it was traded for Machine No. 17-95, a similar asset with an installed cash price of $61,900. A trade-in allowance of $30,110 was received for Machine No. 15-50, and the balance was paid in cash.

Machine No. 17-95's life was predicted to be four years with an $8,200 trade-in value. Double-declining-balance amortization was recorded on each December 31 of its life. On November 2, 2000, it was traded for Machine No. BT-311, which was a dissimilar asset with an installed cash price of $179,000. A trade-in allowance of $27,000 was received for Machine No. 17-95, and the balance was paid in cash.

It was estimated that Machine No. BT-311 would produce 200,000 units of product during its five-year useful life, after which it would have a $35,000 trade-in value. Units-of-production amortization was recorded for the machine for 2000, a period in which it produced 31,000 units of product. Between January 1, 2001, and August 21, 2003, the machine produced 108,000 more units. On the latter date, it was sold for $81,200.

Required

Prepare journal entries to record: *(a)* the purchase of each machine, *(b)* the amortization expense recorded on the first December 31 of each machine's life, and *(c)* the disposal of each machine. (Only one entry is needed to record the exchange of one machine for another.)

Problem 11–7
Analytical essay
(LO 4)

It is January 9, 1996, and you have just been hired as an accountant for Brinks Supply Company. The previous accountant brought the accounting records up to date through December 31, 1995, the end of the fiscal year, including the year-end adjusting entries. In reviewing the entries made last year, you discover the following three items:

a.   An expenditure to have a factory machine reconditioned by the manufacturer so it would last three years longer than originally estimated was recorded as a debit to Repairs Expense, Machinery.

b.   The lubrication of factory machinery was recorded as a debit to Machinery.

c.   The installation of a security system for the building was recorded as a debit to Building Improvements. The new system allowed the company to reduce the number of security guards.

Required

For each of the three items, explain why you think a correction is or is not necessary. Also, describe any correcting entry that should be made.

Problem 11–8
Alternative amortization
methods; retirement of
capital assets
(LO 2, 3, 5)

Part 1. FlatIrons Company purchased and installed a new machine that cost $195,000, had a five-year life, and an estimated $27,300 salvage value. Management estimated that the machine would produce 120,000 units of product during its life. Actual production of units of product was as follows: year 1, 16,800; year 2, 26,400; year 3, 24,000; year 4, 22,800; and year 5, 30,000.

Required

1.   Prepare a calculation showing the number of dollars of this machine's cost that should be charged to amortization over its five-year life.

2. Prepare a form with the following column headings:

Year	Straight Line	Units of Production	Double-Declining Balance

Then show the amortization for each year and the total amortization for the machine under each amortization method.

Part 2. On January 9, Gilman Company purchased a used machine for $68,400. The next day it was repaired at a cost of $8,100 and was mounted on a new cradle that cost $6,300. It was estimated the machine would be used for three years and would then have a $10,800 salvage value. Amortization was to be charged on a straight-line basis. A full year's amortization was charged on December 31 of the first and the second years of the machine's use; and on March 29 of its third year of use, the machine was retired from service.

Required

1. Prepare general journal entries to record the purchase of the machine, the cost of repairing it, and its installation. Assume cash was paid in each case.

2. Prepare entries to record amortization on the machine at the end of the first and second years and on March 29 of the third year.

3. Prepare entries to record the retirement of the machine under each of the following unrelated assumptions: (*a*) the machine was sold for $35,250; (*b*) it was sold for $24,150; and (*c*) it was destroyed in a fire, and the insurance company paid $22,050 in full settlement of the loss claim.

Parker Lewis Company completed the following transactions involving plant assets:

1995

Jan. 2 Purchased on credit from Southwest Equipment an electric packer priced at $19,875. The serial number of the packer was S-67422, its service life was estimated at five years with a trade-in value of $1,875, and it was assigned plant asset No. 420-1.

Apr. 4 Purchased on credit from Southwest Equipment a Donen vibrator priced at $30,705. The serial number of the vibrator was S-33246, its service life was estimated at six years with a trade-in value of $2,625, and it was assigned plant asset No. 430-2.

Dec. 31 Recorded straight-line amortization on the plant equipment for 1995.

1996

Nov. 3 Sold the Donen vibrator to Cement Products for $18,750 cash.

7 Purchased a new Supermix vibrator from Stonework Equipment for $27,000. The serial number of the vibrator was CS-83215, its service life was estimated at eight years with a trade-in value of $3,600, and it was assigned plant asset No. 430-3.

Dec. 31 Recorded straight-line amortization on the plant equipment for 1996.

Problem 11–9
Plant asset records
(LO 2, 4)

Required

1. Prepare general journal entries to record the transactions and post to the proper general ledger and subsidiary ledger accounts.

2. Prove the December 31, 1996, balances of the Plant Equipment and Accumulated Amortization, Plant Equipment accounts by preparing a list showing the cost and accumulated amortization on each item of plant equipment owned by Parker Lewis Company on that date.

Problem 11–10
Real estate costs and partial year's amortization
(LO 1, 2)

In early 1996, Nobles Company paid $975,000 for real estate that included a tract of land on which two buildings were located. The plan was to demolish Building A and build a new factory in its place. Building B was to be used as a company office and was appraised at a value of $315,000, with a useful life of 20 years and a $45,000 salvage value. A lighted parking lot near Building B had improvements valued at $105,000 that were expected to last another five years and have no salvage value. In its existing condition, the tract of land was estimated to have a value of $630,000.

Nobles Company incurred the following additional costs:

Cost to demolish Building A	$ 71,250
Cost to landscape new building site	81,000
Cost to build new building (Building C), having a useful life of 25 years and a $75,000 salvage value	1,125,000
Cost of new land improvements near Building C, which have an 8-year useful life and no salvage value	187,500

Required

1. Prepare a form having the following column headings: Land, Building B, Building C, Land Improvements B, and Land Improvements C. Allocate the costs incurred by Nobles Company to the appropriate columns and total each column.

2. Prepare a single journal entry dated June 1 to record all of the costs incurred, assuming they were all paid in cash.

3. Prepare December 31 adjusting entries to record amortization for the seven months of 1996 during which the assets were in use. Use double-declining-balance amortization for the newly constructed Building C and Land Improvements C and straight-line amortization for Building B and Land Improvements B.

Problem 11–11
Capital asset costs and amortization
(LO 1, 2, 3)

Willo Company recently negotiated a lump-sum purchase of several assets from a road equipment dealer who was planning to change locations. The purchase was completed on September 30, 1995, at a total cash price of $870,000 and included a garage with land and certain land improvements and a new heavy, general-purpose truck. The estimated market values of the assets were: sales garage, $552,750; land, $331,650; land improvements, $100,500; and truck, $20,100.

Required

1. Prepare a schedule to allocate the lump-sum purchase price to the separate assets that were purchased. Also present the general journal entry to record the purchase.

2. Calculate the 1996 amortization expense on the garage using the straight-line method and assuming a 15-year life and a $37,500 salvage value.

3. Calculate the 1995 amortization expense on the land improvements assuming an eight-year life and double-declining-balance amortization.

4. The truck is expected to last five years and have a salvage value of $2,250. Prepare a schedule showing each year's amortization on the truck, assuming (*a*) five-year straight-line amortization and (*b*) double-declining-balance amortization.

The Whitestone Company completed these transactions involving the purchase and operation of delivery trucks:

Problem 11–12
Purchases, betterments, and sales of capital assets
(LO 4, 5)

1995

June 26   Paid cash for a new truck, $34,200 plus $1,710 provincial sales taxes. The truck was estimated to have a four-year life and a $9,000 salvage value.

July 5   Paid $1,890 for special racks and cleats installed in the truck. The racks and cleats did not increase the truck's estimated trade-in value.

Dec. 31   Recorded straight-line amortization on the truck.

1996

June 25   Paid $2,460 to install an air-conditioning unit in the truck. The unit increased the truck's estimated trade-in value by $300.

Dec. 31   Recorded straight-line amortization on the truck.

1997

Mar. 15   Paid $330 for repairs to the truck's fender damaged when the driver backed into a loading dock.

Dec. 31   Recorded straight-line amortization on the truck.

1998

Aug. 31   Traded the old truck and $29,310 in cash for a new truck. The new truck was estimated to have a three-year life and a $9,600 trade-in value, and the invoice for the exchange showed these items:

Price of the truck	$37,200
Trade-in allowance granted	(9,000)
Balance	$28,200
Provincial sales tax	1,100
Balance paid in cash	$29,310

Sept. 4   Paid $3,690 for special cleats and racks installed in the truck.

Dec. 31   Recorded straight-line amortization on the new truck.

Required

Prepare general journal entries to record the transactions.

A company completed the following transactions involving machinery:

Problem 11–13
Amortizing and exchanging plant assets
(LO 4, 5)

Machine No. 366-90 was purchased on May 1, 1996, at an installed cost of $48,600. Its useful life was estimated at four years with a $5,400 trade-in value. Straight-line amortization was recorded on the machine at the end of 1996 and 1997, and on August 5, 1998, it was traded on Machine No. 366-91. A $27,000 trade-in allowance was received, and the balance was paid in cash.

Machine No. 366-91 was purchased on August 5, 1998, at an installed cash price of $63,000, less the trade-in allowance received on Machine No. 366-90. The new machine's life was estimated at five years with a $6,300 trade-in value. Double-declining-balance amortization was recorded on each December 31 of its life; and on January 5, 2003, it was sold for $9,000.

Machine No. 367-10 was purchased on January 6, 1998, at an installed cost of $45,000. Its useful life was estimated at five years, after which it would have a $4,500 trade-in value. Double-declining-balance amortization was recorded on the machine at the end of 1998,

1999, and 2000; and on January 3, 2001, it was traded on Machine No. 367-11. An $8,100 trade-in allowance was received and the balance was paid in cash.

Machine No. 367-11 was purchased on January 3, 2001, at an installed cash price of $53,100, less the trade-in allowance received on Machine No. 367-10. It was estimated the new machine would produce 75,000 units of product during its useful life, after which it would have a $5,400 trade-in value. Units-of-production depreciation was recorded on the machine for 2001, a period in which it produced 7,500 units of product. Between January 1 and October 3, 2002, the machine produced 11,250 more units, and on the latter date it was sold for $36,000.

Required

Prepare general journal entries to record: (*a*) the purchase of each machine, (*b*) the amortization recorded on the first December 31 of each machine's life, and (*c*) the disposal of each machine. Treat the entries for the first two machines as one series of transactions and those of the next two machines as an unrelated second series. Only one entry is needed to record the exchange of one machine for another.

Problem 11–14
Exchange of assets
(LO 5)

Highway Construction had a piece of road equipment which it purchased in January 1994, at a cost of $180,000. The equipment has been amortized over 8 years, assuming no salvage value, on the straight-line method. At the beginning of May 1996, the company exchanged the equipment for a similar machine. No amortization has been recorded on the old machine for 1996. The market value of the new equipment has been estimated at $132,000.

Required

Prepare a journal entry to record the exchange of the equipment assuming that

a. No cash is paid or received.

b. Highway Construction pays $4,000.

c. Highway Construction receives $2,000.

d. Highway Construction receives $15,000.

PROVOCATIVE PROBLEMS

Provocative Problem 11–1
Business communications case
(LO 1, 5)

While examining the accounting records of Fortunato Company on December 15, 1995, you discover two 1995 entries that appear questionable. The first entry recorded the cash proceeds from an insurance settlement as follows:

Apr.	30	Cash	29,000.00	
		Loss on Fire	8,800.00	
		Accumulated Amortization, Machinery	25,200.00	
		Machinery		63,000.00
		Received payment of fire loss claim.		

Your investigation shows that this entry was made to record the receipt of an insurance company's $29,000 cheque to settle a claim resulting from the destruction of a machine in a small fire on April 2, 1995. The machine originally cost $58,800 and was put into operation on January 3, 1992. It was amortized on a straight-line basis for three years, under the assumptions that it would have a seven-year life and no salvage value. During the first week of January 1995, the machine was overhauled at a cost of $4,200. The overhaul did not increase the machine's capacity or its salvage value. However, it was expected that the overhaul would lengthen the machine's service life two years beyond the seven originally expected.

The second entry that appears questionable was made to record the receipt of a cheque from selling a portion of a tract of land. The land was adjacent to the company's plant and had been purchased the year before. It cost $105,000, and another $18,000 was paid for clearing and grading it. Both amounts had been debited to the Land account. The land was to be used for storing finished products but, sometime after the grading was completed, it became obvious the company did not need the entire tract. Fortunato received an offer from a purchaser to buy the north section for $94,550 or the south section for $60,450. The company decided to sell the north section and recorded the receipt of the purchaser's cheque with the following entry:

Nov.	16	Cash	94,550.00	
		Land		94,550.00
		Sold unneeded land.		

Required

Write a memo to the company's Corrections File describing any errors made in recording these transactions. Since the Corrections File is used in making the year-end adjusting journal entries, show the entry or entries needed to correct each error described in your memo.

Manufax Company temporarily recorded the costs of a new plant in a single account called Land and Buildings. Now, management has asked you to examine this account and prepare any necessary entries to correct the account balances. In doing so, you find the following debits and credits to the account:

Provocative Problem 11–2
Financial reporting problem
(LO 1, 2)

Debits

Jan.	4	Cost of land and building acquired for new plant site	$ 564,000
	9	Attorney's fee for title search	1,500
	18	Cost of demolishing old building on plant site	37,500
	30	Nine months' liability and fire insurance during construction	6,075
Sept.	28	Payment to building contractor on completion	819,000
Oct.	1	Architect's fee for new building	25,200
	10	City assessment for street improvements	42,000
	21	Cost of landscaping new plant site	10,500
			$1,505,775

Credits

Jan.	21	Proceeds from sale of salvaged materials from building	$ 7,900
Oct.	5	Refund of one month's liability and fire insurance premium	675
Dec.	31	Amortization at 2-1/2% per year	28,069
			$ 36,644
		Debit balance	$1,469,131

An account called Amortization Expense, Land and Buildings was debited in recording the $28,069 of amortization. Your investigation suggests that 40 years is a reasonable life expectancy for a building of the type involved and that an assumption of zero salvage value is reasonable.

To summarize your analysis, set up a schedule with columns headed Date, Description, Total Amount, Land, Buildings, and Other Accounts. Next, enter the items found in the

Land and Buildings account on the schedule, distributing the amounts to the proper columns. Show credits on the schedule by enclosing the amounts in parentheses. Also, draft any required correcting entry or entries, under the assumption that the accounts have not been closed.

Provocative Problem 11–3
Financial statement analysis case
(LO 1, 2)

Geac

Refer to the annual report for Geac Computer Corporation Limited in Appendix I. Give particular attention to the balance sheet, income statement, and notes to financial statements before answering the following questions:

1. What percentage of the original cost of Geac's fixed assets remains to be amortized as of April 30, 1994, and April 30, 1993? (Assume the assets have no salvage value.)

2. What method of depreciation does Geac use in amortizing its plant assets?

Provocative Problem 11–4
Ethical issues essay

Review the As a Matter of Ethics case on page 534 and write a short essay discussing the situation faced by Sue Ann Meyer. Include a discussion of the alternative courses of action available to Meyer and indicate how you think she should deal with the situation.

ANALYTICAL AND REVIEW PROBLEMS

A&R Problem 11–1

At the last meeting of the executive committee of Kearins, Ltd., Milton Vacon, controller, was severely criticized by both President Kearins and Kate Ryan, vice president of production. The subject of criticism was in the recognition of periodic amortization. President Kearins was unhappy with the fact that what he referred to as "a fictitious item" was deducted, resulting in depressed net income. In his words, "Depreciation is a fiction when the assets being depreciated are worth far more than we paid for them. What the controller is doing is unduly understanding our net income. This in turn is detrimental to our shareholders because it results in the undervaluation of our shares on the market."

Vice President Ryan was equally adamant about the periodic amortization charges; however, she came on from another side. She said, "Our maintenance people tell me that the level of maintenance is such that our plant and equipment will last virtually forever." She further stated that charging amortization on top of maintenance expenses is double-counting—it seems reasonable to charge either maintenance or amortization but not both.

The time taken by other pressing matters did not permit Vacon to answer; instead, the controller was asked to prepare a report to the executive committee to deal with the issues raised by the president and vice president.

Required

The controller asks you, his assistant, to prepare the required report.

A&R Problem 11–2

The Shape Company purchased a large earth-mover four years ago at a cost of $350,000. At that time it was estimated that the economic life of the equipment would be 12 years and that its ultimate salvage value would be $14,000.

Assuming the company uses straight-line amortization, state whether each of the following events requires a revision of the original amortization rate, with reasons for your answer:

a. Due to the persistent inflation, the present replacement cost of the same type of equipment is $410,000.

b.   Because of the higher replacement cost, as described in (*a*) above, the ultimate salvage value is now estimated at $25,000.

c.   The company, in connection with having its line of credit increased, was required by the bank to have the assets appraised. The earth-mover was estimated to have a current value of $315,000.

d.   At the time the appraisal was made in (*c*) above, it was determined that technological change was progressing more slowly than originally estimated and that the earth-mover would probably remain in service for 15 years with the ultimate salvage value as originally estimated at the end of 12 years.

CONCEPT TESTER

Test your understanding of the concepts introduced in this chapter by completing the following crossword puzzle.

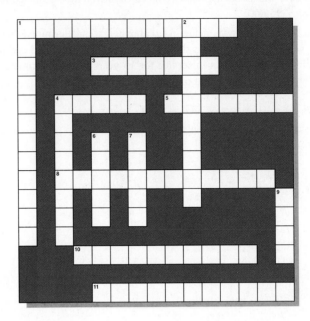

Across Clues

1. Amortization method that allocates an equal amount to each period (2 words).

3. An outlay that produces economic benefits that do not fully expire before the end of the current period (1st of 2 words; also see 11 across).

4. A measure of how efficiently a company uses its assets (1st of 3 words; also see 6 down, 4 down).

5. Expenditures made to keep an asset in normal, good operating condition.

8. A condition in which an asset has lost its usefulness because of new inventions and improvements.

10. A cost incurred to make an asset more efficient.

11. An outlay that produces economic benefits that do not fully expire before the end of the current period (2nd of 2 words; also see 3 across).

Down Clues

1. The expected amount to be recovered at the end of an asset's life (2 words).

2. A condition in which the capacity of an asset becomes too small for the demands of the business.

4. A measure of how efficiently a company uses its assets (3rd of 3 words; also see 4 across, 6 down).

6. A measure of how efficiently a company uses its assets (2nd of 3 words; also see 4 across, 4 down).

7. The original cost of an asset less the accumulated amortization (2nd of 2 words; also see 9 down).

9. The original cost of an asset less the accumulated amortization (1st of 2 words; also see 7 down).

ANSWERS TO PROGRESS CHECKS

11–1 *(a)* office supplies—current assets
(b) office equipment—plant assets
(c) merchandise—current assets
(d) land held for future expansion—long-term investments
(e) trucks used in operations—plant assets

11–2 *(a)* Land
(b) Land Improvements

11–3 $700,000 + $49,000 − $21,000 + $3,500 + $3,000 + $2,500 = $737,000

11–4 Amortization is a process of allocating and charging the cost of plant assets to the accounting periods that benefit from the asset's use.

11–5 *(a)* Book value using straight-line amortization:
$96,000 − [($96,000 − $8,000)/5] = $78,400
(b) Book value using units of production:
$96,000 − [($96,000 − $8,000) × (10,000/100,000)] = $87,200

11–6 ($3,800 − $200)/3 = $1,200
$1,200 × 2 = $2,400
($3,800 − $2,400)/2 = $700

11–7 Machinery 12,000.00
Cash 12,000.00

11–8 A revenue expenditure benefits only the current period and should be charged to the expense of the current period. A capital expenditure has benefit that extends beyond the end of the current period and should be charged to an asset.

11–9 A betterment involves modifying an existing plant asset to improve its efficiency or lengthen its useful life, usually by replacing part of the asset with an improved or superior part. A betterment should be debited to the improved machine's account.

11–10 Amortization Expense 2,500
Accumulated Amortization 2,500
Cash 32,000
Loss on Sales of Equipment 500
Accumulated Amortization 9,500
Equipment 42,000

11–11
Truck 45,000
Loss on Trade-in 3,600
Accumulated Amortization 23,400
Truck 30,000
Cash 42,000

11–12 Total asset turnover:

$$\frac{\$152,156}{(\$149,028 + \$117,872) \div 2} = 1.14 \text{ times}$$

CHAPTER 12

Capital Assets: Natural Resources, Intangible Assets, and Long-Term Investments

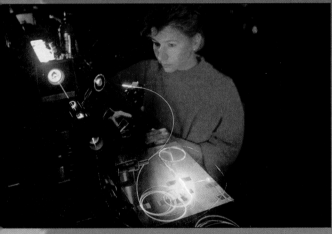

...ompany's assets include many things in addition to tangible equipment and buildings. Patents, ...ural resources, research and development, and outstanding employees all contribute to profits, ...wever, they create unique accounting problems that must be solved.

*K*aren White and Mark Smith are approaching the last chapter dealing with assets. Their instructor has provided some information about Corel Corporation.

In 1993, 1992, and 1991, Corel Corporation, the company that developed and produces CorelDRAW and other related software programs, spent $8.4, $7.2, and $4.4 million on research and development. All of these expenditures were expensed as incurred in accordance with Canadian GAAP. Other assets such as software licences, purchased software, clipart libraries, and photo CD libraries, amounting to $29.0 million, are included in Corel Corporation's Capital Assets.

The above paragraph illustrates an aspect of accounting that is often confusing to the users of financial statements. The amounts incurred to research and develop a valuable asset must be expensed, and the company may not present the asset on the balance sheet. Thus the costs of developing CorelDRAW do not appear on Corel Corporation's statements. However, if a company purchases the rights to produce a product from another party, such as Corel Corporation did with some of its clipart and CD libraries, it may capitalize these costs and show them on the balance sheet.

LEARNING OBJECTIVES

After studying Chapter 12, you should be able to:

1. **Identify assets that should be classified as natural resources or as intangible assets and prepare entries to account for them, including entries to record depletion and amortization.**

2. **State the criteria for classifying assets as long-term investments and describe the categories of securities that are classified as long-term investments.**

3. **Describe the methods used to report long-term securities investments in the financial statements.**

4. **Describe the primary accounting problems of having investments in international operations and prepare entries to account for sales to foreign customers.**

5. **Explain the use of return on total assets in evaluating a company's efficiency in using its assets.**

6. **Define or explain the words and phrases listed in the chapter glossary.**

In Chapters 7 through 9 and 11, you learned about current assets and capital assets. This chapter concludes the focus on assets with a discussion of natural resources, intangible assets, and long-term investments. Natural resources and intangible assets may be particularly important in evaluating the future prospects of some companies. For example, the rights to manufacture computer software products are intangible assets of the companies that developed the products or purchased the rights from the copyright owner.

Many companies make long-term investments in assets such as real estate and debt and equity securities issued by other companies. Also, an increasing number of companies invest in foreign countries or have international operations. The financial statement effects of these investments are often very important. As a result, your study of these topics in this chapter will enrich your ability to understand and interpret financial reports.

NATURAL RESOURCES

LO 1

Identify assets that should be classified as natural resources or as intangible assets and prepare entries to account for them, including entries to record depletion and amortization.

Natural resources include such things as standing timber, mineral deposits, and oil reserves. Because they are physically consumed when they are used, they are known as *wasting assets*. In their natural state, they represent inventories of raw materials that will be converted into a product by cutting, mining, or pumping. However, until the conversion takes place, they are noncurrent assets and appear on a balance sheet under captions such as "Timberlands," "Mineral deposits," or "Oil reserves." Sometimes, this caption appears under the capital asset category of assets and sometimes it is a separate category. **Norcen Energy Resources Limited** combines its natural resources with other fixed assets in one balance sheet item called *Property, plant, and equipment.* However, a note to the financial statements provides more detailed information by separating the total into the following categories: oil and gas, propane marketing, and mineral resources.

Natural resources are initially recorded at cost. Like the cost of capital (or plant) assets, the cost of natural resources is allocated to the periods in which they are consumed. The cost created by consuming the usefulness of natural resources is called **depletion.** On the balance sheet, natural resources are shown at cost less *accumulated depletion.* The amount by which such assets are depleted each year by cutting, mining, or pumping is usually calculated on a units-of-production basis. For example, **Imperial Oil Limited** uses the units-of-production method to amortize the costs of discovering its oil wells.

To illustrate the units-of-production method, assume that a mineral deposit has an estimated 500,000 tonnes of available ore and is purchased for $500,000. The units-of-production depletion charge per tonne of ore mined is $1. Thus, if 85,000 tonnes are mined and sold during the first year, the depletion charge for the year of $85,000 is recorded as follows:

Dec.	31	Depletion Expense, Mineral Deposit	85,000.00	
		Accumulated Depletion, Mineral Deposit		85,000.00
		To record depletion of the mineral deposit.		

On the balance sheet prepared at the end of the first year, the mineral deposit should appear at its $500,000 cost less accumulated depletion of $85,000. Because the 85,000 tonnes of ore were sold during the year, the entire $85,000 depletion charge is reported on the income statement. However, if a portion of the ore had remained unsold at year-end, the depletion cost related to the unsold ore should be carried forward on the balance sheet as part of the cost of the unsold ore inventory, which is a current asset.

The conversion of natural resources through mining, cutting, or pumping often requires the use of machinery and buildings. Because the usefulness of these assets is related to the depletion of the natural resource, their costs should be amortized over the life of the natural resource in proportion to the annual depletion charges. In other words, amortization should be calculated using the units-of-production method. For example, if a machine is installed in a mine and one-eighth of the mine's ore is mined and sold during a year, one-eighth of the machine's cost (less salvage value) should be charged to amortization expense.

INTANGIBLE ASSETS

Some assets represent certain legal rights and economic relationships beneficial to the owner. Because they have no physical existence, they are called **intangible assets.** Patents, copyrights, leaseholds, leasehold improvements, goodwill, and trademarks are intangible assets. We discuss each of these intangible items in more detail in the following sections. Although notes and accounts receivable are also intangible in nature, they are not used to produce products or provide services. Therefore, they are not listed on the balance sheet as intangible assets; instead, they are classified as current assets or investments.

When an intangible asset is purchased, it is recorded at cost. Thereafter, its cost must be systematically written off to expense over its estimated useful life through the process of **amortization.** Generally accepted accounting principles require that the amortization period for an intangible asset be 40 years or less.[1] Companies often disclose the amortization periods they apply to their intangibles. For example, **Onex Corporation's** annual report discloses that it amortizes goodwill principally over 40 years and other intangible assets over their estimated useful lives.

---

[1]*CICA Handbook,* section 3060, "Capital Assets," par. 32.

In many cases, the estimated life of an intangible asset is highly subjective and influenced by a myriad of factors. The selected useful life can have a dramatic impact on reported profits. A few years ago, **Blockbuster Entertainment Corporation** was criticized for changing its amortization period for videotape rights from 9 to 36 months. The change added $3 million, or nearly 20% to Blockbuster's reported income.[2]

Amortization of intangible assets is similar to amortization of plant assets and depletion of natural resources in that all three are processes of cost allocation. However, the straight-line method should be used for amortizing intangibles unless the reporting company can demonstrate that another method is more appropriate. Also, while the effects of depreciation and depletion on the assets are recorded in a contra account (Accumulated Depreciation or Accumulated Depletion), amortization is usually credited directly to the intangible asset account. As a result, the full original cost of intangible assets generally is not reported on the balance sheet. Instead, only the remaining amount of unamortized cost is reported.

Normally, intangible assets are shown in a separate section of the balance sheet that follows immediately after plant and equipment. However, not all companies follow this tradition. The following paragraphs describe several specific intangible assets.

Patents

The federal government grants **patents** to encourage the invention of new machines, mechanical devices, and production processes. A patent gives its owner the exclusive right to manufacture and sell a patented machine or device, or to use a process, for 17 years. When patent rights are purchased, the cost of acquiring the rights is debited to an account called Patents. Also, if the owner engages in lawsuits to defend a patent, the cost of the lawsuits should be debited to the Patents account. However, the costs of research and development leading to a new patent are not debited to an asset account.[3] Instead research costs must be expensed as incurred because of the uncertainty of their future benefits.

Although a patent gives its owner exclusive rights to the patented device or process for 17 years, the cost of the patent should be amortized over its predicted useful life, which might be less than the full 17 years. For example, if a patent that cost $25,000 has an estimated useful life of 10 years, the following adjusting entry is made at the end of each of those years to write off one-tenth of its cost:

Dec.	31	Amortization Expense, Patents	2,500.00	
		Patents		2,500.00
		To write off patent costs over the expected 10-year life.		

The entry's debit causes $2,500 of patent costs to appear on the income statement as one of the costs of the product manufactured and sold under the protection of

---

[2]*Forbes,* June 12, 1989, p. 150.

[3]*CICA Handbook,* section 3450.

the patent. Note that we have followed the convention of crediting the Patents account rather than a contra account.

Copyrights

A **copyright** is granted by the federal government or by international agreement. In most cases, a copyright gives its owner the exclusive right to publish and sell a musical, literary, or artistic work during the life of the composer, author, or artist and for 50 years thereafter. Most copyrights have value for a much shorter time, and their costs should be amortized over the shorter period. Often, the only identifiable cost of a copyright is the fee paid to the Copyright Office. If this fee is not material, it may be charged directly to an expense account. Otherwise, the copyright costs should be capitalized (recorded as a capital expenditure), and the periodic amortization of a copyright should be debited to an account called *Amortization Expense, Copyrights.*

Leaseholds

Property is rented under a contract called a **lease.** The person or company that owns the property and grants the lease is called the **lessor.** The person or company that secures the right to possess and use the property is called the **lessee.** The rights granted to the lessee by the lessor under the lease are called a **leasehold.** A leasehold is an intangible asset for the lessee.

Some leases require no advance payment from the lessee but do require monthly rent payments. In such cases, a Leasehold account is not needed and the monthly payments are debited to a Rent Expense account. Sometimes, a long-term lease requires the lessee to pay the final year's rent in advance when the lease is signed. If so, the lessee records the advance payment with a debit to its Leasehold asset account. Because the usefulness of the advance payment is not consumed until the final year is reached, the Leasehold account balance remains intact until that year. At that time, the balance is transferred to Rent Expense.[4]

Often, a long-term lease gains value because the current rental rates for similar property increase while the required payments under the lease remain constant. In such cases, the increase in value of the lease is not reported on the lessee's balance sheet since no extra cost was incurred to acquire it. However, if the property is subleased and the new tenant makes a cash payment to the original lessee for the rights under the old lease, the new tenant should debit the payment to a Leasehold account. Then, the balance of the Leasehold account should be amortized to Rent Expense over the remaining life of the lease.

Leasehold Improvements

Long-term leases often require the lessee to pay for any alterations or improvements to the leased property, such as new partitions and store fronts. Normally, the costs of these **leasehold improvements** are debited to an account called Leasehold Improvements. Also, since the improvements become part of the property and revert to the lessor at the end of the lease, the lessee must amortize the cost of the

---

[4]Some long-term leases give the lessee essentially the same rights as a purchaser, and result in tangible assets and liabilities reported by the lessee. Chapter 13 describes these leases.

improvements over the life of the lease or the life of the improvements, whichever is shorter. The amortization entry commonly debits Rent Expense and credits Leasehold Improvements.

Goodwill

The term **goodwill** has a special meaning in accounting. In theory, a business has an intangible asset called goodwill when its rate of expected future earnings is greater than the rate of earnings normally realized in its industry. Above-average earnings and the existence of theoretical goodwill may be demonstrated with the following information about Companies A and B, both of which are in the same industry:

	Company A	Company B
Net assets (other than goodwill)	$100,000	$100,000
Normal rate of return in this industry	10%	10%
Normal return on net assets	$ 10,000	$ 10,000
Expected net income	10,000	15,000
Expected earnings above average	$ –0–	$ 5,000

Company B is expected to have an above-average earnings rate compared to its industry and, therefore, is said to have goodwill. This goodwill may be the result of excellent customer relations, the location of the business, the quality and uniqueness of its products, monopolistic market advantages, a superior management and work force, or a combination of these and other factors.[5] Consequently, a potential investor would be willing to pay more for Company B than for Company A. Thus, goodwill is theoretically an asset that has value.

Normally, goodwill is purchased only when an entire business operation is acquired. In determining the purchase price of a business, the buyer and seller may estimate the amount of goodwill in several different ways. If the business is expected to have $5,000 each year in above-average earnings, its goodwill may be valued at, say, four times its above-average earnings, or $20,000. Or, if the $5,000 is expected to continue indefinitely, they may think of it as a return on an investment at a given rate of return, say, 10%. In this case, the estimated amount of goodwill is $5,000/10% = $50,000. However, in the final analysis, the value of goodwill is confirmed only by the price the seller is willing to accept and the buyer is willing to pay.

To keep financial statement information from being too subjective, accountants have agreed that goodwill should not be recorded unless it is purchased. The amount of goodwill is measured by subtracting the fair market value of the purchased business's net assets (excluding goodwill) from the purchase price. In many business acquisitions, goodwill represents a major component of total cost. For example, the **Thompson Corporation's** purchase of **Information Access Company** for

---

[5]Of course, the value of the location may be reflected in a higher cost for the land owned and used by the company.

Intangible Assets

Intangible Assets Disclosed	Number of Companies			
	1992	1991	1990	1989
Goodwill	149	153	149	143
Licences/Broadcast licences	18	20	20	21
Customer lists/circulation	11	10	10	11
Trademarks	11	14	13	12
Patents or patent rights	10	17	15	15
Noncompetition agreements	6	5	4	3
Franchises	4	4	5	5
Publishing rights	4	4	4	4
Technology/Know-how	3	4	5	4

Canadian Institute of Chartered Accountants, *Financial Reporting in Canada, 1993* (Toronto; 1993), p. 120.

$465 million (net of debt acquired) included goodwill of $117 million and other intangibles consisting of publishing rights and circulation of $374 million.

Like other intangible assets, goodwill should be amortized on a straight-line basis over its estimated useful life. However, estimating the useful life of goodwill is very difficult and highly arbitrary in most situations. As a result, you can expect to find companies reporting amortization expense for goodwill based on an estimated useful life of 5 years upward, but not more than 40 years.

Trademarks and Trade Names

Companies often adopt unique symbols or select unique names that they use in marketing their products. Sometimes, the ownership and exclusive right to use such a **trademark** or **trade name** can be established simply by demonstrating that one company has used the trademark or trade name before other businesses. However, ownership generally can be established more definitely by registering the trademark or trade name at the Patent Office. The cost of developing, maintaining, or enhancing the value of a trademark or trade name, perhaps through advertising, should be charged to expense in the period or periods incurred. However, if a trademark or trade name is purchased, the purchase cost should be debited to an asset account and amortized over time.

Amortization of Intangibles

Some intangibles, such as patents, copyrights, and leaseholds, have limited useful lives that are determined by law, contract, or the nature of the asset. Other intangibles, such as goodwill, trademarks, and trade names, have indeterminable lives. In general, the cost of intangible assets should be amortized over the periods expected to be benefited by their use, which in no case is longer than their legal existence. However, as we stated earlier, generally accepted accounting principles require that the amortization period of intangible assets not be longer than 40 years. This limitation applies even if the life of the asset (for example, goodwill) may continue indefinitely into the future.

CLASSIFYING INVESTMENTS

LO 2

State the criteria for classifying securities investments as long-term investments and describe the categories of securities that are reported as long-term investments.

In Chapter 8, you learned how to account for temporary investments in debt and equity securities. (We encourage you to review pages 398–402 before you study this section.) Recall that temporary investments are current assets; they are expected to be converted into cash within one year or the current operating cycle of the business, whichever is longer. In general, temporary investments such as T-bills and term deposits are those that are "capable of reasonably prompt liquidation."[6] They either mature within one year or the current operating cycle or are easily sold and therefore qualify as being *marketable.*

Securities investments that do not qualify as current assets are called **long-term investments.** Long-term investments include investments in bonds and shares that are not marketable or that, although marketable, are not intended to serve as a ready source of cash. Long-term investments also include funds earmarked for a special purpose, such as bond sinking funds, and land or other assets owned but not used in the regular operations of the business. In general, these assets are reported on the balance sheet in a separate *Long-term investments* section.

In Illustration 12–1, the boxes on the left side show the different long-term investments in securities. Note that they include (1) debt securities held to maturity, (2) debt and equity securities available for sale, (3) equity securities which give the investor a significant influence over the investee, and (4) equity securities which give the investor control over the investee. We discuss each of these types of investments in the following sections.

LONG-TERM INVESTMENTS IN SECURITIES

Much of what you learned about temporary investments in Chapter 8 also applies to long-term investments. For example, at the time of purchase, investments are recorded at cost, which includes any commissions or brokerage fees paid to make the purchase. After the purchase, the accounting treatment depends on the type of investment.

---

[6]*CICA Handbook,* par. 3010.02.

Illustration 12-1 Accounting for Long-Term Investments in Securities

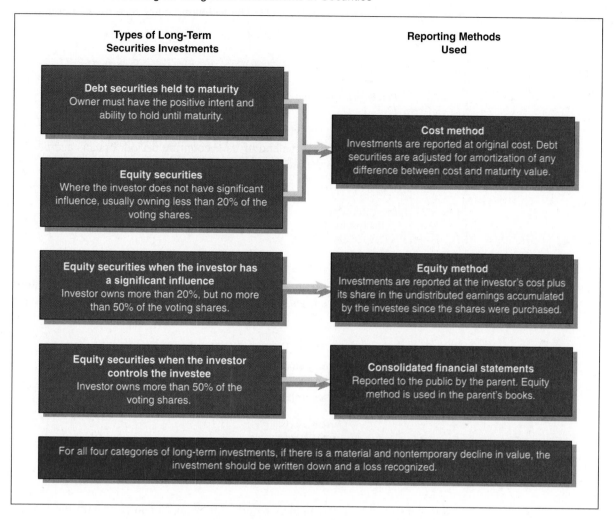

Investments in Debt Securities Held to Maturity

Debt securities held to maturity may be short-term or long-term investments. In either case, the owner should have the intent and the ability to hold the securities until they mature. At the time of purchase, these investments are recorded at cost. Then, interest revenue is recorded as it accrues.

The cost of an investment in debt securities may be more or less than the maturity value of the securities. When the investment is long-term, any difference between cost and maturity value must be amortized over the remaining life of the security. Chapter 13 explains the process of amortizing this difference. In this chapter, however, we assume that the costs of debt investments equal their maturity values.

For example, on August 31, 1996, Francis, Inc., paid $29,500 plus a brokerage fee of $500 to buy $30,000 par value of Candice Corp.'s 7% bonds payable. The bonds pay interest semiannually on August 31 and February 28. The amount of each

LO 3

Describe the methods used to report long-term securities investments in the financial statements.

payment is $30,000 \times 7\% \times 6/12 = \$1,050$. Francis has the intent to hold the bonds until they mature on August 31, 1998. The following entry records the purchase:

1996				
Aug.	31	Investment in Candice Corp. Bonds	30,000.00	
		Cash		30,000.00
		Purchased bonds to be held to maturity.		

On December 31, 1996, at the end of its accounting period, Francis accrues interest receivable with the following entry:

Dec.	31	Interest Receivable	700.00	
		Interest Earned		700.00
		$1,050 \times 4/6 = \$700$.		

In this entry, the $700 represents 4/6 of the semiannual cash receipt for interest. As a result of these entries, Francis's financial statements for 1996 show the following items:

On the income statement for 1996:
Interest earned . . . . $ 700
On the December 31, 1996, balance sheet:
Assets:
   Current assets:
      Interest receivable . . . . $ 700
   Long-term investments:
      Investment in Candice Corp. bonds $30,000

On February 28, 1997, Francis records the receipt of interest with the following entry:

1997				
Feb.	28	Cash	1,050.00	
		Interest Receivable		700.00
		Interest Earned		350.00
		Received 6 months' interest on Candice Corp. bonds.		

When the bonds mature, this entry records the proceeds from the matured bonds:

1998				
Aug.	31	Cash	30,000.00	
		Investment in Candice Corp. Bonds		30,000.00
		Received cash from matured bonds.		

Investments in Equity Securities

The second box on the left side of Illustration 12–1 includes certain equity securities. To be included in this group of long-term investments, the investor in equity securities must not have a significant influence over the investee. Normally, this means that the investor owns less than 20% of the investee corporation's voting shares.[7]

Chapter 8 (pages 398–402) explained the procedures of accounting for temporary investments in equity securities. These same procedures are used for long-term investments accounted for by the cost method. At the time of purchase, the investments are recorded at cost. As dividends are received, they are credited to Dividends Earned and reported in the income statement. When the shares are sold, the proceeds from the sale are compared with the cost of the investment and any gain or loss realized on the sale is reported in the income statement.

Continuing with Francis, Inc., assume that on October 10, 1996, Francis purchased 1,000 common shares of Intex Corp. for $86,000. The following entry records the purchase:

Oct.	10	Investment in Intex Corp. Common Shares	86,000.00	
		Cash		86,000.00
		Purchased 1,000 shares.		

On November 2, Francis received a $1,720 quarterly dividend on the Intex shares. The following entry records the receipt:

Nov.	2	Cash	1,720.00	
		Dividends Earned		1,720.00
		Received dividend of $1.72 per share.		

On December 20, Francis sold 500 of the Intex shares for $45,000, and records the sale with the following entry:

Dec.	20	Cash	45,000.00	
		Investment in Intex Corp. Common Shares		43,000.00
		Gain on Sale of Long-Term Investment		2,000.00
		$86,000/2 = $43,000		

Reporting Long-Term Investments. Long-term investments are shown at cost with market value disclosed even if market value is below cost as long as the decline in value is temporary. However, when there has been a loss in value that

[7]The 20% limit is not an absolute rule. Other factors may overrule. See *CICA Handbook,* section 3050, "Long-Term Investments," par. .04.

is other than temporary, the investment is written down to recognize the loss.[8] The writedown (loss) would be included in determining net income. When a long-term investment has been written down to recognize the loss, the new carrying value is deemed to be the new cost basis for subsequent accounting purposes. A subsequent increase in value would be recognized only when realized (i.e., when the shares are sold). For purposes of calculating a gain or loss on sale of the investment, the cost of the investments sold should be calculated on the basis of the average carrying value (total cost of the shares ÷ number of shares held).[9]

Investment in Equity Securities; Investor Has a Significant Influence or Has Control

Sometimes, an investor buys a large block of a corporation's voting shares and is able to exercise a significant influence over the investee corporation. An investor who owns 20% or more of a corporation's voting shares is normally presumed to have a significant influence over the investee. There may be cases, however, where the accountant concludes that the 20% test of significant influence should be over-ruled by other, more persuasive, evidence.

An investor who owns more than 50% of a corporation's voting shares can dominate all of the other shareholders in electing the corporation's board of directors. Thus, the investor usually has control which is the power to determine the corporation's strategic, operating, investing, and financing decisions without the cooperation of others.[10]

As we stated earlier, the method of accounting for an equity investment depends on the relationship between the investor and the investee. In studying Illustration 12–1, note that if the investor has a significant influence, the *equity method* of accounting and reporting is used. Finally, if the investor controls the investee, the investor uses the equity method in its records, but reports *consolidated financial statements* to the public. We discuss the equity method and consolidated statements in the following sections.

The Equity Method of Accounting for Common Share Investments

If an investor in common shares has significant influence over the investee, the **equity method** of accounting for the investment must be used. When the shares are acquired, the investor records the purchase at cost. For example, on January 1, 1996, Gordon Company purchased 3,000 common shares (30%) of JWM, Inc., for a total cost of $70,650. This entry records the purchase on Gordon's books:

Jan.	1	Investment in JWM Common Shares	70,650.00	
		Cash		70,650.00
		Purchased 3,000 shares.		

[8]Ibid., par. 3050.20.
[9]Ibid., par. 3050.27.
[10]Ibid., par. 1590.03.

Under the equity method, the earnings of the investee corporation not only increase the investee's net assets but also increase the investor's equity claims against the investee's assets. Therefore, when the investee closes its books and reports the amount of its earnings, the investor takes up its share of those earnings in its investment account. For example, assume that JWM reported net income of $20,000 for 1996. Gordon's entry to record its 30% share of these earnings is:

Dec.	31	Investment in JWM Common Shares	6,000.00	
		Earnings from Investment in JWM, Inc.		6,000.00
		To record 30% equity in investee's earnings of		
		$20,000		

The debit records the increase in Gordon Company's equity in JWM. The credit causes 30% of JWM's net income to appear on Gordon Company's income statement as earnings from the investment. As with any other revenue, Gordon closes the earnings to Income Summary.

If the investee corporation incurs a net loss instead of a net income, the investor records its share of the loss and reduces (credits) its investment account. Then, the investor closes the loss to Income Summary.

Under the equity method, the receipt of cash dividends is not recorded as revenue because the investor has already recorded its share of the earnings reported by the investee. Instead, dividends received from the investee simply convert the form of the investor's asset from a share investment to cash. Thus, the equity method records dividends as a reduction in the balance of the investment account.

For example, assume that JWM declared and paid $10,000 in cash dividends on its common shares. Gordon's entry to record its 30% share of these dividends, which it received on January 9, 1997, is:

Jan.	9	Cash	3,000.00	
		Investment in JWM Common Shares		3,000.00
		To record receipt of 30% of the $10,000 dividend		
		paid by JWM, Inc.		

Thus, when the equity method is used, the carrying value of a common share investment equals the cost of the investment plus the investor's equity in the *undistributed* earnings of the investee. For example, after the preceding transactions are recorded on the books of Gordon Company, the investment account appears as follows:

Investment in JWM Common Shares

Date		Explanation	Debit	Credit	Balance
1996					
Jan.	1	Investment	70,650		70,650
Dec.	31	Share of earnings	6,000		76,650
1997					
Jan.	9	Share of dividend		3,000	73,650

If Gordon prepared a balance sheet on January 9, the investment in JWM would be reported as $73,650. This is the original cost of the investment, plus Gordon's equity in JWM's earnings since the date of purchase, less Gordon's equity in JWM's dividends since the date of purchase.

When an equity method share investment is sold, the gain or loss on the sale is determined by comparing the proceeds from the sale with the carrying value (book value) of the investment on the date of sale. For example, suppose that Gordon Company sold its JWM stock for $80,000 on January 10, 1997. The entry to record the sale is:

Jan.	10	Cash	80,000.00	
		Investment in JWM Common Shares		73,650.00
		Gain on Sale of Investments		6,350.00
		Sold 3,000 shares of stock for $80,000.		

Investments that Require Consolidated Financial Statements

Corporations often own shares in and may even control other corporations. For example, if Par Company owns more than 50% of the voting shares of Sub Company, Par Company can elect Sub Company's board of directors and thus control its activities and resources. The controlling corporation, Par Company, is known as the **parent company** and Sub Company is called a **subsidiary.**

Many large companies are parents with subsidiaries. For example, **George Weston Limited** is the parent of several subsidiaries, including Loblaw, Neilson/Cadbury, Zehrmart, E.B. Eddy Paper, and National Grocers.

When a corporation owns all the outstanding shares of a subsidiary, it can take over the subsidiary's assets, cancel the subsidiary's shares, and merge the subsidiary into the parent company. However, there often are financial, legal, and tax advantages if a large business is operated as a parent corporation that controls one or more subsidiary corporations. In fact, many large companies are parent corporations that own one or more subsidiaries.

When a business operates as a parent company with subsidiaries, separate accounting records are maintained by each corporation. From a legal viewpoint, the parent and each subsidiary are still separate entities with all the rights, duties, and responsibilities of individual corporations. However, investors in the parent company indirectly are investors in the subsidiaries. To evaluate their investments, parent company investors must consider the financial status and operations of the subsidiaries as well as the parent. This information is provided in **consolidated financial statements.**

Consolidated statements show the financial position, the results of operations, and the cash flows of all corporations under the parent's control, including the subsidiaries. These statements are prepared as if the business is organized as a single company. Although the parent uses the equity method in its accounts, the investment account is not reported on the parent's financial statements. Instead, the individual assets and liabilities of the affiliated companies are combined on a single balance sheet. Also, their revenues and expenses are combined on a single income statement and their cash flows are combined on a single statement of cash flows.

More detailed explanations of consolidated statements are included in advanced accounting courses.

Progress Check

12-6 What are the similarities and differences in accounting for long-term investments in debt securities that are held to maturity and those that are held as temporary investments?

12-7 What are the three categories of long-term equity investments? Describe the criteria for each category and the method used to account for each.

In today's complex world, many companies conduct business activities in more than one country. In fact, the operations of some large corporations involve so many different countries that they are called **multinational businesses.** The problems of managing and accounting for companies that have international operations can be very complex. Because of this complexity, the following pages present only a brief discussion. A more detailed study of these issues is reserved for advanced business courses.

Two primary problems in accounting for international operations occur because businesses with transactions in more than one country have to deal with more than one currency. These two problems are (1) accounting for sales or purchases denominated in a foreign currency and (2) preparing consolidated financial statements with foreign subsidiaries. To simplify the discussion of these problems, we assume that the companies have a base of operations in Canada and prepare their financial statements in the Canadian dollar. Hence, the **reporting currency** of such firms is the Canadian dollar.

INVESTMENTS IN INTERNATIONAL OPERATIONS

LO 4

Describe the primary accounting problems of having investments in international operations and prepare entries to account for sales to foreign customers.

Exchange Rates between Currencies

Active markets for the purchase and sale of foreign currencies exist all over the world. In these markets, Canadian dollars can be exchanged for U.S. dollars, British pounds, French francs, Japanese yen, or other currencies. The price of one currency stated in terms of another currency is called a **foreign exchange rate.** For example, assume that the current exchange rate for British pounds and Canadian dollars was $2.2770 on January 31, 1996. This rate means that one pound could have been acquired for $2.2770. On the same day, assume that the exchange rate between German marks and Canadian dollars was $0.6917. This number means that one mark could be purchased for $0.6917. Foreign exchange rates fluctuate daily (or even hourly) in accordance with the changing supply and demand for each currency and expectations about future events.

Sales or Purchases Denominated in a Foreign Currency

When a Canadian company makes a credit sale to a foreign customer, a special problem can arise in accounting for the sale and the account receivable. If the sales terms require the foreign customer's payment to be in Canadian dollars, no special accounting problem arises. But, if the terms of the sale state that payment is to be made in a foreign currency, the Canadian company must go through special steps to account for the sale and the account receivable.

For example, suppose that a Canadian company, the Brandon Company, makes a credit sale to London Outfitters, a British company. The sale occurs on December 12, 1996, and the price is £10,000, which is due on February 10, 1997. Naturally, Brandon Company keeps its accounting records in Canadian dollars. Therefore, to record the sale, Brandon Company must translate the sales price from pounds to dollars. This is done using the current exchange rate on the date of the sale. Assuming that the current exchange rate on December 12 is $2.40, Brandon records the sale as follows:

Dec.	12	Accounts Receivable—London Outfitters	24,000.00	
		Sales (10,000 × $2.40)		24,000.00
		To record a sale of £10,000, when the exchange rate equals $2.40.		

Now, assume that Brandon Company prepares annual financial statements on December 31, 1996. On that date, the current exchange rate has increased to $2.45. Therefore, the current dollar value of Brandon Company's receivable is $24,500 (10,000 × $2.45). This amount is now $500 greater than the amount originally recorded on December 12. According to generally accepted accounting principles, the receivable must be reported in the balance sheet at its current dollar value. Hence, Brandon Company must make the following entry to record the increase in the dollar value of the receivable:

Dec.	31	Accounts Receivable—London Outfitters	500.00	
		Foreign Exchange Gain or Loss		500.00
		To record the effects of the increased value of the British pound on our receivable.		

The Foreign Exchange Gain or Loss is closed to the Income Summary account and reported on the income statement.[11]

Assume that Brandon Company receives London Outfitters' payment of £10,000 on February 10, and immediately exchanges the pounds for Canadian dollars. On this date, the exchange rate for pounds has declined to $2.43. Therefore, Brandon Company receives only $24,300 (10,000 × $2.43). The firm records the receipt and the loss associated with the decline in the exchange rate as follows:

Feb.	10	Cash	24,300.00	
		Foreign Exchange Gain or Loss	200.00	
		Accounts Receivable—London Outfitters		24,500.00
		Received foreign currency payment of account and converted it into dollars.		

---

[11] Ibid., section 1650, "Foreign Currency Translation," par. 20.

Accounting for credit purchases from a foreign supplier is similar to the previous example of a credit sale to a foreign customer. If the Canadian company is required to make a payment in a foreign currency, the account payable must be translated into dollars before it can be recorded by the Canadian company. Then, if the exchange rate changes, an exchange gain or loss must be recognized by the Canadian company at any intervening balance sheet date and at the payment date.

Consolidated Statements with Foreign Subsidiaries

A second problem of accounting for international operations involves the preparation of consolidated financial statements when the parent company has one or more foreign subsidiaries. For example, suppose that a Canadian company owns a controlling interest in a French subsidiary. The reporting currency of the Canadian parent is the dollar. However, the French subsidiary maintains its financial records in francs. Before preparing consolidated statements, the parent must translate financial statements of the French company into Canadian dollars. After the translation is completed, the preparation of consolidated statements is not any different than for any other subsidiary.[12]

The procedures for translating a foreign subsidiary's account balances depend on the nature of the subsidiary's operations. In simple terms, the general process requires the parent company to select appropriate foreign exchange rates and then to apply those rates to the account balances of the foreign subsidiary.

Progress Check

12–8   **If a Canadian company makes a credit sale of merchandise to a French customer and the sales terms require payment in francs:**
   a. **The Canadian company will incur an exchange loss if the foreign exchange rate between francs and dollars increases from $0.246 at the date of sale to $0.256 at the date the account is settled.**
   b. **The French company may eventually have to record an exchange gain or loss.**
   c. **The Canadian company may be required to record an exchange gain or loss on the date of the sale.**
   d. **None of the above is correct.**

After studying this and the previous chapters, you have learned about all of the important classes of assets that businesses own. Recall from Chapter 11 that in evaluating the efficiency of a company in using its assets, a ratio that is often calculated and reviewed is total asset turnover. Another ratio that provides information about a company's efficiency in using its assets is **return on total assets.** You can calculate the return on total assets with this formula:

$$\text{Return on total assets} = \frac{\text{Net income}}{\text{Average total assets}}$$

USING THE INFORMATION— RETURN ON TOTAL ASSETS

LO 5

Explain the use of return on total assets in evaluating a company's efficiency in using its assets.

---

[12]The problem grows much more complicated when the accounts of the French subsidiary are maintained in accordance with the French version of GAAP. The French statements must be converted to Canadian GAAP before the consolidation can be completed.

For example, **Canstar Sports Inc.,** the manufacturer of Bauer skates and other sports equipment, earned a net income of $15.3 million during 1993. At the beginning of 1993, Canstar had total assets of $137.2 million, and at the end of the year total assets were $159.2 million. If the average total assets owned during the year is approximated by averaging the beginning and ending asset balances, Canstar's return on total assets for 1993 was:

$$\text{Return on total assets} = \frac{\$15.3}{(\$137.2 + \$159.2)/2} = 10.3\%$$

As we have seen for other ratios, a company's return on total assets should be compared with past performance and with the ratios of similar companies. In addition, you must be careful not to place too much importance on the evaluation of any single ratio. For past performance comparisons, Canstar's return on total assets and total asset turnover over a four-year period were as follows:

Year	Return on Total Assets	Total Asset Turnover
1993	10.3%	1.4
1992	11.5	1.4
1991	7.3	1.3
1990	8.6	1.5

Notice that the change in return on total assets suggests that the company's efficiency in using its assets declined from 1992 to 1993. However, the total asset turnover remained relatively constant. A possible explanation for this might be that Canstar decided to increase expenses at a faster rate than sales in an effort to gain an increasing share of the market for its products. Such a strategy would explain a reduced return on total assets and an increased total asset turnover.

Progress Check

12-9 A company had net income of $140,000 for 1996 and $100,000 for 1997. At December 31, 1996 and 1997, total assets reported were $800,000 and $900,000, respectively. What was the return on total assets for 1997?

SUMMARY OF THE CHAPTER IN TERMS OF LEARNING OBJECTIVES

LO 1. Identify assets that should be classified as natural resources or as intangible assets and prepare entries to account for them, including entries to record depletion and amortization. The cost of a natural resource is recorded in an asset account. Then, depletion of the natural resource is recorded by allocating the cost to expense according to a units-of-production basis. The depletion is credited to an accumulated depletion account. Intangible assets are recorded at the cost incurred to purchase the assets. The allocation of intangible asset cost to expense is done on a straight-line basis and is called amortization. Normally, amortization is recorded with credits made directly to the asset account instead of a contra account.

LO 2. State the criteria for classifying assets as long-term investments and describe the categories of securities that are classified as long-term

investments. Securities investments are classified as current assets if they are held as a source of cash to be used in current operations and if they mature within one year or the current operating cycle of the business or are marketable. All other investments in securities are long-term investments, which also include assets held for a special purpose and not used in operations.

Long-term investments in securities are classified in four groups: (*a*) debt securities held to maturity, (*b*) equity securities where investor has no significant influence, (*c*) equity securities where the investor has a significant influence over the investee, and (*d*) equity securities when the investor controls the investee.

LO 3. Describe the methods used to report long-term securities investments in the financial statements. Debt held to maturity is reported at its original cost adjusted for amortization of any difference between cost and maturity value. Long-term investments in debt and equity securities are reported at cost unless there is a nontemporary decline in value. Then the investment is written down and a loss is recognized.

The equity method is used if the investor has a significant influence over the investee. This situation usually exists when the investor owns 20% or more of the investee's voting stock. If an investor owns more than 50% of another corporation's voting stock and controls the investee, the investor's financial reports are prepared on a consolidated basis.

Under the equity method, the investor records its share of the investee's earnings with a debit to the investment account and a credit to a revenue account. Dividends received satisfy the investor's equity claims, and reduce the investment account balance.

LO 4. Describe the primary accounting problems of having investments in international operations and prepare entries to account for sales to foreign customers. If a Canadian company makes a credit sale to a foreign customer and the sales terms call for payment with a foreign currency, the company must translate the foreign currency into dollars to record the receivable. If the exchange rate changes before payment is received, foreign exchange gains or losses are recognized in the year in which they occur. The same treatment is used if a Canadian company makes a credit purchase from a foreign supplier and is required to make payment in a foreign currency. Also, if a Canadian company has a foreign subsidiary that maintains its accounts in a foreign currency, the account balances must be translated into dollars before they can be consolidated with the parent's accounts.

LO 5. Explain the use of return on total assets in evaluating a company's efficiency in using its assets. Return on total assets is used along with other ratios such as total asset turnover to evaluate the efficiency of a company in using its assets. Return on total assets is usually calculated as the annual net income divided by the average amount of total assets.

The following transactions relate to Brown Company's long-term investment activities during 1996 and 1997. Brown did not own any long-term investments prior to 1996. Show the appropriate journal entries and the portions of each year's balance sheet and income statement that describe these transactions.

DEMONSTRATION PROBLEM

1996

Sept.　9　Purchased 1,000 common shares of Packard, Inc., for $80,000 cash. These shares represent 30% of Packard's outstanding shares.

Oct.   2 Purchased 2,000 common shares of BCE for $60,000 cash. These shares represent less than a 1% ownership in BCE.

       17 Purchased as a long-term investment 1,000 common shares of Apple Computer for $40,000 cash. These shares are less than 1% of Apple's outstanding shares.

Nov.   1 Received $5,000 cash dividend from Packard.

       30 Received $3,000 cash dividend from BCE.

Dec.   15 Received $1,400 cash dividend from Apple.

       31 Packard's 1996 net income was $70,000.

       31 Market values for the investments in equity securities are Packard, $94,000; BCE, $48,000; and Apple Computer, $45,000.

1997

Jan.   1 Packard, Inc., was taken over by other investors, and Brown sold its shares for $108,000 cash.

May   30 Received $3,100 cash dividend from BCE.

June   15 Received $1,600 cash dividend from Apple.

Aug.   17 Sold the BCE shares for $52,000 cash.

       19 Purchased 2,000 shares of Loblaw common shares for $50,000 as a long-term investment. The stock represents less than a 5% ownership in Loblaw.

Dec.   15 Received $1,800 cash dividend from Apple.

       31 Market values of the investments in equity securities are Apple, $39,000 and Loblaw, $48,000.

Planning the Solution

- Account for the investment in Packard under the equity method.
- Account for the investments in BCE, Apple, and Loblaw as long-term investments using the cost method.
- Prepare the information for the two balance sheets by including the appropriate assets and shareholders' equity accounts.

Solution to Demonstration Problem

Journal entries during 1996:

Sept.	9	Investment in Packard Common Shares	80,000.00	
		Cash		80,000.00
		Acquired 1,000 shares representing a 30% equity in Packard, Inc.		
Oct.	2	Investment in BCE Common Shares	60,000.00	
		Cash		60,000.00
		Acquired 2,000 shares as a long-term investment in securities.		
	17	Investment in Apple Common Shares	40,000.00	
		Cash		40,000.00
		Acquired 1,000 shares as a long-term investment in securities.		

Nov.	1	Cash	5,000.00	
		Investment in Packard Common Shares		5,000.00
		Received dividend from Packard, Inc.		
	30	Cash	3,000.00	
		Dividends Earned		3,000.00
		Received dividend from BCE.		
Dec.	15	Cash	1,400.00	
		Dividends Earned		1,400.00
		Received dividend from Apple.		
	31	Investment in Packard Common Shares	21,000.00	
		Earnings from Investment in Packard		21,000.00
		To record our 30% share of Packard's annual earnings of $70,000.		

	Cost	**Market Value**
BCE	$ 60,000	$48,000
Apple	40,000	45,000
Total	$100,000	$93,000

Given the usual fluctuations in market prices, it is reasonable to assume that the reduction is temporary. Therefore, no adjustment is necessary.

December 31, 1996, balance sheet items:

Assets

Long-term investments:
Equity securities, at cost (market value, $93,000) ... $100,000
Investment in Packard, Inc. (market value, $94,000) . 96,000
Total $196,000

Income statement items for the year ended December 31, 1996

Dividends earned .... $ 4,400
Earnings from equity method investment 21,000

Journal entries during 1997:

Jan.	1	Cash	108,000.00	
		Investment in Packard Common Shares		96,000.00
		Gain on Sale of Investments		12,000.00
		Sold 1,000 shares for cash.		
May	30	Cash	3,100.00	
		Dividends Earned		3,100.00
		Received dividend from BCE.		

June	15	Cash	1,600.00	
		Dividends Earned		1,600.00
		Received dividend from Apple.		
Aug.	17	Cash	52,000.00	
		Loss on Sale of Investments	8,000.00	
		Investment in BCE Common Shares		60,000.00
		Sold 2,000 shares for cash.		
	19	Investment in Loblaw Common Shares	50,000.00	
		Cash		50,000.00
		Acquired 2,000 shares as a long-term investment in securities available for sale.		
Dec.	15	Cash	1,800.00	
		Dividends Earned		1,800.00
		Received dividend from Apple.		

	Cost	Market Value
Apple	$40,000	$39,000
Loblaw	50,000	48,000
Total	$90,000	$87,000

December 31, 1997, balance sheet items:

Assets

Long-term investments:
    Equity securities, at cost (market value, $87,000) .. $ 90,000

Income statement items for the year ended December 31, 1997:

Dividends earned	$ 6,500
Gain on sale of investments	12,000
Loss on sale of investments	(8,000)

GLOSSARY

Amortization the process of systematically writing off the cost of an intangible asset to expense over its estimated useful life p. 565

Consolidated financial statements financial statements that show the results of all operations under the parent's control, including those of any subsidiaries; assets and liabilities of all affiliated companies are combined on a single balance sheet, revenues and expenses are combined on a single income statement, and cash flows are combined on a single statement of cash flows as though the business were in fact a single company. p. 576

Copyright an exclusive right granted by the federal government or by international agreement to publish and sell a musical, literary, or artistic work for a period of years. p. 567

Depletion the cost created by consuming the usefulness of natural resources. p. 564

Equity method an accounting method used when the investor has influence over the investee; the investment account is initially debited for cost and then is increased to reflect the investor's share of the investee's earnings and decreased to reflect the investor's receipt of dividends paid by the investee. p. 574

Foreign exchange rate the price of one currency stated in terms of another currency. p. 577

Goodwill an intangible asset of a business that represents future earnings greater than the average in its industry; recognized in the financial statements only when a business is acquired at a price in excess of the fair market value of its net assets (excluding goodwill). p. 568

Intangible asset an asset representing certain legal rights and economic relationships; it has no physical existence but is beneficial to the owner. p. 565

Lease a contract under which the owner of property (the lessor) grants to a lessee the right to use the property. p. 567

Leasehold the rights granted to a lessee by the lessor under the terms of a lease contract. p. 567

Leasehold improvements improvements to leased property made and paid for by the lessee. p. 567

Lessee the individual or company that acquires the right to use property under the terms of a lease. p. 567

Lessor the individual or company that owns property to be used by a lessee under the terms of a lease. p. 567

Long-term investments investments in shares and bonds that are not marketable or, if marketable, are not intended to be a ready source of cash in case of need;

also funds earmarked for a special purpose, such as bond sinking funds, and land or other assets not used in regular operations. p. 570

Multinational business a company that operates in a large number of different countries. p. 577

Parent company a corporation that owns a controlling interest in another corporation (more than 50% of the voting stock is required). p. 576

Patent exclusive right granted by the federal government to manufacture and sell a patented machine or device, or to use a process, for 17 years. p. 566

Reporting currency the currency in which a company presents its financial statements. p. 577

Return on total assets a measure of a company's operating efficiency, calculated by expressing net income as a percentage of average total assets. p. 579

Subsidiary a corporation that is controlled by another corporation (the parent) because the parent owns more than 50% of the subsidiary's voting stock. p. 576

Trademark a unique symbol used by a company in marketing its products or services. p. 569

Trade name a unique name used by a company in marketing its products or services. p. 569

SYNONYMOUS TERMS

Amortization depreciation, depletion.

Natural resources wasting assets.

Equity investment share or stock investment.

QUESTIONS

1. What is the name for the process of allocating the cost of natural resources to expense as the natural resources are used?

2. What are the characteristics of an intangible asset?

3. Is the declining-balance method an acceptable means of calculating depletion of natural resources?

4. What general procedures are followed in accounting for intangible assets?

5. When does a business have goodwill? Under what conditions can goodwill appear in a company's balance sheet?

6. X Company bought an established business and paid for goodwill. If X Company plans to incur substantial advertising and promotional costs each year

to maintain the value of the goodwill, must the company also amortize the goodwill?

7. In accounting for common share investments, when should the equity method be used?

8. Under what circumstances would a company prepare consolidated financial statements?

9. Under what circumstances are long-term investments in debt securities reported at their original cost adjusted for amortization of any difference between cost and maturity value?

10. What are two basic problems of accounting for international operations?

11. If a Canadian company makes a credit sale to a foreign customer and the customer is required to make

payment in Canadian dollars, can the Canadian company have an exchange gain or loss as a result of the sale?

12. A Canadian company makes a credit sale to a foreign customer, and the customer is required to make payment in a foreign currency. The foreign exchange rate was $1.40 on the date of the sale and is $1.30 on the date the customer pays the receivable.

Will the Canadian company record an exchange gain or an exchange loss?

13. Refer to Geac Computer Corporation Limited consolidated balance sheets in Appendix I. What percentage of total assets is represented by goodwill at April 30, 1994?

QUICK STUDY (Five-Minute Exercises)

QS 12–1
(LO 1)

Three Z Mining Co. acquired an ore mine at a cost of $615,000. It was necessary to incur a $60,000 cost to access the mine. The mine is estimated to hold 200,000 tonnes of ore and the estimated value of the land after the ore is removed is $80,000.

a. Prepare the entry to record the acquisition.

b. Prepare the year-end adjusting entry assuming that 46,000 tonnes of ore were removed from the mine this year.

QS 12–2
(LO 1)

Which of the following assets should be reported on the balance sheet as an intangible asset? Which should be reported as a natural resource? (*a*) copper mine, (*b*) copyright, (*c*) building, (*d*) goodwill, (*e*) timberland.

QS 12–3
(LO 1)

In early January of the current year, Big Mountain Ski Shop incurred a $160,000 cost to modernize the shop. The improvements included new floors, lighting, and fitting platforms for rental equipment. These improvements would last for 10 years of use. Big Mountain leases its retail space and has eight years remaining on the lease. Prepare the entry to record the modernization, and the adjusting entry at the end of the current year.

QS 12–4
(LO 2)

On April 1, 1996, Demi Dean purchased 8% bonds of Multi Media Inc. at a cost of $50,000, which equals their par value. The bonds carry an 8% rate of interest to be paid semiannually on September 30 and March 31. Prepare the entries to record the September 30 receipt of interest and the December 31 accrual.

QS 12–5
(LO 2)

On January 2, 1996, Nassau Co. paid $500,000 to acquire 10,000 (10%) of Suffolk Corp.'s outstanding common shares as a long-term investment. On March 25, 1998, Nassau sold half of the shares for $260,000. What method should be used to account for this investment? Prepare entries to record the acquisition of the shares and the sale.

QS 12–6
(LO 3)

Assume the same facts as in QS 12–5 except assume that the shares acquired represented 30% of the shares outstanding. Suffolk Co. paid a $100,000 dividend on October 12, 1996, and reported a net income of $400,000 for the 1996 year. Prepare the entry to record the receipt of the dividend and the year-end adjustment of the investment account.

QS 12–7
(LO 4)

On November 21, 1996, a Canadian company, NCN, made a sale with credit terms requiring payment in 30 days to a German company, Ehlers Inc. The price of the sale was 50,000 marks. Assuming the exchange rate between German marks and Canadian dollars was

$0.6214 on the date of sale and $0.5942 on December 21, prepare the entries to record the sale and cash receipt on December 21.

How is the return on total assets calculated? What does this ratio evaluate?

QS 12–8
(LO 5)

EXERCISES

On March 30, 1996, Clementine Investments paid $7,275,000 for an ore deposit containing 4,850,000 tonnes. The company also installed machinery in the mine that cost $339,500, had an estimated 10-year life with no salvage value, and was capable of removing all the ore in 8 years. The machine will be abandoned when the ore is completely mined. Clementine began operations on July 1, 1996, and mined and sold 582,000 tonnes of ore during the remaining six months of the year. Give the December 31, 1996, entries to record the depletion of the ore deposit and the amortization of the mining machinery.

Exercise 12–1
Depletion of natural resources
(LO 1)

Majestic Productions purchased the copyright to a painting for $369,000 on January 1, 1996. The copyright legally protects its owner for 24 more years. However, the company plans to market and sell prints of the original for only 15 more years. Prepare journal entries to record the purchase of the copyright and the annual amortization of the copyright on December 31, 1996.

Exercise 12–2
Amortization of intangible assets
(LO 1)

Rocky Lane has devoted years to developing a profitable business that earns an attractive return. Lane is now considering the possibility of selling the business and is attempting to estimate the value of the goodwill in the business. The fair value of the net assets of the business (excluding goodwill) is $625,000, and in a typical year net income is about $90,000. Most businesses of this type are expected to earn a return of about 12% on net assets. Estimate the value of the goodwill assuming (a) the value is equal to eight times the excess earnings above average, and (b) the value can be found by capitalizing the excess earnings above average at a rate of 10%.

Exercise 12–3
Estimating goodwill
(LO 1)

During 1996, Stockton Company's investments in securities included five items. These securities, with their December 31, 1996, market values, are as follows:

Exercise 12–4
Classifying equity investments, recording market values
(LO 2, 3)

a. Antel Corporation bonds payable: $167,400 cost; $182,000 market value. Stockton intends and is able to hold these bonds until they mature in 1999.

b. Foxfire, Inc., common stock: 30,800 shares; $132,980 cost; $143,500 market value. Stockton owns 22% of Foxfire's voting stock and has a significant influence on Foxfire.

c. Techcon Corp. common stock: 10,300 shares; $67,900 cost; $73,240 market value. The goal of this investment is to earn dividends over the next few years.

d. Bali common stock: 4,500 shares; $46,120 cost; $45,770 market value. The goal of this investment is an expected increase in market value of the stock over the next three to five years. Bali has 30,000 common shares outstanding.

e. Joskey common stock: 18,400 shares; $57,100 cost; $55,900 market value. This stock is marketable and is held as an investment of cash available for operations.

State whether each of these investments should be classified as a current asset or as a long-term investment.

Exercise 12–5
Investments in securities
(LO 3)

Pratt Company began operations in 1996 and regularly makes long-term investments in securities. The total cost and market value of these investments at the end of several years were:

	Cost	Market Value
On December 31, 1996	$170,000	$164,800
On December 31, 1997	194,000	206,000
On December 31, 1998	264,000	312,000
On December 31, 1999	398,000	354,000

Required

Prepare journal entries to record the LCM of Pratt's investments at the end of each year. Explain the entries you recorded.

Exercise 12–6
Equity investment
transactions; equity
method
(LO 3)

Prepare general journal entries to record the following events on the books of MCM Company:

1996

Jan. 14   Purchased 18,000 common shares of Putnam, Inc., for $156,900 plus broker's fee of $1,000. Putnam has 90,000 common shares outstanding and has acknowledged the fact that its policies will be significantly influenced by MCM.

Oct. 1   Putnam declared and paid a cash dividend of $2.60 per share.

Dec. 31   Putnam announced that net income for the year amounted to $650,000.

1997

Apr. 1   Putnam declared and paid a cash dividend of $2.70 per share.

Dec. 31   Putnam announced that net income for the year amounted to $733,100.

31   MCM sold 6,000 shares of Putnam for $119,370.

Exercise 12–7
Receivables
denominated in a
foreign currency
(LO 4)

On June 2, 1996, Comco Company made a credit sale to a French company. The terms of the sale required the French company to pay 980,000 francs on January 3, 1997. Comco prepares quarterly financial statements on March 31, June 30, September 30, and December 31. The foreign exchange rates for francs during the time the receivable was outstanding were:

June 2, 1996	$0.16720
June 30, 1996	0.17100
September 30, 1996	0.17225
December 31, 1996	0.16885
January 3, 1997	0.17310

Calculate the foreign exchange gain or loss that Comco should report on each of its quarterly income statements during the last three quarters of 1996 and the first quarter of 1997. Also calculate the amount that should be reported on Comco's balance sheets at the end of the last three quarters of 1996.

Donham Company of Montvale, New Brunswick, sells its products to customers in Canada and in the United States. On December 3, 1996, Donham sold merchandise on credit to Swensons, Ltd., of London, Maine, at a price of U.S. $6,500. The exchange rate on that day was $1U.S. equals $1.4685 Canadian. On December 31, 1996, when Donham prepared its financial statements, the exchange rate was $1 U.S. for $1.4230. Swensons, Ltd., paid its bill in full on January 3, 1997, at which time the exchange rate was $1U.S. for $1.4460. Donham immediately exchanged the U.S. $6,500 for Canadian dollars. Prepare journal entries on December 3, December 31, and January 3, to account for the sale and account receivable on the books of Donham.

Exercise 12–8
Foreign currency transactions
(LO 4)

The following information is available from the financial statements of NRE Company:

Exercise 12–9
Return on total assets
(LO 5)

	1996	1997	1998
Total assets, December 31	$320,000	$580,000	$1,200,000
Net income	46,000	75,000	106,000

Calculate NRE's return on total assets for 1997 and 1998. Comment on the company's efficiency in using its assets in 1997 and 1998.

PROBLEMS

Part 1. Five years ago, Zeno Insurance Company leased space in a building for 15 years. The lease contract calls for annual rental payments of $28,000 to be made on each July 1 throughout the life of the lease and also provides that the lessee must pay for all additions and improvements to the leased property. Because recent nearby construction has made the location more valuable, Zeno decided to sublease the space to Bogart & Company for the remaining 10 years of the lease. On June 25, Bogart paid $75,000 to Zeno for the right to sublease the property and agreed to assume the obligation to pay the $28,000 annual rental charges to the building owner, beginning the next July 1. After taking possession of the leased space, Bogart paid for improving the office portion of the leased space at a cost of $90,950. The improvement was paid for on July 8 and is estimated to have a life equal to the 17 years remaining in the life of the building.

Problem 12–1
Intangible assets and natural resources
(LO 1)

Required

Prepare entries for Bogart & Company to record (a) its payment to Zeno for the right to sublease the building space, (b) its payment of the next annual rental charge to the building owner, and (c) payment for the improvements. Also, prepare the adjusting entries required at the end of the first year of the sublease to amortize (d) a proper share of the $75,000 cost of the sublease and (e) a proper share of the office improvement.

Part 2. On February 20 of the current year, Amazon Industries paid $8,700,000 for land estimated to contain 11.6 million tonnes of recoverable ore of a valuable mineral. It installed machinery costing $348,000, which had a 12-year life and no salvage value, and was capable of exhausting the ore deposit in 9 years. The machinery was paid for on May 24, six days before mining operations began. The company removed 744,000 tonnes of ore during the first seven months' operations.

Required

Preparation component:

Prepare entries to record (*a*) the purchase of the land, (*b*) the installation of the machinery, (*c*) the first seven months' depletion under the assumption that the land will be valueless after the ore is mined, and (*d*) the first seven months' amortization on the machinery, which will be abandoned after the ore is fully mined.

Analysis component:

Describe the similarities and differences in amortization, depletion, and depreciation.

Problem 12–2
Goodwill
(LO 1)

Flowers Unlimited has the following balance sheet on December 31, 1996:

Cash	$ 57,800
Merchandise inventory	43,650
Buildings	320,000
Accumulated amortization	(112,000)
Land	101,750
Total assets	$411,200
Accounts payable	$ 9,400
Long-term note payable	124,925
D. E. Flowers, capital	276,875
Total liabilities and owner's equity . .	$411,200

In this industry, earnings average 32% of owner's equity. Flowers Unlimited, however, is expected to earn $100,000 annually. The owner believes that the balance sheet amounts are reasonable estimates of fair market values for all assets except goodwill, which does not appear on the financial statement. In discussing a plan to sell the company, D. E. Flowers has suggested to the potential buyer that goodwill can be measured by capitalizing the amount of above-average earnings at a rate of 12%. On the other hand, the potential buyer thinks that goodwill should be valued at six times the amount of excess earnings above the average for the industry.

Required

1. Calculate the amount of goodwill claimed by Flowers.

2. Calculate the amount of goodwill according to the potential buyer.

3. Suppose that the buyer finally agrees to pay the full price requested by Flowers. If the amount of expected earnings (before amortization of goodwill) is obtained and the goodwill is amortized over the longest permissible time period, what amount of net income will be reported for the first year after the company is purchased?

4. If the buyer pays the full price requested by Flowers, what rate of return on the purchaser's investment will be earned as net income the first year?

Problem 12–3
Accounting for equity
investments
(LO 3)

Austex Company was organized on January 2, 1996. The following transactions and events subsequently occurred:

1996

Jan.   7   Austex purchased 50,000 shares (20%) of Staat, Inc.'s outstanding common shares for $565,500.

Apr. 30   Staat declared and paid a cash dividend of $1.10 per share.

Dec. 31   Staat announced that its net income for 1996 was $480,000. Market value of
the shares was $11.80 per share.

1997

Nov. 30   Staat declared and paid a cash dividend of $0.70 per share.

Dec. 31   Staat announced that its net income for 1997 was $630,000. Market value of
the shares was $12.18 per share.

1998

Jan. 5   Austex sold all of its investment in Staat for $682,000 cash.

Part 1. Assume that Austex has a significant influence over Staat because it owns 20% of
the shares.

Required

1. Give the entries on the books of Austex to record the preceding events.

2. Calculate the carrying value per share of Austex's investment as reflected in the investment account on January 4, 1998.

3. Calculate the change in Austex's equity from January 7, 1996, through January 5, 1998, that resulted from its investment in Staat.

Part 2. Assume that even though Austex owns 20% of Staat's outstanding shares, a thorough investigation of the surrounding circumstances indicates that it does not have a significant influence over the investee.

Required

1. Give the entries on the books of Austex to record the preceding events.

2. Calculate the cost per share of Austex's investment as reflected in the investment account on January 4, 1998.

3. Calculate the change in Austex's equity from January 7, 1996, through January 5, 1998, that resulted from its investment in Staat.

Leling Company's long-term investments portfolio at December 31, 1996, consisted of the following:

Problem 12–4
Accounting for long-term investments
(LO 2, 3)

Long-Term Investments	Cost	Market Value
10,000 shares of Company X common shares	$163,500	$145,000
1,500 shares of Company Y common shares	65,000	62,000
120,000 shares of Company Z common shares	40,000	35,600

Leling made the following long-term investments transactions during 1997:

Jan.   17   Sold 750 common shares of Company Y for $36,000 less a brokerage fee
of $180.

Mar.   3   Purchased 5,000 common shares of Company A for $300,000 plus a brokerage
fee of $1,500. The shares represent a 30% ownership in Company A.

May   12   Purchased 3,000 common shares of Company B for $96,000 plus a brokerage
fee of $400. The shares represent a 10% ownership in Company B.

Dec. 11 Purchased 10,000 common shares of Company D for $89,000 plus a broker-
age fee of $445. The shares represent a 5% ownership in Company D.

20 Sold 10,000 common shares of Company X for $160,000 less a brokerage
fee of $800.

Dec. 31 Company A announced a net profit of $280,000 for the year.

The market values of Leling's investments at December 31, 1997, follow: A, $418,000;
B, $92,000; D, $90,800; Y, $38,200; Z, $31,000.

Required

1. Determine what amount should be reported on Leling's December 31, 1997, balance
sheet for its investments in equity securities.

2. Prepare a December 31, 1997, adjusting entry, if necessary, to record the LCM
adjustment of the long-term investments in securities.

3. What amount of gain or loss on those transactions relating to securities should be
reported on Leling's December 31, 1997, income statement?

Problem 12–5
Foreign currency
transactions
(LO 4)

Lupold Company is a Canadian company that has customers in several foreign countries.
The company had the following transactions in 1996 and 1997:

1996

May 22 Sold merchandise for 15,000 marks to Weishaar Imports of Germany, payment
in full to be received in 90 days. On this day, the foreign exchange rate for
marks was $0.5654.

Sept. 9 Sold merchandise to Campos Company of Mexico for $24,780 cash. The ex-
change rate for pesos was $0.322154.

Aug. 25 Received Weishaar Imports' payment for its purchase of May 22, and exchanged the marks for dollars. The current foreign exchange rate for marks
was $0.5995.

Nov. 29 Sold merchandise on credit to ONI Company located in Japan. The price of
1.1 million yen was to be paid 60 days from the date of sale. The exchange
rate for yen was $0.009195 on November 29.

Dec. 23 Sold merchandise for 158,000 francs to Martinique Company of France, payment in full to be received in 30 days. The exchange rate for francs was
$0.16722.

Dec. 31 Prepared adjusting entries to recognize exchange gains or losses on the annual
financial statements. Rates for exchanging foreign currencies on this day included the following:

Marks (Germany)	$0.5690
Pesos (Mexico)	0.331256
Yen (Japan)	0.010110
Francs (France)	0.16530

1997

Jan. 24 Received full payment from Martinique for the sale of December 23 and immediately exchanged the francs for dollars. The exchange rate for francs was
$0.16342.

30 Received ONI's full payment for the sale of November 29 and immediately
exchanged the yen for dollars. The exchange rate for yen was $0.010290.

Required

Preparation component:

1. Prepare general journal entries to account for these transactions of Lupold.

2. Calculate the foreign exchange gain or loss to be reported on Lupold's 1996 income statement.

Analysis component:

3. What actions might Lupold consider to reduce its risk of foreign exchange gains or losses?

On January 3, Tragor Company purchased 20,000 common shares of Entech Company for $10 per share, or $200,000. Tragor's purchase represents a 30% ownership in Entech. Tragor did not own any investments prior to the Entech stock purchase. Entech did not declare any dividends on its common shares during the year, and on December 31 reported a net loss of $80,000. The market value of the Entech shares on December 31 was $11.00 per share. The accountant for Tragor made the following adjusting entry to update the account balances for the investment in Entech:

Problem 12–6
Analytical essay
(LO 3)

Dec.	31	Long-Term Investments	20,000.00	
		Gain on Investments		20,000.00
		(20,000 × $11) − $200,000 = $20,000		

Explain why this entry is incorrect. Without providing specific amounts, determine what impact the accountant's error had on the financial statements.

Part 1. Five years ago, D. C. Corporation leased space in a building for a period of 20 years. The lease contract calls for $81,000 in annual rental payments on each January 1 throughout the life of the lease and also provides that the lessee must pay for all additions and improvements to the leased property. Recent construction nearby has made the location more valuable; and on December 30, D. C. Corporation subleased the space to T. P., Inc., for the remaining 15 years of the lease, beginning on the next January 1. T. P., Inc., paid $360,000 for the privilege of subleasing the property and in addition agreed to assume and pay the building owner the $81,000 annual rental charges. After taking possession of the leased space T. P., Inc., paid for remodeling the office portion of the leased space at a cost of $270,000. The remodeled office portion is estimated to have a life equal to the remaining life of the building, 25 years, and was paid for on January 10.

Problem 12–7
Intangible assets and
natural resources
(LO 5)

Required

Prepare entries for T. P., Inc., to record: (*a*) T. P., Inc.'s payment to sublease the building space, (*b*) its payment of the annual rental charge to the building owner, and (*c*) payment for the new office portion. Also, prepare the adjusting entries required at the end of the first year of the sublease to amortize (*d*) a proper share of the $360,000 cost of the sublease and (*e*) a proper share of the office remodeling cost.

Part 2. On May 8 of the current year, Huber Company paid $1,080,000 for mineral land estimated to contain 9,000,000 tonnes of recoverable ore. It installed machinery costing $187,500, having an eight-year life and no salvage value, and capable of exhausting the mine in five years. The machinery was paid for on June 28, four days before mining operations began. During the first six months' operations the company mined 720,000 tonnes of ore.

Required

Prepare entries to record (*a*) the purchase of the mineral land, (*b*) the installation of the machinery, (*c*) the first six months' depletion under the assumption that the land will be valueless after the ore is mined, and (*d*) the first six months' amortization on the machinery, which will be abandoned after the ore is fully mined.

Problem 12–8
Goodwill
(LO 5)

Batts Company's balance sheet on December 31, 1996, is as follows:

Cash	$ 170,100
Merchandise inventory	245,700
Buildings	756,000
Accumulated amortization	(198,450)
Land	425,250
Total assets	$1,398,600
Accounts payable	$113,400
Long-term note payable	295,200
Common shares	706,500
Retained earnings	283,500
Total liabilities and owners' equity ..	$1,398,600

In Batts Company's industry, earnings average 11% of common shareholders' equity. Batts Company, however, is expected to earn $198,900 annually. The owners of Batts Company believe that the balance sheet amounts are reasonable estimates of fair market values except for goodwill. In discussing a plan to sell the company, they argue that goodwill should be recognized by capitalizing the amount of earnings above average at a rate of 20%. On the other hand, the prospective purchaser argues that goodwill should be valued at four times the earnings above average.

Required

1. Calculate the amount of goodwill claimed by Batts Company's owners.
2. Calculate the amount of goodwill according to the purchaser.
3. Suppose the purchaser finally agrees to pay the full price requested by Batts Company's owners. If the expected earnings level is obtained and the goodwill is amortized over the longest permissible time period, what will be the net income for the first year after the company is purchased?
4. If the purchaser pays the full price requested by Batts Company's owners, what percentage of the purchaser's investment will be earned as net income the first year?

Problem 12–9
Equity investments—cost
and equity methods
(LO 2, 3)

Ranger Company was organized on January 2, 1996, for the purpose of investing in the shares of other companies. Ranger Company immediately issued 50,000 common shares for which it received $250,000 cash. On January 9, 1996, Ranger Company purchased 10,000 shares (20%) of Trumpe Company's outstanding shares at a cost of $250,000. The following transactions and events subsequently occurred:

1996

Apr. 30 Trumpe Company declared and paid a cash dividend of $1 per share.

Dec. 31 Trumpe Company announced that its net income for the year was $125,000.

1997

Aug.   10   Trumpe Company declared and paid a cash dividend of $0.80 per share.

Dec.   31   Trumpe Company announced that its net income for the year was $95,000.

1998

Jan.   4   Ranger Company sold all of its investment in Trumpe Company for $275,000 cash.

Part 1. Because Ranger Company owns 20% of Trumpe Company's outstanding shares. Ranger Company is presumed to have a significant influence over Trumpe Company.

Required

1. Give the entries on the books of Ranger Company to record the above events regarding its investment in Trumpe Company.
2. Calculate the cost per share of Ranger Company's investment as reflected in the investment account on January 1, 1998.
3. Calculate Ranger Company's retained earnings balance on January 5, 1998, after closing of the books.

Part 2. Although Ranger Company owns 20% of Trumpe Company's outstanding shares, a thorough investigation of the surrounding circumstances indicates that Ranger Company does not have a significant influence over Trumpe Company, and the cost method is the appropriate method of accounting for the investment.

Required

1. Give the entries on the books of Ranger Company to record the above events regarding its investment in Trumpe Company.
2. Calculate the cost per share of Ranger Company's investment as reflected in the investment account on January 1, 1998.
3. Calculate Ranger Company's retained earnings balance on January 5, 1998, after a closing of the books.

Paramount Sales Corporation, a Canadian company that has customers in several foreign countries, had the following transactions in 1996 and 1997:

Problem 12–10
Foreign currency transactions
(LO 5)

1996

June   6   Sold merchandise for 125,000 francs to Poirot Co. of Brussels, payment in full to be received in 60 days. On this day, the foreign exchange rate for francs into dollars was $0.02822.

July   17   Sold merchandise to Nordhoff Distributors of West Germany for $8,880 cash. The exchange rate for marks into dollars was $0.5920.

Aug.   1   Received Poirot Company's payment for its purchase of June 6 and exchanged the francs for dollars. The current foreign exchange rate for francs into dollars was $0.02840.

Oct.   25   Sold merchandise on credit to British Imports, Ltd., a company located in London, England. The price of 3,000 pounds was to be paid 90 days from the date of sale. On October 25, the exchange rate for pounds into dollars was $1.7730.

Nov.   30   Sold merchandise for 350,000 yen to Yamoto Company of Japan; payment in full to be in 60 days. The exchange rate for yen into dollars was $0.007710.

Dec.   31 Prepared adjusting entries to recognize exchange gains or losses on the annual financial statements. Rates for exchanging foreign currencies into dollars on this day included the following:

Francs (Belgium)	$ 0.02833
Marks (W. German)	0.5944
Pounds (England)	1.7125
Yen (Japan)	0.007897

1997

Jan.   23 Received British Imports, Ltd.'s full payment for the sale of October 25 and immediately exchanged the pounds for dollars. The exchange rate for pounds into dollars was $1.7628.

29 Received full payment from Yamoto Company for the sale of November 30 and immediately exchanged the yen for dollars. The exchange rate for yen into dollars was $0.007779.

Required

1. Prepare general journal entries to account for these transactions of Paramount Sales Corporation.

2. Calculate the exchange gain or loss to be reported on Paramount Sales Corporation's 1996 income statement.

PROVOCATIVE PROBLEMS

Provocative Problem 12–1

Business communications case **(LO 2, 3)**

You are the accountant for PCI Company. The owner of PCI, Lester Murphy, has finished reviewing the financial statements you prepared for 1997 and questions the $40,000 loss reported on PCI's sale of its investment in the shares of Runyan Company.

PCI acquired 100,000 shares of Runyan's outstanding common shares on December 31, 1996, at a cost of $500,000. This shares purchase represented a 30% interest in Runyan. The 1997 income statement showed that the investments made by PCI proved to be very profitable and that the earnings from all investments were $340,000. On January 5, 1998, PCI sold the Runyan shares for $580,000. Runyan did not pay any dividends during 1997 and reported $400,000 net income for the year.

Murphy believes that because the purchase price of the Runyan shares was $500,000 and it was sold for $580,000, the 1998 income statement should report an $80,000 gain on the sale.

Draft a memo to Murphy explaining why the $40,000 loss on the sale of the Runyan shares is correctly reported.

Provocative Problem 12–2

Managerial analysis problem **(A review problem)**

UNI Company is considering buying either Riteway Company or Best Company, similar businesses that acquired their equipment and began operating four years ago. In evaluating the two companies, UNI has determined that they have not used the same accounting procedures so their financial statements are not comparable. Over the past four years, Riteway has reported an average annual net income of $197,840 and Best has reported $254,190. The current balance sheets of the two companies show the following:

	Riteway	Best
Cash	$ 131,500	$ 144,400
Accounts receivable	972,400	1,077,000
Allowance for doubtful accounts	(57,000)	–0–
Merchandise inventory	1,268,200	1,666,000
Office equipment	496,800	420,800
Accumulated amortization, office equipment ..	(293,310)	(168,320)
Total assets	$2,518,590	$3,139,880
Total liabilities	$1,176,800	$1,408,600

Riteway has used the allowance method of accounting for bad debts and Best has used the direct write-off method. An examination of each company's accounts revealed that only $30,000 of Riteway's accounts are probably uncollectible and that Best's estimated uncollectible accounts total $54,000.

Because Best uses FIFO, its ending inventory amounts approximate replacement cost. However, Riteway uses LIFO. As a result, Riteway's current inventory is reported $176,000 below replacement cost.

In taking amortization for the past four years, both companies have assumed 10-year lives and no salvage value for their equipment. However, Riteway has used double-declining-balance amortization, while Best has used straight-line. UNI believes that straight-line amortization results in reporting equipment on the balance sheet at its approximate market value.

UNI is willing to pay fair market value for the net assets (including goodwill) of either business. UNI estimates goodwill to be four times the average annual earnings in excess of 14% of the fair market value of the net tangible assets (assets, other than goodwill, minus liabilities).

Required

Prepare the following schedules: (*a*) the net tangible assets of each company at fair market values assessed by UNI, (*b*) the revised net incomes of the companies based on adjusted amounts of bad debts expense, FIFO inventories, and straight-line amortization, (*c*) the calculation of each company's goodwill, and (*d*) the maximum purchase price UNI would pay for each business, if it assumed the liabilities of the purchased business. (Note: Round all calculations to the nearest dollar.)

Examine Geac Computer Corporation Limited's financial statements and supplemental information in Appendix I and answer the following questions:

1. Are Geac's financial statements consolidated? How can you tell?
2. Does Geac have more than one subsidiary? How can you tell?
3. Does Geac have any foreign operations? How can you tell?
4. Is there a foreign exchange gain or loss on the income statement? Provide an explanation for what you find or do not find.
5. What intangible assets does Geac own? Assuming it will not take advantage of any renewal options, what is the maximum time period that Geac can use to amortize these intangibles?
6. Calculate Geac's return on total assets for 1994.

Provocative Problem 12–3

Financial statement analysis case

(LO 1, 4, 5)

Geac

ANALYTICAL AND REVIEW PROBLEMS

A & R Problem 12–1

On January 1, 1996, Tony Company purchases 40% of Danny Company's outstanding voting shares. On December 31, 1997, Tony Company's account Investment in Danny Company showed a balance of $400,000. Danny Company reported the following information for the years of 1996 and 1997:

	Net Income	Dividends Paid
1996	$150,000	$50,000
1997	200,000	50,000

Required

Calculate the purchase price paid by Tony Company for the Danny Company shares.

A & R Problem 12–2

The following is an excerpt from the notes to the financial statements of ABC Sciences Ltd.:

> ABC Sciences holds a 35.4% interest in Halifax-based Eastern Laboratories which develops, manufactures, and distributes chemicals solely in the Canadian market. ABC Sciences accounts for its investment in Eastern Chemicals by the equity method. During 1996, Eastern had a strong year, with revenues increasing 79.6% while net income more than doubled to $7.6 million. ABC Science's share of this net income was . . .

Required

1. Is ABC Sciences using the cost or equity method to account for its investment in Eastern Chemicals? Support your answer.
2. Prepare the journal entry to record ABC Sciences's share of Eastern's net income.
3. If Eastern paid out 50% of its 1996 net income as cash dividends, what entry would ABC Sciences make to record the receipt of cash?

CONCEPT TESTER

Check your understanding of the concepts introduced in this chapter by completing the following crossword puzzle.

Across Clues

1. The process of systematically writing off the cost of an intangible asset.

4. A cost created by consuming the usefulness of a natural resource.

7. A contract under which the owner of the property grants another the right to the property's use.

9. An exclusive right to publish and sell artistic works.

11. An exclusive right to manufacture and sell a product or process.

12. A corporation that holds a controlling interest in another corporation (2 words).

Down Clues

2. A unique symbol used by a company in marketing its product or services.

3. Changes to a leased property made by the lessee (1st of 2 words; also see 6 down).

5. An accounting method used when the investor has influence over the investee (2 words).

6. Changes to a leased property made by the lessee (2nd of 2 words; also see 3 down).

8. An intangible asset of a business represented by future earnings of a business above the norm.

10. A corporation that is controlled by another corporation.

ANSWERS TO PROGRESS CHECKS

12–1 Some possible answers:

    Intangible Assets:

        Patents

        Copyrights

        Leaseholds

        Leasehold Improvements

        Goodwill

        Trademarks

        Exclusive Licenses

    Natural Resources:

        Timberlands

        Mineral Deposits

        Oil Reserves

12–2 $\$650,000 \times (91,000/325,000) = \$182,000$

12–3

Jan.	6	Patents	120,000	
		Cash		120,000
Dec.	31	Amortization Expense	40,000	
		Patents		40,000

12–4 Long-term investments include funds earmarked for a special purpose, bonds and shares that do not meet the test of a current asset, and other assets that are not used in the regular operations of the business.

12–5 An equity investment is classified as a long-term investment if it is not marketable or, if marketable, it is not held as an available source of cash to meet the needs of current operations.

12–6 Long-term investments in debt securities and temporary investments in debt securities are recorded at cost and interest on both is accrued as earned. However, long-term debt securities require amortization of the difference between cost and maturity value.

12–7 Long-term equity investments are placed in the following three categories and accounted for using the method indicated:

   a. Noninfluential holding (less than 20% of outstanding shares) − Cost Method.

   b. Significantly influential holding (20% to 50% of outstanding shares) − Equity Method.

   c. Controlling holding (more than 50%) − Consolidated Statements.

12–8 *d*

12–9 $(\$800,000 + \$900,000)/2 = \$850,000$

     $\$100,000/\$850,000 = 11.8\%$

Despite the risks of being in debt, companies with liabilities enjoy many advantages. For example, sales can be increased if a company agrees to repair or replace defective products under a warranty obligation. Careful borrowing also allows companies to increase their income and assets.

Current and Long-Term Liabilities

Karen White and Mark Smith have been given an assignment to evaluate Safeway's financial condition. They are confused about the nature of the company's liabilities. The balance sheet reports four different categories of liabilities, and the differences between these categories are not clear to Karen and Mark.

Safeway, Inc., is one of the world's largest food retailers. At the end of its 1993 year, Safeway operated approximately 1,080 stores in Canada and the United States. The company's 1993 annual report appears to indicate that Safeway has been successfully emerging from a very difficult period of losses. At the end of its 1989 year, total shareholders' equity was a negative $388.9 million (a deficit). In other words, total liabilities exceeded total assets by $388.9 million. This situation improved each year until, at the end of 1993, total shareholders' equity was a positive $382.9 million.

Safeway Inc. and Subsidiaries
(In millions)

	Year-end 1993	Year-end 1992
Current liabilities:		
Current maturities of notes and debentures	$ 188.6	$ 92.0
Current obligations under capital leases	19.3	20.4
Accounts payable	880.5	811.0
Accrued salaries and wages	216.3	192.5
Other accrued liabilities	406.7	385.9
Total current liabilities	$1,711.4	$1,501.8
Long-term debt:		
Notes and debentures	$2,287.7	$2,736.6
Obligations under capital leases	193.6	199.6
Total long-term debt	$2,481.3	$2,936.2
Deferred income taxes	145.5	176.0
Accrued claims and other liabilities	353.6	368.7
Total liabilities	$4,691.8	$4,982.7

LEARNING OBJECTIVES

After studying Chapter 13, you should be able to:

1. **Define liabilities, explain the difference between current and long-term liabilities, and describe the uncertainties related to some liabilities.**
2. **Describe how accountants record and report estimated liabilities such as warranties and income taxes and how they report contingent liabilities.**
3. **Describe how accountants record and report short-term notes payable.**
4. **Explain and calculate the present value of an amount to be paid at a future date and the present value of a series of equal amounts to be paid at future dates.**
5. **Describe how accountants use present value concepts in accounting for long-term notes, and how liabilities may result from leasing assets.**
6. **Calculate the number of times a company earns its fixed interest charges and describe what it reveals about a company's situation.**
7. **Define or explain the words and phrases listed in the chapter glossary.**

Previous chapters have described liabilities for accounts payable, notes payable, wages payable, and unearned revenues. In this chapter, you will learn about liabilities arising from warranties, income taxes, borrowing, asset purchases and leases. We also describe contingent liabilities and the important concept of present value. As you study this chapter, you will learn how accountants define, classify, and measure liabilities for the purpose of reporting useful information about them.

DEFINING AND CLASSIFYING LIABILITIES

LO 1

Define liabilities, explain the difference between current and long-term liabilities, and describe the uncertainties related to some liabilities.

In general, a liability means that because of a past event, a business has a present obligation to make a future payment. More precisely, liabilities are probable future payments of assets or services that an entity is presently obligated to make as a result of past transactions or events.[1] As shown in the diagram, this definition involves three dimensions in time:

• The company is obligated in the present

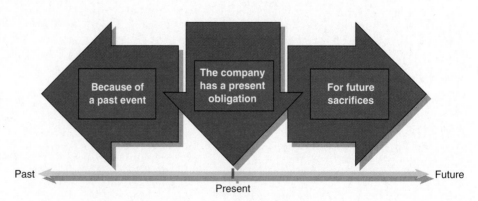

_____

[1] *CICA Handbook*, section 1000, "Financial Statement Concepts," par. 32.

- To pay out assets or deliver services in the future
- Because of an event in the past

This definition also tells us that liabilities do not include all expected future payments. For example, suppose that a company expects to pay wages to its employees in the coming months. These future payments are not liabilities because the company is not presently obligated to pay them. The company is not presently obligated because the employees have not yet earned the future wages. In other words, no past transaction has resulted in a present obligation. The liabilities will be created in the future only when the employees actually perform the work.

Current and Long-Term Liabilities

Information about liabilities is more useful when the balance sheet identifies the liabilities as current and long-term. *Current liabilities* are due within one year or the company's operating cycle, whichever is longer.[2] Typical current liabilities include accounts payable, short-term notes payable, wages payable, warranty liabilities, lease liabilities, payroll and other taxes payable, and unearned revenues.

Obligations that are not expected to be paid within one year (or a longer operating cycle) should be classified as *long-term liabilities*. Typical long-term liabilities include long-term notes payable, warranty liabilities, lease liabilities, and bonds payable. On the balance sheet, these may be presented in a single long-term liabilities section. However, many companies show them as two or more items such as *long-term debt* and *other liabilities*. For example, the liabilities of Safeway Inc., on page 601 include long-term debt, deferred income taxes, and accrued claims and other liabilities. All of these are reported below current liabilities and are understood to be non-current (long-term) liabilities.

Some kinds of liabilities may be either current or long term. A specific debt is assigned to a category on the basis of how soon it will be paid. In fact, a single liability is divided between the two categories if the company expects to make payments in both the near and more distant future. For example, recall the liabilities of **Safeway Inc.** Notice that the first two current liabilities represent the current portions of the two items listed as long-term debt.

A few liabilities do not have a fixed due date because they are payable on the creditor's demand. They are reported as current liabilities because they may have to be paid within the year or a longer operating cycle.

Three important questions concerning liabilities are: Who must be paid? When is payment due? How much is to be paid? In many situations, the answers to these three questions are determined at the time the liability is incurred. For example, assume that Coleman Company has an account payable for precisely $100, payable on August 15, 1996, to R. L. Tucker. There is no uncertainty about any of the questions. The company knows whom to pay, when to pay, and how much to pay. Other types of liabilities may be uncertain with respect to one or more of the three questions.

UNCERTAIN ASPECTS OF SOME LIABILITIES

---

[2]Ibid., section 1510, "Current Assets and Current Liabilities," par. .03.

When the Identity of the Creditor Is Uncertain. Some liabilities have uncertainty about who will be paid. For example, a corporation's board of directors creates a liability with a known amount when it declares a dividend payable to the shareholders. Because the dividend will be paid to the investors who actually own shares on a specified future date, the recipients are not known with certainty until that date. Despite this uncertainty, the corporation has a liability that is reported on the balance sheet.

When the Due Date Is Uncertain. In other situations, a company may have an obligation of a known amount to a known creditor, but not know exactly when the debt must be settled. For example, a copy services company may accept fees in advance from a customer who expects to need copies later. Thus, the copy service company has a liability that will be settled by providing services at an unknown future date. Even though this uncertainty exists, the company's balance sheet is complete only if it includes this liability to its customer. (These obligations are reported as current liabilities because they may have to be settled in the short term.)

When the Amount Is Uncertain. In addition, a company may know that an obligation exists but may not know exactly how much will be required to settle it. For example, a company uses electrical power every day but is billed only after the meter has been read. The cost has been incurred and the liability has been created, even though the bill has not been received. As a result, a liability to the utility company is reported with an estimated amount if the balance sheet is prepared before the bill arrives.

Progress Check

(Answers to Progress Checks are provided at the end of the chapter.)

13–1   What is a liability?

13–2   Is every expected future payment a liability?

13–3   If a liability is payable in 15 months, should it be classified as current or long-term?

ESTIMATED LIABILITIES

LO 2

Describe how accountants record and report estimated liabilities such as warranties and income taxes, and how they report contingent liabilities.

Obligations of uncertain amounts that can be reasonably estimated are called **estimated liabilities.** A common example of an estimated liability involves warranties offered by a seller. Other estimated liabilities are created for contracts to provide future services, income taxes, property taxes, and employee benefits such as pensions and health care.

Warranty Liabilities

An estimated liability is created when a company sells products covered by a warranty. In effect, a **warranty** obligates the seller or manufacturer to pay for replacing or repairing the product when it breaks or otherwise fails to perform within a specified period. For example, a used car might be sold with a warranty that covers parts and labour.

To comply with the *full disclosure* and the *matching principles,* the seller must report the expense of providing a warranty during the same period as the revenue from the sales of the product. The seller must also report the obligation under the warranty as a liability, even though it is uncertain about the existence, amount, payee, and date of its future sacrifices. The seller's warranty obligation does not require payments unless the products break and are returned for repairs. Nonetheless, future payments are probable, and the amount of the liability can be estimated using the company's past experience with warranties.

For example, suppose that a dealer sells a used car for $8,000 on December 1, 1996, with a one-year or 15,000-km. warranty that covers repair parts and labour charges. Experience shows that the warranty expense averages about 4% of a car's selling price. In this case, the expense is expected to be $320 ($8,000 × 4%). The dealer records the expense and liability with this entry:

1996					
Dec.	1	Warranty Expense		320.00	
		Estimated Warranty Liability			320.00
		To record the warranty expense and liability at 4%			
		of the selling price.			

This entry causes the expense to be reported on the 1996 income statement. It also causes the warranty liability to appear on the balance sheet for December 31, 1996.

Now, suppose that the customer returns the car for warranty repairs on January 9, 1997. The dealer performs the work by replacing parts that cost $90 and using labour at a cost of $110. This entry records the partial settlement of the estimated warranty liability:

1997					
Jan.	9	Estimated Warranty Liability		200.00	
		Auto Parts Inventory			90.00
		Cash			110.00
		To record the cost of warranty repairs.			

Notice that this entry does not record any additional expense in 1997. Instead, the entry reduces the balance of the estimated warranty liability. The warranty expense was already recorded in 1996, the year the car was sold under the warranty.

What happens if the total warranty costs actually turn out to be more or less than the predicted $320? In fact, some difference is highly likely for any particular car. Over the long term, management should monitor the actual warranty costs to see whether the 4% rate provides useful information. If actual experience reveals a large difference, the rate should be modified for future sales.

Income Tax Liabilities for Corporations

A proprietorship's financial statements do not include income taxes because they do not pay income taxes; instead, they are assessed directly against the owner. However, corporations are subject to income taxes and must estimate the amount of their income tax liability when they prepare interim financial statements. We explain this process in the following paragraphs. Then, in the next section, we discuss deferred income tax liabilities that arise from temporary differences between GAAP and income tax rules.

Income tax expense for a corporation creates a liability that exists until payments are made to the government. Because the taxes are created by the process of earning income, a liability is incurred as soon as the income is earned. However, the taxes must be paid monthly under federal regulations.

For example, suppose that a corporation, Foster, Inc., prepares monthly financial statements. Based on the income earned in January, the company estimates that it owes income taxes of $12,100. The following adjusting entry records the estimate:

Jan.	31	Income Tax Expense	12,100.00	
		Income Taxes Payable		12,100.00
		Accrued income tax expense and liability based on the estimated income for the month of January.		

The estimated tax liability is paid each month. Assuming the tax installment is paid the next month, the following entry records the payment:

Feb.	10	Income Taxes Payable	12,100.00	
		Cash		12,100.00
		Paid the monthly income taxes based on the estimated income for January.		

The process of accruing and then paying the taxes continues throughout the year. However, by the time the annual financial statements are prepared at the end of the year, the company's accountant knows the amount of income that has been earned and the actual amount of income taxes that must be paid. This information allows the accountant to update the expense and liability accounts.

For example, suppose that Foster, Inc.'s accounts include a $22,000 credit balance in the Income Taxes Liability account at December 31, 1996. Information about the company's income for the year shows that the actual liability should be $33,500. This entry records the additional expense and liability:

Dec.	31	Income Tax Expense	11,500.00	
		Income Taxes Payable		11,500.00
		To record additional tax expense and liability.		

The liability will be settled when the company makes its final payment in 1997.

Deferred Income Tax Liabilities

Another special type of income tax liability may be incurred when the amount of income before taxes reported on a corporation's income statement is not the same as the amount of income reported on its income tax return. These differences arise because income tax laws define income differently from GAAP.[3]

---

[3]The differences between the tax laws and GAAP arise because Parliament uses the tax law to generate revenues, stimulate the economy, and otherwise influence behaviour. GAAP, on the other hand, are intended to provide financial information that is useful for decision making.

Some of the differences between the tax law and GAAP are temporary. These *temporary differences* arise when the tax return and the income statement report a revenue or expense in different years. As an example, for tax purposes, companies are often able to deduct higher amounts of amortization in the early years of an asset's life and smaller amounts in the later years. On their income statements, they often report an equal amount of amortization expense in each year. Thus, in the early years, amortization for tax purposes is more than amortization expense on the income statement. Then, in the later years, amortization for tax purposes is less than amortization expense on the income statement.

When there are temporary differences between taxable income on the tax return and income before taxes on the income statement, GAAP requires corporations to calculate income tax expense based on the income reported on the income statement. In the previous example involving amortization, the result is that the income tax expense reported in the early years is more than the amount of income tax payable. This difference is called **deferred income tax.**

For example, assume that after making and recording its income tax payments, a company determines at the end of the year that an additional $25,000 of income tax expense should be recorded. It also determines that only $21,000 is currently due and $4,000 is deferred to future years. The following entry records the end-of-year adjustment:

Dec.	31	Income Tax Expense	25,000.00	
		Income Taxes Payable		21,000.00
		Deferred Income Tax		4,000.00
		To record tax expense and deferred tax.		

In this entry, the credit to Income Taxes Payable represents the amount that is currently due to be paid. The credit to Deferred Income Tax represents the tax payments that are deferred until future years when the temporary difference reverses.

Many companies report deferred income tax liabilities. For example, **Alcan Aluminium Limited's** December 31, 1994, balance sheet shows that Alcan had a deferred income tax liability of $441 million.

In some circumstances, temporary differences may cause a company to pay income taxes before they are reported on the income statement as an expense. If so, the company usually reports a *deferred income tax debit* on its balance sheet that is similar to a prepaid expense. For example, **Dofasco Inc.'s** December 31, 1994, balance sheet reported deferred income taxes of $14.1 million as a current asset.

Goods and Services Tax and Sales Taxes Payable

Sales tax liabilities arise because the federal government and most provincial governments require businesses to act as collection agencies for the Goods and Services Tax (GST) and provincial sales taxes (PSTs). When a business makes a sale, the customer is charged for the sales tax on top of the selling price, in most cases, and the tax is later paid to the government(s).

Chapter 6 illustrated how the sales taxes would be accumulated in the sales journal. Assume that Superior Clothing Store collected $8,750 of GST and $7,500 of PST during September. At the end of September these amounts would appear on the balance sheet as current liabilities. The entry to pay these taxes during October would be as follows:

Oct.	25	GST Payable	8,750	
		Cash		8,750
		To pay GST for September.		
		PST Payable	7,500	
		Cash		7,500
		To pay PST for September.		

Note that the sales taxes are neither a revenue nor an expense for the enterprise. However, when a business purchases goods and services for its own use, the sales taxes paid become part of the cost of these items. In the case of goods purchased for resale, either the business would be exempt from paying the sales taxes on the purchase or the sales taxes paid could be deducted from the sales taxes collected when determining the amount to be remitted to the government(s).

Progress Check

13-4 Estimated liabilities would include an obligation to pay
  a. An uncertain but reasonably estimated amount to a specific person on a specific date.
  b. A known amount to a specific person on an uncertain due date.
  c. A known amount to an uncertain person on a known due date.
  d. All of the above.

13-5 An automobile was sold for $15,000 on June 1, 1996, with a one-year warranty that covers parts and labour. Based on past experience, warranty expense is estimated at 1.5% of the selling price. On March 1, 1997, the customer returned the car for warranty repairs that used replacement parts at a cost of $75 and labour at a cost of $60. The amount that should be recorded as warranty expense at the time of the March 1 repairs is (a) $0, (b) $60, (c) $75, (d) $135, (e) $225.

13-6 Why would a corporation accrue an income tax liability for interim reports?

CONTINGENT LIABILITIES

Sometimes, past transactions have the effect of requiring a future payment only if some uncertain future event takes place. If the likelihood that the uncertain future event will occur is remote, the company is not required to report a liability in the statements or the notes. However, if the uncertain future event is likely and the amount of the payment can be reasonably estimated, the company is required to report the anticipated payment as a liability.[4]

Contingent liabilities involve situations that fall between these two extremes. One situation is that the uncertain future event is likely but the amount of the payment cannot be reasonably estimated. For example, the company is being sued by a customer but is defending itself and cannot determine what the final outcome will be.

[4]Ibid, section 3290, "Contingencies," par. .06.

The other is that the uncertain future event is not likely but has a reasonable possibility of occurring. The company has guaranteed a loan for an affiliated company and it is unlikely that the loan will go into default. These contingent liabilities are not recorded in the books as liabilities. However, the *full-disclosure principle* requires disclosure of contingent liabilities in the financial statements or in the notes.

Distinguishing between Liabilities and Contingent Liabilities

Contingent liabilities become definite obligations only if some previously uncertain event actually takes place. For example, a typical contingent liability is a discounted note receivable that becomes a definite obligation only if the original signer of the note fails to pay it at maturity. We discussed this example in Chapter 8.

Does a product warranty create a liability or a contingent liability? A product warranty requires service or payment only if the product fails and the customer returns it for service. These conditions make it appear to be like a contingent liability. However, the contingent obligation should be recorded in the books as a liability if the occurrence of the future contingency is likely and if the amount of the liability can be reasonably estimated. Therefore, product warranties are usually recorded as liabilities because: (1) the failure of some percentage of the sold products is likely, and (2) past experience allows the seller to develop a reasonable estimate of the amount to be paid.

Other Examples of Contingent Liabilities

Potential Legal Claims. In today's legal environment, many companies find themselves being sued for damages for a variety of reasons. The accounting question is this: Should the defendant recognize a liability on the balance sheet or disclose a contingent liability in the notes while a lawsuit is outstanding and not yet settled? The answer is that the potential claim should be recorded as a liability only if a payment for damages is likely and the amount can be reasonably estimated. If the potential claim cannot be reasonably estimated or its occurrence is not determinable, it should be described as a contingent liability.

Debt Guarantees. Sometimes a company will guarantee the payment of a debt owed by a supplier, customer, or other company. Usually, the guarantor describes the guarantee in the notes to the financial statements as a contingent liability. However, if it is likely that the original debtor will default, the guarantor needs to record and report the guarantee as a liability.

Other Uncertainties

All companies and other organizations face major uncertainties from future economic events, including natural disasters and the development of new competing products. If these events do occur, they may destroy the company's assets or drive it out of business. However, these uncertainties are not liabilities because they are future events that are not a result of past transactions. Financial statements are not useful if they include speculation about possible effects of events that have not yet occurred.

Be sure to read the comment by Susan Selfe in As a Matter of Opinion. She discusses additional liabilities that companies may need to describe in the future if accounting principles are changed.

As a Matter of Opinion

Susan Selfe (Suominen) is a 1990 graduate of Wilfrid Laurier University's Business Administration CO-OP program. She joined Shell Canada in Toronto as a business analyst and later Household Financial as an internal auditor. In 1993 she was hired by Fidelity Investments Canada as a financial analyst. Fidelity Investments is the 6th largest mutual fund company in Canada and is the Canadian subsidiary of Boston based Fidelity Investments Limited, the world's largest mutual fund company. Since joining Fidelity, Susan obtained her CMA designation and successfully passed the Canadian Securities Course (CSC). In 1995 she was promoted to Senior Financial Analyst where she leads a team that is responsible for reporting the monthly financial and business results to Fidelity's senior management in Canada and the United States. In addition to being involved in project analysis, she also coordinates the quarterly forecast for over 30 cost centres.

Over the past several years, accountants have begun to pay much more attention to the potential future payments that businesses may be obligated to make as a result of current operations. A good example involves the promises of employers to pay health care benefits for their retired employees. The CICA's Accounting Standards Board expects to issue an Exposure Draft in 1996. Companies presently do not report this obligation except by reporting an expense for actual payments they had already made. The Exposure Draft may require them to provide information about their obligations and to recognize the expenses for probable future payments.

Are there other obligations that we presently ignore but someday may have to recognize as liabilities? I would not be surprised. One that comes to mind is potential claims from injuries to product users. Some juries have given large awards many years after a product was sold. Another possible liability is the cost of cleaning up toxic wastes discarded before anyone was aware of the danger.

Nobody can say whether these particular examples will eventually result in new liabilities or disclosures. But, I have no doubt that accounting will continue to evolve in response to an increasing emphasis on the obligations of doing business responsibly.

Susan Selfe, BBA, CMA

Progress Check

13-7   A future payment should be reported as a liability on a company's balance sheet if the payment is contingent on a future event that:
   a. Is not likely but is reasonably possible and the amount of the payment cannot be reasonably estimated.
   b. Is likely and the amount of the payment can be reasonably estimated.
   c. Is not likely but the amount of the payment is known.

13-8   Under what circumstances should a future payment be reported in the financial statements as a contingent liability?

ACCOUNTING FOR KNOWN LIABILITIES

Most liabilities arise in situations with little uncertainty. The procedures used to account for these debts are described in the following sections of the chapter. The topics include:

- Short-term notes payable.
- Long-term notes payable.
- Lease liabilities.

In addition, we introduce you to present value calculations that accountants use when accounting for long-term liabilities and interest expense. Payroll liabilities were discussed in Chapter 10.

A short-term note payable may be created when a company purchases merchandise on credit and then extends the credit period by signing a note that replaces the account. Short-term notes payable also arise when money is borrowed from a financial institution.

SHORT-TERM NOTES PAYABLE

LO 3

Describe how accountants record and report short-term notes payable.

Note Given to Extend a Credit Period

In some cases, a company may create a note payable to replace an account payable. For example, a creditor may ask that an interest-bearing note be substituted for an account that does not bear interest. In other situations, the borrower's weak financial condition may encourage the creditor to obtain a note and close the account to ensure that additional credit sales are not made to this customer.

For example, assume that on August 23, Broke Company asks to extend its past-due $600 account payable to Smart Company. After some negotiations, Smart agrees to accept $100 cash and a 60-day, 12%, $500 note payable to replace the account payable. The accountant for Broke records the substitution with this entry:

Aug.	23	Accounts Payable—Smart Company	600.00	
		Cash		100.00
		Notes Payable		500.00
		Paid $100 cash and gave a 60-day, 12% note to		
		extend the due date on the account.		

Notice that signing the note does not pay off the debt. Instead, the debt's form is merely changed from an account to a note payable. Smart Company may prefer to have the note because it earns interest and because it provides reliable documentation of the debt's existence, term, and amount.

When the note becomes due, Broke will pay the note and interest by giving Smart a cheque for $509.86 and then record the payment with this entry:

Oct.	22	Notes Payable	500.00	
		Interest Expense	9.86	
		Cash		509.86
		Paid note with interest ($500 × 12% × 60/365).		

Note that the interest expense is calculated by multiplying the principal of the note by the original rate for the fraction of the year the note was outstanding.

Borrowing from a Bank

When making a loan, a bank typically requires the borrower to sign a promissory note. When the note matures, the borrower pays back a larger amount. The difference between the two amounts is *interest*. In many situations, the note states that the signer of the note promises to pay the *principal* (the amount borrowed) plus the interest. If so, the *face value* of the note equals the principal.

In other situations, the bank may have the borrower sign a note with a face value that includes both the principal and the interest. In these cases, the signer of the note borrows less than the note's face value. The difference between the borrowed amount and the note's face value is interest. Because the borrowed amount is less than the face value, the difference is sometimes called the **discount on note payable.** To illustrate these two kinds of loans, assume that Robin Goode borrows $2,000 from a bank on behalf of the Goode Company. The loan is made on September 30 and will be repaid in 60 days. It has a 12% annual interest rate.

Face Value Equals the Amount Borrowed. Suppose that the bank requires Goode to sign a loan with a face value equal to the borrowed $2,000. If so, the note will include the following phrase: "I promise to pay $2,000 plus interest at 12% sixty days after September 30." The Goode Company records the increase in cash and the new liability with this entry:

Sept.	30	Cash	2,000.00	
		Notes Payable		2,000.00
		Borrowed cash with a 60-day, 12% note.		

When the note and interest are paid 60 days later, Goode records the event with this entry:

Nov.	29	Notes Payable	2,000.00	
		Interest Expense	39.45	
		Cash		2,039.45
		Paid note with interest ($2,000 × 12% × 60/365).		

Face Value Equals the Amount Borrowed and the Interest. If Goode's bank wishes, it may draw up a note that includes the 12% interest in its face value. If so, the note contains the following promise: "I promise to pay $2,039.45 sixty days after September 30." Notice that the note does not refer to the rate that was used to compute the $39.45 of interest included in the $2,039.45 face value. In all other respects, the note is exactly the same. However, the lack of a stated rate of interest sometimes causes an agreement like this one to be called a **noninterest-bearing note.** In fact, this widely used term is not precise because the note does bear interest, which is included in the face value.

When the face value of the note includes principal and interest, Goode could record the debt with an entry exactly like the previous September 30 entry. However, the more typical practice is to credit Notes Payable for the face value of the note and record the discount in a contra account. The following entry takes this approach:

Sept.	30	Cash	2,000.00	
		Discount on Notes Payable	39.45	
		Notes Payable		2,039.45
		Borrowed cash with a 60-day, 12% note (Discount		
		= $2,000 × 12% × 60/365).		

The Discount on Notes Payable account is contra to the Notes Payable account. If a balance sheet is prepared on September 30, the $39.45 discount is subtracted from the $2,039.45 balance in the Notes Payable account to reflect the $2,000 net amount borrowed.

When the note matures 60 days later on November 29, the entry to record Goode's $2,039.45 payment to the bank is:

Nov.	29	Notes Payable	2,039.45	
		Interest Expense	39.45	
		Cash		2,039.45
		Discount on Notes Payable		39.45
		Paid note with interest.		

If the end of an accounting period falls between the signing of a note payable and its maturity date, the *matching principle* requires the accountant to record the accrued but unpaid interest on the note. For example, suppose that Robin Goode borrowed $2,000 on December 16, 1996, instead of September 30. The 60-day note matures on February 14, 1997. Because the company's fiscal year ends on December 31, the accountant records interest expense for the 15 days in December. The entries depend on the form of the note.

ADJUSTMENTS AT THE END OF THE REPORTING PERIOD

Face Value Equals the Amount Borrowed. If the note's face value equals the amount borrowed, the accrued interest is charged to expense and credited to an Interest Payable account. To illustrate, assume that the $2,000 note signed by Goode on December 16 bears 12% interest. Because 15 out of the 60 days covered by the note have elapsed by December 31, one-fourth (15 days/60 days) of the $39.45 total interest is an expense of 1996. Goode records this expense with the following adjusting entry at the end of 1996:

1996				
Dec.	31	Interest Expense	9.86	
		Interest Payable		9.86
		To record accrued interest on note payable		
		($2,000 × 12% × 15/365).		

When the note matures on February 14, Goode records this entry:

1997				
Feb.	14	Interest Expense ($2,000 × 12% × 45/365)	29.59	
		Interest Payable	9.86	
		Notes Payable	2,000.00	
		Cash		2,039.45
		Paid note with interest.		

The entry recognizes the 45 days of interest expense for 1997 and removes the balances of the two liability accounts.

Face Value Equals the Amount Borrowed and the Interest. Now assume that the face value of the note includes the interest. For example, assume that Goode signed a $2,039.45 noninterest-bearing note on December 15. In recording the note, Goode credited the $2,039.45 face value of the note to Notes Payable and debited the $39.45 discount to a contra account. This adjusting entry is needed to record the accrual of 15 days of interest at the end of 1996:

Dec.	31	Interest Expense	9.86	
		Discount on Notes Payable		9.86
		To record accrued interest on note payable		
		($2,000 × 12% × 15/365).		

Observe that the accrued interest is not credited to Interest Payable. Instead, the entry reduces the balance of the contra account from $39.45 to $29.59. As a result, it increases the net liability to $2,009.46 ($2,039.45 − $29.59).

When the note matures, the following entry accrues the interest expense for the last 45 days of the note and records its payment:

1997				
Feb.	14	Interest Expense	29.59	
		Notes Payable	2,039.45	
		Discount on Notes Payable		29.59
		Cash		2,039.45
		Paid note with interest ($2,000 × 12% × 45/365).		

Progress Check

13-9   **Why would a creditor want a past-due account to be replaced by a note?**

13-10   **A company borrows money for six months by signing a $1,050 note payable. In recording the transaction, the company's bookkeeper correctly debited $50 to Discount on Notes Payable. How much was borrowed? What annual rate of interest was charged?**

LONG-TERM LIABILITIES

In addition to current liabilities, companies often have liabilities that are repaid after one year (or a longer operating cycle). These *long-term liabilities* can arise when money is borrowed from a bank or when a note is issued to buy an asset. A long-term liability also may be created when a company enters into a multiyear lease agreement that is similar to buying the asset. Each of these liability arrangements is described in this chapter. In addition, large companies often borrow money by issuing *bonds* to a number of creditors. These securities are usually long-term liabilities that exist as long as 30 years or more. Accounting for bonds is described in Chapter 17.

Because of the extended lives of long-term liabilities, accounting for them is often more complicated than accounting for short-term liabilities. In particular, the accountant may need to apply present value techniques to measure a long-term liability when it is created and to assign interest expense to each of the years in the liability's life.

Information based on the concept of **present value** enters into many financing and investing decisions. It also enters into accounting for liabilities resulting from those decisions. Therefore, an understanding of present value is important for all business students.

PRESENT VALUE CONCEPTS

LO 4

Explain and calculate the present value of an amount to be paid at a future date and the present value of a series of equal amounts to be paid at future dates.

Because this chapter focuses on liabilities, we explain present value concepts by referring to future cash outflows, payables, and interest expense. However, the same concepts also apply to future cash inflows, receivables, and interest income. The most fundamental present value concept is based on the idea that an amount of cash to be paid (or received) in the future has less value now than the same amount of cash to be paid (or received) today.

For example, $1 to be paid one year from now has a present value that is less than $1. To see why this is true, assume that $0.9259 is borrowed for one year at 8% interest. The amount of interest that will be incurred is $0.9259 × 8% = $0.0741. When the $0.0741 interest is added to the $0.9259, the sum equals the $1 payment that is necessary to repay the debt with interest, as shown here:

Amount borrowed	$0.9259
Interest for one year at 8%	0.0741
Total debt after one year	$1.0000

In this example, the $0.9259 borrowed amount is the present value of the $1 future payment. To state the concept more generally, a borrowed amount is the present value of a future payment if the borrowed amount generates interest at a given rate and the future payment will repay the debt with interest.[5]

To carry this example of present value further, assume that the $1 payment is to be made after two years and the 8% interest is to be compounded annually. Compounding means that interest during the second period is based on the sum of the amount borrowed plus the interest accrued during the first period. In other words,

---

[5]Exactly the same analysis applies to an investment. If $0.9259 is invested at 8%, it will generate $0.0741 interest revenue in one year, thereby amounting to a $1 receipt of principal and interest.

the second period's interest is 8% multiplied by the sum of the original amount borrowed plus the interest earned during the first period.

In this example, where $1 is to be paid back after two years, the amount that can be borrowed (the present value) is $0.8573. The following calculation shows why $0.8573 is the present value:

Amount borrowed during first year	$0.8573
Interest during first year ($0.8573 × 8%)	0.0686
Amount borrowed during second year	$0.9259
Interest during second year ($0.9259 × 8%)	0.0741
Total debt after two years	$1.0000

Notice that the first year's interest is added to the principal amount borrowed so that the second year's interest is based on $0.9259.[6]

Unless otherwise noted, the interest rates used in this text are annual rates and interest is compounded annually.

Present Value Tables

The present value of $1 to be paid after a number of periods in the future can be calculated by using this formula: $1/(1 + i)^n$. The symbol i in the equation is the interest rate per period and n is the number of periods until the future payment must be made. For example, the present value of $1 to be paid after two periods at 8% is $1/(1.08)^2$, which equals $0.8573.

Although you can use this formula to find present values, other techniques are available. For example, many electronic calculators are preprogrammed to find present values. You can also use a **present value table** that shows present values computed with the formula at various interest rates for different time periods. In fact, many students find it helpful to learn how to make the calculations with the tables and then move on to use a calculator when they become comfortable with present value concepts.

Table 13–1 shows present values of a future payment of $1 for up to 10 periods at five different interest rates. The present values in the table have been rounded to four decimal places.[7] (This table is taken from a larger and more complete table in Appendix F at the end of the book.)

To use this table, notice that the first value in the 8% column in Table 13–1 is 0.9259. We used this value in the previous section as the present value of $1 at 8%. Go down one row in the same 8% column to find the present value of $1 discounted at 8% for two years. You should find the value of 0.8573 that we used in the second example. This value means that $0.8573 is the present value of the obligation to pay $1 after two periods, discounted at 8% per period.

---

[6]Benjamin Franklin is said to have described compounding with this expression: "The money money makes makes more money."

[7]Four decimal places are sufficient for the applications described in this book. Other situations may require more precision.

Table 13-1
Present Value of $1

	Rate				
Periods	2%	4%	6%	8%	10%
1	0.9804	0.9615	0.9434	0.9259	0.9091
2	0.9612	0.9246	0.8900	0.8573	0.8264
3	0.9423	0.8890	0.8396	0.7938	0.7513
4	0.9238	0.8548	0.7921	0.7350	0.6830
5	0.9057	0.8219	0.7473	0.6806	0.6209
6	0.8880	0.7903	0.7050	0.6302	0.5645
7	0.8706	0.7599	0.6651	0.5835	0.5132
8	0.8535	0.7307	0.6274	0.5403	0.4665
9	0.8368	0.7026	0.5919	0.5002	0.4241
10	0.8203	0.6756	0.5584	0.4632	0.3855

Using a Present Value Table

To demonstrate how an accountant can measure a liability by using a present value table like Table 13–1, assume that a company plans to borrow cash and then repay it as follows:

To be paid back after one year	$ 2,000
To be paid back after two years	3,000
To be paid back after three years	5,000
Total to be paid back	$10,000

If the company will have to pay 10% interest on this loan, how much will it be able to borrow? The answer is that it can borrow the present value of the three future payments, discounted at 10%. This is calculated in Illustration 13–1 with values from Table 13–1. The illustration shows that the company can borrow $8,054 at 10% in exchange for its promise to make the three payments at the scheduled dates.

Present Values of Annuities

The $8,054 present value of the loan in Illustration 13–1 is the sum of the present values of the three different payments. If the expected cash flows for a liability are not equal, their combined present value must be found by calculating each of their individual present values. In other cases, a loan may create an **annuity,** this is a series of equal payments occurring at equal time intervals. The present value of an annuity can be found with fewer calculations.

For example, suppose that a company can repay a 6% loan by making a $5,000 payment at the end of each year for the next four years. The amount to be borrowed under this loan equals the present value of the four payments discounted at 6%. The present value is calculated in Illustration 13–2 by multiplying each payment by the appropriate value from Table 13–1. The illustration shows that the company can borrow $17,326 under these terms.

Illustration 13-1
Finding the Present
Value of a Series of
Unequal Payments

Years from Now	Expected Payments	Present Value of $1 at 10%	Present Value of Expected Payments
1	$2,000	0.9091	$1,818
2	3,000	0.8264	2,479
3	5,000	0.7513	3,757
Total present value of the payments . .			$8,054

Illustration 13-2
Finding the Present
Value of a Series of
Equal Payments (an
Annuity) by Discounting
Each Payment

Years from Now	Expected Payments	Present Value of $1 at 6%	Present Value of Expected Payments
1	$5,000	0.9434	$ 4,717
2	5,000	0.8900	4,450
3	5,000	0.8396	4,198
4	5,000	0.7921	3,961
Total		3.4651	$17,326

Because the series of $5,000 payments is an annuity, the accountant can determine the present value with either of two shortcuts. As shown in the third column of Illustration 13–2, the total of the present values of $1 at 6% for 1 through 4 periods equals 3.4651. One shortcut multiplies this total of 3.4651 by the $5,000 annual payment to get the combined present value of $17,326. This shortcut requires only one multiplication instead of four.

The second shortcut uses an *annuity table* such as Table 13–2.[8] (Table 13–2 is taken from a more complete table in Appendix F at the end of the book.) Instead of having to take the sum of the individual present values from Table 13–1, you can go directly to the annuity table to find the present (table) value that relates to a specific number of payments and a specific interest rate. Then, you multiply this table value by the amount of the payment to find the present value of all the payments in the annuity.

To continue the example, the second shortcut proceeds as follows: Enter Table 13–2 on the row for four payments and go across until you reach the column for 6%; you will find the value 3.4651. This amount equals the present value of an annuity with four payments of $1, discounted at 6%. Then, multiply 3.4651 times $5,000 to get the $17,326 present value of the annuity.

---

[8]The formula for finding the Table values is: $\dfrac{1 - \dfrac{1}{(1 + i)^n}}{i}$

However, the present values in Table 13–2 can be found by adding the values of the individual payments in Table 13–1. (Because the tables show only four decimal places, there are some ±0.0001 rounding differences between them.)

Table 13–2
Present Value of an
Annuity of $1

	Rate				
Payments	**2%**	**4%**	**6%**	**8%**	**10%**
1	0.9804	0.9615	0.9434	0.9259	0.9091
2	1.9416	1.8861	1.8334	1.7833	1.7355
3	2.8839	2.7751	2.6730	2.5771	2.4869
4	3.8077	3.6299	3.4651	3.3121	3.1699
5	4.7135	4.4518	4.2124	3.9927	3.7908
6	5.6014	5.2421	4.9173	4.6229	4.3553
7	6.4720	6.0021	5.5824	5.2064	4.8684
8	7.3255	6.7327	6.2098	5.7466	5.3349
9	8.1622	7.4353	6.8017	6.2469	5.7590
10	8.9826	8.1109	7.3601	6.7101	6.1446

COMPOUNDING PERIODS SHORTER THAN A YEAR

In the previous examples, the interest rates were applied to periods of one year. However, in many situations, interest is compounded over shorter periods. For example, the interest rate on bonds is usually described as an annual rate but the interest is actually paid every six months. As a result, the present value of the interest payments to be received from these bonds must be based on interest periods that are six months long.

To illustrate a calculation based on six-month interest periods, suppose that a borrower wants to know the present value of a series of ten $4,000 semiannual payments to be made over five years. These payments are to be discounted with an *annual* interest rate of 8%. Although the interest rate is described as an annual rate of 8%, it is actually a rate of 4% per six-month interest period. To find the present value of the series of $4,000 payments, enter Table 13–2 on row 10 and go across to the 4% column. The table value is 8.1109, and the present value of the annuity is $32,444 (8.1109 × $4,000).

Study Appendix F at the end of the book to learn more about present value concepts. The appendix includes more complete present value tables and provides future value tables. It also includes exercises that will help you understand discounting.

Progress Check

13-11 A company enters into an agreement to make four annual payments of $1,000 each, starting one year from now. The annual interest rate is 8%. The present value of these four payments is: *(a)* $2,923; *(b)* $2,940; *(c)* $3,312; *(d)* $4,000; *(e)* $6,733.

13-12 Suppose that a company has an option to pay either $10,000 after one year or $5,000 after six months and another $5,000 after one year. Which choice always has the smaller present value?

APPLYING PRESENT VALUE CONCEPTS TO LONG-TERM NOTES

Earlier in the chapter, we stated that accountants use present value concepts to measure liabilities and to assign or allocate interest expense to each reporting period in a liability's life. In doing this, the liability is initially measured as the present value of the future payments. Over the life of the note, the amount of interest allocated to each period equals the product of multiplying the original interest rate by the balance of the liability at the beginning of the period. The balance at any

LO 5

Describe how accountants
use present value con-
cepts in accounting for
long-term notes and how
liabilities may result from
leasing assets.

point in time equals the original balance plus any allocated interest less any payments.[9]

Interest-Bearing Notes that Require a Single Payment

Suppose that a company buys equipment on January 2 with a fair market value of
$45,000 by issuing an 8%, three-year note, with all of the interest paid at matu-
rity. If the 8% interest is at the prevailing market rate, the face value of the note
should be $45,000. The buyer records the purchase with this entry:

Jan.	2	Store Equipment	45,000.00	
		Notes Payable		45,000.00
		Issued a $45,000, three-year, 8% note payable for		
		store equipment.		

Over the life of the note, the issuer reports annual interest expense equal to the
original interest rate times each year's beginning balance for the liability. Illustration 13–3 shows the interest allocation. Note that the interest is allocated by multiplying each year's beginning balance by the original 8% interest rate. Then, the
interest is added to the beginning balance to find the ending balance, which then
becomes the next year's beginning balance. Because the balance grows through
compounding, the amount of interest allocated to each year increases over the life
of the note. The final ending balance of $56,687 equals the original $45,000 borrowed plus the total interest of $11,687.

Noninterest-Bearing Notes

Earlier in the chapter, we described so-called noninterest-bearing notes, which include the interest in their initial face values. When a noninterest-bearing note is
used to purchase an asset, the note's face value is greater than the asset's fair value.
As a result, the asset and the note should be recorded at the asset's fair value or at
the note's fair value, whichever is more clearly determinable. The note's fair value
can be estimated by finding the present value of its payments discounted at the
market interest rate when it was issued.

For example, suppose that Harborg Company buys machinery on January 2,
1996, by issuing a noninterest-bearing, five-year, $10,000 note payable. The com-
pany's managers conclude that their estimate of the asset's fair value is less reliable than is the current 10% interest rate available to the company.

When the note is issued, its fair value equals the present value of the $10,000
payment due after five years discounted at 10%. Table 13–1 shows us that the present value of 1 discounted at 10% for five years is 0.6209. Thus, the present (fair)
value of the note is calculated as $10,000 × 0.6209 = $6,209. This is also the implied fair value of the asset. The following entry records the purchase:

---

[9]The liability's balance at any date equals the present value of all remaining future payments, discounted at the original interest rate.

Illustration 13-3 Allocation of Interest on a Note with All Interest Paid at Maturity

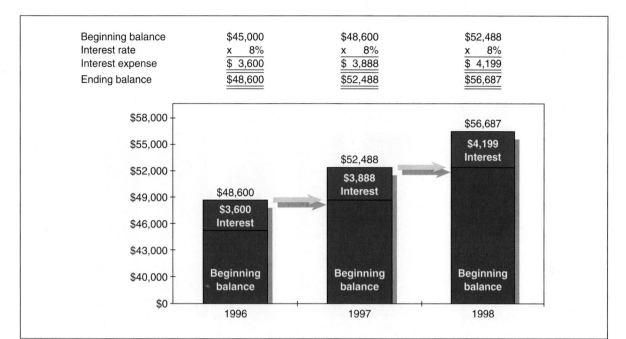

Beginning balance	$45,000	$48,600	$52,488
Interest rate	x 8%	x 8%	x 8%
Interest expense	$ 3,600	$ 3,888	$ 4,199
Ending balance	$48,600	$52,488	$56,687

1996				
Jan.	2	Machinery	6,209.00	
		Discount on Notes Payable	3,791.00	
		Long-Term Notes Payable		
		Cash		10,000.00
		Exchanged a five-year noninterest-bearing note for a machine.		

By recording the maturity value in one account and the discount in a contra account, the entry follows the typical approach of recording a noninterest-bearing note. In the entry, the $3,791 debit to Discount on Notes Payable equals the total amount of interest that must be allocated to the five years in the note's life.

In Illustration 13–4, we calculate each year's interest and show the effect of the allocation on the discount and the net liability. The net liability balance grows over the five years until it reaches the maturity amount of $10,000. Note also that the discount balance decreases to $0 after five years. Because the discount is gradually reduced to zero, this process is often referred to as *amortizing the discount.*

Notice that the process of calculating each year's interest is the same as it was in the previous discussion of interest-bearing notes that require a single payment. The net liability balance at the beginning of each year is multiplied by the 10% interest rate to determine the interest for the year.

The first year's interest and reduction of the discount are recorded when the accountant makes this year-end adjusting entry:

Illustration 13–4   Allocating Interest Expense over the Life of a Noninterest-Bearing Note

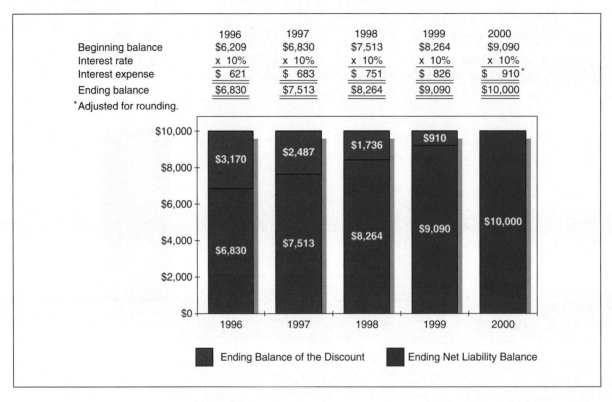

	1996	1997	1998	1999	2000
Beginning balance	$6,209	$6,830	$7,513	$8,264	$9,090
Interest rate	x 10%	x 10%	x 10%	x 10%	x 10%
Interest expense	$ 621	$ 683	$ 751	$ 826	$ 910*
Ending balance	$6,830	$7,513	$8,264	$9,090	$10,000

*Adjusted for rounding.

1996 Dec.	31	Interest Expense	621.00	
		Discount on Notes Payable		621.00
		To record interest expense accrued on a noninterest-bearing note.		

Similar entries are recorded at the end of each year until the balance of the discount account equals $0, and the net liability balance equals $10,000.

When the note matures on January 2, 2001, the issuer records the payment with this entry:

2001 Jan.	2	Long-Term Notes Payable	10,000.00	
		Cash		10,000.00
		Paid noninterest-bearing note.		

LIABILITIES FROM LEASING

As an alternative to purchasing property, companies can lease it by agreeing to make a series of rental payments to the property owner, who is called the *lessor*. Because a lease gives the property's user (called the *lessee*) exclusive control over the property's usefulness, the lessee can use it to earn revenues. In addition, a lease creates a liability if it has essentially the same effect as purchasing the asset on credit.

According to the generally accepted accounting principles described in *CICA Handbook,* section 3065, "Leases," the lessee's financial statements must report a leased asset and a lease liability if the lease qualifies as a **capital lease.** The essence of a capital lease is that the lease agreement gives the lessee the risks and benefits normally associated with ownership. In general, a capital lease covers a number of years and creates a long-term liability that is paid off with a series of equal payments. For example, **Loblaw Companies Limited** reported that its capital leases for equipment and facilities covered assets with a cost of $88.1 million and a book value of $39.8 million as of December 31, 1994. The leases also involved liabilities of $65.6 million.

When a capital lease is created, the lessee recognizes a leased asset and amortizes it over its useful life. The lessee also recognizes a lease liability and allocates interest expense to the years in the lease. The interest allocation process is the same as we have seen for notes payable.

Leases that are not capital leases are called **operating leases.** With an operating lease, the lessee does not report the lease as an asset. The lessee's income statement reports rent expense and does not report either interest or depreciation expense.

Intermediate accounting textbooks describe more details about the characteristics of leases that cause them to be accounted for as capital or operating. They also describe the financial accounting practices used by the lessor and lessee for capital leases.

Progress Check

13-13   On January 1, 1996, Fairview Co. signed a $6,000 three-year note payable bearing 6% annual interest. The original principal and all interest is to be paid on December 31, 1998. The interest will compound every year. How much interest should be allocated to 1997? *(a)* $0; *(b)* $360; *(c)* $381.60; *(d)* $404.50.

13-14   Suppose that a company promises to pay a lender $4,000 at the end of four years. If the annual interest rate is 8% and the interest is included in the $4,000, what is the amount that the company originally borrowed?

13-15   Which one of the following requires the lessee to record a liability?
(a) Operating lease; *(b)* Lessor; *(c)* Contingent liability; *(d)* Capital lease.

A company incurs interest expense when it issues notes or bonds and when it enters into capital leases. Many of these liabilities are long-term obligations that are likely to remain outstanding for a substantial period of time even if the company experiences a decline in sales. As a result, interest expense is often viewed as a fixed cost. That is, the amount of interest is not likely to fluctuate much as a result of changes in sales volume.

Although fixed costs can be advantageous when a company is growing, they create the risk that the company might not be able to pay them if sales decline. The following example shows a company's results for the current year and two possible outcomes for the next year:

USING THE INFORMATION— TIMES FIXED INTEREST CHARGES EARNED

LO 6

Calculate the number of times a company earns its fixed interest charges and describe what it reveals about a company's situation.

	Current Year	Next Year If Sales Increase	Next Year If Sales Decrease
Sales	$600,000	$900,000	$300,000
Expenses (75% of sales)	450,000	675,000	225,000
Income before interest	$150,000	$225,000	$ 75,000
Interest expense (fixed)	60,000	60,000	60,000
Net income	$ 90,000	$165,000	$ 15,000

As we show in the table, expenses other than interest are projected to stay at 75% of sales. In contrast, the interest is expected to remain at $60,000 per year. Note in the second column that the company's income would nearly double if its sales increased by 50%. However, the company's profits would fall drastically if the sales decreased by 50%. These numbers show that a company's risk is affected by the amount of fixed interest charges that it incurs each year.

The risk created by these fixed expenses can be described numerically with the **times fixed interest charges earned** ratio. You can use the following formula to find the ratio:

$$\text{Times fixed interest charges earned} = \frac{\text{Income before interest}}{\text{Interest expense}}$$

For this company's current year, the income before interest is $150,000. Therefore, the ratio is $150,000/$60,000, which equals 2.5 times. This result suggests that the company faces a relatively low degree of risk. Its sales would have to go down by a large amount before the company would not be able to cover its interest expenses. This condition should provide comfort to the company's creditors and its owners.

Care must be taken in calculating the times fixed interest charges earned ratio for a corporation. Because interest is deducted in determining taxable income, the numerator for a corporation can be expressed as follows:

Income before interest = Net income + Interest expense + Income taxes expense

The times fixed interest charges earned ratio is best interpreted in light of information about the variability of the company's net income before interest. If this amount is stable from year to year, or is growing, the company can afford to take on some of the risk created by borrowing. However, if the company's income before interest varies greatly from year to year, fixed interest charges can increase the risk that the owner will not earn a return or that the company will be unable to pay the interest.

Progress Check

13-16 The times fixed interest charges earned ratio
   a. Equals interest expense divided by net income.
   b. Takes on a larger value as the amount of fixed interest charges gets larger.
   c. Is best interpreted in light of information about the variability of the company's net income before interest.

13-17 Two companies each have net income after interest of $100,000. First Company has fixed interest charges of $200,000 and Second Company has fixed interest charges of $40,000. Which one is in a more risky situation in terms of being affected by a drop in sales?

LO 1. Define liabilities, explain the difference between current and long-term liabilities, and describe the uncertainties related to some liabilities. Liabilities are probable future payments of assets or services that an entity is presently obligated to make as a result of past events. Current liabilities are due within one year or one operating cycle, whichever is longer. All other liabilities are long-term liabilities. Potential uncertainties about a liability include the identity of the creditor, the due date, and the amount to be paid.

LO 2. Describe how accountants record and report estimated liabilities such as warranties and income taxes, and how they report contingent liabilities. If an uncertain future payment depends on a likely future event and the amount can be reasonably estimated, the payment should be reported as a liability. The future payment must be described as a contingent liability if (*a*) the occurrence of the future event is not determinable, or (*b*) the event is likely but the amount of the payment cannot be reasonably estimated.

Liabilities for warranties and income taxes are recorded with estimated amounts to be paid. This practice recognizes the expenses in the time period that they are incurred. Deferred income taxes are recognized if temporary differences between GAAP and tax rules result in recording more or less income tax expense than the amount to be currently paid.

LO 3. Describe how accountants record and report short-term notes payable. Short-term notes payable may be interest-bearing, in which case the face value of the note equals the amount borrowed and the note specifies a rate of interest to be paid until maturity. Noninterest-bearing notes include interest in their face value; thus, the face value equals the amount to be paid when the note matures.

LO 4. Explain and calculate the present value of an amount to be paid at a future date and the present value of a series of equal amounts to be paid at future dates. The primary present value concept is that today's value of an amount of cash to be paid or received in the future is less than today's value of the same amount of cash to be paid or received today. Another present value concept is that interest is compounded, which means that the interest is added to the balance and used to determine interest for succeeding periods. An annuity is a series of equal payments occurring at equal time intervals.

LO 5. Describe how accountants use present value concepts in accounting for long-term notes, and how liabilities may result from leasing assets. Accountants may use present value concepts to determine the fair value of assets purchased in return for issuing debt. They also use present value concepts to allocate interest expense among the periods in a note's life by multiplying the note's beginning-of-period balance by the original interest rate. Noninterest-bearing notes are normally recorded with a discount account that is contra to the liability account. The balance of the discount account is amortized in the process of recognizing interest expense over the note's life.

Leases are an alternative to purchases as a means of gaining the use of assets. Capital leases give the lessee essentially the same risks and potential rewards as ownership. As a result, the leases and related lease obligations are recorded as assets and liabilities. Other leases, which are called operating leases, involve recording rent expense as the asset is used.

LO 6. Calculate the number of times a company earns its fixed interest charges and describe what it reveals about a company's situation. Times fixed interest charges earned is calculated by dividing a company's net income before interest by the amount of fixed interest charges incurred. This ratio describes the cushion that exists to protect the company's ability to pay interest and earn a profit for its owners against declines in its sales.

DEMONSTRATION PROBLEM

The following series of transactions and other events took place at the Kern Company during its calendar reporting year. Describe their effects on the financial statements by presenting the journal entries described in each situation.

a. Throughout September 1996, Kern sold $140,000 of merchandise that was covered by a 180-day warranty. Prior experience shows that the costs of fulfilling the warranty will equal 5% of the sales revenue. Calculate September's warranty expense and the increase in the warranty liability and show how it would be recorded with a September 30 adjusting entry. Also show the journal entry that would be made on October 8 to record an expenditure of $300 cash to provide warranty service on an item sold in September.

b. On October 12, Kern arranged with a supplier to replace an overdue $10,000 account payable by paying $2,500 cash and signing a note for the remainder. The note matured in 90 days and had a 12% interest rate. Show the entries that would be recorded on October 12, December 31, and January 10, 1997 (when the note matures).

c. Kern acquired a machine on December 1 by giving a $60,000 noninterest-bearing note due in one year. The market rate of interest for this type of debt was 10%. Show the entries that would be made when the note is created; as of December 31, 1996, and at maturity on December 1, 1997.

Planning the Solution

• For (a), compute the warranty expense for September and record it with an estimated liability. Record the October expenditure as a decrease in the liability.

• For (b), eliminate the liability for the account payable and create the liability for the note payable. Calculate the interest expense for the 80 days that the note is outstanding in 1996 and record it as an additional liability. Record the payment of the note, being sure to include the interest for the 10 days in 1997.

• For (c), measure the cost of the machinery by finding the present value of the $60,000 cash expected to be paid when the note matures. Record the note at its face value, and use a contra-liability account to record the discount. Accrue 30 days' interest at December 31 by reducing the discount account. At maturity, the journal entry should record additional interest expense for 1997, eliminate the note payable account balance, and eliminate the discount account balance.

Solution to Demonstration Problem

a. Warranty expense = 5% × $140,000 = $7,000

Sept.	30	Warranty Expense	7,000.00	
		Estimated Warranty Liability		7,000.00
		To record warranty expense and liability at 5% of sales for the month.		

Oct.	8	Estimated Warranty Liability	300.00	
		Cash		300.00
		To record the cost of the warranty service.		

b. Interest expense for 1996 = 12% × \$7,500 × 80/365 = \$197.26
Interest expense for 1997 = 12% × \$7,500 × 10/365 = \$24.66

Oct.	12	Accounts Payable	10,000.00	
		Notes Payable		7,500.00
		Cash................................		2,500.00
		Paid \$2,500 cash and gave a 90-day, 12% note to extend the due date on the account.		
Dec.	31	Interest Expense	197.26	
		Interest Payable		197.26
		To accrue interest on note payable.		
Jan.	10	Interest Expense	24.66	
		Interest Payable	197.26	
		Notes Payable	7,500.00	
		Cash................................		7,721.92
		Paid note with interest, including accrued interest payable.		

c. Cost of the asset = Present value of the note
Present value of the note = \$60,000 × Table 13–1 value for
$n = 1$ and $i = 10\%$
Present value of the note = \$60,000 × 0.9091 = \$54,546
Discount on the note   = \$60,000 − \$54,546 = \$5,454

Dec.	1	Machinery	54,546.00	
		Discount on Notes Payable	5,454.00	
		Notes Payable		60,000.00
		Exchanged a one-year, noninterest-bearing note for a machine.		

Interest expense for 1996 = 10% × \$54,546 × 1/12 = \$455
Interest expense for 1997 = \$5,454 − \$455 = \$4,999

Dec.	31	Interest Expense	455.00	
		Discount on Notes Payable		455.00
		To accrue interest on noninterest-bearing note payable.		
1997				
Dec.	1	Interest Expense	4,999.00	
		Notes Payable............................	60,000.00	
		Cash		60,000.00
		Discount on Notes Payable		4,999.00
		Paid noninterest-bearing note payable.		

GLOSSARY

Annuity a series of equal payments occurring at equal time intervals. p. 617

Capital lease a lease that gives the lessee the risks and benefits normally associated with ownership. p. 623

Deferred income tax payments of income taxes that are deferred until future years because of temporary differences between GAAP and tax rules. p. 607

Discount on note payable the difference between the face value of a noninterest-bearing note payable and the amount borrowed; represents interest that will be paid on the note over its life. p. 612

Estimated liability an obligation that is reported as a liability even though the amount to be paid is uncertain. p. 604

Noninterest-bearing note a note that does not have a stated rate of interest; the interest is included in the face value of the note. p. 612

Operating lease a lease that is not a capital lease. p. 623

Present value the amount that can be invested (borrowed) at a given interest rate to generate a total future investment (debt) that will equal the amount of a specified future receipt (payment). p. 615

Present value table a table that shows the present values of an amount to be received when discounted at various interest rates for various periods of time, or the present values of a series of equal payments to be received for a varying number of periods when discounted at various interest rates. p. 616

Times fixed interest charges earned the ratio of a company's income before interest and income taxes divided by the amount of interest charges; used to evaluate the risk of being committed to make interest payments when income varies. p. 624

Warranty an agreement that obligates the seller or manufacturer to repair or replace a product that fails to perform properly within a specified period. p. 604

SYNONYMOUS TERMS

Capital lease financing lease

Carrying value of a note book value of a note

Warranty guarantee

QUESTIONS

1. What is the difference between a current and a long-term liability?

2. What is an estimated liability?

3. What are the three important questions concerning the certainty of liabilities?

4. Suppose that a company has a facility located in an area where disastrous weather conditions often occur. Should it report a probable loss from a future disaster as a liability on its balance sheet? Why?

5. Why are warranty liabilities usually recognized on the balance sheet as liabilities even when they are uncertain?

6. What factors affect the present value of a future $2,000 payment?

7. How would a lease create an asset and a liability for the lessee?

8. What proportion of Geac Computer Corporation Limited's liabilities are long-term?

QUICK STUDY (Five-Minute Exercises)

Which of the following items would normally be classified as a current liability for a company that has a 14-month operating cycle?

a. A note payable due in 18 months.

b. Salaries payable.

c. Bonds payable that mature in two years.

d. A note payable due in 10 months.

e. The portion of a long-term note that is due to be paid in 14 months.

QS 13–1
(LO 1)

On December 20, Compu sold a computer for $3,500 with a one-year warranty that covers parts and labour. Warranty expense was estimated at 2% of sales. On March 2, the computer was turned in for repairs covered under the warranty requiring $50 in parts and $30 of labour. Prepare the March 2 journal entry to record the warranty repairs.

QS 13–2
(LO 2)

On December 11, 1996, the Snyder Company borrowed $42,000 and signed a 60-day, 9% note payable with a face value of $42,000. *(a)* Calculate the accrued interest payable on December 31, and *(b)* present the journal entry to record the paying of the note at maturity.

QS 13–3
(LO 4)

Determine the amount that can be borrowed under each of the following circumstances:

a. A promise to pay $50,000 in six years at an interest rate of 10%.

b. An agreement made on January 2, 1996, to make four payments of $4,200 on January 2 of 1997 through 2000. The annual interest rate was 8%.

QS 13–4
(LO 5)

On January 1, 1996, a company borrowed $40,000 in exchange for an interest-bearing note. The note plus compounded interest at an annual rate of 12% is due on January 1, 1999. Determine the amount that the company will pay on the due date.

QS 13–5
(LO 6)

Calculate the times fixed interest charges earned for a company that has income before interest of $462,000 and interest expense of $98,000.

QS 13–6
(LO 7)

EXERCISES

The following list of items might appear as liabilities on the balance sheet of a company that has a two-month operating cycle. Identify the proper classification of each item. In the space beside each item write *C* if it is a current liability, an *L* if it is a long-term liability, or an *N* if it is not a liability.

Exercise 13–1
Classifying liabilities
(LO 1)

___ *a.* Wages payable.

___ *b.* Notes payable in 60 days.

___ *c.* Mortgage payable (payments due after next 12 months).

___ *d.* Notes receivable in 90 days.

___ *e.* Bonds payable (mature in 10 years).

___ *f.* Mortgage payable (payments due in next 12 months).

___ *g.* Notes payable in 6–12 months.

___ *h.* Income taxes payable.

___ *i.*   Accounts receivable.

___ *j.*   Notes payable in 13–24 months.

Exercise 13–2
Warranty expense and liability
(LO 2)

Sassower Co. sold a computer to a customer on December 4, 1996, for $8,000 cash. Based on prior experience, the company expects to eventually incur warranty costs equal to 5% of this selling price. On January 18, 1997, the customer returned the computer for repairs that were completed on the same day. The cost of the repairs consisted of $198 for the materials taken from the parts inventory and $40 of labour that was fully paid with cash.

a.   How much warranty expense should the company report for December for this computer?

b.   How large is the warranty liability for this computer as of December 31, 1996?

c.   How much warranty expense should the company report for January for this computer?

d.   How large is the warranty liability for this computer as of January 31, 1997?

e.   Show the journal entries that would be made to record (1) the sale; (2) the adjustment as of December 31, 1996, to record the warranty expense; and (3) the repairs that occurred in January.

Exercise 13–3
Accounting for income taxes
(LO 2)

McKeag Corp. prepares interim financial statements each month. As part of the process, estimated income taxes are accrued each month as 30% of the company's income for that month. The estimated income taxes are paid in the next month for the amount accrued in the prior month. These facts are known about the last quarter of 1996:

a.   The company determined that the following amounts of net income occurred for these months:

October 1996	$ 8,500
November 1996	6,000
December 1996	10,000

b.   After the tax return was completed in early January, the accountant determined that the Income Taxes Payable account balance should be $7,480 on December 31.

Required

1.   Determine the amount of the adjustment needed to produce the proper ending balance in the Income Taxes Payable account.

2.   Present the journal entries to record the adjustment to the Income Taxes Payable account upon completion of the return and to record the January 15 payment of the fourth-quarter taxes.

Exercise 13–4
Interest-bearing and noninterest-bearing notes payable
(LO 3)

The Knightwood Co. borrowed $50,000 on September 1, 1996, for 90 days at 8% interest by signing a note.

a.   On what date will this note mature?

b.   How much interest expense is created by this note?

c.   Suppose that the face value of the note equals the principal of the loan. Show the general journal entries to record issuing the note and paying it at maturity.

d.   Suppose that the face value of the note includes the principal of the loan and the interest to be paid at maturity. Show the general journal entries to record issuing the note and paying it at maturity.

The Shelby Co. borrowed $30,000 on December 1, 1996, for 90 days at 10% interest by signing a note.

a. On what date will this note mature?

b. How much interest expense is created by this note in 1995?

c. How much interest expense is created by this note in 1996?

d. Suppose that the face value of the note equals the principal of the loan. Show the general journal entries to record issuing the note, to accrue interest at the end of 1996, and to record paying the note at maturity.

e. Suppose that the face value of the note includes the principal of the loan and the interest to be paid at maturity. Show the general journal entries to record issuing the note, to accrue interest at the end of 1996, and to record paying the note at maturity.

Exercise 13–5
Interest-bearing and noninterest-bearing short-term notes payable with year-end adjustments
(LO 4)

On January 1, 1996, a company has agreed to pay $15,000 after three years. If the annual interest rate is 6%, determine how much cash the company can borrow with this promise. Present a three-column table that shows the beginning balance, interest, and ending balance for 1996, 1997, and 1998.

Exercise 13–6
Present value of a future payment and accumulating interest
(LO 4)

Find the amount of money that can be borrowed with each of the following promises:

	Future Payment	Number of Years	Interest Rate
a.	$80,000	1	6%
b.	80,000	5	6
c.	80,000	5	8
d.	60,000	7	10
e.	10,000	1	2
f.	25,000	9	4

Exercise 13–7
Present value of liabilities
(LO 4)

A company recently borrowed money and agreed to pay it back with a series of three annual payments of $10,000 each. The firm also borrowed cash and agreed to pay it back with a series of seven annual payments of $4,000 each. The annual interest rate for the loans was 10%.

a. Use Table 13–1 to find the present value of these two annuities.

b. Use Table 13–2 to find the present value of these two annuities.

Exercise 13–8
Present value of annuities
(LO 4)

A company borrowed cash on January 2, 1996, by promising to make four payments of $3,000 each at June 30, 1996; December 31, 1996; June 30, 1997; and December 31, 1997.

a. How much cash was the company able to borrow if the interest rate was 12%, compounded semiannually?

b. How much cash was the company able to borrow if the interest rate was 16%, compounded semiannually?

c. How much cash was the company able to borrow if the interest rate was 20%, compounded semiannually?

Exercise 13–9
Semiannual compounding
(LO 4)

The Carson Company purchased some machinery on March 10 that had a cost of $56,000. Show the journal entry that would record this purchase under these four separate situations:

a. The company paid cash for the full purchase price.

b. The company gave an interest-bearing note for the full purchase price.

c. The company gave a noninterest-bearing one-year note for $61,600.

Exercise 13–10
Recording an asset purchase in exchange for a note
(LO 5)

Exercise 13–11
Calculations concerning a
noninterest-bearing note
(LO 5)

On January 2, 1996, the Brewster Co. acquired land by issuing a noninterest-bearing note for $20,000. The fair market value of the land was not reliably known, but the company knew that the market interest rate for the note was 6%. The note matures in three years on January 1, 1999.

a. What is the present value of the note at the time of the purchase?

b. What is the initial balance of the discount on the note payable?

c. Prepare a table that shows the amount of interest that will be allocated to each of the three years in the note's life and the ending balance of the net liability for each year.

d. Prepare a table that determines the ending balance of the discount on the note for each of the three years.

Exercise 13–12
Journal entries for a
noninterest-bearing note
(LO 5)

Use the data in Exercise 13–11 to prepare journal entries for these dates:

a. January 2, 1996 (land purchase).

b. December 31, 1996 (accrual entry).

c. December 31, 1997 (accrual entry).

d. December 31, 1998 (accrual entry).

e. January 1, 1999 (the payment of the note).

Exercise 13–13
Times fixed interest
charges earned
(LO 6)

Use the following information for a proprietorship to compute times fixed interest charges earned:

	Net Income or (Loss)	Interest Expense
a.	$ 85,000	$ 16,000
b.	85,000	40,000
c.	85,000	90,000
d.	240,000	120,000
e.	(25,000)	60,000
f.	96,000	6,000

PROBLEMS

Problem 13–1
Estimated product
warranty liabilities
(LO 2)

On November 10, 1996, Bright Beam Co. began to buy and resell high-powered flashlights for $40 each. The flashlights are covered under a warranty that requires the company to replace any nonworking flashlight within 90 days. When a flashlight is returned, the company simply throws it away and mails a new one from inventory to the customer. The company's cost for a new flashlight is only $7. The manufacturer has advised the company to expect warranty costs to equal 8% of the total sales. These events occurred in 1996 and 1997:

1996

Nov. 15   Sold flashlights for $8,000 cash.

30   Recognized warranty expense for November with an adjusting entry.

Dec. 8   Replaced 15 flashlights that were returned under the warranty.

15   Sold flashlights for $22,000 cash.

29   Replaced 40 flashlights that were returned under the warranty.

31   Recognized warranty expense for December with an adjusting entry.

1997

Jan. 14   Sold flashlights for $11,000 cash.

20   Replaced 63 flashlights that were returned under the warranty.

31   Recognized warranty expense for January with an adjusting entry.

Required

1. How much warranty expense should be reported for November and December of 1996?

2. How much warranty expense should be reported for January 1997?

3. What is the balance of the estimated warranty liability as of December 31, 1996?

4. What is the balance of the estimated warranty liability as of January 31, 1997?

5 Prepare journal entries to record the transactions and adjustments.

The Northside Co. entered into the following transactions involving short-term liabilities during 1996 and 1997:

Problem 13–2
Transactions with short-term notes payable
(LO 4)

1996

Mar. 14   Purchased merchandise on credit from Pete Winston Co. for $12,500. The terms were 1/10, n/30.

Apr. 14   Replaced the account payable to Pete Winston Co. with a 60-day note bearing 10% annual interest. Northside paid $3,500 cash, with the result that the balance of the note was $9,000.

May 21   Borrowed $20,000 from Central Bank by signing an interest-bearing note for $20,000. The annual interest rate was 12%, and the note has a 90-day term.

?   Paid the note to Pete Winston Co. at maturity.

?   Paid the note to Central Bank at maturity.

Dec. 15   Borrowed $35,000 from Eastern Bank by signing a noninterest-bearing note for $36,035.62 that matures in 120 days. (This amount is based on a 9% interest rate.)

31   Recorded an accrual adjusting entry for the interest on the note to Eastern Bank.

1997
?   Paid the note to Eastern Bank at maturity.

Required

1. Determine the maturity dates of the three notes just described.

2. Determine the interest due at maturity for the three notes.

3. Determine the interest to be recorded in the adjusting entry at the end of 1996.

4. Determine the interest to be recorded in 1997.

5. Present journal entries for all the preceding events and adjustments.

Sherlock Enterprises is negotiating the purchase of a new building. The seller has offered Sherlock the following three payment plans:

Problem 13–3
Present values of possible liabilities
(LO 4, 5)

Plan A: $100,000 cash would be paid at once.
Plan B: $114,000 cash would be paid after two years.
Plan C: $58,000 cash would be paid at the end of each of the next two years.

The company's owner knows that the market interest rate is 8%.

Required

1. Use the market interest rate to determine present value of each of the three possible payment plans.

2. Show the journal entry that would be made to record the acquisition under each of the three plans. (Assume that the note's face value would include all interest to be paid.)

3. Identify the plan that creates the lowest cost for the company.

4. Assume that Plan B is adopted and the present value of the cash flows is used as the building's cost. Determine the amount of interest expense that will be reported in each of the two years in the note's life.

Problem 13–4
Exchanging a noninterest-bearing note for a plant asset
(LO 5)

On January 2, 1996, Watts Company acquired an item of equipment by issuing a $55,000 noninterest-bearing five-year note payable on December 31, 2000. A reliable cash price for the equipment was not readily available. The market annual rate of interest for similar notes was 4% on the day of the exchange.

Required

(Round all amounts in your answers to the nearest whole dollar.)

1. Determine the initial net liability created by issuing this note.

2. Present a table showing the calculation of the amount of interest expense allocated to each year the note is outstanding and the carrying amount of the net liability at the end of each of those years.

3. Present a table that shows the balance of the discount at the end of each year the note is outstanding.

4. Prepare general journal entries to record the purchase of the equipment, the accrual of interest expense at the end of 1996 and 1997, and the accrual of interest expense and the payment of the note on December 31, 2000.

5. Show how the note should be presented on the balance sheet as of December 31, 1998.

Problem 13–5
Understanding times fixed interest charges earned
(LO 7)

These condensed income statements are for two companies:

Adams Co.		Beene Co.	
Sales	$100,000	Sales	$100,000
Variable expenses (65%) ...	65,000	Variable expenses (85%) ...	85,000
Net income before interest ..	$ 35,000	Net income before interest ..	$ 15,000
Interest (fixed)	25,000	Interest (fixed)	5,000
Net income	$ 10,000	Net income	$ 10,000

Required

Preparation component:

1. What is the times fixed interest charges earned for Adams Co.?

2. What is the times fixed interest charges earned for Beene Co.?

3. What happens to each company's net income if sales increase by 20%?

4. What happens to each company's net income if sales increase by 40%?

5. What happens to each company's net income if sales increase by 80%?

6. What happens to each company's net income if sales decrease by 10%?

7. What happens to each company's net income if sales decrease by 20%?

8. What happens to each company's net income if sales decrease by 50%?

Analysis component:

9. Comment on what you observe and relate it to the ratio values that you found in questions 1 and 2.

Collie Company sells a single product subject to a six-month warranty that covers replacement parts but not labour. The company uses a periodic inventory system to account for merchandise. Prepare journal entries to record the following transactions completed by the company during the month of April:

Problem 13–6
Product warranty expense
(LO 2)

Apr. 2   Purchased 1,200 units of merchandise for $30 per unit, paying cash.

3   Purchased $3,900 of spare parts for making repairs to merchandise that is expected to be returned for warranty work.

8   Sold 500 units of merchandise for $60 per unit, receiving cash.

11   Repaired 30 units of merchandise that customers returned under the warranty. Replacement parts cost $750, and the customers paid $570 for labour.

18   Sold 600 units of merchandise for $65 per unit.

21   Repaired 22 units of merchandise under the product warranty. Replacement parts cost $506, and the customers paid $396 for labour.

29   Recorded warranty expense for April. Past experience shows that 4% of the units sold require warranty work, and the average cost of replacement parts is $24 per unit returned. Average labour charges are $18.50.

Prepare general journal entries to record these transactions of Davies Company:

Problem 13–7
Journalizing notes payable transactions
(LO 3)

1996

Jan. 8   Purchased merchandise on credit from Grant Company, invoice dated January 7, terms 2/10, n/60, $15,600.

Feb. 5   Borrowed money at First Provincial Bank by discounting our own $25,000 note payable for 60 days at 12%. Since the note matures before the end of the year, the discount should be charged to Interest Expense.

Mar. 10   Gave Grant Company $2,100 cash and a $13,500, 60-day, 12% note to secure an extension on our account that was due.

Apr. 5   Paid the note discounted at First Provincial Bank on February 5.

May 10   Paid the note given Grant Company on March 10.

Nov. 1   Borrowed money at First Provincial Bank by discounting our own $30,000 note payable for 90 days at 14%.

Dec. 16   Borrowed money at InterCity Bank by giving a $25,000, 60-day, 15% note payable.

Dec. 31   Made an adjusting entry to record interest on the November 1 note to First Provincial Bank.

31   Made an adjusting entry to record the accrued interest on the December 16 note to InterCity Bank.

1997

Jan. 30   Paid the November 1 note to First Provincial Bank. Also recorded interest expense related to the note.

Feb. 14   Paid the note given InterCity Bank on December 16.

Problem 13–8
Present values of
alternative payment
patterns
(LO 4)

Tropical Adventures is negotiating with a naval architect and shipyard in planning the construction of a 90-foot trimaran that Tropical Adventures expects to acquire and place in charter service. The yacht will be completed and ready for service four years hence. If Tropical Adventures pays for the yacht on completion (Payment Plan A), it will cost $500,500. However, two alternative payment plans are available. Plan B would require an immediate payment of $365,650. Plan C would require four annual payments of $105,850, the first of which would be made one year hence. In evaluating the three alternatives, the management of Tropical Adventures has decided to assume an interest rate of 10%.

Required

Calculate the present value of each payment and indicate which plan Tropical Adventures should follow.

Problem 13–9
Exchanging a noninterest-
bearing note for a capital
asset
(LO 5)

On January 2, 1996, a company gave its own $150,000 noninterest-bearing, five-year note payable in exchange for a machine the cash price of which was not readily determinable. The market rate for interest on such notes on the day of the exchange was 8% annually.

Required

(*Round all amounts in your answers to the nearest whole dollar.*)

1. Prepare a form with the following column headings and calculate and fill in the required amounts for the five years the note is outstanding.

Year	Face Amount of Note	Unamortized Discount at Beginning of Year	Beginning-of-Year Carrying Amount	Discount to Be Amortized Each Year	Unamortized Discount at the End of Year	End-of-Year Carrying Amount

2. Prepare general journal entries to record (*a*) the acquisition of the machine, (*b*) the discount amortized at the end of each year, and (*c*) the payment of the note on January 2, 2001.

3. Show how the note should appear on the December 31, 1998, balance sheet.

Problem 13–10
Installment notes
(LO 5)

On June 30, 1996, Potter Company borrowed $450,000 at the bank by signing a five-year, 12% installment note. The terms of the note require equal semiannual payments beginning December 31, 1996.

Required

(*Round all amounts in your answers to the nearest whole dollar.*)

1. Calculate the amount of the installment payments. (Use Table 13–2 on page 619.)

2. Prepare a table with column headings like the table below. Complete the table for the Potter Company note.

Period Ending	Beginning of Period Principal Balance	Periodic Payment	Interest Expense for Period	Principal Portion of Payment	End of Period Balance

3. Prepare general journal entries to record the first and the last payments on the note.

4. Assume that the note does not require equal payments. Instead, assume the note requires payments of accrued interest plus equal amounts of principal. Prepare general journal entries to record the first and the last payments on the note.

This problem requires you to demonstrate your understanding of noninterest-bearing notes, interest allocation, and present values by explaining how it would be possible to use incomplete information to discover other facts about a loan. Suppose that a company borrowed some cash on January 1, 1996, with a four-year noninterest-bearing note payable. A year later, on December 31, 1996, you know only these two items of information:

a. The net liability (net of the remaining discount) as of December 31, 1996.

b. The interest expense reported for the year ended December 31, 1996.

Write brief explanations of the calculations you would make to identify the following additional facts about the loan:

1. The amount borrowed on January 1, 1996.
2. The market interest rate on January 1, 1996.
3. The amount of interest that will be reported for 1997.

Problem 13–11
Analytical essays
(LO 5)

After a long analysis, the manager of the Greenfield Company has decided to acquire a truck through a long-term noncancellable lease instead of buying it outright. Under the terms of the lease, Greenfield must make regular monthly payments throughout the four-year term of the lease and provide for all the operating costs, including gas, insurance, and repairs. At the end of the lease, the lessor will simply give Greenfield the legal title to the truck. Describe why Greenfield should account for the lease as if it is essentially a purchase.

Problem 13–12
Analytical essay
(LO 5)

PROVOCATIVE PROBLEMS

Sam Ishikawa is the new manager of accounting and finance for a medium-sized manufacturing company. Now that the end of the year is approaching, his problem is determining whether and how to describe some of the company's contingencies in the financial statements. The general manager, Sue Peebles, raised objections to two specific contingencies in his preliminary proposal.

First, Peebles objected to the proposal to report nothing about a patent infringement suit that the company has filed against a competitor. The manager's written comment on his proposal was, "We KNOW that we have them cold on this one! There is no way that we're not going to win a very large settlement!"

Second, she objected to his proposal to recognize an expense and a liability for warranty service on units of a new product that was just introduced in the company's fourth quarter. Her scribbled comment on this point was "There is no way that we can estimate this warranty cost. Besides, we don't owe anybody anything until the products break down and are returned for service. Let's just report an expense if and when we do the repairs."

Provocative Problem 13–1
Business communications case
(LO 2)

Develop a short written response for Ishikawa to the objections raised by the general manager in a one-page memorandum dated December 15.

Provocative Problem 13–2
Financial statement analysis case
(LO 1, 2, 5, 6)

Geac

Answer the following questions by using the information in the financial statements and notes for Geac Computer Corporation Limited that appear in Appendix I at the end of the book:

1. Examine the company's balance sheet to find the amount of long-term debt that it had on April 30, 1994. Also, what is the amount of the company's current notes payable?

2. Examine the statement of operations to find the amount of interest expense during fiscal years 1994 and 1993. Assume that the interest expense represents interest paid. Calculate times fixed interest charges earned for both years and comment on any significant change in the ratio.

3. Does the note on "Commitments and Contingencies" provide information that allows the reader to determine whether the company has entered into any operating or capital leases?

4. What evidence would you look for as an indication that the company has any temporary differences between the income reported on the income statement and the income reported on its tax return? Can you find any evidence of these differences for Geac?

ANALYTICAL AND REVIEW PROBLEMS

A&R Problem 13–1

El Flighter, ace lefthander with the York Bluebirds, is negotiating for renewal of his contract. Prior to making an offer to Flighter, George Megabucks—owner of the team—asks you to check out three alternatives he intends to present to the pitcher. George is only willing to offer a three-year contract but is offering three different payment schemes as follows:

a. $300,000 payable at the end of each year for 10 years.

b. $750,000 payable at the end of each year for 3 years.

c. $1,800,000 payable on signing the three-year contract.

Required

Prepare journal entries for each of the alternatives as of the date of signing the contract and at the end of the first year. Also indicate balance sheet presentation as of the end of the first year. Assume:

1. The going rate of interest is 12%.

2. The company amortizes assets on a straight-line basis.

On September 1, 1996, Chang Company acquired a machine by paying $15,000 cash and signing a two-year note that carried a face amount of $90,000 due at the end of the two-year period; the note did not specify interest. Assume the going rate of interest for this company for this type of loan is 12%. The accounting period ends December 31.

A & R Problem 13–2

Required

Give the entry to record the purchase of the machine and complete a tabulation as follows (round amounts to nearest dollar):

	Straight-Line Method	Interest Method
1. Cash to be paid at maturity	$_____	$_____
2. Total interest expense	$_____	$_____
3. Interest expense on income statement for 1996	$_____	$_____
4. Amount of the liability reported on balance sheet at end of 1996	$_____	$_____
5. Amortization expense for 1996 (assume straight-line, partial year, no residual value, and useful life of five years)	$_____	$_____

CONCEPT TESTER

Test your understanding of the concepts introduced in this chapter by completing the following crossword puzzle.

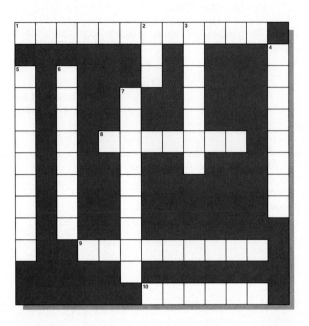

Across Clues

1. The amount, at a given interest rate, that will equate to an amount in the future (2 words).

8. A type of lease that gives the lessee the risks and benefits of ownership.

9. An obligation that is reported even though the amount to be paid is uncertain (1st of 2 words; also see 7 down).

10. Payments of income taxes that arise in future periods due to timing differences (2nd of 3 words; also see 6 down, 2 down).

Down Clues

2. Payments of income taxes that arise in future periods (3rd of 3 words; also see 6 down, 10 across).

3. A series of equal payments occurring at equal time intervals.

4. An agreement that obligates a manufacturer to repair or replace a product that fails to perform.

5. The type of lease that is not a capital lease.

6. Payments of income taxes that arise in future periods due to timing differences (1st of 3 words; also see 10 across, 2 down).

7. An obligation that is reported even though the amount to be paid is uncertain (2nd of 2 words; also see 9 across).

COMPREHENSIVE PROBLEM

The Schwartz Exterminator Company provides pest control services and sells extermination products manufactured by other companies. The following six-column table contains the company's unadjusted trial balance as of December 31, 1996.

Schwartz Exterminator Company (Review of Chapters 1–13)

SCHWARTZ EXTERMINATOR COMPANY
Six-column Table
December 31, 1996

	Unadjusted Trial Balance		Adjustments		Adjusted Trial Balance	
Cash	$ 15,000					
Accounts receivable	24,000					
Allowance for doubtful accounts		$ 3,064				
Merchandise inventory	18,000					
Trucks	22,000					
Accum. amortization, trucks		0				
Equipment	75,000					
Accum. amortization, equipment		21,500				
Accounts payable		6,000				
Estimated warranty liability		1,200				
Unearned extermination services revenue		0				
Long-term notes payable		60,000				
Discount on notes payable	15,898					
Arnold Schwartz, capital		58,800				
Arnold Schwartz, withdrawals	21,000					
Extermination services revenue		70,000				
Interest earned		436				
Sales		135,000				
Purchases	81,000					
Amortization expense, trucks	0					
Amortization expense, equip.	0					
Wages expense	45,000					
Interest expense	0					
Rent expense	16,000					
Bad debts expense	0					
Miscellaneous expenses	6,202					
Repairs expense	11,000					
Utilities expense	5,900					
Warranty expense	0					
Totals	$356,000	$356,000				

The following information applies to the company and its situation at the end of the year:

a.   The bank reconciliation as of December 31, 1996, includes these facts:

Balance per bank	$13,200
Balance per books	15,000
Outstanding cheques	2,600
Deposit in transit	3,500
Interest earned	44
Service charges (miscellaneous expense) . .	17

Included with the bank statement was a canceled cheque that the company had failed to record. (This information allows you to determine the amount of the cheque, which was a payment of an account payable.)

b.   An examination of customers' accounts shows that accounts totaling $2,500 should be written off as uncollectible. In addition, the owner has determined that the ending balance of the Allowance for Doubtful Accounts account should be $4,300.

c.   A truck was purchased and placed in service on July 1, 1996. Its cost is being amortized with the straight-line method using these facts and predictions:

Original cost	$22,000
Expected salvage value	6,000
Useful life (years)	4

d.   Two items of equipment (a sprayer and an injector) were purchased and put into service early in January 1994. Their costs are being amortized with the straight-line method using these facts and predictions:

	Sprayer	Injector
Original cost	$45,000	$30,000
Expected salvage value	3,000	2,500
Useful life (years)	8	5

e.   On October 1, 1996, the company was paid $2,640 in advance to provide monthly service on an apartment complex for one year. The company began providing the services in October. When the cash was received, the full amount was credited to the Extermination Services Revenue account.

f.   The company offers a warranty for all of the products it sells. The expected cost of providing warranty service is 2% of sales. No warranty expense has been recorded for 1996. All costs of servicing products under the warranties in 1996 were properly debited to the liability account.

g.   The $60,000 long-term note is a five-year, noninterest-bearing note that was given to Second National Bank on December 31, 1994. The market interest rate on the date of the loan was 8%.

h.   The ending inventory of merchandise was counted and determined to have a cost of $16,300.

Required

1.   Use the provided information to determine the amounts of the following items:

a.   The correct ending balance of Cash and the amount of the omitted cheque.

b.   The correct ending balance of the Allowance for Doubtful Accounts.

c.   The annual amortization expense for the truck that was acquired during the year (calculated to the nearest month).

d. The annual amortization expense for the two items of equipment that were used during the year.

e. The correct ending balances of the Extermination Services Revenue and Unearned Extermination Services Revenue accounts.

f. The correct ending balances of the accounts for Warranty Expense and the Estimated Warranty Liability.

g. The correct ending balances of the accounts for Interest Expense and the Discount on Notes Payable.

h. The cost of goods sold for the year.

2. Use the results of requirement 1 to complete the six-column table by first entering the appropriate adjustments for items *a* through *g* and then completing the adjusted trial balance columns. (Hint: item *b* requires two entries.)

3. Present general journal entries to record the adjustments entered on the six-column table.

4. Present a single-step income statement, a statement of changes in owner's equity, and a classified balance sheet.

ANSWERS TO PROGRESS CHECKS

13–1 Liabilities are probable future payments of assets or services that an entity is presently obligated to make as a result of past transactions or events.

13–2 No; an expected future payment is not a liability unless an obligation was created by a past event or transaction.

13–3 In most cases, a liability due in 15 months should be classified as long-term. However, it should be classified as a current liability if the company's operating cycle is at least 15 months long.

13–4 *a*

13–5 *a*

13–6 A corporation would accrue an income tax liability for its interim financial statements because income tax expense is incurred when income is earned, not just at the end of the year.

13–7 *b*

13–8 A future payment should be reported as a contingent liability if the uncertain future event is likely and the amount of the payment can be reasonably estimated.

13–9 A creditor might want to have a note payable instead of an account payable in order to (*a*) start charging interest and/or (*b*) have positive evidence of the debt and its terms.

13–10 The amount borrowed was $1,000 ($1,050 − $50). The rate of interest was 5% ($50/$1,000) for six months, which is an annual rate of 10%.

13–11 *c*
$3.3121 \times \$1,000 = \$3,312$

13–12 The option of paying $10,000 after a year always has a lower present value. In effect, it postpones paying the first $5,000 by six months. As a result, the present value of the delayed payment is always less.

13–13 *c*
$[\$6,000 + (\$6,000 \times .06)] \times .06 = \$381.60$

13–14 $\$4,000 \times 0.7350 = \$2,940$

13–15 *d*

13–16 *c*

13–17 The risk can be described by the ratio that shows the number of times the fixed interest charges are covered by the net income *before* interest. The ratio for the first company is only 1.5 [($100,000 + $200,000)/$200,000], while the ratio for the second company is 3.5 [($100,000 + $40,000)/$40,000]. This analysis shows that First Company is more susceptible to the risk of incurring a loss if its sales decline.

Partnership Accounting

As a business enterprise becomes more complex, it needs more human and financial resources. A partnership allows the owners to pool their talents and funds to achieve more than they could individually. A partnership also creates needs for special accounting information.

*F*ive weeks had passed since the instructor asked Karen White and Mark Smith to prepare for a discussion on partnerships. They read the partnership chapter and other related material that came to their attention. They concluded that for their presentation White would take a pro and Smith a con position on the partnership form of business organization.

In summation of positions, White and Smith agreed that:

The partnership form of business organization has many pitfalls and should be entered into only as a last resort. Entry should be made with extreme caution and with as many protective features as can be negotiated.

LEARNING OBJECTIVES

After studying Chapter 14, you should be able to:

1. **List the characteristics of a partnership and explain the concepts of mutual agency and unlimited liability in a partnership.**
2. **Allocate partnership earnings to partners *(a)* on a stated fractional basis, *(b)* in the partners' capital ratio, and *(c)* through the use of salary and interest allowances.**
3. **Prepare entries for *(a)* the sale of a partnership interest, *(b)* the admission of a new partner by investment, and *(c)* the retirement of a partner by the withdrawal of partnership assets.**
4. **Prepare entries required in the liquidation of a partnership.**
5. **Define or explain the words and phrases listed in the chapter glossary.**

The early chapters of this book were devoted, for the most part, to the single proprietorship with only passing references to partnerships and corporations. In this chapter, we examine the partnership form of business in greater detail. The partnership form is widely used, especially in businesses where the owners know each other well. Many professional businesses, including public accounting firms, are organized as partnerships.

CHARACTERISTICS OF PARTNERSHIPS

LO 1

List the characteristics of a partnership and explain the concepts of mutual agency and unlimited liability in a partnership.

Many businesses, such as small retail and service businesses, are organized as partnerships. Also, many professional practitioners—physicians, lawyers, and public accountants—have traditionally organized their practices as partnerships. The provincial Partnership Acts and the Civil Code, with minor variations, define a **partnership** as "the relation which subsists between persons carrying on a business in common with a view of profit." Another definition of a partnership is "an association of two or more competent persons under a contract to combine some or all of their property, labour, and skills in the operation of a business." Both of these definitions say something about the legal nature of a partnership. However, the nature of the partnership form of business becomes clearer when you understand some of the specific features that characterize partnerships.

A Voluntary Association

A partnership is a voluntary association between the partners. All that is required to form a partnership is that two or more legally competent people (that is, people who are of age and of sound mental capacity) must agree to be partners. Their agreement becomes a **partnership contract.** Although it should be in writing, the contract is binding even if it is only expressed orally.

Limited Life

The life of a partnership is always limited. Death, bankruptcy, or anything that takes away the ability of one of the partners to enter into or fulfill a contract automatically ends a partnership. In addition, a partnership may be terminated at will by any one of the partners. Before agreeing to join a partnership, you should understand clearly two important characteristics of a partnership: mutual agency and unlimited liability.

Mutual Agency

Generally, the relationship between the partners in a partnership involves **mutual agency**. Under normal circumstances, every partner is a fully authorized agent of the partnership. As its agent, a partner can commit or bind the partnership to any contract that is within the apparent scope of the partnership's business. For example, a partner in a merchandising business can sign contracts that bind the partnership to buy merchandise, lease a store building, borrow money, or hire employees. These activities are all within the scope of the business of a merchandising firm. On the other hand, a partner in a law firm, acting alone, cannot bind his or her partners to a contract to buy merchandise for resale or rent a retail store building. These actions are not within the normal scope of a law firm's business.

Partners may agree to limit the power of any one or more of the partners to negotiate certain contracts for the partnership. Such an agreement is binding on the partners and on outsiders who know that it exists. However, it is not binding on outsiders who do not know that it exists. Outsiders who are not aware of the agreement have the right to assume that each partner has normal agency powers for the partnership.

Because mutual agency exposes all partners to the risk of unwise actions by any one partner, people should carefully evaluate potential partners before agreeing to join a partnership. The importance of this advice is underscored by the fact that most partnerships are also characterized by unlimited liability.

Unlimited Liability of Partners

When a partnership cannot pay its debts, the creditors normally can satisfy their claims from the *personal* assets of the partners. Also, if some partners do not have enough assets to meet their share of the partnership's debts, the creditors can turn to the assets of the remaining partners who are able to pay. Because partners may be called on to pay all the debts of the partnership, each partner is said to have **unlimited liability** for the partnership's debts. Mutual agency and unlimited liability are the main reasons why most partnerships have only a few members.

Limited Partnerships and Limited Liability Partnerships

Partnerships in which all of the partners have unlimited liability are called **general partnerships**. Sometimes, however, individuals who want to invest in a partnership are not willing to accept the risk of unlimited liability. Their needs may be met by using a **limited partnership**. A limited partnership has two classes of partners, general and limited. At least one partner has to be a **general partner** who must assume unlimited liability for the debts of the partnership. The remaining **limited partners** have no personal liability beyond the amounts that they invest in the business. Usually, a limited partnership is managed by the general partner or partners. The limited partners have no active role except for major decisions specified in the partnership agreement.

A similar form of partnership in some jurisdictions allowing professionals such as lawyers to use is the **limited liability partnership**. This type of partnership is designed to protect innocent partners from malpractice or negligence claims that result from the acts of another partner. When a partner provides service that results in a malpractice claim, that partner has personal liability for the claim. The remaining partners who were not responsible for the actions that resulted in the claim are not personally liable for the claim. However, all partners have personal liability for other partnership debts.

ADVANTAGES AND DISAD-VANTAGES OF A PARTNERSHIP

Limited life, mutual agency, and unlimited liability are disadvantages of a partnership. Yet, there are other reasons why a partnership may be a preferred form of business organization. A partnership has the advantage of being able to bring together more money and skills than a single proprietorship. A partnership is easier to organize than a corporation. Also, a partnership may escape some of the federal and provincial regulations and taxes that are imposed on corporations. Finally, partners may act without having to hold shareholders' or directors' meetings, which are required of a corporation.

PARTNERSHIP ACCOUNTING

Accounting for a partnership does not differ from accounting for a proprietorship except for transactions that directly affect the partners' equity. Because ownership rights in a partnership are divided among the partners, partnership accounting:

- Uses a capital account for each partner.
- Uses a withdrawals account for each partner.
- Allocates net incomes or losses to the partners according to the provisions of the partnership agreement.

When partners invest in a partnership, their capital accounts are credited for the invested amounts. Partners' withdrawals of assets are debited to their withdrawals accounts. In closing the accounts at the end of the year, the partners' capital accounts are credited or debited for their shares of the net income or loss. Finally, the withdrawals account of each partner is closed to that partner's capital account. These closing procedures are like those used for a single proprietorship. The only difference is that separate capital and withdrawals accounts are maintained for each partner.

NATURE OF PARTNERSHIP EARNINGS

Because they are its owners, partners are not employees of the partnership. If partners devote their time and services to the affairs of their partnership, they are understood to do so for profit, not for salary. Therefore, when the partners calculate the net income of a partnership, salaries to the partners are not deducted as expenses on the income statement. However, when the net income or loss of the partnership is allocated among the partners, the partners may agree to base part of the allocation on salary allowances that reflect the relative values of service provided by the partners.

Partners are also understood to have invested in a partnership for profit, not for interest. Nevertheless, partners may agree that the division of partnership earnings should include a return based on their invested capital. For example, if one partner contributes five times as much capital as another, it is only fair that this fact be considered when earnings are allocated among the partners. Thus, a partnership agreement may provide for interest allowances based on the partners' capital balances. Like salary allowances, interest allowances are not expenses to be reported on the income statement.

In the absence of a contrary agreement, the law states that the income or loss of a partnership should be shared equally by the partners. However, partners may agree to any method of sharing. If they agree on how they will share income but say nothing about losses, then losses are shared in the same way as income.

Several methods of sharing partnership earnings can be used. Three frequently used methods divide earnings: (1) on a stated fractional basis, (2) in the ratio of capital investments, or (3) using salary and interest allowances and any remainder in a fixed ratio.

Earnings Allocated on a Stated Fractional Basis

An easy way to divide partnership earnings is to give each partner a fraction of the total. All that is necessary is for the partners to agree on the fractional share that each will receive. For example, assume that the partnership agreement of B. A. Jones and S. A. Meyers states that Jones will receive two-thirds and Meyers will receive one-third of the partnership earnings. If the partnership's net income is $30,000, the earnings are allocated to the partners and the Income Summary account is closed with the following entry:

Dec.	31	Income Summary	30,000.00	
		B. A. Jones, Capital		20,000.00
		S. A. Meyers, Capital		10,000.00
		To close the Income Summary account and allocate the earnings.		

When earnings are shared on a fractional basis, the fractions may reflect the relative capital investments of the partners. For example, suppose that B. Donner and H. Flack formed a partnership and agreed to share earnings in the ratio of their investments. Because Donner invested $50,000 and Flack invested $30,000, Donner will receive five-eighths of the earnings ($50,000/$80,000) while Flack will receive three-eighths of the earnings ($30,000/$80,000).

Salaries and Interest as Aids in Sharing

As we have mentioned, the service contributions and capital contributions of the partners often are not equal. If the service contributions are not equal, salary allowances can compensate for the differences. Or, when capital contributions are not equal, interest allowances can compensate for the unequal investments. When both investment and service contributions are unequal, the allocation of net incomes and losses may include both interest and salary allowances.

For example, in Kathy Stanley and David Breck's new partnership, Stanley is to provide services that they agree are worth an annual salary of $36,000. Breck

DIVISION OF EARNINGS

LO 2

Allocate partnership earnings to earnings to partners *(a)* on a stated fractional basis, *(b)* in the partners' capital ratio, and *(c)* through the use of salary and interest allowances.

Illustration 14-1
Sharing Income When
Income Exceeds
Salary and Interest
Allowances

	Share to Stanley	Share to Breck	Income to Be Allocated
Total net income			$70,000
Allocated as salary allowances:			
Stanley	$36,000		
Breck		$24,000	
Total allocated as salary allowances			60,000
Balance of income after salary allowances . .			$10,000
Allocated as interest:			
Stanley (10% on $30,000)	3,000		
Breck (10% on $10,000)		1,000	
Total allocated as interest			4,000
Balance of income after salary and interest allowances			$ 6,000
Balance allocated equally:			
Stanley	3,000		
Breck		3,000	
Total allocated equally			6,000
Balance of income			$ 0
Shares of the partners	$42,000	$28,000	
Percentages of total net income	60%	40%	

is less experienced in the business, so his service contribution is worth only $24,000. Also, Stanley will invest $30,000 in the business and Breck will invest $10,000. To compensate Stanley and Breck fairly in light of the differences in their service and capital contributions, they agree to share incomes or losses as follows:

1. Annual salary allowances of $36,000 to Stanley and $24,000 to Breck.
2. Interest allowances equal to 10% of each partner's beginning-of-year capital balance.
3. The remaining balance of income or loss is to be shared equally.

Note that the provisions for salaries and interest in this partnership agreement are called *allowances*. These allowances are not reported on the income statement as salaries and interest expense. They are only a means of splitting up the net income or net loss of the partnership.

Under the Stanley and Breck partnership agreement, a first year's net income of $70,000 is shared as shown in Illustration 14–1. Notice that Stanley gets $42,000, or 60% of the income, while Breck gets $28,000, or 40%.

In Illustration 14–1, notice that the $70,000 net income exceeds the salary and interest allowances of the partners. However, the method of sharing agreed to by Stanley and Breck must be followed even if the net income is smaller than the salary and interest allowances. For example, if the first year's net income was $50,000, it would be allocated to the partners as shown in Illustration 14–2. Notice that this circumstance provides Stanley with 64% of the total income, while Breck gets only 36%.

	Share to Stanley	Share to Breck	Income to Be Allocated
Total net income			$ 50,000
Allocated as salary allowances:			
Stanley	$36,000		
Breck		$24,000	
Total allocated as salary allowances			60,000
Balance of income after salary allowances . .			$(10,000)
Allocated as interest:			
Stanley (10% on $30,000)	3,000		
Breck (10% on $10,000)		1,000	
Total allocated as interest			4,000
Balance of income after salary and			
interest allowances			$(14,000)
Balance allocated equally:			
Stanley	(7,000)		
Breck		(7,000)	
Total allocated equally			(14,000)
Balance of income			$ 0
Shares of the partners	$32,000	$18,000	
Percentages of total net income	64%	36%	

A net loss would be shared by Stanley and Breck in the same manner as the $50,000 net income. The only difference is that the income-and-loss-sharing procedure would begin with a negative amount of income because of the net loss. After the salary and interest allowances, the remaining balance to be allocated equally would then be a larger negative amount.

Progress Check

14–1 A partnership is automatically terminated in the event *(a)* the partnership agreement is not in writing; *(b)* a partner dies; or *(c)* a partner exercises mutual agency.

14–2 Mixon and Reed form a partnership by contributing $70,000 and $35,000 respectively. They agree to an interest allowance equal to 10% of each partner's capital balance at the beginning of the year with the remaining income to be shared equally.

14–3 What does the term *unlimited liability* mean when it is applied to a partnership?

In most respects, partnership financial statements are like those of a single proprietorship. On the balance sheet of a partnership, the owner's equity section often shows the separate capital account balance of each partner. The **statement of changes in partners' equity** shows the total capital balances at the beginning of the period, any additional investments made by the partners, the net income or loss of the partnership, withdrawals by the partners, and the ending capital balances. Usually, this statement shows these changes for each partner's capital account and includes the allocation of income among the partners.

PARTNERSHIP FINANCIAL STATEMENTS

Illustration 14–3
A Statement of
Changes in Partners'
Equity

STANLEY AND BRECK
Statement of Changes in Partners' Equity
For Year Ended December 31, 19—

	Stanley		Breck		Total
Beginning capital balances		$ –0–		$ –0–	$ –0–
Plus:					
Investments by owners		30,000		10,000	40,000
Net income:					
Salary allowances	$36,000		$24,000		
Interest allowances	3,000		1,000		
Balance	(7,000)		(7,000)		
Total net income		32,000		18,000	50,000
Total		$62,000		$28,000	$90,000
Less partners' withdrawals		(20,000)		(12,000)	(32,000)
Ending capital balances		$42,000		$16,000	$58,000

For example, recall that Stanley and Breck began their partnership by making investments of $30,000 and $10,000, respectively. During the first year of operations, in which the partnership earned $50,000, assume that Stanley withdrew $20,000 and Breck withdrew $12,000. The statement of changes in partners' equity appears in Illustration 14–3. The inclusion of salary and interest allowances and the allocation of the balances are generally not reported in such a statement. However, the detail in Illustration 14–3 is shown to demonstrate how the division of net income is attained.

WITHDRAWAL OR ADDITION OF A PARTNER

LO 3

Prepare entries for *(a)* the sale of a partnership interest, *(b)* the admission of a new partner by investment, and *(c)* the retirement of a partner by the withdrawal of partnership assets.

A partnership is based on a contract between specific individuals. Therefore, when a partner withdraws from a partnership, the old partnership ceases to exist. Nevertheless, the business may continue to operate as a new partnership among the remaining partners.

The withdrawal of a partner from a partnership may take place in two ways. First, the withdrawing partner may sell his or her interest to another person who pays for the interest by transferring cash or other assets to the withdrawing partner. Second, cash or other assets of the partnership may be distributed to the withdrawing partner in settlement of his or her interest in the partnership.

When a new partner is admitted to a partnership, the old partnership technically ends and is replaced by a new partnership. Similar to the withdrawal of a partner, there are two ways a new partner may be admitted to an existing partnership: First, the new partner may purchase an interest directly from one or more of its partners. In other words, the new partner may pay cash to one or more of the existing partners in exchange for an interest in the partnership. Second, a new partner may join an existing partnership by investing cash or other assets in the business.

Sale of a Partnership Interest

Assume that the Abbott, Burns, and Camp partnership owes no liabilities and has the following assets and owners' equity:

Assets		Owners' Equity	
Cash	$ 3,000	Abbott, capital.............	$ 5,000
Other assets	12,000	Burns, capital..............	5,000
		Camp, capital..............	5,000
Total assets	$15,000	Total owners' equity........	$15,000

Camp's equity in this partnership is $5,000. If Camp sells this equity to Davis for $7,000, Camp is selling a $5,000 recorded interest in the partnership assets. The entry on the partnership books to transfer the equity is

Feb.	4	Camp, Capital	5,000.00	
		Davis, Capital		5,000.00
		To transfer Camp's equity in the partnership to Davis.		

After this entry is posted, the assets and owners' equity of the new partnership are

Assets		Owners' Equity	
Cash	$ 3,000	Abbott, capital.............	$ 5,000
Other assets	12,000	Burns, capital..............	5,000
....		Davis, capital..............	5,000
Total assets	$15,000	Total owners' equity........	$15,000

Two aspects of this transaction are especially important. First, the $7,000 Davis paid to Camp is not recorded in the partnership books. Camp sold and transferred a $5,000 recorded equity in the partnership assets to Davis. The entry that records the transfer is a debit to Camp, Capital, and a credit to Davis, Capital, for $5,000. Furthermore, the entry is the same whether Davis pays Camp $7,000, or $70,000. The amount is paid directly to Camp. Because the partnership is not a party to the transaction, its assets and total equity are not affected by the transaction.

The second important aspect of this transaction is the question of whether Davis's purchase of Camp's interest qualifies Davis as a new partner. In fact, Abbott and Burns must agree if Davis is to become a partner. Abbott and Burns cannot prevent Camp from selling the interest to Davis. But Abbott and Burns do not have to accept Davis as a partner. If Abbott and Burns agree to accept Davis, a new partnership is formed and a new contract with a new income-and-loss-sharing ratio must be drawn.

What if either Abbott or Burns refuses to accept Davis as a partner? Under the partnership acts, Davis gets Camp's share of partnership income and losses. And if the partnership is liquidated, Davis gets Camp's share of partnership assets. However, Davis gets no voice in the management of the firm until being admitted as a partner.

14-4   **PQR are partners. Q sells his interest to his son. Are P and R obliged to take the son into the partnership?**

14-5   **KRJ are partners. With the agreement of K and R, J sells his interest to Z. However, J does not disclose to K and R the amount he received. Is he within his right to withhold such information?**

14-6   **MNO are partners. With the agreement of N and O, M sells her interest to P. P assumes that her sharing of income will be the same as M enjoyed. Do you agree with her assumption?**

Investing Assets in an Existing Partnership

Instead of purchasing the equity of an existing partner, an individual may gain an equity by investing assets in the business. The invested assets then become the property of the partnership. For example, assume that the partnership of Evans and Gage has assets and owners' equity as follows:

Assets		Owners' Equity	
Cash	$ 3,000	Evans, capital	$20,000
Other assets	37,000	Gage, capital	20,000
Total assets	$40,000	Total owners' equity	$40,000

Also, assume that Evans and Gage have agreed to accept Hart as a partner with a one-half interest in the business on his investment of $40,000. This entry records Hart's investment:

Mar.	2	Cash	40,000.00	
		Hart, Capital		40,000.00
		To record the investment of Hart.		

After the entry is posted, the assets and owners' equity of the new partnership appear as follows:

Assets		Owners' Equity	
Cash	$43,000	Evans, capital	$20,000
Other assets	37,000	Gage, capital	20,000
		Hart, capital	40,000
Total assets	$80,000	Total owners' equity	$80,000

In this case, Hart has a 50% equity in the assets of the business. However, he does not necessarily have a right to one-half of its net income. The sharing of incomes and losses is a separate matter on which the partners must agree. As you learned earlier in the chapter, the sharing of profits and losses may be in the ratio of the partners' relative capital contributions. However, the method of sharing also may depend on other factors.

A Bonus to the Old Partners

Sometimes, when the current value of a partnership is greater than the recorded amounts of equity, the partners may require an incoming partner to give a bonus for the privilege of joining the firm. For example, Judd and Kirk operate a partnership business, sharing its earnings equally. The partnership's accounting records show that Judd's recorded equity in the business is $38,000 and Kirk's recorded equity is $32,000. Judd and Kirk agree to accept Lee's $50,000 investment in the business in return for a one-third share of the partnership's earnings and a one-third equity in net assets. Lee's equity is determined with a calculation as follows:

Equities of the existing partners ($38,000 + $32,000) . .	$ 70,000
Investment of the new partner	50,000
Total partnership equity	$120,000
Equity of Lee (⅓ of total)	$ 40,000

Notice that although Lee invested $50,000 in the partnership, his equity in the recorded net assets of the partnership is only $40,000. The $10,000 difference usually is described as a bonus allocated to the existing partners (Judd and Kirk). Therefore, this entry records Lee's investment:

May	15	Cash	50,000.00	
		Lee, Capital		40,000.00
		Judd, Capital		5,000.00
		Kirk, Capital		5,000.00
		To record the investment of Lee.		

Notice that the $10,000 difference between the $50,000 invested by Lee and the $40,000 credited to his capital account is shared by Judd and Kirk according to their income-and-loss-sharing ratio. Such a bonus is always shared by the old partners in their income-and-loss-sharing ratio. This ratio is used because the bonus compensates the old partners for increases in the worth of the partnership that have not yet been recorded as income.

Recording Goodwill

As discussed previously, when a new partner's investment exceeds his or her equity in the partnership's net assets, the entry to record the new partner's admission normally allocates a bonus to the existing partners. Occasionally, however, firms use an alternative method to record the admission of a new partner. The alternative method involves recording goodwill on the books of the partnership. The debit to Goodwill is matched with credits that increase the equities of the existing partners.

The goodwill method of recording a new partner's admission would be used only if the evidence indicates that future earnings of the partnership are large enough to justify the increased partnership equity. Evidence of such future earnings might be provided by a historical record of earnings that are consistently in excess of the average for the industry.

In practice, goodwill is seldom recognized upon the admission of a new partner. Instead, the bonus method usually is used.

Bonus to the New Partner

Sometimes, the members of an existing partnership may be very eager to bring a new partner into their firm. The business may need additional cash or the new partner may have exceptional abilities or business contacts that will increase profits. Thus, the old partners may be willing to give the new partner a larger equity in the business than the amount of his or her investment. In this case, the old partners give a bonus to the new partner.

For example, Jay Moss and Mike Owen are partners with capital account balances of $30,000 and $18,000, respectively. They share incomes and losses in a 2:1 ratio. Anxious to have Kay Pitt join their partnership, the partners will grant her a one-fourth equity in the firm if she invests $12,000. If Pitt accepts, her equity in the new firm is calculated as follows:

Equity of the existing partners ($30,000 + $18,000) . .	$48,000
Investment of the new partner	12,000
Total equity in the new partnership	$60,000
Equity of Pitt (¼ of total)	$15,000

This entry records Pitt's investment:

June	1	Cash	12,000.00	
		Moss, Capital ($3,000 × ⅔)	2,000.00	
		Owen, Capital ($3,000 × ⅓)	1,000.00	
		Pitt, Capital		15,000.00
		To record the investment of Pitt.		

Note that Pitt's bonus is contributed by the old partners in their income-and-loss-sharing ratio. Also remember that Pitt's one-fourth equity does not necessarily entitle her to one-fourth of the earnings of the business. The sharing of income and losses is a separate matter for agreement by the partners.

Withdrawal of a Partner

When a new partnership is formed, the contract should include the procedures to follow when a partner retires from the partnership. These procedures often state that a withdrawing partner shall withdraw assets equal to the current value of the partner's equity. To accomplish this, the procedures may require an audit of the accounting records and a revaluation of the partnership assets. The revaluation places the assets on the books at current values. It also causes the partners' capital accounts to reflect the current value of their equity.

For example, assume that Blue is retiring from the partnership of Smith, Blue, and Short. The partners have always shared incomes and losses in the ratio of one-half to Smith, one-fourth to Blue, and one-fourth to Short. Their partnership agreement provides for an audit and asset revaluation on the retirement of a partner. Just prior to the audit and revaluation, their balance sheet shows the following assets and owners' equity:

Assets			Owners' Equity	
Cash		$11,000	Smith, capital.	$22,000
Merchandise inventory . .		16,000	Blue, capital	10,000
Equipment	$20,000		Short, capital	10,000
Less accum. amort. . .	5,000	15,000		
Total assets		$42,000	Total owners' equity	$42,000

The audit and appraisal indicate that the merchandise inventory is overvalued by $4,000. Also, due to market changes, the partnership's equipment should be valued at $25,000, less accumulated amortization of $8,000. The entries to record these revaluations are

Oct.	31	Smith, Capital	2,000.00	
		Blue, Capital	1,000.00	
		Short, Capital	1,000.00	
		Merchandise Inventory		4,000.00
		To revalue the inventory.		
	31	Equipment	5,000.00	
		Accumulated Amortization, Equipment		3,000.00
		Smith, Capital		1,000.00
		Blue, Capital		500.00
		Short, Capital		500.00
		To revalue the equipment.		

Note in these entries that the partners share the amount of the revaluations in their income-and-loss-sharing ratio. This is fair because revaluations of assets are actually gains and losses. If the partnership were not terminated, these gains and losses would sooner or later show up on the income statement as increases and decreases in net income. The revaluation simply records the effect of the gains and losses earlier than would have occurred.

After the entries revaluing the partnership assets are recorded, the balance sheet for the Smith, Blue, and Short partnership is as follows:

Assets			Owners' Equity	
Cash		$11,000	Smith, capital..............	$21,000
Merchandise inventory ..		12,000	Blue, capital	9,500
Equipment	$25,000		Short, capital..............	9,500
Less accum. amort. ..	8,000	17,000		
Total assets		$40,000	Total owners' equity	$40,000

After the revaluation, if Blue retires and takes cash equal to his revalued equity, this entry records the withdrawal:

Oct.	31	Blue, Capital	9,500.00	
		Cash		9,500.00
		To record the withdrawal of Blue.		

In withdrawing, Blue does not have to take cash in settlement of his equity. He may take any combination of assets to which the partners agree, or he may take the new partnership's promissory note. Also, the withdrawal of Blue generally creates a new partnership between the remaining partners. Therefore, a new partnership contract and a new income-and-loss-sharing agreement may be required.

Withdrawing Partner Takes Fewer Assets than Recorded Equity

Sometimes, when a partner retires, the remaining partners may not wish to revalue the assets on the books of the partnership. Nevertheless, they must determine the current values of the partnership assets to establish the amount of assets to be taken by the retiring partner. For example, the partners may agree that the assets are overvalued. As a result, the retiring partner should receive assets of less value than the book value of his or her equity. Also, even if the assets are not overvalued, a retiring partner may be willing to take less than the current value of his or her equity just to get out of the partnership.

When a partner retires and takes assets of less value than his or her recorded equity, the partner in effect leaves a portion of the equity in the business. The remaining partners share the unwithdrawn equity portion in accordance with their income-and-loss-sharing ratio. For example, assume that partners Black, Brown, and Green share incomes and losses in a $2:2:1$ ratio. Their assets and equities are as follows:

Assets		Owners' Equity	
Cash	$ 5,000	Black, capital..............	$ 6,000
Merchandise inventory	9,000	Brown, capital	6,000
Store equipment	4,000	Green, capital	6,000
Total assets	$18,000	Total owners' equity	$18,000

Brown is anxious to withdraw from the partnership and offers to take $4,500 in cash in settlement for his equity. Black and Green agree to the $4,500 withdrawal, and Brown retires. This entry records the retirement:

Mar.	4	Brown, Capital	6,000.00	
		Cash		4,500.00
		Black, Capital		1,000.00
		Green, Capital		500.00
		To record the withdrawal of Brown.		

In retiring, Brown withdrew $1,500 less than his recorded equity. This is divided between Black and Green in their income-and-loss-sharing ratio. The income-and-loss-sharing ratio of the original partnership was Black, 2; Brown, 2; and Green, 1. Therefore, the ratio for sharing between Black and Green was 2:1, and the unwithdrawn book equity of Brown is shared by Black and Green in this ratio.

Withdrawing Partner Takes More Assets than Recorded Equity

There are two common reasons why a retiring partner might withdraw more assets than his or her recorded equity: First, the partnership assets may be undervalued on the books. Second, the continuing partners may want to encourage the retiring partner to withdraw by giving up assets of greater value than the retiring partner's recorded equity.

When assets are undervalued, the partners may not wish to change the recorded values. A retiring partner allowed to withdraw assets of greater value than that partner's recorded equity is, in effect, withdrawing his or her own equity plus a portion of the continuing partners' equities.

For example, assume that partners Jones, Thomas, and Finch share incomes and losses in a 3:2:1 ratio. The assets and owners' equity of the partnership are as follows:

Assets		Owners' Equity	
Cash	$ 5,000	Jones, capital	$ 9,000
Merchandise inventory	10,000	Thomas, capital	6,000
Equipment	3,000	Finch, capital...............	3,000
Total assets	$18,000	Total owners' equity	$18,000

Finch wishes to withdraw from the partnership. Jones and Thomas plan to continue the business. The partners agree that some of the partnership's assets are undervalued, but they do not wish to increase the recorded values. They further agree that if current values were recorded, the asset total would be increased by $6,000 and the equity of Finch would be increased by $1,000. Therefore, the partners agree that $4,000 is the proper value for Finch's equity and that amount of cash may be withdrawn. This entry records the withdrawal:

May	7	Finch, Capital	3,000.00	
		Jones, Capital	600.00	
		Thomas, Capital	400.00	
		Cash		4,000.00
		To record the withdrawal of Finch.		

DEATH OF A PARTNER

A partner's death automatically dissolves a partnership. As a result, the deceased partner's estate is entitled to receive the amount of his or her equity. The partnership contract should contain provisions for settlement in case a partner dies. Included should be provisions for *(a)* an immediate closing of the books to determine earnings since the end of the previous accounting period and *(b)* a method for determining and recording current values for the assets and liabilities. After these steps are taken, the remaining partners and the deceased partner's estate must agree to a disposition of the deceased partner's equity. This may involve selling the equity to the remaining partners or to an outsider, or it may involve the withdrawal of assets in settlement. We explained the appropriate entries for both cases in the previous paragraphs.

LIQUIDATIONS

LO 4

Prepare entries required in the liquidation of a partnership.

When a partnership is liquidated, its business is ended. The assets are converted into cash, and the creditors are paid. The remaining cash is then distributed to the partners, and the partnership is dissolved. **Partnership liquidations** may follow a variety of different steps. However, we limit the following discussion to three typical situations.

All Assets Are Sold at a Net Gain

One typical partnership liquidation is the situation in which all of the partnership assets are converted into cash at a net gain. Then the cash is distributed and the partnership is dissolved. The following example shows the necessary accounting entries to be made under these conditions.

Ottis, Skinner, and Parr have operated a partnership for a number of years, sharing incomes and losses in a 3:2:1 ratio. Due to several unsatisfactory conditions, the partners decide to liquidate as of December 31. On that date, the books are closed, the income from operations is transferred to the partners' capital accounts, and the partnership's balance sheet appears as follows:

Assets		Liabilities and Owners' Equity	
Cash	$10,000	Accounts payable	$ 5,000
Merchandise inventory	15,000	Ottis, capital	15,000
Other assets	25,000	Skinner, capital	15,000
		Parr, capital	15,000
		Total liabilities and	
Total assets	$50,000	owners' equity	$50,000

In a liquidation, some gains of losses normally result from the sale of noncash assets. These losses and gains are called *losses and gains from liquidation.* Just like any other net incomes or losses, the partners share the losses and gains from liquidation in their income-and-loss-sharing ratio. Assume, for example, Ottis, Skinner, and Parr sell their inventory for $12,000 and their other assets for $34,000. This entry records the sales and the net gain allocation:

Jan.	12	Cash	12,000.00	
		Loss or Gain from Liquidation	3,000.00	
		Merchandise Inventory		15,000.00
		Sold the inventory at a loss.		
	15	Cash	34,000.00	
		Other Assets		25,000.00
		Loss or Gain from Liquidation		9,000.00
		Sold the other assets at a profit.		
	15	Loss or Gain from Liquidation	6,000.00	
		Ottis, Capital		3,000.00
		Skinner, Capital		2,000.00
		Parr, Capital		1,000.00
		To allocate the net gain from sale of assets to the partners in their 3:2:1 income-and-loss-sharing ratio.		

Notice in the last entry that the losses and gains from liquidation were shared in the partners' income-and-loss-sharing ratio. In solving liquidation problems, do not make the mistake of allocating the losses and gains in the ratio of the partners' capital balances.

After the merchandise inventory and other assets of Ottis, Skinner, and Parr are sold and the net gain is allocated, a new balance sheet shows the following:

Assets		Liabilities and Owners' Equity	
Cash	$56,000	Accounts payable	$ 5,000
		Ottis, capital	18,000
		Skinner, capital	17,000
		Parr, capital.	16,000
		Total liabilities and	
Total assets	$56,000	owners' equity	$56,000

Observe that the one asset, cash of $56,000, exactly equals the sum of the liabilities and the equities of the partners.

After partnership assets are sold and the gain or loss shared, the realized cash is distributed to the proper parties. Because creditors have first claim, they are paid first. After the creditors are paid, the remaining cash is divided among the partners. Each partner has the right to cash equal to his or her equity or, in other words, cash equal to the balance of his or her capital account. These entries record the final cash payments and distribution to Ottis, Skinner, and Parr:

Jan.	15	Accounts Payable	5,000.00	
		Cash		5,000.00
		To pay the claims of the creditors.		
	15	Ottis, Capital	18,000.00	
		Skinner, Capital	17,000.00	
		Parr, Capital	16,000.00	
		Cash		51,000.00
		To distribute the remaining cash to the partners according to their capital account balances.		

Notice that after gains and losses are shared and the creditors are paid, each partner receives cash equal to the balance remaining in his or her capital account. The partners receive these amounts because cash is the only remaining partnership asset and a partner's capital account balance represents the partner's equity in that asset. In making the entry to distribute cash to the partners, be sure that you do not make the mistake of distributing it in the partners' income-and-loss-sharing ratio. Gains and losses from liquidations are allocated according to the income-and-loss-sharing ratio; but cash must be distributed to the partners in relation to their capital account balances.

All Assets Are Sold at a Net Loss: Each Partner's Capital Account Is Sufficient to Absorb His or Her Share of the Loss

In a liquidation, the partnership sometimes sells its assets at a net loss. For example, assume that the Ottis, Skinner, and Parr partnership does not sell its assets at a profit. Instead, assume that they sell the inventory for $10,000 and the other assets for $12,000. These entries record the sales and loss allocation:

Jan.	12	Cash	10,000.00	
		Loss or Gain on Liquidation	5,000.00	
		Merchandise Inventory		15,000.00
		Sold the inventory at a loss.		
	15	Cash	12,000.00	
		Loss or Gain on Liquidation	13,000.00	
		Other Assets		25,000.00
		Sold the other assets at a loss.		
	15	Ottis, Capital	9,000.00	
		Skinner, Capital	6,000.00	
		Parr, Capital	3,000.00	
		Loss or Gain on Liquidation		18,000.00
		To allocate the loss from sale of assets to the		
		partners in their income-and-loss-sharing ratio.		

After the entries are posted, a balance sheet shows that the partnership cash exactly equals the liabilities and the equities of the partners:

Assets		Liabilities and Owners' Equity	
Cash	$32,000	Accounts payable............	$ 5,000
		Ottis, capital	6,000
		Skinner, capital	9,000
		Parr, capital	12,000
		Total liabilities and	
Total assets	$32,000	owners' equity	$32,000

The following entries record the distribution of the cash to the proper parties:

Jan.	15	Accounts Payable	5,000.00	
		Cash		5,000.00
		To pay the partnership creditors.		
	15	Ottis, Capital	6,000.00	
		Skinner, Capital	9,000.00	
		Parr, Capital	12,000.00	
		Cash		27,000.00
		To distribute the remaining cash to the partners		
		according to the balances of their capital accounts.		

Notice again that after losses are shared and creditors are paid, the partners receive the remaining cash in the ratio of their capital account balances.

All Assets Are Sold at a Net Loss: A Partner's Capital Account Is Not Sufficient to Cover His or Her Share of the Loss

Sometimes the liquidation losses allocated to a partner exceed that partner's capital account balance. In such cases, the partner must, if possible, cover the deficit by paying cash into the partnership. For example, contrary to the situations described in the previous illustrations, assume that the Ottis, Skinner, and Parr partnership sells its merchandise for $3,000 and sells its other assets for $4,000. These entries record the sales and the loss allocation:

Jan.	12	Cash	3,000.00	
		Loss or Gain on Liquidation	12,000.00	
		Merchandise Inventory		15,000.00
		Sold the inventory at a loss.		
	15	Cash	4,000.00	
		Loss or Gain on Liquidation	21,000.00	
		Other Assets		25,000.00
		Sold the other assets at a loss.		
	15	Ottis, Capital	16,500.00	
		Skinner, Capital	11,000.00	
		Parr, Capital	5,500.00	
		Loss or Gain on Liquidation		33,000.00
		To allocate the loss from sale of assets to the partners in their income-and-loss-sharing ratio.		

After posting the entry to allocate the loss, the capital account of Ottis has a $1,500 debit balance and appears as follows:

Otis, Capital

Date		Explanation	Debit	Credit	Balance
Dec.	31	Balance			15,000.00
Jan.	15	Share of loss on sale	16,500.00		1,500.00 dr.

The partnership agreement states that one-half of all losses or gains should be allocated to Ottis. Therefore, since Ottis's capital account balance is not large enough to absorb his share of the loss, he is obligated to pay $1,500 into the partnership to cover the deficit, or debit balance. If Ottis is able to pay, this entry records the receipt:

Dec.	31	Cash	1,500.00	
		Ottis, Capital		1,500.00
		To record the additional investment of Ottis to cover his share of loss.		

After the $1,500 is received, the partnership has $18,500 in cash. The following entries record the cash distributions to the proper parties:

Jan.	15	Accounts Payable	5,000.00	
		Cash		5,000.00
		To pay the partnership creditors.		
	15	Skinner, Capital	4,000.00	
		Parr, Capital	9,500.00	
		Cash		13,500.00
		To distribute the remaining cash to the partners		
		according to the balances of their capital accounts.		

When a partnership's liquidation loss creates a debit balance in one partner's capital account balance, that partner may be unable to make up the deficit. In such cases, since each partner has unlimited liability, the deficit must be borne by the remaining partner or partners. For example, assume that Ottis is unable to pay the $1,500 necessary to cover the deficit in his capital account. If Ottis is unable to pay, his deficit must be shared by Skinner and Parr in their income-and-loss-sharing ratio. The partners share incomes and losses in the ratio of Ottis, 3; Skinner, 2; and Parr, 1. Therefore, Skinner and Parr share in a 2:1 ratio. This means that Skinner and Parr must share the $1,500 by which Ottis's share of the loss exceeded his capital account balance in a 2:1 ratio. Normally, the defaulting partner's deficit is transferred to the capital accounts of the remaining partners. This is accomplished for Ottis, Skinner, and Parr with the following entry:

Jan.	15	Skinner, Capital	1,000.00	
		Parr, Capital	500.00	
		Ottis, Capital		1,500.00
		To transfer the deficit of Ottis to the capital		
		accounts of Skinner and Parr.		

After the deficit is transferred, the capital accounts of the partners appear as in Illustration 14–4. These entries record the final payments to creditors and distribution to the partners:

Jan.	15	Accounts Payable	5,000.00	
		Cash		5,000.00
		To pay the partnership creditors.		
	15	Skinner, Capital	3,000.00	
		Parr, Capital	9,000.00	
		Cash		12,000.00
		To distribute the remaining cash to the partners		
		according to their capital account balances.		

Illustration 14–4 Allocating Liquidation Loss and Partner's Deficit to Capital Accounts

Otis, Capital

Date		Explanation	Debit	Credit	Balance
Dec.	31	Balance			15,000.00
Jan.	15	Share of loss on sale	16,500.00		1,500.00 dr.
	15	Deficit to Skinner and Parr		1,500.00	–0–

Skinner, Capital

Date		Explanation	Debit	Credit	Balance
Dec.	31	Balance			15,000.00
Jan.	15	Share of loss on sale	11,000.00		4,000.00
	15	Deficit to Skinner and Parr	1,000.00		3,000.00

Parr, Capital

Date		Explanation	Debit	Credit	Balance
Dec.	31	Balance			15,000.00
Jan.	15	Share of loss on sale	5,500.00		9,500.00
	15	Deficit to Skinner and Parr	500.00		9,000.00

Note that Ottis's inability to meet his loss share now does not relieve him of liability. If he becomes able to pay at some future time. Skinner and Parr may collect the full $1,500 from him. Skinner may collect $1,000, and Parr, $500.

The sharing of an insolvent partner's deficit by the remaining partners in their original income-and-loss-sharing ratio is generally regarded as equitable. In England, however, in 1904 in the case of *Garner* v. *Murray,* Judge Joyce ruled that the debit balance of the insolvent partner's capital account is a personal debt due to the other partners and to be borne by them in the ratio of their capital account balances immediately prior to liquidation.

While *Garner* v. *Murray* still appears to be good law, it is considered by most to be inequitable. The decision applies only when the partnership agreement does not cover this situation. It is therefore important to provide in the partnership agreement for the sharing of a partner's debit balance by the remaining partners in their income-and-loss-sharing ratio.

THE PARTNERSHIP AGREEMENT

After studying this chapter, you should appreciate White's and Smith's concluding statement on page 645. The partnership form of business organization is indeed replete with pitfalls. It is, therefore, extremely important that the partnership agreement or contract address possible eventualities, however remote they may seem at the time. The enthusiasm generated by embarking on a new venture should not cause the partners to overlook the importance of the content of the partnership agreement.

Progress Check

14–7 Under what conditions would the existing partners offer a new partner a bonus?

14–8 Why would a new partner's investment exceed his/her equity in a partnership?

14–9 On liquidation of ABC, C's capital balance ends up with a $1,000 debit balance. How is this amount closed out?

LO 1. List the characteristics of a partnership and explain the concepts of mutual agency and unlimited liability in a partnership. A partnership is a voluntary association between the partners that is based on a contract. The life of a partnership is limited by agreement or by the death or incapacity of a partner. Normally, each partner can act as an agent of the other partners and commit the partnership to any contract within the apparent scope of its business. All partners in a general partnership are personally liable for all the debts of the partnership. Limited partnerships include one or more general partners plus one or more (limited) partners whose liabilities are limited to the amount of their investments in the partnership. The risk of becoming a partner results in part from the fact that partnership characteristics include mutual agency and unlimited liability.

LO 2. Allocate partnership earnings to partners *(a)* **on a stated fractional basis,** *(b)* **in the partners' capital ratio, and** *(c)* **through the use of salary and interest allowances.** A partnership's net incomes or losses are allocated to the partners according to the terms of the partnership agreement. The agreement may specify that each partner will receive a given fraction, or that the allocation of incomes and losses will reflect salary allowances and/or interest allowances. When salary and/or interest allowances are granted, the residual net income or loss usually is allocated equally or on a stated fractional basis.

LO 3. Prepare entries for *(a)* **the sale of a partnership interest,** *(b)* **the admission of a new partner by investment, and** *(c)* **the retirement of a partner by the withdrawal of partnership assets.** When a new partner buys a partnership interest directly from one or more of the existing partners, the amount of cash paid from one partner to another does not affect the total recorded equity of the partnership. The recorded equity of the selling partner(s) is simply transferred to the capital account of the new partner. Alternatively, a new partner may purchase an equity by investing additional assets in the partnership. When this occurs, part of the new partner's investment may be credited as a bonus to the capital accounts of the existing partners. Also, to gain the participation of the new partner, the existing partners may give the new partner a bonus whereby portions of the existing partners' capital balances are transferred to the new partner's capital account. Occasionally, goodwill is recorded when a new partner invests in a partnership.

LO 4. Prepare entries required in the liquidation of a partnership. When a partnership is liquidated, losses and gains from selling the partnership assets are allocated to the partners according to their income-and-loss-sharing ratio. If a partner's capital account has a deficit balance that the partner cannot pay, the other partners must share the deficit in their relative income-and-loss-sharing ratio.

SUMMARY OF THE CHAPTER IN TERMS OF LEARNING OBJECTIVES

DEMONSTRATION PROBLEM

The following events affect the partner's capital accounts in several successive partnerships. On a work sheet with six money columns, one for each of five partners and a totals column, show the effects of the following events on the partners' capital accounts:

13/4/92   Kelly and Emerson create K&E Co. Each invests $10,000, and they agree to share profits equally.

31/12/92   K&E Co. earns $15,000 in the year. Kelly withdraws $4,000 from the partnership, and Emerson withdraws $7,000.

1/1/93   Reed is made a partner in KE&R Co. after contributing $12,000 cash. The partners agree that each will get a 10% interest allowance on their beginning capital balances. In addition, Emerson and Reed are to receive $5,000 salary allowances. The remainder of the income is to be divided evenly.

31/12/93   The partnership's income for the year is $40,000, and these withdrawals occur: Kelly, $5,000; Emerson, $12,500; and Reed, $11,000.

1/1/94   For $20,000, Kelly sells her interest to Merritt, who is accepted by Emerson and Reed as a partner in the new ER&M Co. The profits are to be shared equally after Emerson and Reed each receive $25,000 salaries.

31/12/94   The partnership's income for the year is $35,000, and these withdrawals occur: Emerson, $2,500, and Reed, $2,000.

1/1/95   Davis is admitted as a partner after investing $60,000 cash in the new Davis & Associates partnership. Davis is given a 50% interest in capital after the other partners transfer $3,000 to his account from each of theirs. A 20% interest allowance (on the beginning-of-year capital balances) will be used in sharing profits, but there will be no salaries. Davis will get 40% of the remainder, and the other three partners will each get 20%.

31/12/95   Davis & Associates earns $127,600 for the year, and these withdrawals occur: Emerson, $25,000; Reed, $27,000; Merritt, $15,000; and Davis, $40,000.

1/1/96   Davis buys out Emerson and Reed for the balances of their capital accounts, after a revaluation of the partnership assets. The revaluation gain is $50,000, which is divided in the previous 1:1:1:2 ratio. Davis pays the others from personal funds. Merritt and Davis will share profits on a 1:9 ratio.

28/2/96   The partnership had $10,000 of income since the beginning of the year. Merritt retires and receives partnership cash equal to her capital balance. Davis takes possession of the partnership assets in his own name, and the company is dissolved.

Planning the Solution

- Evaluate each transaction's effects on the capital accounts of the partners.
- Each time a new partner is admitted or a partner withdraws, allocate any bonus based on the income-or-loss-sharing agreement.
- Each time a new partner is admitted or a partner withdraws, allocate subsequent net incomes or losses in accordance with the new partnership agreement.

Event	Kelly	Emerson	Reed	Merritt	Davis	Total	Share of Income
13/4/92							
Initial investment	$10,000	$10,000				$ 20,000	
31/12/92							
Income (equal)	7,500	7,500				15,000	$ 15,000
Withdrawals	(4,000)	(7,000)				(11,000)	
Ending balance	$13,500	$10,500				$ 24,000	
1/1/93							
New investment			$12,000			12,000	
31/12/93							
10% interest	1,350	1,050	1,200			3,600	
Salaries		5,000	5,000			10,000	} 40,000
Remainder (equal)	8,800	8,800	8,800			26,400	
Withdrawals	(5,000)	(12,500)	(11,000)			(28,500)	
Ending balance	$18,650	$12,850	$16,000			$ 47,500	
1/1/94							
Transfer interest	(18,650)			$18,650		–0–	
31/12/94							
Salaries		25,000	25,000			50,000	35,000
Remainder (equal)		(5,000)	(5,000)	(5,000)		(15,000)	
Withdrawals		(2,500)	(2,000)			(4,500)	
Ending balance	$ –0–	$30,350	$34,000	$13,650		$ 78,000	
1/1/95							
New investment					$ 60,000	60,000	
Bonuses to Davis		(3,000)	(3,000)	(3,000)	9,000	–0–	
Adjusted balance		$27,350	$31,000	$10,650	$ 69,000	$138,000	
31/12/95							
20% interest		5,470	6,200	2,130	13,800	27,600	127,600
Remain. (1:1:1:2)		20,000	20,000	20,000	40,000	100,000	
Withdrawals		(25,000)	(27,000)	(15,000)	(40,000)	(107,000)	
Ending balance		$27,820	$30,200	$17,780	$82,800	$158,600	
1/1/96							
Gain (1:1:1:2)		10,000	10,000	10,000	20,000	50,000	
Adjusted balance		$37,820	$40,200	$27,780	$102,800	$208,600	
Transfer interests		(37,820)	(40,200)		78,020	–0–	
Adjusted balance		$ –0–	$ –0–	$27,780	$180,820	$208,600	
28/2/96							
Income (1:9)				1,000	9,000	10,000	10,000
Adjusted balance				$28,780	$189,820	$218,600	$227,600*
Settlements				(28,780)	(189,820)	(218,600)	(227,600)**
Final balance				$ –0–	$ –0–	$ –0–	$ –0–

*Total of reported net incomes.
**Total of allocated net incomes.

Solution to the Demonstration Problem

GLOSSARY

General partner a partner who assumes unlimited liability for the debts of the partnership; the general partner in a limited partnership is usually responsible for its management. p. 647

General partnership a partnership in which all partners have unlimited liability for partnership debts. p. 647

Limited partners partners who have no personal liability for debts of the limited partnership beyond the amounts they have invested in the partnership. p. 647

Limited partnership a partnership that has two classes of partners, limited partners and one or more general partners. p. 647

Mutual agency the legal relationship among the partners whereby each partner is an agent of the partnership and is able to bind the partnership to contracts within the apparent scope of the partnership's business. p. 647

Partnership an unincorporated association of two or more persons to carry on a business for profit as co-owners. p. 646

Partnership contract the agreement between partners that sets forth the terms under which the affairs of the partnership will be conducted. p. 646

Partnership liquidations the winding up of a partnership business by converting its assets to cash and distributing the cash to the proper parties. p. 660

Statement of changes in partners' equity a financial statement that shows the total capital balances at the beginning of the period, any additional investments by the partners, the net income or loss of the period, the partners' withdrawals during the period, and the ending capital balances. p. 651

Unlimited liability of partners the legal relationship among general partners of a partnership that makes each general partner responsible for paying all the debts of the partnership if the other partners are unable to pay their shares. p. 647

QUESTIONS

1. Amey and Lacey are partners. Lacey dies, and her son claims the right to take his mother's place in the partnership. Does he have this right? Why?

2. If Roscoe cannot legally enter into a contract, can he become a partner?

3. If a partnership contract does not state the period of time the partnership is to exist, when does the partnership end?

4. As applied to a partnership, what does the term *mutual agency* mean?

5. Kurt and Ellen are partners in operating a store. Without consulting Kurt, Ellen enters into a contract for the purchase of merchandise for the store. Kurt contends that he did not authorize the order and refuses to take delivery. The vendor sues the partners for the contract price of the merchandise. Will the partnership have to pay? Why?

6. Would your answer to Question 5 differ if Kurt and Ellen were partners in a public accounting firm?

7. Can partners limit the right of a partner to commit their partnership to contracts? Would the agreement be binding *(a)* on the partners and *(b)* on outsiders?

8. What does the term *unlimited liability* mean when it is applied to members of a partnership?

9. The partnership agreement of Barnes and Ardmore provides for a two-thirds, one-third sharing of income but says nothing about losses. The first year of partnership operations resulted in a loss and Barnes argues that the loss should be shared equally because the partnership agreement said nothing about sharing losses. What do you think?

10. Ace and Bud are partners who agree that Ace will receive a $50,000 salary allowance after which remaining incomes or losses will be shared equally. If Bud's capital account is credited $1,000 as his share of the net income in a given period, how much net income did the partnership earn?

11. Van, Wink, and York are partners with capital account balances of $7,000 each. Zack pays Van $8,000 for his one-third interest and is admitted to the partnership. The bookkeeper debits Van, Capital, and credits Zack, Capital, for $7,000. Zack objects; he wants his capital account to show an $8,000 balance, the amount he paid for his interest. Explain why Zack's capital account is credited for $7,000.

12. If the partners in Blume Partnership want the financial statements to show the procedures used to allocate the partnership income among the partners, on what financial statement should the allocation appear?

13. After all partnership assets are converted to cash and all liabilities have been paid, the remaining cash should equal the sum of the balances of the partners' capital accounts. Why?

14. Kay, Kat, and Kim are partners. In a liquidation, Kay's share of partnership losses exceeds her capital account balance. She is unable to meet the deficit from her personal assets, and the excess losses are shared by her partners. Does this relieve Kay of liability?

15. A partner withdraws from a partnership and receives assets of greater value than the book value of his or her equity. Should the remaining partners share the resulting reduction in their equities in the ratio of their relative capital balances or in their income-and-loss-sharing ratio?

QUICK STUDY (Five-Minute Exercises)

Fred and Jim entered into a partnership and the first year's operation resulted in the following:

Sales	$510,000
Cost of goods sold	305,000
Operating expenses excluding salaries and wages	45,000
Salaries and wages:	
Two employees	42,000
Fred	30,000
Jim	25,000

Determine the partnership net income.

Fred Earnest and Jackie Magness are partners in a business they started two years ago. The partnership agreement states that Earnest should receive a salary allowance of $15,000 and Magness should receive $20,000. Any remaining income or loss is to be shared equally. Determine each partner's share of the current year's net income of $52,000.

Assume that in QS 14–2 above, the net income was $21,000 instead of $52,000.

Anthony, Bonnie, and Carrie are partners in ABC with respective capital balances on February 1, 1997, of $6,000, $9,000, and $11,000. On that date, Bonnie sold her share to Darwin for $10,000. Anthony and Carrie agreed to accept Darwin as a partner. Prepare the journal entry on the partnership's books to record the transfer of equity from Bonnie to Darwin.

Ken, Lam, and Mat are partners in KLM, sharing net income and loss in 5:3:2 ratio respectively. Lam decides to retire and agreed with Ken and Mat to withdraw from the partnership for a $50,000 cash consideration for his interest. Just prior to withdrawal, the respective capital balances of the partners were $88,000, $56,000 and $44,000. An audit and appraisal indicated that the $50,000 agreed to by Lam represented fair market value of his stake in the partnership. Consequently, decision was to write down the assets to reflect current valuation. Determine capital balances of Ken and Mat in the new partnership.

QS 14–6
(LO 2, 3)

Omni, Paranka, and Quadra are partners in OPQ with respective capital balances of $30,000, $22,000, and $15,000 and income-and-loss-sharing ratio of 3:2:1. Omni and Quadra encouraged Paranka to retire by offering her $30,000 for her stake in the partnership. Paranka accepted the offer. Omni and Quadra agreed that aside from the decrease in the partnership's cash, no other assets would change. Determine the capital balances of Omni and Quadra after the withdrawal of Paranka.

QS 14–7
(LO 2, 3, 4)

Samuel, Amy, and Mary were partners in SAM, sharing income and loss in the 4:3:2 ratio respectively. Their respective capital balances on March 1, 1997, were $65,000, $48,000, and $34,000. On that day they agreed to sell the partnership for an amount sufficient to pay the partnership liabilities and leave $165,000 to be divided by the partners. Determine the amount each partner received.

QS 14–8
(LO 2, 3, 4)

Assume that in 14–7 above, the partnership was sold for an amount that left $120,000 to be divided by the partners. Determine the amount each partner received.

EXERCISES

Exercise 14–1
Journalizing partnership entries
(LO 2)

On February 1, 1996, Young and Olde formed a partnership in which Young contributed $70,000 and Olde contributed land valued at $80,000 and a building valued at $90,000. The partnership also is to assume responsibility for Olde's $30,000 long-term note payable. The partners agreed to share profits as follows: Young is to receive an annual salary allowance of $35,000, each partner is to receive 10% of his or her original capital investment, and any remaining profit or loss is to be shared equally. On November 20, 1996, Young withdrew cash of $40,000 and Olde withdrew $30,000. Present general journal entries to record the initial capital investments of the partners, the cash withdrawals of the partners, and the December 31 closing of the withdrawals accounts and the Income Summary account, which had a credit balance of $68,000.

Exercise 14–2
Income allocation in a partnership
(LO 2)

Newberg and Scampi began a partnership by investing $52,000 and $78,000, respectively. During its first year, the partnership earned $180,000. Prepare calculations that show how the income should be allocated to the partners under each of the following plans for sharing net incomes and losses:

a.   The partners failed to agree on a method of sharing income.

b.   The partners agreed to share incomes and losses in their investment ratio.

c.   The partners agreed to share income by allowing an $85,000 per year salary allowance to Newberg, a $65,000 per year salary allowance to Scampi, 10% interest on beginning capital balances, and the remainder equally.

Exercise 14–3
Income allocation in a partnership
(LO 2)

Assume the partners in Exercise 14–2 agreed to share net incomes and losses by allowing yearly salary allowances of $85,000 to Newberg and $65,000 to Scampi, 10% interest allowances on their investments, and the balance equally. Determine (a) the shares of Newberg and Scampi in a first-year net income of $145,300 and (b) the partners' shares in a first-year net loss of $30,200.

The partners in the Duprix Partnership have agreed that partner Dupont may sell his $70,000 equity in the partnership to Queen, for which Queen will pay Dupont $55,000. Present the partnership's journal entry to record the sale on April 30.

Exercise 14–4
Sale of a partnership interest
(LO 3)

The Hagen-Baden Partnership has total partners' equity of $380,000, which is made up of Hagen, Capital, $300,000, and Baden, Capital, $80,000. The partners share net incomes and losses in a ratio of 75% to Hagen and 25% to Baden. On July 1, Megan is admitted to the partnership and given a 20% interest in equity and in gains and losses. Prepare the journal entry to record the entry of Megan under each of the following unrelated assumptions: Megan invests cash of *(a)* $95,000; *(b)* $115,000; and *(c)* $55,000.

Exercise 14–5
Admission of a new partner
(LO 3)

Hollis, Evans, and Bowen have been partners sharing net incomes and losses in a 3:5:2 ratio. On October 31, the date Bowen retires from the partnership, the equities of the partners are Hollis, $130,000; Evans, $200,000; and Bowen, $50,000. Present general journal entries to record Bowen's retirement under each of the following unrelated assumptions.

Exercise 14–6
Retirement of a partner
(LO 3)

a. Bowen is paid $50,000 in partnership cash for his equity.

b. Bowen is paid $60,000 in partnership cash for his equity.

c. Bowen is paid $45,000 in partnership cash for his equity.

The Whiz-Bam-Boom partnership was begun with investments by the partners as follows: Whiz, $115,600; Bam, $88,600; and Boom, $95,800. The first year of operations did not go well, and the partners finally decided to liquidate the partnership, sharing all losses equally. On December 13, after all assets were converted to cash and all creditors were paid, only $30,000 in partnership cash remained.

Exercise 14–7
Liquidation of a partnership
(LO 4)

Required

1. Calculate the capital account balances of the partners after the liquidation of assets and payment of creditors.

2. Assume that any partner with a deficit pays cash to the partnership to cover the deficit. Then, present the general journal entries on December 31 to record the cash receipt from the deficit partner(s) and the final disbursement of cash to the partners.

3. Now make the contrary assumption that any partner with a deficit is not able to reimburse the partnership. Present journal entries *(a)* to transfer the deficit of any deficient partners to the other partners and *(b)* to record the final disbursement of cash to the partners.

Prince, Count, and Earl are partners who share incomes and losses in a 1:3:4 ratio. After lengthy disagreements among the partners and several unprofitable periods, the partners decided to liquidate the partnership. Before the liquidation, the partnership balance sheet showed total assets, $238,000; liabilities, $200,000; Prince, Capital, $8,000; Count, Capital, $10,000; and Earl, Capital, $20,000. The cash proceeds from selling the assets were sufficient to repay all but $45,000 to the creditors. Calculate the loss from selling the assets, allocate the loss to the partners, and determine how much of the remaining liability should be paid by each partner.

Exercise 14–8
Liquidation of a partnership
(LO 4)

Assume that the Prince, Count, and Earl partnership of Exercise 14–8 is a limited partnership. Prince and Count are general partners, and Earl is a limited partner. How much of the remaining $45,000 liability should be paid by each partner?

Exercise 14–9
Liquidation of a limited partnership
(LO 4)

PROBLEMS

Problem 14–1
Methods of allocating
partnership income
(LO 2)

Del Willis, Lara Hart, and Susan Butler invested $66,400, $58,100, and $41,500, respectively, in a partnership. During its first year, the firm earned $175,500.

Required

Prepare entries to close the firm's Income Summary account as of December 31 and to allocate the net income to the partners under each of the assumptions below. (Round your answers to the nearest whole dollar.)

a. The partners could not agree as to the method of sharing incomes.

b. The partners agreed to share net incomes and losses in the ratio of their beginning investments.

c. The partners agreed to share income by allowing annual salary allowances of $52,000 to Willis, $58,000 to Hart, and $45,000 to Butler; allowing 10% interest on the partners' investments; and sharing the remainder equally.

Problem 14–2
Allocating partnership
incomes and losses;
sequential years
(LO 2)

Linda Meade and Richard Munez are in the process of forming a partnership to which Meade will devote one-third time and Munez will devote full time. They have discussed the following plans for sharing net incomes and losses:

a. In the ratio of their investments which they have agreed to maintain at $33,000 for Meade and $49,500 for Munez.

b. In proportion to the time devoted to the business.

c. A salary allowance of $3,500 per month to Munez and the balance in their investment ratio.

d. A $3,500 per month salary allowance to Munez, 10% interest on their investments, and the balance equally.

The partners expect the business to generate income as follows: year 1, $20,000 net loss; year 2, $60,000 net income; and year 3, $95,000 net income.

Required

1. Prepare three schedules with the following columnar headings:

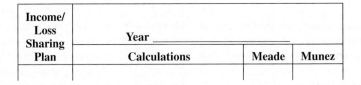

Income/ Loss Sharing Plan	Year _____		
	Calculations	Meade	Munez

2. Complete a schedule for each of the first three years by showing how the partnership net income or loss for each year should be allocated to the partners under each of the four plans being considered. Round your answers to the nearest whole dollar.

Problem 14–3
Allocating partnership
incomes and losses;
sequential years
(LO 2)

Harriet Monroe and Ozzie Young are in the process of forming a partnership to which Monroe will devote one-fourth time and Young will devote full time. They have discussed the following plans for sharing net incomes and losses:

a. In the ratio of their investments which they have agreed to maintain at $49,800 for Monroe and $74,700 for Young.

b. In proportion to the time devoted to the business.

c. A salary allowance of $5,250 per month to Young and the balance in their investment ratio.

d. A $5,250 per month salary allowance to Young, 10% interest on their investments, and the balance equally.

The partners expect the business to generate income as follows: year 1, $30,500 net income; year 2, $82,500 net loss; and year 3, $215,000 net income.

Required

1. Prepare three schedules with the following columnar headings:

Income/ Loss Sharing Plan	Year _____		
	Calculations	Monroe	Young

2. Complete a schedule for each of the first three years by showing how the partnership income for each year would be allocated to the partners under each of the four plans being considered. Round your answers to the nearest whole dollar.

Betty Iris, Jim Dolan, and Bob Carrow formed the IDC Partnership by making capital contributions of $245,000, $280,000, and $175,000, respectively. They anticipate annual net incomes of $390,000 and are considering the following alternative plans of sharing net incomes and losses: (*a*) equally; (*b*) in the ratio of their initial investments; or (*c*) interest allowances of 12% on initial investments, salary allowances of $95,000 to Iris, $46,000 to Dolan, and $60,000 to Carrow, with any remaining balance shared equally.

Problem 14–4
Partnership income allocation, statement of changes in partners' equity, and closing entries
(LO 2)

Required

1. Prepare a schedule with the following column headings:

Income/Loss Sharing Plan	Calculations	Share to Iris	Share to Dolan	Share to Carrow	Totals

Use the schedule to show how a net income of $390,000 would be distributed under each of the alternative plans being considered. Round your answers to the nearest whole dollar.

2. Prepare a statement of changes in partners' equity showing the allocation of income to the partners, assuming they agree to use alternative (*c*) and the net income actually earned is $135,000. During the year, Iris, Dolan, and Carrow withdrew $40,000, $30,000, and $20,000, respectively.

3. Prepare the December 31 journal entry to close Income Summary assuming they agree to use alternative (*c*) and the net income is $135,000. Also close the withdrawals accounts.

Problem 14–5
Partnership income
allocation, statement
of changes in partners'
equity, and closing
entries
(LO 2)

Lou Cass, Red Sanders, and Barbara Archer formed the CSA Partnership by making capital contributions of $116,640, $129,600, and $142,560, respectively. They anticipate
annual net incomes of $195,000 and are considering the following alternative plans of
sharing net incomes and losses: (*a*) equally; (*b*) in the ratio of their initial investments;
or (*c*) salary allowances of $35,000 to Cass, $20,000 to Sanders, and $45,000 to Archer
and interest allowances of 10% on initial investments, with any remaining balance shared
equally.

Required

1. Prepare a schedule with the following column headings:

Income/Loss Sharing Plan	Calculations	Share to Cass	Share to Sanders	Share to Archer	Totals

Use the schedule to show how a net income of $195,000 would be distributed under
each of the alternative plans being considered. Round your answers to the nearest
whole dollar.

2. Prepare a statement of changes in partners' equity showing the allocation of income
to the partners, assuming they agree to use alternative (*c*) and the net income earned
is $85,000. During the year, Cass, Sanders, and Archer withdrew $15,000, $20,000,
and $23,000, respectively.

3. Prepare the December 31 journal entry to close Income Summary assuming they
agree to use alternative (*c*) and the net income is $85,000. Also close the with-
drawals accounts.

Problem 14–6
Withdrawal of a partner
(LO 3)

Part 1. Pushkin, Tolstoy, and Chekhov are partners with capital balances as follows:
Pushkin, $183,750; Tolstoy, $131,250; and Chekhov, $315,000. The partners share incomes
and losses in a 1:2:3 ratio. Prepare general journal entries to record the August 1
withdrawal of Tolstoy from the partnership under each of the following unrelated assumptions.

a. Tolstoy sells his interest to Gogol for $168,000 after Pushkin and Chekhov approve
the entry of Gogol as a partner.

b. Tolstoy gives his interest to a son-in-law, Lermontov. Pushkin and Chekhov accept
Lermontov as a partner.

c. Tolstoy is paid $131,250 in partnership cash for his equity.

d. Tolstoy is paid $194,250 in partnership cash for his equity.

e. Tolstoy is paid $27,250 in partnership cash plus delivery equipment recorded on the
partnership books at $115,000 less accumulated amortization of $63,000.

Part 2. Assume that Tolstoy does not retire from the partnership described in Part 1.
Instead, Nabokov is admitted to the partnership on August 1 with a 25% equity. Prepare
general journal entries to record the entry of Nabokov into the partnership under each of
the following unrelated assumptions:

a. Nabokov invests $210,000.

b. Nabokov invests $157,500.

c. Nabokov invests $262,500.

Maxwell, Adams, and Nelson plan to liquidate their partnership. They have always shared losses and gains in a 1:4:5 ratio, and on the day of the liquidation their balance sheet appeared as follows:

Problem 14–7
Liquidation of a partnership
(LO 4)

MAXWELL, ADAMS AND NELSON
Balance Sheet
June 30, 19—

Assets		Liabilities and Owners' Equity	
Cash	$ 27,500	Accounts payable	$ 52,150
Other assets	180,500	Pam Maxwell, capital	30,500
		Greg Adams, capital	80,350
		Linda Nelson, capital	45,000
		Total liabilities and	
Total assets	$208,000	owners' equity	$208,000

Required

Prepare general journal entries to record the sale of the other assets and the distribution of the cash to the proper parties under each of the following unrelated assumptions:

a. The other assets are sold for $195,250.

b. The other assets are sold for $150,000.

c. The other assets are sold for $85,000, and any partners with resulting deficits can and do pay in the amount of their deficits.

d. The other assets are sold for $75,000, and the partners have no assets other than those invested in the business.

Until May 28, 1996, Block, Sun, and Steen were partners that shared incomes and losses in the ratio of their beginning-of-year capital account balances. On May 28, Sun suffered a heart attack and died. Block and Steen immediately ended the business operations and prepared the following adjusted trial balance:

Problem 14–8
Death of a partner
(LO 3)

BLOCK, SUN AND STEEN
Adjusted Trial Balance
May 28, 1996

Cash	$ 23,625	
Accounts receivable	55,125	
Allowance for doubtful accounts		$ 2,625
Supplies inventory	111,750	
Equipment	70,875	
Accumulated amortization, equipment		18,375
Land	23,625	
Building	262,500	
Accumulated amortization, building		49,875
Accounts payable		15,750
Note payable (secured by mortgage)		52,500
Bob Block, capital		157,500
Joan Sun, capital		157,500
Tim Steen, capital		78,750
Bob Block, withdrawals	8,250	
Joan Sun, withdrawals	8,250	
Tim Steen, withdrawals	8,250	
Revenues		204,750
Expenses	165,375	
Totals	$737,625	$737,625

Required

1. Prepare May 28 entries to close the revenue, expense, income summary, and withdrawals accounts of the partnership.
2. Assume the estate of Sun agreed to accept the land and building and to assume the mortgage note thereon in settlement of its claim against the partnership assets, and that Block and Steen planned to continue the business and rent the building from the estate. Give the partnership's June 15 entry to transfer the land, building, and mortgage note in settlement with the estate.
3. Assume that in place of the foregoing, the estate of Sun demanded a cash settlement, and the business had to be sold to a competitor who gave $355,000 for the noncash assets and assumed the mortgage note but not the accounts payable. Give the June 15 entry to transfer the noncash assets and mortgage note to the competitor, and give the entries to allocate the loss to the partners and to distribute the partnership cash to the proper parties.

Required

1. Prepare general journal entries to record the asset sales, the allocation of the realization loss, and the payment of the creditors.
2. Under the assumption that any partners with capital deficits can and do pay the amount of their deficits on July 17, give the entry to record the receipt of the cash and the distribution of partnership cash to the remaining partners.
3. Under the assumption that any partners with capital deficits cannot pay, give the entry to allocate the deficits to the remaining partners. Then give the entry to distribute the partnership cash to the remaining partners.

Problem 14–9
Analytical essay
(LO 2)

Janet Koppen and Beverly Spikes want to form a partnership and are considering two methods of sharing incomes and losses. Method *a* splits all profits and losses in a 2:3 ratio, or 40% to Koppen and 60% to Spikes. Method *b* depends on the income or loss of the partnership. If the partnership incurs a loss, the partners share it equally. If the income is in the range of $0 to $36,000, it is allocated based on an annual salary allowance of $12,000 to Koppen and $24,000 to Spikes. If the net income exceeds $36,000 the residual after the salary allowances is shared equally.

Spikes has retained you to write an evaluation of the two methods indicating which is most favourable to her. Your discussion should include a comparison of the two methods at each of the three possible net income levels. Also, discuss the importance of asking Spikes to estimate the partnership's future earnings.

Problem 14–10
Analytical essay
(LO 3)

Kay Doobie, Ed Foley, and Brian McKenzie have been operating a partnership for several years. Business has not been good recently, and Doobie is withdrawing from the partnership. The partners agree that the market values of the assets are less than their recorded book values. However, they do not want to change the recorded values at his time. As a result, the partners have agreed that Doobie should withdraw cash in an amount that is less than her capital account balance.

Foley and McKenzie are not sure how to calculate the adjustments to their capital accounts (brought about by the difference between Doobie's equity and the cash she is withdrawing). Foley thinks they should split the difference in the ratio of their capital account balances. McKenzie thinks the adjustments should be calculated using their income-and-loss-sharing ratio. Which partner do you think is correct? Explain why.

PROVOCATIVE PROBLEMS

Lisa White and Joe Black agreed to share the annual net incomes or losses of their partnership as follows. If the partnership earns a net income, the first $50,000 is allocated 25% to White and 75% to Black so as to reflect the time devoted to the business by each partner. Income in excess of $50,000 is shared equally. However, if business operations result in a loss for the year, the partners have agreed to share the loss equally.

**Provocative Problem
14–1**
White and Black
Partnership
(LO 2)

Required

1. Prepare a schedule showing how the 1996 net income of $59,000 should be allocated to the partners.

2. Immediately after the closing entries for 1996 were posted on December 31, 1996, the partners discover $70,000 of unrecorded accounts payable. These accounts payable relate to expenses incurred by the business. Black suggests that the $70,000 should be allocated equally between the partners as a loss. White disagrees and argues that an entry should be made to record the accounts payable and correct the capital accounts to reflect an $11,000 net loss for 1996. (*a*) Present the January 1, 1997, journal entry to record the accounts payable and allocate the loss to the partners according to Black's suggestion. (*b*) Now give the January 1, 1997, journal entry to record the accounts payable and correct the capital accounts according to White's argument. Show how you calculated the amounts in the entry.

3. Which partner do you think is right? Why?

Maddie Hall and Amanda Miller are partners that own and operate The Fitness Place, an exercise and casual wear shop. Hall has a $75,000 equity in the business, and Miller has a $60,000 equity. They share incomes and losses by allowing annual salary allowances of $33,750 to Hall and $27,000 to Miller, with any remaining balance being shared 60% to Hall and 40% to Miller.

**Provocative Problem
14–2**
The Fitness Place
(LO 3)

Susie Hall, Maddie Hall's daughter, has been working in the store on a salary basis. In addition to working in the store, Susie is a popular aerobics teacher and is well known among other aerobics teachers and a number of students. As a result, Susie attracts a great deal of business to the store. The partners believe that a least one-third of the past three years' sales can be traced directly to Susie's association with the store, and it is reasonable to assume she was instrumental in attracting even more.

Susie is paid $1,800 per month but feels this is not sufficient to induce her to remain with the firm as an employee. However, she likes her work and would like to remain in the fitness-wear business. What she really wants is to become a partner in the business.

Her mother is anxious for her to remain in the business and proposes the following:

a. That Susie be admitted to the partnership with a 20% equity in the partnership assets.

b. That she, Maddie Hall, transfer from her capital account to that of Susie's one half the 20% interest; that Susie contribute to the firm's assets a noninterest-bearing note for the other half; and that she, Maddie Hall, will guarantee payment of the note.

c. That incomes and losses be shared by continuing the $33,750 and $27,000 salary allowances of the original partners and that Susie be given a $21,600 annual salary allowance, after which any remaining income or loss would be shared 40% to Maddie Hall, 40% to Amanda Miller, and 20% to Susie Hall.

Prepare a report to Ms. Miller on the advisability of accepting Maddie Hall's proposal. Under the assumption that net incomes for the past three years have been $65,400, $68,500, and $70,500, respectively, prepare schedules showing (a) how net income was allocated during the past three years and (b) how it would have been allocated had the proposed new agreement been in effect. Also, (c) prepare a schedule showing the partners' capital interests as they would be immediately after the admission of Susie.

Provocative Problem 14–3
Venerable Partnership
(LO 3)

The following is the balance sheet of the Venerable Partnership on December 31, 1996:

Assets		Liabilities and Owners' Equity	
Cash	$ 45,250	Hamilton, capital.	$22,750
Other assets	56,250	Adams, capital	33,700
Land	33,750	Hay, capital.	78,750
		Total liabilities and	
Total assets	$135,250	owners' equity	$135,250

The income-and-loss-sharing percentages are: Hamilton, 20%; Adams, 30%; and Hay, 50%. Hamilton wishes to withdraw from the partnership, and the partners finally agree that the land owned by the partnership should be transferred to Hamilton in full payment for his equity. In reaching this decision they recognize that the land has appreciated since it was purchased and is now worth $60,000. If Hamilton retires on January 1, 1997, what journal entries should be made on that date?

Provocative Problem 14–4
Ethical issues essay

Review the "As a Matter of Ethics" case on page 661. Then write a brief essay describing Janis Carpenter's engagement and suggestions you would offer the partners. Your essay should include the reasons why your settlement is fair.

ANALYTICAL AND REVIEW PROBLEMS

A & R Problem 14–1

Jay and Mar entered into a partnership to carry on a business under the firm name of Jay-Mar Sportsland. Prior to the final signing of the agreement Jay asks you to evaluate the "income/loss distribution clause" contained in the agreement.

Your examination revealed that the agreement called for the following: Equal sharing of net income and losses after an initial allocation of $40,000 to Jay and $10,000 to Mar in order to reflect the difference in time and expertise devoted to the business by each partner. The initial allocation would be made regardless of the level of net income/loss.

Required

Prepare a report to Jay on the particular clause of the agreement. Your report should show the consequence on each partner of operating results as follows: (a) net income of $80,000; (b) net income of $20,000; (c) operation at break-even, that is, no net income or loss; (d) loss of $20,000; (e) loss of $80,000.

A & R Problem 14–2

The summarized balance sheet of Bell, Trunk, and Field showed:

Assets		Equities	
Cash	$ 20,000	Liabilities	$ 60,000
Other assets	280,000	Bell, capital	80,000
		Trunk, capital	120,000
		Field, capital	$ 40,000
Total assets	$300,000	Total equities	$300,00

The partnership has operated successfully for nearly 25 years, and Field, because of his age and health, is pushing for sale of the business. In fact, he has found Arn, a buyer who is willing to pay $320,000 cash and take over the liabilities. Both Bell and Trunk are not anxious to sell what they refer to as "our little gold mine."

Field is adamant about getting out and has proposed the following:

1. Either sell to Arn, or Bell and Trunk (a new partnership) Should buy out Field at an amount Field would receive if the business was sold to Arn.

2. Admit Arn to partnership upon the purchase of Field's share for an amount Field and Arn will negotiate.

The present partnership agreement calls for a distribution of net income/loss on a 3:5:2 basis. If Arn is admitted to partnership the ratio would not change; he would be entitled to Field's 20% share of net income/loss. If Bell and Trunk buy out for an amount based on the Arn offer, Bell and Trunk would continue to share net income/loss on the same relative basis. They would (the new partnership of Bell and Trunk) have to borrow sufficient funds from the bank to retain a minimum cash balance of $10,000.

Required

1. Prepare the general journal entry for admission of Arn to the partnership upon his purchase of Field's interest for an undisclosed amount.

2. Prepare the necessary entries to record Field's withdrawal from the partnership. The amount paid to Field is equal to the amount he would have received if the partnership was sold to Arn.

CONCEPT TESTER

Test your understanding of the concepts introduced in this chapter by completing the following crossword puzzle:

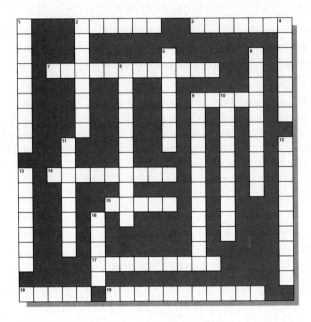

Across Clues

2. Purpose or motive of partnership.
3. A basis for allocation.
7. Characteristic that each partner is able to bind the partnership (2 words).
9. Cause for dissolution of a partnership.
14. Type of association.
15. Reward to new partner.
17. Particulars of partnership.
18. Judge in *Garner* vs *Murray* case.
19. Gain or loss on disposal of partnership assets.

Down Clues

1. Degree of exposure of general partners.
2. Co-owners of an unincorporated business.
4. Liability protection enjoyed by certain partners.
5. Negative balance in a partner's account.
6. Retirement of partner from the partnership.
8. Winding up of a partnership.
9. Final entry on liquidation for disposal of cash.
10. Division of net income/loss.
11. Excess of new partner's investment over her/his equity.
12. Another cause for dissolution of a partnership.
13. Partner(s) with unlimited liability.
16. If not specified, sharing of income/loss.

ANSWERS TO PROGRESS CHECKS

14–1 *b.*

14–2

	Mixon	**Reed**
10% interest	$ 7,000	$ 3,500
Balance	14,750	14,750
Total allocation	$21,750	$18,250

14–3 The creditors may satisfy their claims from personal assets of the partners if partnership assets are not sufficient.

14–4 No. A partnership is a voluntary association requiring an agreement of all potential partners to associate.

14–5 Yes. The transaction is between J and Z and is outside the scope of the other partners.

14–6 No. A new partnership comes into existence with a negotiated sharing ratio that may be different from the ratio used in the replaced partnership.

14–7 The existing partners would offer a bonus if there is a need for additional cash and/or the particular skills that the new partner would bring to the partnership.

14–8 There is evidence of potential superior profitability of the partnership.

14–9 C should contribute $1,000 to the partnership. If C is unable to meet the $1,000 requirement, the deficit would be allocated to A and B before distribution of cash.

Organization and Operation of Corporations

Business corporations that operate as corporations enjoy many advantages, including the ability to grow larger by selling shares to the public. The annual report presents accounting information that helps bridge the gap between a corporation's owners and its professional managers.

Karen White and Mark Smith looked forward to the study of the next two chapters on corporations. They had already acquired a degree of knowledge through examination of the Annual Report of Imperial Oil Limited and the various handouts by the instructor.

When they had finished reading Chapter 15, White and Smith fantasized as to what they would do if they came into money. They wondered what kind of a return they could expect on investments. Snapping out of their daydream, they realized that the questions they contemplated were real and important. Consequently, they decided that the next day they would be back in the library examining not only Imperial's dividend record, but also those of other companies whose names were familiar to them. Karen and Mark decided that they would take with them to the library the stock quotation page from the local newspaper. The next day they compiled the following information:

Company	Common Dividend 1994	Share Prices Feb. 15, 1995
Imperial Oil Limited	$1.80*	$46 ¼
BCE Inc.	2.72	43 ⅜
Anchor Lamina Inc.	0.12	6
Imasco Inc.	1.92	41 ⅜
Hemlo Gold Ltd.	0.20	11 ⅞

*Excludes special dividend of $3.00.

LEARNING OBJECTIVES

After studying Chapter 15, you should be able to:

1. **Explain the advantages, disadvantages, and organization of corporations and the differences in accounting for partnerships and corporations.**
2. **Record the issuance of no-par value shares.**
3. **Record transactions involving share subscriptions and explain the effects of subscribed shares on a corporation's assets and shareholders' equity.**
4. **State the differences between common and preferred shares, and allocate dividends between the common and preferred shares.**
5. **Describe convertible preferred shares and explain the meaning of redemption, book, and market values of shares.**
6. **Calculate dividend yield and explain its meaning.**
7. **Define or explain the words and phrases listed in the chapter glossary.**

Of the three common types of business organizations (proprietorships, partnerships, and corporations), corporations are fewest in number. However, they transact more business than the other two combined. Thus, from an overall economic point of view, corporations are clearly the most important form of business organization. As you study this chapter, you will learn how corporations are organized and operated, and about some of the procedures used to account for corporations.

ADVANTAGES OF THE CORPORATE FORM

LO 1

Explain the advantages, disadvantages, and organization of corporations and the differences in accounting for partnerships and corporations.

Corporations have become the dominant type of business because of the advantages created by their unique characteristics. We describe these characteristics in the following sections.

Corporations Are Separate Legal Entities

Unlike a proprietorship or partnership a corporation is a separate legal entity. Separate and distinct from its owners, a corporation conducts its affairs with the same rights, duties, and responsibilities as a person. However, because it is not a real person, a corporation can act only through its agents, who are its officers and managers.

Shareholders Are Not Liable for the Corporation's Debts

Because a corporation is a separate legal entity, it is responsible for its own acts and its own debts. Its shareholders are not liable for either. From the viewpoint of an investor, this lack of shareholders' liability is, perhaps, the most important advantage of the corporate form of business.

Ownership Rights of Corporations Are Easily Transferred

The ownership of a corporation is represented by shares that generally are easily bought or sold. Also, the transfer of shares from one shareholder to another usually has no effect on the corporation or its operations.[1] Many companies have thousands or even millions of their shares bought and sold every day through major stock exchanges located throughout the world.

---

[1] However, a transfer of ownership can create significant effects if it brings about a change in who controls the company's activities.

Corporations Have Continuity of Life

A corporation's life may continue indefinitely because it is not tied to the physical lives of its owners. In some cases, a corporation's life may be initially limited by the laws of the jurisdiction of its incorporation. However, the corporation's articles of incorporation can be renewed and its life extended when the stated time expires. Thus, a corporation may have a perpetual life as long as it continues to be successful.

Shareholders Do Not Have a Mutual Agency Relationship

The shareholders of a corporation do not have the mutual agency relationship that exists for partners. Thus, a shareholder who is not a manager does not have the power to bind the corporation to contracts. Instead, a shareholder's participation in the affairs of the corporation is limited to the right to vote in the shareholders' meetings. Therefore, if you become a shareholder in a corporation, you may not have to worry about the character of the other shareholders to the same extent that you would if the business were a partnership.

Ease of Capital Accumulation

Buying shares in a corporation often is more attractive to investors than investing in a partnership. Share investments are attractive because (1) shareholders are not liable for the corporation's actions and debts, (2) shares usually can be transferred easily, (3) the life of the corporation is not limited, and (4) shareholders do not have a relationship of mutual agency. These advantages make it possible for some corporations to accumulate large amounts of capital from the combined investments of many shareholders. In a sense, a corporation's capacity for raising capital is limited only by its ability to convince investors that it can use (and has used) their funds profitably. This situation is very different from the one faced by most partnerships, where mutual agency and unlimited liability reduce the number of investors who might be willing to become partners.

Governmental Regulation

Corporations are created by fulfilling the requirements of federal or provincial incorporation laws. These laws subject a corporation to considerable regulation and control. Single proprietorships and partnerships may escape some of these regulations. In addition, they may avoid having to file some governmental reports required of corporations.

Taxation

As business units, corporations are subject to the same property and payroll taxes as single proprietorships and partnerships. In addition, corporations are subject to taxes that are not levied on either of the other two. The most burdensome of these are income taxes which may amount to 50% of a corporation's pretax income. However, the tax burden does not end there. The income of a corporation is taxed twice, first as income of the corporation and again as personal income to the shareholders when cash is distributed to them as dividends. This differs from single proprietorships and partnerships, which are not subject to income taxes as business units. Their income is taxed only as the personal income of their owners.

DISADVANTAGES OF THE CORPORATE FORM

The tax situation of a corporation is generally viewed as a disadvantage. However, in some cases, it can work to the advantage of shareholders. Income taxes may be saved or at least delayed if a large amount of income is divided among two or more tax-paying entities. Thus, an individual who has a large personal income and pays taxes at a high rate may benefit if some of the income is earned by a corporation that person owns, as long as the corporation avoids paying dividends. By not paying dividends, the corporation's income is taxed only once at the lower corporate rate, at least temporarily until dividends are paid. Additionally, the dividend tax credit gives some relief from the effects of double taxation.

ORGANIZING A CORPORATION

A corporation is created by securing a certificate of incorporation or a charter from the federal or provincial government. The requirements that must be met to be incorporated vary among jursidictions. Under the Canada Business Corporations Act, 1975, incorporation is a matter of right. One person, over 18, of sound mind and not bankrupt, may incorporate by submitting completed articles of incorporation and other required documentation to the Director, Corporations Branch, Department of Consumer Affairs. Once the documentation is in order, the Director issues a certificate of incorporation, and a corporation comes into existence.

The newly formed corporation is authorized to issue shares, the number of which may be specified or unlimited. Authorization may also be for the issuance of more than one class of shares. If all the authorized shares have the same rights, they are usually referred to as **common**. However, if there is more than one class, the class(es) that have rights above those of the common, are preferred shares. (We discuss preferred shares later in this chapter.) The sale of shares is recorded by an entry such as

June	5	Cash	30,000.00	
		Common Shares		30,000.00
		Sold and issued 3,000 commom shares.		

The shareholders meet and elect a board of directors who are responsible for guiding the company's business affairs.

ORGANIZATION COSTS

The costs of organizing a corporation, such as legal fees, promoters' fees, and amounts paid to secure articles of incorporation, are called **organization costs**. On the corporation's books, these costs are debited on incurrence to an account called Organization costs. In a sense, this intangible asset benefits the corporation throughout its life. Thus, you could argue that organization costs should be amortized over the life of the corporation, which may be unlimited. Nevertheless, a corporation should make a reasonable estimate of the benefit period, which the CICA recommends should not exceed 40 years, and write off its organization costs over this period.

Although not necessarily related to the benefit period, income tax rules currently permit a corporation to write off 75% of organization costs as a tax-deductible expense at an annual 7% rate on a diminishing balance basis. Consequently, some corporations adopt this same tax period as the period for writing off such costs for financial statement purposes. There is no theoretical justification for this, but it is widely used in practice. Also, because organization costs are usually not material in amount, the *materiality principle* supports the arbitrarily short amortization period.

Although the organizational structures of all corporations are similar, they are not always the same. Illustration 15–1 diagrams two widely used alternatives. In all cases, the ultimate control of a corporation rests with its shareholders. However, this control is exercised only indirectly through the election of the board of directors. Individual shareholders' rights to participate in management begin and end with a vote in the shareholders' meetings, where each of them has one vote for each share owned.

Normally, a corporation holds a shareholders' meeting once each year to elect directors and transact other business as required by the corporation's bylaws. A group of shareholders that owns or controls the votes of 50% plus one share of a corporation's stock can easily elect the board and thereby control the corporation. However, in many companies, very few shareholders attend the annual meeting or even care about getting involved in the voting process. As a result, a much smaller percentage may be able to dominate the election of board members.

Shareholders who do not attend shareholders' meetings must be given an opportunity to delegate their voting rights to an agent. A shareholder does this by signing a document called a **proxy** that gives a designated agent the right to vote the shares. Prior to a shareholders' meeting, a corporation's board of directors typically mails to each shareholder an announcement of the meeting and a proxy that names the existing board chairperson as the voting agent of the shareholder. The announcement asks the shareholder to sign and return the proxy.

A corporation's board of directors is responsible for and has final authority for managing the corporation's activities. However, it can act only as a collective body. An individual director has no power to transact corporate business. Although the board has final authority, it usually limits its actions to establishing broad policy. Day-to-day direction of corporate business is delegated to executive officers appointed by the board.

Traditionally, the chief executive officer (CEO) of the corporation is the president. Under the president, there may be several vice presidents who are assigned specific areas of management responsibility, such as finance, production, and marketing. In addition, the corporate secretary keeps the minutes of the meetings of the shareholders and directors and ensures that all legal responsibilities are fulfilled. In a small corporation, the secretary is also responsible for keeping a record of the shareholders and the transfer of shares among shareholders.

As shown on the right side of Illustration 15–1, many corporations have a different structure in which the chairperson of the board of directors is also the chief executive officer. With this arrangement, the president is usually designated the chief operating officer (COO), and the rest of the structure is essentially the same.

When investors buy a corporation's shares, they may receive a share certificate as proof that they purchased the shares.[2] In many corporations, only one certificate is issued for each block of shares purchased. This certificate may be for any number of shares. For example, the certificate in Illustration 15–2 is for 50 shares. Corporations may use preprinted certificates, each of which represents 100 shares, plus blank certificates that may be made out for any number of shares.

MANAGEMENT OF A CORPORATION

SHARE CERTIFICATES AND THE TRANSFER OF SHARES

---

[2] The issuance of certificates is less common than it used to be. Instead, many shareholders maintain accounts with the corporation or their stockbrokers and never receive certificates.

Illustration 15-1
Alternative Structures
of Authority in a
Corporation

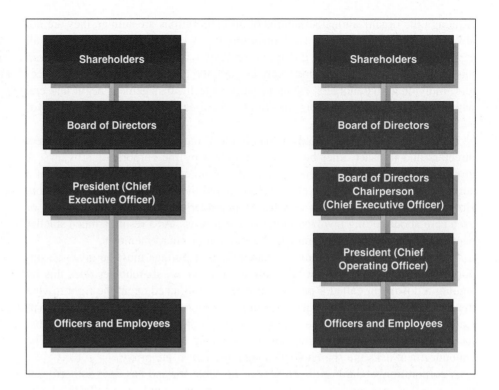

When selling shares of a corporation, a shareholder completes and signs a transfer endorsement on the back of the certificate and sends it to the corporation's secretary or the transfer agent. The secretary or agent cancels and files the old certificate, and issues a new certificate to the new shareholder. If the old certificate represents more shares than were sold, the corporation issues two new certificates. One certificate goes to the new shareholder for the sold shares and the other to the original shareholder for the remaining unsold shares.

Transfer Agent and Registrar

If a corporation's shares are traded on a major stock exchange, the corporation must have a *registrar* and a *transfer agent.* The registrar keeps the shareholder records and prepares official lists of shareholders for shareholders' meetings and for dividend payments. Registrars and transfer agents usually are large banks or trust companies that have the computer facilities and staff to carry out this kind of work.

When a corporation has a transfer agent and a shareholder wants to transfer ownership of some shares to another party, the owner completes the transfer endorsement on the back of the share certificate and sends the certificate to the transfer agent, usually with the assistance of a stockbroker. The transfer agent cancels the old certificate and issues one or more new certificates and sends them to the registrar. The registrar enters the transfer in the shareholder records and sends the new certificate or certificates to the proper owners. Millions of shares are traded each business day on exchanges such as the Toronto Stock Exchange. Illustration 15–3 is a partial list of transactions of February 15, 1995. The information was taken from the February 16, 1995, *Globe and Mail* along with an explanation of how to read the stock tables.

Illustration 15–2   A Share Certificate

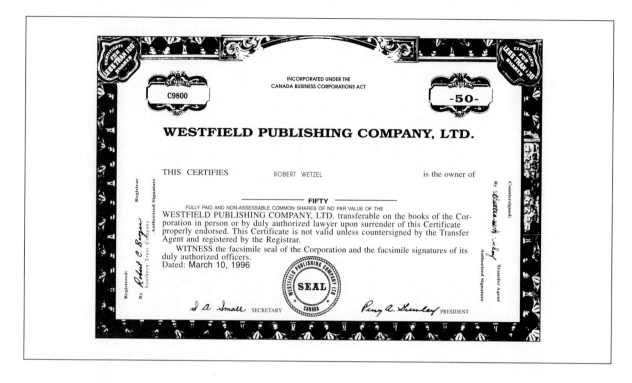

INCORPORATED UNDER THE
CANADA BUSINESS CORPORATIONS ACT

C9800

-50-

WESTFIELD PUBLISHING COMPANY, LTD.

THIS CERTIFIES   ROBERT WETZEL   is the owner of

———————— FIFTY ————————

FULLY PAID AND NON-ASSESSABLE COMMON SHARES OF NO PAR VALUE OF THE

WESTFIELD PUBLISHING COMPANY, LTD. transferable on the books of the Corporation in person or by duly authorized lawyer upon surrender of this Certificate properly endorsed. This Certificate is not valid unless countersigned by the Transfer Agent and registered by the Registrar.

WITNESS the facsimile seal of the Corporation and the facsimile signatures of its duly authorized officers.
Dated: March 10, 1996

SEAL

SECRETARY   PRESIDENT

Registrar
Authorized Signature

Registered:
By
Southern Trust Company
Authorized Signature

Countersigned:
By
Transfer Agent
Authorized Signature

Progress Check

15–1 Which of the following is *not* a characteristic of the corporate form of business?
(a) Ease of capital accumulation.
(b) Shareholders are liable for corporate debts.
(c) Ownership rights are easily transferred.

15–2 Why is the income of a corporation said to be taxed twice?

15–3 What is a proxy?

Accounting for a corporation does not differ from accounting for a proprietorship or a partnership except for transactions that directly affect the owners' equity (shareholders' equity) and recognition of corporate income tax. The shareholders' equity of a corporation is divided into contributed capital and retained earnings. The former represents consideration received by the corporation for the issued shares. The latter, retained earnings, represents the total accumulated net income from the inception of the corporation less losses, if any, and dividends. The separation of contributed capital and retained earnings is required by law.

Financial statements of a corporation consist of a balance sheet, income statement, statement of retained earnings, and a statement of changes in financial position. As indicated earlier in the chapter, corporations are legal entities subject to income tax; therefore, income tax expense is reflected in the income statement. The shareholders' equity section of a corporation's balance sheet reports share authorization, the number of shares issued, and the balance of retained earnings as reported in the statement of retained earnings.

CORPORATION ACCOUNTING

Illustration 15-3   Record of Trades (Partial List) Toronto Stock Exchange February 15, 1995

52-week high	low	Stock	Sym	Div	High	Low	Close	Chg	Vol (1002)	Yield	P/E ratio
0.51	0.25	Amer Leduc	ARL		0.45	0.38	0.40	−0.02	307		40.0
8⅛	4.75	Anchor Lamin	AKC	0.12	6	6	6	+¼	1	2.00	10.9
18	10¾	Anderson	AXL		12¼	12	12¼	+½	8055		27.2
9½	7	Andyne Com	ADY		8⅝	8⅛	8⅝	+⅜	330		43.1
1.35	0.60	Antares Mini	ANZ		0.95	0.90	0.95	+0.02	120		
6¾	5	Anvil Range	ARO		5	5	5	−1¼	51		
1.00	0.65	Apex Land	AXD.A		0.85	0.76	0.85	+0.20	20		6.1
0.95	0.06	Applied Carb	APN		.085	.085	.085		1353		
19¼	12½	Arbor Me	ABO.A	0.07	17½	17½	17½		1	0.40	19.4
23¼	9¼	Archer Res	ARC		9⅞	9¾	9⅞		647		16.5
2.70	1.60	Ariel Res	AU		2.48	2.36	2.36	−0.13	628		84.3
2.03	0.98	Arimetco j	ARX		1.10	1.01	1.01	−0.09	293		
2.70	0.80	Armbro	ARE		1.16	1.16	1.16	+0.01	10		
2.18	0.17	Arrowlink	ARK		0.18	0.17	0.18	+0.01	200		
1.00	0.61	Ascentex En	AEN		0.62	0.62	0.62	+0.01	225		62.0
3.20	0.59	Ashton Minin	ACA		0.68	0.68	0.68		20		
19	12	Astral nv	ACM.A	0.30	15⅛	15⅛	15⅛	+⅜	z 50	1.9	18.4
15⅞	12	Atco nv	ACO.X	0.28	14½	14½	14½		106	1.93	9.8
4.60	2.35	Atcor nv	AKR.A		2.50	2.45	2.45	−0.05	41		12.9
1.85	0.61	Athabaska j	AHB		1.10	1.09	1.10	−0.01	397		
5	3.05	Atlantic Coas	ATC		3.30	3.30	3.30	+0.25	8		41.3
25¾	24⅝	Atltc Sh	ATS.PR.S	2.31	25¼	25¼	25¼		18	9.16	
1.57	1.05	Audrey	AUY		1.25	1.20	1.25	+0.05	25		
19½	14¾	Ault Foods	AUL	0.66	18	17⅞	17⅞		31	3.69	15.1
7½	3.60	Aur j	AUR		4.35	4.25	4.35	+0.05	10176		
1.49	0.90	Aurex Res	AXR		0.95	0.95	0.95		40		
1.13	0.70	Aurizon j	ARZ		0.78	0.78	0.78	−0.01	53		19.5
30⅛	19⅝	Avenor	AVR		28¾	27⅜	28¾	+1¼	2069		
3.85	2.45	Azco Mining	AZC		2.50	2.45	2.45	−0.05	148		
3.35	2.00	Aztec Res	AZL		2.00	2.00	2.00	−0.10	3		8.3
11	9⅜	BAA	BAA	0.09	9⅝	9⅝	9⅝	−1¼	14	1.60	12.2
1.35	0.57	BC Bancorp	BBC		0.66	0.66	0.66	−0.01	13		
16⅛	13⅛	BC Gas	BCG	0.90	13⅝	13¾	13½	+1⅛	290	6.67	13.9
25⅜	24⅝	BC Gas	BGU.PR.B	1.78	25	25	25		28	7.10	
11	7½	BC Sugar	BCS.A	0.40	7⅞	7⅝	7⅞	+¼	987	5.08	17.9
27¾	21½	BC Telecom	BCT	1.24	24⅛	23⅞	24		102	5.17	12.8
52⅞	41⅛	BCE	B	2.72	43¾	43¼	43⅝		2512	6.27	12.3
44	41¼	BCE O	B.PR.O	2.72	41¾	41¾	41¾		9	6.54	
8⅜	0.26	BCE	B.WT		0.55	0.48	0.50	−0.04			
48⅜	35	BCE Mobile	BCX		45¾						
17¼	...	BGR									

52-week high	low	Stock	Sym	Div	High	Low	Close	Chg	Vol (1002)	Yield	P/E ratio
15¾	11½	Hemlo Gold	Hem	0.20	12	11¾	11⅞	+¼	536	1.68	17.7
8⅞	4.00	Hemosol	HML		6¼	6	6	−¼	167		
0.32	0.18	High Bullen	HBR		0.24	0.24	0.24	−0.01	10		
2.97	1.67	High River j	HRG		1.75	1.72	1.75	−0.03	616		
7¾	2.90	Highridge Ex	HRE		3.15	3.15	3.15	+0.05	30		15.8
1.25	0.60	Highwood j	HWD		0.65	0.65	0.65		105		5.4
2.10	1.17	Hillsborough	HLB		1.75	1.70	1.70		353		
17½	11⅝	Hollinger	HLG	0.60	12	11⅝	12	+¼	138	5.00	6.4
0.86	0.45	Hom Ca sb	HCG.B		0.50	0.50	0.50	−0.02	16		8.3
21¼	13⅞	Home Oil	HOC		14¼	13⅞	14⅛	−⅛	2179		88.3
2.10	0.85	Home Prod	HPI		0.95	0.95	0.95	+0.05	10		8.6
22⅛	16⅜	Horsham sv	HSM	A0.06	17⅞	17¾	17¾	−⅛	20	0.47	6.6
32¼	22⅞	Hudsn Bay	HBC	0.92	26½	26¼	26⅜		2076	3.49	7.9
29⅝	16¾	Hummingbir	HUM		25½	24⅞	25⅛	+⅛	104		23.5
7	3.00	Hy & Zels	HZI	0.25	3.25	3.25	3.25	+0.05	10	7.69	4.8
7⅞	4.00	Hyal j	HPC		5⅛	4.90	5⅛		181		
4.10	1.77	Hycroft Res	HYR		1.80	1.77	1.77	−0.03	25		177.0
1.10	0.55	Hydra Captl j	HYX		0.85	0.85	0.85	−0.07	10		85.0
33¼	26⅞	IPL Energy	IPL	2.00	28⅛	27¾	28⅛	+¼	4562	7.11	16.3
15	7⅜	ISG Tech	ISO		8½	8	8	−¼	38		
1.00	.175	Ican j	IMI		0.25	0.23	0.23	−.015	123		
41¾	32	Imasco	IMS	1.92	41¾	41⅜	41⅜	−⅛	532	4.64	9.9
26	21¾	Imperl Lif	IL.PR.D	2.13	24	23½	23½	−½	35	9.04	
1.70	0.55	Imperial Metl	IPM		1.10	1.05	1.05	−0.05	191		105.0
48¾	40⅛	Imperial Oil	IMO	1.80	46⅜	46	46¼	+⅛	2533	3.89	25.0
3.30	0.70	Imutec Corp	IUT		1.00	1.00	1.00	−0.02	120		
43¼	29⅝	Inco	N	A0.4	38⅞	38¼	38¼	−⅜	2470	1.47	
25⅜	23½	Inco	N.PR.B	1.96	25	24½	25	+¼	9	7.85	
7⅞	4.40	Industra Svc	IND	0.08	5⅝	5½	5½	−⅛	7	1.45	78.6
3.35	2.10	Intensity	ITY		2.20	2.10	2.15	−0.01	279		15.4
4.90	2.06	Inter-City	IPR		2.50	2.35	2.40	+0.05	385		
0.75	0.30	Interaction j	INR		0.35	0.35	0.35	−0.01	79		17.5
2.80	1.75	Intl Aqua Food	IAF		2.35	2.30	2.35	+	47		
21¼	8⅜	Intl Colin j	KCN		9½	9½					
1.07	0.16	Intl Contr sv	ICY.A		0.60	0...					
1.95	1.25	Intl Curator Res									

How to read the stock tables

1 2	3	4	5	6	7	8	9	10	11	12	
52-week high low	Stock	Sym	Div	High	Low	Close	Chg	Vol (100s)	Yield	P/E ratio	

Reading Imperial Oil Limited Data

1. Arrow up or down - new 52-week high or low in day's trading

2. 52-week high/low - highest and lowest inter-day price in past 52 weeks — 48¾ 40⅛

3. Stock - abbreviated company name — Imperial Oil

4. Sym - Ticker symbol assigned to issue by exchange; .PR is preferred share, .WT is warrant, .UN is unit, .S means stocks are subject to regulation of the SEC Act,. W means when issued. — IMO

5. Div - Indicated annual dividend (excluding special dividends) — 1.80

6. High - Highest inter-day trading price — 46⅜

7. Low - Lowest inter-day trading price — 46

8. Close - Closing price — 46¼

9. Chg - Change between closing price and previous closing board lot price — +⅛

10. Vol. - Number of shares traded in 100s; z preceding figure indicates sales are reported in full — 2533

11. Yield - expressed as percentage, calculated by dividing the dividend by current market price — 3.89%

12. P/E ratio - Price/earnings ratio; current stock price divided by the company's earnings per share from continuing operations for the latest 12 months — 25

To demonstrate the use of separate accounts for contributed capital and retained earnings as found in corporation accounting and to contrast their use with the accounts used in partnership accounting, assume the following: On January 5, 1996, a partnership involving two partners and a corporation having five shareholders were formed. Also assume that $25,000 was invested in each. In the partnership, J. Olm invested $10,000 and A. Baker invested $15,000. In the corporation, each of the five shareholders bought 500 common shares at $10 per share. Without dates and explanations, General Journal entries to record the investments are:

SHAREHOLDERS' EQUITY ACCOUNTS COMPARED TO PARTNERSHIP ACCOUNTS

Partnership			Corporation		
Cash	10,000		Cash	25,000	
J. Olm, Capital		10,000	Common Shares . .		25,000
Cash	15,000				
A. Baker, Capital . .		15,000			

After the entries are posted, the owners' equity accounts of the two companies appear as follows:

Partnership

J. Olm, Capital

Date	Dr.	Cr.	Bal.
Jan. 5, 1996		10,000	10,000

Corporation

Common Shares

Date	Dr.	Cr.	Bal.
Jan. 5, 1996		25,000	25,000

A. Baker, Capital

Date	Dr.	Cr.	Bal.
Jan. 5, 1996		15,000	15,000

To continue the illustration, assume that during 1996, each company earned a net income of $8,000 and also distributed $5,000 to its owners. According to the partnership agreement, incomes are allocated 40% to Olm and 60% to Baker. The cash distribution to the partners was divided equally. The corporation declared the dividends on December 20, 1996, and both companies made the cash payments to owners on December 25, 1996. The entries to record the distribution of cash to partners and the declaration and payments of dividends to shareholders are

Partnership			Corporation		
J. Olm, Withdrawals	2,500		Dividends Declared	5,000	
A. Baker, Withdrawals . .	2,500		Dividends Payable .		5,000
Cash		5,000	Dividends Payable	5,000	
			Cash		5,000

At the end of the year, the entries to close the Income Summary accounts are

Partnership			Corporation	
Income Summary	8,000		Income Summary	8,000
J. Olm, Capital		3,200	Retained Earnings . .	8,000
A. Baker, Capital . .		4,800		

Finally, the entries to close the withdrawals accounts and the Dividends Declared account are

Partnership			Corporation	
J. Olm, Capital 2,500			Retained Earnings 5,000	
A. Baker, Capital 2,500			Dividends Declared . .	5,000
J. Olm, Withdrawals . .	2,500			
A. Baker, Withdrawals	2,500			

After posting these entries, the owners' equity accounts of the two companies are

Partnership

J. Olm, Capital

Date	Dr.	Cr.	Bal.
5/1/96		10,000	10,000
31/12/96		3,200	13,200
31/12/96	2,500		10,700

A. Baker, Capital

Date	Dr.	Cr.	Bal.
5/1/96		15,000	15,000
31/12/96		4,800	19,800
31/12/96	2,500		17,300

J. Olm, Withdrawals

Date	Dr.	Cr.	Bal.
25/12/96	2,500		2,500
31/12/96		2,500	–0–

A. Baker, Withdrawals

Date	Dr.	Cr.	Bal.
25/12/96	2,500		2,500
31/12/96		2,500	–0–

Corporation

Common Shares

Date	Dr.	Cr.	Bal.
5/1/96		25,000	25,000

Retained Earnings

Date	Dr.	Cr.	Bal. (dr.)
20/12/96	5,000		5,000
31/12/96		8,000	3,000

Dividends Declared

Date	Dr.	Cr.	Bal.
20/12/96	5,000		5,000
31/12/96		5,000	–0–

Observe that in the partnership, after all entries have been posted, the $28,000 equity of the owners appears in the capital accounts of the partnership.

J. Olm, capital	$10,700
A. Baker, capital	17,300
Total owners' equity	$28,000

By comparison, the shareholders' equity of the corporation is divided between contributed capital and the Retained Earnings account, as follows:

Common shares	$25,000
Retained earnings	3,000
Total shareholders' equity	$28,000

Sale of Shares for Cash

When shares are sold for cash and immediately issued, an entry like the following is made to record the sale and issuance:

June	5	Cash	300,000.00	
		Common Shares		300,000.00
		Sold and issued 30,000 common shares at		
		$10 per share.		

Exchanging Shares for Noncash Assets

A corporation may accept assets other than cash in exchange for its shares. In the process, the corporation also may assume some liabilities, such as a mortgage on some of the property. These transactions are recorded with an entry like this:

June	10	Machinery	10,000.00	
		Buildings	65,000.00	
		Land	15,000.00	
		Long-Term Notes Payable		50,000.00
		Common Shares		40,000.00
		Exchanged 4,000 common shares for machinery,		
		buildings, and land.		

A corporation also may give shares of its share capital to its promoters in exchange for their services in organizing the company. In this case, the corporation receives the intangible asset of being organized in exchange for its shares. Record this transaction as follows:

ISSUANCE OF SHARES

LO 2

Record the issuance of common shares.

June	5	Organization Costs	5,000.00	
		Common Shares		5,000.00
		Gave the promoters 500 common shares in exchange		
		for their services in organizing the corporation.		

SALE OF SHARES THROUGH SUBSCRIPTIONS

LO 3
Record transactions involving share subscriptions and explain the effects of shares subscribed on a corporation's assets and shareholders' equity.

Usually, shares are sold for cash and immediately issued. However, corporations sometimes sell their shares through **subscriptions.** For example, when a new corporation is formed, the organizers may realize that the new business has limited immediate need for cash but will need additional cash in the future. To get the corporation started on a sound footing, the organizers may sell shares to investors who agree to contribute some cash now and to make additional contributions in the future. When shares are sold through subscriptions, the investor agrees to buy a certain number of the shares at a specified price. The agreement also states when payments are to be made. When the subscription is accepted by the corporation, it becomes a contract and the corporation acquires an asset. The asset is the right to receive payment from subscribers. At the same time, subscribers gain an equity in the corporation.

To illustrate the sale of shares through subscriptions, assume that Northgate Corporation accepted subscriptions on May 6 to 5,000 common shares at $12 per share. The subscription contracts called for a 10% down payment with the balance to be paid in two equal installments due after three and six months. Northgate records the subscriptions with the following entry:

May	6	Subscriptions Receivable, Common Shares	60,000.00	
		Common Shares Subscribed		60,000.00
		Accepted subscriptions to 5,000 common shares at . .		
		$12 per share.		

At the time that subscriptions are accepted, the firm debits the Subscriptions Receivable account for the total amount of the subscription. This is the amount the subscribers agreed to pay. Notice that the **Common Shares Subscribed** account is credited for the same amount.

The receivables are converted into cash when the subscribers pay for their shares. And when all the payments are received, the subscribed shares will be issued. Northgate records the receipt of the down payment and the two installment payments with these entries:

May	6	Cash	6,000.00	
		Subscriptions Receivable, Common Shares		6,000.00
		Collected 10% down payments on the common shares		
		subscribed.		
Aug.	6	Cash	27,000.00	
		Subscriptions Receivable, Common Shares		27,000.00
		Collected the first installment payments on the		
		common shares subscribed.		

Nov.	6	Cash	27,000.00	
		Subscriptions Receivable, Common Shares		27,000.00
		Collected the second installment payments on the common shares subscribed.		

In this case, the down payments accompanied the subscriptions. Therefore, the accountant could have combined the May 6 entries to record the receipt of the subscriptions and to record the down payments.

When shares are sold through subscriptions, the shares usually are not issued until the subscriptions are paid in full. Also, if dividends are declared before subscribed shares have been issued, the dividends go only to the holders of outstanding shares, not to the subscribers. However, as soon as the subscriptions are paid, the shares are issued. The entry to record the issuance of the Northgate common shares is

Nov.	6	Common Shares Subscribed	60,000.00	
		Common Shares		60,000.00
		Issued 5,000 common shares sold through subscriptions.		

Subscriptions are usually collected in full, but not always. Sometimes, a subscriber fails to pay the agreed amount. When this default happens, the subscription contract is canceled. If the subscriber has made a partial payment on the contract, the amount may be refunded. Or the company may issue a smaller number of shares. Or in some jurisdictions, the subscriber's partial payment may be kept by the corporation to compensate it for any damages.

Subscriptions Receivable and Subscribed Shares on the Balance Sheet

Subscriptions receivable may be reported on the balance sheet as current or long-term assets, depending on when collection is expected. If a corporation prepares a balance sheet after accepting subscriptions to its share capital but before the shares are issued, both the issued shares and the subscribed shares should be reported on the balance sheet as follows:

Common shares, unlimited number of shares authorized, 20,000 shares issued	$200,000
Common shares subscribed, 5,000 shares	60,000
Total common shares issued and subscribed ..	$260,000

Progress Check

15–4   A company issued 7,000 common shares and a $40,000, 5-year, (interest at current market) note payable in exchange for equipment valued at $105,000. The entry to record the transaction would include a credit   *(a)* of $105,000 to Common Shares;   *(b)* of $65,000 to Retained Earnings;   *(c)* of $65,000 to Common Shares.

15–5   The costs of incorporation, such as legal costs, should be expensed in the period of incurrence. Agree?

15–6   On December 31, 1996, XPC Inc. had 100,000 common shares outstanding, issued at $10 per share. The retained earnings balance was $200,000. On January 2, 1997, XPC received confirmed subscriptions for 10,000 shares at $15 per share accompanied by a 25% down payment. XPC accepted all of the subscriptions. Determine   *(a)* the number of common shares outstanding at close of January 2, 1997, and   *(b)* the total shareholders' equity at close of January 2, 1997.

RIGHTS OF COMMON SHAREHOLDERS

LO 4

State the differences between common and preferred shares, and allocate dividends between common and preferred shares.

When investors buy a corporation's common shares, they acquire all the *specific* rights granted by the corporation's charter to its common shareholders. They also acquire the *general* rights granted shareholders by the laws of the jurisdiction in which the company is incorporated. The laws vary, but common shareholders usually have the following general rights:

1. The right to vote at shareholders' meetings.
2. The right to sell or otherwise dispose of their shares.
3. The right to share pro rata with other common shareholders in any dividends declared.
4. The right to share equally in any assets that remain after creditors are paid when the corporation is liquidated.

If desired, the articles of incorporation may provide additional rights. For example, the articles may specifically provide for the **preemptive right,** which holds that no shares of a class shall be issued unless the shares have first been offered to the shareholders holding shares of that class, and that those shareholders have a first opportunity to acquire the offered shares in proportion to their holdings of the shares of that class, at such a price and on such terms as those shares are offered to others.

CLASSES OF SHARES

The Canada Business Corporations Act allows corporations to issue registered no-par-value shares by class and by series of the class so long as there exists one "residual" class of shares that may vote at all meetings of shareholders (except for meetings of specified classes of shareholders) and that may receive the remaining assets of a corporation upon dissolution. The act does not use the adjectives *common* and *preferred* but simply refers to shares in general. Classes of shares may continue to be designated common, preferred, Class A, Class B, and so on. However, the act does require the articles to set out the rights, privileges, restrictions, and conditions attaching to each class and series of shares. Because of their widespread usage, the terms *common* and *preferred* are used throughout this book.

**PREFERRED
SHARES**

If two classes of share capital are issued, one is generally called **preferred** and the other is called *common*.

The term *preferred* is used because the preferred shares have a higher priority (or senior status) relative to common shares in one or more ways. These typically include a preference for receiving dividends and a preference in the distribution of assets if the corporation is liquidated.

In addition to the preferences it receives, preferred share capital carries all the rights of common share capital, unless they are nullified in the articles of incorporation. For example, most preferred shares do not have the right to vote. In effect, this disadvantage is accepted in return for the preferences.

Preferred Dividends

A preference for dividends gives preferred shareholders the right to receive their dividends before the common shareholders receive a dividend. In other words, a dividend cannot be paid to common shareholders unless preferred shareholders also receive one. The amount of dividends that the preferred shareholders must receive is usually expressed as a dollar amount per share. For example, holders of $9 preferred shares must be paid dividends at the rate of $9 per share per year before the common shareholders can receive any dividend. A preference for dividends does not, however, grant an absolute right to dividends. If the board of directors does not declare a dividend, neither the preferred nor the common shareholders receive one.

Cumulative and Noncumulative Preferred Shares

Preferred shares can be either **cumulative** or **noncumulative**. For cumulative, any undeclared dividends accumulate each year until they are received. For noncumulative, the right to receive dividends is forfeited in any year that the dividends are not declared.

When preferred shares are cumulative and the board of directors fails to declare a dividend to the preferred shareholders, the unpaid dividend is called a **dividend in arrears**. The accumulation of dividends in arrears on cumulative preferred shares does not guarantee that they will be paid. However, the cumulative preferred shareholders must be paid both the current dividend and all dividends in arrears before any dividend can be paid to the common shareholders.

To show the difference between cumulative and noncumulative preferred shares, assume that a corporation has outstanding 1,000 of $9 preferred shares issued at $100 per share and 4,000 common shares issued at $50 per share. During 1996, the first year of the corporation's operations, the board of directors declared cash dividends of $5,000. During 1997, it declared $42,000. The allocations of the total dividends are as follows:

	Preferred	Common
Assuming noncumulative preferred:		
1996	$ 5,000	$ 0
1997:		
First: current preferred dividend	$ 9,000	
Remainder to common		$33,000
Assuming cumulative preferred:		
1996	$ 5,000	$ 0
1997:		
First: dividends in arrears	$ 4,000	
Next: current preferred dividend	9,000	
Remainder to common		$29,000
Totals	$13,000	$29,000

Notice that the allocation of the 1997 dividends depends on whether the preferred shares are noncumulative or cumulative. With noncumulative preferred shares, the preferred shareholders never receive the $4,000 that was skipped in 1996. However, when the preferred shares are cumulative, the $4,000 in arrears is paid in 1997 before the common shareholders receive a dividend.

Disclosure of Dividends in Arrears in the Financial Statements

Dividends are not like interest expense, which is incurred as time passes and therefore must be accrued. A liability for a dividend does not come into existence until the dividend is declared by the board of directors. Thus, if a preferred dividend date passes and the corporation's board fails to declare the dividend on its cumulative preferred shares, the dividend in arrears is not a liability. Accordingly, it does not appear as a liability on the balance sheet. However, when preparing the financial statements, the *full-disclosure principle* requires the corporation to report the amount of preferred dividends in arrears as of the balance sheet date. Normally, this information is given in a note. If there is no such disclosure, readers of the financial statements have the right to assume that preferred dividends are not in arrears.

WHY PREFERRED SHARES ARE ISSUED

A corporation might issue nonparticipating preferred shares for several reasons. One reason is to raise capital without sacrificing control of the corporation. For example, suppose that the organizers of a business have $100,000 cash to invest but wish to organize a corporation that needs $200,000 of capital to get off to a good start. If they sold $200,000 of common shares, they would have only 50% control and would have to negotiate extensively with the other shareholders in making policy. However, if they issue $100,000 of common shares to themselves and can sell to outsiders, at $100 per share, 1,000 shares of $8, cumulative preferred shares that have no voting rights, they can retain control of the corporation.

A second reason for issuing preferred shares is to boost the return earned by the common shareholders. Using the previous example to illustrate, suppose that the corporation's organizers expect the new company to earn an annual after-tax income of $24,000. If they sell and issue $200,000 of common shares, this income produces a 12% return on the $200,000 of common shareholders' equity. However, if they sell and issue $100,000 of each kind of shares, retaining the common for themselves, their own return increases to 16% per year, as shown here:

Net after-tax income	$24,000
Less preferred dividends at $(1,000 \times \$8)$	(8,000)
Balance to common shareholders (equal to 16% on their $100,000 investment)	$16,000

In this case, the common shareholders earn 16% because the assets contributed by the preferred shareholders are invested to earn $12,000 while the preferred dividend payments amount to only $8,000.

The use of preferred shares to increase the return to common shareholders is an example of **financial leverage**. Whenever the dividend rate on preferred shares is less than the rate that the corporation earns on its assets, the effect of issuing preferred shares is to increase (or *lever*) the rate earned by common shareholders. Financial leverage also occurs when debt is issued and paid an interest rate less than the rate earned from using the assets the creditors loaned to the corporation.

There are other reasons for issuing preferred shares. For example, a corporation's preferred shares may appeal to some investors who believe that its common shares are too risky or that the dividend rate on the common shares will be too low. Also, if a corporation's management wants to issue common shares but believes the current market price for the common shares is too low, the corporation may issue preferred shares that are convertible into common shares. If and when the price of the common shares increases, the preferred shareholders can convert their shares into common shares.

Progress Check

15-7   In what ways may preferred shares have a priority status to common shares?

15-8   Increasing the return to common shareholders by including preferred shares in the capital structure is an example of *(a)* financial leverage; *(b)* cumulative earnings; *(c)* dividends in arrears.

15-9   MBI Corp. has 9,000 shares at $5, cumulative preferred and 27,000 common shares issued and outstanding. No dividends have been declared for the past two years, but during the current year, MBI declares a $288,000 dividend. The amount to be paid to common shareholders is *(a)* $243,000; *(b)* $153,000; *(c)* $135,000.

CONVERTIBLE PREFERRED SHARES

As mentioned above, an issue of preferred shares can be made more attractive to some investors by giving them the right to exchange the preferred shares for a fixed number of common shares. **Convertible preferred shares** offer investors a higher potential return than do nonconvertible preferred shares. If the company prospers and its common shares increase in value, the convertible preferred shareholders can share in the prosperity by converting their preferred shares into the more valuable common shares.

LO 5

Explain convertible pre-
ferred shares and explain
the meaning of the re-
demption, book, and mar-
ket values of shares.

To see how the conversion of preferred shares is recorded, assume that a corporation's outstanding shares include 1,000 shares of $10 convertible preferred.
The shares were originally issued for $103 per share. Each preferred share is con-
vertible into four shares of common. If all of the preferred shares are converted on
May 1, the entry to record the conversion is

May	1	Preferred Shares	103,000.00	
		Common Shares		103,000.00
		To record the conversion of preferred shares.		

When the preferred shares are converted into common shares, the balance in the
preferred shares account is removed and replaced with an account balance related
to common shares. No gain or loss is recorded.

SHARE VALUES

In addition to an average stated value, shares may have a par value, *call price*, a
market value, and a *book value*.

The Canada Business Corporations Act, 1975, as well as the more recently passed
provincial counterparts, require that all shares be of **no par** or nominal value. These
acts also require the total consideration received by the corporation for each share
issued must be added to the stated capital account maintained for the shares of that
class or series. Some jurisdictions still permit the issuance of par value shares. **Par
value** is an arbitrary value a corporation places on a share of its share capital.

In Canada, the use of par value shares has declined in recent years. As such, we
have not provided examples in the text using par value shares.

Redemption Value of Callable Preferred Shares

Some issues of preferred shares are callable. This means that the issuing corporation has the right to retire the **callable preferred shares** by paying a specified
amount to the preferred shareholders. The amount that must be paid to call and retire a preferred share is its **call price,** or **redemption value**. This amount is set at
the time the shares are issued. Normally, the call price includes the issue price of
the shares plus a premium that provides the shareholders with some additional return on their investment. When the issuing corporation calls and retires preferred
shares, it must pay not only the call price but also any dividends in arrears.

Market Value

The market value of a share is the price at which it can be bought or sold.
Market values are influenced by a wide variety of factors including expected future
earnings, dividends, and events in the economy at large.

Book Value

The **book value of a share** is one share's portion of the corporation's net assets
as recorded in the company's accounts. If a corporation has only common shares,
the book value per share equals the total shareholders' equity divided by the number of outstanding shares. For example, if a company has 10,000 outstanding shares
and total shareholders' equity of $285,000, the book value is $28.50 per share
($285,000/10,000 shares).

Computing the book values of shares is more complex when both common and preferred shares are outstanding. To calculate the book values of each class of shares, you begin by allocating the total shareholders' equity between the two classes. The preferred shareholders' portion equals the preferred share's call price (average stated value if the preferred is not callable) plus any cumulative dividends in arrears. Then allocate the remaining shareholders' equity to the common shares. To determine the book value per share of preferred, divide the portion of shareholders' equity assigned to preferred by the number of preferred shares outstanding. Similarly, the book value per share of common is the shareholders' equity assigned to common divided by the number of outstanding common shares. For example, assume a corporation has the shareholders' equity as shown in Illustration 15–4.

If the preferred shares are callable at $103 per share and two years of cumulative preferred dividends are in arrears, the book values of the corporation's shares are calculated as follows:

Total shareholders' equity		$ 447,000
Less equity applicable to preferred shares:		
Redemption value	$103,000	
Cumulative dividends in arrears ($100,000 × 7% × 2)	14,000	(117,000)
Equity applicable to common shares		$ 330,000
Book value of preferred shares ($117,000/1,000)		$117.00
Book value of common shares ($330,000/10,000)		$ 33.00

In their annual reports to shareholders, corporations sometimes report the increase in the book value of the corporation's shares that has occurred during a year. Also, book value may have significance in contracts. For example, a shareholder may enter into a contract to sell shares at their book value at some future date. However, this agreement may not be wise because book value normally does not approximate market value.

Similarly, book value should not be confused with liquidation value. If a corporation is liquidated, its assets probably will sell at prices that are quite different from the amounts at which they are carried on the books.

Investors buy shares of a company in anticipation of receiving a return from cash dividends and from increases in share value. Shares that pay large dividends on a regular basis are sometimes called *income shares.* They are attractive to investors who want dependable cash flows from their investments. In contrast, other shares pay few or no dividends but are still attractive to investors because they expect the market value of the shares to increase rapidly. The shares of companies that do not distribute cash but use it to finance rapid expansion are often called *growth shares.*

One way to evaluate whether a company's shares should be viewed as income or growth shares is to examine the **dividend yield.** The following formula shows that this ratio is a rate of return based on the annual cash dividends and the share's market value:

USING THE INFORMATION— DIVIDEND YIELD

LO 7
Calculate dividend yield and explain its meaning.

$$\text{Dividend yield} = \frac{\text{Annual cash dividends per share}}{\text{Market value per share}}$$

Illustration 15-4
Shareholders' Equity
with Preferred and
Common Shares

Shareholders' Equity

Share capital:
Preferred, $7, cumulative,
  2,000 shares authorized, 1,000 shares
  issued and outstanding $105,000
Common, no par value, unlimited number of shares
  authorized, 10,000 shares issued and outstanding . . $260,000

Total contributed capital $365,000
Retained earnings   82,000

Total shareholders' equity $447,000

Dividend yield may be calculated on a historical basis using the prior year's actual dividends or on an expected basis. For example, recall from the first page of this chapter the discussion of Imperial Oil and the dividend and share price information for several companies. The dividend yields for those companies were as follows:

Company	Common Dividend 1994	Share Prices Feb. 15, 1995	Current Dividend Yield
Imperial Oil Limited	$1.80*	$46 ¼	3.89%
BCE Inc.	2.72	43 ⅜	6.27
Anchor Lamina Inc.	0.12	6	2.00
Imasco Inc.	1.92	41 ⅜	4.64
Hemlo Gold Ltd.	0.20	11 ⅞	1.68

*Excludes special dividend of $3.00.

An investor can compare these dividend yields to evaluate the relative importance of dividends to the prices of the shares. Current dividends obviously have little impact on **Anchor Lamina** and **Hemlo Gold**. The values of these shares must stem from expected increases in their share prices (and the eventual dividends that may be paid).

On the other hand, **Imasco** and **BCE** pay substantial dividends to yield 4.64% and 6.27%, respectively. These are less than one would expect from investments in corporate debt securities but still high enough to conclude that dividends are a very important factor in establishing their share prices.

SUMMARY OF THE CHAPTER IN TERMS OF LEARNING OBJECTIVES

LO 1. Explain the advantages, disadvantages, and organization of corporations and the differences in accounting for partnerships and corporations. Advantages of the corporate form of business include the following: *(a)* status as separate legal entity; *(b)* lack of shareholder liability for corporate debts; *(c)* a corporation's continuity of life; and *(d)* the fact shareholders are not agents of the corporation. A disadvantage is that corporations are closely regulated by government. Also, the taxable status of corporations is often a disadvantage but sometimes may be an advantage.

A corporation is governed by the shareholders through the board of directors. Officers who manage the corporation include a president, perhaps one or more vice presidents, and a secretary. The chief executive officer may be the president or the board of directors chairperson.

LO 2. Record the issuance of no-par-value shares. When no-par-value shares are issued, the entire proceeds are credited to the share capital account.

LO 3. Record transactions involving share subscriptions and explain the effects of subscribed shares on a corporation's assets and shareholders' equity. If a corporation sells shares through subscriptions, the right to receive payment is an asset of the corporation and the subscribers' equity is recorded in contributed capital accounts. The balance of the Common Shares Subscribed account is transferred to the Common Shares account when the shares are issued, which normally occurs after all payments are received.

LO 4. State the differences between common and preferred shares and allocate dividends between the common and preferred shares. Preferred shares have a priority (or senior status) relative to common shares in one or more ways. Usually, this means that common shareholders cannot be paid dividends unless a specified amount of dividends is also paid to preferred shareholders. Preferred shares also may have a priority status if the corporation is liquidated. The dividend preference for many preferred shares is cumulative, and a few preferred shares also participate in dividends beyond the preferred amount.

LO 5. Describe convertible preferred shares and explain the meaning of the redemption, book, and market values of shares. On the conversion of convertible preferred shares into common shares, the carrying value of the preferred shares is transferred to contributed capital accounts that relate to common shares. No gain or loss is recorded. If preferred shares are callable, the amount that must be paid to retire the share is its call price plus any dividends in arrears. Market value is the price that a share commands when it is bought or sold. The book value of a preferred share is any dividends in arrears plus its stated value, or if it is callable, its redemption price. The residual shareholders' equity is divided by the number of outstanding common shares to determine the book value per share of the common.

LO 6. Calculate dividend yield and explain its meaning. The dividend yield is the ratio between a share's annual dividend and its market value. It describes the rate of return provided to the shareholders from the company's dividends. The yield can be compared with the rates of return offered by other kinds of investments to determine whether the shares should be viewed as income or growth shares.

Barton Corporation was created on January 1, 1996. The following transactions relating to shareholders' equity occurred during the first two years of the company's operations. Prepare the journal entries to record these transactions. Also prepare the balance sheet presentation of the organization costs, liabilities, and shareholders' equity as of December 31, 1996, and December 31, 1997. Include appropriate notes to the financial statements.

DEMONSTRATION PROBLEM

1996

Jan.   1   Authorized the issuance of an unlimited number of shares of no-par-value common shares and 100,000 shares of no-par-value preferred shares. The preferred shares pay a $10 annual dividend and are cumulative.

Jan. 1   Issued 200,000 common shares at $12 per share.

     1   Issued 100,000 common shares in exchange for a building valued at $820,000 and merchandise inventory valued at $380,000.

     1   Accepted subscriptions for 150,000 common shares at $12 per share. The subscribers made no down payments, and the full purchase price was due on April 1, 1996.

     1   Paid a cash reimbursement to the company's founders for $100,000 of organization costs, which are to be amortized over 10 years.

     1   Issued 12,000 preferred shares for $110 per share.

Apr. 1   Collected the full subscription price for the January 1 common shares and issued the shares.

Dec. 31   The Income Summary account for 1996 had a $125,000 credit balance before being closed to Retained Earnings; no dividends were declared on either the common or preferred shares.

1997
June 4   Issued 100,000 common shares for $15 per share.

Dec. 10   Declared dividends payable on January 10, 1998, as follows:

To preferred shareholders for 1996	$120,000
To preferred shareholders for 1997	120,000
To common shareholders for 1997	300,000

     31   The Income Summary account for 1997 had a $1 million credit balance before being closed to Retained Earnings.

Planning the Solution

- Record journal entries for the events in 1996 and 1997.
- Close the accounts related to retained earnings at the end of each year.
- Determine the balances for the 1996 and 1997 balance sheets, including the following amounts to use in the balance sheet and the accompanying note:
  - *a.* The number of shares issued.
  - *b.* The amount of dividends in arrears.
  - *c.* The unamortized balance of organization costs.
- Prepare the specified portions of the 1996 and 1997 balance sheets.

Solution to Demonstration Problem

1996					
Jan.	1	Cash		2,400,000.00	
		Common Shares			2,400,000.00
		Issued 200,000 common shares.			
	1	Building		820,000.00	
		Merchandise Inventory		380,000.00	
		Common Shares			1,200,000.00
		Issued 100,000 common shares.			

1996				
Jan.	1	Subscriptions Receivable	1,800,000.00	
		Common Shares Subscribed		1,800,000.00
		Accepted subscriptions for 150,000 common shares.		
	1	Organization Costs	100,000.00	
		Cash		100,000.00
		Reimbursed the founders for organization costs.		
	1	Cash	1,320,000.00	
		Preferred Shares		1,320,000.00
		Issued 12,000 preferred shares.		
Apr.	1	Cash	1,800,000.00	
		Subscriptions Receivable		1,800,000.00
		Collected balance due on subscribed common shares.		
	1	Common Shares Subscribed	1,800,000.00	
		Common Shares		1,800,000.00
		Issued 150,000 subscribed common shares.		
Dec.	31	Income Summary	125,000.00	
		Retained Earnings		125,000.00
		To close the Income Summary account and update Retained Earnings.		

1997				
June	4	Cash	1,500,000.00	
		Common Shares		1,500,000.00
		Issued 100,000 common shares.		
Dec.	10	Cash Dividends Declared	540,000.00	
		Dividends Payable, Common Shares		300,000.00
		Dividends Payable, Preferred Shares		240,000.00
		Declared current dividends and dividends in arrears to common and preferred shareholders, payable on January 10, 1998.		
	31	Income Summary	1,000,000.00	
		Retained Earnings		1,000,000.00
		To close the Income Summary account and update Retained Earnings.		
	31	Retained Earnings	540,000.00	
		Cash Dividends Declared		540,000.00
		To close to Retained Earnings the Cash Dividends Declared.		

Balance sheet presentations:

	As of December 31,	
	1996	**1997**
Assets		
Organization costs	$ 90,000	$ 80,000
Liabilities		
Dividends payable, common shares		$ 300,000
Dividends payable, preferred shares		240,000
Total liabilities		$ 540,000
Shareholders' Equity		
Share capital:		
Preferred, no par value, $10, cumulative, 100,000 shares authorized, 12,000 shares issued . . .	$1,320,000	$1,320,000
Common, no par value, unlimited number of shares authorized, 450,000 shares issued in 1996, and 550,000 shares in 1997	$5,400,000	$6,900,000
Retained Earnings (see Note 1)	125,000	585,000
Total shareholders' equity	$6,845,000	$8,805,000

Note 1: As of December 31, 1996, there were $120,000 of dividends in arrears on the preferred shares.

GLOSSARY

Book value of a share   one share's portion of the issuing corporation's share capital recorded in its accounts. pp. 702–03

Call price   another name for *redemption value.* p. 702

Callable preferred shares   preferred shares that the issuing corporation, at its option, may retire by paying a specified amount (the call price) to the preferred shareholders plus any dividends in arrears. p. 702

Common shares   shares of a corporation that has only one class of shares, or if there is more than one class, the class that has no preferences over the corporation's other classes of shares. pp. 698–99

Common Shares Subscribed   a shareholders' equity account in which a corporation records the value of unissued common shares that investors have contracted to purchase. p. 696

Convertible preferred shares   preferred shares that can be exchanged for shares of the issuing corporation's common shares at the option of the preferred shareholder. p. 701

Cumulative preferred shares   preferred shares on which undeclared dividends accumulate until they are paid; common shareholders cannot receive a dividend until all cumulative dividends have been paid. p. 699

Dividends in arrears   an unpaid dividend on cumulative preferred shares; it must be paid before any regular dividends on the preferred shares and before any dividends on the common shares. p. 699

Dividend yield   a company's annual cash dividends per share divided by the market value per share. p. 703

Financial leverage   the achievement of an increased return on common shares by paying dividends on preferred shares or interest at a rate that is less than the rate of return earned with the assets invested in the corporation by the preferred shareholders or creditors. p. 701

Noncumulative preferred shares   preferred shares on which the right to receive dividends is forfeited for any year that the dividends are not declared. p. 699

No-par shares   a class of shares that does not have a par value. p. 702

Organization costs   the costs of bringing a corporation into existence, including legal fees, promoters' fees, and amounts paid to secure incorporation. p. 688

Par value   an arbitrary value assigned to a share when the shares are authorized. p. 702

Preemptive right   the right of common shareholders to protect their proportionate interest in a corporation by having the first opportunity to buy additional common shares issued by the corporation. p. 698

Preferred shares   shares that give their owners a priority status over common shareholders in one or more ways, such as the payment of dividends or the distribution of assets on liquidation. pp. 699–702

Proxy   a legal document that gives an agent of a shareholder the power to exercise the voting rights of that shareholder's shares. p. 689

Redemption value   the amount that must be paid to call and retire a preferred share. p. 702

Subscription   a contractual commitment by an investor to purchase unissued shares and become a shareholder. p. 696

SYNONYMOUS TERMS

Call price   redemption value.
Preferred   senior status.

Subscribers   incorporators; founders; promoters.

QUESTIONS

1. Who is responsible for directing the affairs of a corporation?
2. What are organization costs? List several examples of these costs.
3. How are organization costs classified on the balance sheet?
4. What are the duties and responsibilities of a corporation's registrar and transfer agent?
5. List the general rights of common shareholders.
6. What distinguishes preferred shares from common shares?
7. What is the difference between cumulative and non-cumulative preferred shares?

8. What are the balance sheet classifications of these accounts: (a) Subscriptions Receivable, Common Shares, and (b) Common Shares Subscribed?
9. What is the difference between the market value and the book value of a share?
10. Why would an investor find convertible preferred shares attractive?
11. Laws place no limit on the amounts that partners can withdraw from a partnership. On the other hand, laws regulating corporations place definite limits on the amount of dividends that shareholders can receive from a corporation. Why do you think there is a difference?

QUICK STUDY (Five-Minute Exercises)

Of the following statements, which are true for the corporate form of business?

QS 15–1
(LO 1)

a. Capital is often more easily accumulated than with other forms of organization.
b. It has a limited life.
c. Owners have unlimited liability for corporate debts.
d. Distributed income is taxed twice in normal circumstances.
e. It is a separate legal entity.
f. Ownership rights cannot be easily transferred.
g. Owners are not agents of the corporation.

On June 1, YMI Corporation issued 25,000 common shares for $168,000 cash. Present the entry to record this transaction.

QS 15–2
(LO 2)

QS 15–3
(LO 3)

On August 15, Retro Company accepted subscriptions to 12,000 common shares at $10 per share. A 20% down payment was made on this date with the remainder to be paid in six months. Prepare an entry to record this transaction.

QS 15–4
(LO 4)

Nosar Company's shareholders' equity includes 20,000 shares of $1, cumulative, nonparticipating preferred and 200,000 common shares. Nosar did not declare any dividends during the prior year and now declares and pays a $72,000 cash dividend. Determine the amount distributed to each class of shareholders.

QS 15–5
(LO 4)

Prepare journal entries to record the following transactions for Gruene Corporation:

June 15 Declared a $24,000 cash dividend payable to common shareholders.

July 31 Paid the dividend declared on June 15.

Dec. 31 Closed the Cash Dividends Declared account.

QS 15–6
(LO 5)

The shareholders' equity section of Roscoe Company follows:

Shareholders' Equity

Preferred shares, $0.50 cumulative, 20,000 shares authorized, issued, and outstanding	$ 200,000
Common shares, unlimited number of no par-value shares authorized, 150,000 shares issued and outstanding	750,000
Retained earnings	890,000
Total shareholders' equity	$1,840,000

QS 15–7
(LO 6)

The call price of the preferred is $45 and 1 year's dividends are in arrears. Determine the book value per common share. SOS Company expects to pay out a $4.50 per share cash dividend next year on its common shares. The current market price per share is $52.20. Calculate the expected dividend yield on SOS shares.

EXERCISES

Exercise 15–1
Recording issuances of shares
(LO 2)

Prepare General Journal entries to record the following issuances of shares by two different corporations:

1. One thousand common shares are issued for $65,000 cash.

2. Two hundred common shares are issued to promoters in exchange for their efforts in organizing the corporation. The promoters' efforts are estimated to be worth $9,000

Exercise 15–2
Comparative entries for partnership and corporation
(LO 1, 2)

Tom Seabrink and Joan Miller began a new business on February 14 when each of them invested $125,000 in the company. On December 20, it was decided that $48,000 of the company's cash would be distributed equally between the owners. Two cheques for $24,000 were prepared and given to the owners on December 23. On December 31, the company reported a $96,000 net income.

Prepare two sets of journal entries to record the investments by the owners, the distribution of cash to the owners, the closing of the Income Summary account, and the withdrawals or dividends under these alternative assumptions: *(a)* the business is a partnership, and *(b)* the business is a corporation that issued 1,000 no-par-value common shares.

On July 25 United Corporation issued 20,000 common shares for a building and land. The market value of the building and land was $300,000. A comparable land site recently sold for $60,000. Give the entry to record the acquisition.

Exercise 15–3
Accounting for issuance of shares for building and land
(LO 2)

On May 15, Sealtest Dairy Corporation accepted subscriptions to 60,000 no-par-value common shares at $39.00 per share. The subscription contracts called for one-fourth of the subscription price to accompany each contract as a down payment with the balance to be paid on November 15. Give the entries to record *(a)* the subscriptions, *(b)* the down payments, *(c)* receipt of the remaining amount due on the subscriptions, and *(d)* issuance of the shares.

Exercise 15–4
Share subscriptions
(LO 3)

The outstanding share capital of Kuker Realty Corporation includes 47,000 shares of $4 cumulative preferred and 82,000 shares no-par value of common. During its first four years of operation, the corporation declared and paid the following amounts in dividends: first year, $0; second year, $200,000; third year, $420,000; and fourth year, $200,000. Determine the total dividends paid in each year to each class of shareholders. Also determine the total dividends paid to each class over the four years.

Exercise 15–5
Allocating dividends between common and cumulative preferred shares
(LO 4)

Determine the total dividends paid in each year to each class of shareholders of the previous exercise under the assumption that the preferred shares are noncumulative. Also determine the total dividends paid to each class over the four years.

Exercise 15–6
Allocating dividends between common and noncumulative preferred shares
(LO 4)

Four individuals have agreed to begin a new business requiring a total investment of $900,000. Each of the four will contribute $150,000, and the remaining $300,000 will be raised from other investors. Two alternative plans for raising the money are being considered: (1) issue 9,000 common shares at $100 to all investors, or (2) issue 6,000 common shares at $100 to the four founders and 3,000 shares at $100, $7, cumulative preferred to the remaining investors. If the business is expected to earn an after-tax net income of $126,000, what rate of return will the founders earn under each alternative? Which of the two plans will provide the higher return to the four founders?

Exercise 15–7
Effect of preferred shares on rates of return
(LO 4)

How would your answers to Exercise 15–7 be changed if the business is expected to earn an after-tax net income of only $54,000?

Exercise 15–8
Effect of preferred shares on rates of return
(LO 4)

Lakeview Corporation has 6,400 outstanding shares of $8 preferred that is convertible into the corporation's no-par common at the rate of 4 shares of common for 1 share of preferred. The preferred shares were issued at $126 per share. Assume that all shares are presented for conversion.

Longview Manufacturing Corporation has issued 8,000 shares of $25 preferred at $250 per share. Each preferred share is convertible into 20 shares of the corporation's no-par-value common. Assume that one-fourth of the convertible preferred shares were presented for conversion.

Present entries dated March 2 to record the conversions on the books of the two corporations.

Exercise 15–9
Convertible preferred shares
(LO 5)

Exercise 15–10
Per share book value
(LO 5)

The shareholders' equity section from Micro Software Corporation's balance sheet is as follows:

Shareholders' Equity

Share capital:
Preferred share capital, $4, cumulative, $55 call price,
    12,000 shares issued and outstanding . . . . $ 600,000
    Common, no par value, 120,000 shares issued and outstanding . .   1,200,000
    Retained earnings   780,000
    Total shareholders' equity $2,580,000

Required

1. Determine the book value per share of the preferred and of the common under the assumption that there are no dividends in arrears on the preferred shares.

2. Determine the book value per share for each class of shares under the assumption that two years' dividends are in arrears on the preferred shares.

Exercise 15–11
Calculating dividend yield
(LO 6)

Calculate the dividend yield for each of these situations:

	Annual Dividend per Share	Market Price per Share
a.	$6.00	$ 64.00
b.	3.00	30.50
c.	5.50	65.00
d.	0.60	43.00
e.	1.00	25.00
f.	7.50	108.00

PROBLEMS

Problem 15–1
Share subscriptions
(LO 2, 3, 4)

Conrad Corporation is authorized to issue 50,000 shares of $8 cumulative preferred and an unlimited number of no-par-value common shares. Conrad Corporation then completed these transactions:

Apr. 4   Accepted subscriptions to 70,000 common shares at $18 per share. Down payments equal to 25% of the subscription price accompanied each subscription. The balance is due on June 3.

      11   Give the corporation's promoters 1,300 common shares for their services in organizing the corporation. The board valued the services at $26,000.

May 1   Accepted subscriptions to 4,000 preferred shares at $110 per share. The subscriptions were accompanied by 40% down payments. The balance is due on July 31.

June 3   Collected the balance due on the April 4 common subscriptions and issued the shares.

July 1   Accepted subscriptions to 3,000 preferred shares at $112 per share. The subscriptions were accompanied by 40% down payments. The balance is due on August 15.

      31   Collected the balance due on the May 1 preferred subscriptions and issued the shares.

Required

1. Prepare General Journal entries to record the transactions.
2. Prepare the shareholders' equity section of the corporation's balance sheet as of the close of business on July 31. Assume that retained earnings are $23,000.

Ideal Motor Company is authorized by its articles of incorporation to issue an unlimited number of common shares and 50,000 shares of $8, noncumulative convertible preferred. The company completed the following transactions:

Problem 15–2
Shareholders' equity
transactions
(LO 2, 3, 4, 5)

1995

Feb. 2 Issued for cash 210,000 common shares at $1 per share.

28 Gave the corporation's promoters 75,000 common shares for their services in organizing the corporation. The directors valued the services at $80,000.

Mar. 10 Issued 250,000 common shares in exchange for the following assets with the indicated reliable market values: land, $70,000; buildings, $130,000; and machinery, $89,000.

Dec. 31 Closed the Income Summary account. A $61,000 loss was incurred.

1996

Jan. 1 Issued for cash 6,000 preferred shares at $100 per share.

Dec. 1 Ideal Motor Company's preferred shareholders submitted 1,000 shares of their convertible preferred for conversion into common shares on this date. The convertible preferred shareholders accepted 80 common shares for each share of preferred.

31 Closed the Income Summary account. A $196,000 net income was earned.

1997

Jan. 1 The board of directors declared an $8 cash dividend to preferred shares and $0.20 per share cash dividend to outstanding common shares, payable on January 25 to the January 15 shareholders of record.

25 Paid the previously declared dividends.

Nov. 15 Accepted subscriptions to 30,000 common shares at $3.00 per share. Down payments of 25% accompanied the subscription contracts. The balance is due on February 15, 1998.

Dec. 31 Closed the Cash Dividends Declared and Income Summary accounts. A $262,000 net income was earned.

Required

1. Prepare General Journal entries to record the transactions.
2. Prepare the shareholders' equity section of the balance sheet as of the close of business on December 31, 1997.

Sunray Energy Company is authorized to issue an unlimited number of common shares and 200,000 shares of $5, noncumulative, convertible preferred. The company completed the following transactions:

Problem 15–3
Shareholders' equity
transactions
(LO 2, 3, 4, 5)

1995

Feb. 5 Issued 140,000 common shares at $5 for cash.

28 Gave the corporation's promoters 7,500 common shares for their services in organizing the corporation. The directors valued the services at $40,000.

Mar. 3 Issued 88,000 common shares in exchange for the following assets with the indicated reliable market values: land, $80,000; buildings, $210,000; and machinery, $155,000.

Dec. 31 Closed the Income Summary account. A $27,000 loss was incurred.

1996

Jan. 28 Issued 8,000 preferred shares at $50 for cash.

Dec. 15 Sunray Energy Company's preferred shareholders submitted 5,000 of their convertible shares for conversion into common shares on this date. The convertible preferred shareholders accepted nine common shares for each preferred share.

       31 Closed the Income Summary account. A $98,000 net income was earned.

1997

Jan. 1 The board of directors declared a $5 cash dividend to preferred shares and $0.10 per share cash dividend to outstanding common shares, payable on February 5 to the January 25 shareholders of record.

Feb. 5 Paid the previously declared dividends.

Oct. 20 Accepted subscriptions to 8,000 common shares at $7.45 per share. Down payments of 40% accompanied the subscription contracts. The balance is due on January 20, 1998.

Dec. 31 Closed the Cash Dividends Declared and Income Summary accounts. A $159,000 net income was earned.

Required

1. Prepare General Journal entries to record the transactions.
2. Prepare the shareholders' equity section of the balance sheet as of the close of business on December 31, 1997.

Problem 15–4
Calculating book values; allocating dividends between preferred and common shares
(LO 4, 5)

Part 1. The balance sheet of Fiber Filter Company includes the following information:

Shareholders' Equity

Share capital:

Preferred, $5, cumulative, 4,000 shares authorized and issued	$200,000
Common, no-par value, 60,000 shares authorized and issued ..	600,000
Retained earnings	120,000
Total shareholders' equity	$920,000

Required

Assume that the preferred shares have a call price of $55 plus any dividends in arrears. Calculate the book value per share of the preferred and common under each of the following assumptions:

a. No dividends are in arrears on the preferred shares.

b. One year's dividends are in arrears on the preferred shares.

c. Three years' dividends are in arrears on the preferred shares.

Part 2. Since its organization, Newtone Corporation has had 3,200 outstanding shares of $8 preferred and 64,000 shares of no-par-value common. No dividends have been paid this year, and none were paid during either of the past two years. However, the company has recently prospered and the board of directors wants to know how much cash would be required to provide a $1.50 per share dividend on the common. The preferred was issued at $100 per share and the common at $10 per share.

Required

Prepare a schedule that shows the amounts of cash required for dividends to each class of shareholders to provide the desired $1.50 per share dividend under each of the following assumptions:

a. The preferred is noncumulative.
b. The preferred is cumulative.
c. Determine amounts in *(a)* and *(b)* if desired dividend was $2 per common share.

Part 1. The balance sheet of Instant Services Corporation includes the following information:

Problem 15–5
Calculating book values; allocating dividends between preferred and common shares
(LO 4, 5)

Shareholders' Equity

Share capital:
Preferred $8, cumulative, 5,000 shares
authorized and issued . . . . $ 500,000
Common, no-par value, 80,000 shares authorized and issued . . 800,000
Retained earnings 385,000
Total shareholders' equity $1,685,000

Required

Assume that the preferred has a call price of $105 plus any dividends in arrears. Calculate the book value per share of the preferred and common under each of the following assumptions:

a. There are no dividends in arrears on the preferred.
b. One year's dividends are in arrears on the preferred.
c. Three years' dividends are in arrears on the preferred.

Part 2. Since its organization, KPO Corporation has had 14,000 outstanding shares of $11 preferred and 235,000 shares of no-par-value common. No dividends have been paid this year, and none were paid during either of the past two years. However, the company has recently prospered, and the board of directors wants to know how much cash would be required to provide a $1.00 per share dividend on the common. Preferred was issued at $100 per share and the common at $10 per share.

Required

Prepare a schedule that shows the amounts of cash required for dividends to each class of shareholders to provide the desired $1.00 per share dividend to the common shareholders under each of the following assumptions:

a. The preferred is noncumulative.
b. The preferred is cumulative.
c. Determine amounts in *(a)* and *(b)* if desired dividend was $1.50 per common share.

Problem 15–6
Allocating dividends in sequential years between preferred and common shares
(LO 4)

Axcel Bros. Company has 4,000 outstanding shares of $6 preferred and 60,000 shares of no-par-value common. During a seven-year period, the company paid out the following amounts in dividends:

1990	$ –0–
1991	54,000
1992	–0–
1993	30,000
1994	39,000
1995	48,000
1996	90,000

No dividends were in arrears for the years prior to 1990.

Required

1. Prepare two schedules with column headings as follows:

Year	Calculations	Preferred Dividend per Share	Common Dividend per Share

2. Complete a schedule under each of the following assumptions. (Round your calculations of dividends per share to the nearest cent.) The preferred was issued at $50 per share and common at $5 per share.

   a. The preferred is noncumulative.

   b. The preferred is cumulative.

Problem 15–7
Calculation of book values
(LO 5)

Essex Plastics Corporation's common shares are selling on a stock exchange today at $16.80 per share, and a just-published balance sheet shows the following information about the shareholders' equity of the corporation:

Shareholders' Equity

Share capital:	
Preferred, $5, cumulative, 15,600 shares authorized and outstanding	$ 780,000
Common, no par value, 130,000 shares authorized and outstanding	1,650,000
Retained earnings	330,000
Total shareholders' equity	$2,760,000

Required

1. What is the market value of the corporation's common shares?
2. If there are no dividends in arrears, give the book values for
   a. the preferred shares.
   b. the common shares.
3. If two years' dividends are in arrears on the preferred, give the book values for
   a. the preferred shares. (Assume that the preferred shares are not callable.)
   b. the common shares.

Problem 15–8
Analytical essay
(LO 1)

Jan Carston and Carey Glenwood want to create a new software development business. Each of them can contribute fairly large amounts of capital. However, they know that the business will need additional equity capital from other investors after its first year. With respect to their individual activities, they are both planning to devote full-time effort to getting the first products out the door within the year. They plan to hire three employees initially and expect to distribute a substantial amount of cash every year for their personal expenses. Carston has proposed organizing the business as a general partnership, but Glenwood thinks that a corporation offers more advantages. They have asked you to prepare a brief analysis that supports choosing the corporate form. What main points would you include in your analysis?

Refer to the shareholders' equity section of the balance sheet in Problem 15–4. Assume, however, that the common has an unlimited number of shares authorized instead of 60,000. Also, assume that the preferred shares are convertible into common at a rate of eight common shares for each share of preferred. If 1,000 shares of the preferred are converted into common shares, describe how this affects the shareholders' equity section of the balance sheet (immediately after the conversion). If you are a common shareholder in this company, and cash dividends of $487,000 are to be paid out, does it make any difference to you whether or not the conversion takes place? Why?

Problem 15–9
Analytical essay
(LO 4, 5)

PROVOCATIVE PROBLEMS

Jae Xu and Bob Lyle have operated a sports equipment company, X-L Sports, for a number of years as partners sharing net incomes and gains in a 3 to 2 ratio. Because the business is growing, the two partners entered into an agreement with Tom Celic to reorganize their firm into a corporation. The new corporation, X-L Sports, Inc., is authorized to issue 75,000 common shares of no-par-value. On the date of the reorganization, August 15, 1996, a trial balance of the partnership ledger appears as follows:

**Provocative Problem
15–1**
X-L Sports, Inc.
(LO 1, 2)

X-L SPORTS
Trial Balance
August 15, 1996

Cash	$ 38,255	
Accounts receivable	69,750	
Allowance for doubtful accounts		$ 2,625
Merchandise inventory	316,875	
Store equipment	73,500	
Accumulated amortization, store equipment		15,750
Buildings	375,000	
Accumulated amortization, buildings		75,000
Land	93,750	
Accounts payable		41,625
Notes payable		262,500
Jae Xu, capital		339,380
Bob Lyle, capital		230,250
Totals	$967,130	$967,130

The agreement between the partners and Celic carries these provisions:

1. The partnership assets are to be revalued as follows:
   a. The $2,250 account receivable of Blue Tigers is known to be uncollectible and is to be written off as a bad debt.
   b. After writing off the Blue Tigers account, the allowance for doubtful accounts is to be increased to 4% of the remaining accounts receivable.

c. The merchandise inventory is to be written down to $285,000 to allow for damaged and shopworn goods.

d. Insufficient amortization has been taken on the store equipment. Therefore, its book value is to be decreased to $48,750 by increasing the balance of the accumulated amortization account.

e. The building is to be written up to its replacement cost, $487,500, and the balance of the accumulated amortization account is to be increased to show the building to be one-fifth amortized.

2. After the partnership assets are revalued, the assets and liabilities are to be transferred to the corporation in exchange for its shares, with each partner accepting shares at $10 per share for his equity in the partnership.

3. Tom Celic is to buy any remaining authorized shares for cash at $10 per share.

After reaching the agreement outlined, the three principals hired you as accountant for the new corporation. Your first task is to determine the number of shares each person should receive, and to prepare entries on the corporation's books to record the issuance of shares in exchange for the partnership's assets and liabilities and the issuance of shares to Celic for cash. In addition, prepare a balance sheet for the corporation as it should appear after all the shares are issued.

Provocative Problem 15–2
Andrews Corporation
(LO 4)

The management of Andrews Corporation is considering the expansion of its business operations to a new and exciting line of business in which newly invested assets can be expected to earn 20% per year. At present, Andrews Corporation has only 18,000 common shares of no-par-value outstanding, which were issued at $50 per share, no other contributed capital accounts, and retained earnings of $270,000. Existing operations consistently earn approximately $175,000 each year. To finance the new expansion, management is considering three alternatives: (a) Issue 5,000 shares of $13, cumulative preferred. The investment advisors of the company conclude that these shares could be issued at $100 per share. (b) Issue 2,000 shares of $13 cumulative convertible at 3 for 1, preferred. The investment advisors conclude that these shares could be sold for $250 per share. (c) Issue 6,250 common shares at $80 per share.

In evaluating these three alternatives, Andrews Company management asked you to calculate the dividends that would be distributed to each class of shareholder based on the assumption that each year the board of directors will declare dividends equal to the total net income earned by the corporation. Your calculations should show the distribution of dividends to preferred and common shareholders under each of the three alternative financing plans. You should also calculate dividends per share of preferred and dividends per share of common.

As a second part of your analysis, assume that you own 1,000 of the common shares outstanding prior to the expansion and that you will not acquire or purchase any of the newly issued shares. Based on your whole analysis, would you prefer that the proposed expansion in operations be rejected? If not, comment on the relative merits of each alternative from your point of view as a common shareholder.

Provocative Problem 15–3
Reinhold Corporation and Rollins Company
(LO 4, 5)

Having recently inherited $75,000, Brian Parker is thinking about investing the money in one of two securities. They are: Reinhold Corporation common shares or the preferred shares issued by Rollins Company. The companies manufacture and sell competing products, and both have been in business about the same length of time—four years in the case of Reinhold Corporation and five years for Rollins Company. Also, the two companies have about the same amounts of shareholders' equity, as the following equity sections from their latest balance sheets show:

REINHOLD CORPORATION

Common shares, no-par value, unlimited number of shares authorized,
5,000,000 shares issued $5,000,000
Retained earnings 2,000,000
Total shareholders' equity $7,000,000

ROLLINS COMPANY

Preferred shares, $8 cumulative unlimited number,
of shares authorized, 20,000 shares issued $2,000,000*
Common shares, no-par value, unlimited number authorized,
400,000 shares issued 4,000,000
Retained earnings 200,000
Total shareholders' equity $6,200,000

*The current and one prior year's dividends are in arrears on the preferred shares.

Reinhold Corporation did not pay a dividend on its common shares during its first year's operations: however, since then, for the past three years, it has paid a $0.20 per share annual dividend. The shares are currently selling for $1.50 per share. The preferred shares of Rollins Company, on the other hand, are selling for $95 per share. Mr. Parker favours these shares as an investment. He feels the shares are a real bargain since they are selling $21 below book value, and as he says, "Since it is a preferred, the dividends are guaranteed." Too, he feels the common shares of Reinhold Corporation, selling at 7% above book value and 50% above its average stated value, while paying only a $0.20 per share dividend, are overpriced.

Required

a.   Are the preferred shares of Rollins Company selling at a price $21 below its book value, and are the common shares of Reinhold Corporation selling at a price 7% above book value and 50% above their average stated value?

b.   From an analysis of the shareholders' equity sections, express your opinion of the two shares as investments and describe some of the factors Mr. Parker should consider in choosing between the two securities.

Use the information provided in the financial statements of Geac Computer Corporation Limited and the notes (see Appendix I) to answer the following questions:

Provocative Problem 15–4

Financial statement analysis

1.   What classes of shares have been authorized?
2.   How many shares are authorized and outstanding?
3.   Are any shares subscribed?
4.   Did the number of shares of all classes change during 1994? If so, what caused the change?
5.   Did the company pay dividends in 1994?

ANALYTICAL AND REVIEW PROBLEMS

Until March 2 of the current year, Kay, Lace, and Moon were partners sharing losses and gains in a 5:3:2 ratio. On that date they received their certificate of incorporation of KLM Company, Limited. All the assets and liabilities of the partnership were taken over by the new corporation.

A & R Problems 15–1

The trial balance of the partnership just before the transfer and the opening trial balance of the corporation appear below:

KLM COMPANY
Post-Closing Trial Balance
March 2, 19—

Cash	$ 4,500	
Accounts receivable	20,500	
Allowance for doubtful accounts		$ 500
Merchandise inventory	33,000	
Store equipment	13,500	
Accumulated amortization, store equipment		3,500
Land	8,500	
Building	65,000	
Accumulated amortization, building		9,500
Accounts payable		15,500
Mortgage payable		12,000
Kay, capital		45,000
Lace, capital		40,000
Moon, capital		19,000
	$145,000	$145,000

KLM COMPANY, LIMITED
Trial Balance
March 2, 19—

Cash	$ 4,500	
Accounts receivable	20,500	
Allowance for doubtful accounts		$ 1,500
Merchandise inventory	25,000	
Store equipment	8,000	
Land	22,000	
Building	52,000	
Accounts payable		15,500
Mortgage payable		12,000
Share capital, common, no par value, 20,600 shares		103,000
	$132,000	$132,000

Required

How many shares did each shareholder receive? Support your answer.

A&R Problem 15–2 During the first year after incorporation, the following common share transactions were completed:

a. Immediately after incorporation sold 50,000 shares at $40 per share for cash.

b. Near mid-year received a subscription for 1,000 shares at $45 per share, collected 50% in cash, balance due in two equal installments within one year.

c. Two months later issued 500 shares for a used machine that would be used in operations. The machine had cost $30,000 new and was carried by the seller at a book value of $18,000. It was appraised at $24,000 six months previously by a reputable independent appraiser.

d. Collected half of the unpaid subscriptions in (b).

Required

Give entries for each of the above transactions.

CONCEPT TESTER

Test your understanding of the concepts introduced in this chapter by completing the following crossword puzzle.

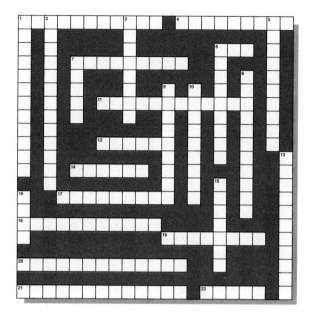

Across Clues

1. Total proceeds credited to share capital account (2 words).
4. Synonym for incorporators.
6. Arbitrary value placed on shares in some jurisdictions.
7. Shares that have senior status.
11. Costs of starting a corporation.
12. Shares with no preference over other classes of shares.
14. Value at which shares issued can be bought.
17. Possible life of a corporation.
18. Issued shares in hands of shareholders.
19. Preferred shares that the corporation has right to retire.
20. Preferred shares that forfeit claim to unpaid dividends.
21. Founders of a corporation.
22. Ratio of annual dividends to market price.

Down Clues

1. Owners of a corporation.
2. Number of shares a corporation is permitted to issue.
3. Achievement of an increased return by use of senior securities.
5. Value at which corporation can call its preferred shares.
6. CEO of a corporation.
7. Legal document that gives voting rights to another individual.
8. Capital invested by shareholders.
9. A type of leverage.
10. Redemption value of preferred shares (2 words).
13. Preferred shares that can be exchanged for common at option of owners.
15. Unpaid dividends on cumulative preferred shares.
16. A type of value of shares.

ANSWERS TO PROGRESS CHECKS

15–1 *b*

15–2 A corporation must pay taxes on its income, and its shareholders must pay personal income taxes on dividends received from the corporation.

15–3 A proxy is a legal document used to transfer a shareholder's right to vote to another person.

15–4 *c*

15–5 No. These costs should be recorded in an asset account, Organization Costs.

15–6 *(a)* $100,000. *(b)* $1,237,500.

15–7 Typically preferred shares have a preference in receiving dividends and in the distribution of assets in the case of a company's liquidation.

15–8 *a*

15–9 *b*

Total dividend	$288,000
To preferred shareholders	135,000*
Remainder to common shareholders	$153,000

*9,000 × $5 × 3 = $135,000

Additional Corporate Transactions; Reporting Income and Retained Earnings; Earnings per Share

*W*hile in the library studying the annual reports of the companies referred to in the previous chapter, Karen White came across an update on one of the companies. This was the three-month report as of November 30, 1994, of Anchor Lamina Inc. She was particularly interested in the remarks of Clare E. Winterbottom, Chairman and CEO:

> In general, we feel that the present is an appropriate time for expansion. We are very adequately financed, thanks to the equity issues placed in 1993. We have also recently concluded new banking relations and arrangements which will add greatly to our financial strength.
> Anchor Lamina is in an expansion mode. It is our intention to make the Company the leader in its industry—and the most profitable.

After reading the remarks, White took the following data to share with Mark Smith.

Astonishing growth of global markets is leading even small companies to customers and investors in other countries. In addition, today's complex world requires complex financial structures.

Anchor Lamina Inc.
Financial Highlights

Year Ended August 31	1994	1993	1992
Consolidated sales	$74,692,601	$59,048,537	$44,706,423
Net income	$ 8,433,081	$ 5,340,942	$ 901,899
Avg. shares outstanding	17,330,199	11,571,467	10,033,865
Earnings per share	49¢	45¢	9¢

3 Months to November 30	1994	1993
Consolidated sales	$30,315,000	$17,162,000
Net income	2,624,000	1,592,000
Avg. shares outstanding	18,096,000	16,143,789
Earnings per share	15¢	10¢

LEARNING OBJECTIVES

After studying Chapter 16, you should be able to:

1. **Record cash dividends, stock dividends, and stock splits and explain their effects on the assets and shareholders' equity of a corporation.**
2. **Record retirement of shares and describe the effect on shareholders' equity.**
3. **Describe restrictions and appropriations of retained earnings and the disclosure of such items in the financial statements.**
4. **Explain how the income effects of discontinued operations, extraordinary items, changes in accounting principles, and prior period adjustments are reported.**
5. **Calculate earnings per share for companies with simple capital structures and explain the difference between basic and fully diluted earnings per share.**
6. **Calculate the price-earnings ratio and explain its meaning.**
7. **Define or explain the words and phrases listed in the chapter glossary.**

We begin this chapter with a discussion of dividends and other transactions between a corporation and its shareholders. In this section of the chapter, you will learn about stock dividends, stock splits, and repurchases of shares by the issuing corporation. The second section of the chapter explains how income and retained earnings information is classified and reported. The third section explains how accountants report the earnings per share of a corporation. Understanding these topics will help you interpret and evaluate corporate financial statements. Note: use of the term *shares* rather than *stock* is preferred in Canada, but in the case of dividends in shares of the issuing corporation, *stock dividend* is normally used instead of *share dividend*. Also, the terms *stock split*, and *stock option*, are in common usage.

CORPORATE DIVIDENDS AND OTHER SHARE CAPITAL TRANSACTIONS

LO 1

Record cash dividends, stock dividends, and stock splits and explain their effects on the assets and shareholders' equity of a corporation.

In Chapter 3, we first described a corporation's retained earnings as the total amount of its net incomes less its net losses and dividends declared since it began operations. Years ago, retained earnings were commonly called **earned surplus**. However, the term is rarely used anymore.

Retained Earnings and Dividends

Most jurisdictions require that a corporation not pay cash dividends unless retained earnings are available. However, the payment of a cash dividend reduces both cash and shareholders' equity. Therefore, a corporation cannot pay a cash dividend simply because it has a credit balance in Retained Earnings; it also must have enough cash on hand to pay the dividend. If cash or assets that will shortly become cash are not available, the board of directors may choose to avoid a dividend declaration even though the Retained Earnings balance is adequate. Even if a corporation has a large Retained Earnings balance, the board of directors may refuse to declare a dividend because the available cash is needed in the operations of the business.

In deciding whether to declare dividends, the board of directors must recognize that operating activities are a source of cash. Perhaps some cash from operating activities should be paid out in dividends and some should be retained for emergencies. In addition, some cash may be retained to pay dividends in years when current operating activities do not generate enough cash to pay normal dividends. Furthermore, management may want to retain some cash from operating activities to finance expanded operations. See page 724 for a discussion of limitations in considering declaration and distribution of a cash dividend.

As was noted in Chapter 15, shareholders enjoy limited liability. Consequently, corporation laws provide for the protection of creditors and others dependent on the continuity of the corporation. To this end, the more recently passed corporations acts include a solvency test. For example, the Canada Business Corporation Act 1975 provides the following in section 40:

> A corporation shall not declare or pay a dividend if there are responsible grounds for believing that
>
> (a) the corporation is, or would after the payment be, unable to pay its liabilities as they become due; or
>
> (b) the realizable value of the corporation's assets would thereby be less than the aggregate of its liabilities and stated capital of all classes.

Entries for the declaration and distribution of a cash dividend were presented in Chapter 15 and need not be repeated here. It should be noted that asset distributions in excess of a credit balance in Retained Earnings are **liquidating dividends**— a return of original investment.

Stock Dividends

Sometimes, a corporation distributes its own unissued shares to its shareholders without receiving any consideration from the shareholders. This type of distribution is called a **stock dividend.** A stock dividend and a cash dividend are very different. A cash dividend transfers assets from the corporation to the shareholders. As a result, a cash dividend reduces the corporation's assets and its shareholders' equity. On the other hand, a stock dividend does not transfer assets from the corporation to the shareholders; it has no effect on assets and no effect on total shareholders' equity.

However, a stock dividend does have an effect on the components of shareholders' equity. To record a stock dividend, you must transfer some of the Retained Earnings balance to contributed capital accounts. For example, assume that Northwest Corporation's shareholders' equity is

---

Shareholders' Equity

Share capital:
Common shares, no-par value, unlimited number
of shares authorized, 10,000 shares issued and
outstanding $108,000
Retained earnings 35,000
Total shareholders' equity $143,000

On December 31, the directors of Northwest Corporation declared a 10%, or 1,000-share, stock dividend distributable on January 20 to the shareholders of record on January 15.

If the market value of Northwest Corporation's shares on December 31 is $15 per share, the dividend declaration is recorded as

Dec.	31	Stock Dividends Declared	15,000.00	
		Common Stock Dividend Distributable		15,000.00
		To record the declaration of a 1,000-share common		
		stock dividend.		

Note that the debit is to Stock Dividends Declared. In previous chapters, when we discussed cash dividends, they were debited to Dividends Declared. However, since a corporation may declare stock dividends as well as cash dividends, a convenient system of accounts would include separate Cash Dividends Declared and Stock Dividends Declared accounts.

In the year-end closing process, close the Stock Dividends Declared account to Retained Earnings as follows:

Dec.	31	Retained Earnings	15,000.00	
		Stock Dividends Declared		15,000.00

On January 20 record the distribution of the shares as follows:

Jan.	20	Common Stock Dividend Distributable	15,000.00	
		Common Shares		15,000.00
		To record the distribution of 1,000 common shares.		

Note that these entries shift $15,000 of the shareholders' equity from retained earnings to contributed capital, or in other words, $15,000 of retained earnings is *capitalized.* Note also that the amount of retained earnings capitalized is equal to the market value of the 1,000 shares issued ($15 × 1,000 shares = $15,000).[1]

As you already learned, a stock dividend does not distribute assets to the shareholders; it has no effect on the corporation's assets. Also, it has no effect on total shareholders' equity and no effect on the percentage of the company owned by each individual shareholder. To illustrate these last points, assume that Johnson owned 100 shares of Northwest Corporation's outstanding shares prior to the stock dividend. The 10% stock dividend gave each shareholder 1 new share for each 10 shares previously held. Therefore, Johnson received 10 new shares.

Illustration 16–1 shows Northwest Corporation's total contributed and retained capital and the book value of Johnson's 100 shares before the dividend and after the dividend.

---

[1]The Canada Business Corporations Act requires that the value of a stock dividend be added to the stated capital account. In other jurisdictions, for example, Ontario, the amount to be capitalized is left to the board of directors.

Before the 10% stock dividend:

Share capital:

Common shares (10,000 shares)	$108,000
Retained earnings	35,000
Total contributed and retained capital	$143,000

$143,000/10,000 shares outstanding = $14.30 per share book value.
Book value of Johnson's 100 shares: $14.30 × 100 = $1,430.

After the 10% stock dividend is distributed:

Share capital:

Common shares (11,000 shares)	$123,000
Retained earnings	20,000
Total contributed and retained capital	$143,000

$143,000/11,000 shares outstanding = $13 per share book value.
Book value of Johnson's 110 shares: $13 × 110 = $1,430.

Illustration 16–1
The Effect of Northwest Corporation's Stock Dividend on Shareholders

Illustration 16–1 shows that before the stock dividend, Johnson owned 100/10,000, or 1/100, of the Northwest Corporation shares, and his holdings had a $1,430 book value. After the dividend, he owns 110/11,000, or 1/100, of the corporation, and his holdings still have a $1,430 book value. In other words, there was no effect on Johnson's investment except that it was repackaged from 100 units into 110. Also, the only effect on the corporation's capital was a transfer of $15,000 from retained earnings to contributed capital. To summarize, there was no change in the corporation's total assets, no change in its total capital or equity, and no change in the percentage of that equity owned by Johnson.

Why Stock Dividends Are Distributed

If stock dividends have no effect on corporation assets and shareholders' equities other than to repackage the equities into more units, why are such dividends declared and distributed? The primary reason for stock dividends is related to the market price of a corporation's common shares. For example, if a profitable corporation grows by retaining earnings, the price of its common shares also tends to grow. Eventually, the price of a share may become high enough to discourage some investors from buying the shares. Thus, the corporation may declare stock dividends to keep the price of its shares from increasing too much. Yet another reason normally cited by management is to preserve cash. For these reasons, some corporations declare stock dividends each year.

Some shareholders may like stock dividends for another reason. Often, corporations that declare stock dividends continue to pay the same cash dividend per share after a stock dividend as before. The result is that shareholders receive more cash each time dividends are declared.

Amount of Retained Earnings Capitalized

The Canada Business Act requires that if a corporation declares a stock dividend, it must capitalize an amount of retained earnings that equals the market value of the shares to be distributed. A requirement to capitalize a specified amount of retained earnings is without justification. If the board of directors can decide the amount of cash dividends, then the power to decide the amount of retained earnings to be capitalized should also be left to their discretion. The authors therefore believe that the provision of the Ontario Corporations Act is correct. That is, the board of directors decides the amount of retained earnings to be capitalized. In the meantime, since there is not consistency in corporate laws regarding the amount of retained earnings to be capitalized, corporations must observe the requirements of the laws of the jurisdiction of incorporation.

Stock Dividends on the Balance Sheet

Because a stock dividend is "payable" in shares rather than in assets, it is not a liability of its issuing corporation. Therefore, if a balance sheet is prepared between the declaration and distribution dates of a stock dividend, the amount of the dividend distributable should appear on the balance sheet in the shareholders' equity section:

Share Capital:	
Common shares, no-par value, unlimited number of shares authorized, shares issued and outstanding	$108,000
Common stock dividend distributable, 1,000 shares	15,000
Total common shares issued and to be issued	$123,000
Retained earnings	20,000
Total shareholders' equity	$143,000

STOCK SPLITS

Sometimes, when a corporation's shares are selling at a high price, the corporation calls them in and issues two, three, or more new shares in the place of each previously outstanding share. For example, a corporation that has shares selling for $375 a share may call in the old shares and issue to the shareholders 4 shares, 10 shares, or any number of shares in exchange for each share formerly held. This is known as a **stock split.** The usual purpose of a stock split is to reduce the market price of the shares and thereby facilitate trading in the shares. Less frequently, a corporation may have a **reverse stock split.** In that case the corporation calls in the old shares and issues 1 new share for each 2 shares, 3 shares, 10 shares, or any number of shares previously held. The usual purpose of a reverse stock split is to cause an increase in the per share market value.

A stock split (or reverse split) has no effect on total shareholders' equity, and no effect on the equities of the individual shareholders. Also, the balances of the Contributed Capital and Retained Earnings accounts are not changed. Thus, a stock split (or reverse split) does not require a journal entry. All that is required is a memorandum entry in the share capital account reciting the facts of the split. For example, such a memorandum might read, "Issued 10 new common shares for each old share previously outstanding." When you prepare the balance sheet, the new number of shares outstanding must be used.

As a Matter of Ethics

Falcon Corporation's board of directors and officers have been meeting to discuss and plan the agenda for the corporation's 1994 annual shareholders' meeting. The first item considered by the directors and officers was whether to report a large government contract that Falcon has just obtained. Although this contract will significantly increase income and cash flows in 1994 and beyond, management decided that there is no need to reveal the news at the shareholders' meeting. "After all," one officer said, "the meeting is intended to be the forum for describing the past year's activities, not the plans for the next year."

After concluding that the contract will not be mentioned, the group has moved on to the next topic for the shareholders' meeting. This topic is a motion for the shareholders to approve a compensation plan that will award the managers the rights to acquire large quantities of shares over the next several years. According to the plan, the managers will have a three-year option to buy shares at a fixed price that equals the market value of the shares as measured 30 days after the upcoming shareholders' meeting. In other words, the managers will be able to buy shares in 1995, 1996, or 1997 by paying the 1994 market value. Obviously, if the shares increase in value over the next several years, the managers will realize large profits without having to invest any cash. The financial vice president asks the group whether they should reconsider the decision about the government contract in light of its possible relevance to the vote on the stock option plan.

Progress Check

16-1 Which of the following statements is correct?
  a. For federally incorporated companies, a stock dividend is recorded by capitalizing retained earnings equal to the market value of the distributable shares.
  b. Stock dividends and stock splits have the same effect on total assets and retained earnings of the issuing corporation.
  c. A stock dividend does not transfer corporate assets to shareholders but does require that retained earnings be capitalized.

16-2 What distinguishes a 100% stock dividend from a 2-for-1 stock split?

16-3 When accounting for a stock dividend an Ontario corporation capitalizes what amount of retained earnings?

RETIREMENT OF SHARE CAPITAL

LO 2

Record retirement of shares and describe the effect on shareholders' equity.

Under the Canada Business Corporations Act, as well as under the more recently passed provincial acts, such as the one in Ontario, a corporation may purchase and retire shares of its own outstanding share capital if it can satisfy a solvency test applicable to cash dividends and cited earlier in this chapter. For example, it was noted in the annual report of **Imasco Limited** that at December 31, 1994, 1,771,400 common shares had been repurchased. These repurchased shares were restored to the status of authorized but unissued shares.

When shares are purchased for retirement, the debit to the stated capital account is the product of the number of shares acquired multiplied by the weighted average per share invested by the shareholders. If the shares are purchased for less than the weighted average per share invested by the shareholders, the difference is credited to an account such as Contributed Capital from Retirement of Shares. On the other hand, if the shares are purchased for more than the weighted average per share invested by the shareholders, the difference is debited to contributed capital from previous credit balances of share retirement transactions to the extent of its balance with any remainder debited to Retained Earnings.

For example, assume a corporation originally issued its no-par-value common shares at an average price of $12 per share. If the corporation later purchased and retired 1,000 of these shares at the price for which they were issued, the entry to record the retirement is

Apr.	12	Common Shares	12,000.00	
		Cash		12,000.00
		Purchased and retired 1,000 common shares at $12 per share.		

On the other hand, if the corporation paid $11 per share instead of $12, the entry for the retirement is

Apr.	12	Common Shares	12,000.00	
		Cash		11,000.00
		Contributed Capital from the Retirement of Common Shares		1,000.00
		Purchased and retired 1,000 common shares at $11 per share.		

If the corporation paid $15 per share, the entry for the purchase and retirement is

Apr.	12	Common Shares	12,000.00	
		Retained Earnings	3,000	
		Cash		15,000.00
		Purchased and retired 1,000 common shares at $15 per share.		

In jurisdictions that have par values when such shares are reacquired for cancellation, all capital items related to the shares being retired are removed from the accounts, and the difference between the purchase price and the weighted average per share invested by the shareholders is treated in a like manner to that illustrated above for no-par-value shares. In addition to the entry to record the reacquisition of shares, corporate statutes require the corporation to **restrict** or appropriate retained earnings equal to the cost of the reacquired shares. This requirement is based on a view that the reacquisition of shares has the same impact as the payment of a cash dividend. The restriction may be accomplished by a note (cross-referenced to the balance sheet) or by a journal entry such as the following:

Retained Earnings	12,000	
Resricted Retained Earnings—Reacquisition of shares		12,000

A corporation may voluntarily designate an amount of retained earnings for some special purpose as a means of explaining to shareholders why dividends are not being declared. In contrast to retained earnings, which carry binding restrictions by law or by contract, **appropriated retained earnings** result from a voluntary action by the board of directors. In earlier years, such appropriations were recorded by transferring portions of retained earnings from the Retained Earnings account to another shareholders' equity account such as Retained Earnings Appropriated for Contingencies or Retained Earnings Appropriated for Plant Expansion. When the contingency or other reason for an appropriation no longer existed, the appropriation account was eliminated by returning its balance to the Retained Earnings account. Today these retained earnings restrictions are usually explained in a letter attached to the financial statements.

VOLUNTARY APPROPRIATIONS OF RETAINED EARNINGS

LO 3

Describe restrictions and appropriations of retained earnings and the disclosure of such items in the financial statements.

REPORTING OF INCOME AND RETAINED EARNINGS INFORMATION

When the revenue and expense transactions of a company consist only of routine, continuing operations, a single-step income statement is adequate. This format shows revenues followed by a list of operating expenses and the net income. Often, however, the activities of a business include items not closely related to its continuing operations. In these cases, the income effects of such items should be separated from the revenues and expenses of continuing operations. Otherwise, the income statement fails to provide readers with clear information about the results of normal business activities.

To see how various income statement items should be classified, look at Illustration 16–2. Observe that the income statement is separated into four sections labeled 1 through 4. The first of the four portions of the income statement shows the revenues, expenses, and income generated by the company's continuing operations. This portion looks just like the single-step income statement we first discussed in Chapter 5. The next income statement section relates to discontinued operations.

Large companies often have several different lines of business operations and deal with different classes of customers. For example, **Imperial Oil Limited** not only produces and sells petroleum products but it also has a major position in the retail fertilizer industry. A company's operations that involve a particular line of business or class of customers may qualify as a **segment of the business.** To qualify as a segment of a business, the assets, activities, and financial results of operations involving a particular line of business or class of customers must be distinguished from other parts of the business.

INCOME STATEMENT ITEMS NOT RELATED TO CONTINUING OPERATIONS

LO 4

Explain how the income effects of discontinued operations, extraordinary items, changes in accounting principles, and prior period adjustments are reported.

DISCONTINUED OPERATIONS

Separating Discontinued Operations on the Income Statement

Normally, the revenues and expenses of all business segments are added together and reported as the continuing operations of the business (as in section 1 of Illustration 16–2). However, when a business sells or disposes of a business segment, the results of that segment's operations must be separated and reported as you see

Illustration 16-2 Income Statement for a Corporation

CONNELLY CORPORATION
Income Statement
For Year Ended December 31, 1996

Net sales		$8,443,000
Gain on sale of old equipment		30,000
Total		$8,473,000
Costs and expenses:		
1 { Cost of goods sold	$5,950,000	
Amortization expense	35,000	
Other selling, general, and administrative expenses	515,000	
Interest expense	20,000	
Income taxes	792,000	(7,312,000)
Unusual loss on sale of surplus land		(45,000)
Infrequent gain on relocation of a plant		72,000
Income from continuing operations		$1,188,000
Discontinued operations:		
Income from operation of discontinued Division A		
(net of $166,000 income taxes)	$ 400,000	
2 { Loss on disposal of Division A (net of $60,000 tax		
benefit)	(150,000)	250,000
Income before extraordinary items and cumulative		
effect of a change in accounting principle		$1,438,000
Extraordinary items:		
Gain on sale of unused land expropriated by the		
state for a highway interchange (net of $35,000		
3 { income taxes)	$ 142,500	
Loss from earthquake damage (net of $310,000		
income taxes)	(670,000)	(527,500)
Net income		$ 910,500
Earnings per common share (250,000 shares outstanding):		
Income from continuing operations		$4.75
4 { Discontinued operations		1.00
Extraordinary items		(2.11)
Net income		$3.64

in section 2 of Illustration 16–2. In the illustration, the results of the discontinued operations are completely separated from the results of other activities. This separation makes it easier for financial statement readers to evaluate the continuing operations of the business.

Separating the Results of Operating a Segment that Is Being Discontinued from the Gain or Loss on Disposal

Within section 2 of Illustration 16–2, note that the income from *operating* Division A (the operation that is being discontinued) during the period is reported separately from the loss on the final *disposal* of Division A. Also, the income tax effects of the discontinued operations are separated from the income tax expense shown in section 1 of Illustration 16–2. Thus, the results of the discontinued operations are reported net of tax. Also, the amount of tax or tax benefit related to each item is disclosed. Similarly, unusual items, items that do not qualify as extraordinary, should be reported separately.

The above discussion summarizes the method of *reporting* the results of discontinued operations and unusual items on the income statement. The detailed requirements for *measuring* the income or losses of discontinued operations are discussed in a more advanced accounting course.

Section 3 of the income statement in Illustration 16–2 reports gains and losses that are extraordinary. The *CICA Handbook* identifies extraordinary items as items that result from transactions or events that have all of the following characteristics: *(a)* they are not expected to occur frequently over several years, *(b)* they do not typify the normal business activities of the entity, and *(c)* they do not depend primarily on decisions or determinations by management or owners.[2] Thus, the essential characteristics of extraordinary items are that they are infrequent and atypical, and they result primarily from nonmanagement decisions. Examples are government expropriation of property or natural disasters. Gains or losses resulting from the risks inherent in an entity's normal business activities, such as losses on accounts receivable or inventories and gains and losses on disposals of long-term assets, may be **unusual** but would not be considered extraordinary.

Each extraordinary item should be disclosed separately and adequately described to allow users of the financial statements to understand the nature of the transactions or events and the extent to which income has been affected.

EXTRAORDINARY ITEMS

Prior period adjustments are accounted for and reported as direct charges (or credits, including disclosure of the applicable income tax) to Retained Earnings; they cause the opening balance of retained earnings to be restated. To qualify as prior period adjustments, items must be rare in occurrence and must meet the specific criteria set out in paragraphs 3600.02–.03 of the *CICA Handbook*. Settlement of lawsuits arising in prior periods and one-time income tax settlements are normally the only items that qualify as prior period adjustments.

PRIOR PERIOD ADJUSTMENTS

Accounting changes (section 1506 of the *CICA Handbook*) include *(a)* accounting errors, *(b)* changes in accounting policy, and *(c)* changes in estimates. The first two types of items—accounting errors arising in prior periods and changes in accounting policy necessitated by a change in circumstances or the development of new accounting principles—receive parallel treatment to that described for prior period adjustments. That is, they are applied **retroactively** with a restatement of the opening Retained Earnings. The latter, change in estimate, is accorded **prospective** treatment. As a company gains more experience in such areas as estimating bad debts, warranty costs, and useful lives of capital assets, there is often a sound basis for revising previous estimates. Such changes affect only the present and

ACCOUNTING CHANGES

---

[2] *CICA Handbook*, section 3480.

Illustration 16–3
Single-Year Statement
of Retained Earnings

CONNELLY CORPORATION
Statement of Retained Earnings
For Year Ended December 31, 1997

Retained earnings, January 1, 1997	$4,745,000
Prior period adjustment for accounting error:	
Cost of the land that was incorrectly charged to expense	
(net of $60,000 income taxes)	130,000
Retained earnings, January 1, 1997, as restated	$4,875,000
Plus net income	937,500
Less cash dividends declared	(240,000)
Retained earnings, December 31, 1997	$5,572,500

future statements. A detailed discussion and comparative statement presentation of items that require retroactive adjustment are left to a more advanced textbook; however, a simple single-year illustration is to be found in Illustration 16–3.

STATEMENT OF CHANGES IN SHAREHOLDERS' EQUITY

In Chapter 5, we explained that some corporations do not present a separate statement of retained earnings. Instead, they present a combined statement of income and retained earnings, an example of which is shown in Illustration 16–4. Other corporations show the statement of retained earnings information in an expanded statement called a *statement of changes in shareholders' equity*. In that statement, the beginning and ending balances of each shareholders' equity account are reconciled by listing all changes that occurred during the year. For example, the annual report of **The Bank of Nova Scotia** for the year ended October 31, 1994, included the financial statement shown in Illustration 16–4.

Progress Check

16–4   Which of the following is an extraordinary item?
   a. A settlement paid to a customer injured while using the company's product,
   b. A loss from damages to a plant caused by a meteorite,
   c. A loss from selling old equipment.

16–5   Identify the four possible major sections of the income statement that might appear below income from continuing operations.

16–6   A company that used FIFO for the past 15 years has decided to switch to LIFO. The effect of this event on past years' net income should be *(a)* reported as a prior period adjustment to retained earnings, *(b)* ignored as it is a change in an accounting estimate, *(c)* reported on the current year's income statement.

EARNINGS PER SHARE

Among the most commonly quoted statistics on the financial pages of daily newspapers is **earnings per share** of common shares. Investors use earnings per share data when they evaluate the past performance of a corporation, project its future earnings, and weigh investment opportunities.

Illustration 16–4   Statement of Shareholders' Equity

Consolidated Statement of Changes in Shareholders' Equity		
For the financial year ended October 31 ($ millions)	**1994**	**1993**
Preferred shares (Note 10)		
Balance at beginning of year	**$1,300**	$1,000
Proceeds of shares issued during the year	**–**	300
Redemption of shares during the year	**(200)**	—
Balance at end of year	**$1,100**	$1,300
Common shares (Note 10)		
Balance at beginning of year	**$1,429**	$1,308
Shares issued to acquire Montreal Trustco Inc. (Note 17)	**280**	—
Shareholder dividend and share purchase plan	**130**	121
Balance at end of year	**$1,839**	$1,429
Retained earnings		
Balance at beginning of year	**$3,175**	$2,771
Net income for the year	**482**	714
Dividends: Preferred	**(97)**	(92)
Common	**(253)**	(233)
Net unrealized foreign exchange gains and losses	**9**	20
Net costs of share issue and redemption	**(14)**	(5)
Balance at end of year	**$3,302**	$3,175

Earnings per share calculations may be simple or complex. The calculations are not as difficult for companies that have simple capital structures. A company has a **simple capital structure** if it has only common share capital and perhaps non-convertible preferred shares outstanding. In other words, to have a simple capital structure, the company cannot have any outstanding options or rights to purchase common shares at a specified price or any securities convertible into common shares.

Calculating Earnings per Share When the Number of Common Shares Outstanding Does Not Change

Consider a company that has only common shares and cumulative nonconvertible preferred shares outstanding.[3] If the number of common shares outstanding does not change during the period, calculate earnings per share as follows:

$$\text{Earnings per share} = \frac{\text{Net income} - \text{Preferred dividends}}{\text{Common shares outstanding}}$$

For example, assume that in 1996 Blackwell Company earned a $40,000 net income and paid its preferred dividends of $7,500. On January 1, 1996, the company

COMPANIES WITH SIMPLE CAPITAL STRUCTURES

LO 5

Calculate earnings per share for companies with simple capital structures and explain the difference between primary and fully diluted earnings per share.

---

[3]If the preferred shares were noncumulative, the deduction from net income would be made only to the extent of the preferred dividends declared. In the case of cumulative preferred, one year's preferred dividends are deducted from net income whether declared or not.

had 5,000 common shares outstanding and this number did not change during the year. Calculate earnings per share for 1996 as follows:

$$\text{Earnings per share} = \frac{\$40,000 - \$7,500}{5,000} = \$6.50$$

However, the calculation becomes more complex if the number of common shares outstanding changes during the period. The number of common shares outstanding may change (1) because the company sells additional shares or reacquires shares or (2) because of stock dividends and stock splits.

Adjusting the Denominator for Sales or Purchases of Common Shares

If additional shares are sold or shares are reacquired during the year, earnings per share is based on the weighted-average number of shares outstanding during the year. For example, suppose that in 1997, Blackwell Company again earned $40,000 and preferred dividends were $7,500. However, on July 1, 1997, Blackwell sold 4,000 additional common shares. Also, on November 1, 1997, Blackwell reacquired 3,000 shares. In other words, 5,000 shares were outstanding for six months; then 9,000 shares were outstanding for four months; then 6,000 shares were outstanding for two months. When such changes occur, calculate the weighted-average number of shares outstanding during 1997 as follows:

Time Period	Shares Outstanding	Weighted by Portion of Year Outstanding
January–June	5,000	$(\%_{12}) = 2,500$
July–October	$(5,000 + 4,000)$	$(\%_{12}) = 3,000$
November–December	$(9,000 - 3,000)$	$(\%_{12}) = 1,000$
Weighted-average common shares outstanding		6,500

An alternative method of calculation is

Time Period	Number of Shares	Weighted by Number of Months Shares Outstanding
January–December	5,000	$\times$ 12 = 60,000
July–December	4,000	$\times$ 6 = 24,000
November–December	(3,000)	$\times$ 2 = (6,000)
		78,000
Weighted-average common shares outstanding 78,000/12 = 6,500		

The calculation of earnings per share for 1997 is

$$\text{Earnings per share} = \frac{\$40,000 - \$7,500}{6,500} = \$5$$

Adjusting the Denominator for Stock Splits and Stock Dividends

A stock split or stock dividend is different from a sale of shares. When shares are sold, the company receives new assets that it uses to generate additional earnings. On the other hand, stock splits and stock dividends do not provide additional assets for the company. Instead, a stock split or stock dividend simply means that the company's earnings must be allocated to a larger number of outstanding shares.

Because of the nature of stock splits and stock dividends, they are treated differently from sales of shares when calculating the weighted-average number of shares outstanding. When a stock split or stock dividend occurs, the number of shares outstanding during previous portions of the year must be retroactively restated to reflect the stock split or dividend. For example, consider the previous example of Blackwell Company. Assume that the share transactions in 1997 included a stock split, as follows:

Jan. 1: 5,000 common shares were outstanding.
July 1: Blackwell sold 4,000 additional common shares.
Nov. 1: Blackwell purchased 3,000 common shares.
Dec. 1: Outstanding common shares were split 2 for 1.

The changes in the number of common shares outstanding during 1997 is the same as in the previous example except for the 2-for-1 stock split. The calculation of the weighted average of common shares outstanding is the same except the resulting number of the former example is multiplied by 2 to arrive at 13,000 shares. The same type of restatement is required for stock dividends. If, for example, the 2-for-1 stock split on December 1 had been a 10% stock dividend, the multiplier would be 1.10 instead of 2. The calculation of Blackwell Company's earnings per share for 1997 is

$$\text{Earnings per share} = \frac{\$40,000 - \$7,500}{13,000} = \$2.50$$

COMPANIES WITH COMPLEX CAPITAL STRUCTURES

Companies with **complex capital structures** have outstanding securities such as bonds or preferred shares that are convertible into common shares. Earnings per share calculations for companies with complex capital structures are more complicated. Often, such companies must present two types of earnings per share calculations. One is called **basic earnings per share**, and the other is called **fully diluted earnings per share**.

Suppose that a corporation has convertible preferred shares outstanding throughout the current year. However, consider what the effects would have been if the preferred shares had been converted at the beginning of the year. The result of this assumed conversion would have been to increase the number of common shares outstanding and to reduce preferred dividends. The net result may have been to reduce earnings per share, or to increase earnings per share. When the assumed conversion of a security reduces earnings per share, the security is said to be **dilutive**; those that increase earnings per share are **antidilutive**. Fully diluted earnings per share are calculated as if all dilutive securities (antidilutive securities are excluded

Illustration 16–5   Reporting Basic and Fully Diluted Earnings per Share

BCE INC. Earnings per Share	1993	1992	1991
Earnings (loss) per share			
Continuing operations	**0.21**	4.52	3.94
Discontinued operations (note 6)	**(2.65)**	(0.31)	0.07
Net earnings (loss) per share (note 3)	**(2.44)**	4.21	4.01
Dividends declared per common share	**2.65**	261	257
Average number of common shares outstanding (millions) . .	**307.0**	307.6	307.6

ANCHOR LAMINA INC.	1994	1993
Basic income per common share (Notes 2&15)	$0.50	$0.47
Fully diluted income per common share (Notes 2&15)	$0.49	$0.46

from the calculation) had already been converted. The complexities of fully diluted earnings per share are left for more advanced accounting courses.

PRESENTATIONS OF EARNINGS PER SHARE ON THE INCOME STATEMENT

Because of the importance attached to earnings per share data, generally accepted accounting principles require that you show this information on the face of published income statements or in the notes to the financial statements cross-referenced to the income statement. Separate earnings per share calculations are normally presented for (1) income before extraordinary items, (2) extraordinary items, and (3) net income. Some corporations provide additional calculations such as unusual items in Illustrations 16–2. Examples from published statements are presented in Illustration 16–5.

Progress Check

16-7   During 1997, FDI Co. had net income of $250,000 and paid preferred dividends of $70,000. On January 1, the company had 25,000 outstanding common shares and purchased and retired 5,000 shares on July 1. 1997 earnings per share are (a) $8.00, (b) $9.00, (c) $10.00.

16-8   How are stock splits and stock dividends treated in calculating the weighted-average number of outstanding common shares?

16-9   What two sets of earnings per share results are reported for a company with a complex capital structure?

USING THE INFORMATION— PRICE- EARNINGS RATIO

You learned in Chapter 15 that share market value is largely affected by the stream of future dividends expected to be paid out to shareholders. Market value is also affected by expected future changes in value. By comparing the company's earnings per share and its market price per share, investors and other decision makers can obtain information about the stock market's apparent expectations for growth in future earnings, dividends, and market values.

Illustration 16–6   Canadian Corporate Reports*

Abitibi-Price

3 months to Dec. 31, 1994		Year ago
Revenue	$568,000,000	$486,000,000
Prof cont ops	10,000,000	(30,000,000)
Prof disc ops	(4,000,000)	(10,000,000)
Net profit	6,000,000	(40,000,000)
Cont. ops./share	0.12	(0.39)
Disc. ops./share	(0.04)	(0.14)
Net profit/share	0.08	(0.53)

Year to Dec. 31, 1994		Year ago
Revenue	$2.11-billion	$1.87-billion
Prof cont ops	(51,000,000)	(98,000,000)
Prof disc ops	(4,000,000)	(13,000,000)
Net profit	(55,000,000)	(111,000,000)
Avg. shares	84,400,000	71,800,000
Cont. ops./share	(0.62)	(1.38)
Disc. ops./share	(0.04)	(0.18)
Net profit/share	(0.66)	(1.56)

Preferred-share dividends were nil vs nil in the quarter and $1-million vs $1-million in the year. Year-earlier results, as well as results for the first three quarters of fiscal 1994, have been restated to reflect the impact of a pact reached last December between Canadian and U.S. taxation authorities.

Accugraph Corp.

Year to Dec. 31, 1994		Year ago
Revenue	$24,806,000	$14,099,000
Net profit	5,090,000	1,075,000
Avg. shares	16,559,000	11,978,000
Net profit/share	0.31	0.09

BMTC Group

3 months to Dec. 31, 1994		Year ago
Revenue	$97,877,000	$87,958,000
Net profit	a2,276,000	3,099,000

Net profit/share	a0.25	0.31

Year to Dec. 31, 1994		Year ago
Revenue	$359,408,000	$306,770,000
Net profit	a9,209,000	7,859,000
Net profit/share	a0.97	0.79

a. Includes a $1,812,000 writedown of goodwill, and a charge of $362,000 related to a change in depreciation policy.

Bedford Capital

6 months to Dec. 31, 1994		Year ago
Revenue	$2,225,469	$782,076
Net profit	500,526	96,221
Avg. shares	6,258,700	3,600,000
Net profit/share	0.08	0.03

Bonar Inc.

Year to Dec. 3, 1994		Year ago
Revenue	$239,668,000	$201,442,000
Net profit	13,116,000	10,227,000
Net profit/share	2.68	2.10

Caribbean Utilities

9 months to Jan. 31, 1995		Year ago
Revenue	$n/a	$a/a
Net profit	7,233,810	5,874,574
Net profit/share	a0.64	0.61

a. Restated to reflect a 2-for-1 stock split in December 1994.

Co-Maxx Energy

Year to Dec. 31, 1994		Year ago
Revenue	$5,667,352	$4,607,035
Cash flow	3,164,956	2,379,108
Net profit	1,584,174	1,265,241
Avg. shares	5,680,000	4,258,000
Cash flow/share	0.56	0.56

Net profit/share	0.28	0.30

Corporate Foods

3 months to Dec. 31, 1994		Year ago
Revenue	$134,500,000	$125,300,000
Net profit	7,800,000	7,500,000
Net profit/share	0.37	0.36

Year to Dec. 31, 1994		Year ago
Revenue	$424,800,000	$360,200,000
Net profit	22,300,000	a21,400,000
Net profit/share	1.06	a1.02

a. Includes a gain of $1.3-million or 6 cents a share.

Doman Industries

3 months to Dec. 31, 1994		Year ago
Revenue	$193,953,000	$164,728,000
Net profit	a24,256,000	1,477,000
Net profit/share	a0.64	nil

Year to Dec. 31, 1994		Year ago
Revenue	$757,502,000	$661,659,000
Net profit	b55,794,000	c40,199,000
Avg. shares	35,691,000	30,498,000
Net profit/share	b1.42	c1.13

a. Includes a refund of duties of $15.2-million or 43 cents a share, and closure costs for the New Westminster sawmill of $1.7-million or 5 cents. b. Includes a refund of duties of $18.4-million or 52 cents a share, and the closure costs of $1.7-million or 5 cents. c. Includes a gain of $7.6-million or 25 cents a share from the sale of an interest.

Preferred-share dividends were $1,215,-000 vs $1,457,000 in the quarter and $5,-218,000 vs $5,803,000 for the full year.

Globe and Mail, February 21, 1995.

Although it would be possible to make this comparison as a rate of return by dividing the earnings per share by the market price per share, the ratio has traditionally been turned upside-down and calculated as the **price-earnings ratio.** Thus, this ratio is found by dividing the share's market price by the earnings per share, as shown in this formula:

LO 6

Calculate the price-earnings ratio and explain its meaning.

$$\text{Price-earnings ratio} = \frac{\text{Market value per share}}{\text{Earnings per share}}$$

The ratio may be calculated using the earnings per share reported in the past period. However, analysts often calculate the ratio based on the expected earnings per share for the next period. Suppose, for example, that the current market price is $100 per share and that its next year's earnings are expected to be $8 per share. Its price-earnings ratio (often abbreviated as the PE ratio) is found as $100/$8, which is 12.5.

Investors normally examine the trend of earnings and the latest reported data such as presented in Illustration 16–6. Note especially the reporting of earnings per share and the detail in the footnotes, for example, Abitibi-Price and the 2-for-1 stock split of Caribbean Utilities.

As a general rule, shares with higher PE ratios (generally greater than 12 to 15) are considered more likely to be overpriced while shares with lower PE ratios (generally less than 5 to 8) are considered more likely to be underpriced. Thus, some investors prefer to sell or avoid buying shares with high PE ratios while they prefer to buy or hold shares that have low PE ratios. Investment decisions are not quite that simple, however, because shares with high PE ratios may prove to be good investments if their earnings increase rapidly. On the other hand, shares with low PE ratios may prove to be low performers. Although the price-earnings ratio is clearly important for investment decisions, it is only one piece of information that investors should consider. For example, Anchor Lamina's 12 PE may be considered as low for a growth company. Investors may have greater confidence in the strategic focus that competing companies are taking.

Progress Check

16-10   Calculate the price-earnings ratio for a company with earnings per share of $4.25 and market value of $34.00.

16-11   Two companies in the same industry face similar levels of risk, have nearly the same level of earnings, and are expected to continue their historical record of paying $1.50 annual dividends per share. Yet, one of the companies has a PE ratio of 6 while the other has a PE ratio of 10. Which company does the market apparently expect to have the highest future growth rate in earnings?

SUMMARY OF THE CHAPTER IN TERMS OF LEARNING OBJECTIVES

LO 1.   Record cash dividends, stock dividends, and stock splits and explain their effects on a corporation's assets and shareholders' equity. Whereas cash dividends transfer corporate assets to the shareholders, stock dividends do not. Stock dividends and stock splits have no effect on assets, no effect on total shareholders' equity, and no effect on the equity of each shareholder. Depending on the jurisdiction, stock dividends are recorded by capitalizing retained earnings equal to the market value of the distributed shares, or capitalizing an amount set by the board of directors.

LO 2.   Record retirement of shares and describe the effect on shareholders' equity. When outstanding shares are repurchased and retired, the stated capital account is debited for the weighted average per share invested by the shareholders. If the purchase price is more or less than the weighted average per share, the difference is debited to Retained Earnings (more) or credited to Contributed Capital, Share Retirements (less).

LO 3.   Describe restrictions and appropriations of retained earnings and the disclosure of such items in the financial statements. In most jurisdictions, retained earnings are legally restricted by an amount equal to the cost of reacquired shares. Retained earnings also may be restricted by contract. Corporations may voluntarily appropriate retained earnings to inform shareholders why dividends are not larger in amount. More often, however, this information is expressed in a letter to the shareholders.

LO 4. Explain how the income effects of discontinued operations, extraordinary items, changes in accounting principles, and prior period adjustments are reported. If management has implemented a plan to discontinue a business segment, the net income or loss from operating the segment and the gain or loss on disposal are separately reported on the income statement below income from continuing operations. Next, extraordinary gains or losses are listed.

Prior period adjustments, which include the income effects of accounting errors made in prior periods and changes in accounting policy or principle, are reported on the statement of retained earnings.

Changes in accounting estimates are made because new information shows the old estimates to be invalid. When an accounting estimate is changed, the new estimate is used to calculate revenue or expense in the current and future periods.

LO 5. Calculate earnings per share for companies with simple capital structures and explain the difference between basic and fully diluted earnings per share. Companies with simple capital structures do not have outstanding securities convertible into common shares. For such companies, earnings per share is calculated by dividing net income less dividends to preferred shares by the weighted-average number of outstanding common shares. In calculating the weighted-average number of shares outstanding, the number of shares outstanding prior to a stock dividend or stock split must be restated to reflect the effect of the stock dividend or stock split.

Companies with complex capital structures have outstanding securities that are convertible into common shares. These companies may have to report both basic earnings per share and fully diluted earnings per share. In calculating basic earnings per share, the denominator is the weighted-average number of common shares outstanding. Fully diluted earnings per share assumes the conversion of all dilutive securities.

LO 6. Calculate the price-earnings ratio and explain its meaning. The price-earnings ratio of common shares is closely watched by investors and other decision makers. The ratio is calculated by dividing the current market value per share by earnings per share. A high ratio may suggest that shares are overvalued while a low ratio may suggest that shares are undervalued. However, selecting shares to buy or sell requires a great deal more information.

Part A

DEMONSTRATION PROBLEM

Maritime Corporation's books on January 31, 1996, showed the following balances (summarized):

Cash	$ 70,000
Other current assets	50,000
Capital assets (net)	470,000
Other assets	110,000
	$700,000
Current liabilities	$ 60,000
Long-term liabilities	120,000
Common, 40,000 shares	420,000
Retained earnings	100,000
	$700,000

The board of directors is considering a cash dividend, and you have been requested to provide certain assistance as the independent accountant. The following matters have been referred to you:

1. What is the maximum amount of cash dividends that can be paid at January 1? Explain.

2. What entries would be made assuming a $1 per share cash dividend is declared with the following dates specified: (*a*) declaration date, (*b*) date of record, and (*c*) date of payment.

3. Assuming a balance sheet is prepared between declared date and payment date, how would the dividend declaration be reported?

Part B

The records of South Corporation showed the following balances on November 1, 1996:

> Common 27,500 shares $770,000
> Retained earnings 390,000

On November 5, 1996, the board of directors declared a stock dividend of one additional share for each five shares outstanding; issue date, January 10, 1997. The market value immediately after the declaration was $36 per share.

Required

Give entries in parallel columns for the stock dividend assuming, for problem purposes, (*a*) market value is capitalized, (*b*) $110,000 is capitalized (amount decided by the board), and (*c*) average paid in is capitalized. Assume the company records the dividend on declaration and credits a Stock Dividends Distributable account (not a liability).

Part C

Complete the following matrix:

	Method of Reflecting the Effect	
	Prospective	**Retroactive**
a. Change in estimate	_____	_____
b. Change in principle or method	_____	_____
c. Correction of error	_____	_____

Part D

Eastern Corporation had outstanding 10,000 no-par common shares sold initially for $20 per share. The Retained Earnings balance is $31,600. The corporation purchased and retired 500 shares of its common at $25 per share.

Required

Give entries to record the reacquired share transactions.

Part E

A company split its common shares three for one on June 30 of its fiscal year ended December 31. Before the split, there were 4,000 common shares outstanding. How many common shares should be used in computing EPS? How many common shares should be used in computing a comparative EPS amount for the preceding year?

Part A

1. The maximum cash dividend that can be paid at January 1 depends in part on the statutory provisions (i.e., solvency test); however, the *cash* available is limiting in this situation. Possible alternatives are:

    a. Limit to cash, $70,000.
    b. Limit to retained earnings, $100,000. This would require property dividends, liability dividends, or generating additional cash through borrowing or other means.

2. a. Date of declaration:

	Dividends Declared (Retained Earnings)	40,000	
	Dividends Payable		40,000
b.	Record date. No entry; prepare list of shareholders.		
c.	Date of payment:		
	Dividends Payable	40,000	
	Cash		40,000

3. Between declaration and payment dates, dividends payable for whatever amount is declared ($40,000) would be reported as a current liability. Retained earnings would be reported as $100,000 − $40,000 = $60,000.

Part B

	Amount Capitalized		
	(a)	*(b)*	*(c)*
		Decision	
	Market	**of the**	**Average**
	Value	**Board**	**Paid in**
November 5, 1996:			
To record declaration:			
Retained Earnings	198,000[b]	110,000[c]	154,000[d]
Stock Dividends			
Distributable			
(5,500 shares)[a]	198,000	110,000	154,000
January 10, 1997:			
To record the share issue:			
Stock Dividend			
Distributable	198,000	110,000	154,000
Common Shares			
(5,500 shares)	198,000	110,000	154,000

Note: Alternative accounting: An equally acceptable alternative manner of accounting and reporting the stock dividend would be to disclose the November 5, 1996, stock dividend declaration in the *notes* to the 1996 financial statements. Then the entry to record the January 10, 1997, issuance of the dividend shares would be the same as the declaration entry given above, except that Common Shares would be credited instead of Stock Dividends Distributable.
[a]27,500 shares outstanding: 27,500 ÷ 5 = 5,500 shares issued for stock dividend.
[b]Capitalize market value; 5,500 shares × $36 = $198,000.
[c]Capitalize amount decided by the board = $110,000.
[d]Capitalize average paid in: $770,000 ÷ 27,500 = $28 per share, average, 5,500 shares × $28 = $154,000.

Part C

	Method of Reflecting the Effect	
	Prospective	**Retroactive**
a. Change in estimate	√	
b. Change in principle or method		√
c. Correction of error		√

Part D

Common Shares (500 shares @ $20)	10,000	
Retained Earnings	2,500	
Cash		12,500

Note: Restriction of Retained Earnings (required by law) for $12,500 (the cost of the reacquired shares) may be recorded by journal entry or disclosed in a note.

Part E

In computing EPS for the year, 12,000 common shares should be used. The *CICA Handbook* prescribes retroactive treatment for stock dividends and stock splits for all periods presented. Therefore, 12,000 shares would also be used to compute EPS (restated) for the preceding year as well. The two EPS amounts are therefore *(a)* comparable and *(b)* both related to the current capital structure.

GLOSSARY

Accounting changes   items that can affect the evaluation or prediction of a firm's earnings. Accounting changes include (*a*) accounting errors, (*b*) changes in accounting policy, and (*c*) changes in accounting estimates. p 733

Antidilutive securities   convertible securities, the assumed conversion of which would have the effect of increasing earnings per share. p. 737

Appropriated retained earnings   retained earnings voluntarily earmarked for a special use as a way of informing shareholders that assets from earnings equal to the appropriations are not available for dividends. p. 731

Basic earnings per share   earnings per share statistics that are calculated for corporations with a simple capital structure and for corporations with complex capital structures before giving effect to the dilutive securities. p. 737

Changes in accounting estimates   adjustments to previously made assumptions about the future such as salvage values and the length of useful lives of buildings and equipment. p. 733

Changes in accounting policy   a change in accounting data caused by a change in one generally accepted accounting principle to another generally accepted accounting principle (i.e., a change from LIFO to FIFO). p. 733

Complex capital structure   a capital structure that includes outstanding rights or options to purchase common shares or securities convertible into common shares. p. 737

Dilutive securities   convertible securities the assumed conversion of which would have the effect of decreasing earnings per share. p. 737

Earned surplus   a synonym for retained earnings, no longer in general use. p. 724

Earnings per share   the amount of net income (or components of income) that accrues to common shares divided by the weighted-average number of common shares outstanding. p. 734

Fully diluted earnings per share   earnings per share statistics that are calculated as if all dilutive securities had already been converted. p. 737

Liquidating dividends   asset distributions in excess of a credit balance in Retained Earnings; a return of original investment. p. 725

Price-earnings ratio   the ratio between a company's current market value and its earnings per share. p. 739

Prior period adjustment   items reported in the current statement of retained earnings as corrections to the beginning retained earnings balance; limited primarily to corrections of errors that were made in past years, settlement of lawsuits that originated in prior years, and one-time income tax settlements. p. 733

Prospective change affects current and future periods. p. 733

Restricted retained earnings retained earnings not available for dividends because of law or binding contract. p. 730

Retroactive change affects prior periods. p. 733

Reverse stock split the act of a corporation to call in its shares and issue one new share in the place of more than one share previously outstanding. p. 728

Segment of a business operations of a company that involve a particular line of business or class of customer, providing the assets, activities, and financial results of the operations can be distinguished from other parts of the business. p. 731

Simple capital structure a capital structure that does not include any rights or options to purchase common shares or any securities that are convertible into common shares. p. 735

Stock dividend a distribution by a corporation of its own shares to its shareholders without the receipt of any consideration in return. p. 725

Stock split the act of a corporation to issue more than one new share in the place of each share previously outstanding. p. 728

Unusual gain or loss a gain or loss (that doesn't qualify as extraordinary) that is abnormal and unrelated or only incidentally related to the ordinary activities and environment of the business. p. 733

SYNONYMOUS TERMS

Basic earnings per share earnings per common share.

Retained earnings earned surplus (no longer in use).

Statement of changes in shareholders' equity statement of shareholders' equity.

QUESTIONS

1. What effect does the declaration of a cash dividend have on the assets, liabilities, and shareholders' equity of the corporation that declares the dividend? What is the effect of the subsequent payment of the cash dividend?

2. What effect does the declaration of a stock dividend have on the assets, liabilities, and total shareholders' equity of the corporation that declares the dividend? What is the effect of the subsequent distribution of the stock dividend?

3. What is the difference between a stock dividend and a stock split?

4. If a balance sheet is prepared between the date of declaration and the date of payment or distribution of a dividend, how should the dividend be shown if it is (a) a cash dividend or (b) a stock dividend?

5. Why do laws place limitations on the reacquisition of a corporation's shares?

6. In the annual income statement of a corporation, what other sections of the statement might appear below income from continuing operations?

7. If a company operates one of its business segments at a loss during much of 1997, and then finds a buyer and disposes of that segment during November of that year, which two items concerning that segment should appear on the company's 1997 income statement?

8. Where on the income statement should a company disclose a gain that is abnormal and unrelated to the ordinary activities of the business and that is not expected to recur more often than once every several years and that occurs as a result of decisions or events outside the corporation?

9. Which of the following items would qualify as an extraordinary gain or loss: (a) operating losses resulting from a strike against a major supplier, (b) a gain from the sale of surplus equipment, or (c) a loss from damage to a building caused by a tornado (a type of storm that rarely occurs in the geographical region of the company's operations)?

10. In past years, Daley Company paid its sales personnel annual salaries without additional incentive payments. This year, a new policy is being instituted whereby they receive sales commissions rather than annual salaries. Does this new policy require a prior period adjustment? Explain why or why not.

11. After taking five years' straight-line amortization on an asset that was expected to have an eight-year life, a company concluded that the asset would last another six years. Does this decision involve a change in accounting principle? If not, how would you describe this change?

12. How is earnings per share calculated for a corporation with a simple capital structure?

13. In calculating the weighted-average number of common shares outstanding, how are stock splits and stock dividends treated?

14. What is the difference between basic earnings per share and fully diluted earnings per share?

15. What is the difference between simple capital structures and complex capital structures?

QUICK STUDY (Five-Minute Exercises)

QS 16–1
(LO 1)

The shareholders' equity section of Maritime Corporation's balance sheet as of June 1 follows:

Common shares, 100,000 shares issued and outstanding	$ 735,000
Retained earnings	422,000
Total shareholders' equity	$1,157,000

On June 1, Maritime (federally incorporated) declares and distributes a 20% stock dividend. On June 1, Maritime's shares were traded at $15 per share. Prepare the shareholders' equity section for Maritime immediately following issuance of the stock dividend.

QS 16–2
(LO 2)

On September 2, Garrett Corporation purchased 2,000 of its own shares for $18,000. The shares were retired. The average stated value per share just prior to the purchase was $5. Prepare the September 2 entry for the purchase and retirement of the shares.

QS 16–3
(LO 3)

Prepare the entry to restrict retained earnings required by law in connection with the purchase and retirement of the 2,000 shares by Garrett in 16–3 above.

QS 16–4
(LO 4)

Answer the questions about each of the following items related to a company's activities for the year:

a. After using an expected useful life of seven years and no salvage value to amortize its office equipment over the preceding three years, the company decided early this year that the equipment will last only two more years. How should the effects of this decision be reported in the current financial statements?

b. In reviewing the notes payable files, it was discovered that last year the company reported the entire amount of a payment on an installment note payable as interest expense. The mistake had a material effect on the amount of income in the prior year. How should the correction be reported in the current year financial statements?

QS 16–5
(LO 5)

On January 1, Star Company had 50,000 common shares issued and outstanding. On April 1, it issued 4,000 additional shares and on June 5, declared a 20% stock dividend. Calculate Star's weighted-average outstanding shares for the year.

QS 16–6
(LO 6)

Calculate a company's price-earnings ratio if its common shares have a market value of $62 per share and if its earnings per share are $6.

EXERCISES

Northridge Corporation's shareholders' equity appeared as follows on August 10:

Share capital:
Common shares, no-par value, unlimited number
authorized, 80,000 shares issued $560,200
Retained earnings   235,000
Total shareholders' equity $795,200

On August 10, when the shares were selling at $9.00, the corporation's directors voted a 20% stock dividend distributable on September 2 to the August 17 shareholders of record. The shares were selling at $7.75 at the close of business on September 2.

Required

1. Prepare General Journal entries to record the declaration and distribution of the dividend.

2. Under the assumption that Cynthia McAllister owned 250 of the shares on August 10 and received her dividend shares on September 2, prepare a schedule showing the number of shares she held on August 10 and on September 2, with their total book values and total market values. Assume no change in total shareholders' equity from August 10 to September 2.

On March 31, 1996, Atlantic Management Corporation's common shares were selling for $45 and the shareholders' equity section of the corporation's balance sheet appeared as follows:

Share capital:
Common shares, no-par value, unlimited number of shares
authorized, 15,000 shares issued $670,450
Retained earnings   298,900
Total shareholders' equity $969,350

Required

1. Assume the corporation declares and immediately issues a 50% stock dividend and capitalizes $25 per share of retained earnings. Answer the following questions about the shareholders' equity of the corporation after the new shares are issued:

   a. What is the retained earnings balance?
   b. What is the total amount of shareholders' equity?
   c. How many shares are outstanding?

2. Assume that instead of declaring a 50% stock dividend, the corporation effects a three-for-two stock split. Answer the following questions about the shareholders' equity of the corporation after the stock split takes place:

   a. What is the retained earnings balance?
   b. What is the total amount of shareholders' equity?
   c. How many shares are outstanding?

Exercise 16–3
Retirement of shares
(LO 2, 3)

On October 31, Sanborn Corporation's shareholders' equity section appeared as follows:

Shareholders' Equity

Share capital:
Common shares, no-par value, unlimited number of shares
authorized, 5,000 shares outstanding $250,000
Retained earnings   220,100
Total shareholders' equity $470,100

On October 31, the corporation purchased and retired 800 shares at $55 per share. Give the entry to record the purchase and prepare a shareholders' equity section as it would appear immediately after the purchase and retirement.

Exercise 16–4
Retirement of shares
(LO 2)

The shareholders' equity section of City Vending, Inc.'s, December 31, 1996, balance sheet is as follows:

Share capital:
Common shares, no-par value, 600,000 shares
authorized, 30,000 shares issued $540,000
Retained earnings   105,800
Total shareholders' equity $645,800

On the date of the balance sheet, the company purchased and retired 400 common shares. Prepare General Journal entries to record the purchase and retirement under each of the following independent assumptions: the shares were purchased for (*a*) $12 per share, (*b*) $18 per share, and (*c*) $24 per share.

Exercise 16–5
Income statement
categories
(LO 4)

The following list of items was extracted from the December 31, 1996, trial balance of Wesson Company. Using the information contained in this listing, prepare Wesson Company's income statement for 1996. You need not complete the earnings per share calculations.

	Debit	Credit
Salaries expense	$66,700	
Income tax expense (continuing operations)	68,380	
Loss from operating segment C (net of $10,200 tax benefit)	24,000	
Sales		$700,240
Total effect on prior years' income of change from declining-balance to straight-line amortization (net of $9,600 tax)		32,400
Extraordinary gain on provincial condemnation of land owned by Wesson Company (net of $24,800 tax)		68,000
Amortization expense	62,100	
Gain on sale of segment C (net of $19,700 tax)		66,000
Cost of goods sold	420,200	

Exercise 16–6
Classifying income
items not related to
continuing operations
(LO 4)

In preparing the annual financial statements for Elite Electronics Company, the correct manner of reporting the following items was not clear to the company's employees. Explain where each of the following items should appear in the financial statements.

a. After amortizing office equipment for three years based on an expected useful life of eight years, the company decided this year that the office equipment should last seven more years. As a result, the amortization for the current year is $8,000 instead of $10,000.

b. This year, the accounting department of the company discovered that last year, an installment payment on their five-year note payable had been charged entirely to interest expense. The after-tax effect of the charge to interest expense was $15,400.

c. The company keeps its repair trucks for several years before disposing of the old trucks and buying new trucks. This year, for the first time in 10 years, it sold old trucks for a gain of $19,900 and then purchased new trucks.

Carefree Footware Inc. reported $261,400 net income in 1996 and declared preferred dividends of $43,000. The following changes in common shares outstanding occurred during the year:

Exercise 16–7
Weighted-average shares outstanding and earnings per share
(LO 5)

January 1:	60,000 common shares were outstanding.
June 30:	Sold 20,000 common shares.
September 1:	Declared and issued a 20% common stock dividend, or 80,000 × 20% = 16,000 additional shares.

Calculate the weighted-average number of common shares outstanding during the year and earnings per share.

Kingsley Production Company reported $741,500 net income in 1996 and declared preferred dividends of $66,500. The following changes in common shares outstanding occurred during the year.

Exercise 16–8
Weighted-average shares outstanding and earnings per share
(LO 5)

January 1:	60,000 common shares were outstanding.
March 1:	Sold 20,000 common shares.
August 1:	Purchased and retired 4,000 shares.
December 1:	Declared and issued a two-for-one stock split.

Calculate the weighted-average number of common shares outstanding during the year and earnings per share.

Northside Corporation's 1996 income statement, excluding the earnings per share portion of the statement, was as follows:

Exercise 16–9
Reporting earnings per share
(LO 5)

Sales		$475,000
Costs and expenses:		
Amortization	$ 51,900	
Income taxes	65,100	
Other expenses	205,000	322,000
Income from continuing operations		$153,000
Loss from operating discontinued business segment (net of		
$23,500 tax benefit)	$ 56,000	
Loss on sale of business segment (net of $9,400 tax benefit) . .	22,000	(78,000)
Income before extraordinary items		$ 75,000
Extraordinary gain (net of $18,400 taxes)		43,200
Net income		$118,200

Throughout 1996, Southside had potentially dilutive securities outstanding. If these particular securities had been converted, the number of common shares outstanding would have increased but the numerators in earnings per share calculations would not have been affected. Assuming the dilutive securities had been converted at the beginning of the year, the weighted-average number of common shares outstanding during the year would have increased by 20,000 to 120,000. Present the earnings per share portion of the 1996 income statement.

Exercise 16–10
Computing the price-
earnings ratio
(LO 6)

Use the following information to calculate the price-earnings ratio for each case:

	Earnings per Share	Market Value per Share
a.	$ 4.50	$ 43.00
b.	18.00	120.00
c.	3.25	45.00
d.	0.75	18.00
e.	5.00	83.00

PROBLEMS

Problem 16–1
Cash dividend, stock
dividend, and stock split
(LO 1)

Last April 30, Fancy Foods Corporation had a $1,035,000 credit balance in its Retained Earnings account. On that date, the corporation's contributed capital consisted of 300,000 shares, which had been issued at $3 and were outstanding. It then completed the following transactions:

May 10 The board of directors declared a $1.50 per share common dividend payable on June 16 to the May 31 shareholders of record.

June 16 Paid the dividend declared on May 10.

Aug. 5 The board declared a 10% stock dividend, distributable on September 2 to the August 20 shareholders of record. The shares were selling at $10.00 per share; this amount was used to capitalize retained earnings.

Sept. 2 Distributed the stock dividend declared on August 5.

   30 Because September 30 is the end of the company's fiscal year, closed the Income Summary account, which had a credit balance of $396,000. Also closed the Cash Dividends Declared and Stock Dividends Declared accounts.

Oct. 12 The board of directors voted to split the corporation's shares two for one. The split was completed on November 17.

Required

1. Prepare General Journal entries to record these transactions and closings.

2. Under the assumption Phillip Bolton owned 5,000 shares on April 30 and neither bought nor sold any shares during the period of the transactions, prepare a schedule with columns for the date, supporting calculations, book value per share, and book value of Bolton's shares. Then complete the schedule by calculating the book value per share of the corporation's and of Bolton's shares at the close of business on April 30, May 10, June 16, September 2, September 30, and October 12. Assume that the only income earned by the company during these periods was the $396,000 earned and closed on September 30.

3. Prepare three shareholders' equity sections for the corporation, the first showing the shareholders' equity on April 30, the second on September 30, and the third on October 12.

Problem 16–2
Calculating net income
from balance sheet
comparison
(LO 1, 2, 3)

The equity sections from the 1996 and 1997 balance sheets of Dylex Corporation appeared as follows:

Shareholders' Equity
(As of December 31, 1996)

Share capital:
    Common shares, no-par value, unlimited number of shares
        authorized, 96,000 shares outstanding . . . . $ 688,000
    Retained earnings   558,608
    Total shareholders' equity   1,246,608

Shareholders' Equity
(As of December 31, 1997)

Share capital:

Common shares, no-par value, unlimited number of shares
authorized, 100,000 shares outstanding .... $ 646,000

Retained earnings, of which $144,000 is restricted—
retirement of shares 459,600

Total shareholders' equity 1,105,600

On March 16, June 25, September 5, and again on November 22, 1997, the board of directors declared $0.20 per share cash dividends on the outstanding common shares. And 20,000 shares were purchased and retired on May 14. On October 5, while the shares were selling for $7.60 per share, the corporation declared a 25% stock dividend on the outstanding shares. The new shares were issued on November 8.

Required

Under the assumption that there were no transactions affecting retained earnings other than the ones given, determine the 1997 net income of Dylex Corporation. Show your calculations. (*Hint:* Remember the impact on retained earnings of repurchase of shares at an amount greater than the per share weighted-average stated value.)

The equity sections from the 1995 and 1996 balance sheets of Henns Corporation appeared as follows:

Problem 16–3
Calculating net income
from balance sheet
comparison
(LO 1, 2, 3)

Shareholders' Equity
(As of December 31, 1995)

Share capital:

Common shares, no-par value, unlimited number of shares
authorized, 350,000 shares issued .... $ 8,750,000

Retained earnings 1,960,720

Total shareholders' equity $10,710,720

Shareholders' Equity
(As of December 31, 1996)

Share capital:

Common shares, no-par value, unlimited number of shares
authorized, 384,000 shares issued .... $ 9,384,000

Retained earnings of which $270,000 is restricted 1,540,640

Total shareholders' equity $10,924,640

On February 11, May 24, August 13, and again on December 12, 1996, the board of directors declared $0.25 per share cash dividends on the outstanding shares: 10,000 shares were purchased at $27 per share and retired on July 6. On November 1, while the shares were selling for $26 per share, the corporation declared a 10% stock dividend on the outstanding shares. The new shares were issued on December 5.

Required

Under the assumption that there were no transactions affecting retained earnings other than the ones given, determine the 1996 net income of Henns Corporation. Show your calculations.

Handy Supply Corporation had several unusual transactions during 1997 and has prepared the following list of trial balance items. Select the appropriate items to use in constructing the 1997 income statement for the company.

Problem 16–4
Classifying income items
in a published income
statement
(LO 4)

	Debit	Credit
Accounts payable		$ 16,600
Loss from operation of Westside Division (net of $14,000 income tax benefit)	$ 32,000	
Sales		392,500
Cost of goods sold	170,600	
Loss on sale of office equipment (an unusual transaction for the company that occurs only when administrative offices are redecorated, which happens about every eight years)	6,300	
Amortization expense, buildings	35,620	
Amortization expense, office equipment	12,450	
Income tax expense	20,950	
Payment received in November of last year on customer account receivable incorrectly recorded in Sales account (net of $4,050 income tax benefit)	16,200	
Gain on sale of investment in land (The land was originally donated to Central Supply by a shareholder. Central Supply has never held land for investment purposes before and has no intention of doing so in the future.) (Net of $7,800 income taxes)		23,400
Loss on customer breach of contract (It is not unusual for companies in this industry, to be involved in breach of contract suits. However, the problem is not expected to arise in the foreseeable future.)	48,700	
Accumulated amortization, buildings		108,000
Accumulated amortization, office equipment		20,900
Gain on sale of Westside Division (net of $3,400 income taxes)		10,750
Interest earned		2,400
Other operating expenses	55,800	
Gain on payment from supplier to compensate for late delivery of materials purchased from supplier. (In this industry, such settlements with suppliers occur quite frequently.)		12,300
Effect on prior years' income of switching from straight-line amortization to accelerated amortization (net of $5,900 income tax benefit)	20,125	

Required

Prepare Handy Supply Corporation's income statement for 1997, excluding the earnings per share statistics.

Problem 16–5
Changes in accounting principles
(LO 4)

On January 1, 1992, Fairfax Industries Inc. purchased a large piece of equipment for use in its manufacturing operations. The equipment cost $280,000 and was expected to have a salvage value of $32,000. Amortization was taken through 1995 on a declining-balance method at twice the straight-line rate, assuming an eight-year life. Early in 1996, the company concluded that given the economic conditions in the industry, a straight-line method would result in more meaningful financial statements. They argue that straight-line amortization would allow better comparisons with the financial results of other firms in the industry.

Required

1. Is Fairfax Industries allowed to change amortization methods in 1996?

2. Prepare a table that shows the amortization expense to be reported each year of the asset's life under both amortization methods and the cumulative effect of the change on prior years' incomes.

3. State the amount of amortization expense to be reported in 1996 and the cumulative effect of the change on prior years' incomes. How should the cumulative effect be reported? Does the cumulative effect increase or decrease net income?

4. Now assume that Fairfax Industries had used straight-line amortization through 1995 and justified a change to declining-balance amortization at twice the straight-line rate in 1996. What amount of amortization expense should be reported in 1996? Does the reporting of the cumulative effect of the change differ from your answer to requirement 3?

Except for the earnings per share statistics, the 1997, 1996, and 1995 income statements of Clear Printing Company were originally presented as follows:

Problem 16–6
Earnings per share calculations and presentation
(LO 5)

	1997	1996	1995
Sales	$998,900	$687,040	$466,855
Costs and expenses	383,570	234,500	157,420
Income from continuing operations	$615,330	$452,540	$309,435
Loss on discontinued operations	(107,325)	—	—
Income (loss) before extraordinary items	$508,005	$452,540	$309,435
Extraordinary gains (losses)	—	80,410	(156,191)
Net income (loss)	$508,005	$532,950	$153,244

Information on common shares:

Shares outstanding on December 31, 1994	14,400
Purchase and retirement of shares on March 1, 1995	− 1,440
Sale of shares on June 1, 1995	+ 6,240
Stock dividend of 5% on August 1, 1995	+ 960
Shares outstanding on December 31, 1995	20,160
Sale of shares on February 1, 1996	+ 2,880
Purchase and retirement of shares July 1, 1996	− 720
Shares outstanding on December 31, 1996	22,320
Sale of shares on March 1, 1997	+ 8,280
Purchase and retirement of shares on September 1, 1997	− 1,800
Stock split of 3 for 1 on October 1, 1997	+57,600
Shares outstanding on December 31, 1997	86,400

Required

1. Calculate the weighted-average number of common shares outstanding during (a) 1995, (b) 1996, and (c) 1997.

2. Present the earnings per share portions of (a) the 1995 income statement, (b) the 1996 income statement, and (c) the 1997 income statement.

The shareholders' equity section of Lang Corporation's balance sheet at September 30 is as follows:

Problem 16–7
Analytical essay
(LO 1, 2)

Share capital:
Common shares, no-par value, unlimited number of shares authorized, 100,000 shares outstanding	$ 650,000
Retained earnings	367,000
Total shareholders' equity	$1,017,000

Assume now that an event occurs on October 1 that impacts Lang's shareholders' equity section, but does not involve net income or additional investment of capital. The following are independent cases in which Lang's shareholders' equity section has been revised to reflect that event.

	Case A	Case B	Case C
Common share capital:			
80,000 shares outstanding	$520,000		
130,000 shares outstanding		$ 800,000	
50,000 shares outstanding			$ 650,000
Retained earnings	317,000	217,000	367,000
Total shareholders' equity	$837,000	$1,017,000	$1,017,000

Required

For each case, describe the differences in the September 30 and the October 1 shareholders' equity sections and state the event that must have occurred.

Problem 16–8
Analytical essay
(LO 5)

Jaspur Company's financial statements for the year ended December 31, 1996, have been completed and submitted to you for review. The shareholders' equity section of Jaspur's balance sheet at December 31 is as follows:

Share capital:	
Preferred shares, $2.80 noncumulative	
10,000 shares authorized, 10,000	
shares issued and outstanding	$ 498,700
Common shares, no-par value, unlimited number of shares	
authorized, 120,000 shares outstanding	946,900
Retained earnings	450,530
Total shareholders' equity	$1,896,130

The only share transactions during 1996 were the purchase and retirement of 24,000 common shares on July 1 and the sale of 12,000 common shares on October 31. Jaspur's 1996 net income was $286,200. A cash dividend on the preferred shares was declared on December 1, but was not paid as of December 31. Earnings per share for 1996 was calculated as follows:

$$\frac{\text{Net income}}{\substack{\text{Common shares} \\ \text{outstanding on Dec. 31}}} = \frac{\$286,200}{108,000} = \$2.65$$

Required

1. Explain what is wrong with the earnings per share calculation, indicating what corrections should be made to both the numerator and the denominator.

2. Explain how your answer to requirement 1 would be different if there had not been a cash dividend declaration to preferred shares and if the purchase and retirement of 24,000 common shares had taken place on January 2, 1996.

Problem 16–9
Analytical essay
(LO 5)

Computex Corporation has tentatively prepared its financial statements for the year ended December 31, 1996, and has submitted them to you for review. The shareholders' equity section of Computex's balance sheet at December 31 is as follows:

Share capital:	
Preferred shares, $2.50, cumulative,	
30,000 shares authorized, 18,000	
shares issued and outstanding	$ 520,100
Common shares, no-par value, unlimited number of shares	
authorized, 132,000 shares outstanding	777,840
Retained earnings	996,200
Total shareholders' equity	$2,294,140

Computex Corporation's 1996 net income was $600,000 and no cash dividends were declared. The only share transaction that occurred during the year was the sale of 24,000 common shares on March 31, 1996. Earnings per share for 1996 was calculated as follows:

$$\frac{\text{Net income}}{\text{Common plus preferred shares outstanding as of Dec. 31}} = \frac{\$600,000}{132,000 + 18,000} = \$4.00$$

Required

1. Explain what is wrong with the earnings per share calculation, indicating what corrections should be made to both the numerator and the denominator.

2. Explain how your answer to requirement 1 would be different if the preferred shares were not cumulative and if the issuance of 24,000 shares had been a stock dividend.

PROVOCATIVE PROBLEMS

On January 1, 1994, Hal Peeks purchased 800 shares of Cornfield Corporation at $45.50 per share. On that date, the corporation had the following shareholders' equity:

Provocative Problem 16–1
Cornfield Corporation
(LO 1, 2, 3)

Common stock, no-par value, unlimited number of shares authorized, 250,000 shares issued and outstanding	$7,000,000
Retained earnings	2,500,000
Total shareholders' equity	$9,500,000

Since purchasing the 800 shares, Mr. Peeks has neither purchased nor sold any additional shares of the company. On December 31 of each year, he has received dividends on the shares held as follows: 1994, $1,408; 1995, $1,672; and 1996, $2,200.

On June 15, 1994, at a time when its shares were selling for $51.25 per share (amount capitalized), Cornfield Corporation declared a 10% stock dividend that was distributed one month later. On October 25, 1995, the corporation split its shares two for one.

Required

Assume that Cornfield Corporation's outstanding shares had a book value of $35.75 per share on December 31, 1994, a book value of $20 per share on December 31, 1995, and a book value of $22.25 on December 31, 1996. Do the following:

1. Prepare statements that show the nature of the shareholders' equity in the corporation at the end of 1994, 1995, and 1996.

2. Prepare a schedule that shows the amount of the corporation's net income each year for 1994, 1995, and 1996. Assume that the changes in the company's retained earnings during the three-year period resulted from earnings and dividends.

Byway (federal incorporation) Company's shareholders' equity on September 15 consisted of the following amounts:

Provocative Problem 16–2
Byway Company
(LO 1)

Common shares, no-par value, unlimited number of shares authorized, 50,000 shares issued and outstanding	$2,875,000
Retained earnings	1,286,000
Total shareholders' equity	$4,161,000

On September 15, when the shares were selling at $100 per share, the corporation's directors voted a 20% stock dividend, distributable on October 5 to the September 25 shareholders of record. The directors also voted a $3.45 per share annual cash dividend, payable on November 23 to the November 15 shareholders of record. The amount of the latter dividend was a disappointment to some shareholders, since the company had for a number of years paid a $4 per share annual cash dividend.

Nancy Cooper owned 1,000 Byway shares on September 25, received her stock dividend shares, and continued to hold all of her shares until after the November 23 cash dividend. She also observed that her shares had a $100 per share market value on September 15, a market value it held until the close of business on September 25, when the market value declined to $90.50 per share.

Required

Give the entries to record the declaration and distribution or payment of the dividends involved here and answer these questions:

a. What was the book value of Cooper's total shares on September 15 (after taking into consideration the cash dividend declared on that day)? What was the book value on October 5 after she received the dividend shares?

b. What fraction of the corporation did Cooper own on September 15? What fraction did she own on October 5?

c. What was the market value of Cooper's total shares on September 15? What was the market value at the close of business on September 25?

d. What did Cooper gain from the stock dividend?

Provocative Problem 16–3

Rutland Corporation

(LO 4)

Rutland Corporation had several rather special transactions and events in 1996 which are described below:

a. Rutland Corporation's continuing operations involve a high technology production process. Technical developments in this area occur regularly, and the production machinery becomes obsolete surprisingly often. Because such developments occurred recently, Rutland decided that it was forced to sell certain items of machinery at a loss and replace those items with a different type of machinery. The problem is how to report the loss.

b. Early last year, Rutland purchased a new type of equipment for use in its production process. Although much of the production equipment is amortized over 5 years, a careful analysis of the situation led the company to decide that the new equipment should be amortized over 10 years. Nevertheless, in the rush of year-end activities, the new equipment was included with the older equipment and amortized on a five-year basis. In preparing adjustments at the end of 1996, the accountant discovered that $90,000 amortization was taken on the new equipment last year, when only $45,000 should have been taken.

c. Rutland has a mining operation in several foreign countries, one of which has been subject to political unrest. After a sudden change in governments, the new ruling body resolved that the amount of foreign investment in the country was excessive. As a result, Rutland was forced to transfer ownership in its mines in that country to the new government. Rutland was able to continue its mining operation in a neighbouring country and was allowed to transfer much of its mining equipment to the neighbouring country. Nevertheless, the price paid to Rutland for its mines resulted in a significant loss.

d. Two years earlier, Rutland Corporation purchased some highly specialized equipment that was to be used in the operations of a new division that Rutland intended to acquire. The new division was in a separate line of business and would have been a separate segment of the business. After lengthy negotiations, the acquisition of the division was not accomplished and the company abandoned any hope of entering that line of business. Although the equipment had never been used, it was sold in 1996 at a loss. Rutland Corporation does not have a history of expanding into new lines of business and has no plans of doing so in the future.

Required

Examine Rutland Corporation's special transactions and events and describe how each one should be reported on the income statement or statement of retained earnings. Also state the specific characteristics of the item that support your decision.

Review the As a Matter of Ethics case on page 729. Discuss the ethical implications of the tentative decision to avoid announcing Falcon Corporation's new government contract. What actions would you take if you were the financial vice president?

Provocative Problem 16–4

Ethical issues essay

The financial statements and related disclosures of Geac Computer Corporation Limited are presented in Appendix I. Based on your examination of this information, answer the following:

Provocative Problem 16–5

Financial statement analysis

Geac

1. Does Geac have a simple or complex capital structure?
2. Did Geac report any extraordinary or unusual gains or losses in 1994 or in 1993?
3. What earnings per share data did Geac report?
4. How did Geac's capital structure change during 1994?
5. How many stock options were outstanding on April 30, 1994?

ANALYTICAL AND REVIEW PROBLEMS

Part 1

The more recent business corporations acts restrict the directors by the "solvency" test in the matter of declaration and payment of dividends in money or property. A similar restriction is not, however, imposed in the case of a stock dividend.

A & R Problem 16–1

Required

Discuss why a restriction is deemed necessary in the former but not in the latter situation.

Part 2

In the case of stock dividends, the Canada Business Corporations Act prescribes that the amount of retained earnings to be capitalized is the product of the number of shares issued as a stock dividend multiplied by the market value of each share. The revised Ontario Business Corporations Act does not stipulate the amount to be capitalized, simply stating that the amount to be added to the stated capital account is the amount declared by the directors.

Required

Can a case be made for either of the positions? Support your answer.

Over the last three years, Commonwealth Enterprises, Inc., has experienced the following income results (all numbers are rounded to the nearest thousand dollars):

A & R Problem 16–2

	1994	1995	1996
Revenues	$11,000	$11,900	$14,600
Expenses	(7,000)	(7,900)	(7,700)
Gains	3,200	2,400	0
Losses	(1,200)	(1,900)	(3,900)
Net income	$ 6,000	$ 4,500	$ 3,000

Part 1

Use the information to develop a general prediction of the company's net income for 1997.

Part 2

A closer analysis of the information shows that the company discontinued a segment of its operations in 1996. The company's accountant has determined that the discontinued segment produced the following amounts of income:

	1994	1995	1996
Revenues	$7,000	$2,600	$1,600
Expenses	(5,000)	(5,000)	(4,000)
Gains		400	
Losses	(1,200)	(1,500)	(900)
Loss on disposal of segment assets			(1,200)

Use the information to calculate the company's income without the discontinued segment and then develop a general prediction of the company's net income for 1997.

Part 3

A more in-depth analysis of the company's activity reveals that the company experienced these extraordinary items during the three years when it retired some of its debts before their scheduled maturity dates:

	1994	1995	1996
Extraordinary gain	$2,200	$2,000	
Extraordinary loss			$(1,700)

Use the information to calculate the company's income from continuing operations and develop a general prediction of the company's net income for 1997.

CONCEPT TESTER

Test your understanding of the concepts introduced in this chapter by completing the following crossword puzzle.

Across Clues

1. Synonym for retained earnings no longer in general use (2 words).

4. Division of shares (2 words).

6. Retained earnings not available for dividends because of contract.

8. Securities which if converted would result in lower EPS.

11. Dividend other than in cash.

13. Line of business or class of customers for which data is compiled.

14. Capital structure that includes stock options.

15. EPS before giving effect to dilutive securities.

16. Type of change resulting from updated assumptions.

17. A change that affects present and future periods.

18. Retained earnings voluntarily earmarked.

19. Dividend that is a return of original investment.

Down Clues

2. Securities which if converted would increase EPS.

3. Test for payment of cash dividend.

5. A change that affects prior periods.

7. Stock split that results in fewer shares outstanding.

9. Items that are rare in occurrence and not typical of business activity.

10. Retained earnings transferred to contributed capital account.

12. Capital structure that does not include convertible securities.

17. Ratio of EPS to market share price.

ANSWERS TO PROGRESS CHECKS

16–1 *a, c*

16–2 A 100% stock dividend doubles the number of shares outstanding and an appropriate amount of retained earnings is capitalized. A 2-for-1 stock split only doubles the number of shares outstanding.

16–3 The amount is set by the board of directors.

16–4 *b*

16–5 The four major sections are continuing operations, discontinued operations, extraordinary items, and earnings per share data.

16–6 *a*

16–7 a ($250,000 − $70,000)/22,500 = $8.00

16–8 The number of shares previously outstanding are retroactively restated to reflect the stock split or stock dividend as if it occurred at the beginning of the year.

16–9 The two sets are basic earnings per share and fully diluted earnings per share.

16–10 $34.00/$4.25 = 8

16–11 The company with the highest PE ratio.

CHAPTER 17

Installment Notes Payable and Bonds

Companies and organizations, including governments, frequently need to borrow money for large, long-term projects, such as building a stadium. Special accounting techniques are used to measure interest expense and the amount of the liabilities.

*A*s part of their next assignment, Karen White and Mark Smith have been asked to evaluate the level of debt for Imperial Oil Limited. Their instructor has provided the following information from Imperial's 1994 annual report.

Imperial's net income has been steadily increasing over the last three years. Imperial has maintained what they believe is a conservative level of debt, given the volatility of the petroleum business.

Imperial Oil Limited (in millions)	**1994**	**1993**	**1992**
Total revenues	$ 9,011	$ 8,903	$ 9,147
Net earnings	359	279	195
Total assets	11,928	12,861	13,192
Long-term debt	1,977	2,030	2,222
Shareholders' equity	5,955	6,566	6,636

LEARNING OBJECTIVES

After studying Chapter 17, you should be able to:

1. **Calculate the payments on an installment note payable and describe their effects on the financial statements.**
2. **Describe the various characteristics of different types of bonds and prepare entries to record bond issuances and retirements.**
3. **Estimate the price of bonds issued at a discount and describe their effects on the issuer's financial statements.**
4. **Estimate the price of bonds issued at a premium and describe their effects on the issuer's financial statements.**
5. **Calculate and describe how to use the ratio of pledged assets to secured liabilities.**
6. **Define or explain the words and phrases listed in the chapter glossary.**

In Chapter 13, you learned that some notes payable require a single payment on the date the note matures. In those cases, the single payment includes the borrowed amount plus interest. You also learned about other notes requiring a series of payments that include interest plus a part of the principal. We begin this chapter with a more complete discussion of these installment notes. Then we turn to bonds, which are securities issued by corporations and government bodies. The discussion explains the nature of long-term debt such as the notes and debentures issued by **Imperial Oil** as part of their long-term debt.

INSTALLMENT NOTES PAYABLE

LO 1

Calculate the payments on an installment note payable and describe their effects on the financial statements.

When an **installment note** is used to borrow money, the borrower records the note with an entry similar to the one used for a single-payment note. That is, the increase in cash is recorded with a debit and the increase in the liability is recorded with a credit to Notes Payable. For example, suppose that a company borrows $60,000 by signing an 8% installment note that requires six annual payments. The borrower records the note as follows:

1995					
Dec.	31	Cash		60,000.00	
		Notes Payable			60,000.00
		Borrowed $60,000 by signing an 8% installment			
		note.			

Installment notes payable like this one require the borrower to pay back the debt with a series of periodic payments. Usually, each payment includes all interest expense that has accrued up to the date of the payment plus some portion of the original amount borrowed (the *principal*). Installment notes generally specify one of two alternative payment patterns. Some notes require payments that include interest and equal amounts of principal while other notes simply call for equal payments.

Installment Notes with Payments of Accrued Interest and Equal Amounts of Principal

Installment note agreements requiring payments of accrued interest plus equal amounts of principal create cash flows that decrease in size over the life of the note. This pattern occurs because each payment reduces the liability's principal balance, with the result that the following period's interest expense is reduced. The next payment is smaller because the amount of interest is reduced. For example, suppose the $60,000, 8% note that we just recorded requires the borrower to make six payments at the end of each year equal to the accrued interest plus $10,000 of principal.

We describe the payments, interest, and changes in the balance of this note in Illustration 17–1. Column *a* of the illustration shows the beginning balance of the note. Columns *b*, *c*, and *d* describe each cash payment and how it is divided between interest and principal. Column *b* calculates the interest expense that accrues during each year at 8% of the beginning balance. Column *c* shows the portion of the payment applied to principal. It shows that each payment reduces the liability with a $10,000 debit to the Notes Payable account. Column *d* calculates each annual payment, which consists of the interest in column *b* plus $10,000. (Notice that the credit to the Cash account equals the sum of the debits to the expense and the liability account.) Finally, column *e* shows the ending balance of the liability, which equals the beginning balance in column *a* minus the principal portion of the payment in column *c*. Over the life of the note, the table shows that the total interest expense is $16,800 and the total reduction in principal is $60,000. Thus, the total cash payments are $76,800.

The graph in the lower section of Illustration 17–1 shows these three points: (1) the total payment gets smaller as the loan balance is reduced, (2) the amount of interest included in each payment gets steadily smaller, and (3) the amount of principal in each payment remains constant at $10,000.

The borrower records the effects of the first two payments with these entries:

1996					
Dec.	31	Interest Expense	4,800.00	
		Notes Payable	10,000.00	
		Cash		14,800.00
		To record first installment payment.		

1997					
Dec.	31	Interest Expense	4,000.00	
		Notes Payable	10,000.00	
		Cash		14,000.00
		To record second installment payment.		

After all six payments are recorded, the balance of the Notes Payable account for the note is eliminated.

Illustration 17-1   Installment Note with Payments of Accrued Interest and Equal Amounts of Principal

	(a)	(b)		(c)		(d)	(e)
		Payments					
Period Ending	**Beginning Balance** *Prior (e)*	*Debit* **Interest Expense** *8% × (a)*	**+**	*Debit* **Notes Payable** *$60,000/6*	**=**	*Credit* **Cash** *(b) + (c)*	**Ending Balance** *(a) − (c)*
Dec. 31, 1996 ..... $60,000		$ 4,800		$10,000		$14,800	$50,000
Dec. 31, 1997 50,000		4,000		10,000		14,000	40,000
Dec. 31, 1998 40,000		3,200		10,000		13,200	30,000
Dec. 31, 1999 30,000		2,400		10,000		12,400	20,000
Dec. 31, 2000 20,000		1,600		10,000		11,600	10,000
Dec. 31, 2001 10,000		800		10,000		10,800	0
Total		$16,800	+	$60,000	=	$76,800	

Payments on the note payable:

Payments decrease.

Interest decreases with each payment.

Each payment includes $10,000 of principal.

Interest   Principal

Installment Notes with Equal Payments

In contrast to the previous pattern, many installment notes require the borrower to make a series of equal payments. These payments consist of changing amounts of interest and principal. To demonstrate this type of note, assume that a $60,000 note requires the borrower to make a series of six equal payments of $12,979 at the end of each year. Illustration 17–2 shows the effects of making the payments on this note. (The payments are $12,979 because $60,000 is the present value of an annuity of six annual payments of $12,979, discounted at 8%. We show you how to make this calculation later in this section.)

Allocating Each Payment between Interest and Principal. Each payment of $12,979 includes both interest and principal. Look at Illustration 17–2 to see how an accountant allocates the total amount of each payment between interest and principal.

Illustration 17-2 Installment Note with Equal Payments

	(a)	(b) Debit Interest Expense 6% × (a)	+	(c) Debit Notes Payable (d) − (b)	=	(d) Credit Cash calculated	(e) Ending Balance (a) − (c)
Period Ending	Beginning Balance Prior (e)						
Dec. 31, 1996 ...... $60,000		$ 4,800		$ 8,179		$12,979	$51,821
Dec. 31, 1997 51,821		4,146		8,833		12,979	42,988
Dec. 31, 1998 42,988		3,439		9,540		12,979	33,448
Dec. 31, 1999 33,448		2,676		10,303		12,979	23,145
Dec. 31, 2000 23,145		1,852		11,127		12,979	12,018
Dec. 31, 2001 12,018		961		12,018		12,979	0
Total		$17,874	+	$60,000	=	$77,874	

Payments on the note payable:

Payments are constant.

Interest decreases with each payment.

Each payment includes an increasing amount of principal.

The table is essentially the same as the table in Illustration 17–1. Again, column *a* shows the liability's beginning balance for each year. Column *b* presents the interest that accrues each year at 8% of the beginning balance. Column *c* calculates the change in the principal of the liability caused by each payment. The debit to the liability account in this column is the difference between the total payment in column *d* and the interest expense in column *b*. Finally, column *e* presents the ending balance after each payment is made.

Even though all six payments are equal, the amount of interest decreases each year because the balance of the liability gets smaller. Then, because the amount of interest gets smaller, the amount of the payment applied to the principal gets larger. This effect is presented graphically in Illustration 17–2. Because the tables in

Illustrations 17–1 and 17–2 show how the principal balance is reduced (or amortized) by the periodic payments, they are often referred to as *installment note amortization schedules.*[1]

The bookkeeper records the effects of the first two payments with these journal entries:

1996 Dec.	31	Interest Expense	4,800.00	
		Notes Payable	8,179.00	
		Cash		12,979.00
		To record first installment payment.		

1997 Dec.	31	Interest Expense	4,146.00	
		Notes Payable	8,833.00	
		Cash		12,979.00
		To record second installment payment.		

The amounts in these entries come from the table in Illustration 17–2. The borrower would record similar entries for each of the remaining payments. Over the six years, the Notes Payable account balance will be eliminated.

To be sure that you understand the differences between the two payment patterns, compare the numbers and graphs in Illustrations 17–1 and 17–2. Notice that the series of equal payments leads to a greater amount of interest expense over the life of the note. This result occurs because the first three payments in Illustration 17–2 are smaller and thus do not reduce the principal as quickly as the first three payments in Illustration 17–1.

Calculating the Equal Periodic Payments on an Installment Note. In the previous example, we simply gave you the size of the equal annual payments on the installment note. Now, we show you how to calculate the size of the payment.

When a note requires a series of equal payments, you can calculate the size of each payment with a present value table for an annuity such as Table 17–2 on page 788.[2] To make the calculation with the table, start with this equation:

$$\text{Payment} \times \text{Annuity table value} = \text{Present value of the annuity}$$

Then, modify the equation to get this version:

$$\text{Payment} = \frac{\text{Present value of the annuity}}{\text{Annuity table value}}$$

---

[1] Many business calculators are programmed to make these amortization calculations for annuities.

[2] Appendix F provides present value tables that include additional interest rates and additional periods (or payments). You should use them to solve the exercises and problems at the end of the chapter.

Because the balance of an installment note equals the present value of the series of payments, the equation can again be modified to become this formula:

$$\text{Payment} = \frac{\text{Note balance}}{\text{Annuity table value}}$$

For this example, the initial note balance is $60,000. The annuity table value in the formula is based on the note's interest rate and the number of payments. The interest rate is 8% and there are six payments. Therefore, enter Table 17–2 on the sixth row and go across to the 8% column, where you will find the value of 4.6229. These numbers now can be substituted into the formula to find the payment:

$$\text{Payment} = \frac{\$60,000}{4.6229} = \$12,979$$

This formula can be used for all installment notes that require equal periodic payments.[3]

Progress Check

(Answers to Progress Checks are provided at the end of the chapter.)

17-1 Which of the following is true for an installment note that requires a series of equal payments?
   a. The payments consist of an increasing amount of interest and a decreasing amount of principal.
   b. The payments consist of changing amounts of principal, but the interest portion of the payment remains constant.
   c. The payments consist of a decreasing amount of interest and an increasing amount of principal.

17-2 How is the interest portion of an installment note payment calculated?

17-3 When a borrower records an interest payment on an installment note, how are the balance sheet and income statement affected?

Business corporations often borrow money by issuing **bonds**.[4] Bonds involve written promises to pay interest at a stated annual rate and to make a final payment of an amount identified on the bonds as the **par value of the bonds**. Most bonds require the borrower to pay the interest semiannually. The par value of the bonds (also known as the *face amount*) is paid at a specified future date called the *maturity date of the bonds*. The amount of interest that must be paid each year is determined by multiplying the par value of the bonds by the stated rate of interest established when the bonds were issued.

Differences between Notes Payable and Bonds

When a business borrows money by signing a note payable, the money is generally obtained from a single lender, such as a bank. In contrast, a group of bonds

BORROWING BY ISSUING BONDS

LO 2

Describe the various characteristics of different types of bonds and prepare entries to record bond issuances and retirements.

---

[3]Business calculators can also be used to find the size of the payments.

[4]Bonds are also issued by nonprofit corporations, as well as the federal government and other governmental units, such as municipalities, provinces, and utilities. Although the examples in this chapter deal with business situations, all issuers use the same practices to account for their bonds.

(often called a *bond issue*) typically consists of a large number of bonds, usually in denominations of $1,000, that are sold to many different lenders. After bonds are originally issued, they often are bought and sold by these investors. Thus, any particular bond may actually be owned by a number of people before it matures.

Differences between Shares and Bonds

Shares and bonds are different types of securities. Shares represent an ownership right in the corporation. For example, a person who owns 1,000 of a corporation's 10,000 outstanding shares controls one-tenth of the total shareholders' equity. On the other hand, if a person owns a $1,000, 11%, 20-year bond, the bondholder has a receivable from the issuer. The bond owner has the right to receive 11% interest ($110) each year that the bond is outstanding and $1,000 when the bond matures 20 years after its issue date. The issuing company is obligated to make these payments and thus has a liability to the bondholder.

ADVANTAGES OF ISSUING BONDS

Companies that issue bonds are usually trying to increase their rate of return on equity. For example, assume a company that has $1 million of equity is considering spending $500,000 to expand its capacity. Management predicts that the $500,000 will allow the company to earn an additional $125,000 of income before paying any interest. The managers are considering three possible plans. Under Plan A, the expansion will not occur. Under Plan B, the expansion will occur, and the needed funds will be obtained from the owners. Under Plan C, the company will sell $500,000 of bonds that pay 10% annual interest ($50,000). Illustration 17–3 shows how the plans would affect the company's net income, equity, and return on equity.

Analysis of the alternatives in the illustration shows that the owners will enjoy a greater rate of return and be better off if the expansion is made and if the funds are obtained by issuing the bonds. Even though the projected net income under Plan C would be smaller than Plan B's income, the rate of return on the equity would be larger because there would be less equity. This result occurs whenever the expected rate of return from the new assets is greater than the rate of interest on the bonds. In addition, issuing bonds allows the current owner or owners of a business to remain in control of the company.

CHARACTERISTICS OF BONDS

Over the years, financial experts have created many different kinds of bonds with various characteristics. We describe some of the more common features of bonds in the following paragraphs.

Serial Bonds

Some companies issue several groups of bonds that mature at different dates. As a result, the bonds are repaid gradually over a number of years. Because these bonds mature in series, they are called **serial bonds**. For example, $1 million of serial bonds might mature at the rate of $100,000 each year from 6 to 15 years after the bonds were issued. There would be 10 groups (or series) of bonds of $100,000 each. One series would mature after six years, another after seven years, and another each successive year until the final series is repaid.

Illustration 17-3
Financing with
Bonds or Shares

	Plan A Don't Expand	Plan B Increase Equity	Plan C Issue Bonds
Income before interest	$ 100,000	$ 225,000	$ 225,000
Interest			(50,000)
Net income	$ 100,000	$ 225,000	$ 175,000
Equity	$1,000,000	$1,500,000	$1,000,000
Return on equity	10.0%	15.0%	17.5%

Sinking Fund Bonds

As an alternative to serial bonds, **sinking fund bonds** all mature on the same date. To reduce some of the risk for owners, these bonds require the issuer to create a *sinking fund*, which is a separate pool of assets used only to retire the bonds at maturity. In effect, the issuer must start to set aside the cash to pay off the bonds long before they mature.

Convertible Bonds

Some companies issue **convertible bonds** that can be exchanged by the bondholders for a fixed number of common shares of the issuing company. These bonds offer issuers the advantage that they might be settled without paying back the cash initially borrowed. Convertible bonds also offer the bondholders the potential to participate in future increases in the market value of the shares. However, if the shares do not appreciate, the bondholders continue to receive periodic interest and will receive the par value when the bond matures. In most cases, the bondholders can decide whether and when to convert the bonds to shares. However, the issuer can force conversion by exercising an option to buy the bonds back at a price less than the market value of the shares.

Registered Bonds and Bearer Bonds

A company that issues **registered bonds** keeps a record of the names and addresses of the bonds' owners. Then, over the life of the bonds, the company makes interest payments by sending cheques to these registered owners. When one investor sells a bond to another investor, the issuer must be notified of the change. Registered bonds offer the issuer the practical advantage of not having to actually issue bond certificates to the investors. This arrangement also protects investors against loss or theft of the bonds.

Unregistered bonds are called **bearer bonds**, because they are payable to whoever holds them (the *bearer*). Since there may be no record of sales or exchanges, the holder of a bearer bond is presumed to be its rightful owner. As a result, lost or stolen bonds are difficult to replace.

Many bearer bonds are also **coupon bonds**. This term reflects the fact that interest coupons are attached to each bond. Each coupon matures on a specific interest payment date. The owner detaches each coupon when it matures and presents it to a bank or broker for collection. At maturity, the owner follows the same process and presents the bond certificates to a bank or broker.

Secured Bonds and Debentures

When bonds are secured, specific assets of the issuing company are pledged (or *mortgaged*) as collateral. This arrangement gives the bondholders additional protection against default by the issuer. If the issuing company fails to pay the interest or maturity value, the secured bondholders can demand that the collateral be sold and the proceeds used to repay the debt.

In contrast to secured bonds, unsecured bonds are potentially more risky because they are supported by only the issuer's general credit standing. Unsecured bonds are also called **debentures**. Because of the greater risk of default, a company generally must be financially strong to successfully issue debentures at a favorable rate of interest.

Sometimes, companies issue debentures that rank below certain other unsecured liabilities of the company. Debentures such as this are called subordinated debentures. In a liquidation, the subordinated debentures would not be repaid until the claims of the more senior, unsecured liabilities were first satisfied.

Bond Market Values

Bonds are securities and can be easily traded between investors. Because they are bought and sold in the market, they have a market value. As a matter of convenience, bond market values are expressed as a percentage of their face value. For example, a company's bonds might be trading at $103\frac{1}{2}$, which means that they can be bought or sold for 103.5% of their par value. If other bonds are trading at 95, they can be bought or sold at 95% of their par value.

THE PROCESS OF ISSUING BONDS

When a company issues bonds, it normally sells them to an investment firm called an *underwriter*. In turn, the underwriter resells the bonds to the public. In some situations, the issuer may sell the bonds directly to investors as the cash is needed.

The legal document that identifies the rights and obligations of the bondholders and the issuer is called the **bond indenture**. In effect, the bond indenture is the legal contract between the issuer and the bondholders. Although the practice is less common today, each bondholder may receive an actual bond certificate as evidence of the company's debt. However, most companies reduce their costs by not issuing certificates to registered bondholders.

If the underwriter sells the bonds to a large number of investors, the bondholders' interests are represented and protected by a *trustee*. The trustee monitors the issuer's actions to ensure that it complies with the obligations in the bond indenture. Most trustees are large banks or trust companies.

Accounting for the Issuance of Bonds

Before bonds are issued, the terms of the indenture are drawn up and accepted by the trustee. If the bonds are to be offered to the general public by the underwriter, they must be registered with the Securities Commission (e.g., the Ontario Securities Commission, or OSC), which means that the issuer must provide extensive financial information in special reports.

For example, suppose that the Barnes Company receives authorization from the OSC to issue $800,000 of 9%, 20-year bonds dated January 1, 1995, that are due on December 31, 2014. They will pay interest semiannually on each June 30 and December 31. Most corporate or government bonds pay interest either quarterly or semiannually. After the bond indenture is accepted by the trustee on behalf of the bondholders, all or a portion of the bonds may be sold to the underwriter. If all the bonds are sold at their par value, Barnes Company makes this entry to record the sale:

1995					
Jan.	1	Cash		800,000.00	
		Bonds Payable			800,000.00
		Sold bonds at par.			

This entry reflects the fact that the company's cash and long-term liabilities are increased.

Six months later, the first semiannual interest payment is made, and Barnes records the payment with this entry:

1995					
June	30	Interest Expense		36,000.00	
		Cash			36,000.00
		Paid semiannual interest on bonds.			
		(9% × $800,000 × 1/2).			

When the bonds mature 20 years later, Barnes Company will record its payment of the maturity value with the following entry:

2014					
Dec.	31	Bonds Payable		800,000.00	
		Cash			800,000.00
		Paid bonds at maturity.			

SELLING BONDS BETWEEN INTEREST DATES

As in the previous example, many bonds are sold on their original issue date. However, circumstances may cause a company to actually sell some of the bonds later. If so, it is likely that the selling date will fall between interest payment dates. When this happens, the purchasers normally pay the issuer the purchase price plus any interest accrued since the issue date or the preceding interest payment date. This accrued interest is then refunded to the purchasers on the next interest date. For example, assume that the Fields Company sold $100,000 of its 9% bonds at par on March 1, 1996, which was two months after the original issue date. The interest on the bonds is payable semiannually on each June 30 and December 31. Because two months have passed, the issuer collects two months' interest from the buyer at the time of the sale. This amount is $1,500 ($100,000 × 9% × 2/12). This situation is represented by the following diagram:

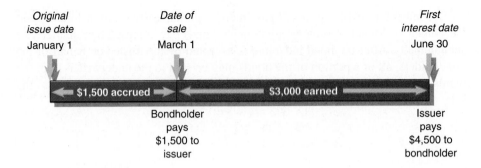

The issuer's entry to record the sale is

Mar.	1	Cash	101,500.00	
		Interest Payable		1,500.00
		Bonds Payable		100,000.00
		Sold $100,000 of bonds with two months' accrued interest.		

Note that the liabilities for the interest and the bonds are recorded in separate accounts.

When the June 30 semiannual interest date arrives, the issuer pays a full six months' interest of $4,500 ($100,000 × 9% × 1/2) to the bondholder. This payment includes the four months' interest of $3,000 earned by the bondholder from March 1 to June 30 plus the refund of the two months' accrued interest collected by the issuer when the bonds were sold. The issuer's entry to record this first payment is

June	30	Interest Payable	1,500.00	
		Interest Expense	3,000.00	
		Cash		4,500.00
		Paid semiannual interest on the bonds.		

The practice of collecting and then refunding the accrued interest with the next interest payment may seem like a roundabout way to do business. However, it greatly simplifies the bond issuer's administrative efforts. To understand this point, suppose that a company sells bonds on 15 or 20 different dates between the original issue date and the first interest payment date. If the issuer did not collect the accrued interest from the buyers, it would have to pay different amounts of cash to each of them in accordance with how much time had passed since they purchased their bonds. To make the correct payments, the issuer would have to keep detailed records of the purchasers and the dates on which they bought their bonds. Issuers avoid this extra record-keeping by having each buyer pay in the accrued interest at the time of purchase. Then, the company pays a full six months' interest to all purchasers, regardless of when they bought the bonds.

The interest rate to be paid by the issuer of bonds is specified in the indenture and on the bond certificates. Because it is stated in the indenture, this rate is called the **contract rate** of the bonds. (This rate is also known as the *coupon rate*, the *stated rate*, or the *nominal rate*.) The amount of interest to be paid each year is determined by multiplying the par value of the bonds by the contract rate. The contract rate is usually stated on an annual basis, even if the interest is to be paid semiannually. For example, suppose that a company issues a $1,000, 8% bond that pays interest semiannually. As a result, the annual interest of $80 (8% × $1,000) will be paid in two semiannual payments of $40 each.

BOND INTEREST RATES

Although the contract rate sets the amount of interest that the issuer pays in *cash*, the contract rate is not necessarily the rate of interest *expense* actually incurred by the issuer. In fact, the interest expense depends on the market value of the issuer's bonds, which depends on the purchasers' opinions about the risk of lending to the issuer. This perceived risk (as well as the supply of and demand for bonds) is reflected in the **market rate** for bond interest. The market rate is the consensus rate that borrowers are willing to pay and that lenders are willing to earn at the level of risk inherent in the bonds. This rate changes often (even daily) in response to changes in the supply of and demand for bonds. The market rate tends to go up when the demand for bonds decreases or the supply increases. The rate tends to go down when the supply of bonds decreases or the demand increases.

Because many factors affect the bond market, various companies face different interest rates for their bonds. The market rate for a specific set of bonds depends on the level of risk investors assign to them. As the level of risk increases, the rate increases. Market rates also are affected by the length of the bonds' life. Long-term bonds generally have higher rates because they are more risky.

Many bond issuers offer a contract rate of interest equal to the rate they expect the market to demand as of the bonds' issuance date. If the contract and market rates are equal, the bonds sell at their par value. However, if the contract and market rates are not equal, the bonds are not sold at their par value. Instead, they are sold at a *premium* above their par value or at a *discount* below their par value. Observe the relationship between the interest rates and the issue price of the bonds' values in this table:

When the contract rate is		The bond sells
Above the market rate	⇒	At a premium
At the market rate	⇒	At par value
Below the market rate	⇒	At a discount

Over the last two decades, some companies have issued *zero-coupon bonds* that do not provide any periodic interest payments. Because this contract rate of 0% is always below the market rate, these bonds are always issued at prices less than their face values.

Progress Check

17-4　Unsecured bonds that are backed only by the issuer's general credit standing are called *(a)* serial bonds, *(b)* debentures, *(c)* registered bonds, *(d)* convertible bonds, *(e)* bearer bonds.

17-5　How do you calculate the amount of interest a bond issuer will pay each year?

17-6　On May 1, a company sold $500,000 of 9% bonds that pay semiannual interest on each January 1 and July 1. The bonds were sold at par value plus accrued interest since January 1. The bond issuer's entry to record the first semiannual interest payment on July 1 should include *(a)* a debit to Interest Payable for $15,000, *(b)* a debit to Interest Expense for $22,500, or *(c)* a credit to Interest Payable for $7,500.

17-7　When the contract rate is above the market rate, do the bonds sell at a premium or a discount? Do the purchasers pay more or less than the par value of the bonds?

BONDS SOLD AT A DISCOUNT

LO 3
Estimate the price of bonds issued at a discount and describe their effects on the issuer's financial statements.

As we described in the previous section, a **discount on bonds payable** arises when a company issues bonds with a contract rate less than the market rate. The expected issue price of the bonds can be found by calculating the *present value* of the expected cash flows, discounted at the market rate of interest.

To illustrate, assume that a company offers to issue bonds with a $100,000 par value, an 8% annual contract rate, and a five-year life. Also assume that the market rate of interest for this company's bonds is 10%.[5] In exchange for the purchase price received from the buyers, these bonds obligate the issuer to pay out two different future cash flows:

1. $100,000 at the end of the bonds' five-year life.
2. $4,000 (4% × $100,000) at the end of each six-month interest period throughout the five-year life of the bonds.

To estimate the bonds' issue price, use the market rate of interest to calculate the present value of the future cash flows. Using an annuity table of present values, you must work with *semiannual* compounding periods. Thus, the annual market rate of 10% is changed to the semiannual rate of 5%. Likewise, the five-year life of the bonds is changed to 10 semiannual periods.

The actual calculation requires two steps: First, you find the present value of the $100,000 maturity payment. Second, find the present value of the annuity of 10 payments of $4,000 each.

The present values can be found by using Table 17–1 (on page 788) for the single maturity payment and Table 17–2 for the annuity. To complete the first step, enter Table 17–1 on row 10 and go across to the 5% column. The table value is 0.6139. Second, enter Table 17–2 on row 10 and go across to the 5% column,

---

[5]The spread between the contract rate and the market rate of interest on a new bond issue is seldom more than a fraction of a percent. However, we use a difference of 2% here to emphasize the effects.

where the table value is 7.7217. This schedule shows the results when you multiply the cash flow amounts by the table values and add them together:

Cash Flow	Table	Table Value	Amount	Present Value
Par value	17–1	0.6139	$100,000	$61,390
Interest (annuity)	17–2	7.7217	4,000	30,887
Total				$92,277

If 5% is the appropriate semiannual interest rate for the bonds in the current market, the maximum price that informed buyers would offer for the bonds is $92,277. This amount is also the minimum price that the issuer would accept.

If the issuer accepts $92,277 cash for its bonds on the original issue date of December 31, 1996, it records the event with this entry:

1996				
Dec.	31	Cash	92,277.00	
		Discount on Bonds payable	7,723.00	
		Bonds payable		100,000.00
		Sold bonds at a discount on the original issue date.		

This entry causes the bonds to appear in the long-term liability section of the issuer's balance sheet as

Long-term liabilities:		
Bonds payable, 8%, due December 31, 2001 ..	$100,000	
Less discount	7,723	$92,277

This presentation shows that the discount is deducted from the par value of the bonds to produce the **carrying amount** of the bonds payable. As we saw in the last chapter for notes payable, the carrying amount is the net amount at which the bonds are reflected on the balance sheet.

Allocating Interest and Amortizing the Discount

In the previous example, the issuer received $92,277 for its bonds and will pay the bondholders $100,000 after five years have passed. Because the $7,723 discount is eventually paid to the bondholders at maturity, it is part of the cost of using the $92,277 for five years. This table shows that the total interest cost of $47,723 is the difference between the amount repaid and the amount borrowed:

Amount repaid:	
Ten payments of $4,000	$ 40,000
Maturity amount	100,000
Total repaid	$140,000
Less amount borrowed	(92,277)
Total interest expense	$ 47,723

The total expense also equals the sum of the 10 cash payments and the discount:

Ten payments of $4,000	$40,000
Plus discount	7,723
Total interest expense	$47,723

In describing these bonds and the interest expense, the issuer's accountant must accomplish two things. First, the total interest expense of $47,723 must be allocated among the 10 six-month periods in the bonds' life. Second, the carrying value of the bonds must be updated for each balance sheet. Two alternative methods accomplish these objectives. They are the straight-line and the interest methods of allocating interest. Because the process involves reducing the original discount on the bonds over the life of the bonds, it is also called *amortizing the bond discount*.

Straight-Line Method.   The **straight-line method** of allocating the interest is the simpler of the two methods. This method allocates an equal portion of the total interest expense to each of the six-month interest periods.

In applying the straight-line method to the present example, the accountant divides the five years' total expense of $47,723 by 10 (the number of semiannual periods in the bonds' life). The result is $4,772 per period.[6] The same number can be found by dividing the $7,723 original discount by 10. That result is $772, which is the amount of discount to be amortized in each interest period. When the $772 of amortized discount is added to the $4,000 cash payment, the total interest expense for each six-month period is $4,772.

When the semiannual cash payment is made, the issuer uses the following entry to record the interest expense and update the balance of the bond liability:

1997				
June	30	Interest Expense	4,772.00	
		Discount on Bonds payable		772.00
		Cash		4,000.00
		To record six months' interest and discount *amortization.*		

---

[6]For simplicity, all calculations have been rounded to the nearest whole dollar. Use the same practice when solving the exercises and problems at the end of the chapter.

Illustration 17–4   Allocating Interest Expense and Amortizing the Bond Discount with the Straight-Line Method

	(a)	(b) Debit Interest Expense	(c) Credit Discount on Bonds	(d) Credit Cash	(e) Ending Balance
Period Ending	Beginning Balance		=	+	
	Prior (e)	$47,723/10	$7,723/10	4% × $100,000	(a) + (c)
June 30, 1997	$92,277	$ 4,772	$ 772	$ 4,000	$ 93,049
Dec. 31, 1997	93,049	4,772	772	4,000	93,821
June 30, 1998	93,821	4,772	772	4,000	94,593
Dec. 31, 1998	94,593	4,772	772	4,000	95,365
June 30, 1999	95,365	4,772	772	4,000	96,137
Dec. 31, 1999	96,137	4,772	772	4,000	96,909
June 30, 2000	96,909	4,772	772	4,000	97,681
Dec. 31, 2000	97,681	4,772	772	4,000	98,453
June 30, 2001	98,453	4,772	772	4,000	99,225
Dec. 31, 2001	99,225	4,775*	775	4,000	100,000
Total		$47,723 =	$7,723 +	$40,000	

*Adjusted for rounding.

Note that the $772 credit to the Discount on Bonds Payable account actually *increases* the bonds' carrying value. The increase comes about by *decreasing* the balance of the contra account that is subtracted from the Bonds Payable account.

Illustration 17–4 presents a table similar to the amortization tables that you have studied for notes payable. It shows how the interest expense is allocated among the 10 six-month periods in the bonds' life. It also shows how amortizing the bond discount causes the balance of the net liability to increase until it reaches $100,000 at the end of the bonds' life. Notice the following points as you analyze Illustration 17–4:

1. The $92,277 beginning balance in column *a* equals the cash received from selling the bonds. It also equals the $100,000 face amount of the bonds less the initial $7,723 discount from selling the bonds for less than par.
2. The semiannual interest expense of $4,772 in column *b* for each row equals the amount obtained by dividing the total expense of $47,723 by 10.
3. The credit to the Discount on Bonds Payable account in column *c* equals one-tenth of the total discount of $7,723.
4. The $4,000 interest payment in column *d* is the result of multiplying the $100,000 par value of the bonds by the 4% semiannual contract rate of interest.
5. The ending balance in column *e* equals the beginning balance in column *a* plus the $772 discount amortization in column *c*. This ending balance then becomes the beginning balance on the next row in the table.
6. The balance in column *e* continues to grow each period by the $772 of discount amortization until it finally equals the par value of the bonds when they mature.

The three payment columns show that the company incurs a $4,772 interest expense each period, but pays only $4,000. The $772 unpaid portion of the expense is appropriately added to the balance of the liability. It is added to the liability by being taken from the contra account balance. This table shows you how the balance of the discount is partially amortized every six months until it is eliminated:

Period Ending	Beginning Discount Balance	Amount Amortized	Ending Discount Balance
June 30, 1997	$7,723	$ (772)	$6,951
Dec. 31, 1997	6,951	(772)	6,179
June 30, 1998	6,179	(772)	5,407
Dec. 31, 1998	5,407	(772)	4,635
June 30, 1999	4,635	(772)	3,863
Dec. 31, 1999	3,863	(772)	3,091
June 30, 2000	3,091	(772)	2,319
Dec. 31, 2000	2,319	(772)	1,547
June 30, 2001	1,547	(772)	775
Dec. 31, 2001	775	(775)*	0
Total		$(7,723)	

*Adjusted for rounding.

Interest Method.   Straight-line allocations of interest used to be widely applied in practice. However, generally accepted accounting principles now allow the straight-line method to be used only if the results do not differ materially from those obtained by using the **interest method** to allocate the interest over the life of the bonds.[7]

The interest method is exactly the same process for allocating interest that you first learned in Chapter 12 for notes payable. Interest expense for a period is found by multiplying the balance of the liability at the beginning of that period by the original market interest rate.

In Illustration 17–5, we present an amortization table for our example. The key difference between Illustrations 17–4 and 17–5 lies in the calculation of the interest expense in column *b*. Instead of assigning an equal amount of interest to each interest period, the interest method assigns an increasing amount of interest over the bonds' life because the balance of the liability increases over the five years. The interest expense in column *b* equals the original 5% market interest rate times the balance of the liability at the beginning of each period. Notice that both methods allocate the same $47,723 of total expense among the five years, but with different patterns.

The amount of discount amortized in any period is the difference between the interest expense in column *b* and the cash payment in column *d*. In effect, the accrued but unpaid portion of the interest expense in column *c* is added to the net liability in column *a* to get the ending balance in column *e*.

In the following table, you can see how the balance of the discount is amortized by the interest method until it reaches zero:

---

[7]FASB, *Accounting Standards—Current Text* (Norwalk, CT, 1994), sec. I69.108. First published in *APB Opinion No. 21,* par. 15. Also see *CICA Re-Exposure Draft,* "Financial Instruments, " par. .170, in *CA Magazine,* April 1994, p. ED27.

Illustration 17-5 Allocating Interest Expense and Amortizing the Bond Discount with the Interest Method

	(a)	(b)	(c)	(d)	(e)
			Payments		
		Debit	**Credit**		
Period	**Beginning**	**Interest**	**Discount**	**Credit**	**Ending**
Ending	**Balance**	**Expense** =	**on Bonds** +	**Cash**	**Balance**
	Prior (e)	*5% × (a)*	*(b) − (d)*	*4% × $100,000*	*(a) + (c)*
June 30, 1997	$92,277	$ 4,614	$ 614	$ 4,000	$ 93,891
Dec. 31, 1997	92,891	4,645	645	4,000	93,536
June 30, 1998	93,536	4,677	677	4,000	94,213
Dec. 31, 1998	94,213	4,711	711	4,000	94,924
June 30, 1999	94,924	4,746	746	4,000	95,670
Dec. 31, 1999	95,670	4,784	784	4,000	96,454
June 30, 2000	96,454	4,823	823	4,000	97,277
Dec. 31, 2000	97,277	4,864	864	4,000	98,141
June 30, 2001	98,141	4,907	907	4,000	99,048
Dec. 31, 2001	99,048	4,952	952	4,000	100,000
Total		$47,723 =	$7,723 +	$40,000	

Period Ending	Beginning Discount Balance	Amount Amortized	Ending Discount Balance
June 30, 1997 . .	$7,723	$ (614)	$7,109
Dec. 31, 1997	7,109	(645)	6,464
June 30, 1998	6,464	(677)	5,787
Dec. 31, 1998	5,787	(711)	5,076
June 30, 1999	5,076	(746)	4,330
Dec. 31, 1999	4,330	(784)	3,546
June 30, 2000	3,546	(823)	2,723
Dec. 31, 2000	2,723	(864)	1,859
June 30, 2001	1,859	(907)	952
Dec. 31, 2001	952	(952)*	0
Total		$(7,723)	

*Adjusted for rounding.

Except for the differences in the amounts, journal entries that record the expense and update the liability balance are the same under the interest method and the straight-line method. For example, the entry to record the interest payment at the end of the first interest period is

1997				
June	30	Interest Expense	4,614.00	
		Discount on Bonds payable		614.00
		Cash		4,000.00
		To record six months' interest and discount amortization.		

Illustration 17-6 Comparing the Straight-Line and Interest Methods of Allocating Interest on a Bond Sold at a Discount

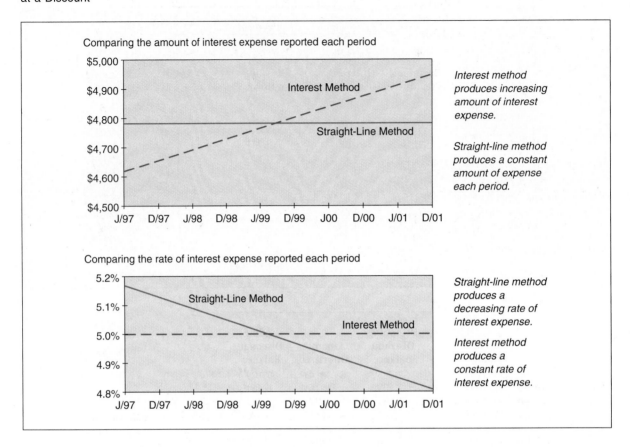

The accountant uses the numbers in Illustration 17–5 to make similar entries throughout the five-year life of the bonds.

Comparing the Straight-Line and Interest Methods. With this background in place, we can now look more closely at the differences between the straight-line and interest methods of allocating interest among the periods in the bonds' life. In Illustration 17–6, the two graphs illustrate the differences for bonds issued at a discount.

The horizontal line in the first graph in Illustration 17–6 represents the amounts of interest expense reported each period under straight-line. The upward sloping line represents the increasing amounts of interest reported under the interest method. The amounts increase because the constant 5% rate is applied to the growing balance of the liability.

The horizontal line in the second graph represents the constant rate of 5% that the interest method uses to determine the interest expense for every six-month period. The downward sloping line represents the changing interest rates produced by the straight-line method when the bond is issued at a discount. The interest rates decrease each period because the amount of interest expense remains constant while the balance of the liability increases.

The interest method is preferred over the straight-line method because it provides a more reasonable description of the growth of the liability and the amount of interest expense incurred each period. As we mentioned, the straight-line method can be used only if the results do not differ materially from those obtained by using the interest method.

Progress Check

A company recently issued a group of five-year, 6% bonds with a $100,000 par value. The interest is to be paid semiannually, and the market interest rate was 8% on the issue date. Use this information to answer the following questions:

17-8   **What is the bonds' selling price?** *(a)* $100,000; *(b)* $92,393; *(c)* $91,893; *(d)* $100,321; *(e)* $92,016.

17-9   **What is the journal entry to record the sale?**

17-10 **What is the amount of interest expense recorded at the time of the first semi-annual cash payment using *(a)* the straight-line method of allocating interest and *(b)* the interest method of allocating interest?**

BONDS SOLD AT A PREMIUM

LO 4

Estimate the price of bonds issued at a premium and describe their effects on the issuer's financial statements.

When bonds carry a contract interest rate that is greater than the market rate, the bonds sell at a price greater than the par value and the difference between the par and market values is called the **premium**. In effect, buyers bid up the price of the bonds until it reaches the level that creates the current market rate of interest. As we explained for the discount situation, this premium market price can be estimated by finding the present value of the expected cash flows from the bonds at the market interest rate.

For example, assume that a company decides to issue bonds with a $100,000 par value, a 12% annual contract rate, and a five-year life. On the issue date, the market interest rate for the bonds is only 10%. Thus, potential buyers of these bonds bid up their market price until the effective rate equals the market rate. To estimate this price, we use the 5% semiannual market rate to find the present value of the expected cash flows. The cash flows consist of:

1. $100,000 at the end of the bonds' five-year life.
2. $6,000 (6% × $100,000) at the end of each six-month interest period throughout the five-year life of the bonds.

The present values can be found by using Table 17–1 (page 788) for the single maturity payment and Table 17–2 for the annuity. To complete the first step, enter Table 17–1 on row 10 and go across to the 5% column. The table value is 0.6139. Second, enter Table 17–2 on row 10 and go across to the 5% column, where the table value is 7.7217. Finally, use these table values to reduce the future cash flows to their present value. This schedule shows the results when you multiply the cash flow amounts by the table values and add them together:

Cash Flow	Table	Table Value	Amount	Present Value
Par value	17–1	0.6139	$100,000	$ 61,390
Interest (annuity)	17–2	7.7217	6,000	46,330
Total				$107,720

If 5% is the appropriate semiannual interest rate for the bonds in the current market, the maximum price that informed buyers would offer for the bonds is $107,720. This amount is also the minimum price that the issuer would accept.

If the issuer does accept $107,720 cash for its bonds on the original issue date of December 31, 1996, it records the event with this entry:

1996				
Dec.	31	Cash	107,720.00	
		Premium on Bonds Payable		7,720.00
		Bonds Payable		100,000.00
		Sold bonds at a premium on the original issue date.		

This entry causes the bonds to appear in the long-term liability section of the issuer's balance sheet as follows:

Long-term liabilities:
  Bonds payable, 8%, due December 31, 2001 .... $100,000
  Plus premium 7,720 $107,720

This presentation shows that the premium is added to the par value of the bonds to produce their carrying amount.

Allocating Interest Expense and Amortizing the Premium

Over the life of these premium bonds, the issuer pays back $160,000, which consists of the 10 periodic interest payments of $6,000 plus the $100,000 par value. Because it borrowed $107,720, the total interest expense will be $52,280. This table shows the calculation:

Amount repaid:
  Ten payments of $6,000 .... $ 60,000
  Maturity amount   100,000
  Total repaid $160,000
Less amount borrowed ......   (107,720)
Total interest expense .... $ 52,280

The following calculation confirms that the total expense also equals the difference between the 10 cash payments and the premium:

Ten payments of $6,000	$ 60,000
Less premium	(7,720)
Total interest expense	$ 52,280

The premium is subtracted because it will not be paid to the bondholders when the bonds mature.

This total interest expense can be allocated over the 10 semiannual periods with either the straight-line or the interest method. Because the interest method is preferred, it is the only one illustrated for these bonds. Illustration 17–7 shows an amortization schedule for the bonds using this method.

Again, column *a* of the illustration shows the beginning balance, and column *b* shows the amount of expense at 5% of the beginning balance. But, the amount of cash paid out in column *d* is larger than the expense because the payment is based on the higher 6% contract rate. As a result, the excess payment over the expense reduces the principal. These amounts are shown in column *c*. Finally, column *e* shows the new ending balance after the amortized premium in column *c* is deducted from the beginning balance in column *a*.

The following table shows how the premium is reduced by the amortization process over the life of the bonds:

Period Ending	Beginning Discount Balance	Amount Amortized	Ending Premium Balance
June 30, 1997	$7,720	$ (614)	$7,106
Dec. 31, 1997	7,106	(645)	6,461
June 30, 1998	6,461	(677)	5,784
Dec. 31, 1998	5,784	(711)	5,073
June 30, 1999	5,073	(746)	4,327
Dec. 31, 1999	4,327	(784)	3,543
June 30, 2000	3,543	(823)	2,720
Dec. 31, 2000	2,720	(864)	1,856
June 30, 2001	1,856	(907)	949
Dec. 31, 2001	949	(949)*	0
Total		$(7,720)	

*Adjusted for rounding.

The effect of premium amortization on interest expense and on the liability can be seen in this journal entry on June 30, 1997, when the issuer makes the first semiannual interest payment:

Illustration 17-7   Allocating Interest Expense and Amortizing the Bond Premium with the Interest Method

Period Ending	(a) Beginning Balance	(b) Debit Interest Expense	+	(c) Debit Premium on Bonds	=	(d) Credit Cash	(e) Ending Balance
	Prior (e)	5% × (a)		(d) − (b)		6% × $100,000	(a) − (c)
June 30, 1997	$107,720	$ 5,386		$ 614		$ 6,000	$107,106
Dec. 31, 1997	107,106	5,355		645		6,000	106,461
June 30, 1998	106,461	5,323		677		6,000	105,784
Dec. 31, 1998	105,784	5,289		711		6,000	105,073
June 30, 1999	105,073	5,254		746		6,000	104,327
Dec. 31, 1999	104,327	5,216		784		6,000	103,543
June 30, 2000	103,543	5,177		823		6,000	102,720
Dec. 31, 2000	102,720	5,136		864		6,000	101,856
June 30, 2001	101,856	5,093		907		6,000	100,949
Dec. 31, 2001	100,949	5,051*		949		6,000	100,000
Total		$52,280	+	$7,720	=	$60,000	

*Adjusted for rounding.

```
1997
June  30  Interest Expense ...........................    5,386.00
              Premium on Bonds Payable ...............       614.00
              Cash ....................................               6,000.00
          To record six months' interest and premium
          amortization.
```

Similar entries are recorded at each payment date until the bonds mature at the end of 2001. However, the interest method causes the company to report decreasing amounts of interest expense and increasing amounts of premium amortization.

ACCOUNTING FOR ACCRUED INTEREST EXPENSE

If a bond's interest period does not coincide with the issuing company's accounting period, an adjusting entry is necessary to recognize the interest expense that has accrued since the most recent interest payment. For example, assume that the bonds described in Illustration 17–7 were issued on September 1, 1996, instead of December 31, 1996. As a result, four months' interest (and premium amortization) accrue before the end of the 1996 calendar year. Because the reporting period ends on that date, an adjusting entry is needed to capture this information about the bonds.

Interest for the four months ended December 31, 1996, equals $3,591, which is 4/6 of the first six months' interest of $5,386. The premium amortization is $409, which is 4/6 of the first six months' amortization of $614. The sum of the interest expense and the amortization is $4,000 ($3,591 + $409), which also equals 4/6 of the $6,000 cash payment that is due on March 1, 1997. The accountant records these effects with this adjusting entry:

1996					
Dec.	31	Interest Expense	3,591.00		
		Premium on Bonds Payable	409.00		
		Interest Payable		4,000.00	
		To record four months' accrued interest and premium amortization.			

Similar entries are made on each December 31 throughout the five-year life of the bonds.

When the $6,000 cash payment occurs on the next interest date, the journal entry recognizes the interest expense and amortization for January and February of 1997 and eliminates the interest payable liability created by the adjusting entry. For this example, the accountant makes the following entry to record the payment on March 1, 1997:

1997					
Mar.	1	Interest Payable	4,000.00		
		Interest Expense ($5,386 × 2/6)	1,795.00		
		Premium on Bonds Payable ($614 × 2/6)	205.00		
		Cash		6,000.00	
		To record two months' interest and amortization and eliminate the accrued interest liability.			

The interest payments made each September are recorded normally because the entire six-month interest period is included within a single fiscal year.

Progress Check

On December 31, 1996, Cello Corporation issued 16%, 10-year bonds with a par value of $100,000. Interest is paid on June 30 and December 31. The bonds were sold to yield a 14% annual market rate of interest. Use this information to solve the following:

17-11   What is the selling price of the bonds?

17-12   Using the interest method of allocating interest expense, Cello would record the second interest payment (on December 31, 1997) with a debit to Premium on Bonds Payable in the amount of *(a)* $7,470; *(b)* $7,741; *(c)* $259; *(d)* $530; or *(e)* $277.

17-13   How would the bonds appear in the long-term liability section of Cello's balance sheet as of December 31, 1997?

RETIRING BONDS PAYABLE

For various reasons, companies may want to retire some or all of their bonds prior to maturity. For example, if market interest rates decline significantly, a company may wish to replace old high-interest debt obligations with new lower-interest debt. Many companies reserve the right to retire bonds early by issuing **callable bonds**. This means the bond indenture gives the issuing company an option to *call* the bonds before they mature by paying the par value plus a *call premium* to the bondholders. When interest rates were high in the 1980s, **Nova Corporation** and

LO 2

Describe the various characteristics of different types of bonds and prepare entries to record bond issuances and retirements.

many other companies issued callable bonds. When market rates dropped dramatically in the early 1990s, many of these bonds were called and retired.

Even if a specific bond issue is not callable, the issuer may be able to retire its bonds by repurchasing them on the open market at the current market price. Whether bonds are called or repurchased, the issuer is unlikely to pay a price that equals the bonds' carrying value. In the case of a repurchase, this is because a bond's market value changes as the market interest rate changes.

If there is a difference between the bonds' carrying value and the amount paid in a bond retirement transaction, the issuer must record a gain or loss equal to the difference. For example, assume that a company issued callable bonds with a par value of $100,000. The call option required the issuer to pay a call premium of $3,000 to the bondholders in addition to the par value. Also assume that immediately after a June 30 interest payment, the bonds had a carrying value of $104,500. Then, on July 1, the issuer called all of the bonds and paid $103,000 to the bondholders. The issuer must recognize a $1,500 gain as a result of the difference between the bonds' carrying value of $104,500 and the retirement price of $103,000. This entry records the bond retirement:

July	1	Bonds Payable	100,000.00	
		Premium on Bonds Payable	4,500.00	
		Gain on Retirement of Bonds		1,500.00
		Cash		103,000.00
		To record the retirement of bonds.		

Although a company generally must call all of its bonds when it exercises a call option, it may retire as many or as few bonds as it desires through open market transactions. If it retires less than the entire set of bonds, it recognizes a gain or loss for the difference between the carrying value of those bonds and the amount paid to acquire them.

MORTGAGES AS SECURITY FOR BONDS AND NOTES

Earlier in this chapter, we said that some bonds are secured by collateral agreements, while others, called *debentures*, are not secured. These risk-reducing arrangements also are widely used for notes payable, including car and home loans. Unsecured bonds and notes are more risky because the issuer's obligation to pay interest and principal has the same priority as all other unsecured liabilities in the event of bankruptcy. If the company's financial troubles leave it unable to pay its debts in full, the unsecured creditors (including the holders of debentures) lose a proportion or all of their balances.

Thus, a company's ability to borrow money with or without collateral agreements depends on its credit rating. In many cases, debt financing is simply unavailable if the borrower cannot provide security to the creditors with a collateral agreement. Even if unsecured loans are available, the creditors are likely to charge a higher rate of interest to compensate for the additional risk. To borrow the funds at a more economical rate, many notes payable and bonds are secured by collateral agreements called *mortgages*.

A **mortgage** is a legal agreement that helps protect a lender if a borrower fails to make the required payments on a note payable or on bonds payable. A mortgage gives the lender the right to be paid out of the cash proceeds from the sale of the borrower's specific assets identified in the mortgage.

A separate legal document, called the *mortgage contract*, describes the terms of a mortgage. The mortgage contract is given to the lender who accepts a note payable or to the trustee for the bondholders. Mortgage contracts usually require a borrower to pay all property taxes on the mortgaged assets, to maintain them properly, and to carry adequate insurance against fire and other types of losses. These requirements are designed to keep the property from losing value and thus avoid diminishing the lender's security. Importantly, mortgage contracts grant the lender the right to *foreclose* on the property if the borrower fails to pay in accordance with the terms of the debt agreement. If a foreclosure occurs, a court either orders the property to be sold or simply grants legal title of the mortgaged property to the lender. If the property is sold, the proceeds are first applied to court costs and then to the claims of the mortgage holder. If there are any additional proceeds, the borrower is entitled to receive them. However, this cash is subject to any claims from the company's unsecured creditors.

Given the relevance of information about a company's security agreements with its lenders, the notes to the financial statements may describe the amounts of assets pledged as security against liabilities. The next section describes a ratio that can be used to assess a borrower's situation with respect to its security agreements.

Progress Check

17-14 Six years ago, a company issued $500,000 of 6%, 8-year bonds at a price of 95. The current carrying value is $493,750. The company retired 50% of the bonds by buying them on the open market at a price of 102 1/2. What is the amount of gain or loss on retirement of the bonds?

17-15 A mortgage is
   a. A promissory note that requires the borrower to make a series of payments consisting of interest and principal.
   b. A legal agreement that protects a lender by giving the lender the right to be paid out of the cash proceeds from the sale of specific assets owned by the borrower.
   c. A company's long-term liability that requires periodic payments of interest and a final payment of its par value when it matures.

As you have learned in this chapter, creditors can reduce their risk with agreements that can force borrowers to sell specific assets to settle overdue debts. Investors who consider buying a company's secured debt obligations need to determine whether the pledged assets of the debtor provide adequate security. One method of evaluating this is to calculate the ratio of **pledged assets to secured liabilities**. This is calculated by dividing the book value of the company's assets pledged as collateral by the book value of the liabilities secured by these collateral agreements:

$$\text{Pledged assets to secured liabilities} = \frac{\text{Book value of pledged assets}}{\text{Book value of secured liabilities}}$$

For example, suppose that a company has assets with a book value of $2,300,000 pledged against loans with a balance of $1,000,000. The ratio is

USING THE INFORMATION— PLEDGED ASSETS TO SECURED LIABILITIES

LO 5

Calculate and describe how to use the ratio of pledged assets to secured liabilities.

$2,300,000/$1,000,000 = 2.3$ to 1. Although there are no hard and fast guidelines for interpreting the values of this ratio, 2.3 to 1 may be sufficiently high to provide the existing secured creditors with some comfort that the debts are safely covered by the assets.

The pledging of assets for the benefit of secured creditors also affects unsecured creditors. As an increasing portion of the assets are pledged, the unsecured creditors are less likely to receive a full repayment. In evaluating their position, unsecured creditors may gain some information from the ratio of pledged assets to secured creditors. For two reasons, an unusually large ratio may suggest that the unsecured creditors are at risk. First, secured creditors may have demanded an unusually large ratio because the value of the assets in liquidation is low. Second, the secured creditors may perceive that the ability of the company to meet its obligations from operating cash flows is weak.

In using this ratio, a creditor must be aware that the reported book value of the company's assets is unlikely to reflect their fair value. Thus, creditors would have better information if they could determine the assets' current market value and then use it in the ratio instead of book value. Major creditors may be able to get this information directly by asking the borrower to provide recent appraisals or other evidence of the assets' fair value. Other creditors may not have this option. In addition, using the ratio requires knowledge about the amounts of secured liabilities and pledged assets. This information may or may not be clearly identified in the financial statements.

Progress Check

17-16   At the end of 1996, A to Z Company has $350,000 of unsecured liabilities and $575,000 of secured liabilities. The book value of pledged assets is $1,265,000. Calculate the ratio of pledged assets to secured liabilities.

17-17   Would the secured creditors or the unsecured creditors be more concerned if A to Z's ratio of pledged assets to secured liabilities was 1.7 to 1 the previous year?

PRESENT VALUE TABLES

Table 17-1
Present Value of $1

	Rate							
Periods	**3%**	**4%**	**5%**	**6%**	**7%**	**8%**	**10%**	**12%**
1	0.9709	0.9615	0.9524	0.9434	0.9346	0.9259	0.9091	0.8929
2	0.9426	0.9246	0.9070	0.8900	0.8734	0.8573	0.8264	0.7972
3	0.9151	0.8890	0.8638	0.8396	0.8163	0.7938	0.7513	0.7118
4	0.8885	0.8548	0.8227	0.7921	0.7629	0.7350	0.6830	0.6355
5	0.8626	0.8219	0.7835	0.7473	0.7130	0.6806	0.6209	0.5674
6	0.8375	0.7903	0.7462	0.7050	0.6663	0.6302	0.5645	0.5066
7	0.8131	0.7599	0.7107	0.6651	0.6227	0.5835	0.5132	0.4523
8	0.7894	0.7307	0.6768	0.6274	0.5820	0.5403	0.4665	0.4039
9	0.7664	0.7026	0.6446	0.5919	0.5439	0.5002	0.4241	0.3606
10	0.7441	0.6756	0.6139	0.5584	0.5083	0.4632	0.3855	0.3220
20	0.5537	0.4564	0.3769	0.3118	0.2584	0.2145	0.1486	0.1037
30	0.4120	0.3083	0.2314	0.1741	0.1314	0.0994	0.0573	0.0334

Table 17-2   Present Value of an Annuity of $1

Payments	Rate							
	3%	4%	5%	6%	7%	8%	10%	12%
1	0.9709	0.9615	0.9524	0.9434	0.9346	0.9259	0.9091	0.8929
2	1.9135	1.8861	1.8594	1.8334	1.8080	1.7833	1.7355	1.6901
3	2.8286	2.7751	2.7232	2.6730	2.6243	2.5771	2.4869	2.4018
4	3.7171	3.6299	3.5460	3.4651	3.3872	3.3121	3.1699	3.0373
5	4.5797	4.4518	4.3295	4.2124	4.1002	3.9927	3.7908	3.6048
6	5.4172	5.2421	5.0757	4.9173	4.7665	4.6229	4.3553	4.1114
7	6.2303	6.0021	5.7864	5.5824	5.3893	5.2064	4.8684	4.5638
8	7.0197	6.7327	6.4632	6.2098	5.9713	5.7466	5.3349	4.9676
9	7.7861	7.4353	7.1078	6.8017	6.5152	6.2469	5.7590	5.3282
10	8.5302	8.1109	7.7217	7.3601	7.0236	6.7101	6.1446	5.6502
20	14.8775	13.5903	12.4622	11.4699	10.5940	9.8181	8.5136	7.4694
30	19.6004	17.2920	15.3725	13.7648	12.4090	11.2578	9.4269	8.0552

LO 1. Calculate the payments on an installment note payable and describe their effects on the financial statements. Typical installment notes require one of two alternative payment patterns: *(a)* payments that include interest plus equal amounts of principal or *(b)* equal payments. In either case, interest is allocated to each period in a note's life by multiplying the carrying value by the original interest rate. If a note is repaid with equal payments, the payment's size is found by dividing the borrowed amount by the annuity table value for the interest rate and the number of payments.

LO 2. Describe the various characteristics of different types of bonds and prepare entries to record bond issuances and retirements. Bonds usually are issued to many investors. Serial bonds mature at different points in time. Companies that issue sinking fund bonds must accumulate a fund of assets to use to pay out the par value of the bonds at the maturity date. Convertible bonds can be exchanged by the bondholders for shares of the issuing company. When bonds are registered, each bondholder's name and address is recorded by the issuing company. In contrast, bearer bonds are payable to whoever holds the bonds.

Some bonds are secured by mortgages on the issuer's assets while other bonds, called debentures, are unsecured. When bonds are sold between interest dates, the accrued interest is collected from the purchasers, who are then refunded that amount on the next interest payment date. Bonds can be retired early by the issuer by exercising a call option or by purchases on the open market. The issuer must recognize a gain or loss for the difference between the amount paid out and the bonds' carrying value.

LO 3. Estimate the price of bonds issued at a discount and describe their effects on the issuer's financial statements. The cash paid to bondholders on semiannual interest payment dates is calculated as one-half of the result of multiplying the par value of the bonds by their contract interest rate. The market value of a bond can be estimated by using the market interest rate to find the present values of the interest payments and the par value. Bonds are issued at

SUMMARY OF THE CHAPTER IN TERMS OF LEARNING OBJECTIVES

a discount when the contract rate is less than the market rate. Then, the issuer records the issuance with a credit to the Bonds Payable account for the par value and a debit to Discount on Bonds Payable. The amount of interest assigned to each interest period can be allocated with the straight-line method if the result is not materially different from the results of applying the interest method. The interest method assigns interest to a period by multiplying the beginning carrying value by the original market interest rate.

LO 4. **Estimate the price of bonds issued at a premium and describe their effects on the issuer's financial statements.** Bonds are issued at a premium when the contract rate is higher than the market interest rate. The issuer records the premium as a credit to Premium on Bonds Payable. The balance of this account is reduced over the life of the bonds through the interest allocation process.

LO 5. **Calculate and describe how to use the ratio of pledged assets to secured liabilities.** Secured and unsecured creditors are both concerned about the relationship between the amounts of assets owned by the debtor and the amounts of secured liabilities. The secured creditors are safer when the ratio of pledged assets to secured liabilities is larger, while the risks of unsecured creditors may be increased in this circumstance.

DEMONSTRATION PROBLEM

The Staley Tile Company patented and successfully test-marketed a new product. However, to expand its ability to produce and market the product, the company needed to raise $800,000 of additional financing. On January 1, 1996, the company borrowed the money under these arrangements:

a. Staley signed a $400,000, 10% installment note that will be repaid with five equal annual installments. The payments will be made on December 31 of 1996 through 2000.

b. Staley issued five-year bonds with a par value of $400,000. The bonds have a 12% annual contract rate and pay interest on June 30 and December 31. The annual market interest rate for the bonds was 10% on January 1, 1996.

Required

1. For the installment note, *(a)* calculate the size of each payment, *(b)* prepare an amortization table, and *(c)* present the entry for the first payment.

2. For the bonds, *(a)* estimate the issue price of the bonds; *(b)* present the January 1, 1996, entry to record issuing the bonds; *(c)* prepare an amortization table using the interest method; *(d)* present the June 30, 1996, entry to record the first payment of interest; and *(e)* present an entry to record retiring the bonds at the call price of $416,000 on January 1, 1998.

Planning the Solution

•   For the installment note, divide the borrowed amount by the annuity table factor (from Table 17–2 on page 788) for 10% and five payments. Prepare a table similar to Illustration 17–2 and use the numbers in the first line for the entry.

•   For the bonds, estimate the issue price by using the market rate to find the present values of the bonds' cash flows. Then, use this result to record issuing the bonds. Next, develop an amortization table like Illustration 17–7, and use it to get the numbers that you need for the journal entry. Finally, use the table to find the carrying value as of the date of the retirement of the bonds that you need for the journal entry.

Part 1:
Payment = Note balance/Table value = $400,000/3.7908 = $105,519
Table value is for 5 payments and an interest rate of 10%.

Table:

Solution to Demonstration Problem

	(a)	(b)		(c)		(d)	(e)
		Payments					
Period Ending	Beginning Balance	Debit Interest Expense	+	Debit Notes Payable	=	Credit Cash	Ending Balance
1996	$400,000	$ 40,000		$ 65,519		$105,519	$334,481
1997	334,481	33,448		72,071		105,519	262,410
1998	262,410	26,241		79,278		105,519	183,132
1999	183,132	18,313		87,206		105,519	95,926
2000	95,926	9,593		95,926		105,519	0
Total		$127,595		$400,000		$527,595	

Journal entry:

1996				
Dec.	31	Interest Expense	40,000.00	
		Notes Payable	65,519.00	
		Cash		105,519.00
		To record first installment payment.		

Part 2:
Estimated issue price of the bonds:

Cash Flow	Table	Table Value	Amount	Present Value
Par value	17–1	0.6139	$400,000	$245,560
Interest (annuity)	17–2	7.7217	24,000	185,321
Total				$430,881

Table value is for 10 payments and an interest rate of 5%.
Journal entry:

1996				
Jan.	1	Cash	430,881.00	
		Premium on Bonds Payable		30,881.00
		Bonds Payable		400,000.00
		Sold bonds at a premium.		

Table:

Period Ending	(a) Beginning Balance *Prior (e)*	**Payments**		(d) Credit Cash *6% × $400,000*	(e) Ending Balance *(a) – (c)*
		(b) Debit Interest Expense *5% × (a)* +	(c) Debit Premium on Bonds = *(d) – (b)*		
June 30, 1996	$430,881	$ 21,544	$ 2,456	$ 24,000	$428,425
Dec. 31, 1996	428,425	21,421	2,579	24,000	425,846
June 30, 1997	425,846	21,292	2,708	24,000	423,138
Dec. 31, 1997	423,138	21,157	2,843	24,000	420,295
June 30, 1998	420,295	21,015	2,985	24,000	417,310
Dec. 31, 1998	417,310	20,866	3,134	24,000	414,176
June 30, 1999	414,176	20,709	3,291	24,000	410,885
Dec. 31, 1999	410,885	20,544	3,456	24,000	407,429
June 30, 2000	407,429	20,371	3,629	24,000	403,800
Dec. 31, 2000	403,800	20,200*	3,800	24,000	400,000
Total		$209,119	$30,881	$240,000	

*Adjusted for rounding.

Journal entries:

1996 June	30	Interest Expense	21,544.00		
		Premium on Bonds Payable	2,456.00		
		Cash		24,000.00	
		Paid semiannual interest on the bonds.			
1998 Jan.	1	Bonds Payable	400,000.00		
		Premium on Bonds Payable	20,295.00		
		Cash		416,000.00	
		Gain on Retirement of Bonds		4,295.00	
		To record the retirement of bonds (carrying value determined as of December 31, 1997).			

GLOSSARY

Bearer bonds bonds that are made payable to whoever holds them (called the bearer); these bonds are not registered. p. 769

Bond a company's long-term liability that requires periodic payments of interest and final payment of its par value when it matures; usually issued in denominations of $1,769. p. 767

Bond indenture the contract between the bond issuer and the bondholders; it identifies the rights and obligations of the parties. p. 770

Callable bonds bonds that give the issuer an option of retiring them before they mature. p. 785

Carrying amount the net amount at which bonds are reflected on the balance sheet; equals the par value of the bonds less any unamortized discount or plus any unamortized premium. p. 775

Contract rate the interest rate specified in the bond indenture; it is multiplied by the par value of the bonds to determine the amount of interest to be paid each year. p. 773

Convertible bonds bonds that can be exchanged by the bondholders for a fixed number of shares of the issuing company's common shares. p. 769

Coupon bonds bonds that have interest coupons attached to their certificates; the bondholders detach the coupons when they mature and present them to a bank for collection. p. 769

Debentures unsecured bonds that are supported by only the general credit standing of the issuer. p. 770

Discount on bonds payable the difference between the par value of a bond and its lower issue price or paying amount; arises when the contract rate is lower than the market rate. p. 774

Installment notes promissory notes that require the borrower to make a series of payments consisting of interest and principal. p. 762

Interest method (interest allocation) a method that allocates interest expense to a reporting period by multiplying the beginning carrying value by the original market interest rate. p. 778

Market rate the consensus interest rate that borrowers are willing to pay and that lenders are willing to earn at the level of risk inherent in the bonds. p. 773

Mortgage a legal agreement that protects a lender by giving the lender the right to be paid out of the cash proceeds from the sale of the borrower's specific assets identified in the mortgage. p. 786

Par value of a bond the amount that the bond issuer agrees to pay at maturity and the amount on which interest payments are based; also called the *face amount.* p. 767

Pledged assets to secured liabilities the ratio of the book value of a company's pledged assets to the book value of its secured liabilities. p. 787

Premium on bonds payable the difference between the par value of a bond and its higher issue price or paying amount; arises when the contract rate is higher than the market rate. p. 781

Registered bonds bonds owned by investors whose names and addresses are recorded by the issuing company; the interest payments are made with checks to the bondholders. p. 769

Serial bonds bonds that mature at different dates with the result that the entire debt is repaid gradually over a number of years. p. 768

Sinking fund bonds bonds that require the issuing company to make deposits to a separate pool of assets; the bondholders are repaid at maturity from the assets in this pool. p. 768

Straight-line method (interest allocation) a method that allocates an equal amount of interest to each accounting period in the life of bonds. p. 776

SYNONYMOUS TERMS

Contract interest rate coupon rate; stated rate; nominal rate.

Principal of a bond par value; face value.

QUESTIONS

1. Describe two alternative payment patterns for installment notes.
2. What is the difference between notes payable and bonds payable?
3. What is the primary difference between a share and a bond?
4. What is the main advantage of issuing bonds instead of obtaining funds from the company's owners?
5. What is a bond indenture? What provisions are usually included in an indenture?
6. What are the duties of a trustee for bondholders?
7. Why does a company that issues bonds between interest dates collect accrued interest from the bonds' purchasers?
8. What are the *contract* and *market interest rates* for bonds?
9. What factors affect the market interest rates for bonds?
10. If you know the par value of bonds, the contract rate, and the market interest rate, how can you estimate the market value of the bonds?
11. Does the straight-line or interest method produce an allocation of interest that creates a constant rate of interest over a bond's life? Explain your answer.

12. What is the cash price of a $2,000 bond that is sold at 98^1/$_4$? What is the cash price of a $6,000 bond that is sold at 101^1/$_2$?

13. Explain why unsecured creditors should be alarmed when the pledged assets to secured liabilities ratio for a borrower has grown substantially.

14. Refer to the financial statements for Geac Computer Corporation Ltd., presented in Appendix I. Is there any indication in the balance sheet that the company has issued bonds?

QUICK STUDY (Five-Minute Exercises)

QS 17–1
(LO 1)

The owner of Ripley's Restaurant borrowed $80,000 from a bank and signed an installment note that calls for eight annual payments of equal size, with the first payment due one year after the note was signed. Use Table 17–2 on page 789 to calculate the size of the annual payment for each of the following annual interest rates: *a.* 5%, *b.* 7%, *c.* 10%

QS 17–2
(LO 2)

Match the following terms and phrases by entering the letter of the phrase that best describes each term in the blank next to the term.

_____ serial bonds	_____ bearer bonds
_____ sinking fund bonds	_____ secured bonds
_____ convertible bonds	_____ debentures
_____ registered bonds	_____ bond indenture

a. Issuer records the bondholders' names and addresses.

b. Unsecured; backed only by the issuer's general credit standing.

c. Varying maturity dates.

d. Identifies the rights and responsibilities of the issuer and bondholders.

e. Can be exchanged for the issuer's common shares.

f. Unregistered; interest is paid to whoever possesses them.

g. Issuer maintains a separate pool of assets from which bondholders are paid at maturity.

h. Specific assets of the issuer are mortgaged as collateral.

QS 17–3
(LO 3)

The Carraway Co. issued 10%, 10-year bonds with a par value of $200,000. On the issue date, the annual market rate of interest for the bonds was 12%, and they sold for $177,059. The straight-line method is used to allocate the interest.

a. What is the total amount of interest expense that will be recognized over the life of the bonds?

b. What is the amount of interest expense recorded on the first interest payment date?

QS 17–4
(LO 4)

The Downhome Co. issued 12%, 10-year bonds with a par value of $60,000 and semiannual interest payments. On the issue date, the annual market rate of interest for the bonds was 10%, and they were sold for $67,478. The interest method is used to allocate the interest.

a. What is the total amount of interest expense that will be recognized over the life of the bonds?

b. What is the amount of interest expense recorded on the first interest payment date?

Use the following information to compute the ratio of pledged assets to secured liabilities for both companies:

	Red Co.	Blue Co.
Pledged assets	$155,000	$ 87,000
Total assets	180,000	300,000
Secured liabilities	90,000	66,000
Unsecured liabilities	140,000	160,000

EXERCISES

When solving the following exercises, round all dollar amounts to the nearest whole dollar. Also assume that none of the companies uses reversing entries.

On December 31, 1996, Acorn Co. borrowed $16,000 by signing a four-year, 5% installment note. The note requires annual payments of accrued interest and equal amounts of principal on December 31 of each year from 1997 through 2000.

a.   How much principal will be included in each of the four payments?

b.   Prepare an amortization table for this installment note like the one presented in Illustration 17–1 on page 764.

Use the data in Exercise 17–1 to prepare journal entries that Acorn Co. would make to record the loan on December 31, 1996, and the four payments starting on December 31, 1997, through the final payment on December 31, 2000.

On December 31, 1996, Gates Co. borrowed $10,000 by signing a four-year, 5% installment note. The note requires four equal payments of accrued interest and principal on December 31 of each year from 1997 through 2000.

a.   Calculate the size of each of the four equal payments.

b.   Prepare an amortization table for this installment note like the one presented in Illustration 17–2 on page 765.

Use the data in Exercise 17–3 to prepare journal entries that Gates Co. would make to record the loan on December 31, 1996, and the four payments starting on December 31, 1997, through the final payment on December 31, 2000.

On January 1, 1996, the Tennyson Co. issued $300,000 of 20-year bonds that pay 8% interest semiannually on June 30 and December 31. The bonds were sold to investors at their par value.

a.   How much interest will the issuer pay to the holders of these bonds every six months?

b.   Show the journal entries that the issuer would make to record (1) the issuance of the bonds on January 1, 1996, (2) the first interest payment on June 30, 1996, and (3) the second interest payment on December 31, 1996.

Exercise 17–6
Journal entries for bond issuance with accrued interest
(LO 2)

On March 1, 1996, the Tennyson Co. issued $300,000 of 20-year bonds dated January 1, 1996. The bonds pay 8% interest semiannually on June 30 and December 31. The bonds were sold to investors at their par value plus the two months' interest that had accrued since the original issue date.

a.   How much accrued interest was paid to the issuer by the purchasers of these bonds on March 1, 1996?

b.   Show the journal entries that the issuer would make to record (1) the issuance of the bonds on March 1, 1996; (2) the first interest payment on June 30, 1996; and (3) the second interest payment on December 31, 1996.

Exercise 17–7
Calculating the present value of a bond and recording the issuance
(LO 3)

The Sesame Co. issued bonds with a par value of $150,000 on their initial issue date. The bonds mature in 15 years and pay 8% annual interest in two semiannual payments. On the issue date, the annual market rate of interest for the bonds turned out to be 10%.

a.   What is the size of the semiannual interest payment for these bonds?

b.   How many semiannual interest payments will be made on these bonds over their life?

c.   Use the information about the interest rates to decide whether the bonds were issued at par, a discount, or a premium.

d.   Estimate the market value of the bonds as of the date they were issued.

e.   Present the journal entry that would be made to record the bonds' issuance.

Exercise 17–8
Straight-line allocation of interest for bonds sold at a discount
(LO 3)

The Columbia Company issued bonds with a par value of $50,000 on January 1, 1997. The annual contract rate on the bonds is 8%, and the interest is paid semiannually. The bonds mature after three years. The annual market interest rate at the date of issuance was 12%, and the bonds were sold for $45,085.

a.   What is the amount of the original discount on these bonds?

b.   How much total interest expense will be recognized over the life of these bonds?

c.   Present an amortization table like Illustration 17–4 on page 777 for these bonds; use the straight-line method of allocating the interest and amortizing the discount.

Exercise 17–9
Interest method allocation of interest for bonds sold at a discount
(LO 3)

The Chatham Company issued bonds with a par value of $30,000 on January 1, 1997. The annual contract rate on the bonds is 8%, and the interest is paid semiannually. The bonds mature after three years. The annual market interest rate at the date of issuance was 10%, and the bonds were sold for $28,477.

a.   What is the amount of the original discount on these bonds?

b.   How much total interest expense will be recognized over the life of these bonds?

c.   Present an amortization table like Illustration 17–5 on page 779 for these bonds; use the interest method of allocating the interest and amortizing the discount.

Exercise 17–10
Calculating the present value of a bond and recording the issuance
(LO 3)

The Allan Co. issued bonds with a par value of $25,000 on their initial issue date. The bonds mature in 15 years and pay 8% annual interest in two semiannual payments. On the issue date, the annual market rate of interest for the bonds turned out to be 6%.

a. What is the size of the semiannual interest payment for these bonds?

b. How many semiannual interest payments will be made on these bonds over their life?

c. Use the information about the interest rates to decide whether the bonds were issued at par, a discount, or a premium.

d. Estimate the market value of the bonds as of the date they were issued.

e. Present the journal entry that would be made to record the bonds' issuance.

The Cypress Company issued bonds with a par value of $40,000 on January 1, 1997. The annual contract rate on the bonds was 12%, and the interest is paid semiannually. The bonds mature after three years. The annual market interest rate at the date of issuance was 10%, and the bonds were sold for $42,030.

Exercise 17–11
Interest method allocation of interest for bonds sold at a premium
(LO 3)

a. What is the amount of the original premium on these bonds?

b. How much total interest expense will be recognized over the life of these bonds?

c. Present an amortization table like Illustration 17–7 on page 000 for these bonds; use the interest method of allocating the interest and amortizing the premium.

On January 1, 1996, the Amsterdam Co. issued $700,000 of its 10%, 15-year bonds at the price of 95$\frac{1}{2}$. Three years later, on January 1, 1999, the company retired 30% of these bonds by buying them on the open market at 105$\frac{3}{4}$. All interest had been properly accounted for and paid through December 31, 1998, the day before the purchase. The company used the straight-line method to allocate the interest and amortize the original discount.

Exercise 17–12
Retiring bonds payable
(LO 2)

a. How much money did the company receive when it first issued the entire group of bonds?

b. How large was the original discount on the entire group of bonds?

c. How much amortization did the company record on the entire group of bonds between January 1, 1996, and December 31, 1998?

d. What was the carrying value of the entire group of bonds as of the close of business on December 31, 1998? What was the carrying value of the retired bonds on this date?

e. How much money did the company pay on January 1, 1999, to purchase the bonds that it retired?

f. What is the amount of the gain or loss from retiring the bonds?

g. Provide the general journal entry that the company would make to record the retirement of the bonds.

The Schaffner Co. issued bonds with a par value of $100,000 and a five–year life on May 1, 1996. The contract interest rate is 7%. The bonds pay interest on October 31 and April 30. They were issued at a price of $95,948.

Exercise 17–13
Straight-line amortization table and accrued interest
(LO 3, 4, 5)

a. Prepare an amortization table for these bonds that covers their entire life. Use the straight-line method of allocating interest.

b. Show the journal entries that the issuer would make to record the first two interest payments and to accrue interest as of December 31, 1996.

PROBLEMS

When solving the following problems, round all dollar amounts to the nearest whole dollar. Also assume that none of the companies uses reversing entries.

Problem 17–1
Installment notes
(LO 1)

On November 30, 1996, the Stanley Company borrowed $50,000 from a bank by signing a four-year installment note bearing interest at 12%. The terms of the note require equal payments each year on November 30.

Required

1. Calculate the size of each installment payment. (Use Table 17–2 on page 789.)
2. Complete an installment note amortization schedule for this note similar to Illustration 17–2 on page 000.
3. Present the journal entries that the borrower would make to record accrued interest as of December 31, 1996 (the end of the annual reporting period) and the first payment on the note.
4. Now assume that the note does not require equal payments but does require four payments that include accrued interest and an equal amount of principal in each payment. Complete an installment note amortization schedule for this note similar to Illustration 17–1 on page 764. Present the journal entries that the borrower would make to record accrued interest as of December 31, 1996 (the end of the annual reporting period) and the first payment on the note.

Problem 17–2
Calculating bond prices and recording issuances with journal entries
(LO 2, 3, 4)

Helmer Co. issued a group of bonds on January 1, 1996, that pay interest semiannually on June 30 and December 31. The par value of the bonds is $40,000, the annual contract rate is 8%, and the bonds mature in 10 years.

Required

For each of these three situations, *(a)* determine the issue price of the bonds and *(b)* show the journal entry that would record the issuance.

1. The market interest rate at the date of issuance was 6%.
2. The market interest rate at the date of issuance was 8%.
3. The market interest rate at the date of issuance was 10%.

Problem 17–3
Straight-line method of allocating interest and amortizing a bond discount
(LO 3)

Abbot Company issued $125,000 of bonds that pay 6% annual interest with two semiannual payments. The date of issuance was January 1, 1996, and the interest is paid on June 30 and December 31. The bonds mature after 10 years and were issued at the price of $108,014.

Required

1. Prepare a general journal entry to record the issuance of the bonds.
2. Determine the total interest expense that will be recognized over the life of these bonds.
3. Prepare the first four lines of an amortization table like Illustration 17–4 based on the straight-line method of allocating the interest.
4. Prepare the first four lines of a separate table that shows the beginning balance of the discount, the amount of straight-line amortization of the discount, and the ending balance.
5. Present the journal entries that the bond issuer would make to record the first two interest payments.

The Martin Company issued $50,000 of bonds that pay 4% annual interest with two semi-annual payments. The date of issuance was January 1, 1996, and the interest is paid on June 30 and December 31. The bonds mature after three years and were issued at the price of $47,292. The market interest rate was 6%.

Problem 17–4
Interest method of allocating bond interest and amortizing a discount
(LO 2, 3)

Required

Preparation component:

1. Prepare a general journal entry to record the issuance of the bonds.
2. Determine the total interest expense that will be recognized over the life of these bonds.
3. Prepare the first four lines of an amortization table like Illustration 17–5 based on the interest method.
4. Prepare the first four lines of a separate table that shows the beginning balance of the discount, the amount of interest method amortization of the discount, and the ending balance.
5. Present the journal entries that the bond issuer would make to record the first two interest payments.

Analysis component:

6. Instead of the facts described in the problem, assume that the market interest rate on January 1, 1996, was 3% instead of 6%. Without presenting any specific numbers, describe how this change would affect the amounts presented on the company's financial statements.

The Jones Company issued $100,000 of bonds that pay 9% annual interest with two semi-annual payments. The date of issuance was January 1, 1996, and the interest is paid on June 30 and December 31. The bonds mature after three years and were issued at the price of $102,619. The market interest rate was 8%.

Problem 17–5
Interest method of amortizing bond premium and retiring bonds
(LO 2, 4)

Required

1. Prepare a general journal entry to record the issuance of the bonds.
2. Determine the total interest expense that will be recognized over the life of these bonds.
3. Prepare the first four lines of an amortization table like Illustration 17–7 based on the interest method.
4. Prepare the first four lines of a separate table that shows the beginning balance of the premium, the amount of interest method amortization of the premium, and the ending balance.
5. Present the journal entries that the bond issuer would make to record the first two interest payments.
6. Present the journal entry that would be made to record the retirement of these bonds on December 31, 1997, at the price of 98.

The Briggs Company issued bonds with a par value of $80,000 and a five–year life on January 1, 1996. The bonds pay interest on June 30 and December 31. The contract interest rate is 8.5%. The bonds were issued at a price of $81,625. The market interest rate was 8% on the original issue date.

Problem 17–6
Bond premium amortization and finding the present value of remaining cash flows
(LO 3, 4)

Required

1. Prepare an amortization table for these bonds that covers their entire life. Use the interest method.

2. Show the journal entries that the issuer would make to record the first two interest payments.

3. Use the original market interest rate to calculate the present value of the remaining cash flows for these bonds as of December 31, 1998. Compare your answer with the amount shown on the amortization table as the balance for that date, and explain your findings.

Problem 17–7
Computing and analyzing ratio of pledged assets to secured liabilities
(LO 5)

On January 1, 1997, Alpha Company issued $45,000 of 10%, five-year bonds secured by a mortgage that specifies assets totaling $75,000 as collateral. On the same date, Beta Company isssued 10%, five-year bonds with a par value of $20,000. Beta is securing its bonds with a mortgage that includes $50,000 of pledged assets. Following is December 31, 1996, balance sheet information for both companies:

	Alpha Co.	Beta Co.
Total assets	$300,000*	$150,000†
Liabilities:		
Secured	$ 70,000	$ 25,000
Unsecured	50,000	55,000
Owners' equity	180,000	70,000
Total liabilities and owners' equity	$300,000	$150,000

*33% pledged
†42% pledged

Required

Preparation component:

1. Calculate the ratio of pledged assets to secured liabilities for each company after January 1, 1997.

Analysis component:

2. Which company's bonds appear to offer the best security? What other information might be helpful in evaluating the risk of the bonds?

Problem 17–8
Analytical essay
(LO 5)

An unsecured major creditor of the Hawkins Company has been monitoring the company's financing activities. Two years before, the ratio of its pledged assets to secured liabilities had been 1.4. One year ago, the ratio had climbed to 2.0, and the most recent financial report shows that the ratio value is now 3.1. Briefly describe what this trend may indicate about the company's activities, specifically from the point of view of this creditor.

Problem 17–9
Installment notes
(LO 1)

Bisk Hardware Manufacturing Company financed a major expansion of its production capacity by borrowing $220,000 from a bank and signing an installment note. The four-year, 14%, $220,000 note is dated April 30, 1996, and requires equal semiannual payments beginning on November 30, 1996

Required

1. Calculate the size of the installment payments. (Use Table 17–2 on page 789.)

2. Complete an installment note amortization schedule for the Bisk Hardware Manufacturing Company note similar to Illustration 17–2.

3. Prepare General Journal entries to record the first and last payments on the note.

4. Now assume that the note requires payments of accrued interest plus equal amounts of principal. Prepare General Journal entries to record the first and last payments on the note.

On December 31, 1996, SONOS Corporation sold $3.7 million of its own 12.9%, 10-year bonds. The bonds are dated December 31, 1996, with interest payable on each June 30 and December 31, and were sold to yield the buyers a 12% annual return. The corporation uses the straight-line method of amortizing the premium.

Problem 17–10
Straight-line method of amortizing bond premium
(LO 4)

Required

1. Calculate the price at which the bonds were sold. (Use present value Tables 17–1 and 17–2, pages 788 and 789.)

2. Prepare a bond premium amortization table similar to Illustration 17–7 but complete only the first two lines.

3. Prepare General Journal entries to record the sale of the bonds and the first two interest payments.

JBC Corporation sold $800,000 of its own 9.7%, five-year bonds on their date of issue, December 31, 1996. Interest is payable on each June 30 and December 31, and the bonds were sold at a price to yield the buyers a 10% annual return. The corporation uses the interest method of amortizing the discount.

Problem 17–11
Interest method of amortizing bond discount
(LO 3)

Required

1. Calculate the price at which the bonds were sold. (Use present value Tables 17–1 and 17–2, page 788.)

2. Prepare a bond discount amortization table similar to Illustration 17–5 but complete only the first two lines.

3. Prepare General Journal entries to record the sale of the bonds and the first two interest payments.

Prepare General Journal entries to record the following bond transactions of Eco Paper Corporation:

Problem 17–12
Interest method of amortizing bond premium; retirement of bonds
(LO 4, 5)

1996

Oct. 1   Sold $2.8 million par value of its own 10.7%, five-year bonds at a price to yield the buyers a 10% annual return. The bonds were dated October 1, 1996, with interest payable on each April 1 and October 1.

Dec. 31   Accrued interest on the bonds and amortized the premium for October through December 1996. The interest method was used to amortize the premium.

1997

Apr. 1   Paid the semiannual interest on the bonds.

Oct. 1   Paid the semiannual interest on the bonds.

1998

Oct. 1   After paying the semiannual interest on the bonds on this date, Eco Paper Corporation purchased one fourth of the bonds at 101¾ and retired them. (Present only the entry to record the purchase and retirement of the bonds.)

Problem 17–13
Comparison of straight-line and interest methods
(LO 3, 4)

On December 31, 1996, Trask Chemical Company sold $7 million of 10-year, 12.5% bonds payable at a price that reflected a 12% market rate of bond interest. The bonds pay interest on June 30 and December 31. Use present value Tables 17–1 and 17–2 (page 788) as needed in calculating your answers.

Required

1. Present a General Journal entry to record the sale of the bonds.

2. Present General Journal entries to record the first and second payments of interest on June 30, 1997, and on December 31, 1997, using the straight-line method to amortize the premium or discount.

3. Present General Journal entries to record the first and second payments of interest on June 30, 1997, and on December 31, 1997, using the interest method to amortize the premium or discount.

4. Prepare a schedule similar to the table in Illustration 17–6 on page 780. It should have columns for the beginning-of-period carrying amount, interest expense to be recorded, and interest expense as a percentage of carrying amount, as calculated under (a) the interest method, and (b) the straight-line method. In completing the schedule, present the amounts for the six-month periods ending on June 30, 1997, and December 31, 1997.

Problem 17–14
Analytical essay
(LO 3, 4, 5)

Review the transactions presented in Problem 17–12 for Eco Paper Corporation. Assume now that on October 1, 1996, the market rate of bond interest was 13% instead of 10%. Describe how the entries to record the sale of the bonds and the December 31, 1996, accrual of interest are different as a result of this change in the facts.

Problem 17–15
Analytical essay
(LO 4, 5)

Review the transactions presented in Problem 17–12 for Eco Paper Corporation. Assume now that on October 1, 1996, Eco sold $2.8 million of its own 10%, 10-year bonds instead of 10.7%, 5-year bonds. Describe how the entries to record the sale of the bonds and the December 31, 1996, accrual of interest are different as a result of this change in the facts.

PROVOCATIVE PROBLEMS

Provocative Problem 17–1
Management decision case
(LO 2, 3, 4)

Star Manufacturing Company is planning major additions to its operating capacity and needs approximately $400,000 to finance the expansion. The company has been considering three alternative proposals for issuing bonds that pay annual interest over the eight years in their lives. The alternatives are:

Plan A: Issue $400,000 of 8% bonds.
Plan B: Issue $450,000 of 6% bonds.
Plan C: Issue $360,000 of 10% bonds.

The market rate of interest for all of these bonds is expected to be 8%.

Required

1. For each plan, calculate:
    a. The expected cash proceeds from issuing the bonds.
    b. The expected annual cash outflow for interest.
    c. The expected interest expense for the first year. (Use the interest method to amortize bond premium or discount.)
    d. The amount that must be paid at maturity.
2. Which plans have the smallest and largest cash demands on the company prior to the final payment at maturity? Which plans require the smallest and largest payment at maturity?

The Angela Company issued $500,000 of zero-coupon bonds on January 1, 1996. These bonds are scheduled to mature seven years later on December 31, 2002. Under the terms of the bond agreement, the company will pay out $500,000 to the bondholders on the maturity date without making any periodic interest payments. The market rate of interest for these bonds was 10% when they were issued.

Provocative Problem 17–2
Financial reporting problem
(LO 3)

Required

1. Estimate the amount of cash that Angela received when it issued these bonds (assume annual compounding).
2. Present the journal entry that Angela's accountant would use to record the issuance of these bonds.
3. Calculate the total amount of interest expense that will be incurred over the life of the bonds.
4. Prepare an amortization table that shows the amount of interest expense that will be allocated to each year in the bonds' life with the interest method.
5. Present the journal entry that Angela's accountant would use to record the interest expense from these bonds for the year ended December 31, 1996.

The following information is taken from the 1995 annual report of The Oshawa Group Limited for the year ended January 28, 1995.

Provocative Problem 17–3
Financial statement analysis case
(LO 1)

Notes to Consolidated Financial Statements (millions)
4. Long-Term Debt

	1995	1994
Series "A" Debentures	$100.0	$100.0
Mortgages and loans payable	23.9	24.5
	123.9	124.5
Less current portion	0.4	0.3
	$123.5	$124.2

The unsecured Series "A" debentures due June 30, 2003, bear interest at a rate of 8.25% per annum and are redeemable in whole or in part, at any time, at the greater of par and a formula price based upon yields at the time of redemption.

The mortgages and loans payable bear interest at an average rate of 9.5% per annum with repayments of less than $2.5 in each of the four years commencing in 1997.

6. Interest

	1995 (53 weeks)	1994 (52 weeks)
Interest on long-term debt	$ 9.8	$6.4
Other interest	1.3	3.0
	$11.1	$9.4

Required

1. Are the debentures secured or unsecured?

2. What is the average interest rate on the mortgages and loans payable?

3. When do the debentures mature?

ANALYTICAL AND REVIEW PROBLEMS

A & R Problem 17–1

On June 30, 1996, Gorge Company issued $500,000 par value 8%, 10-year bonds convertible at the rate of a $1,000 bond for 50 common shares. The bonds were dated June 30, 1996, and were sold at a price to yield investors 10%. Interest was payable annually.

Required

1. Prepare entries on the following dates (Gorge uses straight-line to amortize discounts or premiums): June 30, 1996; December 31, 1996 (year-end); June 30, 1997; and June 30, 1998, to record conversion of 40 of the bonds.

2. On the assumption that Gorge used the interest method for amortization of discounts and premiums prepare entries on the following dates:

    a. December 31, 1996.

    b. June 30, 1997.

    c. June 30, 1998.

A & R Problem 17–2

On May 1, 1996, Tania Torres purchased as a long-term investment 20, $1,000 par value, 10% bonds, due 5½ years from date of purchase. Interest on the bonds is due and payable annually on November 1. Torres does not use discount or premium accounts related to investments of this nature and uses straight-line amortization.

Required

1. On the assumption that Torres' *total* cash outlay for the bonds was $17,040, prepare entries on the following 1996 dates:

    a. May 1, 1996.

    b. November 1, 1996.

    c. December 31, 1996 (year-end).

2. On the assumption that Torres' total cash outlay for the bonds was $22,520 prepare the entries on the following dates:

    a. May 1, 1996.

    b. November 1, 1996.

    December 31, 1996 (year-end).

CONCEPT TESTER

Test your understanding of the concepts introduced in this chapter by completing the following crossword puzzle.

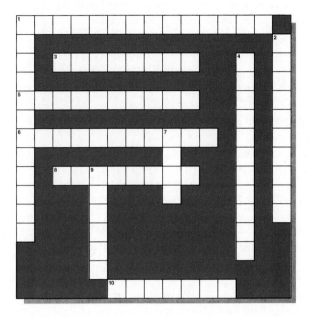

Across Clues

1. The net value of the bonds on the balance sheet (2 words).

3. Type of loan that protects the lender with specific assets of the borrower.

5. Bonds where the names and addresses of the investor are recorded by the issuing company.

6. Bonds that can be exchanged for shares.

8. The difference between the par value of the bonds and the lower issue price.

10. The difference between the par value of the bonds and the higher issue price.

Down Clues

1. The interest charge specified in the bond indenture (2 words).

2. The interest that borrowers are willing to pay and lenders willing to accept (2 words).

4. Bonds that require the borrower to make a series of principal payments.

7. A long-term liability requiring periodic interest payments and payment of principal on maturity.

9. Bonds that mature at different dates.

ANSWERS TO PROGRESS CHECKS

17–1 *c*

17–2 The interest portion of an installment payment equals the beginning balance for the period multiplied by the original interest rate.

17–3 On the balance sheet, the balances of the liability and cash are decreased. On the income statement, interest expense is increased.

17–4 *b*

17–5 Multiply the par value of the bonds by the contract rate of interest.

17–6 *a*

17–7 The bonds sell at a premium, and the purchasers pay more than the par value of the bonds.

17–8 *c.* (Present values of $100,000 and a semiannual annuity of $3,000, both at 4% for 10 semiannual periods.)

17–9 Cash 91,893.00
Discount on Bonds
   Payable 8,107.00
   Bonds Payable 100,000.00

17–10 *a.* $3,811 (Total interest equal to $38,107, or 10 payments of $3,000 plus the $8,107 discount, divided by 10 periods.)
   b. $3,676 (Beginning balance of $91,893 times 4% market interest rate.)

17–11 $110,592 (Present value of $100,000 plus the semiannual annuity of $8,000, both at 7% for 20 semiannual periods.)

17–12 *e.* (On June 30/97: $110,592 × 7% = $7,741 interest expense; $8,000 − $7,741 = $259 premium amortization; $110,592 − $259 = $110,333 ending balance. On Dec 31/97: $110,333 × 7% = $7,723 interest expense; $8,000 − $7,723 = $277 premium amortization.)

17–13 Bonds payable, 16%, due
December 31, 1997 . . . . . . $100,000
Plus premium 10,056* $110,056

*Beginning premium balance of $10,592 less $259 and $277 amortized on June 30/97 and Dec 31/97.

17–14 $9,375 loss (Difference between repurchase price of $256,250 [50% of ($500,000 × 102.5%)] and carrying value of $246,875 [50% of $493,750].)

17–15 *b*

17–16 2.2 to 1 ($1,265,000/$575,000)

17–17 Unsecured creditors. They may be less likely to receive full repayment if the portion of assets pledged increases.

CHAPTER 18

Statement of Changes in Financial Position

Cash flows in and out of a company as the company makes sales, collects receivables, pays expenses, buys and sells assets, borrows cash, issues stock, repays debt, and pays dividends. Information about the cash generated and spent is useful for evaluating the past and predicting the future.

*I*n continuing their study of Imperial Oil Limited's financial statements, Karen White and Mark Smith examined Imperial's Statement of Cash Flows. The excerpt from the statement shows the changing levels of Imperial's cash balances over the last five years. The statement also shows that although Imperial's operating activities provided cash of $783 million, there was a net decrease in cash due to the payment of $930 million in dividends during 1994 and repayment of long-term debt.

It is extremely important that management monitor the levels of cash and its sources and uses. The statement of changes in financial position enables both managers and investors to evaluate how a company has used its cash resources.

IMPERIAL OIL LIMITED—CONSOLIDATED STATEMENT OF CASH FLOWS
(in millions)

Year Ended December 31	1994	1993	1992	1991	1990
Cash: Increase (decrease)	$(196)	$340	$ (21)	$352	$ 34
At beginning of year	605	265	286	(66)	(100)
At end of year	$ 409	$605	$265	$286	(66)

LEARNING OBJECTIVES

After studying Chapter 18, you should be able to:

1. **Explain why cash flow information is important to decision making and describe the information in a statement of changes in financial position (SCFP) and the method used to disclose noncash investing and financing activities.**
2. **Calculate cash inflows and outflows by inspecting the noncash account balances and prepare an SCFP.**
3. **Prepare a working paper for an SCFP.**
4. **Define or explain the words or phrases listed in the chapter glossary.**

Up to this point in your study of accounting, profitability may have seemed to be the sole focus of business managers. Profits certainly are important to business success. However, a business cannot achieve or maintain profitability without carefully managing its cash. Cash is the lifeblood of a business enterprise. In a sense, cash is the fuel that keeps a business moving forward.

Managers and external parties such as investors and creditors pay close attention to a company's cash position and the events and transactions causing that position to change. Information about these events and transactions is reported in a financial statement called the **statement of changes in financial position** or statement of changes in financial position. By studying this chapter, you will learn how to prepare and interpret an SCFP. You will also begin to appreciate the importance of cash flow information as the basis for projecting future cash flows and making a variety of decisions.

WHY CASH FLOW INFORMATION IS IMPORTANT

LO 1

Explain why cash flow information is important to decision making and describe the information in a statement of changes in financial position and the method used to disclose noncash investing and financing activities.

Information about cash flows can influence decision makers in many ways. For example, if a company's regular operations bring in more cash than they use, investors will value the company higher than if property and equipment must be sold to finance operations. Information about cash flows can help creditors decide whether a company will have enough cash to pay its existing debts as they mature. And investors, creditors, managers, and other users of financial statements use cash flow information to evaluate a company's ability to meet unexpected obligations. Cash flow information is used by decision makers outside as well as inside the firm to evaluate a company's ability to take advantage of new business opportunities that may arise. Managers within a company use cash flow information to plan day-to-day operating activities and make long-term investment decisions.

The story of W. T. Grant Co. is a classic example of why cash flow information should be considered in predicting a firm's future stability and performance. From 1970 to 1973, Grant was reporting net income of more than $40 million per year. At the same time, it was experiencing an alarming decrease in cash provided by operations. Net cash *outflow* exceeded $90 million by 1973.[1] In spite of its earnings performance, Grant went bankrupt within a few years.

---

[1]James Largay and Clyde Stickney, "Cash Flow, Ratio Analysis and the W. T. Grant Company Bankruptcy," *Financial Analysts Journal,* July–August 1980, pp. 51–56.

As a Matter of Opinion

Mrs. Hagarty earned a BBA degree with a major in finance and marketing at Wilfrid Laurier University in Waterloo. Upon graduation, she joined the Commercial Banking Group at CIBC where she began her career as an Account Officer. She has also held regional office positions in Quality Management, Project Re-engineering and Marketing Management. Presently, she is a Commercial Account Manager in CIBC's Kitchener office where she manages a lending and investment portfolio of local small businesses.

When I entered the banking industry, there was much talk of "cash flow analysis" but at the end of the day, loan officers focused primarily on profitability and debt/equity ratio when reviewing financial statements. However, in the past few years, the analysis of cash flow has become increasingly important.

We now recognize that a lender must have a complete understanding of a borrower's cash flow in order to better assess borrowing needs and repayment sources. This requires historical and projected information about the major types of cash inflows and outflows.

The bottom line is that cash, and only cash, can repay loans. Accordingly, my job is to determine if a company can generate sufficient cash to service their debt. Over the years I have seen many companies, whose financial statements indicated good profitability, end up experiencing severe financial problems because the owners or managers lacked a good understanding of the company's cash flow. It is my challenge to help my clients properly understand and manage cash flow to their advantage.

Leanne L. Hagarty, BBA

The W. T. Grant investors who relied solely on earnings per share figures in the early 1970s were unpleasantly surprised. In more recent years, investors generally have learned to evaluate cash flows as well as income statement and balance sheet information as they make their investment decisions.[2]

The importance of cash flow information to decision makers has directly influenced the thinking of accounting authorities. For example, the CICA's *Financial Statement Concepts* clearly reflect the importance of cash flow information. The CICA stated that a business's financial statements should include information about

- How it obtains and spends cash.
- Its borrowing and repayment activities.
- The sale and repurchase of its ownership securities.
- Dividend payments and other distributions to its owners.
- Other factors affecting its liquidity or solvency.[3]

To accomplish these objectives, a financial statement is needed to summarize, classify, and report the periodic cash inflows and outflows of a business. This information is provided in a statement of changes in financial position.

---

[2]Marc J. Epstein and Moses L. Pava, "How Useful Is the Statement of Cash Flows," *Management Accounting*, July 1992.

[3]*CICA Handbook*, section 1540, "Statement of Changes in Financial Position," par. .01.

Illustration 18–1   Categories of Information in the Statement of Changes in Financial Position

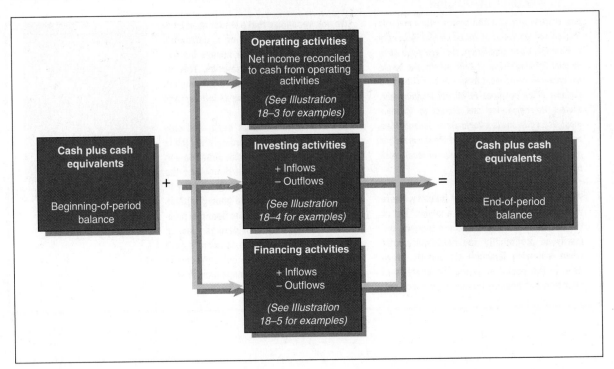

STATEMENT OF CHANGES IN FINANCIAL POSITION

In September 1985, the CICA's Accounting Standards Board revised section 1540 of the *Handbook*. This recommendation requires businesses to include a statement of changes in financial position (SCFP) in all financial reports that contain both a balance sheet and an income statement. The purpose of this statement is to present information about a company's cash receipts and disbursements during the reporting period.

Illustration 18–1 is a diagram of the information reported in an SCFP. The illustration shows three categories of cash flows: cash flows from operating activities, cash flows from investing activities, and cash flows from financing activities. Both inflows and outflows are included within each category. Because all cash inflows and outflows are reported, the statement reconciles the beginning-of-period and end-of-period balances of cash plus cash equivalents.

Direct Method of Presenting Cash Flows from Operating Activities

When preparing a statement of changes in financial position, you can calculate the net cash provided (or used) by operating activities two different ways. One is the *direct method of calculating net cash provided (or used) by operating activities.* The other is the indirect method. When using the direct method, you separately list each major class of operating cash receipts (for example, cash received from customers) and each major class of cash payments (such as payments for merchandise). Then, you subtract the payments from the receipts to determine the net cash provided (or used) by operating activities.

Indirect Method of Presenting Cash Flows from Operating Activities

The indirect method of calculating **net cash provided (or used) by operating activities** is the preferred method in Canada because the *Handbook* indicates that the amount of cash from operations should be reconciled to the income statement.[4] Thus we explain the indirect method.

When using the indirect method, list net income first. Next, adjust it for items that are necessary to reconcile net income to the net cash provided (or used) by operating activities. For example, in the calculation of net income, we subtract amortization expense. However, amortization expense does not involve a current cash payment. Therefore, add amortization expense back to net income in the process of reconciling net income to the net cash provided (or used) by operating activities.

The Format of the Statement of Changes in Financial Position

Illustration 18–2 shows the SCFP for Grover Company calculated using the indirect method. Notice that net income is listed first. It is then adjusted to reconcile its amount to the net amount of cash provided (or used) by operating activities.

Also observe in Illustration 18–2 the other two categories of cash flows reported on the SCFP. In both categories—investing activities and financing activities—we subtract the cash outflows from the cash inflows to determine the net cash provided (or used).

Compare the statement in Illustration 18–2 with the chart in Illustration 18–1. Notice that the beginning and ending balances are called *cash plus cash equivalents* in Illustration 18–1. However, in Illustration 18–2, the beginning and ending balances refer only to *cash*. The balances in Illustration 18–2 are called *cash* because Grover Company does not own any cash equivalents, such as Treasury Bills.

Cash and Cash Equivalents

In section 1540 of the *CICA Handbook,* the Accounting Standards Board concluded that a statement of changes in financial position should explain the difference between the beginning and ending balances of cash and cash equivalents. Prior to this standard, cash equivalents were generally understood to be short-term, temporary investments of cash. As you learned in Chapter 7, however, a *cash equivalent* must satisfy these two criteria:

1. The investment must be readily convertible to a known amount of cash.
2. The investment must be sufficiently close to its maturity date so that its market value is relatively insensitive to interest rate changes.

---

[4]Ibid., par. 1540.12.

Illustration 18-2
Statement of Changes
in Financial Position

GROVER COMPANY
Statement of Changes in Financial Position
For Year Ended December 31, 1997

Cash flows from operating activities:

Net income .... $ 38,000

Adjustments to reconcile net income to net
cash provided by operating activities:

(1)	Increase in accounts receivable	(20,000)	
	Increase in merchandise inventory ...	(14,000)	
	Increase in prepaid expenses	(2,000)	
	Decrease in accounts payable	(5,000)	
	Decrease in interest payable	(1,000)	
	Increase in income taxes payable	10,000	
(2)	Amortization expense	24,000	
(3)	Loss on sale of plant assets	6,000	
	Gain on retirement of bonds	(16,000)	

Net cash provided by operating activities .... $ 20,000

Cash flows from investing activities:

Cash received from sale of plant assets ... $ 12,000

Cash paid for purchase of plant assets .... (10,000)

Net cash provided by investing activities .. 2,000

Cash flows from financing activities:

Cash received from issuing shares .... $ 15,000

Cash paid to retire bonds .... (18,000)

Cash paid for dividends .... (14,000)

Net cash used in financing activities ..... (17,000)

Net increase in cash .... $ 5,000

Cash balance at beginning of 1997 12,000

Cash balance at end of 1997 .... $ 17,000

The idea of classifying short-term, highly liquid investments as cash equivalents is based on the assumption that companies make these investments to earn a return on idle cash balances. Sometimes, however, items that meet the criteria of cash equivalents are not held as temporary investments of idle cash balances. For example, an investment company that specializes in the purchase and sale of securities may buy cash equivalents as part of its investing strategy. Companies that have such investments are allowed to exclude them from the cash equivalents category. However, the companies must develop a clear policy for determining which items to include and which to exclude. These policies must be disclosed in the notes to the financial statements and must be followed consistently from period to period.

CLASSIFYING CASH TRANSACTIONS

On an SCFP, cash and cash equivalents are treated as a single item. In other words, the statement reports the changes in cash plus cash equivalents. Therefore, cash payments to purchase cash equivalents and cash receipts from selling cash equivalents do not appear on the statement. All other cash receipts and payments are classified and reported on the statement as operating, investing, or financing activities. Within each category, individual cash receipts and payments are summarized in a manner that clearly describes the general nature of the company's cash transactions. Then, the summarized cash receipts and payments within each category are netted against each other. A category provides a net cash inflow if the receipts in the category exceed the payments. And, if the payments in a category exceed the receipts, the category is a net use of cash (outflow) during the period.

Operating Activities

Look at the cash flows classified as **operating activities** in Illustration 18–2. Notice that the cash provided by operating activities is $20,000. Net income of $38,000 was modified to exclude those amounts included in the determination of net income but not involved in operating cash inflows or outflows during the period. Net income was also modified to include operating cash inflows and outflows not recorded as revenues and expenses, such as collections of accounts receivable and payments of accounts payable.

Illustration 18–2 shows three types of adjustments to net income. The adjustments grouped under section (1) are for changes in noncash current assets and current liabilities that relate to operating activities. Adjustment (2) is for an income statement item that relates to operating activities but that did not involve a cash inflow or outflow during the period. The adjustments grouped under (3) eliminate gains and losses that resulted from investing and financing activities. These gains and losses do not relate to operating activities.

Adjustments for Changes in Current Assets and Current Liabilities

To help you understand why adjustments for changes in noncash current assets and current liabilities are part of the reconciliation process, we use the transactions of a very simple company as an example. Assume that Simple Company's income statement shows only two items, as follows:

Sales	$20,000
Operating expenses	(12,000)
Net income	$ 8,000

For a moment, assume that all of Simple Company's sales and operating expenses are for cash. The company has no current assets other than cash and has no current liabilities. Given these assumptions, the net cash provided by operating activities during the period is $8,000, which is the cash received from customers less the cash paid for operating expenses.

Adjustments for Changes in Noncash Current Assets

Now assume that Simple Company's sales are on account. Also assume that its Accounts Receivable balance was $2,000 at the beginning of the year and $2,500 at the end of the year. Under these assumptions, cash receipts from customers equal sales of $20,000 minus the $500 increase in Accounts Receivable, or $19,500. Therefore, the net cash provided by operating activities is $7,500 ($19,500 − $12,000).

When we calculate the net cash flow, net income of $8,000 is adjusted for the $500 increase in Accounts Receivable to get $7,500 as the net amount of cash provided by operating activities. The calculations are:

Receipts from customers ($20,000 − $500)	$19,500
Payments for operating expenses	(12,000)
Cash provided (or used) by operating activities	$ 7,500
Net income.	$8,000
Less the increase in accounts receivable	(500)
Cash provided (or used) by operating activities	$7,500

Notice that the increase in Accounts Receivable is subtracted from net income to determine cash provided.

As another example, assume instead that the Accounts Receivable balance decreased from $2,000 to $1,200. Under this assumption, cash receipts from customers equal sales of $20,000 plus the $800 decrease in Accounts Receivable, or $20,800. The net cash provided by operating activities is $8,800 ($20,800 − $12,000). And the $800 decrease in Accounts Receivable is *added* to the $8,000 net income to get $8,800 net cash provided by operating activities.

Adjustments like those for Accounts Receivable are required for all noncash current assets related to operating activities. When a noncash current asset increases, part of the assets derived from operating activities goes into the increase. This leaves a smaller amount as the net cash inflow. Therefore, when you calculate the net cash inflow, subtract the noncash current asset increase from net income. But, when a noncash current asset decreases, additional cash is produced, and you should add this amount to net income. These modifications of income for changes in current assets related to operating activities are

Net income
Add: Decreases in current assets
Subtract: Increases in current assets
Net cash provided (or used) by operating activities

Adjustments for Changes in Current Liabilities

To illustrate the adjustments for changes in current liabilities, return to the original assumptions about Simple Company. Sales of $20,000 are for cash, and operating expenses are $12,000. However, assume now that Simple Company has Interest Payable as its only current liability. Also assume that the beginning-of-year balance in Interest Payable was $500 and the end-of-year balance was $900. This increase means that the operating expenses of $12,000 were $400 larger than the amount paid in cash during the period. Therefore, the cash payments for operating expenses were only $11,600, or ($12,000 − $400). Under these assumptions, the calculation of net cash provided by operating activities is $8,400, or $20,000 receipts from customers less $11,600 payments for expenses. The calculation of $8,400 is net income of $8,000 plus the $400 increase in Interest Payable.

Alternatively, if the Interest Payable balance decreased, for example by $300, the cash outflow for operating expenses would have been the $12,000 expense plus the $300 liability decrease, or $12,300. Then, the calculation of net cash flow is $20,000 − $12,300 = $7,700. Or, the reconciliation is $8,000 − $300 = $7,700. In other words, subtract a *decrease* in Interest Payable from net income.

Adjustments like those for Interest Payable are required for all current liabilities related to operating activities. When a current liability decreases, part of the cash derived from operating activities pays for the decrease. Therefore, subtract the decrease from net income to determine the remaining net cash inflow. And, when a current liability increases, it finances some operating expenses. In other words, cash was not used to pay for the expense and the liability increase must be *added* to net income when you calculate cash provided by operating activities. These adjustments for changes in current liabilities related to operating activities are

Net income
Add: Increases in current liabilities
Subtract: Decreases in current liabilities
Net cash provided (or used) by operating activities

One way to remember how to make these modifications to net income is to observe that a *debit* change in a noncash current asset or a current liability is *subtracted* from net income. And, a *credit* change in a noncash current asset or a current liability is *added* to net income.

Adjustments for Operating Items that Do Not Provide or Use Cash

Some operating items that appear on an income statement do not provide or use cash during the current period. One example is amortization, such as amortization of intangible assets, depreciation, or depletion of natural resources. Another example is bad debts expense.

These expenses are recorded with debits to expense accounts and credits to noncash accounts. They reduce net income but do not require cash outflows during the period. Therefore, when adjustments to net income are made, add these noncash expenses back to net income.

In addition to noncash expenses such as amortization, net income may include some revenues that do not provide cash inflows during the current period. An example is equity method earnings from a share investment in another entity (see Chapter 12). If net income includes revenues that do not provide cash inflows, subtract the revenues from net income in the process of reconciling net income to the net cash provided by operating activities.

The adjustments for expenses and revenues that do not provide or use cash during the current period are

Net income
Add: Expenses that do not use cash
Subtract: Revenues that do not provide cash
Net cash provided (or used) by operating activities

Adjustments for Nonoperating Items

Some income statement items are not related to the operating activities of the company. These gains and losses result from investing and financing activities. Examples are gains or losses on the sale of plant assets and gains or losses on the retirement of bonds payable.

Remember that net income is reconciled to the net cash provided (or used) by operating activities. Therefore, net income must be modified to exclude gains and losses created by investing and financing activities. In making these modifications, subtract gains from financing and investing activities from net income and add losses back to net income:

Net income
Add: Losses from investing or financing activities
Subtract: Gains from investing or financing activities
Net cash provided (or used) by operating activities

Illustration 18-3 summarizes the adjustments to net income or net loss required to determine net cash flows from operating activities.

Investing Activities

Transactions that involve making and collecting loans or that involve purchasing and selling capital assets, other productive assets, or investments (other than cash equivalents) are called **investing activities.** Usually, investing activities involve the purchase or sale of assets classified on the balance sheet as plant and equipment, intangible assets, or long-term investments. However, the purchase and sale of short-term investments other than cash equivalents are also investing activities. Illustration 18–4 shows examples of cash flows from investing activities.

The fourth type of receipt listed in Illustration 18–4 involves proceeds from collecting the principal amount of loans. Regarding this item, carefully examine any cash receipts that relate to notes receivable. If the notes resulted from sales to customers, classify the cash receipts as operating activities. Use this classification even if the notes are long-term notes. But, if a company loans money to other parties, classify the cash receipts from collecting the principal of the loans as inflows from investing activities. Nevertheless, the CICA concluded that collections of interest are not investing activities. Instead, they are included in operating activities.

Net Income or Net Loss	
Plus	**Minus**
Decreases in noncash current assets. Increases in current liabilities.	Increases in noncash current assets. Decreases in current liabilities.
Expenses which do not require a cash outflow during the period.	Income which did not result in a cash inflow during the period.
Losses for investing and financing activities.	Gains from investing and financing activities.

Illustration 18–4
Cash Flows from
Investing Activities

Cash Inflows	**Cash Outflows**
Proceeds from selling productive assets (for example, land, buildings, equipment, natural resources, and intangible assets).	Payments to purchase property, plant, and equipment or other productive assets (excluding merchandise inventory).
Proceeds from selling investments in the equity securities of other companies.	Payments to acquire equity securities of other companies, except cash equivalents.
Proceeds from selling investments in the debt securities of other entities, except cash equivalents.	Payments to acquire debt securities of other entities, except cash equivalents.
Proceeds from collecting the principal amount of loans.	Payments in the form of loans made to other parties.
Proceeds from the sale (discounting) of loans made by the enterprise.	

Financing Activities

The **financing activities** of a business include transactions with its owners and transactions with creditors to borrow money or to repay the principal amounts of loans. Financing activities include borrowing and repaying both short-term loans and long-term debt. However, cash payments to settle credit purchases of merchandise, whether on account or by note, are operating activities. Payments of interest expense are also operating activities. Illustration 18–5 shows examples of cash flows from financing activities.

Some important investing and financing activities do not involve cash receipts or payments during the current period. For example, a company might purchase land and buildings and finance 100% of the purchase by giving a long-term note payable. Because this transaction clearly involves both investing and financing activities, it must be reported in both sections of the SCFP even though no cash was received or paid. That is, the transaction is treated as if two cash transactions occurred simultaneously.

**NONCASH
INVESTING
AND
FINANCING
ACTIVITIES**

Illustration 18-5
Cash Flows from
Financing Activities

Cash Inflows	Cash Outflows
Proceeds from issuing equity securities (e.g., common and preferred shares).	Payments of dividends and other distributions to owners.*
	Repayments of cash loans.
Proceeds from issuing bonds and notes payable.	Payments of the principal amounts involved in long-term credit arrangements.
Proceeds from other short- or long-term borrowing transactions.	

*Some companies treat dividends as an operating activity outflow, while others disclose them in a separate category. Section 1540 of the *CICA Handbook* requires that dividends be disclosed but does not offer any guidance as to their category in the SCFP.

Other investing and financing activities may involve some cash receipt or payment as well as giving or receiving other types of consideration. For example, suppose that you purchase machinery for $12,000 by paying cash of $5,000 and trading in old machinery that has a market value of $7,000. In this case, the SCFP reports a $7,000 cash inflow from the sale of the old machines and a $12,000 cash outflow for the purchase of machinery. Illustration 18–6 shows an example of how a company might disclose its noncash investing and financing activities.

Examples of transactions that must be disclosed as noncash investing and financing activities include the following:

- The retirement of debt securities by issuing equity securities.
- The conversion of preferred shares to common shares.
- The leasing of assets in a transaction that qualifies as a capital lease.
- The purchase of long-term assets by issuing a note payable to the seller.
- The exchange of a noncash asset for other noncash assets.
- The purchase of noncash assets by issuing equity or debt securities.

Progress Check
(Answers to Progress Checks are provided at the end of the chapter.)

18-1   Does an SCFP disclose payments of cash to purchase cash equivalents? Does it disclose receipts of cash from the liquidation of cash equivalents?

18-2   What are the categories of cash flows reported separately on the SCFP?

18-3   Identify the category for each of the following cash flow activities: *(a)* purchase of equipment for cash; *(b)* payment of wages; *(c)* sale of common shares; *(d)* receipt of cash dividends on equity investment; *(e)* collection from customers; *(f)* issuance of bonds for cash.

PREPARING A STATEMENT OF CHANGES IN FINANCIAL POSITION

The information you need to prepare a statement of changes in financial position comes from a variety of sources. These include comparative balance sheets at the beginning and the end of the accounting period, an income statement for the period, and a careful analysis of each noncash balance sheet account in the general ledger. However, because cash inflows and cash outflows are to be reported, you

The company issued 1,000 common shares for the purchase of land and buildings with fair values of $5,000 and $15,000, respectively.

    Investing activity (outflow): Purchase of property for $20,000.
    Financing activity (inflow): Issue of common shares for $20,000.

The company entered into a capital lease obligation of $12,000 for new computer equipment.

    Investing activity (outflow): Acquisition of capital lease assets for $12,000.
    Financing activity (inflow): Capital lease obligation assumed for $12,000.

The company exchanged old machinery with a fair value of $7,000 and a book value of $8,000 for new machinery valued at $12,000. The balance of $5,000 was paid in cash.

    Investing activity (outflow): Acquisition of new machinery for $12,000.
    Investing activity (inflow): Disposal of old machinery for $7,000.

might wonder why we do not focus our attention on the Cash account. For the moment, we should at least consider this approach.

Analyzing the Cash Account

LO 2

Calculate cash inflows and outflows by inspecting the noncash account balances and prepare an SCFP.

All of a company's cash receipts and cash payments are recorded in the Cash account in the General Ledger. Therefore, the Cash account would seem to be the logical place to look for information about cash flows from operating, investing, and financing activities. To demonstrate, review this summarized Cash account of Grover Company:

Summarized Cash Account

Balance, Dec. 31, 1996	12,000		
Receipts from customers	570,000	Payments for merchandise	319,000
Proceeds from sale of plant		Payments for wages and other	
assets	12,000	operating expenses	218,000
Proceeds from issue of shares	15,000	Interest payments	8,000
		Tax payments	5,000
		Payments for purchase of	
		plant assets	10,000
		Payments to retire bonds	18,000
		Dividend payments	14,000
Balance, Dec. 31, 1997	17,000		

In this account, the individual cash transactions are already summarized in terms of major types of receipts and payments. For example, the account has only one debit entry for the total receipts from all customers. All that remains is to determine whether each type of cash inflow or outflow is an operating, investing, or financing activity and then place it in its proper category on the SCFP. The completed SCFP appears in Illustration 18–2 on page 812.

While an analysis of the Cash account may appear to be an easy way to prepare an SCFP, it has two serious drawbacks. First, most companies have so many individual cash receipts and disbursements that it is not practical to review them all. Imagine what a problem this analysis would present for **Stelco, INCO, Loblaw,**

Illustration 18-7 Why an Analysis of the Noncash Accounts Explains the Change in Cash

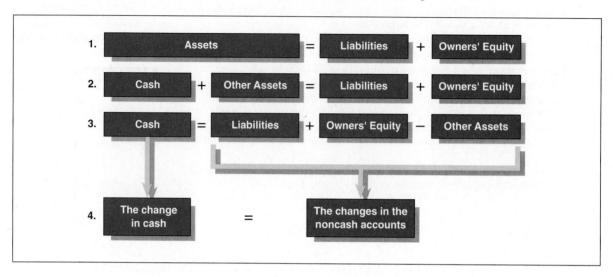

or **Corel,** or even for a relatively small business. Second, the Cash account usually does not contain a description of each cash transaction. Therefore, even though the Cash account shows the periodic postings of debits and credits, you generally cannot determine the type of transaction by looking at the Cash account. Thus, the Cash account does not readily provide the information you need to prepare a statement of cash flows. To obtain the necessary information, you must analyze the changes in the noncash accounts.

Analyzing Noncash Accounts to Determine Cash Flows

When a company records cash inflows and outflows with debits and credits to the Cash account, it also records credits and debits in other accounts. Some of these accounts are balance sheet accounts. Others are revenue and expense accounts that are closed to Retained Earnings, a balance sheet account. As a result, all cash transactions eventually affect noncash balance sheet accounts. Therefore, we can determine the nature of the cash inflows and outflows by examining the changes in the noncash balance sheet accounts. Illustration 18–7 shows this important relationship between the Cash account and the noncash balance sheet accounts.

In Illustration 18–7, notice that the balance sheet equation labeled (1) is expanded in (2) so that cash is separated from the other assets. Then, the equation is rearranged in (3) so that cash is set equal to the sum of the liability and equity accounts less the noncash asset accounts. The illustration then points out in (4) that changes in one side of the equation (cash) must be equal to the changes in the other side (noncash accounts). Part (4) shows that you can fully explain the changes in cash by analyzing the changes in liabilities, owners' equity, and noncash assets.

This overall process has another advantage. The examination of each noncash account also identifies any noncash investing and financing activities that occurred during the period. As you learned earlier, these noncash items must also be disclosed on the SCFP.

Illustration 18-8   Analysis of the Noncash Accounts Explains the Change in Cash

Income Statement Items	Related Balance Sheet Accounts	Possible Cash Flow Effects
Sales	Accounts receivable	Cash receipts from customers
Cost of goods sold	Merchandise inventory, accounts payable	Cash payments to suppliers
Amortization expense	Accumulated amortization	None
Operating expense	Prepaid expenses, accrued liabilities	Cash payments for operating expenses
Gain or loss on sale of capital assets	Capital assets, accumulated amortization, notes receivable	Cash receipts from sale of capital assets
Gain or loss on retirement of bonds payable	Bonds payable, premium or discount on bonds payable	Cash payments for retirement of bonds

When beginning to analyze the changes in the noncash balance sheet accounts, recall that Retained Earnings is affected by revenues, expenses, and dividend declarations. Therefore, look at the income statement accounts to help explain the change in Retained Earnings. In fact, the income statement accounts provide important information that relates to the changes in several balance sheet accounts.

Illustration 18–8 summarizes some of these relationships between income statement accounts, balance sheet accounts, and possible cash flows. For example, to determine the cash receipts from customers during a period, adjust the amount of sales revenue for the increase or decrease in Accounts Receivable.[5] If the Accounts

---

[5]This introductory explanation assumes that there is no bad debts expense. However, if bad debts occur and are written off directly to Accounts Receivable, the change in the Accounts Receivable balance will be due in part to the write-off. The remaining change results from credit sales and from cash receipts. This chapter does not discuss the allowance method of accounting for bad debts since it would make the analysis unnecessarily complex at this time.

Receivable balance did not change, the cash collected from customers is equal to sales revenue. On the other hand, if the Accounts Receivable balance decreased, cash collections must have been equal to sales revenue *plus* the reduction in Accounts Receivable. And, if the Accounts Receivable balance increased, the cash collected from customers must have been equal to Sales *less* the increase in Accounts Receivable.

By analyzing all noncash balance sheet accounts and related income statement accounts in this fashion, you can obtain the necessary information for a statement of changes in financial position. Next, we illustrate this process by examining the noncash accounts of Grover Company.

GROVER COMPANY—A COMPREHENSIVE EXAMPLE

Grover Company's December 31, 1996, and 1997 balance sheets and its 1997 income statement are presented in Illustration 18–9. Our objective is to prepare an SCFP that explains the $5,000 increase in cash, based on these financial statements and this additional information about the 1997 transactions:

a. Net income was $38,000.

b. Accounts receivable increased by $20,000.

c. Merchandise inventory increased by $14,000.

d. Prepaid expenses increased by $2,000.

e. Accounts payable decreased by $5,000.

f. Interest payable decreased by $1,000.

g. Income taxes payable increased by $10,000.

h. Amortization expense was $24,000.

i. Loss on sale of plant assets was $6,000; assets that cost $30,000 with accumulated amortization of $12,000 were sold for $12,000 cash.

j. Gain on retirement of bonds was $16,000; bonds with a book value of $34,000 were retired with a cash payment of $18,000.

k. Plant assets that cost $70,000 were purchased; the payment consisted of $10,000 cash and issuing $60,000 of bonds payable.

l. Sold 3,000 common shares for $15,000.

m. Paid cash dividends of $14,000.

PREPARATION OF THE SCFP

Intuitive Approach

The intuitive approach uses the comparative balance sheets, the income statement, and supplementary data to clarify certain transactions. To illustrate the intuitive approach, we use the financial statements in Illustration 18–9 and the information listed above. The comparative balance sheets show that cash increased by $5,000 during 1997. Therefore, $5,000 must be the amount on the last line before the cash balance at the beginning of 1997 on the SCFP (Illustration 18–2). This change is explained by examining and identifying the causes of the cash inflows and out flows.

Illustration 18-9
Financial Statements

GROVER COMPANY
Balance Sheet
December 31, 1997 and 1996

	1997	1996
Assets		
Current assets:		
Cash	$ 17,000	$ 12,000
Accounts receivable	60,000	40,000
Merchandise inventory	84,000	70,000
Prepaid expenses	6,000	4,000
Total current assets	$167,000	$126,000
Long-term assets:		
Plant assets $250,000		$210,000
Less accumulated amortization 60,000	190,000	48,000 162,000
Total assets	$357,000	$288,000
Liabilities		
Current liabilities:		
Accounts payable	$ 35,000	$ 40,000
Interest payable	3,000	4,000
Income taxes payable	22,000	12,000
Total current liabilities	$ 60,000	$ 56,000
Long-term liabilities:		
Bonds payable	90,000	64,000
Total liabilities	$150,000	$120,000
Shareholders' Equity		
Contributed capital:		
Common shares, no par value .... $ 95,000		$ 80,000
Retained earnings 112,000		88,000
Total shareholders' equity	207,000	168,000
Total liabilities and		
shareholders' equity	$357,000	$288,000

GROVER COMPANY
Income Statement
For Year Ended December 31, 1997

Sales		$ 590,000
Cost of goods sold	$300,000	
Wages and other operating expenses ..	216,000	
Interest expense	7,000	
Income taxes expense	15,000	
Amortization expense	24,000	(562,000)
Loss on sale of plant assets		(6,000)
Gain on retirement of debt		16,000
Net income		$ 38,000

Illustration 18–10

GROVER COMPANY
Statement of Changes in Financial Position
For Year Ended December 31, 1997

		Increase (Decrease)
Cash flows from operating activities:		
Net income for 1997 *(a)*		$ 38,000
Adjustments to reconcile net income to cash provided by operating activities:		
1. Accounts receivable *(b)*	(20,000)	
Merchandise inventory *(c)*	(14,000)	
Prepaid expenses *(d)*	(2,000)	
Accounts payable *(e)*	(5,000)	
Interest payable *(f)*	(1,000)	
Income taxes payable *(g)*	10,000	
2. Amortization expense *(h)*	24,000	
3. Loss on sale of plant assets *(i)*	6,000	
Gain on retirement of debt *(j)*	(16,000)	
Net adjustments		(18,000)
Cash provided by operating activities		20,000
Cash flows from investing activities:		
Cash received from sale of plant assets *(i)*	12,000	
Cash paid for purchase plant assets *(k)*	(70,000)	
Net cash provided by investing activities . .		(58,000)
Cash flows from financing activities:		
Cash received from share issue *(l)*	15,000	
Cash received from bond issue *(k)*	60,000	
Cash paid to retire bonds *(j)*	(18,000)	
Cash paid for dividends *(m)*	(15,000)	
Net cash used in financing activities		43,000
Net increase in cash		$ 5,000
Cash balance at beginning of 1997		12,000
Cash balance at end of 1997		$ 17,000

Analysis of Cash Flows

In order to determine the cash flows from operations, we must adjust the net income figure from Illustration 18–9. First, we add or subtract the changes in the noncash current asset and current liability accounts as shown in Illustration 18–10.

Second, we adjust for the other operating items that do not provide or use cash. From the income statement we can determine that only amortization expense fits into this category. Therefore, we add back the amortization expense.

Third, we adjust for nonoperating items. In Illustration 18–10 these are the loss on sale of plant assets and the gain on retirement of debt.

The net cash provided by financing activities and by investing activities is taken from the additional information. Each item is identified with the corresponding letter from the above list of 1997 transactions, denoted *a* through *m*.

Although the intuitive approach technique may be adequate when doing relatively simple SCFPs, in many cases a more formal method is desirable. This is known as the *working paper approach,* which is illustrated and discussed next.

When a company has a large number of accounts and many operating, investing, and financing transactions, the analysis of noncash accounts can be difficult and confusing. In these situations, a working paper can help organize the information needed to prepare an SCFP. A working paper also makes it easier to check the accuracy of your work.

Illustration 18–11 shows the working paper for Grover Company. Notice that the beginning and ending balance sheets are recorded on the working paper. Following the balance sheets, we enter information in the Analysis of Changes columns about cash flows from operating, investing, and financing activities and about noncash investing and financing activities. Note that the working paper does not reconstruct the income statement. Instead, net income is entered as the first item used in computing the amount of cash flows from operating activities.

Entering the Analysis of Changes on the Working Paper

After the balance sheets are entered, we recommend using the following sequence of procedures to complete the working paper:

1. Enter net income as an operating cash inflow (a debit) and as a credit to Retained Earnings (*a1*) and the change in cash as a debit and credit (*a2*).
2. In the Statement of Changes in Financial Position section, adjustments to net income are entered as debits if they increase cash inflows and as credits if they decrease cash inflows. Following this rule, adjust net income for the change in each noncash current asset and current liability related to operating activities. For each adjustment to net income, the offsetting debit or credit should reconcile the beginning and ending balances of a current asset or current liability.
3. Enter the adjustments to net income for income statement items, such as amortization, that did not provide or use cash during the period. For each adjustment, the offsetting debit or credit should help reconcile a noncash balance sheet account.
4. Adjust net income to eliminate any gains or losses from investing and financing activities. Because the cash associated with a gain must be excluded from operating activities, the gain is entered as a credit in the operating activities section. On the other hand, losses are entered with debits. For each of these adjustments, the related debits and/or credits help reconcile balance sheet accounts and also involve entries to show the cash flow from investing or financing activities.

PREPARING A WORKING PAPER FOR AN SCFP

LO 3
Prepare a working paper for an SCFP.

Illustration 18–11

GROVER COMPANY
Working Paper for Statement of Changes in Financial Position
For Year Ended December 31, 1997

	December 31, 1996	Analysis of Changes Debit	Analysis of Changes Credit	December 31, 1997
Balance sheet—debits:				
Cash	12,000	*(a2)* 5,000		17,000
Accounts receivable	40,000	*(b)* 20,000		60,000
Merchandise inventory	70,000	*(c)* 14,000		84,000
Prepaid expenses	4,000	*(d)* 2,000		6,000
Plant assets	210,000	*(k1)* 70,000	*(i)* 30,000	250,000
	336,000			417,000
Balance sheet—credits:				
Accumulated amortization	48,000	*(i)* 12,000	*(h)* 24,000	60,000
Accounts payable	40,000	*(e)* 5,000		35,000
Interest payable	4,000	*(f)* 1,000		3,000
Income taxes payable	12,000		*(g)* 10,000	22,000
Bonds payable	64,000	*(j)* 34,000	*(k2)* 60,000	90,000
Common stock, no par value	80,000		*(l)* 15,000	95,000
Retained earnings	88,000	*(m)* 14,000	*(a1)* 38,000	112,000
	336,000			417,000
Statement of changes in financial position:				
Operating activities:				
Net income		*(a1)* 38,000		
Increase in accounts receivable			*(b)* 20,000	
Increase in merchandise inventory			*(c)* 14,000	
Increase in prepaid expenses			*(d)* 2,000	
Decrease in accounts payable			*(e)* 5,000	
Decrease in interest payable			*(f)* 1,000	20,000
Increase in income taxes payable		*(g)* 10,000		
Amortization expense		*(h)* 24,000		
Loss on sale of plant assets		*(i)* 6,000		
Gain on retirement of bonds			*(j)* 16,000	
Investing activities:				
Receipts from sale of plant assets		*(i)* 12,000		(58,000)
Purchase of plant assets			*(k1)* 70,000	
Financing activities:				
Payments to retire bonds			*(j)* 18,000	
Receipts from issuance of shares		*(l)* 15,000		43,000
Payments of dividends			*(m)* 14,000	
Receipts from issuance of bonds		*(k2)* 60,000		
Increase in cash balance			*(a2)* 5,000	5,000
		342,000	342,000	

5. After reviewing any unreconciled balance sheet accounts and related information, enter the reconciling entries for all remaining investing and financing activities. These include items such as purchases of plant assets, issuances of long-term debt, sales of shares, and dividend payments.

6. Confirm the accuracy of your work by totaling the Analysis of Changes columns and by determining that the change in each balance sheet account has been explained.

For Grover Company, these steps were performed in Illustration 18–11:

Step	Entries
1	*(a)*
2	*(b)* through *(g)*
3	*(h)*
4	*(i)* through *(j)*
5	*(k)* through *(m)*

Because adjustments *i, j,* and *k* are more complex, we show them in the following debit and credit format. This format is similar to the one used for general journal entries, except that the changes in the Cash account are identified as sources or uses of cash. Note that these are only used on the SCFP working papers and are not entered in the books of Grover.

i.	Loss from Sale of Plant Assets	6,000.00	
	Accumulated Amortization	12,000.00	
	Receipt from Sale of Plant Assets	12,000.00	
	Plant Assets		30,000.00
	To describe the sale of plant assets.		
j.	Bonds Payable	34,000.00	
	Payments to Retire Bonds		18,000.00
	Gain on Retirement of Bonds		16,000.00
	To describe the retirement of bonds.		
k1.	Plant Assets	70,000.00	
	Purchase of Plant Assets Financed by Bonds		70,000.00
	To describe the purchase of plant assets, the cash payment, and the use of noncash financing.		
k2.	Proceeds of Bonds Used to Purchase Plant Assets	60,000.00	
	Bonds Payable		60,000.00
	To show the issuance of bonds payable to finance the purchase of plant assets.		

Progress Check

18–4   **In preparing a working paper for an SCFP, which of the following is true?**
    ***a.* A decrease in accounts receivable is analyzed with a debit in the statement of cash flows section and a credit in the balance sheet section.**

b. **A cash dividend paid is analyzed with a debit to retained earnings and a credit in the investing activities section.**

c. **The analysis of a cash payment to retire bonds payable at a loss would require one debit and two credits.**

d. **Amortization expense would not require analysis on the working paper because there is no cash inflow or outflow.**

18–5   **Determine the net cash provided (or used) by operating activities based on the following data:**

Net income	$74,900
Decrease in accounts receivable	4,600
Increase in inventory	11,700
Decrease in accounts payable	1,000
Loss on sale of equipment	3,400
Payment of dividends	21,500

18–6   **Why are expenses such as amortization of equipment and amortization of goodwill added to net income when cash flow from operating activities is calculated by the indirect method?**

18–7   **A company reports a net income of $15,000 that includes a $3,000 gain on the sale of plant assets. Why is this gain subtracted from net income in calculating cash flow from operating activities according to the indirect method?**

USING THE INFORMATION— CASH FLOWS

LO 1

Explain why cash flow information is important to decision making and describe the information in an SCFP and the methods used to disclose non-cash investing and financing activities.

Numerous ratios are used to analyze income statement and balance sheet data. By comparison, ratios related to the statement of changes in financial position are not widely used.[6] Only one ratio of that nature, cash flow per share, has received much attention. Some financial analysts use that ratio, usually calculated as net income adjusted for noncash items such as amortization. Currently, however, the GAAP does not require reporting cash flow per share, apparently because it might be misinterpreted as a measure of earnings performance.

Leanne Hagarty (As a Matter of Opinion, page 809) typifies the attitude of most managers when she emphasizes the importance of understanding and predicting cash flows. Many business decisions are based on cash flow evaluations. For example, creditors evaluate a company's ability to generate cash before deciding whether to loan money to the company. Investors often make similar evaluations before they buy a company's shares. In making these evaluations, cash flows from investing and financing activities are considered. However, special attention is given to the company's ability to generate cash flows from its operations. The cash flows statement facilitates this by separating the investing and financing activity cash flows from the operating cash flows.

To see the importance of identifying cash flows as operating, investing, and financing activities, consider the following three companies. Assume they operate in the same industry and have been in business for several years.

---

[6]To consider some suggested cash flow ratios, see Don E. Giacomino and David E. Mielke, "Cash Flows: Another Approach to Ratio Analysis," *Journal of Accountancy,* March 1993.

	First Company	Second Company	Third Company
Cash provided (used) by operating activities	$ 90,000	$ 40,000	$(24,000)
Cash provided (used) by investing activities:			
Proceeds from sale of operating assets			26,000
Purchase of operating assets	(48,000)	(25,000)	
Cash provided (used) by financing activities:			
Proceeds from issuance of debt			13,000
Repayment of debt	(27,000)		
Net increase (decrease) in cash	$ 15,000	$ 15,000	$ 15,000

Each of the three companies generated a $15,000 net increase in cash. Their means of accomplishing this, however, were very different. First Company's operating activities provided $90,000, which allowed the company to purchase additional operating assets for $48,000 and repay $27,000 of debt. By comparison, Second Company's operating activities provided only $40,000, enabling it to purchase only $25,000 of operating assets. By comparison, Third Company's net cash increase was obtained only by selling operating assets and incurring additional debt; operating activities resulted in a net cash outflow of $24,000.

The implication of this comparison is that First Company is more capable of generating cash to meet its future obligations than is Second Company; and Third Company is least capable. This evaluation is, of course, tentative and may be contradicted by other information.

Managers analyze cash flows in making a variety of short-term decisions. In deciding whether borrowing will be necessary, managers use the procedures you learned in this chapter to predict cash flows for the next period or periods. These short-term planning situations also may lead to decisions about investing idle cash balances. Another example is deciding whether a customer's offer to buy a product at a reduced price should be accepted or rejected.

Long-term decisions involving new investments usually require detailed cash flow predictions. Companies must estimate cash inflows and outflows over the life of the investment, often extending many years into the future. Other decisions that require cash flow information include deciding whether a product should be manufactured by the company or purchased from an outside supplier, and deciding whether a product or a department should be eliminated or retained.

Progress Check

18–8 Refer to the consolidated statements of changes in financial position for Geac Computer Corporation, in Appendix I. What type and amount of investing activities took place during the year ended April 30, 1994? What was the largest source of cash to finance these activities?

LO 1. Explain why cash flow information is important to decision making and describe the information in a statement of changes in financial position and the methods used to disclose noncash investing and financing activities. Many decisions involve evaluating cash flows. Examples are investor and creditor decisions to invest in or loan money to a company. The evaluations include paying attention to the activities that provide or use cash. Managers evaluate cash flows in deciding whether borrowing is necessary, whether cash balances should be invested, and in a variety of other short-term and long-term decisions.

The SCFP reports cash receipts and disbursements as operating, investing, or financing activities. Operating activities include transactions related to producing or purchasing merchandise, selling goods and services to customers, and performing administrative functions. Investing activities include purchases and sales of noncurrent assets and short-term investments that are not cash equivalents. Financing activities include transactions with owners and transactions to borrow or repay the principal amounts of long-term and short-term debt.

LO 2. Calculate cash inflows and outflows by inspecting the noncash account balances and prepare an SCFP. To identify the cash receipts and cash payments, analyze the changes in the noncash balance sheet accounts created by income statement transactions and other events. To calculate the net cash provided (or used) by operating activities, first list the net income and then modify it for these three types of events: *(a)* changes in noncash current assets and current liabilities related to operating activities, *(b)* revenues and expenses that did not provide or use cash, and *(c)* gains and losses from investing and financing activities.

LO 3. Prepare a working paper for an SCFP. To prepare a working paper, first enter the beginning and ending balances of the balance sheet accounts in columns 1 and 4. Then, establish the three sections of the SCFP. Net income is entered as the first item in the operating activities section. Then, adjust the net income for events *(a)* through *(c)* identified in the preceding paragraph. This process reconciles the changes in the noncash current assets and current liabilities related to operations. Reconcile any remaining balance sheet account changes and report their cash effects in the appropriate sections.

Given the following condensed income statement and a partial list of account balances, calculate the cash provided by operating activities:

BUTTERFIELD COMPANY
Income Statement
For the Year Ended December 31, 1997

Sales		$225,000
Cost of goods sold		130,000
Gross profit from sales		$ 95,000
Operating expenses:		
Salaries and wages	$31,250	
Amortization expense	3,750	
Rent expense	9,000	
Amortization of patents	750	
Office expense	1,000	
Bond interest expense	3,375	49,125
Net income		$ 45,875

Butterfield Company's partial list of comparative account balances as of December 31, 1997 and 1996:

	1997	1996
Cash	$ 2,600	$ 2,200
Accounts receivable (net)	23,200	21,800
Inventory	17,900	19,300
Prepaid expenses	1,200	1,400
Accounts payable	11,400	12,100
Salaries and wages payable	250	650
Interest payable	1,500	750
Unamortized bond discount	500	875

- Prepare a blank section of an SCFP for operating activities.
- Insert the net income figure at the beginning of the schedule.
- Examine each account balance to determine if it has increased or decreased during 1997.
- Adjust net income for increases and decreases in current assets and liabilities.
- Adjust net income for expenses which are not a decrease in cash.
- Compare your answer to the solution.

Planning the Solution

BUTTERFIELD COMPANY
Cash Provided by Operating Activities
For the Year Ended December 31, 1997

Cash provided by operating activities:		
Net income		$45,875
Adjustments to reconcile net income to cash provided by operations:		
Increase in accounts receivable	$(1,400)	
Decrease in inventory	1,400	
Decrease in prepaid expenses	200	
Decrease in accounts payable	(700)	
Decrease in salaries and wages payable	(400)	
Increase in interest payable	750	
Amortization expense	3,750	
Amortization of patents	750	
Amortization of bond discount	375	4,725
Cash provided by operating activities		$50,600

Solution to Demonstration Problem

GLOSSARY

Financing activities transactions with the owners of a business or transactions with its creditors to borrow money or to repay the principal amounts of loans. p. 817

Investing activities transactions that involve making and collecting loans or that involve purchasing and selling capital assets, other productive assets, or investments other than cash equivalents. p. 816

Net cash provided (or used) by operating activities a calculation that begins with net income and then adjusts the net income amount by adding and subtracting items

that are necessary to reconcile net income to the net cash provided or used by operating activities. p. 811

Operating activities activities that involve the production or purchase of merchandise and the sale of goods and services to customers, including expenditures related to administering the business. p. 813

Statement of changes in financial position a financial statement that reports the cash inflows and outflows for an accounting period, and that classifies those cash flows as operating activities, investing activities, and financing activities. p. 808

SYNOMYMOUS TERMS

Cash inflow   source of cash.

Cash outflow   use of cash.

Statement of Changes in Financial Position   statement of cash flows.

QUESTIONS

1. What are some examples of items reported on an SCFP as investing activities?

2. What are some examples of items reported on an SCFP as financing activities?

3. What are some examples of items in the reconciliation for cash flows from operating activities?

4. If a corporation pays cash dividends, where on the corporation's SCFP should the payment be reported?

5. A company purchases land for $100,000, paying $20,000 cash and borrowing the remainder on a long-term note payable. How should this transaction be reported on an SCFP?

6. What is the direct method of reporting cash flows from operating activities?

7. What is the indirect method of reporting cash flows from operating activities?

8. Is amortization a source of cash?

9. On June 3, a company borrowed $50,000 by giving its bank a 60-day, interest-bearing note. On the SCFP, where should this item be reported?

10. If a company reports a net income for the year, is it possible for the company to show a net cash outflow from operating activities? Explain your answer.

11. Refer to Geac Computer Corporation's consolidated statement of changes in financial position shown in Appendix I. What does the change in "non-cash working capital components" represent?

QUICK STUDY (Five-Minute Exercises)

QS 18–1
(LO 1)

Describe the content of a statement of changes in financial position.

QS 18–2
(LO 1)

Classify the following cash flows as operating, investing, or financing activities:

1. Purchased merchandise for cash.
2. Paid interest on outstanding bonds.
3. Sold delivery equipment at a loss.
4. Paid property taxes on the company offices.
5. Collected proceeds from sale of long-term investments.
6. Issued common shares for cash.
7. Received payments from customers.
8. Paid wages.
9. Paid dividends.
10. Received interest on investment.

List three examples of transactions that are noncash financing and investing transactions.   **QS 18–3**
(LO 1)

Use the following information in QS 18–4 through QS 18–9.   **QS 18–4**
(LO 2)

KUNG ATTIRE, INC.
Comparative Balance Sheet

Assets	1997	1996
Cash	$ 47,900	$ 12,500
Accounts receivable (net)	21,000	26,000
Inventory	43,400	48,400
Prepaid expenses	3,200	2,600
Furniture	55,000	60,000
Accumulated amortization, furniture	(9,000)	(5,000)
Total assets	$161,500	$144,500

Liabilities and Shareholders' Equity		
Accounts payable	$ 8,000	$ 11,000
Wages payable	5,000	3,000
Income taxes payable	1,200	1,800
Notes payable (long-term)	15,000	35,000
Common shares, n.p.v. par value	115,000	90,000
Retained earnings	17,300	3,700
Total liabilities and shareholders' equity	$161,500	$144,500

KUNG ATTIRE, INC.
Income Statement
For Year Ended June 30, 1997

Sales		$234,000
Cost of goods sold		156,000
Gross profit		$ 78,000
Operating expenses:		
Amortization expense	$19,300	
Other expenses	28,500	
Total operating expenses		47,800
Net income from operations		$ 30,200
Income taxes		12,300
Net income		$ 17,900

How much cash was received from customers during Year 2?

Refer to the facts in QS 18–4. How much cash was paid for merchandise during 1997?   **QS 18–5**
(LO 2)

Refer to the facts in QS 18–4. How much cash was paid for operating expenses during 1997?   **QS 18–6**
(LO 2)

QS 18–7
(LO 2)

Refer to the facts in QS 18–4 and assume furniture that cost $27,000 was sold at its book value and all furniture acquisitions were for cash. What was the cash inflow related to the sale of furniture?

QS 18–8
(LO 2)

Refer to the facts in QS 18–4 and assume that all shares were issued for cash. How much cash was disbursed for dividends?

QS 18–9
(LO 2)

Refer to the facts in QS 18–4. Calculate cash provided or used from operating activities.

QS 18–10
(LO 3)

When a working paper for an SCFP is prepared, all changes in noncash balance sheet accounts are accounted for on the working paper. Explain why this occurs.

EXERCISES

Exercise 18–1
Classifying transactions
on an SCFP
(LO 1)

The following events occurred during the year. Indicate the proper accounting treatment for each event by placing an *x* in the appropriate column. If the item should appear in more than one section, place an *x* in the appropriate columns.

		Statement of Changes in Financial Position		
		Operating Activities	Investing Activities	Financing Activities
a.	Long-term bonds payable were retired by issuing common shares.	_____	_____	_____
b.	Surplus merchandise inventory was sold for cash.	_____	_____	_____
c.	Borrowed cash from the bank by signing a nine-month note payable.	_____	_____	_____
d.	Paid cash to purchase a patent.	_____	_____	_____
e.	A six-month note receivable was accepted in exchange for a building that had been used in operations.	_____	_____	_____
f.	Recorded amortization expense on all plant assets.	_____	_____	_____
g.	A cash dividend that was declared in a previous period was paid in the current period.	_____	_____	_____

Exercise 18–2
Organizing the SCFP and
supporting schedule
(LO 2)

Use the following information about the 1997 cash flows of Forrest Company to prepare an SCFP.

Cash and cash equivalents balance, December 31, 1996 ...	$ 50,000
Cash and cash equivalents balance, December 31, 1997 ...	140,000
Cash received as interest	5,000
Decrease in salaries payable	35,000
Bonds payable retired by issuing common shares	
(there was no gain or loss on the retirement)	375,000
Cash paid to retire long-term notes payable	250,000
Cash received from sale of equipment	122,500
Cash borrowed on six-month note payable	50,000
Land purchased and financed by long-term note payable ..	212,500
Cash paid for store equipment	47,500
Cash dividends paid	30,000
Increase in accounts payable	40,000
Increase in acounts receivable	80,000
Increase in merchandise inventory	90,000
Net income	265,000
Amortization expense	145,000

In each of the following cases, use the information provided about the 1996 operations of Benzar Company to calculate the indicated cash flow:

Exercise 18–3
Calculating cash flows
(LO 2)

Case A: Calculate cash received from customers:

Sales revenue	$255,000
Accounts receivable, January 1	12,600
Accounts receivable, December 31	17,400

Case B: Calculate cash paid for insurance:

Insurance expense	$ 34,200
Prepaid insurance, January 1	5,700
Prepaid insurance, December 31	8,550

Case C: Calculate cash paid for salaries:

Salaries expense	$102,000
Salaries payable, January 1	6,300
Salaries payable, December 31	7,500

In each of the following cases, use the information provided about the 1996 operations of CNA Company to calculate the indicated cash flow:

Exercise 18–4
Calculating cash flows
(LO 2)

Case A: Calculate cash paid for rent:

Rent expense	$ 20,400
Rent payable, January 1	4,400
Rent payable, December 31	3,600

Case B: Calculate cash received from interest:

Interest revenue	$ 68,000
Interest receivable, January 1	6,000
Interest receivable, December 31	7,200

Case C: Calculate cash paid for merchandise:

Cost of goods sold	$352,000
Merchandise inventory, January 1	106,400
Accounts payable, January 1	45,200
Merchandise inventory, December 31	87,600
Accounts payable, December 31	56,000

Exercise 18–5
Cash flows from
operating activities
(LO 2)

Use the following income statement and information about changes in noncash current assets and current liabilities to present the cash flows from operating activities:

ALAMO DATA COMPANY
Income Statement
For Year Ended December 31, 1996

Sales		$606,000
Cost of goods sold		297,000
Gross profit from sales		$309,000
Operating expenses:		
Salaries expense	$82,845	
Depreciation expense	14,400	
Rent expense	16,200	
Amortization expense, patents	1,800	
Utilities expense	6,375	121,620
Total		$187,380
Gain on sale of equipment		2,400
Net income		$189,780

Changes in current asset and current liability accounts during the year, all of which related to operating activities, were as follows:

Accounts receivable	$13,500 increase
Merchandise inventory	9,000 increase
Accounts payable	4,500 decrease
Salaries payable	1,500 decrease

Exercise 18–6
Cash flows from
operating activities
(LO 2)

Trador Company's 1996 income statement showed the following: net income, $728,000; depreciation expense, $90,000; amortization expense, $16,400; and gain on sale of plant assets, $14,000. An examination of the company's current assets and current liabilities showed that the following changes occurred because of operating activities: accounts receivable decreased $36,200; merchandise inventory decreased $104,000; prepaid expenses increased $7,400; accounts payable decreased $18,400; other payables increased $2,800. Calculate the cash flow from operating activities.

Exercise 18–7
Classifying transactions
on an SCFP
(LO 1, 2)

The following events occurred during the year. Indicate the proper accounting treatment for each event listed below by placing an *x* in the appropriate column.

		Statement of Changes in Financial Position		
		Operating Activities	**Investing Activities**	**Financing Activities**
a.	Land for a new plant was purchased by issuing common shares.	_____	_____	_____
b.	Recorded amortization expense.	_____	_____	_____
c.	Income taxes payable increased by 15% from prior year.	_____	_____	_____
d.	Declared and paid a cash dividend.	_____	_____	_____
e.	Merchandise inventory increased.	_____	_____	_____
f.	Sold plant equipment at a loss.	_____	_____	_____
g.	Accounts receivable decreased during the year.	_____	_____	_____

PROBLEMS

Helix Corporation's 1996 and 1995 balance sheets carried the following items:

Problem 18–1
Statement of changes in
financial position
(LO 1, 3)

Debits	December 31	
	1996	1995
Cash	$116,000	$ 78,000
Accounts receivable	62,000	54,000
Merchandise inventory	406,000	356,000
Equipment.	222,000	198,000
Totals	$806,000	$686,000

Credits		
Accumulated amortization, equipment	$104,000	$ 68,000
Accounts payable.	46,000	64,000
Income taxes payable	18,000	16,000
Common shares, no par value	520,000	480,000
Retained earnings.	118,000	58,000
Totals	$806,000	$686,000

An examination of the company's activities during 1996, including the income statement, shows the following:

a.	Sales		$1,328,000
b.	Cost of goods sold	$796,000	
c.	Amortization expense	36,000	
d.	Other operating expenses	334,000	
e.	Income taxes expense	28,000	1,194,000
f.	Net income		$ 134,000
g.	Equipment was purchased for $24,000 cash.		
h.	Eight thousand common shares were issued for cash at $5 per share.		
i.	The company declared and paid $74,000 of cash dividends during the year.		

Required

Prepare an SCFP working paper.

Refer to the facts about Helix Corporation presented in Problem 18–1. Prepare an SCFP directly from your examination of the financial statements and the other data provided. Do not prepare a working paper.

Problem 18–2
SCFP
(LO 2)

Purcell Company's 1996 and 1995 balance sheets included the following items:

Problem 18–3
SCFP working paper
(LO 1, 3)

Debits	December 31	
	1996	1995
Cash	$ 107,750	$153,250
Accounts receivable	130,000	99,250
Merchandise inventory	547,500	505,000
Prepaid expenses	10,750	12,500
Equipment	319,000	220,000
Totals	$1,115,000	$990,000

| | December 31 | |
Credits	1996	1995
Accumulated amortization, equipment .	$ 69,250	$ 88,000
Accounts payable	176,250	233,250
Short-term notes payable	20,000	12,500
Long-term notes payable	187,500	107,500
Common shares, no par value	402,500	312,500
Retained earnings	259,500	236,250
Totals	$1,115,000	$990,000

Additional information about the 1996 activities of the company follows:

a.	Sales revenue		$992,500
b.	Cost of goods sold	$500,000	
c.	Amortization expense	37,500	
d.	Other expenses	273,000	
e.	Income taxes expense (paid with cash)	24,250	
f.	Loss on sale of equipment	10,250	845,000

The equipment cost $93,750, was amortized by
$56,250, and was sold for $27,250.

g.	Net income		$147,500

h.   Equipment that cost $192,750 was purchased by paying cash of
$50,000 and by signing a long-term note payable for the balance.

i.   Borrowed $7,500 by signing a short-term note payable.

j.   Paid $62,750 to reduce a long-term note payable.

k.   Issued 5,000 common shares for cash at $18 per share.

l.   Declared and paid cash dividends of $124,250.

Required

Preparation component:

1.   Prepare an SCFP working paper.

Analysis component:

2.   Analyze and discuss the information contained in your answer to requirement 1, giving special attention to the wisdom of the dividend payment.

Problem 18–4
Statement of changes
in financial position
(LO 2)

Refer to the facts about Purcell Company presented in Problem 18–3. Prepare an SCFP directly from your examination of the financial statements and the other data provided. Do not prepare a working paper.

Problem 18–5
Analytical essay
(LO 2)

Write a brief essay explaining why, in preparing an SCFP, it is generally better to determine the changes in cash by analyzing the changes in the noncash accounts rather than by examining the Cash account directly. You should include in your essay an explanation of why the changes in cash for the period equal the changes in the noncash balance sheet accounts.

The following items might be found on a working paper for an SCFP. Write a brief essay describing where each item appears on a working paper for an SCFP. Also describe the nature of any debits and/or credits that should be entered in the Analysis of Changes columns next to each item, and any balancing entries.

Problem 18–6
Analytical essay
(LO 3)

a. Accounts receivable.

b. Depreciation expense.

c. Payment for purchase of plant assets.

Cemco Corporation's 1996 and 1995 balance sheets carried the following items:

Problem 18–7
SCFP
(LO 1, 3)

	December 31	
Debits	**1996**	**1995**
Cash	$ 50,400	$ 19,200
Accounts receivable	38,400	43,200
Merchandise inventory	100,800	86,400
Equipment	88,800	72,000
Totals	$278,400	$220,800
Credits		
Accumulated amortization, equipment	$ 21,600	$ 14,400
Accounts payable	40,800	24,000
Income taxes payable	4,800	9,600
Common shares	158,400	144,000
Retained earnings	52,800	28,800
Totals	$278,400	$220,800

Additional information about the company's activities during 1996 follows:

a. Net income was $48,000.

b. Accounts receivable decreased.

c. Merchandise inventory increased.

d. Accounts payable increased.

e. Income taxes payable decreased.

f. Amortization expense was $7,200.

g. Equipment was purchased for $16,800 cash.

h. Twelve hundred shares were issued for cash at $12 per share.

i. The company declared and paid $24,000 of cash dividends during the year.

Required

Prepare an SCFP working paper.

Problem 18–8
SCFP working paper
(LO 3)

Refer to the material in Problem 18–7.

Required

Prepare an SCFP directly from your examination of the balance sheets and the additional information provided about the income statement and other transactions of the company. Do not prepare a working paper.

Problem 18–9
Reconciling net income
to cash flows from
operating activities
(LO 1, 2)

Columbus Corporation's 1996 and 1995 balance sheets included the following items:

Debits	December 31	
	1996	**1995**
Cash	$146,700	$ 38,700
Accounts receivable	72,000	90,000
Merchandise inventory	283,500	288,000
Prepaid expenses	9,000	10,800
Equipment	330,900	231,000
Totals	$842,100	$658,500

Credits		
Accumulated amortization, equipment	$ 54,900	$ 49,200
Accounts payable	193,500	161,100
Short-term notes payable	22,500	13,500
Long-term notes payable	114,000	90,000
Common shares	292,500	225,000
Retained earnings	164,700	119,700
Totals	$842,100	$658,500

Additional information about the 1996 activities of the company follows:

a. Net income was $72,000.

b. Accounts receivable decreased.

c. Merchandise inventory decreased.

d. Prepaid expenses decreased.

e. Accounts payable increased.

f. Amortization expense was $18,900.

g. Equipment that cost $22,200 and was amortized $13,200 was sold for $6,300 cash, which caused a loss of $2,700.

h. Equipment that cost $112,100 was purchased by paying cash of $62,100 and by signing a long-term note payable for the balance.

i. Borrowed $9,000 by signing a short-term note payable.

j. Paid $36,000 to reduce a long-term note payable.

k. Issued 500 common shares for cash at $135 per share.

l. Declared and paid cash dividends of $27,000.

Required

Prepare a schedule that reconciles net income to the net cash provided or used by operating activities.

Problem 18–10
SCFP
(LO 2)

Refer to the information about Columbus Corporation presented in Problem 18–9.

Required

Prepare an SCFP. Do not prepare a working paper. Instead, prepare the statement directly from your examination of the balance sheets and the additional information provided about the income statement and other transactions of the company. Show your supporting calculations.

PROVOCATIVE PROBLEMS

Yaupon, Inc.'s 1996 statement of changes in financial position appeared as follows:

Provocative Problem
18–1
Yaupon, Inc.
(LO 2)

Cash flows from operating activities:

Net income		$111,100
Accounts receivable increase	$(14,700)	
Inventory decrease	47,600	
Prepaid expense increase	(4,600)	
Accounts payable decrease	(16,300)	
Income tax payable increase	4,400	
Amortization expense	12,000	
Loss on disposal of equipment	13,400	
Gain on bond retirement	(7,700)	34,100
Net cash provided by operating activities		$145,200
Cash flows from investing activities:		
Receipt from sale of office equipment	$ 5,100	
Purchase of store equipment	(33,000)	
Net cash used by investing activities		(27,900)
Cash flows from financing activities:		
Payment to retire bonds payable	$(42,300)	
Payment of dividends	(30,000)	
Net cash used by financing activities		(72,300)
Net increase in cash		$ 45,000
Cash balance at beginning of year		45,400
Cash balance at end of year		$ 90,400

Yaupon, Inc.'s beginning and ending balance sheets were as follows:

	December 31	
Debits	**1996**	**1995**
Cash	$ 90,400	$ 45,400
Accounts receivable	114,900	100,200
Merchandise inventory	212,700	260,300
Prepaid expenses	9,000	4,400
Equipment	99,100	108,600
Totals	$526,100	$518,900
Credits		
Accumulated amortization, equipment	$ 18,200	$ 30,200
Accounts payable	58,500	74,800
Income taxes payable	10,900	6,500
Dividends payable	–0–	7,500
Bonds payable	–0–	50,000
Common shares	300,000	300,000
Retained earnings	138,500	49,900
Totals	$526,100	$518,900

An examination of the company's statements and accounts showed:

a.   All sales were made on credit.

b.   All merchandise purchases were on credit.

c.   Accounts Payable balances resulted from merchandise purchases.

d.   Prepaid expenses relate to other operating expenses.

e.   Equipment that cost $42,500 and was amortized $24,000 was sold for cash.

f.   Equipment was purchased for cash.

g.   The change in the balance of Accumulated Amortization resulted from amortization expense and from the sale of equipment.

h.   The change in the balance of Retained Earnings resulted from dividend declarations and net income.

i.   Cash receipts from customers were $772,800.

j.   Cash payments for merchandise inventory amounted to $425,400.

k.   Cash payments for other operating expenses were $169,800.

l.   Income taxes paid were $32,400.

Required

Present Yaupon, Inc.'s income statement for 1996. Show your supporting calculations.

**Provocative Problem
18–2
James Company
(LO 1, 3)**

The following items include the 1996 and 1995 balance sheets and the 1996 income statement of the James Company. Additional information about the company's 1996 transactions is presented after the financial statements.

JAMES COMPANY
Balance Sheet
December 31, 1996 and 1995

	1996		1995	
Assets				
Current assets:				
Cash and cash equivalents	$ 1,000		$ 800	
Accounts receivable	4,500		3,100	
Merchandise inventory	19,000		16,000	
Prepaid expenses	700		600	
Total current assets		$25,200		$20,500
Long-term investments:				
Icahn Corporation common shares		10,000		12,000
Plant assets:				
Land		9,000		4,000
Buildings	$60,000		$60,000	
Less accumulated amortization	38,000	22,000	36,000	24,000
Equipment	$21,000		$16,000	
Less accumulated amortization	6,000	15,000	4,000	12,000
Total assets		$81,200		$72,500

Liabilities

Current liabilities:

Notes payable	$ 5,000	$ 3,500
Accounts payable	9,000	10,000
Other accrued liabilities	5,300	4,200
Interest payable	400	300
Taxes payable	300	500
Total current liabilities	$20,000	$18,500

Long-term liabilities:

Bonds payable, due in 2004	25,000	22,000
Total liabilities	$45,000	$40,500

Shareholders' Equity

Contributed capital:

Common shares	$16,000	$14,000
Retained earnings	20,200	18,000
Total shareholders' equity	36,200	32,000
Total liabilities and shareholders' equity	$81,200	$72,500

JAMES COMPANY
Income Statement
For Year Ended December 31, 1996

Revenues:

Sales	$120,000	
Gain on sale of equity investment	3,000	
Dividend income	500	
Interest income	400	$123,900

Expenses and losses:

Cost of goods sold	$ 50,000	
Other expenses	54,800	
Interest expense	2,000	
Income tax expense	2,500	
Amortization expense, buildings	2,000	
Amortization expense, equipment	4,000	
Loss on sale of equipment	600	
Total expenses and losses		115,900
Net income		$ 8,000

Additional Information

1. Received $5,000 from the sale of Icahn Corporation common shares that originally cost $2,000.

2. Received a cash dividend of $500 from the Icahn Corporation.

3. Received $400 cash from the First National Bank on December 31, 1996, as interest income.

4. Sold old equipment for $1,400. The old equipment originally cost $4,000 and had accumulated amortization of $2,000.

5. Purchased land costing $5,000 on December 31, 1996, in exchange for a note payable. Both principal and interest are due on June 30, 1997.

6. Purchased new equipment for $9,000 cash.

7. Paid $3,500 of notes payable.

8. Sold additional bonds payable at par of $3,000 on January 1, 1996.

9. Issued 1,000 common shares for cash at $2 per share.

10. Declared and paid a $5,800 cash dividend on October 1, 1996.

(The working papers that accompany the text include forms for this problem.)

Required

a. Prepare a working paper for James Company's 1996 SCFP.

b. Prepare the SCFP for 1996.

Provocative Problem 18–3
Financial statement analysis case
(LO 1)

Geac

Look in Appendix I at the end of the book to find Geac Computer Corporation Ltd.'s statement of changes in financial position. Based on your examination of that statement, answer the following questions:

1. During each of the fiscal years 1994 and 1993, was the cash provided by operating activities more or less than the cash paid for dividends?

2. What was the major reason for the difference between net income and cash flow from operating activities?

3. Describe the major cash inflows and outflows during 1994.

4. Describe the major differences in Geac's 1994 cash flows compared to its 1993 cash flows.

ANALYTICAL AND REVIEW PROBLEMS

A & R Problem 18–1

Barrie Company earned $168,000 net income during 1996. Machinery was sold for $232,000, and a $48,000 loss on the sale was recorded. Machinery purchases totaled $660,000 including a July purchase for which a $160,000 promissory note was issued. Bonds were retired at their face value, and the issuance of new common shares produced an infusion of cash. Barrie's comparative balance sheets were as follows (in thousands):

| | December 31 | |
	1996	**1995**
Cash	$ 208	$ 168
Receivables	392	444
Inventory	648	620
Machinery	2,700	2,520
Accumulated amortization	(380)	(420)
Total assets	$3,568	3,332
Accounts payable	$ 476	$ 572
Notes payable	544	420
Dividends payable	64	40
Bonds payable	456	640
Common shares	1,400	1,120
Retained earnings	628	540
Total liabilities and shareholders' equity	$3,568	$3,332

a. What was Barrie's amortization expense in 1996?

b.   What was the amount of cash flow from operations?

c.   What was the amount of cash flow from investing activities?

d.   What was the amount of the cash dividend declared? Paid?

e.   By what amount would you expect the total sources of cash to differ from the total uses of cash?

f.   What was the amount of cash flow from financing activities?

The data below refer to the activities of Banff Limited.

A & R Problem 18–2

Required

For each item, identify both the dollar amount and its classification—that is, whether it would appear as a positive or a negative adjustment to net income in the measurement of cash flow from operations or as some other source or use of cash.

1. Declared a $22,000 cash dividend; paid $19,000 during the year.

2. Sold for $120,000 cash land that had cost $95,000 two years earlier.

3. Sold for cash 2,000 shares for $14 a share.

4. Bought machinery for $37,000 in exchange for a note due in eight months.

5. Bought a computer that had a fair value of $140,000 by giving in exchange real estate that had cost $95,000 in an earlier period.

6. Equipment amortization, $56,000.

7. Issued for cash on December 31, 1993, 10-year, 10% $500,000 no-par-value bonds at $24,000 discount.

8. Bought its own shares for $12,500 and immediately canceled them.

9. Paid a lawyer $13,500 for services performed, billed, and recorded correctly in 1995.

10. Reported net income of $86,000 for the year ended December 31, 1996.

Adjustments to derive cash flow from operations:

A & R Problem 18–3

	Income Element	Adjust By	
		Adding	**Subtracting**
1.	Changes in current assets:		
	a. Increases		
	b. Decreases		
2.	Changes in current liabilities		
	a. Increases		
	b. Decreases...........................		
3.	Amortization of plant assets		
4.	Amortization of intangible assets		
5.	Interest expense:		
	a. Premium amortized....................		
	b. Discount amortized....................		
6.	Sale of noncurrent asset:		
	a. Gain		
	b. Loss		

Required

Indicate by an *x* in the appropriate column whether an item is added or subtracted to derive cash flow from operations.

CONCEPT TESTER

Test your understanding of the concepts introduced in this chapter by completing the following crossword puzzle.

Across Clues

1. Transactions to borrow money or repay debit (1st of 2 words; also see 5 across).

3. The statement that reports the cash inflows and outflows for the period (abbreviation).

4. Transactions that involve the purchase and sale of goods and services in the ordinary course of business (1st of 2 words; also see 5 across).

5. See 1 across, 2 down and 4 across for clues (2nd of 2 words).

Down Clues

2. Transactions that involve the purchase or sale of capital assets (1st of 2 words; also see 5 across).

ANSWERS TO PROGRESS CHECKS

18–1 No. The SCFP reports changes in the sum of cash plus cash equivalents. It does not report transfers between cash and cash equivalents.

18–2 The three categories of cash inflows and outflows are operating activities, investing activities, and financing activities.

18–3 a. Investing
b. Operating
c. Financing
d. Operating
e. Operating
f. Financing

18–4 a

18–5 $74,900 + $4,600 − $11,700 − $1,000 + $3,400 = $70,200

18–6 In the calculation of net income, expenses such as amortization are subtracted. However, these expenses do not require current cash outflows. Therefore, adding these expenses back to net income eliminates noncash items from the net income number, converting it to a cash basis.

18–7 In the process of reconciling net income to net cash provided or used by operating activities, a gain on sale of plant assets is subtracted from net income because a sale of plant assets is not an operating activity; it is an investing activity.

18–8 Investing activities during the year ended April 30, 1994, used net cash of $14,866 ($ in thousands). Cash outflows that contributed to this include net additions to fixed assets for $5,435, additions to capitalized software development of $5,385, and acquisitions of $5,572. The foreign exchange adjustment provided $1,526. The largest source of cash to finance these activities was a common share issue for $2,245.

Analyzing Financial Statements

Financial reports are highly summarized descriptions of complex organizations. Analyzing and understanding the information they present requires a lot of effort; the people who prepare reports need to know what their readers are looking for and how to help them find it.

Karen White and Mark Smith were given an article about a group of hi-tech wizards who have a vision and a desire to create a computer software corporation. In their enthusiasm, they have told a few potential investors that their proposed company was likely to be so successful it would rival the current companies in the industry. Corel corporation was named as an example of what the new venture was likely to become. The investors were quite familiar with the history of Corel and suggested that the wizards might be wise to be a little more moderate in their expectations. When the wizards disagreed, the investors pointed out that Corel was formed in 1985 and by 1994 had revenues of $67.5 million. It ships its products through a network of more than 160 distributors in 60 countries worldwide.

In concluding the conversation, the investors gave the wizards a copy of Corel's 1994 annual report and suggested that they study it carefully to see if it really represented a goal they could achieve. Karen and Mark prepared the following schedule:

COREL CORPORATION Growth percentages—increases	Year Ended November 30			
	1994	1993	1992	1991
Sales	56%	56%	29%	79%
Net income	56%	149%	-26%	62%
Earnings per share	40%	105%	-77%	50%
Book value per share	32%	-37%	-9%	37%

LEARNING OBJECTIVES

After studying Chapter 19, you should be able to:

1. **Explain the relationship between financial reporting and general purpose financial statements.**
2. **Describe, prepare, and interpret comparative financial statements and common-size comparative statements.**
3. **Calculate and explain the interpretation of the ratios, turnovers, and rates of return used to evaluate (*a*) short-term liquidity, (*b*) long-term risk and capital structure, and (*c*) operating efficiency and profitability.**
4. **State the limitations associated with using financial statement ratios and the sources from which standards for comparison may be obtained.**
5. **Define or explain the words and phrases listed in the chapter glossary.**

Chapter 19 demonstrates how to use the information in financial statements to evaluate the activities and financial status of a business. By explaining how you can relate the numbers in financial statements to each other, this chapter expands your ability to interpret the ratios we described in previous chapters.

FINANCIAL REPORTING

LO 1

Explain the relationship between financial reporting and general purpose financial statements.

Many people receive and analyze financial information about business firms. These people include managers, employees, directors, customers, suppliers, current and potential owners, current and potential lenders, brokers, regulatory authorities, lawyers, economists, labour unions, financial advisors, and financial analysts. Some of these, such as managers and some regulatory agencies, are able to gain access to specialized financial reports that meet their specific interests. However, the others must rely on the **general purpose financial statements** that companies publish periodically. General purpose financial statements include the (1) income statement, (2) balance sheet, (3) statement of changes in shareholders' equity (or statement of retained earnings), (4) statement of changes in financial position, and (5) notes related to the statements.

Financial reporting is intended to provide useful information to investors, creditors, and others for making investment, credit, and similar decisions. The information should help the users assess the amounts, timing, and uncertainty of prospective cash inflows and outflows.

Financial reporting includes communicating through a variety of means in addition to the financial statements. Some examples are reports filed with the Securities Commissions, news releases, and management letters or analyses included in annual reports. For an example, in Appendix I look at the section of **Geac Computer Corporation's** annual report called Management Discussion and Analysis of Financial Condition and Results of Operations.

Progress Check

19-1 Who are the intended users of general purpose financial statements?

19-2 What statements are usually included in the general purpose financial statements published by corporations?

In analyzing financial information, individual items usually are not very revealing. However, important relationships exist between items and groups of items. As a result, financial statement analysis involves identifying and describing relationships between items and groups of items and changes in those items.

You can see changes in financial statement items more clearly when amounts for two or more successive accounting periods are placed side by side in columns on a single statement.[1] Statements prepared in this manner are called **comparative statements.** Each financial statement can be presented in this comparative format.

In its simplest form, a comparative balance sheet consists of the amounts from two or more successive balance sheet dates arranged side by side. However, the usefulness of the statement can be improved by also showing each item's dollar amount of change and percentage change. When this is done, large dollar or percentage changes are more readily apparent. Illustration 19–1 shows this type of comparative balance sheet for Corel Corporation.

A comparative income statement is prepared in the same way. Amounts for two or more successive periods are placed side by side, with dollar and percentage changes in additional columns. Look at Illustration 19–2 to see **Corel Corporation's** comparative income statement.

COMPARATIVE STATEMENTS

LO 2

Describe, prepare, and interpret comparative financial statements and common-size comparative statements.

Calculating Percentage Increases and Decreases

To calculate the percentage increases and decreases on comparative statements, divide the dollar increase or decrease of an item by the amount shown for the item in the base year. If no amount is shown in the base year, or if the base year amount is negative (such as a net loss), a percentage increase or decrease cannot be calculated.

In this text, percentages and ratios typically are rounded to one or two decimal places. However, there is no uniform practice on this matter. In general, percentages should be carried out far enough to be meaningful. They should not be carried out so far that the important relationships become lost in the length of the numbers.

Analyzing and Interpreting Comparative Statements

In analyzing comparative data, study any items that show significant dollar or percentage changes. Then, try to identify the reasons for each change and, if possible, determine whether they are favorable or unfavorable. For example, in Illustration 19–1, the first item, Cash and short-term investments, shows a $28.6 million increase (50.2%). To a large extent, this may be explained by the increase in two other items: the $21.6 million increase in share capital and the $32.5 million increase in Retained earnings.

Note that **Corel's** liabilities increased by $5.4 million. In light of this, the $28.6 million increase in Cash and short-term investments might appear to be an excessive investment in highly liquid assets that usually earn a low return. However, the

[1]*CICA Handbook,* section 1500, "General Standards of Financial Statement Presentation," par. .09.

Illustration 19–1

COREL CORPORATION
Consolidated Balance Sheets
November 30, 1994, and November 30, 1993

	November 30 1994	November 30 1993	Amount of Increase or (Decrease) in 1994	Percent of Increase or (Decrease) in 1994
	(in thousands)			
Assets				
Current assets:				
Cash and short-term investments	$ 85,618	$ 57,000	$28,618	50.2
Accounts receivable				
Trade	50,586	36,327	14,259	39.3
Other	2,264	2,185	79	3.6
Inventory	13,417	7,361	6,056	82.3
Prepaid expenses	1,348	812	536	66.0
Total current assets	153,233	103,685	49,548	47.8
Capital assets	38,189	28,605	9,584	33.5
Total assets	$191,422	$132,290	$59,132	44.7
Liabilities and shareholders' equity				
Current liabilities:				
Accounts payable	$ 8,487	$ 5,391	$ 3,096	57.4
Accrued liabilities	10,722	6,073	4,649	76.6
Income taxes payable	4,930	7,400	(2,470)	(33.4)
Total current liabilities	24,139	18,864	5,275	28.0
Deferred income taxes	2,330	2,192	$ 138	6.3
Total liabilities	26,469	21,056	5,413	25.7
Shareholders' equity:				
Common share capital	89,380	67,792	21,588	31.8
Contributed surplus	352	352	0	0.0
Foreign currency adjustment		372	(372)	(100.0)
Retained earnings	75,221	42,718	32,503	76.1
Total shareholders' equity	164,953	111,234	53,719	48.3
Total liabilities and shareholders' equity	$191,422	$132,290	$59,132	44.7

company's very strong and liquid financial position indicates an outstanding ability to respond to new opportunities such as the acquisition of other companies.

Now look at the comparative income statement for Corel in Illustration 19–2. Corel's rapid growth is reflected by its 56.4% increase in sales. In fact, we should point out that the growth in 1994 continued a very strong trend established in prior years. (Later, we present data showing that sales in 1994 were 562% of sales in 1990.) Perhaps the most fundamental reason for this is the company's commitment to research and development. Note that research and development expenses were $10.9 million in 1994, up $4.6 million from 1993.

Illustration 19–2

	Years Ended November 30		**Amount of Increase or (Decrease) in 1994**	**Percent of Increase or (Decrease) in 1994**
COREL CORPORATION **Consolidated Statements of Income** **For Years Ended November 30, 1994, and 1993**				
	1994	**1993**		
	(in thousands)			
Sales	$164,313	$105,027	$59,286	56.4
Cost of sales	35,940	24,310	11,630	47.8
Gross profit	128,373	80,717	47,656	59.0
Expenses:				
Advertising	34,390	20,579	13,811	67.1
Selling, general and administrative	30,833	18,005	12,828	71.2
Research and development	10,888	6,256	4,632	74.0
Depreciation and amortization ...	6,137	4,079	2,058	50.5
Loss (gain) on foreign exchange ..	1,546	(480)	2,026	422.1
Total expenses	83,794	48,439	35,355	73.0
Income from continuing operations	44,579	32,278	12,301	38.1
Interest income	2,861	2,389	472	19.8
Income from continuing operations before income taxes	47,440	34,667	12,773	36.8
Income taxes	14,937	13,814	1,123	8.1
Net income	$ 32,503	$ 20,853	$11,650	55.9

All of the income statement items (except foreign exchange) reflect the company's rapid growth. The increases ranged from 67.1 to 19.8%. Especially note the large $13.8 million or 67.1% increase in Advertising. This suggests the company's leadership and strong response to competition in the software industry. Although the dollar increase in Interest income was only $.5 million, this amounted to a 19.8% increase. This is consistent with the increase in Cash and short-term investments reported on the balance sheet.

Trend Percentages

Trend percentages (also known as *index numbers*) can be used to describe changes that have occurred from one period to the next. They are also used to compare data that cover a number of years. To calculate trend percentages:

1. Select a base year and assign each item on the base year statement a weight of 100%.

2. Express each item from the statements for the other years as a percentage of its base year amount. To determine these percentages, divide the amounts in the nonbase years by the amount of the item in the base year.

For example, consider the following data for Corel Corporation:

	1994	1993	1992	1991	1990
Sales	$164,313	$105,027	$67,515	$52,242	$29,230
Cost of sales	35,940	24,310	19,459	7,735	6,015
Gross profit	$128,373	$ 80,717	$48,056	$44,507	$23,215

Using 1990 as the base year, we calculate the trend percentages for each year by dividing the dollar amounts in each year by the 1990 dollar amounts. When the percentages are calculated, the trends for these items appear as follows:

	1994	1993	1992	1991	1990
Sales	562.1%	359.3%	231.0%	178.7%	100.0%
Cost of sales	597.5	404.2	323.5	128.6	100.0
Gross profit	553.0	347.7	207.0	191.7	100.0

Illustration 19–3 presents the same data in a graph. A graph can help you identify trends and detect changes in their strength or direction. For example, note that the gross profit line was bending upward from 1990 to 1991 but was essentially flat from 1991 to 1992. The gross profit increased at a lower rate from 1991 to 1992 but then parallels the sales line from 1992 to 1994.

A graph also may help you identify and understand the relationships between items. For example, the graph in Illustration 19–3 shows that through 1993, cost of sales increased at a rate that was somewhat more than the increase in sales. Further, the differing trends in these two items had a clear effect on the percentage changes in gross profit. That is, gross profit increased each year at a somewhat slower rate than sales.

The analysis of financial statement items also may include the relationships between items on different financial statements. For example, note the following comparison of Corel's total assets and sales:

	1994	1990	1994 Amount as a Percentage of 1990
Sales	$164.3	$29.2	562.7%
Total assets (fiscal year-end)	191.4	41.9	456.8

The rate of increase in total assets was not quite as large as the increase in sales. Was this change favourable? We cannot say for sure. It might suggest that the company is no longer able to use its assets as efficiently as in earlier years. On the other hand, it might mean that the company can expect slower growth in future years. Financial statement analysis often leads the analyst to ask questions, without providing one clear answer.

Illustration 19-3 Trend Lines Showing Percentage Changes in Net Revenues, Cost of Revenues, and Gross Profit

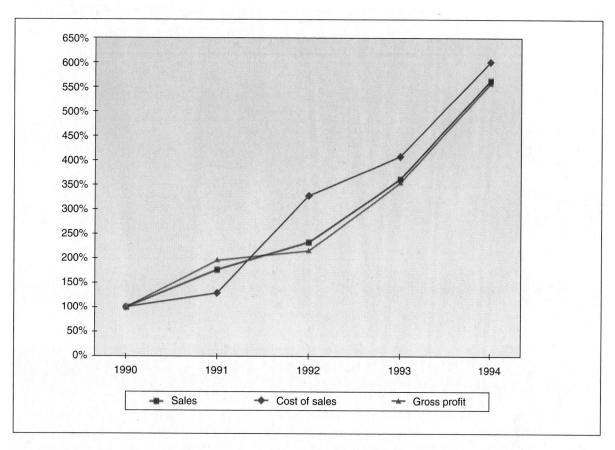

Common-Size Comparative Statements

Although the comparative statements illustrated so far show how each item has changed over time, they do not emphasize the relative importance of each item. Changes in the relative importance of each financial statement item are shown more clearly by **common-size comparative statements.**

In common-size statements, each item is expressed as a percentage of a *base amount.* For a common-size balance sheet, the base amount is usually the amount of total assets. This total is assigned a value of 100%. (Of course, the total amount of liabilities plus owners' equity also equals 100%.) Then, each asset, liability, and owners' equity item is shown as a percentage of total assets (or total liabilities plus owners' equity). If you present a company's successive balance sheets in this way, changes in the mixture of the assets or liabilities and equity are more readily apparent.

For example, look at the common-size comparative balance sheet for Corel in Illustration 19–4. Note that Cash and short-term investments amounted to 43.1% of total assets at the end of the 1993 fiscal year. By comparison, they were 44.7% of total assets at the end of 1994.

Illustration 19–4

	November 30		Common-Size Percentages	
	1994	1993	1994	1993
	(in thousands)			
CORE L CORPORATION — Common-Size Comparative Balance Sheet — November 30, 1994, and November 30, 1993				

COREL CORPORATION
Common-Size Comparative Balance Sheet
November 30, 1994, and November 30, 1993

	November 30		Common-Size Percentages	
	1994	**1993**	**1994**	**1993**
	(in thousands)			
Assets				
Current assets:				
Cash and short-term investments	$ 85,618	$57,000	44.7	43.1
Accounts receivable				
Trade	50,586	36,327	26.4	27.4
Other	2,264	2,185	1.2	1.7
Inventory	13,417	7,361	7.0	5.6
Prepaid expenses	1,348	812	0.7	0.6
Total current assets	153,233	103,685	80.0	78.4
Capital assets	38,189	28,605	20.0	21.6
Total assets	$191,422	$132,290	100.0	100.0
Liabilities and shareholders' equity				
Current liabilities:				
Accounts payable	$8,487	$5,391	4.4	4.1
Accrued liabilities	10,722	6,073	5.6	4.6
Income taxes payable	4,930	7,400	2.6	5.6
Total current liabilities	24,139	18,864	12.6	14.3
Deferred income taxes	2,330	2,192	1.2	1.6
Total liabilities	26,469	21,056	13.8	15.9
Shareholders' equity				
Common share capital	89,380	67,792	46.7	51.2
Contributed surplus	352	352	0.2	0.3
Foreign currency adjustment		372		0.3
Retained earnings	75,221	42,718	39.3	32.3
Total shareholders' equity	164,953	111,234	86.2	84.1
Total liabilities and shareholders' equity	$191,422	$132,290	100.0	100.0

In producing a common-size income statement, the amount of net sales is usually the base amount and is assigned a value of 100%. Then, each statement item appears as a percentage of net sales. If you think of the 100% sales amount as representing one sales dollar, the remaining items show how each sales dollar was distributed among costs, expenses, and profit. For example, the comparative income statement in Illustration 19–5 shows that for each dollar of sales during 1994, research and development expenses amounted to 6.6 cents. In 1993, research and development consumed 6.0 cents of each sales dollar.

Common-size percentages help the analyst see any potentially important changes in a company's expenses. For Corel, the relative size of each expense changed very little from 1993 to 1994. A common problem with the percentages is that the totals do not foot because of rounding. However, these slight errors, which are 0.1%, do not usually cause serious difficulties.

Illustration 19-5

	Years Ended November 30		Common-Size Percentage	
	1994	1993	1994	1993
	(in thousands)			
Sales	$164,313	$105,027	100.0	100.0
Cost of sales	35,940	24,310	21.9	23.1
Gross profit	128,373	80,717	78.1	76.9
Expenses:				
Advertising	34,390	20,579	20.9	19.6
Selling, general and administrative	30,833	18,005	18.8	17.1
Research and development	10,888	6,256	6.6	6.0
Depreciation and amortization	6,137	4,079	3.7	3.9
Loss (gain) on foreign exchange	1,546	(480)	0.9	(0.5)
Total expenses	83,794	48,439	51.0	46.1
Income from continuing operations	44,579	32,278	27.1	30.7
Interest income	2,861	2,389	1.7	2.3
Income from continuing operations before income taxes	47,440	34,667	28.9	33.0
Income taxes	14,937	13,814	9.1	13.2
Net income	$ 32,503	$ 20,853	19.8	19.9
Earnings per share	$ 0.63	$ 0.45		
Weighted-average shares outstanding	51,768	46,146		

COREL CORPORATION
Common-Size Comparative Income Statement
For Years Ended November 30, 1994 and 1993

Many corporate annual reports include graphic presentations such as those in Illustration 19–6 from Corel's 1994 Annual Report. The pie chart on the left side of the illustration shows the sales generated by each of the company's geographic regions in 1993. The pie chart on the right shows the revenues by sales channel. In that chart, OEM refers to original equipment manufacturers. In the annual report, the data for these charts did not appear in the financial statements. Instead, they were included as part of the discussion and analysis by management.

Progress Check

19-3 On common-size comparative statements, which of the following is true? *(a)* Each item is expressed as a percentage of a base amount. *(b)* Total assets is assigned a value of 100%. *(c)* Amounts from two or more successive periods are placed side by side. *(d)* All of the above are true.

19-4 What is the difference between the percentages shown on a comparative income statement and those shown on a common-size comparative income statement?

19-5 Trend percentages *(a)* are shown on the comparative income statement and balance sheet; *(b)* are shown on common-size comparative statements; or *(c)* are also known as index numbers.

858   Chapter 19

Illustration 19-6   Pie-Chart Presentations, Corel Corporation

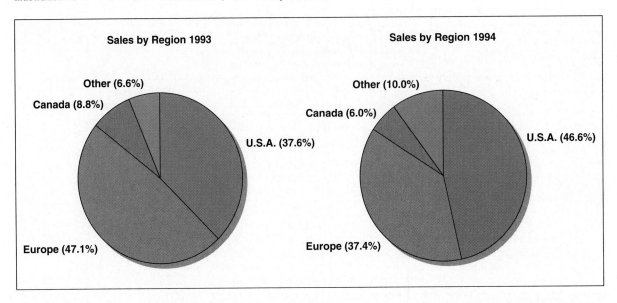

ANALYSIS OF SHORT-TERM LIQUIDITY

LO 3

Calculate and explain the interpretation of the ratios, turnovers, and rates of return used to evaluate *(a)* short-term liquidity, *(b)* long-term risk and capital structure, and *(c)* operating efficiency and profitability.

The amount of current assets less current liabilities is called the **working capital** or *net working capital* of a business. A business must maintain an adequate amount of working capital to meet current debts, carry sufficient inventories, and take advantage of cash discounts. Indeed, a business that runs out of working capital cannot meet its current obligations or continue operations.

Current Ratio

When evaluating the working capital of a business, you must look beyond the dollar amount of current assets less current liabilities. Also consider the relationship between the amounts of current assets and current liabilities. Recall from Chapter 3 that the *current ratio* describes a company's ability to pay its short-term obligations. The current ratio relates current assets to current liabilities, as follows:

$$\text{Current ratio} = \frac{\text{Current assets}}{\text{Current liabilities}}$$

For example, using the information in Illustration 19–1, Corel's working capital positions and current ratios at the end of its 1994 and 1993 years were:

	November 30, 1994	November 30, 1993
(In millions)		
Current assets	$153,233	$103,685
Current liabilities	24,139	18,864
Working capital	$129,094	$84,821
Current ratio:		
$153,233/$24,139 . .	6.35 to 1	
$103,685/$18,864 . .		5.50 to 1

A high current ratio generally indicates a strong position because a high ratio suggests the company is capable of meeting its current obligations. On the other hand, a company might have a current ratio that is too high. This condition means that the company has invested too much in current assets compared to its needs. Normally, current assets do not generate very much additional revenue. Therefore, if a company invests too much in current assets, the investment is not being used efficiently.

Years ago, bankers and other creditors often used a current ratio of 2 to 1 as a rule of thumb in evaluating the debt-paying ability of a credit-seeking company. A company with a 2 to 1 current ratio was generally thought to be a good credit risk in the short run. However, most lenders realize that the 2 to 1 rule of thumb is not a good test of debt-paying ability. Whether a company's current ratio is good or bad depends on at least three factors:

1. The nature of the company's business.
2. The composition of its current assets.
3. The turnover rate for some of its current assets.

Whether a company's current ratio is adequate depends on the nature of its business. A service company that has no inventories other than supplies and that grants little or no credit may be able to operate on a current ratio of less than 1 to 1 if its sales generate enough cash to pay its current liabilities on time. On the other hand, a company that sells high-fashion clothing or furniture may occasionally misjudge customer demand. If this happens, the company's inventory may not generate as much cash as expected. A company that faces risks like these may need a current ratio of much more than 2 to 1 to protect its liquidity.

Therefore, when you study the adequacy of working capital, consider the type of business under review. Before you decide that a company's current ratio is too low or too high, compare the company's current ratio with ratios of other successful companies in the same industry. Another important source of insight is to observe how the ratio has changed over time.

Keep in mind that the current ratio can be affected by a company's choice of an inventory flow assumption. For example, a company that uses LIFO tends to report a smaller amount of current assets than if it uses FIFO. Therefore, consider the underlying factors before deciding that a given current ratio is acceptable.

Also consider the composition of a company's current assets when you evaluate its working capital position. Cash and short-term investments are more liquid than accounts and notes receivable. And, short-term receivables normally are more liquid than merchandise inventory. Cash can be used to pay current debts at once. But, accounts receivable and merchandise inventory must be converted into cash before payments can be made. Therefore, an excessive amount of receivables and inventory could weaken the company's ability to pay its current liabilities.

One way to take the composition of current assets into account is to evaluate the acid-test ratio. We discuss this next; then, we examine the turnover rates for receivables and inventories.

Acid-Test Ratio

Recall from Chapter 5 that an easily calculated check on current asset composition is the *acid-test ratio,* also called the *quick ratio.* Quick assets are cash, short-term investments, accounts receivable, and notes receivable. These are the most liquid types of current assets. Calculate the ratio as follows:

$$\text{Acid-test ratio} = \frac{\text{Quick assets}}{\text{Current liabilities}}$$

Using the information in Illustration 19–1, we calculate Corel's acid-test ratios as follows:

(In millions)	November 30, 1994	November 30, 1993
Cash and short-term investments	$ 85,618	$ 57,000
Accounts receivable, trade	50,586	36,327
Total quick assets	$136,102	$ 93,327
Current liabilities	$ 24,139	$ 18,864
Acid-test ratio:		
$136,102/$24,139	5.64 to 1	
$93,327/$18,864		4.95 to 1

A traditional rule of thumb for an acceptable acid-test ratio is 1 to 1. However, as is true for all financial ratios, you should be skeptical about rules of thumb. The working capital requirements of a company are also affected by how frequently the company converts its current assets into cash. Thus, a careful analysis of a company's short-term liquidity should include additional analyses of its receivables and inventories.

Accounts Receivable Turnover

One way to measure how frequently a company converts its receivables into cash is to calculate the accounts receivable turnover. As you learned in Chapter 8, this is calculated as follows:

$$\text{Accounts receivable turnover} = \frac{\text{Net sales}}{\text{Average accounts receivable}}$$

Although this ratio is widely known as accounts receivable turnover, all short-term receivables from customers normally are included in the denominator. Thus, if a company has short-term notes receivable, those balances should be included with the accounts receivable. In the numerator, the calculation would be more precise if credit sales were used. Usually, however, net sales is used because information about credit sales is not available.

Applying the formula to Corel's 1994 fiscal year results, the company's accounts receivable turnover was

$$\frac{\$164,313}{(\$50,586 + \$36,327)/2} = 3.78 \text{ times}$$

If accounts receivable are collected quickly, the accounts receivable turnover is high. In general, this is favorable because it means that the company does not have to commit large amounts of capital to accounts receivable. However, an accounts receivable turnover may be too high. This might occur when credit terms are so restrictive they negatively affect sales volume.

Sometimes, the ending accounts receivable balance can substitute for the average balance in calculating accounts receivable turnover. This is acceptable if the effect is not significant. Also, some analysts prefer using gross accounts receivable before subtracting the allowance for doubtful accounts. However, balance sheets may report only the net amount of accounts receivable.

Days' Sales Uncollected

Accounts receivable turnover is only one way to measure how frequently a company collects its accounts. Another method is to calculate the days' sales uncollected, which we defined in Chapter 7 as

$$\text{Days' sales uncollected} = \frac{\text{Accounts receivable}}{\text{Net sales}} \times 365$$

Although this formula takes the usual approach of placing accounts receivable in the numerator, short-term notes receivable from customers should be included. To illustrate, we refer to the information about Corel in Illustrations 19–1 and 19–2. The days' sales uncollected on November 30, 1994, was

$$\frac{\$50,586}{\$164,313} \times 365 = 112.4 \text{ days}$$

Days' sales uncollected has more meaning if you know the credit terms. A rule of thumb is that days' sales uncollected: *(a)* should not exceed one and one-third times the days in the credit period, if discounts are not offered; *(b)* should not exceed one and one-third times the days in its discount period, if discounts are offered.

Turnover of Merchandise Inventory

Working capital requirements are also affected by how long a company holds merchandise inventory before selling it. This effect can be measured by calculating merchandise turnover, which we defined in Chapter 9 as:

$$\text{Merchandise turnover} = \frac{\text{Cost of goods sold}}{\text{Average merchandise inventory}}$$

Using the cost of revenues and inventories information in Illustrations 19–1 and 19–2, we calculate Corel's merchandise turnover during 1994 as follows (cost of goods sold is called *cost of sales* on Corel's income statement):

$$\frac{\$35,940}{(\$13,417 + \$7,361)/2} = 3.46 \text{ times}$$

In this calculation, the average inventory was estimated by averaging the beginning and the ending inventories for 1994. In case the beginning and ending inventories do not represent the amount normally on hand, an average of the quarterly inventories may be used, if that is available.

From a working capital point of view, a company with a high turnover requires a smaller investment in inventory than one that produces the same sales with a low turnover. On the other hand, the merchandise turnover may be too high if a company keeps such a small inventory that sales volume is restricted.

Days' Stock on Hand

Recall from Chapter 9 that days' stock on hand is another means of evaluating the liquidity of a company's inventory. It relates to inventory in a similar fashion as day's sales uncollected relates to receivables. The calculation is

$$\text{Days' stock on hand} = \frac{\text{Ending inventory}}{\text{Cost of goods sold}} \times 365$$

Applying the formula to Corel's 1994 information, we calculate days' stock on hand as:

$$\frac{\$13,417}{\$35,940} \times 365 = 136.3 \text{ days}$$

Assuming the particular products in inventory are those customers demand, the formula estimates that the inventory will be converted into receivables (or cash) in 136.3 days. If all of Corel's sales were credit sales, the conversion of inventory to receivables in 136.3 days plus the conversion of receivables to cash in 112.4 days would suggest that the inventory would be converted into cash in about 249 days (136.3 + 112.4 = 248.7).

Progress Check

19-6   The following is taken from the December 31, 1996, balance sheet of Paff Company: cash, $820,000; accounts receivable, $240,000; inventories, $470,000; plant and equipment, $910,000; accounts payable, $350,000; and income taxes payable, $180,000. Calculate the *(a)* current ratio and *(b)* acid-test ratio.

19-7   On December 31, 1995, Paff Company (see 19–6) had accounts receivable of $290,000 and inventories of $530,000. Also, during 1996, net sales amounted to $2,500,000 and cost of goods sold was $750,000. Calculate the *(a)* accounts receivable turnover, *(b)* days' sales uncollected, *(c)* merchandise turnover, and *(d)* days' stock on hand.

ANALYSIS OF LONG-TERM RISK AND CAPITAL STRUCTURE

LO 3

Calculate and explain the interpretation of the ratios, turnovers, and rates of return used to evaluate (*a*) short-term liquidity, (*b*) long-term risk and capital structure, and (*c*) operating efficiency and profitability.

An analysis of working capital evaluates the short-term liquidity of the company. However, analysts are also interested in a company's ability to meet its obligations and provide security to its creditors over the long run. Indicators of this ability include *debt* and *equity* ratios, the relationship between *pledged assets* and *secured liabilities,* and the company's capacity to earn *sufficient income to pay its fixed interest charges.*

Debt and Equity Ratios

Financial analysts are always interested in the portion of a company's assets contributed by its owners and the portion contributed by creditors. This relationship is described by the debt ratio you learned about in Chapter 2. Recall that the debt ratio expresses total liabilities as a percentage of total assets. The **equity ratio** provides complementary information by expressing total shareholders' equity as a percentage of total assets.

We calculate the debt and equity ratios of Corel Corporation as follows:

	1994	1993
a. Total liabilities	$ 26,469	$ 21,056
b. Total shareholders' equity	164,953	111,234
c. Total liabilities and shareholders' equity	$191,422	$132,290
Percentages provided by creditors: (a/c)	13.8%	15.9%
Percentages provided by shareholders: (b/c)	86.2%	84.1%

Corel's financial statements reflect very little debt compared to most companies. It has only one long-term liability and, at the end of the 1994 year, its current liabilities provide only 13.8% of the total assets. In general, a company is less risky if it has only a small amount of debt in its capital structure. The larger the portion provided by shareholders, the more losses can be absorbed by shareholders before the remaining assets become inadequate to satisfy the claims of creditors.

From the shareholders' point of view, however, including debt in the capital structure of a company may be desirable, so long as the risk is not too great. If a business can earn a return on borrowed capital that is higher than the cost of borrowing, the difference represents increased income to shareholders. Because debt can have the effect of increasing the return to shareholders, the inclusion of debt is sometimes described as financial leverage. Companies are said to be highly leveraged if a large portion of their assets is financed by debt.

Pledged Assets to Secured Liabilities

In Chapter 17, we explained how to use the ratio of pledged assets to secured liabilities to evaluate the risk of nonpayment faced by secured creditors. Recall that the ratio also may provide information of interest to unsecured creditors. The ratio is calculated as follows:

$$\text{Pledged assets to secured liabilities} = \frac{\text{Book value of pledged assets}}{\text{Secured liabilities}}$$

Regardless of how helpful this ratio might be in evaluating the risk faced by creditors, the information needed to calculate the ratio is seldom presented in published financial statements. Thus, it is used primarily by persons who have the ability to obtain the information directly from the company managers.

The usual rule-of-thumb minimum value for this ratio is 2 to 1. However, the ratio needs careful interpretation because it is based on the book value of the pledged assets. As you know, book values are not intended to reflect the amount that would be received for the assets in a liquidation sale. Also, the long-term earning ability of the company with pledged assets may be more important than the value of the pledged assets. Creditors prefer that a debtor be able to pay with cash generated by operating activities rather than with cash obtained by liquidating assets.

Times Fixed Interest Charges Earned

As you learned in Chapter 13, the times fixed interest charges earned ratio is often calculated to describe the security of the return offered to creditors. The amount of income before the deduction of interest charges and income taxes is the amount available to pay the interest charges. Calculate the ratio as follows:

$$\text{Times fixed interest charges earned} = \frac{\text{Income before interest and income taxes}}{\text{Interest expense}}$$

The larger this ratio, the greater the security for the lenders. A rule of thumb for this statistic is that creditors are reasonably safe if the company earns its fixed interest charges two or more times each year. Look in Illustration 19–2 and observe that Corel did not report interest expense as a separate item. Apparently interest expense is not material; probably it is offset against interest income. Also recall from Illustration 19–1 that Corel did not have any long-term debt. Furthermore, few if any of the company's current liabilities would be likely to generate interest expense. As a result, we are not able to calculate a times fixed interest charges earned ratio for Corel. Yet, we should again recognize that there appears to be little risk for Corel's creditors.

ANALYSIS OF OPERATING EFFICIENCY AND PROFITABILITY

Financial analysts are especially interested in the ability of a company to use its assets efficiently to produce profits for its owners and thus provide cash flows to them. Several ratios are available to help you evaluate operating efficiency and profitability.

Profit Margin

The operating efficiency of a company can be expressed in two components. The first is the company's *profit margin*. As you learned in Chapter 4, this ratio describes a company's ability to earn a net income from sales. It is measured by expressing net income as a percentage of net sales. For example, we can use the information in Illustration 19–2 to calculate **Corel's** 1994 profit margin as follows:

$$\text{Profit margin} = \frac{\text{Net income}}{\text{Revenues}} = \frac{\$32,503}{\$164,313} = 19.8\%$$

To evaluate the profit margin of a company, consider the nature of the industry in which the company operates. For example, a publishing company might be expected to have a profit margin between 10 and 15%, while a retail supermarket might have a normal profit margin of 1 or 2%. Low margin businesses rely on high sales volume to be successful.

Total Asset Turnover

The second component of operating efficiency is *total asset turnover,* which describes the ability of the company to use its assets to generate sales. In Chapter 11, you learned to calculate this ratio as follows:

$$\text{Total asset turnover} = \frac{\text{Net sales}}{\text{Average total assets}}$$

In calculating Corel's total asset turnover for 1994, we follow the usual practice of averaging the total assets at the beginning and the end of the year. Taking the information from Illustrations 19–1 and 19–2, the calculation is:

$$\frac{\$164{,}313}{(\$191{,}422 + \$132{,}290)/2} = 1.015 \text{ times*}$$

*Carried to three decimal places to avoid later rounding error.

Both profit margin and total asset turnover describe the two basic components of operating efficiency. However, they also evaluate management performance because the management of a company is fundamentally responsible for its operating efficiency.

Return on Total Assets

Because operating efficiency has two basic components (profit margin and total asset turnover), analysts frequently calculate a summary measure of these components. This summary measure is the *return on total assets* that we discussed in Chapter 12. Recall that the calculation is:

$$\text{Return on total assets} = \frac{\text{Net income}}{\text{Average total assets}}$$

Applying this to Corel's 1994 year, we calculate return on total assets as

$$\frac{\$32{,}503}{(\$191{,}422 + \$132{,}290)/2} = 20.1\%$$

Corel's 20.1% return on total assets appears very favourable compared to most businesses. However, you should make comparisons with competing companies and alternative investment opportunities before reaching a final conclusion. Also, you should evaluate the trend in the rates of return earned by the company in recent years.

Earlier, we said that the return on total assets summarizes the two components of operating efficiency—profit margin and total asset turnover. The following calculation shows the relationship between these three measures. Notice that both profit margin and total asset turnover contribute to overall operating efficiency, as measured by return on total assets.

Profit margin	$\times$	Total asset turnover	$=$	Return on total assets
$\dfrac{\text{Net income}}{\text{Net sales}}$	$\times$	$\dfrac{\text{Net sales}}{\text{Average total assets}}$	$=$	$\dfrac{\text{Net income}}{\text{Average total assets}}$
For Corel Corporation:				
19.8%	$\times$	1.015	$=$	20.1%

Return on Common Shareholders' Equity

Perhaps the most important reason for operating a business is to earn a net income for its owners. The *return on common shareholders' equity* measures the success of a business in reaching this goal. In Chapter 1, we simplified this calculation by basing it on the beginning balance of owners' equity. However, many companies have frequent transactions that involve issuing and perhaps repurchasing stock during each year. Thus, you should allow for these events by calculating the return based on the average shareholders' equity, as follows:

$$\text{Return on common shareholders' equity} = \frac{\text{Net income} - \text{Preferred dividends}}{\text{Average common shareholders' equity}}$$

Recall from Illustration 19–1 that Corel did not have any preferred shares outstanding. As a result, we determine Corel's 1994 return as follows:

$$\frac{\$32,503}{(\$164,953 + \$111,234)/2} = 23.5\%$$

When preferred shares are outstanding, the denominator in the calculation should be the book value of the common shares. In the numerator, the dividends on cumulative preferred shares must be subtracted whether they were declared or are in arrears. If the preferred is not cumulative, the dividends are subtracted only if declared.

Price Earnings Ratio

Recall from Chapter 16 that the price earnings ratio is calculated as follows:

$$\text{Price earnings ratio} = \frac{\text{Market price per share}}{\text{Earnings per share}}$$

Sometimes, the predicted earnings per share for the next period is used in the denominator of the calculation. Other times, the reported earnings per share for the most recent period is used. In either case, the ratio is an indicator of the future growth of and risk related to the company's earnings as perceived by investors who establish the market price of the shares.

During the last three months of Corel's 1994 year, the market price of its common shares ranged from a low of $14.50 to a high of $23.25. Using the $0.63 earnings per share that was reported after the year-end, the price earnings ratios for the low and the high were

$$\text{Low: } \frac{\$14.50}{\$0.63} = 23.0 \qquad \text{High: } \frac{\$23.25}{\$0.63} = 36.9$$

In its 1994 annual report, Corel's management reported that it did not expect the 1995 revenue growth rates to be as high as those for 1994. Management also indicated that operating expenses as a percentage of revenues might increase. Nevertheless, the price earnings ratios are much higher than for most companies. No doubt, Corel's high ratios reflect the expectation of investors that the company would continue to grow at a much higher rate than most companies.

Dividend Yield

As you learned in Chapter 15, *dividend yield* is a statistic used to compare the dividend-paying performance of different investment alternatives. The formula is

$$\text{Dividend yield} = \frac{\text{Annual dividends per share}}{\text{Market price per share}}$$

Some companies may not declare dividends because they need the cash in the business. For example, Corel's 1994 annual report stated that the company had not declared any dividends.

Progress Check

19–8 Which ratio describes the security of the return offered to creditors? *(a)* Debt ratio; *(b)* Equity ratio; *(c)* Times fixed interest charges earned; *(d)* Pledged assets to secured liabilities.

19–9 Which ratio measures the success of a business in earning net income for its owners? *(a)* Profit margin; *(b)* Return on common shareholders' equity; *(c)* Price earnings ratio; *(d)* Dividend yield.

19–10 If BK Company has net sales of $8,500,000, net income of $945,000, and total asset turnover of 1.8 times, what is BK's return on total assets?

To evaluate short-term liquidity, use these ratios:

$$\text{Current ratio} = \frac{\text{Current assets}}{\text{Current liabilities}}$$

$$\text{Acid-test ratio} = \frac{\text{Cash} + \text{Short-term investments} + \text{Current receivables}}{\text{Current liabilities}}$$

$$\text{Accounts receivable turnover} = \frac{\text{Net sales}}{\text{Average accounts receivable}}$$

$$\text{Days' sales uncollected} = \frac{\text{Accounts receivable}}{\text{Net sales}} \times 365$$

$$\text{Merchandise turnover} = \frac{\text{Cost of goods sold}}{\text{Average merchandise inventory}}$$

$$\text{Days' stock on hand} = \frac{\text{Ending inventory}}{\text{Cost of goods sold}} \times 365$$

To evaluate long-term risk and capital structure, use these ratios:

$$\text{Debt ratio} = \frac{\text{Total liabilities}}{\text{Total assets}}$$

$$\text{Equity ratio} = \frac{\text{Total shareholders' equity}}{\text{Total assets}}$$

$$\text{Pledged assets to secured liabilities} = \frac{\text{Book value of pledged assets}}{\text{Secured liabilities}}$$

$$\text{Times fixed interest charges earned} = \frac{\text{Income before interest and taxes}}{\text{Interest expense}}$$

To evaluate operating efficiency and profitability, use these ratios:

$$\text{Profit margin} = \frac{\text{Net income}}{\text{Net sales}}$$

$$\text{Total asset turnover} = \frac{\text{Net sales}}{\text{Average total assets}}$$

$$\text{Return on total assets} = \frac{\text{Net income}}{\text{Average total assets}}$$

REVIEW OF FINANCIAL STATEMENT RATIOS AND STATISTICS FOR ANALYSIS

$$\text{Return on common shareholders' equity} = \frac{\text{Net income} - \text{Preferred dividends}}{\text{Average common shareholders' equity}}$$

$$\text{Price earnings ratio} = \frac{\text{Market price per common share}}{\text{Earnings per share}}$$

$$\text{Dividend yield} = \frac{\text{Annual dividends per share}}{\text{Market price per share}}$$

STANDARDS OF COMPARISON

LO 4
State the limitations associated with using financial statement ratios and the sources from which standards for comparison may be obtained.

After computing ratios and turnovers in the process of analyzing financial statements, you have to decide whether the calculated amounts suggest good, bad, or merely average performance by the company. To make these judgments, you must have some bases for comparison. The following are possibilities:

1. An experienced analyst may compare the ratios and turnovers of the company under review with *subjective* standards acquired from past experiences.
2. For purposes of comparison, an analyst may calculate the ratios and turnovers of a selected group of competing companies in the same *industry*.
3. *Published* ratios and turnovers (such as those provided by Dun & Bradstreet) may be used for comparison.
4. Some local and national trade associations gather data from their members and publish *standard* or *average* ratios for their trade or industry. When available, these data can give the analyst a useful basis for comparison.
5. *Rule-of-thumb* standards can be used as a basis for comparison.

Of these five standards, the ratios and turnovers of a selected group of competing companies normally are the best bases for comparison. Rule-of-thumb standards should be applied with great care and then only if they seem reasonable in light of past experience and the industry's norms.

Progress Check

19-11 Which of the following would not be used as a basis for comparison when analyzing ratios and turnovers?
 a. Companies in different industries.
 b. Subjective standards from past experience.
 c. Rule-of-thumb standards.
 d. Averages within a trade or industry.

19-12 Which of the typical bases of comparison is usually best?

SUMMARY OF THE CHAPTER IN TERMS OF LEARNING OBJECTIVES

LO 1. Explain the relationship between financial reporting and general purpose financial statements. Financial reporting is intended to provide information that is useful to investors, creditors, and others in making investment, credit, and similar decisions. The information is communicated in a variety of ways, including general purpose financial statements. These statements normally include an income statement, balance sheet, statement of changes in shareholders' equity or statement of retained earnings, statement of changes in financial position, and the related notes.

LO 2. Describe, prepare, and interpret comparative financial statements and common-size comparative statements. Comparative financial statements show amounts for two or more successive periods, sometimes with the changes in the items disclosed in absolute and percentage terms. In common-size statements, each item is expressed as a percentage of a base amount. The base amount for the balance sheet is usually total assets, and the base amount for the income statement is usually net sales.

LO 3. Calculate and explain the interpretation of the ratios, turnovers, and rates of return used to evaluate (*a*) short-term liquidity, (*b*) long-term risk and capital structure, and (*c*) operating efficiency and profitability. To evaluate the short-term liquidity of a company, calculate a current ratio, an acid-test ratio, the accounts receivable turnover, the days' sales uncollected, the merchandise turnover, and the days' stock on hand.

In evaluating the long-term risk and capital structure of a company, calculate debt and equity ratios, pledged assets to secured liabilities, and the number of times fixed interest charges were earned.

In evaluating operating efficiency and profitability, calculate profit margin, total asset turnover, return on total assets, and return on common shareholders' equity. Other statistics used to evaluate the profitability of alternative investments include the price earnings ratio and the dividend yield.

LO 4. State the limitations associated with using financial statement ratios and the sources from which standards for comparison may be obtained. In deciding whether financial statement ratio values are satisfactory, too high, or too low, you must have some bases for comparison. These bases may come from past experience and personal judgment, from ratios of similar companies, or from ratios published by trade associations or other public sources. Traditional rules of thumb should be applied with great care and only if they seem reasonable in light of past experience.

DEMONSTRATION PROBLEM

Use the financial statements of Precision Co. to satisfy the following requirements:

1. Prepare a comparative income statement showing the percentage increase or decrease for 1996 over 1995.
2. Prepare a common-size comparative balance sheet for 1996 and 1995.
3. Compute the following ratios as of December 31, 1996, or for the year ended December 31, 1996:

   a. Current ratio.
   b. Acid-test ratio.
   c. Accounts receivable turnover.
   d. Days' sales uncollected.
   e. Merchandise turnover.
   f. Debt ratio

   g. Pledged assets to secured liabilities.
   h. Times fixed interest charges earned.
   i. Profit margin.
   j. Total asset turnover.
   k. Return on total assets.
   l. Return on common shareholders' equity.

PRECISION COMPANY
Comparative Income Statement
For Years Ended December 31, 1996 and 1995

	1996	1995
Sales	$2,486,000	$2,075,000
Cost of goods sold	1,523,000	1,222,00
Gross profit from sales	$ 963,000	$ 853,000
Operating expenses:		
Advertising expense	$ 145,000	$ 100,000
Sales salaries expense	240,000	280,000
Office salaries expense	165,000	200,000
Insurance expense	100,000	45,000
Supplies expense	26,000	35,000
Amortization expenses	85,000	75,000
Miscellaneous expense	17,000	15,000
Total operating expenses	$ 778,000	$ 750,000
Operating income	$ 185,000	$ 103,000
Less interest expense	44,000	46,000
Income before taxes	$ 141,000	$ 57,000
Income taxes	47,000	19,000
Net income	$ 94,000	$ 38,000
Earnings per share	$ 0.99	$ 0.40

PRECISION COMPANY
Comparative Balance Sheet
December 31, 1996, and December 31, 1995

	1996	1995
Assets		
Current assets:		
Cash	$ 79,000	$ 42,000
Short-term investments	65,000	96,000
Accounts receivable (net)	120,000	100,000
Merchandise inventory	250,000	265,000
Total current assets	$ 514,000	$ 503,000
Capital assets:		
Store equipment (net)	$ 400,000	$ 350,000
Office equipment (net)	45,000	50,000
Buildings (net)	625,000	675,000
Land	100,000	100,000
Total plant and equipment	$1,170,000	$1,175,000
Total assets	$1,684,000	$1,678,000
Liabilities		
Current liabilities:		
Accounts payable	$ 164,000	$ 190,000
Short-term notes payable	75,000	90,000
Taxes payable	26,000	12,000
Total current liabilities	$ 265,000	$ 292,000
Long-term liabilities:		
Notes payable (secured by		
mortgage on building and land)	400,000	420,000
Total liabilities	$ 665,000	$ 712,000

Shareholders' Equity

Contributed capital:

Common share, no par value	$ 475,000	$ 475,000
Retained earnings	544,000	491,000
Total shareholders' equity	$1,019,000	$ 966,000
Total liabilities and shareholders' equity	$1,684,000	$1,678,000

- Set up a four-column income statement; enter the 1996 and 1995 amounts in the first two columns, and then enter the dollar change in the third column and the percentage change from 1995 in the fourth column.

- Set up a four-column balance sheet; enter the 1996 and 1995 amounts in the first two columns, and then compute and enter the amount of each item as a percent of total assets.

- Compute the given ratios using the provided numbers; be sure to use the average of the beginning and ending amounts where appropriate.

Planning the Solution

1.

PRECISION COMPANY
Comparative Income Statement
For Years Ended December 31, 1996 and 1995

Solution to Demonstration Problem

	1996	1995	Increase (Decrease) in 1996 Amount	Percent
Sales	$2,486,000	$2,075,000	$411,000	19.8
Cost of goods sold	1,523,000	1,222,000	301,000	24.6
Gross profit from sales	$ 963,000	$ 853,000	$110,000	12.9
Operating expenses:				
Advertising expense	$ 145,000	$ 100,000	$ 45,000	45.0
Sales salaries expense	240,000	280,000	(40,000)	(14.3)
Office salaries expense	165,000	200,000	(35,000)	(17.5)
Insurance expense	100,000	45,000	55,000	122.2
Supplies expense	26,000	35,000	(9,000)	(25.7)
Amortization expense	85,000	75,000	10,000	13.3
Miscellaneous expenses	17,000	15,000	2,000	13.3
Total operating expenses	$ 778,000	$ 750,000	$ 28,000	3.7
Operating income	$ 185,000	$ 103,000	$ 82,000	79.6
Less interest expense	44,000	46,000	(2,000)	(4.3)
Income before taxes	$ 141,000	$ 57,000	$ 84,000	147.4
Income taxes	47,000	19,000	28,000	147.4
Net income	$ 94,000	$ 38,000	$ 56,000	147.4
Earnings per share	$ 0.99	$ 0.40	$ 0.59	147.5

2.

PRECISION COMPANY
Common-Size Comparative Balance Sheet
December 31, 1996, and December 31, 1995

	December 31		Common-Size Percentages	
	1996	**1995**	**1996***	**1995***
Assets				
Current assets:				
Cash	$ 79,000	$ 42,000	4.7	2.5
Short-term investments	65,000	96,000	3.9	5.7
Accounts receivable (net)	120,000	100,000	7.1	6.0
Merchandise inventory	250,000	265,000	14.8	15.8
Total current assets	$ 514,000	$ 503,000	30.5	30.0
Capital assets:				
Store equipment (net)	$ 400,000	$ 350,000	23.8	20.9
Office equipment (net)	45,000	50,000	2.7	3.0
Buildings (net)	625,000	675,000	37.1	40.2
Land	100,000	100,000	5.9	6.0
Total plant and equipment	$1,170,000	$1,175,000	69.5	70.0
Total assets	$1,684,000	$1,678,000	100.0	100.0

	December 31		Common-size Percentages	
	1996	**1995**	**1996***	**1995***
Liabilities				
Current liabilities:				
Accounts payable	$ 164,000	$ 190,000	9.7	11.3
Short-term notes payable	75,000	90,000	4.5	5.4
Taxes payable	26,000	12,000	1.5	0.7
Total current liabilities	$ 265,000	$ 292,000	15.7	17.4
Long-term liabilities:				
Notes payable (secured by mortgage on building and land)	400,000	420,000	23.8	25.0
Total liabilities	$ 665,000	$ 712,000	39.4	42.4
Shareholders' Equity				
Contributed capital:				
Common share, no par value	$ 475,000	$ 475,000	28.2	28.3
Retailed earnings	544,000	491,000	32.3	29.3
Total shareholders' equity	$1,019,000	$ 966,000	60.5	57.6
Total liabilities and equity	$1,684,000	$1,678,000	100.0	100.0

*Columns may not foot due to rounding.

3. Ratios for 1996:

a. Current ratio: $514,000/$265,000 = 1.9 to 1

b. Acid-test ratio: ($79,000 + $65,000 + $120,000)/$265,000 = 1.0 to 1

c. Average receivables: ($120,000 + $100,000)/2 = $110,000
   Accounts receivable turnover: $2,486,000/$110,000 = 22.6 times

d. Days' sales uncollected: ($120,000/$2,486,000) $\times$ 365 = 17.6 days

e. Average inventory: ($250,000 + $265,000)/2 = $257,500
   Merchandise turnover: $1,523,000/$257,500 = 5.9 times

f. Debt ratio: $665,000/$1,684,000 = 39.5\%$

g. Pledged assets to secured liabilities:
($625,000 + $100,000)/$400,000 = 1.8 to 1

h. Times fixed interest charges earned: $185,000/$44,000 = 4.2 times

i. Profit margin: $94,000/$2,486,000 = 3.8\%$

j. Average total assets: ($1,684,000 + $1,678,000)/2 = $1,681,000
Total asset turnover: $2,486,000/$1,681,000 = 1.48 times

k. Return on total assets: $94,000/$1,681,000 = 5.6\%$ or $3.8\% \times 1.48 = 5.6\%$

l. Average total equity: ($1,019,000 = $966,000)/2 = $992,500
Return on common shareholders' equity: $94,000/$992,500 = 9.5\%$

GLOSSARY

Common-size comparative statements comparative financial statements in which each amount is expressed as a percentage of a base amount. In the balance sheet, the amount of total assets is usually selected as the base amount and is expressed as 100%. In the income statement, net sales is usually selected as the base amount. p. 855

Comparative statement a financial statement with data for two or more successive accounting periods placed in columns side by side, sometimes with changes shown in dollar amounts and percentages. p. 851

Equity ratio the portion of total assets provided by shareholders' equity, calculated as shareholders' equity divided by total assets. p. 862

Financial reporting the process of providing information that is useful to investors, creditors, and others in making investment, credit, and similar decisions. p. 850

General purpose financial statements statements published periodically for use by a wide variety of interested parties; include the income statement, balance sheet, statement of changes in shareholders' equity (or statement of retained earnings), statement of changes in financial position, and related notes. p. 850

Working capital current assets minus current liabilities. p. 858

QUESTIONS

1. Explain the difference between financial reporting and financial statements.

2. What is the difference between comparative financial statements and common-size comparative statements?

3. Which items are usually assigned a value of 100% on a common-size comparative balance sheet and a common-size comparative income statement?

4. Why is working capital given special attention in the process of analyzing balance sheets?

5. What are three factors that would influence your decision as to whether a company's current ratio is good or bad?

6. Suggest several reasons why a 2 to 1 current ratio may not be adequate for a particular company.

7. What does a relatively high accounts receivable turnover indicate about a company's short-term liquidity?

8. What is the significance of the number of days' sales uncollected?

9. Why does merchandise turnover provide information about a company's short-term liquidity?

10. Why is the capital structure of a company, as measured by debt and equity ratios, of importance to financial statement analysts?

11. Why must the ratio of pledged assets to secured liabilities be interpreted with caution?

12. Why would a company's return on total assets be different from its return on common shareholders' equity?

13. What ratios would you calculate for the purpose of evaluating management performance?

14. Using the financial statements for Geac Corpora- tion in Appendix I, calculate Geac's return on total assets for the fiscal year ended April 30, 1994.

QUICK STUDY (Five-Minute Exercises)

QS 19–1
(LO 1)

Which of the following items are means of accomplishing the objective of financial reporting but are not included within general purpose financial statements? *(a)* Income statements; *(b)* Company news releases; *(c)* Balance sheets; *(d)* Certain reports filed with the Securities Commission; *(e)* Statements of changes in financial position; *(f)* Management discussions and analyses of financial performance.

QS 19–2
(LO 2)

Given the following information for Moyers Corporation, determine *(a)* the common-size percentages for gross profit from sales, and *(b)* the trend percentages for net sales, using 1995 as the base year.

	1995	1996
Net sales	$134,400	$114,800
Cost of goods sold	72,800	60,200

QS 19–3
(LO 3)

a. Which two terms describe the difference between current assets and current liabilities?

b. Which two short-term liquidity ratios measure how frequently a company collects its accounts?

c. Which two ratios are the basic components in measuring a company's operating efficiency? Which ratio is the summary of these two components?

QS 19–4
(LO 4)

What are five possible bases of comparison you can use when analyzing financial statement ratios? Which of these is generally considered to be the most useful? Which one is least likely to provide a good basis for comparison?

EXERCISES

Exercise 19–1
Calculating trend percentages
(LO 2)

Calculate trend percentages for the following items, using 1993 as the base year. Then, state whether the situation shown by the trends appears to be favourable or unfavourable.

	1997	1996	1995	1994	1993
Sales	$377,600	$362,400	$338,240	$314,080	$302,000
Cost of goods sold	172,720	164,560	155,040	142,800	136,000
Accounts receivable	25,400	24,400	23,200	21,600	20,000

Where possible, calculate percentages of increase and decrease for the following:

Exercise 19–2
Reporting percentage
changes
(LO 2)

	1995	1994
Short-term investments	$145,200	$110,000
Accounts receivable	28,080	32,000
Notes payable	38,000	–0–

Express the following income statement information in common-size percentages and assess whether the situation is favourable or unfavourable:

Exercise 19–3
Calculating common-size
percentages
(LO 2)

CLEARWATER CORPORATION
Comparative Income Statement
For Years Ended December 31, 1995 and 1994

	1995	1994
Sales	$960,000	$735,000
Cost of goods sold	576,000	382,200
Gross profit from sales	$384,000	$352,800
Operating expenses	216,000	148,470
Net income	$168,000	$204,330

TGA Company's December 31 balance sheets included the following data:

Exercise 19–4
Evaluating short-term
liquidity
(LO 3)

	1996	1995	1994
Cash	$ 61,600	$ 71,250	$ 73,600
Accounts receivable, net	177,000	125,000	98,400
Merchandise inventory	223,000	165,000	106,000
Prepaid expenses	19,400	18,750	8,000
Plant assets, net	555,000	510,000	459,000
Total assets	$1,036,000	$890,000	$745,000
Accounts payable	$ 257,800	$150,500	$ 98,500
Long-term notes payable secured by mortgages on plant assets	195,000	205,000	165,000
Common shares, no par value (32,500 shares issued) ..	325,000	325,000	325,000
Retained earnings	258,200	209,500	156,500
Total liabilities and shareholders' equity	$1,036,000	$890,000	$745,000

Required

Compare the short-term liquidity positions of the company at the end of 1996, 1995, and 1994 by calculating: (*a*) the current ratio and (*b*) the acid-test ratio. Comment on any changes that occurred.

Refer to the information in Exercise 19–4 about TGA Company. The company's income statements for the years ended December 31, 1996, and 1995 included the following data:

Exercise 19–5
Evaluating short-term
liquidity
(LO 3)

	1996	1995
Sales	$1,345,000	$1,060,000
Cost of goods sold	$ 820,450	$ 689,000
Other operating expenses	417,100	267,960
Interest expense	22,200	24,600
Income taxes	17,050	15,690
Total costs and expenses	$1,276,800	$ 997,250
Net income	$ 68,200	$ 62,750
Earnings per share	$ 2.10	$ 1.93

Required

For the years ended December 31, 1996, and 1995, assume all sales were on credit and calculate the following: *(a)* days' sales uncollected, *(b)* accounts receivable turnover, *(c)* merchandise turnover, and *(d)* days' stock on hand. Comment on any changes that occurred from 1995 to 1996.

Exercise 19–6
Evaluating long-term risk and capital structure
(LO 3)

Refer to the information in Exercises 19–4 and 19–5 about TGA Company. Compare the long-term risk and capital structure positions of the company at the end of 1996 and 1995 by calculating the following ratios: *(a)* debt and equity ratios, *(b)* pledged assets to secured liabilities, and *(c)* times fixed interest charges earned. Comment on any changes that occurred.

Exercise 19–7
Evaluating operating efficiency and profitability
(LO 3)

Refer to the financial statements of TGA Company presented in Exercises 19–4 and 19–5. Evaluate the operating efficiency and profitability of the company by calculating the following: *(a)* profit margin, *(b)* total asset turnover, and *(c)* return on total assets. Comment on any changes that occurred.

Exercise 19–8
Evaluating profitability
(LO 3)

Refer to the financial statements of TGA Company presented in Exercises 19–4 and 19–5. This additional information about the company is known:

Common share market price, December 31, 1996	$30.00
Common share market price, December 31, 1995	28.00
Annual cash dividends per share in 1996	.60
Annual cash dividends per share in 1995	.30

Required

To evaluate the profitability of the company, calculate the following for 1996 and 1995: *(a)* return on common shareholders' equity, *(b)* price earnings ratio on December 31, and *(c)* dividend yield.

Exercise 19–9
Determining income effects from common-size and trend percentages
(LO 2)

Common-size and trend percentages for a company's sales, cost of goods sold, and expenses follow:

	Common-Size Percentages			Trend Percentages		
	1996	1995	1994	1996	1995	1994
Sales	100.0%	100.0%	100.0%	106.5%	105.3%	100.0%
Cost of goods sold	64.5	63.0	60.2	104.1	102.3	100.0
Expenses	16.4	15.9	16.2	96.0	94.1	100.0

Required

Determine whether the company's net income increased, decreased, or remained unchanged during this three-year period.

PROBLEMS

The condensed statements of Stellar Company follow:

Problem 19–1
Calculating ratios and
percentages
(LO 2, 3)

STELLAR COMPANY
Comparative Income Statement
For Years Ended December 31, 1996, 1995, and 1994
($000)

	1996	1995	1994
Sales	$148,000	$136,000	$118,000
Cost of goods sold	89,096	85,000	75,520
Gross profit from sales	$ 58,904	$ 51,000	$ 42,480
Selling expenses	$ 20,898	$ 18,768	$ 15,576
Administrative expenses	13,379	11,968	9,735
Total expenses	$ 34,277	$ 30,736	$ 25,311
Income before taxes	$ 24,627	$ 20,264	$ 17,169
Income taxes	4,588	4,148	3,481
Net income	$ 20,039	$ 16,116	$ 13,688

STELLAR COMPANY
Comparative Balance Sheet
December 31, 1996, 1995, and 1994
($000)

	1996	1995	1994
Assets			
Current assets	$24,240	$18,962	$25,324
Long-term investments	–0–	250	1,860
Plant and equipment	45,000	48,000	28,500
Total assets	$69,240	$67,212	$55,684
Liabilities and Shareholders' Equity			
Current liabilities	$10,100	$ 9,980	$ 9,740
Common shares	36,000	36,000	27,000
Other contributed capital	4,500	4,500	3,000
Retained earnings	18,640	16,732	15,944
Total liabilities and shareholders' equity ..	$69,240	$67,212	$55,684

Required

Preparation component:

1. Calculate each year's current ratio.
2. Express the income statement data in common-size percentages.
3. Express the balance sheet data in trend percentages with 1994 as the base year.

Analysis component:

4. Comment on any significant relationships revealed by the ratios and percentages.

Problem 19–2
Calculation and analysis
of trend percentages
(LO 2)

The condensed comparative statements of Jasper Company follow:

JASPER COMPANY
Comparative Income Statement
For Years Ended December 31, 1997–1991
($000)

	1997	1996	1995	1994	1993	1992	1991
Sales	$797	$698	$635	$582	$543	$505	$420
Cost of goods sold	573	466	401	351	326	305	250
Gross profit from sales	$224	$232	$234	$231	$217	$200	$170
Operating expenses	170	133	122	90	78	77	65
Net income	$ 54	$ 99	$112	$141	$139	$123	$105

JASPER COMPANY
Comparative Balance Sheet
December 31, 1997–1991
($000)

	1997	1996	1995	1994	1993	1992	1991
Assets							
Cash	$ 34	$ 44	$ 46	$ 47	$ 49	$ 48	$ 50
Accounts receivable, net	240	252	228	175	154	146	102
Merchandise inventory	869	632	552	466	418	355	260
Other current assets	23	21	12	22	19	19	10
Long-term investments	0	0	0	68	68	68	68
Plant and equipment, net	1,060	1,057	926	522	539	480	412
Total assets	$2,226	$2,006	$1,764	$1,300	$1,247	$1,116	$902
Liabilities and Equity							
Current liabilities	$ 560	$ 471	$ 309	$ 257	$ 223	$ 211	$136
Long-term liabilities	597	520	506	235	240	260	198
Common shares	500	500	500	420	420	320	320
Other contributed capital	125	125	125	90	90	80	80
Retained earnings	444	390	324	298	274	245	168
Total liabilities and equity	$2,226	$2,006	$1,764	$1,300	$1,247	$1,116	$902

Required

Preparation component:

1. Calculate trend percentages for the items of the statements using 1991 as the base year.

Analysis component:

2. Analyze and comment on the situation shown in the statements.

The 1996 financial statements of Oltorf Corporation follow:

Problem 19–3
Calculation of financial
statement ratios
(LO 3)

OLTORF CORPORATION
Income Statement
For Year Ended December 31, 1996

Sales		$697,200
Cost of goods sold:		
Merchandise inventory, December 31, 1995 ..	$ 64,800	
Purchases	455,800	
Goods available for sale	$520,600	
Merchandise inventory, December 31, 1996 ..	62,300	
Cost of goods sold		458,300
Gross profit from sales		$238,900
Operating expenses		122,700
Operating income		$116,200
Interest expense		7,100
Income before taxes		$109,100
Income taxes		17,800
Net income		$ 91,300

OLTORF CORPORATION
Balance Sheet
December 31, 1996

Assets		Liabilities and Shareholders' Equity	
Cash	$ 18,000	Accounts payable	$ 32,600
Temporary investments	14,700	Accrued wages payable	4,200
Accounts receivable, net	55,800	Income taxes payable	4,800
Notes receivable (trade)	6,200	Long-term note payable,	
Merchandise inventory	62,300	secured by mortgage on	
Prepaid expenses	2,800	plant assets	125,000
Plant assets, net	306,300	Common shares, no par value ..	180,000
		Retained earnings	119,500
		Total liabilities and	
Total assets	$466,100	shareholders' equity	$466,100

Assume that all sales were on credit. On the December 31, 1995, balance sheet, the assets totaled $367,500, common shares were $180,000, and retained earnings were $86,700.

Required

Calculate the following: (*a*) current ratio, (*b*) acid-test ratio, (*c*) days' sales uncollected, (*d*) merchandise turnover, (*e*) days' stock on hand, (*f*) ratio of pledged assets to secured liabilities, (*g*) times fixed interest charges earned, (*h*) profit margin, (*i*) total asset turnover, (*j*) return on total assets, and (*k*) return on common shareholders' equity.

Problem 19–4
Comparative analysis of
financial statement ratios
(LO 3)

Two companies that compete in the same industry are being evaluated by a bank that can lend money to only one of them. Summary information from the financial statements of the two companies follows:

	Payless Company	Capital Company
Data from the current year-end balance sheets:		
Assets		
Cash	$ 37,400	$ 66,000
Accounts receivable	73,450	112,900
Notes receivable (trade)	16,200	13,100
Merchandise inventory	167,340	263,100
Prepaid expenses	8,000	11,900
Plant and equipment, net	568,900	606,400
Total assets	$ 871,290	$1,073,400
Liabilities and Shareholders' Equity:		
Current liabilities	$ 120,200	$ 184,600
Long-term notes payable	159,800	210,000
Common shares, no par value	350,000	410,000
Retained earnings	241,290	268,800
Total liabilities and shareholders' equity ...	$871,290	$1,073,400
Data from the current year's income statements:		
Sales	$1,325,000	$1,561,200
Cost of goods sold	970,500	1,065,000
Interest expense	14,400	23,000
Income tax expense	24,840	38,700
Net income	135,540	210,400
Beginning-of-year data:		
Accounts receivable, net	$ 57,800	$ 106,200
Notes receivable	0	0
Merchandise inventory	109,600	212,400
Total assets	776,400	745,100
Common shares, no par value	350,000	410,000
Retained earnings	189,300	181,200

Required

1. Calculate the current ratio, acid-test ratio, accounts (including notes) receivable turnover, merchandise turnover, days' stock on hand, and days' sales uncollected for the two companies. Then, identify the company that you consider to be the better short-term credit risk and explain why.

2. Calculate the profit margin, total asset turnover, return on total assets, and return on common shareholders' equity for the two companies. Assuming that each company paid cash dividends of $2.00 per share and each company's shares can be purchased at $25 per share, calculate their price earnings ratios and dividend yields. Payless has 70,000 shares and Capital has 82,000 shares outstanding. Also, identify which company's shares you would recommend as the better investment and explain why.

Metro Corporation began the month of March with $750,000 of current assets, a current ratio of 2.5 to 1, and an acid-test ratio of 1.1 to 1. During the month, it completed the following transactions:

Problem 19–5
Analysis of working capital
(LO 3)

Mar. 4   Bought $85,000 of merchandise on account. (The company uses a perpetual inventory system.)

10   Sold merchandise that cost $68,000 for $113,000.

12   Collected a $29,000 account receivable.

17   Paid a $31,000 account payable.

19   Wrote off a $13,000 bad debt against the Allowance for Doubtful Accounts account.

24   Declared a $1.25 per share cash dividend on the 40,000 outstanding common shares.

28   Paid the dividend declared on March 24.

29   Borrowed $85,000 by giving the bank a 30-day, 10% note.

30   Borrowed $100,000 by signing a long-term secured note.

31   Used the $185,000 proceeds of the notes to buy additional machinery.

Required

Prepare a schedule showing Metro's current ratio, acid-test ratio, and working capital after each of the transactions. Round calculations to two decimal places.

The condensed statements of Tradent Corporation follow:

Problem 19–6
Calculating ratios and percentages
(LO 2, 3)

TRADENT CORPORATION
Comparative Income Statement
For Years Ended December 31, 1996, 1995, and 1994
($000)

	1996	1995	1994
Sales	$98,000	$82,400	$71,000
Cost of goods sold	54,500	43,300	33,800
Gross profit from sales	43,500	39,100	37,200
Selling expenses	13,100	10,350	10,900
Administrative expenses	9,800	10,450	9,500
Total expenses	22,900	20,800	20,400
Income before taxes	20,600	18,300	16,800
Income taxes	7,210	6,405	5,880
Net income	$13,390	$11,895	$10,920

TRADENT CORPORATION
Comparative Balance Sheet
December 31, 1996, 1995, and 1994
($000)

	1996	1995	1994
Assets			
Current assets	$22,600	$12,500	$14,900
Long-term investments		700	5,700
Plant and equipment	51,000	53,000	39,200
Total assets	$73,600	$66,200	$59,800

Liabilities and Capital

Current liabilities	$11,000	$ 9,200	$ 7,700
Common shares	19,600	19,600	16,000
Retained earnings	43,000	37,400	36,100
Total liabilities and capital	$73,600	$66,200	$59,800

Required

1. Calculate each year's current ratio.

2. Express the income statement data in common-size percentages.

3. Express the balance sheet data in trend percentages with 1994 as the base year.

4. Comment on any significant relationships revealed by the ratios and percentages.

Problem 19–7
Calculation and analysis
of trend percentages
(LO 2)

The condensed comparative statements of Clear River Company, Ltd., follow:

CLEAR RIVER COMPANY, LTD.
Comparative Income Statement
For Years Ended December 31, 1996–1990
($000)

	1996	1995	1994	1993	1992	1991	1990
Sales	$450	$470	$460	$490	$530	$520	$560
Cost of goods sold	190	197	194	208	219	212	214
Gross profit from sales	$260	$273	$266	$282	$311	$308	$346
Operating expenses	200	207	205	224	231	235	255
Income before taxes	$ 60	$ 66	$ 61	$ 58	$ 80	$ 73	$ 91

CLEAR RIVER COMPANY, LTD.
Comparative Balance Sheet
December 31, 1996–1990
($000)

	1996	1995	1994	1993	1992	1991	1990
Assets							
Cash	$ 30	$ 33	$ 32	$ 36	$ 45	$ 42	$ 46
Accounts receivable, net	92	103	99	101	112	110	118
Merchandise inventory	143	149	147	156	159	169	162
Other current assets	20	21	22	24	23	26	28
Long-term investments	80	60	40	87	87	87	90
Plant and equipment, net	362	368	372	287	292	297	302
Total assets	$727	$734	$712	$691	$718	$731	$746
Liabilities and Capital							
Current liabilities	$162	$169	$152	$121	$143	$171	$216
Long-term liabilities	130	145	160	175	190	205	220
Common shares	205	205	205	205	205	205	205
Retained earnings	230	215	195	190	180	150	105
Total liabilities and capital	$727	$734	$712	$691	$718	$731	$746

Required

1. Calculate trend percentages for the items of the statements using 1990 as the base year.

2. Analyze and comment on the situation shown in the statements.

The year-end statements of Tooner Corporation follow:

Problem 19–8
Financial statement ratios
(LO 3)

TOONER CORPORATION
Income Statement
For Year Ended December 31, 1996

Sales		$805,000
Cost of goods sold:		
Merchandise inventory, December 31, 1995 . .	$ 62,800	
Purchases	500,700	
Goods available for sale	$563,500	
Merchandise inventory, December 31, 1996 . .	48,200	
Cost of goods sold		515,300
Gross profit from sales		$289,700
Operating expenses		227,800
Operating income		$ 61,900
Interest expense		9,500
Income before taxes		$ 52,400
Income taxes		15,720
Net income		$ 36,680

TOONER CORPORATION
Balance Sheet
December 31, 1996

Assets		Liabilities and Shareholders' Equity	
Cash	$ 18,500	Accounts payable	$ 40,700
Temporary investments	20,400	Accrued wages payable	5,200
Accounts receivable, net	43,400	Income taxes payable	5,800
Notes receivable	8,800	Long-term note payable,	
Merchandise inventory	49,200	secured by mortgage	
Prepaid expenses	4,800	on plant assets	95,000
Plant assets, net	272,100	Common shares, 160,000 shares . .	160,000
		Retained earnings	110,500
		Total liabilities and	
Total assets	$417,200	shareholders' equity	$417,200

Assume all sales were on credit. On the December 31, 1995, balance sheet, the assets totaled $360,600, common shares were $160,000, and retained earnings was $89,700.

Required

Calculate the following: *(a)* current ratio, *(b)* acid-test ratio, *(c)* days' sales uncollected, *(d)* merchandise turnover, *(e)* ratio of pledged plant assets to secured liabilities, *(f)* times fixed interest charges earned, *(g)* profit margin, *(h)* total asset turnover, *(i)* return on total assets employed, and *(j)* return on common shareholders' equity.

Two companies that operate in the same industry as competitors are being evaluated by a bank that may lend money to each one. Summary information from the financial statements of the two companies is provided below:

Problem 19–9
Comparative analysis of
financial statement ratios
(LO 3)

Data from the Current Year-End Balance Sheets

	Zesta Corporation	Festa Corporation
Assets		
Cash	$ 30,200	$ 57,100
Accounts receivable	105,500	118,500
Notes receivable	18,000	16,500
Merchandise inventory	98,700	133,300
Prepaid expenses	15,700	17,900
Plant and equipment, net	332,900	340,100
Total assets	$601,000	683,400

Liabilities and Capital		
Current liabilities	$113,400	$141,800
Long-term notes payable	120,000	135,000
Common shares*	182,000	212,000
Retained earnings	185,600	194,600
Total liabilities and capital ...	$601,000	$683,400

Data from the Current Year's Income Statements

Sales	$703,500	$992,100
Cost of goods sold	518,000	708,200
Interest expense	14,100	17,800
Income tax expense	22,500	42,700
Net income	54,200	74,700

Beginning-of-Year Data

Accounts receivable, net	$ 98,000	$100,500
Notes receivable	–0–	–0–
Merchandise inventory	118,200	93,900
Total assets	514,300	600,000
Common shares*	182,000	212,000
Retained earnings	158,700	151,700

*All shares were issued at $20 per share.

Required

1. Calculate current ratios, acid-test ratios, accounts (and notes) receivable turnovers, merchandise turnovers, and days' sales uncollected for the two companies. Then state which company you think is the better short-term credit risk and why.

2. Calculate profit margins, total asset turnovers, returns on total asset employed, and returns on common shareholders' equity. Assuming that each company paid cash dividends of $3 per share and each company's shares can be purchased at $45 per share, calculate price earnings ratio and dividend yield. Also state which company's shares you would recommend as the better investment and why.

Problem 19–10
Analysis of working capital
(LO 3)

Ft. Mason Corporation began the month of March with $286,000 of current assets, a current ratio of 2.2 to 1, and an acid-test ratio of 0.9 to 1. During the month, it completed the following transactions:

Mar. 3   Sold for $55,000 merchandise that cost $36,000.

  5   Collected a $35,000 account receivable.

  10   Bought $56,000 of merchandise on account. (The company uses a perpetual inventory system.)

  12   Borrowed $60,000 by giving the bank a 60-day, 12% note.

15   Borrowed $90,000 by signing a long-term secured note.

22   Used the $150,000 proceeds of the notes to buy additional machinery.

24   Declared a $1.75 per share cash dividend on the 40,000 shares of outstanding common shares.

26   Wrote off a $14,000 bad debt against Allowance for Doubtful Accounts.

28   Paid a $45,000 account payable.

30   Paid the dividend declared on March 24.

Required

Prepare a schedule showing the company's current ratio, acid-test ratio, and working capital after each of the foregoing transactions. Round to two decimal places.

PROVOCATIVE PROBLEMS

Kerbey Company and Telcom Company are similar firms that operate within the same industry. The following information is available:

Provocative Problem 19–1
Analytical essay
(LO 3)

	Kerbey			Telcom		
	1996	**1995**	**1994**	**1996**	**1995**	**1994**
Current ratio	1.8	1.9	2.2	3.3	2.8	2.0
Acid-test ratio	1.1	1.2	1.3	2.9	2.6	1.7
Accounts receivable turnover	30.5	25.2	29.2	16.4	15.2	16.0
Merchandise turnover . . .	24.2	21.9	17.1	14.5	13.0	12.6
Working capital	$65,000	$53,000	$47,000	$126,000	$98,000	$73,000

Required

Write a brief essay comparing Kerbey and Telcom based on the preceding information. Your discussion should include their relative ability to meet current obligations and to use current assets efficiently.

Snowden Company and Comet Company are similar firms that operate within the same industry. Comet began operations in 1994 and Snowden in 1988. In 1996, both companies paid 7% interest to creditors. The following information is available:

Provocative Problem 19–2
Analytical essay
(LO 3)

	Snowden			Comet		
	1996	**1995**	**1994**	**1996**	**1995**	**1994**
Total asset turnover	3.3	3.0	3.2	1.9	1.7	1.4
Return on total assets . .	9.2	9.8	9.0	6.1	5.8	5.5
Profit margin	2.6	2.7	2.5	3.0	3.2	3.1
Sales	$800,000	$740,000	$772,000	$400,000	$320,000	$200,000

Required

Write a brief essay comparing Snowden and Comet based on the preceding information. Your discussion should include their relative ability to use assets efficiently to produce profits. Also comment on their relative success in employing financial leverage in 1996.

**Provocative Problem
19–3**
Financial statement
analysis case
(LO 2, 3)

In your position as controller of Skinner Company, you are responsible for keeping the board of directors informed about the financial activities and status of the company. In preparing for the next board meeting, you have calculated the following ratios, turnovers, and percentages to enable you to answer questions:

	1996	1995	1994
Sales trend	137.00	125.00	100.00
Selling expenses to net sales	9.8%	13.7%	15.3%
Sales to plant assets	3.5 to 1	3.3 to 1	3.0 to 1
Current ratio	2.6 to 1	2.4 to 1	2.1 to 1
Acid-test ratio	0.8 to 1	1.1 to 1	1.2 to 1
Merchandise turnover	7.5 times	8.7 times	9.9 times
Accounts receivable turnover	6.7 times	7.4 times	8.2 times
Total asset turnover	2.6 times	2.6 times	3.0 times
Return on total assets	8.8%	9.4%	10.1%
Return on shareholders' equity . .	9.75%	11.50%	12.25%
Profit margin	3.3%	3.5%	3.7%

Required

Using the preceding data, answer each of the following questions and explain your answers:

a. Is it becoming easier for the company to meet its current debts on time and to take advantage of cash discounts?

b. Is the company collecting its accounts receivable more rapidly?

c. Is the company's investment in accounts receivable decreasing?

d. Are dollars invested in inventory increasing?

e. Is the company's investment in plant assets increasing?

f. Is the shareholders' investment becoming more profitable?

g. Is the company using its assets efficiently?

h. Did the dollar amount of selling expenses decrease during the three-year period?

**Provocative Problem
19–4**
Financial statement
analysis
(LO 2, 3)

Refer to the financial statements of Geac Computer Corporation, Ltd., in Appendix I, to answer the following questions:

a. Calculate common-size percentages for 1994 and 1993 for the following categories of assets: total current assets; fixed assets; and other assets.

b. Calculate the 1994 and 1993 common-size percentages for sales, total expenses, and net income.

c. Calculate the high and low price earnings ratio for 1994. Geac's share prices were 18⅞ high and 11⅞ low.

d. Calculate the debt and equity ratios for 1994.

ANALYTICAL AND REVIEW PROBLEMS

On the basis of the information given, complete the balance sheet.

A & R Problem 19–1

VIDIO COMPANY LIMITED
December 31, 1996

Assets		Liabilities and Capital	
Cash	$_____	Current liabilities	$_____
Accounts receivable	_____	8% bonds payable	_____
Inventory	_____	Common shares	15,000
Plant and equipment	_____	Retained earnings	_____
. . . .		Total liabilities and	
Total assets	$_____	capital	$_____

Sales (all credit)	$40,000
Cost of goods sold	24,000
Expenses	13,000
Income taxes	1,000
Net income	2,000
Net income/shareholders' equity	10%
Bonds payable/shareholders' equity	1 to 4
Inventory turnover	4 times
Accounts receivable collection period (360-day year) . .	45 days
Current ratio	2 to 1
Total asset turnover	1.25 times

A & R Problem 19–2

A company began the month of May with $200,000 of current assets, a 2-to-1 current ratio, and a 1-to-1 acid-test (quick) ratio. During the month it completed the following transactions:

		Current Ratio			Acid-Test Ratio		
		Inc.	Dcr.	No Change	Inc.	Dcr.	No Change
a.	Bought $20,000 of merchandise on account (the company uses a perpetual inventory system)						
b.	Sold for $25,000 merchandise that cost $15,000						
c.	Collected an $8,500 account receivable						
d.	Paid a $12,000 account payable						
e.	Wrote off a $1,000 bad debt against the allowance for doubtful accounts						
f.	Declared a $1 per share cash dividend on the 10,000 shares of outstanding common shares						
g.	Paid the dividend declared in (f)						
h.	Borrowed $12,000 by giving the bank a 60-day, 10% note						
i.	Borrowed $30,000 by placing a 10-year mortgage on the plant						
j.	Used $20,000 of proceeds of the mortgage to buy additional machinery						

Required

1. Indicate the affect on *(a)* current ratio and *(b)* working capital of each transaction. Set up a chart in your answer similar to that shown above and use check marks to indicate your answers. (Working capital is defined as "current assets minus current liabilities.")

2. For the end of May, calculate the
   a. Current ratio.
   b. Acid-test ratio.
   c. Working capital.

CONCEPT TESTER

Test your understanding of the concepts introduced in this chapter by completing the following crossword puzzle:

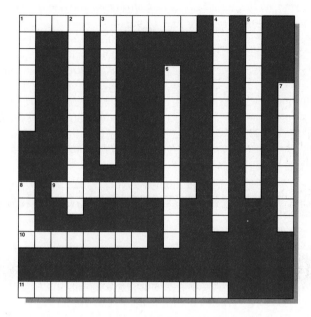

Across Clues

1. When data is presented for two or more accounting periods (1st of 2 words; also see 7 down).

9. The process of providing information that is useful to the users of statements (1st of 2 words; also see 3 down).

10. Cost of goods sold divided by average inventory (2nd of 2 words; also see 5 down).

11. Dividends per share divided by market price per share (2 words).

Down Clues

1. Ratio of current assets to current liabilities.

2. Net income divided by net sales (2 words).

3. The process of providing information that is useful to the users of statements (2nd of 2 words; also see 9 across).

4. Ratio of market price per share to earnings per share (2 words).

5. Cost of goods sold divided by average inventory (1st of 2 words; also see 10 across).

6. The proportion of total assets provided by shareholders' equity (2 words).

7. When data are presented for two or more successive accounting periods (2nd of 2 words; also see 1 across).

8. Ratio of total liabilities to total assets.

ANSWERS TO PROGRESS CHECKS

19–1   General purpose financial statements are intended for the large variety of users who are interested in receiving financial information about a business but who do not have the ability to require the company to prepare specialized financial reports designed to meet their specific interests.

19–2   General purpose financial statements include the income statement, balance sheet, statement of changes in shareholders' equity (or statement of retained earnings), and statement of changes in financial position, plus notes related to the statements.

19–3   *d*

19–4   Percentages on a comparative income statement show the increase or decrease in each item from one period to the next. On a common-size comparative income statement, each item is shown as a percentage of net sales for a specific period.

19–5   *c*

19–6   (*a*) ($820,000 + $240,000 + $470,000)/($350,000 + $180,000) = 2.9 to 1

      (*b*) ($820,000 + $240,000)/($350,000 + $180,000) = 2 to 1

19–7   (*a*) $2,500,000/[($290,000 + $240,000)/2] = 9.43 times

      (*b*) ($240,000/$2,500,000) × 365 = 35 days

      (*c*) $750,000/[($530,000 + $470,000)/2] = 1.5 times

      (*d*) ($470,000/$750,000) × 365 = 228.7 days

19–8   *c*

19–9   *b*

19–10   Profit margin × Total asset turnover = Return on total assets ($945,000/$8,500,000) × 1.8 = 20%

19–11   *a*

19–12   The ratios and turnovers of a selected group of competing companies.

Present and Future Values: An Expansion

After studying Appendix F, you should be able to:

1. Explain what is meant by the present value of a single amount and the present value of an annuity and be able to use tables to solve present value problems.
2. Explain what is meant by the future value of a single amount and the future value of an annuity and be able to use tables to solve future value problems.

The concept of present value is introduced and applied to accounting problems in Chapters 13 and 18 (Volume II). This appendix supplements those presentations with additional discussion, more complete tables, and additional homework exercises. In studying this appendix, you also learn about the concept of future value.

The present value of a single amount to be received or paid at some future date may be expressed as:

$$p = \frac{f}{(1 + i)^n}$$

where

p = Present value
f = Future value
i = Rate of interest per period
n = Number of periods

PRESENT VALUE OF A SINGLE AMOUNT

LO 1
Explain what is meant by the present value of a single amount and the present value of an annuity, and be able to use tables to solve present value problems.

For example, assume that $2.20 is to be received one period from now. It would be useful to know how much must be invested now, for one period, at an interest rate of 10% to provide $2.20. We can calculate that amount with this formula:

$$p = \frac{f}{(1 + i)^n} = \frac{\$2.20}{(1 + .10)^1} = \$2.00$$

Alternatively, we can use the formula to find how much must be invested for two periods at 10% to provide $2.42:

$$p = \frac{f}{(1 + i)^n} = \frac{\$2.42}{(1 + .10)^2} = \$2.00$$

Note that the number of periods (n) does not have to be expressed in years. Any period of time such as a day, a month, a quarter, or a year may be used. However, whatever period is used, the interest rate (i) must be compounded for the same period. Thus, if a problem expresses n in months, and i equals 12% per year, then 1% of the amount invested at the beginning of each month is earned during that month and added to the investment. Thus, the interest is compounded monthly.

A present value table shows present values for a variety of interest rates (i) and a variety of numbers of periods (n). Each present value is based on the assumption that the future value (f) is 1. The following formula is used to construct a table of present values of a single future amount:

$$p = \frac{1}{(1 + i)^n}$$

Table F–1 on page AP–8 is a table of present values of a single future amount and often is called a *present value of 1* table.

Progress Check

F-1 Lamar Company is considering an investment that will yield $70,000 after six years. If Lamar requires an 8% return, how much should it be willing to pay for the investment?

FUTURE VALUE OF A SINGLE AMOUNT

LO 2

Explain what is meant by the future value of a single amount and the future value of an annuity, and be able to use tables to solve future value problems.

The following formula for the present value of a single amount can be modified to become the formula for the future value of a single amount with a simple step:

$$p = \frac{f}{(1 + i)^n}$$

By multiplying both sides of the equation by $(1 + i)^n$, the result is:

$$f = p \times (1 + i)^n$$

For example, we can use this formula to determine that $2.00 invested for one period at an interest rate of 10% will increase to a future value of $2.20:

$$f = p \times (1 + i)^n$$
$$= \$2.00 \times (1 + .10)^1$$
$$= \$2.20$$

Alternatively, assume that $2.00 will remain invested for three periods at 10%. The $2.662 amount that will be received after three periods is calculated with the formula as follows:

$$f = p \times (1 + i)^n$$
$$= \$2.00 \times (1 + .10)^3$$
$$= \$2.662$$

A future value table shows future values for a variety of interest rates (i) and a variety of numbers of periods (n). Each future value is based on the assumption that the present value (p) is 1. Thus, the formula used to construct a table of future values of a single amount is:

$$f = (1 + i)^n$$

Table F–2 on page AP–9 is a table of future values of a single amount and often is called a *future value of 1* table.

In Table F–2, look at the row where $n = 0$ and observe that the future value is 1 for all interest rates because no interest is earned.

Observe that a table showing the present values of 1 and a table showing the future values of 1 contain exactly the same information because both tables are based on the same equation:

$$p = \frac{f}{(1 + i)^n}$$

This equation is nothing more than a reformulation of:

$$f = p \times (1 + i)^n$$

Both tables reflect the same four variables, p, f, i, and n. Therefore, any problem that can be solved with one of the two tables can also be solved with the other table.

For example, suppose that a person invests $100 for five years and expects to earn 12% per year. How much should the person receive after five years? To solve the problem using Table F–2, find the future value of 1, five periods from now, compounded at 12%. In the table, $f = 1.7623$. Thus, the amount to be accumulated over five years is $176.23 ($100 × 1.7623).

Table F–1 shows that the present value of 1, discounted five periods at 12% is 0.5674. Recall that the relationship between present value and future value may be expressed as:

$$p = \frac{f}{(1 + i)^n}$$

This formula can be restated as:

$$p = f \times \frac{1}{(1 + i)^n}$$

In turn, it can be restated as:

$$f = \frac{p}{\dfrac{1}{(1 + i)^n}}$$

Because we know from Table F–1 that $1/(1 + i)^n$ equals 0.5674, the future value of $100 invested for five periods at 12% is:

$$f = \frac{\$100}{0.5674} = \$176.24$$

In summary, the future value can be found two ways. First, we can multiply the amount invested by the future value found in Table F–2. Second, we can divide the amount invested by the present value found in Table F–1. As you can see in this problem, immaterial differences can occur between these two methods through rounding.

PRESENT VALUE OF AN ANNUITY

LO 3

Explain what is meant by the present value of a single amount and the present value of an annuity, and be able to use tables to solve present value problems.

An annuity is a series of equal payments occurring at equal intervals, such as three annual payments of $100 each. The present value of an annuity is defined as the present value of the payments one period prior to the first payment. Graphically, this annuity and its present value (p) may be represented as follows:

One way to calculate the present value of this annuity finds the present value of each payment with the formula and adds them together. For this example, assuming an interest rate of 15%, the calculation is:

$$p = \frac{\$100}{(1 + .15)^1} + \frac{\$100}{(1 + .15)^2} + \frac{\$100}{(1 + .15)^3} = \$228.32$$

Another way calculates the present value of the annuity by using Table F–1 to compute the present value of each payment then taking their sum:

First payment:	$p = \$100 \times 0.8696 = \$\ 86.96$
Second payment:	$p = \$100 \times 0.7561 =\ \ \ \ 75.61$
Third payment:	$p = \$100 \times 0.6575 =\ \ \ \ 65.75$
Total:	$p = \$228.32$

We can also use Table F–1 to solve the problem by first adding the table values for the three payments and then multiplying this sum by the $100 amount of each payment:

From Table F–1:	$i = 15\%, n = 1, p =\ \ \ 0.8696$
	$i = 15\%, n = 2, p =\ \ \ 0.7561$
	$i = 15\%, n = 3, p =\ \ \ 0.6575$
	2.2832
	$2.2832 \times \$100 = \$228.32$

An easier way to solve the problem uses a different table that shows the present values of annuities like Table F–3 on page AP–10, which often is called a *present value of an annuity of 1* table. Look in Table F–3 on the row where $n = 3$ and $i = 15\%$ and observe that the present value is 2.2832. Thus, the present value of an annuity of 1 for three periods, discounted at 15%, is 2.2832.

Although a formula is used to construct a table showing the present values of an annuity, you can construct one by adding the amounts in a present value of 1 table.[1] Examine Table F–1 and Table F–3 to confirm that the following numbers were drawn from those tables:

From Table F–1		From Table F–3	
$i = 8\%, n = 1$	0.9259		
$i = 8\%, n = 2$	0.8573		
$i = 8\%, n = 3$	0.7938		
$i = 8\%, n = 4$	0.7350		
Total	3.3120	$i = 8\%, n = 4$	3.3121

The minor difference in the results occurs only because the numbers in the tables have been rounded.

In addition to the preceding methods, you can use preprogrammed business calculators and spreadsheet computer programs to find the present value of annuities.

Progress Check

F–3 Smith & Company is considering an investment that would pay $10,000 every six months for three years. The first payment would be received in six months. If Smith & Company requires an annual return of 8%, they should be willing to invest no more than: *(a)* $25,771; *(b)* $46,229; *(c)* $52,421.

FUTURE VALUE OF AN ANNUITY

Just as an annuity has a present value, it also has a future value. The future value of an annuity is the accumulated value of the annuity payments and interest as of the date of the final payment. Consider the earlier annuity of three annual payments of $100. These are the points in time at which the present value (p) and the future value (f) occur:

Note that the first payment is made two periods prior to the point at which the future value is determined. Therefore, for the first payment, $n = 2$. For the second payment, $n = 1$. Since the third payment occurs on the future value date, $n = 0$.

One way to calculate the future value of this annuity uses the formula to find the future value of each payment and adds them together. Assuming an interest rate of 15%, the calculation is:

$$f = \$100 \times (1 + .15)^2 + \$100 \times (1 + .15)^1 + \$100 \times (1 + .15)^0 = \$347.25$$

---

[1]The formula for the present value of an annuity of 1 is:

$$p = \frac{1 - \frac{1}{(1 + i)^n}}{i}$$

Another way calculates the future value of the annuity by using Table F–2 to find the sum of the future values of each payment:

First payment: $f = \$100 \times 1.3225 = \$132.25$
Second payment: $f = \$100 \times 1.1500 = 115.00$
Third payment: $f = \$100 \times 1.0000 = \underline{100.00}$
Total: $f = \underline{\underline{\$347.25}}$

A third approach adds the future values of three payments of 1 and multiplies the sum by $100:

From Table F–1: $i = 15\%, n = 2, f = 1.3225$
$i = 15\%, n = 1, f = 1.1500$
$i = 15\%, n = 0, f = \underline{1.0000}$
Sum $= \underline{3.4725}$
Future value $= 3.4725 \times \$100 = \underline{\underline{\$347.25}}$

A fourth and easier way to solve the problem uses a table that shows the future values of annuities, often called a *future value of an annuity of 1* table. Table F–4 on page AP–11 is such a table. Note in Table F–4 that when $n = 1$, the future values are equal to 1 ($f = 1$) for all rates of interest because the annuity consists of only one payment and the future value is determined on the date of the payment. Thus, the future value equals the payment.

Although a formula is used to construct a table showing the future values of an annuity of 1, you can construct one by adding together the amount in a future value of 1 table like Table F–2.[2] Examine Table F–2 and Table F–4 to confirm that the following numbers were drawn from those tables:

From Table F–2		From Table F–4	
$i = 8\%, n = 0$	1.0000		
$i = 8\%, n = 1$	1.0800		
$i = 8\%, n = 2$	1.1664		
$i = 8\%, n = 3$	1.2597		
Total	4.5061	$i = 8\%, n = 4$	4.5061

Minor differences may occur because the numbers in the tables have been rounded.

You can also use business calculators and spreadsheet computer programs to find the future values of annuities.

Observe that the future value in Table F–2 is 1.0000 when $n = 0$ but the future value in Table F–4 is 1.0000 when $n = 1$. Why does this apparent contradiction arise? When $n = 0$ in Table F–2, the future value is determined on the date that the single payment occurs. Thus, no interest is earned and the future value equals the payment. However, Table F–4 describes annuities with equal payments occurring

---

[2]The formula for the future value of an annuity of 1 is:

$$f = \frac{(1 + i)^n - 1}{i}$$

each period. When $n = 1$, the annuity has only one payment, and its future value also equals 1 on the date of its final and only payment.

Progress Check

F-4 **Syntel Company invests $45,000 per year for five years at 12%. Calculate the value of the investment at the end of five years.**

SUMMARY OF THE APPENDIX IN TERMS OF LEARNING OBJECTIVES

LO 1. Explain what is meant by the present value of a single amount and the present value of an annuity, and be able to use tables to solve present value problems. The present value of a single amount to be received at a future date is the amount that could be invested now at the specified interest rate to yield that future value. The present value of an annuity is the amount that could be invested now at the specified interest rate to yield that series of equal periodic payments. Present value tables and business calculators simplify calculating present values.

LO 2. Explain what is meant by the future value of a single amount and the future value of an annuity, and be able to use tables to solve future value problems. The future value of a single amount invested at a specified rate of interest is the amount that would accumulate at a future date. The future value of an annuity to be invested at a specified rate of interest is the amount that would accumulate at the date of the final equal periodic payment. Future value tables and business calculators simplify calculating future values.

Table F-1 Present Value of 1 Due in *n* Periods

Periods	1%	2%	3%	4%	5%	6%	7%	8%	9%	10%	12%	15%
1	0.9901	0.9804	0.9709	0.9615	0.9524	0.9434	0.9346	0.9259	0.9174	0.9091	0.8929	0.8696
2	0.9803	0.9612	0.9426	0.9246	0.9070	0.8900	0.8734	0.8573	0.8417	0.8264	0.7972	0.7561
3	0.9706	0.9423	0.9151	0.8890	0.8638	0.8396	0.8163	0.7938	0.7722	0.7513	0.7118	0.6575
4	0.9610	0.9238	0.8885	0.8548	0.8227	0.7921	0.7629	0.7350	0.7084	0.6830	0.6355	0.5718
5	0.9515	0.9057	0.8626	0.8219	0.7835	0.7473	0.7130	0.6806	0.6499	0.6209	0.5674	0.4972
6	0.9420	0.8880	0.8375	0.7903	0.7462	0.7050	0.6663	0.6302	0.5963	0.5645	0.5066	0.4323
7	0.9327	0.8706	0.8131	0.7599	0.7107	0.6651	0.6227	0.5835	0.5470	0.5132	0.4523	0.3759
8	0.9235	0.8535	0.7894	0.7307	0.6768	0.6274	0.5820	0.5403	0.5019	0.4665	0.4039	0.3269
9	0.9143	0.8368	0.7664	0.7026	0.6446	0.5919	0.5439	0.5002	0.4604	0.4241	0.3606	0.2843
10	0.9053	0.8203	0.7441	0.6756	0.6139	0.5584	0.5083	0.4632	0.4224	0.3855	0.3220	0.2472
11	0.8963	0.8043	0.7224	0.6496	0.5847	0.5268	0.4751	0.4289	0.3875	0.3505	0.2875	0.2149
12	0.8874	0.7885	0.7014	0.6246	0.5568	0.4970	0.4440	0.3971	0.3555	0.3186	0.2567	0.1869
13	0.8787	0.7730	0.6810	0.6006	0.5303	0.4688	0.4150	0.3677	0.3262	0.2897	0.2292	0.1625
14	0.8700	0.7579	0.6611	0.5775	0.5051	0.4423	0.3878	0.3405	0.2992	0.2633	0.2046	0.1413
15	0.8613	0.7430	0.6419	0.5553	0.4810	0.4173	0.3624	0.3152	0.2745	0.2394	0.1827	0.1229
16	0.8528	0.7284	0.6232	0.5339	0.4581	0.3936	0.3387	0.2919	0.2519	0.2176	0.1631	0.1069
17	0.8444	0.7142	0.6050	0.5134	0.4363	0.3714	0.3166	0.2703	0.2311	0.1978	0.1456	0.0929
18	0.8360	0.7002	0.5874	0.4936	0.4155	0.3505	0.2959	0.2502	0.2120	0.1799	0.1300	0.0808
19	0.8277	0.6864	0.5703	0.4746	0.3957	0.3305	0.2765	0.2317	0.1945	0.1635	0.1161	0.0703
20	0.8195	0.6730	0.5537	0.4564	0.3769	0.3118	0.2584	0.2145	0.1784	0.1486	0.1037	0.0611
25	0.7798	0.6095	0.4776	0.3751	0.2953	0.2330	0.1842	0.1460	0.1160	0.0923	0.0588	0.0304
30	0.7419	0.5521	0.4120	0.3083	0.2314	0.1741	0.1314	0.0994	0.0754	0.0573	0.0334	0.0151
35	0.7059	0.5000	0.3554	0.2534	0.1813	0.1301	0.0937	0.0676	0.0490	0.0356	0.0189	0.0075
40	0.6717	0.4529	0.3066	0.2083	0.1420	0.0972	0.0668	0.0460	0.0318	0.0221	0.0107	0.0037

Rate

Table F-2 Future Value of 1 Due in *n* Periods

Periods	1%	2%	3%	4%	5%	6%	7%	8%	9%	10%	12%	15%
0	1.0000	1.0000	1.0000	1.0000	1.0000	1.0000	1.0000	1.0000	1.0000	1.0000	1.0000	1.0000
1	1.0100	1.0200	1.0300	1.0400	1.0500	1.0600	1.0700	1.0800	1.0900	1.1000	1.1200	1.1500
2	1.0201	1.0404	1.0609	1.0816	1.1025	1.1236	1.1449	1.1664	1.1881	1.2100	1.2544	1.3225
3	1.0303	1.0612	1.0927	1.1249	1.1576	1.1910	1.2250	1.2597	1.2950	1.3310	1.4049	1.5209
4	1.0406	1.0824	1.1255	1.1699	1.2155	1.2625	1.3108	1.3605	1.4116	1.4641	1.5735	1.7490
5	1.0510	1.1041	1.1593	1.2167	1.2763	1.3382	1.4026	1.4693	1.5386	1.6105	1.7623	2.0114
6	1.0615	1.1262	1.1941	1.2653	1.3401	1.4185	1.5007	1.5869	1.6771	1.7716	1.9738	2.3131
7	1.0721	1.1487	1.2299	1.3159	1.4071	1.5036	1.6058	1.7138	1.8280	1.9487	2.2107	2.6600
8	1.0829	1.1717	1.2668	1.3686	1.4775	1.5938	1.7182	1.8509	1.9926	2.1436	2.4760	3.0590
9	1.0937	1.1951	1.3048	1.4233	1.5513	1.6895	1.8385	1.9990	2.1719	2.3579	2.7731	3.5179
10	1.1046	1.2190	1.3439	1.4802	1.6289	1.7908	1.9672	2.1589	2.3674	2.5937	3.1058	4.0456
11	1.1157	1.2434	1.3842	1.5395	1.7103	1.8983	2.1049	2.3316	2.5804	2.8531	3.4785	4.6524
12	1.1268	1.2682	1.4258	1.6010	1.7959	2.0122	2.2522	2.5182	2.8127	3.1384	3.8960	5.3503
13	1.1381	1.2936	1.4685	1.6651	1.8856	2.1329	2.4098	2.7196	3.0658	3.4523	4.3635	6.1528
14	1.1495	1.3195	1.5126	1.7317	1.9799	2.2609	2.5785	2.9372	3.3417	3.7975	4.8871	7.0757
15	1.1610	1.3459	1.5580	1.8009	2.0789	2.3966	2.7590	3.1722	3.6425	4.1772	5.4736	8.1371
16	1.1726	1.3728	1.6047	1.8730	2.1829	2.5404	2.9522	3.4259	3.9703	4.5950	6.1304	9.3576
17	1.1843	1.4002	1.6528	1.9479	2.2920	2.6928	3.1588	3.7000	4.3276	5.0545	6.8660	10.7613
18	1.1961	1.4282	1.7024	2.0258	2.4066	2.8543	3.3799	3.9960	4.7171	5.5599	7.6900	12.3755
19	1.2081	1.4568	1.7535	2.1068	2.5270	3.0256	3.6165	4.3157	5.1417	6.1159	8.6128	14.2318
20	1.2202	1.4859	1.8061	2.1911	2.6533	3.2071	3.8697	4.6610	5.6044	6.7275	9.6463	16.3665
25	1.2824	1.6406	2.0938	2.6658	3.3864	4.2919	5.4274	6.8485	8.6231	10.8347	17.0001	32.9190
30	1.3478	1.8114	2.4273	3.2434	4.3219	5.7435	7.6123	10.0627	13.2677	17.4494	29.9599	66.2118
35	1.4166	1.9999	2.8139	3.9461	5.5160	7.6861	10.6766	14.7853	20.4140	28.1024	52.7996	133.176
40	1.4889	2.2080	3.2620	4.8010	7.0400	10.2857	14.9745	21.7245	31.4094	45.2593	93.0510	267.864

Table F-3 Present Value of an Annuity of 1 per Period

Periods	1%	2%	3%	4%	5%	6%	7%	8%	9%	10%	12%	15%
1	0.9901	0.9804	0.9709	0.9615	0.9524	0.9434	0.9346	0.9259	0.9174	0.9091	0.8929	0.8696
2	1.9704	1.9416	1.9135	1.8861	1.8594	1.8334	1.8080	1.7833	1.7591	1.7355	1.6901	1.6257
3	2.9410	2.8839	2.8286	2.7751	2.7232	2.6730	2.6243	2.5771	2.5313	2.4869	2.4018	2.2832
4	3.9020	3.8077	3.7171	3.6299	3.5460	3.4651	3.3872	3.3121	3.2397	3.1699	3.0373	2.8550
5	4.8534	4.7135	4.5797	4.4518	4.3295	4.2124	4.1002	3.9927	3.8897	3.7908	3.6048	3.3522
6	5.7955	5.6014	5.4172	5.2421	5.0757	4.9173	4.7665	4.6229	4.4859	4.3553	4.1114	3.7845
7	6.7282	6.4720	6.2303	6.0021	5.7864	5.5824	5.3893	5.2064	5.0330	4.8684	4.5638	4.1604
8	7.6517	7.3255	7.0197	6.7327	6.4632	6.2098	5.9713	5.7466	5.5348	5.3349	4.9676	4.4873
9	8.5660	8.1622	7.7861	7.4353	7.1078	6.8017	6.5152	6.2469	5.9952	5.7590	5.3282	4.7716
10	9.4713	8.9826	8.5302	8.1109	7.7217	7.3601	7.0236	6.7101	6.4177	6.1446	5.6502	5.0188
11	10.3676	9.7868	9.2526	8.7605	8.3064	7.8869	7.4987	7.1390	6.8052	6.4951	5.9377	5.2337
12	11.2551	10.5753	9.9540	9.3851	8.8633	8.3838	7.9427	7.5361	7.1607	6.8137	6.1944	5.4206
13	12.1337	11.3484	10.6350	9.9856	9.3936	8.8527	8.3577	7.9038	7.4869	7.1034	6.4235	5.5831
14	13.0037	12.1062	11.2961	10.5631	9.8986	9.2950	8.7455	8.2442	7.7862	7.3667	6.6282	5.7245
15	13.8651	12.8493	11.9379	11.1184	10.3797	9.7122	9.1079	8.5595	8.0607	7.6061	6.8109	5.8474
16	14.7179	13.5777	12.5611	11.6523	10.8378	10.1059	9.4466	8.8514	8.3126	7.8237	6.9740	5.9542
17	15.5623	14.2919	13.1661	12.1657	11.2741	10.4773	9.7632	9.1216	8.5436	8.0216	7.1196	6.0472
18	16.3983	14.9920	13.7535	12.6593	11.6896	10.8276	10.0591	9.3719	8.7556	8.2014	7.2497	6.1280
19	17.2260	15.6785	14.3238	13.1339	12.0853	11.1581	10.3356	9.6036	8.9501	8.3649	7.3658	6.1982
20	18.0456	16.3514	14.8775	13.5903	12.4622	11.4699	10.5940	9.8181	9.1285	8.5136	7.4694	6.2593
25	22.0232	19.5235	17.4131	15.6221	14.0939	12.7834	11.6536	10.6748	9.8226	9.0770	7.8431	6.4641
30	25.8077	22.3965	19.6004	17.2920	15.3725	13.7648	12.4090	11.2578	10.2737	9.4269	8.0552	6.5660
35	29.4086	24.9986	21.4872	18.6646	16.3742	14.4982	12.9477	11.6546	10.5668	9.6442	8.1755	6.6166
40	32.8437	27.3555	23.1148	19.7928	17.1591	15.0463	13.3317	11.9246	10.7574	9.7791	8.2438	6.6418

Rate

Table F-4 Future Value of an Annuity of 1 per Period

Periods	1%	2%	3%	4%	5%	6%	7%	8%	9%	10%	12%	15%
							Rate					
1	1.0000	1.0000	1.0000	1.0000	1.0000	1.0000	1.0000	1.0000	1.0000	1.0000	1.0000	1.0000
2	2.0100	2.0200	2.0300	2.0400	2.0500	2.0600	2.0700	2.0800	2.0900	2.1000	2.1200	2.1500
3	3.0301	3.0604	3.0909	3.1216	3.1525	3.1836	3.2149	3.2464	3.2781	3.3100	3.3744	3.4725
4	4.0604	4.1216	4.1836	4.2465	4.3101	4.3746	4.4399	4.5061	4.5731	4.6410	4.7793	4.9934
5	5.1010	5.2040	5.3091	5.4163	5.5256	5.6371	5.7507	5.8666	5.9847	6.1051	6.3528	6.7424
6	6.1520	6.3081	6.4684	6.6330	6.8019	6.9753	7.1533	7.3359	7.5233	7.7156	8.1152	8.7537
7	7.2135	7.4343	7.6625	7.8983	8.1420	8.3938	8.6540	8.9228	9.2004	9.4872	10.0890	11.0668
8	8.2857	8.5830	8.8923	9.2142	9.5491	9.8975	10.2598	10.6366	11.0285	11.4359	12.2997	13.7268
9	9.3685	9.7546	10.1591	10.5828	11.0266	11.4913	11.9780	12.4876	13.0210	13.5795	14.7757	16.7858
10	10.4622	10.9497	11.4639	12.0061	12.5779	13.1808	13.8164	14.4866	15.1929	15.9374	17.5487	20.3037
11	11.5668	12.1687	12.8078	13.4864	14.2068	14.9716	15.7836	16.6455	17.5603	18.5312	20.6546	24.3493
12	12.6825	13.4121	14.1920	15.0258	15.9171	16.8699	17.8885	18.9771	20.1407	21.3843	24.1331	29.0017
13	13.8093	14.6803	15.6178	16.6268	17.7130	18.8821	20.1406	21.4953	22.9534	24.5227	28.0291	34.3519
14	14.9474	15.9739	17.0863	18.2919	19.5986	21.0151	22.5505	24.2149	26.0192	27.9750	32.3926	40.5047
15	16.0969	17.2934	18.5989	20.0236	21.5786	23.2760	25.1290	27.1521	29.3609	31.7725	37.2797	47.5804
16	17.2579	18.6393	20.1569	21.8245	23.6575	25.6725	27.8881	30.3243	33.0034	35.9497	42.7533	55.7175
17	18.4304	20.0121	21.7616	23.6975	25.8404	28.2129	30.8402	33.7502	36.9737	40.5447	48.8837	65.0751
18	19.6147	21.4123	23.4144	25.6454	28.1324	30.9057	33.9990	37.4502	41.3013	45.5992	55.7497	75.8364
19	20.8109	22.8406	25.1169	27.6712	30.5390	33.7600	37.3790	41.4463	46.0185	51.1591	63.4397	88.2118
20	22.0190	24.2974	26.8704	29.7781	33.0660	36.7856	40.9955	45.7620	51.1601	57.2750	72.0524	102.444
25	28.2432	32.0303	36.4593	41.6459	47.7271	54.8645	63.2490	73.1059	84.7009	98.3471	133.334	212.793
30	34.7849	40.5681	47.5754	56.0849	66.4388	79.0582	94.4608	113.283	136.308	164.494	241.333	434.745
35	41.6603	49.9945	60.4621	73.6522	90.3203	111.435	138.237	172.317	215.711	271.024	431.663	881.170
40	48.8864	60.4020	75.4013	95.0255	120.800	154.762	199.635	259.057	337.882	442.593	767.091	1,779.09

EXERCISES

Exercise F–1
Present value of an amount
(LO 1)

Jasper Company is considering an investment which, if paid for immediately, is expected to return $172,500 five years hence. If Jasper demands a 9% return, how much will it be willing to pay for this investment?

Exercise F–2
Future value of an amount
(LO 2)

LCV Company invested $529,000 in a project expected to earn a 12% annual rate of return. The earnings will be reinvested in the project each year until the entire investment is liquidated 10 years hence. What will the cash proceeds be when the project is liquidated?

Exercise F–3
Present value of an annuity
(LO 1)

Cornblue Distributing is considering a contract that will return $200,400 annually at the end of each year for six years. If Cornblue demands an annual return of 7% and pays for the investment immediately, how much should it be willing to pay?

Exercise F–4
Future value of an annuity
(LO 2)

Sarah Oliver is planning to begin an individual retirement program in which she will invest $1,200 annually at the end of each year. Oliver plans to retire after making 30 annual investments in a program that earns a return of 10%. What will be the value of the program on the date of the last investment?

Exercise F–5
Interest rate on an investment
(LO 1)

Kevin Smith has been offered the possibility of investing $0.3152 for 15 years, after which he will be paid $1. What annual rate of interest will Smith earn? (Use Table F–1 to find the answer.)

Exercise F–6
Number of periods of an investment
(LO 1)

Laura Veralli has been offered the possibility of investing $0.5268. The investment will earn 6% per year and will return Veralli $1 at the end of the investment. How many years must Veralli wait to receive the $1? (Use Table F–1 to find the answer.)

Exercise F–7
Number of periods of an investment
(LO 2)

Tom Albertson expects to invest $1 at 15% and, at the end of the investment, receive $66.2118. How many years will elapse before Albertson receives the payment? (Use Table F–2 to find the answer.)

Exercise F–8
Interest rate on an investment
(LO 2)

Ed Teller expects to invest $1 for 35 years, after which he will receive $20.4140. What rate of interest will Teller earn? (Use Table F–2 to find the answer.)

Exercise F–9
Interest rate on an investment
(LO 1)

Helen Fanshawe expects an immediate investment of $9.3936 to return $1 annually for 13 years, with the first payment to be received in one year. What rate of interest will Fanshawe earn? (Use Table F–3 to find the answer.)

Exercise F–10
Number of periods of an investment
(LO 1)

Ken Priggin expects an investment of $7.6061 to return $1 annually for several years. If Priggin is to earn a return of 10%, how many annual payments must he receive? (Use Table F–3 to find the answer.)

Steve Church expects to invest $1 annually for 40 years and have an accumulated value of $95.0255 on the date of the last investment. If this occurs, what rate of interest will Church earn? (Use Table F–4 to find the answer.)

Exercise F–11
Interest rate on an investment
(LO 2)

Bitsy Brennon expects to invest $1 annually in a fund that will earn 8%. How many annual investments must Brennon make to accumulate $45.7620 on the date of the last investment? (Use Table F–4 to find the answer.)

Exercise F–12
Number of periods of an investment
(LO 2)

Bill Lenehan financed a new automobile by paying $3,100 cash and agreeing to make 20 monthly payments of $450 each, the first payment to be made one month after the purchase. The loan was said to bear interest at an annual rate of 12%. What was the cost of the automobile?

Exercise F–13
Present value of an annuity
(LO 1)

Stephanie Powell deposited $4,900 in a savings account that earns interest at an annual rate of 8%, compounded quarterly. The $4,900 plus earned interest must remain in the account 10 years before it can be withdrawn. How much money will be in the account at the end of the 10 years?

Exercise F–14
Future value of an amount
(LO 2)

Sally Sayer plans to have $90 withheld from her monthly paycheque and deposited in a savings account that earns 12% annually, compounded monthly. If Sayer continues with her plan for 2½ years, how much will be accumulated in the account on the date of the last deposit?

Exercise F–15
Future value of an annuity
(LO 2)

Stellar Company plans to issue 12%, 15-year, $500,000 par value bonds payable that pay interest semiannually on June 30 and December 31. The bonds are dated December 31, 1996, and are to be issued on that date. If the market rate of interest for the bonds is 10% on the date of issue, what will be the cash proceeds from the bond issue?

Exercise F–16
Present value of bonds
(LO 1)

Travis Company has decided to establish a fund that will be used 10 years hence to replace an aging productive facility. The company makes an initial contribution of $150,000 to the fund and plans to make quarterly contributions of $60,000 beginning in three months. The fund is expected to earn 12%, compounded quarterly. What will be the value of the fund 10 years hence?

Exercise F–17
Future value of an amount plus an annuity
(LO 2)

McCoy Company expects to earn 10% per year on an investment that will pay $756,400 six years hence. Use Table F–2 to calculate the present value of the investment.

Exercise F–18
Present value of an amount
(LO 1)

Comet Company invests $216,000 at 7% per year for nine years. Use Table F–1 to calculate the future value of the investment nine years hence.

Exercise F–19
Future value of an amount
(LO 2)

ANSWERS TO PROGRESS CHECKS

F–1 $70,000 × 0.6302 = $44,114

F–2   *c* $299,850/$150,000 = 1.9990
        Table F–2 shows this value for nine years at 8%.

F–3   *c* $10,000 × 5.2421 = $52,421

F–4 $45,000 × 6.3528 = $285,876

Accounting Principles and Conceptual Framework

After studying Appendix G, you should be able to:

1. **Explain the difference between descriptive concepts and prescriptive concepts.**
2. **Explain the difference between bottom-up and top-down approaches to the development of accounting concepts.**
3. **Describe the major components in the Accounting Standards Board's "Financial Statement Concepts."**

Accounting principles or concepts are not laws of nature. They are broad ideas developed as a way of *describing* current accounting practices and *prescribing* new and improved practices. In studying Appendix G, you will learn about some new accounting concepts that the Accounting Standards Board (AcSB) developed in an effort to guide future changes and improvements in accounting.

ACCOUNTING PRINCIPLES AND CONCEPTUAL FRAMEWORK

To fully understand the importance of financial accounting concepts or principles, you must realize that they serve two purposes. First, they provide general descriptions of existing accounting practices. In doing this, concepts and principles serve as guidelines that help you learn about accounting. Thus, after learning how the concepts or principles are applied in a few situations, you develop the ability to apply them in different situations. This is easier and more effective than memorizing a very long list of specific practices.

Second, these concepts or principles help accountants analyze unfamiliar situations and develop procedures to account for those situations. This purpose is especially important for the Accounting Standards Board, which is charged with developing uniform practices for financial reporting in Canada and with improving the quality of such reporting.

In prior chapters, we defined and illustrated several important accounting principles. These principles, listed together here for convenience, describe in general terms the practices currently used by accountants.

DESCRIPTIVE AND PRESCRIPTIVE ACCOUNTING CONCEPTS

LO 1

Explain the difference between descriptive concepts and prescriptive concepts.

Generally Accepted Principles

Business entity principle	Going-concern principle	Revenue recognition
Conservatism principle	Matching principle	principle
Consistency principle	Materiality principle	Time-period principle
Cost principle	Objectivity principle	Unit of measure
Full-disclosure principle		assumption

The listed principles (defined on pages 20–23) are useful for teaching and learning about accounting practice and are helpful for dealing with some unfamiliar transactions. As business practices have evolved in recent years, however, these principles have become less useful as guides for accountants to follow in dealing with new and different types of transactions. This problem has occurred because the principles are intended to provide general descriptions of current accounting practices. In other words, they describe what accountants currently do; they do not necessarily describe what accountants should do. Also, since these principles do not identify weaknesses in accounting practices, they do not lead to major changes or improvements in accounting practices.

In order to improve accounting practices, principles or concepts should not merely *describe* what was being done, they should *prescribe* what ought to be done to make things better.

Before we examine the concepts enunciated in the conceptual framework, we need to look more closely at the differences between descriptive and prescriptive uses of accounting concepts.

THE PROCESSES OF DEVELOPING DESCRIPTIVE AND PRESCRIPTIVE ACCOUNTING CONCEPTS

LO 2

Explain the difference between bottom-up and top-down approaches to the development of accounting concepts.

Sets of concepts differ in how they are developed and used. In general, when concepts are intended to describe current practice, they are developed by looking at accepted specific practices and then making some general rules to encompass them. This bottom-up approach is diagrammed in Illustration G–1 which shows the arrows going from the practices to the concepts. The outcome of the process is a set of general rules that summarize practice and that can be used for education and for solving some new problems. For example, this approach leads to the concept that asset purchases are recorded at cost. However, these kinds of concepts often fail to show how new problems should be solved. To continue the example, the concept that assets are recorded at cost does not provide much direct guidance for situations in which assets have no cost because they are donated to a company by a local government. Further, because these concepts are based on the presumption that current practices are adequate, they do not lead to the development of new and improved accounting methods. To continue the example, the concept that assets are initially recorded at cost does not encourage asking the question of whether they should always be carried at that amount.

In contrast, if concepts are intended to *prescribe* improvements in accounting practices, they are likely to be designed by a top-down approach (Illustration G–2). Note that the top-down approach starts with broad accounting objectives. The process then generates broad concepts about the types of information that should be reported. Finally, these concepts should lead to specific practices that ought to be used. The advantage of this approach is that the concepts are good for solving

Illustration G–1 A Bottom-Up Process of Developing Descriptive Accounting Concepts

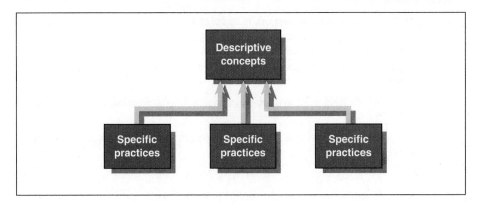

Illustration G–2 A Top-Down Process of Developing Prescriptive Accounting Concepts

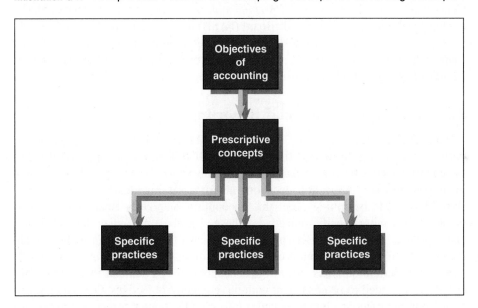

new problems and evaluating old answers; its disadvantage is that the concepts may not be very descriptive of current practice. In fact, the suggested practices may not be in current use.

Since the AcSB uses accounting concepts to prescribe accounting practices, the Board used a top-down approach to develop its conceptual framework. The Board's concepts are not necessarily more correct than the previously developed concepts. However, the new concepts are intended to provide better guidelines for developing new and improved accounting practices. The Board has stated that it will use them as a basis for its future actions and already has used them to justify important changes in financial reporting.

THE CONCEPTUAL FRAMEWORK

LO 3

Describe the major components in the Accounting Standards Board's "Financial Statement Concepts."

During the 1970s the accounting profession in both Canada and the United States turned its attention to the apparent need for improvement in financial reporting. In 1980 *Corporate Reporting: Its Future Evolution,* a research study, was published by the Canadian Institute of Chartered Accountants, and in 1989 "Financial Statement Concepts," section 1000 of the *CICA Handbook,* was approved. In the United States the Financial Accounting Standards Board (FASB) published, in the 1978–85 period, six statements regarded as the most comprehensive pronouncement of the conceptual framework of accounting. FASB *(SFAC 1)* and Accounting Standards Board *(CICA Handbook,* section 1000) identified the broad objectives of financial reporting.

The Objectives of Financial Reporting

"Financial Statement Concepts" identified the broad objectives of financial reporting. The most general objective stated in the *CICA Handbook,* par. 1000.12, is to "communicate information that is useful to investors, creditors, and other users in making resource allocation decisions and/or assessing management stewardship." From this beginning point the Accounting Standards Board (AcSB) expressed other, more specific objectives. These objectives recognize that (1) financial reporting should help users predict future cash flow and (2) in making such predictions, information about a company's resources and obligations is useful if it possesses certain qualities. All of the concepts in the "Financial Statement Concepts" are intended to be consistent with these general objectives. Of course, present accounting practice already provides information about a company's resources and obligations. Thus, although the conceptual framework is intended to be prescriptive of new and improved practices, the concepts in the framework are also descriptive of many current practices.

The Qualities of Useful Information

The AcSB discussed the fact that information can be useful only if it is understandable to users. However, the users are assumed to have the training, experience, and motivation to analyze financial reports. With this decision, the Board indicated that financial reporting should not try to meet the needs of unsophisticated or other casual report users.

The AcSB said that information is useful if it is (1) relevant, (2) reliable, and (3) comparable. Information is *relevant* if it can make a difference in a decision.

As a Matter of Opinion

Ms. Gordon received a B.A. in economics and commerce and both an M.A. and a Ph.D. in economics at Simon Fraser University, where she has been a member of the faculty of business administration since 1981. Ms. Gordon teaches financial accounting and is engaged in research in the areas of positive accounting theory, the accounting-economics interface, social responsibility accounting, and issues in accounting education. She has been a member of CGA-Canada Research Committee since 1984 and was president of the Canadian Academic Accounting Association for 1988-1989.

While my university degrees all carry economics in the title, my Ph.D. courses, thesis, and subsequent research have heavily emphasized accounting issues ranging from pensions to internal control to accounting theory.

Accounting research is fundamentally interdisciplinary in character. It is this breadth of character that initially sparked my interest and has held it over time. Additionally, in a world where accounting standard setters' decisions are made which have an effect on differing cultures, societies, economic systems, and individuals, this interdisciplinary emphasis is vital. The link between the research of individual accounting academics and standard setting is both important and a "two-way street." Without continuing accounting research, the standard setting process might lack the background or new ways to view our rapidly changing world. As well this linkage gives a purpose to much of the ongoing accounting research.

Irene M. Gordon, CGA

Information has this quality when it helps users predict the future or evaluate the past, and when it is received in time to affect their decisions.

Information is *reliable* if users can depend on it to be free from bias and error. Reliable information is verifiable and faithfully represents what is supposed to be described. In addition, users can depend on information only if it is neutral. This means that the rules used to produce information should not be designed to lead users to accept or reject any specific decision alternative.

Information is *comparable* if users can use it to identify differences and similarities between companies. Comparability is possible only if companies follow uniform practices. However, even if all companies uniformly follow the same practices, comparable reports do not result if the practices are not appropriate. For example, comparable information would not be provided if all companies were to ignore the useful lives of their assets and amortize all assets over two years.

Comparability also requires consistency, which means that a company should not change its accounting practices unless the change is justified as a reporting improvement. Another important concept discussed is materiality.

Elements of Financial Statements

Another important step in developing the conceptual framework was to determine the elements of financial statements. This involved defining the categories of information that should be contained in financial reports. The AcSB's discussion of financial statement elements includes definitions of important elements such as assets, liabilities, equity, revenues, expenses, gains, and losses. In earlier chapters, we referred to many of these definitions when we explained various accounting procedures.

Recognition and Measurement

The AcSB, in paragraphs 36-47 of section 1000, established concepts for deciding (1) when items should be presented (or recognized) in the financial statements, and (2) how to assign numbers to (or measure) those items. In general, the Board concluded that items should be recognized in the financial statements if they meet the following criteria:

- Definitions. The item meets the definition of an element of financial statements.
- Measurability. It has a relevant attribute measurable with sufficient reliability.
- Relevance. The information about it is capable of making a difference in user decisions.
- Reliability. The information is representationally faithful, verifiable, and neutral.

The question of how items should be measured raises the fundamental question of whether financial statements should be based on cost or on value. Since this question is quite controversial, the AcSB's discussion of this issue is more descriptive of current practice than it is prescriptive of new measurement methods. However, before we consider alternative accounting valuation systems, let us review and expand upon the accounting concepts or principles.

ACCOUNTING PRINCIPLES

An understanding of accounting principles begins with the recognition of the broad concepts as to the nature of the economic setting in which accounting operates.

The Business Entity Principle

Every business unit or enterprise is treated in accounting as a separate entity, with the affairs of the business and those of the owner or owners being kept entirely separate.

The Going-Concern Principle

Unless there is strong evidence to the contrary, it is assumed that a business will continue to operate as a going concern, earning a reasonable profit for a period longer than the life expectancy of any of its assets.

The Time-Period Principle

The environment in which accounting operates—the business community and the government—requires that the life of a business be divided into relatively short periods and that changes be measured over these short periods. Yet, it is generally agreed that earnings cannot be measured precisely over a short period and that it is impossible to learn the exact earnings of a business until it has completed its last transaction and converted all its assets to cash.

Cost Principle

The cost principle specifies that cash-equivalent cost is the most useful basis for the initial accounting of the elements that are recorded in the accounts and reported on the financial statements. It is important to note that the cost principle applies to the initial recording of transactions and events.

The cost principle is supported by the fact that at the time of a completed arm's-length business transaction, the market value of the resources given up in the transaction provides reliable evidence of the valuation of the item acquired in the transaction.

When a noncash consideration is involved, cost is measured as the market value of the resources given or the market value of the item received, whichever is more reliably determinable. For example, an asset may be acquired with a debt given as settlement. Cost in this instance is the present value of the amount of cash to be paid in the future, as specified by the terms of the debt. The cost principle applies to all of the elements of financial statements, including liabilities.

The cost principle provides guidance at the original recognition date. However, the original cost of some items acquired is subject to depreciation, depletion, amortization, and write-down in conformity with the matching principle and the conservatism constraint (discussed in the sections that follow).

Revenue Recognition Principle

The revenue recognition principle specifies when revenue should be recognized in the accounts and reported in the financial statements. Revenue is measured as the market value of the resources received or the product or service given, whichever is the more reliably determinable.

Under the revenue recognition principle, revenue from the sale of goods is recognized according to the sales method (i.e., at the time of sale) because the earning process usually is complete at the time of sale. At that time, the relevant information about the asset inflows to the seller would be known with reliability.

Under revenue recognition principle, revenue from the sale of services is recognized on the basis of performance because performance determines the extent to which the earning process is complete.

The revenue recognition principle requires accrual basis accounting rather than cash basis accounting for revenues. For example, completed transactions for the sale of goods or services on credit usually are recognized as revenue in the period in which the sale or service occurred rather than in the period in which the cash is eventually collected.

Matching Principle

A major objective of accounting is the determination of periodic net income by matching appropriate costs against revenues. The principle recognizes that streams of revenues continually flow into a business, and it requires (1) that there be a precise cutoff in these streams at the end of an accounting period, (2) that the inflows of the period be measured, (3) that the costs incurred in securing the inflows be determined, and (4) that the sum of the costs be deducted from the sum of the inflows to determine the period's net income.

The Objectivity Principle

The objectivity principle holds that changes in account balances should be supported to the fullest extent possible by objective evidence.

   Bargained transactions supported by verifiable business documents originating outside the business are the best objective evidence obtainable, and whenever possible, accounting data should be supported by such documents.

Full-Disclosure Principle

The full-disclosure principle requires that the financial statements of a business clearly report all of the relevant information about the economic affairs of the enterprise. This principle rests upon the primary characteristic of relevance. Full disclosure requires (a) reporting of all information that can make a difference in a decision and (b) that the accounting information reported must be understandable (i.e., not susceptible to misleading inferences). Full disclosure also requires that the major accounting policies and any special accounting policies used by the company be explained in the notes to the financial statements.

The Consistency Principle

In many cases two or more methods or procedures have been derived in accounting practice to accomplish a particular accounting objective. While recognizing the validity of different methods under varying circumstances, it is still necessary, in order to ensure a high degree of comparability in any concern's accounting data, to insist on a consistent application in the company of any given accounting method, period after period. It is also necessary to insist that any departures from this doctrine of consistency be fully disclosed in the financial statements and the effects thereof on the statements be fully described.

The Principle of Conservatism

The principle of conservatism holds that the accountant should be conservative in his or her estimates and opinions and in the selection of procedures, choosing those that neither unduly understate nor overstate the situation.

The Principle of Materiality

A strict adherence to accounting principles is not required for items of little significance. Consequently, the accountant must always weigh the costs of complying with an accounting principle against the extra accuracy gained thereby, and in those situations where the cost is relatively great and the lack of compliance will have no material effect on the financial statements, compliance is not necessary.

   There is no clear-cut distinction between material and immaterial items. Each situation must be individually judged, and an item is material or immaterial as it relates to other items. As a guide, the amount of an item is material if its omission, in the light of the surrounding circumstances, makes it probable that the judgment of a reasonable person would have been changed or influenced.

Implementation Constraints

Two of the principles listed, materiality and conservatism, are different from the other principles. In fact, some regard these as constraints which exert a modifying influence on financial accounting and reporting. The two other constraints are cost-benefit and industry peculiarities.

The cost of preparing and reporting accounting information should not exceed the value or usefulness of such information. Accounting focuses on usefulness and substance over form. Thus, pecularities and practices of an industry may warrant selective exceptions to accounting principles and practices. These exceptions are permitted for specific items where there is a clear precedent in the industry based on uniqueness and usefulness.

Departure from the strict application of accounting principles and concepts must be fully disclosed whether it be on the basis of (*a*) materiality, (*b*) conservatism, (*c*) cost-benefit, or (*d*) industry peculiarity.

Unit-of-Measure Assumption

The unit-of-measure assumption specifies that accounting should measure and report the results of the entity's economic activities in terms of a monetary unit such as the Canadian dollar. The assumption recognizes that the monetary unit of measure is an effective means of communicating financial information. Thus, money is the common denominator—the yardstick used in accounting. Using money allows dissimilar things to be aggregated.

Unfortunately, use of a monetary unit for measurement purposes poses a dilemma. Unlike a yardstick which is always the same length, the dollar changes in value. Therefore, during times of inflation or deflation, dollars of different size are entered in the accounts and intermingled as if they possessed equal purchasing power. Because of the practice of ignoring changes in the purchasing power of a dollar, accounting implicitly assumes that the magnitude of change in the value of the monetary unit is not material. This is incorrect. However, this problem and the efforts of the accounting profession to develop alternative valuation systems that report the effects of changes in prices is beyond the scope of this textbook.

Progress Check

G-4 **That a business should be consistent from year to year in its accounting practices most directly relates to the AcSB's concept that information reported in financial statements should be:** *(a)* relevant; *(b)* material; *(c)* reliable; *(d)* comparable.

G-5 **What are the characteristics of accounting information that make it reliable?**

G-6 **What is the meaning of the phrase *elements of financial statements*?**

SUMMARY OF APPENDIX G IN TERMS OF LEARNING OBJECTIVES

LO 1. Some accounting concepts provide general descriptions of current accounting practices. Other concepts prescribe the practices accountants should follow. These prescriptive concepts are most useful in developing accounting procedures for new types of transactions and making improvements in accounting practice.

LO 2. A bottom-up approach to developing concepts examines current practices and then develops concepts to provide general descriptions of those practices. In contrast, a top-down approach begins by stating accounting objectives and from there, develops concepts that prescribe the types of accounting practices accountants should follow.

LO 3. The AcSB's financial statement concepts identify the broad objectives of financial reporting and the qualitative characteristics accounting information should possess. The elements contained in financial reports are defined and the recognition and measurement criteria to be used are identified.

QUESTIONS

1. Why are concepts developed with a bottom-up approach less useful in leading to accounting improvements than those developed with a top-down approach?

2. What is the starting point in a top-down approach to developing accounting concepts?

3. What is the starting point in a bottom-up approach to developing accounting concepts?

4. What are the basic objectives of external financial reporting according to "Financial Statement Concepts"?

5. What is implied by saying that financial information should have the qualitative characteristic of relevance?

6. What are the characteristics of accounting information that make it reliable?

PROBLEM

Problem G–1
Analytical essay
(LO 1, 2, 3)

Write a brief essay that explains why a top-down approach to developing descriptive accounting concepts is not likely to be effective. Also explain why a bottom-up approach is more likely to be effective. Finally, explain why the conceptual framework reflects a top-down approach to developing concepts.

ANSWERS TO PROGRESS CHECKS

G–1 *c*

G–2 A top-down approach to developing accounting concepts begins by identifying appropriate objectives of accounting reports.

G–3 A bottom-up approach to developing accounting starts by examining existing accounting practices and determining the general features that characterize those procedures.

G–4 *d*

G–5 To have the qualitative characteristic of being reliable, accounting information should be free from bias and error, should be verifiable, should faithfully represent what is supposed to be described, and should be neutral.

G–6 The elements of financial statements are the objects and events that financial statements should describe, for example, assets, liabilities, revenues, and expenses.

Accounting for Corporate Income Taxes

After studying Appendix H, you should be able to:

1. **Explain why income taxes for accounting purposes may be different from income taxes for tax purposes.**

2. **Prepare an income tax schedule and journal entries for a company where timing differences exist between accounting and taxable income.**

Financial statements for a business should be prepared in accordance with generally accepted accounting principles. Income tax returns, on the other hand, must be prepared in accordance with income tax laws. As a result, a corporation's *income before taxes* measured in accordance with generally accepted accounting principles is almost never the same as *taxable income* calculated on income tax returns.

You have already learned how to determine net income under GAAP for a profit-oriented entity. However, the determination of taxable income for a corporation, while starting with the accounting net income, is done using the Canadian Income Tax Act. Almost always, this results in taxable income being different from the GAAP accounting income.

A major difference between accounting income and taxable income results from what are known as timing differences. These arise because some items are included as revenue or expense in one period under GAAP, whereas they are included in a different period under the income tax rules. For example:

1. The application of accounting principles for installment sales requires that gross profit on these sales is recognized in accounting income before it is recognized in taxable income under the income tax rules.

2. Accounting principles require an estimate of future costs, such as costs of making good on guarantees; they also require a deduction of such costs from revenue in the year the guaranteed goods are sold. However, tax rules do not permit the deduction of such costs until they are actually incurred.

3. Reported net income also differs from taxable income because the taxpayer uses a method or procedure believed to fairly reflect periodic net income for accounting purposes, but is required to use a different method of procedure for tax purposes. For example, the last-in, first-out inventory method of cost allocation may be used for accounting purposes, but is not permitted for tax purposes. Likewise, many companies use straight-line amortization of capital assets for accounting purposes but are required to use a different procedure, called *capital cost allowances,* for tax purposes.

LEARNING OBJECTIVES

ACCOUNTING AND TAXABLE INCOME

LO 1
Explain why income taxes for accounting purposes may be different from income taxes for tax purposes.

CAPITAL COST ALLOWANCES

Depreciation (amortization) accounting has been greatly influenced by income tax laws. The 1948 Income Tax Act replaced the complex body of rules that had developed for the purpose of limiting the amount of amortization allowed for tax purposes. The act defined and set a limit on amounts which could be deducted, for tax purposes, in respect to the cost of amortizable assets. These amounts are known as *capital cost allowances* (CCA).

The capital cost allowances are identical in nature and purpose with the accountants' concept of amortization and are based on the declining-balance method, discussed in Chapter 11. For tax purposes, the taxpayer may claim the maximum allowed or any part thereof in any year regardless of the amortization method and the amounts used in the accounting records.

Although capital cost allowances are based on the declining-balance method, certain procedures have been set out by the Regulations of the Act. The more important of these are as follows:

1. All amortizable assets are grouped into a comparatively small number of classes and a maximum rate allowed is prescribed for each group. The assets most commonly in use are set out below according to the class to which they belong, with the maximum rate of allowance for each such class (as at the time of writing).

   Class 1 (4%): Buildings or other structures.
   Class 7 (15%): Ships, scows, canoes, and rowboats.
   Class 8 (20%): Machinery, equipment, and furniture.
   Class 10 (30%): Automobiles, trucks, tractors, and computer hardware.

2. The assets of a designated class are considered to form a separate pool of costs. The costs of asset additions are added to their respective pools of unamortized capital cost. When assets are disposed of, the proceeds (up to the original cost) received from disposal are deducted from the proper pool. The balance of each pool of costs is also diminished by the accumulated capital cost allowance claimed. A capital cost allowance is claimed on the balance, referred to as the *unamortized capital cost* (UCC), in the pool at the end of the fiscal year. However, when there are net additions to the pool, only one half of the amount added is used in the calculation of CCA in the year of the net additions. The effect is that the assets are assumed to have been acquired halfway through the fiscal year.

3. "Losses" and "gains" on disposal of individual assets disappear into the pool of unamortized capital costs except when an asset is sold for more than its capital cost. In this case, proceeds of disposal in excess of the capital cost of the asset are normally treated as a capital gain. Where the proceeds of disposal (excluding the capital gain, if any) exceed the unamortized capital cost of the class immediately before the sale, the amount of the excess is treated as a "recapture" of capital cost allowances previously taken. Such a recapture is considered as ordinary income. When all of the assets in a class are disposed of and the proceeds are less than the unamortized capital cost of the class immediately before the sale, the proceeds less the unamortized capital cost may be deducted in determining the year's taxable income.

Companies must, with few exceptions, use capital cost allowances for tax purposes, but commonly use straight-line amortization in their accounting records. A problem arising from this practice is discussed in the next section.

TAXES AND THE DISTORTION OF NET INCOME

LO 2

Prepare an income tax schedule and journal entries when timing differences exist.

When one accounting procedure is required for tax purposes and a different procedure is used in the accounting records, a problem arises as to how much income tax expense should be deducted each year on the income statement. If the tax actually incurred in such situations is deducted, reported net income often varies from year to year due to the postponement and later payment of taxes. Consequently, in such cases, since shareholders may be misled by these variations, many accountants are of the opinion that income taxes should be allocated in such a way that any distortion resulting from postponing taxes is removed from the income statement.

To appreciate the problem involved here, assume that a corporation has installed a $100,000 machine, the product of which will produce a half-million dollars of revenue in each of the succeeding four years and $80,000 of income before amortization and taxes. Assume further that the company must pay income taxes at a 40% rate (round number assumed for easy calculation) and that it plans to use straight-line amortization in its records but the capital cost allowance for tax purposes. If the machine has a four-year life and a $10,000 salvage value and if the maximum permitted capital cost allowance rate on this particular machine is 50%, annual amortization calculated by each method will be as follows:

Year	Straight-Line	Capital Cost Allowance
1996	$22,500	$25,000
1997	22,500	37,500
1998	22,500	18,750
1999	22,500	8,750*
Totals	$90,000	$90,000

*Use $8,750 in order to match salvage value.
CCA allowed is $9,375.

In the year of acquisition, only one-half of the CCA otherwise allowed may be claimed. In subsequent years, CCA may be claimed up to the maximum amounts allowed.

Since the company uses capital cost allowance for tax purposes, it will be liable for $22,000 of income tax on the first year's income, $17,000 on the second, $24,500 on the third, and $28,500 on the fourth. The calculation of these taxes is shown in Illustration H–1.

Furthermore, if the company were to deduct its actual tax payable each year in arriving at income to be reported to its shareholders, it would report the amounts shown in Illustration H–2.

Observe in Illustrations H–1 and H–2 that total amortization, $90,000, is the same whether calculated by the straight-line or the declining-balance method. Also

Illustration H-1
Calculation of Income Taxes

Annual Income Taxes	1996	1997	1998	1999	Total
Income before amortization and income taxes	$80,000	$80,000	$80,000	$80,000	$320,000
Amortization for tax purposes (declining-balance)/CCA	25,000	37,500	18,750	8,750	90,000
Taxable income	$55,000	$42,500	$61,250	$71,250	$230,000
Annual income taxes (40% of taxable income).	$22,000	$17,000	$24,500	$28,500	$ 92,000

Illustration H-2 Calculation of Remaining Income

Income after Deducting Actual Tax Liabilities	1996	1997	1998	1999	Total
Income before amortization and income taxes.	$80,000	$80,000	$80,000	$80,000	$320,000
Amortization per books (straight-line) . . .	22,500	22,500	22,500	22,500	90,000
Income before taxes	57,500	57,500	57,500	57,500	230,000
Income taxes (actual liability of each year)	22,000	17,000	24,500	28,500	92,000
Remaining income	$35,500	$40,500	$33,000	$29,000	$138,000

note that the total tax paid over the four years, $92,000, is the same in each case. Then note the distortion of the final income figures in Illustration H–2 due to the postponement of taxes.

If this company should report successive annual income figures of $35,500, $40,500, $33,000, and then $29,000, some of its shareholders might be misled as to the company's earnings trend. Consequently, in cases such as this, many accountants think income taxes should be allocated so that the distortion caused by the postponement of taxes is removed from the income statement. These accountants advocate that

> when one accounting procedure is used in the accounting records and a different procedure is used for tax purposes, the tax expense deducted on the income statement should not be the actual tax liability but the amount that would be payable if the procedure used in the records were also used in calculating the tax.

If the foregoing is applied in this case, the corporation will report to its shareholders in each of the four years the amounts of income shown in Illustration H–3.

In examining Illustration H–2, recall that the company's taxes payable are actually $22,000 in the first year, $17,000 in the second, $24,500 in the third, and $28,500 in the fourth, a total of $92,000. Then observe that when this $92,000 liability is allocated evenly over the four years, the distortion of the annual net incomes due to the postponement of taxes is removed from the published income statements.

Illustration H–3 Tax Expense Based on Accounting Income

Net Income That Should Be Reported to Shareholders	1996	1997	1998	1999	Total
Income before amortization and income taxes.	$80,000	$80,000	$80,000	$80,000	$320,000
Amortization per books (straight-line) . . .	22,500	22,500	22,500	22,500	90,000
Income before taxes	57,500	57,500	57,500	57,500	230,000
Income taxes (amounts based on straight-line amortization).	23,000	23,000	23,000	23,000	92,000
Net income.	$34,500	$34,500	$34,500	$34,500	$138,000

When income taxes are allocated as in Illustration H–3, the tax payable for each year and the deferred income tax are recorded with an adjusting entry. The adjusting entries for the four years of Illustration H–2 and the entries in General Journal form for the payment of the taxes (without explanations) are as follows:

ENTRIES FOR THE ALLOCATION OF TAXES

1996	Income Tax Expense	23,000	
	Income Taxes Payable		22,000
	Deferred Income Tax		1,000
	Income Taxes Payable	22,000	
	Cash		22,000
1997	Income Tax Expense	23,000	
	Income Taxes Payable		17,000
	Deferred Income Tax		6,000
	Income Taxes Payable	17,000	
	Cash		17,000
1998	Income Tax Expense	23,000	
	Deferred Income Tax	1,500	
	Income Taxes Payable		24,500
	Income Taxes Payable	24,500	
	Cash		24,500
1999	Income Tax Expense	23,000	
	Deferred Income Tax	5,500	
	Income Taxes Payable		28,500
	Income Taxes Payable	28,500	
	Cash		28,500

Note: To simplify the illustration, it is assumed that the entire year's tax liability is paid at one time. However, corporations are usually required to pay estimated taxes on a monthly basis.

In the entries the $23,000 debited to Income Tax Expense each year is the amount that is deducted on the income statement in reporting annual net income. Also, the amount credited to Income Taxes Payable each year is the actual tax liability of that year.

Observe in the entries that since the actual tax payable in each of the first two years is less than the amount debited to Income Tax Expense, the difference is credited to *Deferred Income Tax*. Then note that in the last two years, because the actual liability each year is greater than the debit to Income Tax Expense, the difference is debited to Deferred Income Tax. Now observe in the following illustration of the company's Deferred Income Tax account that the debits and credits exactly balance each other out over the four-year period:

Deferred Income Tax

Year	Explanation	Debit	Credit	Balance
1996			1,000	1,000
1997			6,000	7,000
1998		1,500		5,500
1999		5,500		–0–

In passing, it should be observed that many accountants believe the interests of government, business, and the public would be better served if there were more uniformity between taxable income and reported net income. However, since the federal income tax is designed to serve other purposes in addition to raising revenue, it is apt to be some time before this is achieved.

Before concluding this appendix on income taxes, we should mention some additional features of the rules that govern accounting for income taxes.

1. In the example above, we assumed an income tax rate of 40% in each year. However, if the income tax rate changes, we use the rate in effect for that year. When the timing difference reverses, the average rate over the accumulation period should be used to avoid throwing the deferred tax amount into a debit balance (this point is covered more thoroughly in later courses).

2. In the example, 1996 income before taxes was *more than* taxable income because of a timing difference that was expected to reverse in 1998 or 1999. As a result, we recognized a deferred tax balance on the December 31, 1996, balance sheet. In other situations, just the opposite kind of timing difference may occur. In other words, a timing difference that will reverse in the future may cause income before taxes to be *less than* taxable income. These latter situations may, under certain conditions, result in the recognition of a deferred tax debit.

3. The Deferred Income Tax account balance may be reported as a long-term liability or as a current liability, depending on how far in the future the amount will reverse.

4. Federal tax laws generally require corporations to estimate their current year's tax liability and make advance payments of the estimated amount before the final tax return is filed. As a result, the end-of-year entries to record income taxes, such as those shown above, often have to be altered to take

into consideration any previously recorded prepayments.

5. The income tax rate varies depending on the type of organization, small or large, and manufacturing or nonmanufacturing.

LO 1 Explain why income taxes for accounting purposes may be different from income taxes for tax purposes. Accounting income and taxable income will differ when revenues and/or expenses may be included in one period for accounting purposes and in a different period for tax purposes.

LO 2 Prepare an income tax schedule and journal entries for a company where timing differences exist between accounting and taxable income. Reconcile accounting and taxable income by adding or subtracting the items which constitute timing differences. Income tax expense is based on accounting income, income tax payable on taxable income, and the debit or credit to deferred taxes on the net timing differences.

SUMMARY OF APPENDIX H IN TERMS OF LEARNING OBJECTIVES

EXERCISES

Indicate which of the following items might cause timing differences for a corporation:

a. Sales on account.
b. Capital cost allowances.
c. Wages paid to employees.
d. Property taxes.
e. Installment sales.
f. Cost of goods sold.
g. Warranty expenses.
h. Rents received in advance.
i. Cash sales.

Exercise H–1
Timing differences
(LO 1)

a. Explain why accounting income is usually different from taxable income.
b. What reasons can you give for the two sets of rules?

Exercise H–2
Taxable vs. accounting income
(LO 1)

Vacon Inc. began operations on January 1, 1996. During 1996, Vacon's operations resulted in a current tax payable of $350,000. In addition, Vacon sold land for $210,000 that had cost $70,000. The sale qualified as an installment sale for tax purposes, so the gain was subject to tax as cash was received. The purchaser agreed to pay for the land on June 1, 1997. Present the December 31, 1996, entry to record Vacon Inc.'s income taxes. Assume a tax rate of 45% and that the profit on the land is fully taxable.

Exercise H–3
Recording corporate income tax expense
(LO 2)

Buster Corporation would have had identical accounting and taxable income for the three years 1996–1998 were it not for the fact that for tax purposes an operational asset that cost $24,000 was amortized $3/6$, $2/6$, $1/6$ (assumed for problem purposes to be acceptable), whereas for accounting purposes, the straight-line method was used. The asset has a three-year op-

Exercise H–4
Recording corporate income tax expense
(LO 2)

erational life and no residual value. Income before amortization and income taxes for the years concerned follow:

	1996	1997	1998
Pretax accounting income (before amortization)	$40,000	$45,000	$50,000

Assume an income tax rate of 40% for each year.

Required

1. Calculate the accounting and taxable income for each year.
2. Prepare journal entries to record the income tax expense for each year.

Exercise H–5
Analyze timing differences; entries
(LO 2)

Castor Corporation reports the following information for the year ended December 31, 1996:

Revenue	$525,000
Expenses	390,000
Net income before tax	$135,000

Additional information:

a.   Revenues (above) do not include $30,000 of rent which is taxable in 1996 but was earned at the end of 1996.

b.   Capital cost allowances for 1996 are $32,000 greater than the amortization expense included above.

c.   Expenses (above) include $12,000 of estimated warranty expenses which are not deductible for tax purposes in 1996.

d.   Assume an income tax rate of 40%.

Prepare a journal entry to record income taxes for Castor Corporation on December 31, 1996.

Exercise H–6
Timing differences; entries
(LO 2)

Income tax returns on Vastly Corporation reflected the following:

	Year Ended Dec. 31		
	1996	1997	1998
Royalty income	$180,000		
Investment income	30,000	$20,000	$40,000
Rent income	10,000	10,000	10,000
	$220,000	$30,000	$50,000
Deductible expenses	30,000	20,000	20,000
Taxable income	$190,000	$10,000	$30,000

Assume the average income tax rate for each year was 40%.

The only differences between taxable income on the tax returns and the pretax accounting income relate to royalty income. For accounting purposes, royalty income was recognized ratably (equally) over the three-year period.

Required

Give journal entries such as would appear at the end of each year to reflect income tax and allocation.
(CGA adapted)

Geac

ANNUAL REPORT
1994

FINANCIAL HIGHLIGHTS

5 YEAR FINANCIAL INFORMATION

(millions of dollars, except per share amounts)	1994	1993	Years Ended April 30 1992	1991	1990
Revenues	152.2	105.1	85.3	82.2	73.5
Income from operations before unusual items & taxes	26.9	17.9	12.7	5.0	5.2
Unusual items	-	(10.7)	-	(9.8)	4.7
Income (loss) before income taxes	26.9	7.2	12.7	(4.8)	9.9
Net income (loss)	22.9	4.5	11.1	(5.5)	8.2
Cash	53.3	40.9	32.0	24.4	13.5
Earnings (loss) per share	$ 0.81	$ 0.17	$ 0.50	$ (0.25)	$ 0.38

SALES BY REGION
for the years ended April 30, 1994 (1993)

Canada 13.7% (18.0%)

USA 44.2% (38.4%)

Europe 24.9% (33.8%)

Australasia 17.2% (9.8%)

SALES BY DIVISION
for the years ended April 30, 1994 (1993)

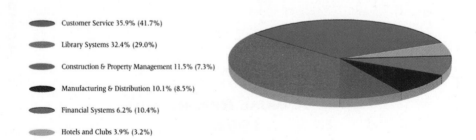

Customer Service 35.9% (41.7%)

Library Systems 32.4% (29.0%)

Construction & Property Management 11.5% (7.3%)

Manufacturing & Distribution 10.1% (8.5%)

Financial Systems 6.2% (10.4%)

Hotels and Clubs 3.9% (3.2%)

FINANCIAL REVIEW

MANAGEMENT DISCUSSION AND ANALYSIS OF FINANCIAL CONDITION AND RESULTS OF OPERATIONS

Acquisitions

During fiscal 1994, Geac acquired a number of new businesses:

Assets of New Tech Hospitality Systems Pty Ltd., an Australian developer and marketer of hotel and resort software, effective June 30, 1993. Geac initially entered the hotel software market as part of the Jonas and Erickson acquisition in fiscal 1991.

Claymore Systems Group, a Canadian developer of asset valuation software for the real estate industry, effective June 30, 1993. This complements Geac's property management software.

ECI Computer, Inc., a USA based developer of hotel management software with a worldwide customer base, effective August 4, 1993. ECI's advanced Informix based product is targeted at major chains and larger full service hotels.

Datamark International Limited, a New Zealand developer and marketer of manufacturing and distribution software, its Australian subsidiary, Dmark International Pty Limited, both effective September 30, 1993, and the assets of Convergent Solutions Pty Ltd., Datamark's main Australian distributor, effective November 1, 1993. Together with previous strategic acquisitions, these make Geac the largest provider of hardware, software, consulting and support solutions to manufacturers in the fast growing Australasian region.

Assets of Hotel Systems Pty Limited in Australia and Hotel Computer Systems Limited in New Zealand, effective January 31, 1994. Together with New Tech and the Australasian customers of ECI, this makes Geac the largest supplier of hotel and resort management solutions in the region.

These eight acquisitions were made for a total cash consideration of $5.7 million. After their respective dates of acquisition, they contributed about $11 million to fiscal 1994 sales and achieved approximately breakeven operating income. Because of the restructuring and integration of the acquired businesses with Geac's existing business, sales and profitability of the acquired businesses prior to their respective dates of acquisition are not meaningful.

As a result of these acquisitions, Geac included on its balance sheet as other assets $2.2 million of acquired software development and $5.6 million of goodwill. The nature of the assets acquired requires that they be capitalized in accordance with generally accepted accounting principles in Canada.

Results of Operations

Geac reported a net income of $22.9 million for fiscal 1994 compared to a net income of $4.5 million in fiscal 1993. During fiscal 1993, the Company expensed as an unusual item $10.7 million of purchased software research. Income from operations before the unusual item and income taxes increased to $26.9 million (17.9% of sales) from $17.9 million (17.4% of sales) in 1993.

Sales revenue was $150.3 million in fiscal 1994 compared to $102.7 million in fiscal 1993. Service revenue, primarily contracted support of customers' hardware and licensed software, increased to $73.0 million compared to $55.1 million in the prior year. Service revenue represented 49% of sales compared to 54% in fiscal 1993, as new product sales increased more rapidly in a stronger economy. Computer hardware represents about 20% of sales. Higher margin software licences and consulting sold to new and existing customers account for over 30% of sales.

Interest income decreased to $1.8 million from $2.4 million in the prior year due to generally declining average interest rates worldwide.

 9

Provision for income taxes was $4.0 million compared to $2.8 million in fiscal 1993. Geac operates through wholly owned subsidiaries in several countries. The tax consequences of these operations vary significantly based on the results of each legal entity and the tax laws of each country. Future effective tax rates on operating income are likely to be substantially lower than the combined basic Canadian federal and provincial rate of 44% because most countries in which Geac operates have lower effective tax rates and the subsidiaries have a total of $26 million of tax losses and $4 million of favourable timing differences to apply against future income. The utilization of tax losses and timing differences depends on the financial results of individual subsidiaries and, because individual subsidiary future earnings are not certain, some tax losses may expire before they can be used.

Liquidity and Capital Resources

Cash balances of $53.3 million at April 30, 1994 increased by $12.4 million during the year. The Company has no bank borrowings and no long-term debt. Current cash balances and future operating cash flows are more than sufficient to cover foreseeable cash requirements. Commitments at April 30, 1994 consist primarily of lease obligations for office space. No significant fixed asset expenditures are anticipated. In the 1995 fiscal year, cash potentially may be used for the repurchase of the Company's outstanding common shares under a Normal Course Issuer Bid and for the acquisition of new businesses.

Cash is invested in short-term, low risk financial instruments, such as treasury bills and bankers' acceptances. Cash is held in various countries and currencies according to anticipated future needs. Foreign exchange gains included in operations were $0.8 million in fiscal 1994 and $0.1 million in fiscal 1993. Substantially all cash is freely remittable to Canada.

Outlook

Geac's historical and ongoing emphasis is to provide a total solution consisting of hardware, software, service and support to customers in selected vertical markets. Vertical markets are specific groups of current and potential customers where the Company provides complete integrated application software solutions to meet critical system requirements. Vertical markets in which Geac participates include academic and public libraries, leasing and asset finance, consumer banking institutions including credit unions, savings banks and savings and loans, manufacturing and distribution, construction, property management, hotels and clubs.

Geac generally enjoys long-term relationships with its customers, providing hardware and software service, support, maintenance and upgrades as well as consulting in the years following the initial sale. On average, subsequent revenues exceed the initial hardware and software sale. As a result, more than 50% of Geac's annual revenue has been relatively stable. Geac's well established worldwide service network and strong financial position give new and existing customers confidence that Geac support will continue over the life of their systems.

Since 1990, Geac has offered its products on a broad range of industry standard hardware platforms which support a Unix-based Open Systems environment. Geac is now a large worldwide vendor of Unix vertical market application software. Customers benefit from Open Systems solutions because the market for RISC/Unix hardware and peripherals is highly competitive and prices continue to decline rapidly as technology advances. As a result, Geac's revenue from selling equivalent computer processing power has continued to decline. Since the highly competitive hardware market limits hardware revenue and margins, there is a trend towards software and services forming an increasing portion of Geac's sales mix. The primary market trend affecting the Company is the continuing decline in hardware prices. Management continues to focus on operating efficiencies by controlling direct operating expenses and overheads.

MANAGEMENT'S REPORT

The consolidated financial statements and other financial information in this annual report were prepared by management of Geac Computer Corporation Limited, reviewed by the Audit Committee and approved by the Board of Directors.

Management is responsible for the consolidated financial statements and believes that they fairly present the Company's financial condition and results of operations in conformity with generally accepted accounting principles. Management has included in the Company's consolidated financial statements amounts based on estimates and judgements that it believes are reasonable under the circumstances.

To discharge its responsibilities for financial reporting and safeguarding of assets, management believes that it has established appropriate systems of internal accounting control which provide reasonable assurance that the financial records are reliable and form a proper basis for the timely and accurate preparation of financial statements. Consistent with the concept of reasonable assurance, the Company recognizes that the relative cost of maintaining these controls should not exceed their expected benefits. Management further assures the quality of the financial records through careful selection and training of personnel, and through the adoption and communication of financial and other relevant policies.

The shareholders have appointed Deloitte & Touche to audit the consolidated financial statements. Their report outlines the scope of their examination and their opinion.

Stephen J. Sadler
President and
Chief Executive Officer

David G.B. Scott
Vice President,
Finance and Administration

AUDITORS' REPORT

To the Shareholders of Geac Computer Corporation Limited:

We have audited the consolidated balance sheets of Geac Computer Corporation Limited as at April 30, 1994 and 1993 and the consolidated statements of operations, retained earnings and changes in financial position for the years then ended. These financial statements are the responsibility of the Company's management. Our responsibility is to express an opinion on these financial statements based on our audits.

We conducted our audits in accordance with generally accepted auditing standards. Those standards require that we plan and perform an audit to obtain reasonable assurance whether the financial statements are free of material misstatement. An audit includes examining, on a test basis, evidence supporting the amounts and disclosures in the financial statements. An audit also includes assessing the accounting principles used and significant estimates made by management, as well as evaluating the overall financial statement presentation.

In our opinion, these consolidated financial statements present fairly, in all material respects, the financial position of the Company as at April 30, 1994 and 1993 and the results of its operations and the changes in its financial position for the years then ended in accordance with generally accepted accounting principles.

Chartered Accountants
Markham, Canada
June 17, 1994

CONSOLIDATED BALANCE SHEETS

		April 30
(thousands of dollars)	1994	1993
Assets		
Current assets:		
Cash and short-term investments	$ 53,327	$ 40,943
Accounts receivable	29,389	21,277
Unbilled receivables	7,437	7,591
Inventory (note 2)	16,269	16,166
Prepaid expenses	1,878	2,534
	108,300	88,511
Fixed assets (note 3)	16,083	15,196
Other assets (note 4)	24,645	14,165
	$ 149,028	$ 117,872
Liabilities		
Current liabilities:		
Accounts payable and accrued liabilities	$ 24,327	$ 21,830
Income taxes payable (note 9)	1,761	218
Deferred sales revenue	25,996	25,146
	52,084	47,194
Shareholders' Equity		
Share capital (note 5):		
Common shares	63,611	61,366
Convertible preference shares	-	269
Retained earnings	32,041	9,277
Cumulative foreign exchange translation adjustment (note 6)	1,292	(234)
	96,944	70,678
	$ 149,028	$ 117,872

Approved by the Board of Directors:

Donald C. Webster
Chairman of the Board

Stephen J. Sadler
President and Chief Executive Officer, Director

CONSOLIDATED STATEMENTS OF OPERATIONS

	Years ended April 30	
(thousands of dollars, except per share amounts)	**1994**	*1993*
Revenues:		
Sales (note 8)	**$ 150,335**	$ 102,718
Interest income	**1,821**	2,356
	152,156	105,074
Expenses:		
Costs, excluding amounts shown below	**113,137**	77,152
Research and development expenses	**8,469**	8,233
Research and development grants and investment tax credits (note 9)	**(2,093)**	(2,012)
Depreciation and amortization	**5,632**	3,695
Interest expense	**79**	129
	125,224	87,197
Income from operations before unusual item and income taxes	**26,932**	17,877
Unusual item:		
Purchased software research (note 11)	**-**	(10,674)
Income before income taxes	**26,932**	7,203
Provision for income taxes (note 9)	**4,000**	2,750
Net income for the year	**$ 22,932**	$ 4,453
Earnings per share:		
Basic	**$ 0.81**	$ 0.17
Fully diluted	**$ 0.80**	$ 0.17

CONSOLIDATED STATEMENTS OF
RETAINED EARNINGS

	Years ended April 30	
(thousands of dollars)	**1994**	*1993*
Retained earnings at the beginning of the year	**$ 9,277**	$ 4,824
Premium on redemption of Series 2 preference shares (note 5)	**(168)**	-
Net income for the year	**22,932**	4,453
Retained earnings at the end of the year	**$ 32,041**	$ 9,277

13

CONSOLIDATED STATEMENTS OF CHANGES IN FINANCIAL POSITION

	Years ended April 30	
(thousands of dollars)	1994	1993
Operating activities		
Net income for the year	$ 22,932	$ 4,453
Adjusted for amounts not affecting cash:		
Depreciation of fixed assets	5,352	3,662
Amortization of other assets	2,763	624
Purchased software research (note 11)	-	10,674
	31,047	19,413
Changes in non-cash working capital components	(5,605)	(1,064)
Cash provided by operating activities	25,442	18,349
Investing activities		
Additions to fixed assets, net	(5,435)	(3,341)
Additions to capitalized software development	(5,385)	(1,403)
Acquisitions less cash acquired (note 11)	(5,572)	(21,231)
Foreign exchange translation adjustment	1,526	(267)
Cash used in investing activities	(14,866)	(26,242)
Financing activities		
Issue of common shares	2,245	16,938
Issue of preference shares	-	93
Conversion of preference shares	(74)	(222)
Redemption of Series 2 preference shares	(363)	-
Cash provided by financing activities	1,808	16,809
Cash and short-term investments		
Net cash increase during the year	12,384	8,916
Cash position at the beginning of the year	40,943	32,027
Cash position at the end of the year	$ 53,327	$ 40,943

NOTES TO CONSOLIDATED FINANCIAL
STATEMENTS

1. ACCOUNTING POLICIES

Accounting principles
These consolidated financial statements are prepared in conformity with accounting principles generally accepted in Canada.

Basis of consolidation
These consolidated financial statements comprise the financial statements of Geac Computer Corporation Limited and its subsidiary companies.

Inventory
Finished goods inventory is stated at the lower of cost on a first-in first-out basis and net realizable value. Maintenance and service parts are recorded net of a provision for obsolescence which amortizes their cost over an estimated useful life of four to six years.

Fixed assets
Fixed assets are recorded at cost and are depreciated as follows:
- Computers, processing and office equipment - declining balance at rates ranging between 18.5% and 20%.
- Leasehold improvements - straight-line over the lease term.

Goodwill
Goodwill represents the excess of purchase consideration over fair market value of net identifiable assets acquired, and is amortized on a straight-line basis over forty years.

Revenue recognition
The Company's activities are the design, manufacture, sale, service and rental of computer systems and software. System sales revenues are recognized at the time of shipment or upon customer acceptance. The timing of revenue recognition often differs from contract payment schedules, resulting in revenues that have been earned but not billed. These amounts are included in unbilled receivables. Service and rental revenues are recognized rateably over applicable contractual periods or as services are performed. Amounts billed but not yet earned are recorded as deferred revenue.

Research and development costs
Research and development costs relate principally to computer software intended for licensing to end-user customers. All costs up to the date on which the software is considered technically and commercially viable, as well as software maintenance and documentation, are expensed as incurred, net of government grants and other amounts recoverable. Software development, after technical and commercial viability is established, is deferred and amortized on a straight-line basis over its expected useful life, not exceeding four years. The amortization is included in research and development expenses in the statement of operations.

Foreign exchange
All of the Company's foreign subsidiaries are considered self-sustaining. Assets and liabilities of these subsidiaries are translated into Canadian dollars at exchange rates in effect at the balance sheet dates. Income and expense items are translated at average exchange rates for the periods. Accumulated net translation adjustments are included as a separate component of shareholders' equity.

The monetary assets and liabilities of the Corporation which are denominated in foreign currencies are translated at the year-end exchange rates. Revenues and expenses are translated at rates of exchange prevailing on the transaction dates. All exchange gains or losses are recognized currently in earnings.

2. INVENTORY

(thousands of dollars)	April 30 1994	April 30 1993
Finished goods	$ 4,914	$ 4,960
Maintenance and service parts	11,355	11,206
	$ 16,269	$ 16,166

3. FIXED ASSETS

(thousands of dollars)

	Cost	Accumulated Depreciation	1994 Net	April 30 1993 Net
Computers and processing equipment	$ 39,413	$ 29,184	$ 10,229	$ 9,986
Office equipment	9,104	5,620	3,484	3,499
Leasehold improvements	4,596	2,226	2,370	1,711
	$ 53,113	$ 37,030	$ 16,083	$ 15,196

4. OTHER ASSETS

(thousands of dollars)

	1994	April 30 1993
Acquired capitalized software development (note 11)	$ 7,736	$ 5,510
Capitalized software development	6,788	1,403
Less: Accumulated amortization	(3,074)	(591)
Net capitalized software development	11,450	6,322
Goodwill (note 11)	13,508	7,876
Less: Accumulated amortization	(313)	(33)
Net goodwill	13,195	7,843
	$ 24,645	$ 14,165

5. SHARE CAPITAL

The Company is authorized to issue an unlimited number of common shares and preference shares, issuable in series, each without par value.

As final settlement under the Definitive Proposals accepted by the creditors in 1988, an additional 4,037 Series 2 preference shares were issued during the 1993 fiscal year. Between May 1 and June 15, 1993, 6,108 Series 2 preference shares were converted into 54,972 common shares. The remaining 12,097 Series 2 preference shares were redeemed for $362,910. The premium on this transaction of approximately $168,000 was charged to retained earnings in fiscal 1994.

On May 10, 1994, the Company filed notice of its intention to make a Normal Course Issuer Bid for its common shares through the facilities of The Toronto Stock Exchange. The Company may purchase up to a maximum of 1,436,996 common shares, being 5% of the 28,739,921 common shares outstanding at April 29, 1994. The price at which the Company may purchase such shares will be the market price at the time of any particular transaction. The bid commenced on May 13, 1994 and will terminate on May 12, 1995, unless the maximum number of common shares purchasable thereunder has been acquired before that time. There have been no repurchases as of June 17, 1994.

An analysis of the capital stock account is as follows:

	Number of shares 1994	1993	Thousands of dollars 1994	1993
Common Shares				
Balance at the beginning of the year	27,948,409	22,472,157	$ 61,366	$ 44,428
Issued for cash	741,831	5,311,741	2,171	16,716
Converted from Series 2 preference shares	54,972	164,511	74	222
Balance at the end of the year	28,745,212	27,948,409	$ 63,611	$ 61,366
Series 2 Convertible Preference Shares				
Balance at the beginning of the year	18,205	32,447	$ 269	$ 398
Converted to common shares	(6,108)	(18,279)	(74)	(222)
Issued under Definitive Proposals	-	4,037	-	93
Redeemed for cash	(12,097)	-	(195)	-
Balance at the end of the year	-	18,205	$ -	$ 269

Stock Ownership Plan

An Employee Stock Ownership Plan under which employees may make quarterly purchases of shares in the Company at a 10% discount from the prevailing market price has been in existence since 1984. During 1994, 20,981 shares were issued to employees under this plan (1993 - 25,741) and 120,000 shares were cancelled. The aggregate number of shares still available to be issued under this plan is 115,580 (1993 - 256,561).

Stock Options

Options have been granted to management personnel to purchase common shares at or above the prevailing market price at the time of the grant under the Employee Stock Option Plan. These options are vested or vest at various times over the next 3 years and expire 5 years after vesting.

An analysis of the stock options is as follows:

(thousands of shares)	1994	1993
Balance at the beginning of the year	1,334	1,821
Options granted	767	171
Options exercised at option prices from $1.10 to $9.25	(720)	(606)
Options cancelled or expired	(68)	(52)
Balance at the end of the year	1,313	1,334

The outstanding options as at April 30, 1994 were granted at prices from $1.10 to $14.50 (1993 - $1.10 to $11.75) per common share.

In addition, other options to senior management personnel to purchase 80,000 common shares at $1.60 per share were outstanding at the beginning of the year and remain outstanding at the end of the year.

6. CUMULATIVE FOREIGN EXCHANGE TRANSLATION ADJUSTMENT

(thousands of dollars)	April 30 1994	1993
Cumulative unrealized gain (loss) at the beginning of the year	$ (234)	$ 33
Unrealized gain (loss) for the year on translation of net assets	2,190	(495)
Realized (gain) loss on dividends and return of capital paid by foreign operations	(664)	228
	$ 1,292	$ (234)

7. COMMITMENTS AND CONTINGENCIES

The Company has operating leases on rental equipment for varying terms up to a maximum of four years and has entered into leases for rental of premises for varying terms up to a maximum of thirteen years. Aggregate lease payments in each of the five years ending April 30, 1999 and subsequent are as follows:

(thousands of dollars)	
1995	$ 4,965
1996	4,041
1997	3,359
1998	2,440
1999	1,797
2000 and subsequent	5,169
	$ 21,771

As at April 30, 1994, letters of credit are outstanding for approximately $378,000. The Company is potentially liable for approximately $16 million of performance bonds which are routinely issued on its behalf by insurance companies and other third parties in connection with outstanding contracts with various public sector customers. There has never been a claim under any of the Company's performance bonds and any estimated outstanding contract obligations are provided for in the accounts.

There are certain legal actions pending against the Company which management believes are without merit and will not result in any material liability. No benefit has been recorded for certain pending legal actions by the Company against others, the outcome of which cannot be reasonably determined.

8. SEGMENTED INFORMATION

The business of the Company is carried on in one industry segment: the design, manufacture, sale, service and rental of computer systems and software products.

Revenues are derived from system sales and from service and rental agreements, as follows:

(thousands of dollars)	Years ended April 30 1994	1993
System sales	$ 77,291	$ 47,657
Service and rental	73,044	55,061
Total sales revenues	$ 150,335	$ 102,718

The Company operates in four geographic segments as follows:

Year ended April 30, 1994

(thousands of dollars)	Canada	USA	Europe	Australasia	Eliminations	Total
Segment revenue:						
Sales revenues	$ 20,629	$ 66,451	$ 37,425	$ 25,830	$ -	$ 150,335
Transfers between segments	2,065	-	-	-	(2,065)	-
	$ 22,694	$ 66,451	$ 37,425	$ 25,830	$ (2,065)	$ 150,335
Segment operating income	$ 8,483	$ 12,121	$ 6,783	$ 1,982	$ -	$ 29,369
Expenses (income):						
Corporate expenses						4,179
Interest, net						(1,742)
Provision for income taxes						4,000
Net income for the year						$ 22,932
Total identifiable assets	$ 44,056	$ 52,605	$ 36,388	$ 15,979	$ -	$ 149,028

Year ended April 30, 1993

(thousands of dollars)	Canada	USA	Europe	Australasia	Eliminations	Total
Segment revenue:						
Sales revenues	$ 18,485	$ 39,409	$ 34,678	$ 10,146	$ -	$ 102,718
Transfers between segments	4,313	15	-	100	(4,428)	-
	$ 22,798	$ 39,424	$ 34,678	$ 10,246	$ (4,428)	$ 102,718
Segment operating income (loss)	$ 9,519	$ 4,546	$ 5,985	$ (785)	$ -	$ 19,265
Expenses (income):						
Corporate expenses						3,615
Interest, net						(2,227)
Unusual item						10,674
Provision for income taxes						2,750
Net income for the year						$ 4,453
Total identifiable assets	$ 32,721	$ 37,442	$ 39,889	$ 7,820	$ -	$ 117,872

9. INCOME TAXES

Substantially all of the Company's activities are carried out through operating subsidiaries in a number of countries. The income tax effect of operations depends on the tax legislation in each country and the operating results of each subsidiary and the parent Company.

In fiscal 1994, the Company recognized the benefit of $1,800,000 (1993 - $1,800,000) of previously unrealized investment tax credits as their realization became reasonably assured due to the earnings history of the relevant subsidiary. The benefit is included in the statement of operations as a reduction of expense under the caption "Research and development grants and investment tax credits". The Company has remaining unrealized investment tax credits of approximately $4,000,000 (1993 - $5,000,000) which are available to reduce income taxes payable in future years and expire as shown in the table below. The benefit of unrealized investment tax credits will be included in the statement of operations as a reduction in research and development expense when realization is reasonably assured.

The Company has non-capital losses of approximately $26,000,000 (1993 - $30,000,000) which are available for carryforward against taxable income in future years, which expire as shown in the table below and will be recognized when realized by a reduction in the provision for income taxes.

The Company has net favourable timing differences of approximately $4,000,000 (1993 - $4,000,000) which may be applied against taxable income of future years. The timing differences relate primarily to contract revenues, accrued expenses, deferred revenue and depreciation and amortization of assets which are recognized in the financial statements in periods other than those in which they are included in taxable income in accordance with the tax laws of the countries in which the Company and its subsidiaries operate. Timing differences do not expire. When realized, they will be recognized by a reduction in the provision for income taxes.

(thousands of dollars)	Non-capital losses	Investment tax credits
1995	$ -	$ 300
1996	800	1,000
1997	3,800	600
1998	1,000	600
1999 - 2009	5,000	1,000
Losses without expiry date	15,400	500
	$ 26,000	$ 4,000

The provision for income taxes reflects an effective tax rate which differs from the corporate tax rate for the following reasons:

		Years ended April 30	
(thousands of dollars)		1994	1993
Combined basic Canadian federal and provincial income tax rate		44%	44%
Provision for income taxes based on above rate	$	11,850	$ 3,170
Increase (decrease) resulting from:			
Permanent differences -			
Purchased software research expensed		-	4,600
Other		1,000	200
Lower rate on earnings of foreign subsidiaries		(80)	(140)
Losses of subsidiaries not tax effected		700	500
Benefit of previously unrecognized losses and timing differences realized in the year		(9,000)	(4,900)
Other		(470)	(680)
Provision for income taxes per statement of operations	$	4,000	$ 2,750

10. RELATED PARTY TRANSACTIONS

During the year the Company paid $225,000 (1993 - $310,000) for management services including investigation of potential acquisitions to Helix Investments (Canada) Inc. (formerly Helix Investments Limited), a significant shareholder.

11. ACQUISITIONS

Year ended April 30, 1994

During the year ended April 30, 1994, the Company acquired for cash the businesses shown in the table below. New Tech, Convergent, and Hotel Systems were asset purchases. In each of the other acquisitions, the Company acquired all of the issued and outstanding shares of the companies. Acquisitions are accounted for by the purchase method with the results of operations of each business included in the financial statements from the respective dates of acquisition.

The total purchase price was $5,673,000. The acquired businesses included, at fair value, $101,000 of cash, $2,798,000 of other current assets, $2,226,000 of software development which met the Company's criteria for capitalization (note 4), $804,000 of fixed assets, and $5,888,000 of current liabilities.

The difference between the total purchase price and the net fair value of all identifiable assets and liabilities acquired was $5,632,000 and is accounted for as goodwill.

Acquisition	Effective Date
Assets of New Tech Hospitality Systems Pty Ltd.	June 30, 1993
957024 Ontario Inc. (operating as Claymore Systems Group)	June 30, 1993
ECI Computer, Inc.	August 4, 1993
Datamark International Limited	September 30, 1993
Dmark International Pty Limited	September 30, 1993
Assets of Convergent Solutions Pty Ltd.	November 1, 1993
Assets of Hotel Systems Pty Limited	January 31, 1994
Assets of Hotel Computer Systems Limited	January 31, 1994

Year ended April 30, 1993

During the year ended April 30, 1993, the Company acquired for cash the businesses shown in the table below. Albion and McDonnell Douglas Information Systems were asset purchases. In each of the other acquisitions, the Company acquired all of the issued and outstanding shares of the companies. Acquisitions are accounted for by the purchase method with the results of operations of each business included in the financial statements from the respective dates of acquisition.

The total purchase price was $22,421,000. The acquired businesses included, at fair value, $1,190,000 of cash, $25,305,000 of other current assets, $5,510,000 of software development which met the Company's criteria for capitalization (note 4), $5,419,000 of fixed assets and $33,553,000 of current liabilities.

In the CLSI acquisition, $10,674,000 of the purchase price was allocated to purchased software research related to new products which had not achieved technical and commercial viability.

The difference between the total purchase price and the net fair value of all identifiable assets and liabilities acquired, including the purchased software research, was $7,876,000 and is accounted for as goodwill.

Acquisition	Effective Date
Assets of Albion Computing Australia Pty Limited	June 1, 1992
Assets of McDonnell Douglas Information Systems Canada, Inc.	November 30, 1992
CLSI, Inc. and its UK, France, Netherlands and Canadian affiliates	November 30, 1992
Mentat Computer Systems Pty Ltd.	February 26, 1993
Concord Management Systems, Inc.	February 28, 1993
Computer Library Services International Pty Limited and its subsidiary Aldis Pty Limited	March 31, 1993
NBI Canada, Inc., subsequently renamed Geac (Canada) Services Limited	April 30, 1993
MAI United Kingdom Limited	April 30, 1993
Tekserv Computer Services Limited	April 30, 1993

12. COMPARATIVE FIGURES

Certain of the prior year's figures have been reclassified to conform with the current year's presentation.

Comprehensive List of Accounts Used in Exercises and Problems

Current Assets

101	Cash
102	Petty cash
103	Cash equivalents
104	Temporary investments
105	Allowance to reduce temporary investments to market
106	Accounts receivable
107	Allowance for doubtful accounts
108	Legal fees receivable
109	Interest receivable
110	Rent receivable
111	Notes receivable
115	Subscriptions receivable, common shares
116	Subscriptions receivable, preferred shares
119	Merchandise inventory
120	_____ inventory
121	_____ inventory
124	Office supplies
125	Store supplies
126	_____ supplies
128	Prepaid insurance
129	Prepaid interest
130	Prepaid property taxes
131	Prepaid rent
132	Raw materials inventory
133	Goods in process inventory, _____
134	Goods in process inventory, _____
135	Finished goods inventory

Long-Term Investments

141	Investment in _____ shares
142	Investment in _____ bonds
144	Investment in _____
145	Bond sinking fund

Capital Assets

151	Automobiles
152	Accumulated amortization, automobiles
153	Trucks
154	Accumulated amortization, trucks
155	Boats
156	Accumulated amortization, boats
157	Professional library
158	Accumulated amortization, professional library
159	Law library
160	Accumulated amortization, law library
163	Office equipment
164	Accumulated amortization, office equipment
165	Store equipment
166	Accumulated amortization, store equipment
167	_____ equipment
168	Accumulated amortization, _____ equipment
169	Machinery
170	Accumulated amortization, machinery
173	Building _____
174	Accumulated amortization, building _____
175	Building _____
176	Accumulated amortization, building _____
179	Land improvements _____
180	Accumulated amortization, land improvements _____
181	Land improvements _____
182	Accumulated amortization, land improvements _____
183	Land

Natural Resources

185   Mineral deposit
186   Accumulated depletion, mineral deposit

Intangible Assets

191   Patents
192   Leasehold
193   Franchise
194   Copyrights
195   Leasehold improvements
196   Organization costs
197   Deferred income tax debits

Current Liabilities

201   Accounts payable
202   Insurance payable
203   Interest payable
204   Legal fees payable
205   Short-term notes payable
206   Discount on short-term notes payable
207   Office salaries payable
208   Rent payable
209   Salaries payable
210   Wages payable
211   Accrued payroll payable
214   Estimated warranty liability
215   Income taxes payable
216   Common dividend payable
217   Preferred dividend payable
218   UI payable
219   CPP payable
221   Employees' medical insurance payable
222   Employees' retirement program payable
223   Employees' union dues payable
224   PST payable
225   GST payable
226   Estimated vacation pay liability

Unearned Revenues

230   Unearned consulting fees
231   Unearned legal fees
232   Unearned property management fees
233   Unearned _____ fees
234   Unearned _____
235   Unearned janitorial revenue
236   Unearned _____ revenue
238   Unearned rent _____

Long-Term Liabilities

251   Long-term notes payable
252   Discount on notes payable
253   Long-term lease liability
254   Discount on lease liability
255   Bonds payable
256   Discount on bonds payable
257   Premium on bonds payable
258   Deferred income tax credit

Owners' Equity

301   _____, capital
302   _____, withdrawals
303   _____, capital
304   _____, withdrawals
305   _____, capital
306   _____, withdrawals

Corporate Contributed Capital

307   Common shares
309   Common shares subscribed
310   Common stock dividend distributable
313   Contributed capital from the retirement of common shares
315   Preferred shares
317   Preferred shares subscribed

Retained Earnings

318   Retained earnings
319   Cash dividends declared
320   Stock dividends declared

Revenues

401   _____ fees earned
402   _____ fees earned
403   _____ services revenue
404   _____ services revenue
405   Commissions earned
406   Rent earned
407   Dividends earned
408   Earnings from investment in _____
409   Interest earned
410   Sinking fund earnings
413   Sales
414   Sales returns and allowances
415   Sales discounts

Cost of Goods Sold Items

501   Amortization of patents
502   Cost of goods sold
503   Depletion of mine deposit
505   Purchases
506   Purchases returns and allowances
507   Purchases discounts
508   Transportation-in

Manufacturing Accounts
520 Raw materials purchases
521 Freight-in on raw materials
530 Factory payroll
531 Direct labour
540 Factory overhead
541 Indirect materials
542 Indirect labour
543 Factory insurance expired
544 Factory supervision
545 Factory supplies used
546 Factory utilities
547 Miscellaneous production costs
548 Property taxes on factory building
550 Rent on factory building
551 Repairs, factory equipment
552 Small tools written off
560 Amortization of factory equipment
561 Amortization of factory building

Standard Cost Variance Accounts
580 Direct material quantity variance
581 Direct material price variance
582 Direct labour quantity variance
583 Direct labour price variance
584 Factory overhead volume variance
585 Factory overhead controllable variance

Expenses

Amortization (Depreciation and Depletion Expenses)
601 Amortization expense, _____
602 Amortization expense, copyrights
603 Depletion expense, _____
604 Amortization expense, boats
605 Amortization expense, automobiles
606 Amortization expense, building _____
607 Amortization expense, building _____
608 Amortization expense, land improvements _____
609 Amortization expense, land improvements _____
610 Amortization expense, law library
611 Amortization expense, trucks
612 Amortization expense, _____ equipment
613 Amortization expense, _____ equipment
614 Amortization expense, _____
615 Amortization expense, _____

Employee Related Expenses
620 Office salaries expense
621 Sales salaries expense
622 Salaries expense
623 _____ wages expense
624 Employees' benefits expense
625 Payroll taxes expense

Financial Expenses
630 Cash over and short
631 Discounts lost
633 Interest expense

Insurance Expenses
635 Insurance expense, delivery equipment
636 Insurance expense, office equipment
637 Insurance expense, _____

Rental Expenses
640 Rent expense
641 Rent expense, office space
642 Rent expense, selling space
643 Press rental expense
644 Truck rental expense
645 _____ rental expense

Supplies Expense
650 Office supplies expense
651 Store supplies expense
652 _____ supplies expense
653 _____ supplies expense

Miscellaneous Expenses
655 Advertising expense
656 Bad debts expense
657 Blueprinting expense
658 Boat expense
659 Collection expense
661 Concessions expense
662 Credit card expense
663 Delivery expense
664 Dumping expense
667 Equipment expense
668 Food and drinks expense
669 Gas, oil, and repairs expense
671 Gas and oil expense
672 General and administrative expense
673 Janitorial expense
674 Legal fees expense
676 Mileage expense
677 Miscellaneous expenses
678 Mower and tools expense
679 Operating expenses
681 Permits expense
682 Postage expense
683 Property taxes expense
684 Repairs expense, _____
685 Repairs expense, _____
687 Selling expenses
688 Telephone expense
689 Travel and entertainment expense

690	Utilities expense
691	Warranty expense
695	Income taxes expense

Gains and Losses

701	Gain on retirement of bonds
702	Gain on sale of machinery
703	Gain on sale of temporary investments
704	Gain on sale of trucks
705	Gain on _____
801	Loss on disposal of machinery
802	Loss on exchange of equipment
803	Loss on exchange of _____
804	Loss on market decline of temporary investments
805	Loss on retirement of bonds
806	Loss on sale of investments
807	Loss on sale of machinery
808	Loss on sale of _____
809	Loss on _____
810	Loss or gain from liquidation

Clearing Accounts

901	Income summary
902	Manufacturing summary

NOTES

NOTES

NOTES

NOTES

NOTES